P3
BUSINESS ANALYSIS
STUDY TEXT

ACCA

Edition 3, Version 1

ISBN 978-1-84808-215-1

Published by

Get Through Guides Ltd.
Unit – 2, 308A Melton Road
Leicester LE47SL
United Kingdom

Website: www.GetThroughGuides.com

Email: info@GetThroughGuides.com

Student Support Forum: http://GetThroughGuides.co.uk/forum

We are grateful to Pearson Education Limited for permission to reproduce some definitions from their book "Exploring Corporate Strategy" written by Gerry Johnson, Kevan Scholes and Richard Whittington. This book is referred to throughout the text as JSW.

Limit of liability / Disclaimer of warranty: While the publisher has used its best efforts in preparing this book, it makes no warranties or representations with respect to the accuracy or completeness of contents of this book and specifically disclaims any implied warranties of merchantability or fitness for any specific or general purpose. No warranty may be created or extended by sales or other representatives or written sales material. Each company is different and the suggestions made in this book may not suit a particular purpose. Companies/individuals should consult professionals where appropriate. The publisher shall not be liable for any loss of profit or other commercial damages including but not limited to special, incidental, consequential or other damages.

We are grateful to the Association of Chartered Certified Accountants for permission to reproduce past examination questions. The answers to past examination questions have been prepared by Get Through Guides Ltd.

All rights reserved. No part of this publication may be reproduced, stored in a retrieval system or transmitted, in any form or by any means, electronic, mechanical, photocopying, scanning or otherwise, without the prior written permission of Get Through Guides Ltd.

The publisher has made every effort to contact the holders of copyright material. If any such material has been inadvertently overlooked the publishers will be pleased to make the necessary arrangements at the first opportunity.

No responsibility for any loss to anyone acting or refraining from action as a result of any material in this publication can be accepted by the author, editor or publisher.

Please check the back of this book for any updates / errata. Further live updates / errata may also be found online on the Get Through Guides Student Support Forum at: http://getthroughguides.co.uk/forum. Students are advised to check both of these locations.

© Get Through Guides 2011

STUDY CONTENTS

P3 - BUSINESS ANALYSIS

About the paper — i - vii

Section A — Strategic position

1. The need for, and purpose of, strategic and business analysis — 1 - 18
2. Environmental issues affecting the strategic position of an organisation — 19 - 44
3. Competitive forces affecting an organisation — 45 - 72
4. Marketing and the value of goods and services — 73 - 88
5. The internal resources, capabilities and competences of an organisation — 89 - 102
6. The expectations of stakeholders and the influence of ethics and culture — 103 - 140

Section B — Strategic choices

1. The influence of corporate strategy on an organisation — 141 - 172
2. Alternative approaches to achieving competitive advantage — 173 - 194
3. Alternative directions and methods of development — 195 - 208

Section C — Strategic action

1. Organising and enabling success — 209 - 228
2. Managing strategic change — 229 - 254
3. Understanding strategy development — 255 - 272

Section D — Business process change

1. The role of process and process change initiatives — 273 - 286
2. Improving the processes of the organisation — 287 - 314
3. Software solutions — 315 - 334

Section E — Information technology

1. Principles of e-business — 335 - 358
2. E-business application: upstream supply chain management — 359 - 380
3. E-business application: downstream supply chain management — 381 - 398
4. E-business application: customer relationship management — 399 - 418

Section F — Project management

1. The nature of projects — 419 - 444
2. Building the business case — 445 - 456
3. Managing and leading projects — 457 - 468
4. Planning, monitoring and controlling projects — 469 - 482
5. Concluding a project — 483 - 490

Section G — Financial analysis

1. The link between strategy and finance — 491 - 500
2. Finance decisions to formulate and support business strategy — 501 - 510
3. The role of cost and management accounting in strategic planning and implementation — 511 - 532
4. Financial implications of making strategic choices and of implementing strategic actions — 533 - 564

STUDY CONTENTS

P3 - BUSINESS ANALYSIS

Section H — People

1. Strategy and people: leadership   565 - 574
2. Strategy and people: job design   575 - 588
3. Strategy and people: staff development 589 - 602

Glossary   1 - 4
Index   1 - 4

Total Page Count: 618

Syllabus

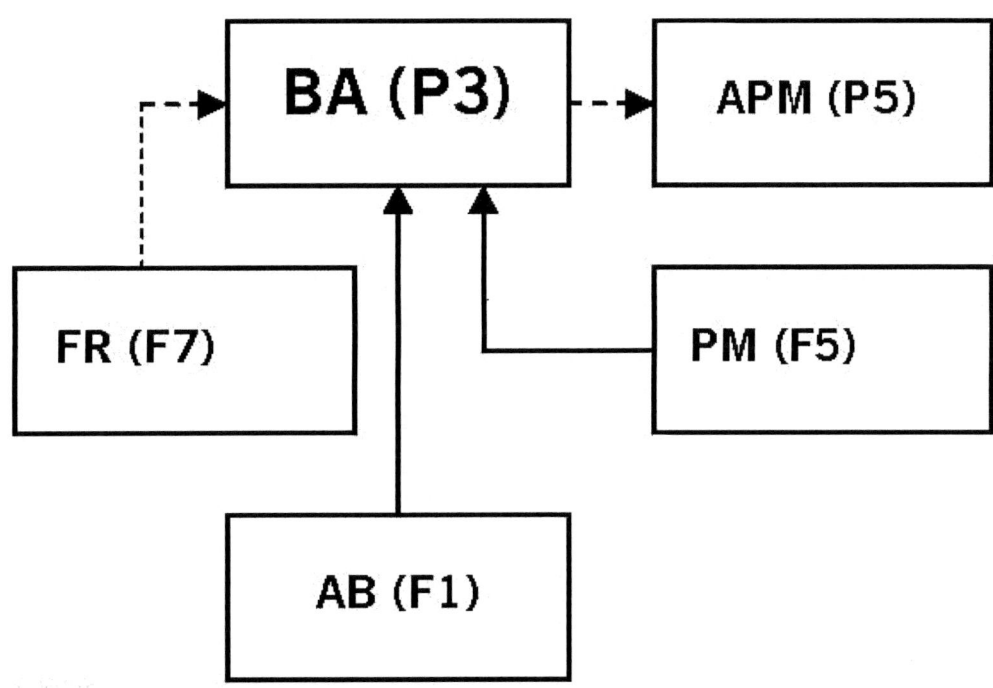

AIM

To apply relevant knowledge, skills and exercise professional judgement in assessing strategic position, determining strategic choice and implementing strategic action through beneficial business process and structural change; coordinating knowledge systems and information technology and by effectively managing quality processes, projects and people within financial and other resource constraints.

MAIN CAPABILITIES

On successful completion of this paper, candidates should be able to

A   Assess the strategic position of an organisation
B   Evaluate the strategic choices available to an organisation
C   Discuss how an organisation might go about its strategic implementation
D   Evaluate and redesign business processes and structures to implement and support the organisation's strategy taking account of customer and other major stakeholder requirements
E   Integrate appropriate information technology solutions to support the organisation's strategy
F   Advise on the principles of project management to enable the implementation of aspects of the organisation's strategy with the twin objectives of managing risk and ensuring benefits realisation
G   Analyse and evaluate the effectiveness of a company's strategy and the financial consequences of implementing strategic decisions
H   Assess the role of leadership and people management in formulating and implementing business strategy

RELATIONAL DIAGRAM OF MAIN CAPABILITIES

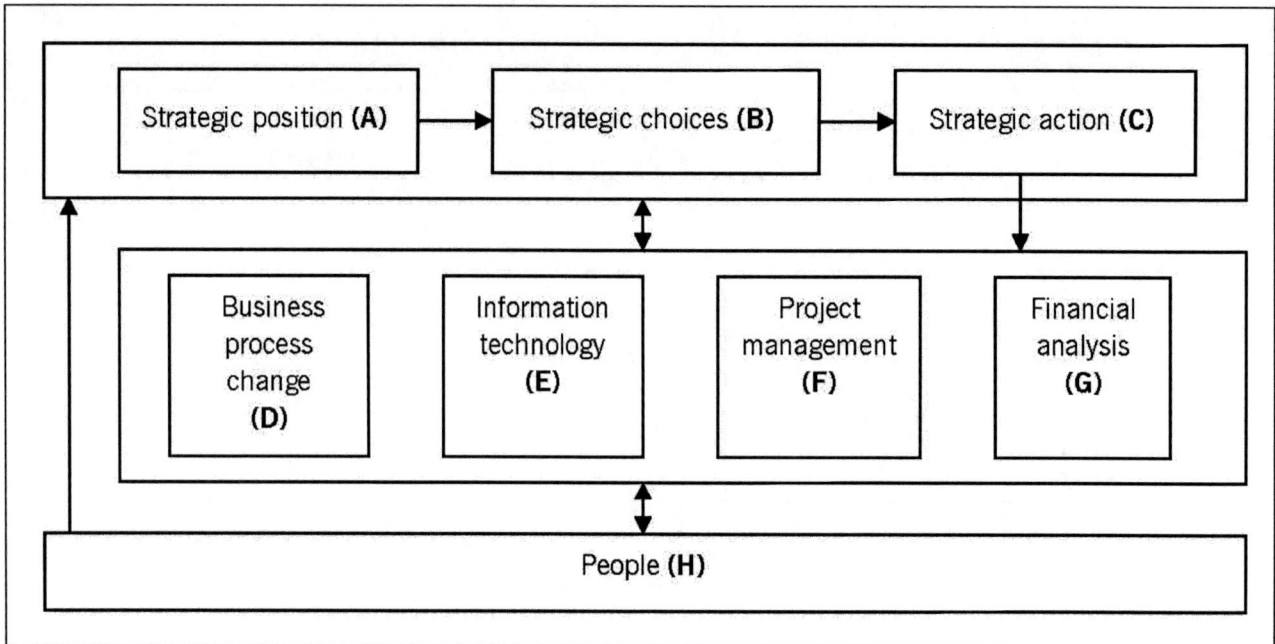

RATIONALE

The syllabus for Paper P3, Business Analysis, is primarily concerned with two issues. The first is the external forces (the behaviour of customers, the initiatives of competitors, the emergence of new laws and regulations) that shape the environment of an organisation. The second is the internal ambitions and concerns (desire for growth, the design of processes, the quality of products and services, the competences of employees, the financial resources) that exist within an organisation. This syllabus looks at both of these perspectives, from assessing strategic position and choice to identifying and formulating strategic action and its formulation. It identifies opportunities for beneficial change that involve people, finance and information technology. It examines how these opportunities may be implemented through the appropriate management of programmes and projects.

The syllabus begins with the assessment of strategic position in the present and in the future using relevant forecasting techniques and is primarily concerned with the impact of the external environment on the business, its internal capabilities and expectations and how the organisation positions itself under these constraints. It examines how factors such as culture, leadership and stakeholder expectations shape organisational purpose. Strategic choice is concerned with decisions which have to be made about an organisation's future and the way in which it can respond to the influences and pressures identified in the assessment of its current and future strategic position.

Strategic action concerns the implementation of strategic choices and the transformation of these choices into organisational action. Such action takes place in day-to-day processes and organisational relationships and these processes and relationships need to be managed in line with the intended strategy, involving the effective coordination of information technology, people, finance and other business resources.

Companies that undertake successful business process redesign claim significant organisational improvements. This simply reflects the fact that many existing processes are less efficient than they could be and that new technology makes it possible to design more efficient processes. Strategic planning and strategy implementation has to be subject to financial benchmarks. Financial analysis explicitly recognises this, reminding candidates of the importance of focusing on the key management accounting techniques that help to determine strategic action and the financial ratios and measures that may be used to assess the viability of a strategy and to monitor and measure its success.

Throughout, the syllabus recognises that successful strategic planning and implementation requires the effective recruitment, leadership, organisation and training and development of people.

INTELLECTUAL LEVELS

The syllabus is designed to progressively broaden and deepen the knowledge, skills and professional values demonstrated by the student on their way through the qualification.

The specific capabilities within the detailed syllabuses and study guides are assessed at one of three intellectual or cognitive levels:

Level 1: Knowledge and comprehension
Level 2: Application and analysis
Level 3: Synthesis and evaluation

Very broadly, these intellectual levels relate to the three cognitive levels at which the Knowledge module, the Skills module and the Professional level are assessed.

Each subject area in the detailed study guide included in this document is given a 1, 2, or 3 superscript, denoting intellectual level, marked at the end of each relevant line. This gives an indication of the intellectual depth at which an area could be assessed within the examination. However, while level 1 broadly equates with the Knowledge module, level 2 equates to the Skills module and level 3 to the Professional level, some lower level skills can continue to be assessed as the student progresses through each module and level. This reflects that at each stage of study there will be a requirement to broaden, as well as deepen capabilities. It is also possible that occasionally some higher level capabilities may be assessed at lower levels.

Examination Structure

The syllabus is assessed by a three-hour paper based examination.

Section A

This section contains one multi-part question based on a case study scenario. The question is worth 50 marks..

Section B:

This section will consist of three discrete questions each worth 25 marks. Candidates must answer two questions from this section.

Total 100 marks

Reading and planning time

For all three hour examination papers, ACCA has introduced 15 minutes reading and planning time.

This additional time is allowed at the beginning of each three-hour examination to allow candidates to read the questions and to begin planning their answers before they start writing in their answer books. This time should be used to ensure that all the information and exam requirements are properly read and understood.

During reading and planning time candidates may only annotate their question paper. They may not write anything in their answer booklets until told to do so by the invigilator.

DETAILED SYLLABUS

A Strategic position

1. The need for and purpose of, strategic and business analysis
2. Environmental issues affecting the strategic position of an organisation
3. Competitive forces affecting an organisation
4. Marketing and the value of goods and services
5. The internal resources, capabilities and competences of an organisation
6. The expectations of stakeholders and the influence of ethics and culture

B Strategic choices

1. The influence of corporate strategy on an organisation
2. Alternative approaches to achieving competitive advantage
3. Alternative directions and methods of development

C Strategic action

1. Organising and enabling success
2. Managing strategic change
3. Understanding strategy development

D Business process change

1. The roles of process and process change initiatives
2. Improving the processes of the organisation
3. Software solutions

E Information technology

1. Principles of e-business
2. E-business application: upstream supply chain management
3. E-business application: downstream supply chain management
4. E-business application: customer relationship management

F Project management

1. The nature of projects
2. Building a business case
3. Managing and leading projects
4. Planning, monitoring and controlling projects
5. Concluding a project

G Financial Analysis

1. The link between strategy and finance
2. Finance decisions to formulate and support business strategy
3. The role of cost and management accounting in strategic planning and implementation
4. Financial implications of making strategic choices and of implementing strategic actions

H People

1. Strategy and people: leadership
2. Strategy and people: job design
3. Strategy and people: staff development

SECTION A: STRATEGIC POSITION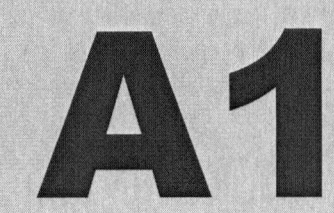

STUDY GUIDE A1: THE NEED FOR AND PURPOSE OF STRATEGIC AND BUSINESS ANALYSIS

Get Through Intro

Imagine you have had enough of working for other people and you want to start up your own business. You have always wanted to set up your own radio station and you have heard that the local government is tendering licences.

You need to decide how you are going to convince the government to give you the licence, instead of other people with more experience. In order to do this, you need to show the government your strategy – who your station will be for, how you will finance it and how long it will take to become profitable.

In fact, any business you join will always be looking at where they currently are, and where they want to be in the future. An important role for you will be to help shape that strategy. The more you understand how a strategy is built, the more important and useful you will be to the organisation.

This book will teach you the building blocks of how to build a good strategy, maintain it and expand it to stay ahead of your competitors. It will also ensure that you progress well in your career too!

Learning Outcomes

a) Recognise the fundamental nature and vocabulary of strategy and strategic decisions.
b) Discuss how strategy may be formulated at different levels (corporate, business level, operational) of an organisation.
c) Explore the Johnson, Scholes and Whittington model for defining elements of strategic management - the strategic position, strategic choices and strategy into action.
d) Analyse how strategic management is affected by different organisational contexts.
e) Compare three different strategy lenses (Johnson, Scholes and Whittington) for viewing and understanding strategy and strategic management.
f) Explore the scope of business analysis and its relationship to strategy and strategic management in the context of the relational diagram of this syllabus.

2: Strategic Position

Introduction

Case Study

Richard Branson is well known as being an entrepreneur. At the age of 15 he set up a magazine called School. He also noticed that young people liked listening to music, but often could not afford to buy records as it was too expensive. He noticed that across the English Channel in France, records sold for lower prices. So he started going across the Channel and bringing back van-loads of records. He sold these under the banner 'virgin' as no one had ever done this before.

Since then, Richard Branson has had an ability to see a gap in the market and provide a product that fills it. He has been famously quoted as saying "I don't go into ventures to make a fortune. I do it because I'm not satisfied with the way others are doing business."

This was certainly the case with Virgin Airlines. It was the first airline that treated economy passengers well and gave them a number of benefits e.g. individual TV screens, computer games to play on board, better food, a travel pack etc. It managed to do this and also be competitive on price.

The above case study shows that Richard Branson was quick at spotting a gap and then forming the strategy to take advantage of that gap. This chapter will show you how to come up with strategies for your business ideas – both in the exam and in real life!

1. Recognise the fundamental nature and vocabulary of strategy and strategic decisions.[2]
[Learning Outcome a]

1.1 The fundamental nature of strategy

At its most fundamental level, strategy can be said to be linked to and involved with setting the long term direction for an organisation. It requires an organisation to not only examine and assess its present position but also its desired future position. Strategy then becomes the bridge that will help enable organisations to go from "where we are now" to "where we want to be in the future".

Diagram 1: Strategy

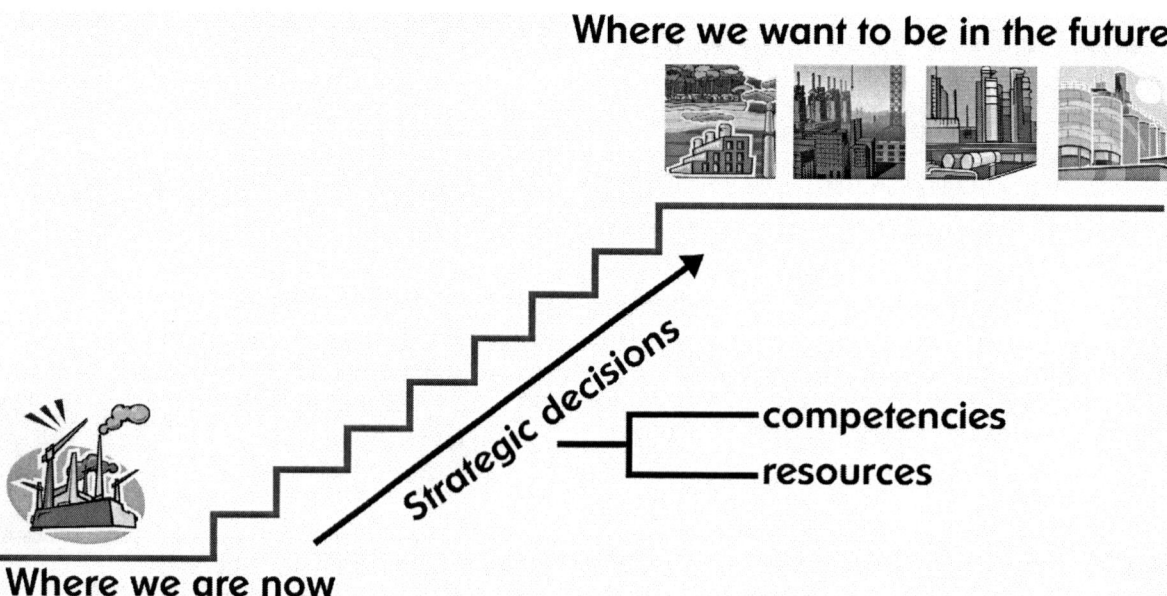

Building upon this base, it can be stated that the fundamental nature of strategy is that it is a process of using a company's internal resources to respond to its external environment in order to be successful. Broadly speaking this means an organisation deciding upon how it will meet its goals. More specifically it translates into a methodology through which a firm:

➢ outlines its long term objectives and
➢ decides upon the deployment of its resources (i.e. allocation of people, budgets etc)

The latter leads an organisation into following what is commonly referred to as the "resource based view" of strategy. This approach involves an organisation examining its resources (what it has) and its competencies (what it is good at) against the background of what is being demanded (in terms of goods and services) from the market place.

The main idea or end objective here is for an organisation to create a "strategic fit" with its business environment. By this what is meant is that an organisation should find a match between what goods and services they can best provide, against what goods and services are being demanded (or are likely to be demanded) by potential customers.

Example

Research undertaken by Bank 1 has shown that a greater number of automobile purchasers are choosing to lease rather than purchase a car with each passing month.

➢ Bank 1 then analyses whether it should introduce lease financing as a new product.

➢ Bank 1 has a large customer base that they can market this product to. However their rates will not be as competitive as those offered by dealerships.

➢ Bank 1 decides to go ahead and offer lease financing as a product. To compensate for the higher rates, Bank 1 will offer a longer payback period.

However no organisation can afford to formulate and base its strategy solely on the analytical procedures described above. Along with examining its capabilities and the external environment, organisations must also take into account the values and expectations of all their stakeholders. Johnson, Scholes and Whittington ("JSW") define stakeholders as being "individuals or groups who depend on the organisation to fulfill their own goals and on whom in turn the organisation depends". Common examples of the types of external stakeholders include:

➢ banks and other creditors

➢ suppliers

➢ governments and local communities

The internal stakeholders include:

➢ owners / investors of the business

➢ employees of the business

Therefore if an organisation and its chosen strategies are to have any chance of success they must have the support of stakeholders.

Example

Confederate Cars is a relatively small manufacturer of custom sports cars. Management of the organisation has recently come up with a strategy to change from producing small numbers of a large variety of models to the opposite of producing large volumes of a small number of models thereby increasing production efficiencies and subsequently profitability.

To further improve production efficiencies, management would like to automate much of the manufacturing process. This would result in a significant number of redundancies amongst shop floor workers. The factory employees immediately oppose this strategy and obtain the support of the organisation's office and clerical staff all of whom threaten to strike.

Therefore management will not be able to implement their proposed strategy (at least in the short turn) unless they can convince their employees of the value and benefits of following this new direction.

Therefore taking all of the above into account, strategy can be thought of and defined in the words of JSW as being "the direction and scope of an organisation over the long term, which achieves advantage in a changing environment through its configuration of resources and competences with the aim of fulfilling stakeholder expectations".

SUMMARY

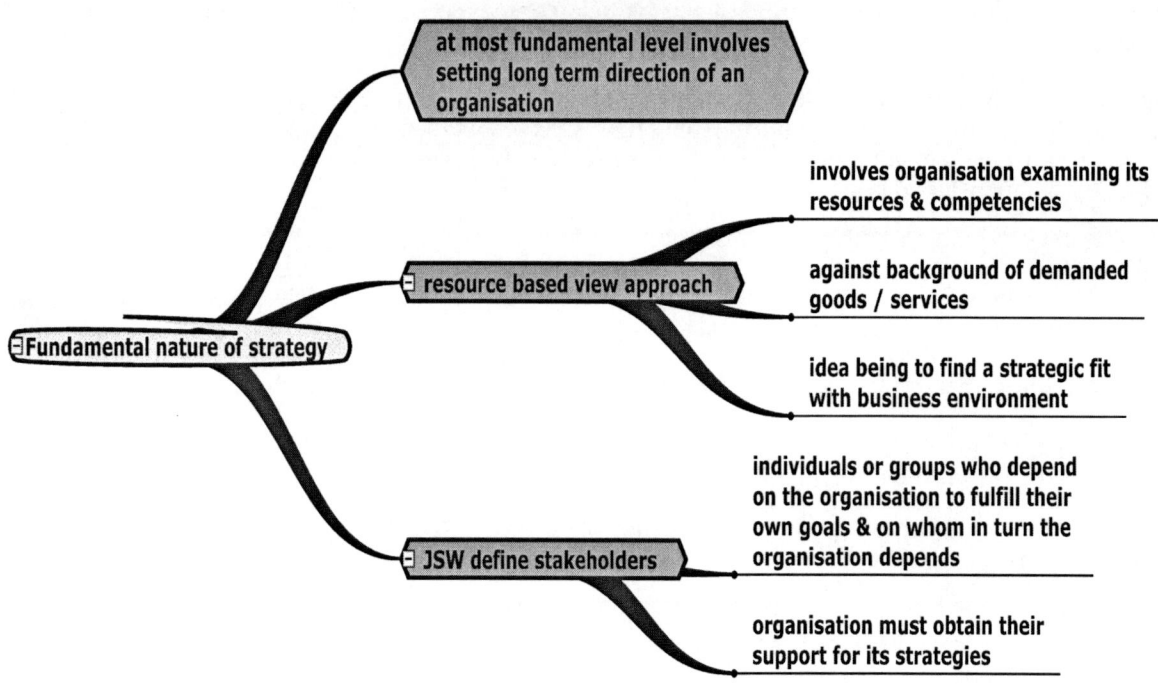

1.2 The vocabulary of strategy

As the above definition indicates, strategy is a process rather than just a "one-off" activity and like all processes has a vocabulary consisting of key terms such as:

a) mission statement

b) vision

c) goal

d) objective

e) resources

f) capabilities

Mission statements are written to help explain the purpose behind the particular organisation and where the organisation is going at present. They should include a description of what the organisation does as well as why it does it. This has also been discussed in the Ashridge Mission Model in learning outcome 1 of Study Guide B1.

Example

For instance, the Federal Express mission statement declares "FedEx is committed to our People-Service-Profit Philosophy. We will produce outstanding financial returns by providing totally reliable, competitively superior, global, air-ground transportation of high-priority goods and documents that require rapid, time-certain delivery."

The purpose of a **vision statement** is to define and describe what the organisation is aspiring to be for the future. It typically reflects an ambitious and optimistic view of what management believes the organisation can and should achieve.

Example

For instance the vision statement for Toastmasters International is "To empower people to achieve their full potential and realize their dreams. Through our member clubs, people throughout the world can improve their communication and leadership skills, and find the courage to change".

JSW define **goals** as being a "general statement of aim or purpose" and objectives as being a "quantification (if possible) or more precise statement of the goal."

> **Example**
>
> To illustrate the goal for an organisation in the service industry could be to enhance consumer satisfaction. A subsequent objective could be that the number of customer complaints should decrease by 20 percent over a one year period.

1.3 Strategic decisions

The old German proverb of "what's the use of running if you are not on the right road" best illustrates the purpose and value of strategic decisions. As mentioned earlier, an organisation's strategy can be thought of as a bridge that links "where it is at present" to "where it would like to be in the future". Strategic decisions represent the steps that an organisation takes in order to reach the end of this bridge.

1. **The mechanics to making strategic decisions involve organisations assessing the factors and decisions that will enable the firm to meet its objectives.** These include:

   a) Assessing what the scope of the organisation's focus should be.

   b) Forecasting shifts and trends in the business environment.

   c) Analysing the company's strengths and weaknesses against the background of the above two factors.

Therefore strategic decisions are the decisions that help an organisation to chart its path or direction to follow in order to achieve its long term objectives and strategy. They represent the process by which management / executives identify obstacles which are preventing an organisation from realising its long term objectives and attempt to overcome them.

2. **Characteristics of strategic decisions are that they:**

   a) Determine an organisation's long term goals and direction.

   b) Determine the scope of an organisation' activities (e.g. which products / services to provide).

   c) Are general or "big picture" decisions (e.g. decision to enter a new market).

   d) Apply to the entire organisation.

> **Example**
>
> Organisation TWS manufactures laptop computers. TWS' long term objective and strategy is to work towards producing the world's most technologically advanced laptops. Towards achieving this ambition TWS has taken the strategic decision to outsource all their non-core tasks such as handling customer complaints, IT maintenance etc. The rationale being that this will allow the organisation to focus its resources (it is also believed that outsourcing will result in costs savings) and energies on research and development and manufacturing.

SUMMARY

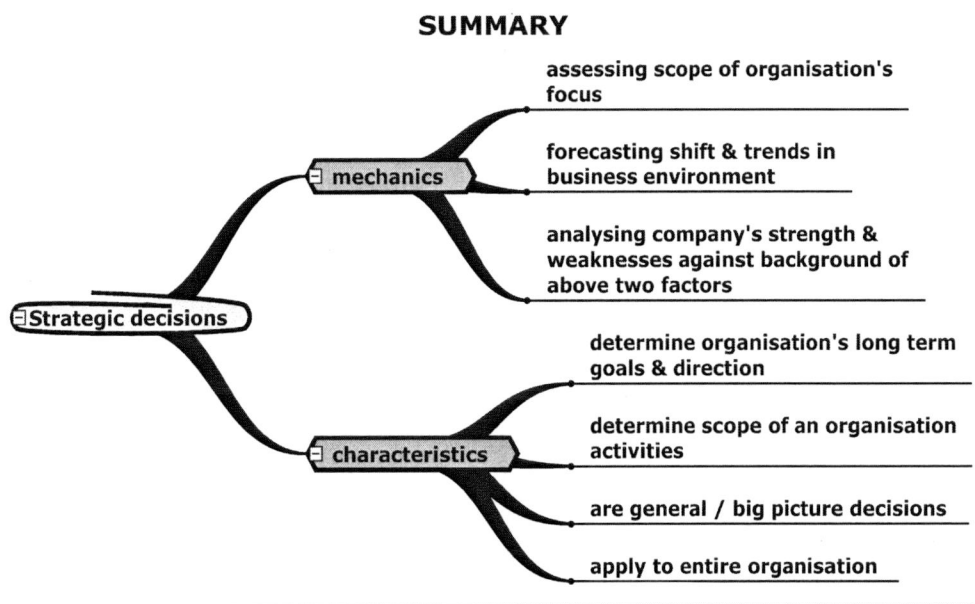

> **Test Yourself 1**
>
> Explain the resource based view of strategy?

2. Discuss how strategy may be formulated at different levels (corporate, business level and operational) of an organisation. [2]

[Learning Outcome b]

In general strategy formulation involves a company following the steps illustrated below:

Diagram 2: General strategy formulation and management

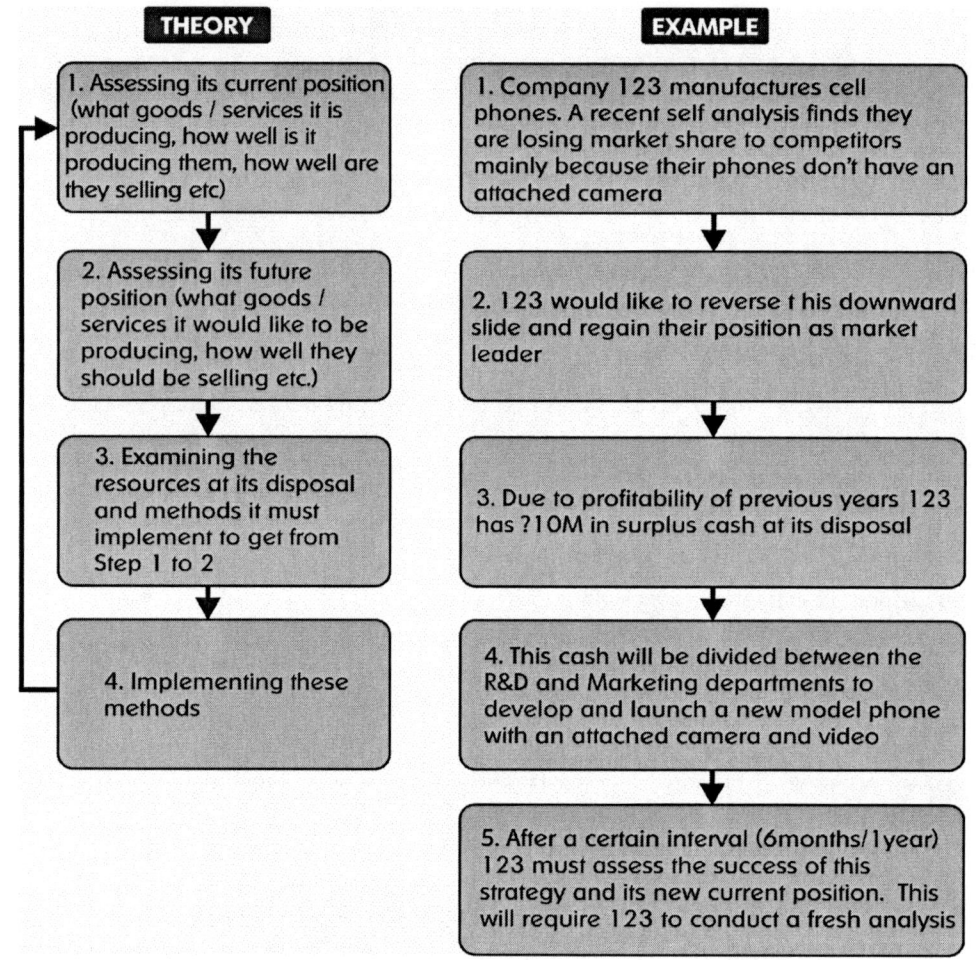

As the arrows suggest, strategic management is a fluid on-going process rather than a static detailed one-off plan. It should be thought of as a general set of directions rather than a specific map. Strategic Management can be broadly broken down into the three components diagrammed below.

Diagram 3: Components of Strategy and Strategic Management

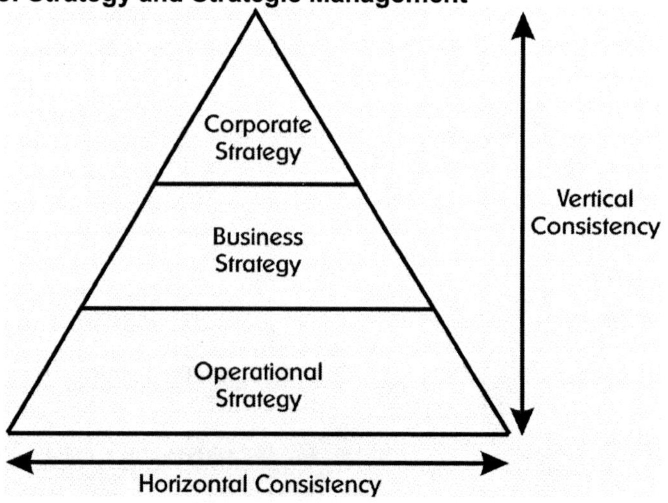

In simplified terms the differences between the three strategies are:

- **Corporate Strategy:** Corporate strategy looks at the overall suite of businesses / products of an organisation. It involves an organisation asking itself what kind of business should I be in? For instance should I be an orange or an apple seller?

- **Business Strategy:** Business strategy is usually at the Strategic Business Unit (SBU) level and involves an organisation asking itself how it can achieve its corporate strategy? For instance how can I be a better orange or apple seller?

- **Operational Strategy:** Involves an organisation asking itself how it can implement its business strategy? For instance how do I now go about selling oranges or apples?

As the above indicates there is a hierarchy of strategy for most organisations. At the top of the hierarchy is corporate strategy. Corporate strategy is in essence the "macro" and overreaching strategy of the organisation. More specifically, corporate strategy involves an organisation deciding upon what industries and markets it should be in and is typically set by the top executives or board of directors.

The next level strategy is business strategy which is the more focused or "micro" strategy for the organisation. It involves an organisation assessing how it should compete in the markets and industries identified at the corporate strategy level. Business strategies are normally formulated by management as they set about implementing the organisation's corporate strategy.

The lowest level of the strategy hierarchy is operational strategy. Operational strategy has a very narrow focus and is concerned with the day to day operating activities of the organisation. It represents how an organisation implements the strategies set at the preceding business level. This type of strategy is formulated by the employees / management of an organisation.

Example

A bank's Board of Directors will determine and set lending guidelines for the bank. These guidelines will specify which industries the bank is interested in financing.

(Corporate strategy)
↓
The executives of the bank will then identify which companies in these industries they would be interested in dealing with.

(Business strategy)
↓
The management of the bank would then target and market these companies.

(Operational strategy)

SUMMARY

Different levels of strategy formulation

- **corporate strategy**
  - the macro & overreaching strategy of organisation
  - set by the top executives / board of directors

- **business strategy**
  - more focused or micro strategy for organisation
  - set by management

- **operational strategy**
  - narrow focus & concerned with day to day activities of organisation
  - set by employees/management

Test Yourself 2

Tasty Burgers is an established chain of fast food outlets in London which began operation in 20X4. Initially it had only a few outlets. The company grew rapidly and now has 15 outlets in the UK.

The company has recently appointed Mack Dellas as the CEO who is also responsible for the company's global operations.

Dellas has started working towards the long-term objectives of the company. He has prepared a list of challenges to be met in order to achieve the company's goals. The key elements of Dellas' strategy are as follows:

- opening a further 500 outlets over the next 5 years, both within the UK and abroad
- identifying a suitable market position and promoting the brand name through extensive advertising
- offering high value to customers by providing efficient and quality services
- increasing the existing range of meals by offering new menu items including special low price meals to increase market penetration

In addition, instead of managing each outlet individually, Mr. Dellas has decided that entering into franchising agreements would be a cost effective strategy. Franchising is an arrangement whereby Tasty Burgers would grant its dealers (or franchisees), the right to sell the fast food products in exchange for some consideration. However, if any of the franchisees performs poorly, this could adversely affect the reputation of the entire group.

Required:

From the above scenario, explain the strategy which has been adopted by Dellas. Also explain the level / type of the strategy adopted, stating the reasons for its adoption.

---

3. Explore the Johnson, Scholes and Whittington model for defining elements of strategic management – the strategic position, strategic choices and strategy into action.[3]
[Learning Outcome c]

JSW state that the aim of strategic management is to take a holistic as opposed to a department specific view of the issues facing an organisation. The objective is to understand the overall obstacles that face an organisation and to then decide upon the long term direction for the organisation in this context.

3.1 Elements of strategic model

In their model, JSW break down the strategic model into 3 main elements:

- understanding the strategic position of the organisation;
- understand what are its strategic choices for the future and
- turning the strategy that is chosen into action

1. Understanding the strategic position

This part of the model involves an organisation looking at the following factors:

a) the impact a strategy will have on the external environment and vice versa;

b) the organisation's strategic capability and

c) the expectations and influences of stakeholders

Diagram 4: Strategic position of an organisation

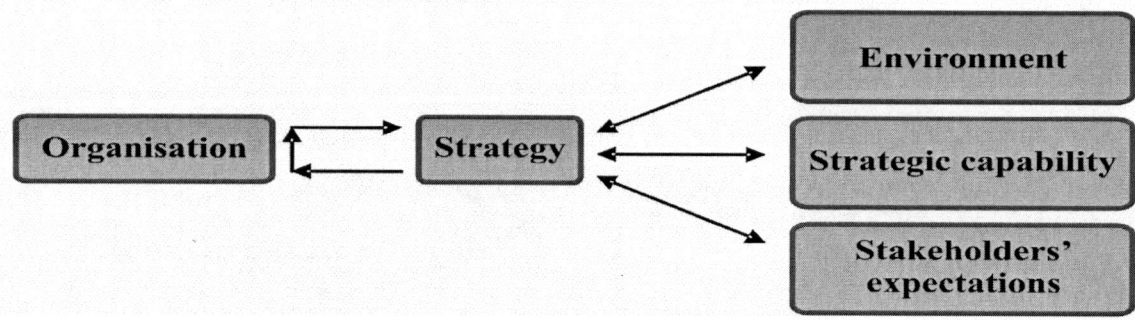

In regards to the external environment it should be remembered that no organisation exists in a vacuum. An organisation will exist as part of an industry which in turn is a subset of a much larger society. This society (and in turn the organisation) will be shaped by a host of factors that include:

i. political (e.g. government taxes and or regulation);
ii. economic (e.g. inflation, rising interest rates);
iii. social (e.g. changing demographics and consumer mindsets);
iv. technological (e.g. invention of new technologies such as wi-fi);
v. environmental (e.g. lobbying by environmental activists) and
vi. legal (e.g. legislation requiring more stringent financial reporting)

(The strategic capability of an organisation has been described in earlier sections of this Study Guide)

JSW define stakeholders as "those individuals or groups who depend on the organisation to fulfil their own goals and on whom, in turn the organisation depends". Examples of different stakeholders for an organisation include:

- owners
- employees
- customers
- suppliers
- unions
- financial institutions

Naturally they have a very real interest in the firm, the strategies it is following and its overall continued well being. They also have the capability to influence the direction a firm is heading or intends to head. Therefore it is important to predict how they will respond to a new strategy. An organisation must ask will they accept the strategy or oppose it. If any of the stakeholder groups oppose a strategy, the probability of its success automatically lowers.

Example

In 1985, without adequate customer research, Coca Cola executives decided to change the formula of their existing coke drink. However, the new Coke was strongly rejected by consumers (the company received 400,000 protest calls and letters within three months). The New Coke was then quickly replaced by Coke Classic (which kept the original recipe).

2. Strategic Choice

Strategic choice is about appreciating what factors will influence the future direction an organisation is to take. It involves an understanding about what is at the core of developing strategy for an organisation at both the corporate and strategic business unit ("SBU") level.

Corporate strategy centres on outlining the scope of an organisation. This involves decisions on determining:

➢ What **products** to sell / **services** to provide (e.g. should the organisation specialise in a few products / services or offer an entire portfolio);	➢ The working **relationship** between itself and its various SBUs (e.g. should marketing / operational policy be dictated or should autonomy be given);
➢ The **geographic** areas where they are to be marketed (e.g. should the organisation be a regional, national or international player);	➢ The possibility of creating **synergies** (e.g. streamlining the number of suppliers used across all the SBUs to achieve economies of scale).

Strategic choice at the business level requires identifying areas where an organisation can differentiate itself from competitors and therefore achieve a competitive advantage. It involves companies performing a self analysis to answer questions such as:

- What are the goods / services that an organisation provides that differentiate it from competitors;
- Which of the organisation's goods / services currently being offered are superior to those of competitors and
- Are there any needs of customers that are currently not being met (identifying of market niches).

3. Strategy into action

JSW define turning strategy into action as "being concerned with ensuring that strategies are working in practice". Three elements that will help an organisation better implement its strategies are:

a) Adequate structuring in terms of organisation structures, processes and relationships and their subsequent interactions.

b) Enabling or matching the strategies of an organisation with its resources (e.g. people, processes, finances etc).

c) Managing the change that following any new strategy will bring to an organisation.

SUMMARY

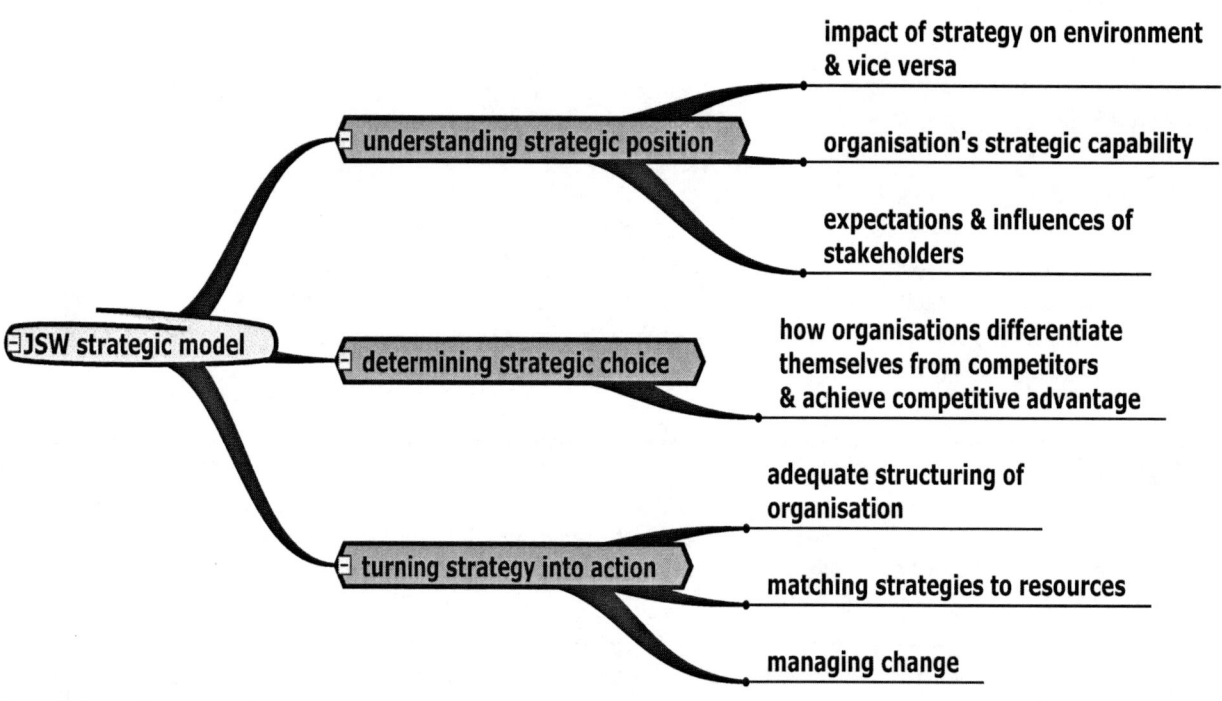

Test Yourself 3

Peter Parker started an accounting firm in 20X5 and within two years his fee income was in excess of £50K a year. He had nearly 50 clients mostly acquired through word of the mouth. Peter noticed that smaller businesses which employ 20 people or less, usually do not receive the best services from their accountants. Peter thought that this was an opportunity to expand his business. However, it was difficult to increase his client base on the basis of his existing strengths. Therefore, Peter appointed four part-time accountants and took care of most of the business himself, in order to control the operating costs.

Peter met Kevin Watts, who ran an accounting firm of a similar size to Peter's. He suggested to Kevin that the two firms should enter into a partnership and Kevin agreed. They decided that the partnership firm, called Parker & Watts, would be launched in 20X8. Kevin would look after the business development and Peter would focus on managing the day-to-day office affairs.

Initial research suggested that in addition to small and micro-businesses, the new firm could target the retail market since this was largely untapped.

Peter and Kevin knew that their target to achieve income of £2 million within the next 3 years would only be achieved if they could reduce costs significantly. Both partners agreed to establish a subsidiary in India in order to benefit from lower employee costs.

Required:

What are the advantages and disadvantages to Parker and Watts of creating and implementing a strategic plan (despite the fact that small firms are generally reluctant to carry out strategic planning)?

4. Analyse how strategic management is affected by different organisational contexts.[3]
[Learning Outcome d]

Strategic management is an important if not vital function for almost all businesses. However its process and product (the organisation's strategy) will vary across both organisational and industry lines. There is no "one size fits all" concept when it comes to strategy formulation and strategic management.

As mentioned before there are a number of factors that contribute to and affect an organisation's strategy and strategic management. One such factor is a business' organisational context. An organisational context refers to characteristics such as:

- the organisation's size
- the organisation's type
- the organisation's structure
- the organisation's purpose
- the organisation's culture

Characteristics such as how large an organisation is, the types of goods / services it sells as well as why it is in existence will all influence its strategic process, choices and management. For instance there will be a marked contrast in the type and level of strategic management followed by organisations of varying sizes.

To illustrate, small businesses such as owner / operated firms must function in a context of limitations and constraints. These types of firms typically can only offer a limited number of products / services. In addition they also have limited money and management resources.

Therefore in this "Small Business Context" strategic management is a rather informal and limited process. These types of firms do not have the resources to engage in lengthy strategic planning processes. Nor do they see the point in doing so as there only a limited number of options (in regards to providing goods / services) open to them.

At the other end of the spectrum are multinational corporations who are almost faced with an agony of choice. These types of organisations have the resources (money and management personnel) to pursue a multitude of strategic options as there are a multitude of products / services they can develop. Strategic management here is a much more formal process as these organisations typically have entire dedicated departments to perform strategic planning and management.

Multinational corporations such as Nike, Toshiba and BMW have offices, plants and facilities in several different countries and continents. One of the main (and unique) strategic management issues that they face is deciding upon organisation structure. More specifically these types of organisations must decide upon the level of control that its Head Office should have over its overseas subsidiaries as well as how resources should be allocated across all the different business units.

Example

Joe's Accountancy Practice is a small owner / operated firm. Joe is the only ACCA in the organisation and is supported by a staff of three assistants. The majority of work he takes on is preparing and filing individual tax returns. Given this scenario, Joe's strategic management activities are limited to determining how he can find more clients (e.g. deciding on how much expenditure should be spent on advertising). He has neither the time nor resources to think strategically on matters such as whether he should diversify or expand his business.

Accenture is a multinational corporation that describes itself as a "global management consulting, technology services and outsourcing company". The organisation has offices and operations in 49 countries and offers clients a variety of services and expertise in the areas of consulting (e.g. change and financial management), technology (e.g. enterprise and infrastructure solutions) and outsourcing (e.g. application and business process outsourcing). The types of strategic management issues that Accenture must concentrate on include deciding which types of services to offer, which countries to offer them in and how resources should be allocated across its various divisions and offices.

The second aspect of a business' organisational context is the type of goods / services it provides. Organisations that provide different types of goods / services will have different operational methods, customer types, marketing needs etc and therefore will require different types of strategic management.

For instance for the manufacturing industry, strategic management is typically product centred. The strategic management focus for these types of organisations is on factors such as capacity (how much to produce), type (what features / quality goods should have) as well as operations (how the goods should be produced).

Service organisations on the other hand are those whose output is not a tangible product but an intangible experience. This feature of intangibility is what differentiates the strategic management practiced by the service industry from its manufacturing counterpart. Unlike manufacturing organisations, for service providers the main activity occurs in combination with and not away from their customers. Therefore the main focus of strategic management becomes concerned with how to manage and ensure the quality of the experience for the customer.

Example

Core strategic management activities for an aircraft manufacturer would centre on how the plane is to be designed, built and marketed to potential customers. For instance many organisations in the aerospace industry have taken the strategic direction of outsourcing much of their supply chain. Organisations such as Boeing now see themselves as being more of large-scale systems integrators rather than airplane manufacturers.

Core strategic management activities for an airline carrier centre on how to deliver a satisfactory flight experience for their passengers. Some organisations such as Virgin focus their strategic management on how they can be a high quality service provider that ensure a passenger's flight is as a comfortable and luxurious as possible. Other "no-frills" airline carriers focus their strategic management on how to be able to get their passengers from one destination to another at the lowest possible price.

Lastly as important a factor for determining a business' organisational context is its purpose or more specifically the reason why it was created and is in existence. Firms that were started and run for a profit motive will differ in strategic management from public sector as well as voluntary and non-profit organisations.

Public sector organisations are set up and run by governments for the purpose of providing goods or services to the people of a society. Although they often charge for these services they are guided by motives other than profitability. Therefore their strategic management will be influenced by a number of other factors such as maximising social welfare.

Not-for-profit and voluntary organisations are started and run for the purpose of providing benefits. These benefits may be provided on an individual level or to society as a whole. Again their strategic management focus will differ from those of commercial (for profit) organisations. Here the emphasis will be on matters such as broad development, fundraising and volunteer management.

Example

Although government hospitals charge their patients for treatment and medicine, their strategic management cannot be dictated by or focus on profitability. This is because they main purpose is to provide health care for their constituents and therefore they cannot engage in activities such as offering only those services that provide a profit for the organisation.

Similarly organisations such as the Royal Society for Prevention of Cruelty to Animals will focus their strategic management on issues such as how to build and develop awareness and support (donations and volunteers) for their cause.

Test Yourself 4

Fleetguard Plc is a medium-sized company which manufactures automobile components. The company's immediate objective is to expand its domestic operations. In the future it plans to globalise.

Teleguard Plc is an established telecom service provider in the UK and is planning to expand its operations globally.

Required:

Explain why the strategic management and processes followed by Fleetguard Plc will differ from those followed by Teleguard Plc (which is in the service industry).

5. Compare three different strategy lenses (Johnson, Scholes and Whittington) for viewing and understanding strategy and strategic management. [3]

[Learning Outcome e]

1. There are three main ways an organisation can formulate a strategy:

a) by design (strategy is thought through and penned out by management)

b) through experience (strategy evolves out of the past experiences and culture of an organisation's employees)

c) through innovation (strategy comes out of employees' new ideas)

2. JSW identifies three different ways or strategy lenses that can be used to view and understand the strategy and subsequent strategic management of an organisation.

a) Strategy as design

Here the strategic direction of an organisation is decided through using a formalised planning process. The strategic position and choices of an organisation are analytically analysed and a future path for the organisation to follow is chosen. This method of strategy development is common in traditional, rigid and large corporations such as HSBC.

b) Strategy as experience

Here the experience of managers and employees as well as the successes of past strategies influence the future direction of the organisation. New directions arise out of amendments to or deviations from existing strategies. FMCG (fast moving consumer goods) companies such as Procter & Gamble use this type of strategy development.

c) Strategy as ideas

Here strategies arise emerge out of the day to day operations of employees. The role of top management here is to maintain an environment that encourages innovative thinking so as new directions for the organisation can be found. The IT Company Google is an example of an organisation that follows this type of strategy development.

Test Yourself 5

Which one of the three strategy lenses identified by JSW would a large, established bank such as Citibank follow?

6. Explore the scope of business analysis and its relationship to strategy and strategic management in the context of the relational diagram of this syllabus. [3]

[Learning Outcome f]

Diagram 5: Relationship between business analysis and strategy

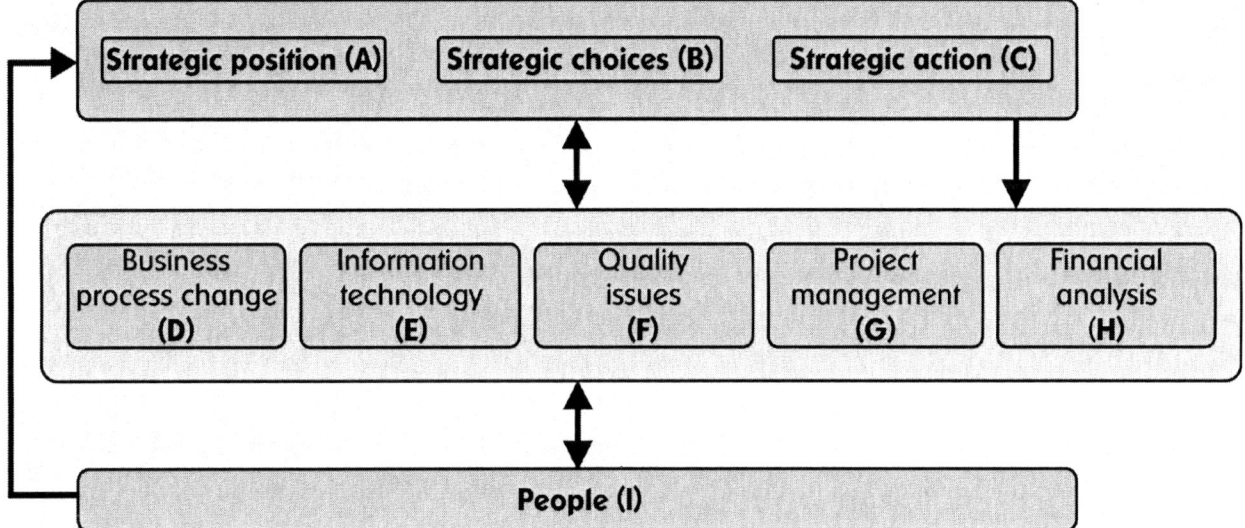

Business analysis requires an organisation to look internally. It calls for an organisation to examine what products are being produced and for whom. As importantly an organisation must ask itself why it is that their customers buy their products.

This will provide an organisation with a clear indication of its present position. Unfortunately this level of analysis alone is not sufficient given the dynamic and competitive environment that most organisations operate in today.

As mentioned before, no organisation operates in a vacuum. Their external environment will undoubtedly evolve and change over the course of time. Against this backdrop, an organisation must assess its strategic position. This assessment will provide an organisation with an idea of how well positioned they are to adapt to the changes in the external environment that are likely to take place.

In addition, analysing its strategic position will also help an organisation formulate its strategic choices. An organisation's strategic choices represent the future directions it can take. Once a strategic choice has been finalised, the organisation is at the strategic action stage. At this stage, the corresponding strategy is implemented, then monitored / adapted or even changed as time progresses.

Answers to Test Yourself

Answer to TY 1

The resource-based view of strategy involves an organisation examining its resources (what it has) and its competencies (what it can do well) against the background of what is being demanded (in terms of goods and services) from the marketplace. The resource based view explains the competitive advantage for an organisation in terms of its strategic capabilities. These resources could be tangible (such as plant or labour) or intangible (such as knowledge or intellectual resources).

The distinctive capabilities (or core competencies) of an organisation explain the competitive advantages it enjoys. These distinctive capabilities explain why certain organisations are able to perform better than the others. The more successful organisations could possess resources and competencies which enable them to reduce their cost of production or generate a superior product. For example, a manufacturing company might have gained certain core competencies on the basis of unique methods of production which gives the company a competitive advantage.

Answer to TY 2

Strategy, in a broader sense, can be considered the key in setting the long-term direction for an organisation. It requires an organisation not only to examine and assess its present position but also its desired future position. The strategy is the bridge that will help an organisation to progress from "where we are now" to "where we want to be in the future". In the case in question, the management has a strategic plan to expand globally with the vision of providing high quality products under its brand name.

Tasty Burgers' strategy is a **corporate strategy** which often involves the organisation questioning the kind of business the organisation should be in.

Corporate strategies represent the long-term direction of the organisation. They could include diversification plans, acquisition, divestment, strategic alliances and the formulation of new business ventures. The organisation's long-term expansion plan is part of its corporate strategy.

Corporate strategies deal with plans for the entire organisation and change in accordance with industry and market conditions. Penetrating the global market is a part the organisation's corporate strategy.

Since the company has decided its long-term objectives, it needs to focus on how to achieve these objectives. The key points of Dellas's strategy indicate the organisation's corporate strategy as they give an insight regarding the following:

➢ The business mission, i.e. to expand globally, has already been stated by the directors (top management). This is the long-term strategic plan which would need to be implemented.

➢ The CEO's long-term performance target is to expand the operations globally and devise a strategic plan which forms a part of the organisation's corporate strategy.

It should be noted that top management has the primary decision making responsibility in developing corporate strategies and the managers are directly responsible to shareholders.

Answer to TY 3

Although small firms are often reluctant to do so, it is sometimes necessary to prepare a strategic plan in order to obtain financial support. The advantages and disadvantages to Parker and Watts of creating and implementing a strategic plan would be as follows:

Disadvantages

- **Improved performance**: it is difficult to measure whether carrying out strategic planning leads to improved performance or not.
- **The time involved**: It is time consuming to create a strategic plan which is one reason why small firms are reluctant to do so. Day-to-day operational issues prevent them from planning for the future.
- **Restrict flexibility**: strategic plans may also restrict the firm's flexibility in responding to the changing business environment. The firm can miss profitable business opportunities.
- **Lack of skills**: strategic planning requires certain skills and is often viewed as a process carried out by large firms. Owners of small companies are much less aware of strategic management tools.
- **Lack of trust**: owner / managers may be reluctant to involve others in the planning process, as giving them access to key information about the business could be a risk. Owners may prefer to limit the size of their organisation so that it will remain under their personal control.

Advantages

- A commitment to strategic planning results in fast decision making
- The organisation is better able to respond changes and there is increased scope for innovation.
- Strategic planning may result in a higher growth rate and profits, giving the firm a competitive advantage.

For Parker and Watts to be a successful business, it must follow its strategic plan very strictly.

Answer to TY 4

Strategic management is a vital function of all businesses. However, the strategic management of each organisation will vary according to the industry in which the organisation operates and its products and processes etc.

The main factors which affect the strategic management of an organisation are:

a) the size of the organisation
b) the type of the organisation
c) the structure of the organisation
d) the culture of the organisation
e) the purpose of the organisation

a) The size of the organisation

Even though strategic management is a vital function for every organisation, it is not as predominant in a small organisation as it is in a big organisation. The reasons why the size of an organisation affects its strategic management are as follows:

- Small and medium-sized firms typically offer only a limited number of products / services in comparison to their larger counterparts. They also have limited funds and management resources.
- Small firms do not have the resources to engage in lengthy strategic planning processes.
- As small firms have limited options, these options restrict the scope of strategic management.
- On the other hand, strategic management in multinationals is a much more formal process as these organisations typically have departments dedicated to performing strategic planning and management. This is necessary due to the vast range of strategic options available to the organisation.

b) The type of the organisation

Organisations that provide different types of goods / services will have different operational methods, customer types, marketing needs etc. and will therefore require different types of strategic management. As discussed above, the goods / services provided by an organisation affect its strategic management in the following manner.

- In the manufacturing industry, strategic management is typically product-centred.
- Service organisations, on the other hand, are those whose output is not a tangible product but intangible in nature. This feature of intangibility is what differentiates the strategic management practised by the service industry from its manufacturing counterpart.

c) The purpose of the organisation

Yet another important factor in determining a business's organisational context is its purpose or, more specifically, the reason why it was created. Firms which are run for a profit motive will differ in strategic management from public sector as well as voluntary and non-profit organisations. Hence the strategic management changes accordingly. Mission statements are written to explain the purpose behind the particular organisation and where the organisation is going at present.

Answer to TY 5

JSW identify three different ways or strategy lenses that can be used to view and understand the strategy and subsequent strategic management of an organisation. These are strategy as design, strategy as experience and strategy as ideas.

A large, traditional and rigid organisation such as Citibank is likely to follow the strategy as a design method. Here the strategic direction of an organisation is decided through using a formalised planning process. The strategic position and choices of an organisation are analysed analytically and a future path for the organisation to follow is chosen.

Quick Quiz

1. What is the relationship of an "objective" to a "goal"?

2. List the three different levels strategy is formulated at?

3. List the three main elements of the JSW Strategic Model?

4. What are the three different strategy lenses identified by JSW

Answers to Quick Quiz

1. An objective is a quantification or more precise statement of a goal.

2. Corporate, business and operational

3. Understanding the strategic position of an organisation, understanding what its strategic choices for the future are and turning the selected strategy into action.

4. Strategy as design, strategy as experience and strategy as ideas

Self Examination Questions

Question 1

Tony is an engineer running a small workshop where he manufactures special-purpose machine tools for a few large clients. He is one of the very few manufacturers of such tools and has witnessed high growth in this business in the last few years.

Due to the tremendous growth in business over a significant period of time, Tony decided to convert his proprietary firm into a private limited company. By this time he was facing competition from new players in the market.

Tony started manufacturing more machine tools in his assembly line. He continued to take ad-hoc decisions on his own without understanding the impact of the external environment on his business and consulting experienced strategic advisors. This resulted in the failure to earn higher profits in spite of committing to higher investments. Later, Tony realised that strategy is very important for any business.

Required:

(a) Explain why an overall strategy is important for any business.

(b) Which factors other than analytical problems should be taken into account before formulating a strategy?

Question 2

Relentless Ltd is a manufacturer of electronic components with some 100 employees which aims to double its turnover over the next three years. The company was set up three years ago as a spin out company by two research professors from a major university who now act as its joint managing directors. The company has not been growing in line with its strategic plan due to competition from other companies in the same business.

Required:

Identify the questions that the company needs to ask itself for improving its competitive position in the market.

Answers to Self Examination Questions

Answer to SEQ 1

(a) All organisations are created for the purpose of providing goods and/or performing a service to potential customers. At the time of a company's creation, it will be operating under a certain set of industry and environmental conditions. These include factors such as customer mindsets, bargaining power of buyers / suppliers, strengths of competitors, technological advances and government intervention / regulation.

However this is not a static setting. The business world of today is a very dynamic one, evolving and changing at an almost unprecedented pace. Change is no longer a probability but a certainty. Invariably over the course of time, customer preferences, competitor behaviour and a host of other factors will change. This in turn will change the industry and environment the firm operates in. So it is no longer enough for Tony to know and understand his business's present position.

Tony must take a long-term view. He should try to ascertain how the environment will change over time. He should not only know where he stands but also where he will need to be in the future. This outlines and identifies why strategy is not just important but essential for an organisation.

Strategy, at its most fundamental level, can be said to be linked to and involved with setting the long-term direction of an organisation. It requires an organisation not only to examine and assess its present position but also its desired future position.

Building upon this base strategy then requires an organisation to examine its resources (e.g. men, materials, money) and its competencies (e.g. what goods / services it produces best) against the background of what is being demanded (in terms of goods and services) from the market place.

The organisation's objective is to create a "strategic fit" with its business environment. This means that an organisation should attempt to synthesise what goods and services it can best provide against what goods and services are being demanded (or are likely to be demanded) by potential customers.

(b) It is important to note that no organisation can afford to formulate and base its strategy solely on the analytical procedures described above. Along with examining its capabilities and the external environment, organisations must also ensure that they take into account the values and expectations of all their stakeholders. If an organisation and its chosen strategies are to have any chance of success, they must have the support of its stakeholders (e.g. owners, employees, creditors).

One way to achieve this is to ensure that an organisation's strategy is in line with its published mission and vision statements. Mission statements describe the purpose behind an organisation and the direction to which its strategies should ultimately lead. Vision statements describe what the organisation is aspiring to be for the future and typically reflect an ambitious and optimistic view of what management believes the organisation can and should achieve.

Overall it can be said that strategy is important because it is a function that helps an organisation to set its direction and scope of activities over the long term while taking into account changes in the external environment as well as the needs and expectations of its various stakeholders.

Answer to SEQ 2

The company should consider whether it has developed a niche product segment which is difficult for its competitors to emulate. The company can consider the following questions to analyse its competitive position:

1. How have its competitors performed over the last three years?

2. How has the company tackled competition during this period?

3. What does the present and expected global competitive environment look like?

4. What are the plans to overcome the competitive challenges?

SECTION A: STRATEGIC POSITION

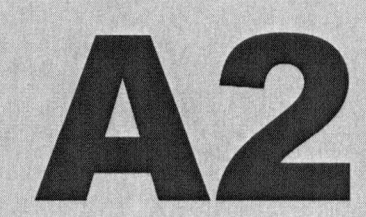

STUDY GUIDE A2: ENVIRONMENTAL ISSUES AFFECTING THE STRATEGIC POSITION OF AN ORGANISATION

Get Through Intro

Before launching a new product, it is really important to study the environment in which you will be launching your product. This includes looking at if there are political or legislative factors which could stop you from doing so, or even encourage you to do so. For example, if you were looking at manufacturing a device that could decrease carbon emissions from factories, it is likely that the government may support your product. In addition, people are becoming more environmentally friendly, so the product would be welcomed.

Having said that, if you were looking at manufacturing a new brand of cigarettes, you may find that the environment does not react so positively as smoking is generally seen as a bad habit, which causes cancer.

This chapter will help you understand how to analyse the environment and see the affect it has on your product. This is essential if your product is to succeed

Learning Outcomes

a) Assess the macro-environment of an organisation using the PESTEL.
b) Highlight the key drivers of change likely to affect the structure of a sector or market.
c) Explore, using Porter's Diamond, the influence of national competitiveness on the strategic position of an organisation.
d) Prepare scenarios reflecting different assumptions about the future environment of an organisation.
e) Evaluate methods of business forecasting used when quantitatively assessing the likely outcome of different business strategies.

20: Strategic Position

Introduction

Case Study

Looking at data collected in various censuses carried out over the past years, it is fairly clear that Europe has an ageing population and India has an extremely youthful one.

Just with this knowledge, we can start to make some assumptions on what products may or may not be in demand in the future, e.g. in 2030.

For Europe, there is likely to be a rise of medicines and medical equipment needed for elderly people. Homes for the elderly, clothing geared towards the elderly and skincare creams which decrease wrinkles are all growth markets.

If we consider India on the other hand, with a likely population of 500m people under 40, there will be much more demand for young fashionable clothes. There will be a huge need for schools, universities and colleges. There will also be a need for bars, restaurants and clubs.

The above details show that it is important to look at demographic factors when making decisions about the future. There are many other areas that should be looked at and this chapter will show you them!

1. Assess the macro-environment of an organisation using PESTEL. [3]

[Learning Outcome a]

An organisation operates within the boundaries of an economic environment. The nature and condition of this external environment is influenced and shaped by a number of different factors. These factors will impact upon organisations and need to be considered as part of the strategic planning process.

Before discussing the different factors influencing the macro-environment in depth, let us first look at the meaning of macro-environment.

1.1 Macro-environment

The macro-environment comprises all **external environmental forces** which affect the operation of an organisation but which are beyond its control. These forces include – political, economic, social / sociocultural, technological, environmental and legal forces.

1.2 PESTEL

It is essential for an organisation to effectively and constantly analyse its external environment because, as the environment changes, the strategies of the organisation change. One of the best methods of **analysing the external environment** is to use the **PESTEL method**.

Analysing the external environment is not an easy task for the managers of an organisation. There are innumerable variables in existence that could potentially affect the future of an organisation. The PESTEL method classifies those variables within the following framework:

➤ Political
➤ Economic
➤ Social
➤ Technological
➤ Environmental
➤ Legal

PESTEL helps to simplify matters by forcing managers to **categorise factors into appropriate slots** (e.g. political, economic, legal etc.). The factors in each slot can then be **further classified in terms of the probable impact** they will have on an organisation. For instance, would they cause a change in demand for the goods / services produced or require the organisation to change the way it operates.

For exam purposes it is best to use PESTEL as a framework to gauge the positive and negative impacts that these factors might impart upon the organisation.

Strategic planners use PESTEL to assess whether the environmental climate is attractive or attractive for the organisation or a part of the organisation and to estimate changes in the environmental climate that might impact upon the organisation.

1. Political

Political factors are caused by the **role that the government plays in shaping the environment** within which the organisation operates. They represent the nature and type of external environment within which the organisation must operate.

Example

On the domestic front, examples include regulations such as the introduction of new taxes. On the international front, an example could be integration of the nation into the EU (for European countries) or the introduction of NAFTA (for US and Canadian companies). New taxes make the product or service an organisation offers more expensive. The increased price could result in a decrease in demand for the particular product or service. The main purpose of bodies such as the EU and NAFTA is to increase trade between their member countries by removing tariffs, duties etc. that exist and thereby allowing a free flow of goods and services between countries. This would result in organisations facing greater competition from their foreign competitors (as their goods or services would become more accessible).

A country's political system and government policy will **set the rules and regulations of the external environment** within which all organisations must operate. In turn, the combination of these rules and regulations will create the **economic, social and political conditions** that organisations must work under. Naturally, these conditions will **affect the business and strategic choices** that an organisation can and does make. They will influence decisions the organisation makes such as:

- what goods or services to produce and market
- how to produce and market these goods and services
- what prices to charge
- where to market these goods and services

Furthermore these conditions will change over the course of time, either making life simpler or more difficult for an organisation.

Example

An import duty or tax is imposed on a particular product. For instance in India, a 115% import duty is levied on any new, imported car. The existence of this tax is beneficial for local car manufacturers that produce the same product because their foreign competitors' goods become more expensive. This has also led to some of the premium car manufacturers taking the strategic decision to start manufacturing in India, in order to avoid the import duty – Mercedes Benz and General Motors, for example, have recently opened new manufacturing plants in India to service the domestic market.

a) Political factors affecting an organisation

i. **Government policies**: each organisation needs to comply with the government policies applicable to it. While assessing the environment, an organisation has to forecast possible changes in the environment as these changes could affect the strategic actions and strategic position of the company.

ii. **Stability and tenure of government:** each government has its own beliefs and strategies. For example, one government might be for outsourcing and another might be against it. Therefore, if the government of a country is stable, this makes it easier for organisations to form their strategies.

iii. **Pressure groups:** these groups may put pressure on companies to change their strategies. For example, the pressure group Greenpeace puts pressure on companies to become more environmentally-friendly.

iv. **Government's planned strategy:** planned reforms, implications of regional government's plans and actions on the nation's strategy and subsidies awarded by the government are factors which change the organisation's external environment.

b) Questions for assessment (questions that an organisation needs to ask itself):

i. How does a change in the political situation affect an organisation?

ii. Who will win the next election?

iii. What are the political views of that party?

2. Economic

Economic factors refer to the **macroeconomic factors** that will shape the broader economic environment within which the firm operates. They represent **the financial condition** of the external environment within which the organisation must operate.

Example

An economic example of how the political system and government policy affects an organisation is when interest rates are increased. Rising interest rates make it more expensive for an organisation to borrow capital. This could potentially result in an organisation having to reconsider any planned acquisitions or large item purchases. In addition, if this increase also results in an extra cost for an organisation's suppliers, it could also increase the cost of raw materials for an organisation. Rising interest rates will also normally mean that consumer spending will reduce leading to a contraction of demand.

---

a) Economic factors affecting an organisation

i. GDP

Gross Domestic Product is the market value of all the goods and services produced within the country. A country's GDP is an indicator of its market size. Low GDP means that the country is still developing. An organisation has to keep such economic factors it in mind while forming its marketing strategies.

ii. Taxes

A change in the government's taxation policy will affect the organisation's plans. A change in tax leads to a change in cash flow. However this is a micro-environmental change. If the government declares any area to be a tax-free region, then the organisation can take strategic decisions accordingly. Organisations might enter into the production or sale of tax-free goods.

iii. Exchange rates

Organisations which conduct cross-border business such as the import or export of goods are affected by fluctuations in exchange rates. Fluctuations in exchange rates are considered to be micro-environmental changes except when such differences affect strategic decisions such as where to set up a factory for manufacturing goods.

iv. Unemployment

Unemployment is directly linked to the purchasing power of consumers. It is also one of the indicators of a recession. Since demand for organisations' goods and services is dependent on the market conditions, organisations have to predict changes in the economy and plan accordingly.

v. Trade factors and tariffs

Each country has its own rules on import and export. Some countries enter into free trade agreements (e.g. the US and Canada). These trade factors and tariffs control the supply of foreign goods in the nation and consequently their sale. Favourable rules increase the demand for the organisation's goods internationally. Therefore these factors change the macro-environment of an organisation by changing its market share.

vi. Monopolistic practices

If an organisation has a monopoly on a particular product, the organisation has control over the market. If the monopoly is accompanied by cost effectiveness through mass production, it does not result in the exploitation of consumers. On the other hand, if the monopoly does result in the exploitation of consumers, the government will interfere.

b) Questions for assessment (questions that an organisation needs to ask itself):

i. Is the economy towards a recession or a boom?

ii. How are the current economic conditions affecting the organisation?

iii. Are there any changes expected in the economic conditions and will they have an impact on the organisation?

3. Social

Social factors refer to factors such as changing demographic patterns, changing consumer tastes and preferences and overall societal trends. They represent the **tastes and demands** of the external environment within which the organisation must operate.

Example

An article published by BBC news online magazine described changes which have taken place in the ageing population in the UK. The article recognised two types of pensioners: those who are in poor health or have a low income and those who are in good health or have a high income. Organisations are learning slowly that the aged population is a group of customers which is increasing day by day and which could even determine the future of the UK.

The UK company Saga has benefited tremendously from this demographic change: Saga arranges trips for elderly people who have a love of travelling and exploring new places and who were unable to visit those places in their youth. The organisation aims to provide facilities to these elderly customers which make them feel at home and more comfortable.

a) **Social factors affecting an organisation**

i. **Population growth:** population growth has an impact on the market share and the purchasing power of consumers. An increase in population is directly linked to an increase in demand for essential goods and services. If this growth is accompanied by a reduction in per capita income, then it leads to reduced demand for luxury goods and services.

ii. **Population profile and education levels:** the population profile relates to the education levels of the population. Organisations demanding highly-skilled workers are interested in environments in which such people are available. The unavailability of such an environment could affect an organisation's strategic decisions such as whether or not to outsource a particular function.

iii. **Age and health of the population:** the ratio of the working population to the dependants, such as the elderly and the young population, affects the organisation's strategy as it affects the demand for essential goods and luxury goods. If there is a large population of elderly people, then is there is a high demand for the goods required by these people, such as medicines. All these factors help the organisation in planning its strategic actions.

iv. **Disposable income levels:** high disposable income which is the result of low deductions from salaries means high purchasing power. High purchasing power results in an increase in the market volume. The disposable income levels of consumers affect an organisation's strategic decisions such as what to produce and the selling prices of its products.

v. **Social trends:** social trends in fashions, lifestyle and religion have a huge impact on an organisation's environment. These factors are directly related to strategic decisions such as what to produce and what prices to charge.

b) **Questions for assessment (questions that an organisation needs to ask itself):**

i. What socio-cultural factors are affecting the organisation?

ii. Will change in these factors have an impact on the organisation?

4. Technological

Technological factors take into account the **effect that technology has** on the way an organisation makes and delivers its goods and services. In addition to looking at present technology, organisations also need to look at upcoming technology and how it will affect the current way of business.

Example

Amazon.com Inc was one of the first companies which sold its products over the internet. This organisation became popular during the dot com bubble of the late 1990s. The organisation launched the model using advanced technology immediately after the bubble burst, but it earned its first profit only in the year 2003.

The organisation initially sold books online. Later on, with the development of technology, it expanded its scope of business. It started selling electronics, MP3s, DVD's, CDs, computer software etc. online.

Every organisation needs to continually assess these influences to see if they are changing the external environment within which it operates. If these forces are **significant in changing the external environment**, then the organisation may have to **significantly change the way** it does business.

a) **Technical factors affecting an organisation**

i. **Rate of change and new developments in technology:** the rate at which technology is changing is really amazing. Every year, manufacturers of electronic goods and automobiles introduce new models with added features using new technology or even completely new products. Organisations have to keep up with the new market trends and form their strategies keeping in mind that their existing products might become obsolete. Toyota's invention of the hybrid car in response to strategic risk is an example of an organisation changing its strategy because of its external environment.

ii. **Patents granted**: an organisation which introduces new technology to the market, takes out a patent on the technology. This means that if another organisation wants to use the same technology then it has to either invent the technology itself or pay a large amount to the patent holder as copyright fees.

iii. **Diffusion of technology:** as technology spreads throughout the market, organisations are forced to update their products in order to prevent them from becoming obsolete. Organisations survive due to the profit on the sale of their products and if an organisation's products become obsolete this could signal the end of the organisation. Therefore organisations have to modify their strategies according to the market conditions.

b) **Questions for assessment (questions that an organisation needs to ask itself):**

i. How is technology changing?
ii. Has the technology we are using become obsolete?
iii. How have changes in technology affected market conditions and marketplaces?

5. Environmental

Consumers are becoming increasingly concerned with the protection of the environment in which they live. This is, in part as a result of the tremendous surge in media attention directed to such issues as: climate change, carbon emission, waste disposal and recycling, they desire that their environment should be prevented from all harmful effects so that it does not deteriorate over time. In the present era, along with the consumers, the government is also becoming much more concerned about the environment. This has resulted in the introduction of large amounts of legislation designed to protect the environment and encourage its conservation.

Example

Railways are one of the most environmentally-friendly modes of transport because the rate at which harmful gases are emitted is comparatively less than other modes of transport. In addition, the resources used by railways are generally renewable in nature.

Network Rail is involved in protecting the largest number of sites of Special Scientific Interest (SSSIs) near railway tracks in the UK.

Protection of the environment is essential because it is a source of resources needed for the production of goods. Harmony between man and the environment is the essence of healthy life and growth. To the organisation its also a source of competitive advantage, e.g., the environmentally friendly organisation may find it easier to win and retain customers, to recruit staff and to encourage investment (ethical investors).

a) **Environmental factors affecting an organisation**

i. **Trends:** what are the environmental standards in the area? How is waste disposed of? All these trends are important. If there are no specific laws governing environmental issues such as waste disposal, an organisation should follow the practices prevalent in the industry.

ii. **Penalties for abuse:** there are huge penalties for non-adherence to environmental laws.

iii. **Competitive advantage:** companies which adopt environmentally-friendly practices such as planting trees or adopting special measures to reduce pollution, have a competitive advantage.

b) **Questions for assessment (questions that an organisation needs to ask itself)**

i. What are the current rules and regulations affecting the organisation?

ii. What are the environmental standards published by the government?

iii. Is the organisation complying with these rules?

iv. Are there any alternatives for carrying out the organisation's activities?

6. Legal

Legal factors represent the **legislative framework** within which the organisation must operate. They represent the "laws of the land" that the organisation must follow. Organisations have to follow the law framed by the legislatives and always operate within the boundaries of the legal framework.

There are various laws which affect **all organisations** such as company law, environment law, employment law, tax law, competition law, law relating to health and safety etc.

Example

Examples include employment laws such as fair hiring practices, health and safety standards for work, and minimum quality standards for products. For instance, in the UK, the advertising standards agency has ruled that no advertisements for "junk foods" will be allowed during the hours in which children's programmes are broadcast. This effectively means that products such as Pepsi and Coke cannot show their advertisements during these times.

a) **Legal factors affecting an organisation**

i. **Employment law:** organisations have to follow laws on employment such as those related to equal opportunity. Some companies which are engaged in the production of arms, aeroplanes or other products related to national security have to follow special rules prescribed by the government.

ii. **Business, health and safety law, company law**

iii. **Marketing laws:** organisations have to follow the marketing laws which have been formed to protect the customers. Organisations should not advertise or give misrepresentations to the public in order to sell their products. Such misrepresentation is punishable under the law.

iv. **Monopolies / restraint of law:** in a monopoly, one company or a small number of companies with similar interests has sole control of the market. This situation is harmful to society. Therefore the government forms laws to prevent organisations from forming monopolies.

v. **National versus international laws:** every organisation has to follow both national and international laws. The European Community has its own laws formed for the social and economic benefit of the members of the EC. In most cases, international laws take precedence over national laws if these laws contradict each other. Organisations have to follow both laws while forming their strategies.

b) **Assessment questions: (questions that an organisation needs to ask itself)**

i. What expected or possible changes might there be in laws and regulations?

ii. What impact could such changes have on the organisation?

1.3 Overall assessment (questions that an organisation needs to ask itself)

What are the environmental factors affecting the organisation?

The PESTEL framework poses this question to organisations as part of their overall assessment. Each organisation works in a different environment. The way an organisation interacts with its environment also varies. Every organisation has to conduct an assessment of its environment, including the factors that affect or can affect the organisation.

Another question that PESTEL asks is: which of these factors are the most important at the present time and which will be the most important over the next few years?

Each organisation demands its strategy makers to anticipate future problems and act upon them in advance so that they will not take place. This process of forecasting can be carried out with the help of the factors outlined in the PESTEL framework

SUMMARY

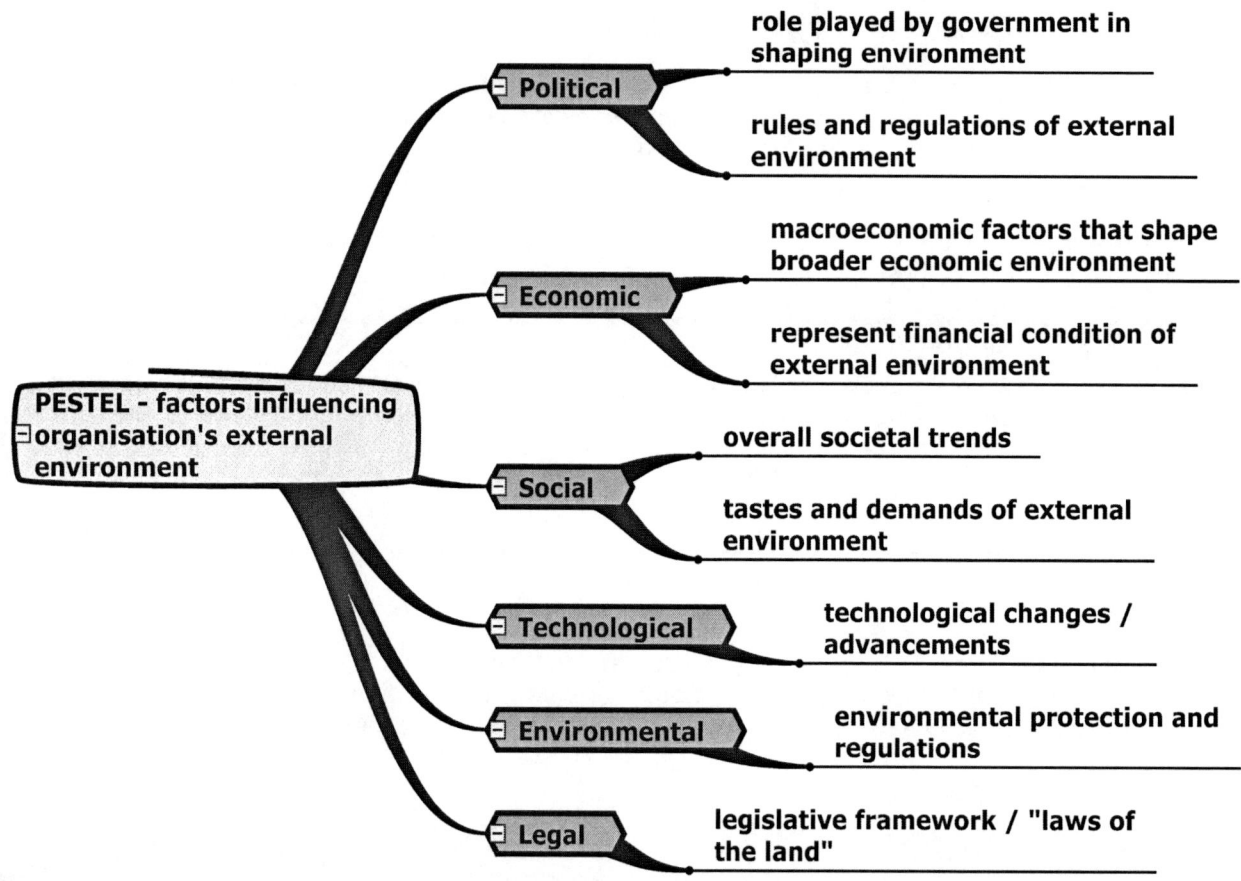

All these factors are just the starting point and will reveal the prospective impacts and changes that might affect in an organisation. It is important to analyse the **impact of all these factors on the organisation**. Planners must also assess how these factors will affect their organisation and the way in which business is currently operated. What must be identified here are the **key drivers of change** i.e. the factors that may change the structure of the organisation and its industry.

For instance, only listing those interest rates which may rise is not sufficient as an economic factor. What also has to be considered is the impact these higher interest rates will have on the organisation. Rising interest rates will mean that it will become more expensive for the organisation to raise capital. This could result in any planned expansions or purchases having to be reconsidered.

In addition, if this results in an extra cost for its suppliers, the cost of the raw materials the organisation purchases may also increase.

Diagram 1: External environmental forces.

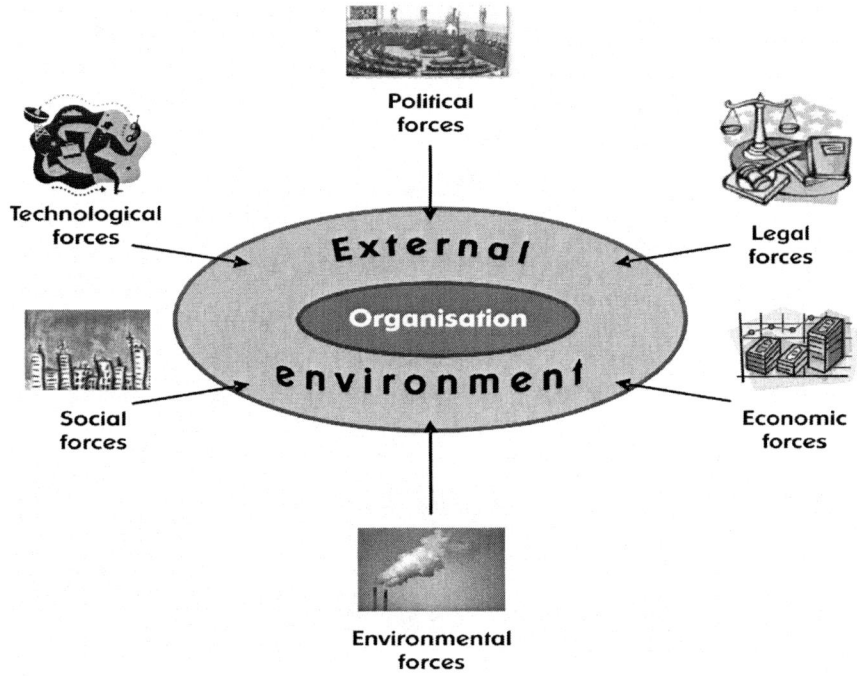

Example

PESTEL analysis for an IT company in India

Micro tech is an Indian software solutions company. The organisation writes customised software programs for large corporate and multinational firms based abroad (predominantly in Europe and the U.S.A). Although Micro tech delivers quality products; their main selling point is their cost advantage. Micro tech bills clients at the rate of $20 per hour whereas their western competitors charge an average of $100 per hour.

PESTEL analysis for the IT industry in India

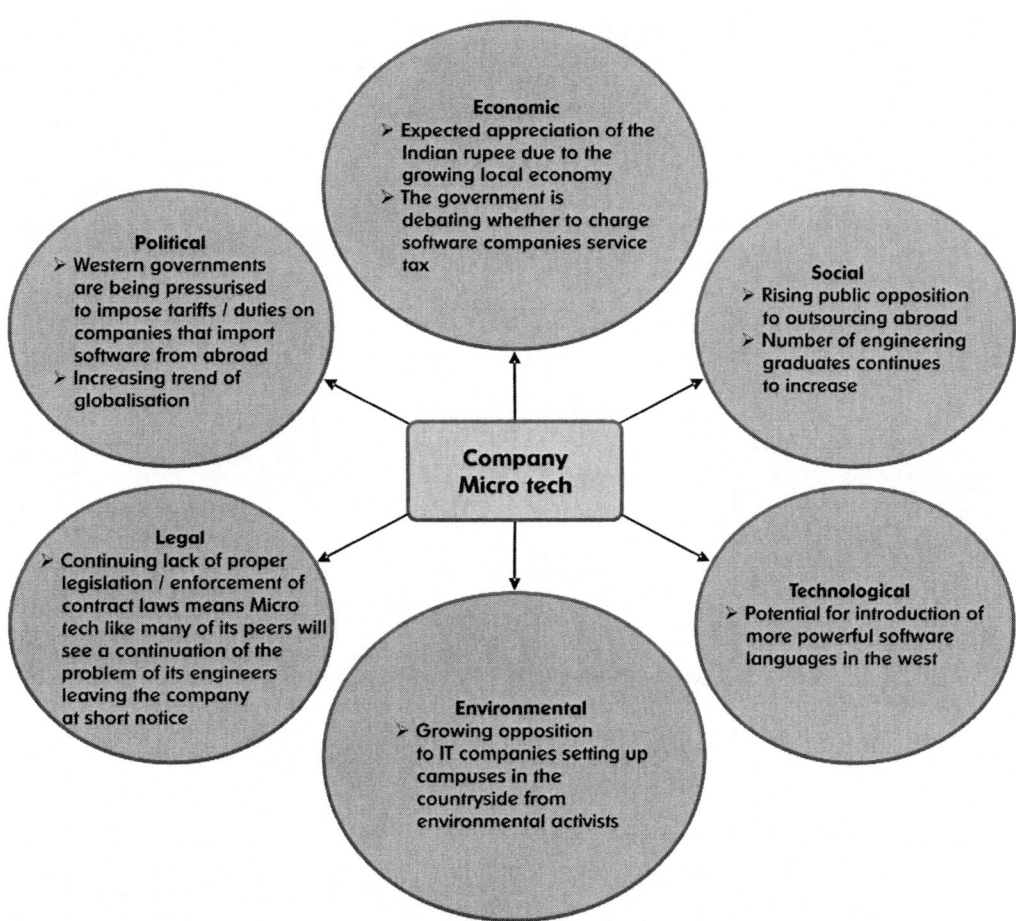

28: Strategic Position

Test Yourself 1

Excellence Ltd is a publishing house which develops and publishes books for international qualifications. Excellence carries out the whole work related to writing and printing in one country and sells its books worldwide. The price for the books is quoted in dollars. The input required for Excellence is authors and stationery items. Excellence can hire the authors from within the country itself. The company is new and there are large, established publications worldwide for the same qualifications.

The economy of the country in which Excellence operates is expanding fast. In addition, the domestic currency is strengthening. However, in order to control inflation, the central bank of the country has increased the rates of interest. The government of the country is involved in the international trade agreement and aims to establish free trade. The population of the country is predominantly young adults and the education level of the country is high.

Excellence has also planned an innovative product i.e. providing an e-learning facility to students. Management is keen to produce quality material and therefore has implemented six-sigma techniques to improve quality.

Required:

Assess the external macro-environment and its impact on organisational strategy of Excellence Ltd using PESTEL analysis.

---

2. Highlight the key drivers of change likely to affect the structure of a sector or market. [3]
[Learning Outcome b]

2.1 What is a sector?

A sector is a group of organisations which produce the **same** products or services e.g. all the organisations producing cloth material constitute the textile sector.

2.2 What is a market?

A market is a social arrangement where buyers and sellers can obtain information about each other's needs and offerings and then carry out a voluntary exchange of goods or services. It is a group of various organisations which have different characteristics and compete **on different bases such as quality, price.**

Example

Simon purchased a new house in April. He wanted to design his home and wanted it to include every luxury such as a television, refrigerator, washing machine, furniture etc. The market where he can find all these things is known as the consumer durables market.

Simon decides to invest his spare cash in the shares of listed companies. The place where he can purchase shares is called a stock market.

2.3 drivers of change

Key drivers of change are those forces which affect the structure of a sector, industry or market.

Example

All supermarkets now have organic sections, where people can buy goods which have been grown without preservatives, additives and in more natural conditions. This has come about because customers have demanded it – therefore the customers are the drivers of change. Often, however, one group does not cause the change – the drivers of change could be many groups working together or independently.

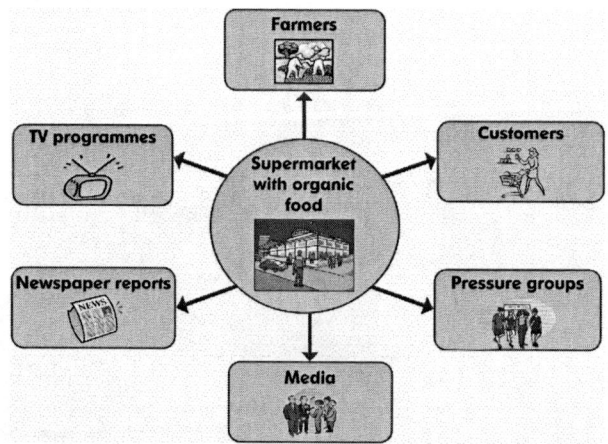

In the present era, globalisation is increasing day by day. The key drivers which result in increasing globalisation are as follows:

Diagram 2: Key drivers of change

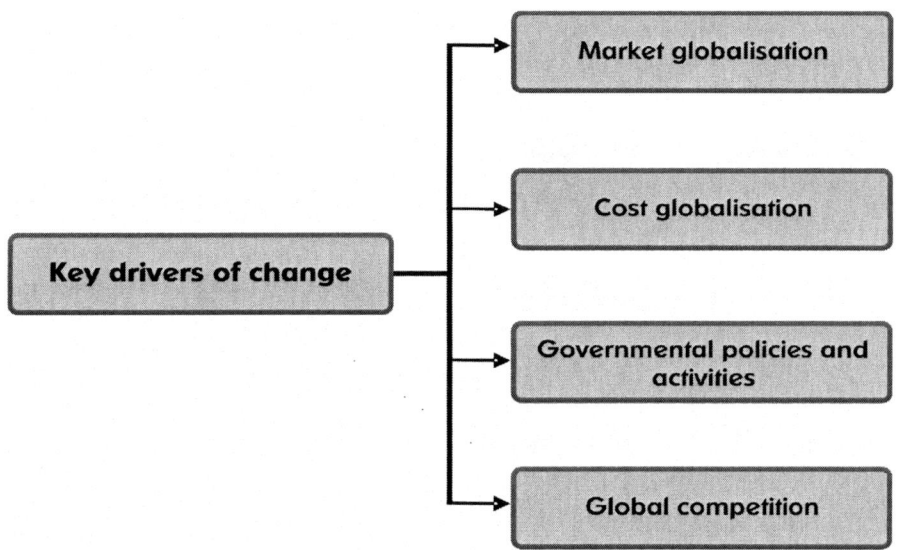

1. **Market globalisation**

Market globalisation is taking place for the following reasons:

a) Customer needs and tastes are becoming similar in many markets; in particular developing nations such as India, China, Nigeria and Brazil are aspiring to western style consumption practices.

b) When some of the markets globalise, those who operate in such global markets become global customers and in return they are in search of global suppliers.

c) The increase in operations through global communication and distribution channels has led to the emergence of global markets.

Example

Many organisations have started to sell their products over the internet. The customers can place their orders on the organisation's websites, pay money online using credit cards and even obtain the product without actually meeting the supplier personally, as in the case of Amazon.

d) The possibilities for transference of marketing lead to the emergence of global brands. Here, transference of marketing means the transfer of marketing techniques from one nation to other nations which results in the product being globally recognised.

e) The development of global advertisements, marketing policies and brand names gives rise to global demands and expectations from customers.

f) Improvements in marketing cost advantages via economies of scale can accrue for global operators.

2. **Cost globalisation**

a) Cost advantages are enjoyed by organisations which operate on a large scale and those which have standardisation of production.

b) Cost advantages are enjoyed by organisations which have experience in large scale operations (economies of scale).

c) Costs can be reduced if requisitions are obtained from the lowest-cost suppliers across the world, also known as central sourcing efficiencies.

d) Country-specific costs lead to a reduction in cost.

e) Product development costs are high when businesses operate fewer products globally.

30: Strategic Position

3. Governmental policies and activities

a) Government is formulating such trade policies which encourage free trade between nations.

b) Technical standardisation between countries have encouraged globalisation (technical standardisation means the standards of production or rendering services are common or same among the two countries which lead to increase in trade).

c) Host governments encourage global operators to base themselves in their countries.

Tip
In many countries, country-specific rules exist which state the extent of entering into global strategies. For example, Hong Kong and the UK entered into a taxation agreement in which shipowners in either country are required to pay tax on their income in either of the two countries only.

4. Global competition

a) When the trade between different nations are high in a free trade market, the level of competition in a global market is increased.
b) When a business operates globally, customers also operate on a global scale and, as a result, competitors are encouraged to operate globally.
c) The interdependence of an organisation's operations leads to the globalisation of its competitors.

All the four key drivers of change will be distinct for different industries and sectors. The effect of these drivers will also vary across industries and sectors.

To remember these four key drivers of change, memorise the following:

Tip
Market is **C**ostly, **G**o and **G**et it now.

Test Yourself 2
There is a growing level of economic interdependence between different countries across the world. The volume and types of cross border transactions are increasing. There is a greater flow of capital and technology across the world.

We frequently hear about the effects of 'globalisation'.

Required:

When does market globalisation take place? Explain with the help of an example.

---

3. Explore, using Porter's Diamond, the influence of national competitiveness on the strategic position of an organisation.[2]
[Learning Outcome c]

3.1 What is meant by strategic position?

There are three elements of strategic management:
➤ strategic position
➤ strategic choices
➤ strategic action

To remember these three elements, remember this:

Tip
It is a **P**rivate **C**ar parking **A**rea.

1. Strategic position

> **Definition**
>
> Johnson, Scholes and Whittington define **strategic position** as follows: "It is concerned with the impact on strategy of the external environment, an organisation's strategic capability (resources and competences) and the expectations and influence of stakeholders."
>
> (Source: JSW)

Strategic position is explained in depth in Study Guide A1.

2. National competitiveness

> **Definition**
>
> The National Competitiveness Council defines **national competitiveness** as the ability to achieve success in markets leading to better standards of living for all.
>
> (Source: http://www.forfas.ie/ncc/reports)

3.2 Traditional theorists' view of competitiveness

Traditional economic theory believes that the following factors enable a country to achieve a sustainable competitive advantage over other nations:

- land
- location
- natural resources
- labour
- local population size

Therefore, according to classical theorists, the competitive advantage depends upon the abovementioned five factors. Michael Porter, however, strongly disagrees with this view.

In his book, 'The competitive advantage of nations', published in 1990, he argues that there are very few cases of countries where sustained economic growth has come about because of these factors. He is of the opinion that factors of production such as labour, arable land (land that can be cultivated for growing crops), natural resources, capital and infrastructure are nothing more than the inputs to compete in any industry. These are clearly important but less vital to success than before.

3.3 Overview of Porter's Diamond

- Michael Porter is a famous Harvard business professor. He made a detailed study of ten nations to learn what leads to success.
- He believes that standard traditional theories on competitive advantage are insufficient or even wrong.
- According to Porter, a nation attains a competitive advantage only when its firms are competitive. He further believes that firms become competitive through innovation. Innovation means modernisation and it includes technical improvements to the product or to the production process.

SUMMARY

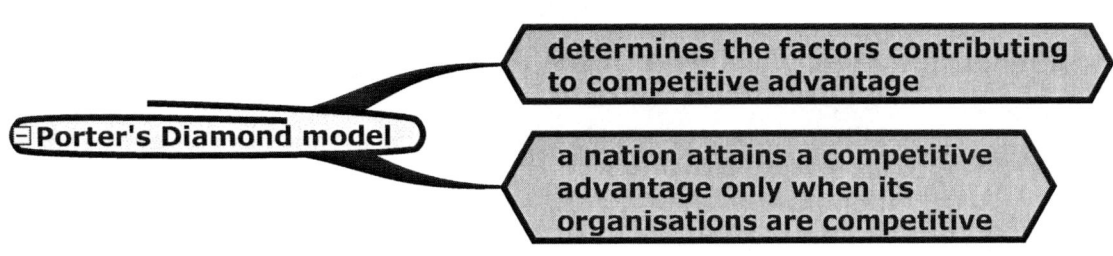

3.4 Porter's Diamond

Porter argues that a country achieves a sustainable competitive advantage when its companies / industries achieve a sustainable competitive advantage on a global scale. There are **four factors** which constitute Porter's Diamond. These factors suggest that there are inherent reasons why some nations are more competitive than others and why some industries within nations are more competitive than others.
These factors are as follows:

- firm strategy, structure and rivalry
- demand conditions
- related and supporting industries
- factor conditions

Diagram 3: Porter's Diamond

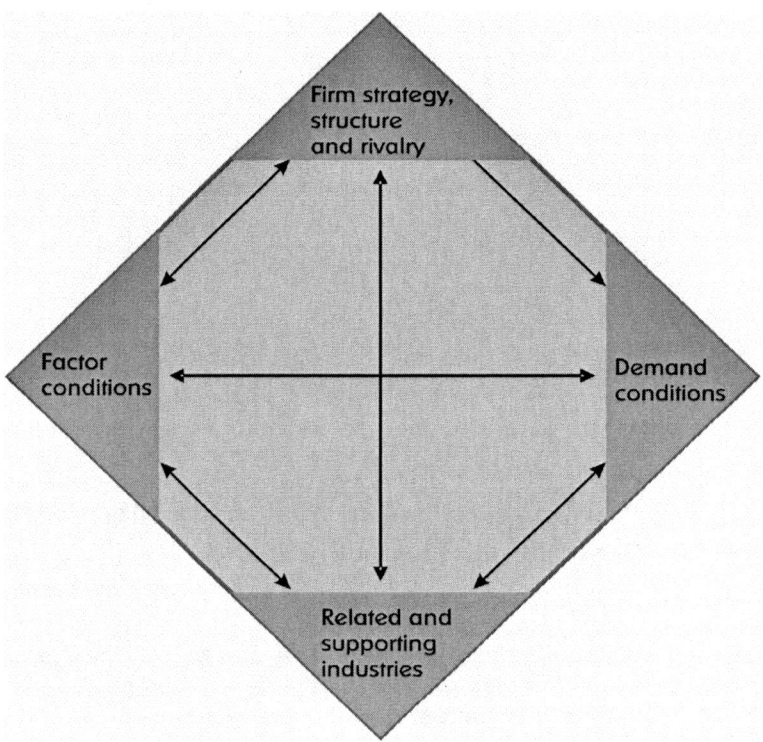

To remember these four factors, memorise this:

> **Tip**
>
> **P**eter, **F**irst **D**o **R**eading **F**ast.

1. **Firm strategy, structure and rivalry** (i.e. conditions for organisations and the nature of domestic rivalry)

The first factor refers to the **local competitive structure** for a country's industries. Companies that can operate and survive in a highly competitive local environment can be prepared to compete in the global environment. These companies are forced to become, efficient and innovative in order to succeed in a global environment. This factor refers to how the firms manage to cope with the competition.

> **Example**
>
> An example often cited is that of Japanese electronics companies such as Sony. Sony has managed to excel not only in the small and ultra-competitive Japanese market but also worldwide because of its ability to develop pioneering and technologically advanced products (e.g. the Sony Walkman) over the years. There are many other Japanese electronics companies such as Mitshubishi, Sharp, Murata and Nippondenso which means Sony has to be efficient in its operations and innovative in terms of new product development. Sony pioneered the production of electronic products in the country and gained national competitiveness.

Domestic rivalry and the search for competitive advantages within a nation can help provide organisations with bases for achieving such an advantage on a more global scale.

2. **Demand conditions** (i.e. sophisticated customers in home market)

Demand conditions refer to the **sophistication of local consumers**. The more demanding and discerning a country's customers, the more demanding they will be on suppliers of their local goods and services. When the customers within the country are more demanding and sophisticated, then organisations will be forced to ensure their products are of high quality and differentiated from the competition. Moreover, when the nation's discerning values spread to other countries, it becomes easier for the local firms to compete in the global market. In other words, when the culture or the habits of one country are adopted by other countries, it becomes easier to sell the products into that nation.

Example

Japanese are very fussy about their electronics – they want the latest, the smallest, and the most advanced products. So they ensure that electronic companies consistently innovate to give them what they need.

3. **Related and supporting industries**

The term **"related and supporting industries"** refers to the existence of organisations that serve similar industries and can collaborate. This usually means they are part of the industry supply chain. This increases the possibility of an **ongoing exchange of ideas**. If there is success in one industry, it is advantageous for the success of the other industry. In the case of related industries, an organisation would prefer home suppliers rather than foreign suppliers because home suppliers can provide co-operation and timely availability of resources. These organisations help each other and the industry as a whole can grow. When industries are related, the firms can co-operate with each other and hence attain a competitive advantage.

The supporting industries are not the same as the related industries. The former includes the suppliers and the latter includes the strategic alliances.

Example

Japan has achieved remarkable growth in the low cost consumer electronics industry with the help of related and supporting industries. Government of Japan has simplified the procedures for obtaining approvals for business purposes. The human resources such as skilled electrical engineers also play an important role in it. The industry structures and supporting institutions promote continuous and long-term technical and process improvements.

4. **Factor conditions** (i.e. the nation's position in factors of production, such as skilled labour and infrastructure)

Factor conditions are production for inputs such as:

a) human resources such as skilled labour
b) money market (Bond market, repo market) / capital market (debt market, equity market)
c) physical resources such as availability of good quality raw materials
d) intellectual resources such as computer
e) infrastructural resources such as transport system

These factor conditions help in forming the basis of advantage on a national level. It is not sufficient for a nation to have an enormous amount of resources; instead it is essential to **deploy these available resources to the optimum level**. Where there is an abundance of resources, it leads to their wastage whereas if there is a scarcity of resources, it may lead to innovation. Nations which do not have the required resources make efforts to innovate and create those resources. The key requirement is for the nation's resources to be deployed to offer their maximum advantage.

Example

Companies in Japan appoint highly qualified and technically trained managers. Past studies indicate that approximately 75% of the CEOs in Japanese manufacturing firms are professional engineers. Moreover, Japanese firms take advantage of their existing infrastructural facilities, skilled labour force and advanced production technologies to achieve a low cost of production, higher quality products and availability of the products in short periods of time.

Porter distinguishes between general and specialised factor conditions. **General factor conditions** are the conditions that can be **easily replicated** across nations. Examples include unskilled labour and raw materials.

Examples of **specialised factor conditions** are skilled labour and good infrastructure. **These cannot be easily replicated** across nations (at least not without heavy investment). Specialised factors involve heavy, sustained investment. They are more difficult to replicate. This leads to a **competitive advantage** because if other firms cannot easily replicate these factors, they become valuable.

Example

The number and the quality of Japanese engineers are the factor conditions that have helped its electronics industry earn a reputation for technological excellence.

Test Yourself 3

Given below is the scenario of a software industry of country Z.

The industry has shown a rapid growth in past 15 years and most of the companies have been established recently. There is a cut-throat competition prevailing in the industry. The domestic market for software is small but demanding. The country has a pool of well educated and trained engineers. The customers have high expectations about the quality of software solutions provided by the software companies. The other industries such as hardware and ITES are competitive and have performed well in recent years. The structure of the software companies is flat and decision making is fast.

Required:

Explain whether country Z has achieved national competitive advantage in software industry and if yes how.

---

4. Prepare scenarios reflecting different assumptions about the future environment of an organisation.[3]

[Learning Outcome d]

4.1 What is meant by a scenario?

A scenario is an **account or synopsis of a projected course of action, event or situation**. It is a **detailed view regarding the business environment** of an organisation and how that organisation will develop in the future based on all the key environmental influences and drivers of change about which there is a high level of uncertainty. Scenarios are widely used by organisations to help in understanding the different ways that future events could unfold and how these might impact on the firm's position and profitability.

Scenario planning or scenario thinking is a complex business process related to futures studies. Scenario development is used in policy planning, product pricing and marketing strategy, organisational development and, generally, when organisations wish to test strategies against uncertain future developments.

Understanding past change is helpful in anticipating future change. Scenario building is a powerful tool for the process of decision making which brings together participants from all levels. By motivating creative ways of thinking, scenarios help everyone from local farmers to national policy makers in making decisions based on various possible futures.

1. Forecasting

One of the methods that organisations use to prepare for the future environment is **forecasting**. Supporters of forecasting state that it improves organisational effectiveness. Forecasting differs entirely from planning.
Planning is when an organisation develops its future strategies whereas forecasting estimates the results the organisation can hope to achieve by following these strategies.

Forecasting is not feasible for long periods of time, for example 15 years. However, forecasting would be feasible for a period of around 5 years. Forecasting depends upon the level of uncertainty involved in a particular industry. Each scenario is different from the other and so when different scenarios are shared or discussed among the managers, it helps them to learn new ideas or form opinions from the other planned scenarios.

2. Levels of forecasting

There are three main levels of forecasting:
- economic forecasting
- environmental forecasting
- market and product forecasting

a) The first level is economic forecasting

In economic forecasting, planners try to forecast what the **condition of the economy as a whole** will be in the future. Factors such as the GDP, inflation, interest rates, exchange rates and the unemployment rate will be estimated along with other macroeconomic indicators. This forecast will provide a picture of the economic health of the environment in which the organisation operates.

b) The second level is an environmental forecast

This would involve examining factors covered in a **PESTEL** (political, economic, social, technological, environmental and legal) analysis. The forecast of several of these factors will depend upon the outcome of the economic forecast (e.g. political involvement from the government is much more likely in the case of a recession).

c) The third level consists of market and product forecasts

Market forecasting will involve **predicting how the overall market for a product will grow**. Product forecasting involves predicting how well the product itself will sell. Again, results from the previous two levels of forecasts will influence the predictions made under this level.

SUMMARY

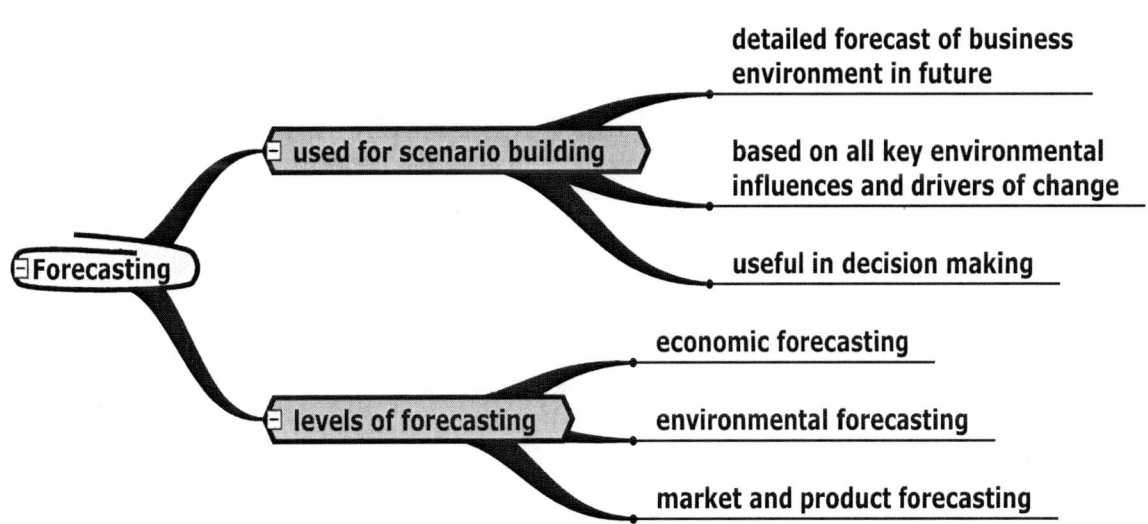

3. Methods of forecasting

Forecasting methods can be divided into two main groups:
- subjective methods such as surveys and opinion polls
- objective methods based on various statistical methodologies

1. Subjective methods

The **subjective approach** allows **individuals to participate** in the forecasting decision to arrive at a forecast based on their **feelings, ideas, and personal experiences**. Many organisations in the United States have started using the subjective approach. When subjective methods are internally used, they sometimes take the form of "**brainstorming sessions**", in which managers, executives, and employees work together to develop new ideas or to solve complex problems.

The subjective approach may also be in the form of a **survey of the organisation's salespeople**. This approach, which is known as the sales force composite or grass roots method, is relied on because, generally, salespeople interact directly with purchasers and they have a good vision of which products will or will not sell and the quantity of sales for the various products.

It is advantageous to use the salespeople's forecasts because it is presumed that the salespeople are the most qualified to explain the demand for products, especially in their own territories.

There is also a disadvantage in that the salespeople tend to be optimistic in their estimates if they believe that a low estimate might lead to them losing their jobs. However, it is also true that one should not rely blindly on the opinions of salespeople to the exclusion of all others because they may not be aware of future changes in other areas, such as the availability of raw materials, the entrance of a competitor into the market in the near future or national economic developments.

2. Objective methods

Objective methods are much more **scientific in nature** and are more widely used by organisations. Three very commonly used objective methods are:

- exponential smoothing
- correlation
- multiple regression and factor analysis

i. With exponential smoothing past data is "weighted". The rationale to this method is that **the more recent the data, the more valid it is**.

Example
If a company uses its last 5 years' sales data to forecast sales for the 6th year, not all the years' data would be given an equal weighting. Data from year 4 would be given a greater weighting than data from year 5, and so forth.

ii. Correlation is a statistical technique for evaluating the **relationship between two independent sets of data**. The first set of data is often called the dependent variable and is the forecasted item. The second set of data is the independent variable and is used to explain the movement of the first.

Example
Taking two variables into consideration, unemployment and inflation, many economists believe that a fall in the unemployment rate will lead to a rise in the inflation level.

iii. Multiple regressions is similar to correlation but involves the **use of more than one independent variable**.

Example
Demand for real estate will depend upon several factors such as the state of the economy, the level of interest rates, etc. Multiple regression attempts to measure the effect each of these will have on the demand for real estate.

SUMMARY

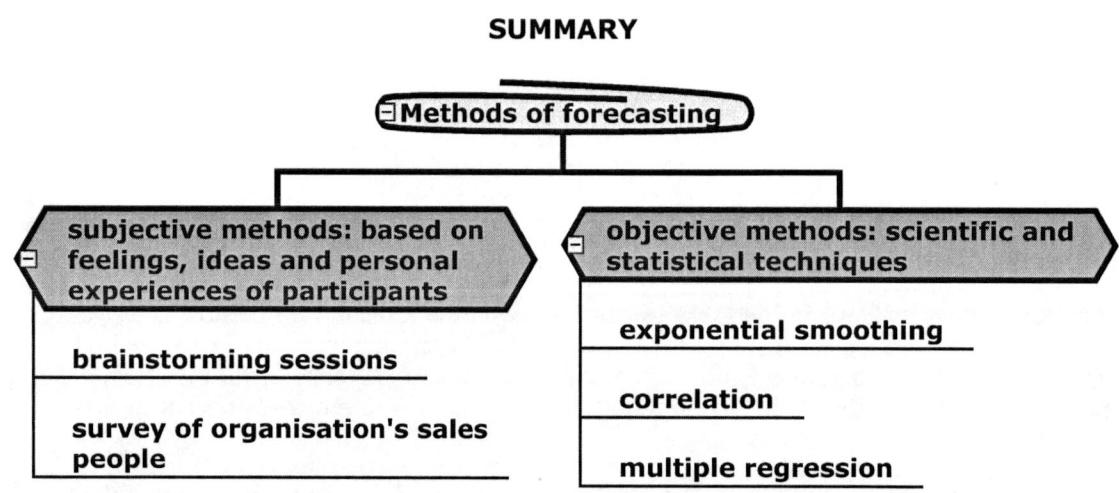

4. Scenario planning

Another subjective forecasting technique is scenario planning. The basic methodology here is that a group of analysts generate different scenarios or situations for the planners of an organisation.

These scenarios will be set in the future and include known and forecasted factors.

Example

Examples of known factors are demographics, presence of competitors, product mix etc. These factors are kept constant and played out against a number of possible social, economic, technical and political trends.

The main objective here is to provide planners with scenarios that are both likely and that will put a strain on the organisation (e.g. technological advances that will force the organisation to change the way it operates, unfavourable government regulations).

Corporate strategies can then be evaluated in terms of how well they prepare the organisation for these possible events. Scenario planning becomes a tool that managers / planners can use to identify upcoming potential risks as well as how to prepare for them.

5. Types of scenario building

There are two types of scenario building:

a) **Macro scenario**: while building this type of scenario, all possible environmental factors are taken into consideration.

b) **Industry scenario**: here, individual industry conditions are taken into consideration in more detail.

SUMMARY

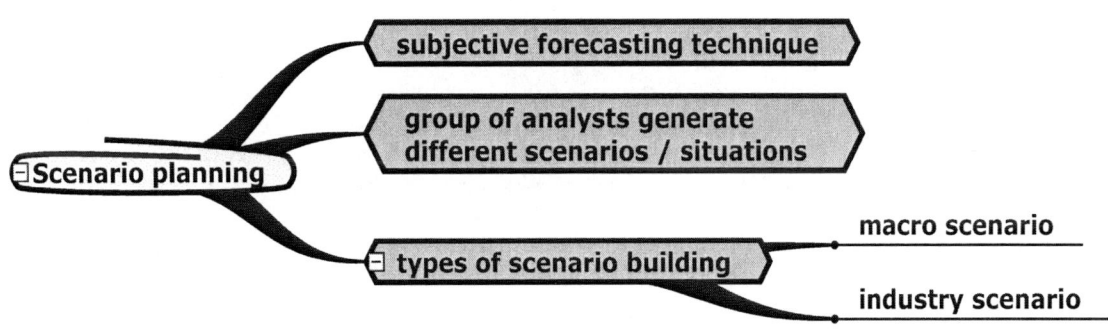

Test Yourself 4

Perfect Sports Ltd, a leader in designing and developing high performance running footwear, apparel and accessories, is planning to sell specialised sports gear targeted towards professional sportsmen, in addition to general sports goods. The company has worldwide sales offices in more than ten countries. The company is relying on its regional sales force to forecast incremental sales from its specialised sports gear.

Required:

Briefly discuss the objective methods that the regional sales team can use to forecast incremental sales from the new product line.

---

5. Evaluate methods of business forecasting used when quantitatively assessing the likely outcome of different business strategies.

[Learning Outcome e]

Business strategies are usually formulated and implemented over a long period of time. The strategic choices to be made by an organisation will be affected by many variables, both economic and non-economic. Firms would ultimately like to know the demand for the product or service they sell and the cost of resources that they need to deliver the product. The variables that may affect both can be categorised as follows:

Economic Factors:

a) Impact of business cycles over the life cycle of the product
b) Interest rates, deposit rates
c) Inflation rates for selling prices and input costs
d) Foreign currency rate fluctuations
e) Changes in the economic law
f) Availability of factors of production
g) Entry of competition

Non-Economic Factors

a) Changes in technology
b) Socio-cultural changes that may affect consumer behaviour
c) Political factors
d) Changes in the legal structure affecting the way the business could be run

As business strategies are formulated for implementation over a long period of time, the above factors would make the task of forecasting very complex. The objective of business forecasting is to come out with the likely outcomes of the plan variables like sales volume, prices, costs etc.

The forecasting techniques used by corporates should help achieve this objective and also should be robust enough to build the risk factors in the model so that the estimates are close to reality. Some important quantitative forecasting methods are discussed below.

Quantitative forecasting techniques

1. **Time series:** A time series is a series of data points i.e. figures or values recorded over time that indicate the trend of the data series, for example, monthly sales volume over the last five years or sales during a particular season over the last ten years etc.

   Time series analysis is one of the quantitative techniques of forecasting that attempt to understand the trend of the data collected at regular intervals over a period of time, in order to project the trend for the future period. Under this method the past data is collected to understand its behaviour and is projected into the future to estimate the variable under consideration. This method builds in different trends such as secular, cyclical, seasonal and irregular variations. Based on the trends revealed, the forecasts are prepared using moving averages.

   You may recall the discussion on this method in paper F5. The method is useful only for relatively shorter terms and only in situations where the business model does not change significantly. For new projects or business initiatives, this method is of little help. Furthermore, it assumes that the past trend is likely to reflect the future, which is not fully correct.

2. **The Survey Method:** The planners get market and other data from market research and tests carried out either by the internal staff or an outsourced agency. The company lists the variables to be captured for each of the data parameters and gets the survey done. The data so collected is then analysed and used to prepare forecasts. However, this method suffers from subjectivity and personal biases.

3. **Precursor method:** Some organisations use analogies or learning from their previous experiences for forecasting their new ventures. They carry an in depth analysis of the outcomes of their previous forecasts based on the locations covered.

4. **Regression method:** This method is useful when assessing the impact of more than two independent variables that affect business. It is flexible as one may decide to include or exclude one or more factors while performing the regression analysis. However, the relationship between the business and the variables may not always be linear. In such a case non-linear method of forecasting is used.

5. **Smoothing method:** If the time series analysis does not reveal any specific trend or shows up irregular variations, the smoothing method helps to decompose these variations and arrive at a smooth trend that can be used to develop a business forecast.

6. **Simulation method:** This method helps to assess the impact of variations in the factors affecting business. For example, one may simulate the quantity demanded using different price brackets, or one may choose to evaluate profitability under different assumptions of technological changes.

7. **Probabilistic models:** The concept of probability is helpful in evaluating the risks associated with forecasts. By attaching probability to the expected outcomes as the chance of occurrence, companies can find out the values of the most likely outcome. One can resort to the Monte Carlo simulation technique.

Forecasting cannot be free from errors. Regardless of which method of forecasting is adopted, it is necessary to assess the forecasting error by applying the statistical technique of measures of dispersion like standard deviation or coefficient of variation.

Modern day forecasting is done by using the power of computer spreadsheets with features of "what if" analysis built into them.

SUMMARY

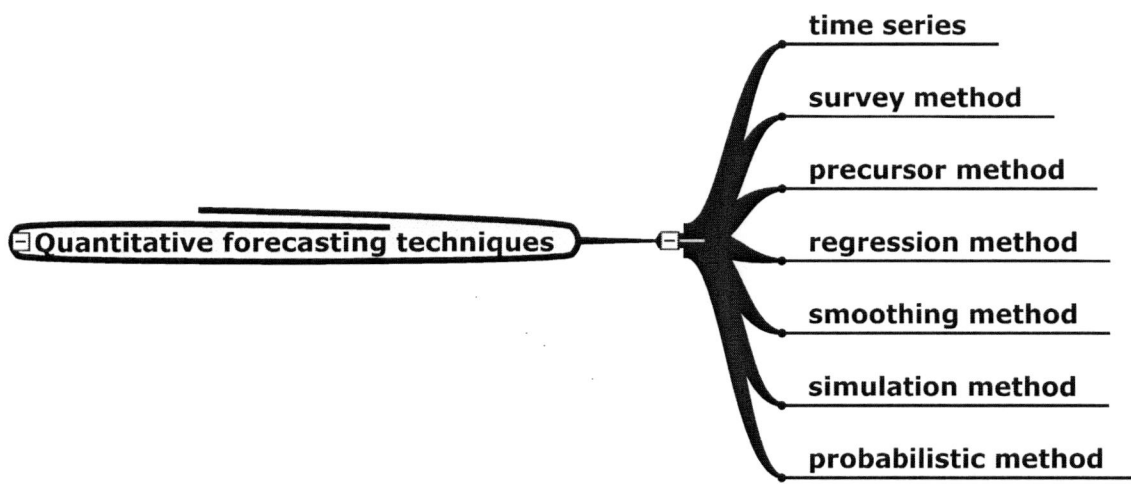

Answers to Test Yourself

Answer to TY 1

PESTEL stands for political, economic, social, technological, environmental and legal. These are the external factors which influence an organisation's decision-making and performance. The external macro-environment of an organisation is often unstable and unfriendly. PESTEL analysis is a tool that helps to identify and understand key external influences which will have an impact upon the organisation's strategy.

1. **Political**

Political factors are caused by the role that the government plays in shaping the environment within which the organisation operates. Since the government of the country in which Excellence operates is keen on free trade policies, there will be lower or no tariffs or duties on exports. This will help Excellence to reduce the price of its books in order to compete with established publications.

As the interest rates in the country have been increased, it will be expensive for Excellence to borrow money which may affect its strategy regarding the volume of production, or the decision to open new divisions etc.

2. **Economic**

Economic factors refer to the macroeconomic factors that will shape the broader economic environment within which the organisation operates. The strengthening of the domestic currency will affect the pricing strategy of Excellence. This is because the organisation is spending in domestic currency, i.e. a strong currency, but will receive revenue in dollars which will be lower in terms of domestic currency. This will ultimately affect the profitability of the company and could even take the company into losses.

3. **Social**

Social factors refer to the overall societal trends. Since the predominant age group in the country is young adults and the education level is high, Excellence can easily hire qualified authors from within the country itself at low rates. In addition, there will also be a large market for its publications within the country itself, which may not have been considered a lucrative market before.

4. Technological

Technological factors take into account the effect of technology on the way an organisation makes and delivers its goods and services. Changes in technology affect the demand for a product. Nowadays, e-learning is popular in the education field; therefore Excellence has decided to include this in its strategy.

In addition, it is aiming to produce a quality product and is therefore adopting six-sigma techniques. This will give Excellence a cost advantage and therefore a price advantage.

5. Environmental

Environmental factors refer to environmental protection and regulations. Excellence does not cause any direct harm to the environment but it uses paper which is made from wood. Assuming its social responsibility, Excellence can opt to use environmentally-friendly paper for printing its books.

6. Legal

Legal factors represent the legislative framework within which the organisation must operate. Excellence must take into consideration the effect of a range of legislation on its strategy. Since Excellence is involved in the writing and publishing business, effective enforcement of the Copyright Act is essential. The organisation has to comply with all applicable legal regulations to ensure the smooth functioning of operations.

Answer to TY 2

1. Market globalisation takes place for the following reasons:

a) Customer needs and tastes are becoming similar in some of the markets.

b) When some of the markets globalise, those who operate in such global markets become global customers and, in return, they are in search of global suppliers.

c) The increase in operations through global communication and distribution channels has led to the emergence of global markets.

d) The possibilities of transference of marketing leads to the emergence of global brands.

e) The development of global advertisements, marketing policies and brand names gives rise to global demands and expectations from customers.

f) Improvement in marketing cost advantages for global operators.

2. Example: In recent years, Mc-Donalds outlets have opened in many countries. As a result, the fast food habits of the customers have become homogeneous. This has resulted in market globalisation.

Answer to TY 3

To analyse whether country Z has achieved national competitive advantage, one has to apply Porter's diamond model. Porter's diamond model relates to why some nations have competitive advantage over other nations in particular industries. It helps in understanding competitive position of a nation on global scale with the help of four factors. These factors in relation to country Z's software industry can be explained as follows:

1. Firm strategy, structure and rivalry

The high local rivalry in country Z's software industry impels firms to be more productive and innovative. The flat organisational structure helps software companies to be quick and outwit the competition.

2. Demand conditions

The domestic market of country Z's software industry is very demanding. The demanding and sophisticated local market puts pressure on software companies to improve constantly and deliver high quality software solutions.

3. Related and supporting industries

The related and supporting industries of software industry are competitive and successful. This facilitates exchange of ideas and information and availability of cost effective and innovative inputs for country Z's software industry.

4. Factor conditions

Country Z has crated its own important factor conditions such as skilled resources and technology base. The software industry possesses specialised factor conditions in the form of skilled labour.

These factors suggest that country Z has achieved national competitive advantage in software industry. These four factors lead to national competitive advantage for country Z.

Answer to TY 4

Perfect Sports Ltd has decided to enter into a new product line which focuses on high-performance products targeted towards professional sportsmen. The forecasting process should be aligned to support the strategic direction of the company.

The company should establish an independent forecasting group, reporting directly to the management and co-ordinating input from various departments such as sales, marketing, product development and production.

Based on past data and statistics, the regional sales team can forecast sales for the new product line using the following objective methods:

1. Correlation

The sales team can forecast sales for the new product line by establishing a relationship between sales of newly introduced products in the past with the market share that the product currently demands. This will help the team to assess the growth rate of the product since its introduction, which can give a fair estimation of market response.

2. Multiple Regressions

This method uses several variables to predict the sales forecast. The sales team may use variables such as the level of interest, production capacity, state of economy, etc., to make a more accurate forecast of sales from the new product line.

3. Exponential smoothing

This method is more suitable for predicting the future sales of established product lines. However, the sales team can analyse competitors' past data for the new product line. By applying adequate weights to each year that is considered for forecasting, the sales forecast for a new product line can be predicted.

Quick Quiz

1. One of the elements of PESTEL analysis is 'ethics'. Is this statement correct? If it is, then explain the statement. If not, then what do the two 'e's stand for?
2. Which model helps in analysing the influence of national competitiveness on the strategic position of an organisation?
3. State the levels of forecasting in scenario building.
4. What are the different levels of forecasting?

Answers to Quick Quiz

1. No. The two 'e's stand for 'economic' and 'environment'.
2. The Porter's Diamond model helps in analysing the influence of national competitiveness on the strategic position of an organisation.
3. Three main levels of forecasting are:
   A. economic forecasting
   B. environmental forecasting
   C. market and product forecasting
4. There are three main levels of forecasting:
   A. economic forecasting
   B. environmental forecasting
   C. market and product forecasting

Self Examination Questions

Question 1

Nikoles Furniture Co is a major producer of furniture within the UK. Nikoles Furniture is a subsidiary of Dick Furniture Inc - a global, vertically integrated furniture manufacturing and retailing company, based within the USA but with interests all over the world.

Nikoles Furniture has a reputation as a producer of high quality furniture, but at competitive prices. It has also maintained a good relationship with many furniture distributors throughout the UK, particularly the main retailers group. Nikoles Furniture decided for on-site development. Nikoles Furniture caters to the two major market segments - the commercial (offices and industries) market and the household market. In the household market, it offers a wide range of products from luxury furniture down to cheaper products.

Nikoles Furniture's total annual turnover is currently £90 million of which commercial furniture contributes up to 30%. During the late 19X0s the turnover of the company was growing at 9% per annum, but since 20X4 sales have dropped by 6% per annum, in real terms.

Dick Furniture is worried about the recent decline in furniture sales. It has recognised that the increasing concentration within the European furniture manufacturing sector has led to aggressive competition within a low growth industry. It does not consider the overseas sales growth of Nikoles Furniture to be an attractive proposition, as this would mean that Nikoles Furniture would be competing with other Dick Furniture companies. It is concerned about the trade barriers in the market. The technology used for the production of furniture should be highly advanced for producing superior designs of furniture. It does, however, consider the vertical integration into retailing (as already practised within the USA) to be a serious option. This would give Nikoles Furniture increased control over its sales and reduce its exposure to competition. The president of the parent company has asked George Taylor, managing director of Nikoles Furniture, to address this issue and provide guidance to the US board of directors. As the parent company has large cash reserves on its (SOFP) balance sheet, there are no funding problems.

Required:

(a) Acting in the capacity of George Taylor, you are required to undertake an external environmental analysis concerning the key external influences which could impact upon Nikoles Furniture's decision.
(b) What is the purpose of PESTEL analysis?

Question 2

Describe Porter's Diamond and its key factors for assessing competitive advantage. What are the uses of this model?

Answers to Self Examination Questions

Answer to SEQ 1

(a) The external environment in which an organisation operates is complex, dynamic and increasingly global. The external environmental analysis enables an understanding of the current and potential changes taking place in the organisation's external environment. It provides strategic intelligence and is an essential prerequisite for determining the organisation's strategies. It enables the organisation to identify and understand the key external and uncontrollable influences which will have an impact upon the organisation's strategy. External factors need to be taken into consideration within the planning process.

The PESTEL analysis of Nikoles Furniture's macro-environment will influence its decision on whether it should concentrate on the UK or seek diversification elsewhere, either in products or markets. The PESTEL analysis is a framework used to scan the external macro-environment, covering the following environments: political, economic, social, technological, environmental and legal.

Possible factors likely to have an impact on Nikoles Furniture's decision are as follows:

1. **Political / legal:** the role that the government plays in shaping the environment in which the organisation operates. These factors refer to the "laws of the land" that the organisation must follow. A country's political system and government policy will set the rules and regulations of the external environment. In this case, the government's policy on site-development and planning would affect Nikoles Furniture's decision.

2. **Economic:** future economic policies, interest rates, taxation policies, income distribution, unemployment and trade barriers.

3. **Social:** customer tastes and preferences, the trend of purchasing furniture from superstores or out-of-town sites.

4. **Technological**: how developments in technology will affect the way business is conducted. Nikoles Furniture has to analyse whether the retailing technology available is expensive or reasonable.

5. **Environmental:** much legislation has been passed to protect the environment. Rules and regulations have to be strictly followed when the organisation dispose of the waste generated from the production of furniture.

(b) The external macro-environment of an organisation is often unstable and unfriendly and it is therefore essential for an organisation to analyse this environment effectively. PESTEL analysis is a framework used to analyse the external macro-environment in which an organisation operates. PESTEL analysis helps to identify and understand the key external influences (Political, Economic, Social, Technological, Environmental and Legal) which will have an impact upon the organisation's strategy. If the organisation does not have knowledge of the environmental factors, it is possible that there may be enormous changes in future policies.

The purposes of a PESTEL analysis are as follows:

- It is a useful tool which provides a 'big picture' of the environment in which an organisation operates. When an organisation has knowledge of its environment, it can take advantage of the opportunities available and take efforts to reduce threats.

- Effective use of PESTEL analysis ensures that the decisions and actions of the organisation are aligned positively with the powerful and uncontrollable forces affecting its external environment. The organisation is therefore in a better position to gain a competitive advantage over others by taking advantage of change.

- Actions that are predestined to fail for reasons beyond the organisation's control can be avoided with the help of PESTEL analysis.

- When the organisation starts operating in a new country or region, PESTEL helps the organisation to get rid of unconscious assumptions and quickly adapt to the realities of the new environment.

- PESTEL analysis enables the organisation to position itself appropriately in response to the external environment and the competition. With the help of PESTEL analysis, organisations can cope with the competition prevailing in the industry.

Answer to SEQ 2

Michael Porter introduced a model which helps in analysing why some nations are more competitive than others and why some industries within nations are more competitive than others. This model, known as Porter's Diamond, determines the factors which contribute to competitive advantage. According to Porter, a nation attains a competitive advantage only when its firms are competitive. He believes that firms become competitive through innovation. Porter's Diamond is a model that can help in understanding the competitive position of a nation / organisation in global competition. In order to gain a sustainable competitive advantage over others, an organisation has to analyse an international business environment.

Traditional economic theory believed that competitive advantage resides in factors such as land, location, natural resources, labour, and the size of the local population. Michael Porter strongly disagrees with this view. He argues that a country only achieves a sustainable competitive advantage when its companies / industries achieve a sustainable competitive advantage on a global scale. He suggests that the national home base of an organisation plays an important role in shaping the extent to which it is likely to achieve advantage on a global scale.

There are four interconnected key elements which constitute Porter's Diamond. These factors support or hinder organisations from attaining advantages in global competition. These four factors / key elements are described below:

Firm strategy, structure and rivalry

This refers to the **local competitive structure** for a country's industries. These are the factors relevant for competition in particular industries. Domestic competition encourages organisations to strategise, increase productivity and innovate. Companies that can operate and survive in a highly competitive local environment become better prepared to compete in the global environment.

Demand conditions

These are the factors that describe the state of **domestic demand**. The demand conditions within the nation form the basis upon which the characteristics of the organisation's competitive advantage are shaped. A more demanding local market leads to a national competitive advantage. When the customers within the country are more demanding and sophisticated, then the possibility of selling high quality goods in the global market arises.

Related and supporting industries

There is opportunity for an ongoing **exchange of ideas**. The supporting industries work in co-operation with the other industries and hence, if there is success in one industry, it ultimately leads to success in the other related industries.

Factor conditions

These include **production factors** such as human resources, capital resources, physical resources, intellectual resources and infrastructural resources, which are relevant to competition in particular industries. These factor conditions help in forming the basis of advantage on a national level. It is not sufficient for a nation to have an enormous amount of resources; instead it is essential to deploy these available resources to the optimum level.

Uses of Porter's diamond

a) Porter's Diamond helps in identifying the extent to which organisations can build on national advantages to create a competitive advantage on a global front.
b) On national level, governments can use this model to consider the policies that they need to follow to establish national advantages.

SECTION A: STRATEGIC POSITION

STUDY GUIDE A3: COMPETITIVE FORCES AFFECTING AN ORAGNISATION

Get Through Intro

Competition is what keeps companies innovating and coming up with better products. You must have noticed that if a particular sector has a monopoly, often prices are higher and services are not so good. Let's take the case of the telephone sector in the UK. Until 1981, British Telecom or BT was a monopoly. Until then, it could often take a number of days or weeks to get a phone connection and prices for calls were high. Once the market opened up, competitors came into the market and offered immediate connections and calls for free subject to monthly rentals. BT had to reconsider its strategy as its profits were plummeting.

This chapter will teach you the importance of competitors and analysing competitor actions. This will help ensure that your business does well, but keeping you one step ahead of the competition!

Learning Outcomes

a) Discuss the significance of industry, sector and convergence.
b) Evaluate the sources of competition in an industry or sector using Porter's five forces framework.
c) Assess the contribution of the lifecycle model and the cycle of competition and associated costing implications to understanding competitive behaviour.
d) Analyse the influence of strategic groups and market segmentation.
e) Determine the opportunities and threats posed by the environment of an organisation.

46: Strategic Position

Introduction

Case Study

Parker Pens are very smart elegant pens, generally priced slightly expensively. The question is, who is Parker Pens' competition? At first glance, many would say any other pen companies eg Sheaffer Pens, Cross Pens or Waterman pens – all well known brands. Actually when analysis was carried out, it was discovered that most purchases of pens were not for personal use, but for giving as gifts to other people. Hence actually, Parker Pens' competition were not just the branded pen companies, but chocolates, gift vouchers, CDs, DVDs etc are all considered competition.

From the above case study, you should realise that competitors could be a much wider group than you initially thought. Parker pens had to advertise and market their product to compete with other gifts, rather than stressing the benefits of why it was a good writing instrument. Hence they introduced nice presentation boxes for pens and different colours to be more eye catching.

This Study Guide will help you identify who your competitors are and how you can strengthen your position as compared to them!

1. Discuss the significance of industry, sector and convergence.[3]

[Learning Outcome a]

1.1 What is meant by an industry?

An industry is a **group of organisations** which produce **similar products** or products which are **close substitutes** of each other; strictly speaking substitutes are in another industry. It is a group of different organisations which share a **common method of generating profits, production techniques and product offerings**. The term is used to cover any form of economic activity. Industries are classified as those belonging to the primary, secondary or tertiary sectors. Primary sector industries or extractive industries are those that get their source of income from naturally occurring resources like agriculture, fishing, mining. The secondary sector refers to the manufacturing or processing industries which typically uses the outputs of the primary industries and then converts them into other usable or finished goods like textiles, food processing etc. service industries such as banking, insurance, finance and others come under the tertiary sector

1.2 What is meant by sector?

A sector is a **part of** a market, society, industry or economy, whose components have **similar characteristics**. In the business world, it is a general practice to categorise different types of organisations which have similar features. There are two broad methods of dividing sectors:

1. on the basis of ownership e.g. public sector and private sector
2. on the basis of the type of product they produce e.g. primary sector, secondary sector and service sector

Example

Type of sector	Industries
Public sector organisation	Electricity sector, educational institutions run by government
Private sector	Textile sector operated by private organisations
Primary sector	Mining and farming
Secondary sector	Manufacturing
Service sector	Insurance organisations

SUMMARY

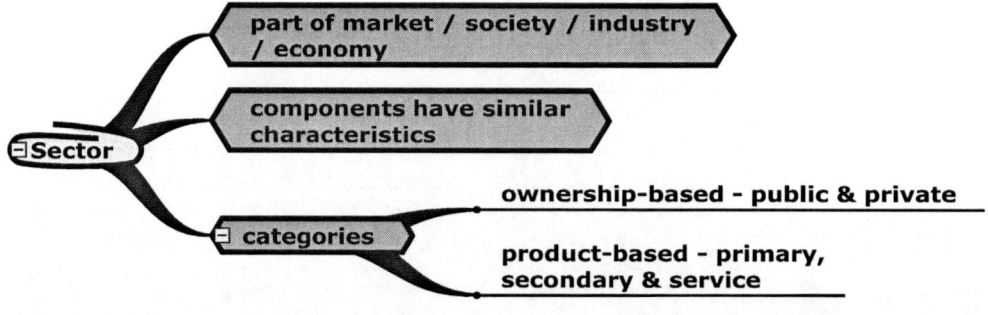

1.3 Significance of industry / sector

1. It allows managers to understand the competitive forces at work in a particular sector

> **Example**
>
> Competitive pressures and the need for greater profits are pushing automobile manufactures like Skoda and Volkswagen to re-evaluate their supply chain activities. Automobile manufacturers are going in for mass customisation by introducing a wide variety of products which, in turn, is leading to escalating costs and complexity in manufacturing processes.

2. It informs important decisions about product / market strategy

Although organisations belonging to an industry produce similar products, they vary in many aspects such as work culture, capabilities etc. These organisations also share many common features e.g. exposure to major changes in the external environment which impact upon all the organisations in a particular industry.

> **Example**
>
> After the September 11 attacks on the twin towers in New York, domestic and business demand for air travel dropped considerably which created problems for the tourism and airline industries.

1.4 Convergence

The meaning of convergence is "to come together or unite".

It refers to the **coming together of two or more different entities or phenomena**. It is a process which increases similarities and decreases differences.

> **Definition**
>
> Johnson, Scholes and Whittington describe **convergence** as occurring "where previously separate industries begin to overlap in terms of activities, technologies, products and customers".
>
> (Source: JSW)

Convergence is a way to explain the **"coming together"** of voice, data, video, wireless and collaboration on enterprise networks today.

> **Example**
>
> The launch of the Napster website was seen as a serious threat to the survival of the music industry. Napster's file sharing service allowed tens of thousands of users to simultaneously open their hard drives and freely exchange copyrighted songs amongst themselves.
>
> The Recording Industry Association of America filed a suit against the company. They stated that this file swapping was copyright infringement and could lead to a large loss of revenue to the music industry. On March 6, 2001 a federal judge ordered Napster to prohibit any copyrighted material from being swapped.
>
> However, the ruling has not prevented dozens of similar sites from opening. To combat this problem, many music labels are now offering customers the chance to purchase music electronically.
>
> Hence, till the launch of the Napster website, music and internet were totally separate. Napster created an example of convergence between the internet and music and opened up the possibility for different users to hear different music.
>
> Similarly, the Virgin Group, owned by Sir Richard Branson, is using convergence technology to fuse the internet and voice communication businesses; it is hoped that this will provide customers with a broader range of internet services that can be accessed via mobile telephones.
>
> The above case studies indicate that industries will always be in a state of change. One force that alters the industry in which an organisation operates is the process of convergence. Convergence can be caused by regulatory changes, technological changes or market changes.

48: Strategic Position

Market convergence occurs when the functional characteristics or nature of an existing product is changed. This often takes place when the product of one industry becomes a substitute for products from other industries.

Example

Personal computers have become technologically advanced and now have the capabilities to serve as DVD players and stereos.

What are the reasons for convergence?

There are two main reasons which lead to convergence.

1. Supply-led

When the supplier of one industry finds some **link or connection** with the supplier of other industries, they can join together to build a new market or sector. Supply-led convergence is popular in the case of public sector organisations where the government compels the entities to work together.

2. Demand-led

Here, the consumers behave as if the industries have converged. The consumers substitute products for one another.

Example

Consumers prefer to substitute televisions with PCs, since increasing technological changes have enabled them to view movies and sitcoms through the PC. Changes in the screen size of the computer monitors also make viewing more pleasurable and similar to the experience associated with viewing televisions.

Moreover, consumers prefer to have complementary products in order to enjoy improved facilities.

Example

In the case of the travel industry, consumers prefer to have a holiday package which combines air travel and hotel facilities.

SUMMARY

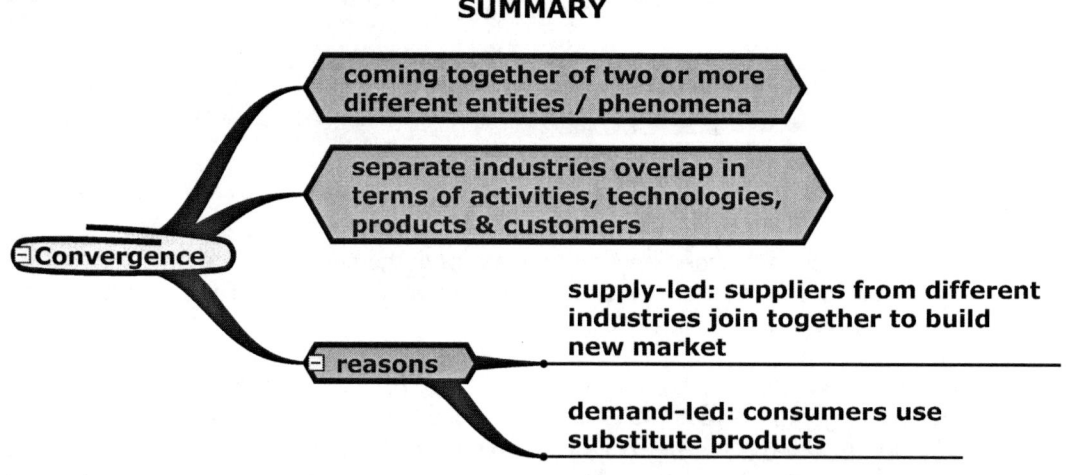

Test Yourself 1

Destiny Ltd, a mobile phone company, is a key player in the market. The mobile market is rapidly growing and developing and continuously introducing advanced technology and additional features. Destiny Ltd introduces a new model of mobile phone called Amazing. Amazing allows customers to access the Internet and email accounts and has a keyboard which helps the customer to write emails easily. Its RAM capacity is more than any other mobile, allowing the customer to store emails, films, photos and songs on it. Amazing also has a good camera which enables customers to take photographs and record videos. The model has a large screen so that customers can view their emails, films and photos very clearly. As a result of all these features, customers can use Amazing as a substitute for a computer and/or camera and it has become a best-seller. Destiny Ltd's shares in mobile market have increased accordingly.

Required:

Explain what convergence is and when market convergence occurs. With the help of above case study, explain the main reasons for convergence.

2. Evaluate the sources of competition in an industry or sector using Porter's five forces framework.[3]

[Learning Outcome b]

Meaning of competition

Competition refers to a force which motivates organisations to achieve dominance or attain a reward or goal. It denotes a dynamic process of rivalry among firms in which only the fittest survive and succeed.

Example

Talk more Ltd, a mobile phone company, reduced its call charges by 1% from its current rate to compete with the prices of another mobile company, Comfort Ltd.

Here, the two companies compete on the basis of price to gain more customers and expand their market.

2.1 Overview of Porter's five forces

Michael Porter of Harvard University and the author of " Competitive Strategy (1980) developed the Strategic Management Model known as the **five forces of competition** which explains the five key factors which must be analysed when evaluating a business's profitability in the future.

By applying the five forces model, the market factors can be analysed so that an organisation can make a strategic assessment of its competitive position in a particular market. Michael Porter's five forces framework provides a simple outlook for **assessing and analysing the competitive strength and position** of a business organisation.

2.2 Important points to be considered before applying this model

1. These forces must be considered for specific strategic business units (SBUs) and not for the organisation as a whole because organisations operate in different industries and therefore the influence of these forces may be different on each unit.
2. These five forces are dependent on each other.
3. It is essential to understand the link between the competitive forces and the key drivers in the macro-environment because these environmental factors may influence the competition in the industry.

2.3 Sources of competition using Porter's five forces framework

There are five main factors that influence the level of competitiveness in an industry or sector. These factors or forces have been identified by Michael Porter in his famous "five forces" model as the:

1. threat of potential entrants
2. existence of substitutes
3. bargaining power of buyers
4. bargaining power of suppliers
5. intensity of rivalry among existing firms

An ideal industry would be one where:

➢ there is little or no possibility of new organisations entering because of significant barriers to entry
➢ buyers will pay whatever prices the organisation sets
➢ suppliers will sell at whatever prices the organisation sets
➢ there are no substitute products
➢ there is no competition from any other organisation i.e. a monopoly exists

In the above example, all of the five forces are weak; it therefore represents a very profitable or almost ideal industry to enter into. However, this ideal only exists in theory. In practice, every industry usually has at least one strong force. The greater the number or strength of these forces, the more competitive the industry or sector is.

Diagram 1: Porter's five forces model

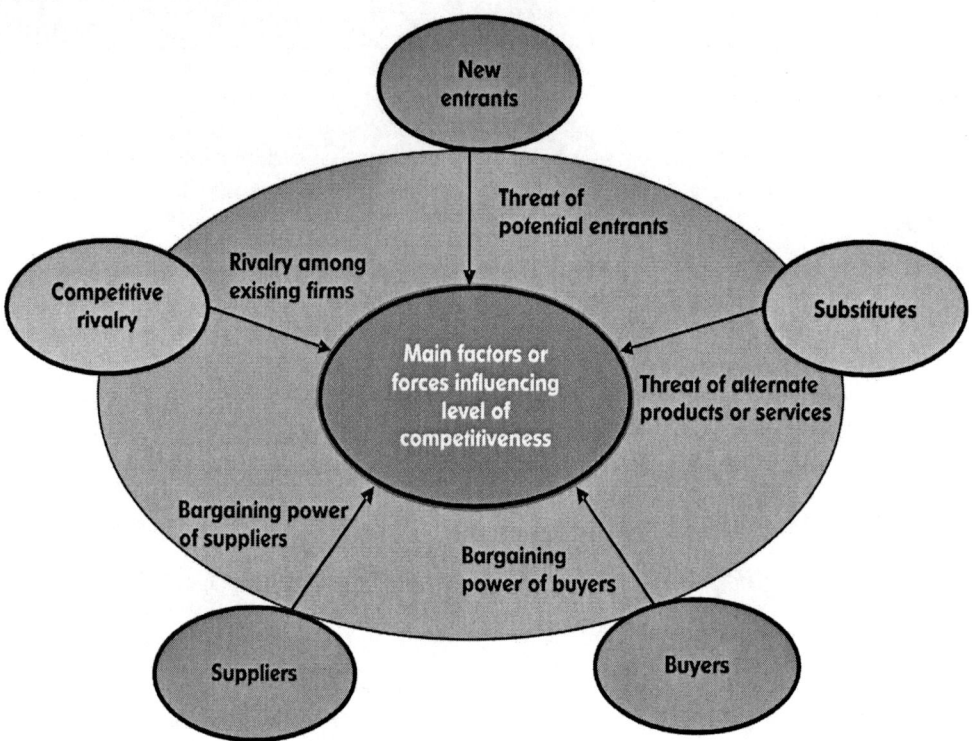

1. Threat of new entrants

One of the biggest worries for the organisations of any industry is the possibility that other firms will enter their industry. The **more firms that enter an industry, the more competitive the industry** is likely to become. The more competitive the industry, the lower the level of profits likely to be earned by its organisations. Naturally it is easier to enter some industries than others.

> **Example**
>
> It is much more difficult for an organisation to enter a capital intensive industry such as oil exploration than it is for it to enter into the field of IT consultancy. This is because to enter into the oil exploration business an organisation would have to purchase very expensive assets such as oil rigs, drills etc and acquire mining exploration rights. To become an IT consultancy business, an organisation would only need an office space and computers.

The above example illustrates a **barrier to entry** (i.e. high capital cost requirements). How high the threat of potential or new entrants is will depend upon how many barriers to entry there are. Examples of barriers to entry include:

a) whether existing organisations have achieved **economies of scale** (this is particularly prevalent in manufacturing industries): an organisation that has achieved economies of scale is producing very large numbers of a product at a low per unit cost. Therefore, it is **harder for a new organisation** to launch in this industry as it may not gain the economies of scale and therefore will not be able to sell products as competitively.

b) whether there is high capital / **start up costs**: these result in the organisation having to endure a **longer time period** to recoup their investment. Hence many organisations may not be able to afford to wait for a long period before they can gain a return on their investment. This, in turn, would reduce the likelihood of new firms entering the industry.

c) limited access to supply / distribution channels

d) patent agreements

e) access to specialised and unique skills or capabilities

Example

Although there are a few other cola manufacturers alongside Coke and Pepsi, they have a very limited share of the market. One of the reasons for this is that they have difficulty getting their product to a mass market. This, in turn, is partly because Coke and Pepsi have a long history of not allowing vending machines that sell their products to stock any other cola thereby limiting other cola manufacturers' access to supply / distribution channels. Pepsi and coke also have very strong brand identities.

f) **strong customer loyalty** to existing products: any new tobacco manufacturer will have a difficult time getting customers to change over from their existing brands.

g) organisations that **enter the industry earlier** have **more experience and exposure** to the market and therefore have an advantage over others in this respect. This is known as the experience effect and will allow the existing firms to operate more efficiently and competitively.

h) **product differentiation**: organisations within an industry have created **goodwill** in the market by earning **customer loyalty** and building a **brand name** for their products.

Example

Subway is a leading fast food chain which offers foot long and six-inch sandwiches filled with assorted meat, vegetable and other toppings, which it promotes as a healthy alternative to burgers. This formula has enabled Subway to capture a sizeable portion of the fast food market.

i) **Government action or legislation**: the government enacts various legislation to regulate the markets and takes action to control competition.

SUMMARY

- **Threat of new entrants**
  - the more new entrants, the more competitive the industry
  - depends upon number of entry barriers
    - economies of scale achieved by existing organisations
    - high capital / start up costs
    - limited access to supply and distribution channels
    - strong customer loyalty to existing organisations
    - existing organisations have more experience and exposure to market
    - product differentiation by existing organisations
    - government action / legislation

2. Threat of substitutes

The threat of substitutes depends upon the **ease at which a customer can switch to an alternative product**. In an industry where there are many substitutes, organisations need to understand why their product might be substituted for a competitor's and then take steps to ensure that their product is differentiated in some way in the minds of their customers.

What is a substitute?

A substitute is a product from one industry that can perform the same function required in another industry. Examples include butter and margarine; and ferries and low cost airlines.

It is important to note that there are different **forms of substitution**. These include:

a) **Product for product substitution**

It occurs because of two reasons - convergence and availability of complementary products.

Example

An example of this type of substitution is when a man travels to work by train but decides to switch to a coach service.

b) **Substitution of need**

In this instance a new product renders an existing one obsolete.

Example

The fax machine made the telex redundant and it (the fax machine) has also become obsolete because of email.

c) **Generic substitution**

This occurs with products / services that compete for a small portion of a customer's disposable income. The consumers may also decide to do without the particular product.

Example

White goods such as toasters and kettles are common examples of where generic substitution occurs. Consumers typically see little performance or quality difference between brands in these types of goods. Therefore, at the time of purchase, they often buy any available model or make.

SUMMARY

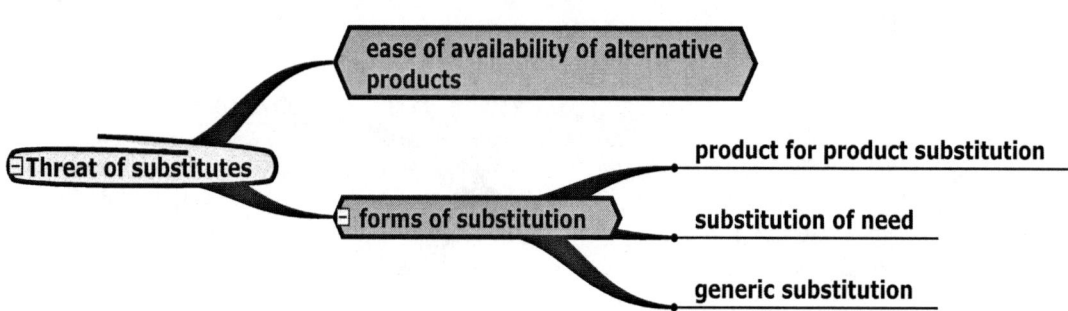

3. Bargaining power of buyers

If buyers have high bargaining power then an organisation will be **restricted in the price** that it can charge for its goods or services. Situations where the bargaining power of buyers will be high are when:

a) There is a **concentration of buyers (the industry is dominated by just a few customers) and the volumes they are purchasing are large.**

Example

For instance, the multinational Unilever has operations and subsidiaries all over the globe. Recently the organisation has begun consolidating its purchasing for all its companies from one central location. This has resulted in the organisation achieving cost efficiencies and economies of scale as it now mass orders the goods it requires.

b) The cost of switching to an alternative supplier is low and involves little risk. A switching cost is the financial and emotional cost associated with changing suppliers.

Example

Long distance phone rates in the US are relatively very low because of the ease at which customers can switch from one long distance carrier to another (over the phone and at no charge with immediate effect). This means that the phone companies must be extremely competitive in order to remain in business. This was not always the case however; only a few years ago, carriers could levy large cancellation charges and ask for extensive paperwork to be completed if a customer wished to switch carrier. The financial penalty together with the time required to complete the paperwork deterred many customers from changing their carrier.

c) The **buyer has the ability to either buy products from another company or produce the same product / service in-house)**. If the suppliers do not offer a reasonable price or good quality, the buyers may produce the products themselves. This is known as **backward integration**. The threat of backward integration is not desirable.

Example

Sainsbury's (a UK supermarket chain) is able to negotiate discounts from Heinz and other ketchup manufacturers because they also produce their own brand of tomato ketchup. Having a readily available substitute product means they can negotiate a reduction in the price of other manufacturers' ketchups. Given the quantity of this product that is sold, this translates into a significant cost saving for the organisation.

d) When buyers have better **information levels**, they are capable of bargaining with suppliers and hence can force the supplier to sell the product at a lower price.

e) Buyers enjoy high bargaining power when they are aware of the **product differentiation** available in the market. Differentiation is the process of distinguishing a product from competitors' products to gain a competitive advantage. The buyers possess knowledge of the value of the product by differentiation and hence can effectively bargain with the supplier regarding its price.

f) When the buyers are aware of the **quality of products** provided by the supplier and its competitors, they are in a better position to bargain on price with their supplier.

SUMMARY

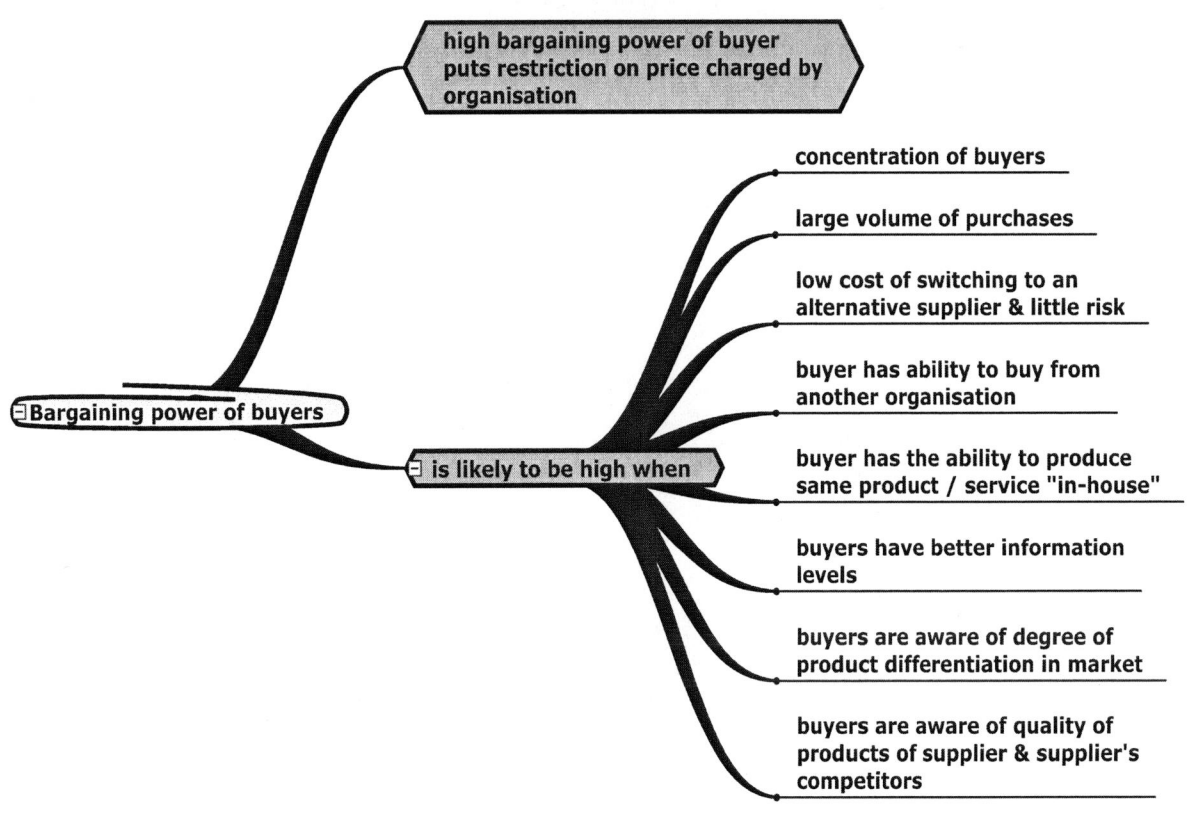

4. Bargaining power of suppliers

When the bargaining power of suppliers is high, firms normally end up paying a relatively **high cost for the raw materials** and other inputs (remember that labour is also a supplier) they need to be able to produce their goods or services. This, in turn, restricts the price that they can charge for their product or service. For instance, if the cost of their raw materials increases, firms in all probability will have to pass this cost on to their customers (at the risk of losing business).

Situations where the bargaining power of suppliers will be high are when:

a) there is a **concentration of suppliers and a large number of buyers**.

Example

The few large chemical companies that supply to the glass manufacturing industry enjoy this advantage. This is because the special chemical they supply is essential to the glass manufacturing process. This chemical is produced by only a few companies whereas there are a large number of glass manufacturers willing to buy the product.

b) **Switching costs of a consumer are high**.

Example

Switching to an alternative operating system would be difficult for most computer users given the almost universal usage of Windows. Therefore consumers have very little or no bargaining power when it comes to purchasing the Windows operating system.

c) If the suppliers do not get the prices they want for their products and they have the ability to directly compete with the buyers. This is known as **forward integration**. An example would be a mobile phone manufacturer operating its own retail shops.

d) When suppliers can use the **substitute inputs** for their products, they are in a better position to bargain on price because they can insist on lower prices or else purchase the substitute.

e) Buyers can force suppliers to reduce the prices when they desire to purchase the inputs in **larger quantities**. If the prices are not reduced, they may even cancel the contract for the purchase of inputs which is very costly for the supplier.

f) Suppliers enjoy high bargaining power when they are aware of the **product input differentiation** available in the market. Differentiation is a process of distinguishing the product input from competitors' product inputs to gain a competitive advantage. When suppliers possess knowledge of the value of the product input by differentiation, they can effectively bargain on its price.

SUMMARY

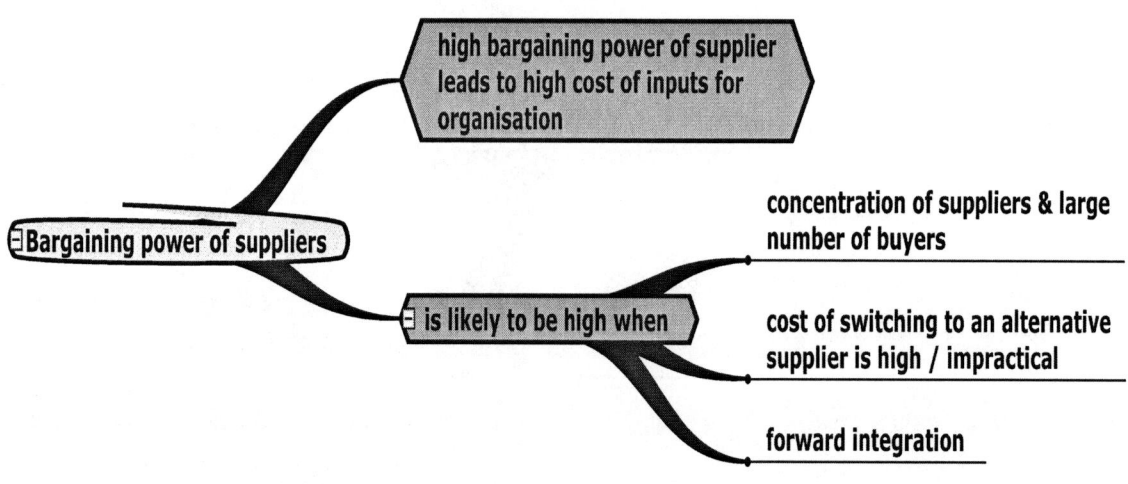

5. Competitive rivalry

As important as the number of firms that exist in an industry is the intensity of rivalry that exists between them. The **more competitive the rivalry** that exists between firms, **the lower the level of profits** that typically will be earned by firms in that industry (as firms will attempt to outdo each other in terms of offering lower prices and/or greater quality).

Situations where there will be intense rivalry between competing organisations (when organisations offer similar products/services to the same group of customers) are when:

a) the **competitors are in balance** (i.e. they have roughly the same size and capabilities).

Example
The Canadian banking industry is said to be amongst the most competitive in the world. The industry is dominated by 5 "major" banks that have approximately the same size, product offerings and reach. In many instances, branches of these banks will almost face each other. Therefore competition for customers is fierce between these banks as they all offer similar products, services and quality.

b) competing organisations are **operating in a mature market** (a market that is not growing). Here the only way for an organisation to achieve growth is by gaining market share from one or more of its rivals.

c) there are **high fixed costs**. Fixed costs are constant costs that an organisation has to incur in a particular period regardless of the level of activity it engages in for that period. Even if an organisation does not produce any goods or services, it will still have to pay its fixed costs for that particular period. A common fixed cost is the rent that organisations pay for their office premises.

Example
Airlines routinely offer discounts and promotional packages as their fixed costs are regular and high (i.e. a scheduled flight must take off regardless of how many seats are empty). Therefore airlines need to fill as many seats as possible for a scheduled flight even if some of the seats are sold at discounted prices.

Continental Airlines is an airline that offers discounts and promotional packages

d) there are **many exit barriers**. When organisations cannot leave an industry easily, this leads to increased competition. An organisation may be unable to exit an industry because government regulations, heavy investment in fixed assets or large staff redundancy costs.

e) a **variety of products is available**. As a result, customers have a range of choices and so they may shift to competitors to purchase their requirement.

f) the **competitors' responses are aggressive**. Each organisation tries to gain a competitive advantage over the others, leading to intense rivalry.

SUMMARY

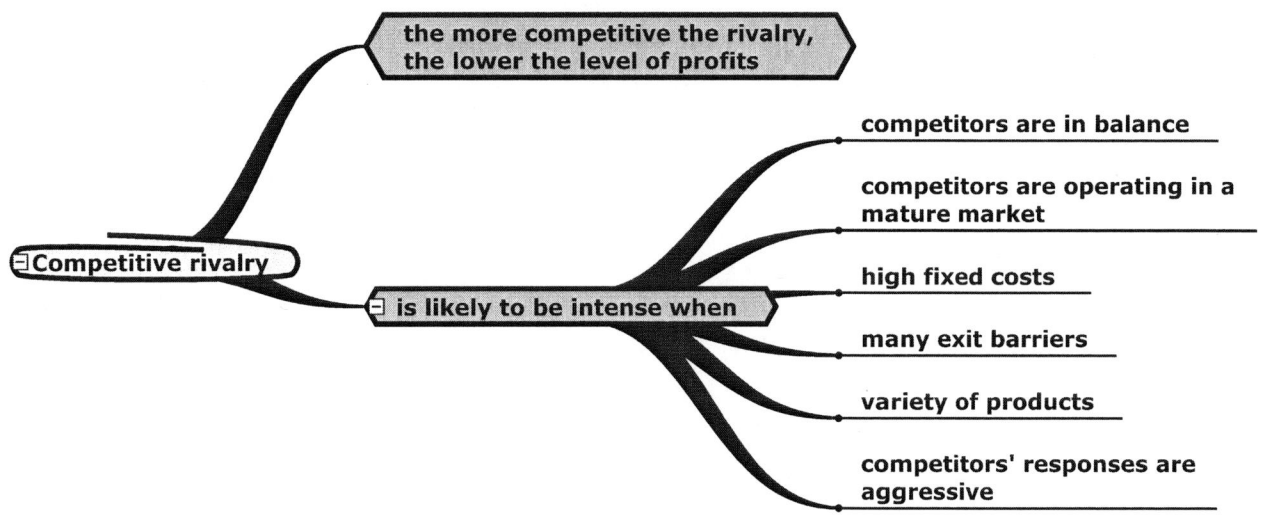

Case Study

Porter's five forces: consumer products

The five forces concept is perhaps best explained through example. Let's briefly examine the household consumer-products industry by considering rival firms Clorox CLX, Kimberly-Clark KMB, Colgate-Palmolive CL, and Procter & Gamble PG in terms of Porter's five forces:

Buyer power: consumer-products companies face weak buyer power because customers are fragmented (NOT CONCENTRATED) and have little influence on price or product. But if we consider the buyers of consumer products to be retailers rather than individuals, then these firms face very strong buyer power. Retailers like Wal-Mart WMT and Target TGT are able to negotiate for pricing with companies like Clorox because they purchase and sell so much of Clorox's products. Verdict: Strong buyer power from retailers.

Supplier power: more than likely, consumer-products companies face some amount of supplier power simply because of the costs they incur when switching suppliers. On the other hand, suppliers that do a large amount of business with these companies--supplying Kimberly-Clark with raw materials for its diapers, for instance--also are somewhat beholden to their customers, like Kimberly-Clark. Nevertheless, bargaining power for both the firms and their suppliers is probably limited. Verdict: Limited supplier power.

Threat of new entrants: given the amount of capital investment needed to enter certain segments in household consumer products, such as manufacturing deodorants, we suspect the threat of new entrants is fairly low in the industry. In some segments within the household consumer-products industry, this may not be the case since a small manufacturer could develop a superior product, such as a detergent, and compete with Procter & Gamble. The test is whether the small manufacturer can get its products on the shelves of the same retailers as its much larger rivals. Verdict: Low threat of new entrants.

Threat of substitutes: within the consumer-products industry, brands succeed in helping to build a competitive advantage, but even the pricing power of brands can be eroded with substitutes such as store-branded private-label offerings. In fact, some of these same store-brand private-label products are manufactured by the large consumer-products firms. The firms believe that if they can manufacture and package a lower-price alternative themselves, they would rather accept the marginal revenue from their lower-priced items than risk completely losing the sale to a private-label competitor. Verdict: High threat of substitutes.

Degree of rivalry: consumers in this category enjoy a multitude of choices for everything from cleaning products to bath washes. While many consumers prefer certain brands, switching costs in this industry are quite low. It does not cost anything for a consumer to buy one brand of shampoo instead of another. This, along with a variety of other factors, including the forces we've already examined, makes the industry quite competitive. Verdict: High degree of rivalry.

Examining an industry through the framework of Porter's five forces helps illustrate the different dynamics at work. It's not always clear-cut, either, so one wouldn't expect all of the firms in this industry to fall into one big bucket labelled wide moat or narrow moat. Instead, there are firms with distinct, long-term advantages and wide moats, like Procter & Gamble and Colgate, while others have advantages that we think may be less sustainable, such as Clorox and Kimberly-Clark.

(Source: www.news.morningstar.com)

Test Yourself 2

Flintstone Ltd is a book publishing company. Flintstone has a monopoly in the market for CFA (Chartered Financial Analyst) books.. Flintstone sells its books at a very low cost, which no other competitors can afford. Flintstone gives its distributors a high commission on the condition that they sell only Flintstone books and not any other competitors' books. The Marketing and Advertising department of Flintstone is very strong which helps to increase the sales of Flintstone.

Required:

Explain what an ideal industry is, with reference to the above case study.

> **3. Assess the contribution of the lifecycle model and the cycle of competitive costing implications to understanding competitive behaviour.**[3]

3.1 Lifecycle model

This model is a tool to analyse the **effects of an industry's growth on competitive** evolution consists of five phases. The stages of the lifecycle model have a significant impact upon strategy and performance.

Phases of lifecycle model:

1. development
2. growth
3. shakeout
4. maturity
5. decline

Diagram 2: Lifecycle model

	Development	Growth	Shakeout	Maturity	Decline
Products	Introduction and basic	Improving and better	Improved and streamlined	Highly standardised	Quality deteriorated
Buyers	Few and eager to be adopters	Many and curious to try products / services	Numerous selection before purchase	Expanded market and brand loyalty	Reduction in purchase
Competitors	Few competitors	Many new entrants try to obtain share	Increased competition Weak competitors leave the industry	Reduction in cost Aim to maintain share	Few competitors exit the industry

1. Development stage
There is only a few or perhaps even only one organisation in operation. Naturally competition is very low or nonexistent. There is little customer loyalty.

2. Growth stage
At this stage, competition has built up as more organisations have entered the industry. The level of competitive behaviour is not intense as the overall market is growing. Organisations do not need to steal customers from each other to achieve growth.

3. Shakeout stage
At this stage, the size of the market has peaked and many more firms are now operating in the industry. Competition intensifies as the "strong" or efficient organisations strive to drive out the "weak" or inefficient firms.

4. Maturity stage
The intensity of competition remains as the market size looks set to decline. The only way for organisations remaining in the industry to increase sales is by stealing market share from competing firms. Customer loyalty is high.

5. Decline stage
The intensity of competition declines as more organisations decide to exit the industry given the declining market size.

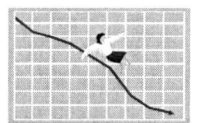

lifecycle of the 'walkman' product very closely follows this model. Sony was the pioneering company as they were the first to market the concept of portable music players with their Walkman tape player. However, within a short time span, other Japanese consumer electronics companies such as Sharp, Sanyo, Aiwa, Toshiba and Panasonic also followed suit, entering the market with their own brands of walkmans.

Over time the market grew with many other consumer electronics companies such as Philips also entering the market. Competition and price wars between the companies intensified.

By the late nineties, walkmans were beginning to show signs of obsolescence and the market size started to decline. Cassettes were avoided in favour of music in CD, DAT and MiniDisc formats. The invention of portable digital music players such as the IPOD has further escalated this trend.

However, Sony and a few other companies still continue to make cassette-based walkmans in limited numbers.

SUMMARY

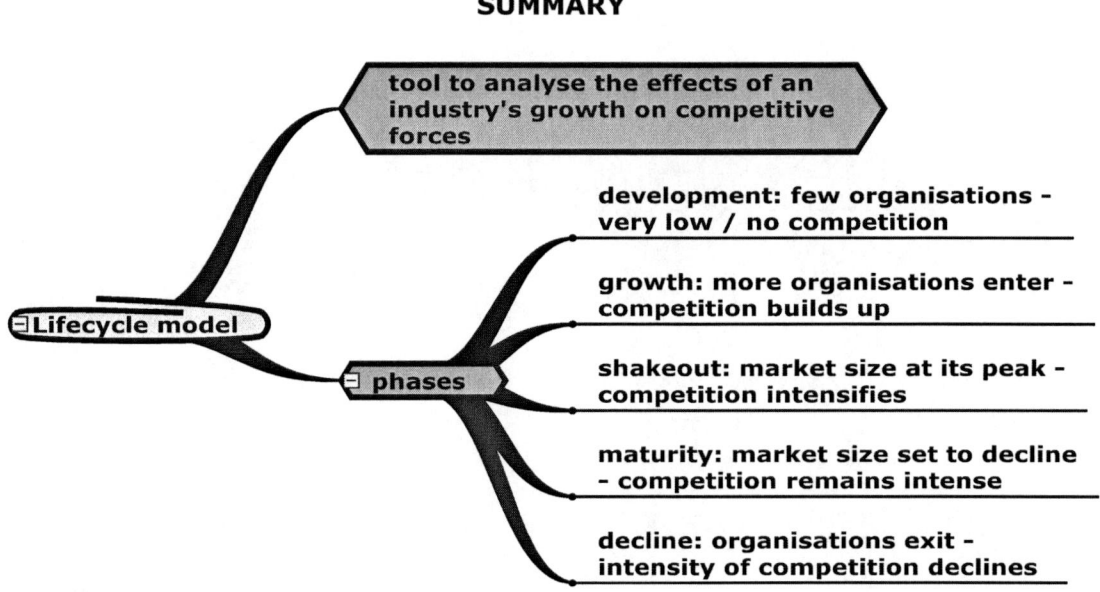

3.2 Cycle of competition

This model shows the relationship between an established firm and a new entrant. The nature of competition that prevails in an industry is uncontrollable and each competitor will have its own influence in the industry. The competitive forces that a five forces analysis will identify are not static in nature. They change and evolve over the course of time. In particular, the barriers to entry for an industry are never permanent. They simply act as a delaying factor. Other organisations will, over time, find a way to overcome them and enter a particular industry.

Technological breakthroughs or changes in government regulation are examples of factors that will erode the entry barriers to an industry. When a new entrant enters an industry, the following interaction that occurs between itself and the incumbent organisation is referred to as the cycle of competition.

How does cycle of competition operate?

The established firm builds entry barriers for the entrant. If an entrant plans to enter the industry, it must overcome the barriers. The new entrant first attacks the firm which is of the same size and nature so that the impact of the attack is fruitful for the new entrant. The entrant firm attacks the existing firm on a particular geographical area, a market segment or on their technology. If the existing firm **does not respond** to this attack, the entrant widens its scope of attack.

However, if the existing firm **responds** to such an attack, it may be by reinforcing its barriers of entry. It may reinforce the entry barriers by spending more on technology etc.

Once the barriers are reinforced, the entrant now begins the price war. As a result, the entrant faces a reduction in margins.

Once the price is reduced by the entrant, the existing firm faces a tremendous challenge and so it may in turn cut down its prices in the prevailing (home) market to force the new entrant to leave the market and make an entry in some other market.

Diagram 3: Cycle of competition

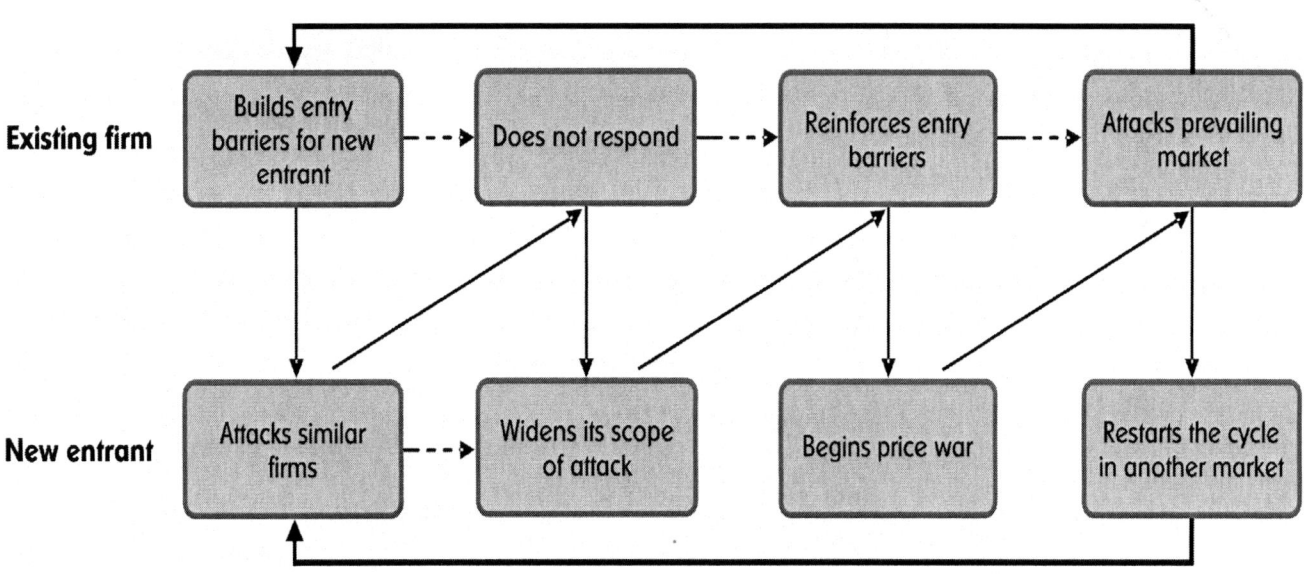

Effects of attack by new entrant or the counter attack by existing firm

- When the new entrant or the existing firm attacks, it requires a huge amount of cash and skill.
- When the entrant makes an entry in a new geographical area, it involves high risk and huge costs.

Example

In 1929, there were 241 motorcycle manufacturers operating in the United States. By 1954 they had all gone out of business / exited the industry except for one, Harley Davidson. The market presence of Harley Davidson was a significant barrier to entry for the American motorcycle market.

During this time, Honda was looking to expand its motorcycle business overseas. It had identified Europe and the States as two key markets. Despite the strong brand image of Harley Davidson, it decided to enter the American market (as it represented one large single market).

Honda entered the US market with its larger motorcycle products (the 250 and 350cc models). It only imported its much smaller end product (the supercub 50cc) for the personal use of its employees and managers.

The 250 and 350cc models were plagued with reliability and quality problems. They failed to receive any demand or interest from American consumers. This and the fact that Harley only produced motorcycles of 1000cc and above meant that their entry provoked no response.

However, the public did notice the 50cc bikes that employees used to drive themselves. Interest and demand for these machines grew to such an extent that Honda was forced to start selling them. As time progressed, Honda started producing bigger and better quality machines and began competing with Harley.

In the 1980s, Honda (and the other Japanese companies such as Kawasaki that followed them) was winning. Their bikes were of better quality, more reliable and cheaper than Harleys. In 1972, Harley Davidson had a 100 per cent share of the market for motorcycles with engines of 1000cc or more. By 1982 their market share had dropped to 15 per cent.

Harley Davidson's response was to then prioritise all efforts and focus on improving the quality of their machines. They became one of the first American companies to introduce the Just in Time inventory system.

They also started an aggressive advertising campaign that promoted the company's heritage with the slogan "motorcycles by the people and for the people". They created an inclusive company culture that welcomed customers to join.

Today, Harley's share of the 650cc and above market is close to 50 per cent. Furthermore the company is also present in many other countries including Japan.

3.3 Hypercompetition

This concept relates to the speed of the competition cycle. If the cycle moves slowly, the competition in an industry settles down many times in a well-established manner. On the other hand, if the speed of competition cycle is high, it is called hypercompetition. This results in frequent competitive change.

Example

There is high level of competition among the mobile phone manufacturers like Nokia, Motorola and Samsung with each of them vying for market share by introducing new and upgraded products.

SUMMARY

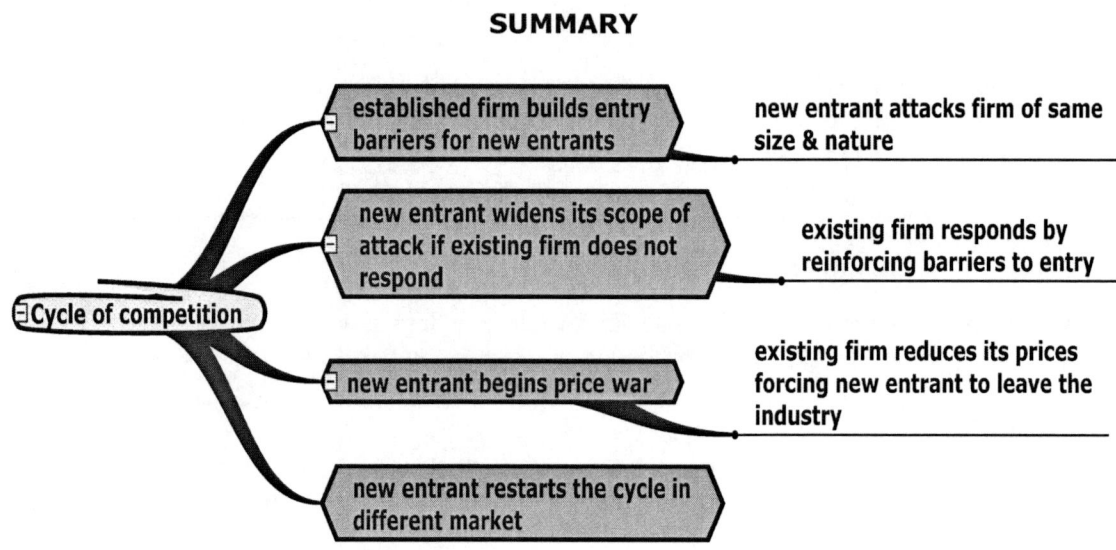

In order to formulate successful business strategies, firms strive for the best fit decision alternatives. In a competitive market, every firm would try to gain a distinct competitive advantage by building the strategies that embody the cost implication over the life cycle of the product or service as well as the competition cycle.

The strategist will have to consider the following cost implications.

3.4 Cost Implications of Life Cycle Model:

a) Costs involved at different stages of a product life-cycle

For each of the business functions at each stage of the life-cycle of each product, costs keep on being incurred. Let us try to identify the possible costs at each stage of the life-cycle:

1. At **the introduction and development stage**: research and development cost, costs of product design, capital equipment etc.

2. At **the growth and maturity stage:** these stages witness both growth and maturity in sales. All the manufacturing, marketing (customer service, promotion etc.), selling and distribution costs (transport and handling) are incurred at this stage.

3. At **the decline stage:** as discussed earlier, the demand for the product declines at this stage. The producers may be required to provide after sales service for the products sold in the past. Costs that are incurred in this stage include all costs relating to after sales service including provision of spares, expert services and costs of abandonment and disposal of the product.

b) Conceptualising customer life-cycle costing

A different notion of life-cycle costs is **customer life-cycle costs.** Customer life-cycle costs include the total costs incurred by a customer to acquire and use a product or service until it is replaced. Customer life-cycle costs for a car, for example, include the cost of car itself plus the costs of operating and maintaining the car less the disposal price of the car. Customer life-cycle costs can be an important consideration in the pricing decision.

Cost Implications of a Competition Cycle Model

i. When a new product is introduced in the market for the first time, the firm producing it will create barriers of entry for the competition. This could be done through pricing policies, technology barriers, distribution channels, after sales service, spares etc. Building these barriers could entail huge costs. Firms will have to keep incurring these costs if they want to keep the competition at bay. These costs could be related to R & D efforts, advertising & promotional efforts, continuous technology upgrading costs, warranty costs etc.

ii. If a firm wants to enter into new markets with the existing products, the costs of promoting the product, highlighting the unique features, running promotional schemes, introducing higher sales incentives etc. could be very high. Many European car makers have recently entered Asian markets with a bang. Although they are well known international brands, they had to spend a lot to ensure that the cars would suit the conditions and consumer preferences of these countries.

iii. In hyper competitive market situations, the product profitability may start eroding and if the firms still want to compete with the other players, they will have to incur huge selling, distribution and service costs. The 3G mobile industry is the best example of this scenario.

iv. Many companies, in order to be competitive, shift their manufacturing base to low cost countries. This at times is a good strategy as it can bring about long term cost reduction. Automakers the world over have shifted their manufacturing bases to Eastern Europe, South East Asia, India etc. to take advantage of this.

SUMMARY

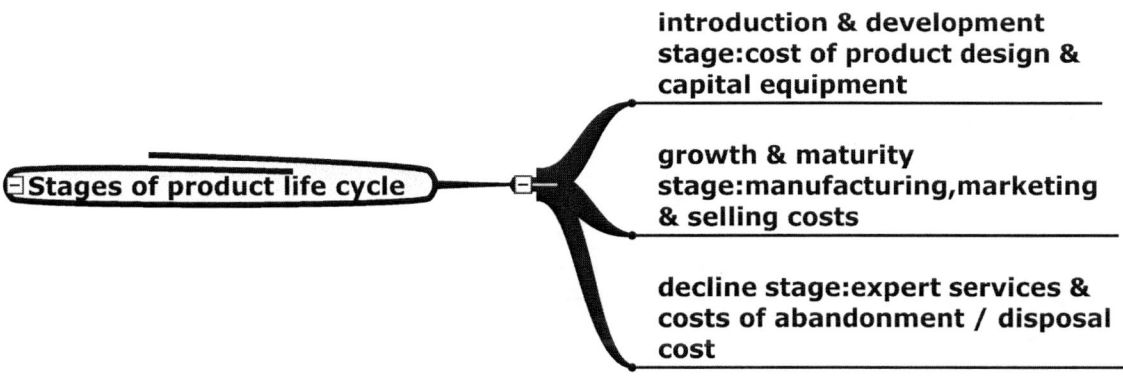

Test Yourself 3

Balamory Ltd was the only computer monitor manufacturing company in its region in the mid nineties. However, within a short time other companies like Baywatch Ltd and Blur Ltd also launched computer monitors into the market within the same region. Competition and price wars intensified between the companies.

The market had grown and each company endeavoured to use the latest, advanced technology in their products.

By the start of the 21st century, monitors were becoming less popular and their market size started to decline. Many technological alternatives became available, including flat screens, lap-tops etc. Balmory did not introduce any advanced technology into its products, whereas Baywatch continuously upgraded its products according to new technology.

Required:

Explain the phases of the lifecycle model. From the above case study, explain how the lifecycle model helps in understanding competitive behaviour.

---

4. Analyse the influence of strategic groups and market segmentation.[3]

[Learning Outcome d]

To understand the concept of competition, the level of industry or sector is very general. In order to understand competition more fully, it is necessary to analyse the markets.

4.1 Strategic groups

Definition

JSW defines a **strategic group as:**
"Organisations within an industry with similar strategic characteristics, following similar strategies or competing on similar bases".

(Source: JSW)

Therefore, strategic groups are the subgroups within an industry that reduce the number of competitors in each market normally each strategic group will have a similar marketing and strategic approach.

Diagram 4: Strategic group within an industry

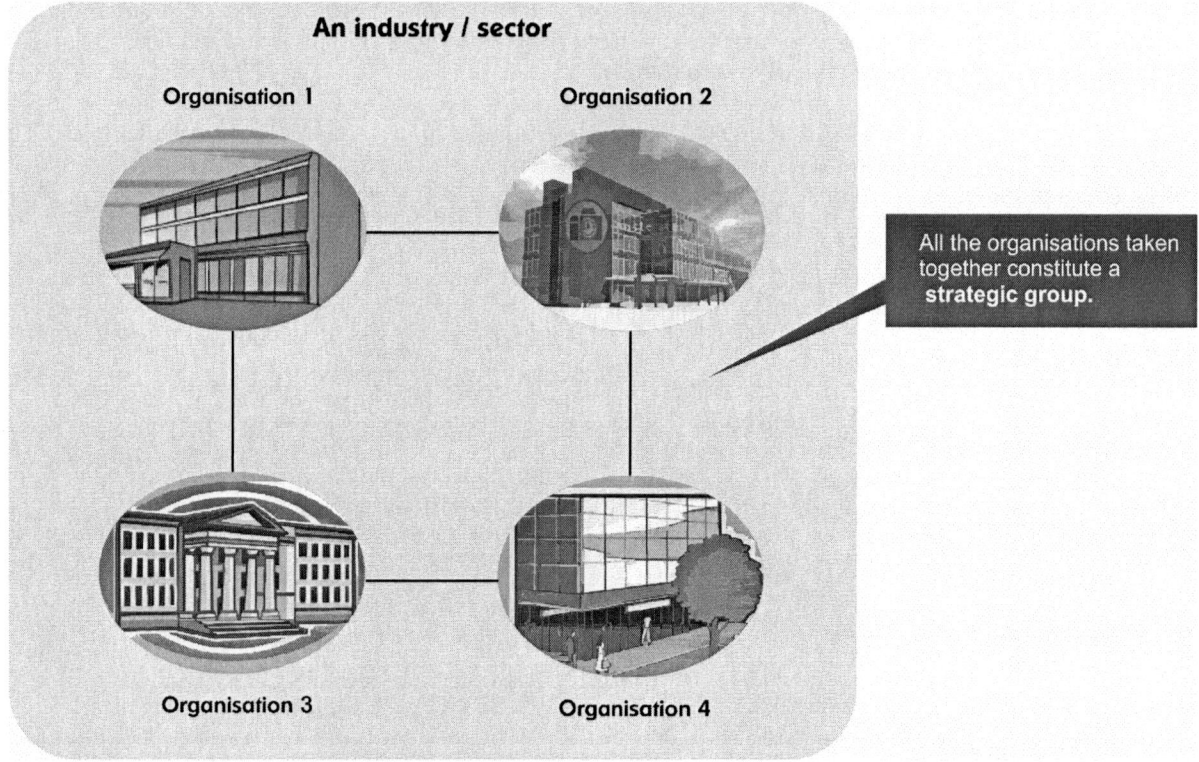

There may be more than one strategic group within an industry, each with different characteristics.

Diagram 5: Strategic groups

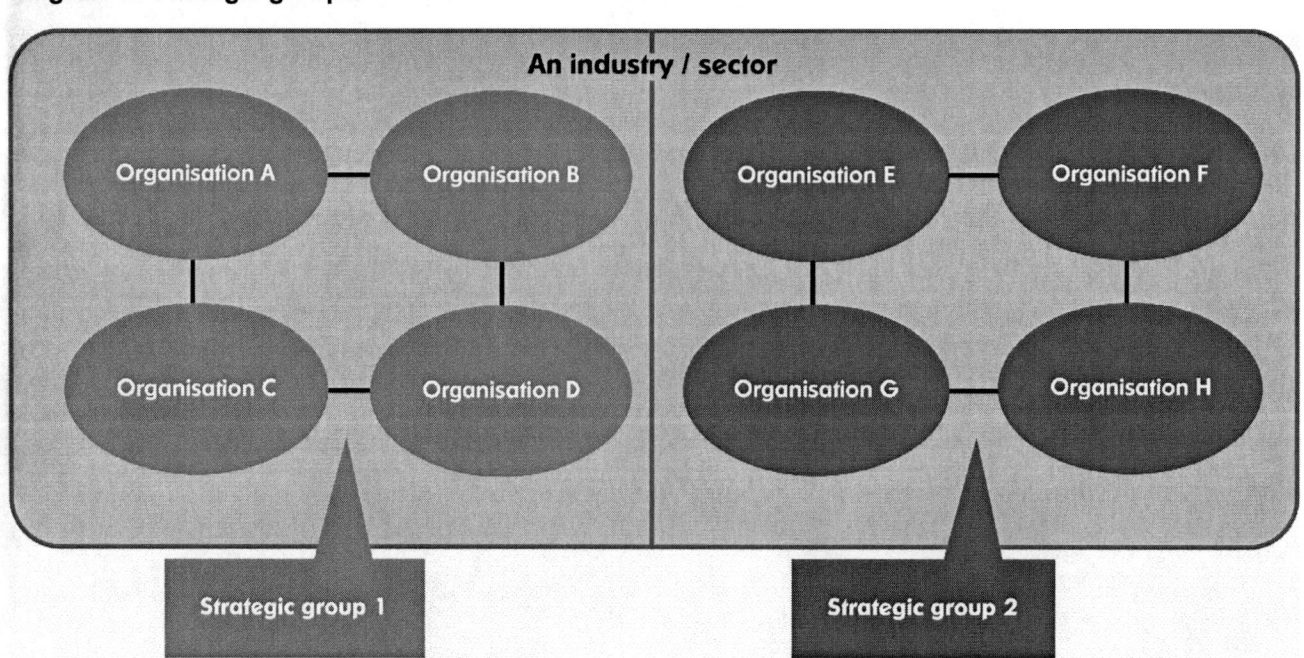

The aim of strategic group analysis (SGA) is to **identify organisations with similar strategic characteristics, following similar strategies or competing on similar bases**.

These groups can be identified on the basis of the following characteristics:

1. extent of product (or service) diversity
2. geographic coverage
3. distribution channels
4. extent of branding
5. number of market segments served
6. marketing effort
7. product (or service) quality
8. pricing policy

Example

In the telecom industry, there are two strategic groups based on the technology used in the mobile phones. One strategic group uses CDMA technology, the other uses GSM technology. Both these strategic groups have different characteristics of usage etc.

Uses of strategic groups

- Members can identify competitors who are in **direct competition** with them.
- Members have common interests and so possess negotiating power.
- Members can recognise future opportunities and threats to their organisation.
- Members can identify any competitive rivalry.
- Within strategic groups, it becomes possible for organisations to move from one strategic group to another strategic group.

The mobility of an organisation depends upon the entry barriers between one group and another.
Identifying the specific strategic group to which it belongs is a beneficial exercise for an organisation. It helps an organisation to identify:

- which firms are its closest or most direct competition
- what the mobility barriers for entering a different strategic group are

Mobility barriers are the entry barriers that have to be overcome if an organisation wishes to shift strategic position from one strategic group to another.

Example

If Suzuki wishes to enter the same strategic group as Ferrari it will have to increase the quality of its automobiles to match the standard set by these manufacturers. On the other hand, if Ferrari wishes to enter the same strategic group as Toyota it will have to greatly expand its product range to serve a mass market.

In addition to understanding themselves and the competitive forces of their industry, organisations must also understand their customers. Ultimately an organisation's profitability will depend upon how well they are able to satisfy their customers.

4.2 Market segmentation

Definition

JSW defines a **market segment** as:
A market segment is a group of customers who have similar needs that are different from customer needs in other parts of the market.

(Source: JSW

Therefore a market segment is a subgroup of people or organisations which share one or more characteristics and have **similar product needs, in other words they are homogeneous (the overall market is heterogeneous)**. As organisations can be categorised into different industries, customers can also be placed into different market segments. All organisations in a particular industry are not the same; neither are all customers in a particular market. All segments are either consumer or industrial markets.

...ion is the process of **dividing a particular market into a collection of submarkets based** ...**needs or product preferences**. When an individual market segment is homogeneous on the ...s and attitudes, there is the possibility of responding similarly to a given marketing strategy.

...n aim of market segmentation is to identify groups of similar customers and prospective customers in ...to gain a better understanding of their behaviour, to prioritise the groups to address and to respond with appropriate marketing strategies that satisfy the different preferences of each segment.

Example

The automobile industry has different segments based on its compact cars, luxury and sports car models. The markets for these are based on its price, utility and the lifestyle they want to imply.

1. Need for market segmentation
a) Understanding customers and satisfying their needs better.
b) Identifying viable segments, for example, those segments where his competition is not strong.
c) By **target marketing:** once a viable segment has been identified, specific marketing plans can be set in train to meet the precise customer needs
d) When the needs of the customers are common, there is opportunity for adequate and clear communication between the customers and organisations.
e) When the market is segmented, if any need of the customer is not fulfilled then an organisation can take measures to satisfy this need by applying new methods.
f) When the market provides whatever is needed by the consumer, the consumer in turn is ready to pay even a high price for it which results in a rise in the profits of the organisation.

2. Bases of market segmentation
The consumer market is often segmented on the basis of the following characteristics:
a) geographic
b) behaviouralistic
c) demographic
d) psychographic

a) Geographic segmentation

The market is divided on the basis of:
i. geographical region such as country, state or continent
ii. climatic conditions according to weather patterns
iii. type of population such as rural, urban or suburban

Example

Coolbreeze Ltd sells air conditioners across the country. It has divided its market into two broad regions. One region has an average high temperature throughout the year and the other has a relatively low temperature throughout the year. Hence, Coolbreeze Ltd follows geographic market segmentation.

b) Behaviouristic segmentation

This type of segmentation is based on the consumer behaviour regarding the products. The characteristics of segmentation are as follows:
i. user status i.e. whether the user of the particular product is a first time user, a prospective user or a regular user
ii. customer's readiness to buy the product
iii. usage rate i.e. how often the consumer uses the product
iv. brand loyalty i.e. the customer's dependence on and confidence in a particular product's brand
v. holidays and events that inspire customers to buy the products

c) Demographic segmentation

This type of segmentation is made on the basis of the following variables:
i. sex / gender
ii. age group
iii. family size
iv. education
v. income
vi. occupation
vii. religion
viii. social class
ix. nationality
x. health

> **Example**
>
> Woodworld Ltd manufactures a variety of household furniture items. It has divided its market on the basis of the level of income of its consumers. It offers luxury furniture items to high income group consumers and low cost furniture items to low income group consumers. Hence, it follows demographic market segmentation.

d) Psychographic segmentation

Here, the segmentation is made on the basis of the consumer's lifestyle. The variables are as follows:

i. Interests

The interests of the customers are varied. Some have traditional interests while some others have modern interests. The market has to be segmented according to the interests of the customers.

ii. Attitudes and values

Some customers assign a high value to luxury goods whereas, for other customers, luxury goods are not of any importance, i.e. they do not give much value to them. Therefore the market has to be segmented accordingly.

iii. Opinions and activities

The opinion of every individual varies. A product which is necessity for one customer may be unimportant to another customer and the segmentation varies accordingly.

SUMMARY

- **Market segmentation**
  - dividing market into submarkets based on similar customer needs / preferences
  - **bases**
    - geographical
    - behaviouralistic
    - demographic
    - psychographic

3. Segmentation of industrial markets

Industrial customers purchase their product requirements in large quantities. The decision to purchase the industrial products is taken by a large group of people. Many of the variables of consumer markets also apply to industrial markets. The other variables of segmentation are as follows:

a) type of organisation: whether the organisation is a manufacturing or a service organisation

b) product or service grouping / type

c) location of the organisation: when the needs of particular firms in an industry are common, they come together in a particular area

d) behavioural features: consumers in an industrial market have different patterns of purchasing compared to consumers in a consumer market. In an industrial market, the consumer's purchase decision is based on the opinion of many people in an organisation. The variables of segmentation are the usage rate and the buyer's status (first time buyer, prospective buyer or regular buyer)

A detailed discussion on marketing and the value of goods and services is given in the next Study Guide, A4.

Test Yourself 4

Destiny Ltd is a mobile phone company which offers a variety of mobile phones. It has divided its market on the basis of its customers' levels of income. Destiny has introduced a model called Amazing which is a Cell phone and has a high range. Customers can use Amazing to access the Internet and emails. The target customers for Amazing are businessmen.

Destiny has also introduced the Best model. The target customers for Best are young people who want their mobile to look good and incorporate advanced technology at a competitive price. Best is a slimline model with a high storage capacity which allows the user to store films or songs. It has a megapixel camera which can be used as a substitute for a digital camera.

The third model which Destiny has introduced is called Angels and is targeted at the general public whose mobile usage is very limited and who are more concerned with prices rather than look or technology.

Required:

Explain what market segmentations are and explain the need for market segmentation in the case of Destiny Ltd.

---

5. Determine the opportunities and threats posed by the environment of an organisation. [2]
[Learning Outcome e]

Opportunities and threats are the **external forces** which influence the organisation's strategic planning.

Opportunity

A **favourable condition** in an organisation's environment which enables it to strengthen its position. It is a situation whereby the demand for a product or service increases.

Threat

An **unfavourable condition** in an organisation's environment which causes damage or risk to the organisation's position. A threat may be a constraint or a barrier.

Opportunities and threats posed by the environment

1. **Political threats and opportunities**

a) When a government enacts **regulations** which are favourable to an organisation, this creates opportunities for the organisation. However, if the regulations are strict and unfavourable this is a threat to the organisation.

Example

If a government enacts any regulation which expands the benefits of exemption relating to export duty and also direct tax benefits for export-oriented undertakings, then this is an opportunity for those organisations who export their products.

---

b) If **government policies** are such that they benefit the organisation, this is an opportunity whereas if governmental policies are not beneficial and impose various conditions to be fulfilled, this is a threat.

c) Where the **government changes** during a period and the new government passes favourable policies then this is an opportunity for an organisation, whereas if the new government passes strict regulations unfavourable to the organisation, this is a threat.

d) **Government spending programmes**: if the government undertakes to spend a fix amount on any particular project, the organisations in that industry will have an opportunity as the government will bear the burden of spending to some extent.

2. Economic threats and opportunities

a) If the **tax provisions** are beneficial for an organisation, this is an opportunity whereas if they are strict and take away any exemptions or benefits, this is a threat.

b) If the **interest rates** on borrowings are low this is an opportunity whereas if these rates are high this is a threat.

Example
In the year 2006, the rate of interest on borrowings was 9%. In the current year, 2007, financial institutions have reduced the rate of interest to 8%. For organisations who intend to acquire a loan from financial institutions, this is an opportunity because, in the current year, by paying less interest, they can obtain a larger loan.

c) Where **inflation rates** are high, this is a threat because when inflation exists in an economy, people do not purchase as much as their purchasing power reduces, and so this is a threat. On the other hand, if the inflation rate is low, the purchasing power increases and hence creates an opportunity for an organisation.

d) When the government enacts an **anti-monopoly regulation**, this is an opportunity for an organisation who desires to enter the particular market whereas it is a threat for an existing firm in that industry because, after the enactment of this regulation, new competitors will enter the industry.

3. Social threats and opportunities

a) **Social changes**

Example
When there is a change in the age distribution of the population. If an organisation produces a product targeted at the elderly but the age distribution of the population changes so that there are a greater proportion of young people, this is a threat for the organisation.

b) **Cultural changes** such as changes in the leisure activities of the people.

4. Technological threats and opportunities

Advancement in technology is an opportunity for an organisation because it leads to an increase in production and ultimately increased profits. On the other hand, if there is technological development in a competitor's organisation, this is a threat because the competitor's production will increase and ultimately their profits will rise.

Opportunities and threats are the elements of **SWOT analysis**. SWOT stands for strength, weakness, opportunities and threats. Strengths and weaknesses are internal forces whereas opportunities and threats are external forces. SWOT analysis is explained in detail in Study Guide A5.

SUMMARY

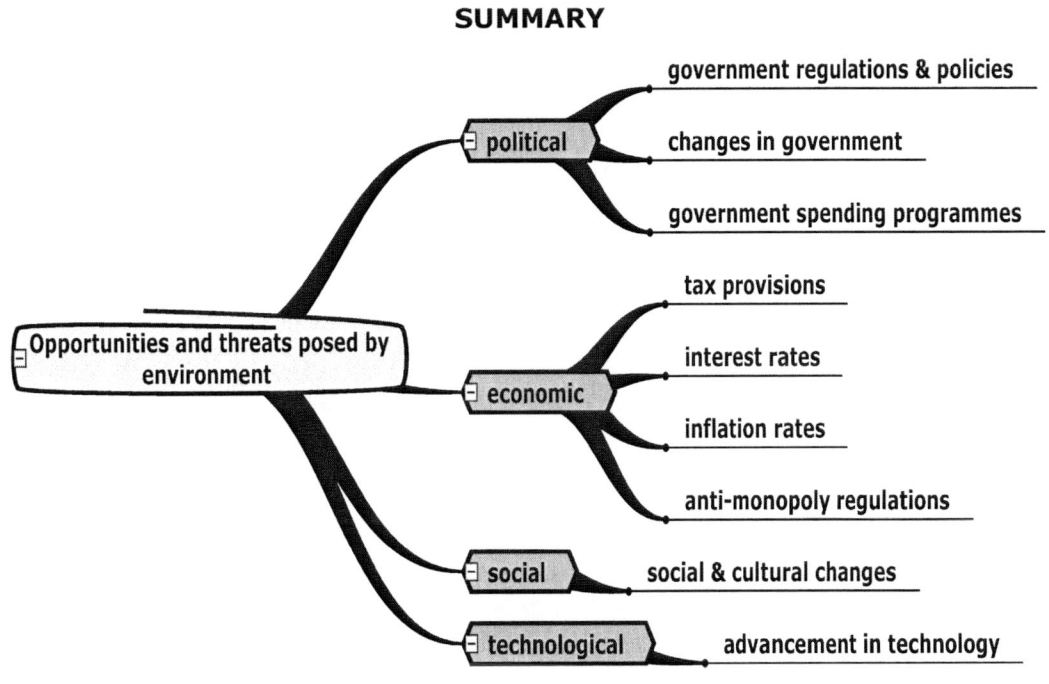

Test Yourself 5

Crusoe Ltd is a steel manufacturing company, involved in exporting stainless steel pipes and other steel material for industrial use. Previously, Crusoe was exempted from paying duty on exports. Nowadays due to the increasing cost of stainless steel, the government has imposed a heavy export duty on stainless steel products.

Due to this, Crusoe Ltd will now need to sell its goods at a high rate. This may affect its market sales as well as its profit earnings. Previously, due to its exemption from export duty, Crusoe Ltd was able to sell its goods at lower cost and still earn a good amount of profits.

Required:

Explain what opportunity and threat mean and how they affect the business of Crusoe.

Answers to Test Yourself

Answer to TY 1

Convergence is a process in which similarities increase and differences decrease. It refers to the coming together of two or more different technologies.

Market convergence occurs when the functional characteristics or nature of an existing product is changed. This often takes place when the product of one industry becomes a substitute for products from other industries.

There are two main reasons which lead to convergence.

1. Supply-led

When the supplier of one industry finds some link or connection with the supplier of other industries, they can join together to build a new market or sector. Supply-led convergence is popular in the case of public sector organisations where the government compels the entities to work together.

2. Demand-led

The consumers substitute products for one another. The consumers behave as though the industries have converged.

In the case of Destiny Ltd, convergence is supply-led. Destiny has added many features to its mobile functions. The Amazing model which Destiny has created can be used as a substitute for a computer and/or camera. Its memory capacity is very good where customer can use it as to save movie clips, photos, e-mail and other details. Mobile camera giving the replacements for camera functions where customer have not need to carry a separate camera or video camera's they can clicks the photos as well as they can shoot anything according to their wish.

Answer to TY 2

An ideal industry is one in which:

- there is no possibility of new organisations entering
- buyers will pay whatever prices the organisation sets
- suppliers will sell at whatever prices the organisation sets
- there are no substitute products
- there is no competition from any other organisation

Flintstone Ltd is enjoying a monopoly in the market for CFA books, but there are other competitors in the market. Buyers are paying whatever prices Flintstones sets but these prices are very low and no other competitor can sell its books at such low prices. There are substitute products in the market, but the prices of the books are very high compared to the cost of Flintstone's books. The marketing and advertising department of Flintstone is very strong which helps the organisation to increase its sales continuously.

An ideal industry only exists in theory. In practice, every industry has at least one strong force. The greater the number or strength of these forces, the more competitive the industry or sector is.

Answer to TY 3

The phases of the lifecycle model are: development, growth, shakeout, maturity and decline.

The lifecycle model links the intensity of competition in a particular industry with the growth of that industry. It is a tool used to analyse the effects of an industry's growth on competitive forces. All industries go through different stages of a lifecycle. Various organisations within the same industry can go through lifecycle stages at different times. The strategies of an organisation and its competitors vary depending on their stages within the lifecycle. The following are the five phases of the evolution of an industry in relation to its level of competition:

1. **Development**

A new product is developed and introduced at this stage. An industry is in its infancy and there is only one organisation or very few organisations in operation. Therefore competition is very low or nonexistent at this phase.

2. **Growth**

This phase indicates the fast growth of the industry. Competition builds up as more new entrants join the industry. However, the level of competitive behaviour is not intense as the overall market is growing.

3. **Shakeout**

At this stage, many more organisations start operating in the industry. Competition intensifies as the "strong" or efficient organisations strive to drive out the "weak" or inefficient organisations.

4. **Maturity**

There are usually fewer firms, and those that survive are larger and more dominant. The only way for organisations remaining in the industry to increase sales is by stealing market share from competing organisations.

5. **Decline**

The intensity of competition declines as organisations that did not leave during the maturity stage exit the industry at this stage. Market size declines at a faster rate. Yet, some organisations remain competing in the smaller market.

At the development stage, Balamory Ltd was the only company manufacturing computer monitors in its region, and it did not face any competition. As soon as other organisations entered the industry, competition intensified; the overall market was at the growth stage. At the shakeout stage, competition increased, which meant that only strong and efficient organisations that were able to satisfy customer demands were able to survive. At the maturity stage, organisations that provided advance technology for their existing products, or introduced a new product (like flat screen monitors or laptops) were able to survive. At the decline stage, organisations that were weaker, or those that had not improved their products according to market demands, lost their market.

Balmory lost business whilst Baywatch became the key player because it had consistently introduced new products into market and had applied the most advanced technology.

Answer to TY 4

Market segmentation is the process of dividing a particular market into a collection of submarkets based upon similar needs or product preferences. The main aim of market segmentation is to identify groups of similar customers, understand their needs and respond with appropriate marketing strategies and products for each segment, which satisfy the customer demands.

Market segmentation takes place as follows:

1. The organisation first needs to understand the customers' requirements and satisfy their demands.
2. The organisation then carries out market research to identify viable segments where competition is not strong.
3. After identifying viable segments, specific market plans are set to fulfil specific customer needs.

Destiny Ltd has applied market segmentation by identifying viable segments and introducing products which are appropriate for these segments. Destiny has introduced the Amazing model by considering business class people who are ready to pay cost against technology which satisfy their business needs. Amazing is made in such a way which functions as a mini computer for them. Best mobile has specifically make by considering young people who wants advance technology as well as look to their mobile. Best has provided them mobile as well as it has function like IPOD where they can hear a song or they can see the movie by storing them into their mobile. It has mega pixel camera which can be the substitute for digital cameras. Angel mobile is satisfying the need of general class people who are keen for product cost rather than the technology use in it.

Answer to TY 5

Opportunity means a favourable condition in an organisation's environment which helps it to strengthen its position. It is a situation where the demand for a product or service increases.

Threat means an unfavourable condition in an organisation's environment which causes damage or risk to the organisation's position. A threat may be a constraint or a barrier.

Crusoe enjoyed an opportunity when the government gave it an exemption from paying duty on exports. Crusoe sold its goods at a low cost which enabled it to make high profits. The government's decision to impose a heavy duty on exporting stainless steel goods may affect the business of Crusoe. Crusoe may now need to sell its goods at a high cost with low profit. Previously the government's favourable policies created an opportunity for Crusoe whereas its unfavourable export policy is creating a threat to its business.

Quick Quiz

1. _____ occurs "where previously separate industries begin to overlap in terms of activities, technologies, products and customers".

2. Which model is useful for assessing the factors that influence the level of competitiveness in an industry or sector?

3. At which phase of the lifecycle model is there no or very low competition?

4. Opportunities and threats are internal forces. Is the statement correct?

Answers to Quick Quiz

1. Convergence

2. Porter's five forces model provides a framework for assessing competitive forces / factors that influence the level of competitiveness in an industry or sector.

3. Development stage

4. No. Opportunities and threats are external forces.

Self Examination Questions

Question 1

The Supersaver supermarket operates its business through more than 3,000 large retail stores. It has grown substantially over recent years, and has experienced global expansion. However it has a presence in relatively few countries worldwide. Supersaver positions itself as a high volume, low cost, low margin, cash-based supermarket grocery chain. It has a reputation for value for money, convenience and offering a wide range of products all in one store. Its business success depends heavily on tight cost control, stock management, flexible pricing strategies and efficient buying and merchandising operations. None of Supersaver's competitors is able to beat its "Low Prices" philosophy.

Supersaver head office staff undertakes all major buying, merchandising, marketing and financial activities leaving store management largely concerned with day-to-day operations such as staffing, customer service, cash handling and store security. Supersaver has a focused strategy in place for human resource management and development. People are key to Supersaver's business and it invests time and money in training, retaining and developing them.

Supersaver has a core competence involving its use of information technology to support its domestic and international logistics system. For example, management can see at a glance how individual products are performing country-wide and store-wide. IT also supports Supersaver's efficient procurement.

Based at head office is the Supersaver computer centre where mainframe systems manage the communications network of small in-store computers located at each supermarket. In-store computers undertake electronic point of sale (EPOS) and point of receipt (POR) processing and associated stock control routines. Each computer is on-line to the centre mainframe for the purposes of data transfer for store operations.

Supersaver deals with more than 50,000 small and a few large suppliers. At head office order / purchasing systems provide daily on-line order requirements to suppliers, calling off quantities against bulk supply contracts. Frequent delivery takes place direct from the supplier to each individual store allowing only the minimum levels of stock to be carried by each store. Supersaver sees no major current competitive advantage in the EPOS / POR systems as these are now fully utilised by all of its competitors. The next stage of development will however be key in maintaining a competitive edge.

Supersaver has proven to be the top retailer in the domestic retailing industry. Its quest is to dominate the international market. Even though Supersaver has what seems to be a flawless business model, there is still a major problem with making profits in potential international markets. Supersaver tried to duplicate its domestic business model in the international market. It led to several challenges and problems when it attempted this transition as the industry domestically is quite different than internationally.

Required:

Using an appropriate model and the data from the scenario, provide competitive forces analysis of Supersaver to assess its current strategic position.

Question 2

Coronation Ltd is an organisation which is involved in manufacturing deodorant Coronation was the first company in its region to introduce deodorant into the market. Cosby Ltd is another company which has recently entered the market. Coronation is an established firm and has a monopoly in the market. Coronation's prices are very competitive and it is difficult for Cosby to sell its products at such low prices. Cosby also needs to compete with Coronation on many different aspects, as Coronation's goodwill as well as the marketing and advertising of its products are very strong.

The management of Cosby has held a staff meeting to identify solutions to how it can compete with Coronation and establish itself in the market. The management wants to explain to its employees the significance of the industry / sector, the cycle of competition and how the organisation can overcome these problems.

Required:

(a) Explain what is meant by an industry and the significance of the industry / sector to Cosby staff.

(b) Explain the cycle of competition and how it operates.

(c) Suggest solutions which will help Cosby to compete with Coronation.

Answers to Self Examination Questions

Answer to SEQ 1

Porter's five forces model is a useful means of analysing the competitive environment. It provides a framework to assess competitive forces in terms of threats of new market entrants and threats of substitutes, buyer and supplier bargaining power, and the degree of competition from existing players in the market. These are the five main factors that influence the level of competitiveness in an industry or sector and shape an organisation's environment. The five forces model is used to analyse Supersaver's strategic position.

1. Threat of new entrants

Entry barriers are relatively high, as Supersaver has an outstanding procurement, inventory management and distribution systems, locations, brand name and financial capital to fend off potential competitors. Supersaver does not face the threat of new entrants because it has economies of scale. It often has an absolute cost advantage over other competitors. Due to its "low prices" philosophy, the competitors are unable to beat Supersaver. Supersaver also has access to distribution channels with secure distribution for its products. Its information systems are being used to lock in suppliers and buyers. Technology plays an important role in helping Supersaver stay customer-focused and gain customer loyalty. There are high barriers of entry for organisations aspiring to come into the retail industry because of the resources that Supersaver possesses.

2. Threat of substitutes

Supersaver provides a wide range of products at a low price all under one roof. Its customers have the option of going to specialty stores to get their desired products. There are not many substitutes that offer convenience and low pricing like Supersaver. Moreover, its information systems are being used to maintain the value of the supply chain to reduce the risk of substitutes.

However, online shopping over the internet proves another alternative for customers because it is more convenient and the customer can gain price advantages. (In this case the company does not necessarily have to have a brick and mortar store, passing the savings onto the consumer.) Supersaver can use the existing technology base to add value to customers and to extend the range of their products and services over the internet.

3. Bargaining power of buyers

The individual buyer can apply little or no pressure on Supersaver. Buyers do not have to bargain with Supersaver for low prices, higher quality or more services because it has already established the philosophy of low prices, higher quality and more services. The customers could shop at a competitor / specialty store which offers comparable products but the convenience and the price advantage is lost.

4. Bargaining power of suppliers

Suppliers can exert power by threatening to raise prices or reduce the quality of goods and services supplied by them. This will not happen in the case of Supersaver as it holds a large market share and offers a lot of business to manufacturers and wholesalers. This gives Supersaver a lot of power as it could threaten to switch to a different supplier. However Supersaver does deal with some large suppliers who have more bargaining power than small suppliers.

5. Competitive rivalry

There is no intensity of rivalry among Supersaver and its competitors in the domestic retail industry because Supersaver excels in this sector. No competitor is able to sell at prices equal to or lower than those of Supersaver. It has proven to be the top retailer in the domestic retailing industry.

However, since Supersaver sells products across many sectors, it may not have the flexibility of some of its more focused competitors. The Supersaver stores are currently trading in a relatively small number of countries. Therefore there are tremendous opportunities for future business in expanding consumer markets. However, Supersaver is facing problems in entering the international market.

Major competitors of Supersaver can try to tap the international market and steal Supersaver's opportunity for globalisation. Although the competitive rivalry for Supersaver is low in the domestic market, it will be comparatively high in the international market.

Competitive advantage arises when a business positions itself in a way which makes maximum use of the positive capabilities which distinguish it from its competitors. It follows that competitive advantage is dynamic in the sense that advantages are temporary and a business must always be seeking new areas for advantage. Supersaver is pursuing an overall cost leadership strategy which demands high levels of information systems capability to manage logistical processes, to exploit cost advantage through strategic pricing and to maintain tight cost control.

Answer to SEQ 2

(a) Coronation and Cosby are both working in the deodorant industry. An industry is a group of organisations which produce similar products i.e. products which are close substitutes for each other. In addition, organisations in an industry share a common method of generating profits and production techniques.

The industry / sector is significant as it allows managers to understand the competitive forces at work in a particular sector and helps them to take important decisions about the product / market strategy.

Cosby's management needs to re-evaluate its production cost as well as its selling cost. It needs to make a proper plan before introducing the new product. It needs to plan the aspects on which it will compete with Coronation. It should build a strong marketing and advertising team in order to attract consumers. It needs to study the common features as well as the work culture of both the companies.

(b) The cycle of competition shows the relationship between an established firm and a new entrant. Each competitor will have its own influence in the industry. An established firm builds entry barriers for new entrants. A new entrant attacks a firm of the same size and nature; if the existing firm does not respond then it widens its scope of attack and the existing firm responds by reinforcing the barriers to entry. This results in a price or technology war. The new entrant then restarts the cycle in a different market.

(c) Cosby needs to identify the area where it needs to compete with Coronation. Both companies are selling the same product and price is the main issue. Cosby needs to reduce its production costs and can use advanced technology which will help it to reduce the production cost, so that it can also sell its product at as low a price as Coronation. Cosby should give its employees free deodorants as a way of advertising its products. It can also start an aggressive advertising campaign to promote its products. Cosby needs to identify its target customers and concentrate on advertising its products to these customers. It also needs to increase its range of products. In this way it may capture market share and increase its business and profit.

SECTION A: STRATEGIC POSITION

STUDY GUIDE A4: MARKETING AND THE VALUES OF GOODS AND SERVICES

■ Get Through Intro

Many of you, in future years, will go on to start your own businesses. You may believe that you have an unbeatable product that will sell and hopefully make you millions. However, without customers, it can not happen. You need to ensure that the customers want your product, they value it and they are willing to pay enough to give you a decent profit. It sounds easy, but it can not be done without analysing your customers, identifying why your product meets their needs and maximising the value you are giving them.

This chapter will teach you to do just that. You probably did not know that Windows 1.0 operating system was not a success as there were many bugs in it. Many customers were not interested as it did not meet their needs and much preferred the Apple Mac. However, if Bill Gates had given up then, what the world be like today?

■ Learning Outcomes

a) Analyse customers and markets.
b) Establish appropriate critical success factors (CSF) and key performance indicators (KPI) for products and services.
c) Explore the role of the value chain in creating and sustaining competitive advantage.
d) Advise on the role and influence of value networks.
e) Assess different approaches to benchmarking an organisation's performance.

Introduction

Case Study

The best examples are often the ones in front of you. For this case study we are going to look at a real life example that you know something about - Get Through Guides!

Before we started writing our Text books, the GTG team had to analyse who our customers were and what our markets were. You may think that the answer to this is simple – surely students who are already studying the ACCA qualification. However, this is not true. Many students who are studying will already be going to a college which may recommend certain non GTG text books and bundle this in to the price of the course. Hence these students will not want to buy an additional text book. So initially GTG concentrated on students who were not going on courses and were studying by themselves.

GTG then had to decide what the critical success factors should be. Through focus group discussions with students studying on their own, students revealed that they felt the current products in the markets did not give sufficient examples of the theory and consequently students found it hard to apply the theory. Price was also an issue for many of them, which is why they did not go on courses. Finally, many students said they felt parts of the syllabus seemed to have been left out in other textbooks.

So GTG decided to emphasise practical examples after each major part of theory. GTG also priced competitively and finally addressed each learning outcome from the syllabus.

By pricing competitively, GTG needed to ensure that all costs incurred were as low as possible, In order to do this, GTG used value chain analysis to see where the value was being added and maximise this. At the same time, GTG saw where costs could be cut.

Every year, GTG reviews what competitors are doing and also tries to come up with innovative ways of making studying more fun and less of a chore. This is how we believe we will keep our competitive edge.

The above case study hopefully shows you that all companies need to think about these important areas if their businesses are going to succeed. Study this area well as your business could depend on it in the future!

1. Analyse customers and markets.[2]

[Learning Outcome a]

A customer can be defined as being any party (individual or organisation) who purchases or intends to purchase and / or use a final product / service. The traditional description of a market was that of being a physical location that brought together buyers and sellers for the purpose of discovering information as well as making purchases and sales. Today the need for a market to have a tangible presence has disappeared due to the existence of delivery channels such as the phone and internet. Therefore a market is now said to exist whenever a transaction can or does takes place between customers and suppliers of a product / service.

However it is important to note that not all customers of a particular product / service will have the same needs or purchase the product / service for the same reasons. Organisations that provide products / services must take this factor into account and identify the different types or groups of customers they have. This leads into the area of market segmentation. Market segmentation involves an organisation dividing its market (total number of customers and potential customers) into various segments. Each segment would contain a particular group of customers with a particular set of needs. The markets are heterogeneous (made up of many different segments) and the segments are homogeneous.

The **main methods of segmentation** are as follows:

- geographic
- behaviouralistic
- demographic
- psychographic

All these methods are explained in detail in Study Guide A3.

Example

BMW is a leading automobile manufacturer. The organisation produces a variety of different models each of which is aimed for a particular market segment. For instance its top end models of luxury sedans (the 7 series) are aimed for executives / businesspersons. These models are designed to satisfy their needs for luxury and prestige. On the other hand their sports models (the M series) are targeted towards driving enthusiasts and are designed to satisfy their needs for speed and other aspects of performance driving.

Organisations also need to identify the different types of customers they have and subsequently how they should sell to each type of customer they have. For instance mobile phone manufacturers do not sell their phones directly to the end user (the individuals who use them). Instead they sell to organisations such as retail and department stores that display and subsequently sell the phones on to the end consumers.

Therefore organisations such as Nokia and Motorola have and must satisfy the needs of two very different types of customers. Their commercial customers industrial markets) would place an emphasis and greater value on how the mobiles are packaged and presented (e.g. they would want them to be "eye catching") whereas consumers (consumer markets) would emphasise and place a greater value on the phone's features and price.

Both types of customers and both types of needs are important. The end consumer is naturally very important because it is this group that eventually purchases the phones and will account for sales. However the commercial customers are also important because if the phones are poorly displayed then sales will get adversely affected.

Organisations must not only take this step of distinguishing between the different types of customers they have but must also determine which is their "strategic customer". Johnson, Scholes and Whittington ("JSW") state "the strategic customer is the person(s) at whom the strategy is primarily addressed because they have the most influence over which goods or services are purchased".

Mobile phone manufacturers are well aware of this fact and attempt to meet the needs of their strategic customers through attractive packaging as well as offering display units and advertising material such as pamphlets and brochures. However it is important to note that this is not done at the expense of ignoring the needs of the end customer (mobile phone models are continually upgraded with better and more features).

Overall organisations must determine:

➢ the different types of customers they have;

➢ the different market segment each of these groups of customers represent and

➢ what the needs of each segment are.

SUMMARY

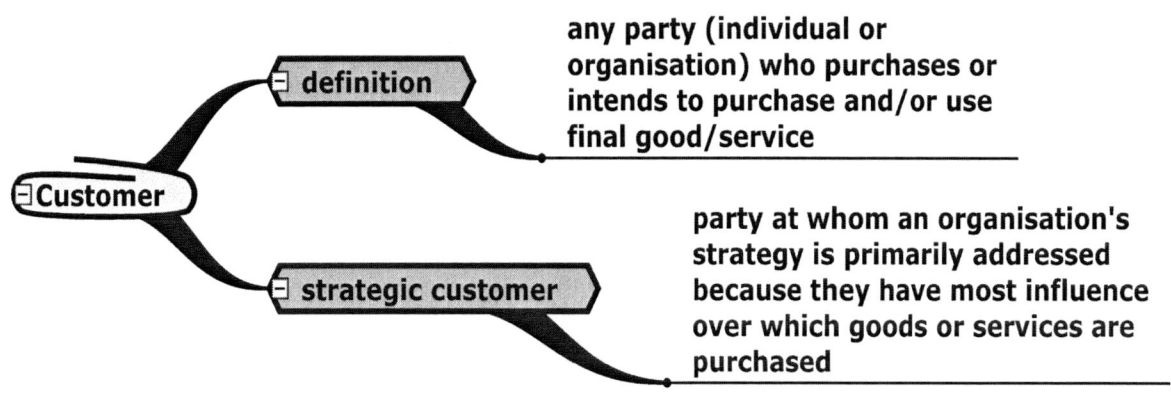

76: Strategic Position

SUMMARY

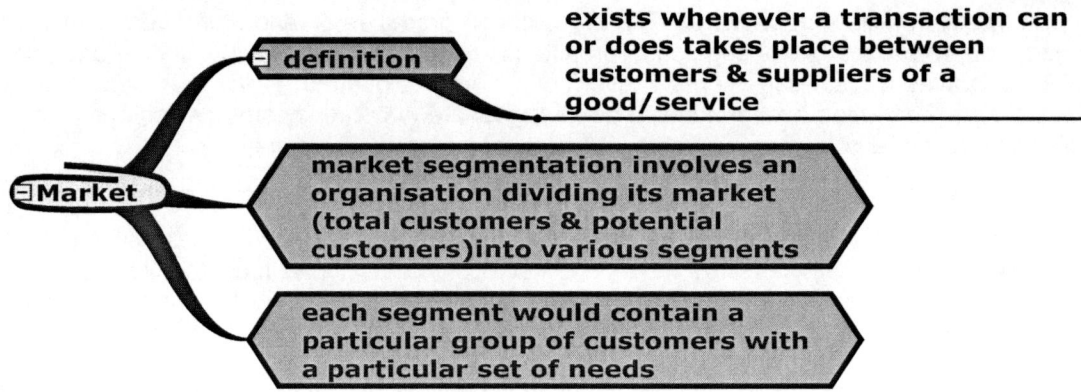

Test Yourself 1

Gadget Ltd is a global leader in automobile manufacture with operations in Europe and Asia. The organisation produces a variety of models of motorbike which are aimed at particular market segments. The latest models manufactured are:

- Model IX Pleasure Scooter with contemporary styling and the components aesthetically nested in the front body. 115cc engine with an output of 6bhp. 1 year warranty. Price $867.
- Model XIX Pure Rider which comes in various styles and has a 166cc engine with an average output of 9bhp. 1 year warranty. Price $1,089.
- Model XX Super Bluster bike with newly designed headlight translucent visor. Fuel efficient 200cc engine with an average output of 12bhp. 3 year warranty. Price $1,346.

These products are designed to satisfy customers' needs and their increasing demands. Gadget has two types of customer: industrial market customers and end users.

Required:

How should Gadget Ltd identify its different types of customer and sell its products to each type of customer according to their needs and demands?

---

2. Establish appropriate critical success factors CSF) and key performance indicators (KPI) for products and services.[2]

[Learning Outcome b]

As mentioned in the previous section, organisations will have different types of customers and/or customers with different types of needs. This leads to the need for organisations to divide their customers into sets of different market segments.

Organisations must then determine why each segment is purchasing its product / service. This question is normally answered by determining the features of the product / service that customers value in general as well as more specifically its critical success factors.

Critical Success Factors (CSFs) are the specific features of a particular product / service that customers or segments attach the most importance to when making their purchase decisions. Johnson, Scholes and Whittington expand upon this definition and state that "Critical success factors are those product features that are particularly valued by a group of customers and, therefore where the organisation must excel to outperform the competition".

Example

Au Natural is an ice cream manufacturer that specialises in making fruit flavoured ice creams. To differentiate itself, Au Natural ensures that they only use fresh fruits when preparing their ice creams. Their customers purchase their ice creams for their taste (the general quality they value) and more specifically because of their fresh fruit content (the critical success factor).

A tool that can be used to identify how customers value different features of the same product / service provided by competing organisations is the strategy canvass. A strategy canvass is basically a line graph where the horizontal axis lists the various features / qualities of a product / service. The vertical axis in turn depicts a range of values to quantifiably measure how effectively each particular feature / quality is being delivered.

A strategy canvass is completed by plotting and connecting a series of dots for each organisation (each dot represents how well a particular organisation is delivering a particular feature / quality).

Diagram 1: Strategy canvass

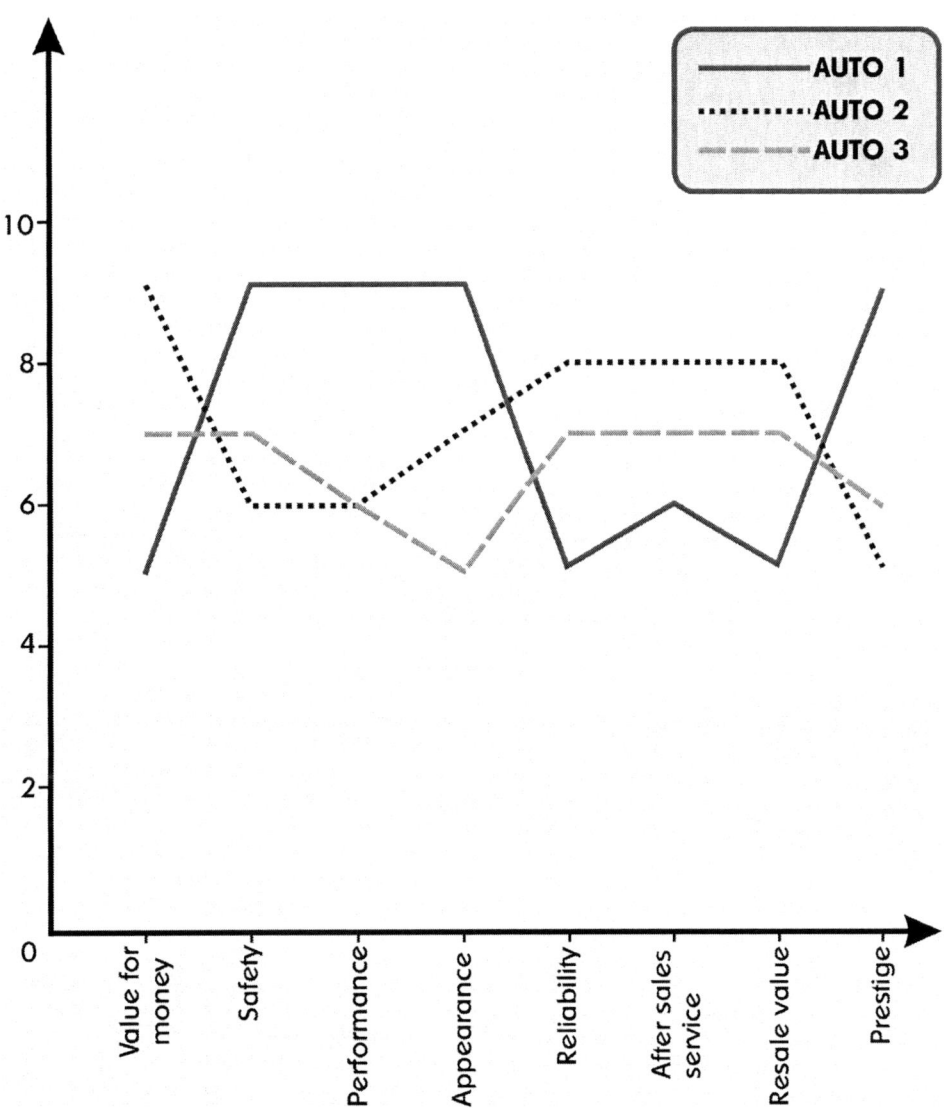

As can be seen a strategy canvas allows each organisation to see which strategy it as well as its competitors are currently following. With the above diagram, Auto1 which is a premier automobile manufacturer such as BMW is focusing on offering high end performance, prestige and safety for its customers but at a high price.

Other **advantages of a strategy canvas** are that it:

➤ identifies areas where an organisation is differentiating itself from the competition.
➤ identifies areas where customer needs are not being met.

Disadvantages of a strategy canvas are that:

➤ It is not always easy to construct in practice as it is often difficult to determine why consumers have purchased a particular product / service.

➤ Organisations often have difficulty in determining who exactly are their strategic customers. For instance many manufacturers are separated from the final end user by several intermediary distributors.

➤ The features / qualities that customers value will change over time due to factors such as technological advances, new competitive offerings and socio-economic changes.

SUMMARY

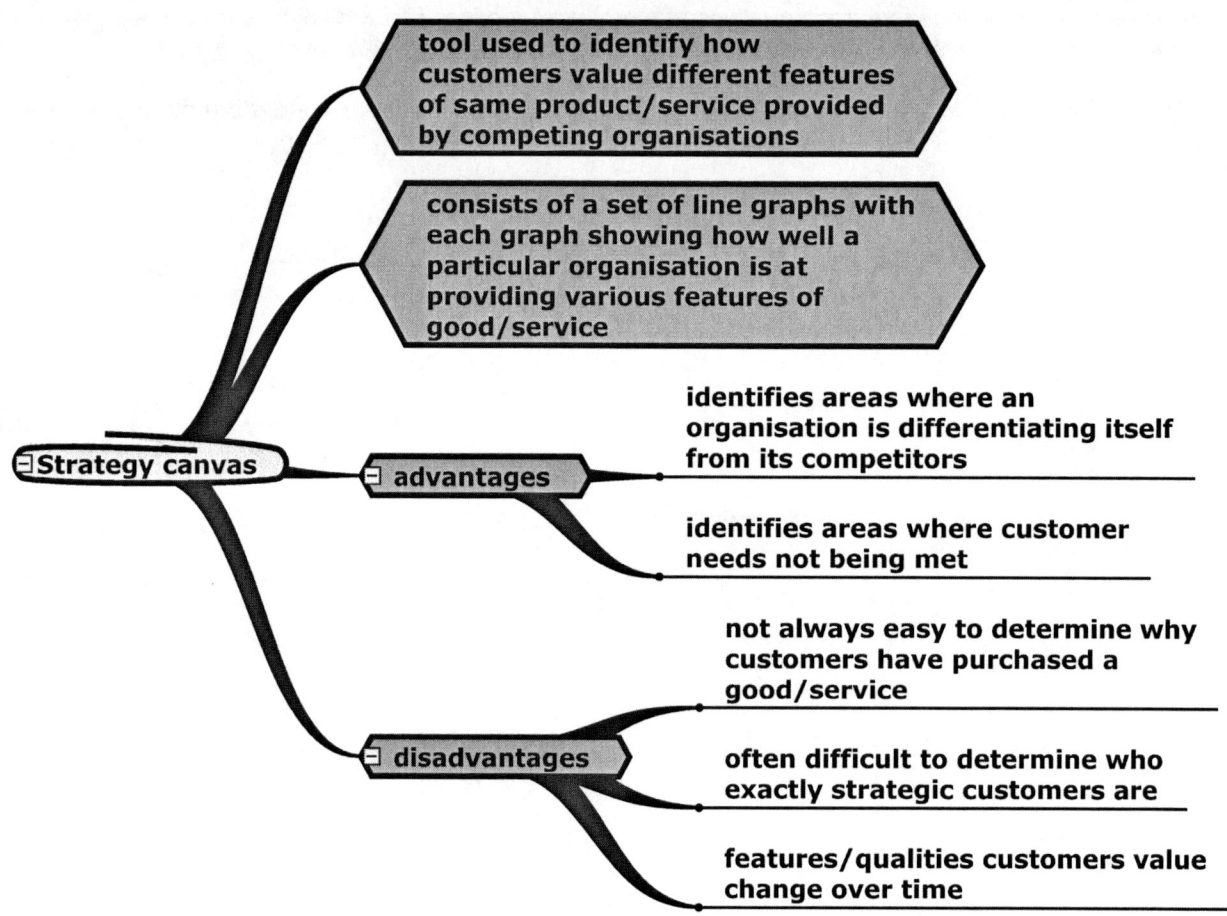

Test Yourself 2

Pure Herb Plc is an herbal product manufacturer that specialises in the production of hair shampoo, hair oil and body lotion. Pure Herb Plc ensures that the products it manufactures are handmade and do not contain any chemical or synthetic additives.

Required:

How can Pure Herb Plc attract customers to purchase its products and satisfy the different needs of the customers?

---

3. Explore the role of the value chain in creating and sustaining competitive advantage.[2]
[Learning Outcome c]

The main reason why consumers purchase a product / service is because they believe it has some value. They may derive this value from either using the product / service or re-selling it to another party at a profit. Therefore organisations need to understand how they create this value when they are producing a product / service.

A value chain is a technique that can be used by organisations to identify how the various activities that go into producing a product / service create value. This model was developed by Michael Porter and describes activities within and around an organisation, which when performed in sequence go on to create a final product / service by adding incremental value at each stage.

Diagram 2: Value chain

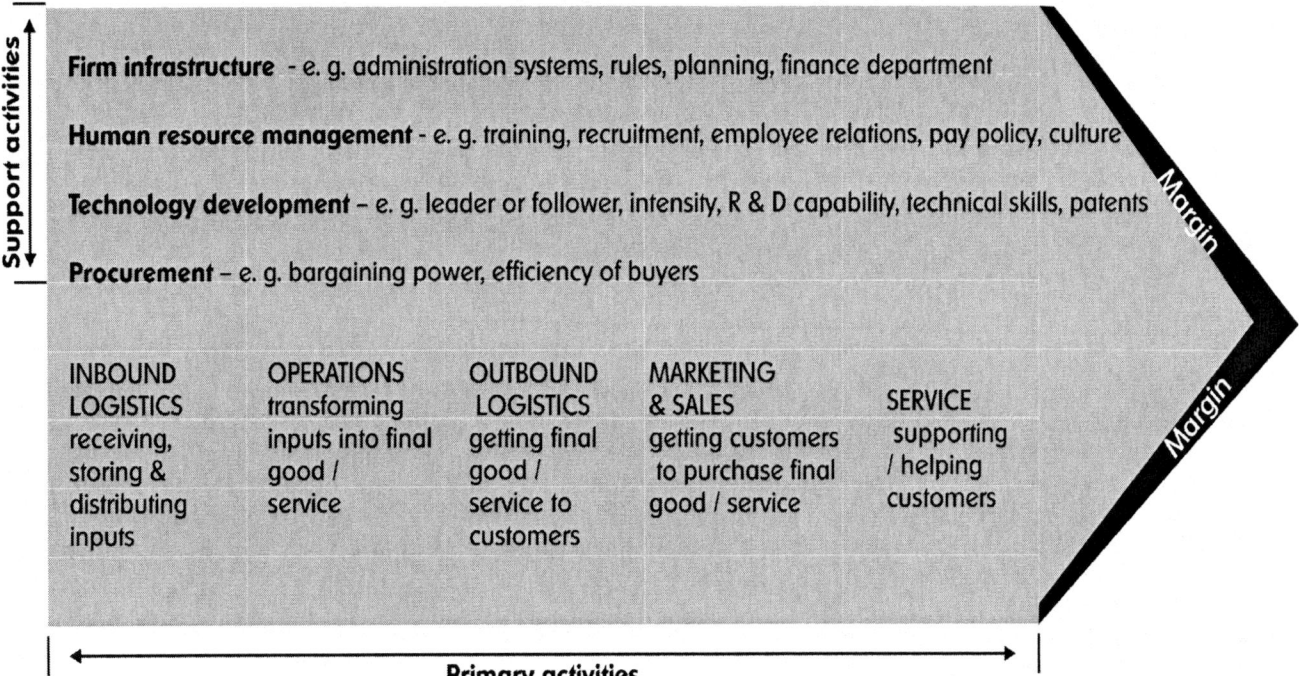

As can be seen from the above diagram these activities fall into one of two major groups – primary activities and secondary activities. Primary activities include functions such as production, marketing, logistics and after sales functions. They are labelled "primary" because these activities are directly involved with producing and/or bringing a product / service one stage closer to the customer. The value chain is only one way of carrying out internal analysis. There are other ways of carrying out internal analysis, such as using an activity system. An activity system is a system which comprises connected circles that represent key value-driving activities. If the connections between the circle / activity are high or the relationships are close, it becomes more difficult for the market competitors to imitate the strategy selected by the organisation. An activity system is used to identify the areas where value could be added either through differentiation or cost leadership. It is also used to assess how easily operating systems can be imitated.

Secondary activities are those that serve as a support function to the organisation's primary activities. Their purpose is to help an organisation to improve the efficiency / effectiveness of its primary activities. One of the support activities is **firm infrastructure**. This includes administration systems, planning, procedures, rules and the finance department of the organisation. Firm infrastructure is an important support system in an organisation, for example, the **administration system** enables the smooth functioning of the organisation's operations. If any of the staff members require something in order to complete a task, the administration personnel assist him with the desired requirement. In the same way, the **finance department** is also of utmost importance to any organisation because the finance department satisfies the financial needs of each department of the organisation.

Naturally each of these activities will involve an organisation incurring some costs but they should in turn deliver some value back to the organisation. Ideally each activity should return a value that outweighs its costs. Organisations need to focus on how they can increase the value created by / reduce the amount each activity costs. Organisations that can perform key activities better (derive greater value) and/or at a lower cost than their competitors will be able to create and sustain a competitive advantage.

Overall a value chain should be thought of as a chain of activities that need to be undertaken in sequence to produce a final product / service. A product / service must pass each activity in turn with each activity attaching some additional value. The ultimate goal being that the sum of values from all activities should exceed the total costs incurred thereby generating a profit margin for the organisation.

It is to be noted here that one of the most important uses of the value chain is to align the whole firm to a generic strategy. So, if the firm is a cost leader, it would look to cut costs throughout the value chain. On the other hand, if the firm is a differentiator, it would look to add quality throughout the value chain.

Example

Tables and Trees Limited (TTL) is an organisation that manufactures and sells coffee tables. Its value chain is as follows:

Inbound logistics: TTL sources and imports high quality lumber from various S. American countries.

Operations: this lumber is then cut into a variety of sizes and shapes. Each piece of lumber then represents a particular part of the coffee table (e.g. leg, top etc). These parts are then joined to form the final coffee table.

Outbound logistics: the coffee tables are then packed, packaged and shipped out to various retail outlets where they are sold.

Marketing and sales: TTL's salesforce are constantly contacting retail outlets to obtain orders for the organisation's tables.

Service: each of TTL's tables comes with a customer complaint form. A service department goes through all returned forms and passes their feedback onto the operations department.

TTL creates value by taking a raw material (lumber) and transforming into a usable end product (a coffee table). Further value is then added by packing the end product and shipping it outlets where it can be easily purchased by its end user (the customer). Naturally at each stage where value is added, the cost of the product is also correspondingly increased. For instance the cost of the coffee table will be more than the cost of the lumber that was used to manufacture it.

Parts and Pieces (PNP) is also an organisation that manufactures coffee tables. However it follows a different method of operation from TTL and therefore has a different value chain.

Inbound logistics: PNP sources pre-ordered coffee table parts (e.g. legs, top) directly from other organisations that when assembled will create the final product.

Operations: these parts are then placed into a single package along with an instruction sheet on how they should be assembled.

Outbound logistics: these packages are then shipped out to various retail outlets where they are sold.

Marketing and sales: PNP's sales force are constantly contacting retail outlet to obtain further orders.

Service: each of PNP's tables comes with a customer complaint form. A service department goes through all returned forms and passes their feedback onto the operations department.

PNP creates value by taking its raw material (coffee table parts) and transforming into a package where they can be easily assembled into the final product by the consumer. Further value is then added by shipping these packages to outlets where they can be easily purchased by its end user (the customer). However since the assembly of the coffee table is done by the consumer, PNP's tables sell at a discount ($60 versus TTL's $100 for a table).

Test Yourself 3

Hi-fashion Ltd is a newly launched small textile company that manufactures designer shirts. The company is finding it difficult to withstand the competition and expand its business. The organisation needs to find out how to add value to its products.

Required:

Explain how the company can use the value chain to add value to its products.

4. Advise on the role and influence of value networks.[3]

[Learning Outcome d]

As the value chain indicates, getting a final product / service to the customer requires a number of different stages / activities to be completed. However it is rare to find an organisation today that undertakes and completes each one of these activities internally; it is usually a collaborative process.

Organisations typically have their own (but limited) value chain and are also part of a much larger value network. This network typically consists of an organisation and all of its suppliers and distributors. Johnson, Scholes and Whittington define a value network as being "the set of inter-organisational links and relationships that are necessary to create a product or service".

Diagram 3: Amazing Electrical Ltd

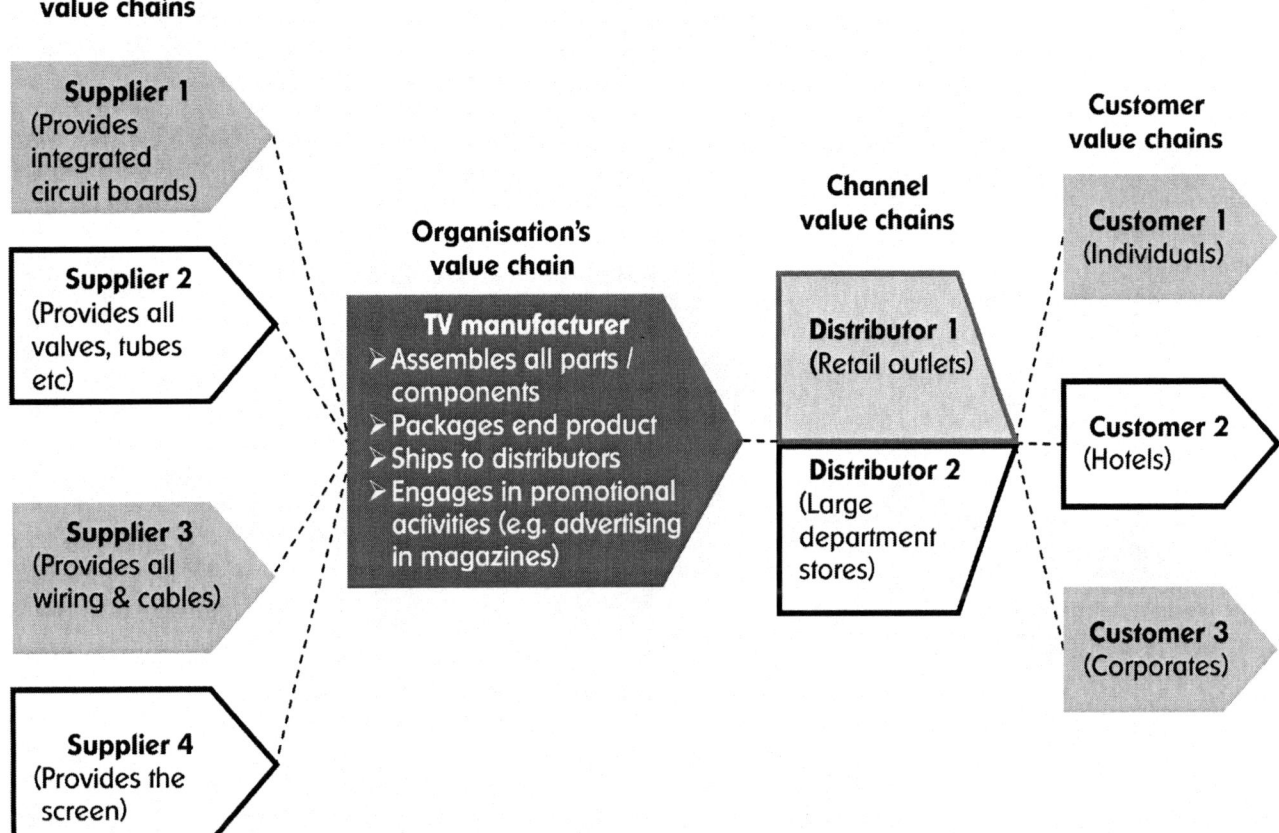

As can be seen from the above diagram it is as important for an organisation to manage its relationship with its suppliers and distributors as it is for it to complete its own activities.

This is because for a value network to be successful each member must contribute and receive value so that both its own success and that of the entire network can be sustained.

Other **advantages of value networks** are that they:

➢ enable an organisation to identify where their costs and values are being created

➢ identify the relationships which are important to the organisation and its strategy

➢ identify "profit pools / sanctuaries" (areas that offer an organisation the potential to earn greater profit margins)

➢ identify which (if any) areas of the value network should be exited

Test Yourself 4

Amazing Electrical Ltd is a TV manufacturer which has a production department which assembles all parts / components used in the manufacturing process. It also has a packaging department which packs the finished product, a distribution department which arranges shipping of the finished goods and promotional departments which advertise the products.

Reliable Ltd supplies Amazing Electrical with integrated circuit boards, tubes, other valves, wiring, cables and screens.

Amazing Electrical has two distributors of its products in the UK: Sam Store which is a retail outlet and Shopee, the largest departmental store in the UK.

The organisation has three types of customer: individual customers, hotels and corporates.

Required:

What features of the value network would be identified by Amazing Electrical?

---

5. Assess different approaches to benchmarking an organisation's performance.[3]
[Learning Outcome e]

The quality or value of most products / services is a relative matter. By this what is meant is that how highly a product / service is valued typically depends upon how its quality compares to that of similar products.

Similarly, the strategic capability of an organisation is also relative and has to be assessed against the strategic capabilities of other organisations. A technique that helps organisations to carry out this procedure is benchmarking.

The term benchmarking has its origins in surveying. It describes the practice where a notch or mark was made to denote a specific altitude. Other heights would then be calibrated or "benchmarked" against this measurement.

In an organisational context, benchmarking involves comparing the standard of one organisation against another. Factors of an organisation that can be benchmarked include:

➢ **Performances** (where specific performances or achievements such as profitability of one organisation are compared against others)
➢ **Products / services** (where specific product offerings of different organisations are compared against each other)
➢ **Processes** (where methods and practices of performing business are compared across organisations)
➢ **Strategies** (where strategic choices made by different organisations are evaluated and compared)

The 3 main types of benchmarking

1. Historical benchmarking

Here an organisation compares or "benchmarks" one aspect of its present performance with those of its past years. For instance the profitability earned on a current year's product model is compared to the profitability of models from earlier years.

The main advantage of historical benchmarking is that it is relatively easy for an organisation to conduct as the needed is readily available and comparable. The main disadvantage is that the practice offers limited value. The main reason being that it is far more beneficial for an organisation to benchmark itself against its competitors / other organisations. It also fails to take into account market trends and changes.

2. Industry / sector benchmarking

With industry benchmarking an organisation compares itself with its competition (i.e. other organisations operating in the same industry). This involves an organisation comparing aspects such as its products, services, processes against those of its competition. With sector benchmarking an organisation compares itself against organisations that provide very similar products / services.

For instance industry benchmarking for Ferrari may involve comparing its performance against those of all other car manufacturers. Sector benchmarking would involve making comparisons only with organisations such as Porsche, Lotus, Lamborghini and Aston Martin.

The main advantage of this type of benchmarking is that it offers an organisation a much wider and better assessment of its performance than historical benchmarking. One of the main disadvantages is that even this type of benchmarking is much harder to conduct as competitors may be unwilling to share information. In addition it also may no longer be sufficient by itself as there is an increasing trend of blurring between industry lines. For instance today many mobile phones also have an attached camera.

3. Best in class benchmarking

With this type of benchmarking an organisation compares itself to another organisation that has a reputation for excellence for a particular process, function or practice. Here the target organisation often does not come from the same sector or even industry.

This because there are many business processes that are undertaken by variety of organisations from different industries. It is therefore considered good practice for organisation to compare one of its processes with those of an organisation from another industry that has a reputation for excellence or "best in class" for that particular process.

Example

For instance when Xerox (a manufacturer of photocopiers and office equipment) wanted to find an organisation to benchmark their warehousing and materials handling processes they chose L.L. Bean (LLB).

LLB is a mail order and retail organisation that specialises in clothing and outdoor equipment. Although their products are very dissimilar, both organisations need to have effective warehousing systems that can manage products that come in a variety of sizes, shapes and designs.

After studying LLB's processes, Xerox went on to implement many of their practices. This resulted in a more rapid flow of materials and their picker travel distance being minimised.

The main advantage of "best in class" benchmarking is that it offers the highest potential for discovering innovative practices and / or greatest improvements as the practice forces "out of the box" thinking. For instance British Airways was able to improve turnaround times for its aircraft after studying how Formula 1 racing teams conduct their pit stops.

The main disadvantage to this type of benchmarking is that it is a difficult tool to implement. Lessons learnt cannot always be easily transferred from one industry to another. For instance many European and American organisations have not been able to implement the supply chain management techniques of the Japanese firms they benchmarked.

This was mainly because these firms were members of a "keiretsu". A keiretsu is the Japanese word used to describe a set of organisations (e.g. manufacturers, suppliers and distributors) that have not only a common set of objectives but also ownership (each organisation owns shares in all of the other member organisations).

	Historical benchmarking	Industry / sector benchmarking	Best in class benchmarking
Method	An organisation compares its present performance against those of previous years	An organisation compares itself to other organisations in the industry / main competitors	An organisation compares itself to another organisation that has a reputation for excellence for a particular process
Advantages	Data is readily available and easily comparable	Offers an organisation a much wider and better assessment than historical benchmarking	Offers the highest potential for discovering innovative practices / greatest improvements as the practice forces "out of the box" thinking
Disadvantages	Practice offers limited value	Is a much harder technique to implement than historical benchmarking	Is a difficult tool to implement

SUMMARY

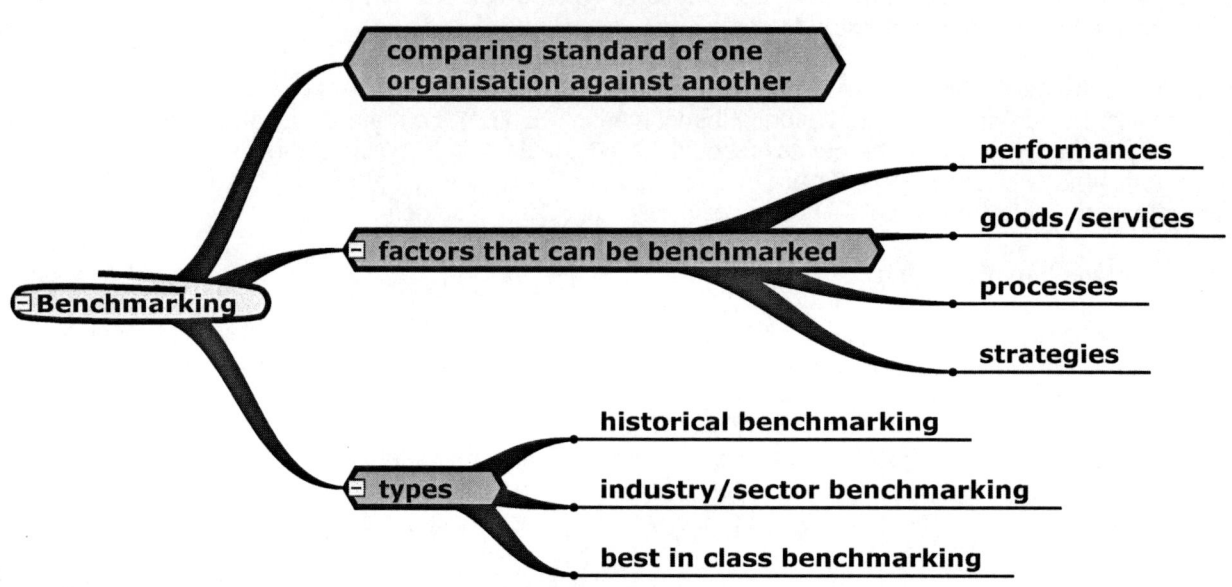

Test Yourself 5

Polymaker Ltd is a manufacturer of plastic products and its competitor is Tony Plastic group. Polymaker is considering the need to assess and compare its strategic capabilities with those of Tony Plastic group through benchmarking. It wants to examine the role of key performance drivers such as quality, supply chain management, distribution and pricing with the similar factors pertaining to its competitors.

Required:

What is benchmarking? Why does Polymaker Ltd need to benchmark and what type of benchmarking is suitable for it?

Answers to Test Yourself

Answer to TY 1

One of the most important functions of any organisation is 'segmentation' of the market i.e. identifying the different types or groups of customers. Market segmentation involves an organisation dividing its market into different segments containing a particular group of customers with particular needs.

Gadget Ltd does not sell its product directly to the end user. Instead it sells its product to wholesalers, retailers and showrooms that display the products and sell them to the end users.

Therefore Gadget Ltd must satisfy the needs of two different types of customers: the customers of the industrial market and the customers who are the end user of the product.

Needs and demands of customers

1. **Commercial market customer:** The customers of the commercial market will focus on the design, style, packaging and presentation of the product.

   The main focus of commercial market customers is the features and presentation of the product as these aspects will attract the end user.

2. **End user:** For the end users, the most important aspects of the product are the product features and the price. End users look for a product with the maximum number of features for minimum cost.

   Therefore Gadget should be able to identify the end users of its products and satisfy their requirements.

Answer to TY 2

Every organisation has different types of customers with different needs. In order to encourage customers to purchase their products, it is important to specify the features of the particular product as this is what customers will look for before purchasing.

The critical success factors for Pure Herb Plc are the specific features of its shampoo, hair oil and body lotion that customers attach the most importance to when making their purchase decisions. These features are as follows:

1. **Price of product:** does it offer value for money?
2. **Brand or make of the product:** is the brand well-known? Does it have a reputation for reliability?
3. **Ingredients of the product:** does the product contain herbal extracts? Does it contain any chemical or synthetic additives?
4. **Outcome of the product:** will using the products improve the condition of the customer's hair / skin? Is the product free of any undesirable side-effects?

The company can consider the above features to provide value to its customers.

Answer to TY 3

Hi-fashion needs to identify how the various activities that go into producing its goods add value. This is called a 'value chain'. A value chain divides the organisation's activities into the areas of designing, producing, marketing and distributing products. By performing the activities within the value chain efficiently, Hi-fashion can generate value and gain a competitive advantage.

The activities of the value chain are divided into primary and support activities.

1. Primary activities

The primary activities of Hi-fashion are directly related to the production of the designer shirts. The primary activities are divided into:

- **Production:** Production includes the whole process from the purchase of raw materials until the completion of the final product. Hi-fashion will require high quality fabric, thread and buttons as raw materials for the manufacturing of designer shirts. It will also require the latest sewing machinery, embroidery machinery and other equipment in the production processes.

    The activities carried out by the production department will include selecting the appropriate fabric, cutting the fabric to the required size and sending it to the sewing team for sewing. After this process, the shirts will be passed on to the embroidery team and then the button sewing team where the shirts will be given the complete designer look. This is the end of the manufacturing process. The product lot will then be sent for packaging.

- **Logistics:** Logistics involve the efficient storing, distributing and transporting of the product for inventory control. Inbound and outbound logistics carry out the following processes:

    - the primary activities of collecting, storing, and physically distributing the designer shirts to the buyers
    - in the warehouse, keeping track of the products issued and keeping receipts for further follow-up (which includes finished goods warehousing, material handling, delivery vehicle operations, order processing and timing)
    - giving a clear inventory report to Hi-fashion
    - providing adequate transportation for export of Hi-fashion designer shirts and providing accuracy of deliveries hence gaining customer satisfaction
    - shipping operations, freight cost and settlement for foreign trade
    - verifying and receiving raw material (inbound logistics)

- **Marketing and sales functions:** The marketing and sales department of Hi-fashion will be involved in advertising the designer shirts, which may involve hiring models and promotional staff and advertising on hoardings. The marketing team must market the product to various shops and shopping malls so that they can achieve good sales. They must also determine suitable prices so that they can earn profits.

2. Support activities

These activities support the primary activities through:

- **Firm infrastructure:** Hi-fashion's infrastructure will support the entire value chain; i.e. not only the particular primary activities carried out by the company. It involves the activities that are essential to support the administration system. The planning and the financial support needed should given by the management. If any additional resources are required for the manufacturing, packaging or marketing processes, this work will be carried out by the administration department.

- **Human resource management:** The HR department will be concerned with activities such as the recruitment, training and development of different types of employees. If Hi-fashion requires any designer or other highly skilled employee to increase the company efficiency or any training is required for the new employees, the HR manager must look into this and come up with the best conclusion. This will affect Hi-fashion's competitive advantage since it can identify employees' skill and enthusiasm.

- **Technological development:** Technological development will help Hi-fashion to improve its product and process. The activities will include research into the fabric, process equipment design and implementation of the process. It is important for a Hi-fashion to create a competitive advantage.

- **Procurement:** Procurement will support the function of buying inputs i.e. raw material, sewing and embroidery machinery that are used in the company's value chain. The availability of raw materials, supplies and other consumable items are categorised in procurement. Plant and machinery, office equipment and industrial area are also included under procurement activities.

The support activities help the organisation to improve the efficiency / effectiveness of its primary activities.

Answer to TY 4

A value network is a complicated set of social and technological resources which work together to create economic value. It accounts for the overall value of the products manufactured by Amazing Electrical Ltd. Amazing Electrical has both an internal value chain and an external value network. The external value network includes customers, stakeholders, distributors and suppliers and the internal value network includes production of goods and order fulfilment.

The features of the value network that would be identified by Amazing Electrical are as follows:

1. **Managing relationships:** one of the important value networks for Amazing Electrical is managing relationships. This focuses on managing and gathering information about the following people:
    - Customers: Amazing Electrical must find out its customers' requirements and whether its customers are satisfied with the product. If its customers aren't satisfied, it should find out what improvements are suggested by them.
    - Suppliers: Amazing Electrical must negotiate the delivery of the raw material and also the payment terms with its supplier, Reliable.
    - Distributors: Amazing Electrical needs to manage its relationship with its distributors (Sam Store and Shopee) regarding the product display, sales and other cost requirements.
    - Other business partners: the company should also communicate the company's progress and achievements to its stakeholders.

2. **Business networking:** relevant value networking for Amazing Electrical is proper deployment of the available resources. For example, the company should make proper use of the available resources to transport the TV sets at the agreed time. These resources should also be used for marketing Amazing Electrical products.

Answer to TY 5

The term benchmarking has its origins in surveying. It involves comparing the standards of one organisation with those of another. Benchmarking involves examining the performance and training of other organisations in order to adopt considerably better practices that lead to better performance.

Benchmarking goes beyond comparing with competitors to understand the practices that lie behind the performance gaps. It does not only involve copying the methods or the procedures carried out by competitors but also looking for better processes outside the industry. It refers to the activity of establishing genuine benchmarks and 'best' practices.

Polymaker Ltd needs to benchmark to attain the following benefits:

1. It will provide real and attainable goals.
2. It allows employees to imagine the improvement, which may be a powerful motivator for change.
3. It creates a sense of necessity for improvement.
4. It helps to identify weaker areas and specify the methods to improve them.

Therefore benchmarking is the only real way of assessing industrial competitiveness and determining how one company's process performance compares to other companies.

Suitable benchmarking for Polymaker Ltd

Benchmarking practices are not mutually exclusive and an organisation can choose any combination to meet its objectives. Industry / sector benchmarking is the first to be chosen as it will allow Polymaker Ltd to compare its products, services and processes with those of its competitor, Tony Plastic group.

Polymaker must begin benchmarking by considering the needs and expectations of the customer. It should measure customer satisfaction and the gaps between the company's performance and its customers' standards. Here Polymaker may compare its performance in terms of product quality, pricing of products and distribution against Tony plastic Plastic.

Benchmarking must be a continuous process with the extent and scope of the project being dependent on the resources that the company has available.

Quick Quiz

1. Explain what is meant by the term strategic customers.
2. Define critical success factors (CSFs).
3. What is the role of a value chain?
4. A value network typically consist of an organisation and its -------------
5. Name three different approaches to benchmarking.

Answers to Quick Quiz

1. A strategic customer is the person(s) at whom an organisation's strategy is primarily addressed because they have the most influence over which goods or services are purchased.
2. Critical success factors are the specific factors of a particular product / service that customers attach the most importance to when making their purchase decisions.
3. A value chain is a technique that can be used by an organisation to identify how the various activities that go into producing a product / service create value.
4. Suppliers and distributors
5. Historical benchmarking, Industry / sector benchmarking and Best in class benchmarking

Self Examination Questions

Question 1

McDonald's is the largest and best-known fast-food retailer and one of the two best-known and most powerful brands in the market. The company has expanded its leadership position through convenience, superior value and excellent operations.

Carlson Hotels is a five-star chain of gourmet restaurants that offers culinary delights prepared by gourmet chefs and five-star services to visitors.

Compare the value chain for both a five-star gourmet restaurant and for a fast-food retailer such as McDonald's.

Question 2

Discuss how the use of CSFs can help determine the information requirements of an organisation.

Self Examination Questions

Answer to SEQ 1

McDonald's outlets pride themselves on their speedy service, low prices and ability to serve very large volumes of customers on a daily basis.

- **Inbound logistics:** McDonald's sources its raw materials (e.g. burgers, buns, lettuce) from a variety of carefully chosen suppliers. Suppliers are required to ship these materials directly to the various outlets. In addition all goods must meet stringent quality requirements.

- **Operations:** The method of operation that each outlet has to follow is highly standardised. Exact procedures have to be followed from how customers are to be greeted, how the various food items are to be prepared, right up to how the outlet's signs are to be displayed

- **Outbound logistics:** There are no outbound logistics as customers must come to a McDonald's outlet, except for some home delivery orders.

- **Marketing and sales:** Apart from advertising heavily McDonald's often engages in several promotional activities such as tying up with popular films (e.g. children are given a free toy linked to the particular film with every meal purchased).

- **Service:** Although McDonald's is predominantly a self-service restaurant, the organisation goes a long way in establishing a "family" atmosphere at its outlets.

McDonald's creates value in three stages. First, through its operations by transforming the various raw materials / ingredients into a meal. Second, through its marketing activities, McDonald's has built a brand so that their customers believe they are not just purchasing a meal but an experience. Lastly through service, its outlets have become a place where customers can enjoy a value meal in a hygienic, friendly and family atmosphere.

On the other hand, a 5 Star gourmet restaurant would place a strict emphasis on the quality (both in appearance and taste) of its meals.

- **Inbound logistics:** With gourmet restaurants, the raw materials / ingredients are usually sourced directly by the head chef.

- **Operations:** The method of operation here would be that a fresh menu is created on a daily basis. Therefore operations are completely un-standardised and instead reflect the character and working style of the head chef.

- **Outbound logistics:** There are no outbound logistics as customers must come to the restaurant.

- **Marketing and sales:** These types of restaurants engage in very limited or no marketing. They gain business through "word of mouth" referrals and from critical reviews in magazines / newspapers.

- **Service:** Gourmet restaurants sell not only a meal but a complete dining experience. Service levels extend to the point of almost pampering customers.

Answer to SEQ 2

The CSF approach is based on the premise that an organisation pursues certain goals and that specific factors are crucial in achieving these goals. Appropriate management controls should be established for these factors. By focusing attention on the CSFs, the management highlights those areas where it is crucial to have an effective management information system. Information subsystems can then be developed to serve these critical factors. The CSF approach recognizes that the purpose of providing information is to serve corporate goals. The CSF's provide an important link between the business strategy and the information systems strategy.

SECTION A: STRATEGIC POSITION

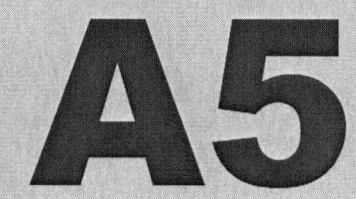

STUDY GUIDE A5: THE INTERNAL RESOURCES, CAPABILITIES AND COMPETENCES OF AN ORGANISATION

■ Get Through Intro

Every organisation has resources. How well you use those resources helps define how successful the company will be. If you deploy your resources effectively, use them innovatively and to the maximum of their ability, you are likely to develop a successful business.

However, remember that it is not enough any more to be as good as a competitor – this will only help you survive. In order to succeed and thrive, you must be better than your competitors, so develop distinctive competences which prove this.

Let's take Josh, a man in your office. He is employed as a book-keeper in the accounting department and is known for being inaccurate when posting figures on to the accounting system. Occasionally he is responsible for making phone calls to clients, to chase payments. You notice that he has an excellent way with clients and often can convince them to pay their outstanding bills immediately. You realise that he could be better placed as part of the marketing team, due to his persuasive nature. When you speak to him, he is really happy to be given an opportunity in another area as he also realised that he was not suited to accounting.

As a result of the job switch, your marketing team is going to gain a person with competence in dealing with people. Your accounting department will lose someone who was not adding sufficient value to the team. Hence you have increased the overall competence of the business!

■ Learning Outcomes

a) Discriminate between strategic capability, threshold resources, threshold competences, unique resources and core competences.
b) Discuss from strategic perspective the continuing need for effective cost management and control systems within organisations.
c) Discuss the capabilities required to sustain competitive advantage.
d) Explain the impact of new product, process, and service developments and innovation in supporting business strategy.
e) Discuss the contribution of organisational knowledge to the strategic capability of an organisation.
f) Identify opportunities for managing the strategic capability of an organisation.
g) Determine the strengths and weaknesses of an organisation and formulate an appropriate SWOT analysis.

Introduction

Case Study

Samsung mobiles - The transformation of Samsung mobiles has been amazing. Over the years, it has gone from being a cheap imitator of other electronics companies, to a market leader in certain markets.

How did this happen? It has been widely reported that in 1995, Kun-Hee Lee, the Chairman of Samsung sent some mobile phones as new year presents to his friends. The friends politely called/returned the phones as they did not work properly. Lee was incensed and went to the plant that manufactured the phones. He apparently organised a bonfire of the entire inventory (about $15 - $50 million dollars, depending which article you read) and burnt it all, in front of all the employees. Here came the turning point for Samsung.

The 3 key areas Samsung focused on from then on were R&D, Quality management and technology innovation. Since then, Samsung mobiles have become leaders in many markets, but most so in their home market of Korea.

The above case study shows how Samsung turned its fortunes around in the mobile phone business, by improving its core competences and potentially turning some of them eg innovation into distinctive competences. Samsung introduced the first MP3 phone and the world's slimmest phone.

This Study Guide will teach you how to identify your core and distinct competences, so you can strengthen your lead over competitors – both in the exam and in real life!

> 1. **Discriminate between strategic capability, threshold resources, threshold competences, unique resources and core competences.**[3]
> **Discuss the contribution of organisational knowledge to the strategic capability of an organisation.**[2]
> **Identify opportunities for managing the strategic capability of an organisation.**[2]
> [Learning Outcomes a, e and f]

Definition

Johnson, Scholes and Whittington define strategic capability as being "the adequacy and suitability of the resources and competences of an organisation for it to survive and prosper."

As this definition indicates, the strategic capability of an organisation is determined by its resources and competences. Resources represent the assets of an organisation or what it owns. They can be tangible in nature such as the physical assets of an organisation such as plant, property and equipment. Organisations also often command intangible resources that represent its non physical assets such as brand name, patents, staff capabilities or reputation in the marketplace.

As important as the type, amount and quality of resources, an organisation has, is how these resources are utilised. For instance it will be of little benefit for an organisation to purchase state of the art machinery if the equipment will not subsequently be used correctly or efficiently. These resources have to be effectively harnesses by management in order to be able to generate competitive advantage.

This is where the concept of competences comes into play. Competences represent what the entire organisation can do. They represent all the various activities and / or processes an organisation carries out to produce its end goods and / or services.

Definition

As Johnson, Scholes and Whittington further explain "competences are the activities and processes through which an organisation deploys its resources effectively".

Therefore, to summarise the above, the strategic capability of an organisation should be thought of as the way it uses the resources and competences at its disposal to provide products and / or services that will be valued and purchased by its customers.

These customers today are what Kotler and Keller describe as being "value maximisers". Therefore they will only purchase goods and / or services they perceive to have some form of inherent value. These values can be threshold values or in other words the bare minimum features / qualities a good / service should possess. Or they can be the critical success factors of the same good / service (the product features particularly valued by a group of customers).

Therefore, there is a **difference between resources and competence levels**.

Sr. no.	Resources	Competences
1.	Resources represent the assets of an organisation or what it owns	Competences represent what the entire organisation can do, i.e. its skills
2.	Resources may be the tangible or intangible assets which an organisation has	Competence is necessarily intangible
3.	Resources are assets which have to be utilised effectively	Competences are skills inherent in the activities and processes through which an organisation effectively deploys its resources

Example

The threshold values for a mobile phone today would be factors such as clear connectivity and the ability to send and receive messages. These features are what all phones are expected to have as a bare minimum. Critical success factors would be features such as a camera and the ability to play MP3 files.

Threshold resources therefore are the resources that an organisation needs and uses to meet the threshold requirements of its customers. For instance, for a manufacturing firm, its threshold resources would be its property, plant and equipment as these are the base resources the organisation needs to produce its goods.

Similarly **threshold competences** are the minimum levels of competence that an organisation must posses so that it can meet the threshold requirements of their customers. They represent the abilities and skills an organisation must possess just to be able to "stay in the game". For instance, for mobile phone manufacturers, threshold competences would represent the processes and activities needed to produce mobile phones capable of making and receiving both telephone calls and mail messages.

However the main objective for most organisations is not to merely "stay in the game" but to outperform their competitors. This requires that organisations possess either unique resources and / or core competencies. **Unique resources** are those resources that no other organisation possesses. For instance, an organisation holding the exclusive right to search and drill for oil in a particular region would be an example of a unique resource. Unique resources can act as a barrier to interest.

Core competences represent the skills and abilities an organisation possesses to "get ahead of the game". They represent an organisation's ability to conduct business and deploy resources more efficiently and effectively than their competitors.

Example

In the 1970s, the core competences of Japanese photocopying manufacturers were allowing them to sell their photocopying machines at the price it cost their main competitor, Xerox to build one.

Strategic capability

Given the existence of the knowledge economy, core competencies today are very often based upon the knowledge an organisation possesses. This organisational knowledge stems from the skills, abilities and information that employees hold as well as the process / activities that have been put into place by the organisation that allow their employees to use and apply this knowledge. For instance, engineers at Google are given free reign and a budget to design and develop projects of their own choosing.

Therefore **organisational knowledge** is of paramount importance when it comes to determining and developing an **organisation's strategic capabilities**. For today most organisations operate in hyper competitive markets. Any advantages they enjoy because of unique resources and / or core competencies are relatively short lived.

For instance with televisions, the superior quality offered by plasma screens was quickly ousted by the picture quality of LCD screens which in turn are now being surpassed by High Definition television sets. Organisations today need to be able to move quickly from developing one core competence to the next in order to **maintain their strategic capabilities**. The factor that will help them achieve this the most is their **organisational knowledge**.

Along with organisational knowledge another important aspect to managing an organisation's strategic capability is the **external environment** it operates in. This external environment will change over time due to a multitude of factors such as changing consumer tastes, government regulations and technological advances. This change can either bring about opportunities (the potential to increase sales and profitability) or threats (the possibility that sales and profitability will decline) for an organisation.

This then leads to the concept of "**strategic fit**". A strategic fit occurs when an organisation adapts or amends its competences and resources (i.e. its strategic capabilities) to meet the new demands and tastes of the changed external environment. For instance many traditional retailers have implemented an electronic sales and delivery channel giving their customers the option to make their purchases over the internet.

The polar opposite to the concept of "strategic fit" is the concept of "**strategic stretch**". Here an organisation changes the external environment it operates in rather than changing itself. It does this by "stretching" its strategic capabilities to offer new products / services to the marketplace. For instance a "strategic stretch" was created when firms such as Haagen-Dazs and Ben & Jerry's used their strategic capabilities to develop and launch a premium quality ice cream. Therefore the practices of **both strategic fit and strategic stretch** are examples of opportunities of **how an organisation can manage its strategic capability**.

SUMMARY

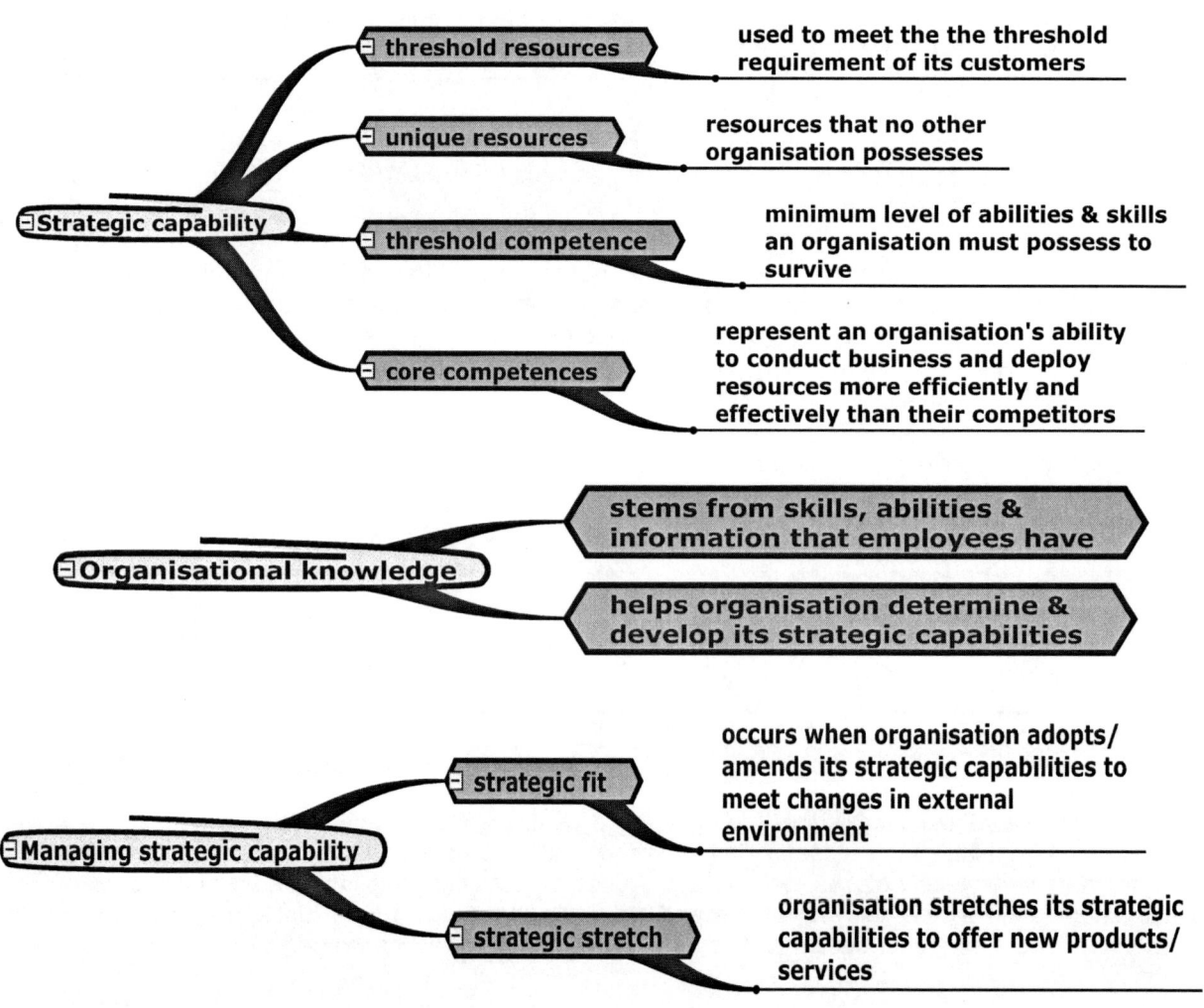

Test Yourself 1

Mobile Technology Ltd was established in 19W3. It is engaged in researching and developing the production and sales of mobile phones. Now the organisation has a large research team that is involved in advancing its product from time to time. Currently, the organisation has more than 250 workers, including 10 senior management staff, 15 scientific researchers, 100 trainees, more than 25 bachelors, 8 masters, and 30 sales personnel.

Mobile Technology Ltd made a huge profit in the past but in the last few years it has suffered losses, so now it needs to bring strategic capability into the organisation.

Required:

What is strategic capability and how should the organisation bring strategic capability into the organisation?

---

2. Discuss from strategic perspective the continuing need for effective cost management and control systems within organisations [3]

[Learning Outcome b]

As mentioned before consumers today are what Kotler and Keller label as being "value maximisers". This means that they expect the products / services they purchase to continually offer greater and greater value. This in turn translates into organisations having to continually compete to ensure that their products / services are offering the greatest value for money.

Therefore **cost efficiency** has become an **essential activity for almost every organisation**. Achieving cost efficiency **involves reducing the operational costs that an organisation incurs when producing a good / service without having to sacrifice on quality**. The good / service can then be offered to customers at a cheaper price.

Some of the ways that organisations achieve cost efficiency is through achieving economies of scale / scope and progressing along the experience curve. Economies of scale are achieved when an organisation manages to lower the per-unit cost of manufacturing a particular good through increasing output.

This is mainly because the production of a good usually involves both fixed and varied costs. If variable costs can be held constant whilst increasing production numbers, then the fixed costs involved are divided amongst a much larger base thereby reducing the per unit manufacturing cost of each good.

Economies of scope occur when an organisation achieves cost savings from producing an increasing number of different goods. Synergy is achieved here as the joint total cost of producing two or more goods is lower than what it would have cost the organisation to produce each good independently and at different times. The main cause of economies of scope is the ability to share its investments and costs (e.g. advertising) across more than one product group or strategic business unit (SBU).

Example

The Virgin Group is a private company which was incorporated in the UK in 1989. Virgin is a holding company which runs under the brand of British business tycoon, Sir Richard Branson. It has many subsidiary companies. Each company operating under the Virgin brand is a separate entity and provides different goods or services. Some of the subsidiary companies are wholly owned by Branson; in others, he holds minority or majority stakes.

Progressing along the experience or learning curve also usually gives rise to opportunities for achieving cost efficiencies. This is because typically as an organisation produces the same good over a period of time it learns from mistakes and identifies areas for improvement / lower cost.

A combination of these can lead to the organisation being able to produce goods more efficiently or cheaply over time and, therefore, being able to earn cost efficiencies. For instance, car manufacturers such as Toyota and Honda have over the years introduced increasing levels of automation into their factories due to the increases in efficiency and productivity it brings.

Lastly, regardless of the method(s) chosen achieving cost efficiency will be an on-going battle for almost all organisations. This is because in the hyper competitive economic environment of today, achieving cost efficiency has become a threshold and not a core competence.

SUMMARY

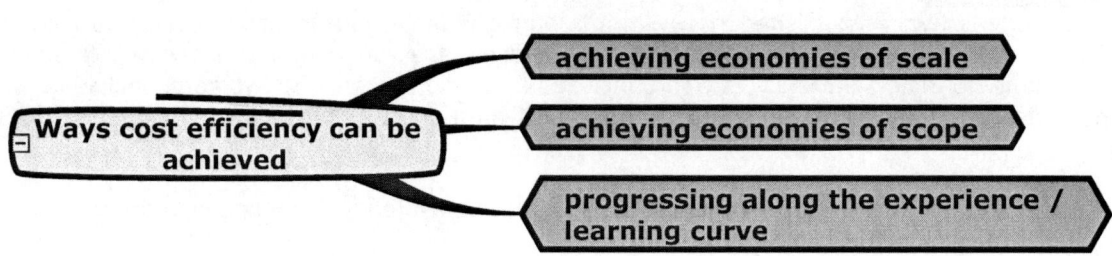

The need for strategic cost management (SCM) from the strategic angle could be justified in the following areas:

a) **Permanent Cost efficiency**: this helps in making the organisations' processes cost effective by eliminating non-value adding activities.
b) **Operational & strategic excellence**: This can be achieved through value analysis, value engineering, business process re-engineering, benchmarking, activity based management model, life cycle model etc. Cost is the pivot in all such techniques. When properly formulated and implemented, these cost initiatives would be extremely useful for companies to achieve their strategic objectives.
c) **Customer satisfaction**: Cost management tools provide important information regarding the costs the companies spend on providing customers what they want on an on-going basis.
d) **Value creation**: The SCM recognises the need to create value for the stakeholders of the organisation. Value is the function of benefits and costs. The SCM tools help organisations to monitor whether the benefits are increasing and the cost are reducing.

Management control system (MCS) of an organisation is an internal, self-regulating mechanism that governs the activities of individual components of the organisation that help to achieve the enterprise-wide objectives and goals. The MCS usually includes the following steps:

a) Set a target or a benchmark (this could be a standard of performance or budget).
b) Measure the actual performance.
c) Compare it with the targets set and find deviations.
d) Diagnose and analyse the reasons for the variations.
e) Take corrective action.

There are different ways in which such control systems are practised by companies. These include developing a policy manual giving operational rules for different functions of the organisation. Some companies also adopt Standard Operating Practices manual (SOP), Total Quality Management methodology or Six Sigma methodology, ERP systems etc.

The need for control systems in an organisation can be seen from the following strategic perspectives:

a) **Clarity of operations**: The control systems lay down rules and regulations which the managers have to adhere to. This provides clarity to the entire team and leaves no room for confusion. However, too much of bureaucratic control could result in delays in decision making that can cause harm to the firms.
b) **Goal congruence**: The control system will ensure that the individual targets set are properly linked with the organisational goals.
c) **Performance management**: A well laid MCS will ensure assessment of performance of individual parts of an organisation and the organisation as a whole. This can be helpful in establishing a good reward system for employees.
d) **Quality management**: MCS will foster the quality of performance as the system will ensure that the deviations are diagnosed at an early stage and the cost of corrections is reduced.
e) **Ethical standards**: the effective control systems will facilitate ethical behaviour.
f) **Information systems**: Modern MCS such as ERP solutions help create extremely robust MIS that helps organisations take decisions.
g) **Avoiding fraud and mismanagement**: Efficient MCS minimise the instances of fraud and mismanagement as the exceptional activities immediately get highlighted to the relevant levels of management and corrective action can be taken in time.

Test Yourself 2

Rock Baby was launched in 19W5. The company specialises in manufacturing and exporting fashion garments for toddlers. The fashion garments are very popular and there is a demand for the company to start manufacturing baby products. The company decided to expand its establishment and, in 20X5, the company expanded its product range to include baby blankets, baby bottles covers, baby cushions, baby diapers and towels.

However, the company wants to ensure cost efficiency while venturing into new products, so that it can withstand competition in the market.

Required:

Suggest how Rock Baby can achieve cost efficiency.

---

3. Discuss the capabilities required to sustain competitive advantage.[2]
[Learning Outcome c]

An organisation is said to have achieved competitive advantage when it has earned higher than average profits for its particular industry. If the organisation continues to maintain this level of profitability then it is said to have a sustainable competitive advantage.

Organisations that achieve a competitive advantage do so because they have superior resources and/or competencies. However, in practice, organisations that achieve a sustainable competitive advantage are typically able to do so because they possess superior competencies and not resources.

This is because the same resources get acquired / imitated by competitors over the course of time. For instance, having an outlet / store in a prime locality would be short lived unique resource for a retailer as competitors would eventually open their stores in the same location.

Porter identifies two main ways or types of competitive advantages organisations can achieve through their competences. The first is achieving a cost competitive advantage where an organisation is able to deliver a product / service (of the same quality) more cheaply than its competitors. Ways organisations can do this have been discussed in the previous learning outcome.

Alternatively organisations can achieve a differentiation competitive advantage. This occurs when an organisation is able to deliver a superior quality product / service offering from its competitors but at the same cost. Prahalad and Hamel state that one of the main ways organisations achieve this is through developing core competencies that represent management's ability to consolidate technology, production skills and various other activities / functions into competencies.

Overall any sustainable competitive advantage will gradually diminish and then disappear over the course of time. However there are certain factors that will help an organisation to preserve the sustainability of its competitive advantage. These include the:

➢ **Durability of the competency / resource** (e.g. if competitive advantage is based upon owing a state of the art machine then its sustainability will be limited as the technological superiority of the machine will diminish over time)

➢ **Transparency of the competency / resource** (e.g. the less transparent or obvious the competency is the less likely it is to be copied by competitors)

➢ **Transferability of the competency / resource** (e.g. if the competence / resource happens to be a key employee then it is highly transferable as the employee can be recruited by competitors)

➢ **Ability to replicate the competency / resource** (e.g. if an organisation's competitive advantage is based upon having a large sales force then this will be short lived as the basis for the advantage can easily be replicated by competitors)

SUMMARY

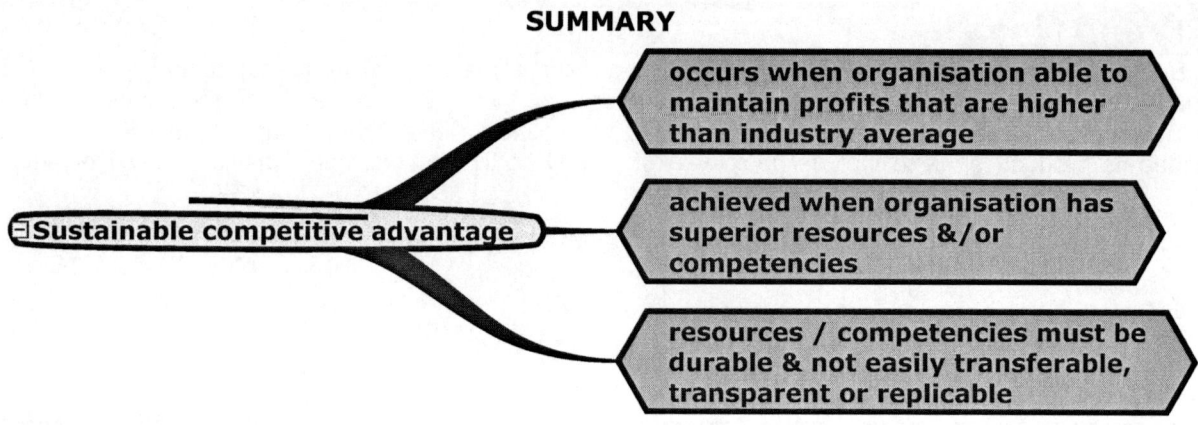

Test Yourself 3

Mommy Milk & Milk Products Marketing Ltd is the country's largest food products marketing organisation which works with 15 milk producers. The company's daily milk collection totals about 8 million litres. It aims to serve the interests of its consumers by providing quality products that are a value for money.

Mommy Milk & Milk Products Marketing Ltd markets products such as bread spreads, cheeses, chocolates & confectionery, ice creams, infant milk, milk powder, fresh milk, condensed milk, yoghurt products, and health drinks.

Mommy has achieved a competitive advantage and has earned higher than average profits in the last five years. The average profit earned by the company is $500 per year.

Year	Profit $ (in million)
20X2-20X3	550
20X3-20X4	620
20X4-20X5	687
20X5-20X6	934
20X6-20X7	1156

However, the company needs to have a sustainable competitive advantage in order to maintain its level of profitability.

Required:

What factors would help Mommy Milk to preserve the sustainability of its competitive advantage?

---

4. Explain the impact of new product, process and service developments and innovation in supporting business strategy.[2]

[Learning Outcome d]

Creation of a new product involves beginning the functions of designing, manufacturing and marketing completely from scratch. There are three basic types of new products / services an organisation can introduce:

1. New to the market (e.g. plasma televisions when they were first introduced to the home entertainment market)
2. New to the organisation (e.g. Microsoft with its X-Box)
3. New to the world (e.g. Virgin Galatica's plans to offer commercial passenger suborbital spaceflight)

Modified products may also be introduced e.g. a new version of a car model. The introduction of any new product, process or strategy will invariably be tied up with the business strategy an organisation is following. Organisations can either adopt a proactive or reactive approach in this regard.

A proactive approach occurs when an organisation uses its resources and capabilities to identify and develop new products / services to target unmet customer needs. A reactive approach is when an organisation introduces a new product / service in response to a competitor having introduced a similar product / service.

Regardless of the approach it follows, the introduction of any new product, process or service will influence and be influenced by the business strategy the organisation is following. As mentioned previously the ultimate objective of business strategy is to enable an organisation to earn a competitive advantage over its competitors. This can be a cost competitive advantage or a differentiation competitive advantage.

Porter identifies three basic types of strategies organisations follow in order to earn competitive advantage. These are:

a) A **differentiator strategy** (where an organisation attempts to create products / services that are different from ones offered by their competitors. Apple's introduction of its IPOD is an example of an organisation following this kind of strategy)

b) A **cost leadership strategy** (where an organisation attempts to produce and sell its product / service at a lower price than what its competitors charge. Wal-Mart is an example of an organisation that follows this kind of strategy)

c) A **focus strategy** (where an organisation concentrates on servicing a specific market niche and customer segment. Bentley with its ultra high end automobiles is an example of an organisation that follows this kind of strategy). Focus strategy can be either differentiation or cost leadership orientated.

Naturally introduction of new products will have the highest impact on organisations that are following a differentiator strategy as factors such as their quality, suitability, marketability etc will ultimately determine whether the organisation's strategy succeeds or not. Therefore for these types of organisations, the relationship between the business strategy being followed and new "introductions" is a two way street. The introduction of new products / services supports the business strategy being followed and vice versa. Here, it is significant to note that core competences that are operational in nature can serve cost leadership firms such as a new production line system. Operational efficiencies tend to reduce costs and, therefore, help to keep costs at the lowest level. In this manner the firm can retain its leadership on the cost front.

Example

Sony is an example of an organisation that follows the differentiator strategy. The organisation enjoys a reputation for engineering excellence and bringing groundbreaking products to market. As a result of and to support this strategy Sony has continually launched many innovative products over the decades such as the walkman, the Compact Discs, Magnetic Discs and Lithium-Ion batteries.

Organisations typically amend existing processes or create new ones in an effort to reduce costs and improve efficiency. This then allows the organisation to offer their product / service at a cheaper price to their customers. For a manufacturing organisation this might include introducing a new production method or technology into the production process. For service organisations, process innovations centre around being able to service customers more efficiently.

Example

Many banks today have "centralised" much of their administration and customer service functions in an efficiency drive. This new method of operation involves many "paper based" processing functions such as direct debits, standing orders, customer complaints being removed from individual branches and conducted into one large back-office operation.

Lastly, the activity that has the highest potential for impacting an organisation's business strategy is innovation. Innovation can be described as being an organisation's ability to design, create and bring to market a novel product / service. This is because an innovative product / service can not only transform the strategy an organisation must follow but also the industry itself.

Given that the business environment of today is widely referred to as being the "knowledge economy", innovation is considered to be of paramount importance. Organisations today need to be innovative in all areas including marketing, distribution and supply chain management in addition to developing / improving their products / services in order to grow and prosper.

Example

It is commonly cited that one of the reason for Google's success is the emphasis the organisation's business strategy places on innovation. This strategy believes that innovation can come from any employee / level of the organisation. Therefore Google engineers are given "free thinking time" which means that they are expected to spend one day a week on their own pet projects.

SUMMARY

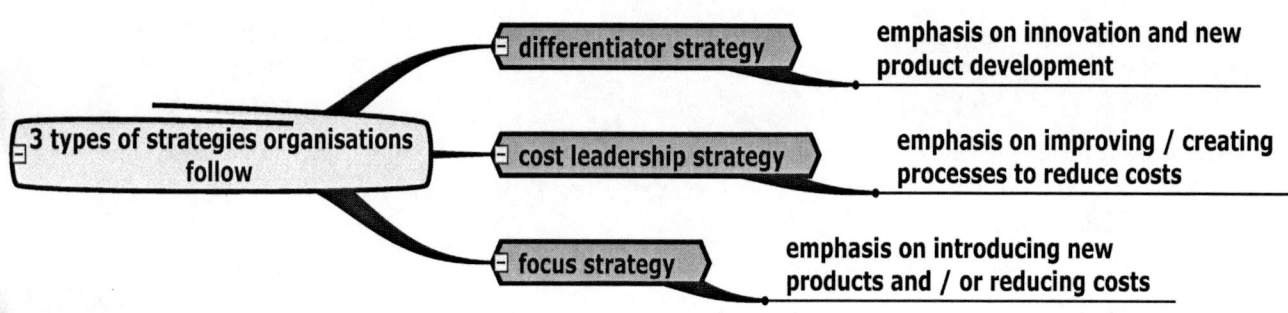

Test Yourself 4

Famous Noodles & Co was established in New Zealand and is a specialist in flavoured noodles since 19W0. Its innovative packing designs and its quality are very popular. The company has grown rapidly by offering a wide variety of flavoured noodles. It introduced a new variety and range of products by including soup and noodle mixes of various flavours in attractive packages.

Required:

What are the business strategy requirements while introducing a new range of products by Famous Noodles & Co?

---

5. Determine the strengths and weaknesses of an organisation and formulate an appropriate SWOT analysis.[2]

[Learning Outcome g]

A SWOT analysis is a strategic planning tool that organisations use to identify their strengths, weaknesses, opportunities and threats (hence the acronym). Conducting a SWOT involves an organisation carrying out both an internal and an external analysis.

With the internal analysis an organisation identifies it strengths and weaknesses. Strengths are attributes of the organisation that can help it achieve a competitive advantage. Weaknesses on the other hand are attributes of the organisation that would hinder it in achieving a competitive advantage.

Identifying opportunities and threats that potentially face the organisation is what constitutes an external analysis. Opportunities are external conditions or situations that could potentially benefit an organisation. Threats are external conditions or situations that could potentially harm an organisation's business.

SWOT analysis is best used as a snapshot of **strategic position** after the organisation has done an internal and external analysis.

Diagram 1: S.W.O.T Analysis

	Useful to achieving the objective	Detrimental to achieving the objective
Internal origin (attributes of the organisation)	Strengths	Weaknesses
External origin (attributes of the environment)	Opportunities	Threats

1. Some of the factors that an organisation examines when conducting a SWOT are its / current:

   - structure
   - culture
   - human resources: staff capabilities, training policy, retention
   - financial resources
   - competitors
   - customers
   - government legislations
   - socio-economic trends

2. Overall the benefits that conducting a SWOT analysis offers are that it helps an organisation to:

   - match its resources and capabilities to its competitive environment
   - identify strategies that it can follow to achieve a competitive advantage

Example

Tech1 is an organisation that manufactures and markets mainframe computers. It recently conducted a SWOT analysis and identified the following:

Strengths: highly motivated and technically competent sales force
Weaknesses: designs of existing products are all over three years old
Opportunities: the government is set to introduce a tax break for organisations that purchase mainframe computers
Threats: a number of micro computer manufacturers are planning to start manufacturing mainframe computers

As an outcome of the SWOT, Tech1 decides to design a fresh model so as to better position themselves to compete against the new firms that are planning to enter their industry.

SUMMARY

Test Yourself 5

Health Cure Ltd is an international pharmaceutical company operating worldwide. The company is involved in pharmaceutical research. The products manufactured by the company are prescribed in chronic therapy areas like cardiology, psychiatry, neurology and respiratory medicine.

Required:

Conduct a SWOT analysis for Health Cure Ltd.

Answers to Test Yourself

Answer to TY 1

Strategic capability represents the way in which an organisation uses the resources and competences at its disposal to provide products / services that will be valued and purchased by its customers.

Strategic capability refers to the competencies, knowledge, and skills that an organisation can apply to achieve success in a competitive environment. An understanding of strategic capability is important because it is concerned with whether an organisation's strategy continues to respond to it environment, opportunities and threats. Strategic capability is derived from a core competencies approach and is seen as a pillar of strategic management which mainly focuses on the ability to provide products that are valued by customers, who are the value maximisers.

Strategic capability includes threshold resources, threshold competencies, unique resources and core competencies. Mobile Technology Ltd needs to bring strategic capability into the organisation. It needs:

a) **Threshold resources:** these are the resources that the organisation needs and utilise to meet the threshold requirements of its customer. The threshold resources for Mobile technology Ltd would be its land, plants and machinery, research equipment, raw material, and transport. These are the base resources the organisation needs in the production and sale of its products.

b) **Threshold competences:** these are the minimum levels of competence that the organisation possesses to meet the threshold requirement of its customers. It represents the ability and skill of the employees in the organisation. The threshold competence for Mobile technology Ltd would present the processes and the activities needed to produce mobile phones that have all the basic facilities, such as making and receiving calls and text messages, and advance features like a camera, mp3 player, etc.

c) **Core competences:** the main aim of any organisation is not only to run its business but also to **outsmart** its competitors. Core competence refers to the skills and abilities within Mobile Technology Ltd which can enable it to get ahead. It represents the ability to conduct research and development for the production and sales of mobile phones and to deploy resources more efficiently and effectively than the company's competitors.

Answer to TY 2

Managing costs requires both resources and competencies. Cost efficiency reduces the operational costs incurred by the organisation in the production of goods without sacrificing quality. If a company increases the price of its products, the sale would reduce and the competitors would enter the market with their low price product. Therefore, for a company to run in its business and beat its competitors, cost efficiency is very important.

Achieving cost efficiency involves economies of scale, which are achieved when a company manages to lower the cost per unit of manufacturing a particular product by increasing output.

Rock Baby Co needs to lower its per unit cost of manufacturing products by installing updated machinery and equipment which can increase the production output. By reducing unit costs in this way, the company can achieve cost efficiency without compromising on quality.

Rock Baby saves on costs by producing an increasing number of new products; therefore economies of scope are created. Synergy is achieved, as the cost for producing new products is lower than the cost of producing a single product independently. The main reason for economies of scope is the ability to share investments and costs for more than one product group or strategic business unit (SBU).

Answer to TY 3

Mommy has achieved a competitive advantage and earned a higher profit than its average profit per year. Now the company needs to maintain the same level of profitability. The company has achieved high profits because of its superior resources and competencies.

Mommy wants to preserve the sustainability of its competitive advantage, which requires superior competencies more than resources, as the resources may be acquired by competitors.

Factors that might help Mommy to preserve its competitive advantages include:

a) **durability of the competency / resource:** as the competitive advantage is based on the technological superiority of the processing unit, the sustainability of the processing unit will be of a longer duration. The company should always be on the lookout for better technology to process and store the milk products, and competent manpower.
b) **transparency of the competency / resource:** the company should maintain less transparency of the competency so that it cannot be copied by competitors.
c) **transferability of the competency / resource:** the company should keep knowledge about important processes limited to select employees, and take extra precautions for retaining these employees so that employees who have competencies are not recruited by competitors.

d) **ability to replicate the competency / resource:** the main base of achieving competitive advantages for Mommy could be, for example, a group of dairy cooperatives who keep supplying good quality milk This may be short-lived and can be easily be replicated by competitors. The company has to find ways to strengthen its network of cooperatives.

Answer to TY 4

The introduction of a new variety or product is significant to the growth and success of any company, but carries a high risk. Introduction of soup mix and noodle mix would involve completely new process and market requirements for Famous Noodles.

Development and process requirement for the new range of product

1. Broadcasting is necessary to decide whether or not to allocate the funds to the current project.
2. Market judgment is necessary to judge the requirements of the market demand for the users.
3. Technical judgement: it is necessary to judge the technical quality and problems of the project. The problems that arise during development should be handled promptly.
4. Financial requirement is necessary to judge the financial resources available for product development.
5. Internal testing of the product is necessary in order to do a lab test for the production of genuine product.
6. Production start-up (the start-up of full-scale or commercial production) - production is carried out in a formal process with better coordination among employees and different units
7. Market launch (the launch of the product, on a full-scale and / or commercial basis - an identifiable set of marketing activities specific to this product). A market with long term potential is required.
8. Experienced employees - more experienced employees with better facilities should be introduced for effective work.
9. Time and effort expectations should increase.
10. Management support – finally, there should be support from the management.

The success of the company's new soup and noodles mixes cannot be guaranteed but there is certainly sufficient reason for giving more thought to the way new products are considered and developed.

Answer to TY 5

a) **Strengths**
   - Chemical and other constituents are of a better quality than those of the competitors.
   - Drugs are available at a cheaper cost than the competitors.
   - Products are available worldwide.
   - Many skilled employees and scientist have been hired.
   - Research for drugs has been carried out for 24 hours.
   - Good relationship between employee and management, and employee and customer.
   - Good management capability to perform tasks.
   - Standard trademark.
   - Strengthening market share and keeping customer focus remains a high priority for the company.

b) **Weaknesses**
   - No attention to customer complaints.
   - Reliability of the service provided not up to mark.

c) **Opportunities**
   - Demand for drugs at cheaper rate (which the company can provide).

d) **Threats**
   - High tax rate.
   - Strict quality checks regarding the right composition of drug contents for consumers' benefit.

Quick Quiz

1. Which type of competences represent the minimum levels of competence that an organisation must possess?
2. Identify three ways an organisation can achieve cost efficiency?
3. What are the two types of competitive advantages an organisation can achieve through their competences?
4. What are the three types of new products / services an organisation can introduce?
5. S.W.O.T analysis involves an organisation conducting both an _____ and an _____ analysis.

Answers to Quick Quiz

1. Threshold competences

2. Achieving economies of scale, achieving economies of scope and / or progressing along the experience curve

3. Cost competitive advantage and a differentiation competitive advantage

4. New to the market, new to the organisation and new to the world

5. Internal and external

Self Examination Questions

Question 1

Techno Ltd is a medium-sized IT company which creates customised software solutions for companies based in the US and Europe. It develops software solutions in India, thereby benefiting from relatively low labour costs.

However the company has recently experienced intense competition from suppliers who have even lower cost bases. The CEO of the company has decided that the company will benefit if it focuses on niche areas that can provide higher profit margins.

He has decided to target customers in the banking and financial services industry. Increasingly companies in the banking and financial services sector are demanding software solutions that incorporate the ever-changing business needs and risk management frameworks. The company now needs to develop a suitable marketing strategy to succeed in this new area and maintain a sustainable competitive advantage.

Required:

Conduct a SWOT analysis for Techno Ltd..

Question 2

Explain the meaning of strategic capability in a business context.

Answers to Self Examination Questions

Answer to SEQ 1

Strengths	➢ Existence of labour arbitrage (i.e. the ability to create a customised software solution in India at a much lower cost) ➢ Large availability of skilled English speaking engineers ➢ Time zone differential means work and testing of the program can be done on a 24 hour basis.
Weaknesses	➢ Reputation for being a low cost (and not high quality) service provider ➢ Cultural / national differences with customers ➢ Not updated on the very latest technologies / programming languages.
Opportunities	➢ Large number of untapped organisations still present in the US and Europe. ➢ Potential to move up the software value chain with existing clients
Threats	➢ Appreciating Indian rupee which makes developing software in India more expensive for American / European organisations. ➢ Increasing competition from organisations in other countries who are also able to exercise labour arbitrage (e.g. Russia).

Answer to SEQ 2

Strategic capability refers to the competencies, knowledge, and skills that an organisation can apply to achieve success in a competitive environment. The concept is considered to be derived from the core competencies approach to corporate strategy. It is looked upon as one of the main pillars of strategic management and focuses on the ability to provide products that provide value to customers.

SECTION A: STRATEGIC POSITION

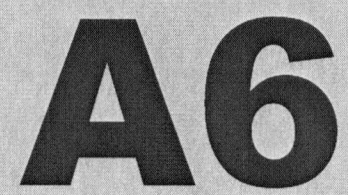

STUDY GUIDE A6: THE EXPECTATIONS OF STAKEHOLDERS AND THE INFLUENCE OF ETHICS AND CULTURE

■ Get Through Intro

Once upon a time, the sole focus of business was to make a profit. In fact it was to make as much profit as possible. Companies strived to give the highest returns to their shareholders, who were the only group of important stakeholders. That time has long gone and the majority of businesses have learnt the importance of considering other stakeholders. Profit is no longer the sole goal; employee satisfaction, thriving local communities and even satisfied suppliers are now considered reasonable goals to have.

This chapter is an important one as it should show you that there is more to life than just earning money. It is possible to earn a little less money sometimes and make a lot of other people very very happy. In the long run, this can earn you even more money as people see you as an ethical organisation which cares about a wider range of stakeholders.

■ Learning Outcomes

a) Advise on the implications of corporate governance on organisational purpose and strategy.
b) Evaluate, through stakeholder mapping, the relative influence of stakeholders on organisational purpose and strategy.
c) Assess ethical influences on organisational purpose and strategy.
d) Explore the scope of corporate social responsibility.
e) Assess the impact of culture on organisational purpose and strategy.
f) Prepare and evaluate a cultural web of an organisation.
g) Advise on how organisations can communicate their core values and mission.

Introduction

Case Study

Has slavery ended in Europe and America?

Many people in Europe and America have enjoyed the falling prices of quality clothing over the past decade. It is now possible to pick up a pair of Jeans for $6 in many countries. T-shirts can be bought for $2 and 100% wool suits for $100. This was unheard of 20 years ago. Whilst many shoppers are happy to shop at stores which sell clothes at these prices (Tesco, Asda and Primark included), charities, television companies and the rest of the media are eager to bring the plight of those who make the clothes to the attention of the world.

Many factories in developing countries employ children under 15, pay less than the minimum local wage and force overtime without compensation. Some of the factories are run in appalling conditions, where light is low, temperatures are high and managers regular antagonise workers (often physically). According to an article in The UK Daily Mail (June 08), ' Tesco's fashion has come under fire, too. It was accused by War on Want [a charity] of using 'slave labour' after an investigation found that a textile factory, used by the company, in Bangalore, India, sources goods from a factory where workers are paid just 16 pence an hour.'

However, the large supermarkets and clothing stores are making steps to improve this situation. They realise that they are making huge profits and perhaps they should be considering their suppliers too – not treating them as slaves. They also realize that their customers will start making ethical choices and perhaps may choose to shop away from them in the future. Most of the supermarkets have now introduced fair trade coffee and other products, to show that they are concerned and are ethical.

The above case study shows that other stakeholders are becoming increasingly important and businesses will have to consider them in the equation when deciding on which strategy to pursue. This chapter will give you an idea of who the different stakeholders are and what kind of importance businesses place on them. This is an important chapter for the exam as you will have to apply your knowledge of this to the given scenarios.

1. Advise on the implications of corporate governance on organisational purpose and strategy.[2]

[Learning Outcome a]

1.1 What is corporate governance?

Corporate governance represents the set of policies and procedures that determine how an organisation is **directed, administered and controlled**. It sets the broad framework or parameters within which the organisation must operate. It provides the structure and process to ensure companies are managed in the interests of their owners.

Corporate governance sets out what an organisation is supposed to do thereby providing a **benchmark** against which the future performance and actions of managers / executives can be measured and evaluated by shareholders and other stakeholders.

Definition

The OECD (Organisation for Economic Co-operation and Development) defines corporate governance as "the system by which business corporations are directed and controlled".

There are various **participants** in corporate governance structure such as the board, managers, shareholders and other stakeholders (i.e. employees, customers, suppliers, government and the society at large). The corporate governance structure specifies the allocation of **rights and responsibilities** among these different participants in the corporation and spells out the rules and procedures for making decisions on corporate affairs. It therefore provides a code of conduct for the Board of Directors. By doing this, it also provides the structure through which the company objectives are set, and the means of attaining those objectives and monitoring performance.

Tip

Corporate governance is about promoting corporate fairness, transparency and accountability.

> **Example**

Although the contents of corporate governance will vary from organisation to organisation, almost all will have the following components:

a) **Accountability:** managers, executives and the board of directors are ultimately responsible to shareholders and must always act with the best interests of shareholders (and other stakeholders) in mind.

b) **Compliance:** managers, executives and the board of directors must always comply with all laws and regulations including industry codes of conduct and the common law.

c) **Transparency:** information on the financial performance and position of the organisation as well as any activities the organisation is engaged in should always be available and known to shareholders.

d) **Integrity:** managers, executives and the board of directors must always behave in an ethical manner. Their actions and decisions should represent not only what is legal but also what is morally right.

The emergence of Corporate Governance as an important business discipline is linked to two major theories:

Firstly the views of **Milton Friedman** who famously stated that the only responsibility a business had were to its shareholders (so long as it acted within the law).

Secondly, the concept of stakeholder theory which asserts that businesses have a responsibility to all their stakeholders, not just its shareholders.

Stakeholder theory recognises the groups of stakeholders of an organisation. The theory also details the methods by which the top management of the organisation can give due importance to these groups.

SUMMARY

Corporate governance
- set of policies and procedures that determine how organisations are directed and controlled
- extends to organisation's stakeholders
- contents
  - accountability: towards shareholders
  - compliance: with all laws and regulations
  - transparency: in financial information
  - integrity: ethical actions and decisions

1.2 Hierarchy of governance / the governance chain

Parties involved in corporate governance include **the chief executive officer, the board of directors, management, shareholders and other stakeholders** which include suppliers, employees, creditors, customers, tax authorities and the community at large.

> **Definition**

The persons who affect or are affected by the success or the failure of the organisation's effort to achieve its objective are known as the stakeholders.

In corporations, the shareholder delegates the right to make decisions to the managers who are required to act in the company's best interests. In larger organisations it is simply not practical for shareholders to effectively run the firm. Professional managers are given the responsibility of managing the organisation but they have less interest in the ownership of the organisation (unless they have incentives such as share schemes). This **separation of ownership from control** involves a loss of effective control by shareholders over managerial decisions.

Partly as a result of this separation between the two parties, a system of corporate governance is implemented **to assist in aligning the incentives of managers with those of shareholders**. With the significant increase in equity holdings of investors, an opportunity has arisen for a reversal of the separation of ownership and control and problems have occurred due to ownership and control not being separated. Hence, when management and ownership are separated, the professional managers act as the agents of the owners i.e. the shareholders.

Diagram 1: Separation of ownership and control

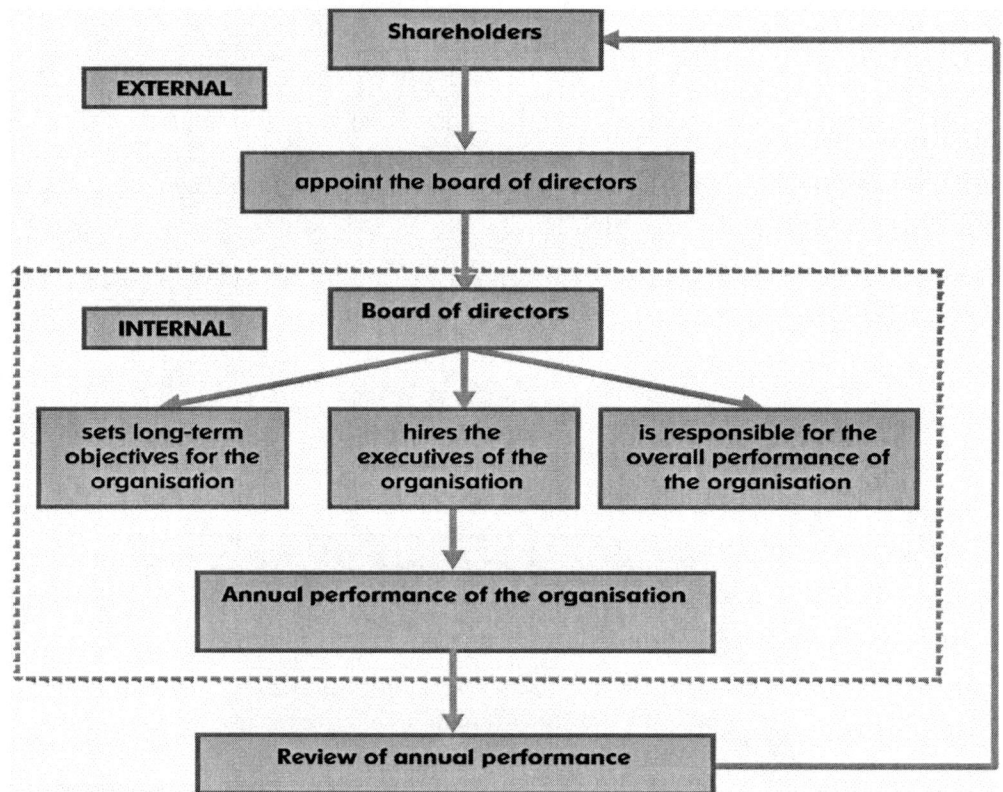

A **board of directors** often plays a **key role** in corporate governance. It is their responsibility to endorse the organisation's strategy, develop directional policy, appoint, supervise and remunerate senior executives and to ensure **accountability of the organisation** to its owners and authorities.

All parties to corporate governance have an interest, whether direct or indirect, in the effective performance of the organisation. Generally they receive some form of consideration (benefit). Directors, workers and management receive salaries, benefits and reputation, while shareholders receive capital return. Customers receive goods and services; suppliers receive compensation for their goods or services. In return, these individuals provide value in the form of natural, human, social and other forms of capital.

A key factor in an individual's decision to contribute to an organisation (by investing) is that they will receive a fair share of the organisation's returns commensurate with their inputs. If some parties receive more than their fair return then the investors may choose to leave the organisation and the organisation will collapse.

Corporate governance functions in a chain. Managers are answerable to senior managers. Senior managers are answerable to the board of directors. The board of directors is accountable to individual shareholders and institutional investors. This governance chain is characterised by **vertical integration**. The hierarchical levels differ from organisation to organisation.

For a small organisation, the board of directors is the agent of the shareholders and so in this type of organisation, few levels are in operation in the governance chain. On the other hand, in the case of large organisations, the hierarchical levels are many.

Diagram 2: Vertical integration of governance chain

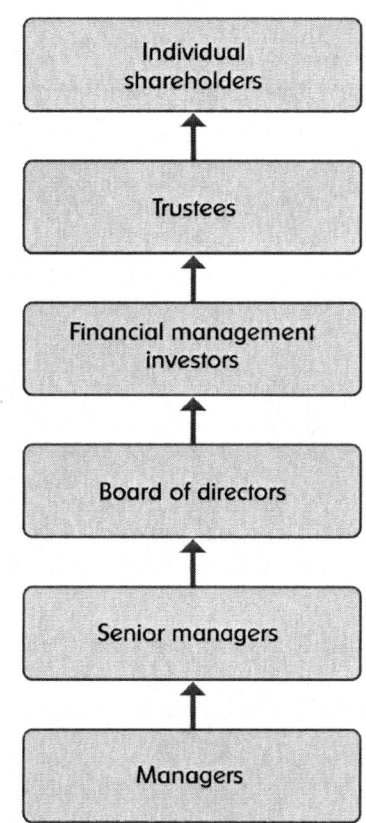

The managers are appointed to manage the operations of an organisation, so they act as an **agent** of the shareholders. The relationship between the two can be studied by the **agency model**. This model is based on the assumption that the agent works in good faith for the benefit of the principal. The agency model suffers from various problems e.g. managers may not act in the best interests of shareholders; they may be self serving. For example, managers may spend money on perquisites and pet projects and avoid risk which might mean they do not pursue projects that carry the greatest returns. The performance of managers and their behaviour also needs to be reviewed i.e. by an internal audit which, itself, is an agency cost.

Example

Sun Ltd is a manufacturing organisation engaged in the production of electrical wires. Peter and Sam are the senior managers of the organisation. The organisation obtains an order from a customer for a thousand metres of wire to be supplied within two days. The managers have to decide whether to accept the proposal or not and also whether it will be possible to deliver the order in two days' time. Here, as the senior managers are looking after the day-to-day operations of the organisation, they act as an agent of the stakeholders.

The governance chain raises the following important points relating to the organisational purpose and strategy:

1. The **responsibilities of directors** towards shareholders. It is always important to consider whether directors are held directly accountable to shareholders only or whether they are also accountable to stakeholders.

2. The **agency model** operates on the basis of the **targets and budgets** of the organisation. It helps in identifying the behaviour of senior managers and in knowing the extent to which shareholders' interests are safeguarded.

3. The governance chain requires that the senior managers and the members of the board of directors should be **aware of shareholders' expectations.**

4. There are **differences in opinion relating to the interests** of different groups in corporate governance and also differences in opinion between managers and directors because they aim to keep a balance between these different interests. Some directors work in their own interests rather than in the interests of the shareholders at large.

5. When the directors regularly inform the stakeholders of the position of the organisation, this influences the strategies to be framed for the organisation.

SUMMARY

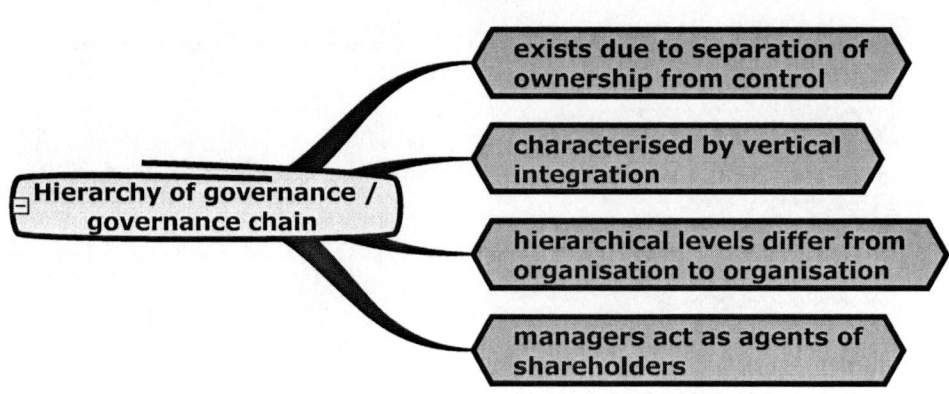

1.3 Functions of governing body

In the private sector, the governing body is the board of directors. In the public sector, a similar body with a larger coverage that is accountable to the shareholders regarding the functioning of the organisation is the governing body. The main function of the governing body is to **satisfy the owners of the organisation**.

The operations of the board of directors differ in different countries. Hence, there are **four models** of corporate governance:

1. the Anglo-Saxon model
2. the Rhine model
3. the Japanese model
4. the Latin model

Sr. no.	Models	Country where used	Features	Weaknesses
1.	Anglo-Saxon	USA, UK, Australia	➢ single-tier board ➢ both executive and non-executive directors included ➢ institutional shareholders are more powerful than individual shareholders ➢ organisations following this model are more globalise and have huge funds at their disposal ➢ organisations are market-oriented	➢ short-term view of organisational strategies and policies ➢ insufficient governance standards ➢ unstable
2.	Rhine model	Switzerland, Germany, The Netherlands	➢ two tier board - a two tier system is a model whereby independence is accomplished by the division of supervisor and supervisee into two different boards that work independently of each other. ➢ motivates effective employee representation on governing body ➢ gives rise to combined decision-making healthy corporate governance procedures	➢ difficult to globalise ➢ inflexible
3.	Japanese model		➢ Directors anticipate interests of employees and promote these interests	➢ slow decision-making process ➢ responsibility is weak ➢ low returns for shareholders
4.	Latin model	Italy, Spain, France	➢ Enormous state involvement in business. ➢ Government influences industrial policies. ➢ Investment is stable. There is uniformity in economic, political or administrative goals.	➢ Excessive involvement of government gives rise to political problems.

1.4 Influences of corporate governance on strategies

The development of an organisation depends upon effective strategies which aim for the success of the organisation. The success or failure of an organisation's strategies depends upon its governance. Governance here means the board of directors.

1. The board may exercise a **stewardship role** where it assigns the work to executives. The board will have to make sure that the executives are working in the interests of the stakeholders and not their own interests.

2. The board may also be a **participant with management** in the process of strategic management. In this case, problems may arise such as a lack of sufficient time and the lower understanding level of the non-executive directors.

3. The members of the board keep **watch** on whether the work performed by the executives is in the interests of the stakeholders.

4. The members must be self-sufficient and they operate independently i.e. **able to participate freely in the decision-making** process. Their decisions should not be influenced by management.

5. The board should have **sufficient time** to perform their duties effectively.

Due to the separation between the ownership and control of large entities, corporate governance has been introduced. Corporate governance keeps a check on the working practices of those who are in control of the entity i.e. management. It sets the **broad framework** within which the entity must operate.

1.5 Objectives of governance

The main purpose of corporate governance is to align the interests of managers, executives and the board of directors with those charged with governance. The objectives of corporate governance include:

1. to **protect the interests of shareholders** by aligning the interests of the board with shareholders' interests

The primary objective of corporate governance is to protect the interests of shareholders. This requires the business to be run honestly and ethically.

Corporate governance aims to align the interests of the board of the entity with the interests of the shareholders.

2. to **meet the organisational objectives** by directing and controlling the organisation

An organisation is a set of people chasing certain objectives. To meet these objectives, the set of people should be lead by managers, who will give **proper direction and control** to all activities. Corporate governance entrusts various responsibilities to managers to supervise, control and direct the company. Governance provides assurance to the shareholders and management that the entity is chasing its objectives.

Corporate governance sets out what an organisation is supposed to do thereby providing a **benchmark** against which the future performance and actions of managers / executives can be measured and evaluated. When discussing the organisation's objectives, it should be remembered that the need for a system of corporate governance stems from the concept of separation of ownership and control. For many businesses and especially for large publicly traded organisations, the concept of separation of ownership and control has resulted in one set of individuals owning the business and another set running the business.

Case Study

Tyco International

The board of Directors of Tyco International is comprised of world class leaders with high experience. The Board has adopted the best governance practices and procedures which results in setting higher standards of honesty, integrity and excellence in the organization. Moreover, the Board has adopted new and advanced governance principles for higher standards of corporate governance. The organisation has also adopted new memorandum for revised benefit programs and compensation and a new Tyco guide for employees for ethical consideration which results in building higher value for the stakeholders of the company and ultimately gains market trustworthiness.

The Board of directors has the mission to enhance the value of the organisation for the better interests of their stakeholders.

Therefore, in a broad sense, the objectives of corporate governance can be said to be to provide the necessary structure and rules through which the:

- interests of an organisation's board of directors, executives and management can be aligned with those of its shareholders (e.g. an organisation holds an annual general meeting so that shareholders can vote in the board of directors who in turn appoint the executives / management of an organisation);

- activities of the organisation can be directed and controlled (e.g. an organisation has its management provide detailed reports on its major activities and expenditures to shareholders on a quarterly basis); and

- effectiveness, efficacy and ethics of the board of directors, executives and managers as well as the organisation as a whole can be measured (e.g. an organisation has a written mandate to donate 10 per cent of its profits to charities).

Overall, corporate governance involves organisations being **transparent and honest in all their dealings,** be they with customers, suppliers, investors, employees or any type of stakeholder or shareholder. This factor, given the recent high profile accounting frauds (e.g. Enron), makes corporate governance especially relevant today.

In addition, the traditional view that corporate governance is an internal and private matter for an organisation has disappeared. Today legislation such as the Sarbanes-Oxley Act introduced in the year 2002 (following the Enron Scandal in the year 2001) in the United States and the Combined Code in the UK are placing many basic requirements on listed companies in regards to their corporate governance systems.

Example

The UK Combined Code states that for a publicly listed company, the number of non-executive directors should comprise no less than one third of the total number of directors serving on the organisation's board. Non-executive directors are defined as directors who have no operational responsibility for the organisation. Therefore they are much more likely to take an independent and unbiased view of the organisation's policies and performance. They also bring specialist expertise.

Lastly the **importance of having an effective system of corporate governance** is that it:

- builds **investor and shareholder confidence** in the organisation (e.g. research has found that investors worldwide are willing to pay more for shares of an organisation that has a reputation for good corporate governance);

- **demonstrates the commitment** an organisation has towards being ethical, efficient and effective (e.g. an organisation conducts an audit on all of its directors' expenses claims on an annual basis);

- helps an organisation's board of directors, executives and management to take **ethical decisions** (e.g. all strategies have to be evaluated not only in terms of their potential profitability but also as to how ethical they are); and

- provides a **system of checks and balances** so that neither management nor large shareholders can abuse their power at the expense of other shareholders or the organisation (e.g. an organisation has a policy that at least 50 per cent of its board must consist of non-executive directors).

Test Yourself 1

Hi-Fashions Ltd has been manufacturing clothes for 20 years. The business is owned and operated by the Smith family. The business has been expanding rapidly since its inception. Hi-Fashions have been a successful venture in terms of profitability. It also enjoys an excellent reputation in the clothing market.

The Smith family has recently decided to try to capitalise on these factors and list the organisation on a local stock exchange. The board of directors is aware that, in order to have a successful listing, they will first need to have a system of corporate governance in place.

You are working as a consultant in Apex Consultancy Group. The directors of Hi-Fashions are unfamiliar with the term "corporate governance" and want to know what good corporate governance entails for their organisation and themselves. They have come to you for advice and guidance on this matter.

Required:

Write a letter to the board of directors:

(a) explaining what corporate governance is
(b) explaining why it becomes particularly relevant if they are considering listing their business
(c) explaining why it is important to have a system of corporate governance

2. Evaluate, through stakeholder mapping, the relative influence of stakeholders on organisational purpose and strategy.[3]

[Learning Outcome b]

2.1 Who are the stakeholders?

There are some groups which are not a part of the governance chain. These groups are consumers, suppliers, the government, the public, employees etc. These parties, who may be either internal to or external to the organisation, are known as stakeholders.

Definition

Johnson, Scholes and Whittington define a **stakeholder** as:

Stakeholders are those individuals or groups who depend on an organisation to fulfill their own goals and on whom, in turn, the organisation depends.

(Source: JSW)

To understand the different stakeholder groups, it is not sufficient to learn only about the formal structure of the organisation; students must also be aware of the informal and indirect relationships.

Categories of stakeholders

One of the methods of identifying the groups of stakeholders is by using a model consisting of internal and external circles.

Diagram 3: Stakeholders

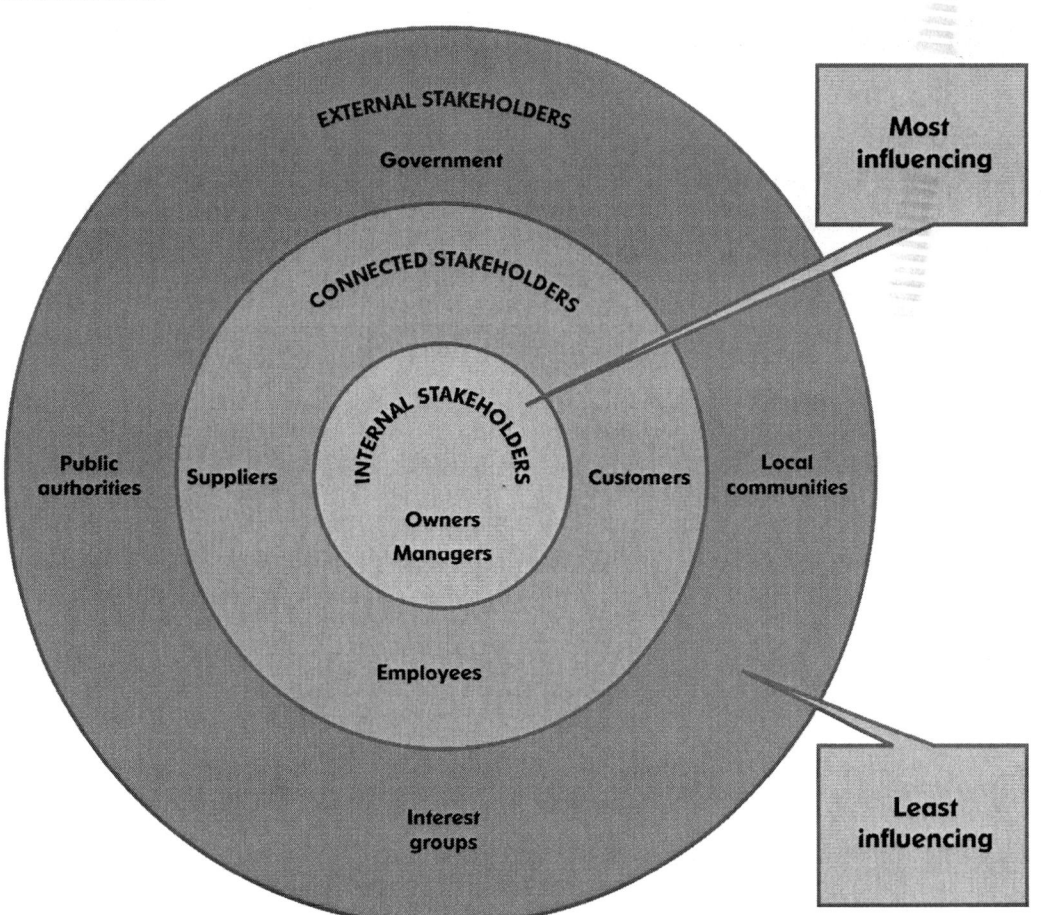

In this model, the innermost circle consists of the important stakeholders i.e. the stakeholders who have most influence over the organisation. The stakeholders located in the middle circle have influence over the organisation but this influence is weaker than that of the most important stakeholders. The outer circle consists of that stakeholder group which has influence on the organisation but the weakest influence as compared to the other groups of stakeholders.

From the above it is clear that the stakeholder groups can be divided into two categories:

> **Internal stakeholder groups** are management and employees.

> **External stakeholder groups** are customers, suppliers, local communities, government, public authorities, interest groups, competitors etc.

The external stakeholders may be further categorised on the basis of the nature of their association / relationship with the organisation. Customers, suppliers, competitors etc. are categorised as stakeholders from the market environment. All these types of stakeholders are present in Porter's five forces model. Government authorities, local communities, public authorities etc. are stakeholders from the political / social environment.

Also, according to the Mendelow Matrix, stakeholders are classified on the basis of power and interest. This matrix is explained in the following paragraphs under stakeholder mapping. Stakeholder mapping is a way of presenting the relationship of a stakeholder with the organisation on the basis of the stakeholder's power and level of interest.

2.2 What are the expectations of stakeholders?

Stakeholders have various expectations from the organisation which need to be satisfied.

Sr. no.	Stakeholders	Expectations
1.	Managers	> adequate authority for performance of duty
2.	Employees	> adequate training > job satisfaction > healthy working conditions > adequate incentives and motivation > quality of work life > job security > empowerment to practise new ideas > ability to pursue a good career
3.	Suppliers	> timely payment of their consignment > availability of regular orders
4.	Customers	> provision of goods / services at low cost > high quality products > proper communication channels in case of difficulty
5.	Shareholders	> good returns on their investments > satisfactory other benefits
6.	Government	> timely payment of taxes > compliance with all regulations
7.	Public at large	> provide donations to the needy > protect environment from hazards

Example

John supplies automobile components to Best Cars Plc. He is an external stakeholder of Best Cars. Best Cars expects John to make timely delivery of components of the prescribed quality. In the same way, John expects Best Cars to make timely payment of his bills and also to recommend him to other companies looking for suppliers.

As there are various types of stakeholders, their expectations also vary according to their needs. Quite often there is the **possibility of conflicts** between the expectations of the stakeholders. As described in the previous sections, an organisation's stakeholders will come from a variety of backgrounds. This diversity will result in different stakeholders having not only **very different but often contradictory objectives**.

> **Example**
>
> In an organisation, staff will desire higher wages but shareholders might want low wages which lowers organizational costs so that the organisation's profit will be higher (of course, in the long run this would not be a good strategy).

One of the most important challenges for an organisation is to ensure that it balances the interests of these conflicting groups, as these groups will simultaneously pull the organisation in different directions.

> **Example**
>
> An organisation's customers would like it to charge the lowest possible price for its goods and services. Shareholders would like it to charge the highest possible price, as they will make more money.
>
> Management and unions are two of an organisation's stakeholders that are frequently at loggerheads. Management's priorities are maximising profits / shareholder value whilst the focus for unions is protecting their employee members (better wages, work hours, job security etc).
>
> In most cases, their different agendas are settled by talks and compromise. However, in extreme cases when communication breaks down, the results are walkouts and strikes.

SUMMARY

- **Stakeholders**
  - **individuals / groups**
    - who depend on organisation to fulfil their goals
    - and on whom, in turn, organisation depends
  - **categories**
    - internal stakeholders
    - external stakeholders
  - different stakeholders have different & contradictory objectives

2.3 Stakeholder mapping

The stakeholders influence the organisational purposes and strategies. The impact of such an influence depends upon the nature of the relationship between the organisation and the stakeholder. Stakeholder mapping was derived by Mendelow. Stakeholder mapping is a way of presenting the relationship of a stakeholder with the organisation on the basis of the stakeholder's power and level of interest. Here, interest refers to interest in exerting power and power is over resources and key decisions.

Diagram 4: Mendelow's stakeholder mapping matrix

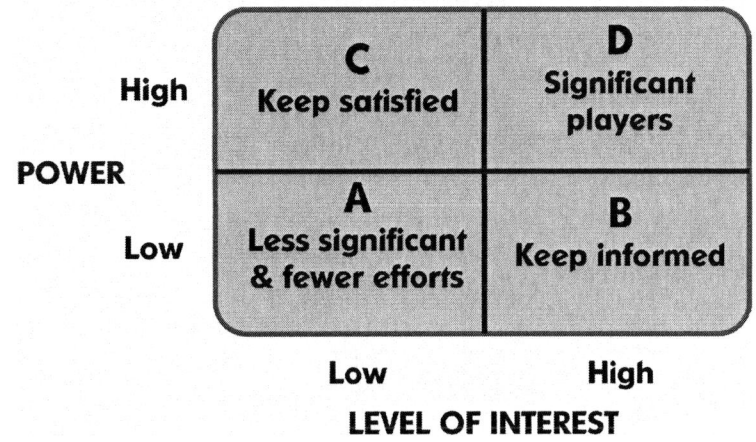

A. Low interest-low power

Stakeholders with low interest and low power are of **low importance** to the organisation.

Example

An office cleaner would be an example of such a stakeholder. Although he meets the definition of an internal stakeholder, his work is of minimal consequence to the success of the organisation. In turn, such stakeholders typically have very little interest in the activities or success of the organisation.

B. High interest-low power

Stakeholders with high interest but low power are of **medium importance** to an organisation.

Example

A common example of such a stakeholder is the average individual investor for a large publicly-traded corporation. This type of stakeholder is very interested in the operations and performance of the organisation as the value of his investment depends upon it. However, given that the extent of his holdings is typically only a few hundred shares or a tiny percentage of the organisation, he can exert very little influence over the organisation. However, the company needs to keep him informed or he may lose interest and sell his shares.

C. Low interest-high power

Stakeholders with low interest but a high level of power would be of **medium importance** to an organisation.

Example

Governments are typically not interested in the operations of an organisation. However, they will intervene if laws are being broken or the organisation is detrimentally affecting society as a whole. For instance, many governments have taken Microsoft to court when they believed Microsoft was following monopolistic practices. Microsoft therefore needs to keep the government satisfied.

D. High interest-high power

The **most important** stakeholder groups are those with a high interest in the organisation and a high level of power over the organisation.

Example

For General Motors, Kirk Kerkorian would fit into this category. Kerkorian is a billionaire investor who has bought millions of the company's shares. His holdings amount to close to 10 per cent of General Motors' stock. Kerkorian closely follows the operations of the company and actively pushes for reforms. General Motors, in return, listens and acts on what he says.

SUMMARY

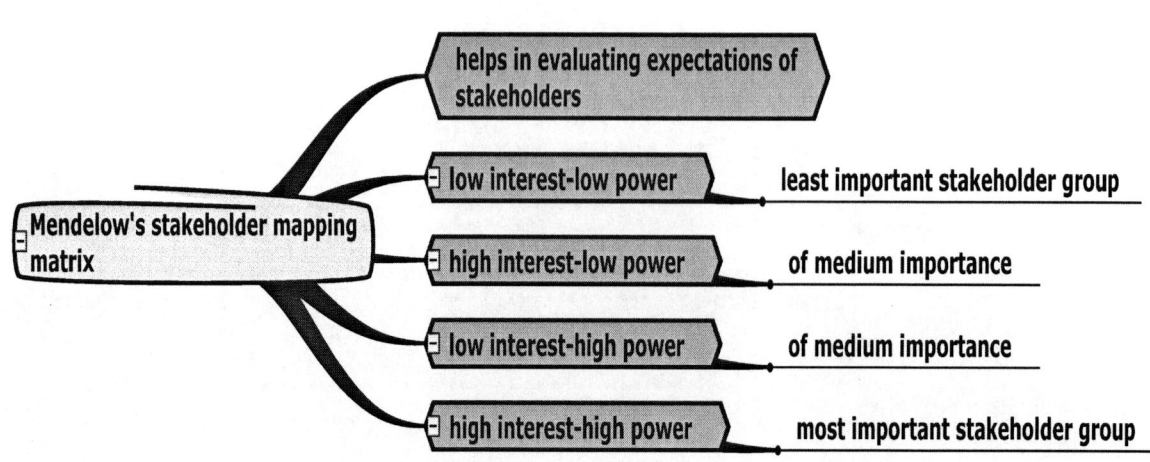

The stakeholders influence the strategies of the organisation. The extent of such influence depends upon their **power and interest**. The stakeholder mapping matrix is a useful mode of understanding the features of each stakeholder group. With the help of this matrix, the expectations of stakeholders can be effectively evaluated.

Example

Sun Ltd wants to move its branch office in the month of June. There is the possibility that the local authorities may influence their decision to move the office.

1. Shareholders' influence

The shareholders of an organisation have **immense influence on the strategies** of an organisation. In the case of small organisations, the shareholders are in direct communication with the managers and in some cases, the shareholders are even the directors of the organisation. As a result, they have a strong influence on the organisation's purpose and strategy. On the other hand, in the case of large organisations, the shareholders holding a small percentage of shares do not have any standing in the organisation's management and so have negligible influence on the organisation's strategies. Any shareholder holding a large percentage of shares may have immense influence on the organisation.

2. What is power?

Power is an authority that enables a person to control the behaviour of others.
Determinants of power

- extent to which stakeholders can cause the organisational policies to be changed
- extent to which the organisation's plans can be disrupted by stakeholders
- position of stakeholders in the organisation
- organisation depends upon stakeholders for its needs
- stakeholders' control over the organisation's strategy formulation
- ability and skills of stakeholders
- extent of stakeholders' investment in the organisation

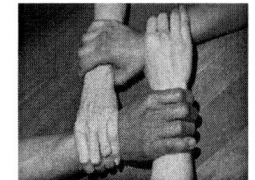

3. The French and Raven model recognises five types of power. These are:

- **Referent power**: referent power is person-oriented. This type of power is exerted as a function of the regard and respect for an individual in an organisation, on account of his personal attributes or charisma in the eyes of others.
- **Expert power**: this type of power is a kind of referent power which is exerted on the basis of recognised expertise in the organisation.
- **Legitimate power**: legitimate power is exerted on the basis of authority enjoyed by the person as a result of his position in the organisation. This type of power is not person-oriented.
- **Reward power**: this type of power is exerted when there is the capability to grant positive support for the desired behaviour.
- **Coercive power**: this type of power is exerted when there is the capability to impose punishment on a subordinate person in the organisation.

Test Yourself 2

You have just been appointed as an operations manager of Good Eats Ltd, a medium-sized company that produces ready-to-eat food products. The company sells its products directly to retailers on a wholesale basis. The following two issues have been raised:

1. The association of local retailers has proposed to arrange an event for the promotion of local supermarkets on the occasion of its annual day. It has asked Good Eats to provide sponsorship for this event.
2. A local sports club has approached Good Eats to provide sponsorship for a rugby match. Good Eats, in turn, can advertise and sell its products during the match.

Both the events will be happening in the same month. The amount of funds required for sponsoring both the events is same. The prospective returns from sponsorship of both the events in terms of the marketing of Good Eats' products will be same. The finance department has informed you that the budget has been approved for sponsoring any one of the events.

Required:

With the help of stakeholder mapping, decide which event will be more appropriate for Good Eats to sponsor.

3. Assess ethical influences on organisational purpose and strategy.[3]

[Learning Outcome c]

3.1 The term "ethics" comes from the Greek word "ethikos". Ethikos literally translated means **theory of living**. This definition has evolved over time and now refers to abiding by a set of written and unwritten rules based on both **legality and morality.**

Definition
Ethics can be defined as abiding by a set of written and unwritten rules based on both legality and morality.

Legality, because ethics involves obeying the laws of a country. Morality, because ethics involves doing what a society believes is just and correct.

Example
Although cheating while playing sports or cards with a friend is not illegal, it is considered unethical. This is because it is widely believed that people should be honest in all their activities.

Ethics also involves having a **permanent commitment** to abiding by these rules. A person cannot claim to be ethical by following ethics in some situations, but not in others.

Example
Sam is an honest employee and a law-abiding citizen. However, if Sam lies about the condition of a car he is selling he becomes unethical, despite his ethical behaviour in other situations.

Very broadly speaking, ethics involves doing **what is right and what will not harm the interests of others.** Having a system of ethics is very important to people on both an individual and a collective level. Individuals have a basic level of trust with one another because they expect others to have a basic set of ethics. This trust level sets the foundation on which people interact with each other on social and business levels. It is also what allows society to function as a whole. Having a system of ethics is as important as having a legal system.

Example
Most people do not commit murder, not just because it is illegal but also because they feel it is immoral.

SUMMARY

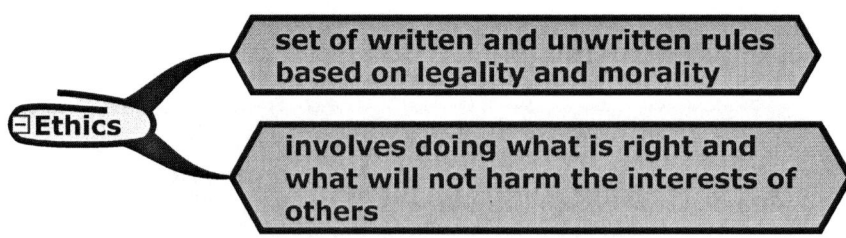

3.2 Ethics also has a very **important place in commerce**. Remember that the business world comprises and is run by people. Even the world's largest organisations are all ultimately controlled by one individual. How ethical an organisation is, will depend upon how ethical its employees are.

Definition
Business ethics can be defined as the branch of ethics that examines rules and principles within a commercial context.

The original view of organisations was that their only ethical responsibility was to maximise profits for their owners or shareholders so long as they behaved lawfully (Friedman). The belief was that profitability should be the only criterion used to evaluate decisions.

This view later changed to the belief that organisations also have an ethical **responsibility towards their various stakeholders** (e.g. their employees, suppliers, customers etc).

Friedman famously stated that the only responsibility a business had was to its shareholders (so long as it acted within the law).

Friedman supports the 'shareholder value' view. The Friedman doctrine states that the social responsibility of any business is to increase its profits so long as it acts lawfully. Freeman supports the stakeholder theory of the firm which recognises the groups of stakeholders within an organisation. R. Edward Freeman, in his book, Strategic Management, defined stakeholders as "those groups who can effect, or are affected by, the achievement of an organisation's purpose."

The theory also details the methods by which the top management of the organisation can give due importance to these respective groups.

Any decision now needs to be considered in terms of both profitability and also whether it will detrimentally affect the interests of any of the organisation's stakeholder groups. Decisions that would hurt the interests of any stakeholder group would be **unethical** despite the level of profits they would bring to the organisation.

Example
It would be unethical for an organisation to exaggerate or lie about the features of one of its products, regardless of how heavily this tactic would increase sales.

Today, organisations are expected to have an ethical responsibility to their **shareholders and stakeholders, as well as to society at large**. Organisations are expected not to take decisions or engage in activities that will hurt the interests of any of these groups. In addition, organisations are expected to also **"give something back"** to society through donations or by sponsoring welfare activities.

Example
IBM, through its Used Technology Donation Program has provided over 5,000 used personal computer systems to over 1,000 non-profit organisations. These organisations provide education, training, and computer literacy skills to adults and children with disabilities.

It should be noted that there is also a **strong economic justification** for organisations to behave ethically. Experience has shown that being ethical makes good business sense for the organisation in the long run. For example, suppliers are more willing to deal with organisations that have an established reputation for behaving ethically; staff are more motivated if they are treated well and the local community feel valued if there are community-corporate links.

Research has also shown that people are more willing to work for or buy products from an ethical organisation. Behaving ethically across all levels will promote the overall efficiency of both the organisation and society as a whole.

Example
The purchase managers of the organisation Trust1 have a well-earned reputation for not accepting bribes. Therefore, the organisation's suppliers offer this bribe amount as a legitimate discount to the organisation instead.

Trust1 also follows a very strict policy of not discriminating against candidates on any level when recruiting. This has led to the organisation having great success in hiring the most suitable candidates for its job openings over the years.

Trust1 has also itself followed a policy of not giving bribes to win government contracts. By following this policy, it has earned credibility with both the government and the public, which has led to the organisation being awarded several large construction projects.

Lastly and most importantly **in today's world, organisations have to be ethical.** Society and governments will no longer tolerate unethical behaviour from organisations. Stakeholders are increasingly showing their frustrations via activism including: industrial action in the case of employees; boycotts in the case of consumers and blacklisting in the case of suppliers. Just as individuals are expected to abide by a code of ethics, so too are organisations.

Although an organisation may "get away" with unethical practices in the short run, in the long run it will see its sales, profitability and share price decline because of this type of behaviour.

Case Study

Nike

Nike Inc is the largest producer and seller of footwear, clothing, equipment and accessory products in the sports and athletic market. The organisation produces these products both in its home country (the USA) and internationally through a network of 700 contract factories.

The employment conditions in these contract factories have been a never-ending controversy for Nike. Its main critics, which include labour groups such as Oxfam's Nike Watch and the Clean Clothes Campaign, state that Nike:

➢ does not pay fair wages;
➢ does not have adequate working conditions for its factory workers; and
➢ employs child labour.

Nike's response has been to implement a global code of conduct for all its suppliers (which strictly prohibit child labour) and work with the NGO Global Alliance to review 21 of their factories. Nike also states that its auditing of factories will continue.

However, this has not been enough for its critics who want independent inspections. Nike has refused, explaining that it will be better able to monitor the conditions in these factories by using independent third parties on a confidential basis.

So, despite these efforts along with continual reporting on its website, criticisms of Nike continue.

SUMMARY

Business ethics emerge on three **levels**:

1. macro level
2. corporate level
3. individual level

1. Macro level

At this level, the responsibility of the organisation is put in a wider context. The organisation has to exercise ethical considerations in the international business environment.

2. Corporate social responsibility (Corporate level)

In the second learning outcome, it was explained that the expectations of stakeholders conflict because every stakeholder has its own expectations which an organisation needs to satisfy. So, an organisation is under an obligation to manage the expectations of all the stakeholders.

This is explained in more details in the next section.

3. Individual level

An organisation is responsible for the individual behaviour of its employees in the workplace. Employee behaviour in the workplace is an example of ethics at an individual level.

Every organisation has certain goals to achieve, which are referred to as the mission of the organisation. While operating for the attainment of a goal, organisations are under an obligation to follow the **norms and standards** which are in existence. The managers of the organisation have to frame the decisions according to the ethical considerations prevailing in the society. They have no right to make any policy which is unethical and against the interests of the stakeholders at large.

Examples of **unethical acts** include corruption, bribery, coercion, undue influence, dishonesty etc. Some people commit unethical acts for the following reasons:

- A person is aware of the right thing to do but it needs **courage and willpower** to do the right thing.
- A person has to carry out **many tasks** at a time in a short span of time.
- A person may even commit unethical acts by **mistake**.
- When there are many people engaged in a particular task, they **all agree** together to perform the work unethically.
- Sometimes, in an organisation, it is essential to **complete the task** but the managers are unable to achieve the target unless they apply unethical means.

SUMMARY

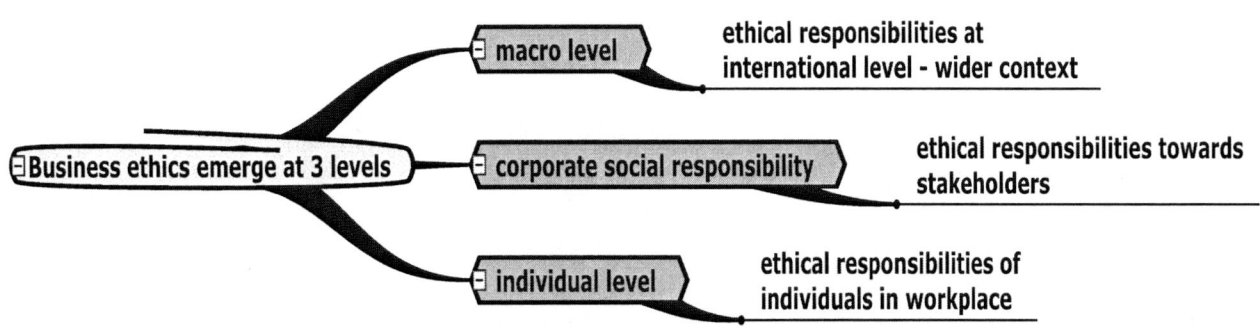

Test Yourself 3

Mega Construct is a construction company. Mega has an annual turnover of $25 million. Mega's management has worked on several construction projects which were mostly government projects. It's rumoured that Mega secured these projects through bribery. Recently some third party investigations into these cases have been undertaken by government officials. There are some complaints regarding the quality of the work done by Mega Ltd. Mega Ltd is now no longer receiving construction contracts from the government.

Beck Ltd is another construction company. As a result of the action against Mega Ltd and Beck's ethical reputation, Beck has now received a contract worth $25 million from the government.

Required:

Explain the importance of ethics for contemporary organisations.

4. Explore the scope of corporate social responsibility.[3]

[Learning Outcome d]

1. What is corporate social responsibility?

As the term suggests, 'corporate social responsibility' refers to the **social** responsibility of organisations towards stakeholders. In fact, it refers to the social as well as **environmental** responsibilities towards all the groups of stakeholders.

Definition

It is an idea where the organisations voluntarily incorporate environmental and social concerns in their business dealings and in their relations with the stakeholders.

Corporate social responsibility cannot be detached from business strategy and purposes. It has to be combined with the two so that organisational goals can be achieved smoothly. There are different stakeholder groups in and around an organisation. They have various expectations according to their needs. The organisation has to aim to satisfy the needs of all the stakeholders. It has to prioritise the expectations of different stakeholders.

SUMMARY

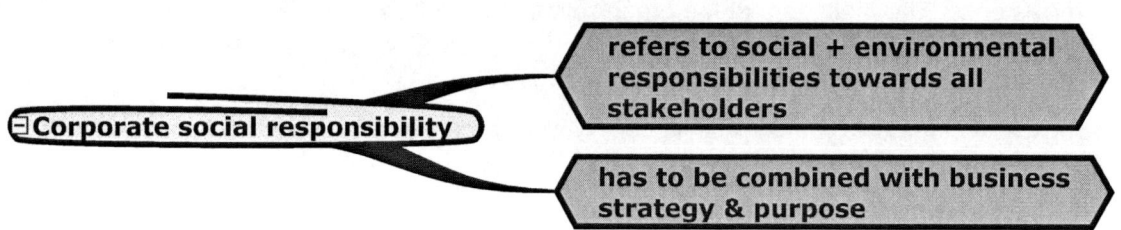

2. Scope of corporate social responsibility

In Learning Outcome 2, it was explained that there are two types of stakeholder groups: internal stakeholders and external stakeholders. These stakeholder groups can also be referred to as corporate and community stakeholders. This categorisation is made on the basis of the stakeholders' legal relationship with the organisation.

Corporate stakeholders have a legal relationship with the organisation whereas community stakeholders do not have a legal relationship and hence they do not enjoy legal protection from the organisation. Corporate stakeholders are employees, customers and suppliers. Community stakeholders are local communities, pressure groups, public authorities etc.

One problem with the concept of corporate social responsibility is that it is somewhat of an oxymoron. Responsibility is a human trait but an organisation is a bundle of assets and liabilities, so how can one expect it to be responsible? It is the officers who can be held responsible but it is difficult to ensure that they are and so controls and regulations are frequently required.

Corporate social responsibility gives **more importance to community stakeholders**. Organisations have to take care of the environment in which they exist because if this environment is destroyed, they will be unable to survive. The organisation's strategies should be framed in such a way that the organisation **protects resources** which are scarce or resources which are difficult to renew.

If an organisation is a manufacturing concern, it has to formulate its strategies in such a way that the waste generated from its factories and the machines does not cause harm to the public at large and is also not hazardous to the environment. There must be policies and strategies regarding the recycling of the available resources.

Over the last five decades, organisations have grown. They have grown in terms of their numbers as well as in terms of size. Today, the largest multinational organisations have an economic strength equivalent to that of a small country.

Therefore the impact of their decisions on society and their respective stakeholders is much greater. Organisations need to be aware of this as well as the fact that their actions are under greater scrutiny than ever before.

In addition, there has been a shift in thinking in the minds of all stakeholders as well as the public in general. Today, the widespread and almost global belief exists that organisations (regardless of their size) only prosper because society allows them to. Therefore, an organisation should not just profit from society but should also serve society by **"giving something back"**.

As usual, there is also a **business as well as a moral case** to be made for organisations meeting their social and environmental responsibilities. Organisations that follow good corporate governance and engage in activities to promote corporate social responsibilities, better the conditions of a society and those who live in it.

The better the quality of a life in a society, the more stable its political and social environment. A stable political and social climate is a necessity for all organisations that wish to do business.

Organisations now acknowledge that, along with sharing an economic environment with their stakeholders, they share a natural environment with them. All groups live and are maintained by the same fragile eco-system. In addition, all groups also use and draw from the same set of finite natural resources.

Along with all their stakeholder groups and all other members of society, organisations have a responsibility towards this natural environment. They have a responsibility to **not pollute or damage** it as well the obligation to **preserve** it for current and future generations.

SUMMARY

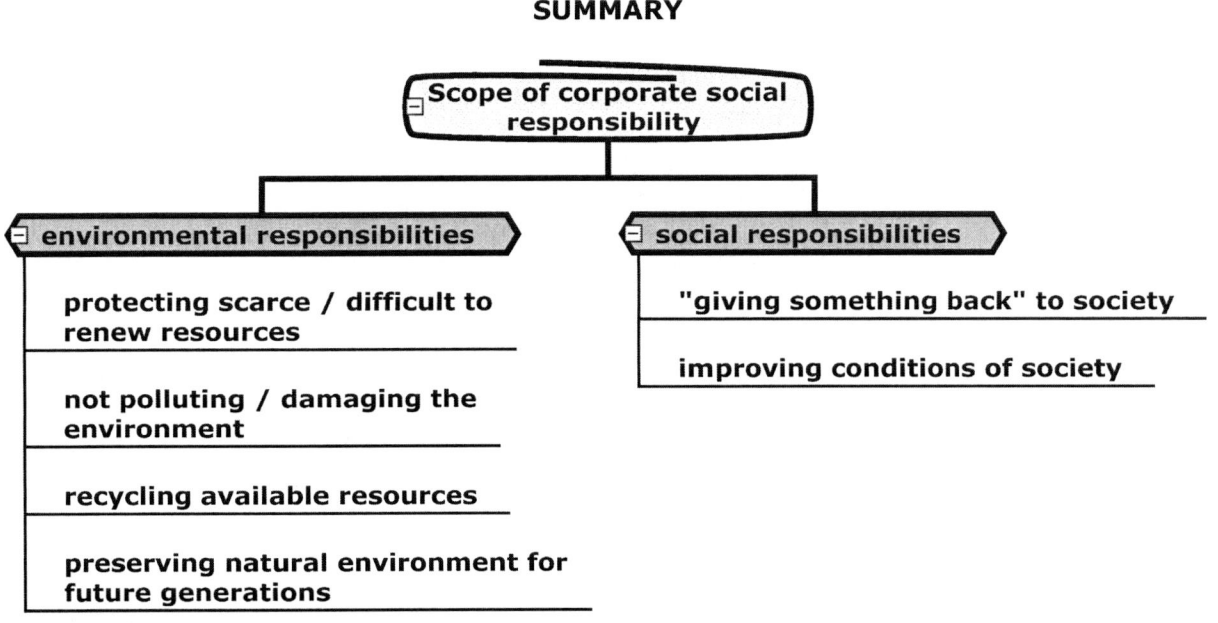

Example

In call centre organisations, many employees suffer from health problems because they have to work night shifts. Their way of living changes completely because they work at night and sleep during the day. Due to long working hours and stress, their work-life balance is also affected. Many call centre employees don't have a social life and cannot spend time with their families. In some call centre organisations, employees have to do overtime. They may even work for more than 14 hours a day due to which there is high risk of them falling ill.

Many organisations have understood that regular night shifts / overtime are not healthy and have decided to provide nutritious food in their staff canteens. Hence, organisations have realised the importance of corporate social responsibility.

3. Corporate governance and corporate social responsibility

Organisations have a responsibility to two main groups: their shareholders and their stakeholders. Shareholders constitute the **owners** of the organisation and are what gives the organisation (through their capital) its existence. Stakeholders represent the group that **supports the organisation** in its activities, helping it to be successful.

An organisation needs to maintain appropriate standards of corporate governance to help ensure that managers, executives and the board of directors **act in the best interests of the shareholders**.

An organisation needs to maintain an appropriate standard of corporate social responsibility to ensure that the organisation **does not take any actions / decisions that will go against the interests of their stakeholders and society.**

Organisations need to establish these standards so that their actions and decisions remain ethical, moral and in line with the interests of their shareholders, stakeholders and society at large. As mentioned before, an organisation cannot survive without their support and so needs to support them in return.

CSR according to Carroll's model

Carroll's model defined CSR as a pyramid of principles, consisting of four parts: economic at the base or foundation, then legal, followed by ethical and philanthropic responsibilities at the top of the pyramid.

Diagram 5: Carroll's model

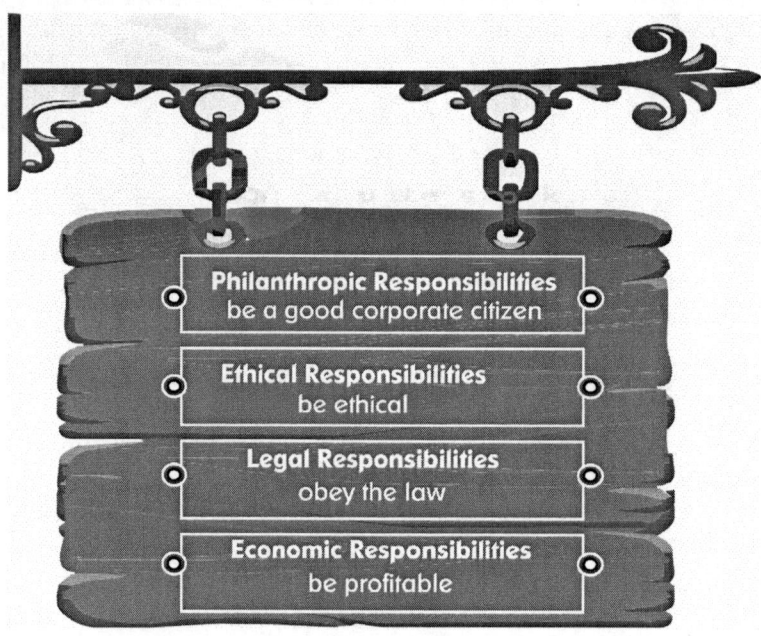

Diagram 6: Corporate governance and social responsibility

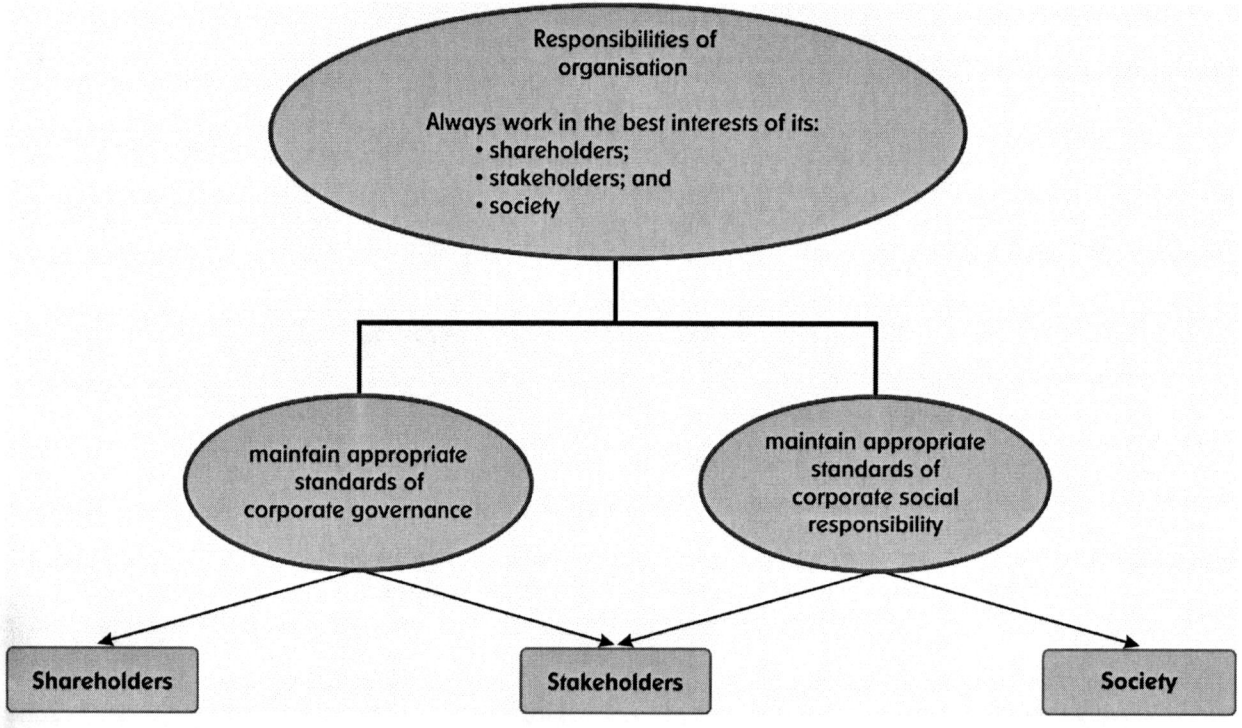

Initially, establishing these standards was only a **moral responsibility** for an organisation. However, it is quickly becoming a **legal requirement** as well. Therefore, corporate social responsibility includes social and environmental responsibilities.

Example

The most recent example is the Sarbanes-Oxley Act passed in the USA in 2002. The Act was passed in response to the public's outrage over the Enron and WorldCom financial scandals. Some of the provisions of the act call for:

➢ the establishment of a public accounting oversight board (a private sector non-profit organisation created to oversee the auditing of public companies)
➢ the independence of auditors (the auditors of a firm cannot have any other dealings with the firm)
➢ much greater detail and disclosure in financial statements

With regard to social responsibility, this is no longer just desired by society, but demanded by it. Organisations that behave unethically will find themselves becoming the target of outspoken written criticism, protests and boycotts from special interest groups and members of the public.

SUMMARY

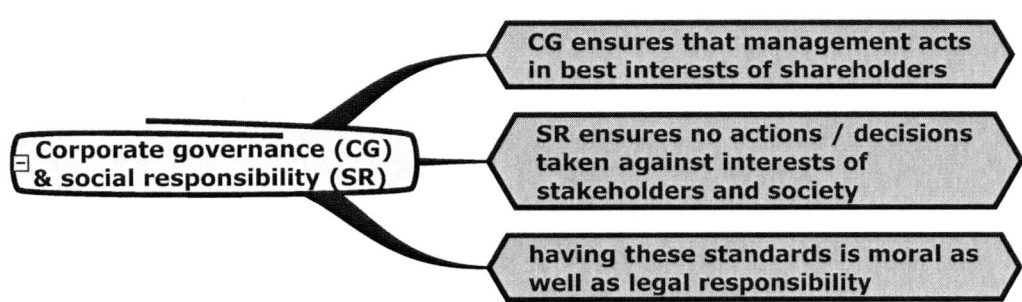

4. **Benefits of corporate social responsibility**

- encourages more people to join the organisations as their employees
- provides awareness about loopholes to overcome inefficiencies in the production process
- builds goodwill, reputation and brand name in the market
- results in improving quality of the product
- enables recognition of weaknesses in the strategic management and operations
- develops selling and marketing strategies of the products
- results in improving overall competitiveness
- encourages dialogue with key stakeholders
- Attracts capital as some investors favour ethical investments

Test Yourself 4

Megachem Ltd manufactures chemicals used in the cosmetics industry. The management of Megachem is considering setting up an additional plant at its current location to increase production. By doing this, the cost per unit of chemical produced would reduce considerably.

The present waste treatment and disposal facilities of Megachem are not adequate to handle the waste that would be generated by the new plant. The new plant could still comply with the government standards for waste management but would not meet the fairly high industry standards. If the waste treatment facilities were to be upgraded according to the industry standards, the estimated cost per unit of chemical would increase. Megachem's closest competitor does not have any waste treatment facilities.

Considering these facts, the management of Megachem has decided not to upgrade its waste treatment facilities.

Required:

Explain whether the decision taken by Megachem's management is the correct decision in the light of its social responsibility.

5. Assess the impact of culture on organisational purpose and strategy.[3]
[Learning Outcome e]

5.1 What is culture?

Culture refers to the customs, traditions and the way of life of a particular community.

Definition

The Oxford English Dictionary defines culture as "the arts, customs, ideas etc. of a nation, people or group".

This definition also applies to the culture of an organisation.

In practice, culture is an **intangible resource** for the company. It provides a **framework** that enables employees to work together in achieving their own departmental goals as well as the goals of the company.

The foundation of this framework is the **basic assumptions and values that all employees share**. These common standards are developed over time through a system of **collective learning**. The culture of an organisation will represent and reflect how it operates and functions.

> **Example**
>
> Organisations with an informal culture have a very relaxed working atmosphere. Managers will typically keep their office doors open, be easily accessible and on a first name basis with their subordinates.
>
> In contrast, organisations with a formal culture have a much more rigid working atmosphere. Subordinates typically have to schedule an appointment to see their seniors and would refer to them by their last names.

Culture is explained pictorially as consisting of four separate layers rather like the texture of an onion.

Diagram 7: Four layers of culture

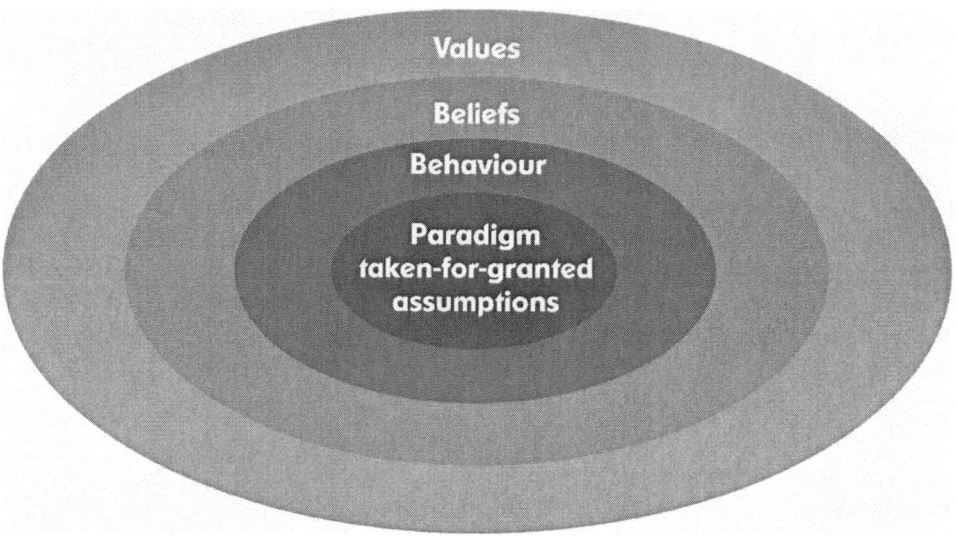

a) Values

Values are often formally documented by top management in the form of aims, objectives, vision or mission statements. These statements are typically very broad-ranging and cover the **long-term objectives** of the organisation. The values of an organisation are often unclear but indicate what the firm stands for and rates as being right and justifiable.

> **Example**
>
> Wal-Mart defines its values or core beliefs as being "respect for the individual; service to the customer; equal benefits to all and strive for excellence".

b) Beliefs

Beliefs are the **views and feelings** held by the employees of the organisation. These are more precise. These are the opinions on a particular matter which can be easily discussed. These often flow from the values of the organisation.

> **Example**
>
> Staff at Virgin Atlantic Airways is known for the effort they put into making flights a pleasurable experience for their passengers. This behaviour communicates their employees' belief that they are working for a focused but fun organisation.

c) Behaviour

Behaviour represents the visible **day-to-day operations** of the organisation. These include items such as work routines, the way employees interact and even dress.

d) Paradigm (taken for granted assumptions)

Paradigm refers to the **set of assumptions that are held in common and taken for granted** by the employees of an organisation.

It is important to note here that the paradigm is far more representative of an organisation's culture than its values. The paradigm is the **core of a company's culture** and is what enables employees to pull together and work towards a common goal.

SUMMARY

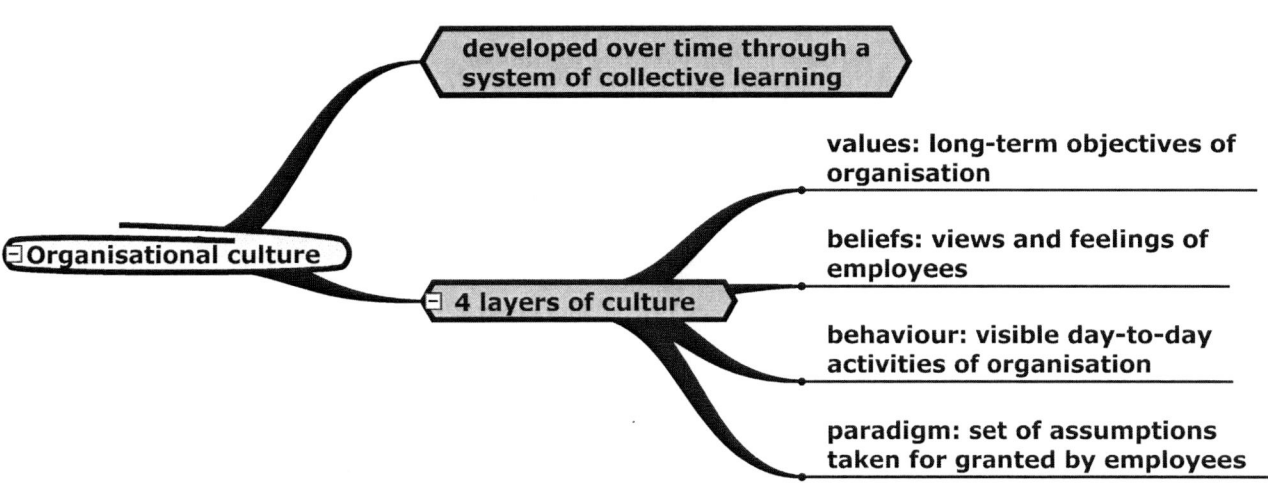

The Handy model of cultural types is based on a four quadrant model which names Apollo, Athena, Dionysus and Zeus for the four cultures of role, task, people and power respectively.

> **Role culture** - The responsibilities are assigned on the basis of the official position in the organisation. The style of communication is formalised.
> **Task culture** - The task culture is friendly and co-operative because it is not hierarchical. The style of communication is open and relaxed. The organisation is structured according to tasks and processes.
> **People culture** - The people culture focuses on the needs of the individual first and makes the organisation the source for individual skills and talents. The style of communication is personal.
> **Power culture** - Power culture is focused on the leader. This type of culture performs effectively when the organisation is relatively smaller in size and the leader is efficient enough to lead the team as a group. The style of communication is formal and generally based on the procedures and systems applied.

5.2 Factors that shape organisational culture

The main factor that shapes the culture of an organisation is the **system of collective learning** amongst employees. This collective learning occurs as employees work together to solve problems and overcome difficulties. Successful methods and practices go on to become the generally held assumptions and values of the organisation.

Example

ANB Inc is a relatively small bank that specialises in offering finance to small owner-operated organisations. The bank also offers personal banking products such as mortgages and car loans. The commercial department of the bank has always been very successful, the personal division much less so.

However, over time, ANB's personal division has found that it has the highest success rates in its marketing efforts when representatives from both the commercial and personal divisions make a joint sales call. Over time, this has grown to become standard operating practice for the bank and now reflects the teamwork culture present in the organisation.

Culture is reflected both internally and externally by the organisation:

> internally, in terms of employee attitudes, morale and motivation
> externally, by the way staff deal with customers, suppliers and other stakeholders

Other factors that determine the culture of an organisation include:

a) **the industry** the organisation belongs to
b) **the type of environment** it operates in

Example

Advertising companies typically have cultures that develop and support a creative environment. An open door policy is followed across the organisation to promote cross-lateral thinking and the flow of ideas as well as information across all divisions. Inter-departmental cooperation and teamwork is the normal behaviour.

This is in direct contrast to the culture found in most governmental agencies. Here, employees are regimented into following strictly laid out policies and procedures. Deviation from these procedures and teamwork or even cooperation among divisions is minimal.

c) **the size and nature of the organisation** (e.g. large publicly traded organisations typically have a formal work culture involving factors such as strict dress codes, timings, routines etc. whereas smaller privately held organisations tend to have a much more informal work culture)
d) **the type of customers it has** (e.g. organisations such as Accenture that have only corporate clients have a very task-focused, goal-focused and competitive culture whereas a small owner-operated grocery store would have a more people-oriented and relaxed culture)
e) **the diversity of its workforce** (the more minorities, ethnic groups and nationalities present in an organisation's workforce, the more diverse its culture is likely to be)
f) **the character and working style of top management** (the policies, procedures and work practices set by top management will form the foundation on which the culture of the organisation is formed)

SUMMARY

Factors shaping organisational culture
- system of collective learning
- organisation's industry
- type of external environment
- size and nature of organisation
- type of customers
- diversity of workforce
- character & working style of top management

5.3 Organisational strategy and culture

Culture is one of the determinants of the individual's behaviour. The impact of culture on organisational purpose and strategy are as follows:

1. In the case of organisational strategic management, the managers have to **integrate the culture** of the organisation with the strategy so that the strategy can be **successfully implemented**.

2. For **excellent performance** and **achievement of goals**, culture cannot be ignored because if **behavioural values** are not considered then strategies cannot be effectively implemented.

3. Culture influences the **formulation of strategies** in the organisation.

There are some researchers who are of the different view that culture has a negligible impact on strategy formulation or implementation.

5.4 Significance of organisational culture

- It is important for performance, growth and success of the organisation.
- It promotes product innovation.
- It is reflected in the mission
- It facilitates team work.
- It is the centre of all aspects of organisation.
- It supports strategy innovation.
- Through collective learning, employees obtain more knowledge.
- Employees share knowledge which leads to creativity.

Case Study

General Electric

In 1981, General Electric ("GE") named Jack Welch as their new CEO. At the time the company had a market capitalisation of approximately $12 billion. When Welch stepped down as CEO in 2000, GE's market value was close to $500 billion.

One of the main reasons for the company's success is because of the cultural change Welch implemented and drove throughout the organisation. Before Welch's tenure, GE was a very bureaucratic organisation. Managers had to fill numerous forms and seek various approvals before taking decisions.

Welch changed all this by empowering managers to build up their units in an entrepreneurial fashion. Managers in turn were also expected to empower their subordinates and involve them in the running of the business unit. As Welch put it "the best way to manage people is just to get out of their way".

This "boundary-less culture" still remains at GE today where employees from all levels involve themselves in innovation and problem solving".

Test Yourself 5

Green Bus Co used to be a subsidiary company and a regional operating division of a public corporation - Red Bus Corp. As part of the privatisation strategy of the national government, all the operating divisions of Red Bus Corp have been separately sold by tender-based offer for sale. The Green Bus division has been acquired through a management buyout led by the existing general manager of Green Bus Co, Mark Clark.

The newly privatised Green Bus Co will have the freedom to extend its route network nationally if it wishes and to expand into commercial operations. Green Bus Co's existing bus routes are contracted to it for a period of two years, after which other operators will be allowed to run services on these routes. Mark is aware of the fact that Green Bus Co's competition will become intense as soon as the routes become fully competitive in two years' time.

Although the company has first class experience of bus operations, it has a number of weaknesses such as the absence of a marketing department, the lack of internal management accounting (as most management reports were directed at Red Bus Corp's management team), overstaffing and unionism. Mark is deeply concerned about the prevailing culture of Green Bus Co. Few, if any, of its managers, supervisors or employees have any real idea about customer care, quality or competitive advantage. In fact, there has been very limited formal management training and development.

Required

Why do you think Mark Clark believes that organisational culture is so important for the success of his plans?

---

6. Prepare and evaluate a cultural web of an organisation.[2]

[Learning Outcome f]

6.1 Culture is difficult to define in exact words but is present in an organisation and influences how the work is carried out and the strategy formulation and implementation in an organisation.

In the previous learning outcome, it was explained that there are four layers of culture: values, beliefs, behaviour and paradigm. The cultural web is the internal two layers: behaviour and paradigm.

When there is a merger of two organisations, there may be clashes of culture among the organisations. In addition, when an organisation grows, the culture followed before may become irrelevant which leads to failures instead of achievements. The culture may be inappropriate for its new business situation. Hence, there may be a need to change the organisational culture.

The culture of an organisation is varied, so regular analysis of what makes a corporate culture effective and what measures need to be taken to change the culture is required.

Gerry Johnson and Kevan Scholes provided an approach in 1992, called the cultural web which helps in **analysing the organisational culture and changing the culture if required**. Johnson and Scholes defined cultural web as:

Definition

The **cultural web** is a representation of the taken-for-granted assumptions, or paradigm, of an organisation and the physical manifestations of organisational culture.

(Source: JSW)

SUMMARY

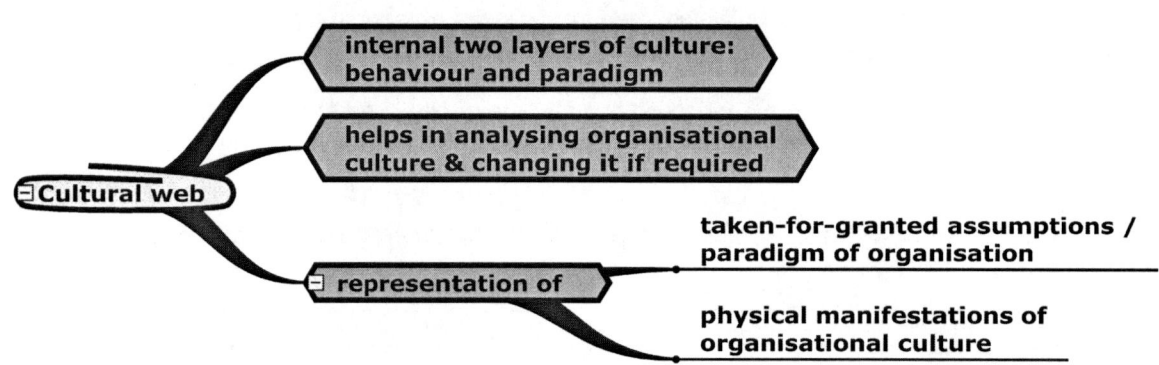

6.2 Elements of cultural web

There are **six elements** of the cultural web. The analysis of the factors in each of the elements helps in viewing the bigger picture of the organisational culture, the pros and cons of this culture and how the culture can be changed.

1. **Symbols**: these are the **pictorial representations** of the nature of the organisation. Organisations use **logos** with the name of their organisation. They use specific **languages** in the organisation. **Dress codes** may be specified sometimes according to specific days. They have status symbols. All these aspects reflect the culture of an organisation.

2. **Stories**: the members of an organisation talk about past events to outsiders and newly joined members of the organisation and also **tell stories to each other which tell the story** of the organisation to internal members of an organisation as well as outsiders. These stories reflect the views of what is of value to the organisation and what results in good behaviour.

3. **Rituals and routines**: routine means the **day-to-day behaviour** of the members of an organisation. It helps to ensure the smooth functioning of the organisation as the behaviour of members is analysed daily. This behaviour is second nature to the long-term staff members but the new staff members have to learn the behaviour e.g. the fact that monthly meetings are held in the organisation.

   Rituals mean the **special programmes** which are undertaken within an organisation to emphasise what is essential and useful for the organisation. Rituals may be training programmes, appraisals, promotions, marketing seminars etc. which explain the correct method of carrying out a task and why this method is valued by senior management.

4. **Power structures**: there are various hierarchies in an organisation. Power of decision making rests with a few senior managers. They are the planners and policy makers in an organisation. These senior managers influence the organisational decisions and operations.

5. **Organisational structures**: there are formal and informal structures in an organisation. Formal structures include organisational charts. In informal structures, the allocation of power is undefined. Both types of structure have influence on the organisation. The cultural web indicates which structure has the most influence.

6. **Control systems**: the financial system, reward system, quality systems and measurement system help in analysing which areas of the organisation it is important to supervise.

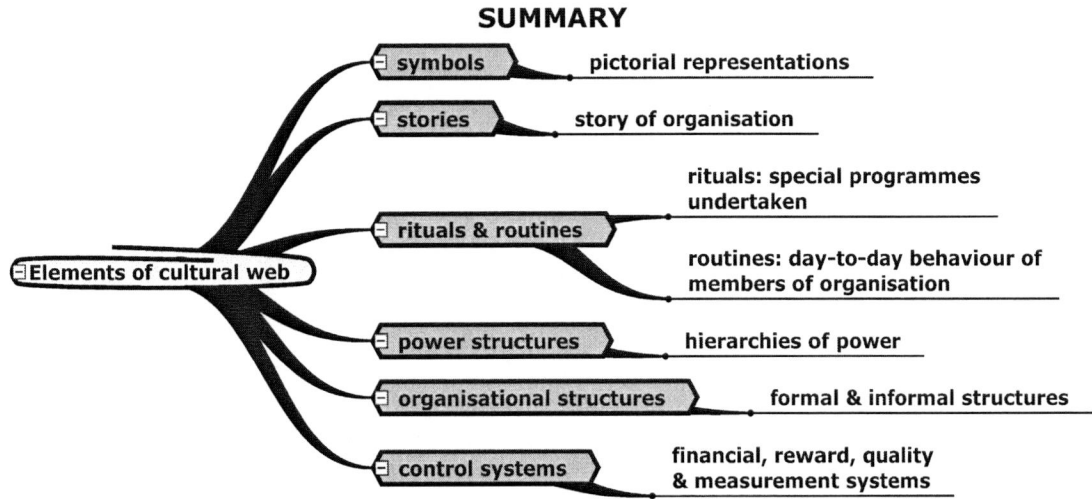

SUMMARY

Elements of cultural web
- symbols — pictorial representations
- stories — story of organisation
- rituals & routines
  - rituals: special programmes undertaken
  - routines: day-to-day behaviour of members of organisation
- power structures — hierarchies of power
- organisational structures — formal & informal structures
- control systems — financial, reward, quality & measurement systems

6.3 Uses of cultural web

- analyses organisational culture (present culture)
- helps in understanding how managers desire the organisation's culture to be (future culture)
- highlights the differences between the organisation's present and future cultures

Once the differences between the present position and the future position have been studied, it is essential to make a plan of action to eradicate the differences between the two and to follow an effective culture in an organisation.

Example

Super Bank has been operating in the UK for the last 20 years. The analysis of the factors in each element of the cultural web helps in viewing the bigger picture of the bank's culture. It helps in understanding the pros and cons of the culture present in the bank and also helps in changing the culture. The elements of the cultural web of Super Bank are as follows:

Symbols

- logo -
- formal dressing by all employees
- posters, banners and pamphlets
- branch layout

Stories

- We have a reputation as being the best bank in the country.
- We are known for our variety of products / schemes designed to suit the needs of different types of customers.
- We are known for our wide branch network spread throughout the country.
- Staff members talk about the managing director, because of whom the bank achieved its current position.

Rituals and routines

- weekly team meetings
- employees are expected to work 12 hours a day
- customers expect a newspaper and coffee while they wait
- training programmes

Power structures

- managing directors
- regional heads
- branch managers

Organisational structure

- tall and formal structure

Continued on the next page

130: Strategic Position

Control systems

- tight controls
- weekly reporting
- use of advanced technology
- audit
- circulars
- incentives to employees on achievement of targets

Test Yourself 6

Star is a chain of supermarkets. In addition to food items, Star sells a variety of items including kitchenware, clothes, toys, electronic goods and pharmaceuticals. Star's present culture is a little different from the culture of other companies. Star is a family-owned business and most of Star's management consists of family members. Star's culture represents family values. Star's staff consists mainly of students at the nearby university. Star gives them free groceries up to the value of one day's salary as well as medical insurance. Every customer who visits a Star supermarket is greeted with "Hello".

Star's management values education and offers various types of help to these students. Star also supports international students by offering them part-time jobs. Star also actively participates in local charities.

Star's staff are unhappy and are accusing Star of not giving talented staff the opportunity to participate in the management.

Required:

Explain the elements of the cultural web and discuss the advantages and disadvantages of Star's culture.

7. Advise on how organisations can communicate their core values and mission.[3]
[Learning Outcome g]

7.1 What are mission statements and core values?

Mission statements

Mission statements are written to explain the **purpose behind the particular organisation** and where the organisation is going at present. They should include a description of what the organisation does as well as why it does it. A mission statement explains 'why' the organisation is in existence or its raison d'etre.

Some organisations even use vision statements in place of mission statements. A vision statement is written to define and describe what the organisation is aspiring to be in the future. It typically reflects an ambitious and optimistic view of what management believes the organisation can and should achieve.

The Ashridge mission model states that the managers and the employees of the organisation search for a purpose and a sense of identity. They are always in pursuit of more than just pay i.e. the opportunities to enhance their skills and capabilities. They are in need of a "sense of mission". According to the Ashridge mission model, there are various functions that an organisation can perform. They include internal and external functions:

- allocate resources efficiently
- provide guidance and direction
- manage balance between conflicting stakeholders
- motivate managers and employees and thereby improve performance
- take measures to improve organisational performance

The elements of Ashridge mission model are as follows:

- Strategy: it is the commercial logic of the organisation.
- Values: norms and behavioural standards in the organisation. They are the beliefs and moral principles of an organisation.
- Behavioural standards: they are the policies which assist people to take decisions as what to be done on a daily basis.

Core values

> **Definition**
>
> Johnson and Scholes define **core values** as:
> Core values are the principles that guide an organisation's actions.
>
> **(Source: JSW)**

Core value statements explain how an organisation will value its suppliers, customers and employees. The values of all the members of the organisation are essential to form the corporate culture.

7.2 How to communicate organisation's core values and mission?

Core values and mission are important for an organisation. Once they have been defined by management, it is essential to communicate the core values and mission to the employees of the organisation. Communication of values and mission is often done through **team building activities** i.e. the leader of the team communicates the core values and mission to all the employees in a group. The leader must ensure that these values are implemented in practice i.e. the values are actually exercised in day-to-day operations.

Although there are various technological modes of communication, **face-to-face communication or written communication** is essential for better cooperation in an organisation.

The communication is to be made **at the time of recruitment** because, before joining the organisation, the prospective employee should be aware of the values and mission of the organisation so that if his values do not match the organisational values, he can consider this carefully before joining; the employer may of course, feel that his values do not match those of the organization and therefore an offer of employment may not be made.

> **Example**
>
> Bright Ltd is engaged in the production and development of software programs. The organisation aims to increase its sales of software in the outskirts of the city. It has prepared a mission statement and has specified its core values. Bright Ltd wants to communicate the core values and mission to the members of the organisation. It can do so in the following manner:
>
> 1. printing them in the employee handbook and company's quarterly / annual reports
> 2. printing them on posters and banners
> 3. posting them on the company website
> 4. including them in automatic signature statements and footers at the end of every outgoing e-mail
> 5. printing them on company stationery such as letterheads, business cards and notepads
> 6. including them in the recruiting process and in the training and induction programme for new employees
> 7. introducing them in staff meetings

SUMMARY

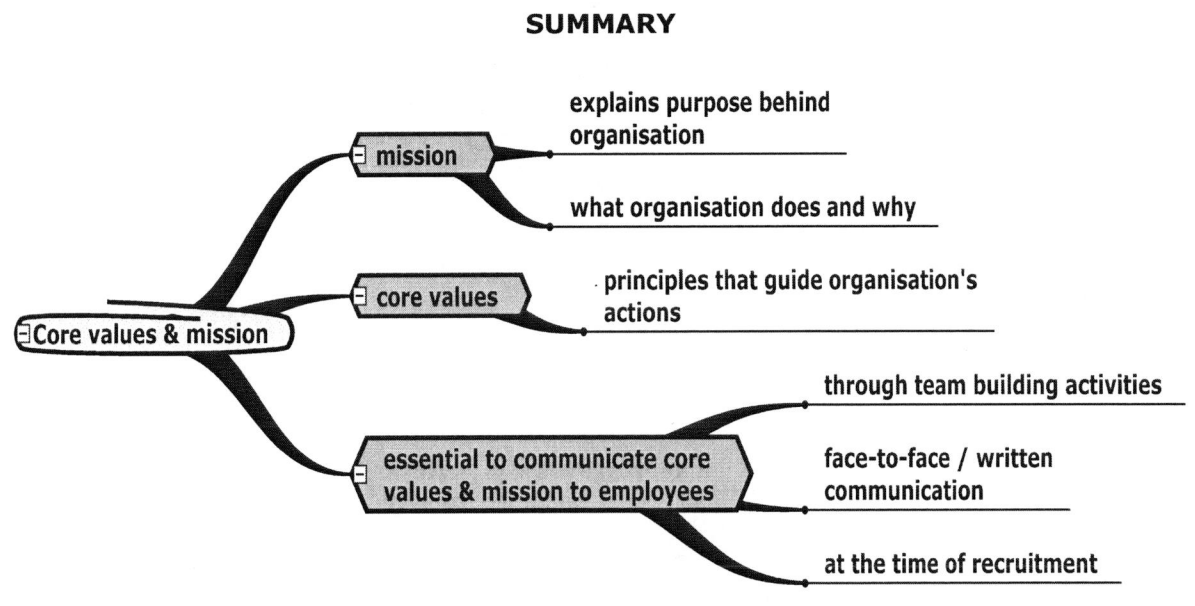

Test Yourself 7

Eduworld is an educational institution. James Hack is the founder of Eduworld. Teaching is his passion. He started Eduworld with the mission statement 'Every child has a right to education.' For James, Eduworld is more than just a business. He offers scholarships to many students who can't afford to study.

James encourages his staff members to teach in order to improve their students' knowledge and understanding and not just to get them through exams. Recently Eduworld opened a new branch which will specialise in giving education to mentally disabled children. James has hired new staff for this branch and wants to convey to them the core values of his institution.

Required:

Discuss how James Hack can communicate the core values and mission of Eduworld to the new staff.

Answers to Test Yourself

Answer to TY 1

To: The board of directors, Hi-Fashions Ltd

Dear Sir,

The term "good corporate governance" is definitely a buzz world in the business world of today and one that you will hear repeatedly going forward. In essence, it represents the set of policies and procedures that determine how an organisation is directed, administered and controlled. The main objective of a corporate governance system is to align the interests of an organisation's board of directors and its management with those of its shareholders.

Businesses today are expected to implement a system of sound corporate governance so that the organisation has a benchmark against which the actions and performance of managers / executives can be measured and evaluated. An effective system will set out a broad framework and parameters within which all managers and employees must operate. It also provides the process through which the company objectives are set, and the means of attaining those objectives and monitoring performance are established.

This helps an organisation to be transparent and honest in all of its dealings – be they with customers, suppliers, employees and especially investors. It is important to remember that the need for a system of corporate governance stems from the concept of separation of ownership and control.

Given that you are considering listing your organisation, you must always bear in mind that you will be asking people to invest their money into a business they are not running or controlling. Having a strong system of corporate governance in place will increase investor confidence in your business as well as the possibility of a successful listing.

Lastly, the importance of having an effective system of corporate governance is that it:

- builds investor confidence in the organisation
- demonstrates the commitment an organisation has towards being ethical, efficient and effective
- helps an organisation's board of directors, executives and management to take ethical decisions
- provides a system of checks and balances so that neither management nor large shareholders can abuse their power at the expense of other shareholders or the organisation

Overall, designing and implementing a system of good corporate governance will require investment on your part, in terms of both time and money. However, once such a system is in place, I am very confident that you will find that the returns far outweigh the costs.

Yours,

(_____)

Answer to TY 2

The retailers' association and the sports club are stakeholders of Good Eats. The retailers are customers of the company. The sports club falls under the category of local community. As the costs and benefits of sponsoring both the events are same, it is necessary to identify which of the two stakeholders is more important for Good Eats. The stakeholder mapping matrix is a useful mode by which to understand the features and relative importance of different stakeholder groups.

The association of retailers is a high interest-high power stakeholder of the organisation. High interest because its members are customers of Good Eats. High power because it is an association of all local retailers and in turn has high bargaining power over Good Eats. Hence it is of high importance to the company. This type of stakeholder is one which the company needs to "keep satisfied". The sports club is a low interest-low power stakeholder of the company. Low interest because it doesn't deal with Good Eats and doesn't have any connection with it. Low power because it can't exercise any power over the company. Hence it is of low importance to the company. The company needs to take only minimal efforts for this type of stakeholder.

Considering the importance and influence of the retailers' association, it is more appropriate for Good Eats to sponsor the event organised by it.

Answer to TY 3

Ethics has a very important place in commerce. Today organisations are expected to have an ethical responsibility to their shareholders and stakeholders, as well as to society at large. There is a strong economic justification for organisations to behave ethically. Experience has shown that being ethical makes good business sense for the organisation in the long run. Being ethical is important for contemporary organisations for the following reasons:

- Potential employees are more willing to work for an ethical organisation.
- Customers are more willing to buy products from an ethical organisation.
- Suppliers are more willing to deal with an ethical organisation.
- Potential business collaborators are more willing to associate with an organisation that has an established reputation for behaving ethically.
- Ethical behaviour across all levels promotes the overall efficiency of the organisation.
- Although an organisation may "get away" with unethical practices in the short run, they are likely to affect the organisation adversely when these are discovered.
- In the long run, an unethical organisation will see its sales, profitability and share price decline.

Answer to TY 4

Corporate social responsibility refers to the social as well as environmental responsibilities of an organisation towards its stakeholders. Organisations have a responsibility to not pollute or damage the natural environment they operate in. A manufacturing concern has to formulate its strategies in a way whereby the waste generated from the factories and the machinery does not cause harm to the public at large and is also not hazardous for the environment. Corporate social responsibility is no longer just desired by society, but demanded by it.

Although Megachem's new plant of could meet the lenient government standards, the fact remains that the present waste treatment and disposal facilities are not adequate to handle the waste products that would be generated by the new plant. The new plant would not meet more stringent industry standards. The waste generated by the new plant would therefore to harm the environment and adversely affect the citizens residing nearby.

The fact that additional treatment facilities will increase Megachem's expenditure and its competitor has not set up waste treatment facilities, does not justify Megachem's decision to not upgrade its waste treatment facilities. The company cannot have a casual attitude towards the environment.

Hence the decision of Megachem to not upgrade its waste treatment facilities is not correct in the light of its social responsibility.

Answer to TY 5

Culture means the system of basic assumptions and values shared by all employees of an organisation. It provides a framework that enables employees to work together in achieving their own, departmental and company's goals. It has become widely accepted that the culture of an organisation is as important as the type of goods or services it produces.

Corporate culture can have a huge impact on an organisation's work environment and output. There is a view that successful organisational culture leads to excellence in performance. Culture is also closely linked to strategy as it provides a framework for both strategy formulation and implementation. Culture can be positive, a drive for excellence, or negative, resistance to necessary strategic change.

The culture at Green Bus Co has evolved to fit the requirements of a public sector organisation. Mark feels that this culture is not suitable for changes which he must make in the next two years to give Green Bus Co a competitive edge so that it can survive. Privatisation has repositioned Green Bus Co within its environment and fundamental strategic change is now required. Mark will have to frame the strategy of Green Bus so as to create a culture of growth, innovation, customer care and competitive instincts. There might be greater negative responses to such change in Green Bus Co where there has been a stable culture over a long period of time and hence little history of change. Hence the new strategy of Green Bus after privatisation must be supported by the culture of the organisation if it is to be successfully implemented.

Answer to TY 6

A cultural web has six elements:

1. **Symbols** are the pictorial representations of the nature of the organisation such as the organisation's logos. They convey information such as the language used in the organisation and the organisation's dress code.

2. **Stories**: the members of an organisation tell stories to each other, outsiders and newcomers about the organisation's history. These stories reflect the views of what is of value to the organisation and what constitutes good behaviour.

3. **Rituals and routines**: routine means the **day-to-day behaviour** of the members of an organisation. It helps to ensure the smooth functioning of the organisation as the behaviour of members is analysed daily. This behaviour is second nature to the long-term staff members but the new staff members have to learn the behaviour e.g. the fact that monthly meetings are held in the organisation.

    Rituals mean the **special programmes** which are undertaken within an organisation to emphasise what is essential and useful for the organisation. Rituals may be training programmes, appraisals, promotions, marketing seminars etc. which explain the correct method of carrying out a task and why this method is valued by senior management.

4. **Power structures**: there are various hierarchies in an organisation. The power to take important decisions rests with a few senior managers. They are the planners and policy makers in an organisation. These senior managers influence the organisational decisions and operations.

5. **Organisational structures**: there are formal and informal structures in an organisation. Formal structures include organisational charts. In informal structures, the allocation of power is undefined. Both types of structure have an influence on the organisation. The cultural web indicates which structure has the most influence.

6. **Control systems**: the financial system, reward system, quality systems and measurement system help in analysing which areas of the organisation it is important to supervise.

Star is a family business and all the power lies with the family. Star's culture is good and the organisation has social standing as Star has engaged in charitable activities. Star helps university students to earn while learning. As most of the staff members are young, Star's work culture is also enthusiastic.

As all the management members are from the family, Star is depriving itself of outside talent. Moreover the existing members who are not satisfied with Star may leave it. Star's culture might not be viewed as suitable for long-term employment.

Answer to TY 7

Core value statements explain how an organisation will value its customers, suppliers and employees.

In the case of Eduworld, the core value statement will explain that Eduworld values all students and describe the mission for its employees. Once the management is sure about the core values and mission, it has to communicate these to the employees. This can be done through the following activities.

➢ Team-building activities i.e. the leader of the team communicates the core values and mission to all the employees in a group. The leader must ensure that these values are implemented in practice i.e. in the day-to-day operations.
➢ Face-to-face communication, which promotes better cooperation in the organisation.
➢ Written communication through e-mail and letters is also effective at improving communication.
➢ Recruitment: organisation's core values should be communicated at the time of recruitment. Prospective employees should be aware of the organisation's values and mission, so that if their values do not match the organisation's values, they can consider this before joining. If the organisation thinks that the prospective employee's value do not match the organisation's values, then it should not offer an employment letter to him.

Quick Quiz

1. What are the components of corporate governance?

2. Give examples of different stakeholders of an organisation and list their categories.

3. What is the core of a company's culture?

4. List the elements of a cultural web.

Answers to Quick Quiz

1. Corporate governance is the system which informs investors of the internal matters of the company. It protects the interests of the company.

The following are the components of corporate governance:

➢ **Accountability:** accountability means all the managers, directors, executives are responsible for the tasks of the organisation which must be aligned with the interests of shareholders.
➢ **Compliance:** managers, executives and directors should comply with all laws and regulations.
➢ **Transparency:** transparent in the sense that all the information on financial performance and the different activities of the organisation should be disclosed to the shareholders. Shareholders should be aware of all the information and internal matters of the company.
➢ **Integrity:** managers, executives and directors should behave with integrity and in an ethical manner. They should support the employees of the organisation legally and morally.

2.

	Stakeholders	Category
1.	Customers	External stakeholders
2.	Managers	Internal stakeholders
3.	Suppliers	External stakeholders
4.	Employees	Internal stakeholders
5.	Government	External stakeholders
6.	Local communities	External stakeholders

3. The paradigm is the core of a company's culture. It enables employees to pull together and work towards a common goal.

4. The elements of a cultural web are: symbols, stories, rituals and routines, power structures, organisational structures and control systems.

Self Examination Questions

Question 1

William Sheldon is the chairman and chief executive of FunToy Plc, a medium-sized company specialising in making educational toys for young children. These are simple, high quality toys intended to stimulate the imagination of children and to help them develop their visual and coordination abilities.

William started the company in the early 1980s. He had initially made toys in his garage for his own children. He soon was persuaded to expand his activities. To his surprise the demand for his products grew at a faster rate than he had expected. The company was operating in a growing niche market, in which it was a significant participant. The company has pursued a growth strategy based on the aggressive acquisition of a number of smaller toy manufacturing units. This growth has gone down well with shareholders of FunToy, but a significant slowdown in sales has resulted in falling profits, dividends and, as a consequence, its share price.

William was convinced that his unique experience in the educational toy-making industry would be sufficient to guide the company through its current misfortunes. The company and its board of directors were completely under the control and dominance of William. He accepted little input from others in making decisions and his decisions were rarely challenged at board level. He felt no need for any non-executive directors drawn from outside the company to be on the board. His idiosyncratic and arrogant style of management had been associated with a reluctance to accept criticism from any quarter and to pay little attention to communicating with shareholders.

Shareholders were already asking questions about William's lavish lifestyle at company expense, which regularly made the headlines in the popular press. As a result of the downturn in the company's fortunes, some of his acquisitions have been looked at more closely and there are, as yet, unsubstantiated claims that FunToy's share price had been maintained through premature disclosure of proposed acquisitions and evidence of insider trading. William had amassed a personal fortune through the acquisitions, share options and above average performance-related bonuses, which had on occasion been questioned at the shareholders' Annual General Meeting. Recently, there has been concern expressed in the financial press that the auditors appointed by FunToy, some twenty years ago, were also providing consultancy services on his acquisition strategy and on methods used to finance the deals.

Required:

What corporate governance issues are raised by the management style of William Sheldon?

Question 2

CineGold was established in 1960 as a charitable trust to promote and increase public awareness of the cinema as an entertainment and cultural medium. CineGold is managed through a part-time board of governors drawn from representatives of the film industry, from government nominees and from elected nominees of the membership of the CineGold film institute. The board of governors delegate executive responsibility to a chief executive officer (CEO). CineGold has five major activity areas or operational divisions each of which has its own manager. These are:

1. The multi-screen Film Theatre (FT) which provides performances for the general public of new releases, classic films and minority interest films.

2. The Museum of the Cinema (MoC) which provides a permanent exhibition of the history and development of the film industry.

3. The Globe restaurant, bars and cafeteria which are open to cinema-goers and to the general public.

4. The Film Archive Unit (FAU) which is concerned with the transfer of old film archive material to video as a means of long-term preservation.

5. The CineGold Film Institute (CFI), membership of which is open to members of the public by annual subscription. Members receive preferential bookings to events, seat discounts and a free copy of CineGold monthly magazine, 'Movie Magic'. The magazine and associated publishing activities also form part of the responsibilities of the film institute.

In addition to the five business units, there are also three support units which provide common support services as follows:

a) administration: office services, finance, personnel, computing.
b) buildings: building maintenance, cleaning, security, repairs and renewals
c) maintenance: technical and technician support for the repair and maintenance of capital equipment

The three support units come under the control of a head of support services.

CineGold is partly funded by government grant and partly funded from its own commercial activities. However, as a part of government policy to reduce the contribution to the arts, the grant to CineGold will, over the next three years, be reduced by 20%.

Peter Jones has recently taken over as the chief executive officer of CineGold. He has been recruited from a senior position in an international media business. The board of governors at CineGold was directed by the government to bring in an external CEO as a result of a series of management problems which have attracted considerable adverse publicity, as detailed below:

➢ A failure to stay within the government financial guideline of not operating an annual financial deficit.
➢ Press criticism regarding the loss of archive film due to the failure to speed up the transfer to video tape.
➢ Further press criticism on the recent imposition of an admission charge to the Museum of the Cinema.
➢ Reports of poor quality service and expensive food in the Globe restaurants.
➢ Persistent labour relations problems with the public sector staff trade union which represents almost all the non-managerial museum, film theatre, clerical and catering staff.
➢ Complaints from the CFI membership that the film season has concentrated too much on popular income earning mainstream films with a subsequent fall in the number of showings of classic and non-English language films.

Peter realises that he faces major challenges in revitalising the CineGold organisation and dealing with the proposed sharp reduction in government funding. He believes that what CineGold needs is a vision of its role and priorities plus management control systems which link performance to clear-cut divisional objectives. He has offered you a one year management consultancy contract to assist him.

Required:

Peter's background is in profit-seeking organisations in which objectives and goals seemed much more clear-cut than at CineGold. To clarify the 'vision' of the organisation, Peter has decided to undertake an analysis of all the internal and external stakeholder groups at CineGold.

Select and identify four different CineGold stakeholder groups, indicating for each, its potential power and influence and its likely expectations of CineGold.

Question 3

Jack Winfrey is a CEO of Superior Machines Inc, company manufacturing machinery used in the textile industry. In its initial phase, the company grew at a rapid rate. The successful demand within the domestic market led the company into a false sense of security. It completely neglected market development. Recently, the company has been experiencing a financial crisis. Profits have been low for a number of years but now small losses are occurring. The company is under a heavy debt burden which is undermining its cash flow.

Superior Machines desperately needs funds in order to continue its operations and pursue its strategy of capturing foreign markets. It began talks with financial institutions, with the intention of borrowing funds. However, considering the current financial position of the company, most of the financial institutions offered Superior Machines a very high rate of interest.

Easy Finance Corp is keen on providing funds to Superior Machines at a considerably low rate of interest. Bill Smith, chairman of Easy Finance, is aggressively involved in political activities. During the meeting between Jack and Bill, Bill agreed to grant funds to Superior Machines on the condition that Jack donates $100,000 to Bill's political campaign fund. Jack has never made a political contribution of this sort and it would certainly attract press attention in Bill's next campaign fund report.

Required:

What are the ethical issues at stake considering the offer made by Bill Smith to facilitate sanction of the loan?

Question 4

Spice Hub is a £3 billion UK-based company providing catering services. It is a distributor of foods to professional catering organisations. Operating from 35 locations throughout the country, it supplies a complete range of fresh, chilled and frozen food products including not only the ingredients needed to prepare meals, but also numerous ancillary preparation and serving items. Its customers include restaurants, fast food chains, hotels, motels, schools, colleges, nursing homes and hospitals. Wholesale food distribution is very much a price-driven service, in which it is very difficult to differentiate Spice Hub's service from its competitors. Diana Rhodes is Spice Hub's vice president of operations.

Spice Hub operates a fleet of 1,000 delivery vehicles to distribute food products to its customers. Each vehicle produces the equivalent of its own weight in pollutants over the course of a year without the installation of expensive pollution control systems. The larger customers of Spice Hub are looking for their distributors to become more socially and environmentally responsible. Diana is also aware of the government's growing interest in promoting good corporate social responsibility practices and encouraging companies to achieve the international quality standard for environmentally responsible operations.

Diana is planning to develop and implement a company-wide environmental management and social responsibility strategy including the achievement of the international quality standard. However, her concern is not shared by her fellow managers responsible for the key distribution functions including purchasing, logistics, warehousing and transportation. They argued that time spent on corporate responsibility issues would be time wasted and simply added to costs.

Diana has decided to propose the appointment of a project manager for this purpose. You have been appointed as project manager for Spice Hub's "corporate social responsibility" project.

Required:

Suggest the measures that Spice Hub can take so as to become socially responsible and add to its competitive advantage.

Answers to Self Examination Questions

Answer to SEQ 1

Corporate governance sets out what an organisation is supposed to do thereby providing a benchmark against which the future performance and actions of managers / executives can be measured and evaluated by shareholders. In corporations, the shareholder delegates the right to make decisions to the manager who is required to act in the company's best interests. Professional managers are given the responsibility of managing the organisation and they have less interest in the ownership of the organisation. This separation of ownership from control involves a loss of effective control by shareholders over managerial decisions.

Managers are appointed to manage the operations of an organisation, so they act as an agent of the shareholders. The relationship between the two can be studied by the agency model. This model is based on the assumption that the agent works in good faith for the benefit of the principal. Corporate governance requires that the senior managers and the members of board of directors should be aware of the expectations of the shareholders.

The chairman, William, tells the difference between the theoretical maximisation of shareholders' wealth and the actual implementation of strategies in the organisation. In practice, it can be seen that most of the directors work to benefit their own interests rather than the interests of shareholders. The managers aim to achieve many goals at a time. Due to this, it becomes difficult to achieve the main organisational goal itself. Often managers are unable to cope with multiple tasks at the same time and ultimately they end up losing the desired goal.

Agency theory aims to work for the benefit of shareholders. The managers are appointed to manage the operations of an organisation, so they act as an **agent** of the shareholders. The relationship between the two can be studied by the **agency model**. This model is based on the assumption that the agent works in good faith for the benefit of the principal. In FunToy Plc, William was dominating and arrogant in his behaviour and so the organisation and its board of directors were under his control. The stakeholders accepted his behaviour unwillingly. The organisation is heading towards a crisis because its sales have slowed down, and it profits and share price have fallen. The large stakeholders may take strict action against the behaviour of William. They may even decide to change the chairman of the organisation.

If the crisis situation in FunToy continues, then the stakeholders may decide to quit the organisation.

Answer to SEQ 2

Stakeholders are the individuals or groups who depend on an organisation to fulfil their goals and in turn the organisation also depends upon them.

There are two stakeholders groups: internal and external stakeholders.

For CineGold the stakeholder groups are:

1. Trade union

Trade unions have a great impact on an organisation because they influence the members who are working in the organisation. A trade union exercises its power on the organisation through discussions, meetings and negotiation procedures. When the trade union has influence over the organisation, there is the possibility of withdrawal of employees from the organisation or employees not cooperating with management i.e walkouts and strikes.

Expectations: good working conditions, promotions, no extra working hours, handsome pay packages, employment protection

2. Government

The government influences the organisation in that the organisation has to comply with various legal provisions. The government exercises power by providing funds to the organisation and by nominating the board of governors.

Expectations: timely payment of taxes by the organisation.

3. Film institute members

Film institute members can exercise power through electing the board of governors.

Expectations: low fares for seats, easy availability of tickets, more availability of shows during weekends.

4. Public at large

The public at large are the customers of CineGold. They can be any group i.e. customers of the museum, theatre, globe restaurant or bar.

Other stakeholder groups are management, banker, financial institutions, film producers, board of governors and film distributors.

Answer to SEQ 3

Today, organisations are expected to assume an ethical responsibility to their shareholders and stakeholders, as well as to society at large. Organisations are expected not to take decisions or engage in activities that would hurt the interests of any of these groups. Decisions that would hurt the interests of any stakeholder group would be unethical despite the level of profits they would bring to the organisation.

Jack needs to be very careful while negotiating the borrowing terms with Easy Finance. If Jack raises the money for Bill, he can easily obtain finance at a low interest rate for his company but risks his reputation and becomes a target for legal and political investigations. It would not only be unethical for Jack to seek financial advantage by arranging for Bill's campaign fund, it would also be illegal. His donation would appear on Bill's campaign finance disclosure statement and could be easily linked to the loan sanctioned to Superior Machines, proving an embarrassment for Jack, as well as grounds for indictment and conviction.

Jack must recognise that, in his position, he has to safeguard the interests of all stakeholders. He cannot ethically compensate for the poor management decisions that have brought his company into its current difficulties by opting for bribery. He must be careful not to be seen to be protecting his own position at the expense of the rest of the company.

Certainly, shareholders also have a stake in the decision. The revelation of a campaign contribution to Bill could adversely impact stock prices of Superior Machines. The interests of members of the society in their role as deposit holders with Easy Finance (those who have kept money with Easy Finance as deposits) and its shareholders also need to be considered. Ultimately they are the ones who will suffer due to the low interest paid by Superior Machines as it will adversely affect the profitability of Easy Finance.

Corporate social responsibility (CSR) refers to attaining a balance between the interests of all of an organisation's stakeholders within its strategic planning and operations. It is a concept whereby organisations integrate social and environmental concerns in their business operations and in their interaction with their stakeholders on a voluntary basis.

Contemporary organisations recognise that they cannot be successful without the support of their stakeholders. It has been witnessed that more and more organisations are incorporating systems of CSR into their very frameworks. Today, CSR is widely seen a management strategy option. Spice Hub are, therefore, correct in seeing environmental standards as a positive step towards becoming more, not less, competitive. Building in positive social responsibility strategies can help Spice Hub differentiate itself from other professional catering organisations and through improved resource productivity become more competitive. Spice Hub's decision to give high priority to CSR can be reflected in a number of aspects of its activity.

Food safety and quality assurance

Spice Hub needs to make sure that the food products it supplies have been produced in an environmentally responsible way, that animal welfare standards are adhered to and that the products are safe. It should have a food safety and quality assurance programme in place, designed to maintain the highest standards of food quality in accordance with international practices. Food safety not only relates to the wellbeing of Spice Hub's customers, but also to the success and reputation of its customers and itself.

Employee relations

Motivated, respected and well-remunerated employees are more productive than dissatisfied employees. Spice Hub can set up various employee training, development and welfare programmes to assist staff to do their job and maintain a suitable quality of life. For example, free meals for employees, medical servicing, organisation of employee transportation, workplace safety, scholarship programmes and rewards and gifts.

Supply chain integrity

Spice Hub can set up codes of conduct to ensure supply chain integrity. The supplier selection and evaluation process should adhere to strict criteria. Spice Hub needs to design a code of practice for socially responsible sourcing which covers issues such as health and safety, equal opportunities and the protection of children. It can avoid "food miles" and support local farmers and producers of meat.

Preservation of environment

Key stakeholders of Spice Hub in the form of both government and customers are looking to it to become more 'green'. Spice Hub needs to continually upgrade its fleet so that its vehicles are safer, more efficient and produce fewer emissions. It needs to take measures to route delivery vehicles more efficiently which can reduce engine emissions. It also needs to ensure minimum damage to the environment through using energy-efficient, environmentally-friendly warehouse and vehicle refrigeration, fuel and fuel storage systems and warehouse equipment.

Social initiatives

CSR is often equated with a business's interaction with the local community in this respect; Spice Hub can support different humanitarian and charity projects and make donations for the wellbeing of the local community.

SECTION B: STRATEGIC CHOICES

STUDY GUIDE B1: THE INFLUENCE OF CORPORATE STRATEGY ON AN ORGANISATION

Get Through Intro

Many companies in the Western world realise that in order to succeed in today's environment, they need to sell more. Local competition may be intense, so often companies think about going abroad to increase sales. China and India, known as Chindia, are seen as great potential markets, due to the fact that they have respective populations of over 1 billion people. Hence corporate strategy needs to be adapted to bring in opportunities abroad, as well as in the home market.

However, products that are successful in the home market may not always be successful in foreign markets. For example, McDonalds' staple product throughout the world is beef and for many years, the majority of the menu was geared to meat-eaters. In India, however, the cow is sacred – so McDonalds needed to adapt to make products that were predominantly vegetarian and certainly not with beef.

Equally, the way one operates the company in a home market may not be acceptable in a foreign market. In many parts of the Middle East, the weekend is Friday and Saturday (it used to be Thursday and Friday). Whilst the head office in Europe may want local staff in the Middle East to work Monday to Friday, this would meet with resentment from local staff.

Finally it is dangerous for a company to put all its eggs in 1 basket and only concentrate on 1 product or 1 market. Just because a product is successful today, the company should not sit back and relax – it should ensure it has other products in the pipeline to potentially take over if the main product starts to decrease in value.

This chapter explains what you will need to think about when coming up with an international corporate strategy and how you can ensure your company has a solid long term future!

Learning Outcomes

a) Explore the relationship between a corporate parent and its business units.
b) Assess the opportunities and potential problems of pursuing different corporate strategies of product / market diversification from a national, international and global perspective.
c) Assess the opportunities and potential problems of pursuing a corporate strategy of international diversity, international scale operations and globalisation.
d) Discuss a range of ways that the corporate parent can create and destroy organisational value.
e) Explain three corporate rationales for adding value - portfolio managers, synergy managers and parental developers.
f) Explain and assess a range of portfolio models (the growth / share (BCG) matrix, the public sector portfolio matrix, market attractiveness / SBU strength matrix, directional policy matrix, Ashridge Portfolio Display) that may assist corporate parents manage their business portfolios.

Introduction

Case Study

Japanese Mobile Phone Failed To Move in China

According to an article in the China TMT review (on the net at market Avenue), Japan's leading electronics conglomerate, Kyocera, has become the latest Japanese mobile phone company to withdraw from the Chinese market in early 2008. The article also states that, Toshiba, Panasonic, NEC and Mitsubishi have all exited the Chinese market since 2005. It certainly seems strange that Japanese companies, which are considered the best in the world for research and development should fail in the Chinese market.

The following are extracts from the article:

Not about technologies

In terms of product quality, few companies can compete with the Japanese manufacturers, but that cannot guarantee Japanese mobiles' market shares in China. In China, mobiles are not only communication devices, but also symbols for individual identity and status. In addition to good functionalities, phones should also have magnificent appearances. For example, design superiority has been one of the reasons for Korean Samsung to gain popularity among Chinese consumers. Therefore Japanese mobiles, which have insisted on its long-held "functionally useful" mindset, are difficult to attract Chinese consumers.

Both Panasonic and NEC, which introduced many cutting-edge technologies into China in the past, have seen their mobile phone sales plummeted in China, further demonstrating that technologies are not the reasons for Japanese phones to fail in China. On the other hand, as technologies like phone camera and GPS are becoming more and more mature in recent years, Japanese companies are also gradually losing their technological competitive advantage.

Management culture

Due to historical reasons, many Japanese phone companies have come to China via joint ventures with state-owned Chinese companies, but most Chinese executives don't have decision-making authorities in their JV companies. It is not uncommon for Chinese executives to rise to the top in European and American JV companies, but that's not the case for Japanese JV companies.

Even if Chinese executives can unusually rise to the top, they will still be constrained by their headquarters in Japan. For example, NEC appointed Mr Lu Lei, a professional manager from Motorola, as its China CEO in 2004, but Lu didn't bring any expected changes to NEC's China operation. In his one year-plus tenure, apart from setting his own sales strategies in a limited scope, Lu seemed not to have much authority. Under the hierarchical approval processes, the Chinese team's decision making mechanism existed in name only. For fast moving consumer products such as mobile phones, slow decision making will inevitably lead to losing sales.

Unlike European and American companies which can timely adjust their strategies to suit the changing Chinese market, Japanese phones' rigid product strategy is also another reason for their failure in China. In terms of product development, Western companies can usually launch almost 40 new models in a year, compared to the 10-20 models by Japanese brands, which are relatively insensitive to market positioning. Many of them did know the market, but were slow to launch new products. And the matter got worse when they were also slow to develop distribution channels.

But the Chinese mobile communication market is predominantly operating under a phone-SIM separation model, thus Chinese consumers have lots of choices. While Japanese companies can still dominate the premium electronics market of China with their advanced technologies, it will be difficult for them to dominate the mobile phone market, where technologies don't account for much competitive advantage, simply with product durability. Therefore the lack of both market strategies and product strategies has doomed the failure of Japanese mobile companies in China.

Ms Han Xiaobing, a senior analyst from Norson IT Consulting, attributed the reasons for Japanese mobile phone failure in China as follows: lack of localisation, Japanese executives dominating decision-making process with little understanding of the Chinese market; lack of product range and market responsiveness, with most R&D centres still located in Japan rather than in China; lack of economies of scale, with high costs leading to little price competitiveness.

(Source: www.marketavenue.cn)

The above case study shows that a company could have the most technically advanced product, but it will not necessarily sell in certain markets. It also shows that the head office needs to be sensitive to the differences in culture. This chapter will help guide you through all these areas.

1. Explore the relationship between a corporate parent and its business units.[2]
[Learning Outcome a]

Within every organisation there is said to be a hierarchy of objectives as illustrated below

Diagram 1: Hierarchy of objectives in an organisation

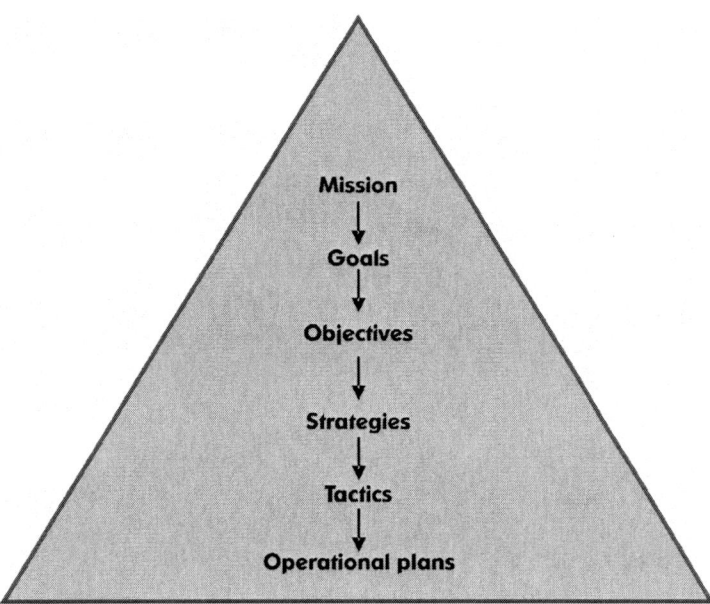

As the level in the hierarchy increases, the aims become relevant to a **greater proportion of the organisation's activities**.

Mission statements are written to explain the **purpose behind the particular organisation** and where the organisation is going at present. They should include a description of what the organisation does as well as why it does it. A mission statement explains 'why' the organisation is in existence or its raison d'être.

Some organisations even use vision statements in place of mission statements. A vision statement is written to define and describe what the organisation is aspiring to be in the future. It typically reflects an ambitious and optimistic view of what management believes the organisation can and should achieve.

The Ashridge mission model states that the managers and the employees of the organisation search for a purpose and a sense of identity. They are always in pursuit of more than just pay i.e. the opportunities to enhance their skills and capabilities. They are in need of a "sense of mission".

According to the Ashridge mission model, there are various functions that an organisation can perform. They include internal and external functions:

➢ allocate resources efficiently
➢ provide guidance and direction
➢ manage balance between conflicting stakeholders
➢ motivate managers and employees and thereby improve performance
➢ take measures to improve organisational performance

The elements of the Ashridge mission model are as follows:
➢ **Strategy:** the commercial logic of the organisation
➢ **Values:** the norms and behavioural standards in the organisation. They are the beliefs and moral principles of the organisation.
➢ **Behavioural standards:** the policies which assist people to take decisions as what is to be done on a daily basis.

The mission, as stated previously, encompasses the activities of the entire organisation.

Example

One of the PepsiCo's goals is no doubt to "beat Coke". Its mission is to be a world famous producer of consumer products, with particular focus on convenience foods and beverages. It aims to provide attractive financial rewards to its investors and opportunities for the development of its employees, the society in which it exists and its business partners. In everything it does, it makes an effort to behave with truthfulness and integrity.

1.1 Corporate strategy

Corporate strategy is the **direction and scope** of an organisation over the **long term.** It is not changed frequently. Therefore, other decisions, including investment proposals have to be **fine-tuned to the organisation's corporate strategy.**

In rare cases, corporate strategy may be changed if an excellent investment opportunity arises which does not match the existing corporate strategy.

1.2 Objectives and strategy

As depicted in the above diagram, strategy formulation can only take place once the organisation's objectives have been **clearly identified**. These objectives relate directly to the organisation's **broad based goals** and, ultimately, to its **mission**. Objectives tell managers and employees precisely what they are supposed to achieve.

Strategy and strategic thinking have their origins in the military domain. Strategy can be defined as a **course of action**, including the specification of resources, necessary to achieve an objective. In other words, it is a means to an end; it tells managers how to go about achieving objectives.

1. **Strategic decisions normally involve the following matters**

b) What should the long-term direction of the organisation be? Which products should it sell and in which geographical areas?
c) Achieving a competitive advantage: how should the company develop and retain unique features in its products and services which competitors will find difficult to match?
d) What should the company's brands be and how should they be positioned?
e) How can the organisation use its resources and competencies in the best possible manner?
f) How can the values and expectations of the stakeholders be balanced?

2. **Strategic management has three levels**

a) **top level – corporate level**
b) **middle level – business level**
c) **bottom level – functional level**

1.3 What is a business unit?

Definition

According to JSW, an SBU is a part of an organisation which has a different external market for goods or services which is distinct from any another strategic business unit.

In the current era, customers are highly educated and their needs are varied and sophisticated. To satisfy these needs, there are various markets. Organisations have different business units which compete in different markets. A business unit is a part of an organisation and so each business unit formulates its own strategy.

Example

Virgin Group is a private company which was incorporated in the UK in 1989. The company operates in various sectors including airlines, trains, beverages, financial services, Internet, music, radio, jewellery, cosmetics, retail and mobile phones. Virgin Group has generated more than 200 branded companies all over the world.

1.4 Relationship between corporate parent and its business units

The corporate parent establishes and incorporates the business units. The parent forms the board of directors and the members of management, pronounces the purposes of business of the business units and also **controls** the units.

The corporate parent has the authority of **policy decision-making** and deciding whether to maintain the SBU as a separate unit or not. The corporate parent sets the mission for the organisation. The business units have their own goals and they function to achieve these goals. The corporate parent supports the business units in all respects e.g. by providing business units with skills, capabilities and financial support. The corporate parent encourages the business units to achieve the organisational mission.

1.5 Why are strategic business units established?

1. The corporate parent aims to start a new area of operation that is not connected to the existing business line.
2. There is high scope for profits in the new business area.
3. High risk is involved in the new business which may affect the existing business areas. So, if SBUs are established, the risk in the existing business may be minimised to a greater extent.
4. The corporate parent is not willing to engage existing assets in the new business area hence the desire to establish a separate business unit.
5. The parent's shareholders are not to be disturbed by the operations of new business units.
6. There are possibilities of grouping the business territorial.
7. When businesses are grouped on the basis of similar business operations, it helps in strategic planning because the policies can be set for the same business lines and synergies may be found.
8. Each business unit has its own competitors so that the parent corporate is not affected.

Example

The Inland Revenue was a department of the British Government responsible for administration and collection of direct taxes. Her Majesty's Customs and Excise (HMCE) was a department of the British Government responsible for administration and collection of indirect taxes. In 2005, the Inland Revenue was merged with HMCE to form a new department, HM Revenue and Customs (HMRC). HMRC is responsible for collection and administration of direct taxes and indirect taxes as well as paying tax credits and child benefit. The single combined department, HMRC, has the added benefits of producing greater efficiencies, reducing the tax gap, providing a greater customer focus, measuring tax compliance costs more accurately and setting a proper target for reducing them.

SUMMARY

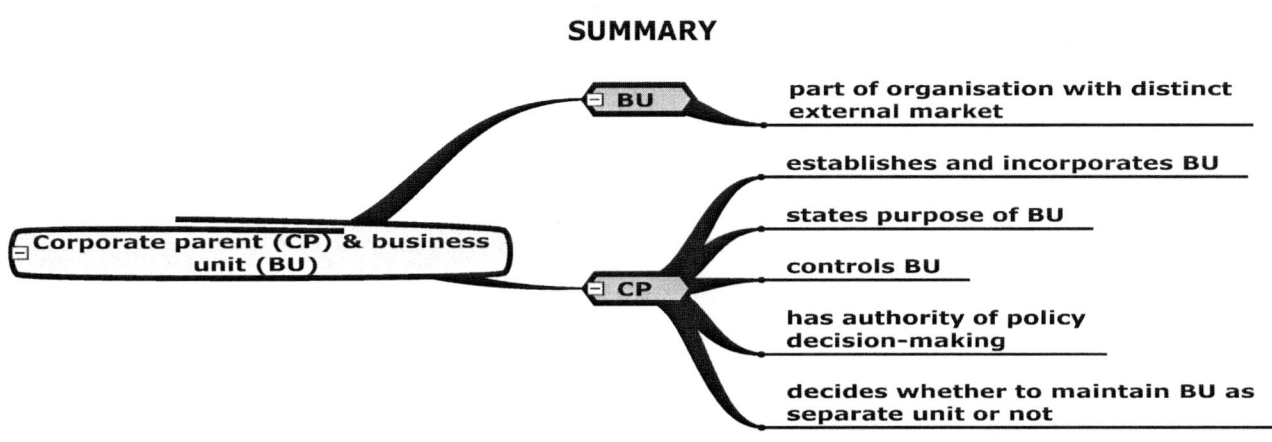

Test Yourself 1

Tech Mat is a UK business group. Tech Mark's business operates in the area of steel, automobiles, tires, chemical, and information technology. Tech Mat has recently acquired another company, Techno World based in the USA. Tech Mat has expansion plans in Asia too. It is looking for a strategic partner in India and China. Tech Mat wants to expand its automobile business in these regions.

To smooth out its expansion plan, Tech Mat has introduced the concept of business units.

Required:

State any five reasons why a corporate parent establishes a business unit.

> 2. Assess the opportunities and potential problems of pursuing different corporate strategies of product / market diversification from a national, international and global perspective.[3] Assess the opportunities and potential problems of pursuing a corporate strategy of international diversity, international scale operations and globalisation.[3]
>
> [Learning Outcomes b and c]

2.1 What is diversification?

Diversification is a **marketing strategy** for an organisation. It can take place either at the corporate level or the business unit level. At the corporate level, diversification is undertaken by entering into a new business area, an area altogether different from the existing business area. On the other hand, at the business unit level, diversification is undertaken as a new segment within an industry in which the business is already operating. The organisation diversifies because it aims to **increase its profitability** by increasing revenues through entering into new products or new markets.

Example

Johnson & Johnson is a multi-national US-based manufacturer of pharmaceutical, medical devices and consumer packaged goods, founded in 1886. Since the 1900s, the company has pursued steady diversification. It added consumer products in the 1920s and created a separate division for surgical products in 1941.

Consumer products: baby products (wipes, shampoos, cotton buds etc); wound care (Band-Aid); feminine hygiene (Carefree, Stayfree); reach dental products

Medical: non-prescription drugs (Tylenol, Pepcid AC); prescription drugs; surgical products; Accuvue contact lenses

In recent years, Johnson & Johnson has expanded into areas as diverse as biopharmaceuticals, orthopedic devices and internet publishing.

The diversification of Johnson & Johnson is depicted below:

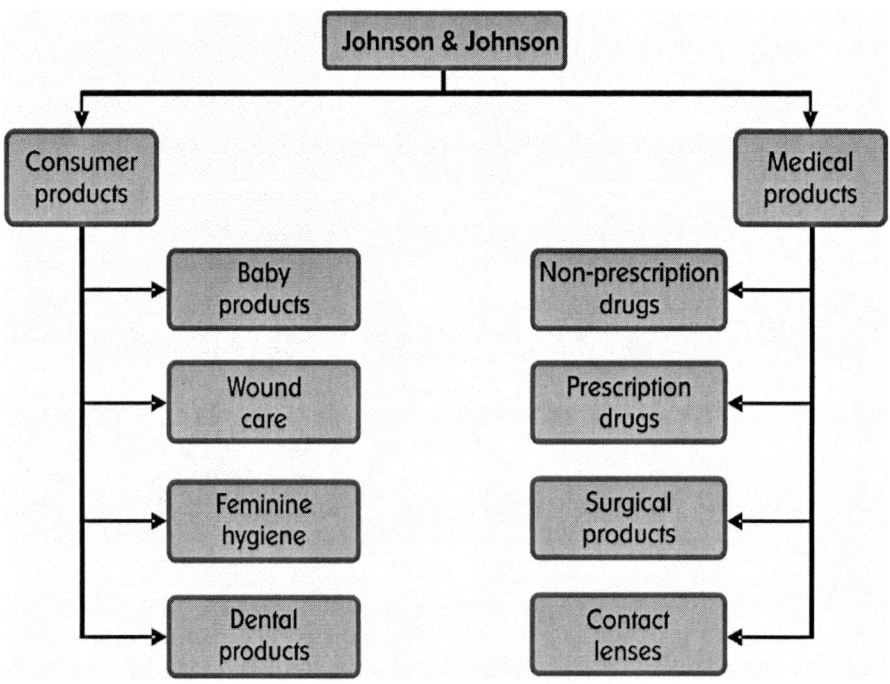

The Ansoff matrix is a model that helps guide managers to understand which markets and specific customer groups (segments) to target for expansion. It explains the meaning of diversification in relation to products. Ansoff is of the opinion that when diversification is undertaken, it demands new technologies, new facilities, new talents etc.

The matrix is shown as follows

Diagram 2: Ansoff matrix

	Products	
Markets	Present	New
Present	Market penetration	Product development
New	Market development	Diversification

As the above diagram depicts, there exist four possible product / market combinations or **strategic options** available to an organisation. These are:

- **market penetration**
- **market development**
- **product development**
- **diversification**

A market penetration strategy is followed when an organisation uses its existing product lines to increase sales and profitability from existing customers. It does this by either "poaching" customers from competitors and / or increasing sales levels from existing customers. Common tactics associated with this type of strategy include advertising, sales promotion such as special offers and price cutting.

Product development occurs when an organisation develops a new product(s) to sell to its existing customer base. This is often called switch selling. It is important to note here that this strategy calls for the product to be either entirely new or an existing product that has been very significantly modified or improved. Simply adding additional features to an existing product does not qualify as product development.

The market development strategy occurs when an organisation attempts to market products to an entirely new market segment for its existing products. Existing products must be targeted towards and launched to an entirely new customer base for the organisation.

Diversification is when an organisation moves into entirely new products and markets. In other words, diversification occurs when an organisation develops an entirely new product and markets it to an entirely new customer base. A diversification can be either a related diversification (where the newly developed product bears some connection / similarity to the organisation's existing product lines and core competences) or an unrelated diversification.

Among all the marketing strategies, the diversification strategy is the most **risky** as all of its features are new i.e. new product, new market, new facilities and new skills. As there are high risks involved in diversification, organisations may make several attempts before they succeed. A good example of an organisation which carried out successful diversification is Canon, a manufacturer of cameras, which diversified into producing a new range of office equipment.

2.2 Reasons for diversification

1. **Economies of scope in contrast to economies of scale:** an organisation may achieve economies of scope by increasing its number of SBUs so that its total costs are spread over a greater number of business units. The cost per business unit therefore falls. In this manner, diversification takes place.

2. **Benefits of synergy:** the benefits of synergy refer to the benefits arising out of working together of two or more parts. The benefits arise because the result is greater than the sum of their individual effects or capabilities.

...te managerial core competences: the skills of managers at different levels vary. The managers ... corporate level have the core competences to share the resources available for the new markets ... products which the operational managers lack.

Increase in market power: when organisations diversify into new products or markets, they have a diverse range of products or customers which results in increased market power. If one of the products earns huge profits and results in surpluses and another product incurs losses, then the surpluses can be cross-subsidised i.e. used for the improvement of product which resulted into losses.

These are the main **value-generating reasons** for diversification. There are also other reasons but they tend to benefit the managers more than the shareholders.

5. **Respond to environmental change:** sometimes an organisation may have to diversify because the environment demands it. For example, if technology is developed or there is a convergence of technologies in the product market, an organisation may have to add new features to its products by utilising the new technology available, otherwise existing products will become obsolete. In order to add new features, the organisation may have to buy technologies from a business which is utilising them or buy the business itself (i.e. integrate with the other business).

Example

Enjoy More Ltd has been producing mobile phones for the last ten years. It has a huge market share and a good reputation.

In recent years, some competitors have started to produce mobile phones which include a camera feature. In order to face this competition, Enjoy More Ltd must produce mobile phones which meet the needs of the market i.e. phones with camera features. To incorporate this feature, the organisation will have to possess the necessary skills and technologies. If the skills and technologies are not readily available, then Enjoy More Ltd may decide to takeover another organisation which produces cameras. In this case, technological convergence and the needs of customers are the reasons for diversification.

---

6. **Spread risk across a range of businesses:** organisations aim to earn profits. They always make an effort to develop and expand their business. In a market, there is always a risk of incurring losses. To reduce this risk, organisations diversify their business area and scope so that, if losses are incurred in one area, they can be compensated by the profits earned in other area of business.

   In the case of investors, they invest their funds in such a way that, if any organisation gives lower returns, these low returns can be compensated by the higher returns from other organisations.

7. **Expectations of shareholders:** to meet shareholders' expectations of earning higher returns, organisations decide to diversify in product or market.

SUMMARY

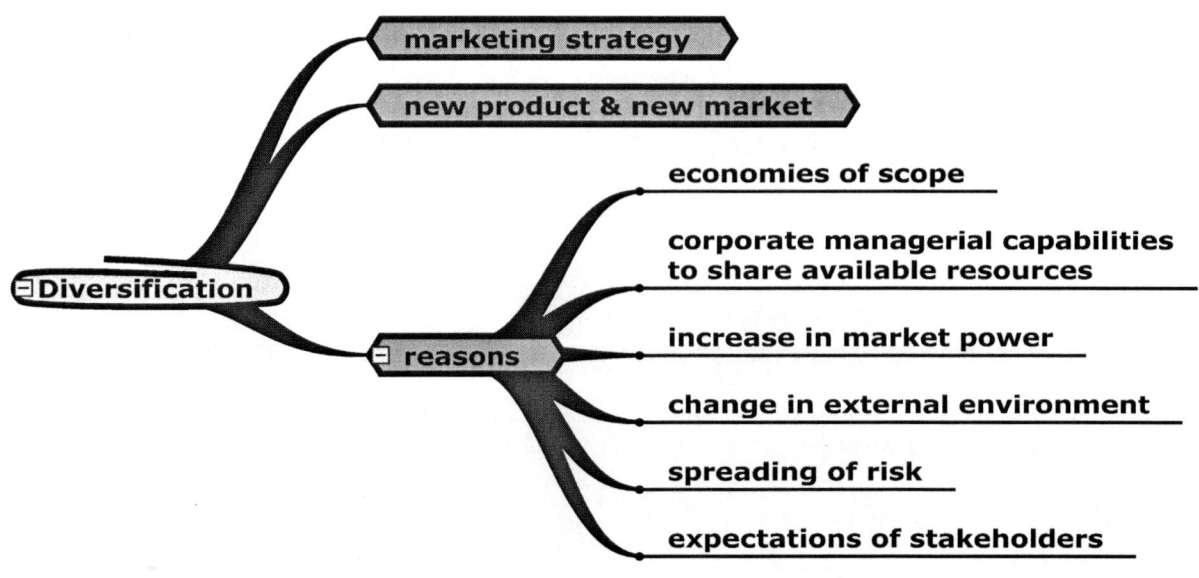

2.3 Forms of diversification

Diagram 3: Forms of diversification

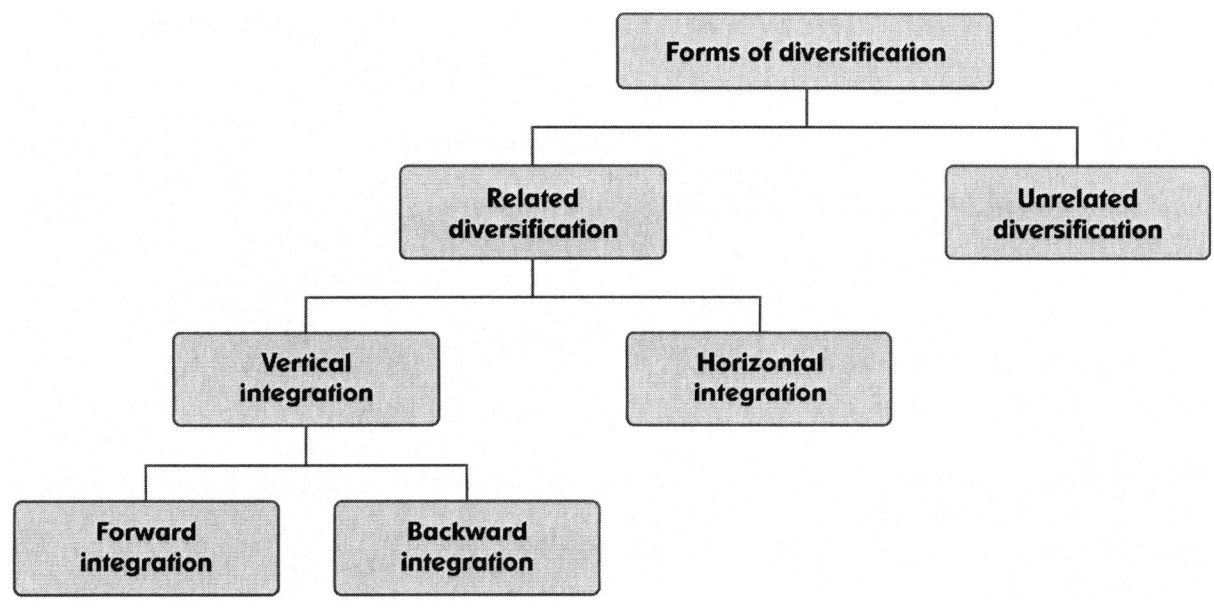

1. Related diversification

> **Definition**

According to JSW, **related diversification** is strategy development beyond existing products and markets, though within the capabilities or value network of the organisation.

Related diversification is **within the capacities, core competences or value network** of the organisation.

Reasons for related diversification:

- Help to spread risk over business products.
- Leads to cost savings.
- Possibility of transferring skills and capabilities from one business to another.
- International development of organisation's brand name.
- Helps to build core competences.
- Organisations can have control over markets.

> **Example**

Gillette exercised related diversification because it diversified from its chief business of the production of razors and razor blades to the production of related items such as toothbrushes, toiletries etc.

In this example, diversification is within the value network of the company because the capabilities required for the two types of production, i.e. the production of razors and razor blades and the production of toothbrushes and toiletries, are different. They require different raw materials, varied skills etc. Gillette diversified within its value network because it sold its new, diversified products to largely the same group of customers.

> **Example**

Procter & Gamble is an organisation which has exercised related diversification.

- Haircare: Pantene, Head & Shoulders, Clairol
- Household cleaning / care: Flash, Febreze, Fairy
- Laundry: Daz, Ariel, Fairy, Bounce
- Paper: Bounty, Pampers, Always
- Beauty: Oil of Olay, Max Factor

Here, diversification is within both the capabilities and the value network of the organisation.

There are different forms of related diversification on the basis of the organisation's **value network**.

a) Vertical integration: this is integration in **adjacent activities** in a value system.

It may be of two types

i. Forward integration

> **Definition**
>
> According to JSW, forward integration is expansion into activities which are related with the organisation's outputs.

This type of integration extends control over **downstream distribution operations**; those areas of the value system which are closer to end users.

> **Example**
>
> Forward integration took place in the securities industry. Shearson Lehman Brothers bought E.F Huton. Huton was having strong network of retail brokers and Sherson was attracted by it.

ii. Backward integration

> **Definition**
>
> According to JSW, backward integration is expansion into activities related with the inputs into the organisation's existing business.

This type of integration involves extending control over **upstream operations**; those areas of the value system which are further from the end user.

> **Example**
>
> Hi Tech Ltd is a computer manufacturer in the UK. It decided to acquire Superb Ltd, a spare parts manufacturer.
>
> This is backward integration because Hi Tech is producing outputs and it intends to acquire a business which is its raw material manufacturer i.e. which produces inputs.

> **Example**
>
> Shell is a worldwide group of oil, gas and petrochemical companies. The company's main business is the exploration for and the production and trading in a range of energy resources. The company has extensive vertical integration. It conducts exploration, production, transportation, refining, retail distribution and sale of fuel.
>
> The vertically integrated business model gave significant economies of scale to Shell and provided it with the opportunity to establish barriers to entry both geographically and on a more global scale.

b) Horizontal integration: this is integration in **complementary activities** in a value system. It results in the production of substitute products.

Horizontal integration is **useful** in the following ways
:
- economies of scope
- reduction in competition
- fulfilment of customer expectations
- availability of substitutes
- economies of scale

SUMMARY

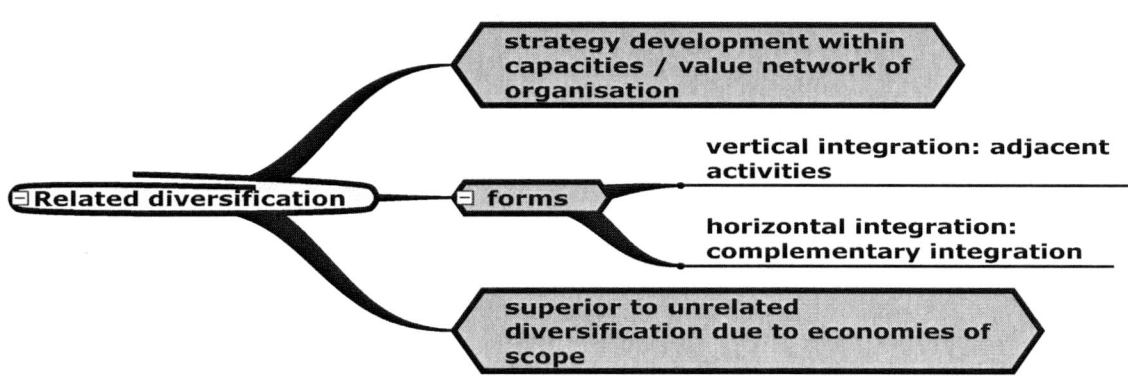

2. Unrelated diversification

Unrelated diversification is the development of products or services **beyond the current capabilities or value network** of the organisation. It is referred to as 'conglomerate strategy'.

Features of unrelated diversification:

- There is value chain interrelationship.
- Organisations penetrate into any business where they think they can earn profits.
- There is a corporate strategy policy.

Advantages of unrelated diversification

- The financial resources of the organisation can be utilised to the fullest extent in the industry where higher profits can be earned.
- There is the opportunity to maximise the utilisation of underutilised resources or competencies.
- The risk involved in business is spread over different industries.

Example

Virgin is one of the world's most recognised and respected brands. Conceived in 1970 by Sir Richard Branson, the Virgin Group has gone on to grow very successful businesses in sectors ranging from mobile telephony, to transportation, travel, financial services, leisure, music, holidays, publishing and retailing.

The businesses owned by Virgin are as follows:

- Virgin Travel (& Virgin Holidays)
- Virgin Retail (Music & Entertainment)
- Virgin Investments (computer products, promotional blimps, property development)
- Virgin Hotels Group (clubs & hotels in UK, Spain & Virgin Islands)
- Virgin Communications (Virgin Interactive Entertainment, Publishing, Radio, TV)

SUMMARY

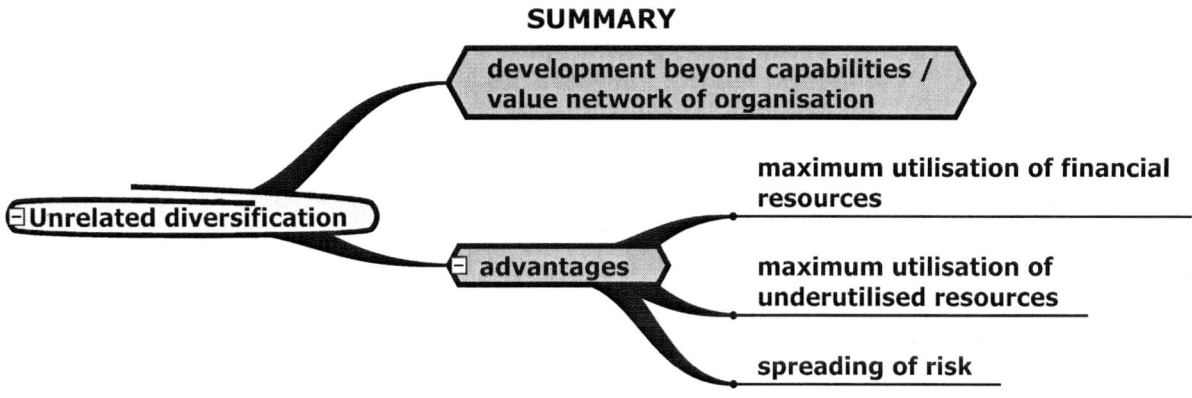

It is a matter of debate whether diversified organisations perform better than undiversified organisations.

Related diversification is superior to unrelated diversification because it usually creates economies of scope. However, there are some problems associated with related diversification such as:

- It is time-consuming.
- It is expensive.
- Difficulties may arise in sharing resources.

2.4 Difference between related and unrelated diversification

Basis of difference	Related diversification	Unrelated diversification
Definition	Diversification is **within** the capacities or value network of the organisation	Diversification is the development of products or services **beyond** the current capabilities or value network of the organisation
Economies of scope	There are (usually) **economies of scope**	There are USUALLY **no** economies of scope, (but this is not always the case, e.g. Virgin attempts unrelated diversification but there are still some common HO functions).

There are cases where organisations diversify only to save managerial jobs, share the risk and / or safeguard the status of the organisation. Organisations that exercise related diversification benefit a lot compared to undiversified or unrelated diversified organisations. The relationship between diversification and performance can be depicted as an inverted U-shape because limited diversification is beneficial for an organisation but too much diversification is not.

Diagram 4: Relationship between the diversification and performance

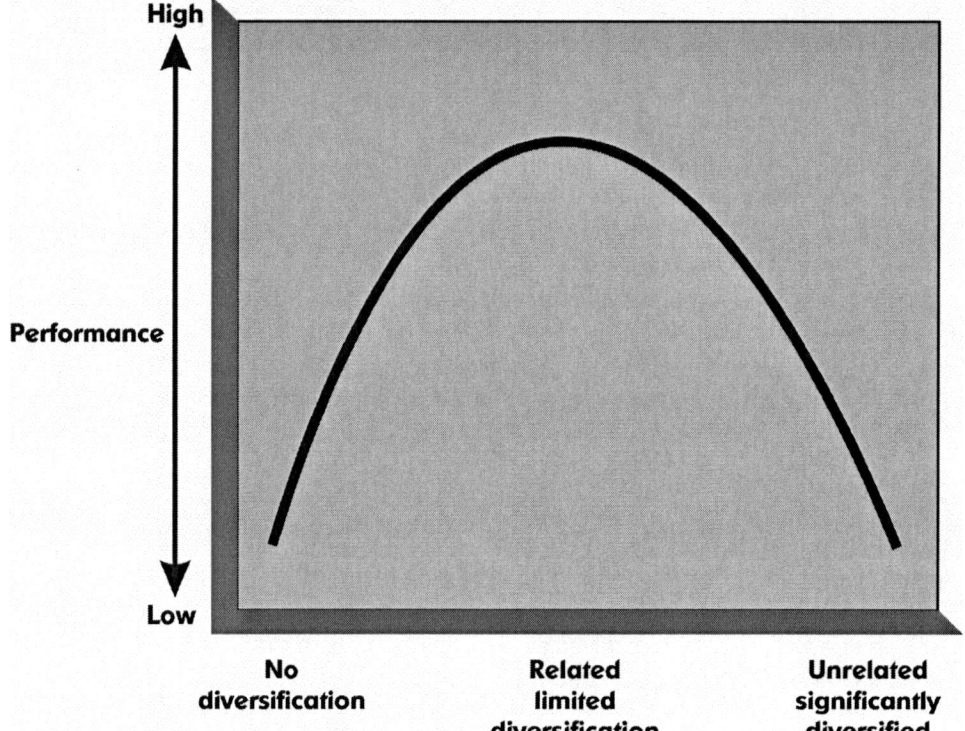

This relationship is general. There are a few **exceptions**:

➢ Organisations in developing economies perform well.

➢ Some managers are skilful and hence have improved in developing unrelated diversification.

➢ Organisations which diversify significantly tend to perform poorly in the long run if senior managers leave the organisation and therefore their skills are no longer available.

2.5 Market diversification from international perspective

Organisations aim to increase their profits. Profits can be increased by increasing sales. To increase sales, organisations tend to improve their products or produce new products for their existing customers i.e. through product diversification. Organisation may **increase sales** by selling their products in a **new market** i.e. to new customers, possibly foreign customers. This is called market diversification from an international perspective.

It is not easy to operate in an international market. Organisations have to comply with various legal requirements when they decide to sell their products internationally. They have to follow the principles which they use in the domestic market. In addition, there are some factors which have to be taken into consideration while operating in foreign markets which are overlooked in domestic markets.

> **Example**
>
> The air conditioners used in the UK may not be suitable for use in Asia, as the temperatures in Asia are much higher consistently than in Europe

Requirements of selling products internationally

1. The international market must be given importance because, like domestic customers, foreign customers also tend to buy products from a reputed buyer who provides high quality products. The international market should not be taken for granted. Organisations have to be **committed to their work**.

2. Organisations should not be rigid i.e. they should be **prepared to change** according to the requirements of the foreign customers. When organisations produce new products and their customers desire specific features to be incorporated in the product, the organisations should be willing to make the required modifications.

Organisations may have to adopt **different promotional and marketing policies and pricing strategies** to sell their products in the international market effectively. The buying habits of foreign customers will be different from domestic customers and hence organisations have to aim to satisfy their varied needs. To be successful in the international market, an organisation must know where it should sell its products and how it should sell the products.

> **Example**
>
> In America, people tend to buy in larger lots so that they don't have to purchase frequently. On the other hand, in European countries, people tend to buy in smaller lots and hence they purchase goods very often. Therefore, an organisation which wishes to sell its products in Europe should provide many distribution centres as its customers have the habit of frequent buying.

SUMMARY

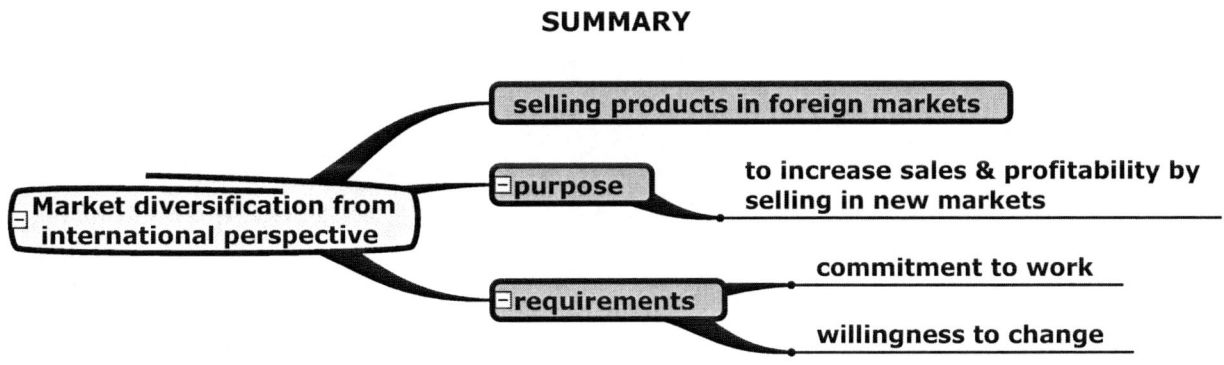

2.6 International diversity and corporate strategy

1. Strategy of internationalisation

Organisations pursue the strategy of internationalisation for the following reasons:

a) Competition has led to internationalisation because, due to domestic competition, organisations aim to increase their profits by selling their products in the international market.

b) Markets have become global markets because the tastes and demands of customers across the globe have grown homogeneous.

c) When organisations develop internationally, they can circumvent the shortfalls in the domestic market.

d) Organisations may benefit from their strategic capabilities in the following ways:

i. They can widen their market size. When organisations have greater strategic capabilities, they can operate effectively in the domestic as well as in foreign markets.

ii. When organisations provide value-adding activities to foreign customers, there is the possibility of the strategies and capabilities developed being exploited in the domestic market. This could create competitive advantages for these organisations.

e) Organisations which expand internationally, develop their skills and knowledge bases which leads to an improvement in the industry overall e.g. the IT industry in the USA.

f) Organisations may also enjoy various economic benefits such as the following:

i. Market size increases which leads to **economies of scale**. As customers across the world have similar tastes and needs, this leads to enormous production and hence national economy benefits.
ii. As sales increase, **income** across the globe also **increases**.

2. Opportunities that influence organisations to operate internationally

a) Emergence of new markets

In the present era there has been immense technological development on a global scale. People's income has increased heavily due to which their purchasing power has also increased. Due to income growth, people wish to have luxurious lifestyles and therefore their demands have increased and varied. To satisfy these **new and varied demands,** organisations have an opportunity to emerge into new markets in foreign nations.

b) Fast growth in new markets

Some organisations have the potential to grow at a rapid pace in the new markets compared to the existing domestic market.

c) Higher profits

Organisations have realised that selling products in foreign markets will allow them to earn **higher profits** because the prices charged may be higher and / or the labour charges or raw material costs may be lower compared to the domestic market. The demand for the products may be higher with less competition. This may give rise to voluminous sales which lead to higher profits.

d) Emergence of new products for the local market

When organisations sell new products in the foreign market, some consumers might purchase the products and wish to obtain the same products in the domestic market. For example, French wines have a good market in the US Therefore, organisations may have the opportunity to expand their scope of production in the domestic market and obtain a competitive advantage over others.

e) Development of new technology

Organisations utilise modern technology due to which **production is fast** and takes less time. The cost of production can be reduced and hence the margin of profit can be maintained and **economies of scale** can be enjoyed. Hence, organisations are encouraged to operate in foreign markets and domestic markets too.

Example

With the invention of the steam engine in the late nineteenth century, travelling times reduced. As a result, the transportation cost of products and people reduced immensely.

In the mid-twentieth century, the bulk production of telephones and cars resulted in the reduction of the costs of technology due to which many people were able to purchase these products.

f) Globalisation of financial markets

Organisations are attracted to **grow internationally** because they have the funds needed for expansion in foreign markets. In other words the growth in finance availability has led to the development of international markets.

Example

The International Monetary Fund was established by the United Nations in 1945 to provide financial assistance to World Trade and the World Bank which gives and promotes loans to developing and under-developed nations.

SUMMARY

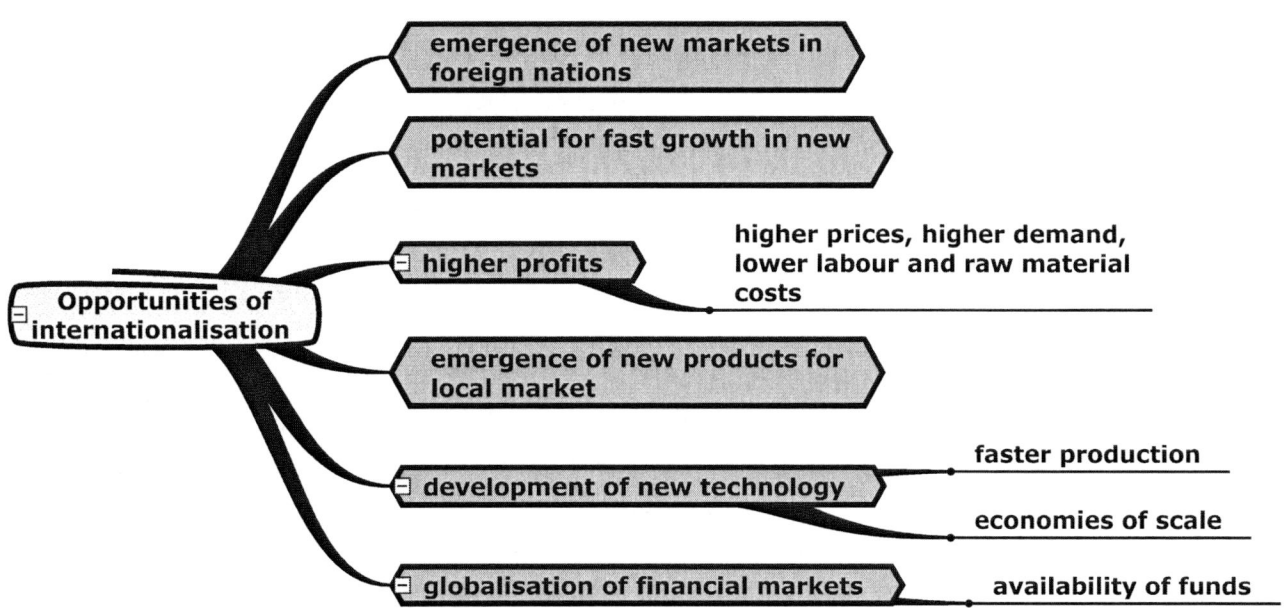

3. Problems that organisations face while operating internationally

a) Organisations operating internationally have to follow the **legal provisions of all nations in which they operate** i.e. they have to abide by the rules of both the domestic as well as the foreign governments.

b) Organisations have to **deal in different currencies** for which they have to comply with various conditions.

c) When organisations concentrate on foreign markets, there is the possibility that the **demand in the home market may be hampered** which will result in an increase in imports.

d) **Declining demand in the domestic market:** a product passes through various stages in its lifecycle such as inception, growth, maturity and recession. The demand for the product may be low in the domestic market because the market may be saturated or in recession.

4. Market entry

An organisation is always keen to enter a market which is beneficial to it and to enter through a mode which is the most attractive and profitable. The choice of mode of entry is made on the basis of PESTEL analysis. The PESTEL framework is explained in Study Guide A2. The factors which influence an organisation's selection of mode of market entry are the market conditions, competitive advantages and factors at the macro-level.

The factors which influence the selection of mode of market entry are:

➢ cultural features
➢ social factors
➢ transportation and infrastructure facilities
➢ legal compliances in the foreign nation
➢ political barriers
➢ macro-economic conditions such as purchasing power of the customers in the foreign market, the gross domestic product (GDP)

Example

Labour costs form a large part of the total costs of an organisation's products or services. Organisations seek to keep these costs low in order to survive. This is why US companies are outsourcing many jobs to far eastern countries such as Japan, Taiwan, South Korea and China, as the labour cost in these countries is cheaper.

Additionally, in the last ten years, a great deal of inexpensive labour has come from India. Compared to their counterparts in the United States and other developed nations, workers in Indian companies are both plentiful and inexpensive to employ.

2.7 Locational advantages

An organisation's decision on whether or not to operate in an international market depends upon the emergence of new markets as well as on where the **elements of the organisation's value chain are located**. Organisations can benefit by locating the elements of the value chain in places where they can perform effectively. The effective performance of value chain elements can be achieved through **global outsourcing, joint ventures** etc. Global outsourcing means obtaining the elements required for production or procuring services from a place where they are available at low cost.

When organisations purchase materials or services from a location where they are readily available, this results in the following advantages:

- comparatively lower labour charges
- lower transportation and communication costs
- considerable financial resources
- government tax concessions
- extraordinary capabilities which allow an organisation to gain competitive advantage over others
- liberal economic policies

Although organisations have to consider locational advantages, importance has to be given to managerial and management considerations while evaluating international investment decisions.

Test Yourself 2

Luxury Travels Ltd is a medium-sized company which has been in the travel and tourism business for the last 10 years. It operates in a small country which has spectacular beaches. The company has secured consistent revenue since its inception, as the country is one of the top tourist destinations around the globe.

Recently, a series of hurricanes devastated the country's beaches. The hurricanes swept away billions of dollars of potential tourism business in the country. This has had a great impact on Luxury Travels as there has been a sharp decline in revenue after this event.

Required:

What strategies should Luxury Travels explore to minimise the risk of unexpected events?

> 3. **Discuss a range of ways that the corporate parent can create and destroy organisational value.**[2]
> **Explain three corporate rationales for adding value—portfolio managers, synergy managers and parental developers.**[3]
>
> [Learning Outcomes d and e]

3.1 International strategies

Global organisational design is undertaken to build structures which are suitable for varied locations and able to respond to the market demands.

There are two international strategies.

1. Multi-domestic strategy

Operational and strategic decisions are allocated to strategic business units in respective nations. The value-adding activities are located in the domestic market. The products and services are produced and marketed according to the local requirements. Control is decentralised and local decision-making takes place. The product is customised for each market. This strategy has many advantages e.g. minimised political risk, local responsiveness, local knowledge etc.

Example

Philips followed a multi-domestic strategy. This strategy benefited the company in the following way:

- customised products for individual countries
- innovation from domestic research and development
- backward integration giving rise to high quality products
- organisational strength

The organisation also had to face various challenges as a result of following a multi-domestic strategy:
- Innovation from domestic R&D led to the products becoming R&D driven and not market demand driven.
- Costs were enormously high as the products were customised.

2. Global strategy

Operational and strategic decisions are comparatively stable across the markets. The products are produced in a single location i.e. their production is centralised. Here, the main focus is on value-adding activities and economies of scale. Control is centralised and hence local level management has little authority to take decisions. Under this strategy, the product is the same in all markets. The benefits of this strategy are fast product development, lower costs etc.

Example

Matsushita Electric Industrial Co Ltd is a worldwide leader in the development and manufacture of electronics products for a wide range of consumer, business and industrial needs. It produces products under a variety of brand names including Panasonic, National, Techniques and Quasar.

Matsushita followed a global strategy. The features were:
- excessive functional R&D
- global distribution network
- easy availability of market
- financial control

The organisation had to face various challenges by following global strategy:
- excessive dependency on one product i.e. VCR
- the problem of the strong Yen

Diagram 5: Types of international strategies

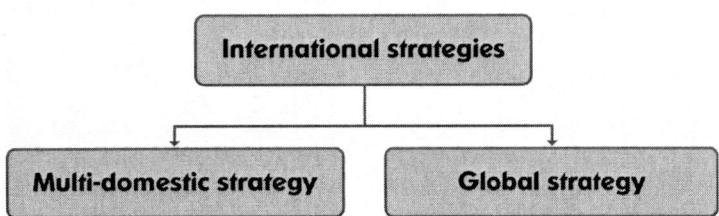

In Learning Outcome 2, it was seen that the relationship between the diversification (product / service) and performance can be depicted as an inverted U-shape because limited diversification is beneficial for an organisation but too much diversification is not. In the same way, the relationship between international diversification and performance can also be shown as an inverted u-shape.

3.2 Creation of values by corporate parent

An investor wishes to put his money in safe hands. An investor invests in an organisation in order to earn attractive profits. Before investing, an investor will always evaluate the financial position and the goodwill of the organisation in the market.

1. Strategic management has three levels:

- top level – corporate level
- middle level – business level
- bottom level – functional level

A corporate parent creates value which encourages a potential investor to invest his funds. Corporate parent helps in the development of confidence and trust in an organisation. The corporate parent does not have direct contact with customers or suppliers. It has to manage the business units within an organisation.

Michael Goold, Andrew Campbell and Marcus Alexander explain the concept of parenting. They are of the view that the corporate parent not only adds value to the organisation but should endeavour to **add more value** to the organisation as compared to other corporate parents. This is termed **parenting advantage**.

2. **Parenting advantage** recognises the following features that lead to the creation of value:

a) The corporate parent should have **parenting characteristics** – it should possess the resources or should have the capacity to support the performance of an organisation.
b) The corporate parent should have **opportunity** to support the organisation in its performance.
c) The corporate parent must have the **willingness to serve the business**. It should be in a position to understand the control factors and the ways to achieve the goals of the organisation.
d) The corporate parent should **possess distinguishing features** with special skills that make it more effective than other corporate parents.

3. **Value-adding activities**

According to Johnson, Scholes and Whittington (JSW), there are three roles in which a corporate parent can add value:
a) **envisioning**
b) **intervening**
c) **offering central services and resources**

a) **Envisioning:** it is essential for a corporate parent to be clear about its intention relating to the goals or expectations of an organisation, for the following reasons:

i. Focus: the value added to the units should be commensurate with the cost incurred for that activity. When the goal is focused, the cost incurred is effective and thereby adds value to the business unit.

ii. Clarity to business units: it is of the utmost importance that the business unit managers are aware of the activities undertaken by the parent. If they are not aware of the parent's activities, unit managers may have the idea that the parent is nothing but a cost burden. The business unit managers may therefore operate and frame strategic decisions to attain their business goal rather than to achieve the corporate goal. If the corporate parent is clear about its strategies, this results in a clearer understanding of stakeholders' expectations.

iii. Clarity to external stakeholders:

Definition

The persons who affect or are affected by the success or the failure of the organisation's effort to achieve its objective are known as the stakeholders.

It is essential that the external stakeholders are informed of the organisation's goals and the strategies to attain these goals. The investors / government (in the case of a public sector organisation) must be informed about the units within a business portfolio.

b) **Intervening**: the role of the corporate parent is to improve the performance of the business units. It has to intervene between the business units to ensure their development. This is done in the following manner:

i. If, after regular monitoring, it appears that some action needs to be taken to improve of the units, then the corporate has to take the necessary actions e.g. disinvesting from units which are not adding to the turnover of the organisation as a whole or appointing new managers.
ii. Some standards and policies are framed by the corporate parent; therefore it must ensure that these are properly adhered to.
iii. By providing training and incentives to the managers and staff of the business units.
iv. By motivating the business units to expand their scope of work from domestic to international level.
v. By sharing resources and capabilities among the business units to develop their performance.

c) The corporate parent may **offer central services and resources** to support business units. When corporate parents possess expertise in any area, they provide their expertise to business units in various ways:

i. If any unit is in need of resources for production or rendering of services, then these resources are provided by the corporate parent.
ii. The parent provides funds when needed e.g. if any business unit newly incorporates then the corporate parent invests in this unit.
iii. If one manager is capable of managing an activity more skillfully than another, then the corporate parent may transfer such managerial capabilities across the different business units.
iv. If a corporate parent is an expert in any particular area, it may provide help to the business units.
v. When skills and ideas are shared among the business units, this helps in the learning process and moreover helps to generate new ideas.

Example

Unilever has operations located across the globe with each subsidiary having its own purchasing department to meet its individual requirements.

Recently, the organisation has begun consolidating its purchasing for all its companies from one central location. At the "war room" in Greenwich, Connecticut the company has begun centralising purchasing through implementing standard e-procurement, online auction, purchasing management and demand planning systems.

Continued on the next page

The underlying rationale behind this reorganisation is that Unilever believes it will result in cost efficiencies and economies of scale in purchasing. For example, by mass ordering common items such as box packaging, the organisation can negotiate better prices from suppliers.

These efforts have resulted in the organisation rolling out consistent, collaborative procurement processes across the company on a global basis. Unilever has already saved close to US$2 billion and expects the benefits to continue.

SUMMARY

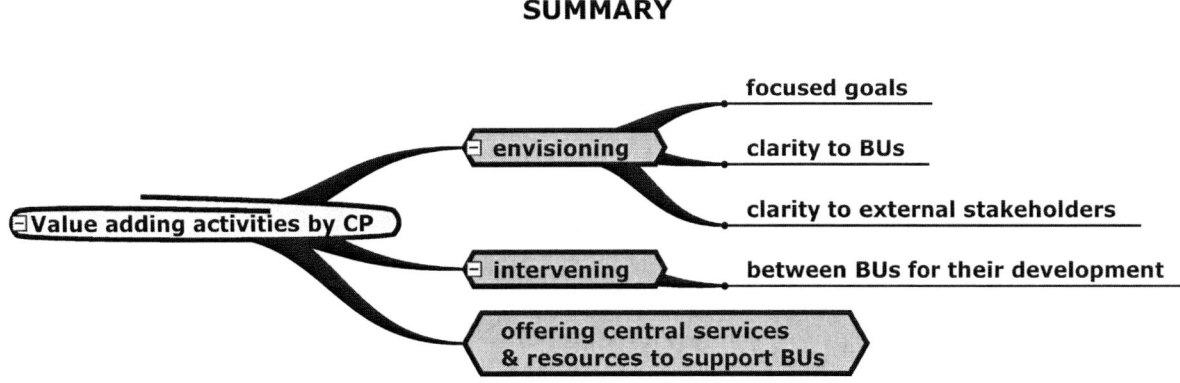

3.3 Value-destroying activities

Sometimes, inadvertently, a corporate parent may destroy any of the values of an organisation. This may happen in any of the following ways:

> The corporate parent builds unnecessary (financial) safety coverage for the executives due to which executives do not understand the problems in actual practice.
> Sometimes the size and varied operations of the organisation hamper the development of the organisation and may mislead the clear vision of the organisation.
> Managers are at the top of the organisational hierarchy. There is the possibility that the corporate hierarchy will give importance to the goals of managers instead of the goals of business units. This results in the development of managers as opposed to the development of the organisation as a whole.
> A corporate parent may increase the cost of operations or may create delays in decision-making. It may even create unnecessary bureaucracy.

SUMMARY

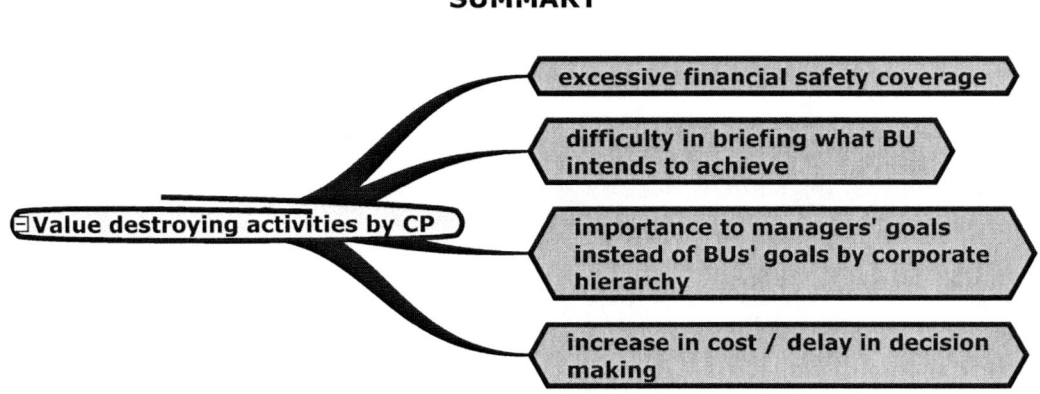

3.4 Corporate rationales for adding value

1. **Portfolio managers**

A corporate parent acts as an **agent on behalf of financial markets and shareholders**. It performs the activity of recognising under-valued businesses or assets and adopts methods to develop them. The managers of business units (chief executives) enjoy a high level of independence. Portfolio managers aim to lower the costs of the centre. They have to reward the chief executives who achieve targets and vice-versa.

These managers are involved in the **central assessment** of the organisation's goals and forming the organisation's financial targets and evaluations relating to investing or divesting funds. They are not directly involved in product or market strategies. As a result, they can manage many business units. Where a corporate parent acts as a portfolio manager, this is an extreme form of a multi-domestic strategy, because parents are involved in the activities relating to financial transactions / relationships between two markets and other areas of business are to be handled by business units themselves.

SUMMARY

2. Synergy managers

A synergy manager is a corporate parent which aims to improve and develop value by **managing synergies** among business units. The value can be developed among the business units in the following ways:

a) Skills or competences may be shared

The value-adding activities among the business units may be common even if the products or services within an industry are different. Hence, by sharing these skills or competences, the performance of the business may be improved.

b) Activities or resources may be shared

When the different business units have the same technological requirements, they may share the technology needed among the business units. In addition, when the business units are situated in different geographical areas, they may share product distribution facilities.

Synergy managers practise economies of scope. There are some conditions which organisations must fulfil to obtain synergetic benefits.

i. When business units share resources, activities or skills, this involves **huge cost**.

ii. The business units may not cooperate fully as they may be interested in their own business focus. The managers of business units are rewarded on the basis of the performance which they achieve in their business units.

iii. As business units may be located in different geographical areas, there may be **differences in the local conditions**. For example, the customer demand and the market forces may be different in different geographical areas.

iv. The staff of the corporate parent must be committed to achieving synergies through the sharing of skills and competences which demands accurate business knowledge. The corporate parent may be required to **participate in the strategic planning or control.**

v. There is the possibility that the synergies may only be imaginary i.e. there may be an **illusion of synergy**. In some cases, although the skills and competences may be present; they may not add value to the organisation.

vi. When business units share activities or resources, it should be **convenient for them to do so.** Sometimes the cultures followed in two different business units may be different and hence sharing may not be appropriate.

Example

When there are various business units and the raw materials required by one unit are the output of another unit, the transfer price for the raw materials is to be fixed. A business unit will add its margin and then transfer its output to the other unit.

The units do not cooperate with the corporate parent in fixing the price. The unit fixes a price which is beneficial for it and not for the organisation as a whole.

3. Parental developers

Definitions

According to JSW, **a parental developer** is a corporate parent looking to employ its own competences as a parent to append value to its businesses and construct parenting abilities that are appropriate for its portfolio of business units.

From the above definition, it is clear that the corporate parent employs its own competences. Unlike a synergy manager, it does not have to worry about the sharing or transferring of skills, resources or activities.

Parental developers have to work for the **improvement and / or development of business units**. To do this, the corporate parent should possess accurate knowledge about the resources, activities, skills and business levels. Where parenting competences exist, "parenting opportunity" must be identified by the corporate manager.

Corporate parents have different competences. Some have good negotiation capability, some are financially strong and some have excellent mobility across the world in order to conduct business.

These are some problems which corporate parents face while improving / developing business units through a parental developer.

a) The corporate parent may be unsure of the **type of parenting to be adopted**. There may be **confusion** regarding whether to act as a synergy manager or parental developer or both. The corporate manager and the manager of the business units may be unclear of the goals to be achieved and moreover the cost involved may be high.

b) When the parental developer is to be followed, the managers / executives of the corporate parent must possess **sufficient knowledge of the business**.

c) As the parent seeks to employ its own competences, it is essential to identify the **capabilities of the parent**.

d) There are various business units. The parent may **add little value** to some of the business units. Some business units might be self-sufficient in performing well in the business. Although the corporate parent is not adding any value, cost is incurred and so this **destroys value**.

e) Sometimes the capacities of corporate parents are recognised. If the capabilities are not applied in the manner for which they were established, they can become costly.

Test Yourself 3

Glenbex Ltd is a leading healthcare provider engaged in the production of medicines and vaccines. The company has strong competences in research and development and a state-of-the-art, multi-disciplinary research facility. Gemini Ltd, a business unit of Glenbex, produces low calorie food for patients undergoing treatment for different diseases. Glenbex's R&D division provides full support to Gemini in research and development of the low calorie food. Apart from R&D, Glenbex does not intervene in Gemini to improve performance or to develop business unit strategy.

Required:

Which corporate role is adopted by Glenbex as a corporate parent?

...nd assess a range of portfolio models (the growth / share (BCG) matrix, the public ...rtfolio matrix, market attractiveness / SBU strength matrix, directional policy ...shridge Portfolio Display) that may assist corporate parents manage their business portfolios.[3]

[Learning Outcome f]

An organisation aims to earn large returns. It always expects to operate in those lines of business which give profits. An organisation comprises different business units. Whether or not to invest in a business depends upon the profit-generating capacity of that particular business. A **business portfolio** is a collection of businesses and products. The businesses and products taken together form an organisation. A suitable business portfolio is one which best suits the organisation's strengths and weaknesses to opportunities in the environment.

4.1 Portfolio analysis

Portfolio analysis is a method of helping management to identify and evaluate the different businesses or product groups within an organisation. It is a set of techniques which helps in strategic decision-making relating to products or businesses in an organisation. It is basically used for strategic planning and analysing the competitive advantage of an organisation with different business units. As such it is a corporate planning tool.

With the application of different business portfolio models, the organisation may decide which business to include and which one to exclude from its portfolio. Whether or not to include a particular business unit in a portfolio depends upon the following criteria:

- balance of portfolio
- extent to which the SBU is "fit" for an organisation
- how attractive the SBU is in terms of profit-earning capacity

4.2 Portfolio models

1. BCG Matrix

The Boston Consulting Group identified a matrix based on relative **market share and market growth,** which is called a growth / share matrix. It focuses on the cash inflow and outflow effects. In this matrix, four important terms suggest the different types of businesses in a portfolio. The terms are stars, question marks, cash cows and dogs.

The matrix is presented as follows:

Diagram 6: BCG matrix

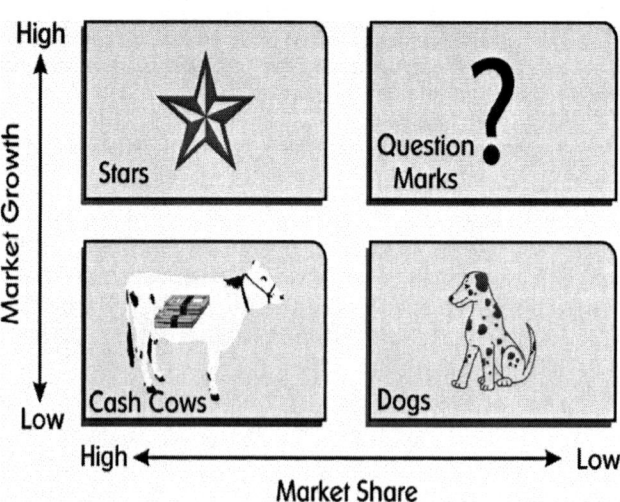

a) Stars

From the above diagram, it is clear that when a **market is growing**, a business unit which enjoys **high market share** is termed a star business unit. To gain market share, the expenditure may be high but gradually the costs may be reduced.

Here, the business unit is at the **growth phase**. The business risks are very high as the industry is fast growing and therefore expensive. This business unit is established in the market and to expand further it may require funds from different sources. It has to build market share by continued investment and has to wait for the industry to slow down until it moves into the cash cow quadrant.

b) Question marks

A business unit with a **low market share** in a **growing market** is termed a question mark. There may be high expenditure to raise the market share but there is the possibility that the business unit may not achieve cost reduction benefits. Such units require a large amount of cash to retain their market share. The strategy is invest or divest (sell or abandon) as the business risks are very high i.e. large net cash outflow. These business units are not established in the market; they are in the **beginning phase** of their life cycle. The investment requirements of these units are very high. They fulfil their fund requirement from **equity** sources. They try to improve their market share by spending money on marketing and research and development etc.

c) Cash cows

A business unit with a large **market share** in a market with **low market growth** is termed a cash cow. These units are successful and established. As growth is low and its market share is high, it requires less investment. As the unit has a large market share, its cost levels are expected to be below its competitors. In the long run, when the market growth rate reduces, star business units become cash cows. These business units are the units which have reached the **maturity phase**. They have higher amounts of surplus cash at their disposal. They have fewer business risks as they are well established in the market. As there is a high level of surplus, there are higher retained earnings. In this type of business unit, it is preferable to obtain funds from both **debt and equity** because the surplus earned by the business can be used to pay the interest incurred by the debt. The financial risk with debt funds is higher than with equity funds. The strategy to be followed should be harvest i.e. obtain profits without spending too much on investment as the product is towards the end of the product / industry lifecycle. The business unit should direct some of the funds towards new product development and help in the development of question marks and stars in the portfolio. It should hold market share by promotion or differentiation etc.

d) Dogs

These are business units which have a **low market share** in a market with **low market growth rate**. They do not have sufficient cash reservoir for the future. There is also the possibility that they may not have enough cash to survive. Business units of this sort may be reduced by liquidation or divestment. This business unit is the worst among all other business units. Here, business units are in the **declining phase**. It is difficult for the organisation to fund its needs from equity sources. For this type of unit, it is preferable to **borrow** money for its funding requirements. Units borrow funds by retaining some of the organisation's left over assets as security but it is not wise to invest in a dog. The strategy adopted is divest if possible but exit costs like redundancies and lease settlements may be prohibitive.

This matrix helps in strategic planning. As it shows the relationship between market share and market growth, it considers the lifecycle development of that market.

There are some important issues with this method.

➢ Analysis to be applied only to strategic business units and not to markets.
➢ "Business units of the dog category are not considered important all of the time".

This is not correct because sometimes dogs may find an important place in an organisation's portfolio. The dog may be trying hard to make its place in the market after completing its products. It should be used as a loss leader i.e. the product should be continued even though it is loss making, as it helps advertise the master brand and therefore may help other products in the portfolio. The organisation may also attempt to buy other dog businesses in the same industry and merge them together to create a cash cow unit. The organisation may also attempt to rebrand the product in order to increase the market share. This is very difficult to do in the mature / decline phase of the product lifecycle as customer loyalties to selected suppliers tend to be strong.

The **features of the BCG matrix** at a glance:

Business units	Profit	Required investment	Net cash flow	Strategy
Stars	High	High	Modest	Hold / invest
Question marks	Negative	Very high	Very negative	Invest / divest
Cash cows	High	Low	High	Hold
Dogs	Low / negative	Disinvest	Positive (from disinvestment procedure)	Hold / divest

2. Public sector portfolio matrix

This matrix helps in analysing the portfolio of public sector organisations. It is based on factors such as the ability to serve effectively and the public need and support.

Diagram 7: Public sector portfolio matrix

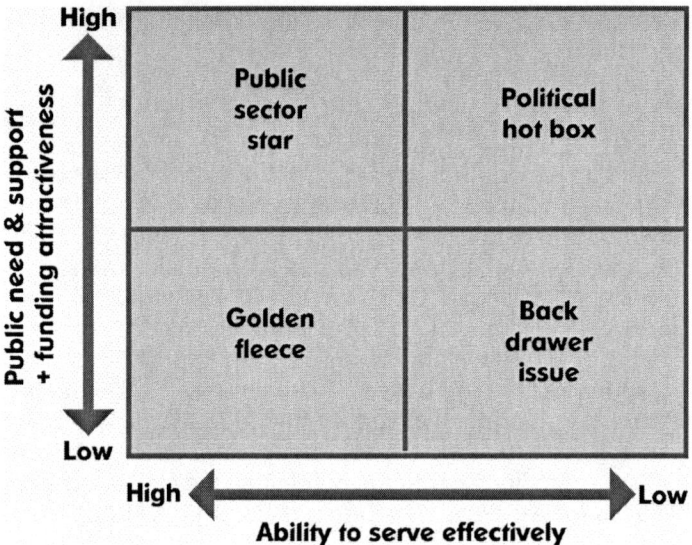

a) When the ability to serve effectively and the need and support both are high, it is a public sector star.
b) When the ability to serve effectively is low, but the public need and support are high, it is a political hot box
c) When public need and support are low but the ability to serve effectively is high, it is referred to as 'the golden fleece'.
d) The last combination in the matrix is where the ability to serve effectively and the public need and support are both low. It is referred to as a back drawer issue. It is similar to a dog in the BCG matrix. As in case of dogs, the strategy to be pursued is disinvestment. Likewise, in the case of the public sector portfolio matrix, these types of services are left out.

Management may face the following problems:

➢ The organisation has to provide services which are necessities but which do not provide any returns.
➢ Management may have difficulty in realising surplus funds for investment purposes.

3. Market attractiveness / SBU strength matrix and directional policy matrix

In the case of the market attractiveness matrix, the analysis is made for **one particular strategic business unit** whereas, in the case of the directional policy matrix, the analysis is made on the basis of the **industry as a whole**.

The market attractiveness matrix identifies and groups the business units on the basis of having good forecasts and less good forecasts i.e. the strengths of their forecasts. The two factors considered in this matrix are:
➢ the market attractiveness; and
➢ the competitive potential of the business units

a) Indicators of market attractiveness

i. **Market growth rate** i.e. growth achieved by the organisation from its inception to its present condition. This may be analysed on a percentage basis e.g. what was the percentage growth in the years 2005, 2006 and the current year 2007.

ii. **Inflation rate** i.e. the rate at which the prices increase in the market. When there is a high inflation rate, the prices in the market rise at a greater pace and hence the market is not attractive to customers.

iii. **Segmentation** i.e. the division of the market on various bases like geographical areas and customer needs. When the market is segmented on a basis which is favourable to the customers, the market is attractive to the customers.

iv. **Distribution system** (e.g. retail, direct, wholesale) – when the goods and services are easily available to the customers through a convenient distribution system, the market is attractive to the customers.

v. **Technology:** when the market uses advanced technologies to produce goods and provide services, customers are attracted to the market by the highly modernised goods and services on offer.

vi. **Overall risk or returns in the industry:** before investing in any market, investors are interested in knowing the risk and returns from the particular investment. If the returns are high and the risk is low, the market is more attractive.

vii. **Opportunity to differentiate products and services:** customers are attracted towards a market where there is immense scope to provide new and better facilities by modifying the products or by applying differentiation techniques.

Some other factors are

- Regulations
- political factors
- environmental factors
- social factors
- market size
- pricing trends
- legal factors
- competitive intensity / rivalry

These indicators suggest whether the market is attractive or not.

b) **Indicators of strength of business units**

i. **Customer loyalty:** when business units develop and maintain a good relationship with their customers.

ii. **Market share and distribution:** when business units have high market share and many distribution centres to facilitate smooth flow of goods across the nation.

iii. **Relative brand strength:** when the brand name of the unit is well-known in the market.

iv. **Research and development:** when the business unit undertakes efficient and cost effective research and development activities which result in future benefits to the organisation.

v. **Good financial standing:** when the financial capacity and the creditworthiness of the business unit are strong in the market.

vi. **Sales force:** when the unit possesses a skilled and effective sales force.

vii. **Relative cost structure compared to competitors:** when cost analysis is favourable compared to competitors.

This matrix gives a combination of business units which have competitive strength within an organisation and attractive conditions within a market place.

Diagram 8: Directional policy matrix

	High	**Medium**	**Low**
High (Industry attractiveness)	Invest & growth	Selective growth	Selectivity
Medium	Selective growth	Selectivity	Harvest / Divest
Low	Selectivity	Harvest / Divest	Harvest / Divest

Business strengths

The matrix suggests that the units with the highest business strengths and with the highest industry attractiveness are the business units where the decision relates to **investing**. On the other hand, business units with the lowest industry attractiveness and the lowest business strengths are the business units where the decision relates to **divesting**.

SUMMARY

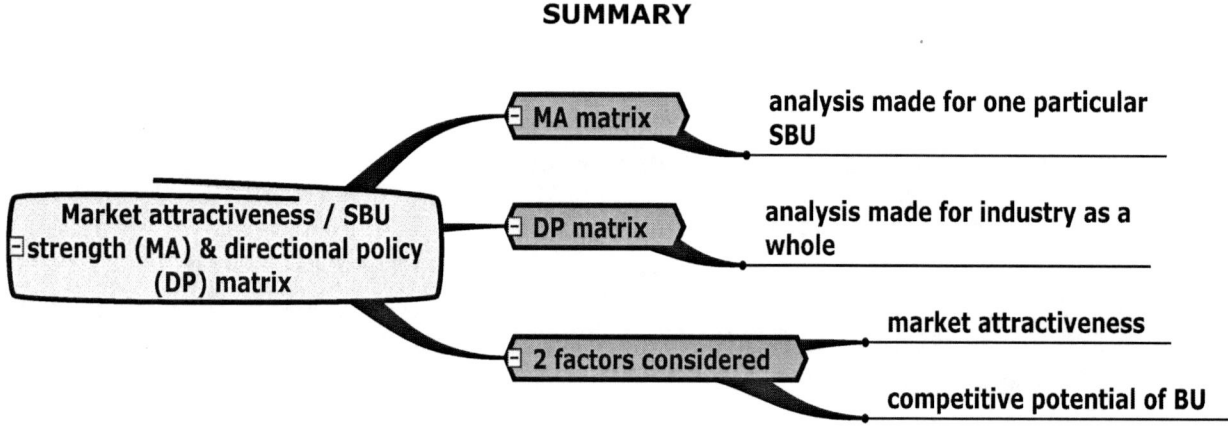

Market attractiveness / SBU strength (MA) & directional policy (DP) matrix
- MA matrix — analysis made for one particular SBU
- DP matrix — analysis made for industry as a whole
- 2 factors considered — market attractiveness; competitive potential of BU

4. Ashridge Portfolio Display

The Ashridge Portfolio Display was developed by Michael Goold and Andrew Campbell. This model takes into account **'strategic fit'**. In this matrix, the corporate parent plays the role of **parental developer**. The term parental developer has been explained in the previous learning outcome.

The basis of this model is that the organisation should have a portfolio which fits the skills and ability of the corporate parent and the corporate parent should possess and develop such skills which benefit the strategic business units of a portfolio.

The organisations can gain 'fit' elements from the following:
➤ The corporate parent should have an appropriate **'feel' for SBUs' businesses** because these SBUs will form the portfolio. There should be a fit between the capabilities of the corporate parent and the critical success factors of the business units.
➤ The business unit should benefit from the corporate parent i.e. there should be **parenting opportunity**.

The assessment of fit elements is made to reduce the problems faced by the business units. This is done by evaluating the **critical success factors of SBUs**. When there are high fit elements, this leads to a low risk of problems and vice-versa.

A parenting opportunity means the opportunity that business units can obtain from the resources and capabilities of the corporate parent.

SUMMARY

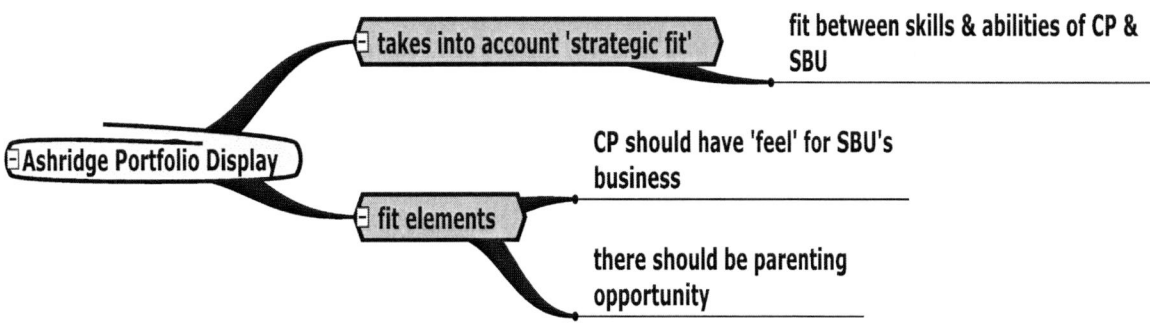

The Ashridge portfolio is depicted as follows:

Diagram 9: Ashridge Portfolio Display

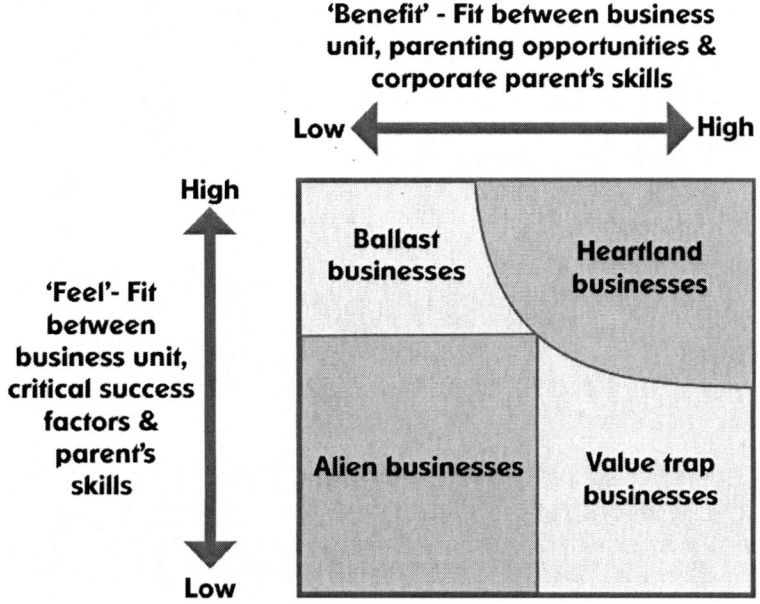

The above diagram shows that, in this type of model, there are four kinds of business units:

a) **Heartland business**

This type of business unit **benefits** from the corporate parent, as 'feel' and benefit are both high. There is no risk of harm of any type. Therefore a heartland business should be included in future strategy.

b) **Ballast business**

The parents have a **high feel** for the business of the units. They have knowledge about the critical success factors of SBUs.

c) **Value trap business**

Business units have **high parenting opportunity** but, at the same time, very **low feel** for the business of SBUs. So the corporate parent's support may be **harmful** rather than beneficial. It will be essential for the corporate parent to incorporate new skills, resources or capabilities.

d) **Alien business**

In this type of business unit, **both feel and benefit are low**. The corporate parents do not have an appropriate understanding of business or the critical success factors of the business unit. There is **a lack of parenting opportunity**. It is advisable for the business unit to leave the organisation.

168: Strategic Choices

This model explains the benefits and value which the corporate parent adds to the strategic business units.

There are some problems which parents come across:

i. It is difficult for the parent to understand the value-adding activities at the **business unit level**.
ii. It is difficult for the parent to understand the value-adding activities at the **corporate level**.
iii. There should be a **balance** between the value added to the unit and the cost incurred by the parent.
iv. The corporate parent will have to **review the portfolio**. Taking all the factors of 'feel' and benefits into account, it has to evaluate which business units should be included in the portfolio and which should be excluded.

SUMMARY

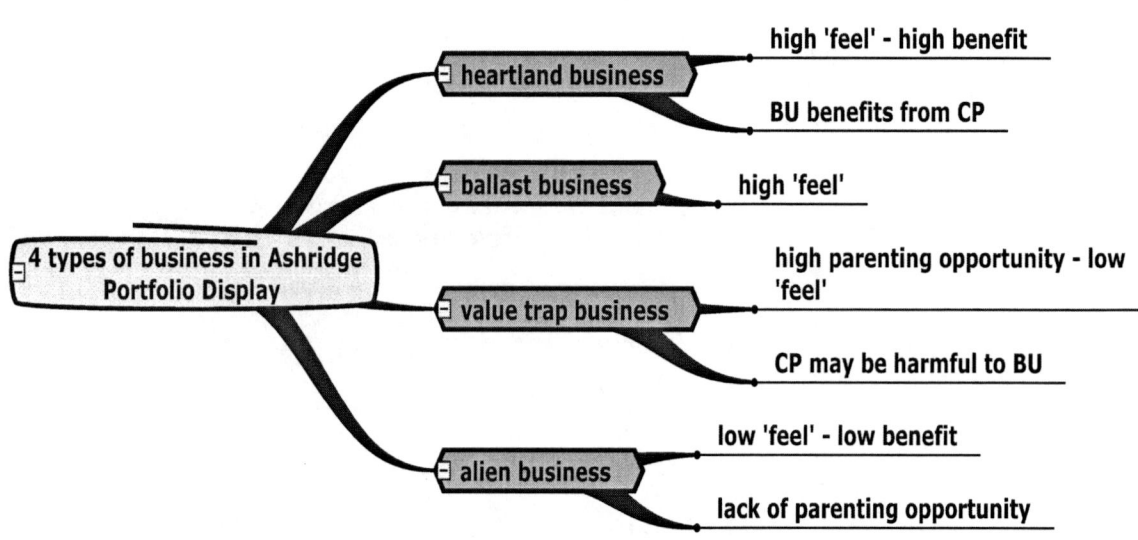

Test Yourself 4

Axis Corp produces four products: QA, QB, QC and QD. Axis has average business strength for producing QA and its business sector prospects are also average. QB belongs to an unattractive market and the company has weak competitive capabilities in its production. QC is an unattractive market but Axis has strong business strength in its production. Axis' competitive capabilities for QD are average and it is in an attractive sector.

Required:

What would be the possible strategic choices of Axis for its products based on the directional policy matrix?

Answers to Test Yourself

Answer to TY 1

A business unit is a part of an organisation for which different strategies are formulated. As an organisation grows in size and complexity, it may establish and control one or more business units. There are many reasons why a corporate parent may establish a business unit:

➢ The corporate parent desires to start a new line of business which is completely different from the existing one.
➢ There is high potential for profits in the new business line.
➢ The corporate parent does not wish to engage its existing assets in the new business line.
➢ The parent's shareholders are not to be affected by the operations of new business line.
➢ Possibilities of grouping the businesses area wise.

Answer to TY 2

Luxury Travels' geographic market was focused on only one specific region. Diversification will minimise the organisation's risk and increase the probability of it surviving in the long term. Diversification is a form of growth marketing strategy. It is defined as a strategy which takes the organisation into new markets and products / services. It seeks to increase profitability through greater sales volume obtained from new products or new markets.

Strategically, Luxury Travels has to look to new geographic travel markets i.e. markets that will allow it to **expand** in addition to being compatible with the current markets it is serving. The diversification tactic will allow Luxury Travels to reduce the risk that an unexpected event in a single market will hurt it significantly.

Answer to TY 3

Glenbex is assuming the role of a parental developer. The parental developer seeks to employ its own competences as a parent to add value to its businesses and help them in their operations and development. Glenbex is using its specific research and development skills to add value to Gemini. Here, the issue is not so much about how it can help create or develop benefits across business units or transfer capabilities between business units.

Answer to TY 4

The directional policy matrix provides the portfolio of business units on the basis of an SBU's strength and market attractiveness.

- QA may require some investment support. Axis should carefully analyse QA in order to determine whether it is worth the investment required to increase its market share.
- QB might be incurring losses. Axis should minimise its losses by divesting. It should continue with QB only if it supports a more profitable part of its business, otherwise it should be liquidated.
- The profits and cash generated by QC are high and the investments needed are low. Axis should use the cash generated from QC to fund QA and QD.
- Axis may resort to external financing in order to increase its business strength and bring QD to a position of leadership. However it should consider carefully before investing funds in QD.

Quick Quiz

1. Name two international strategies.

2. Development of new technologies is a(n) _____ that influence organisation willing to operate internationally.
   A. Opportunity
   B. Threat

3. What are the three corporate rationales for adding value?

4. In the BCG Matrix, what does "B" stand for?
   A. Bankruptcy
   B. Boston
   C. Balance
   D. Boom

5. What is the difference between the market attractiveness / SBU strength matrix and the directional policy matrix?

Answers to Quick Quiz

1. Two international strategies are: multi-domestic strategy and global strategy.

2.
(a) – Development of new technology leads to faster production and economies of scale.

3. The corporate rationales for adding value are – portfolio managers, synergy managers and parental developers.

4.
(b) Boston.

5. In the case of the market attractiveness matrix, the analysis is made for one particular strategic business unit whereas in the case of the directional policy matrix, the analysis is made on the basis of the industry as a whole.

Self Examination Questions

Question 1

Refreshing Drinks Co produces a range of carbonated, sweetened beverages of different flavours. It sells its products directly to supermarkets, shops and restaurants. It has its own well-established distribution network throughout the country. Refreshing Drinks has strong brand recognition in the country. The company is known for its aggressive marketing and advertising strategies.

Refreshing Drinks recently acquired Gold Dairy Ltd, a company producing dairy products such as skimmed milk, yoghurt, butter and cheese. Gold Dairy is a medium-sized company that does not have a presence throughout the country. Refreshing Drinks is to manage the marketing, sales and distribution of Gold Dairy. Gold Dairy can use Refreshing Drinks' extensive distribution system for its products.

What would be Refreshing Drinks' rationale for adding value? What could be the difficulties in achieving this rationale?

Question 2

FIXIT Adhesives Ltd is a UK-based company that manufactures a range of adhesives for sale to a wide range of customers. FIXIT's products range from adhesives used for household purposes to high performance adhesives, used for industrial purposes. It has three factories manufacturing three broad categories of products.

The first category is contact adhesive products. Contact adhesives are used in laminates which are supplied to furniture and footwear manufacturers in the UK. FIXIT's market share for this product group is 10% which has been consistent for the last few years. FIXIT's major competitor for contact adhesives has a reputation for aggressive product innovation.

The second category of FIXIT's products is reactive adhesives used to prevent loosening of bolts and screws in automobile engines. FIXIT's competition in this category is of a smaller size and not regarded as being particularly innovative. FIXIT has had success in meeting the particular adhesive needs of car makers in their new car model programmes. FIXIT has to satisfy the demanding quality standards required by each car manufacturer.

The third category is drying adhesives, which are typically used for household applications. The move into drying adhesives is very recent, aimed at the apparently ever-increasing demand for drying adhesives in the domestic market. The technology to produce drying adhesive was imported from abroad with an ultra-modern factory built to manufacture these products. After setting up the factory, FIXIT faced the dual problem of excess industry capacity and sales of low priced adhesives in Europe by low cost US producers. FIXIT's market share for this product category is expected to increase rapidly. The main competitor for FIXIT in this category is an American company with access to lower cost raw materials and a 35% share of the UK market.

FIXIT's current sales and financial performance

	Contact adhesives £' 000	Reactive adhesives £' 000	Drying adhesives £' 000
Sales	1,700	4,510	3,100
Cost of sales	980	2,593	2,650
Gross profit	720	1,917	450
R & D	Low	High	Moderate
Market share	10%	40%	8%

The financial health of FIXIT looks reasonably sound, if not exciting. Sales and costs seem to be increasing more or less in line with one another. However, closer analysis of the performance of the individual factories or product groups reveals some disturbing differences.

Required:

Evaluate the performance of the three product groups of FIXIT using the BCG matrix.

Answers to Self Examination Questions

Answer to SEQ 1

The acquisition gave Refreshing Drinks the opportunity to diversify its product portfolio. Refreshing Drinks would be a synergy manager. A synergy manager enhances value across business units by managing synergies. It can do so in a number of ways. One of these ways is by **sharing resources or activities**. In this case, Gold Dairy can share the extensive distribution system of Refreshing Drinks. The synergy manager can also add value by sharing skills and competences. Refreshing Drinks can add value to Gold Dairy by sharing its marketing skills and competences, thereby improving its performance.

However Refreshing Drinks may come across some difficulties while achieving this rationale:

➤ There may be substantial costs involved in undertaking such integration. For example, Refreshing Drinks will have to spend heavily on the storage, distribution and marketing of dairy products.
➤ Sharing and bringing synergy may be problematic if the systems and culture of Gold Dairy are different from Refreshing Drinks.
➤ The managers of Gold Dairy may not cooperate in such change and sharing because of their self-interests.
➤ Refreshing Drinks' skills and competences in marketing may not add value to Gold Dairy. Refreshing Drinks has expertise in marketing for beverages whereas the skills and competences required for marketing dairy products are different.

Therefore, being a synergy manager, Refreshing Drinks needs to be determined to ensure that synergy is actually achieved. To do this, it may need to intervene in Gold Dairy in terms of strategic direction and control.

Answer to SEQ 2

The BCG matrix suggests the different types of businesses in a portfolio. The BCG matrix offers a very useful map in analysing corporate parent's business units or product lines. The BCG matrix emphasises the relationship between an organisation's growth and market share. It is based on the observation that a company's business units can be ranked into four categories on the basis of their relative market shares and growth rates. These categories are: question marks (high growth, low market share), stars (high growth, high market share), cash cows (low growth, high market share) and dogs (low growth, low market share). A company with a portfolio of products could expect some to be in low growth industries and others to be in industries achieving high rates of growth.

BCG matrix for FIXIT Adhesives Ltd

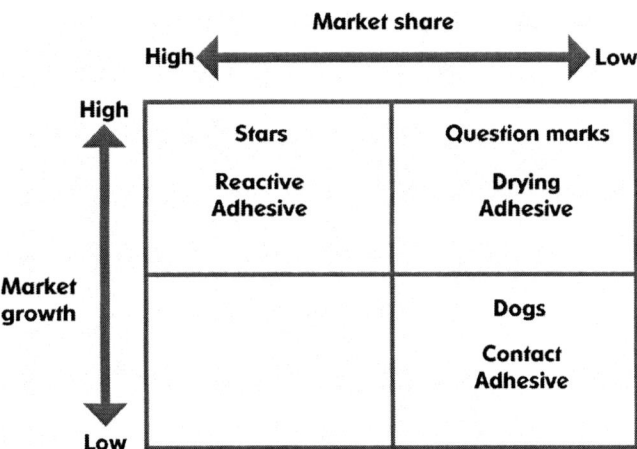

FIXIT's contact adhesives product group can be classified as a dog. It has a low market share (10%) in a mature industry. It also has a low growth rate as the market share has been consistent for the last few years. The cost of sales and the R&D cost of contact adhesives are low compared to the other two categories. Therefore it neither generates nor consumes a large amount of cash for FIXIT. FIXIT should avoid having a dog in the organisation.

Reactive adhesives product group can be classified as a star. It has a high market share (40%) in a fast-growing industry. It generates large amounts of cash but also consumes large amounts of cash to sustain its market leadership. FIXIT should make sure to maintain its large market share for reactive adhesives as it will become a cash cow when the market growth rate declines.

The drying adhesives product group of FIXIT can be classified as a question mark. It consumes large amounts of cash as it is growing rapidly. However, it does not generate much cash because it has a low market share (8%). The drying adhesives group has the potential to gain market share and become a star, and eventually a cash cow when the market growth slows. If nothing is done to change the market share, the question mark will simply absorb great amounts of cash and later, as the growth stops, will degenerate into a dog. FIXIT must analyse the drying adhesives group carefully in order to determine whether it is worth the investment required to increase its market share.

The overall goal of this ranking is to help organisations decide which of their business units to fund and how much funding to put into them; and which units to sell.

SECTION B: STRATEGIC CHOICES

B2

STUDY GUIDE B2: ALTERNATIVE APPROACHES TO ACHIEVING COMPETITIVE ADVANTAGE

■ Get Through Intro

When starting a business or working for a company, it is important to understand on what basis you are competing. Is it price or is it on quality. Are you creating a premium brand, or do you not care about the brand, but just want to sell as many as possible? For instance, if you need to buy a matchbox or a lighter, would you ask for a particular brand? It is likely you would not. Hence most matchbox makers do not spend money on advertising and keep costs to a minimum. One of the major matchbox makers made a fortune by shaving about half a penny of the cost of a box of matches by only putting the fire strip on one side of the match box. On a product that at that time sold for 5 pence, it was a significant saving.

This chapter will explain to you what approaches you or your company may take, in order to be competitive. It will also explain the relative advantages and disadvantages. This will ensure that you can help your company meet its goals by ensuring you are one step ahead of the competition!

■ Learning Outcomes

a) Evaluate, through the strategy clock, generic strategy options available to an organisation.
b) Advise on how price-based strategies, differentiation and lock-in can help an organisation sustain its competitive advantage.
c) Explore how organisations can respond to hypercompetitive conditions.
d) Assess opportunities for improving competitiveness through collaboration.

Introduction

Case Study

An example of low cost

Ryanair was one of the world's first no frills airlines. Originally started by the Ryan family with a share capital of just £1, 1 plane, 1 route and 25 staff, the airline now has 5000 staff and 163 new aircraft (with 99 more planes already ordered), running over 713 routes.

RyanAir has always been known for its frugal behaviour and its appetite to cut costs where at all possible. This is necessary, according to the company, to maintain their position as a low cost airline and create the competitive advantage of offering flights at the lowest costs.

Michael O Leary, the Chief Executive is known for cutting all costs. He once famously said in an interview that he did not allow his staff to buy pens – he preferred them to go to stores like Argos (a catalogue store) where pens were freely available and pick them up for free!

In addition, according to the Guardian Newspaper, Ryanair does not let its staff charge their mobile phones in the office (saving 1.4p each charge) and it makes staff pay for their uniform, meals and training!

The above case study shows how one airline has really taken the meaning of cutting costs to the maximum level, in order to ensure it can offer fares at £1 for customers flying.

1. Evaluate, through the strategy clock, generic strategy options available to an organisation.[3]

[Learning Outcome a]

1.1 Strategy clock

The strategy clock was developed by Cliff Bowman. It is an extension of Porter's generic strategy model. Like Porter, Bowman considered competitive advantage in relation to cost advantage or differentiation advantage. According to the strategy clock, an organisation can achieve competitive advantage by **satisfying the customer needs better than the competitors**.

Customers have the opportunity to select suppliers from which they will purchase the products on the basis of cost benefit analysis, i.e. by analysing how much benefit they will receive in return for paying a certain amount of money (and also other inputs such as their time spent on the purchasing process).

The strategy clock represents different positions adopted by customers on the basis of selling price and perceived benefits. The most important aspect considered in all strategies is the organisation's cost (compared to competitors).

The strategy clock is depicted as follows:

Diagram 1: The strategy clock

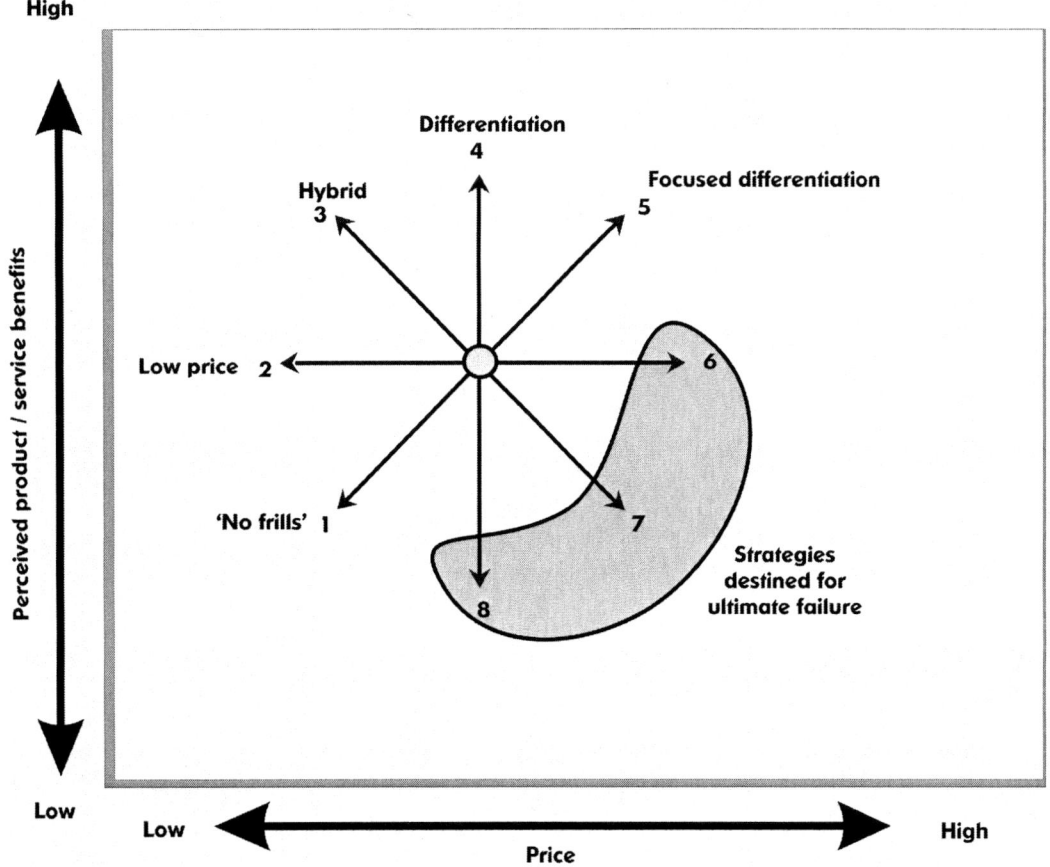

The **numbers** in the diagram above indicate the **positions of the customers** in the market. It is essential to recognise the **critical success factors** in each position of the clock. The two axes considered in the clock are price and perceived (apparent) product / service benefits. The positions in brief are:

➢ **Positions 1 and 2 – No frills and low price** respectively - low price and low perceived benefits (position 1): customers are very concerned with the price. This is the position (1) where low price is the main consideration. This may happen in a market which deals in commodities (commodities are goods and services where it is very hard to differentiate, e.g., glass, aluminium, steel, sugar beet etc). Position 2 gives comparatively more importance to perceived benefits than position 1.

➢ **Position 3 – Hybrid -** low price and high perceived benefits: the strategy aims to provide higher benefits to customers than competitors at low price. This position is a combination of differentiation and low price.

➢ **Position 4 – Differentiation strategies:** the aim of this strategy is to provide better products or services than competitors at the same or higher prices. This is usually achieved by offering a different product or service benefit that is desired by the customer; marketers sometimes refer to these differences as **Unique Selling Points** (USPs)..

➢ **Position 5 – Focused differentiation:** this strategy aims to provide higher benefits to customers but at a higher price. These products are called premium products and the extra profit that accrues is referred to as a price premium. These are marketed to a specific segment (niche) of the market.

➢ **Position 6, 7 and 8 – Failure strategies:** these strategies result in providing lower benefits to customers at higher prices and are destined to fail as they produce unattractive cost benefits ratios for the customer.

Each position in the clock is explained in detail below.

1. **Price-based strategies (Positions 1 and 2)**

a) **A 'no frills' strategy** is a strategy whereby the **prices are very low** and the **benefits to the customers are also very low**. The target customers are very conscious of the prices.

Features of the strategy

i. This strategy is a useful strategy for a commodity-like market. Customers purchase products from a supplier who can provide benefits at lower prices. So, 'money' is the crucial factor in assessing competitive advantages.

Example

Suzy has bought a new house and wishes to buy a range of appliances including a refrigerator, a dishwasher, a washing machine and a television. She wants to purchase all the items at low prices.

Jackson Ltd and Michael Plc are two dealers in household appliances. They have both been operating in the market for many years. In recent months, many new entrants have established their firms in the market.

Jackson Ltd is an organisation which possesses managers with excellent strategic skills. In response to the new entrants in the market, its managers decided to follow a strategy of reducing the prices by lowering the costs of the products.

On the other hand, Michael Ltd followed the strategy of improving the product quality and providing more benefits by increasing the prices.

Here, as Suzy is interested in purchasing all her requirements at low prices, she will prefer to buy the appliances from Jackson Ltd. the strategy followed by Jackson Ltd is a 'no frills' strategy.

ii. The customers may be not willing to pay more to obtain better perceived benefits. There may be cases where customers are not able to pay more. These types of customers are very sensitive to price elasticity.
iii. This type of strategy is a helpful tool for market entry. New entrants can enter the market at low prices.
iv. It is a challenging task to build customer loyalty because customers may move to competitors if prices are increased by suppliers.

Example

For the airline industry, European low cost no frills airlines are an example of a no frills strategy.

After 11th September 2001, the airline industry suffered tremendously. The prices of tickets reduced considerably. Many of the airlines suffered heavily, especially flagship carriers (national airlines) e.g. Swiss air. Generally, they had cut costs to the maximum possible extent.

However, the airlines which followed a low cost strategy coped admirably with the problems and actually ended up gaining customer confidence. Ryan air and Easy jet have generally remained cost-effective and are operating at their fullest capacity. These airlines have managed to function offering low fares by reducing their cost to a minimum. At present, to withstand competition in the market, the airline industry has had to manage itself by lowering their costs as far as possible.

Ryanair has adopted a strategy of no frills which resulted not only in reducing the members of cabin crew but has also managed quicker pre-flight groundwork, on top of continuously reducing fares for passengers.

b) **A low price strategy** aims to provide **better perceived benefits** as compared to competitors and charge **lower prices** than competitors. It may give rise to a price war in the market amongst the competitors and, in turn, may lead to a reduction in the profit margins.

When a business unit decides to adopt a low price strategy, it may do so in two different ways:

i. It may enter a market where **competitors are not attracted**. As a result, the unit does not have to worry about the price. An attractive profit margin is therefore likely.
ii. It may enter a market segment where there are **many competitors** competing on the basis of prices. Pressure on profit margins is therefore likely.

There are many challenges involved in applying a low price strategy:
➤ A low price strategy results in price reduction because, to survive in the market, the organisation will have to reduce its profit margin.
➤ Reducing prices is not an easy task. In order to reduce prices, organisations first have to **reduce costs**. Moreover, the costs should be reduced in such a way that competitors are unable to acquire knowledge about the method of cost reduction.

The third position in the strategy clock is a hybrid strategy. To understand this strategy, it is first necessary to understand the meaning of a differentiation strategy.

2. Differentiation strategy (Position 4)

This strategy aims to provide **better products or services** than competitors at **relatively higher prices** or at the **same prices**. In addition, the organisation's aim is to gain a competitive advantage by providing perceived **benefits** that are **different** from those provided by its competitors. Differentiation can be achieved through many different methods including marketing, branding, advertising, core competences and enhancing product features and benefits. It should be noted here that the customers do not buy features; they buy benefits.

An organisation should recognise the scope of its competitors in the market. This is because knowing competitors' scope will help the organisation to make choices as to how it should differentiate itself for the benefit of customers. The art of differentiation strategy involves understanding the customer needs; finding out which of those needs are not yet offered in the market; using core competences and skills to satisfy those needs and thus taking a price premium.

Example

BMW is an example of an organisation which has followed a differentiation strategy. BMW serves a comparatively wide range of the total market but its cars are differentiated in the eyes of the customers who are ready to pay a higher price for a BMW than for a Toyota, for instance, of similar specification.

BMW differentiates itself from the rest of the automobile market, by manufacturing cars with fine handling which offer a unique driving experience. New cars such as the Accura TL are often referenced in comparison to a BMW product that has set the standards. BMW has also maintained, besides its technical and luxury features, the category of its automobiles, which are large, luxury cars.

BMW produces a car that is unique in the speed, power and status it offers customers as compared to its competitors. Customers are attracted to BMW for its reputation for performance, handling, and enjoyable driving. The BMW name is synonymous with luxury, craftsmanship, and all round excellence.

In the past, BMW has carefully avoided the smaller car market. However, in recent years, BMW has opted to diversify its range to include the small to medium-sized car market.

3. Hybrid strategy (Position 3)

A hybrid strategy, as the name suggests, is a combination of two things. Specifically, a hybrid strategy is the **combination of differentiation and low prices strategies**. The strategy aims to achieve competitive advantage by providing **higher perceived benefits by lowering the prices**. This strategy aims to maintain differentiation by earning huge profits. There is the possibility of developing various differentiations i.e. new features in the products.

The benefits of hybrid strategy are as follows

a) If the markets for the products or services are larger than the competitors' markets, the profit margin can be increased to a greater extent.

b) This strategy is best suited to a situation where an organisation can differentiate and sell products at low prices. For example, if an organisation understands the needs of its customers and accordingly differentiates into the required area, it can gain from this strategy by lowering the cost.

c) When an organisation desires to enter a market, it may do so by introducing a product which is not strongly sold by the competitors due to loopholes (drawbacks) in their operations. Here, the organisation should sell a better quality product than its competitors and, if possible, it should make every effort to lower its price. This strategy is applied by organisations which enter a new geographical area where competitors do not function effectively.

Organisations can achieve high quality at low prices by adopting just-in-time and total quality management systems.

i. Just-in-time

Just-in-time is an inventory control system that prevents the blockage of funds in inventory and reduces carrying costs. In JIT, items are procured as and when required i.e. 'just in time'. This leads to a reduction in storage space and costs. JIT helps organisations to achieve high quality, lowering the prices and provides the following benefits:

- It reduces the set up times in the factory.
- It reduces the carrying costs of the inventory.
- Highly skilled employees can be engaged in more challenging tasks.
- The reduction in costs may lead to reductions in the prices charged to the ultimate customers.

ii. Total quality management

Management comprises of planning, directing, organising, control and assurance. TQM is a tool to manage the total quality in an organisation. Thus, it is a management tool which controls the quality assurance in all managerial processes. It is a process which involves lowering prices and improving quality, resulting in customer satisfaction.

Example

Toyota, the Japanese car manufacturer, follows a hybrid strategy combining low cost production with cars which are differentiated on the basis of their quality and reliability. Toyota Motor Corporation is primarily engaged in business in the automotive industry. Toyota also conducts business in finance and other industries.

Toyota has three business segments: automotive operations, financial services operations and all other operations. The automotive operations include the manufacturing, designing, assembling and selling of passenger cars, recreational and sport utility vehicles and trucks. It also operates in accessories and related parts.

Toyota follows a combination of cost leadership and differentiation strategies where economies of scopes are relevant. A combined attention on both cost leadership and differentiation strategies is often required across the different segments of the value chain.

The production system of Toyota is considered the most efficient in the world. This efficiency enables Toyota to follow a low cost strategy in the global car industry. Moreover, Toyota has differentiated its cars from those of its competitors on the basis of high quality and advanced design. This superiority permits the company to charge a premium price for many of its famous models. Hence, Toyota seems to be following both a low cost and a differentiated business level strategy simultaneously.

4. Focused differentiation (Position 5)

This strategy aims to provide **higher benefits to customers at higher prices**. These products are called premium products. Organisations following this strategy concentrate in a specific segment of the market. They tend to satisfy unique customer needs and, try to build brand loyalty for the products in the market. Every organisation aims to accomplish the overall organisational goal. So, it is difficult to follow a focused strategy for **a part** of an organisation's overall strategy.

5. Failure strategies (Positions 6, 7 and 8)

These strategies are not beneficial to customers. There are **no perceived benefits** to the customers. The price is high and the perceived benefits are low. Adoption of these strategies will lead to the failure of the organisation.

- **Position 6**: the price is high as depicted in the clock above. There is **no corresponding increase in benefits**. This strategy is common in monopolies.

- **Position 7**: the price is higher than the competitors and there is a **reduction in perceived benefits** to the customers as compared to position 6.

- **Position 8**: there is a **higher reduction in perceived benefits** to the customers but the price is maintained. When organisations are following failure strategies, they try to leave the market (divest). In such a situation, public service organisations are attracted to enter the market as political forces desire to continue the services.

SUMMARY

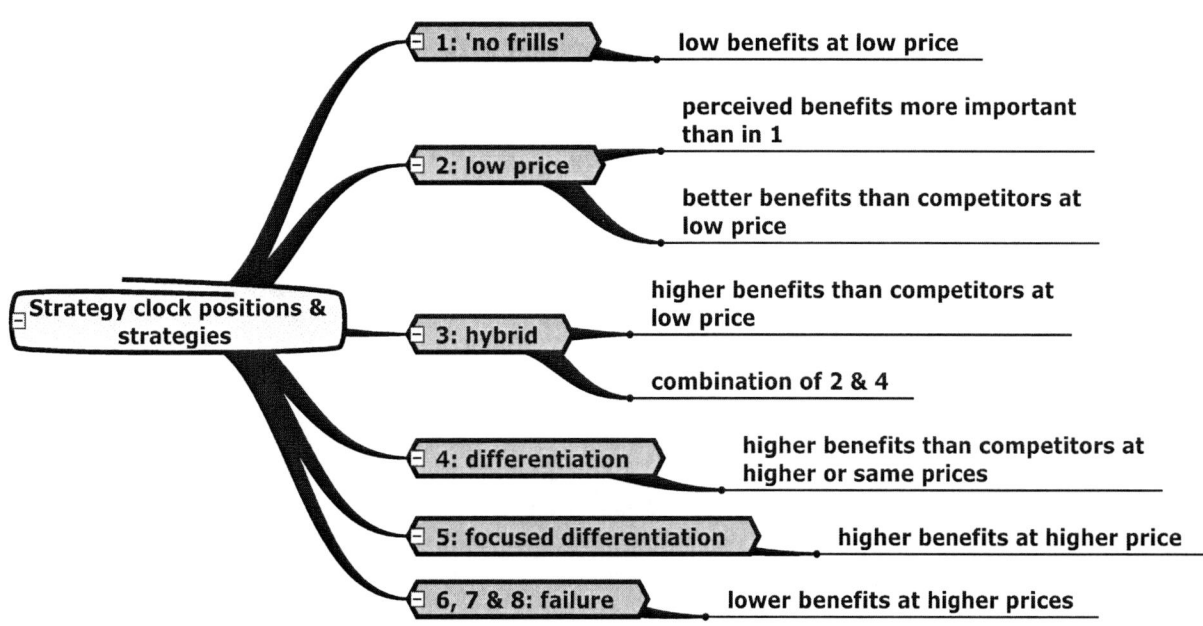

1.2 Generic strategy

According to Porter, an organisation can **achieve competitive advantage** through three generic strategies cost leadership, differentiation and focus (cost focus and differentiation focus). Achieving a competitive advantage means gaining an edge over competitors. Competitive advantage refers to the ways and means by which an organisation can increase its sales and earn higher profits compared to its competitors.

Diagram 2: Porter's generic strategies

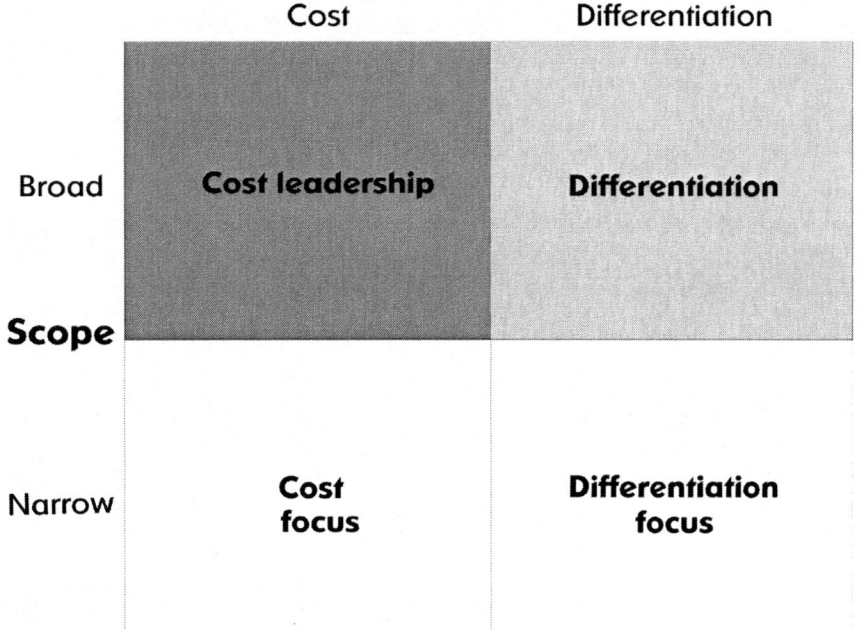

1. Cost leadership strategy

The organisation is the leader in the industry or market in terms of cost. A competitive advantage is gained by reducing the cost to the organisation. It is essential that the organisation attempts to have the lowest cost base in the industry because only producing the products at a **low price is not sufficient** to gain the advantage. The products should also be produced at the **lowest cost**.. However, if the technique of cost reduction becomes known to competitors, they can also apply this technique to produce at low cost.

Tip

This strategy emphasises the reduction of the **cost to the organisation** of producing and delivering products or services. It is not concerned with the price paid by the customers.

The cost can be reduced by the organisation in the following ways:
- using cheap labour
- using advanced technologies to increase production
- reducing overhead expenses incurred on production
- reducing cost by producing in large quantities i.e. economies of scale

Example

Wal-Mart has followed a cost leadership strategy from the inception of its business. It started its operations in 1962. Wal-Mart was founded by a determined entrepreneur, Sam Walton (Walton), who believed that retailing was a quantity-driven business and his company could grow and achieve goals only by offering better perceived value to its customers. Walton always tried to obtain products at the lowest possible prices from suppliers. During the first two decades, Wal-Mart established discount stores in small towns and tried to gain control over a significant market share.

In the year 1980, the company made heavy investments in information technology to improve its supply chain and tried to expand its scope of operations into bigger cities. When the company realised that the discount stores business was developing at a good pace, in the late 1980s, it decided to enter into the business of food retailing by introducing supercentres.

In the late 1990s, the company launched exclusive grocery shops and chemists in the US, which were commonly known as 'neighbourhood markets'. With its expansion into grocery shops and chemists, the company faced a lot of criticism from competitors regarding its strategies.

Wal-Mart followed the strategy of low cost. It gave the benefits of this strategy to its customers by charging them lower prices and providing them with the maximum perceived benefits for their money. A technical analysis of companies clarifies that Wal-Mart's products were usually priced 20% lower than those of its competitors. Wal-Mart earned brand loyalty from rural customers as it provided good quality products at lower prices compared to competitors in the market. The company followed the strategy of earning higher profits by selling in huge volumes.

Efficiency and economies of scale are the two key factors which form the basis of Wal-Mart's strategy. Wal-Mart has earned a reputation as a supplier of high quality products at the lowest price in the market. In this way, the company eliminates competitors from the market and improves revenues and market share.

---

2. **Differentiation strategy**

The organisation aims to produce products which are **different** from those produced by its competitors **and are unique**. However, differentiation is only worthwhile if the difference is desired by customers. The products may be developed in terms of their features, durability or functioning.

The organisation may achieve successful differentiation by:
- incorporating new facilities into the product
- emphasising better research and development
- improving marketing, branding and advertising facilities to make customers aware of the new features provided by the products.

The **Garvin model** is a quality model. It can be applied to the differentiation strategy. This model shows the relationship between quality and performance. According to Garvin, "quality is defined from the point of view of customers." There are various **dimensions** of the quality of a product including performance, features, reliability, conformance, durability, serviceability, aesthetics and perceived quality.

a) **Performance:** the general characteristics of the product are satisfactory to the customers. The organisation provides superior products which include advanced features to its customers.

b) **Features:** the product possesses "extra" features on top of the basic features, which provide enhanced facilities to the customers.

c) **Reliability:** the customers can assume that the product is of good quality and will operate for a specific number of years.

d) **Conformance:** the product is produced or the service is provided according to the design specified by the customer i.e. the organisation produces the product according to pre-established standards.

e) **Durability:** the organisation provides products which last for a reasonable duration of time.

f) **Serviceability:** this refers to the ease with which the customers may obtain various services. The service quality depends upon the following features:

- **courtesy** i.e. how the employees treat the customer
- **timeliness** i.e. whether or not the task given by the customer is completed on time
- **completeness** i.e. whether or not the customer receives what they desire
- **accuracy** i.e. whether or not the task is completed perfectly as demanded by the customer
- **consistency** i.e. whether or not the services provided to the customers are consistent
- **convenience** i.e. whether or not the services are provided according to the comfort of the customers

g) **Aesthetics:** the physical features of the product are attractive and of good quality e.g. appearance and sound.

h) **Perceived quality:** the customers expect that the product should be safe to use i.e. it should not cause any harm or injury to the user.

The Garvin model emphasises that improving the reliability and conformance of a product results in a reduction in service costs, scrap costs and manufacturing costs which leads to better productivity and ultimately higher profits.

3. **Focus strategy**

The organisation concentrates on only **one market segment or niche**. There are two types of focus strategies i.e. a cost focus strategy and a differentiation focus strategy. Organisations can produce low-priced and specified goods for customers. Concentrating on a particular niche area enables them to build brand loyalty.

If an organisation decides to apply a focus strategy it will have to choose between cost focus and differentiation focus. While using cost or differentiation focus, the most important consideration is whether the strategy is beneficial to the niche area.

Example

Martin-Brower follows a focus strategy. An organisation that follows a focus strategy concentrates on satisfying the specialised needs of its customers. Products and services can be designed to suit the requirements of the customers.

An approach to focusing is to service either industrial buyers or consumers, but not both. Martin-Brower, the third-largest food distributor in the United States, serves only the eight leading fast-food chains. With its limited customer list, Martin-Brower need only stock a limited product line; its ordering procedures are adjusted to match those of its customers; and its warehouses are located so as to be convenient to customers.

Example

Another example of differentiation focus is Morgan sports cars. They are one of the UK's largest established Sportscar manufacturers. They provide all types of services including sales, repairs, after sales services and provision of accessories. They appeal to a very narrow segment: primarily middle age but wealthy consumers with a sporty outlook.

a) **Cost focus:** the strategy to be applied where the organisation is a **cost leader** in a **particular market segment**.

b) **Differentiation focus:** the organisation applies the strategy of **differentiation** in a **particular market segment**.

The focus strategy has many advantages and disadvantages. The advantages include:

- **Closer to customer:** as the organisations produce at low prices and in accordance with customers' needs, the organisations are very close to the customers. The needs of the customers are given special attention and the products required by them are provided to them with ease.
- **Targeted marketing:** the focus strategy aims to concentrate on only one market segment. This concentration on a particular niche area enables the organisation to build strong brand loyalty in the market and offer outstanding customer care.

The disadvantages for an organisation of following a focus strategy are as follows:

- **Limited economy of scale:** as the focus is on a particular market segment, the economy of scale is limited to that segment only.
- If, due to environmental factors, the niche disappears, then the organisation loses a wide range of customers on which its business depended.

SUMMARY

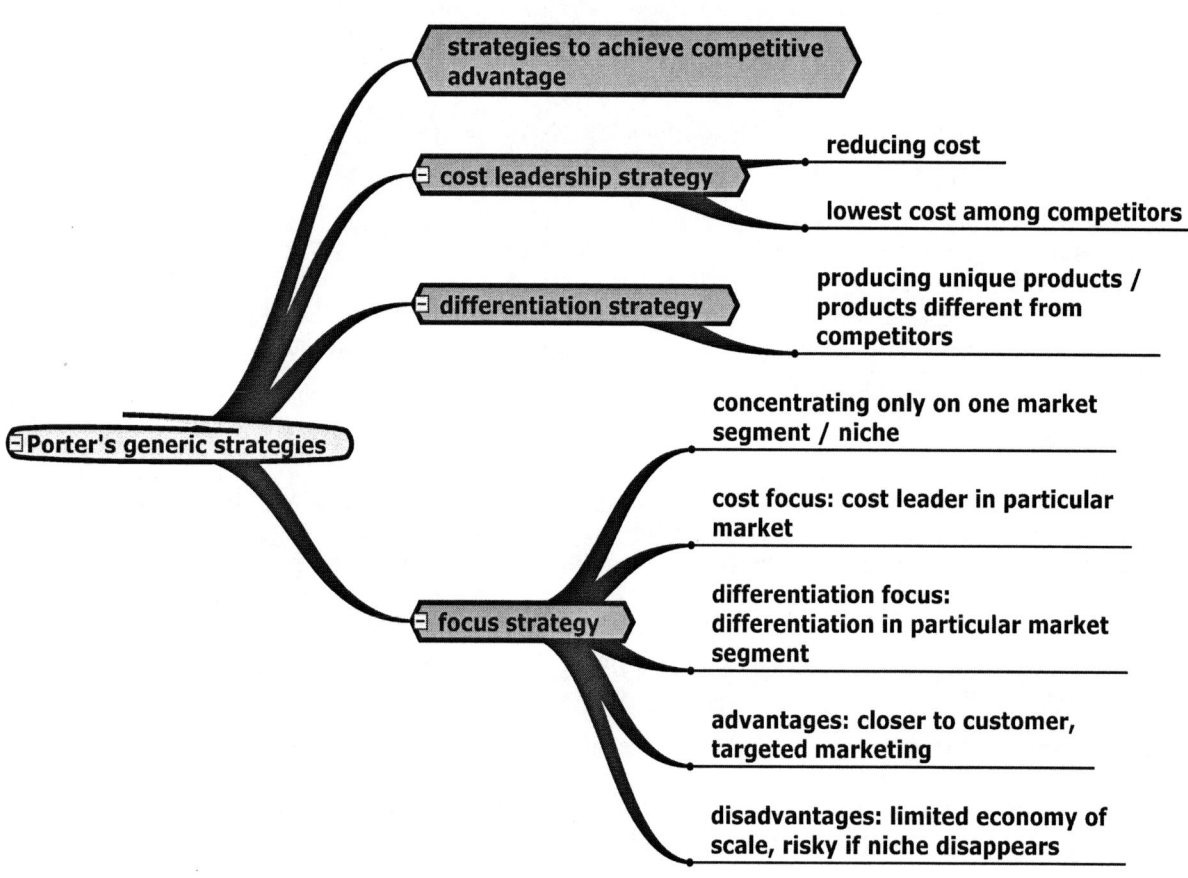

1.3 Choice of strategy

Selection of an appropriate strategy is essential for an organisation because all the other strategic decisions depend upon the type of strategy applied. The selection of strategy should take into consideration the strengths and weaknesses of the organisation. Different strategies have different essential requirements e.g. a cost leadership strategy requires complete knowledge and awareness of the organisation's operations and future plans. A differentiation strategy, on the other hand, requires specialisation and creativity in an organisation.

Test Yourself 1

Cherry Delight Ltd is a newly started ice cream producing company. There are several established ice cream brands in the market. The company has decided to enter the market by offering its products at prices lower than its competitors with the help of effective cost control techniques. Moreover the ice cream flavours being produced by the company are completely different from any of the flavours produced by established ice cream producers.

Required:

State the kind of strategy from the strategy clock which is being followed by Cherry Delight Ltd.

2. Advise on how price-based strategies, differentiation and lock-in can help an organisation sustain its competitive advantage.[3]

[Learning Outcome b]

2.1 What is a competitive advantage?

Definition

Hill and Jones defined competitive advantage as "a '**profit rate**' that is higher than the average".

When an organisation earns profit which **exceeds the average** for that industry, the organisation possesses a competitive advantage over other organisations. An important issue here is **sustaining the competitive advantage**. 'Sustain' means to maintain over time. Organisations aim to achieve sustainable competitive advantages. Competitive advantages lead to better value for an organisation's customers and higher profits for the organisation itself and may be generated / created using core competences, capabilities or resources.

2.2 Price-based strategies and sustainability of competitive advantage

Price-based strategies are mainly focused on the '**price**' element. An organisation is said to sustain competitive advantages when they offer the **same perceived benefits** as their rivals but **at a lower prices**.

1. An organisation may sustain competitive advantage by entering into '**price war**'. A price war refers to the strategy whereby the organisation reduces its price below that of its competitors. The organisation tries to lower costs to a level where competitors are unable to stay in the market. Price war is a **short-term strategy**. The competitor may respond by lowering its price even further and in this way a price war is waged. It is important to note here that to be successful in a price war, an organisation needs to have greater resources at its disposal compared to its competitors and that, ultimately, prices may go up once competitors are forced to leave.

2. An organisation may concentrate on those **market segments** where **low-price products** are in high demand. A disadvantage associated with a low price strategy is that, when customers find that the product has a low price, they may also assume that the quality of the product is low.

3. An organisation may **lower** its **margins**. Reduced margins refer to reductions in the prices charged to customers whereas the cost may be relatively high. Organisations accept such reduced margins because the lower margins are per head and therefore by increasing the volume of sales, they can increase their overall profitability. They can even increase their profitability by cross-subsidising i.e. by compensating for the loss of one business unit with the profits of another business unit.

4. An organisation may try to **lower its cost.** It may do this by applying advanced technologies, skilled labour, good quality raw materials etc. or by adopting innovative ideas. It should be careful to avoid wastage in the production process. To sustain the cost advantages, it is essential that competitors are not able to obtain the same benefits that may lead to a reduction in their cost of production.

Example

As a nation, it is very difficult to enter into a price war with China. China is best known for its low-cost manufacturing as a result of low wages. However, manufacturers in China are starting to focus on quality as a means of increasing their competitive advantage.

SUMMARY

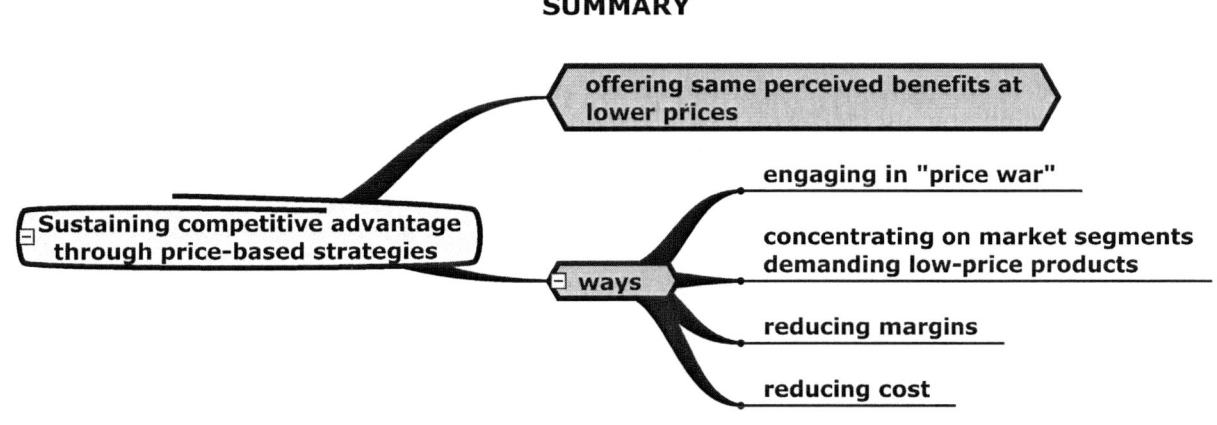

2.3 Differentiation strategies and sustainability of competitive advantage

Differentiation strategies are mainly focused on the **'product'** element. The kind of differentiation adopted by organisations may be different in different industries. Differentiation is of any advantage only if it creates **value** for the customers.

Differentiation can be related to the product itself, the after-sales services provided to the customers, the marketing techniques adopted, the delivery system etc. When product features are added, there is the possibility that the production, distribution or marketing costs may be higher than the costs for an undifferentiated product. So, the customer must be ready to pay a **higher price** in the case of differentiation. An organisation is said to sustain competitive advantages when it offers **better perceived benefits** as compared to competitor's products.

What are the conditions required to sustain competitive advantages through differentiation strategies?

1. The organisation should protect the **resources** that are important for the organisation to sustain differentiation advantages. Some of these resources, such as the innovative skills possessed by managers, should be preserved so that competitors do not obtain these resources. Competitors may offer attractive incentives to managers to encourage managers to join them. In this case, the organisation must prevent their resources from going to competitors.

    However, there are some resources which are difficult for competitors to obtain i.e. **immobile resources**. The organisation enjoys added advantages from these resources follows:

    a) When the organisation enters into a contract with a customer to provide some **specific services**, in this case the capabilities and the specialisations offered by the organisation to the customer cannot be easily taken by competitors.
    b) Sometimes the customer wants to obtain the product or service from a particular organisation only. He is unwilling for any other supplier to satisfy his demand. In this case, as the organisation has become an accredited supplier, the competitor cannot easily obtain the organisation's customers.
    c) The goodwill which an organisation possesses in the market cannot be easily obtained by competitors. In some cases, competitors propose to purchase the organisation to obtain the goodwill. Here also, the competitors cannot readily take advantage of the organisation's goodwill because customers will not rely on the new ownership easily.

2. **Imitation** may reduce the perceived (proposed) differences between the organisation's product and a competitor's product. If the competitor manages to incorporate the same features as the organisation's product, then the advantage cannot be sustained. So, organisations must add **those product features that are difficult for others to imitate**.

3. Organisation must be aware of **changes in the customer tastes**. The tastes in the current year might not be the same in the next year. The product must be differentiated on a **regular basis** "in accordance with the market trend otherwise competitors may take advantage of the fact that the organisation's products are outdated. The organisations must conduct market research programmes to keep themselves aware about the trend existing in the market. Also, the organisations should provide the customers with customer care services because these kinds of facilities add value to the organisation's product. The customer care department can solve the queries of the customers immediately without causing any trouble to the customer. These services are available to the customers at all time i.e. twenty-four hours.

4. Organisations must try to **reduce their costs** as compared to those of competitors. When cost is reduced, the possibility of earning good margins arises. The **surplus can be invested** in the products that need to be differentiated.

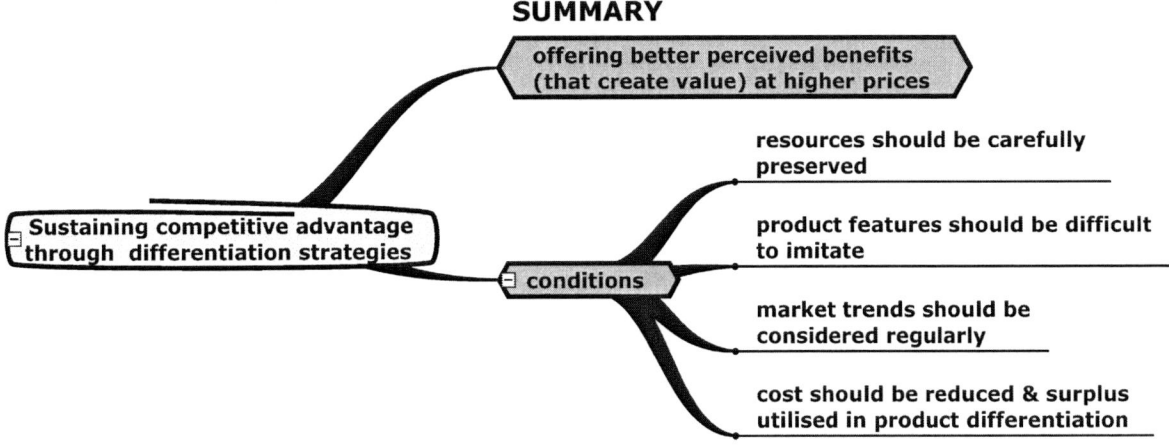

2.4 Lock-in strategies and sustainability of competitive advantage

The lock-in strategy is an idea originated by Arnoldo C. Hax and Dean L. Wilde. Lock-in is an approach towards sustaining competitive advantages for both price-based and differentiation strategies. Lock-in is a situation whereby the organisation's product is at the top position in an industry and it becomes an **industry standard**.

The lock-in strategy is also called the Delta model. The Delta model links strategy with execution by selecting a distinctive strategic position and then integrating it with a company's collective processes. An organisation's actions must be completely aligned with its strategic position, and the results must give feedback on adapting the strategy.

Factors affecting lock-in are as follows:

1. **First-mover advantage:** the industry standard is set when a new product is introduced in the market and not at the maturity of the product.

2. **Accurate enforcement:** when the product gains the position as an industry standard, competitors will try to attack this position and the organisation, in turn, will rigorously defend its standard position.

3. **Market dominance:** prospective competitors or other organisations will conform the industry standard if they believe that the standard setter has a significant market share in the industry.

4. **Own-reinforcement:** when an organisation obtains the position of industry standard, it is essential for the organisation to maintain its standards in order to remain at the top position in the market.

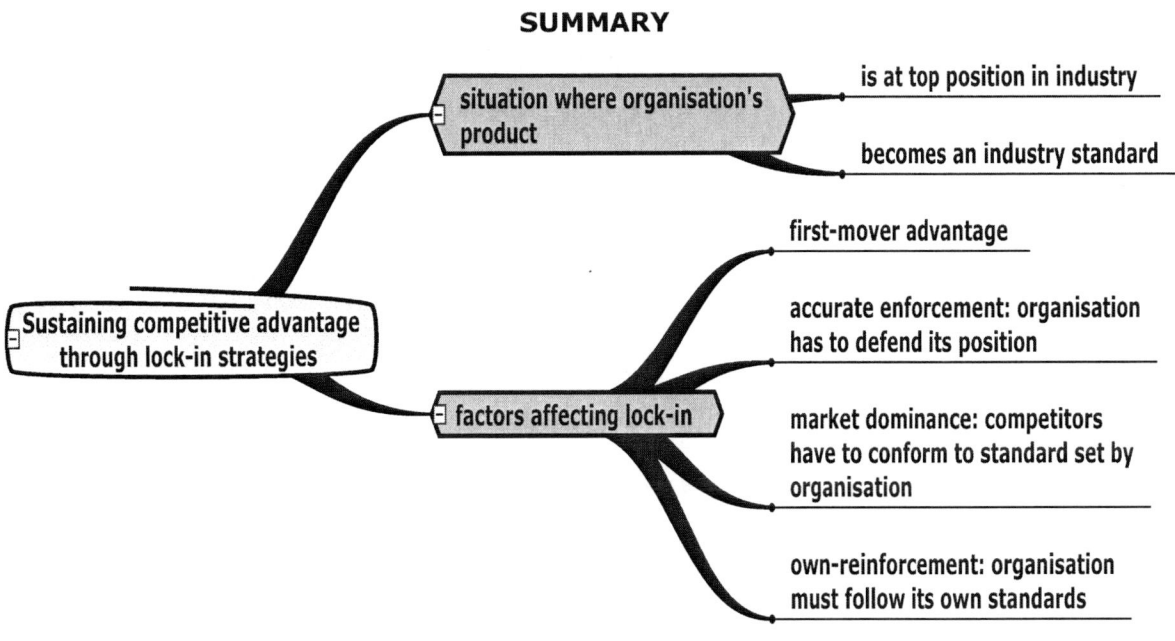

Test Yourself 2

Digi-Tech Corp is a multinational company providing customer-focused information technology and communications solutions. The company was a pioneer in developing video density technology (VDT). This technology is used to provide crystal-clear video quality for digital videos from the smallest amount of video data. VDT is Digi-Tech's best-selling product. The company has approximately 90% of the market share in the VDT market. Most of Digi-Tech's business comes from licensing VDT to electronics manufacturers operating throughout the globe. As the technology became successful, other IT companies tried to produce and market similar kinds of technology but found it difficult to break into the market. The few other companies that are operating in the VDT market have to consider Digi-Tech's standard while producing and marketing their product.

Required:

Identify the way in which Digi-Tech attempts to sustain a competitive advantage.

---

3. Explore how organisations can respond to hypercompetitive conditions.[2]
[Learning Outcome c]

3.1 What is hypercompetition?

Hypercompetition is a state of competition in which the level of competition is growing rapidly. In this fast-changing environment, it is impossible to sustain traditional advantages.

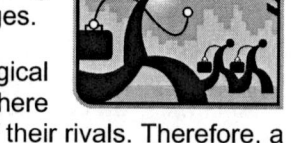

Hypercompetition is **high velocity competition** due to quick changes in the technological environment. Hypercompetition refers to strong and rapid competition moves, where competitors move quickly to obtain new advantages and to eradicate the advantages of their rivals. Therefore, a **fast-changing and growing** level of competition is called hypercompetition. When rapid development in technology is taking place, there may also be rapid development in product features. As a result, in hypercompetitive conditions, technology becomes outdated more quickly and therefore the product life cycle becomes shorter. This means that competitive advantages may not last for a long period of time.

Sustaining competitive advantages in normal competitive conditions has been discussed in the previous Learning Outcome. In the case of hypercompetitive conditions, competitive advantages will be of a **temporary nature**. Sustaining the advantages will be a matter of an organisation's capability and willingness to cope with the changing conditions in the environment. The organisation's capability will be in terms of flexibility, adaptability, creativity and speed.

Example

Hindustan Unilever Ltd, the Indian subsidiary of Unilever Ltd is a reputed company producing branded products in the consumer goods market. The company has various strengths including strong management processes and an attractive distribution chain that give it a competitive advantage over others.

In the last few years, companies like Hindustan Unilever Ltd have not been in a position to price their products on the basis of their own strategies. The prices of the products have been market-driven. However, HUL has managed to hold its position in the market because it has much strength and has taken great efforts to lower its costs throughout its supply chain.

3.2 Which strategies are to be followed in the case of hypercompetitive conditions?

The nature of the strategy to be followed in the case of hypercompetitive conditions depends upon the following:
➢ significant capabilities that the organisation possesses in terms of speed, flexibility, ability to change etc.
➢ the goals and core competences of an organisation

Diagram 3: Strategies in hypercompetitive conditions

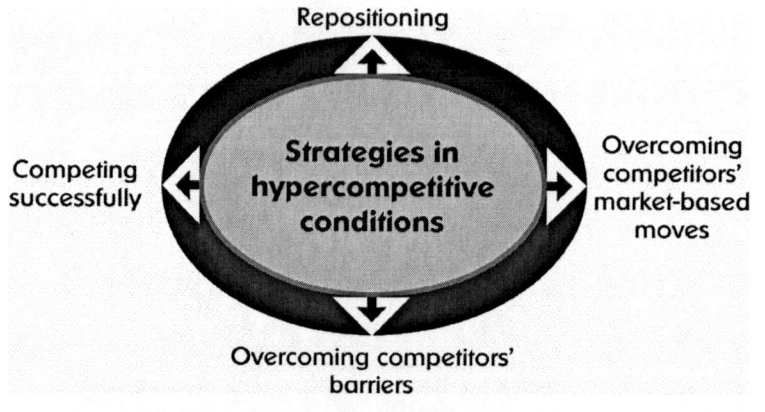

1. Repositioning

A repositioning strategy may be adopted to cope with hypercompetitive conditions. A repositioning strategy refers to **reconsidering the position on the strategy clock**. The positions on the strategy clock have been explained in detail in Learning Outcome 1.

If an organisation is positioned in position 1, i.e. the 'no frills' position, where both perceived benefits and prices are low, it can move towards position 2, i.e. the 'low price' position, where price is low but the perceived benefits are comparatively higher than in position 1. Furthermore, the organisation may take efforts to move towards the 'hybrid' position i.e. position 3 in the strategy clock where price is low but the perceived benefits are high.

There are some risks associated with the adoption of a repositioning strategy such as customer confusion and internal deficits. When an organisation lowers the price and simultaneously provides low perceived benefits and then, after some time, lowers the price further and provides higher benefits, this creates confusion among customers about the strategy followed by the organisation. There may also be the risk of internal deficit. This is because once the organisation lowers the price and provides perceived benefits to its customers, and then further lowers the price, it is possible that the organisation may incur financial deficits.

2. Overcoming competitors' market-based moves

a) The organisation may attempt to gain a competitive advantage by **preventing the first-movers** from dominating the market. Organisations may enter a market segment by following a 'no frills' strategy where price is low and the perceived benefits are also low. They may try to attract a small segment by offering low prices. Organisations may plan to capture market gradually by penetrating the market with a new product and block the advantages of the first-mover.

b) As, in the case of hypercompetitive conditions, the competition is moving very fast, organisations have to cope with competition at a higher speed. Another way of overcoming a competitor's market-based move is by copying the competitor's products. Here, copying refers to **imitating the products** produced by the competitor. So, organisation should produce the products with some better features incorporated in it.

3. Overcoming competitors' barrier

a) The organisation can gain an advantage over others through **economies of scale** in production. The organisation may try to produce in large quantities, which the new entrant would not be able to do due to a shortage of funds. The new entrant won't have the capacity to compete with the organisation. In this situation, the new entrant should make an attempt to develop interest in customers in the home market first and then gradually grow globally.

b) When there are **technological advancements**, there may be rapid developments in product features. The **product life cycle becomes shorter** because the technology quickly becomes outdated in hypercompetitive conditions. This means that competitive advantages may not last for a long period.

The organisation may try to control the market by blocking new entrants through building **strong entry barriers**. For example, an organisation may patent its products or build a relationship with its suppliers which enable it to obtain raw materials at a lower price than its competitors. In this situation, competitors may try to attract customers by providing facilities to the customers either at **low price or free of cost**.

c) Competition may be overcome through a **price war**. Competitors may try to **reduce prices** below the price prevailing in the market to gain a competitive advantage and attract customers.

Example

Enjoy More Ltd has been producing mobile phones for the last ten years. It has a huge market share and a good reputation. In recent years, some competitors have started to produce mobile phones which allow users to take photos and to access the internet.

Enjoy More Ltd has to produce mobile phones with camera and internet facilities in order to meet the demands of the market. Due to technological advancements, mobile phones without these facilities have become outdated.

4. Elements of successful hypercompetitive strategies

In the introductory paragraph, it is mentioned that a characteristic of hypercompetitive conditions is rapid change. As a result, organisations have to be capable of changing their strategies according to the conditions prevailing in the market.

a) The organisation must always try to **improve / develop its products** in terms of features, quality, durability etc.
b) The organisation **should not imitate** its competitors. It should have its own innovative ideas for production.
c) The organisation **should not attack** the competitor's weaknesses because this may make a competitor aware of its strengths and weaknesses and, in turn, may assist the competitor to frame or modify its future strategies to its advantage.
d) The organisation **should not disclose its future strategies** otherwise competitors will be able to frame their strategy accordingly. Hence the results of the strategies may not be as predicted.

SUMMARY

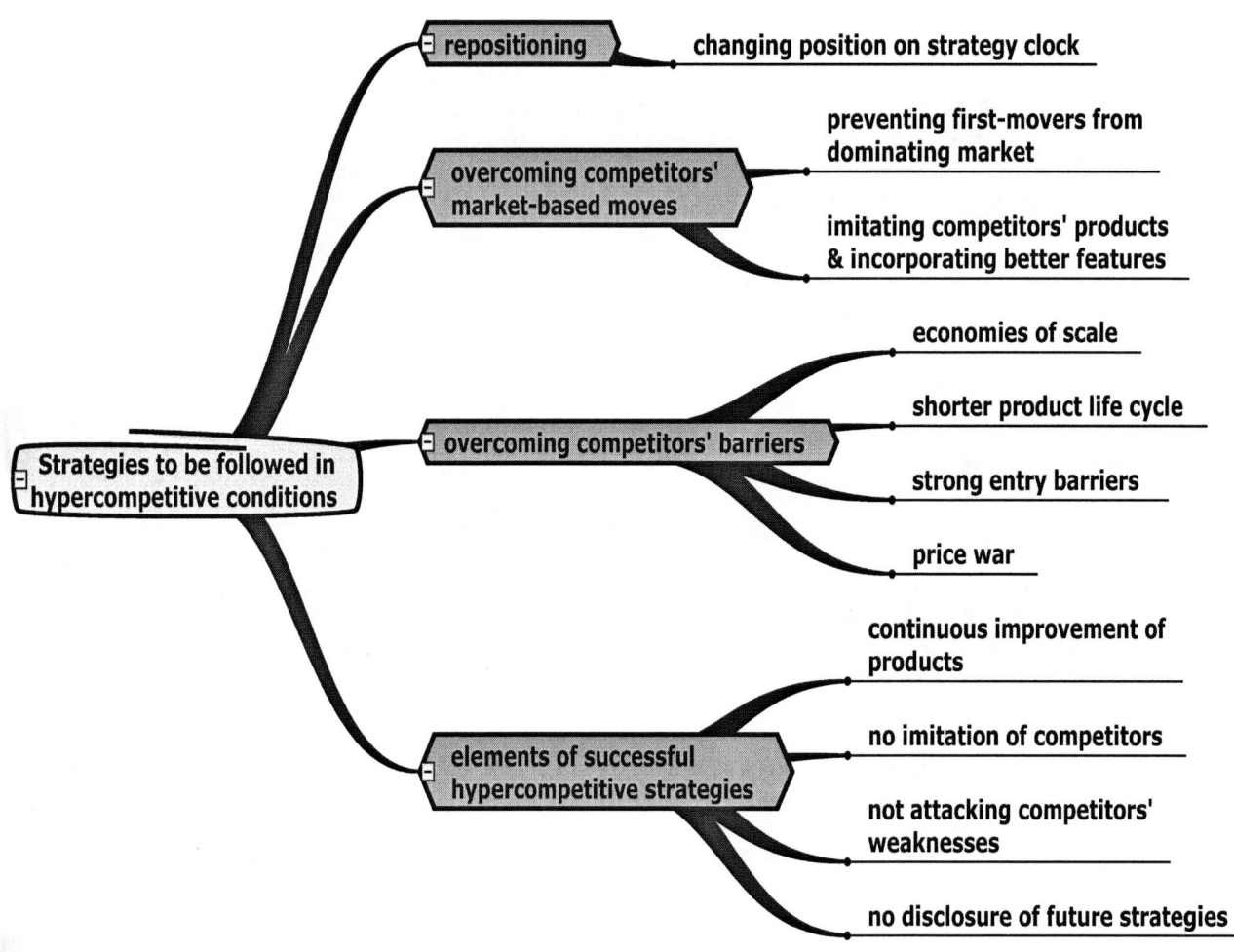

Test Yourself 3

Angel Ltd is a leading manufacturer of skin and hair care products for women such as soaps, lotions, shampoo and body wash. Angel's products are high quality products made from pure natural ingredients and with minimum usage of chemicals. The prices charged by Angel are higher than those charged by its competitors who do not make as much use of natural ingredients in their products. Recently, the company has started to lose its competitive advantage due to increased levels of competition, a fast-changing business environment and aggressive moves by its competitors.

Required:

Explain how Angel Ltd can respond to these conditions through repositioning.

4. Assess opportunities for improving competitiveness through collaboration.[3]
[Learning Outcome d]

4.1 What is collaboration?

Collaboration is when two or more organisations come together to cooperate with each other in order to **pursue mutual objectives**. Collaboration is a **strategic option** which provides assistance to the organisation in achieving its goals. Collaboration is beneficial to the organisation if the costs of purchase of business are less than the costs of self-operation.

Definition
Strategic alliances

Pyka and Windrum define a strategic alliance as being a "cooperative agreement between two or more autonomous firms pursuing common objectives or working towards solving common problems through a period of sustained interaction".

Examples of strategic alliances include research and development coalitions, marketing and distribution agreements and franchising.

An organisation will typically join forces with another organisation(s) and form a strategic alliance when it wants to enter a particular industry or market with a particular type of product / service but does not, individually, have all the required resources and/or competences.

Therefore, through a strategic alliance, an organisation changes its structure in order to achieve its objective of being able to deliver a particular product / service. It is of vital importance that the organisation effectively manages its relationships with the other organisation(s) participating in the strategic alliance.

Example
Eurofighter project

Four nations (Germany, Italy, Spain and the UK) signed a contract in December 2004 to produce Eurofighter Typhoon, the world's most advanced swing-role combat aircraft. This strategic alliance will enable Germany, Italy, Spain and the UK to meet the demands of their air forces by combining their expertise in cutting-edge electronics and computing.

Collaboration should not be confused with outsourcing. Outsourcing aims to obtain products or services at a cheaper rate than producing these goods/services in-house. Collaboration aims to share knowledge, capabilities and risks amongst different organisations.

4.2 Opportunities for improving competitiveness through collaboration

Collaboration improves the competitiveness of organisations in the following ways:

1. **Increasing buying power:** purchasing large quantities requires huge funds. When small retailers desire to purchase larger quantities, they may do so by collaborating with others.

2. **Increasing selling power:** while purchasing any products, quality is of the utmost importance. When the buyer has confidence that the supplier will supply a good quality product, the buyer and seller may collaborate with each other for the supply of the product. Hence, the seller may increase its selling power. The collaboration may make it possible to design new products and may also lead to a large reduction in research costs.

3. **Low risk of substitution:** in a market, organisations always have a fear of substitute products. If an organisation is unable to satisfy the customer needs, its competitors will try to produce a substitute product. When an organisation collaborates with another organisation, the organisations may combine their funds for research and development to make the product more sophisticated and in line with the needs of the customer. In this way, collaboration may help to prevent substitution in the market and overcome competition.

4. **Sharing of knowledge:** two organisations collaborate to achieve a mutual goal. These organisations possess managers with different skills and capabilities. In this situation, knowledge may be shared between the two organisations. The sharing of knowledge may give rise to innovative ideas for use in product development and product innovation.

5. **Increase in building entry barriers:** when organisations collaborate, they share their operational and technical knowledge. In doing so, they gain the potential to satisfy customer needs. Sometimes new entrants in the market may try to attract the customers of the organisations. In this situation, the collaborated organisations will try to build barriers for the new entrants so that they are forced to leave the market. In this way, competition is reduced through collaboration.

6. **Introduction in new markets:** sometimes organisations collaborate to enter into a new market. It may be the case that an organisation wants to expand its scope geographically. This is possible only when it has knowledge of the conditions of the geographical area into which it wants to expand. To enter a market, an organisation requires knowledge, skill and competences. It can gain knowledge from an organisation that is already in existence in the particular market. Thus, collaboration also increases the economies of scale in operations.

In some cases, the government itself induces organisations to collaborate with other organisations. In the case of development in the area of information systems, infrastructure facilities etc., it is advantageous for two organisations to collaborate and operate together so that they can share their knowledge and expertise in their respective fields.

Diagram 4: Collaboration and competitiveness

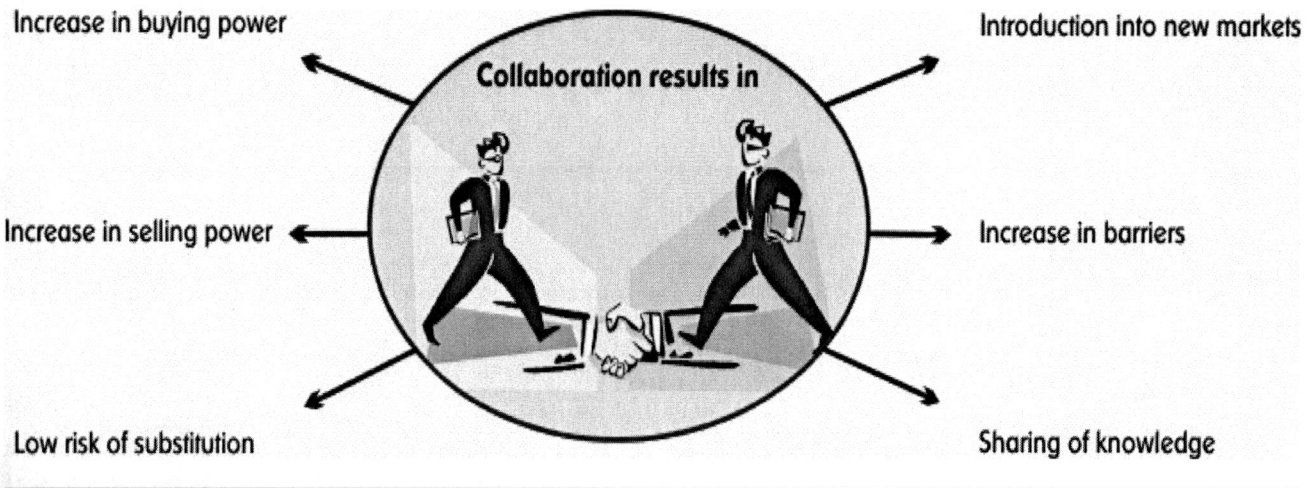

Example

Collaboration between Sony Ericsson and Google

Sony Ericsson Mobile Communications entered into a deal with Google to integrate the search engine company's blogger and web search into Sony Ericsson mobile phones. When the phones are pre-loaded with the software, subscribers to Blogger.com can update their personal blogs from their mobile phones.

Nowadays, people use the internet very often. When a mobile phone offers internet facilities, more and more customers are attracted to it. By providing Google services in its phones, the Sony Ericsson team offers a quick and easy way for customers to blog and thereby attracts more customers to its phones.

The collaboration between Sony Ericsson and Google makes Google web search the standard search engine for all Sony Ericsson phones. The search is highly customised and allows searches from within any page being browsed on the phone.

SUMMARY

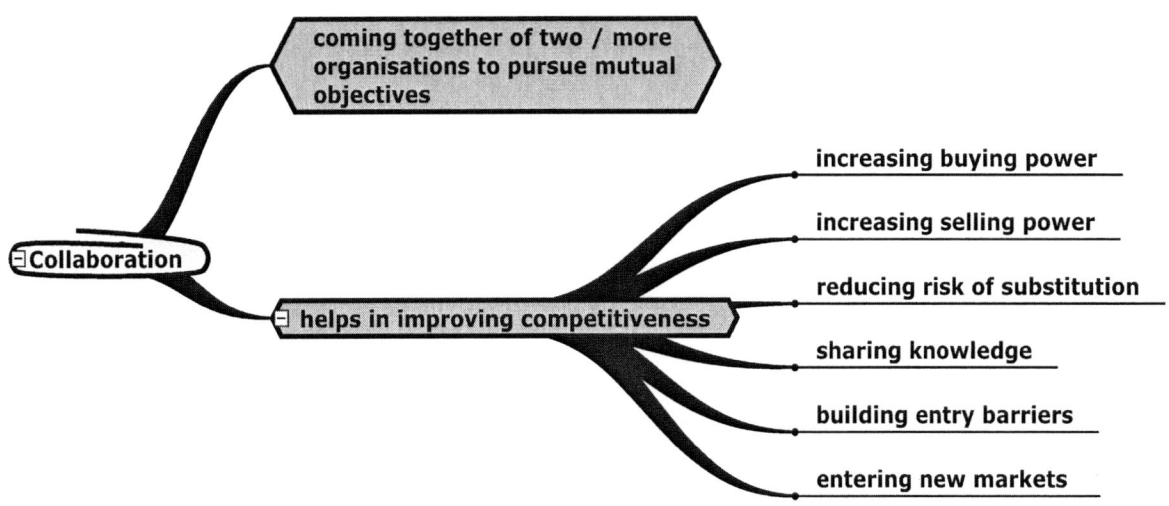

Test Yourself 4

Auto Suppliers Alliance is a trade association of manufacturers who supply transmission system devices to automobile manufacturers. The association was primarily established for the purpose of trade promotion and upgrading of technology. Recently the market for transmission system components has been very competitive due to an increase in outsourcing from automobile manufacturers. Existing automobile components suppliers are facing fierce competition from new entrants. A significant number of new entrants are likely to enter the industry in the near future.

Required:

Explain how collaboration can help the automobile components suppliers to cope with increased competition from new entrants.

Answers to Test Yourself

Answer to TY 1

Cherry Delight has adopted a hybrid strategy. It is at position 3 on the strategy clock. A hybrid strategy is an optimal balance between price and the added value perceived by the customer. A hybrid strategy seeks to achieve differentiation and a price lower than that of competitors simultaneously. In a differentiation strategy, an organisation produces a product that is perceived to be unique in the market. Cherry Delight's products are unique as the flavours being offered by it are different from those offered by its competitors. In addition, the company aims to keep its prices lower than its competitors with the help of cost control techniques. Therefore the company seeks to achieve differentiation together with a reduction in prices.

Answer to TY 2

Digi-Tech attempts to sustain a competitive advantage through lock-in. In the case of lock-in, an organisation becomes an industry standard. Lock-in is a position whereby the prospective competitors and other organisations have to conform to the standard in order to grow in the industry. Therefore, the other companies operating in the VDT market have to relate to Digi-Tech's standard while producing and marketing their product.

Digi-Tech was a pioneer in developing VDT, its best-selling product. The company has a monopoly in the VDT market. Other organisations are not able to break into the VDT market. Digi-Tech became the industry standard for VDT by achieving a lock-in position. This is evident from the fact that the efficiency of the products of Digi-Tech's competitors is judged against the standard set by Digi-Tech.

Answer to TY 3

Angel Ltd is currently facing hypercompetitive conditions. It can sustain its competitive advantage and respond to these conditions by following the repositioning strategy i.e. by changing its position on the strategy clock.

The company is currently following a differentiation strategy. The perceived benefits from Angel's products are better and different from those of its competitors and the price charged is relatively high. However, the company will not be able to sustain a competitive advantage in hypercompetitive conditions with this strategy. Angel Ltd can change its competitive strategy from differentiation (position 4) to hybrid (position 3). A hybrid strategy aims to provide higher perceived benefits while lowering prices. Angel Ltd is already providing high perceived benefits to its customers. In order to sustain its competitive advantage, it also needs to reduce its prices.

Answer to TY 4

Automobile components suppliers are facing a threat from new entrants. Collaboration can help them to reduce competitive pressure from new entrants. For example, Auto Suppliers Alliance can reduce competitive pressure by building barriers to entry. Entry barriers are the factors that prevent a new organisation from entering the industry. In addition:

➢ Existing organisations can collaborate to invest heavily in research and development so as to produce high technology components that can be produced by only those organisations with access to that technology. It can also help organisations to reduce their per unit cost.

➢ Auto Suppliers Alliance can set stringent technical standards and make it mandatory for any manufacturer operating in the industry to meet these standards.

➢ Auto Suppliers Alliance can build close links with automobile manufacturers so as to make arrangements that only members of the association are authorised to supply components to automobile manufacturers.

➢ Existing organisations in collaboration may adopt predatory pricing policies by lowering prices to a level that would force new entrants to operate at a loss.

Quick Quiz

1. A hybrid strategy is a combination of _____ and _____ strategies.

   A. differentiation and low price
   B. low price and no frills
   C. differentiation and no frills
   D. focused differentiation and differentiation

2. What is meant by competitive advantage? Is it necessary to sustain it? If yes, why?

3. What is meant by lock-in? State the factors affecting a lock-in strategy.

4. What are the strategies that can be followed in hypercompetitive conditions?

5. Organisations collaborate to make their product more sophisticated and in line with the needs of the customer so as to reduce the risk of _____.

Answers to Quick Quiz

1.
   A differentiation and low price

2. When an organisation earns profit exceeding the average profits for that industry, it is said to have a competitive advantage over other competitors. Yes, it is essential to sustain a competitive advantage because a competitive advantage leads to the creation of better value for an organisation's customers and higher profits for the organisation itself.

3. Lock-in is a situation where the organisation's product is at the top position in an industry and it becomes an **industry standard**. The lock-in strategy is also called the Delta model. The factors affecting lock-in are:

   ➢ first-mover advantage
   ➢ accurate enforcement
   ➢ market dominance
   ➢ own-reinforcement

4. Repositioning, Overcoming competitors' market-based moves, Overcoming competitors' barriers, Competing successfully

5. Substitution.

Self Examination Questions

Question 1

(a) Premium Electronics Corp manufactures a range of consumer electronics products including television sets, refrigerators, CD / DVD players and washing machines. Although there are many big players in the consumer electronics market, Premium Electronics is able to gain a competitive advantage due to its brand image. The company is known for its innovative products that provide new convenience, features or benefits to consumers through technology. The company is also known for its excellent after-sales service which none of its competitors is currently providing. Hence consumers prefer to buy Premium Electronics' products even though its prices are slightly higher than its competitors.

(b) Spicy-Bite Plc is a chain of fast-food restaurants primarily selling burgers, sandwiches, breakfast items, cold drinks, milkshakes and desserts. There are several similar fast-food restaurants competing with Spicy-Bite, however Spicy-Bite is known for providing good quality food at a low price. The company has a significant share in the fast food market. Spicy-Bite's business success depends on its low cost base. Its restaurants are very basic, located in low rent areas and offer a standardised menu. Spicy-Bite positions itself as a high volume, low cost, low margin fast-food restaurant chain.

Required:

Identify the types of strategies that are being followed by Premium Electronics Corp and Spicy-Bite Plc.

Question 2

Ryan Brandon is the managing director of Aircon Plc, a medium-sized company, manufacturing and marketing central heating and air-conditioning systems. Aircon manufactures and installs building control systems and has a strong reputation within the European market. About 70% of Aircon's sales are focused on the industrial and business sectors with the remainder going to the household consumer.

In the last few years, the market within Europe has been very difficult. The recession has curtailed new industrial and commercial building projects and competition is becoming increasingly dictated by price. Ryan believes that future growth will not be strong in Europe but that South-East Asia offers the most attractive opportunities. Ryan has the approval of the management team (and the financial support) to develop an entry strategy into South East Asia.

Fresh-Care Ltd is a medium-sized company, based in one of the South-East Asian countries, that manufactures air conditioning systems for businesses and households. The company has a good network and presence throughout South East Asia. The committee appointed by Ryan suggested collaborating with Fresh-Care as an effective entry strategy.

Required:

Explain how the collaboration with Fresh-Care would help Aircon. In addition, state what the possible difficulties in such collaboration could be.

Answers to Self Examination Questions

Answer to SEQ 1

(a) Premium Electronics follows a differentiation strategy. The company's aim is to achieve a competitive advantage by offering better products at higher prices. The features that Premium's products offer are different from those of its competitors. The company adds enough value to the product to justify its relatively high price. Premium Electronics also offers superior after-sales service. Consumers are prepared to pay a higher price as Premium's products are differentiated in the eyes of the consumers and are widely valued by them.

(b) Spicy-Bite follows a low-price strategy. It provides good quality fast-food items at low prices. Its low price strategy is supported by a low cost base. Spicy-Bite's products are basic and are produced at a relatively low cost and made available to a very large customer base. By producing high volumes of standardised products, the company takes advantage of economies of scale. Although its prices are low, Spicy-Bite preserves a reasonable margin by keeping cost low.

Answer to SEQ 2

Collaboration is a business relationship between two or more organisations whereby they share resources, capabilities and activities to pursue a set of mutual goals while remaining independent organisations. Collaboration enables organisations to gain competitive advantage through sharing of resources, including products, distribution channels, markets, technologies, people, manufacturing capabilities, project funding, capital equipment, knowledge, expertise and intellectual property.

The entry strategy of collaboration with Fresh-Care will be helpful to Aircon in the following manner:

- Aircon can achieve expansion in South East Asia more rapidly through using the manufacturing plant and distribution network of Fresh-Care, which is already in place. This expansion will also require less initial capital outlay.

- Aircon can access the distribution channels and market presence of Fresh-Care in South East Asia.

- Aircon can gain local market knowledge from Fresh-Care. Aircon can make use of Fresh-Care's market expertise as the trading customs, culture and the general external environment in South East Asia will be considerably different to that of Europe.

- Aircon can increase its brand awareness in South East Asia through Aircon's channels.

- Buyers, governments and other critical influencers will prefer to deal with a joint venture company rather than with an exclusively foreign supplier.

The possible difficulties or problems involved with the collaboration could be as follows:

- There may be disputes concerning pricing strategies, particularly inter-company transfers which might be used to minimise tax liabilities.

- There may be disputes regarding sharing of resources.

- The skills, experiences and cultures of Aircon will be different than those of Fresh-Care. There may be difficulties in learning and understanding the cultural differences between the companies.

- There may be differences in the corporate objectives and dividend payout policies of Aircon and Fresh-Care.

- Aircon may work with an organisation which does not have the manufacturing expertise or quality standards which might be considered essential.

- Fresh-Care may desire to adopt a reinvestment policy whereas Aircon may wish to repatriate a larger level of profits.

- Aircon will lose flexibility and autonomy in decision-making.

SECTION B: STRATEGIC CHOICES

B3

STUDY GUIDE B3: ALTERNATIVE DIRECTIONS AND METHODS OF DEVELOPMENT

■ Get Through Intro

Imagine that you have a successful upmarket clothing manufacturing and selling business in Romania. You export to Europe and to the United States of America, but you realise that a huge potential market for you is Asia. You have no idea about Asia and no idea how to set up. You have researched the market and identified Japan as a country which has high disposable income and a taste for your style of clothing. You have a number of options for expansion. You could send a trusty member of staff out to Japan to look at setting up an office for you. Alternatively, you could try to find an agent out there. You do realise that the Japanese are slimmer and smaller than their American counterparts too. So you could also perhaps find a local manufacturing company which could potentially manufacture your designs, whilst adjusting for the height and weight differences to the Americans!

Whatever your decision, you have to make sure the decision is suitable for your company, acceptable to the stakeholders and feasible financially/operationally. If not, you are heading for problems!

So many options are open to you. Which will you choose? This chapter will help you decide what will be the right decision for your company and why it would be so.

■ Learning Outcomes

a) Determine generic development directions (employing an adapted Ansoff matrix and a TOWS matrix) available to an organisation.
b) Assess how internal development, mergers, acquisitions and strategic alliances can be used as different methods of pursuing a chosen strategic direction.
c) Establish success criteria to assist in the choice of a strategic direction and method (strategic options).
d) Assess the suitability of different strategic options to an organisation.
e) Assess the feasibility of different strategic options to an organisation.
f) Establish the acceptability of strategic options to an organisation through analysing risk and return on investment.

Introduction

Case Study

Toyota – a company that tries everything

Toyota, the motor company, is not averse to trying different forms of relationships, depending what suits its strategy best.

For example, it formed a joint venture with China's biggest automaker and began production of Toyota's Prius hybrid cars in China. The joint venture, Sichuan FAW Toyota Motor Co was the first time the model had been produced outside Japan.

In 2005, Toyota also formed a strategic alliance with Fuji Heavy Industries – the makers of Subaru, which according to the Asian Wall Street Journal was to ensure increased capacities at some plants in the USA and also to have Subaru send engineers to Toyota in Japan to coordinate production capabilities.

However, Toyota is not averse to expanding by itself either. In Canada, the USA and Brazil, Toyota has opened its own plants which are producing huge numbers of cars for the local markets. The latest in June 2008, was the announcement of a $1 billion second car plant in Brazil, which will produce over 200,000 cars per year, in addition to engines. The plant would be ready in 2010.

The above case study should show you that it is possible for 1 company to have many different ways of tackling different markets. Where it needed internal expertise and in order to meet regulations (China), it formed a joint venture. Where less red tape existed and a clear need for products, Toyota built its own plants. Where it lacked expertise in a certain area, it formed a strategic alliance.

Hopefully you will be able to identify the best route in the exam, using this example and the rest of the chapter!

1. Determine generic development directions (employing an adapted Ansoff matrix and a TOWS matrix) available to an organisation.[2]

[Learning Outcome a]

As mentioned previously the strategy that an organisation decides upon and subsequently follows can be thought of as a **"bridge"** that will help enable it to go from **"where I am now"** to **"where I want to be in the future"**. Therefore at the most fundamental level the concept of strategy comprises of two components:

- **setting the direction** an organisation should be taking (i.e. what types of products / services it should be offering); and

- **choosing the method(s)** the organisation should be employing (i.e. how it should go about producing and marketing its goods / services)

The main factor that determines the type of strategy an organisation chooses is what Johnson, Scholes and Whittington label as being **"motives"**. They further explain that there are three basic types of motives:

1. Environment based motives	Here an organisation formulates its strategy in response to changes in the external business environment. An example here could be an automobile manufacturer deciding to produce hybrid cars in response to society's growing concern over the environment.
2. Capability based motives	Here an organisation formulates and bases its strategy around its competencies and resources. An example here would be an organisation that manufactures computer screens decides to use its resources and capabilities to also start manufacturing televisions.
3. Expectation based motives	Here an organisation arrives at a strategy as a response to the expectations that have been placed on it by important stakeholders. An example here would be of an organisation that expands its manufacturing facilities to increase production output by 20 percent because its shareholders expect sales of the organisation to increase by this amount.

Therefore as can be seen the motive behind an organisation's strategy will set what Johnson, Scholes and Whittington label as being its "development directions".

Definition

Development directions are "the strategic options available to an organisation, in terms of p coverage".

In addition to deciding upon its goods / services mix, organisations must also decide upon how they will go about delivering these products.

There are two management tools / techniques an organisation can use to decide upon its development directions and the methods it will have to utilise to get to its intended destination. These are;

- the **Ansoff matrix** and
- the **TOWS matrix**.

1. The Ansoff matrix

The Ansoff matrix was developed to help organisations decide upon the type of products it should be developing and for which markets and segments. It is important to note that the term products and services, is used to denote any item intended for sale to a customer and markets, the total number of potential customers. This matrix is in essence a pictorial representation of the strategic options available to an organisation and can be used to help decide upon their strategic choices (i.e. what goods / services to offer and to whom).

Diagram 1: The Ansoff Matrix

	Existing Products	New Products
Existing Markets	Market Penetration	Product Development
New Markets	Market Development	Diversification

As the above diagram depicts, there exists four possible product / market combinations or strategic options available to an organisation. These are:
- market penetration
- product development
- market development
- diversification

a) A **market penetration strategy** is followed when an organisation uses its existing product suite to increase sales and profitability. It does this by either "poaching" customers away from competitors and / or increasing sales levels from existing customers. Common tactics associated with this type of strategy include advertising, price cutting, product revisions, etc.

b) **Product development** occurs when an organisation develops a new product(s) to sell to its existing customer base. This is also known as switch selling. An example of switch selling is when a bank tries to sell personal loans to its existing retail clients who have a personal savings account with the bank. It is important to note here that this strategy calls for the product to be either entirely new or an existing one that has been very significantly modified or improved. Simply adding additional features to an existing product does not qualify as product development.

) The **market development strategy** occurs when an organisation finds an entirely new market segment for its existing products. Existing products must be targeted towards and launched to an entirely new customer base for the organisation. An example of this is when a company decides to focus more on internet selling than retail selling

d) **Diversification** is when an organisation moves into entirely new products and markets. In other words it occurs when an organisation develops an entirely new product and markets it to an entirely new customer base. Diversifications can be either a related diversification (where the newly developed product bears some connection / similarity to the organisation's existing product suite or to its core competencies or an unrelated diversification (which is risky).

Example

Bank1 is a large and traditional multinational bank that offers a comprehensive range of financial services such as personal banking, corporate banking, trade finance and treasury. Bank1 wants to select a strategy that would result in an increase in both sales and profitability (to meet their shareholders' expectations). Using the Ansoff matrix, Bank1 identifies the following four strategic choices that are available to the organisation:

Market penetration: To assign a relationship manager to all of the bank's high networth personal and corporate clients. The primary duty of the relationship manager would be to extract more business (increase "walletshare") from each customer.

Market development: To open branches in countries / cities where Bank1 does not already have a presence.

Product development: To introduce lease financing as an alternative to customers who are interested in obtaining car loans from the bank.

Diversification: To launch a wholly owned subsidiary that will engage in investment banking and venture capital financing activities

2. **The TOWS matrix**

As mentioned previously organisations can use a SWOT (strengths, weaknesses, opportunities and threats) analysis to identify their current strategic position. As a next step an organisation can then use a TOWS matrix as pictured below to help identify strategies that will capitalise on their strengths and opportunities and / or mitigate against their weaknesses and threats

Diagram 2: The TOWS matrix

External Factors (Opportunities & Threats) \ Internal Factors (Strenghs & Weaknesses)	Strenghs (S)	Weaknesses (W)
Opportunities (O)	SO Strategies	WO Strategies
Threats (T)	ST Stretegies	WT Strategies

A TOWS matrix is a technique designed to help an organisation match its **internal strengths** and **weaknesses** to the **threats** and **opportunities** that are present in its **external environment**. This matching helps an organisation to identify and choose from the strategic choices at is disposal.

There are four main types of strategic choices that an organisation can choose from. These four are:

➢ Strengths and Opportunities (SO) strategies

➢ Strengths and Threats (ST) strategies

- Weaknesses and Opportunities (WO) strategies
- Weaknesses and Threats (WT) strategies

With an SO strategy an organisation focuses on how it can use its existing **strengths to capitalise** on opportunities that exist in the external environment. This represents the ultimate position organisations wish to be in as all major weaknesses and threats have been mitigated against. The remaining three strategies can be viewed as "stepping stone" strategies that will help an organisation to reach this position.

An ST strategy focuses on how existing strengths can be used to **mitigate against current or upcoming threats**. The obvious objective being for an organisation to be able to devise a strategy that will use its strengths to manage or even remove threats that it is facing.

With a WO strategy an organisation focuses on how it can **use opportunities** that have presented themselves in the **external environment** to overcome its existing weaknesses. With this type of strategy an organisation typically focuses on how it can overcome weaknesses that are preventing it from taking advantage of any present or upcoming opportunities.

A WT strategy focuses on **minimising existing weaknesses** so as to help protect an organisation from current and anticipated threats. Organisations employing this strategy are typically in a very weak competitive position and may even be fighting for their survival.

Example

Tech1 is an organisation that manufactures and markets mainframe computers. It recently conducted a SWOT analysis and identified the following:

Strengths: Highly motivated and technically competent sales force.

Weaknesses: Designs of existing products are all over three years old.

Opportunities: The government is set to introduce a tax break for organisations that purchase mainframe computers.

Threats: A number of micro computer manufacturers are planning to start manufacturing mainframe computers.

Using the above information, management of Tech1 come up with the following strategic choices:

SO Strategy: To increase the incentive payments it makes to its salespersons to encourage them to market even more aggressively to take advantage of the increased demand for mainframe computers that should arise out of the government tax break.

ST Strategy: To offer various innovative financing schemes (e.g. zero percent down and payments to be made in monthly instalments) which its sales force will aggressively market to existing and potential customers to help minimise the threat of them buying from a new entrant organisation.

WO Strategy: To have the R&D department work in collaboration with the sales force to quickly arrive at a new mainframe computer design that is in line with current market demands and tastes.

WT Strategy: To design a new mainframe computer so as to be better prepared to compete against the new entrants when they enter the mainframe market.

SUMMARY

Test Yourself 1

Drywear is an organisation that manufactures and sells wet suits designed for scuba divers. The organisation realises that it is operating in a mature market but would still like to increase sales and profitability. It therefore reduces the prices of all its products and makes this fact known to all customers through an advertising campaign.

Required:

Which one of Ansoff's strategic options has Drywear chosen?

---

2. Assess how internal development, mergers, acquisitions and strategic alliances can be used as different methods of pursuing a chosen strategic direction.[3]

[Learning Outcome b]

As mentioned before, the strategy of an organisation will comprise of two components: **direction** and **method**. Direction represents the types of goods / services an organisation has decided to produce and for which markets. Method represents the way the organisation will go about producing its selected goods / services. There are three basic methods available to an organisation:

➢ internal development
➢ mergers and acquisitions
➢ strategic alliances

1. Internal development

With the internal development method an organisation will use its existing resources and competencies to produce its **newly targeted goods / services**. However if the organisation does not currently possess the needed resources and competencies it must go about developing / acquiring them.

Example

LLT Manufacturers is an organisation that designs and manufactures high end leather handbags. Based on the success LLT has enjoyed in recent years, management decides to also start designing and manufacturing leather shoes that will match their handbags. However management realises that their current designers do not have the capabilities and experience to design shoes. Management must then either train their current designers or hire new ones who have the capabilities and experience needed.

Internal development is also often referred to as organic development and represents the most common strategic method organisations employ to move forward. Reasons for this include:

a) many organisations believe developing their products / services themselves better prepares and positions them to market the same more effectively

b) marketing their goods / services directly (instead of using intermediaries such as agents) in turn better positions an organisation to understand the tastes and demands of their customers

c) Inadequate resources for acquisitions or inability to identify suitable organisations to form alliances with

d) Internal development though a much slower development method avoids organisations having to deal with issues of compatibility that arise out of both mergers and alliances

2. Mergers and acquisitions

As mentioned above, the internal development route is a relatively slow way for an organisation to obtain the **resources / competencies** it needs. This coupled with the existence of a rapidly and continually changing external environment leads many organisations to pursue the mergers and acquisitions route. An acquisition occurs when one organisation buys over and takes ownership of all the resources (and consequently capabilities) of another organisation. A merger occurs when two organisations pool all their resources (and consequently capabilities) together into a newly combined third entity.

Therefore mergers and acquisitions represent a much faster strategic method for organisations to obtain the resources and capabilities they need. They also offer the potential for management to create additional value by creating synergies between the acquiring organisation and the target organisation. In addition, often the key resources of an organisation will consist of intangible assets (e.g. brand name, reputation in the marketplace) which are difficult if not impossible for another organisation to replicate. Mergers and acquisitions therefore represent a way that these unique resources can be obtained.

An organisation will initiate a merger or acquisition either to consolidate or diversify its present position. Consolidation mergers / acquisitions are carried out because an organisation wants to strengthen its current market position. The underlying rationale being that the new combined entity due to its larger size and organisational power should be able to gain advantages such as increased bargaining power over suppliers and achieve operating synergies and economies of scope.

Example

BT Discs and KT Discs are two organisations that manufacture blank compact discs. The organisations are of a similar size and produce approximately 1 million discs per year. After merging, the new entity of BKT Discs is able to produce 2.5 million discs a year as the production methods both organisations use get amalgamated into a more efficient and effective new process. In addition, given that BKT buys raw materials in greater bulk sizes it is able to negotiate a 10 percent discount from all its suppliers enabling it to sell its compact discs at a cheaper price and gain market share.

Diversification mergers / acquisitions are carried out because an organisation wants to branch out its current market position and expand its products / services offer mix. The main motives behind a diversification merger / acquisition is to reap benefits such as:

- being able to offer their customers a different products / services mix
- obtaining a revenue stream from a different source
- acquiring a different set of resources and competencies
- achieving economies of scope

Example

BOW Enterprises is an organisation that manufacturers fuel injection valves. These valves are the organisation's only product and can be only used in petrol engines. BOW wishes to diversify its position and enter the diesel energy industry. Therefore they decide to acquire KOW Enterprises an organisation that makes turbo chargers (a component that is used in diesel engines). Once the acquisition is finalised BOW will be able to service both the petrol and diesel engine markets.

However despite the motives behind them, all mergers and acquisition have several barriers to overcome if they are going to create synergies and ultimately value. These include incorporating two different sets of human resources, work cultures and work processes into one entity. In addition the two organisations also have to develop ways that they can learn from each other to successfully adopt each other's best practices (and other lessons learned from their respective experience curves).

3. Strategic Alliances

Definition

Johnson, Scholes and Whittington state that a strategic alliance occurs when "two or more organisations share resources and activities to pursue a strategy".

It typically occurs when two or more organisations want to enter a particular industry or market with a particular type of good / service but do not individually have all the needed resources and / or competences.

One of the main types of a **strategic alliance** is a **joint venture**. Here the participating organisations remain independent of each other and instead form a jointly owned special purpose firm. The resources and work each participating organisation is then expected to contribute is explicitly spelled out and formally agreed upon.

Example

Life1 is an American organisation that manufacturers soaps, deodorants and other personal care products. The organisation wants to be able to service the Chinese market but does not have the necessary local presence or knowledge to do so. Therefore it enters into a joint venture with a local company calling the new organisation LifeChina. Life1 will provide LifeChina with all the necessary products which will then be marketed and sold by the sales force and distributors of their local partner.

Another type of a strategic alliance is a **network**. A network occurs when two or more organisations agree to work upon a particular activity in collaboration. Co-branding is a common example of a network and occurs when a single product or service is associated with more than one organisation.

Example

The Senseo coffeemaker carries both the Philips (appliances) and Douwe Egberts (coffee) brands.

Other types of **strategic alliances** are franchising and subcontracting. McDonalds is an example of an organisation that works on the franchise business model. All corporate activities such as marketing and brand building are handled by the McDonalds organisation. The individual owner / operators of outlets (the franchisees) are responsible for all operations and running their individual outlets.

With subcontracting, an organisation typically contracts out part of its work / activities to another organisation. Subcontracting is a fairly common practice in the construction industry (e.g. construction of a building is done by one firm which then subcontracts out installing all the necessary wiring and electrical points to another organisation).

Motives or benefits for organisations to form strategic alliances include:

- the costs and risks of **producing a new good / service** can be shared
- the opportunity for each participating organisation to **concentrate on its core competencies**
- the opportunity for each organisation to **learn from the other participating organisations**
- the opportunity to gain entry into markets / industries that would other otherwise be inaccessible

SUMMARY

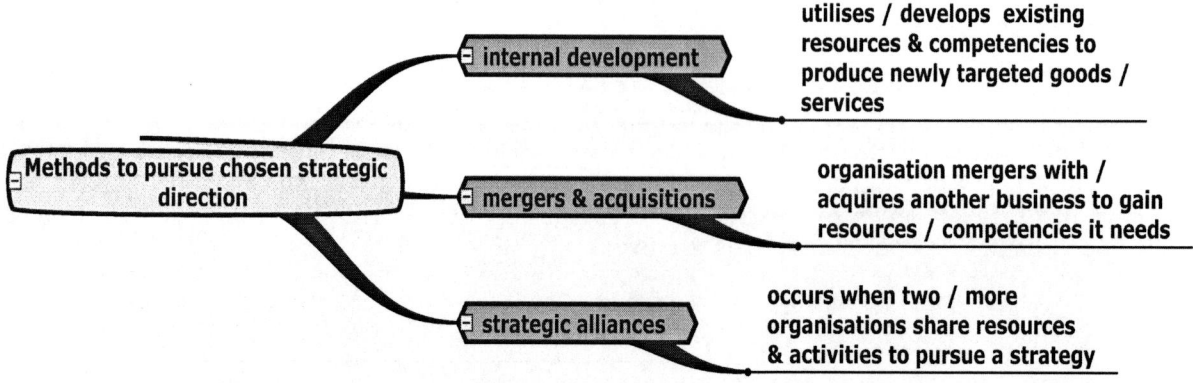

Test Yourself 2

AllBase is an American organisation that manufacturers and sells baseball equipment and apparel (bats, shoes, t-shirts, hats, etc). BasketB is also an American firm but manufactures and sells basketball equipment and apparel (balls, hoops, shoes, etc). Given the growing popularity of soccer, the organisations decide to combine forces and form a third organisation AB Sports that will produce soccer equipment and apparel. Employees from AllBase will be temporarily assigned to the new organisation to design and manufacture the products and employees from BasketB to do marketing and sales.

Required:

What type of arrangement is this?

---

3. **Establish success criteria to assist in the choice of a strategic direction and method (strategic options).**[2]
   Assess the suitability of different strategic options to an organisation.[3]
   Assess the feasibility of different strategic options to an organisation.[3]
   Establish the acceptability of strategic options to an organisation through analysing risk and return on investment.[3]

   [Learning Outcomes c, d, e and f]

Almost every organisation at some point will come to a "crossroads" or in other words be in a position where it has to choose from a number of strategic options. Each of these options will identify a certain strategic direction the organisation should be taking. Therefore organisations need tools that will help management to **evaluate the validity** of each of these choices.

These techniques basically involve the organisation examining each strategy from the perspective of how:

- beneficial the strategy is likely to be (e.g. how will it improve the financial condition and performance of the organisation)
- risky the strategy is likely to be (e.g. what are the potential consequences to the organisation if the strategy fails)
- likely the strategy is to succeed

Or in other words they establish a set of success criteria that a strategy should fulfil if it is to be adopted by an organisation. Johnson, Scholes and Whittington establish 3 main success criteria against which a proposed strategy should be measured. These are the **suitability**, **acceptability** and **feasibility criteria.**

The suitability criteria attempts to determine if the **proposed strategy addresses** and is relevant to the particular **circumstances an organisation is operating under**. An acceptability criteria attempts to determine **if the risk and return components** of the strategy are in line with the expectations of the organisation's important stakeholders. Lastly, the feasibility criteria attempts to determine whether the proposed **strategy is realistic in practice**.

Diagram 3: Success criteria for evaluating strategies

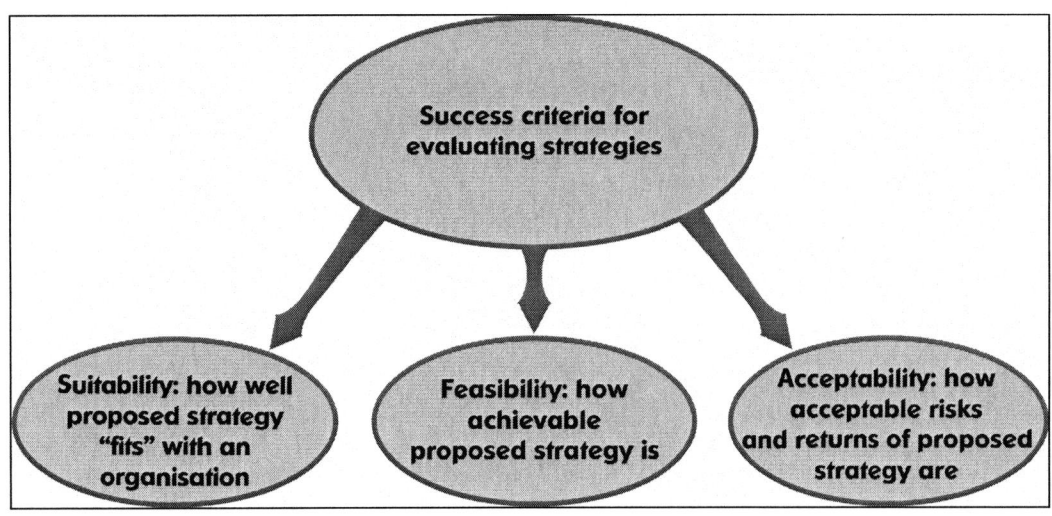

1. Suitability

As its name suggests the suitability criteria **attempts to assess** how well a proposed strategy fits in with an organisation. More specifically it examines the underlying rationale behind the strategy by asking questions such as:

➤ does the strategy address the circumstances / problems currently facing the organisation
➤ will the strategy enable the organisation to successfully adapt to expected changes in the external environment
➤ does the strategy take advantage of the organisation's strengths and / or mitigate its weaknesses
➤ will the strategy enable the organisation to capitalise on opportunities and / or mitigate against threats
➤ will the strategy enable the organisation to compete more efficiently and gain a competitive advantage

Overall it looks at whether the proposed strategy will enable the organisation to use its resources and capabilities to successfully adapt to the external environment and outperform its competitors.

2. Feasibility

The feasibility **criteria evaluates** a proposed strategy from the angle of whether an organisation has the resources and capabilities needed to implement it. In other words it attempts to determine how practical or even realistic a proposed strategy is.

Naturally one of the first and foremost resources that needs to be examined are finances to determine if the organisation has / will be able to obtain the financing the strategy needs. One method that can be used here is funds flow forecasting which involves determining the amount / type of funding a strategy will require and from where / when this funding will come. For instance if a particular strategy requires an organisation to purchase machinery, then the organisation needs to determine if it has the ready cash or whether it will be able to obtain a loan to purchase the needed machines.

In addition to examining resources such as finance and assets (e.g. does the organisation have the necessary infrastructure), organisation also need to look at their capabilities. More specifically organisations need to assess if they currently have the capabilities to meet at least the threshold requirements of the new product / service offering associated with the proposed strategy. These include looking at whether their human resources have the necessary skills and experience and if the organisation has the necessary processes / activities in place to produce the new goods / services.

Overall the feasibility approach involves an organisation asking itself if it has the necessary:

➤ funds / funding to carry out the strategy
➤ people and processes to carry out the strategy
➤ organisation structure, infrastructure and culture to carry out the strategy

3. Acceptability

The acceptability approach **focuses on the expected return** a proposed strategy will bring to an organisation in combination with the risks that will be faced in following the particular strategy. In other words it helps an organisation to determine if the returns following a proposed strategy promises justifying taking the risks that will correspondingly accompany it.

Therefore it involves assessing a strategy from the lens of:

➤ how attractive the expected returns (both financial and non financial) of the proposed strategy are
➤ how likely or possible is it for the organisation to achieve these returns
➤ how risky is the strategy (e.g. what are the possible consequences to the organisation if the strategy fails)

a) Returns

Returns can be thought of as the benefits that an organisation will derive from following a particular strategy. These benefits can be either financial in nature (e.g. increased sales / profitability) or non-financial (e.g. enhanced brand / reputation in the market place). Although there is no standard measure available to determine what constitutes an acceptable return there are certain tools / techniques available to help management in evaluating the acceptability of a proposed strategy.

One such method is looking at the ROCE (return on capital employed) of a proposed strategy. As the name suggests this method looks at how much an organisation would have to invest to follow a proposed strategy and what the expected payoff of following the strategy is expected to be. For instance, if a strategy required an investment of $100 and the expected payoff was $8 then the ROCE would be 8%. This technique allows management to either accept / reject proposed strategies by setting a "hurdle rate" (e.g. rejecting any strategy that does not offer a return of less than 8%).

Another method is to examine what the discounted cash flows of the proposed strategy would be. Discounted cash flows represent the revenues that are expected to be generated in future time periods (usually years). These flows are then "discounted" back to show what level of revenue they would be equivalent to in the current period. Again this technique allows management to set a "hurdle rate" (e.g. reject any strategy whose discounted cash flows are not greater than the revenue the organisation is currently earning).

Lastly, organisations should also look at what intangible benefits following a proposed strategy could be. For instance a proposed strategy may be to spend 10 percent of profits each year on training and development for employees. Although this strategy will not bring about any direct (and measurable) revenues it may bring non tangible benefits such as an increased commitment to the organisation by its employees.

b) Risks

The concept of risk on the other hand concerns itself with the probability and consequences of a proposed strategy failing. It is important to note here that just as in the case of returns, both the financial (e.g. reduced profitability or even losses) and non financial risks (damaged reputation / ruined brand name) of following a particular strategy need to be assessed. Again there is no standard measure available to determine what constitutes an acceptable risk but there are certain tools / techniques available to help management in evaluating the acceptability (in terms of risk) of a proposed strategy.

One method that can be used is a break even analysis. Here the organisation must assess the volume of sales (or other types of revenue) an organisation must be able to generate to payback the investment it has made in following a particular strategy. For instance if following a particular strategy requires $100,000 to spent on training its salesforce then the organisation must determine if it is realistic to expect its sales to also increase by at least $100,000. Alternatively, the discounted payback method can also be used.

Organisations also need to assess how following a particular strategy will affect its SOFP (balance sheet). More specifically they need to ascertain how it will affect their liquidity and leverage. Liquidity represents an organisation's ability to meet its short tem debt obligations (e.g. payments to suppliers). If a proposed strategy reduces the liquidity of an organisation, then there exists the risk that if the strategy does not bring about its proposed returns it may affect the ability of the organisation to continue operations.

Leverage represents the amount of debt an organisation has in relation to its net worth. The higher the leverage the higher the level of debt. Again the risk associated with strategies that increase an organisation's leverage is that if expected returns do not materialise then the organisation may not be able to service its debt requirements going forward and may have to cease operating.

Lastly, organisations also have to look at the non-financial risks associated with a strategy. For instance, a proposed strategy may call for an organisation to open a "call centre" or customer servicing department in India due to the cheaper operating costs. However taking this option may go against the "tide of public opinion" that feel that offshoring results in local job losses and damages the local economy which may in turn damage the organisation's reputation, goodwill and even sales.

SUMMARY

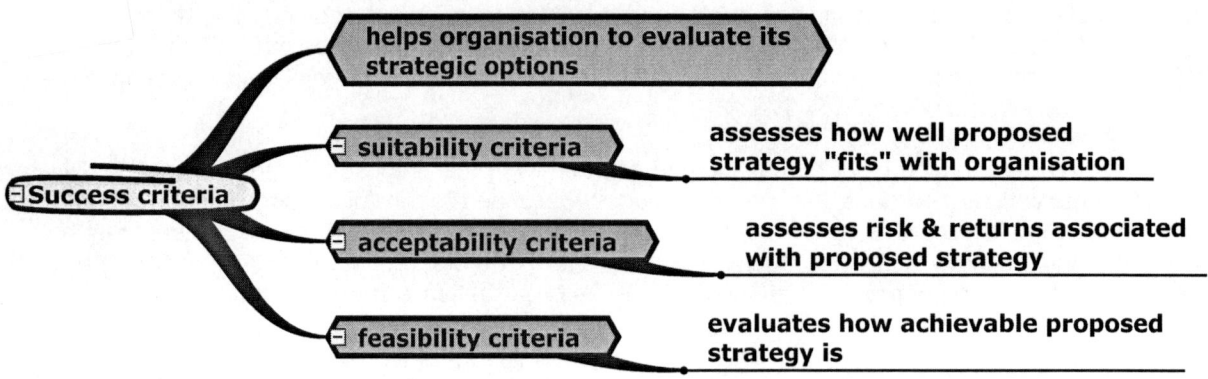

Test Yourself 3

Valvo is an organisation that designs and manufactures industrial safety valves. At present the manufacturing process is very labour intensive. Management is currently considering a strategy that will enable the organisation to increase productivity and efficiency. The strategy calls for much of the production process to be automated. This would require a heavy capital investment for purchase of machinery as well as an intensive training program for employees to use the new machines. Management subsequently determines that they do not have the necessary financial resources and reject the strategy.

Required:

Which one of the three success criteria did the proposed strategy not meet?

Answers to Test Yourself

Answer to TY 1

Market penetration. This particular strategy is followed when an organisation uses its existing product suite to increase sales and profitability. It does this by either "poaching" customers away from competitors and / or increasing sales levels from existing customers. Common tactics associated with this type of strategy include advertising and price cutting.

Answer to TY 2

A joint venture which is a type of strategic alliance. A strategic alliance occurs when two or more organisations share resources and activities to pursue a strategy. It typically occurs when two or more organisations want to enter a particular industry or market with a particular type of good / service but do not individually have all the needed resources and / or competences.

With a joint venture participating organisations remain independent of each other and instead form a jointly owned special purpose firm. The resources and work each participating organisation is then expected to contribute is explicitly spelled out and formally agreed upon.

Answer to TY 3

The feasibility test. This criteria evaluates a proposed strategy from the angle of whether an organisation has the resources and capabilities needed to implement it. In other words it attempts to determine how practical or even realistic a proposed strategy is. Naturally one of the first and foremost resources that needs to be examined are finances to determine if the organisation has / will be able to obtain the financing the strategy needs

Quick Quiz

1. According to the Ansoff matrix what are the four possible product / market combinations or strategic options available to an organisation?

2. A joint venture is a form of a_____.

3. Name the three success criteria that can be used to evaluate a strategic option.

Answers to Quick Quiz

1. The four strategic options available to an organisation are

    - market penetration
    - market development
    - product development
    - diversification

2. strategic alliance

3. Suitability, acceptability and feasibility criteria

Self Examination Questions

Question 1

WST is an Indian IT organisation that creates customised software solutions for businesses from Europe and America. The organisation has just finished a SWOT analysis on itself and identified the following:

1. **Strengths:** Existence of labour arbitrage (i.e. the ability to create a customised software solution in India at a much lower cost than its counterparts in Europe and America).
Large availability of skilled English speaking engineers.
Time zone differential means work and testing of a program can be done on a 24 hour basis.

2. **Weaknesses:** Reputation for being a low cost (and not high quality) service provider.
Cultural / national differences with customers.
Not updated on the very latest technologies / programming languages.

3. **Opportunities:** Large number of untapped organisations still present in the US and Europe.
Potential to move up the software value chain with existing clients.

4. **Threats:** Appreciating Indian rupee is making WST services more expensive for its customers
Increasing competition from organisations in other countries who are also able to exercise labour arbitrage (e.g. Russia).

Using a TOWS matrix identify four different strategic options available to WST.

Question 2

Briefly explain the market penetration strategy of the Ansoff matrix and state some of its objectives.

Answers to Self Examination Questions

Answer to SEQ 1

1. **SO Strategy:** Target existing customers to obtain more "high end" software creation and programming assignments. Main marketing ploy to be that this work can be done more cost effectively by WST then its counterparts in America and Europe (who are currently getting such assignments).

2. **ST Strategy:** Reduce prices / rates in accordance with how the Indian rupee appreciates to ensure that costs for software development remain constant for customers. Although this will reduce profitability it will also reduce the risk of customers / potential customers having their software developed elsewhere.

3. **WO Strategy:** Introduce training and developing programs that will have staff updated on the latest technologies / programming. Use this as a basis for marketing to existing customers to obtain more "high end" software creation and programming assignments.

4. **WT Strategy:** Hire either expatriate or local managers with Western experience / exposure to serve as intermediaries between WSN programmers and customers (thereby helping to bridge the cultural gap that exists between the two groups).

Answer to SEQ 2

A market penetration strategy is a strategy where an organisation focuses on selling existing products in existing markets. It seeks to achieve the following objectives:

- **Maintaining / increasing the market share of current products:** this can be achieved by a combination of competitive pricing strategies, advertising, sales promotion, etc.

- **Restructuring by elimination of competitors:** this requires a highly aggressive promotional campaign, supported by a pricing strategy designed to make the market unattractive for competitors.

- **Increasing usage by existing customers:** this can be achieved by introducing loyalty schemes.

SECTION C: STRATEGIC ACTION

STUDY GUIDE C1: ORGANISING AND ENABLING SUCCESS

■ Get Through Intro

Up until recently, many companies saw employees as just numbers and operated with employees in a strict hierarchy. Many new companies, however, see employees for what they are: the catalysers of change and efficiency. Hence companies structure their organisation to make the best use of employees in order to deliver their strategy.

For example, IT companies are known for their flat structures and team leaders, as opposed to bosses. It is the same in advertising agencies and marketing companies. The question is, why are they structured in this way? What was wrong with the old fashioned hierarchical structure?

This chapter will help show why a particular structure is suitable to a particular strategy, so you will be able to use this knowledge in real life.

■ Learning Outcomes

a) Advise on how the organisation can be structured to deliver a selected strategy.
b) Explore generic processes that take place within the structure, with particular emphasis on the planning process.
c) Discuss how internal relationships can be organised to deliver a selected strategy.
d) Discuss how external relationships (outsourcing, strategic alliances, networks and the virtual organisation) can be structured to deliver a selected strategy.
e) Explore (through Mintzberg's organisational configurations) the design of structure, processes and relationships.

Introduction

Case Study

According to a press release in June 2008, GlaxoSmithKline PLC, the world's second-largest drug maker said it is cutting around 2 percent of its research staff, as part of an ongoing restructuring plan aimed at boosting productivity.

Glaxo had also confirmed plans to restructure its research and development operations into smaller units. The aim would be for these units to focus on specific diseases. It was also reported that the units would be rewarded based on performance.

Glaxo had previously split its research operations into therapeutic areas in a move to boost innovation and bring new drugs into the market.

The above case study shows that companies are constantly changing their structures to better reflect their strategies. This Study Guide will help explain how they do this and why.

1. Advise on how the organisation can be structured to deliver a selected strategy.[3]
[Learning Outcome a]

Definition

An organisation in the most basic sense can be defined as being a collection of people jointly working towards achieving a shared objective or purpose.

This objective is usually characterised by the organisation's vision / mission statement which highlights the reason why the organisation was created in addition to all that it wishes to achieve and become.

Example

Sony's mission statement in the early 1950s was "Become the company most known for changing the worldwide poor-quality image of Japanese products".

Correspondingly then the selected strategy of an organisation represents how it intends to achieve these objectives. More specifically it outlines the direction an organisation wishes to take (i.e. the type and quality of goods / services it will produce) and the methods that will be employed (i.e. how it will produce its target goods / services).

Johnson, Scholes and Whittington identify three different ways through which organisations determine or arrive at the final strategy that they are going to adopt. These three approaches are strategy selection through innovation, strategy selection through experience or strategy selection through design. With the innovation or "ideas" approach, an organisation selects and bases its strategy solely around an innovation or innovative idea that has emerged out of the organisation.

Whereas strategy selection through design represents a highly rational and top-down approach to strategic development and management. Here the top management / executives of an organisation determine the strategy an organisation will assume through a formal planning process. This strategy will then be communicated to and implemented by the rest of the organisation.

Lastly with the experience approach, the strategy an organisation finally selects is one that has not been formally planned but rather has emerged as a result of individual and collective experiences. Here strategy selection occurs "in the doing". By this what is meant is that an organisation begins with a general strategic route it would like to take which is then amended as and when necessary. Therefore the final strategy selected is not an outcome of a formal planning process but rather a result of experimentation and "learning on the run".

As important as the type of strategy an organisation is implementing is the type of organisation structure it has. This is because as Professor John C. Camillus states: "A key enabler for effective strategy implementation is the ability to align organisational structure with strategic goals and objectives. The structure and strategy of the organisation must be complementary."

The structure of an organisation determines how an organisation will go about delivering the goods / services it has targeted in its strategy. More specifically organisation structures determine which parts of an organisation will perform which activities / functions and how. They also define the conditions that exist in an organisation such as the:

- formal reporting relationships and communication channels
- responsibilities of individuals, groups and departments
- grouping of departments / activities
- type and numbers of hierarchical levels
- span of control of managers
- uses of processes and systems

The four main ways an organisation can choose to structure itself include:

- structuring itself around its functions
- structuring itself around its customers
- adopting a matrix structure
- adopting a network structure

1. **Function focused structure:** an organisation that has a functional structure is divided into a series of departments. Each of these divisions is responsible for carrying out a specific function or activity of the organisation. Each employee of the organisation is then placed into one of these departments and is assigned a specific set of roles and responsibilities to carry out.

Diagram 1: Function focused structure

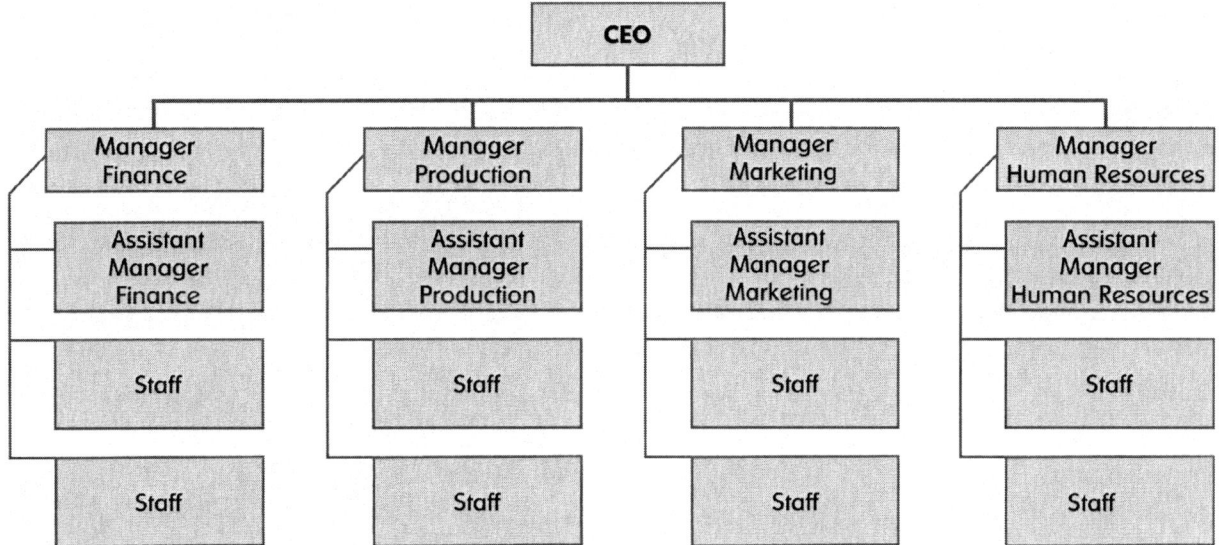

Advantages to this type of structure include that it:

- helps top management in coordinating and controlling the entire organisation to follow a uniform strategic direction
- clarifies the roles / responsibilities and what is expected of each employee
- allows each department to focus on its own work / activities
- provides clear accountability at both the departmental and individual level

Disadvantages to this type of structure include that it:

- creates a rigid and slow moving organisation
- leads to a loss of innovation and innovative thinking as employees become more process oriented (focused on following correct procedures and protocol) rather than results oriented
- does not allow for sharing of information / ideas across departmental lines (which is viewed as being especially important in today's knowledge economy)

This type of structure is typically suited for an organisation that produces a limited set of goods / services and / or operates in a stable environment.

2. **Customer focused structure:** an organisation that has adopted a "customer focus" will also have a hierarchical structure in place (similar to that of the functional organisation). However here the organisation will be departmentalised along either product, geographical or project lines. Each of these departments then becomes responsible for servicing and meeting the needs of a particular type / group of the organisation's customers.

Diagram 2: Customer focused structure

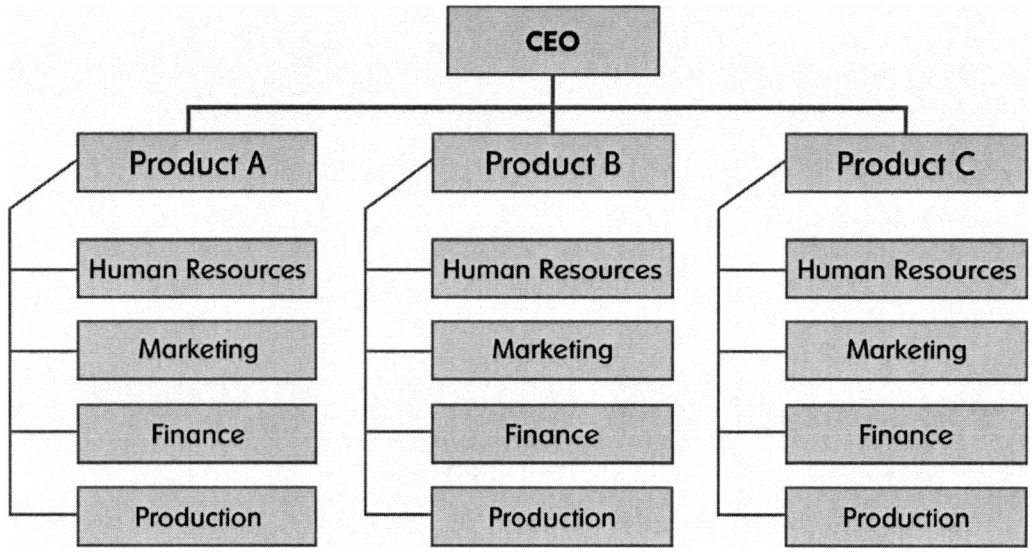

Advantages to this type of structure include that it:

➢ enables an organisation to be more aligned with the needs of its customers
➢ promotes innovation and innovative thinking as the organisational culture becomes more focused on problem solving / meeting customer needs than following processes and protocol

Disadvantages to this type of structure include:

➢ individual departments can become too autonomous which makes setting and coordinating a single strategic direction to be followed difficult
➢ it limits the sharing of information / ideas across the organisation lines (which is viewed as being especially important in today's knowledge economy)

This type of structure is typically suited to an organisation that has multiple sets of customers and operates in a rapidly changing environment.

3. **Matrix structure:** a matrix structure is adopted when an organisation combines elements of a functional and customer focused structure.

Diagram 3: Matrix structure

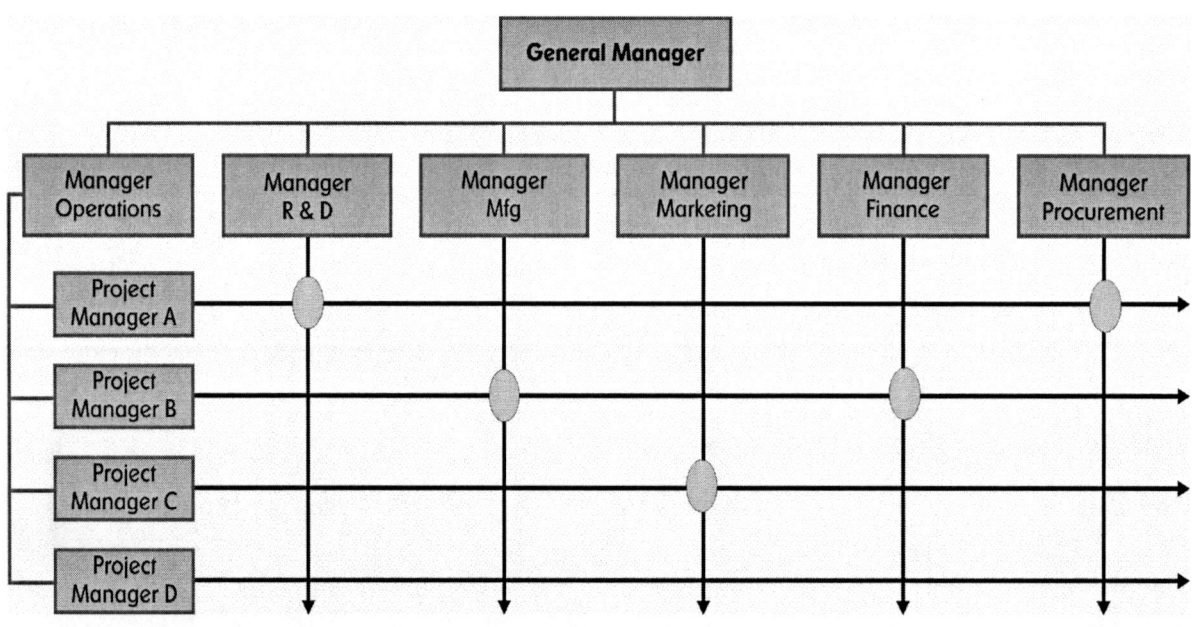

Advantages to this type of structure include that it:

- facilitates cross organisational learning and coordination as people and resources are shared across the organisation
- makes communication across the organisation more efficient and effective
- creates a flexible organisation as it calls for different functions and divisions to work together
- motivates staff so employees constantly learn new tasks and skills
- encourages innovation and promotes differentiation

Disadvantages to this type of structure include that:

- it can lead to confusion as areas of authority and accountability often overlap between different functions and divisions
- employees can often be unclear on their exact roles and responsibilities as they typically have two bosses and so they can get frustrated
- it makes it difficult to set and coordinate a single strategic direction for the organisation to follow
- it is difficult for firms in stable environments

This type of structure is typically suited for organisations that have multiple product / service lines as well as customer groups and / or operate in diverse geographic regions. In addition, this type of structure is suited to innovative firms such as Intel and Microsoft.

4. **Network structure :** as mentioned in Study Guide A4, in addition to having their own value chain more and more organisations today are also members of a value network.

Definition

A value network is a network of organisations which have entered into business with each other or have a business relationship with each other so as to create a particular product or service.

Therefore organisations operating in this context will maintain a bare minimum organisation structure that allows it to concentrate on performing its core competencies. The other aspect of the way the organisation will be structured will be to enable it to manage relationships with the other organisation / suppliers in its value network.

Diagram 4: Network structure

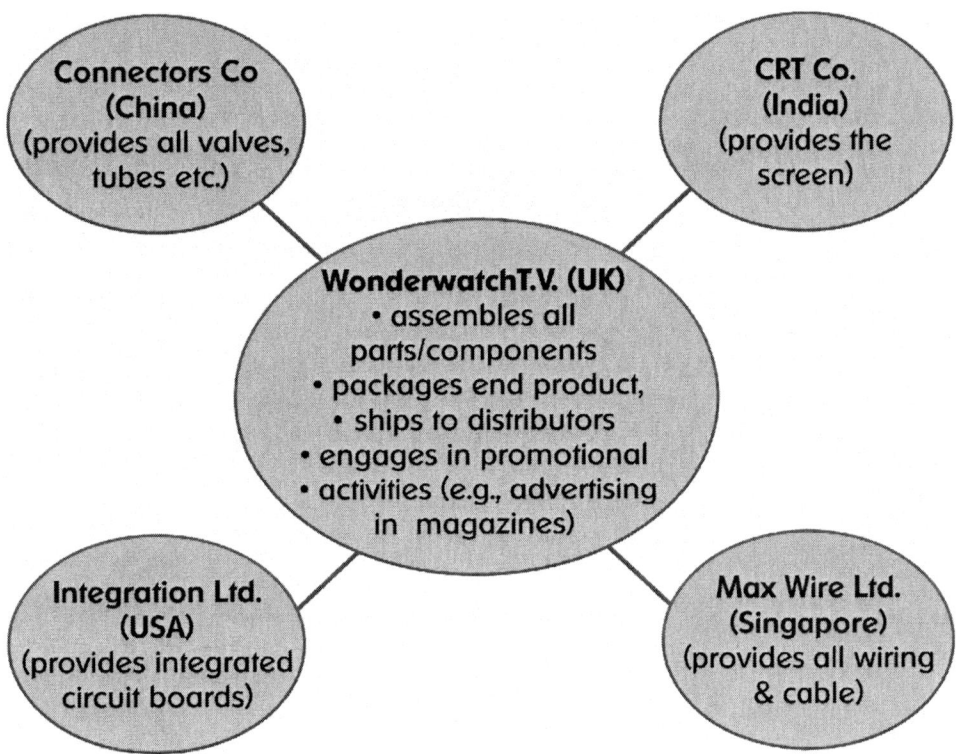

Advantages to this type of organisation structure are that it allows an organisation to:

➢ be highly flexible
➢ concentrate on its core competencies
➢ to share information and learn from multiple other parties

Disadvantages to this type of organisation structure are that:

➢ coordination becomes difficult given the multiple parties / organisations involved
➢ an organisation loses control over much of the activities / functions that go into providing its product / service

This type of organisation structure is suited for organisations that operate in very dynamic and rapidly changing markets.

Overall when it comes to selecting an organisation structure, firms need to follow a system of "backward integration". By this what is meant is that organisations must first consider the type of goods / services they would like to offer. The next step involves identifying what types of activities and work would be required to produce these goods / services. From here the organisation can then determine the type of structure it should adopt to deliver the goods / services associated with its selected strategy.

For instance a functional organisation structure would be most appropriate for a small engineering firm that produces a single product on a mass production scale and in a stable environment. Whereas for a multinational organisation such as Unilever whose strategy calls for it to operate on an almost global scale and offer a multitude of different products, a matrix organisation structure would be most appropriate.

SUMMARY

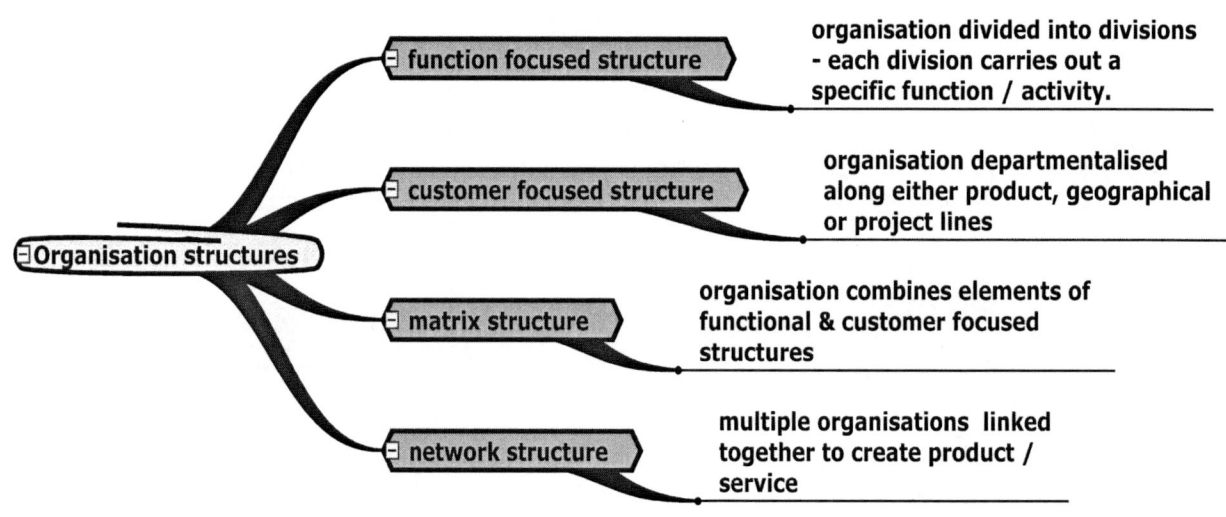

Test Yourself 1

Addon is an organisation that manufactures industrial adhesive products. Every employee of Addon is a member of one of its four departments, which include finance, production, marketing and human resources. Each of these departments is headed by a manager who reports to the CEO of the organisation.

Required:

(a) Explain which type of organisational structure Addon has adopted.

(b) What are its advantages and disadvantages?

> **2. Explore generic processes that take place within the structure, with particular emphasis on the planning process.**[3]
>
> [Learning Outcome b]

As covered in the previous learning outcome, structure represents the way an organisation has set itself up to undertake all the work / activities needed to produce its goods / services. Processes represent the way an organisation wants its employees to carry out the necessary work / activities to produce its targeted goods / services. Or to put it another way, processes represent how an organisation attempts to control the way its employees work and interact.

There are six main or generic processes organisations can implement. These are:

- direct supervision
- planning processes
- self control and motivation
- cultural processes
- performance targeting processes
- market processes

1. Direct supervision

Direct supervision occurs when the employees of an organisation are almost "micro-managed". With this process, the strategy an organisation is to follow is set by top management. In addition, the way the strategy is to be implemented is also decided upon and closely monitored by top management. Obviously this approach is must suited to small owner-operated firms, where the owner thoroughly knows and understands how each type of work/activity needs to be performed.

2. Planning processes

With this approach, the strategy that is to be followed is also determined by top management and then reproduced in a plan or budget. The plan details the targets / results that are expected to be achieved from the organisation's various divisions or groups. It also allocates the resources (e.g. capital, staff, equipment etc) to each of these groups to enable them to achieve the targets that have been set.

The divisions are then required to report to top management on how they will use these resources in order to achieve their targets. Top management then adopts a monitoring role to help ensure that these resources are used effectively and efficiently and the department achieves the desired results.

Example

An organisation's plan calls for its sales department to increase sales from their current level of $5 million a year to $10 million a year. To help the manager of the department achieve this "jump", a new budget has been assigned to the department that will enable him to hire 5 additional sales persons.

The manager is allowed the flexibility to deploy the sale force how ever he wishes (e.g. which sales person is to be assigned to which area / customers). Top management however continually monitor the progress made by the department to ensure that sales are increasing by $500,000 on a monthly basis.

This type of process is appropriate for organisations that have adopted a functional organisational structure and/or operate in a stable external environment.

Organisations plan formal processes to review the work of their employees. One of these processes is appraisals.

An **appraisal** is a structured, formal interaction between an employee and his or her supervisor. Appraisals may be conducted annually or more frequently, depending on the organisation's planning. Appraisals are conducted on a regular basis to review the performance of employees and to judge whether or not they are being paid appropriately. Hence, performance appraisals may result in a rise or fall in an employee's salary.

3. Self control and personal motivation

The self control and personal motivation approach involves empowering employees. Employees become empowered when their organisation grants them a relatively high level of flexibility and autonomy when it comes to planning and performing their work. Here the processes focus on creating the right conditions for employees to be able to use their initiative to help the organisation achieve its goals.

Example

There is an increasing trend of "corporate entrepreneurship" taking place amongst organisations today. Corporate entrepreneurship occurs when an organisation provides its employees the freedom and (if necessary) the funding to pursue any new ideas they have developed that will help the organisation to achieve its strategy.

4. Cultural processes

Johnson, Scholes and Whittington state that "cultural processes are concerned with organisational culture and the standardisation of norms." It is important to note here that the culture of an organisation symbolizes the way employees work and relate to each other. Therefore it reflects how an organisation operates and functions and the way employees expect work of the organisation to be carried out. These processes represent a form of tacit control as they expect employees to abide by the "unwritten" rules of the organisation.

Example

For instance software engineers at Infosys (an Indian IT organisation) are required by the culture of the organisation to make themselves available to clients well after office hours (this is in addition to completing the normal working day). This expectation is drilled into new recruits as being an essential requirement of what it means to be an "Infoscion".

However having strong cultural processes can be a "double edged sword" for organisations. This is because it may be difficult for top management to change a firmly rooted culture even it is no longer effective or valid in the environment the organisation operates in.

5. Performance targeting processes

This type of approach focuses on attempting to control work done by the organisation by setting employees / divisions targets for their output. Examples of targets could be number of units of a particular good to be produced, the quality level of a good that is produced (e.g. zero defects) or the amount of revenue to be brought in to the organisation.

Performance targets are also often referred to as key performance indicators. Once implemented, the performances of employees, divisions and even the organisation as a whole can be measured against whether these key performance indicators are being met. Although key performance indicators will differ from organisation to organisation, industry to industry, they typically represent the critical success factors of an organisation.

Example

A key performance indicator for a customer service department of an organisation (that cites client servicing as one of its competitive advantages) might be that the maximum response time for any inquiry will not exceed two days. Whereas a key performance indicator for a private school (that cites quality of teaching as one of its competitive advantages) may be that the pass-out or graduation rate for its students should not fall below ninety percent.

This type of control again provides employees with a relatively high degree of latitude in planning and performing their work as the main focus is on their outputs. However it is important to note here that for this type of control to work, the key performance indicators must be quantifiable. This is because if targets are not quantified, then it becomes difficult (if not impossible) for an organisation to effectively determine if they are being met or not.

6. Market processes

When an organisation deals with external parties (i.e. its customers, suppliers etc) it cannot rely on any of the processes discussed above. What regulates the interactions and transactions between them are market forces.

For instance if an organisation operates in a competitive market it may not be able to raise its prices at its discretion. This is because many of its customers would in all probability switch over and purchase the same good / service from one of their competitors. Organisations that comprise of a number of business units can implement a similar process internally to control the way these individual units operate and perform.

Example

BSF Enterprises is a conglomerate that consists of two business units. The first unit builds ships and the second unit speed boats. The manufacturing processes that both of these units use require steel as one of their raw materials.

Continued on the next page

The organisation recently went through a "backward integration" exercise and added a third business unit that produces steel. Management at BSF decide that rather than setting detailed performance targets for this unit (how much steel it should sell to the other two business units and at what price) it will allow the market to regulate this unit's performance.

Or in other words, there is no compulsion for BSF's ship and speed boat divisions to buy the steel they require internally. Therefore they will only buy their raw material from the third unit if its price and quality is competitive.

SUMMARY

Six main / generic processes:

- **direct supervision** — strategy is decided by top management & employees "Micro managed"
- **planning processes** — strategy is determined by and reproduced in a plan/ budget for employees to follow
- **self control & motivation** — employees empowered
- **cultural processes** — work controlled by culture of organisation
- **performance targeting processes** — employees / divisions set targets for their output
- **market processes** — relationships between individual business units controlled by market forces

Test Yourself 2

Technocrat is an organisation that manufactures motherboards for personal computers. The current capacity is 3,000 motherboards per month. The organisation wishes to increase production in order to meet the increasing in the market and decides to increase production by 2,000 motherboards per month. Therefore, the total production per month will become 5,000. The organisation's new strategic plan has taken this factor into account and given the production department a new output target along with additional resources.

Required:

Explain how the organisation can manage the expansion process.

3. Discuss how internal relationships can be organised to deliver a selected strategy.[2]
[Learning Outcome c]

There are two main aspects to consider when examining the internal relationships that exist in an organisation:

- the extent to which it is centralised / decentralised
- the role of the corporate centre or head office in relation to individual business units

3.1 Centralisation and Decentralisation

The concepts of centralisation and decentralisation deal with how decision making authority is divided / distributed across an organisation. More specifically they identify the extent to which important strategic decisions are made at the lower (operational and tactical) levels of the organisation.

Centralisation calls for the top management or executives of an organisation to assume all decision making authority. This results in a policy of standardisation spreading throughout the organisation as all employees end up following a single set of directives. Middle management and operational staff are given very little autonomy in terms of decision making but are instead expected to simply execute the directions that flow from above.

Centralisation typically results in an organisation becoming more efficient. This is because it helps avoid / reduce duplication of work and efforts across different divisions and enables an organisation to follow a focused strategic direction in a coordinated and clear manner. Other advantages are that it helps to promote a uniform corporate image and vision as well as helping to ensure a standard level of quality is maintained for an organisation's goods / services.

Decentralisation is not as it name suggests the complete opposite of centralisation. Rather it calls for some, but not a complete re-distribution of power and authority from top to middle management and operational staff. It calls for middle management and supervisors to be granted a limited amount of decision making authority.

The underlying rationale behind decentralisation is that it will enable an organisation to adapt to changes in the external environment much more rapidly. It will also empower the employees of the business thereby helping to create a more flexible and innovative organisation.

This leads to the question of which is the better system for which however there is no simple answer. Which of the two systems an organisation should adopt depends upon the particular set of circumstances and conditions it is operating under. For instance decentralisation is particularly beneficial when an organisation has to deal with a great deal of diversity such as a multinational corporation that has subsidiaries / business units in many different countries. However if there is a great deal of interdependence among business units, then a policy of centralisation will benefit the organisation more.

In addition when deciding between the two an organisation also needs to examine factors such as:

- the participation it wants from different levels of the organisation
-
- the way it wants information to flow across the organisation

Naturally the greater the participation from employees and / or flow of information an organisation would like, the greater the extent of decentralisation that will exist in the organisation. Decentralisation will also result in an organisation having a "flat" organisation structure. Flat organisations have relatively few managerial layers and numbers of managers. Consequently each manager then has a wide span of control and a much greater level of independence is given to each employee. Here, control refers to a mechanism to regulate the functioning of an organisation. Therefore, control is any practice, policy or procedure framed to provide considerable assurance that the organisation's objectives and goals will be achieved.

Correspondingly centralisation results in creating a "tall" organisation structure. Generally, tall organisations have a much larger number of managerial layers but each manager has a relatively narrow span of control. Employees have much less independence as their roles and responsibilities are typically very well defined.

Centralisation and a tall organisation structure therefore would suit an organisation that wishes to follow a strategy of offering a single or limited product / service mix and operates in a stable environment. Whereas decentralisation would be more appropriate for organisations that follow a strategy of offering multiple products / services and / or operate in dynamic and diverse markets.

3.2 Role of the corporate centre

Goold and Campbell identify three generic strategies a corporate centre or head office can adopt in relation to dealing with its individual business units. These three strategies are:

- financial control
- strategic planning
- strategic control

This model can be explained with the help of a graph, as follows:

Diagram 5: Role of the corporate centre

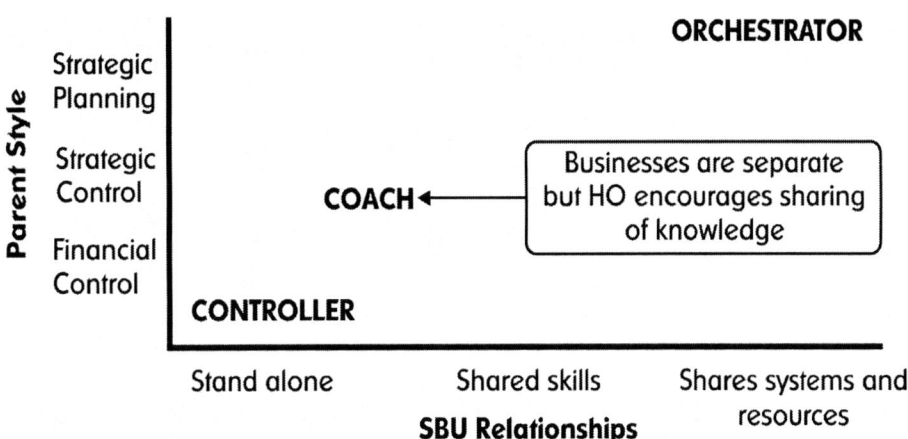

1. Financial control

With this type of strategy, the corporate centre acts as a provider of finance or banker to the individual business units. Its involvement is typically limited to setting financial targets (e.g. achieving a ROCE of 8%) and monitoring the progress made by the business units in achieving these targets.

The business units are therefore granted a relatively high degree of autonomy as they are left free to formulate and implement strategies of their choice. The corporate centre will adopt a "management by exception" approach meaning that it will only intervene if a business unit is not meeting its targets. If the non-performance continues, the corporate centre may "pull the plug" by discontinuing funding and divesting the unit.

2. Strategic planning

With this type of strategy the corporate centre acts as a planner by setting an all encompassing strategy for the entire organisation. This strategy is usually developed around a "theme" or strategic direction the corporate centre and all the business units are expected to follow. Here business units are granted a relatively low degree of autonomy as the role each unit has to play in achieving the overall strategy is spelled out by the centre.

3. Strategic control

With this type of strategy the corporate centre acts as a shaper by setting both financial and strategic targets for the business units. However coming up with the "nuts and bolts" of the strategy is then left up to each particular business unit. Business units are given a fair degree of latitude as long they achieve the predetermined financial targets and they do not deviate too far from the overall organisational strategy.

Test Yourself 3

3. Glassperfect is a small organisation that provides finished stainless glass window panes. The organisation has 4 main divisions or departments: purchasing, manufacturing (where the glass is cut into standard shapes and sizes), human resources and finance.

All marketing and strategic decisions are handled by the CEO of the organisation.

Required:

(a) Is Glassperfect a decentralised organisation or a centralised organisation?

(b) Discuss the advantages of both types of organisational structures.

---

4. Discuss how external relationships (outsourcing, strategic alliances, networks and the virtual organisation) can be structured to deliver a selected strategy.[2]

[Learning Outcome d]

As important as the structure, processes and internal relationships present in an organisation is the way it manages the relationships it has with important external stakeholders and parties. This is because almost every organisation needs to transact and / or collaborate with some external party (e.g. suppliers) in order to be able to deliver the target goods / services it has identified in its strategy. Amongst the most important external parties and/or activities of an organisation are:

- outsourcing
- strategic alliances
- networks
- virtual organisations

1. Outsourcing

Outsourcing occurs when an organisation hires an external party to provide goods / services that it previously produced internally. It began in the early 1980s with organisations typically contracting out their non core or support activities such as training to an external party that specialised in providing that particular service, product or function.

Some of the benefits that outsourcing brings are that it:

- lowers costs

- allows the organisation to concentrate on its core functions and competencies (resulting in a more efficient use of the organisation's time and resources)

- results in the outsourced function being performed more effectively and efficiently (as the outsourcer typically has a greater skill set in this particular area)

- the outsourcer can take advantage of economies of scale and, as a result, can charge cheaper prices

However it is important to note that even though an activity has been outsourced, the responsibility for its successful completion still rests with the organisation. This is the main reason why it is important for an organisation to manage the relationship it has with any external party it has outsourced to.

Example

For instance, an organisation's responsibility for ensuring that its employees receive their salaries on time does not end simply because it has outsourced this function to an external party. Employees will still hold the organisation responsible if they are not paid on time.

This is especially important today as outsourcing is becoming increasingly seen as being an integral part of an organisation's business strategy and not just as a transaction that has resulted out of the need for achieving cost savings. Types of activities / functions now being outsourced include financial and engineering services as well as data mining and management.

Outsourcing is gaining in popularity because when utilised effectively it allows organisations to:

- manage their labour and supply costs more effectively

- concentrate on their core competencies and develop a competitive advantage

Example

Outokumpu Stainless is one of the largest producers in the world of hot rolled plate. The organisation has outsourced all of its corrective and maintenance activities for its factory located at Degerfors in Sweden to ABB Service.

Outokumpu state that outsourcing this function has enabled the organisation (from 2001) to:

- reduce staff by 30%

- decrease total maintenance costs by 24%

- reduce maintenance cost per produced ton by 58%

- achieve their current customer satisfaction score of 91.2%

Therefore organisations need to not only manage relationships but also partner with external parties they have outsourced to. Organisations should ensure that these parties not only understand the strategic direction they are following but also work in sync with them to help them achieve their strategies.

2. Strategic Alliances

> **Definition**
>
> Pyka and Windrum define a strategic alliance as being a "cooperative agreement between two or more autonomous firms pursuing common objectives or working towards solving common problems through a period of sustained interaction".

Examples of strategic alliances include research and development coalitions, marketing and distribution agreements and franchising.

An organisation will typically join forces with another organisation(s) and form a strategic alliance when it wants to enter a particular industry or market with a particular type of good / service but does not individually have all the needed resources and / or competences.

Therefore a strategic alliance represents the way an organisation is changing its structure in order for it to achieve its strategy of being able to deliver a particular good / service. Again it is of vital importance that an organisation effectively manages the relationships it has with the other organisation(s) participating in the strategic alliance.

This is because the targeted good / service have to be produced in collaboration. For the collaboration to be an effective effort each organisation will have to:
- understand the operations and activities it is expected to perform
- perform these operations and activities up to the standard expected by the other participating organisations
- coordinate and liaise with the other participating organisations to ensure that their operations and activities are completed effectively

(For more information and examples on strategic alliances please refer to Study Guide B3 of this study text)

3. Networks

Most organisations today not only have a value chain but are also members of a much larger value network. This is because they do not typically carry out all of the activities and functions needed to provide a good / service. This network therefore consists of an organisation and all of its suppliers and distributors.

> **Definition**
>
> A value network is a network of organisations which have entered into business with each other or have a business relationship with each other so as to create a particular product or service.

Again as with strategic alliances, an organisation enters into a network when it wants to enter a particular industry or market with a particular type of good / service but does not individually have all the needed resources and / or competences. Therefore networks also represent the way an organisation is changing its structure (i.e. having an external party carry out some the needed activities / functions) in order for it to achieve its strategy of being able to deliver a particular good / service.

(for more information and examples on strategic alliances please refer to Study Guide A4 of this study text)

4. Virtual organisations

A virtual organisation is an organisation formed by partnership, collaboration and networking. It is not characterised by a formal structure or the physical proximity of the employees. Therefore virtual organisations represent a collection of individuals and / or organisations who are all working jointly towards achieving a common purpose (i.e. being able to provide a particular good / service).

The virtual organisation can be said to be a logical extension of outsourcing, networking and strategic alliances. Here the resources that this type of organisation will own and the activities it will carry out will represent its bare minimum (or strictly its core competencies only).

> **Example**
>
> Terry Smith has decided to start an organisation that will produce athletic shoes. He chooses that his business TSS, will be a virtual organisation. Terry decides that the only activities that he and his staff of three will perform will be marketing and promotion. The design of the shoes will be contracted out to individual designers on a contract basis.
>
> Once the design of a particular shoe has been finalised it will be sent to a manufacturing firm in Malaysia. This organisation will then produce the shoes in the quantities Terry has specified and then have the order shipped to Terry's office in London.
>
> At TSS, Terry's staff will then attach the organisation's label and logo to the shoes. Once this has been done, Terry will focus on his core competency of marketing the shoes to sports shops and athletic department stores.

SUMMARY

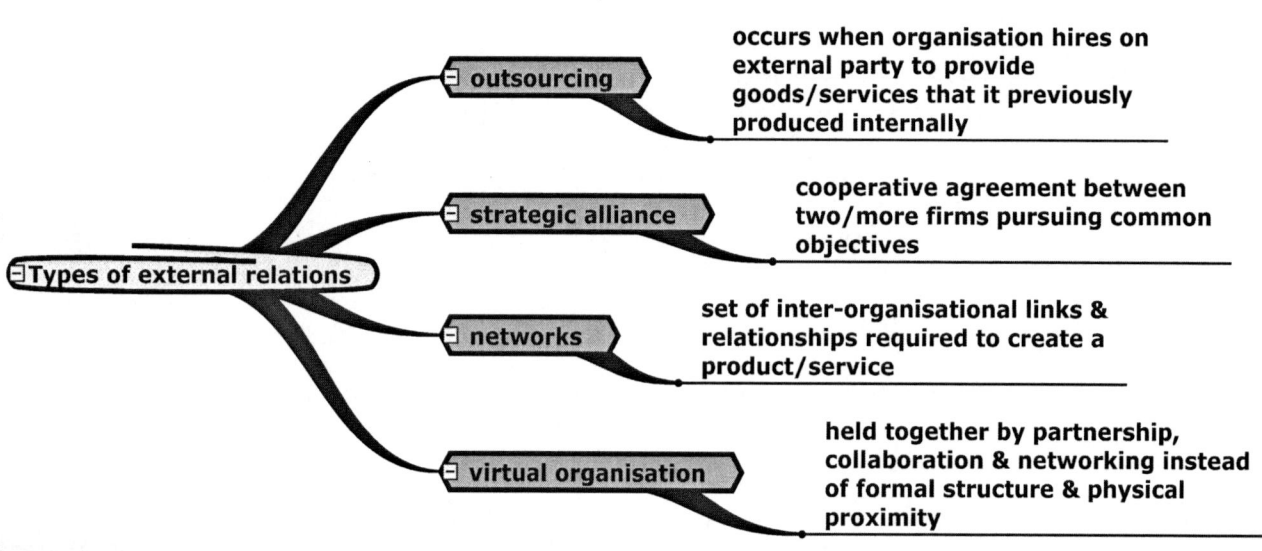

Types of external relations
- **outsourcing** — occurs when organisation hires on external party to provide goods/services that it previously produced internally
- **strategic alliance** — cooperative agreement between two/more firms pursuing common objectives
- **networks** — set of inter-organisational links & relationships required to create a product/service
- **virtual organisation** — held together by partnership, collaboration & networking instead of formal structure & physical proximity

Test Yourself 4

Wizardsoft is an IT organisation that specialises in creating software products for the engineering industry. The business has been enjoying steady growth and profitability over the last few years. After the expansion, the company's need for technical support has increased e.g. initial installation of software and subsequent help to users of the software.

It has been suggested that the company should expand its technical support manpower, leading to an increase in manpower costs by up to 40%, and other related costs by 15%. However, customer satisfaction cannot be guaranteed. Therefore, the company is struggling hard to come up with suitable solutions.

Required:

Suggest possible solutions to help Wizardsoft resolve its current problem.

---

5. Explore (through Mintzberg's organisational configurations) the design of structure, processes and relationships.[3]

[Learning Outcome e]

As mentioned in the previous learning outcomes, an organisation's structure determines which parts of the business will perform which activities / functions and how. Its processes represent the way employees are expected to carry out their necessary activities / functions to produce the targeted goods / services. Finally its relationships define how employees work and interact with each other as well as with any external parties that deal with the organisation.

These three elements go into establishing an organisation's configuration. This configuration will then establish how the organisation operates through integrating the knowledge and activities present in the different parts of the business to effectuate its strategy. Naturally the more aligned an organisation's configuration is with its strategy the greater the probability that the strategy will succeed.

Mintzberg identifies six different types of generic configurations an organisation can adopt. Which configuration an organisation should adopt will depend upon factors such as it's:

- external environment
- type of industry
- culture
- targeted goods / services

1. Simple Configuration

Here the organisation has no formal structure and centres itself around one dominant individual (e.g. the CEO or owner of the organisation). The organisation's direction, activities and functions are all controlled and coordinated by this individual. Work behaviours and processes are all highly informal. This type of configuration is typically found in small entrepreneurial organisations.

2. Machine Configuration

Here the organisation's structure is based around its main functions / departments. Work behaviours and processes are highly formal as all work / activities are planned out in advance by top management. Decision making is very centralised resting only at the apex of the organisation. This type of configuration is usually found in organisations that produce a limited range of goods / service and/or operate in stable environments.

3. Professional Bureaucracy

This type of organisational configuration is suited to professional firms such as law offices or accounting practices which typically have two main groups of employees. The first group is the professional staff of the organisation and the second is the remaining employees who are there to support them in their work. Work processes and relationships rest on the professionals concentrating on their core competencies to meet the needs of their clients whilst the support staff provides them with the necessary assistance.

4. Divisionalised

Here the organisation structures itself around a series of divisions. Each division has its own "head" or general manager. Each division's head then reports to the CEO or overall head of the organisation who assigns them their respective strategic and financial targets. Decision making is relatively decentralised as each division is given the autonomy to decide how to achieve its set goals. This type of configuration is most appropriate for large scale organisations that are diverse and offer multiple products / services (e.g. multinational corporations).

5. Adhocracy

This type of configuration is most appropriate for organisations that operate in a climate of continual change and innovation. Work processes and relationships here revolve around all the projects the organisation has taken on board. Resources such as people and funds are assigned to one particular project for its duration and then subsequently re-assigned to another project. Consulting and software development firms are examples of organisations that typically adopt this type of configuration.

6. Missionary

This type of configuration is most suited to organisations that have a clear and distinctive purpose that all of its employees believe in. These types of organisations will then rely upon cultural processes rather than formal structures to conduct their work / activities. Employees work with a minimum amount of controls / supervision and rely on a system of networks to achieve the organisation's mission. Charity and volunteer organisations typically adopt this type of configuration. According to Mintzberg, this is a difficult type of structure to maintain, since the external environment can dilute the ideology that forms the basis of the organisation. Perhaps this is the reason why these organisations are rare.

SUMMARY

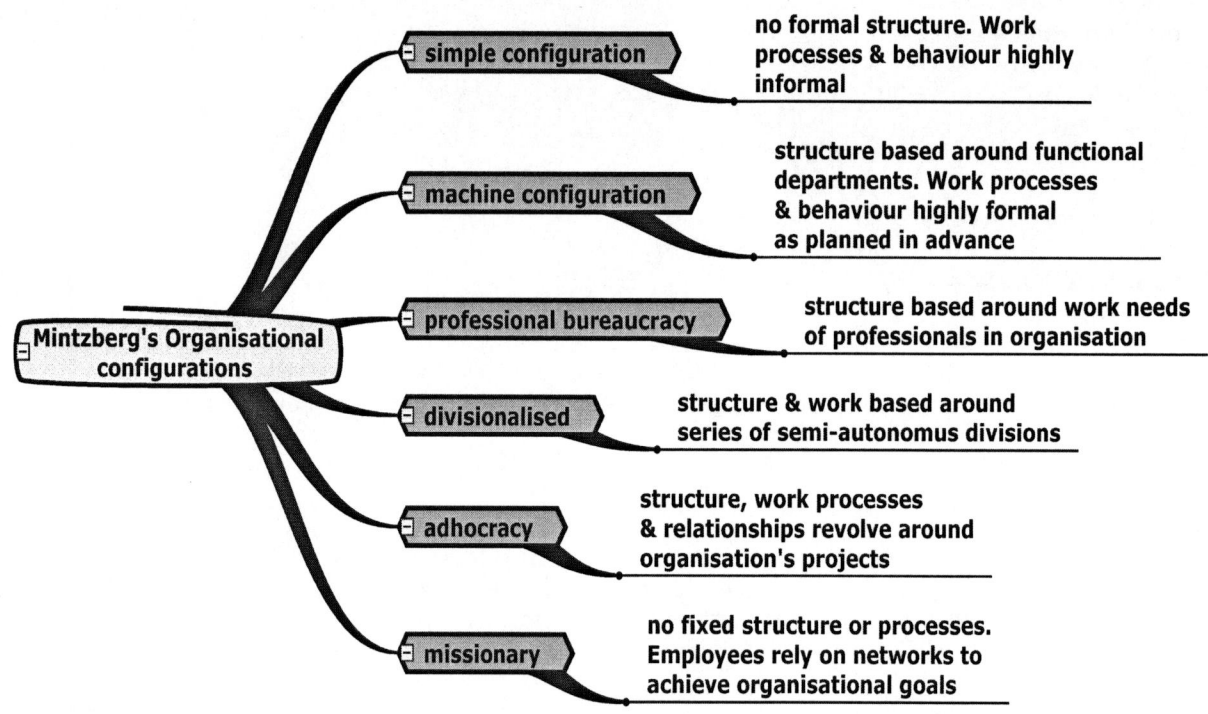

Answers to Test Yourself

Answer to TY 1

(a) The ways in which an organisation can choose to structure itself are:

- function focused structure
- customer focused structure
- matrix structure
- network structure

Here, Addon has adopted a function focused organisational structure because the organisation is divided into four divisions or departments. Each department is then made responsible for carrying out a specific function / activity for the organisation. Subsequently, each employee is then placed into one of these departments and is assigned a specific set of roles and responsibilities. As Addon is the manufacturer of industrial adhesive products, a functional structure is the most suitable structure for this organisation.

(b) **Advantages and disadvantages of functional structure organisation**

Advantages	Disadvantages
1. each department focuses on its own work and activities	1. creates a rigid and slow-moving organisation.
2. helps management to coordinate and control the entire organisation in a strategic way	2. time required for coordination may be too long
3. identifies role and responsibility for each employee	3. leads to loss of innovation and innovative thinking as employees become more process-oriented
4. provides clear accountability at both the departmental and individual levels	4. does not allow sharing of information or ideas across departments

Answer to TY 2

Technocrat manufactures motherboards for personal computers and, due to the increase in demand, it needs to increase production. But Technocrat needs to implement generic processes to manage the work carried out by its employees.

Here, Technocrat plans to produce 5,000 motherboard per month from the current quantity of 3,000 motherboards. Technocrat needs to conduct a proper planning of the process.

When Technocrat carries out its planning and budgeting, it will be able to determine the resources required. For example, Technocrat may require an addition ten skilled employees, two or three new pieces of equipment, one project manager and some additional raw materials. The planning also determines the targets for timing and the quantity of work that needs to be completed. The management also needs to supervise the work to ensure that available resources are utilised properly.

Due to the management's continuous monitoring, the company can ensure that the required production target is achieved.

Answer to TY 3

(a) Glassperfect is a small organisation where all strategic decisions are made by the CEO. Therefore, we can deduce that Glassperfect is a centralised organisation. The divisions of the organisation are expected simply to execute the directions and directives that the CEO sets.

(b) Advantages of having a centralised organisation and a decentralised organisation:

Advantages of having a centralised organisational structure:

- The CEO enjoys total control over the organisation.

- The CEO makes all decisions and the decisions are considered beneficial to the whole organisation, not only to particular department.

- Strong self-initiative and incentive which responds rapidly to the requirements of the organisation.

- The financial structure allows professional risks to be taken by the organisation.

- Use of standardised systems could save cost and make a profit.

Advantages of having a decentralised organisational structure:

- The CEO only concentrates on the very important decisions to be made for company and all other decisions are made by other department managers of the organisation.

- Decentralised decision-making tends to increase enthusiasm and also increases staff output.

- Create a flat organisational structure with few managerial layers.

Answer to TY 4

One possible solution which could help Wizardsoft to come out of predicament is outsourcing. The decision to outsource must be taken at a strategic level and the board should give approval for this.

Wizardsoft should outsource technical support and other suitable functions to an organisation that specialises in these activities. This will allow proper utilisation of resources and thereby will help the organisation to manage the growth of the company more effectively.

Outsourcing technical support services would benefit Wizardsoft in several ways:

1. **Cost effective services:** outsourcing technical support services will provide the same services with the same level of quantity and quality but at a lower cost. It will save substantial amounts of money. The company would benefit as it would receive a high quality service at a cost-effective price.

2. **Specialised service provider:** outsourcing enables a company to obtain specialised services. These will not affect the core competency of the company and at the same time, the company will be able to benefit from specialised service providers.

3. **Concentration on the core business:** with outsourcing, Wizardsoft will be able to fully concentrate on its core business of manufacturing software only. The employees can concentrate and give their 100% which could lead to huge growth in the core business. Other non-core functions of the business can be carried out by the outsourcing partner.

4. **Customer satisfaction:** outsourcing delivers high-quality services which can impress customers and can also increase customers' satisfaction, which increases the chances of customer loyalty.

5. **Increased work efficiency:** outsourcing increases work efficiency. Non-core business functions can be performed efficiently by an outsourcing partner and the core business can be carried out efficiently in the organisation. Therefore, Wizardsoft can achieve overall efficiency and profitability will increase.

6. **Increase in revenue and profits:** outsourcing will increase the saving capacity of the business and will therefore increase profits. Outsourcing helps to save time, effort, infrastructure, manpower and also avoids unnecessary investment. These savings will increase business revenue.

7. **Increase in business value:** outsourcing the technical support service will also increase productivity, quality and profitability. It will help in every aspect of the business. The overall value of the business will increase.

Quick Quiz

1. What type of structure requires an organisation to be divided into a number of divisions each of which is responsible for a specific function or activity?

2. Which approach focuses on attempting to control work done in an organisation by setting employees / divisions targets for their output?

3. What are the three generic strategies identified by Goold & Campbell that can be used by a corporate centre can adopt in relation to dealing with its individual business units?

4. What type of organisation can be said to be a logical extension of outsourcing, networking and strategic alliances?

Answers to Quick Quiz

1. Function focused structure.

2. Performance targeting processes.

3. Financial control, strategic planning and strategic control.

4. Virtual organisation

Self Examination Questions

Question 1

Everyday News Publisher is one of the leading business news providers. It is the first choice for business readers. It publishes newspapers in all counties of the UK. Everyday News Publisher believes in liberal, reasonable and self-sufficient journalism and strives to inspire these values in its editorial staff. The journalism practised by Everyday News puts prioritises on features, reliability and accurateness of their published news.

The company has one of the country's best economic journalists and columnists working for it. Editing is done by one of the best business journalists who earlier undertook and completed and highly successful revamp of the News Times and was also responsible for the organisation's growth.

Apart from a business newspaper, Everyday News wants to introduce several bulletins, including fashion magazines, sports magazines etc.

Required:

Explain why both the strategy and the organisational structure are important for the success of Everyday News Publisher.

Question 2

Briefly explain the role which a corporate centre or head office can adopt while dealing with its individual business units.

Answers to Self Examination Questions

Answer to SEQ 1

Organisational strategy outlines the direction taken by the organisation for the type of product or service provided to consumers and also for the method employed in the production of target goods or services.

However, organisational structure determines how an organisation will go about delivering the goods and services it has targeted in its strategy. The structure of an organisation defines the activities and the functions performed by each part of the organisation. It also defines the relationship and communication within and outside the organisation, the responsibility of employees, departments and the management, the control of managers, proper utilisation of processes and systems.

Therefore, organisational strategy is influenced by the type of structure the organisation uses. The structure and the strategy of the organisation must be complementary. An organisation can be structured in the following ways:

➢ structuring itself around its functions

➢ structuring itself around its customers

➢ adopt a matrix structure

➢ adopt a network structure

Everyday News Publisher will have a customer-focused organisational structure. Organisations will be departmentalised along either product, geographical or project lines. The departments will therefore become responsible for servicing and meeting the needs of a particular group of customers.

The following represents the hierarchical structure of Everyday News Publisher:

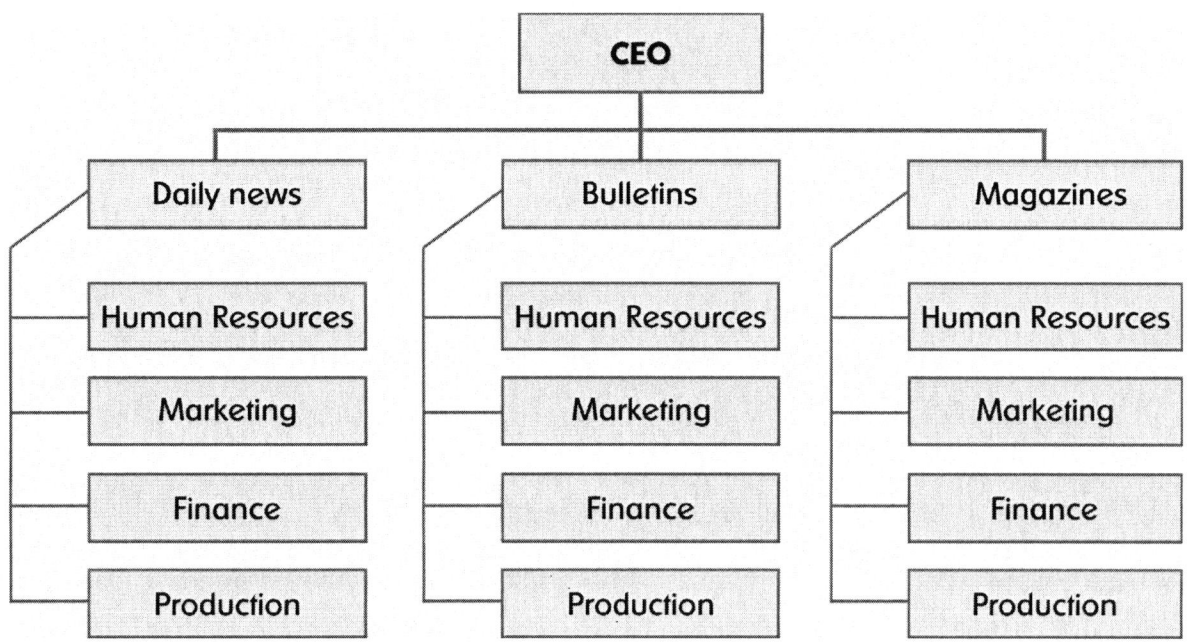

A customers-focused organisational structure will enable Everyday News Publisher to be more aligned with the needs of its customers. It will promote innovation and innovative thinking as Everyday News will be able to focus on meeting the needs and requirements of its customers.

Answer to SEQ 2

1. **Financial control:** the corporate centre aims to provide a better investment performance.

2. **Strategic control:** the centre coordinates and reviews the strategy and attempts to create links between businesses to create competitive advantage.

3. **Strategic planning:** the centre coordinates the actions and creates links between the units.

SECTION C: STRATEGIC ACTION

C2

STUDY GUIDE 2: MANAGING STRATEGIC CHANGE

■ Get Through Intro

Imagine you are working for a company and there are 10 people in the office. The bosses sit on another floor. There are tea and coffee facilities and the atmosphere is jovial. Then management come in to tell you that the office is moving to another building in another part of town. It will be open plan and everyone will be sitting together. Infact you will be sitting next to the CEO and her Personal Assistant. There are also no tea of coffee facilities, but there is a coffee shop on the ground floor.

What are your first comments? Are you happy with the news? You need to remember that generally people do not like change. It is unsettling and makes people insecure. However, change is necessary in a lot of situations. Managing change is crucial in order to get the support of others in the organisation. This Study Guide will help you in making the changes that are needed to improve your business.

■ Learning Outcomes

a) Explore different types of strategic change and their implications.
b) Determine the organisational context of change and use the cultural web to diagnose this organisational context.
c) Establish potential blockages and levers of change.
d) Advise on the style of leadership appropriate to manage strategic change.
e) Specify organisational roles required to manage strategic change.
f) Discuss levers that can be employed to manage strategic change.

Introduction

Case Study

Managing Change at a museum - Auckland War Memorial was going through an extensive expansion project. The completion of this project meant the structure needed to change in order to effectively deliver new programmes wanted by the museum board and the public.

Here, the museum director, Dr Vitali started the change by spending three months chatting to employees in large and small groups. She also studied other NZ museums and also spoke to other stakeholders, the board, the taumata (Maori advisory group) and donors.

According to the article, she said that when these talks began, 'restructuring was not yet a goal. As a result of these talks, employees produced a list of their key outputs, which were assembled into a chart so complex and shapeless staff have come to call it "the amoeba".

Dr Vitali stressed that transparency and dialogue were the fundamental tenets of successful change management. Transparency means explaining the process in full to everyone and telling people the goals all along the transition. Dialogue means engaging in discussion about the complexity of delivering museum services, about differing priorities and tasks.

Excerpts from (http://www.nzherald.co.nz) article by Roy Stager Jacques

The above case study shows us what the most important elements of the change process management are. Hopefully by reading this Study Guide you will be able to apply change management techniques in real life and in the exam.

1. Explore different types of strategic change and their implications.[2]
[Learning Outcome a]

1.1 Strategic change

Change is ever present in our society and a fact of organisational life. **Change** is necessary if an organisation wishes to prosper in an uncertain, complex and volatile environment. Strategic changes happen due to the forces at work in the environment, which may be internal or external. A strategic change may be needed to:

- keep up with competitive pressures which are either in terms of cost leadership or differentiation
- adapt to change in regulations
- take advantage of new products and emerging markets
- meet demand and ensure supply
- adopt new technology

Example

Kathy Ltd manufactures bubble bath liquid which it sells for $10 in its domestic market and $8 in the international market. Recently, Clean Soft Ltd has entered the same market and has started to capture Kathy's market share. Clean Soft has adopted the pricing strategy of selling its bubble bath liquid at $8 in the domestic market. Quality surveys of the products of Kathy and Clean Soft show that the products are of the same quality. In this case, to maintain its existing market share, Kathy has decided to sell its product at $7. Often high demand could justify the lower prices or reduced margins per unit as the fixed costs have been allocated to a large number of units resulting in an overall profit. For example, the allocation of $100 to 10 units will add $10 as a fixed cost to the cost of the goods whereas the allocation of $100 to 20 units will add only $5 as a fixed cost per unit. Kathy may follow this policy until Clean Soft has been forced out of the market.

1.2 Types of strategic change

Strategic change is dependent on the forces that influence the change. As a result, there is never one right method or way for all changes to take place. Change can be analysed on the two axes of velocity and mass. The **velocity** of change could be both incremental and built on existing policies or could be a '**big bang**' approach when rapid changes are needed. **Mass** is the extent of change, where the question is whether change can be accomplished within the existing paradigm (**realignment**) or a more fundamental change (**transformational**) is required.

> **Example**
>
> Rayan Ltd is a company which produces chocolate. Due to the competition in the market, Rayan has to take a decision regarding its cost policy and starts working towards reducing the cost of goods sold. Here the velocity of the change is incremental as it has to change its cost policy and mass i.e. the extent of the change is dependent on the existing cost structure and the scope for the savings without reducing the quality of the goods.

Balogun and Hope Hailey came up with four different types of strategic change that can occur. These are as follows:

1. **Adaptation** is change that happens **incrementally** and does not involve any fundamental changes to an organisation's thinking.

> **Example**
>
> Sainsbury's has successfully introduced an organic section in all its outlets to take advantage of customers' demands for organic produce. The change is adaptive in the sense that it has not involved any major rehauling of the products that Sainsbury's inventories.

2. **Reconstruction** is change that requires a **major overhauling** of an organisation's policies to counter competitive pressures or a falling bottom line. The emphasis in such a change is on speed.

> **Example**
>
> Kids Shoppe manufactures and sells toys. Previously it sold the toys only nationally. Recently its business has increased and now it sells the toys in three main regions. Managing this increased business by following the traditional hierarchy structure is difficult, so Kids Shoppe has decided to reconstruct its business around the matrix structure. Each region has been given a controller who is responsible for that cost / profit centre. This has brought about a large change in Kids Shoppe's policies.

3. **Evolution is change that happens over a long period of time and is transformational**. Managers may anticipate the need for such a change and take steps to achieve the change over time. Evolutionary change is gradual, linear and usually sequential.

> **Example**
>
> E-Learning has evolved since computers were first used in the field of education. Companies involved in publishing text books at present have to slowly evolve to adapt to the scenario where all learning will be through the medium of the internet.

4. **Revolution** is change that is not only **rapid** but involves **fundamental changes** to the organisation's goals and beliefs. This may happen when **pressures for change are extreme** e.g. when the demise of the organisation is to be avoided. This path of transformational change may not be linear or sequential.

> **Example**
>
> New developments such as computer reservation systems, flight booking on the internet, internet auctions and electronic ticketing have radically transformed the travel business. Travel agencies are forced to find survival strategies because airlines have started to sell tickets directly via the internet or call centres. They have to change their business from just selling tickets to modularised systems that meets the needs of the individual customers.
>
> Online ticketing has now replaced the traditional systems for booking tickets. Travel agents have to change over quickly to the new systems or be forced out of business.

SUMMARY

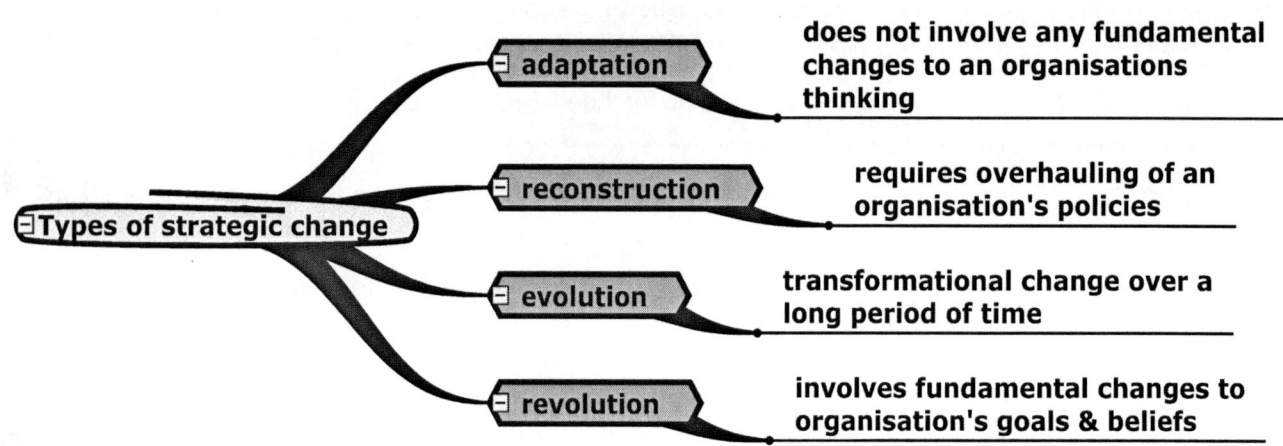

1.3 Implications of change on stakeholders

Any change alters the clarity and stability of roles within an organisation, often creating chaos. There are costs associated with strategic change because it draws resources from an organisation, interrupts its operations and tampers with its legitimacy i.e. brings changes in its existing control structure / environment. In addition, implementing the change involves enormous risk and is usually met with resistance from employees and often other stakeholders. Organisational inertia is one cause of this resistance, and it serves to limit organisational adaptive flexibility. This requires realignment and renegotiation of formal patterns of relationships as the previous roles of the employees may be changed. Sometimes such change might result in the reduction of human resources or a negative change in an individual's responsibilities. Such change may also cause employees to lose self-confidence.

Hence it is essential for them to be involved in planning and executing change and to have opportunities for developing the new skills needed by the change.

The stakeholders who may be affected by the proposed strategic change would be:

1. **Shareholders and Lenders:** sometimes there may be a need to inject a large amount of capital when a reconstruction of the organisation is taking place. Dilution of their interest and returns may not be welcomed by the shareholders unless the future revenue from such a change is clearly stated. Lenders are more concerned about the security of their holdings.

2. **Customers:** incremental changes involving the price and quality of goods and services will affect both existing and new customers. Unless the proposed change takes into account their interests, the organisation may stand to lose its customer base.

3. **Employees:** one of the main groups of stakeholders which is affected by any type of change is the employees of the organisation. Any change which will affect their job security, pay and conditions or job satisfaction will be greeted with hostility. Effective communication will go a long way to increasing their commitment to the proposed change.

4. **General public**: their main concern regarding the proposed strategic change is whether such a change is going to cause any inconveniences which did not previously exist and how the organisation plans to address this. An example of such planning could be preparation to obtain planning permission from the government.

5. **Government agencies:** their primary concern would be whether the proposed change comes within the ambit of all regulatory agencies and whether the organisation is geared up towards meeting them.

Test Yourself 1

Joy Ltd is engaged in the production and sale of medicines. It also has one branch which is engaged in researching new medicines and the side effects of existing medicines which have not yet been brought into the market. Recently, Happy Ltd took over the research wing of Joy Ltd. Immediately after this acquisition, Happy came to the conclusion that some of the research activities should be discontinued in view of the government's decision to ban the use of certain drugs. Consequently, Happy decided to reduce the human resources.

Required:

A Explain the implications of the reduction of human resources on the stakeholders.
B Explain the types of strategic change with reference to their scope and nature.

2. Determine the organisational context of change and use the cultural web to diagnose this organisational context.[3]

[Learning Outcome b]

The management of change depends on the context in which change occurs. When contexts differ, approaches to managing change also differ. Managing change in an NGO where the members themselves are motivated would be very different from managing change in a public limited company. Motivating the members of the public limited company is also a challenging task.

2.1 The contextual features of change which affect the approach to the management of change are as follows:

1. **Time:** the time needed for change will depend on how soon the organisation reacts to environmental pressures that it is facing.

> **Example**
>
> Yoyo is a political party which is preparing for the elections that are going to be held early next year. Yoyo has decided to change the structure of its party for the election campaign. Yoyo has very little time to make this change as it must do so before the election campaign gets underway.

2. **Preservation:** which of the organisational resources and capabilities need to be retained to make change easier?

3. **Diversity:** different views, opinions or cultures in different functions within an organisation may assist the change process. A uniform view, on the other hand, may lead to resistance to change.

4. **Capability:** are the staff and management capable of handling change? Past experience may help to assess this.

> **Example**
>
> Gbang Ltd is a manufacturing company. It has three different factories producing three different products. Gbang has decided to close down one of the factories and automate one of the remaining factories. The workers have started to challenge the company on these issues. How Gbang's management handles this issue will determine how mature and capable the management is. Whether its staff is capable of working with the changed technology will influence management's approach towards handling the change.

5. **Capacity:** Are there enough resources in terms of finance and management time to effect change?

> **Example**
>
> Denis Inc is a pharmaceutical company. Due to the FDA (US Food and Drug Administration) guidelines, Denis has had to withdraw its best-selling medicine from the market. What's more, Denis has had to pay damages in the form of monetary compensation to the individuals who used the medicine. It is now considering producing a new medicine. In this case, the management of the change is dependent on Denis's financial and managerial capacity to handle the change. For example, having paid huge damages, does it have enough resources to invest in a new product?

6. **Readiness:** Are the staff and management ready to effect change or are they not still convinced of the need for change?

7. **Power:** Who has the power to make the proposed changes without facing much resistance? Is there the required support for the change?

An analysis of the features leads to the following questions:

- Is the proposed change **achievable** in terms of capacity, capability and readiness?
- What are the **means** by which change can be managed and how does the context affect this?
- How much of the context needs to be **changed** before beginning the change process?
- Will the proposed change have to be managed **all at once** or can it be done **one step at a time**?

Using the cultural web to diagnose the organisational context

The cultural web may be used to assess the current culture of the organisation and to identify the differences that would be needed if change were to be effected. We use the cultural web first of all to compare the organisational culture as it is now and the organisational culture desired in future, and then to identify the differences between the two. These differences are the changes that need to be made to achieve the desired future strategy. The cultural web can be used to diagnose the organisational context, as the elements considered in 2.1 above are in some way influenced by the corporate culture. For example, a hierarchical power structure may affect an organisation's capability to bring about change due to its rigid outlook. The different elements of the cultural web are:

1. **Symbols:** the ways in which the organisation is represented. These may include logos, dress codes, office space and cars. For example, the organisation might have the culture of requiring its employees to wear formal dress except on Fridays where casual dress is allowed. Or it may have a parking system in which anyone can park anywhere depending on the available spaces.

2. **Stories and myths and legends:** a means of perpetuating traditions and creating role models.

Example

Rachel Inc is the market leader in women's perfume. Its employees always tell the story of how Rachel started the company with a capital of $20,000 and how it grew to become the biggest company in the country. Stories of how she invented the specific perfumes, her work style, how she took past decisions and how the company has benefited from them are famous Rachel has become a role model for the current management and the company's work culture is influenced by the stories about her.

3. **Power structure:** refers to both the formal and informal power structure. An employee may gain power by holding a position of authority, gaining access to resources or through knowing who's who in the business and political world.

4. **Routines:** how things are done in an organisation which, in turn, guides the behaviour of staff internally as well as externally.

5. **Control systems:** the systems in place to monitor activities e.g. a budgetary control system.

6. **Organisational culture:** the hierarchy and the authority and responsibility associated with the roles within the organisation.

2.2 Analysing culture as it is now

Start by looking at each element separately, and asking questions that help to determine the dominant factors in each element. Elements and related questions are shown below, along with examples from a shoe manufacturing company.

1. **Stories**

   - Which stories about the organisation do employees currently tell?
   - What image is communicated to customers and other stakeholders?
   - What do employees talk about when they think of the history of the company?
   - Who are the role models?

Example

- The company is known for its cheap goods.
- Staff members talk about the founder starting the company in his garage.
- The message conveyed is that the company does things in the cheapest way possible.

2. **Symbols**

   - Is company-specific logo or language used?
   - Are there any status symbols or dress codes?

3. **Power structures**

   - Who has the real power in the organisation?
   - Who makes or influences decisions?
   - How is this power used or abused?

Example
- The owner has the real power and he believes in a low cost, high profit model.
- Power is preserved through access to resources.

4. Organisational structure

- Is the structure flat or hierarchical?
- Where are the formal lines of authority?
- Are there informal lines?

Example
- Hierarchical structure - owner, senior managers, staff.
- The PA to the CEO has informal authority over a lot of decisions.

5. Control systems

- Which process or procedure has the strongest controls? Weakest controls?
- Are employees rewarded for good work or penalised for poor work?
- Which reports are issued to keep control of operations, finance, etc.?

Example
- Costs are highly controlled through detailed budgeting and cost control reports.
- Getting the work done with the lowest amount of direct costs is given priority over quality.
- Employees are penalised for delays in reacting to customer complaints.

6. Rituals and routines

- What do customers expect when they enter a retail outlet?
- What do employees expect?
- What behaviour do these routines encourage?
- When a new problem is encountered, what rules do employees apply when solving it?

Example
- Customers expect to be attended to immediately.
- Employees expect to have to just quietly attend to their work without asking any questions.
- There is a lot of focus on money, and especially on how to cut costs.
- If a problem is encountered, then employees are encouraged to deal with it on their own without consulting seniors.

Diagram 1 Analysing existing culture

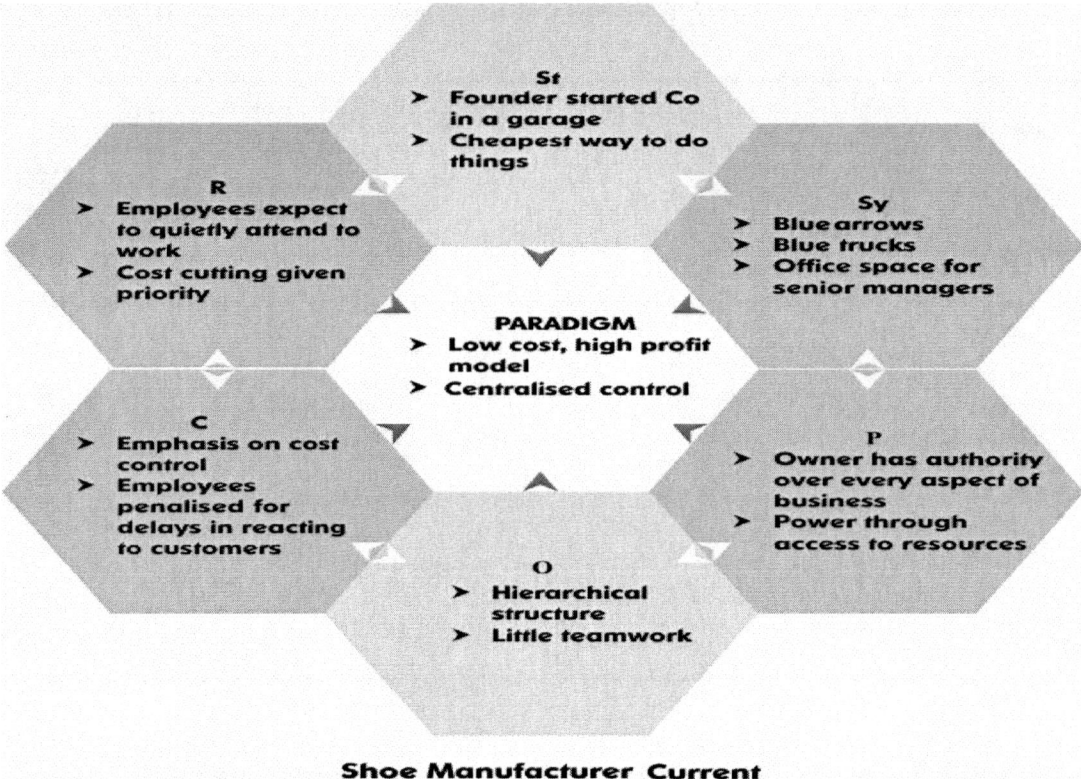

Shoe Manufacturer Current

2.3 Analysing the desired, future culture

As these questions are answered, a picture of the corporate culture emerges. In the illustration given above, the common theme is cost control with low levels of employee and customer satisfaction. With the picture of the current cultural web complete, the process is repeated to identify the future culture that would be the ideal corporate culture aiming for high quality goods at economic prices.

Diagram 2: Analysing Future web

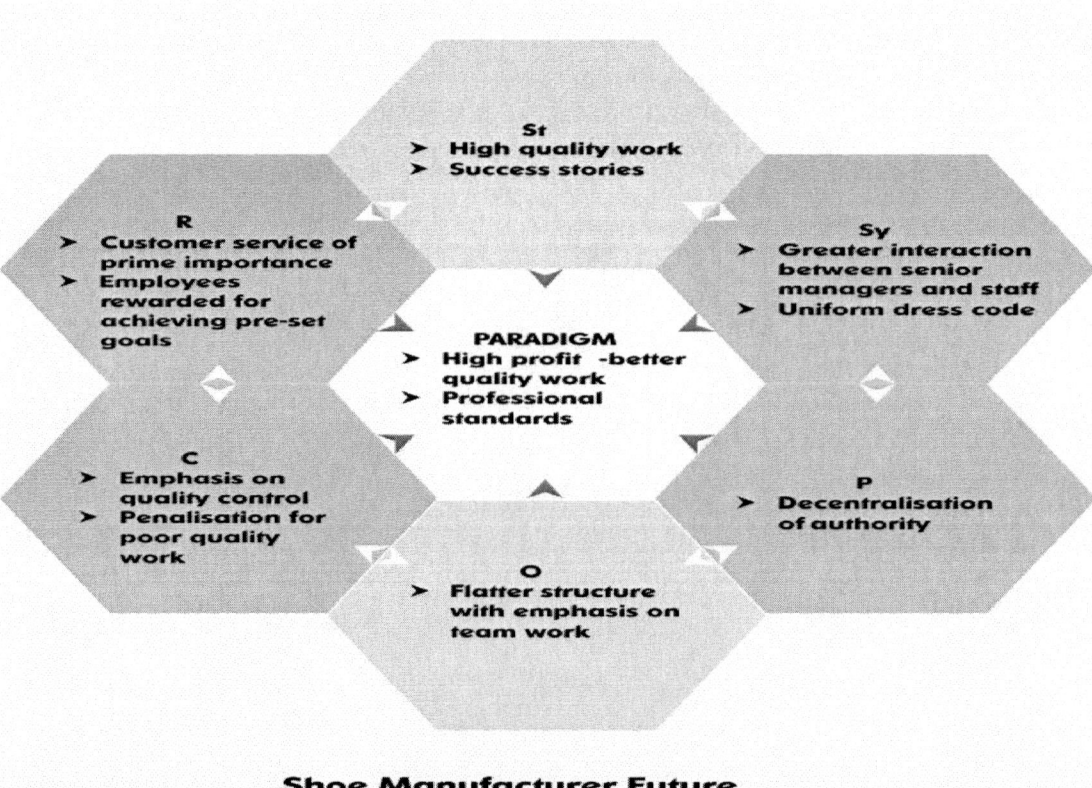

Shoe Manufacturer Future

2.4 Mapping the differences between the two

The next step is to compare the two cultural web diagrams, and identify the differences between the two. Considering the organisation's strategic goals, the following questions should be answered:

- Which cultural strengths have been highlighted by the analysis of the current culture?
- Which factors are hindering strategy and which factors need to be reinforced?
- Which factors are detrimental to the productivity of the workplace?
- Which factors need to change?

In this way, the cultural web can be used to achieve a more conducive environment for growth and success.

Test Yourself 2

Jack used to manufacture his own noodles at home and now owns a small organisation called Zaggi Noodles. His noodles are very famous in his hometown, because of their quality and low price. Jack has a very good relationship with his employees and customers. However, when a problem is encountered, his employees deal with it on their own without consulting seniors which sometimes causes problems. Jack attends to his customers immediately and provides high quality service. The organisational structure is flat as the organisation consists of only the owner and his employees. The employees are happy as they can deal directly with the boss. They are rewarded for punctuality. All authority naturally vests with the owner.

Required:

Jack is now planning to expand his business all over the country. As his management consultant, advise him on the future culture of the organisation and what changes will need to be made to attain this future culture.

3. Establish potential blockages and levers of change.[2]
[Learning Outcome c]

One of the considerations in diagnosing change is to identify the factors that encourage the change (levers) and the factors that may hinder the change (blockages).

3.1. Forcefield analysis

Kurt Lewin's 'forcefield analysis' is a guide to identifying the factors that will assist or hinder change. It is a study of those aspects of the current situation that might aid change in the desired direction and how can they be reinforced, and those aspects that block the change and how these can be weakened or overcome. These conflicting factors are represented by opposing arrows. The thickness of the arrow indicates the strength of the factor. Alternatively, scores can be assigned to denote the strength of the factors. Here the elements of the cultural web are usually the factors that aid or hinder change. Changes can be effected by strengthening the levers and weakening the blockages. The steps involved in force field analysis are as follows:

- describe the current situation in the centre of the diagram
- list all the forces for change in one column and all forces against the change in another column
- assign a score to each force – say 1 (weak) to 5 (strong)
- decide how to strengthen the assisting forces and weaken the restricting forces
- make an action plan

Forcefield analysis will help to improve the profitability of the project by presenting two options:

a) empowering the factors that are assisting the change

b) overcoming the resistance of the restraining forces

The second option is better as addressing the negative forces first will increase commitment to the change whereas attempting to force the change may make the staff uncooperative.

If the above project were to be implemented, then the following changes may be needed:

- It may be necessary to train staff in order to eliminate the fear of technology.
- To compensate for loss of overtime, wages may be increased to reflect the increased productivity.
- It may be useful to explain to staff that the change will make their jobs less monotonous. If necessary, the fact that the equipment is needed to cope with competitive pressures and to ensure that the company remains in business may be communicated to the staff.

When the blockages have been overcome and the assisting factors have been reinforced, the manager can go ahead with his plan of installing the new equipment.

Tip

Force field analysis is a useful technique for looking at all the forces for and against a plan. It helps you to weigh the importance of these factors and decide whether a plan is worth implementing.

In addition, when you have decided to carry out a plan, force field analysis helps you to identify changes that you could make to improve it.

Case Study

Christ Hospital is the second largest hospital in its area. Just like any other hospital, Christ's nursing staff work in three shifts. Christ has a lot of problems with miscommunication caused by changes in nurses' shifts. A few of the patients who should have received new medication were given their old medication. Recently, there were three cases where patients filed complaints against the nursing staff who failed to carry out patients' requests because of shift changeovers. Even a few of the doctors were annoyed because of the nurses' behaviour and miscommunication between staff. An increase in the number of such problems became a threat to the hospital's reputation.

The hospital decided to change its traditional shift changeover system. It carried out a force field analysis of the changeover and identified the driving and restraining forces for the change. The driving forces included the support of some staff members such as ward managers, peers, patients, and doctors' arguments in favour of change. The most important driving force was the determination to see the change take place. Amongst the restraining forces were the lateness of employees and the lack of an overlap between shifts. Lack of information and the uncertainty surrounding the change were also restraining forces.

Christ Hospital managed restraining forces by opening communication with its employees, and employees were given freedom to express their opinions and to participate in the decision-making process.

Diagram3: Forcefield analysis of the above case study

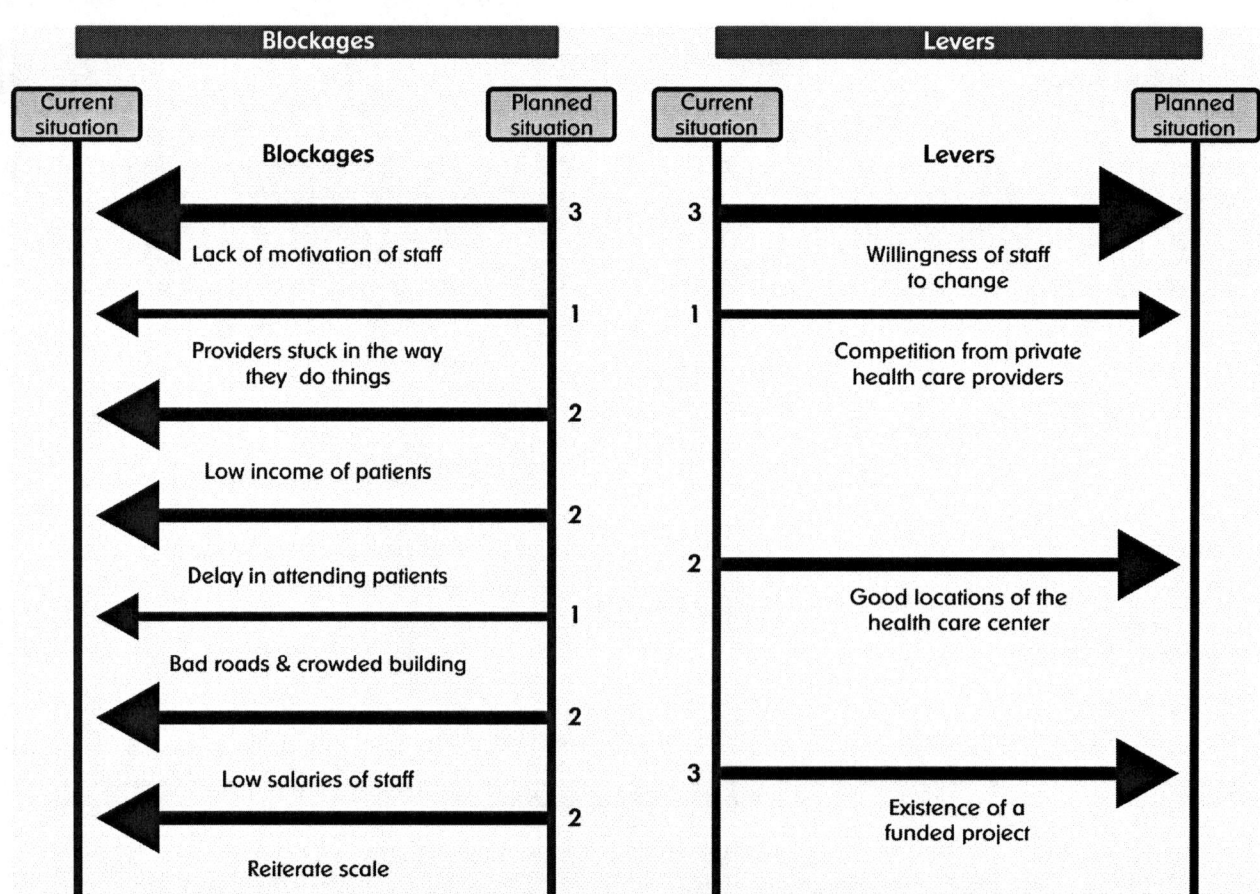

Total = 13   Total = 9

SUMMARY

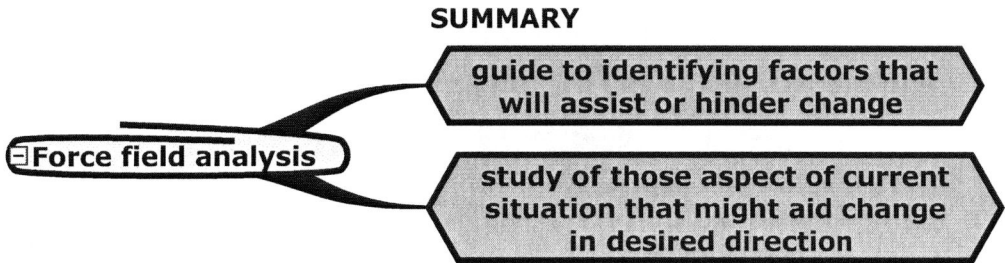

Test Yourself 3

The Rosalind Health Centre is a **privately funded** clinic that serves a community of 10,000 who belong mainly to the low income group. The staff is made up of a director, a team of doctors, nurses and health assistants, a pharmacist, administration staff and laboratory technicians. There are no inpatient facilities. Patients are treated and then sent home. Services provided by the clinic include: laboratory services, primary health care, immunisation, maternal and paediatric services. It also operates a pharmacy which dispenses medicines at low costs. Although the clinic is always busy, it reaches only a small proportion of the population. The clinic now wants to increase its coverage by improving the quality of services offered by ensuring the health service building is clean and the staff is cordial and professional. A task force comprising some of the staff members has been formed to formulate and implement the plan.

Required:

If you were a member of the task force, how would you identify the factors hindering or assisting the health centre in its achievement of the proposed mission?

---

4. Advise on the style of leadership appropriate to manage strategic change.[2]
[Learning Outcome d]

4.1 Styles of managing change

This section deals with the different styles of management that may be adopted under different organisational contexts. The different styles of managing change are:

1. **Communication and coaching**

This style of managing change involves communicating the **reason for the change as well as the way in which the change is going to be implemented**. This approach works well when the change is incremental in nature. Education may eliminate any misconceptions or miscommunication and will help to increase commitment to the change. Coaching explains the need to learn and the best way to do it, so that the individual understands and accepts the need to change. The communication and coaching style is often used in conjunction with other styles. One-to-one coaching is more effective than class-based.

2. **Participative / supportive**

In this approach, **those affected by the proposed change are involved in its planning and development** to foster a positive attitude towards the change by building capability and readiness. Individuals and teams know their part in the change process and are also made aware of the bigger picture. Getting their input on the given task and explaining its significance will give them a sense of value. This is the ideal approach but it may delay the change process. There is also an inherent risk of trying to incorporate the change within the existing set-up, without exploring the need for exploring outside the present culture. The very basis of participation involves trust between management and staff. This style is suited for an evolutionary type of change.

Example

A company has decided a new staffing policy which recommends that employees should not work after the office hours. If they do so, they will not be paid overtime.). Before implementing this policy, the company will need to take into consideration the views of the current staff. Fears about job security and demotions can be eliminated through effective communication.

3. Intervention / delegation

This usually **involves a change agent** who will be in charge of the change process. Some elements of the proposed change are delegated to other individuals or teams within the organisation for greater effectiveness. The delegated groups are responsible for planning and implementation to some extent. The expectations of the delegated group are made clear from the outset and the deadlines for completion are agreed. The lines of accountability and monitoring of the delegated task are also specified. Control and responsibility is retained by the change agent. This is the ideal style to be adopted in a situation which calls for incremental change.

4. Directive / persuasive

The management decides the strategy and the method for change in this approach. It works well in a hierarchical structure when there are numerous employees involved in the process or a tight deadline looms. There is both clarity of vision and speed in implementation. The leader often answers the employees questions regarding why, where, what, how and when change is to be accomplished. Communication must be detail-oriented, unambiguous and set specific standards and expectations. It is ideal when change is transformational in nature.

Example

A company wants to introduce a new system of processing receipts by using an ERP tool. In this case, the persuasive style may be appropriate. Management should hold a meeting and explain to the relevant staff how the company will be benefit from implementing the ERP tool and how the work of the employees who are currently processing the receipts will change. The method of implementing the system should also be explained to them.

5. Autocratic

In this approach, **change is imposed by use of power**. This is the most useful style when the organisation is facing a crisis but it is also the least popular. Here the leader tries to control work to the maximum extent. Frequent audits are carried out to ensure strict adherence to procedures.

SUMMARY

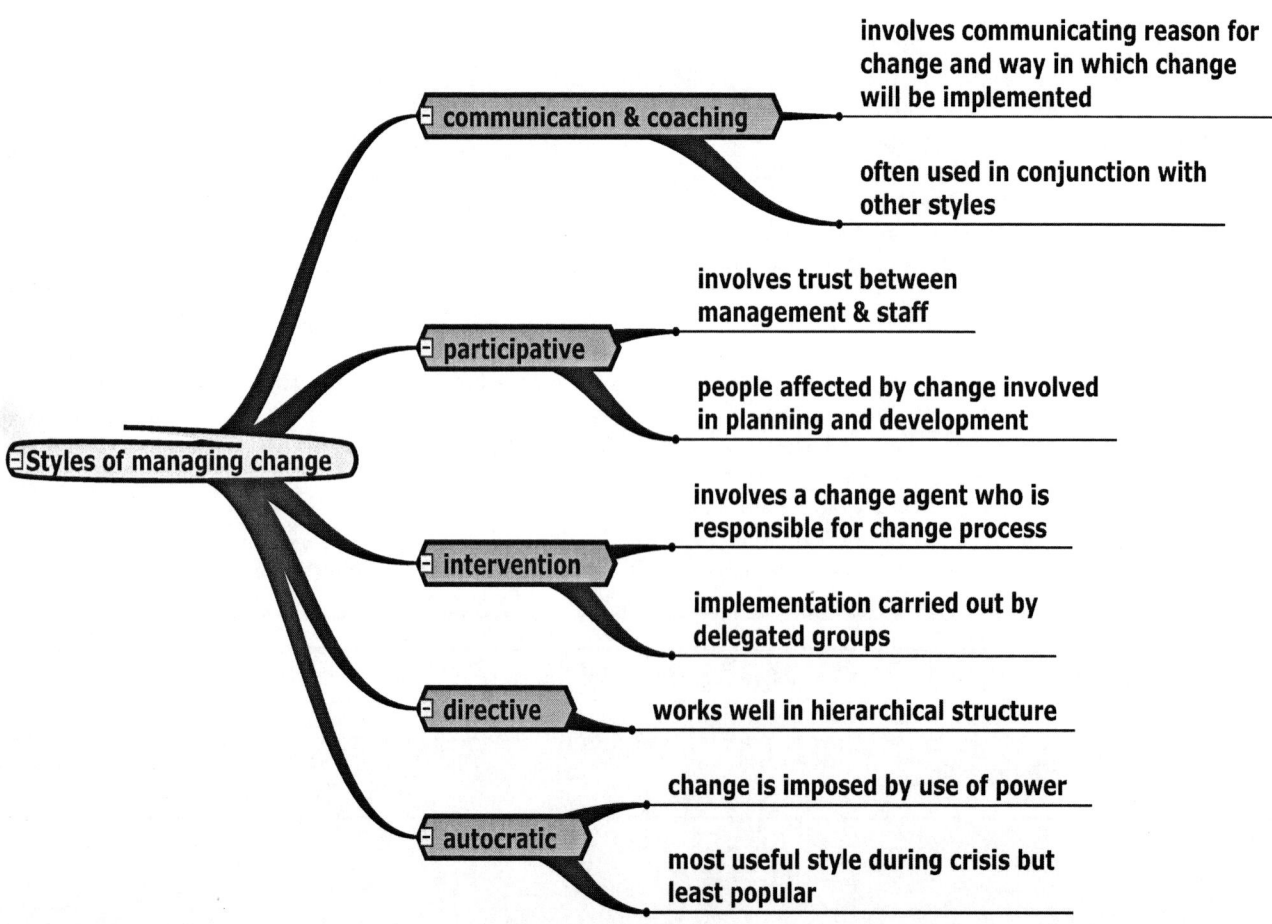

4.2 Appropriate styles under different contexts

Different styles of change may be adopted under different contexts irrespective of who is managing the change. A combination of styles will work better in a change process. The different styles under different criteria are enumerated below:

1. **Types of strategic change:** for strategic changes that are adaptive in nature, a participative style is appropriate since this style will foster greater commitment to the change and help build readiness and capability. Where a revolutionary change is required, a directive style may be appropriate since this will help to provide a clear insight in how to undertake the process of change as well as enable faster implementation. For a reconstructional or evolutionary change, a combination of participative and directive style will work better.

2. **Power structures:** a directive style will work when the organisational structure is hierarchical. A participative style or interventional style is suitable for a flatter organisation.

3. **Managerial personality:** styles adopted by different personality types will be the ones they are most comfortable with, but the best managers will easily adopt different styles.

4. **Contextual features:** styles may differ according to the contextual features of the organisation. When change is to be accomplished in a short span of time, a directive style will work best. An organisational context resembling a military mission will require a directive style. A participative or interventional approach is best suited for developing capabilities such as making employees ready to use new technology. Different departments or functions may need different styles. Different groups of stakeholders may also need to be approached by adopting different management styles.

Test Yourself 4

Sharon is the managing director of Great Looks Ltd which manufactures herbal beauty products. The company has done well locally because of its innovative herbal products and posts a moderate margin on sales. Sharon also has a team of experts whom she has personally trained. The company has 20 outlets currently which are headed by trained experts. She now wants to expand to national and international markets. Her plan is to increase the number of outlets by 25% each year for the next 5 years. Such growth will place a considerable strain on the existing organisation and its resources. Each outlet is to have its own management team, sales personnel and administration. Great Looks is planning to employ an additional 500 people at various functional levels.

Required:

Sharon needs to inform her staff of her plans regarding the company's growth over the next five years and is concerned about the staff's approach towards the company and its growth plans. What management style(s) can she adopt to successfully implement the changes?

---

5. Specify organisational roles required to manage strategic change.[2]
[Learning Outcome e]

Change management programmes are undertaken by change agents who may be strategic leaders, middle managers or outsiders. A change agent is an individual or group of individuals who have the conviction and ability to bring about change in the desired direction. Their role is essentially to bring order out of chaos. Outsiders playing the role of change agents may be one or more of the following:

➢ A new chief executive or chairman or a new set of managers who have been appointed to bring fresh approaches and new ideas into the organisational setup.

➢ Consultants who have been appointed to help in the planning and development of strategy. They are effective as change agents as they are not constrained by existing routines and can analyse them independently.

➢ Other stakeholders who have the capacity to act as change agents by virtue of their power and influence over the organisation.

Change agents need to employ a number of skills:

a) **Analytical skills:** to be able to analyse clearly and then persuasively defend their analyses to the organisation. They should have clarity of vision and be sensitive to the external and organisational contexts of change.

b) **Communication skills:** to be able to work with teams to inspire and stimulate employees.

c) **Networking skills:** to develop and maintain useful relationships with a wide variety of individuals and clients so as to be able to influence change in positive directions.

d) **Diagnostic skills:** to be able to 'deconstruct' an organisation or process and then reconstruct it in innovative ways. They also need to understand the financial impacts of change and speak many languages – marketing, finance, systems management and motivational skills.

5.1 Strategic leaders

Definitions

Strategic leadership can be described as visionary leadership in which the leader has to give overall direction to the organisation as a whole. A strategic leader is more involved with performing macro-management, i.e. delegating day-to-day implementation responsibilities to other senior executives. His role is to lead others on the path i.e. identify directions, evaluate different strategies and implement the right strategy for the organistion as well as inspire the other employees to achieve the organisation's strategic goals.

A strategic leader must create the vision which will provide a corporate sense of being and a sense of enduring purpose. As he develops clarity, he can start the process of educating, generating support and building momentum for change. The need then arises to formally announce and communicate the vision. Successful change starts when people take a hard look at the organisation's performance in the face of competitive pressures, market position and technological advances. When unpleasant facts are bought out in the open, then comes the willingness and need to change. Along with the vision, the strategic plan for action to change the vision into reality should also be communicated. It is then the duty of the strategic leader to remove blocks to change and call for new behaviour that will be consistent with the plan.

5.2 Leaders often fall under two categories

1. Charismatic leaders

They articulate the vision, communicate high expectations and show the determination to succeed. They inspire, instill, energise and reassure their employees. They are concerned with the long-term vision and goals of the organisation. These leaders are often referred to as transformational leaders.

Example

Donald Trump is an example of how effective decision-making and sharp communication skills can transform an organisation into an empire. He is a man of great vision and strength. He encourages his people to reach greater heights in their areas of expertise and helps them grow in experience. He comes across as a man intolerant of carelessness. His vitality and thirst for success are inspiring.

2. Transactional leaders

Their focus is on developing, communicating and controlling the organisation's activities. They are concerned with the current situation and how this can be changed to ensure success and growth.

Example

Several well-known universities including Harvard and IIM are analysing the Indian Railways Minister Laloo Prasad Yadav's style of management. Laloo Prasad achieved a turnaround in the Indian railways. One of his successful strategies was to give railway officers complete independence. He has a lot of common sense and realised that to succeed, his officers had to be given freedom. He has selected a few advisors who give him the right advice and he has given them the authority to work without fear or favour.

5.3 Leadership approaches

Whatever the type, the leadership approaches to manage change are different. The different leadership approaches are as follows:

1. **Planning:** a leader following this approach will concentrate on planning and may delegate the day-to-day operations and management of change to other managers.

Example

In most cases, the directors of a company participate in the planning phase of the company's strategic activities. Managing the day-to-day operations and the management of change is left to the managing director.

2. **Human resources:** a leader adopting this style will concentrate on getting the right type of people and developing their capabilities to enable them to handle change. The strategic management in this case is left to other managers.

3. **Core competences:** this approach involves the leader building and improving the areas of competences to attain a competitive advantage. The management of change is based on the core competences of the individual managers.

Example

The leadership approach based on core competences exists mainly in professional businesses such as law firms where the leader is busy in building and improving professional competencies amongst the staff and the management of change is handled based on the core competencies of the individual managers.

4. **Control:** here the leader is involved in formulating control measures and monitors performance. Other managers are also involved in control procedures and policies. Change management, needless to say, is strictly monitored at every step.

5. **Continuous development:** this approach emphasises continual change through communication channels. Other managers take the role of change agents.

Diagram 4: Leadership approaches

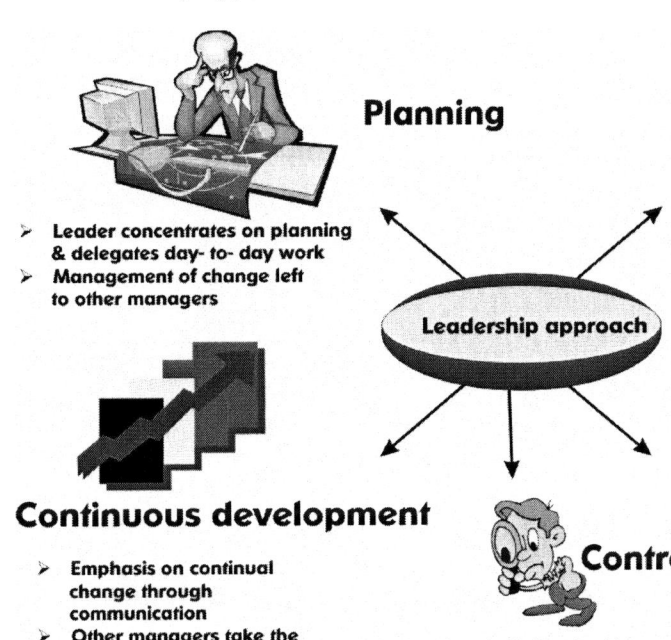

5.4 Middle managers

The involvement of the middle managers in effecting a successful change is very important as they are the link between top management and the rest of the organisation. Their role can be summarised as follows:

- Implementing the necessary changes in their functional areas.
- Controlling and monitoring the change process.
- Translating the strategy into ways that are relevant to their departments. Also, since they are in day-to-day control of operations, they are involved in the adjustment of the strategic responses. Balanced scorecards are used to align the organisation's activities to the organisation's larger visions or strategies.
- Advising top management on the blockages that may arise and the changes required to tackle them.

However, the middle managerial role in formulating strategy and facilitating its articulation is fundamentally undervalued and misunderstood in many organisations. It is important for senior management to realise that championing change will not ensure success. They need to develop the people in the middle management to drive the programme forward on a day-to-day basis. On their part, middle managers need to move away from day-to-day operations and think like senior managers to understand the business strategy. They can take on the role of 'ace mediators' between senior management and staff. Middle managers know the difficulties faced in day-to-day operations and if they know the strategies of the organisations, they can communicate it in a better way to the staff and motivate them to work according to the organisation's strategy. Problems which persist can be pointed out to higher management. Higher management is in a better position to take any corrective action or change certain strategies. They can be good role models and re-engineer success through overcoming organisational barriers to success.

Test Yourself 5

Spice is a family-owned restaurant run by the Beckhams, specialising in continental cuisine. It has been doing average business but is now threatened by the arrival of a competitor in the vicinity. The Beckhams decide to hire a professional, Mr Smith, to initiate changes and make the restaurant attractive to its customers so as to maintain its client base. The family has adequate funds at its disposal to implement the changes that may be needed.

Required:

What are the skills needed by Mr Smith to make the restaurant more popular and thereby increase the turnover and hence profits?

---

6. Discuss levers that can be employed to manage strategic change.[2]
[Learning Outcome f]

In this section, the levers that can be employed to manage change are discussed. As mentioned in section 3.1, levers are the facilitating factors that enable the organisation to successfully implement the change process. The elements of the cultural web are normally the levers for change. Handling the strategic change is always difficult for employees, including management. If the strategic change is not handled carefully, it could result in the closure of the entire business. Below are some levers which could be applied to a situation of strategic change to enable the successful implementation of the change.

6.1 Turnaround strategy

A turnaround strategy is adopted when there is a need for quick changes to ensure business survival. The objective of a turnaround strategy is to bring an underperforming company to acceptable levels in terms of profitability, cash flows and solvency. This is normally achieved through cost control techniques or revenue improvement measures. The elements of a successful turnaround strategy are as follows:

1. Disaster mitigation

Control measures are instituted to avert organisational disasters. Focus is on rapid implementation of cost reduction techniques and revenue improvement methods. Cost reduction has the fastest impact on the bottom line. This may be achieved through cutting direct or overhead costs. Cost reduction may lead to retrenchment of employees, especially if salary and wages form a large chunk of the organisation's operational costs. Working capital reductions are common to most turnaround strategies. Revenue enhancement measures focus on increasing turnover by improved product mix, new products and new markets and effective after-sales service to improve customer satisfaction. Revenue improvement measures are normally undertaken after implementing cost reduction methods, since they take a longer time to have effect. Portfolio disinvestment often takes place to raise additional resources for implementing the turnaround and to retreat to core business.

2. Management changes

Normally a new set of top and middle management is introduced into the organisation to provide a fresh perspective. Since they are not saddled with the baggage of the existing culture, they are able to think and act proactively which is what is needed to initiate change processes. A change agent with experience in restructuring similar enterprises and the ability to draw on staff from such enterprises is well placed to bring about structural change. Reorganisation is often required to ensure the success of other elements such as cost reduction, revenue improvement and market repositioning.

> **Example**
>
> In the organisational context of billion dollars write-offs coming from bad mortgages, Citigroup chose Vikram Pandit as the leader of the new generation. Vikram Pandit is famous for his ability to think strategically and has worked as the chief of the investment banking division of Citibank. Citigroup opted for Vikram Pandit instead of going for a person with more experience. He has the ability to consider Citi's processes from a fresh perspective. This decision by Citigroup could be viewed as the lever used to handle the situation of strategic change.

3. Stakeholder backing

The issues of different stakeholder groups such as lenders and employees can be tackled by effective communication throughout the period of change.

> **Example**
>
> There could be conflicts between different stakeholders such as employees and shareholders. Employees might want an increase in monetary benefits and better working conditions whereas shareholders / directors might be experiencing financial problems. Such problems could be resolved by effective communication.
>
> Where the lenders are insisting on the adherence to certain procedures and quality improvement from the workers, problems might arise as employees might show their resistance to these demands. Such problems could be resolved by effective communication.

They need to be informed of the change processes being implemented because their power and backing is essential for a successful turnaround. Stakeholders often require short-term results before approving a longer term plan.

4. Strategic repositioning

A successful turnaround is likely to require abandoning unprofitable operations and refocusing on the target market. Strategic repositioning is changing the mission of the organisation by changing what products are offered to what markets and how they are offered. This may be done by growing, shrinking or just refocusing. Sometimes this shrinking may also entail a tremendous exit cost in terms of redundancies or non-cancellable leases.

> **Example**
>
> Baywatch Ltd manufactures and sells three different products. The cost department of Baywatch has found out that product C is running at a loss and is eating into the profits from product A and product B. Consequently, the management of Baywatch has decided to discontinue production of product C. This is called strategic repositioning.

Shrinking would entail removing unprofitable product lines. Growth, on the other hand, may entail additional investment in terms of technology and people which may not be a viable option, especially if the business is in severe difficulties.

5. New financial arrangements

The financial structure may be changed by opting for long-term borrowings or renegotiating with creditors so that immediate cash outflows are reduced.

6. Focus on important improvement areas

Those areas which will give quick results can be given priority while implementing a turnover strategy. Extensive training is a crucial element of a successful turnaround.

A successful turnaround strategy should be implemented in two stages:

a) First, stabilise the business by executing reorganisation, cost reduction and asset reduction measures to improve the cash flow.
b) Then, having gained stakeholder support, go in for major restructuring measures such as revenue enhancement or market repositioning using long-term borrowings.

Example

A leading consumer electronics company whose head office was overseas was suffering from depressed consumer prices that had started to erode its profitability. However, due to cost-effective production and strong management the company started to yield satisfactory financial results. The sponsor provided the necessary finances to hire a first rate management team, hired enthusiastic, well-educated people to implement new technical and marketing know-how. Thanks to the sponsor's initiation of the turnaround strategy, issues of stakeholder commitment and financial restructuring were solved.

SUMMARY

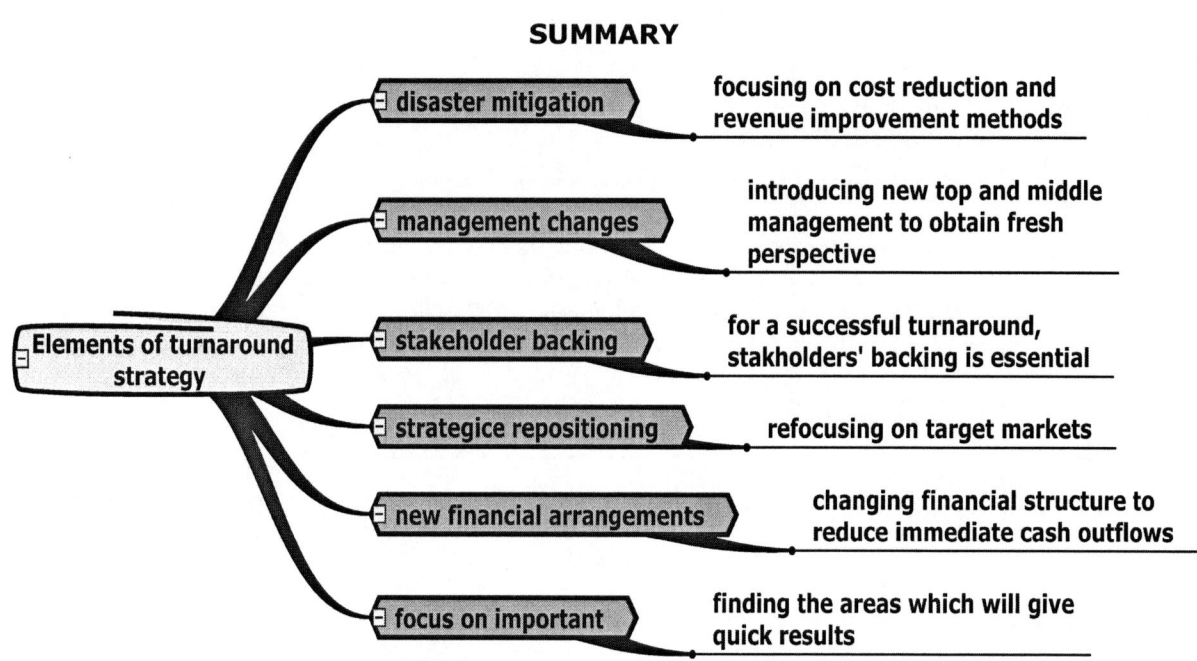

6.2 Challenging the existing assumptions

One of the major levers for change is to challenge the existing mindset. Research shows that most often revolutionary changes are required to pull an organisation out of its inertia. A lot of persistence is needed to make people realise that the existing set-up is not working anymore. This can be done through analytical workshops or by exposing staff to the day-to-day realities.

Example

Most organisations assume that fresh graduates with the required education have more knowledge of the practical work than the workers. This assumption is not correct. The graduates have not been exposed to practical work during their studies. Therefore, on entering the business world, they need to be exposed to the day-to-day business activities of the organisation. It is unfair to expect good results from them without giving them scope to acquaint themselves with the practical world.

6.3 Changing organisational routines and symbols

Routines are the way things are done in an organisation. Changing routines can signal strategic change in everyday terms and hence is relevant to people throughout the organisation. Changing routines are relatively easier than changing the mindset. It is an incremental process and may be subtly used initially and then actively changing the existing way of doing things. Symbols are objects, acts which relate to status and physical settings that reflect the power associated with a manager's authority or just meaningful everyday things. Myths, stories, rituals and behaviours are important levers for culture change. A symbolic physical gesture is literally removing the symbols associated with the old, non-functional organisation to signal the birth of the new organisation. Changing the office location or altering office spaces are powerful symbols of change.

> **Example**
>
> Often organisations choose to relocate their business in order to overcome some of its strategic problems. They may intend to maximise profitability by reducing cost. Many organisations have transferred their manufacturing, production or maintenance providing activities to developing countries where the cost of production is low. They have maximised their profitability by changing the location of the business.

The behaviour of the change agents should be in accordance with the envisaged change in order to convey the message to the rest of the organisation. Special importance is to be given to the language used by the change agents for it is the vehicle for expressing mindsets. A poor choice of language such as problem solver may signal that the old status quo still stands. Inconsistencies in language can lead to confusion about the nature of change.

> **Example**
>
> **Continuing the previous example**
>
> When a company relocates to another country to benefit from the low cost of production, its management has to ensure that problems will not arise due to the different languages used in the two countries. The reduction in cost should not be at the expense of quality problems requiring cost expenditure.

6.4 Power systems

The implementation of changes requires the support of those people who wield power over the organisation. In this context, it is important for change agents to gather and broaden the power base and overcome the resistance of influential groups. Control over resources, creation of specialists and team building are some means by which influence over the change process may be maintained.

6.5 Communicating and monitoring change

The key to change is communication. This can be brought about by educating and / or involving people in the planning process. Different media e.g. e-mails, general notices or one-to-one communication methods can be used depending upon the complexity of the matter to be communicated. The idea here is to clarify the need for change so that implementation is successful.

6.6 Change tactics

1. Some important levers of change are:

a) **Timing:** choosing the right time to promote change is important. In times of crisis, it is easier to make fundamental changes. The introduction of a new CEO or the launch of a new product could provide the opportunity to introduce changes. Messages about the timing of the change must be in accordance with the nature of the change.

b) **Job losses:** a strategic change programme often brings with it the issue of redundancy of workers and job losses. Identifying the individual(s) who need to go is very important. Typically they are the people who are blocking the change. A sympathetic approach to job losses must be taken by the change levers to signal to the rest of the organisation that they care. An open and transparent plan, including retraining and outplacement for redundant workers, is likely to facilitate major staff reductions.

Creating short-term wins: short-term pay-offs will inspire and motivate people to go through the entire change process. Available resources can be used on those areas which will give immediate results.

> **Example**
>
> **Continuing the example of Baywatch Ltd**
>
> Employees might show their resistance to Baywatch's plan to close down factory C. In such a case, Baywatch could offer a monetary benefit, such as $10,000, to each employee who is going to lose his employment. This could motivate the staff to accept the change i.e. they might withdraw their resistance towards the closure of the factory in return for an immediate financial benefit.

2. Potential pitfalls

To avoid the failure of a change programme, it would be useful to be aware of the potential pitfalls.

For example, sometimes change becomes a purely **ritualistic process** which signifies very little to the rest of the organisation. Changes may sometimes be **superficial** when senior executives fail to understand ground realities.

Change will be accepted by people only if it serves their **own self-interests**. People will not change if they are happy with their present state of affairs. Furthermore, admitting that the previous situation was wrong or no longer relevant can be a major setback for people. So the change may be reinvented according to the old culture.

> **Lack of self-confidence:** In those who have to implement the change is a major hindrance since they may try to fight off change. The adherence to the old ways seems safe and secure.
>
> Change agents may not have the **requisite knowledge** or the problem itself may not have been defined properly.

6.7 7s model

McKensey's 7s model is also helpful in making an ineffective organisation effective. An organisation has to consider the seven areas given in this model. These elements are interrelated and if the organisation failed to give enough attention to any of it, it will suffer. This tool will help in analysing the effects of the strategic change in any organisation.

Diagram 5: Mckensey's 7s model

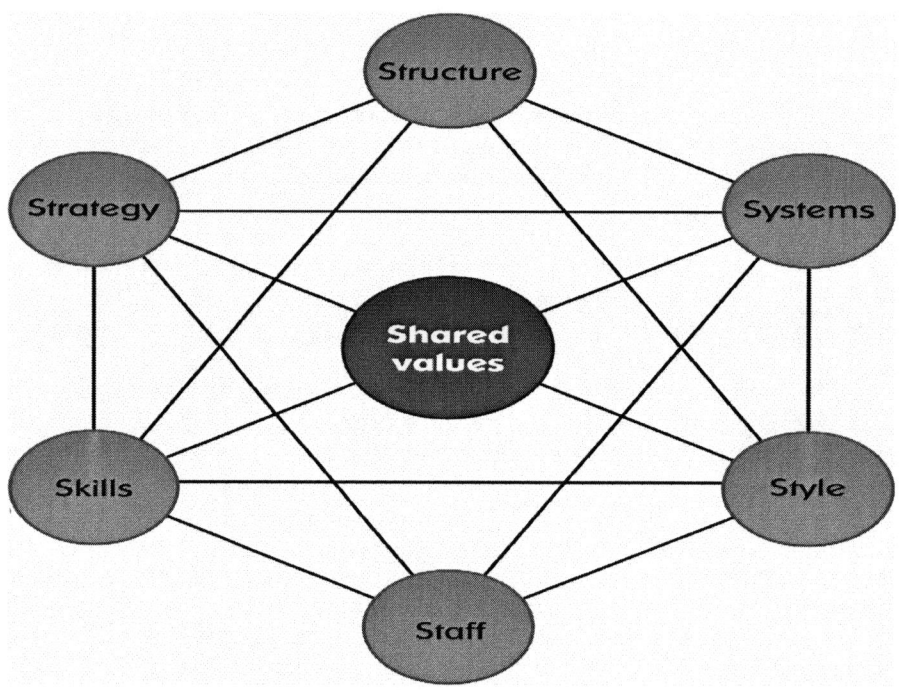

7s as described by the Mckinsey model are as follows:

1. **Strategy:** organisation's long term plan of action. Strategy is the path the organisation has taken to achieve its objectives.
2. **Structure:** factors which fall under structure include the way organisation is organised, whether it is centralised or decentralised, matrix or traditional form, its reporting styles, departments.
3. **Systems:** the policies and procedures that govern the organisation's work and systems such as information systems, performance management systems, finance, marketing systems.
4. **Skills:** capability and competencies that exists within the organisation.
5. **Shared values:** values that are believed and followed by the members of the organisation.
6. **Staff:** size and types of the workforce
7. **Style:** cultural styles such as 'cognitive' which are followed by managers in achieving objectives.

Case Study

Angel Shoe Plaza is a chain of retail shoe sellers, which has made its impact on the shoe industry over the last 10 years. Since its inception, Angel has made remarkable progress. Angel owns the majority of shares in the shoe market. Its shoes are very popular amongst teenagers, young people and the middle-aged population. For the first time, in early 20X6, the company noticed that its market share was reducing. For the first time in its history, Angel recorded a loss in one quarter of the previous year. The management of Angel took this very seriously, and appointed a committee to take care of the issue of reduced profits and reduced market share.

This committee took the following actions to resolve this issue:

- analysed the causes for the decline in Angel's profits and for the reduction in market share
- identified triggers or events responsible for generating these reasons
- analysed current trends of the shoe market
- studied predictions regarding future trends and customer preferences
- analysed the challenges faced by the shoe industry and the steps taken by other shoe retailers to overcome this

This committee then drafted a plan of action which comprised the process redesign and introduction of new and overhauled products to align them to changing market demands and customer preferences. Angel modified its strategy according to this committee's suggestions. In the following year, Angel noticed a turnaround effect and again became the leader of the shoe market.

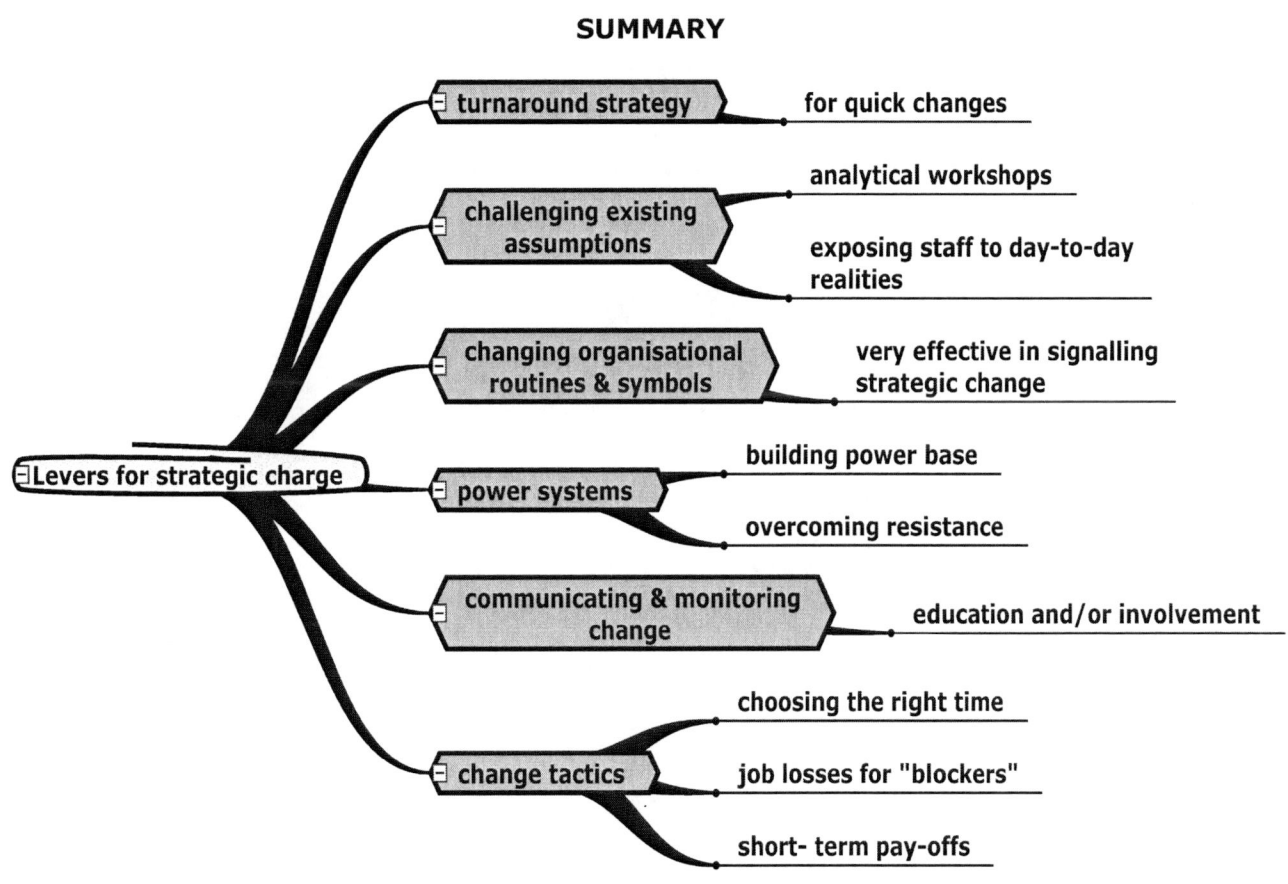

Test Yourself 6

Sally International is a large export house which specialises in buying a wide variety of manufactured products from the USA for resale in Latin America. In recent years, the company has been facing competition from stronger manufacturing companies, which have started to provide a similar sales service. The competitors do not like the idea of export houses selling their products and making profits on them.

Last year, Sally International developed a number of strategies to overcome this problem. It tried to increase its product base, supply base and consumer base simultaneously. To minimise conflict with suppliers, it also entered into major collaborative agreements. However, none of these strategies seem to have worked.

Required:

Prepare a report to identify the reasons why the selected strategies may not have been successful.

Answers to Test Yourself

Answer to TY 1

A   Implications of reduction of human resources on the stakeholders:

Shareholders and lenders: shareholders and lenders who have invested or lent money to Happy might be affected adversely as they might have invested the money in the hope of the existing research proving successful. If this is the case, they will be disappointed. The reduction in human resources could be interpreted as a reduction in non-productive costs or it may lead to doubts about whether or not Happy is going to continue Joy's research wing.

Customers: Happy's customers are internal i.e. they are within the firm. Therefore they will not be greatly affected by Happy's decision to reduce its human resources. External customers could have benefited from Happy's research.

Employees: Happy's decision to reduce its human resources is likely to have a negative effect on its employees. The employees might feel insecure. It will be a challenge for Happy's management to handle such a change. Happy's management has to communicate effectively with its employees in order to reduce their resistance to the change.

General public: the general public will be deprived of the findings which would have resulted from the continuing research.

Government agencies: the government agencies will be satisfied as Happy has stopped the research involving the banned drugs. However, the reduction in human resources will be of concern to them, because Happy is not looking into other research options. Lay-offs signal the slowing down of the economy. It's the government's responsibility to take measures to prevent the economy from slowing down.

B   The types of strategic changes with reference to scope and nature are as follows:

- **Adaptation** is change that happens incrementally and does not involve any fundamental changes to an organisation's thinking.

- **Reconstruction** is change that requires a major overhauling of an organisation's policies to counter competitive pressures or a falling bottom line. The emphasis in such a change is on speed.

- **Evolution** is change that happens over a long period of time and is transformational. Managers may anticipate the need for such a change and take steps to achieve the change over time. Evolutionary change is gradual, linear and usually sequential.

- **Revolution** is change that is not only rapid but involves fundamental changes to the organisation's goals and beliefs. This may happen when pressures for change are extreme i.e. when the survival of the organisation is at stake. This path of transformational change may not be linear or sequential.

Answer to TY 2

Jack, the owner of Zaggi Noodles, wants to expand his organisation all over the country. The current culture of the organisation seems to be a low cost, high profit model with a high level of employee and customer satisfaction. While considering the future culture, Jack will have to make sure that satisfaction levels of both employees and customers are maintained. The factors that need to change are those that will enable team work and coordination between different functions. Authority will be delegated to at least the senior managers who will need to have more power to enable the smooth functioning of the retail outlets.

The cultural elements of Zaggi Noodles, assuming the expansion plan is implemented, will change as follows:

1. As the organisation grows, there will be an increase in the number of employees both in the staff and in the managerial level. New symbols to represent the organisation such as uniforms for the staff will be needed. In addition, senior managers may be given the use of company cars as a privilege.
2. The employees can expect to be rewarded for jobs well done. Flexible working schedules can be adopted so that outlets can remain open for longer times and thereby ensure increased sales. Managers can be offered incentives which are based on the volume of sales achieved. Also management needs to offer training to employees.

3. The organisational structure will become hierarchical – owner, senior managers, managers and staff. Team work will need to be emphasised to ensure success. If required Jack could add more layers which will depend upon the size of the organisation.
4. To maintain the high level of customer satisfaction, customer complaints need to be attended to promptly. Freebies such as newspapers and magazines can be offered so that customers are entertained during their waiting time.
5. Cost control measures such as budgeting and MIS reports have to be put in place. Quality audits need to be undertaken to ensure the high standards are not compromised because of increased volume. The organisation will have to change to a high volume, high profit model.

Answer to TY 3

Force field analysis can be used to identify the factors that will aid or hinder the change.

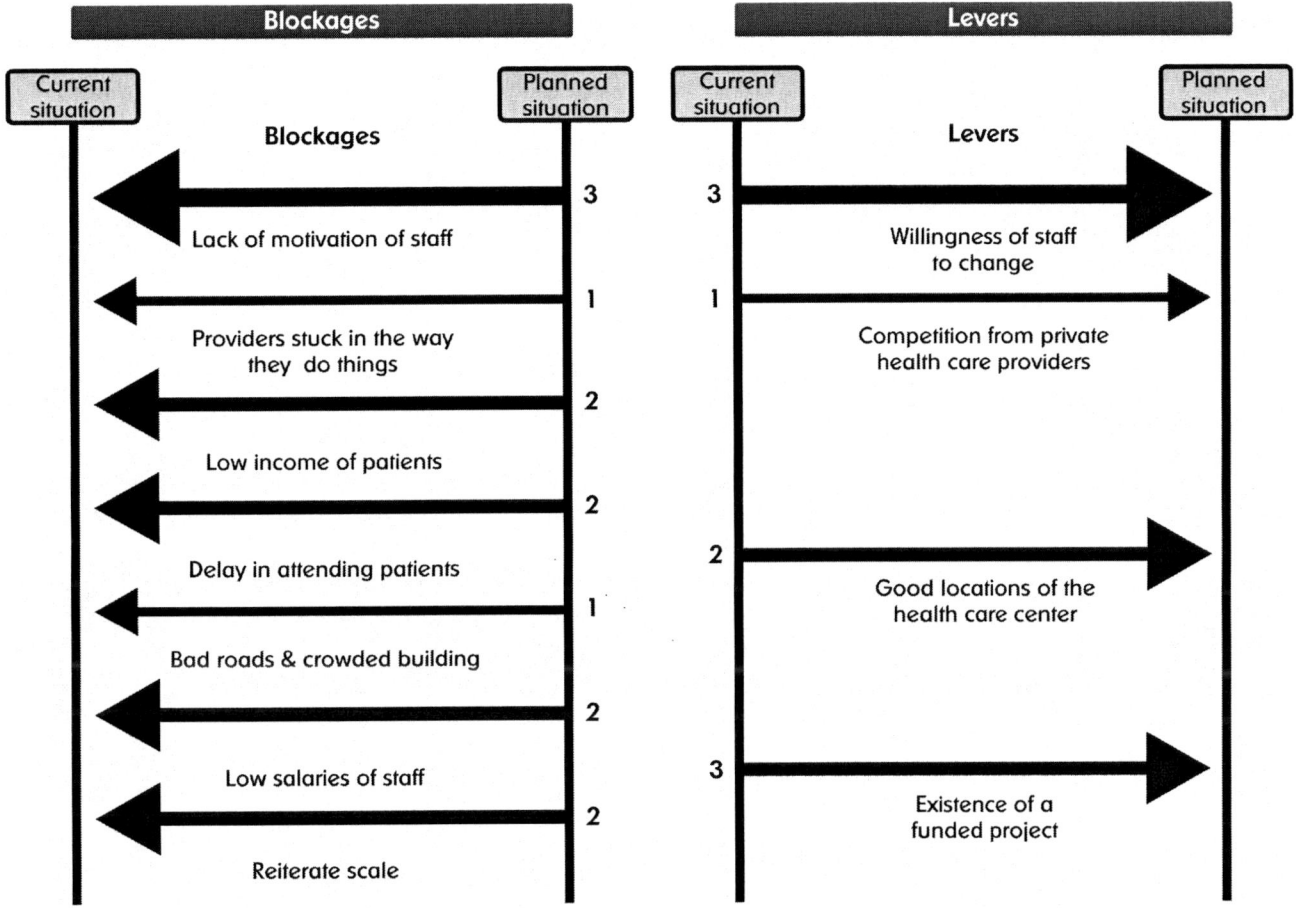

- An analysis of the factors shows that the major factors restraining the change come from the staff itself - either through lack of motivation or low salaries. These factors can be taken care of by motivating staff through incentives (such as trips), more training and better resolution of problems. This should improve the quality of services offered by the healthcare centre.

- Pay rises can be made on the basis of merit.

- Mass communication through posters and pamphlets can be carried out to educate the users about the new changes in the facility.

- Better marketing of the health centre's facilities so that users know about the services offered by them.

Answer to TY 4

The management styles Sharon can adopt to successfully implement the change include communication, participation, direction and compulsion. The success of the chosen strategy will be influenced to a large extent by the managing style adopted.

Continued on the next page

Education / communication is repeatedly argued to be the best style when there is a need to clarify misconceptions about job security, staff changes etc. The change at Great Looks is a significant change and will affect everyone in the organisation. Hence communication of the expansion plans to the staff will help in getting them to accept the change process. Jobs changes may happen but they are likely to be favourable to the staff as they will be able to benefit from their experience at Great Looks. Also there might be promotions for existing staff and job enrichment is possible with the corresponding increase in salary.

A directive / participative style will help as Sharon has a clear vision of where she wants to be in 5 years and how she is going to achieve this. She seems to have her team's loyalty, so she can involve her team of experts to tackle problems arising regionally. She needs their cooperation and commitment to the change process and this can be done by providing incentives such as a share in profits in accordance with the volume of turnover in their respective regions. A coercive approach may not work as it may set the staff against the management and have a number of unexpected and adverse consequences.

Answer to TY 5

Mr. Smith has to possess the skills needed by a successful change agent.

a) The customer is king in this business and he has to frame his strategy keeping in mind their expectations. He has to find out customer preferences and whether the restaurant has enough resources in terms of finance and human resources to meet them. Analytical and evaluation skills will enable him to achieve the desired outcome.

b) He has to understand which of the old entity's processes are not in line with the desired strategy and how he can address them. It may be that the interior décor of the restaurant is unoriginal. Here his creative skills will come into play. He can change the décor to reflect an open, spacious and lively ambience.

c) He may introduce an alternative type of cuisine if there is a market for this cuisine locally. To do this he may need to get chefs with culinary skills in that cuisine. Networking skills will help him to find the right staff.

d) He has to set about communicating to the staff the need to introduce changes. He has to get the message across that customer service is of prime importance. Once the restaurant takes off he can motivate them by offering incentives which are based on the feedback received from customers.

Answer to TY 6

There are a number of reasons why Sally International has not been able to successfully implement the strategic changes.

A major problem seems to be the absence of any priority over which of the numerous strategies were to be adopted first. This may have led to confusion for both staff and suppliers. Resources seem to have been utilised without deciding which strategy would have yielded short-term pay-offs.

In attempting to juggle too many strategies, the monitoring system seems to have been inadequate. Most of the actions seem to be reactive. The organisational structure is rigid and hence actions are delayed. Intermediate milestones to measure the amount of progress made have not been initiated, so remedial actions could not be taken.

Resistance to change from employees and suppliers is not surprising under these circumstances. Issues such as timescales, management priorities, risk factors and the impact of such changes on the staff and organisational structure seem to have been ignored. Stakeholder commitment to the changes should have been obtained by clearly allocating responsibility and accountability by giving them individual targets

Quick Quiz

1. How is force field analysis useful in thinking about strategic change?
2. Why is understanding the organisational context important in managing strategic change?
3. When is strategic change likely to be successful in circumstances of (a) incremental change and (b) sudden, rapid change?
4. What is the role of middle managers in the strategic management process?

Answers to Quick Quiz

1. Force field analysis provides a way of identifying the forces aiding and blocking the change and how the aiding factors can be empowered and the restraining factors overcome.

2. Strategic change differs according to the organisational context and there is no single correct formula that can be applied to all organisations, each will have different cultures, structures, finances etc

3. In circumstances of incremental change, strategic change is likely to be successful when it is accepted and owned by those who will implement it such as stakeholders.
   In circumstances of sudden, rapid changes, a directive style in which there is clarity of vision regarding the intended change as well as the authority to quickly implement it, will be successful.

4. Middle managers are responsible for implementing the strategies determined by the top management. They act as a bridge between the senior management and the lower staff and can therefore ensure that change is brought about. They can advise management regarding the barriers encountered and the ways to tackle them. They can interpret and adapt strategies to suit local requirements.

Self Examination Questions

Question 1

Simon Clark is Head of the Department of Business at a local public sector college which provides professional training on a part-time basis for students who are already in employment. The students are mainly studying for professional qualifications in accountancy, marketing or personnel. A number of students are also studying for general management qualifications. Increasingly, the college is experiencing competition from a newly established private sector organisation. This private sector organisation is able to deliver programmes more efficiently and effectively than the older, established college because of its more flexible work contracts and working practices. The traditional method of tuition has been on a part-time basis (with students being given one day or one half-day a week off work, to study at the college). With local companies becoming more reluctant to give their staff time off on a regular basis to study, Simon is proposing that more of the training should be carried out on a distance-learning basis, often being supplemented by weekend teaching programmes. This will involve the staff in writing study material and working weekends.

The staff of Simon's college have, in recent years, had to adapt to new situations including organisational structure changes and syllabus changes. However, they are most unhappy about the current proposals which could result in their conditions of service worsening. They are reluctant to work on weekends without additional payments. This would make the college uncompetitive. The private sector college, although it employs high quality staff, is able to absorb the high costs by employing lecturers on a freelance basis and by having larger class sizes, the students being drawn from a larger catchments area. Simon is becoming frustrated by his staff's apparent opposition to accept the proposed changes, and he is contemplating what to do next.

Required:

Simon has arranged a meeting with his staff to discuss weekend working and study material production. Identify and discuss the different tactics which Simon could adopt in dealing with this conflict.

Question 2

Suhana is a manufacturing company which sells consumer electronics and home appliances. Although the company saw phenomenal growth until the 1990s, recently its profits have started to decline. A combination of factors are responsible for this situation. The company has grown both in size and in the number of employees. Although the majority of its sales are from overseas operations, the company did not have a global management structure to coordinate its operations. The accounting system was outdated. Its business units focused on market share rather than profitability. The company was facing stiff competition and even as its production costs were rising, the prices were falling.

Required:

Prepare a strategic plan to show what changes need to be instituted to bring it back to acceptable profitability levels.

Answers to Self Examination Questions

Answer to SEQ 1

The environment under which Simon is operating is a traditional environment which hasn't changed much over the years. The teaching staff in his college have already undergone changes which seem to have increased their work load. The competitive pressure from the private sector teaching organisations have increased their fears of job security. These factors seem to compound the problem that Simon is currently facing.
There are many ways through which Simon can tackle the situation:

Denying the existence of the problem and hoping it will vanish will not work in this situation as the problem is so major that it is threatening to destroy its customer base. Simon can suppress the problem and institute changes at a slow rate so as not to antagonise the staff. However, this may backfire because the staff will probably see through this tactic. Alternatively, he can be coercive and insist on the staff adapting to the new service conditions. Both these tactics are likely to lead to resentment and the staff may become uncooperative by not providing quality lectures which will affect the students and thereby the college's reputation.

Participation and collaboration seems to be the other option. There will definitely be a need for compromise both on the parts of the staff and management. The staff will have to give up some of their privileges by working at weekends and management can compensate for this by offering flexible working schedules and other incentives which need not be of a monetary nature such as vacation time equivalent to hours worked on Sundays. Alternatively he can hire new staff who are prepared work on Sundays.

Simon has to take a positive approach to the problem and not take out his frustration on the staff arbitrarily. He can emphasise the need for immediate change to ensure business survival and can enter into a dialogue with the staff to find common ground.

Answer to SEQ 2

A radical change in vision is required to get the company back on track, since its core business area is itself suffering from falling prices. A new management team with fresh ideas would be the first step required to shake the company from its inertia. A strong, centralised global headquarters to coordinate and manage its various business units would be needed.

The company has to embark on cost reduction methods. The labour costs of the company could be reduced by job cuts. Selling unprofitable units would not only bring in additional resources but also reduce the costs associated with those units.

Revenue enhancement will happen only if some new products are introduced. Here the company should explore the option of environmentally-friendly products since the consumer electronics division is experiencing a downturn. The company needs to focus more on business value and profitability than sales. Keeping the stakeholders informed through effective communication methods will help in getting their commitment to the change process.

Last but not least is understanding of the relationship of the 7s defined by the Mckinsey. These 7s are strategy, structure, systems, skills, staff, style and shared value. These elements are interrelated to each other. Suhana Ltd needs to analyse its 7s and relationship on the strategy.

New management change to what Suhana is planning should be consistent with its strategy. Policies of cost reduction and job cuts should be according to the interdependencies of these elements. Just looking at one area might misguide the company. So Suhana needs to look at the overall picture.

SECTION C: STRATEGIC ACTION — C3

STUDY GUIDE 3: UNDERSTANDING STRATEGY DEVELOPMENT

■ Get Through Intro

At Get Through Guides, our aim, as you know, is to produce easy to read material which can help you get through the ACCA exams. As a result we have amassed a lot of very good material, which we have used in the text books. You also know that the market for us is ACCA students who want to pass their exams. That is what we thought too. Except, it appears that this is not the only market for our ACCA books. Many students who are studying accounting, finance and commerce at university are looking for easy to understand textbooks. Some of these students have stumbled upon the GTG books at local libraries and through friends. They are now also buying our textbooks. This is not a market that GTG initially thought about going into. However, now that we can see demand, it makes sense for us to fulfil this demand.

Universities buying GTG textbooks is an example of an emergent strategy. It was not our intended strategy, but it has emerged as a way to increase business.

Whenever your company makes a product or provides a service, there are a number of emergent strategies that could come up. You will need to understand how to deal with them, as some may not be profitable for you. This study guide will give you an insight into how strategy develops and how you can make the best use of it!

■ Learning Outcomes

a) Discriminate between the concepts of intended and emergent strategies.
b) Explain how organisations attempt to put an intended strategy into place.
c) Highlight how emergent strategies appear from within an organisation.
d) Discuss how process redesign, quality initiatives and e-business can contribute to emergent strategies.
e) Assess the implications of strategic drift and the demand for multiple processes of strategy development.

Introduction

Case Study
Ice cream cones!

The history of the ice cream cone is an interesting one. The ice cream cone was invented at the St Louis world fair which was held in St.Louis in 1904. It's hard to identify the real inventor of the ice cream cone. There were many ice cream shops at the fair. One of the ice cream sellers ran out of paper plates. Just next to his shop was a pastry seller. The pastry seller suggested to the ice cream seller that he serve the ice cream on his waffle pastries. Soon almost every ice cream shop at that fair sold ice cream in that particular cone-shaped waffle pastry. That is how our favourite ice cream cones were invented.

In this case study, the sellers' intended strategy was to sell ice cream. Serving the ice cream in the cone-shaped pastry was their emergent strategy.

1. Discriminate between the concepts of intended and emergent strategies.[3]
[Learning Outcome a]

1.1 Intended and emergent strategies

The literal meaning of 'intended' is proposed, planned, deliberate, and intentional. 'Strategy' is a direction or a course of action taken in order to accomplish some future objective. Strategy is like a game of chess: it is all about positioning your own pieces to gain an advantage. The meaning and purpose of strategy is explained in detail in Study Guide A1.

Intended strategies, as the name suggests, are strategies that are **planned and deliberate**. This is a set of planned acts that have the intention of achieving a prospective goal. The goal that needs to be achieved is pre-determined and set in advance, before the strategy is implemented. An intended strategy is also referred to as a **deliberate strategy**. Deliberate strategy means that the managers must plan and think before they act. Deliberate strategy is a visualisation of effective strategy formulation that emphasises the advantages of performing intentionally. It does not imply that deliberate strategies are totally blind to uncertain conditions or unexpected developments in the organisation.

There is often a question about whether intended strategies are realised strategies.
The answer to this question is 'yes' and 'no'; there is no single answer.

When deliberate and intended plans are **realised completely**, intended strategies result in **realised strategies**. It may be that the resultant strategy is **completely different** from the strategies that were intended and planned – these are **unrealised strategies**. There may be a third situation where the resultant strategy was **not perfectly executed (according to its intentions), but also did not completely deviate** from the intended actions, called as **emergent strategy**. Emergent strategy is a set of actions or behaviour which becomes a realised pattern and is **not expressly intended** at the time of planning the strategy.

Example
Excellence University decides to appoint students from a new high school. This appointment becomes the intended strategy of the university.

When the actual appointment process is implemented, it is realised that the students who responded effectively to recruitment were students from community colleges. Therefore, the recruitment process was modified to attract more college students. This became Excellence University's emergent strategy.

Diagram 1: Intended and emergent strategies

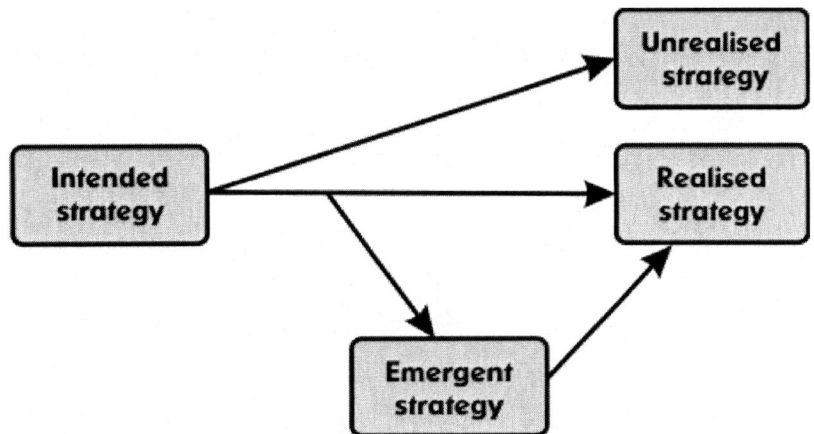

From the above diagram, we can see that the intended strategy can be realised or unrealised, but the emergent strategy is only ever a realised strategy. Emergent strategy results when intentions do not followed through completely but, in the process of accomplishing the goal, some unintentional strategies emerge; these are called emergent strategies. According to the Mintzberg, this is like a potter making a pot. Emergent strategy is a result of the day-to-day activities and processes of organisations.

Distinction between intended and emergent strategies

	Intended strategy	Emergent strategy
1	Strategy is planned and deliberate	Strategy is unplanned and not deliberate
2	Goal to be achieved are pre-determined	Goal to be achieved are accidental and incidental
3	Intended strategy may be realised or unrealised strategy	Emergent strategy is always realised strategy
4	Intended strategy may lead to emergent strategy	Emergent strategy never leads to intended strategy
5	Intended strategy gives an organisation a sense of focused direction	Emergent strategy implies that an organisation gains knowledge of what works in actual practice

Test Yourself 1

Healthy Drinks Co is a producer of prepackaged juices made from a combination of vegetables, fruits and herbs. The company is based in country A. One of the main goals of Healthy Drinks is to satisfy health-conscious consumers. The company has had enormous success in country A because of the health benefits offered by its juices. As a part of its growth strategy, Healthy Drinks decided to enter a significant untapped market for prepackaged juices. The company formed a committee to analyse the possibilities of market expansion. Based on the recommendations of the committee, a market survey was conducted in country B and the company decided to implement its strategy of entering the new market. However, the company was not able to sell as well in country B as in country A because of the different tastes and preferences of consumers in country B. Eventually, Healthy Drinks starts producing and selling only fruit juices in country B in order to satisfy all kinds of consumers, including health-conscious consumers.

Required

Explain whether the strategy followed by Healthy Drinks is intended / emergent / realised / unrealised.

2. Explain how organisations attempt to put an intended strategy into place.[2]
[Learning Outcome b]

2.1 Development of intended strategy

An organisation forms an intended strategy when it wants to achieve some **specific goals** in future. Every organisation has its own intended strategy. The formulation of intended strategy relates to its **strategic planning systems**.

Abraham Lincoln said, "If we could first know where we are, then whither we are tending, we could then decide what to do and how to do it." Strategic planning is a managerial process which raises three important questions:

➢ Where are we today?
➢ Where do we wish to arrive, and when?
➢ How do we get from here to there?

In Section A of this text, we have seen that there are three stages in strategy development.

➢ strategic analysis
➢ strategic choice
➢ strategic implementation

A strategic planning system is a **process of strategic implementation**. It explains how strategies are formulated. The stages in the strategic planning cycle are:

1. **Planning guidelines**: this is the first step in the process of planning a cycle. The organisation forms the guidelines for what the plan should be for the benefit of the organisation. It assesses the conditions prevailing in the external environment and studies the factors that are going to affect it adversely. The organisation forms guidelines for how it will tackle problems. The organisation plans its priorities to attain future objectives.

2. **Prepare a rough business plan:** when the guidelines are set, the next step is preparing the business plan. The divisions and business groups within the organisation set their business plans. The business plan contains the goals that need to be achieved by different business processes.

3. **Consultation with the senior level managers:** the business plans formulated by divisions and businesses are discussed with the corporate managers. Generally, this discussion occurs in face-to-face meetings because it is beneficial for managers to resolve issues by communicating and clarifying doubts in person.

4. **Review the business plan:** if, after discussion, the corporate managers form the opinion that the business plan needs to be revised, then the plan is revised accordingly.

5. **Prepare estimate budgets:** the next step is the preparation of the annual budgets. The managers prepare the budget relating to the funds required for capital expenditure and operating expenditure. This provides an overview of the organisation's fund requirement.

6. **Prepare a final corporate plan:** business plans, when taken together, form a corporate plan. A corporate plan is prepared for the accomplishment of corporate goals.

7. **Take approval from the board of directors:** when the corporate plan is prepared, it needs to be approved by the corporate board of directors.

8. **Annual performance targets and review:** the corporate managers plan performance targets for the organisation on an annual basis.

9. **Performance appraisal:** once the targets are set, corporate managers compare the actual goals achieved with the targets set. The organisation is inclined to scrutinise the performance of the strategic-level managers using the balanced scorecard.

Example

Gotcha Ltd, a manufacturing company, has its branch offices in many countries. Each country is represented by the managing director of the company located in that region. These managing directors receive their revenue targets from Gotcha's head office in London. These managing directors have the freedom to develop their own strategies to achieve their respective targets. Gotcha, while conducting performance appraisals, compares the managing director's performance against the given targets.

Diagram 2: Stages in strategic planning cycle

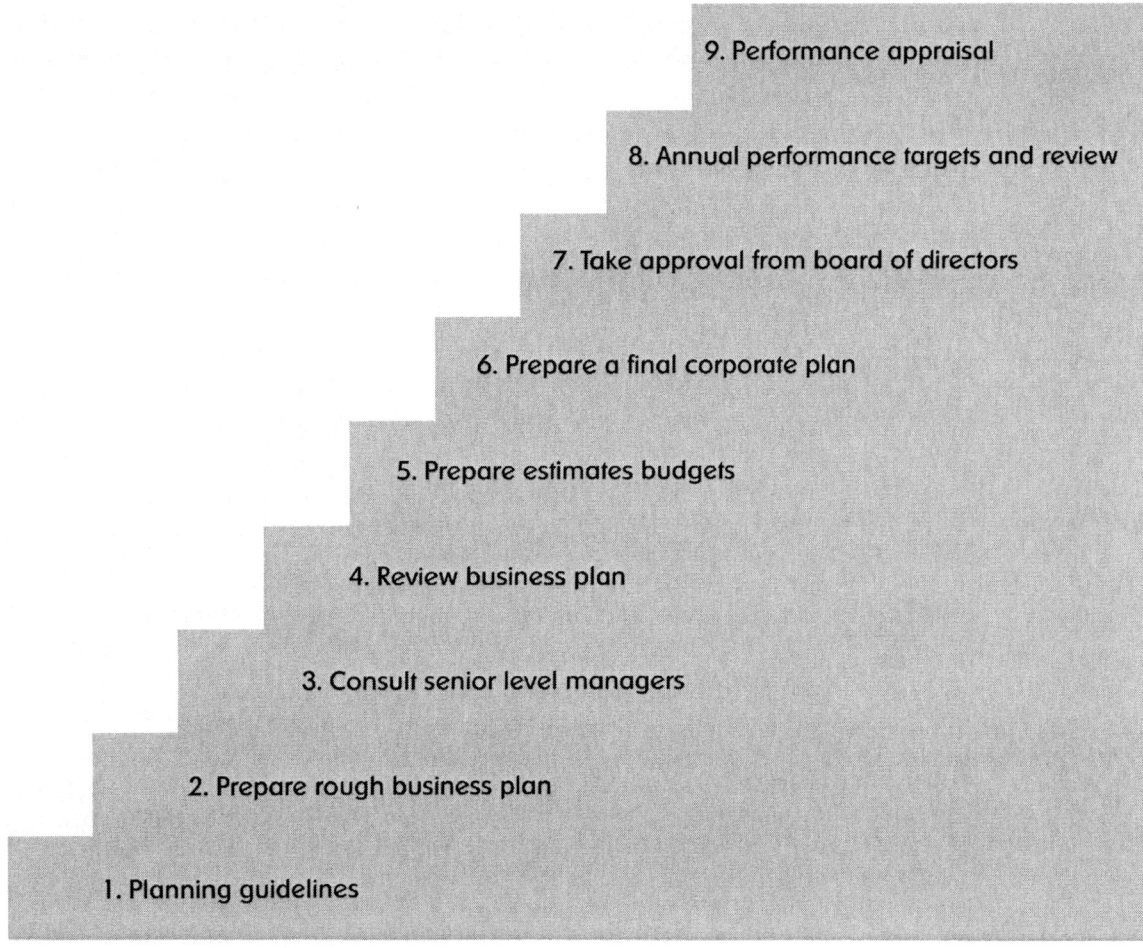

2.2 Benefits of a strategic planning system

1. It helps to **prioritise future objectives** according to their importance. It suggests which objective should be fulfilled first and provides ways to achieve them.

2. It promotes the **optimum utilisation of resources,** be it financial resources or human resources.

3. It provides a **performance measurement** because the actual goal achieved can be compared with the planned goal.

4. When the objectives are specified clearly, it helps to form an **effective analysis** and to think of ways to achieve them.

5. It helps to create a **sense of co-operation** and togetherness in the organisation because, when business plans are compiled together, they form an overall corporate strategic plan.

6. When plans and objectives are fixed, it encourages managers to operate and **perform effectively** to achieve their goals.

7. Once the planning is done, the senior managers can exercise **effective control** over lower level managers and staff in case they deviate from the set objectives.

2.3 Problems in strategic planning systems

1. There is a possibility that the **right strategy may not be planned for** in the planning process.

2. When the planning process results in the formulation of a strategy, there is a chance that the mangers may not think beyond the planned activity. Therefore, the planning process may **hinder managers' innovative and analytical thinking**.

3. Sometimes the planning process and budgetary control processes are considered the same. This is incorrect because budgetary control deals with financial aspects and strategic planning is a wide concept which considers all the aspects in an organisation.

4. When the planning system is **complicated**, it is **difficult for staff** to understand and implement it.

5. Sometimes the implementation of the strategic planning system becomes difficult because operational managers are so busy in their day-to-day activities that they cannot find time to implement strategic plans effectively.

6. In the case of extensive planning systems, the information collected may be voluminous, which may lead to an overburdening of information and wastage of managerial time. This may result in the neglect of important strategic issues. In addition, if the planning takes too long, the firm may not be able to devote sufficient time to market operations,

2.4 Strategy workshops and project teams

A strategic planning system is referred to as a **top-down approach,** as the planning is done by the top level managers and the implementation of the plan is carried out by strategic managers in the lower level of the organisational hierarchy. The concept of strategy workshops has become popular.

In the case of strategy workshops, some of the organisation's managers can come together and establish a group that organises **workshops for informing the top, strategic level staff about the organisation's strategy**. The managers who conduct the workshop explain the corporate strategy and ask for any suggestions or different plans that might benefit the organisation.

Generally, strategy workshops are for the top level managerial personnel, but they may be conducted for any level of the organisation's staff. The management can decide to take staff away from its usual work place for few days in order to discuss issues relating to the organisation's strategy which are known as the 'away days'.

The nature of strategy workshops differs between organisations and also depends on the purpose it is conducted for. These purposes could include the following:

1. **To formulate the organisational strategy:** when the top management wants to plan the strategy, it may conduct a workshop which involves taking its staff away to another location for a day or two.
2. **To carry out the strategic analysis:** the workshop conductors may analyse the implementation of strategies and take measures in case of deviations from the plans.
3. **To check the development of strategy**: once the planning is done, the managers need to implement the strategy. It is essential to continuously monitor the progress of strategy by the organisation's staff.
4. **To formulate the plans for implementing strategy:** this provides guidelines for methods and procedures that need to be adopted for the actual implementation of strategies. Implementation is the responsibility of all employees (not only of the top management) and these workshops can provide guidance on organisational strategy implementation for all members of staff.
5. **To overcome barriers to strategic implementation:** these workshops support the managers in solving any problems or to face challenges to strategy implementation.
6. **To obtain new and unique ideas from other level managers**: the workshop provides a ground upon which other staff members can give innovative ideas and solutions for strategies.
7. **To raise queries about the guidelines provided in the strategic planning process**: members of the organisation can argue in an organised manner on any of the issues raised by the top management during the strategic planning process in the evaluation meetings.

Example

Members of the Senate and the House of Representatives generally get to participate in strategy workshops. When the budget is announced in the Senate, it is discussed between its members and then only can strategic matters such as the budget be finalised.

Benefits of a strategy workshop

a) It creates a **sense of participation** in the strategy formulation of the organisation and unifies the organisation and prevents strategic drift.
b) It is beneficial for staff to **understand the objectives** of the organisation as this motivates them.
c) These groups make the management aware of any **problems faced by the staff** by discussing issues openly.

SUMMARY

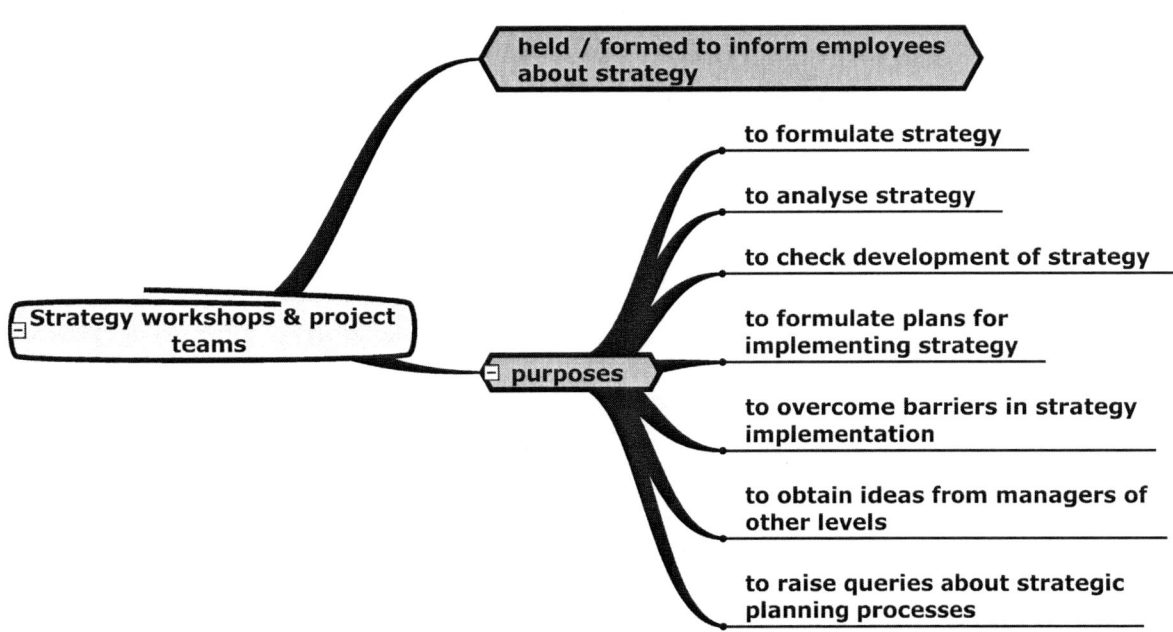

2.5 Strategy consultants

Strategy consultants are the external firms who assist in the strategy development of an organisation. Strategy consultants possess **specialised and innovative knowledge** about strategic management. Being external parties, they can form better opinions and judgements about strategy formulation; they are **experts in solving problems** that relate to different strategic issues and are impartial. Such firms help the managers of the organisation with strategy analysis and development by providing different ideas and views about the new strategy that the organisation can adopt to benefit the organisation.

The various **roles** played by strategy consultants are as follows:

1. **Analysis of strategy and generating options:** strategy consultants provide assistance to the organisation's managers with their strategy analyses. Sometimes the managers are not able to solve an issue or form a rational judgement about a strategy, in which case the consultants support them in a strategic analysis. In case of confusion among the organisation's managers, the consultants provide various options so that managers can select the options suitable for their organisational strategy.

2. **Provide knowledge and perspective:** the consultants provide different perspectives to their clients. They can support their clients with the expert knowledge they have gained from dealing with various kinds of organisations.

3. **Reviewing client's strategy if required:** when the strategic planning process of an organisation as already been undertaken by the managers, the consultant helps his client by reviewing their work, if necessary.

4. **Assists in strategic decision-making:** strategy consultants provide assistance for making decisions to the client organisation. This gives the organisation ideas and perspectives about the future consequences of particular decisions. While the consultant is promoting and supporting the decision-making process, an important point to remember is that the consultant should not influence the managers although consultants can express their opinion and narrate the facts to the client. The consultants can assist and support but should in no way impose a decision on the organisation's managers since they work in an advisory capacity only.

5. **Implementation of strategic change:** the consultants play a vital role in implementing strategic changes in an organisation by providing training and coaching. This is because, they possess consulting experience with various types of organisations and so have the ability to enhance the knowledge base of the firm which might help introduce new and more competitive practices.

Diagram 3: Roles played by strategy consultants

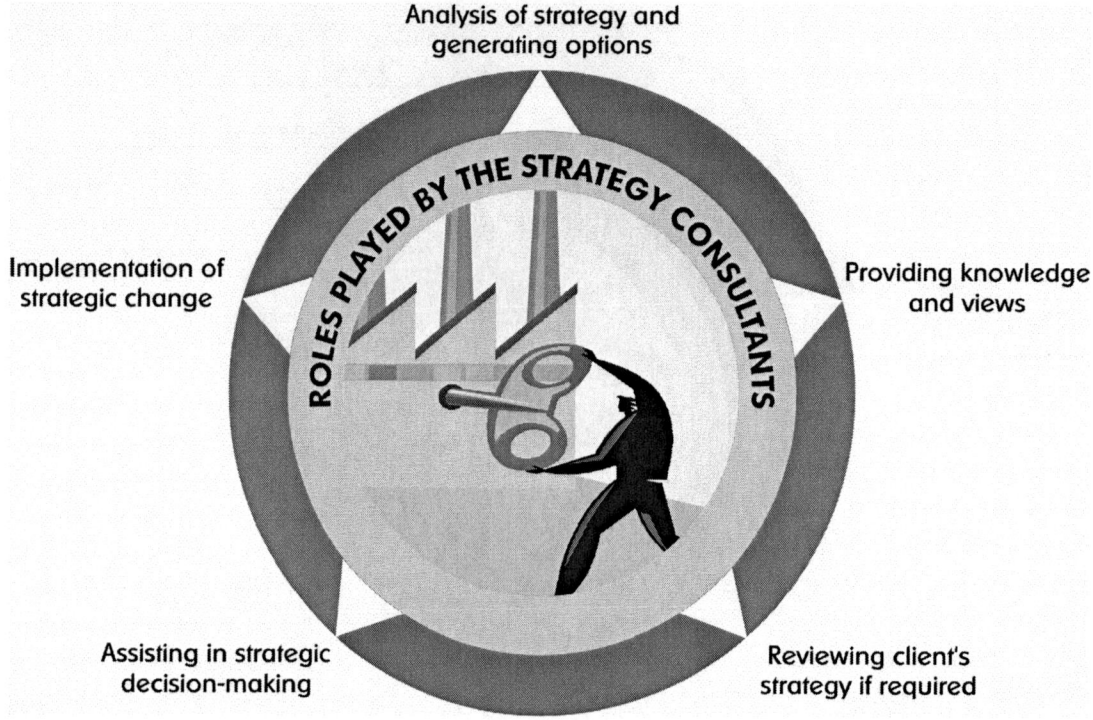

> ### Example

McKinsey is a global consultancy firm that provides companies with innovative and unique ideas which can be applied for achieving organisational goals. The firm help companies to analyse complex problems and identify the opportunities for improvement.

2.6 Imposed strategy

Imposed strategy, as the name suggests, is a strategy which is **imposed by an external force**. Here, the external force is the **external stakeholders** who have significant influence over an organisation's strategy. Therefore, imposed strategy is not an intention of the managers of the organisation but it is a strategy forced by external stakeholders.

Externally imposed strategy is normally found in cases relating to **public sector organisations** because the government can exercise immense influence on their policies and strategies by imposing various rules and regulations. Also, the government may pass certain directives or provisions to be complied with by the industry as a whole. The government can also consider any organisation or industry for rivatisation or deregulation.

The possibility of externally-imposed strategy does, however, exist in the case of **private sector organisations too**. When an organisation exports its products, the government may impose various provisions relating to the export of goods or providing services abroad and may therefore impose certain strategies on the organisation.

> ### Example

An example of a government- imposed strategy is the government's control on aeroplane production companies which also manufacture fighter aeroplanes.

> ### Test Yourself 2

Summit Info Ltd is in the business of researching and developing different kinds of guides, such as those relating to travel, food, shopping, finance and health. Summit Info has an alliance with a media publishing company that funds its data collection efforts. The company is not getting suitable monetary compensation from its alliance partner. Summit Info plans to expand its operations to other locations, which cannot be funded by its existing alliance.

Considering these factors, Summit Info wants to form a new alliance that can fund operations in other locations and also help in the leveraging of the existing content across several media. Furthermore, the company wants to venture into a new business area but there is a lack of clarity over which category of business would be most suitable for the company. The company has appointed Zenith Ltd as its strategy consultant for these purposes.

Continued on the next page

Required:

Assuming the role of strategy consultant, explain the possible ways in which Zenith Ltd could help Summit Info Ltd.

---

3. Highlight how emergent strategies appear from within an organisation. [3]
[Learning outcome c]

Emergent strategies

When strategy emerges out of intended strategy, is termed emergent strategy. It is not planned or deliberate. Emergent strategy is explained in depth in Learning Outcome 1.

3.1. Logical incrementalism

Logical incrementalism has been explained by James Brian Quinn (1980). According to Quinn, effective strategic management involves a continuous integration of **simultaneous incremental processes of strategy formulation and implementation**. Quinn believes that the implementation of strategic change in a big organisation is difficult and time-consuming. So, a fully expressed strategic plan may not be possible in practice. In the case of the incremental approach, managers do not directly come to a decision; they undertake a **step by step** iterative process. The incremental approach states that every issue in a particular subsystem must be identified by the members. If the organisation's objectives are announced at the very beginning of the planning process, then there is a possibility of losing innovative ideas, new perspectives and opinions, resulting in limited flexibility. Strategy formulation and implementation are linked together in a **continuous improvement cycle**. This emphasises the need to analyse, plan and implement the strategy incrementally. Quinn was extensively influenced by Braybrooke and Lindblom and hence his theory of strategic decisions includes both random and logical elements. Managers are inclined to formulate strategic decisions on the basis of **incremental opportunities** that would add value to strategic management. Logical incrementalism provides sufficient opportunities to learn new and innovative things.

Quinn's observations are as follows:

1. The objectives are **general in nature**. If only specific objectives are announced during the planning phase, then there would be no need to experiment. The managers have a generalised view of the organisation's future prospects and therefore move ahead incrementally.
2. Managers who have exposure and experience of strategic management are aware that there may be environmental changes which could have an impact on strategic change. So, Quinn states that strategic managers cannot ignore **environmental changes**; they should continuously monitor environmental factors.
3. All the employees participate in the development of strategy. There are different departments in the organisation which facilitate production. The members of these departments are the groups that are known as '**subsystems**' which work together to plan the strategy for the organisation.
4. Strategies are formulated by the top management by discussing issues with subsystems in a formal or informal manner.

SUMMARY

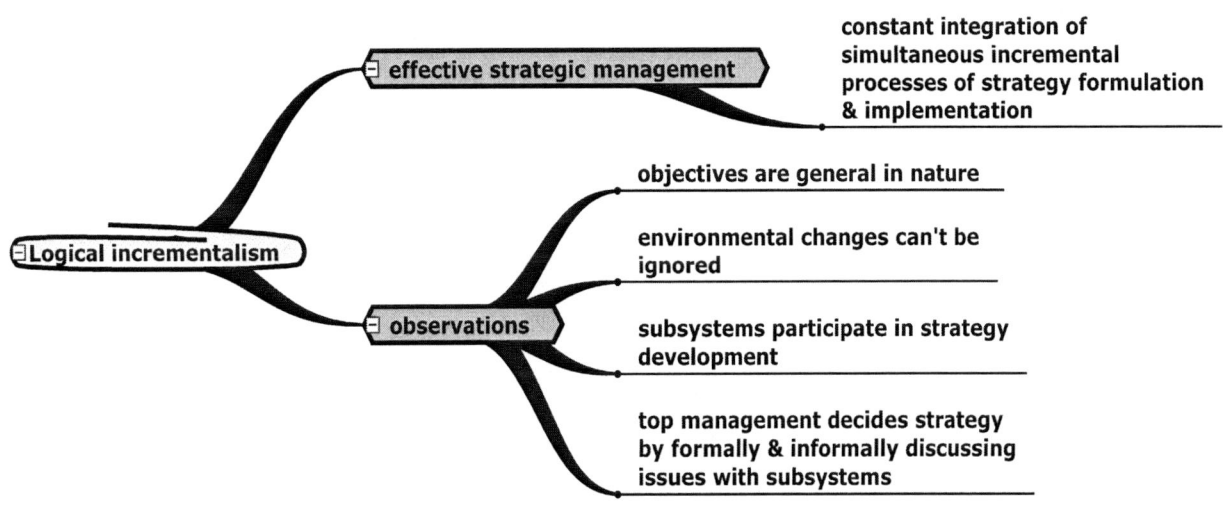

3.2. Resource allocation routines

Emergent strategies may arise out of organisational routines. Routines are activities that strengthen the smooth functioning of companies. Emergent strategies are formed without explicit analysis by the top level management. Routines are the day-to-day operations of an organisation. When the results for the allocation of resources are confirmed, it gives rise to the emergence of different strategies, other than the strategies that were planned previously.

The process of strategy development is explained by Bower and Burgelman in a different way. Strategy development may take place through the **routine activities** of an organisation. Bower and Burgelman are of the view that substantial changes in strategic behaviour take place when conventional routines fail to address new and unknown situations, resulting in **changes in strategies**. As these routines are interlinked, any change in one set of activities has an impact on other sets of activities, which affects organisational strategies in an unpredictable way.

If managers in an organisation want to achieve a particular mission, they will have to deploy the resources available to them at that time. Decision-makers will measure the benefits they gained from their previous use of resources and consider the manager's proposed use of resources before making a decision. Hence, the strategy may change according to the manager's proposal

3.3. Cultural Processes

Culture includes patterns of behaviour that are difficult to define in exact words but are present in an organisation. This influences how work is done, and how strategy is formulated and implemented in an organisation. There are four layers of culture: values (ideas about the appropriate standards), beliefs (such as stories or myths), behaviours (behavioural patterns) and paradigms (role models). The culture of an organisation is ambiguous, so analysis is needs to be done regularly to identify what makes a corporate culture effective and what measures need to be implemented in order to change the culture.

When there is a merger of two organisations, there may be a clash of cultures between the organisations. Furthermore, where there is growth in an organisation, the culture previously followed by the organisation may become irrelevant, which leads to failures instead of achievements. Hence, there may be a need to change the organisational culture.

Changes in cultural processes lead to strategy development because assumptions (such as who should perform specific work) that were previously taken for granted may change, which would result in a strategic change. The culture of an organisation may influence the strategies that need to be formulated. So, managers are influenced by an organisation's cultural processes. When strategy is changed on the basis of cultural forces, it is likely that the change has been influenced by the experiences of the people in the organisation. Therefore, in a nutshell, strategic change due to cultural processes may not relate to environmental changes and may lead to strategic drift.

3.4. Imposed politics

What are politics?

Politics are a means of identifying and integrating competing interests within an organisation.

How does this influence emergent strategy?

Strategy development is influenced by the **interests of different stakeholders** (internal or external). Strategy must be developed by managers in a way that protects the interests of the stakeholders. So, political influence creates a negative impact on strategic development because there is no scope for effective study and logical analysis by the top level managers.

As there may be political influence, strategy can be influenced by highly knowledgeable individuals or powerful in terms of the French and Raven model. Strategy which is influenced by political factors is emergent strategy and not intended strategy. Political influence also has a positive impact because managers can be provided with new and innovative ideas.

Test Yourself 3

Duncan Ltd a fashion boutique which is one of the key players in its market. The company wishes to restructure itself. Duncan finds it difficult to run the organisation according to its current intended strategy, as customer responses and market trends in fashion industries are always changing.

Required:

Advise Duncan on the strategy it needs to follow for the organisation's continuous improvement and explain the advantages of the suggested strategy.

---

4. Discuss how process redesign, quality initiatives and e-business can contribute to emergent strategies.[2]

[Learning Outcome d]

4.1 Contribution of process redesign, quality initiatives and e- business

These activities are similar to each other as each one involves a review and change in existing processes. The way in which these activities contribute towards emergent strategies is explained below.

1. Process redesign, quality initiatives and e-business activities bring fundamental changes to the processes implemented by an organisation.

2. These activities bring about cultural changes in an organisation. An organisation has to know what is going on in actual practice. The process of learning or gaining knowledge about actual practice is implied in emergent strategies. Process redesign, quality initiatives and e-business require the organisation to learn new ways of doing business. Such learning implies the existence of emergent strategies.

3. Logical incrementalism, the process of incremental formulation and implementation of strategy makes the use of emergent strategies. Strategies get formulated and implemented through the decision to implement process redesigns, quality initiatives and e-business.

Example

Joseph Ltd is a bookseller Joseph decides to implement an e-business and begins its e-business development efforts. At the stage of formulating and implementing an e-business strategy, Joseph Ltd comes up with the innovation of selling books in their digital forms by the giving the option to download the book from the internet. This development can be termed emergent strategy.

---

4. Resources are planned on the basis of intended strategies. Managers have to implement their mission with the available resources, which might be different from the planned resources. Strategies are modified on the basis of available resources. Such modified strategies become the emergent strategies of an organisation. While implementing the process redesign, quality initiatives, or e-business, a manager might come across measures relating to quality, speed and cost that are different from the measures outlined in the intended strategy.

Example

Babita Ltd is an automobile accessories manufacturing company. Babita has begun process redesign efforts to streamline its production costs. Here, streamlining the cost of production is the company's intended strategy. But while implementing this strategy, Babita may see some scope for quality improvement and redirect its efforts towards this. The company could also try to add a product to its sales line. Quality improvement or adding another more product to the company's product data would be considered emergent strategies.

---

5. Emergent strategies may come from organisational routines. Activities such as process redesign, e-business, and quality initiatives bring changes in the organisational routine. Such changes in routines give birth to new emergent strategies.

Example

Continuous quality improvement efforts or quality standards such as ISO 9000 could bring changes to an organisation's routine and new emergent strategies may be developed from such changes.

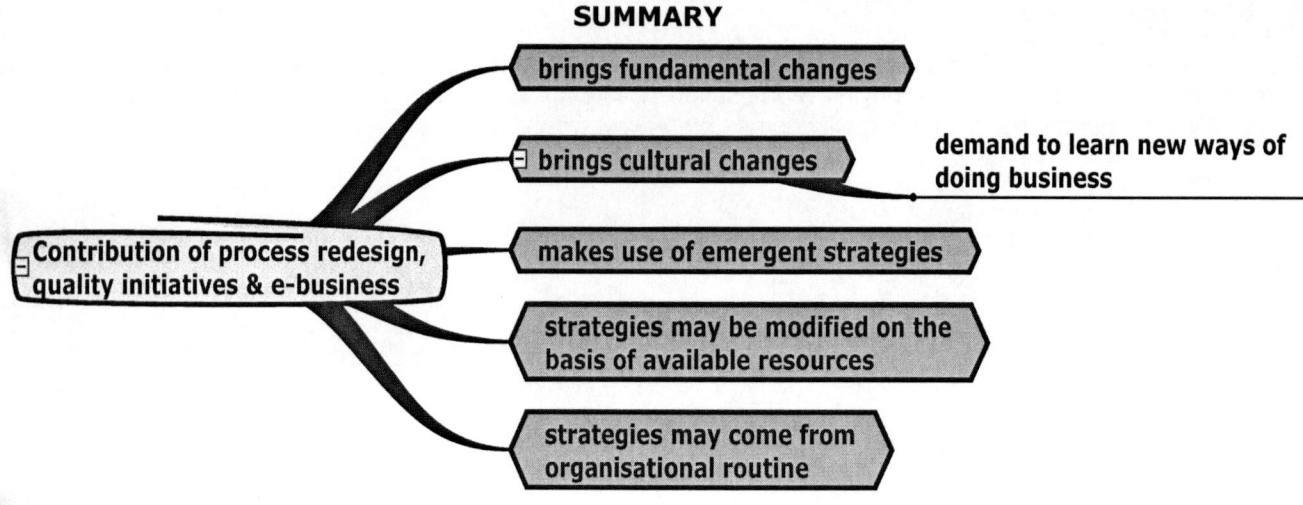

Test Yourself 4

Melanie's Pizzeria is a restaurant that has been making a loss continuously for the past three years. The owner, Peter, is frustrated with the situation and wants to redesign the structure of the business so that he can overcome losses and start making profits.

Required:

Explain to Peter the ways in which process redesign, quality initiatives and e-business can contribute to emergent strategies.

---

5. Assess the implications of strategic drift and the demand for multiple processes of strategy development.[3]

[Learning Outcome e]

5.1 Strategic drift

Strategic drift is a situation:

➤ where the organisation exists for a long period of time with little or no change in its established strategies; and

➤ these strategies progressively or continuously fail to achieve a strategic position for the organisation, which shows a deterioration in performance.

Example

Baywatch Ltd has a hotel business near a sea beach. Baywatch wants to attract a lot of tourists and strategically wants to achieve the number one position in its local market, so that tourists will recognise Baywatch as the best hotel in the area. Baywatch's strategy is to advertise in newspapers and through agents. Baywatch has been following this strategy for many years. In the absence of modern advertising techniques such as internet advertisement (e.g. advertising on websites such as priceline.com), Baywatch has continuously failed to meet its target and is a long way from reaching its intended strategic position. This could be described as a situation of strategic drift.

An organisation might change its strategies but the directions in which it is moving may not be very clear. This situation is known as 'flux'. As the direction is not clear, organisations may find themselves following the same pattern of failures. Organisations might make a dramatic change in their strategies – known as a transformational change. Transformational change is a rare phenomenon in an organisation's lifecycle. Such change may be positive, in which case it progresses the strategic position of the company, or negative, in which case an organisation may need to close its business.

Diagram 4: Strategic drift

Organisation has not made any changes leading to a strategic drift situation.

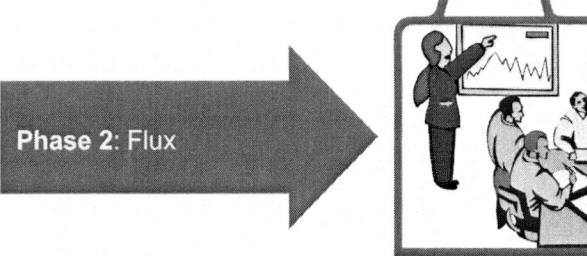

Little change with no clear direction in strategies.

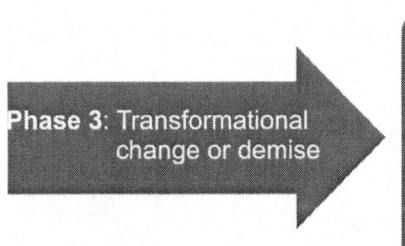 

Turn-around changes in strategy leading to dramatic results.

5.2 Implications of strategic drift

Incremental change in an organisation's strategy may not be responsive to the changes in its environment. This kind of situation could throw the organisation out of business. The changes in the environment may be so rapid that an incremental change may not be sufficiently effective and the organisation may have to use transformational techniques.

Example

Kitchen Depot sells utensils and cooking equipment. All the goods that Kitchen Depot sells have not changed in their specifications for many years. Although there are few changes in specifications, they are not at par with the environment. Modern cooking styles require the use of oven proof, microwave proof and dishwasher proof utensils. This kind of situation could throw Kitchen Depot out of its market.

Sometimes organisations change their strategies in order to react to environmental changes. These organisations do not take any initiative to find new ideas or apply new innovations. Such organisations are self-satisfied and are not ready to explore new opportunities.

Example

Continuing the previous example

Kitchen Depot could decide to stock goods to meet market specifications. Such an action could be considered reactive to the environment. Here, Kitchen Depot is losing opportunities available through initiatives like internet sale or e-business. Kitchen Depot should try to create new ideas or innovate new opportunities. Envisaging the future trends of the market and acting upon them could take Kitchen Depot to a new level.

5.3 Factors demanding multiple processes of strategy development

1. Stagnant environment

An environment where there is little technological change and the market conditions need little strategic development. In such environments, most of the time change is predictable and organisations can prepare themselves well in advance to face changes. So, organisations have enough time for choosing the right strategy and planning its implementation.

2. Rapidly changing environments

It's hard for strategy-makers to choose the right strategy when environments keep changing. Strategies need to be formed by projecting the likely future. Strategies can change very often in such organisations. Such organisations have to plan to meet the needs of upcoming environments. Such organisations try to build an awareness of future developments in every employee and encourage an atmosphere of organisational learning. Coping with ever-changing environments is a challenge for strategy-makers.

3. Multifaceted environments

Multifaceted environments are, by nature, difficult to understand. Such environments can be stagnant or rapidly changing. Environments which are both difficult to understand and rapidly changing are a challenge for strategy-makers.

Processes required for strategy developments will vary across different situations. Organisations have to go through many situations and processes in order to develop strategies which will be successful. Organisations that face rapidly changing environments may have to choose different processes of strategy development each time. Sometimes organisations might experience a strategic drift and the situation may demand the use of new strategy development processes. There are different kinds of strategies, including those that are intended or emergent. Intended strategies are formed by the strategy–makers, generally by an organisation's directors. Senior executives have to plan how to implement these strategies. Emergent strategies may be developed from the lower levels. Organisations have to change their strategy development processes.

> **Example**
> Software companies or electronic companies experience a rapid change in their environments. New software tools and languages are emerging constantly, making old ones obsolete. So there is a risk that before the development of an organisation's software is complete, the latest development in the software industry will make such software obsolete. This is also true for electronic products. Digital camcorders, DVD players, etc., have made older electronic products such as camcorders and VCRs obsolete. These companies have to follow different processes of strategy development, such as developing strategies to overcome competition each time there is a change in the environment.

SUMMARY

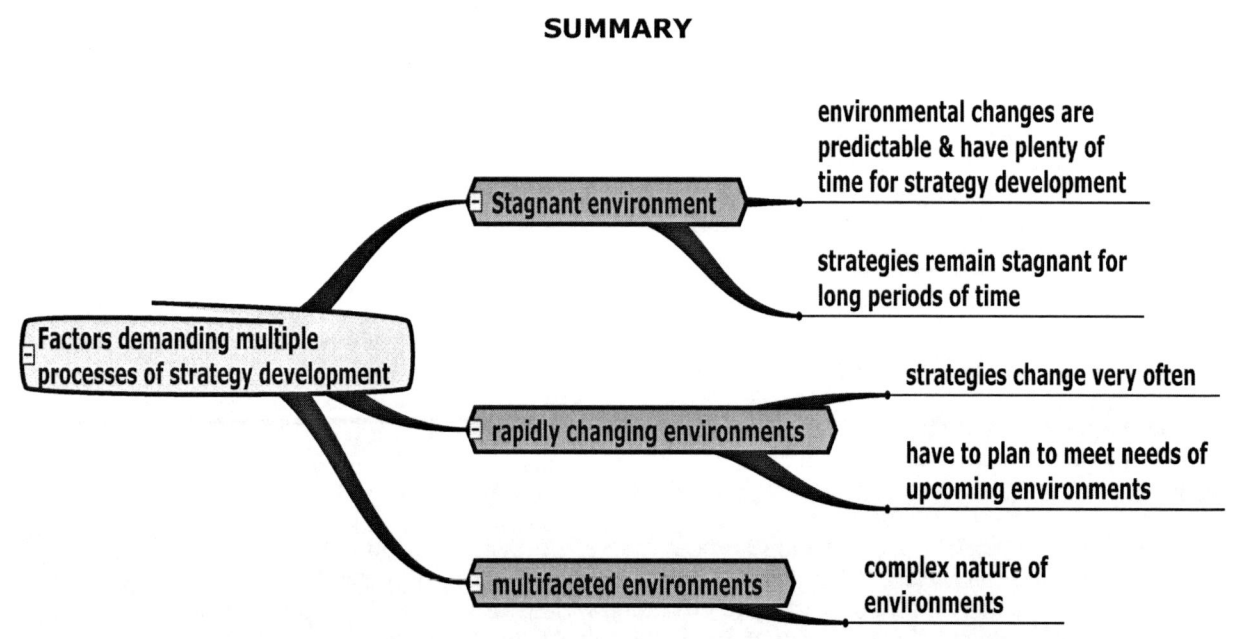

Test Yourself 5

Tygra Ltd, a motorcycle manufacturing company, runs its business through traditional management structures and spends very little on its research and development activities. The company has never analysed its market conditions and never tried to improve its existing products. This management strategy has affected the company and it has started making a loss. Tygra's management has realised its strategic drawbacks and has tried to implement a new technology which was not sufficient for the organisation to overcome its losses.

In the current year, management changes have been made at Tygra. The new management is more advanced and understands the importance of research and development activities. It knows how essential it is for any organisation to analyse its position in relation to market conditions, and how important it is to improve products according to customers' demands.

With the help of new technology, Tygra introduces a new bike to the market and provides good customer support for this. As a result, Tygra begins to earn profits.

Required:

Consider the above case study and explain the implications of strategic drift. How does strategic drift affect Tygra?

Answers to Test Yourself

Answer to TY 1

Healthy Drinks' strategy in country A is an intended strategy as it is planned and deliberate. Its act of producing juices made from the combinations of vegetables, fruits and herbs is intended to achieve the predetermined goal of satisfying health-conscious consumers. This shows Healthy Drinks' sense of focused direction. At the same time, it is evident from the success of Healthy Drinks in country A that its strategy is a realised strategy. The company's deliberate and intended plans are realised completely in country A.

Healthy Drinks' strategy in country B is an emergent strategy as it is unplanned and not deliberate. Its goal to satisfy all types of consumers in country B is accidental and incidental, as the company's juices that were made from vegetable, fruits and herbs failed in country B. The resultant strategy of Healthy Drinks to sell only fruit juices in country B is not perfect according to its intentions but does not completely deviate from intended actions. The emergent strategy of Healthy Drinks implies that the company began to understand that what works in country A may not work in country B. This is a realised strategy, as emergent strategy is always realised strategy.

Answer to TY 2

Strategy consultants are the external firms that assist in the strategy development of an organisation. They may play various roles in strategy development, such as analysing strategy and generating options, providing knowledge and views, reviewing a client's strategy if required and assisting in strategic decision-making. The consultants bring external experience and impartiality to the firm.

In the case of Summit Info Ltd, the strategy consultant can provide assistance to the company in making decisions about forming new strategic alliances and venturing into new business areas. The consultant can offer expert knowledge and perspectives for arriving at these decisions.

Zenith Ltd can help Summit Info to identify the best possible exit option from its existing alliance. Simultaneously, Zenith Ltd can analyse and identify the best business organisation to ally with, based on synergies in business and funding capabilities. Zenith Ltd can analyse the present capabilities of Summit Info and assist the company in identifying the best business category to venture into.

Answer to TY 3

Duncan needs to follow logical incrementalism in which the management is continuously integrating the simultaneous incremental processes of strategy formulation and the implementation of such processes. Duncan will be able to form its strategy according to the current market trends and simultaneously implement it, which would beneficial for the company.

Advantages of logical incrementalism:

- objectives are general in nature
- management always needs to keep an eye on environmental changes and accordingly needs to make changes to plans and policies
- strategy is up to date
- subsystems participate in strategy development
- top management discusses with subsystems formally and informally to formulate strategy which motivates employees and increases team sprit

This will help Duncan since the entire subsystem, including the senior management, management, workers, creative and non-creative teams will be participating in the decision-making process and in the development of strategy. This will give employees responsibilities and help to increase the employees' creativity. The organisation will come across different ideas, views, customer tests and current market trends. This will help the organisation to create a strategy and to implement it. The process will indirectly help to improve the quality and quantity of production and increase the profits of the organisation.

Answer to TY 4

Peter needs to review the strategy followed by the company and change its processes by elevating the efficiency of the existing processes and / or by incorporating e-business.

Process redesign, quality initiatives and e-business bring fundamental changes to the processes implemented by an organisation. These factors will contribute to the development of emergent strategies in the following ways:

- Bring cultural changes and allow the organisation to learn new ways of doing business. Therefore, the strategy of organisational learning may emerge from it.
- Emergent strategies might take place during the implementation of process redesign, quality initiatives or e-business as these processes incorporate new ways of doing business
- Emergent strategies that emerge from the organisation's routine are generally changed during the implementation of process redesign, quality initiatives or e-business.
- Resource availability may restrict the changes suggested in the process redesign, quality initiative and e-business. Such changed processes become the emergent strategy of an organisation.
- Process redesign which has resulted from workplace learning may become an emerged strategy

Peter needs to change the work culture and display ads for his restaurant, perhaps by creating his own website. Peter needs to inform customers about pricing as well as the kind of food and beverages that are available at the restaurant. He can offer them a service for ordering food and beverages online, so that customers can get a home delivery – this will lead to an increase in the number of customers.

Apart from its regular menu items, Melanie needs to analyse the market trends and try to incorporate new items in its menu. For this, Peter requires qualified employees. He can start training and development programmes for existing employees. All this will change Pizzeria's routine and will contribute towards the inauguration of emergent strategy.

Answer to TY 5

Strategic drift is a situation where:

- an organisation has made little or no change in its strategies
- an organisation fails to achieve a strategic position because of the non-implementation of progressive strategies and therefore shows a deterioration in performance

When the management of Tygra adopted a strategy in which it did not analyse itself and neglected product development, the company lost business continuously and became a loss-making company. Although afterwards the management tried to implement changes, it was not sufficient and did not help the organisation to make up for its losses. Therefore, strategic drift made Tygra a loss-making company.

The new management of Tygra started implementing research and development activities and adopted new technology. By making a transformational change in its strategies (such as by introducing a new product into the market and providing good customer support) the company was able to make up for losses and become a profit-making company. It was able to recover its position and reverse the strategic drift.

Quick Quiz

1. Intended strategy is always realised strategy. State whether this is true or false.
2. Effective strategic management involves continuous and simultaneous integration of the _____ process of strategy formulation and implementation.
3. Explain what is meant by a multifaceted environment.
4. Explain the similarities between what process redesign, quality initiatives and e-business activities aim to do.

Answers to Quick Quiz

1. False - intended strategy may be realised or unrealised strategy. Emergent strategy is always realised strategy.
2. Incremental

Continued on the next page

3. A multifaceted environment is complex in nature. Such environments can be stagnant or rapidly changing.
4. The contribution of process redesign, quality initiatives and e- business activities are similar to each other as each one contains a review and change of the existing processes.

Self Examination Questions

Question 1

Wonder Ltd publishes a daily newspaper. The management of Wonder Ltd wants to expand the business. It starts to publish a weekly book which provides general information and a part of this is dedicated to economic news. After six months, the management observes that its economic news section is the most popular part of the book.

The management has reviewed its organisational strategy and wishes to adopt a new strategy where Wonder can start a daily economics newspaper as well its weekly publication.

Required:

(a) Explain whether this is intended strategy or emergent strategy.
(b) Explain the stages Wonder needs to go through in its strategic planning cycle.

Question 2

Judith Ltd, a bags manufacturing company, has acquired the Alistair Ltd, which is another manufacturer of bags.

For the past six years, Alistair has been incurring losses and has earned a reputation of being a loss-making company. Alistair's management finally decided to sell Alistair to Judith Ltd. The committee which was appointed to evaluate the proposal of Alistair's acquisition made the following observations:

- Alistair formed its intended strategy a long time ago and after that it never analysed its strategy. A strategic drift had occurred in Alistair's case.
- Alistair never conducted any market research and did not make necessary changes to its strategy.
- Alistair's management made small changes in its strategy in order to gain some profit. But the changes did not have a clear direction.
- Alistair's culture did not encourage organisational learning and the development of innovative ideas.
- Alistair never introduced new technology into its business.

Judith's culture is different from the Alistair's culture. Judith conducts strategy workshops and analyses its strategy according to the changes in its environment. Judith's management has always ensured that Judith remains a technologically advanced company. Judith entered e-business a long time ago. Judith regularly conducts training and development programmes for its employees. Judith's management always tries hard to improve the performance of its employees and tries to motivate them.

Now Judith's management wants Alistair's employees to follow Judith's work culture. Judith also wants to revise its strategy and form a new strategy in the view of the acquisition.

Required:

(a) Explain how the implications of strategic drift affect Alistair's business.
(b) Explain to Alistair how cultural processes and the absence of strategy development affected the progress of the organisation.
(c) Explain the factors that demand multiple processes of strategy development.

Answers to Self Examination Questions

Answer to SEQ 1

(a) Intended strategy is planned and deliberate, whereas emergent strategy is unplanned and not deliberate.

Wonder wants to adopt a new strategy to start a daily economics newspaper as well as its weekly publication. Wonder has made this decision after collecting and analysing the response from the customers. Here, starting the weekly newspaper is the intended strategy of Wonder and starting the economic newspaper is the emergent strategy of the organisation.

To start a daily economics newspaper is the organisation's emergent strategy. Wonder has not previously planned this activity. The organisation wants to launch its new idea after observing customer interest in the economics section of its weekly publication.

Continued on the next page

(b) To launch a daily economics newspaper as well as its weekly publication, Wonder needs to do some strategic planning. The following are the stages of strategic planning cycle:

- **Planning guidelines**: the organisation forms the guidelines for its future plan and sets priorities for achieving its future objectives.
- **Prepare a rough business plan**: after setting the guidelines, the organisation makes its business plan. The business plan contains the goals that need to be achieved by different businesses.
- **Consultation with senior level managers**: the business plan set by the organisation is discussed with the corporate managers in a face-to-face meeting. These meetings are beneficial because they clarify issues and doubts more quickly by allowing one-to-one communication.
- **Review the business plan**: in the meeting, if the corporate managers want to revise the plan, it will be revised accordingly.
- **Prepare estimate budgets**: in this stage, organisation prepares the budget relating to the required funds for capital expenditure and operating expenditure. This provides an overview of fund requirements.
- **Prepare a final corporate plan**: collectively, all the business plans form a corporate plan. This is prepared for the accomplishment of corporate goals.
- **Approval from board of directors**: Corporate plan requires the approval of the board of directors.
- **Annual performance targets and review**: the corporate managers plan performance targets for the organisation on an annual basis using the balanced scorecard approach.
- **Performance appraisal**: an organisation is inclined to scrutinise the performance of strategic-level managers. The organisation compares the actual goals achieved with the targets set.

Wonder Ltd must follow these stages before launching the new product. The company first needs to set its guidelines and, according to that, a plan of future objectives can be formed. First, the company needs to consult and review its plan with corporate managers. It needs to prepare the estimated budgets as well as the corporate plan and then take the approval of the board of directors. After launching the new product, the organisation can review its performance and analyse its achieved targets with the set goals.

Answer to SEQ 2

(a) Alistair's management did not analyse its strategy and the effect of this on the organisation's growth.
Alistair did not keep itself at par with market trends and consequently failed to satisfy its customers' preferences. Even after the incurring losses for six years, the company failed to carry out any product development. It did come out of the strategic drift situation, but it failed to bring transformational change with regard to its losses. Finally, Alistair sold its business to Judith Ltd.

Therefore, the strategic drift finally led Alistair to sell its business.

(b) Alistair's work culture needs a lot of improvement. Alistair should have conducted market research and, based on that, it should have concentrated on product development. Every organisation needs to change the processes of strategy development according to the changes in its environment. Adopting market trends and starting an e-business could have helped Alistair. Improving the performance of employees and motivating them to work efficiently are two things that Alistair's HR neglected to do. Alistair should have provided training and development opportunities to its employees.

Judith's work culture has contributed and is still contributing towards Judith's success and recent expansion, whilst Alistair has had to sell its business.

(c) Below are the factors that demand multiple processes of strategy development. Processes of strategy development are different under the following situations:

1. **Stagnant environment**: organisations experiencing little or no change in their environments (such as technological environments, market conditions, etc.) need very little strategy development. Processes for strategy development under such situations are simple. Even if these environments experience change, most of the time it is predictable. Hence, processes required for strategy development are fairly simple.

2. **Rapidly changing environments**: such environments keep changing every now and then. Processes used for strategy development under such situations are different to the ones used for stagnant environments. Organisations that are facing such environments have to change their strategy according to changes in these environments.

3. **Multifaceted environments**: these complex environments are hard to understand. Such environments might be stagnant or rapidly changing. Environments which are complex and rapidly changing demand frequent changes in strategy development. Processes used for strategy development are different for the development of each strategy.
Strategies go through different phases in their lifecycles. Strategies might come from the top down or might come from lower levels such as emergent strategies. Each development in strategy might need different processes for strategy development.

SECTION D: BUSINESS PROCESS CHANGE — D1

STUDY GUIDE 1: THE ROLE OF PROCESS AND PROCESS CHANGE INITIATIVES

Get Through Intro

Many of you will join large organisations which have been running for years. You may be heading up a team or department, which has many people in it. Often, when you first join, you will quickly see some ways of improving the way business can be conducted. It may be that you have 50 people reporting directly to you, which is time-consuming. You may reorganise them into smaller teams, with a team leader and have the team leaders report to you. This will help streamline the business and helps your staff have more of a reporting structure. It also frees you up to concentrate on the bigger picture.

This Study Guide will help you think about how and why you may need to change the way processes are run within a business, whether it is changing the organisational structure, or making a product in a different way, using different machinery or a different centre (e.g. outsourcing production of components to China).

Learning Outcomes

a) Advise on how an organisation can reconsider the design of its processes to deliver a selected strategy.
b) Appraise business process change initiatives previously adopted by organisations.
c) Establish an appropriate scope and focus for business process change using Harmon's process-strategy matrix.
d) Explore the commoditisation of business processes.
e) Advise on the implications of business process outsourcing.
f) Recommend a business process redesign methodology for an organisation.

Introduction

Case Study

Genpact

Whilst you may not have heard their name, you certainly know their clients: Aon, BUPA, Cadbury Schweppes, GE, GlaxoSmithKline, Invensys, Westpac and the list goes on...

According to their website, 'Genpact manages business processes for companies around the world. The company combines process expertise, information technology and analytical capabilities with operational insight and experience in diverse industries to provide a wide range of services using its global delivery platform. Genpact helps companies improve the ways in which they do business by applying Six Sigma and Lean principles plus technology to continuously improve their business processes. Genpact operates service delivery centres in India, China, Hungary, Mexico, the Philippines, the Netherlands, Romania, Spain and the United States. Earlier this year Genpact was named 'Best Performing BPO' and 'Best in Human Capital Development' by industry consultants NeoIT and Global Services magazine.'

Genpact have over 35,000 people working for them around the globe and their revenues in 20X7 were $877 million dollars. They have won countless awards for outsourcing and are currently looking at being able to outsource now for where they have large local presences like India and China.

The success of Genpact highlights the thirst for companies to outsource activities where they cannot add value themselves. Genpact performs finance and accounting functions for many clients, where Genpact staff do everything from supplier statement reconciliation up to the point where they prepare the final financial statements and provide management analysis. This leaves the client with time to concentrate on its core activities.

This Study Guide will help you identify when it may be appropriate to outsource services and hopefully save your company a lot of money!

> 1. Advise on how an organisation can reconsider the design of its processes to deliver a selected strategy.[3]
> Appraise business process change initiatives previously adopted by organisations.[3]
> [Learning Outcomes a and b]

As mentioned in previous Study Guides an organisation can be thought of as being a collection of people working towards achieving a shared objective and purpose. In addition it can also be described as being a resource processing machine. By this what is meant is that an organisation will take resources such as labour, money, materials etc and through its processes convert them into usable products / services.

The processes of an organisation represent how an organisation controls / wants its work to be done. More specifically as Davenport states they are "a specific ordering of work activities across time and space, with a beginning, an end, and clearly identified inputs and outputs". For instance ordering raw materials from a supplier would be an example of a process for a manufacturing organisation.

Business processes therefore then become sets of logically related tasks that use an organisation's resources to provide the goods / services its customers want and will enable the organisation to achieve its objectives. For instance developing and marketing a new product would be examples of business processes for a FMCG (fast moving consumer goods organisation).

Therefore given how integral an organisation's processes are to its success, improving existing processes has and in all probability will always be a recurring theme for most businesses. In fact improving business processes has not only benefited individual performances but has also helped to revolutionise entire industries in the past.

Example

A very commonly cited example is how Henry Ford managed to revolutionise the automobile industry by creating a brand new production process (the assembly line).

Amongst the first of the major breakthroughs in improving business processes came with the introduction of Total Quality Management ("TQM"). Toyota introduced the concept of TQM in 1980 by appraising and improving their fundamental methods of production which were initially called "Total Productive Maintenance" or TPM. The main principles of the TQM are namely management commitment, employee empowerment, continuous improvement, customer focus and fact based decision making.

The main concept behind TQM is to focus on achieving a standardisation of the processes present in an organisation. The underlying rationale being that once processes have been redesigned / improved so that they are performed in a standardised way, an organisation will be able to achieve a certain desired level of consistency in its output.

Another method, organisations have used to focus on ways of improving and controlling the quality of their outputs is through obtaining an ISO 9000 certification. ISO refers to the International Organisation for Standardisation. An organisation is ISO 9000 certified when it has a sufficient number of well documented policies and procedures in place for each activity that it undertakes. Again this implies by following these documented and policies and procedures an organisation will achieve consistency its processes and therefore in the quality of the output of its goods / services.

Although widely adopted in the 1980s, these types of quality focused process change initiatives came under criticism for only resulting in incremental gains in productivity. This paved the way for the Business Process Reengineering ("BPR") movement that began in the 1990s.

Definition

Hammer and Champy define reengineering as being "the fundamental rethinking and redesign of business processes to achieve dramatic improvements in critical, contemporary measures of performance, such as cost, quality, service and speed".

Therefore BPR can be thought of as the analysis and redesign of workflow within and between organisations. The underlying belief here being that an organisation's processes should all be radically redesigned and or reconstructed.

The widely believed way to achieve these objectives was through effective use of Information Technology ("IT") and Information Systems ("IS"). Organisations would need to think in terms of comprehensive and continuous processes that resulted in an end product / service rather than "zeroing in" on single functions or activities. The rapid advancements that had been made in IT and IS would enable organisations to transcend across departmental and divisional lines and integrate all the various activities and functions. One of the key features of BPR is the rearrangement of the business processes along strategic lines and is customer / staff focused rather than around functions e.g. departments.

However during this same period another "guru" of BPR, Rummler advocated that organisations should focus on human process improvements. More specifically he felt that organisations should redesign themselves and structure their processes and activities in such a way that they would enable employees to function effectively.

The Rummler-Brache Matrix identifies nine different and separate issues that need to be addressed whenever an organisation undertakes changing one of its processes. The objective of the matrix is to get organisations to consider not only how processes should be designed but also how they must be managed and eventually measured in terms of success / effectiveness.

Diagram 1: Rummler-Brache Matrix

	Goal	Design	Management
Organisational level	Organisation Goals	Organisation Design	Organisation Management
Process Level	Process Goals	Process Design	Process Management
Job/Performer Level	Job Goals	Job Design	Job Management

However despite the number of its advocates, BPR's success rate never matched the hype that accompanied it. Hammer identifies and outlines three main reasons for this:

- A lack of sustained management commitment and leadership
- Unrealistic scope and expectations on the part of top management / executives
- Resistance to change from employees
- Association with staff downsizing although this is not the objective of BPR

Therefore in the new millennium focus switched from PBR to Enterprise Resource Planning ("ERP") systems. ERP systems represent software application packages such as SAP and PeopleSoft which are designed to help an organisation to integrate its various departments / functions by allowing information to freely flow across the business.

Example

For instance an organisation's MIS might consist of three separate software applications for its accounting, inventory control and human resources functions. An ERP system would integrate the systems used by these departments to enable the organisation to operate them all from the same software platform.

Overall the focus behind using ERP systems is to automate existing processes as far as possible and replace existing department specific software with one all encompassing and integrated program. However just as with BPR the results derived from implementing ERP systems has not matched the accompanying hype.

This has led to the present day emphasis on business process change initiatives. The current thinking is that organisations should not only focus on improving business processes but should also ensure that the new processes are properly aligned with the overall goals and strategy of the organisation. Therefore business processes should be improved / redesigned not only so that work and activities are performed more efficiently and effectively but also so that they are in line with corporate strategies and managerial objectives.

SUMMARY

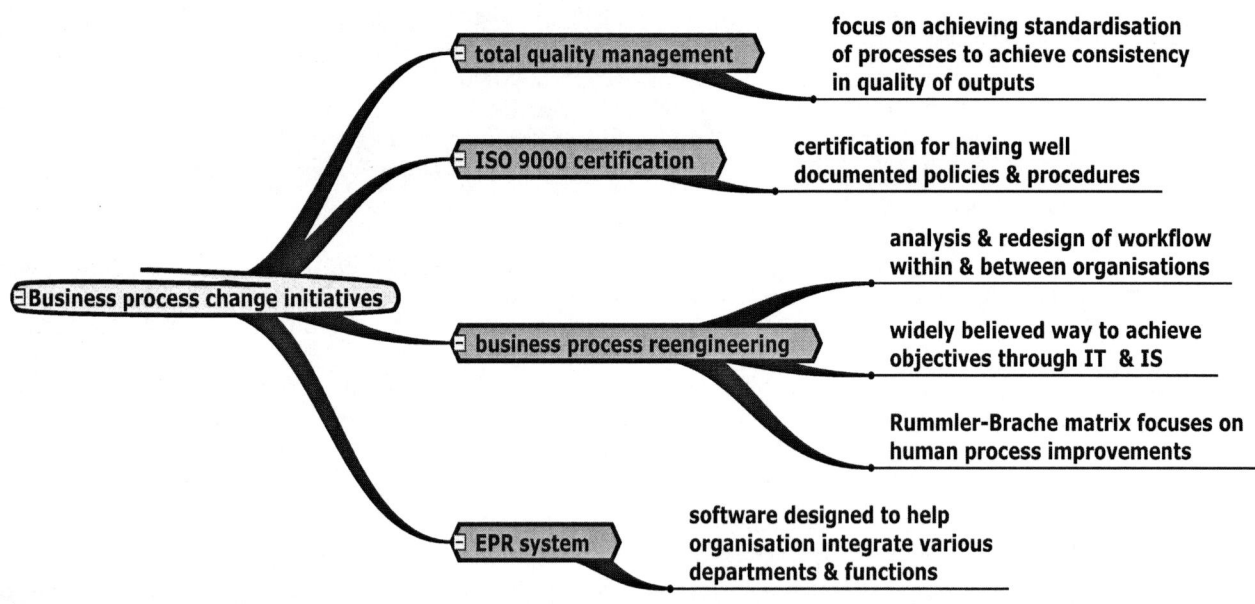

Test Yourself 1

Extendinghands is a manufacturing organisation that specialises in developing robotic arms. The business has adopted a simple functional organisation structure dividing itself into four main departments. These departments are manufacturing, finance and accounting, human resources and marketing. Each department at present has its own MIS consisting of a specialized off-the shelf software package (e.g. manufacturing uses CADCAM and accounting ACCPAC). This has restricted information flows and data exchanges across the divisions and made it more difficult for the organisation to perform as a cohesive whole.

Required:

Suggest a business process change technique Extendinghands can implement?

2. Establish an appropriate scope and focus for business process change using Harmon's process-strategy matrix.[3]

[Learning Outcome c]

Harmon's process-strategy matrix is a technique that organisations can use to identify and categorise their various processes as well as ways in which these processes can be improved. The X axis of the matrix measures how complex / straightforward and dynamic / static a particular process is whereas the Y-axis considers its strategic importance to the organisation.

The first step in using this tool is to identify and list out all of the processes of an organisation. Each process should then in turn be analysed and rated on how complex, dynamic and strategically important it is to the organisation. The results of this analysis will determine which of the four quadrants of the matrix the process should be placed into.

For each of the quadrants, Harmon also states how best the process should be changed in order to be improved. For instance Harmon states that a process that is straightforward, static and strategically important to an organisation such as an assembly line should be automated whenever possible.

It is important to note here that the terms complexity and straightforward as well as dynamic and static are used to cover and describe the types of tasks and work a particular process involves. For instance a process can be labelled as being straightforward if it requires little initiative / decision making and a routine set of procedures to be carried out (e.g. filing reports). A process may be considered static if its function is unlikely to change over the course of time (e.g. payroll).

The term strategic importance in the context of this matrix is used to cover and describe how much value a particular process adds to the production of the organisation's final good / service. For instance a key question would be if the process represents a core competence of the organisation or is merely a support activity.

Diagram 2: Harmon's Process Matrix

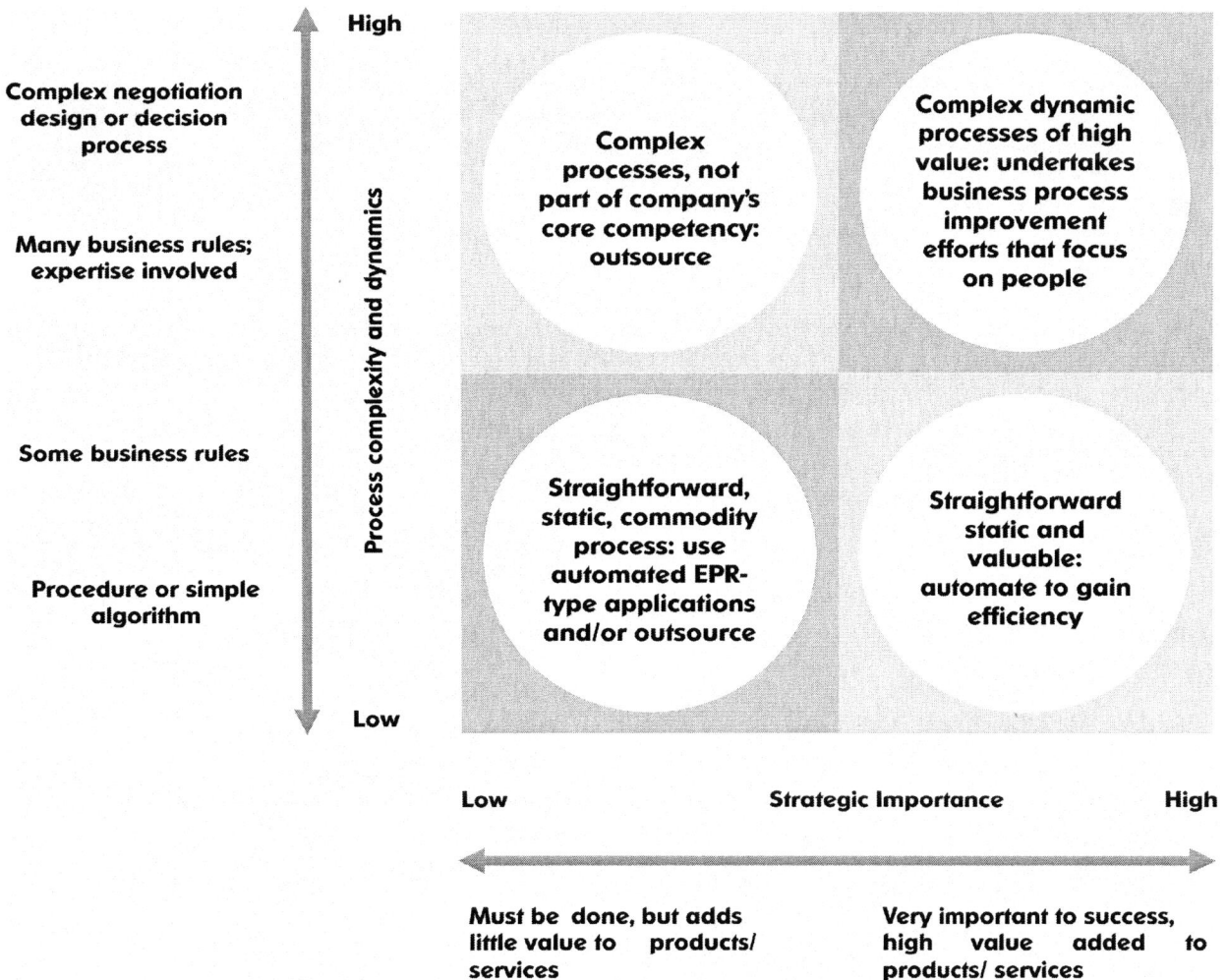

Test Yourself 2

A Explain how Harmon's process-strategy matrix measures whether a particular process is static or dynamic with regards to its strategic importance to an organisation.

B Explain, with an example, why Harmon's process-strategy matrix is not the same for all organisations.

3. Explore the commoditisation of business processes.[3]

[Learning Outcome d]

A business process represents the way an organisation conducts its operations or in simpler terms, the way it does its work. It relates to the set of activities prescribed for employees to follow when they are carrying out their respective functions.

Commoditisation in economic theory is the term used to describe the transformation that occurs when a previously unique and branded product / service becomes so widely and commonly available that it's only distinguishing feature then becomes its price.

Therefore the commoditisation of business processes can be said to occur when there is no significant difference in the way different organisations perform the same function. There are 3 main factors and reasons why business processes are becoming increasingly commoditised today:

1. The growth in use of business process management systems
2. The growth in adoption of process standards
3. The increasing use of outsourcing and internal factors such as concentration on strategic ignoring the routine functions.

a) Growth in use of business process management systems

Business process management systems are integrated software solutions or packages that help organisations to set and control the processes that will drive their business. Common examples include ERP systems such as SAP and PeopleSoft. Setting up an effective business process management system involves an organisation:

➢ Identifying where its critical decisions are being made
➢ Identifying the processes that lead up to and control these decisions
➢ Finding ways to automate and control these decisions

Therefore as more and more organisations begin purchasing and implementing the same systems to automate and control their processes, the more and more alike their processes or way of working will become. However achieving such a competitive advantage is not an easy task.

b) Growth in adoption of process standards

The main objective of process standards is to help an organisation to standardise its business processes. A process is said to be standardised when it is performed the same way each time it is carried out (regardless of which employee is driving the process).

Organisations are increasingly attempting to achieve standardisation because it will:

➢ Help the business to perform as a more cohesive whole.
➢ Facilitate communication flows across the organisation.
➢ Enable comparative measures of performance to be made across the business.

Example

For instance standardising the procurement function would involve establishing:

➢ what key activities are to be undertaken and in what order?
➢ how much time, money and resources should be consumed in performing each activity?
➢ what the minimum output or results should be on completion of each activity?

c) Increasing use of outsourcing

Traditionally organisations carried out each and every one of their processes internally. However from the 1980s organisations began outsourcing some of their secondary or support function such as payroll processing or training to external parties that specialised in performing that particular function.

This trend has continued and grown as today many organisations have also started outsourcing some of their major capabilities to an external party. For instance, Kodak and Dupont have both outsourced their IT management functions. In addition Nike has outsourced the great majority of its manufacturing to factories located outside the United States.

Outsourcers like other organisations are also increasingly standardising their processes. This in turn means that the outsourced work of more and more organisations will also be performed using standard or commoditised business processes across the board. Outsourcing helps organisations in the following ways:

- gaining economies of scale by reducing the cost of obtaining the service
- focusing on core business areas
- reduction in the staff (headcount) required for performing the outsourced tasks
- Increase in quality and productivity
- Improved services

However, outsourcing suffers from the following pitfalls:

- loss of managerial control
- could be a possible threat to the security and confidentiality
- loss of flexibility for responding to changing business conditions
- presence of hidden switching costs

SUMMARY

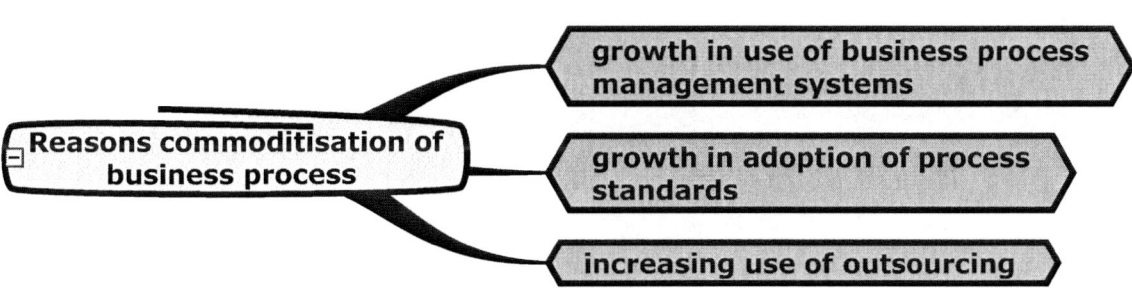

Test Yourself 3

Why has the growing trend of outsourcing led to the increasing commoditisation of business processes?

---

4. Advise on the implications of business process outsourcing.[3]

[Learning Outcome e]

Business process outsourcing ("BPO") occurs when an organisation contracts out an entire business function to an external party. Today this external party is very often domiciled in a foreign country. Popular destinations or sites of BPO organisations include India, Brazil, the Philippines, Dominica, Israel, China, Romania and the Russian federation.

There are two main categories of BPO

1. **back office outsourcing** where internal functions such as billing and purchasing are contracted out
2. **front office outsourcing** where customer related services such as telemarketing and technical support are contracted out

In addition BPO today covers an entire range of functions and industries such as:

- financial and banking services (e.g. processing of credit card applications)
- insurance (e.g. processing application claims)
- human resources (e.g. hiring and recruiting)

Factors that have led to this increase of BPO activity include:

- advancements in Information Technology and Information Systems
- the decline in the cost of telecommunications
- the spread of Internet accessibility and usage
- flexibility offered by outsourcing (e.g. the need for hiring staff is eliminated thereby saving costs)
- the existence labour arbitrage (e.g. the ability to have the same business process performed in a foreign country at a significantly lower cost due to cheaper labour costs)

Research has shown that most organisations that engage in BPO have reported cost savings ranging from 30 to 60% as well as productivity gains ranging from 15 to 25%. However it should be noted that today taking the BPO option is no longer viewed as being a pure cost cutting exercise but also as a strategic initiative.

Outsourcing a business process enables the management of an organisation to spend more time and resources on concentrating on their core competencies. This in turn increases the possibility that the organisation will be able to earn a competitive advantage. The functions that are more likely to be outsourced include the routine and mundane functions such as payroll processing, customer service, etc. However, the core and strategic functions such as production, tax planning, etc are not outsourced.

Furthermore, the fact that many BPO organisations have "proved themselves" to their customers through a combination of lowering overhead costs whilst simultaneously improving quality and productivity levels has enabled them to move up the value chain. Today more and more high end value processes such as on-line training and product design are being outsourced by organisations. This trend shows absolutely no signs of reversing especially with the onset and growth of the KPO (knowledge process outsourcing) industry. KPO firms are engaged in providing niche processes, advanced analytical skills and business expertise, rather than just process expertise as provided by BPO's.

Overall the increasing use of BPO will mean that as time goes forward greater and greater numbers of organisations will become leaner and more flexible (as they will be able to spend more time concentrating on their core competencies) and the external environment they operate in will become more and more globalised (as in all probability the outsourcing organisation will be domiciled in a foreign country).

SUMMARY

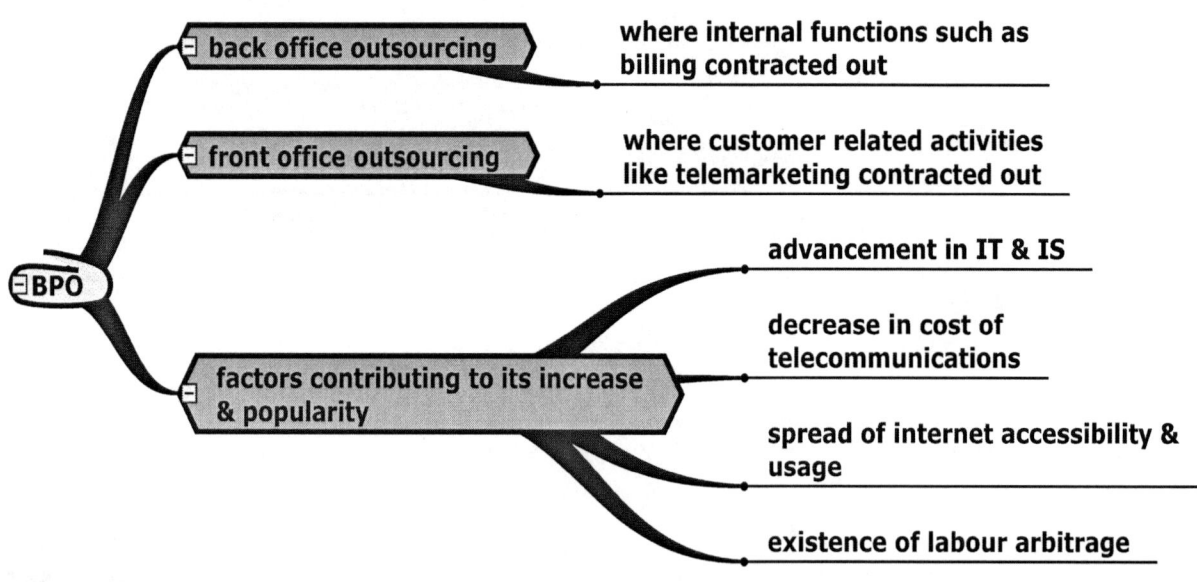

Test Yourself 4

Outsourcing human resource functions

Human resource (HR) outsourcing is a relatively recent phenomenon in the area of outsourcing. HR managers look at the process of managing human resources as a strategic process since people are the most valuable resources of a company. Companies should take a broad view of HR outsourcing and its effects on workforce planning and other issues that have a major impact on business performance and profitability.

Employees expect efficient and proactive services from their HR department. However, a typical HR department usually lacks the capabilities to deal with issues like savings plans, retirement funds, health plans and other benefits. Hence HR operations in some companies tend to be a time-consuming process.

Required:

Continued on the next page

A Explain how HR outsourcing can improve an organisation's services and the factors that promote an outsourcing activity in general.
B State the strategic advantage that a company could enjoy by outsourcing its HR function.

---

5. Recommend a business process redesign methodology for an organisation.[2]
[Learning Outcome f]

The previous sections of this Study Guide discussed the importance for an organisation to understand why it should always strive to better its performance by continually identifying business processes that could be improved upon. However this only represents "half the battle" for the next stage then becomes actually redesigning the selected process(es).

To aid organisations in this matter, Harmon has developed a generic methodology that can be used by organisations when they are redesigning a particular process. However Harmon cautions that this approach should only be used when an organisation is attempting "to undertake a major overhaul of a value chain (activity) or a major business process".

This methodology consists of a 5 stage plan consisting of the following phases:

1. Planning a process redesign effort
2. Analysis of an existing process
3. Design of a new or improved process
4. Development of resources for an improved process
5. Managing the implementation of the new process

In addition, Harmon advises that organisations should create a specific purpose team to carry out this project. This team should comprise of managers and employees from each of the departments / functions involved in the process as well as IT and HR specialists. Harmon also recommends that a facilitator be appointed to help ensure that discussions that go on during the planning stages remain on track.

Diagram 3: Harmon's 5 stage plan for process redesigning

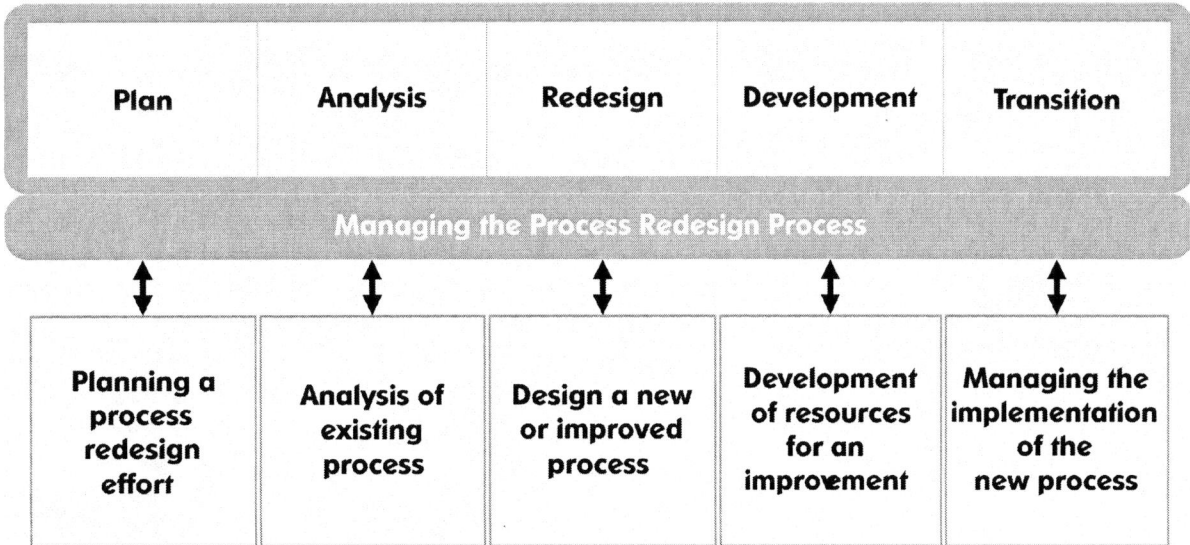

Phase 1: Planning a process redesign effort

This initial phase involves the redesign team formulating a plan for the entire redesign process. The plan should outline goals as well as a schedule for the entire process. The plan should also highlight the particular aspects of the organisation's overall strategy that the new process will contribute to as well as how it will interact and / or affect the organisation's other processes and external parties (e.g. customers, suppliers, distributors etc).

Phase 2: Analysis of an existing process

During this phase the workings of the process to be redesigned are thoroughly analysed and documented thus providing a starting point for the actual redesigning effort. Here specific activities and flows associated with the targeted process are identified and then reproduced in diagrammatic form (this will make it easier for team members to identify the particular steps in the process that need to be improved upon). This diagram should also identify:

Continued on the next page

- all activities
- all sub-activities
- where all the inputs come from
- where all the outputs go

Phase 3: Design of a new or improved process

Here the team will identify specific opportunities or places where existing activities can be improved upon as well as how these activities should be improved upon. The end result or objective of this phase is to have the targeted process completely redesigned and therefore significantly bettered. The team at this point must also specify how roles and responsibilities of employees / managers will change when the new process is implemented.

Phase 4: Development of resources for an improved process

This phase requires the team to detail how the new redesigned process is to be implemented and begin working on the same. Types of activities that will need to be carried out include:

- acquiring any additional space and resources that may be needed
- providing any necessary additional training for employees who will be involved with the process (this responsibility will fall upon the HR specialised member(s) of the team
- integrating the new processes into the organisation's existing MIS (this responsibility will fall upon the MIS specialised member(s) of the team

Specific goals and / or performance measures for the new process will also be set here.

Phase 5: Managing the transition to a new process

The final phase represents the actual implementation of the redesigned process. It requires the team to monitor and ensure that all relevant managers / employees begin following all of the activities involved with the new process (and not revert to the "old way" of doing things). To help them in this regard team members should ensure that all managers and employees involved with the new process have been made to understand how and why the previous process was redesigned.

Test Yourself 5

LINK petrochemicals Ltd supplies petrochemicals. The company is planning to redesign its logistics operations across all its plants.

The existing procedures followed by the company, from inspecting and loading a truck to completing all the commercial formalities, have a turnaround time of one hour per truck. However, in practice, the turnaround time is significantly higher than the planned turnaround time. Consequently, there is a significant variance between the planned and actual dispatch time of finished goods. The higher turnaround time is also a cause of concern for the transporters.

A systematic analysis of the situation revealed the reasons for the significantly higher turnaround time. As a consequence of this analysis, it was felt that deploying additional resources, optimising the activity processing time, sub-contracting some of the routine activities and extensive automation of the process would only marginally reduce the turnaround time.

The company is planning to reduce the turnaround time to one minute per truck within the next three years. In order to reduce the turnaround time substantially, the company needs to redefine its operations substantially.

Required:

Explain how the existing process could be redesigned using the 5 stage plan developed by Harmon.

Answers to Test Yourself

Answer to TY 1

Extendinghands should examine implementing an ERP system. ERP systems represent software application packages such as SAP and PeopleSoft which are designed to help an organisation to integrate its various departments / functions by allowing information to freely flow across the business.

Answer to TY 2

A The strategy component of the matrix describes how much value a particular process adds to the production of the goods or services produced by the organisation. Before discussing Harmon's process-strategy matrix and how organisations can use it to identify and categorise their various processes, it is necessary to understand the meaning of static and dynamic processes.

Static process: a process may be considered static if its function is unlikely to change over the course of time (e.g. payroll).

Dynamic process: a process may be considered dynamic if it keeps changing rapidly in response to changes in the environment e.g. changes in the external environment such as changes in regulations. For example, being a member of a bank's loan processing unit, whose process includes an activity that assigns risk premiums.

When considering process complexity and dynamics, it is necessary to consider the type of task and how it is of strategic importance to the organisation. This can be viewed in the following table:

Quadrant in Harmon's process strategy matrix	Nature of the process in terms of adding value in the organisation	What it implies in matrix
Lower-left	Processes that must be carried out but add little value and are straightforward in nature.	These tasks need to be automated in the most efficient manner possible
Lower-right	Processes that are high-value processes and are straightforward	These processes should be automated to reduce costs and to increase efficiency
Upper-left	Processes that are complex and critical in nature, but don't add much direct value to the company's product or services	If these processes are not carried out they could cause certain problems since they are complex and difficult to outsource
Upper-right	High value processes that are complex in nature	These processes often involve human expertise – like design of a new product – and are difficult to automate

B Harmon's process-strategy matrix enables processes to be differentiated according to the complexity, dynamics and strategic importance of the process to the organisation.

It should be noted that Harmon's process-strategy matrix is different for different companies, even if the processes are the same in both organisations. For example, one company's strategic process is another company's routine process. A primary concern of company AAA, which manufactures sports shoes, will be its manufacturing process, as this is a core business activity. Shipping of the goods, on the other hand, is a routine process for AAA and not a core business activity. However, for a shipping company, shipping is its core business activity and hence it is a strategic process.

In conclusion, the same process exercised by different organisations has different levels of strategic importance.

Answer to TY 3

Today organisations are not only organisation outsourcing their secondary or support functions but also some of their major capabilities to an external party. However outsourcers like other organisations are also increasingly standardising their processes. This in turn means that the outsourced work of more and more organisations will also be performed using standard or commoditised business processes across the board.

Answer to TY 4

A The outsourcer can provide effective and efficient HR solutions by using user-friendly technology. Modern technology allows employees to update their benefit selections, retirement contributions and payroll deductions using interactive voice response technologies. This is not only more efficient for employees, who get timely and accurate information, but it reduces the company's costs.

The most frequently outsourced HR functions include compensation planning, payroll, benefits administration, recruiting and outplacement services, savings plans and retirement plans, management development and training programmes. Most of these functions could be performed effectively and efficiently if outsourced thereby minimising the costs for the organisation and increasing employee productivity.

The following factors have encouraged organisations to outsource their activities:

- advances in information technology and information systems
- the decline in the cost of telecommunications
- the spread of internet accessibility and usage
- the existence of labour arbitrage (e.g. the ability to have the same business process performed in a foreign country at a significantly lower cost due to cheaper labour costs)

B Research has shown that most organisations that engage in BPO have reported cost savings ranging from 30% to 60% as well as productivity gains ranging from 15% to 25%. However, the strategic advantages connected with the outsourcing of HR are as follows:

- provides greater administrative efficiency
- provides an opportunity to focus more on the core business
- helps to maintain a competitive edge in the industry
- increases shareholder value
- improves service quality
- helps company to meet changing customer demands

Answer to TY 5

In the given case, the team could follow the 5 stage plan developed by Harmon to redesign its existing logistics operations and reduce its turnaround time substantially. The process for the in-plant logistics operations could be redesigned in phases as follows:

Phase 1: Planning the process redesign

In this phase, the redesign team should formulate a plan for the entire redesign process which includes:

- **Deciding a goal:** the goal should be to redesign the existing process in order to reduce the delay in turn around time significantly.

- **Ascertain the contribution of the goal to the organisation's strategy:** the removal of bottlenecks in operations will improve profitability by reducing the variance between the planned and actual dispatch time of finished goods.

Phase 2: Analysis of the existing process

In this phase, the process steps to be redesigned are thoroughly analysed and documented thus providing the starting point for the actual redesigning exercise. Specific activities and flows associated with the targeted process are identified and then reproduced in diagrammatic form. This diagram should also identify:

- all the activities involved in the logistics operations (every minute activity from inspecting, loading and completing the required commercial formalities to the final dispatch should be analysed)
- all sub-activities which are a part of the main activities (e.g. the security check is a sub-activity of the inspection process)
- where all the inputs come from
- where all the outputs go

The analysis of the process may reveal the following:

- The loading operation is not the major contributor to truck turnaround time. Instead, other related activities are holding up the system.
- The bottleneck activity is the security and vehicle check.
- There is a mismatch between the budgeted time and the actual time for the critical activities.
- The truck driver has to stop at 8 locations before leaving the complex.
- There is a substantial room for automation.

Phase 3: Designing of a new and improved process

Here the team will identify specific opportunities or areas where the existing activities can be improved upon as well as how these activities should be improved. The objective of this phase is to completely redesign the targeted process.

Approach towards alternatives: based on the above set of observations, it is possible to generate several alternatives by which the turnaround time can be improved.

Continued on the next page

Several solutions to reducing the truck turnaround time such as automation, deployment of additional resources, simplification of processes and reduction of activities (e.g. reducing the number of checks) should be considered.

The team at this point must also specify how the roles and responsibilities of employees and managers will change when the new process is implemented.

Phase 4: Development of resources for an improved process

This phase requires the team to detail how the new, redesigned process should be implemented and start working on its implementation. The following points will need to be ensured:

- The revised process should ensure that the truck stops only once inside the plant for material loading. Changes to the internal plant designs should be made accordingly.
- The new process should be information technology enabled.

During phase 4 of Harmon's business process methodology, the business process team will have to develop any additional resources that the new improved process will require. This will involve:

- providing any necessary additional training for employees who will be involved with the process (this responsibility will fall upon the member(s) of the team specialising in HR)
- integrating the new processes into the organisation's existing MIS (this responsibility will fall upon the member(s) of the team specialising in the MIS).

Phase 5: Managing the transition to a new process

The final phase represents the actual implementation of the redesigned process. It requires the team to monitor all managers / employees concerned to ensure that they start following the activities included in the new process.

The team members should ensure that all managers and employees involved with the new process understand how and why the previous process was redesigned.

Quick Quiz

1. Cite 3 reasons why the success of BPR did not match its hype.
2. What is the first step in using Harmon's process-strategy matrix?
3. What are the three main reasons for the commoditisation of business processes?
4. What are the two main categories of BPO?
5. What is the third phase in Harmon's business process redesign methodology?

Answers to Quick Quiz

1.
    i. Lack of sustained management commitment and leadership
    ii. Unrealistic scope and expectations on part of top management and leadership
    iii. Resistance to change from employees.

2. To identify and list out all of the processes of an organisation

    i. Growth in use of business process management systems
    ii. Growth in adoption of process standards
    iii. Increase use of outsourcing.

3. Back office outsourcing & front office outsourcing.

4. Design of a new or improved process.

Self Examination Questions

Question 1

Rollingstone Recordings is a small record label that specialises in discovering developing fresh talent. The organisation signs up new artists who it believes will have the potential to achieve commercial success.

Continued on the next page

The organisation then has the artist record a music album from which a CD is cut. Rollingstone then promotes and sells the album to various radio stations and music stores. Once the artist has achieved a certain degree of success, Rollingstone sells his / her contract one of the major record labels.

The processes Rollingstone follows are:

- Scouting for fresh talent
- Developing albums for their signed artists (letting artists record their songs in the studio)
- Manufacturing these albums (i.e. placing the songs recorded in the studio onto a CD)
- Storing and warehousing these albums
- Promoting and marketing these albums (to radio stations and music stores)
- Selling these albums (i.e. over the phone sales to individuals)
- Negotiating with major labels for sale of artists' contracts

Required:

Place each of these processes into one of the four quadrants present in the Harmon's process-strategy matrix.

Question 2

State the elements of business process outsourcing. Briefly explain the meaning of the terms offshore and onshore outsourcing in the context of a BPO.

Answers to Self Examination Questions

Answer to SEQ 1

Quadrant 1 Straightforward, static, commodity processes	- Storing and warehousing these albums - Selling these albums (i.e. over the phone sales to individuals) - Manufacturing these albums (i.e. placing the songs recorded in the studio onto a CD)
Quadrant 2 Straightforward, static and valuable	- Developing albums for their signed artists (letting artists record their songs in the studio)
Quadrant 3 Complex processes, not part of company's core competency	- None
Quadrant 4 Complex, dynamic processes of high value	- Scouting for fresh talent - Promoting and marketing these albums (to radio stations and music stores) - Negotiating with major labels for sale of artists' contracts

Answer to SEQ 2

The elements of a BPO are:

- front office processing
- back-office transaction processing services
- IT outsourcing
- Finance and Accounting (F&A) outsourcing
- Human Resource (HR) outsourcing
- Knowledge Process Outsourcing (KPO)

When a BPO is contracted outside a company's country of operation, this is called "offshore" outsourcing; when it is contracted within the company's country of operation, this is called "onshore" outsourcing

SECTION D: BUSINESS PROCESS CHANGE

D2

STUDY GUIDE 2: IMPROVING THE PROCESS OF THE ORGANISATION

Get Through Intro

In the last Get Through Intro, we wrote of you entering a new company and wanting to make some changes to the structure of your 50 staff who directly report to you. However, the first question we should be asking is why do we want to make any changes? There is an old expression, 'if it is not broken, then don't try to fix it.'

Generally due to increased competition or increased costs (prices of materials and labour), changes in business are inevitable. We may have been profitable selling a product at $10, but now, due to increased competition, many competitors are offering the same product at $8. We will need to change our processes so we can be as competitive, or change our product to show some sort of differentiation which is why it is worth paying another $2 for the product.

This Study Guide will explain how we analyse our processes, with the aim of improving them. There are different methods and by learning them, you could save your company a lot of money and also score very well in the exam by applying your knowledge!

Learning Outcomes

a) Evaluate the effectiveness of current organisational processes.
b) Describe a range of process redesign patterns.
c) Establish possible redesign options for improving the current processes of an organisation.
d) Assess the feasibility of possible redesign options.
e) Assess the relationship between process redesign and strategy.

Introduction

Case Study

Colin Thurston and Kevin Smith

The following extracts show how Laboratory Information Management Systems (LIMS) are helping to decrease costs and increase productivity, whilst at the same time ensuring optimum product quality and regulatory compliance.

It is obvious that companies need to extract the maximum oil from each well that they dig. Basically, LIMS gives feedback quickly and accurately as to what the potential is in oil and gas exploration and production. There has been therefore a rapid increase in the number of analyses and samples that are run, which leads to a need for efficient data management.

It is also common knowledge that due to the scarcity of resources, often large oil and gas companies locate their exploration and production processes in harsh and isolated areas. It often makes it hard to set up research facilities in these areas.

By now integrating LIMS within the systems, there have been many benefits. This includes, according to the article, 'the elimination of human error and data duplication, better data quality, considerable time savings and earlier generation of result reports. In addition, immediate data flow between the laboratory and the rest of the operations facilitates faster, data-driven business decision-making.

By centralising and consolidating IT and technical support personnel, enterprise-wide LIMS integration lowers the total cost of ownership significantly. Standardising on a central LIMS allows organisations to store SOPs, specification limits and have immediate alerts sent out when a sample tests out of specification. An integrated LIMS approach helps companies identify trends and monitor product quality more rapidly with greater ease, dramatically improving their overall quality control process and maintaining the highest quality standards.'

(http://www.engineerlive.com)

The above case study shows that by analysing business processes, many benefits can be received. But how does one decide what needs to be improved and how it could be improved? This Study Guide will answer these questions… and more!

1. Evaluate the effectiveness of current organisational processes. [3]

[Learning Outcome a]

An organisation, whether it is a manufacturer, trader, service provider, governmental or semi-governmental body, is created to achieve a certain objective. To meet this objective, it needs to put in place certain procedures and practices in its day-to-day interactions with customers and other stakeholders.

A business process is a set of procedures and practices which collectively realise a business objective or policy goal, normally within the context of the organisation. The flow or sequence of actions usually defines the functional roles and relationships.

The types of business processes which evolve over a period of time show the allocation of responsibilities and coordination between functions in fulfilling organisational goals.

The types of business processes are as follows:

- **Management processes** are carried out by top management which defines the organisation's objectives. Management processes consist of corporate governance or strategic management and provide direction and support to the organisation. For example, the preparation of a performance budget involves determining the organisation's performance goals. It also involves assessing and arranging for the infrastructure, capital, manpower and facilities needed to achieve the goals.

- **Supporting processes** are functions such as purchasing, accounting, inventory management, recruitment and IT support.

- **Operational processes** are a set of activities relating to receiving raw materials and components and converting them into finished products or services. These activities are also referred to as production activities. Production activities are preceded by the preparation of a production plan which is again an extension of the organisational goal relating to the production function.

Support processes and operational processes are monitored by management through the management control mechanism. For example, inventory management processes which ensure that sufficient inputs are procured to produce the required output quantity and meet sales targets. These support processes are part of the value chain.

These procedures and practices are known as 'organisational processes'. These are also referred to as 'business processes'. Nevertheless, both these terms convey the same meaning.

For the convenience of the organisation, the responsibilities for managing processes are divided among managers looking after corporate business processes and managers looking after functional activities.

Example

The sales department of an airline has the responsibility to book flights for customers. Hence the sales department will need call centre staff to talk to customers, take bookings and collect payments. However a separate team may look after internet bookings via the company's website. The call centre and the website are 2 separate business processes for the company.

These processes are designed to help organisations conduct their daily activities effectively. They are also designed to ensure that the organisation delivers quality products and services to its customers at the desired speed. These processes also have to meet the expectations of stakeholders and other categories of associates such as suppliers, contractors and employees of the organisation.

We will discuss the various aspects of evaluation of effectiveness of the processes in this Study Guide.

1.1 Why is there a need to evaluate the effectiveness of processes?

Every organisational process is aimed at incorporating efficient and effective procedures and practices for managing business operations. The business may involve manufacturing products and/or providing services. However, the processes have to achieve the aims of offering economical prices and delivering as quickly as possible, all at the lowest possible cost. The process has to ensure that these objectives are achieved without compromising on the quality of the products or services provided.

These processes are designed to operate under certain known and anticipated circumstances, generally known as the business environment. Unfortunately, the foreseeable business environment considered at the time of designing the business processes cannot be expected to occur over the plan period. The business environment changes due to numerous factors.

The effects of changing business environments are explained below:

➢ An increase in the purchasing power of customers leading to more business opportunities has been a prominent change in developing countries in Asia over the last decade. As a result, the market places have changed from department stores to big malls. Companies have started to adopt more aggressive marketing and selling practices. Counter service is being replaced by self-service. The old business processes have lost their effectiveness in the changed business scenario.

➢ Technological advancements such as the development of the internet and mobile telephones have enabled economically advanced countries to achieve cost reduction by employing the services of qualified, low cost manpower in developing countries such as India, China and the Nigeria.

➢ Technological advancements have also provided Asian businessmen with the opportunity of setting up business process outsourcing businesses. Hence, to reduce their costs, many organisations need to change their processes and come up with new ways of performing processes to ensure that their processes were effective. Likewise, to take advantage of the new business opportunity, businessmen in many countries need to understand and implement processes related to business process outsourcing.

➢ The electronic goods industry has experienced an increase in the number of customers preferring products with advanced features at higher prices. The result is that businesses producing electronic goods with advanced features are flourishing whereas many old brand names are experiencing difficulties. The organisations which are losing business are driven to evaluate the effectiveness of their business processes.

➢ The need for cost cutting in Europe and the US resulted in many businesses offloading work to Asian countries (outsourcing). This has changed the business environment in the UK and the US as well as in Asian countries.

> **Example**
>
> Availability of cheaper and better products in the market: for example, many low cost airlines (such as Ryanair) have come into existence over recent years. This has led to extra competition for traditional carriers, e.g. British Airways, and forced them to think about costs and revenues, due to falling profits. Consequently, British Airways has had to adapt its business processes to cope with this increased competition. This has included cutting its prices, becoming more efficient in plane turnaround times and putting more resources into website bookings.

Therefore, due to the constantly changing business environments, the organisation has to manage the processes to ensure that the organisational processes serve the purpose for which they were designed.

1. **It is therefore necessary to understand what is meant by 'effectiveness of the processes'.**

As mentioned earlier, every process has to fulfil certain needs of the organisation in a timely, efficient and economical manner. When the processes fulfil the aim for which they were designed, we can say that 'they are effective'. However, most of the time, 'effectiveness of processes' is not achieved automatically.

Hence, to ensure that the processes are effective even in a constantly changing business environment, there has to be an effective process management system in place. The process management system essentially monitors the results of the process against the goal measures applicable to ensure that the process is serving its purpose, and thereby proving it to be effective: The measurement of the 'effectiveness of the processes' will also be influenced by the performance results of the same processes by competitors.

> **Example**
>
> According to the current process, Gymnast Built Plc has to deliver a treadmill at a price of $1,899 within a period of 15 days from the date of online order and payment. If competitors are selling a similar product at $1,785 within 10 days of online order and payment, Gymnast Built Plc will have to re-examine its processes.

1.2 Assessment and evaluation of effectiveness

As seen above, the changing business environment makes it necessary for every organisation to establish **business process management** procedures involving managers concerned. A change in one or more factors such as the ones mentioned earlier affects the usefulness of the results or outputs of certain processes. Hence, the organisation needs the system in place to constantly collect information on process results and evaluate the process results to ensure that the processes are meeting the requirements of the organisation.

Business process managers are required to be alert and quickly understand the effect of various changes and trends in the business environment available through news bulletins, economic reviews published by the government and customer feedback etc.

> **Example**
>
> Airline operators (e.g. British Airways, Lufthansa) collect 'ratings' by their customers regarding the quality of services provided by them and invite suggestions for improving the services.

Recently, authorised automobile service providers of reputed car manufacturers have adopted the practice of requiring their customers to fill in a form rating the quality of various services provided by them and also the behaviour of the attendants during their interactions. Confirmatory calls are also made by the service providers after 2 days of service to assess whether the vehicle serviced by them is working properly.

Such practices are also put in place by hospitals, malls and other service providers where customers are invited to write 'Suggestions for improving the services' in the register meant for the purpose or by filling in questionnaires.

The **management of organisational processes** needs business process managers and functional managers to monitor the process results or process outputs on a regular basis. This is done through the regular generation of MIS reports by the managers responsible for the corporate and other functions showing the actual performance against the plans and its review by senior management.

For a given period, these reports cover the information about the planned versus actual performance of the major parameters such as orders received or quantity produced, The analysis of the MIS reports reveals the 'external' and 'internal' factors influencing the organisational performance.

In addition to published reviews, customer feedback is also used for the assessment of product quality as perceived by customers. The information and data collected through these practices provides a foundation for assessment and evaluation. The information collected is then systematically analysed to identify the strengths and weaknesses of the product / service, repeated complaints regarding products / services and repeated suggestions by customers and employees for improvements.

It also possible that the analysis and evaluation of information will confirm that the processes are adequately effective and efficient, even in changing business environments. Normally, the analysis and evaluation of information highlights a need for changing processes to meet changing business needs in order to maintain the supremacy of organisational processes.

Keeping in mind the objectives of the organisational processes, it is also important to assess and evaluate whether there is any weakness in the process which cannot or may not prevent deterioration in performance. This is done to ascertain the effectiveness of the process and ways in which to improve it. Challenging the needs of the company's own processes will involve assessing whether the process is required at all and evaluating the effectiveness of the given process. Likewise, questioning the processes in the functions which have exceeded the planned performance will reveal the causes e.g. error in planning goals or a favourable change in the business environment leading to better opportunity for growth.

Through detailed analysis of the information collected through external and internal information channels, management has to determine the deficiencies in the processes and the quality of the product or services provided and decide improvement parameters for the processes affected by the changing business environment.

The process of collecting the information via external and internal information channels and analysing it to ascertain the usefulness of current processes in relation to desired effects on organisational processes under the changed business environment is known as 'assessment and evaluation of effectiveness'.

Example

The case study is an example of effective organisational process management and the re-designing of the organisational process relating to Account Opening which has a major negative impact on High Net Worth customers of the organisation.

The company is a multi-product entity. Recently, it has been facing a loss of customers resulting in reduced business volumes and profits.

The company's current process of opening customer accounts is overly complex and outdated. It involves different software applications and a paper-based manual process of document verification. It consumes a lot of time and cost and renders most of the customers dissatisfied.

In redesigning this process, the process architecture team is focused on solving the problems with the existing multiple mechanisms that customers use when opening accounts and document processing practices by back office support service.

After several brainstorming sessions between the team and management, the team's objectives were decided as:

- to simplify the online account opening process
- to integrate processes to reduce the time taken and to eliminate irritation caused by slow processes
- to facilitate adoption and integration of contemporary hardware and software
- to speed up the document verification and validation process

The process architecture team studied both the manual and the automated processes. On mapping and analysing the current processes, it observed that:

a) the processes of online account opening can be simplified by introducing separate processes for normal customers and high net worth customers.

b) The customer had to switch from one step to another which involved following tedious processes again and again. This was due to the adoption of different hardware and software at different times. As a result the processes remained unintegrated.

Finally, the processes were redesigned using contemporary hardware and software:

a) The outdated hardware and software were replaced with a single system on a WebSphere process server.

b) The integrated processes run smoothly and do not involve switchovers.

c) The redesigned processes were simplified by introducing separate processes for normal customers and high net worth customers.

d) The speed of document verification and validation process was enhanced by reducing the applicability of document verification. The requirements for document verification and validation for HN customers were redefined as 25% of customers in lower brackets and 100% of customers in the top end bracket.

e) Back office support was made available on request.

Therefore the objectives of the redesign were achieved by redefining the requirements, changing the methods of operation and adopting contemporary technology.

Test Yourself 1

High Music Plc manufactures CD players and music systems. The products are marketed through supermarkets and electrical product retailers in Europe. The company implemented a quality management system (total quality management, also referred to as TQM) 3 years ago and, until recently, has been enjoying a good brand image.

However, for the last 15 months, the company has been facing the following problems:

➢ The number of new sales has been falling for the last three quarters.

➢ The number of complaints of product failure has been increasing over the last year.

➢ The increased cost of free repairs and replacements has further reduced already declining profits.

High Music Plc's management is surprised that, despite the implementation of TQM, there is an increased level of faults. Management is trying to improve the quality of High Music's products in order to regain the company's good brand image.

Required:

Explain why the implementation of TQM in the company 3 years ago did not prevent High Music's current problems from arising. Highlight the importance of maintaining effective business processes through a process management mechanism.

---

2. Describe a range of process redesign patterns.[2]
[Learning Outcome b]

We have seen in the previous section that the designs of organisational processes always aim to ensure the efficient and effective management of product manufacture and/or service provision. The aim is to deliver products and/or services at economical prices, delivering as quickly as possible and at the lowest possible cost without compromising on the quality of the products or services provided.

These processes are designed under certain known and anticipated 'business environments'. In reality, the business environment changes constantly. Hence, to minimise the adverse effects of the changing business environment and also to take advantage of emerging opportunities, management must ensure that the effectiveness of the processes is maintained. For this purpose, management continuously monitors and evaluates the effectiveness of the existing processes.

As an outcome of the evaluation of processes, management may have to redesign certain processes to meet the needs of the changing business environment.

In this section, various process patterns are discussed.

2.1 Process redesign patterns

Definition

The techniques or approaches evolved over a period of time for redesigning a process are called '**process redesign patterns**'.

There has been constant rethinking regarding the ways of enhancing the efficiency and effectiveness of processes. In the recent past, various patterns have often been used to achieve the desired results. It is also important to understand that it is not always possible to achieve the ultimate results of the redesign of processes by using any particular technique or pattern in isolation. It will often be necessary to apply different redesign patterns in combination to achieve the desired results.

We can trace the need for the periodical redesign of processes and techniques to the Industrial Revolution. In spite of the need for a different approach, fresh thinking and updating to contemporary techniques, organisations are using outdated methodologies that have been in use for many years.

Whatever the choice of process redesign pattern, it has to satisfy the technological, financial or economical and administrative viabilities.

We find the following process redesign patterns are generally implemented by the business world, which we will discuss in detail:

- business process re-engineering (BPR)
- value-added analysis
- gaps and disconnects
- simplification

Diagram 1: Process redesign pattern

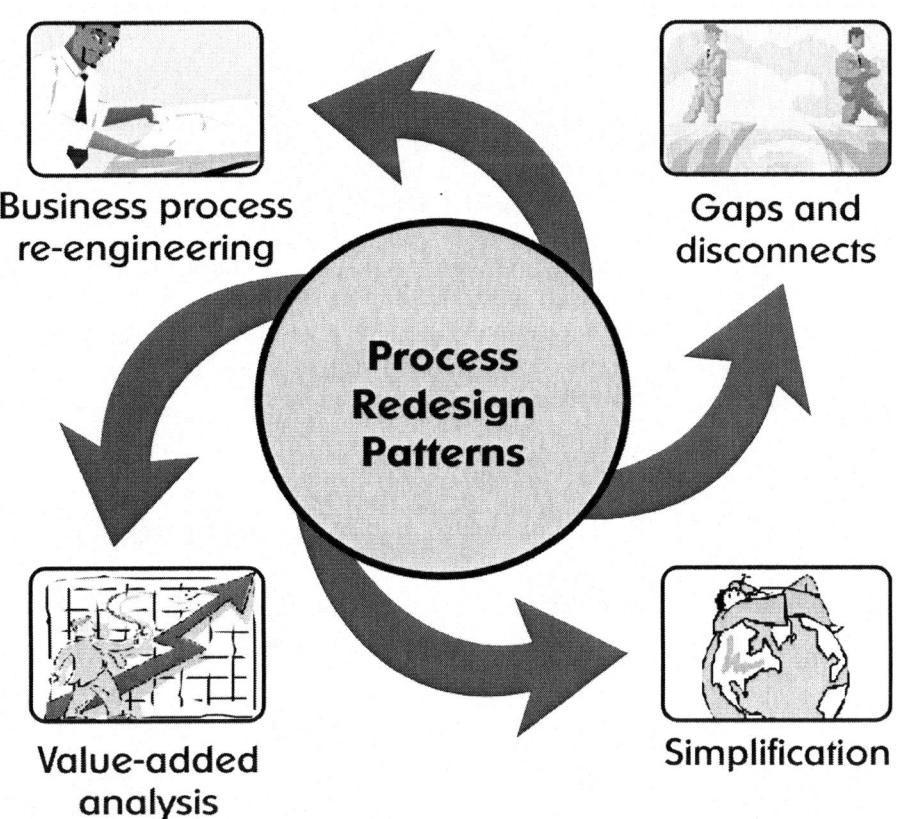

1. Business process re-engineering

Business process re-engineering is one of the most popular techniques of process redesign. It involves 'wiping the slate clean and starting again from scratch'. It is undertaken with the management belief that a drastic step is necessary to lower costs and increase the quality of products and services. It undertakes process analysis afresh ignoring the existing processes and redesigns the workflow within and between organisations. Business process re-engineering is sometimes called **"organisational redesign". Refer to Hammer and Champney.**

This technique goes through the steps of questioning work flow sequences, work, motion and method study and linking operational measures to organisational goals. In line with technological advancements, it also questions the appropriateness of technology in use. Its aim is to specify a fresh process or best practices to suit the current business environment. Its focus is on the complete integration of cross-functional processes into organisational processes and maintaining the supremacy of organisational processes. It stresses the importance of functions and responsibilities rather than roles.

In the last few decades, many banking organisations have redesigned their processes and introduced the latest computer technologies. The redesigned processes involve completely new products such as cash deposits (sealed envelope deposits), cheque deposits - CDM (Cheque Deposit Machines) and cash withdrawals (ATM). The processes were integrated to provide information technology enabled facilities such as internet banking. Process redesign of this nature is not possible unless the start to finish approach of business process re-engineering is adopted. This forced the entire banking world to redesign its processes by choosing the option of BPR. The banks redesigned and integrated their processes to overcome the major challenge posed by competition.

The effect of the changing business environment on current business processes is illustrated in the following example.

Example

Allfin Bank Plc, a leading multinational bank, offers a wide range of consumer banking, corporate banking and treasury services.

The bank has been operating for more than 4 decades. It has been performing quite well. Over the last year, however, it has been facing competition from new private banks and banks with aggressive globalisation strategies. Customers' expectations are growing and the bank's reputation in the market is at stake.

The bank decided to carry out business process redesign to meet customer expectations and maintain its standing in the market.

The objective of the business process redesign project was defined as shown below:

- evaluate possible ways to face the competition and make use of business opportunities
- evaluate technological applications and upgrade existing applications to facilitate new processes
- improve service quality
- redefine cross-functional processes in terms of roles and responsibilities
- reduce costs
- determine and minimise operating risks

A study group comprising senior managers and consultants was formed to identify the areas requiring improvements to meet the objectives.

The study group, after interactions with functional heads, staff and customers; stressed the need for the company to keep up-to-date with the changing business environment. To fulfil the objectives set by the management, it came up with the following recommendations:

- redefine roles and responsibilities of front-office and back-office workers
- redefine roles and responsibilities of workers in branches, regional offices and head office
- establish new low cost and customer-friendly channels for providing customer services
- devise better ways of providing preferential treatment for high-net-worth (HNW) customers
- redesign products and services to provide value-addition
- introduce computerised credit limit-monitoring and administration procedures
- improve coverage, timeliness and quality of management information system
- introduce perpetual financial control and strategic planning

The business process re-engineering project was completed keeping in mind the objectives of the redesign project and the concerns and findings of the study group. The project was monitored by a managing team (the Steering Committee) .The MIS was redesigned to ensure that reliable information was available on time and corrective actions could be taken.

The BPR project has proved to be beneficial to Allfin Bank in the following ways:

a) **Customer service:** customers visiting branches are attended to personally. High net worth customers are treated with special attention. Due to improved processes, the customers using call centre (outsourced) services are now provided better services at lower costs. New products in the area of housing, finance and business loans have been developed to meet the needs of different classes of customers.

Continued on the next page

b) **Business growth:** improved customer service has helped to retain customers and attract new customers through the introduction of new products. The business is growing satisfactorily.

c) **Low cost sales channels:** low cost call centre services abroad are used to provide services to customers. This arrangement has resulted in substantial reductions in expenses. The services are provided according to the redesigned processes without compromising on quality.

d) **Speed and quality of service:** the speed and quality of transaction processing has substantially improved. The reorganised set-up also helped to speed up administrative and approval processes through implementing these processes in regional offices instead of routing them through the head office.

Example

e) **Resource utilisation:** the streamlined processes have enabled the relocation of employees to achieve customer proximity to the workplace and enhance customer service quality. The time of skilled personnel is effectively utilised in building customer relationships.

f) **Reduced operating risk:** the newly designed comprehensive MIS provides real time operational data to managers without depending on assistants to collect data and compile reports. The processes of planning, monitoring and reviewing performance and taking corrective action are now more efficient.

g) **Technology updating:** the choice of contemporary software and hardware to support the operations has ensured uninterrupted services to customers.

As a result of redesigning its business processes, Allfin Bank managed to overcome the challenge posed by the changing business environment and regain its position in the industry.

The BPR concept gained popularity in the business world in the mid nineties. However, it suffered due to:

- lack of sustained management commitment and leadership,
- unrealistic scope,
- high expectations,
- long duration,
- high cost of implementation and
- resistance to changes by employees since it often associated with staff downsizing, although this was never the objective of BPR.

The situation has often prompted management to abandon the concept of BPR and adopt new process redesign methodologies such as Enterprise Resource Planning (ERP).

The organisations which implemented BPR were certainly benefited by the introduction of 'best practices' and the creation of efficient and effective organisational processes. The processes were integrated to eliminate duplications of operations in different functions as well as delays in transferring information to cross-functional entities. Accurate information could be generated at high speed. Therefore, apart from overall organisational efficiency, BPR implementation resulted in the saving of process time and process costs while maintaining overall organisational process goals.

In spite of its benefits, BPR is not free from problems. It has earned a bad reputation because such projects have often resulted in massive layoffs. This reputation is not altogether unfair, since companies have often downsized under the banner of re-engineering. Further, re-engineering has not always lived up to expectations. It is aimed at start to finish redesign and its implementation involves a tremendous volume of work, takes between 10 to 15 months and involves very high costs. It is also a matter of concern for management that due to constant interruptions and obstructions in work flow during implementation, resentment may develop among the employees. Senior management support also fades away over the period. It is these human aspects of the changes which are often significantly more complex to manage than any technological changes. As a result, BPR implementation often leads to complete failure.

Example

Leather World Plc is an internationally renowned leather goods manufacturer. Products manufactured by the company are receiving good customer ratings. Market research conducted by Leather World has shown that the demand for designer purses is increasing and there is an unfulfilled demand for about 50,000 purses annually. The business potential has been found to be quite encouraging. Leather World Plc has therefore introduced a new product line: designer purses.

Continued on the next page

A designer purse being a luxury item, the company has to consider new business processes for purses. The company therefore considers the options available. In addition, the company obtains advice from consultants on the business process redesign technique suitable for the new product.

The options evaluated included:

➢ revamping current business processes to incorporate the requirements of business processes for purses
➢ partially redesigning current business processes to meet the majority of the new requirements.
➢ creating completely new business processes for the new product

Example

The team of managers and consultants unanimously agrees that the new product is a luxury item and hence very sensitive to quality issues. Any major problems with design, delivery and after sales services may affect the company's market image. The team has stressed that decisions regarding the methodology of the business process redesign should be taken carefully. The decisions should take into account the importance of different departments (such as marketing, sales, design, manufacturing) in meeting customer expectations.

Having considered these aspects, the team concludes that it will be in the best interests of the company to design entirely new business processes for the new product. This will ensure that the product quality is not compromised for the sake of reducing the efforts needed to redesign the processes. The company might save some time by modifying the current processes, but this is a trial and error process and may not meet the requirements of a luxury item such as a designer purse.

Accordingly, Leather World Plc has implemented business process re-engineering methodology for their new luxury product.

SUMMARY

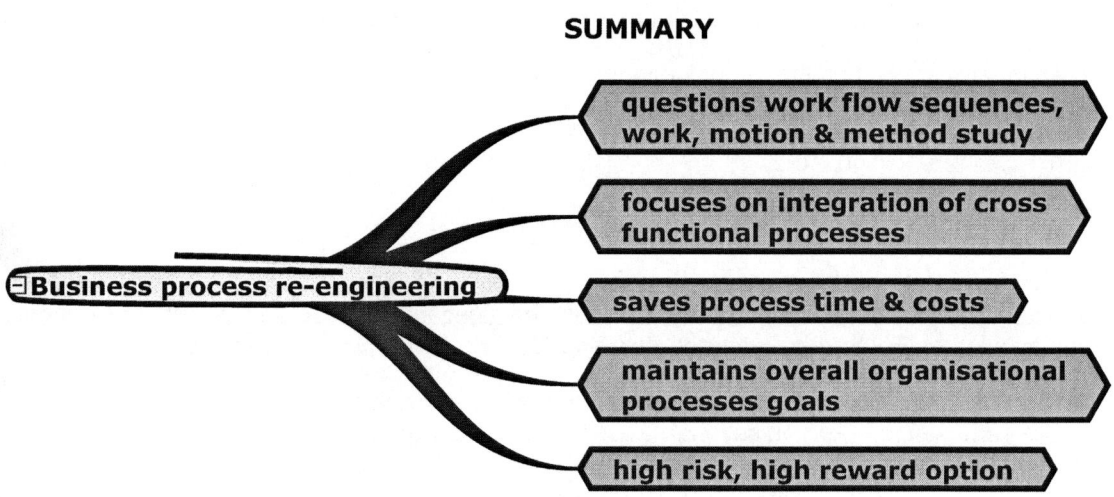

2. Value-added analysis

'The systematic analysis of organisational processes to identify the steps in any process that add value, rather than simply adding cost' – is the fundamental thought process of this technique. Although apparently simple, it is very strict in its approach to ensure the desired results. It challenges the necessity of every process element of cost, materials, manpower, methods of work, machines used, movement of materials and workmen and support function processes. It also questions the adequacy of every step by step process result.

The process must add value or enable value addition from the customers' perspective or the organisational perspective. The term 'customers' encompasses both external and internal customers. For example, the direct production functions are customers of the support functions.

In this exercise, processes which do not add value or do not enable value addition, redundant processes, duplications and inefficient people, machines and methods are brought to the surface and corrective measures are taken to ensure appropriate and effective processes are put in place.

The simple test for a 'value-added process' is that the customer is willing to pay for it without hesitation, the process is being performed differently and gives desired results without adversely affecting other related processes and it is performed effectively, giving results in the first attempt.

Example

High Tech Projects Co undertakes projects all over the country. It procures proprietary products from authorised dealers from any region by receiving and evaluating quotations. The order is placed with the dealer who offers the lowest prices and is also located near the project site. On detailed analysis, it was established that the rate advantage of buying from the dealers in the regions near the project site was negligible compared to the cost involved in speedy transportation of small quantities, insurance formalities, claims and complying with the tax laws of different regions. Therefore the procurement process, instead of adding value, was actually destroying value and hence was eliminated. Instead, procurement of these products was managed centrally through the company's HQ located in the large industrial town.

The best part of this technique is that its implementation involves moderate efforts, time and cost. It does not burden the organisation with the impact of a 'start to finish' approach while assuring a modest to major increase in process efficiencies. If the existing processes contained numerous duplications and redundancies, the outcome of this technique will boost the morale of management and employees.

SUMMARY

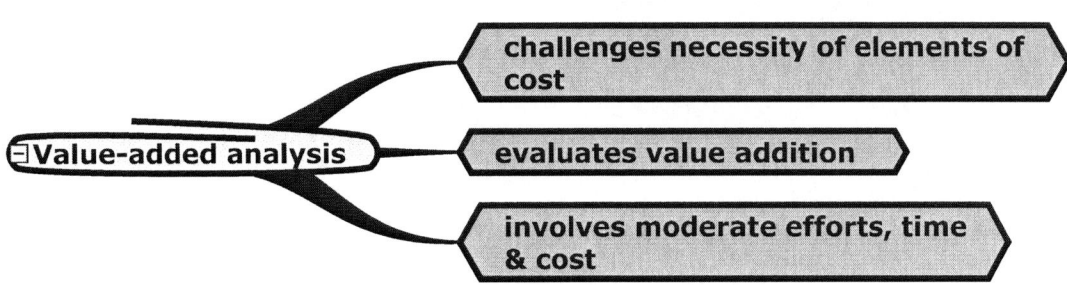

3. Gaps and disconnects

This technique was evolved by professionals to tackle the process failures arising out of 'failure of proper and timely communication' among the concerned processes, divisions of the organisation and within the process itself. The basic principle of this technique is recognising and satisfying customer needs – both external and internal - and maintaining the processes of management alignment through a properly laid down hierarchy and responsibility.

The term 'failure in communication' has been used to express a broader meaning i.e. covering 'missing connections and coordination between processes, within the process itself and process management'. It focuses on the repeated failure to share / transfer accurate information or knowledge to the user or cross-functional departments or to the persons responsible for performing activities in the chain of processes.

Example

The process of inventory management does not create information immediately when inventory items reach reorder level. This information is extracted by the staff in inventory accounting and sent to the procurement department. If the procurement department fails to act promptly on this information, this will lead to obstructions in production flow or stoppages. There is no mechanism to ensure that the procurement department is taking action on inventory requests received from the inventory accounting dept. Thus, there is a lack of proper and timely communication, coordination and action.

The implementation of this process redesign technique is therefore aimed at correcting such gaps and disconnects. These gaps and disconnects are often the result of handing over incorrect or incomplete information and lack of timely coordination and feedback among managers.

Naturally, the failure of processes to perform effectively results in the failure of management processes, raising doubts about the success of management alignment and generally leading to a very dissatisfactory environment in the organisation.

The implementation of this process redesign pattern requires, as a first step, detailed evaluation of the present organisational chart, existing processes, their linkage with organisational goals, performance measures of these processes and process management.

The technique emphasises the identification of points of intersection or crossing of a process with another process or functional area. Hence, the present process and system flow charts are converted into an improved system flow chart and process flow charts. These improved charts are used to highlight the importance of previously neglected inter-functional 'connections' and specify improvements in these areas.

The improvements, once implemented, result in a proper linkage between related processes for smoother movement of material, information and coordination among the managers concerned. They also increase awareness of the consequences of process failure in the people responsible for proper performance of the given processes.

This process redesign pattern involves modification of existing processes to incorporate desirable process connections and remove undesirable disconnects. It involves moderate efforts, time and cost. It certainly improves process efficiencies. The extent of improvement can be modest to major, depending mainly on the extent of gaps and disconnects in the existing processes.

SUMMARY

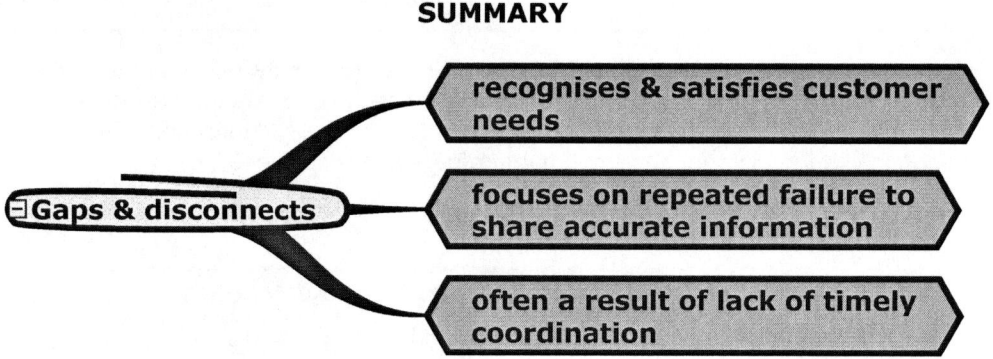

4. Simplification

'**Simplification**' is another well-known process redesign pattern. In this pattern, the approach is non-radical. It attempts to improve the processes or sub-processes by identifying and eliminating 'redundancies' and 'duplications'.

The implementation of this pattern involves in-depth analysis of existing processes and sub-processes. The processes are validated by evaluating the need to perform given processes. It sternly questions the existence of a process by asking 'If not what happens?' and 'If yes is it the best?'

It is the general experience of process evaluators that functional managers always try to justify the need for the processes performed in their departments, even though the results of the given processes are available from other processes. The management representative and evaluators have to take a very realistic view to resolve conflicts of this nature. The decision is obvious - one of the processes has to be eliminated as it is duplicate or redundant.

The simplification pattern usually does not have the objective of evaluating each and every process in the organisation. In this approach, the focus mostly shifts to functional processes. Hence, it has an element of risk due to neglecting the integration and alignment of organisational processes and functional processes towards organisational goals. This, however, needs be taken care of by ensuring the 'effectiveness of redesigns' from the organisational perspective.

Example

Multi-cord Co produces musical instruments of different kinds. The quantity of each batch is decided based on the requirements for the following month. The cost data for products are generated through three accounting channels: one for material consumed from stores, the second for material procured and directly used in the production and the third for sub-contract services utilised. The transactions contain the description of the product and cost allocations to different production batches. There are often errors in cost allocations. The process fails to allocate cost in proportion to the order quantity of different production batches. The allocation process is repeated in order to rectify the errors. As a result, a lot of time and efforts are wasted in allocation and rectification of cost allocations.

Management wants to improve the cost allocation process by ensuring that costs are allocated correctly the first time round and thereby eliminating any need to repeat the process.

The company collects and analyses the details of incorrect entries. The analysis reveals that errors in cost data have been caused due to two reasons: lack of information in the transactions regarding product batch and batch quantity and secondly, human errors in cost allocation.

Management determines ways of improving the quality of entries to enable the proper calculation of cost. The first step is to ensure that every cost accounting transaction includes mandatory information such as product number, batch number and batch quantity. This mandatory information entered is cross-checked and validated by a computer program. The computer program uses information from the relevant bill of material / process sheet and allocates the cost to batches of relevant products.

The process has been simplified by introducing 'mandatory information' and using computer programs to verify this information. The process has also been improved through the removal of duplication of work

It is now an easier task to compile reliable cost data and takes a shorter period of time.

This technique is less radical in its approach towards process redesign. The validation process, being based on the rationale of 'removal of redundancies and duplication' is not subject to severe resistance by employees. It takes a short to moderate time period (say 6 to 8 months) and low to moderate cost depending on the determined scope of 'simplification'. It improves the processes moderately.

SUMMARY

- **Simplification**
  - improves processes eliminating redundancies & duplications
  - processes are validated by evaluating need of processes

Test Yourself 2

Bright Steels Ltd is one of the largest suppliers of iron in the UK. The company is divided into three profit centres, also called product units: Bright Pipes, Bright Sheets and Bright Bars. Documents such as supply orders, delivery advice and invoices are prepared by the Product Units.

The orders received by the company are adequate to meet the sales targets. The production for the last 6 months is 90% of the targeted production, without any quality or management control issues.

The product units are facing problems in meeting their sales targets. The number of complaints of delayed deliveries is increasing every fortnight. Sales have also been falling short of targets for the last six months. Management is worried about the profit targets. There is already a shortfall in profits for the first half of the year. The processes in these functions are reasonable. The exceptions are customer order processing and management control areas.

Management is planning to implement business process re-engineering to improve the efficiency of certain departments.

Required:

Determine weaknesses in the processes and explain to the management of Bright Steels Ltd why business process re-engineering is not suitable under the given circumstances.

---

3. Establish possible redesign options for improving the current processes of an organisation.[2]
Assess the feasibility of possible redesign options.[3]
[Learning Outcomes c and d]

We have studied so far the purpose of the organisational processes, the need for continuous monitoring of the effectiveness of the processes, business process redesign as a tool for achieving improvements and different process redesign patterns.

In this section, we will examine the possible options available to organisations implementing process redesigns.

3.1. Redesign options

There are various options available to organisations, when it comes to redesigning organisational processes. The choice of options is greatly influenced by the objectives of redesign, the resources available and the degree of management commitment, to name a few. The expected results of redesign will have to be determined by management and consultants, taking into account the circumstances leading to the redesign decision.

Some of these options are discussed below.

1. Replace existing processes by designing completely new processes

This option is in line with business process re-engineering (BPR). This is a 'start to finish' approach. It is exercised under very special circumstances e.g. to provide a major boost to overall efficiencies, to achieve major cost cutting or to overcome a major threat by competitors using innovative business processes.

Example

The recession which began in the late 1990s, led by US slowdown, impacted most economies. During this period, organisations were struggling for survival. Under the reduced business volumes, cost cutting was their top priority. Many major organisations therefore opted for business process re-engineering as the solution to achieve an increase in process efficiencies, downsizing and thereby cost reduction.

Example

The growth of the internet and the willingness of customers to acquire browsers and interact online, led a number of companies to create radically new business models by replacing the existing ones. The power of the internet also led to the concept of 'internet banking' and banks were forced to add entirely new process packs by the early 1990s.

2. Major revamp of vital processes

This option is a moderately modified version of BPR. It does not adopt a 'start to finish' approach. However, it involves the major exercise of evaluating existing processes. The objective here is to identify the weaknesses in the existing processes and change them suitably to increase their efficiencies. Compared to BPR, it demands less time and cost and may result in moderate improvement in processes.

Example

If the organisation decides to redesign the processes to integrate materials management, inventory management, supplier payment and customer collection, it will involve substantial effort, time and cost. However, it still does not cover the remaining operational areas such as production, sales and other administrative functions.

3. Change existing process to some extent

This option may require identifying the processes affected by the changes in circumstances and effecting suitable changes. This exercise applies generally to selected operations and not to large areas of operation. This is comparatively a small exercise involving little time, low workload, fewer resources and lower costs.

Example

The UK government has changed the rate of Value Added Tax (VAT) from 15% to 17.5%. This change will require a comparatively small process redesign exercise in limited business processes. The processes affected by the VAT change are order processing in sales, the billing process and delivery documentation in warehouses.

4. Switchover to Enterprise Resource Planning (ERP) like solutions

This option offers the scope to choose off-the-shelf software such as ERP or CRM (Customer Relationship Management) and use the process as it is or with little changes. Some are tailored for specific industries and some are generic.

Companies looking for a packaged supply chain application may opt for SAP, for example, which provides maps that show how the company organises its modules to support supply chain systems in different industries. SAP is an integrated ERP software that deals with the business software requirements of organisations across various industries and sectors.

All of the leading packaged software vendors offer modules to support multi-industry operations. Similarly, some are designed to actually automate processes and others are designed to monitor processes and report to managers.

These packages have gone through substantial improvements over recent years. As a result, this option can save substantial work volume, time and can give reasonably good results at reasonably low cost.

Recently developed organisational process tools such as ERP systems, supply chain management and customer relationship management systems have embedded ideologies of cross-functional process integration and elimination of duplication to enhance the effectiveness of processes. There is an increasing trend among small and medium organisations to adopt these tools to meet their selective process redesign needs

Example

Mycar Auto Comp Plc, a medium-sized organisation, has not been meeting the delivery schedules for components which it has committed to its customers. The inventory of finished components has also been increasing over the last two years. The sales are very erratic. Profitability is declining and cash flows are irregular.

The management of Mycar conducted an initial assessment and has found that:

- adequate information on pending customer orders (order backlog) is not available
- there is a lack of coordination between the sales and production functions
- the production plan is unable to follow proper delivery commitments
- material procurement is based on the judgement of the purchase head
- components not due for delivery are manufactured, resulting in the build up of inventory

Management considered the following approaches to this situation:

- replacing the current processes with completely new processes (i.e. business process re-engineering)
- revamping vital processes
- changing the existing processes to some extent
- using off-the-shelf ERP solutions

After considering the various impacts of each of the options, the decision was taken to redesign operational processes and to implement an off-the-shelf ERP solution. The ERP product comprised all standard processes for:

- processing customer orders
- preparing a delivery plan
- generating information on the pending deliveries
- preparing a production plan
- calculating the material requirement for a given production plan
- raising purchase orders
- updating inventory information (raw materials and finished components)
- raising invoices of components delivered
- reporting on payments receivable from customer with due dates
- reporting on payments due to suppliers etc.

The process redesign carried out through implementing the ERP solution in core operational processes solved Mycar's problems to a great extent.

5. Outsourcing

This option involves companies using the services of business process outsourcing vendors to conduct part or full routine processes involving little decision-making. Processes which are frequently outsourced include accounting data entry and various database operations such as sales activities and collection of customer feedback.

Companies have been experimenting with outsourcing for the last decade. Depending on the requirement, a company may hire a vendor to manage a single application, or more. As a broad trend, companies have been more willing to outsource processes. There has been a move on the part of larger, more sophisticated outsourcers such as IBM, EDS and Unisys to offer to manage major business processes.

There is an increasing need to reduce operational cost. As a result, businesses in the US and Europe are offloading (outsourcing) standard business processes to service vendors in Asian countries. The business processes outsourced include attending to customer enquiries and booking customer orders. The cost of one assistant in the US is $18,000 per annum, whereas an assistant with similar skills in an Asian country costs $5,500 per annum. Organisations in the US and the UK have been substantially reducing their costs through outsourcing for about a decade.

As explained in the Allfin Bank case in Learning Outcome (b), outsourcing of business processes has been resorted to by organisations from Europe and the UK. Through selected business process redesign to suit the outsourcing option, these organisations have achieved cost reduction without compromising on the quality of their services to customers. However, it is unadvisable to outsource core competencies.

This option involves a partial redesign of relevant processes. It can prove to be highly beneficial due to creating large cost reductions and needing comparatively fewer resources to make the changes.

In short, there cannot be one ideal solution for improving processes for all organisations every time. Different types of problems require different solutions. In making a choice amongst different redesign options, consideration must be given to the type and size of organisation, its financial capabilities and the environment in which it operates etc.

SUMMARY

Redesign options

- **replace existing processes by designing new processes**
  - to provide major boost to overall efficiencies
  - to achieve major cost cutting
  - use of innovative business processes
- **major revamp of vital processes to a large extent**
  - identifies weaknesses & changes processes to increase efficiencies
  - demands less time & cost
- **change existing process to some extent**
  - applied to selected operations
  - involves little time, low workload
- **switchover to ERP like solutions**
  - scope to choose off-the-shelf software
- **outsourcing**
  - companies choose outsourcing to conduct part or full routine processes

In the last section, we have seen the effective use of business process redesign as a tool to achieve improvements and the different redesign options available to organisations.

In this section, we discuss the 'feasibility' aspects of redesign options.

3.2 Feasibility

Feasibility can be described as 'the evaluation of the possibility of achieving the objectives (success) of a given project within the estimated time and costs and with the means or resources allocated to it by the organisation.'

The following redesign options were discussed in detail in the previous section:

- replace existing processes by designing completely new processes
- major revamp of vital processes to a large extent
- change existing process to some extent
- switchover to ERP-like solutions
- outsourcing

The considerations dominating 'feasibility' in relation to these options are as follows:

1. **Major considerations**

   a) objectives of redesigning process in light of reasons for process redesign decision
   b) estimated time required for implementation
   c) employee attitude towards redesign project
   d) availability of personnel with desired skills
   e) training needs of existing employees
   f) extent of workflow distortions
   g) availability of technical services for hardware and software identified with redesign
   h) statement of cost benefit analysis

2. **Secondary considerations**

   a) investments required for hardware and software
   b) estimated cost of technical services for hardware and software
   c) estimated cost of implementation

Example

Secure Net Worth Insurance Co is a leading insurance company in the UK. To meet its objective of continuous growth, three years ago it acquired and merged two insurance companies which were doing good business in an area of the UK. The company's growth over the last two years has not been as expected. The company has faced severe competition from emerging insurance companies with new products and efficient services.

The company decides to reorganise its business to overcome the effects of competition. Two teams supported by consultants are created to look into the matter. One team is to focus on business strategy and the second on business process improvements.

The business process improvement team discovers the following information:

➤ The two newly merged companies have different products.
➤ Even common products have different processes, leading to customer confusion.
➤ The information technology used in these two companies is quite old and requires operators with special skills.
➤ Interruptions caused by the failure of old systems are very high. Maintenance cost has also been increasing for each of the last two years.
➤ There is a need for business process redesigning to ensure uniformity across the organisation

The team has taken into account the following feasibility considerations in arriving at recommendations for process redesigning:

Sr no	Feasibility considerations	Evaluation of feasibility considerations	Feasibility risk assessment
1	Organisation's capabilities	The organisation should have / arrange for managerial talent in required numbers	Weakness in management leadership, functional leadership and management processes as a whole may result in failure
2	Objectives of redesigning process in light of reasons for process redesign decision	The objectives of the process improvement are fully justified. The management has to maintain its commitment and support until objectives are fulfilled.	Withdrawal of management commitment and support will lead to failure
3	Estimated time required for implementation	The process improvement will have to be undertaken applying business process re-engineering (BPR) techniques. It may take 10 to 12 months.	Pressure for early completion may result in process quality being compromised. This may defeat the purpose of the exercise.
4	Employee attitude towards redesign project	Management should ensure employee involvement and support. This is vital for the successful implementation of BPR.	Lack of employee support may result in problems and shortcomings in implementation. May lead to failure.

Example

5	Manpower required	Additional manpower required only during BPR implementation have been considered on an assignment basis. They are available at 1.25 times the normal employee cost.	A shortage in the desired manpower may delay the implementation. The longer the duration of the shortage, the higher the risk of failures.
6	Availability of manpower with desired skills	Additional employees will be needed at different locations. Such manpower is available at reasonable cost.	A shortage in the desired manpower may result in underutilisation of the improved facility at some locations. This may defeat the purpose of the exercise.
7	Training needs of existing employees	The employees needing training should attend the training programmes arranged by software vendors.	Employee resistance to undergo training may result in ineffectiveness of improved facility.
8	Extent of workflow distortions	BPR considered here includes processes and technology applications. Work flow distortions are inevitable.	Management and employees will have to cooperate. If they do not, this may result in withdrawal of the exercise mid-way and failure.
9	Availability of technical services for hardware and software identified with redesign	The technology is contemporary and widely used. The technical services are available at competitive rates at all locations.	Unavailability of services may lead to the selection of relatively unsuitable technology and process quality being compromised.
10	Estimated cost of technical services for hardware and software	These are estimated based on our assessment. No major variation is expected.	Any abnormal increase over estimated expenses may result in withdrawal of the exercise mid-way and failure.
11	Estimated investment and cost of implementation	These are estimated based on our information. No major variation is expected.	Any abnormal increase over estimates may result in withdrawal of the exercise mid-way and failure.

If any of the major considerations is unlikely to meet the measure set for it, we can safely say that the feasibility of the project is in serious doubt. The extent of failure will be determined by the adverse effect that the consideration can have on the success of the project. The non-fulfilment of expectations by major considerations may lead to the total failure of the project.

The secondary considerations are also important as far as feasibility is concerned. However, an increase in these costs slightly above the tolerable limit may not affect the feasibility so seriously as to amount to failure, as long as the objectives of the project are fulfilled.

The redesign option has a bearing on every element mentioned above. The intensity of the impact on these aspects varies according to the redesign option chosen. At the same time, successful implementation of the selected option has to meet the expectations of the organisation in terms of meeting the objectives determined.

The secondary considerations are related to investment and the cost of implementation. If the organisation is convinced of the benefits and is able to raise additional funds if required, the project will achieve its objective of improved processes but at additional cost. Therefore, when the risk of secondary considerations is confirmed to be the most likely situation, the project as a whole may become unfeasible.

Whereas, if the assessment of the possibility of achieving the objectives of the redesign project gives a negative result on any of the secondary considerations it is supposed to produce, this will mean that the redesign option chosen is not feasible on that count, but the overall feasibility may still be positive.

3.3 Depending on the evaluation of the expected results on various considerations of feasibilities, they are called organisational feasibility, technical feasibility, financial feasibility, social feasibility and environmental feasibility. We will now discuss in detail, the important feasibility tests the process redesign project has to pass through.

1. Organisational feasibility

The organisational feasibility is the organisation's ability to convert organisational objectives into reality within the given period and with the given resources. This will require the organisational strengths to be reassessed.

The strength of an organisation lies in:

- the adequacy of its managerial talent
- the availability of managers in the desired numbers in different functions
- the organisation's monitoring and control system
- management's ability to lead a team of employees and consultants
- the organisational culture

If the organisation is weak in any of these areas, and undertakes a process redesign project, there is the possibility that the organisation will fail to achieve the objective. Under such conditions, the project can be said to be organisationally unfeasible.

The objectives of the organisation will reveal the circumstances leading to the process redesign decision. Usually, organisations decide to redesign their business processes either to gain a competitive advantage or to face competition. Goals such as taking advantage of opportunities and achieving substantial growth in business volumes and profits in the next 2-3 years will require reassessment of organisational strengths and weaknesses. A positive capability assessment of the factors mentioned above will satisfy the test for 'organisational feasibility'.

Example

Smart Sales Ltd has current sales of $500 million. The company is managed by three partners. The partners have identified an opportunity for business growth and aim to double the company's sales in the next three years. They are prepared to redesign the company's business processes to meet this objective. For reasons of cost saving and economic business operations, they are hesitant to recruit senior managers.

In future, the partners plan to expand the business over multiple locations as against one location currently. The size of business operations is rapidly expanding. The managers conducting business processes also need a minimum level of expertise in order to succeed.

Until the company acquires new managers in adequate numbers, it is likely to under-perform and may remain exposed to the risk of organisational infeasibility.

2. Technical feasibility

Careful assessment is necessary to ascertain whether the hardware, software and support services (including those required for the redesign of production processes) are available at reasonable notice and at reasonable cost. The availability of technical manpower with the right expertise to operate these machines should be assessed, and, if required, training of the existing personnel should be considered. There is also a need to ensure that there will not be 'compatibility issues' and bottlenecks when the outputs of various processes form the inputs of the next process in an integrated process environment. A positive assessment of these measures will satisfy the 'technical feasibility test' of the project.

Example

A manufacturer of polythene bags is considering buying an additional production unit in order to manufacture larger polythene tubes. The tubes are converted into bags after printing a design of the customer's choice. Hence the output of the tube-producing unit is the input to the printing machine. The capacity and specifications of the printing machine are based on the existing tube size and manufacturing capacity. The size and quantity of the tubes produced by the new production unit will not match the size and quantity of tubes that the present printing machine can print. Therefore, considering the present printing facility, the proposal will not be technically feasible.

3. Financial feasibility

The project of process redesign is based on certain financial commitments and the cost benefit ratio approved by management. Although the benefits are expressed in intangible terms e.g. simplification of work, saving of time, reduction in errors and reduction in reworking; the benefits are always converted in terms of value with the help of functional heads and outside consultants. When the value of the benefits is equal to or higher than the costs involved, the business process redesign project is said to satisfy the financial feasibility test.
If investments and costs involved are beyond the capacity of the organisation to raise funds, the project will not satisfy the test of 'financial feasibility'.

Example

Temptation Foods Ltd needs $200 million to implement its business process redesign project. It has $100 million in a free reserve to support the funding for the project. The financers are unwilling to provide funds beyond the free reserves of the company. Under these circumstances, the company cannot proceed with the project. The project does not satisfy the test of financial feasibility, although the company may have a favourable cost benefit ratio.

4. Social feasibility

This feasibility assessment involves a close look at human-related issues and their impact on business process redesign project implementation and post-implementation operations. The business process redesign project requires complex personnel management.

The feasibility assessment starts with an assessment of management's commitment to the project. Additional aspects such as mentioned below are key factors for success of the project. They are-

- employee attitude towards the project
- availability of manpower with the desired skills
- capability and preparedness of existing employees to undergo requisite training
- labour union cooperation on matter of manpower reduction

Positive outcomes on these aspects will confirm the 'social feasibility' of the project.

5. Environmental feasibility

In very unusual circumstances, the redesign of the production process may result in the generation of harmful substances causing health concerns for employees and residents of the surrounding area. This is a serious matter for which the organisation has to provide a satisfactory solution acceptable to the government authority concerned, the labour union and the Member of Parliament representing the constituency.

SUMMARY

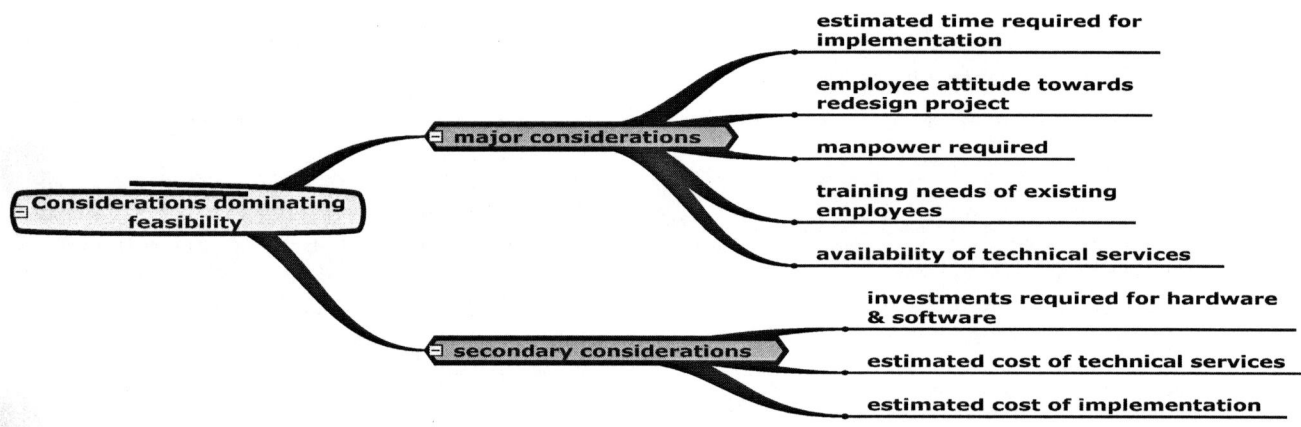

Test Yourself 3

Kidz Wears Ltd is a manufacturer of children's clothes. Although Kidz Wears Ltd is not a well-known brand, its products are popular with customers. The company sells its products through outlets at ten locations in England. The management of the company is considering expanding the business to major towns all over the UK.

Due to the heavy cost involved, the company decides that opening outlets in major towns is an unviable proposition. The company therefore considers selling the products through mixed brand outlets in ten more cities.

Required:

Explain the factors that the company will have to take into account to ascertain the feasibility of the business expansion plan.

The answer should assess the major risks the company is exposed to as a result of the plan to expand the business by selling through mixed brand outlets.

What are the important feasibility tests of a business process redesign project?

4. Assess the relationship between process redesign and strategy.[3]
[Learning Outcome e]

Until the early 1970s, business strategy formulations were mainly focused on financial measures. The most popular strategies focused on growth in revenue, sound cash flow, increase in profits and high return on investment (ROI). In these strategies, there was no specific attention given to the customer and his requirements, the quality of the products and services provided to the customer and the internal processes designed for the purpose. There was also little importance given to keeping infrastructure and employees up-to-date with the latest developments in technology.

The weakness of these kinds of strategies was first highlighted by Robert Kaplan and David Norton in the mid 1960s. They introduced the concept of the 'balanced scorecard' to reduce undue emphasis on financial measures. They redefined Key Performance Indicators (KPIs) of strategy by including other Performance Indicators relating to important functions which were earlier ignored in strategy formation.

The focus of the balanced scorecard concept was on specifying and monitoring KPIs as follows:

Functional areas	Key performance indicators
Financial	Revenue growth, cash flow and profitability
Customer	Identify specific market segment, specific groups of customers and specify goals and measures for each group
Internal business processes	Specify measures of internal business process success
Innovation and learning	Specify measures of technical infrastructure and employees with required skills and knowledge

The concept of the balanced scorecard highlighted the importance of the relationship between strategy and business processes along with the other non-traditional KPIs. It measures:

- leading v lagging indicators;
- internal v external indicators; and
- quantitative v non-quantitative indicators.

The strategy finalised by the management team can be a combination of goals such as the following:

a) Enhanced market share
b) Broadened product line
c) Increased profits
d) Reductions in delivery time
e) Improved product / service qualities

The strategy is implemented throughout the organisation. Communication of this kind helps to create a feeling of belongingness, to ensure awareness and to garner the support of middle management, functional supervisors, operating staff and workers.

The organisational strategy is divided into functional goals, activities and measures of performance, helping to clarify the Key Performance Indicators (KPIs) applicable. The share of each function forms a very small portion of the total organisational goal.

It becomes imperative that business processes and infrastructure are adequately updated to support the functional activities, enabling functions to perform effectively and to produce results that satisfy the applicable KPIs.

Example

Mr. Rousing and Mr. Clerk are friends who run a business supplying processed food to a chain of restaurants in the city. They have agreed an organisational strategy to double the business volume over the next two years by expanding into larger cities nearby.

The customer feedback collected through an agency has revealed that 35% of customers have ordered the food based on recommendations from their friends and relatives. Mr. Rousing and Mr. Clerk are reaping the benefits of customer satisfaction.

Continued on the next page

The expansion plan is based on the customer loyalty enjoyed by the company's products. However, in order for the plan to be successful, the partners will have to take into account the requirements against factors such as the following:

- organisation structure for the expanded operations
- managerial talent required at headquarters and business locations
- method of sales (direct or through franchisees)
- business process redesign
- quality control mechanism at locations
- management control mechanism
- additional investments
- marketing of new venture
- estimate of increased revenue and operating expenses
- availability of employees with desired skills

For the strategy of the business partners to be successful, it will have to be linked to the expected goals of functional areas and the results of activities. This linkage is made by taking appropriate actions to fulfil the needs highlighted by evaluating the following factors:

Factors	Likely actions
Management team	Reconsideration of the capabilities of the management team consisting of the two friends. The team will now require reasonably experienced city managers to manage the business in the larger cities. This is a restructuring of management.
Organisational processes	Current organisational processes designed for business in one city and managed by two partners will be converted into multi-city operations managed by city managers with information flowing to Head Office.
Production capacity	Expansion of the current production facility or creation of new facilities in every city to be served. If a franchisee is set up it should conform to a desired standard.
Delivery management	Several new dimensions will be added to the delivery of products. The actions required will vary depending on the location(s) of production, points of service and distances involved and the availability of a dependable transport contractor or ability to maintain own vehicles.
Quality management	It will not be an easy task to maintain the food quality in an expanded production facility or at different locations. The strong 'quality reputation' is at stake.
Control system	The new organisational structure with operations at multiple locations will require a proper monitoring and control system
Investment	All the decisions from 1 to 6 above will involve additional expenses and investments, the effects of which will have to be evaluated properly

The business processes have to support the organisational strategy and functional goals. Hence, there is a need to constantly monitor and modify or update the processes. This objective is achieved through business process management which involves continuous process monitoring and improvement.

Test Yourself 4

Jack and Jill run a business providing travel services to tourists. They operate in one state and have a reputation for providing quality service. They plan to double business profits over the next three years by expanding their business into other states. They have employed the services of professional business consultants to assess their business's potential for expansion and enhancement of profits. The consultants' report has projected high growth potential for their business in neighbouring states. The partners are delighted and decide to implement the expansion plan.

Required:

Explain to Jack and Jill the need for partners to integrate business strategy and redesign of business processes. What are the factors they need to consider in doing so?

Answers to Test Yourself

Answer to TY 1

High Music Plc's management implemented TQM practices three years ago. Customers are unhappy over the increased level of faults. The company has been facing serious problems for the last 15 months. New sales have been declining over the last three quarters, complaints about product failure have been increasing for the last year and there is substantial pressure from the increased cost of free repairs and replacements on already declining profits.

Management has been trying to improve the quality of their products to regain its favourable brand image.

The company has conducted investigations and the findings are as follows:

➢ Process management practices (monitoring of process results) have failed to alert management of the seriousness of their problems,
➢ Major reasons for product failure have been attributed to faults in product design and product quality control processes.
➢ The increased number of products with high specifications available on the market has had knock-on effects on the expectation of High Music's customers. It has enhanced customer expectations over the last two years.
➢ The sales function has been slow to process information about the heightened consumer expectations and forward it to the management team. Furthermore, the new customer expectations had not initially been taken seriously by management.
➢ Lowering the price of the product may help to retain the firm's market share.

The company has taken the following actions to solve these problems and to minimise the risk of such drawbacks in the future. It has:

➢ prioritised product redesign.
➢ decided to reinforce TQM practices paying particular attention to process management practices
➢ reduced product prices temporarily by 10% to regain market share.

Despite the implementation of TQM practices, the effectiveness of processes in sales, quality control and process management practices have failed to fulfil process objectives. Compliance with process management practices should have highlighted the seriousness of the matter much earlier. This is a case of the failure of the process management system to maintain effectiveness of processes under a changing business environment.

As a conclusion, maintaining business process effectiveness requires the continuous monitoring of results and evaluation of the effectiveness of the process. When required, changes should be made to the current process to meet changing business needs and to maintain efficiency in processes.

Answer to TY 2

The orders received by Bright Steels Ltd are sufficient to meet sales targets. The root of problem is failure to process orders on time, which has resulted in reduced sales and profits. The number of complaints about delayed deliveries increases every fortnight. The performance of the production department has been reasonable and the warehouse is adequately equipped to handle the number of deliveries within the fortnightly targets; the processes performed by these functions are satisfactory. The only exceptions are the customer order processing and management control areas.

The evaluation of business processes and analysis of its deficiencies has been carried out. The business process evaluation exercise includes a recommendation on whether Business Process Re-engineering will help to solve the problems faced by the company.

The findings are as follows:

➢ The production unit does not have to track incomplete customer orders. As a result the entry such orders has been omitted from the supply order module.
➢ There is a delay in recording complete customer orders in the supply order module
➢ The information system does not provide details of supply orders due for delivery in upcoming weeks; this information is compiled by warehouse staff based on a hard copy of supply orders received.
➢ There is no system to track missing supply order which have not been received by the warehouse.
➢ The information system does not provide information uncompleted supply orders.

The findings above reveal the weakness in customer order handling and management control practices

In this case, the implementation of Business Process Re-engineering (BPR) will not be desirable because the process improvement required in the company only relates to certain functions.

The recommendations are as follows:

➢ Incomplete customer orders should be tracked by the sales department. A suitable computer program should be installed to compliment the process.
➢ The missing information on incomplete orders should be collected by contacting customers through email or telephone.
➢ Orders which have been put on hold for longer than 3 days whilst further information is sought should be reviewed by respective senior managers.
➢ A fortnightly dispatch plan should be generated using an IT system.
➢ Orders not completed within the promised delivery date should be reviewed by senior managers in the sales function.
➢ In the case of unavoidable delays, the customers who will be effected should be informed in advance.

Thus, instead of Business Process Re-engineering, Bright Steels Ltd should opt for selective process redesign in order to improve its performance over next nine months.

Answer to TY 3

Kidz Wears Ltd is a manufacturer of childrenswear and is not a particularly well-known brand. It is not viable for the firm to open its own outlets in major towns due to the heavy cost involved, The company is considering selling its products through the mixed-brand outlets in ten more cities.

The company's management needs to consider the following major factors for its feasibility assessment-

Sr. No	Factors considered for feasibility	Evaluation of feasibility risk	Feasibility risk assessment
1	Organisational capability	The company is already operating in ten cities so managerial talent may not be a crucial risk factor for the company.	With the current business model of the company as it is, managerial talent does not appear to a major feasibility risk for the company.
2	Financial strength	The plan may require the expansion of manufacturing capacity, long term marketing arrangements, and advance payment towards rent of multi-brand outlets. The ability of the company to raise adequate funds will be vital for the plan to go ahead.	If the company is not able to raise adequate funds for the implementation of the expansion plan it will not be feasible.
3	Marketing	The firm needs an aggressive marketing strategy to achieve high sales in its multi-brand outlets. The marketing budget will have to be increased for the next 2 years. Depending on the customer response the firm may be able to revert back to its original marketing budget.	Creative marketing to draw customers to new products is required. In addition, marketing activity is going to cause an additional financial burden disproportionate unsupportable by the additional revenue. Possible failure of the marketing campaign to create sufficient demand and the withdrawal of financial support are crucial risks.
4	Manufacturing capacity and product quality	Production volume is likely to double as the new location is added. Additional investment required to create this added capacity has to be accounted for. Subcontracting should be considered as an alternative to creating additional capacity.	If additional investment is only limitedly available, subcontracting may be the best option. The risk of ensuring quality products from subcontractors may create further difficulties.
5	Prompt delivery of products	Securing reliable transportation and delivery would be helpful in achieving periodical sales targets.	This activity requires administration and is not a major feasibility risk.
6	Profitability	The return on capital at at least 10% in the first two years and 15% thereafter is considered as a reasonable level of profitability	There are huge additional costs involved in the implementation of the expansion plan. If the return on capital falls below the minimum expectation the plan will not be feasible.

The considerations of the major feasibility factors relating to the company's business expansion plan have been laid out in the table above. As in the table, if the risk assessment is positive for any of the factors, the plan will not be feasible.

Answer to TY 4

The business strategy of doubling profits has to be carefully studied. It is necessary to determine the long lasting effects this strategy will have on the methods of doing business in comparison to the present business. Jack and Jill will have to take into account the following interdependent factors and achieve the integration of related business processes to ensure the smooth working and management of a large business.
The factors considered are as follows:

1. **Management processes:** after the business expansion, the two partners will not be able to run their business alone. They will require a management team consisting of regional managers, state managers, branch managers, fleet managers and administrators. They will also need a large number of operating supervisors and staff to run the business. Naturally, human resource management will form an important part of the management function.

   The form of management will change from a partnership firm to a professionally managed business. This transition will require a hierarchy to be defined, setting out the roles, responsibilities, procedures, practices, performance objectives and measures applicable to all the functions and activities under the functions.

2. **Organisational processes:** the organisational objective is to double the profits over the next three years. The organisational processes will have a huge impact on every functional area e.g. business management and control, field operations, customer service, fleet management, human resource management, accounts and finance and general administration. The processes applicable to these functions today will not be adequate to conduct day-to-day activities and ensure the flow of information to a larger management group spread over many states.

   The 'organisational chart', with a properly defined hierarchy of managerial and functional responsibilities, has to be communicated to the managers concerned. Replicating the processes in a number of states will present a number of challenges and will demand flexible solutions without losing the supremacy of organisational processes.

3. **Control system:** as the business spreads over multiple states, a proper control system will have to be evolved. The system will now involve a large number of managers and staff. Therefore the system will have to be well defined and goals and measures properly communicated and monitored.

   It will be ideal to have online data access and data transfer features built into the new system. If this is not possible, at a minimum a periodical reporting system has to be designed and implemented to ensure flow of reliable information in time.

4. **Service quality management:** when the business was limited to one state, the business earned a reputation for service quality. Even under the changed business model, Jack and Jill will have to ensure passenger (guest) safety, baggage security and arrangement of timely pick up and drop facility, provision of refreshment, reasonable fare, etc. Management should maintain the service quality and should take regular feedback from their customers for further improvement. As the business's reputation for service quality has prompted the expansion, this reputation has to be maintained through a proper monitoring system.

5. **Investments:** investment is one of the most important functions requiring proper assessment. The financial impact will vary depending on whether the partners decide to buy or hire additional buses. Without additional buses, all the above functions are not possible. Huge investment is required during expansion and careful analysis should be made before investing. It should also be ensured that sufficient sources of funds are available to implement the plan without the risk of fund starvation.

   This involves a substantial change of processes. The organisation will have to address this by introducing and monitoring proper procedures and practices for the corporate management function, which was, until now, a very small function for the partners.

   In each of the above factors, the redesign of business processes must ensure that the process fulfils the requirement of supporting the organisational objectives. The process management function will have to monitor results to ensure the efficient performance of processes. It will have to effect suitable changes to processes to maintain their effectiveness under changing business environments.

Quick Quiz

1. What is meant by a business process?
2. How is business process management organised?
3. What is the distinct approach of BPR towards process redesign?
4. What are the disadvantages of business process re-engineering in terms of implementation?
5. What are the considerations dominating feasibility in relation to the possible redesign options?
6. What is a balanced scorecard?
7. What are the additional functional perspectives highlighted by the balanced scorecard approach?

Answers to Quick Quiz

1. All types of organisation need to put in place certain procedures and practices in order to conduct their day-to-day interactions with customers and others concerned. These procedures and practices are known as 'business processes'.

2. The management of business processes is a continuous activity of monitoring results and evaluating the effectiveness of the processes. This activity is organised and managed by the business process manager. As and when required, either at the initiative of functional heads or the business process manager, re-evaluation of the relevant processes is conducted. The desirable changes are then effected in the processes to meet the needs of the changing business environments and maintain the effectiveness of the processes.

3. BPR is a radical approach towards process redesign. It is a 'start to finish' exercise whose aim is to replace existing processes with entirely new processes i.e. it does not involve redesigning the existing processes.

4. Business process re-engineering implementation has many admirable advantages. However, it also has the following disadvantages:

    A. It is a 'start to finish approach'. This means that it aims to replace existing processes i.e. not to redesign them.
    B. Its implementation requires huge investments, costs, manpower, time and workload.
    C. It has earned a bad reputation because a project of this sort often results in a massive reduction of manpower.
    D. Companies have often downsized under the banner of re-engineering.
    E. High workload and disrupted workflows during implementation may lead to discontentment among employees.
    F. Due to the long duration of implementation, management support may also fade.
    G. It is a very high risk and high reward option.

5. There are major and secondary considerations dominating feasibility. They are as follows:

    Major considerations
    - objectives of process redesigning
    - estimated time required for implementation
    - employee attitude towards redesign project
    - manpower required
    - availability of manpower with desired skills
    - training needs of existing employees
    - extent of workflow distortions
    - availability of technical services for hardware and software
    - statement of cost benefit analysis

    Secondary considerations
    - investments required for hardware and software
    - estimated cost of technical services for hardware and software
    - estimated cost of implementation

6. The balanced scorecard is the management concept used extensively mainly in business and industry to align business activities with the organisation's strategy and to monitor organisational performance.

    The concept of 'balanced scorecard' introduced by Robert Kaplan and David Norton resulted in the reduction of undue emphasis on financial measures (return on investment). They redefined key performance indicators (KPIs) of strategy by including other performance indicators relating to important functions which were earlier ignored in strategy formation.

Improving the process of the Organisation: 313

7. Additional functional perspectives highlighted through the concept of balanced scorecard are as follows:
   - the financial perspective relates to revenue growth, cash flow and profitability
   - the customer perspective relates to identifying market segment, specifying groups of customers and the goals and measures of each group
   - the internal business process perspective measures the success of internal business processes
   - the innovation and learning perspective measures technical infrastructure and employees with the required skills and knowledge

Self Examination Questions

Question 1

PGI manufactures various parts for the automobile industry. The parts manufactured include body and engine components for motorcycles and cars. Orders are received regularly and about 2-3 weeks in advance of when the components are needed.

The company has eight main customers who assemble and paint products prior to selling them to dealers. It has been profitable for the last 10 years.

Management, in response to customer demand, has been updating itself with recent technological changes. The company has in place general accounting, inventory accounting and finished component inventory control systems. It has also implemented on-line ordering systems for customers via Electronic Data Interchange (EDI).

BAL and ASCO, two customers of PGI, have been approached by a company running a portal for various services. The portal company intends to popularise the procurement requirements of the customers of both companies and invite secret on-line bids. The customers can see the bids and place purchase orders on selected suppliers through the portal company's website. It is possible that PGI's other customers will also start to use the services of e-commerce rooms in the next 9-12 months. This may gradually bring to an end the practice of placing orders directly with manufacturers.

In this process, naturally, bidders will have no knowledge of other bids, which will affect the likelihood of PGI getting contracts / orders. PGI has a good reputation with its customers but this may not help it to get orders in this situation.

Required:

Explain the effects that the use of e-commerce rooms is likely to have on PGI's business and the business process redesign requirements under the changed business scenario.

Question 2

Summer Thunder Plc is a soft drink manufacturer. It sells its products through agencies on a commission basis. The company has designed a system in which agents are paid according to the sales achieved and payments collected from customers in a limited geographical area. The company has designed its business processes very carefully and they have been found to be adequate for the organisation.

The company has now decided to expand its business to over ten major towns and has recruited 50 employees for this purpose. Management has expressed doubts about the adequacy of the current business processes and the ability of the management control system to manage the expanded business. In order to overcome this, the management has decided to adopt business process redesigning.

Required:

Explain the circumstances leading to business process redesigning, when the company already has proven business processes in place and the possible deficiencies of the current processes in the changed circumstances. Also explain the factors management will consider in opting for selective business process redesigning.

Answers to Self Examination Questions

Answer to SEQ 1

The gradual switch to the use of e-commerce room services by PGI's customers over the next 9-12 months will have the following effects on the orders received by PGI as well as its business processes and IT infrastructure:

1. The number of orders PGI receives from its current customers is likely to decrease.
2. PGI may have to create a website to attract prospective customers so that it can find new customers to maintain its profits during the lean periods, as order flow may not be even over the period.
3. Production scheduling and material requirement planning may need additional system support in planning and monitoring production, raw material inventory and process components inventories etc.

4. If PGI decides to register with the portal, it will have to install hardware and software to support e-commerce.
5. The quotation process in particular will undergo a major change. The determination of the minimum bid price for a quotation will require careful cost analysis.
6. Technology support staff will have to be recruited and sales staff will have to be trained in the usage and monitoring of e-commerce processes.
7. Business processes will have to be re-evaluated to improve results and achieve cost savings. This is essential for PGI to be competitive in the changed scenario.
8. There is a remote possibility of PGI getting access to the prices charged by competitors. If this information can be obtained, a monitoring and tracking system to include a success ratio showing the orders won and lost and prices quoted can become a base for policy decisions.
9. PGI's IT infrastructure has to be as robust as possible with adequate backups of connectivity, servers, power supply and data storage etc.
10. The management information system should be modified to include new data building requirements for pricing and a management control mechanism.
11. The entire system involves a lot of confidential information flowing to and from the e-commerce room. Adequate protection has to be provided to ensure that information is not accessed by competitors.

The factors mentioned above show that the use of e-commerce rooms will have major effects on business processes in the areas of sales, production planning under erratic order flow, IT services, IT infrastructure and management control. There may not be major changes in production processes just because the customer orders are received through an e-commerce room.

Under these circumstances, PGI will have to find new customers to compensate for the uncertainty of orders for about a year. During this period, PGI will have to put in place effective processes within the least possible time. Hence, business process re-engineering is not a desirable approach for business process redesigning. PGI should therefore undertake selective business process redesigning. Through this process, it is possible to modify the affected processes stated above in a short time with comparatively less investment and cost.

Answer to SEQ 2

Summer Thunder's business model is changing in two ways. First of all, business expansion has been planned to ten new cities and secondly, the agencies are being replaced by the company's own employees. The company is satisfied with its current business processes and management information system. However, the company is planning to take advantage of a business opportunity which will lead to a change in its circumstances.

This has necessitated reconsideration of the following factors:
1. There will be a substantial increase in customers and product sales.
2. Management will not have reliable information on sales and up-to-date information on receivables for the new locations.
3. It will be necessary to monitor employee performance in the new locations.
4. Due to the large number of customers, staff will face difficulties in customer order processing and coordinating sales.
5. It will not be possible for management to monitor profit according to location.
6. The effectiveness of the current business processes will have to be reassessed.
7. A decision will need to be taken regarding the selection of business process redesigning methodology.

The adequacy or effectiveness of business processes, which have so far been satisfactory, may be adversely affected under changing business situations, as has happened at Summer Thunder.

Different business process redesigning methodologies are available to the company such as business process re-engineering (BPR), a major revamp of business processes, selective process redesigning and the adoption of generic software.

The company is not going to face problems in every business process but only those listed above. Therefore the company will not be compelled to choose BPR, a major revamp of business processes or the adoption of a generic software solution. Instead, this is a case in which making suitable changes in selective business processes such as order processing (online, as far as possible), location-wise accounting of sales, customer collections, customer outstandings and expenses is enough.

The redesigning of processes will be completed in a comparatively short time and at lower cost. The results of the redesigned processes will be very close to the expected ones. Hence the redesigning of selective processes and the management information system in light of the changed circumstances will resolve the problems envisaged by management.

The primary aim of Summer Thunder Plc's management information system is to ensure that complete system assistance is provided in planning, organising, monitoring and controlling operations, even under the redesigned management information system.

SECTION D: BUSINESS PROCESS CHANGE

D3

STUDY GUIDE 3: SOFTWARE SOLUTIONS

Get Through Intro

Can we live without computers? No – we cannot! Think about this text book. How was it created? Qualified people wrote the Study Guides after masses of researching (with a lot on the Internet). They then typed it into a computer. Another programme formatted the Study Guide so all Study Guides had a similar look and feel. Then an index was made by a computer programme picking up key words in each Study Guide. Then a contents page was generated. Once the whole book was completed, it was sent digitally to the printer, who then entered it into his printing machinery computer system and printed the books. The books were then picked up and sent to the warehouse where they were logged onto a system. Then they were sold, mainly through the on-line shoppinbg cart on the Get Through Guides site. Wow! Could we have done it without computers? It would have been extremely difficult, if not impossible, especially if we wanted to keep the prices low.

The purpose of this Study Guide is to show you how software solutions can help streamline your business and reduce costs. It can also help improve quality. This should help you in the future when you have to analyse how to improve a system using computers.

Learning Outcomes

a) Establish information system requirements required by business users.
b) Assess the advantages and disadvantages of using a generic software solution to fulfil those requirements.
c) Establish a process for evaluating, selecting and implementing a generic software solution.
d) Explore the relationship between generic software solutions and business process redesign.

Introduction

Case Study

A growing business around the world is Electronic Medical Record (EMR) systems for doctors. Through these systems, doctors can track appointments, maintain medical information, see drugs prescribed and much more. Without a generic system, this is an extremely paper intensive business.

"I see in the next five to 10 years you'll see [doctor] offices installing EMR the way they have electronic billing today," said Robert Ontolchik, president of Maritec Medical Systems, a Westlake, Ohio-based solution provider that implements EMR and office automation systems in physician offices in Ohio, Michigan and California. "There's tremendous potential for EMR," he said. He went on to state that generic applications can cost around $5,000 but with customisation can cost between $20,000 and $50,000.

(http://www.crn.com/healthcare)

The above case study shows you that the use of computers is diverse. It also shows that whilst standard generic systems may be acceptable, as a business becomes larger, it will need to customise to meet the needs of the business and also the clients.

In the previous sections, we have discussed the fast changing business environment and its impact on the organisational processes. We have also discussed the redesign techniques available to businesses and the suitability as well as feasibility considerations relating to these techniques.

In this section, we will study the information system, its constituents and the requirements of an information system. The information system requirements have two dimensions. The first is the magnitude of the data and deciding the outcome or results expected from the system and the second is the configuration of constituents suitable to meet the processing and storage needs of the information system. The assessment of system requirements also includes resolution of conflicts influencing the decisions regarding constituents of the information system.

We will have to keep in mind that the word information system covers the terms 'management information system' (MIS) and 'business information system'.

1. Establish information system requirements required by business users.[2]
[Learning Outcome a]

Establishing the information system requirements of business users requires an understanding of the constituents of an information system and its needs in relation to a business organisation. The following diagram outlines the constituents of an information system and their contribution to fulfilling the requirements of business users.

1.1. Assessment of hardware and software requirements

The organisation will have to make a choice about hardware and software depending on volume of data, data processing and storage needs. There are special application devices such as voice data entry, light pens and touch screens, MICR, barcode readers, digital cameras. The organisation may opt not to use voice data entry, light pens and touch screens, MICR, barcode readers, digital cameras and software relating to systems and applications as part of its information system, depending on its nature of business and process requirements.

1.2. Information system configuration

The information system requirements must be identified considering the size and nature of the business. The information system features (configurations) are also determined based on considerations such as whether processing is centralised or distributed, and whether network components are based on local area networking (LAN) or wide area networking (WAN), arrangements.

The centralised processing involves installation of mainframe computers, large in size and a kind of complicated machines. Decentralised processing involves decentralised hardware and software support to individual end users of system.

The local area networking enables selective access to system by the end users within the organisation. The access can be provided to and from the computer on adjacent table in the office and also the computer in workshop of the company. The wide area network arrangement enables the access to and from computers of the organisation in different cities and even beyond the national boundaries. Most of the banks have their computers supported with WAN arrangements.

Options such as client server networking, usage of, internet, intranet and extranet also hold importance in deciding hardware software requirements of the information system.

1. Client-server network

A client-server arrangement separates a client (user) from a server, and is almost always implemented over a computer network. A client-server network establishes interactions between two computer programs in which the client program makes a service request and the server fulfils the request. This allows the client's devices to share files, information and programs on the server. Although the client-server idea can be used by programs within a single computer, it is a more important idea in a network. In a network, the client-server model provides a convenient way to interconnect programs that are distributed across different locations. Online transactions using the client-server model are very common. For example, when you check your bank account over the internet, a client program in your computer forwards your request to a server program at the bank. That program may, in turn, forward the request to its own client program which sends a request to a database server at another bank computer to retrieve your account transactions. The transactions are returned to the bank data client which, in turn, transfers this information to the client in your personal computer. Your computer displays the information for you. Most businesses nowadays use the client-server model. The distinction between client-server network computing and centralised mainframe computing has almost disappeared as mainframes and their applications have also turned to the client-server model and become part of network computing.

SUMMARY

- Client/server network
  - interaction between user computer & server
  - user access to files & programs on server & vice-versa

2. Internet, intranet and extranet

The internet enables computers all over the world to connect to each other. This connectivity enables information and resources to be shared between people and companies. The term intranet refers to an internal network that functions like a private internet for use by an organisation. If access to an intranet is extended to people outside the organisation, this is called an extranet. In other words, an extranet is a type of private internet that isn't entirely internal but an extended intranet.

There are firms which provide virtual private network (VPN) services to organisations. These firms have developed advanced applications to provide their clients with secure, high-performance, fully managed VPNs on privately owned networks. A private internet is protected by a firewall and can be extended to the public internet so that clients can make use of the expanded reach of the internet while benefiting from the privacy and security of a private network. VPN services are available at varying speeds depending on location. Companies requiring applications such as customer relationship management (CRM), supply chain management (SCM) and enterprise resource planning (ERP) will find these speedy and secure services suitable. These services have a worldwide reach and are available at a reasonable cost.

3. Database management

The advantages and disadvantages of databases and database management systems, office automation, access to e-mail, facsimile (fax), teleconferencing and video conferencing have varying levels of importance in new age business models.

There are three main database architectures: network, hierarchical and relational. The Data Base Management systems (DBMS) that follow the relational architectural concepts are known as Relational Data Base Management system (RDBMS). RDBMS are supposed to be superior in design and performance to the other two database architectures. Therefore, most of the functional DBMS follow RDBMS.

One advantage of RDBMS is that RDBMS allow the data to be queried based on any column in any table. It is not necessary to create an index or keys in order to query data. As a result, relational data is easier to query than hierarchical data or the data provided by some other model. Secondly, relational model results are quite accurate. SQL servers have been developed for RDBMS applications.

The configuration will also be guided by considerations such as the size of the business, the geographical spread of business activities, the complexity of the business, the complexity of the information systems, resources and expenditure, intended system users, time constraints and mission requirements. Above all, the skills of the organisational leadership in establishing and maintaining the information system will determine its successful implementation.

SUMMARY

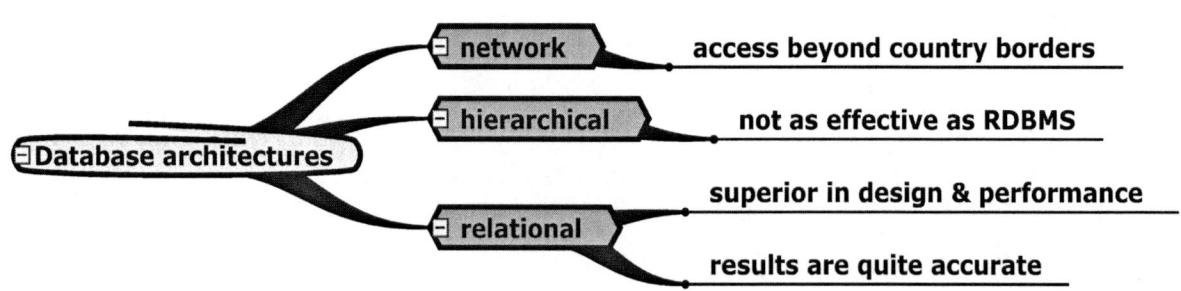

1.3. Why is the information system needed?

In the olden days, the requirement of business information was limited in nature. Traders were content to know the numbers of their cash sales at the end of the day. This information, alongside information on customers who had not paid their bills for a long time and items and quantities of inventory for replenishment in the week ahead, was considered to be adequate for running the business.

Since the industrial revolution, businesses have adopted the organisational form of large partnerships. During the last two decades, due to remarkable developments in technology and means of communication and transportation, our planet has been reduced to a small village. As a result, business organisations are also taking the shape of multinational, giant corporate houses.

The increasingly complex nature of businesses and the emergence of large business operations involving huge investments, wide geographical areas and complex human-related matters have changed the business environment substantially. Naturally, managing businesses under these complex circumstances is not an easy task for business owners and managers.

Businesses are set up to earn and, wherever possible, maximise profits. If a business is not aware of whether its objective of earning profits or profit maximisation has been achieved, the purpose of setting up the business may be unlikely. The realisation that the objective has been achieved should not come as a pleasant surprise. Likewise, finding out that the objective has not been achieved should not come as a shock. Instead, surprises or shocks should be avoided through regular monitoring of business performance.

The monitoring of business performance requires an arrangement for collecting and monitoring business performance data. This arrangement is known as an information system. It is also aptly called a business intelligence mechanism.

For this purpose, management establishes processes to generate, process and share business data on various performance parameters, on a periodic basis. The data compiled in this way enable management to evaluate business performance in comparison to pre-determined objectives. Any variation on important measures works as an alarm and management is in a position to take timely corrective actions. Generating or collecting information and monitoring and evaluating the information are the key activities of an information system.

An information system may be designed to collect information regarding actual performance against functional goals in the form of quantity produced, wastages of material, idle labour, labour efficiency, quantity sold by divisions, inventory levels, delay in receiving payments from customers, delay in paying suppliers, wastage of power, product failures, customer complaints, customer satisfaction etc.

'The customer is king'. Many businesses have adopted this approach towards customers and have introduced quality management and customer care functions into their organisational structure. Through the information system mechanism, customer care and loyalty is ensured.
A sound information system enables management to fulfil its control function and to conduct business effectively.

The example below will clarify the functional goals and information system requirements for monitoring actual performance.

Example

A large business house runs a business selling fashionable clothes. It has three clothes divisions – men, women and children. The organisation has set the objective of achieving annual sales worth $1 billion. It aims to make $440 million in sales over four months i.e. January, October, November and December 20X8. The balance sales figure is split evenly over the remaining months. The company objective is further split into divisional goals.

The division-wise monthly objectives are given in the table below:

($million)

Month	Children	Women	Men	Total
January	35	30	25	90
February	25	25	20	70
March	25	25	20	70
April	25	25	20	70
May	25	25	20	70
June	25	25	20	70
July	25	25	20	70
August	25	25	20	70
September	25	25	20	70
October	40	35	30	105
November	45	40	30	115
December	50	45	35	130
Total				1,000

If there are no processes in place to generate, process and share monthly sales data with the corporate management, management will most probably fail to monitor correctly the achievements of the divisions against the given objectives and may not be able to take the corrective measures required, if any.

Therefore, the company has to ascertain whether its sales performance is in line with the objectives and hence must have an information system to provide reliable data on actual divisional sales on daily, weekly and monthly bases.

Management evaluates and reviews the business information available through the business intelligence mechanism in order to make decisions. This process is part of the management control system.

Businesses need different kinds of information relating to business activities. This information may be available through sources within the organisation (internal) or outside the organisation (external).

Information on the results of activities within the organisation generated and processed in the normal course of business is available to the business internally. The information has to be collected and processed by a particular function in the organisation before it can be used in decision-making.

Example

Examples of information available through internal sources are as follows:

➢ The quantity of products produced during the month or year is available through the production statement generated by the production department.
➢ The quantity of products sold during the month or year is available through the sales statement generated by the sales department.

Information that is available outside the organisation (often appearing in the media) is known as external information.

Example

Examples of information available through external sources are as follows:

➢ Information on banks offering finance at reduced interest rates. This information will be of great importance to a business as it will enable the finance and accounts department to restructure the business's finance.
➢ Information on reduction of product prices by competitors. Using this information, the marketing and sales department will have to adopt a suitable strategy to counter the situation.

The examples highlight that information which has an impact on business performance is required by businesses. However, every business organisation will have to determine the kind of information it will require and who will collect, process and make use of this information. It is also necessary to lay down the procedure to be followed when using information to make decisions.

Businesses are exposed to stronger and more technologically advanced competitors. In this competitive world, accuracy and speed of decision-making has gained tremendous importance. What's more, a business management team cannot take correct and timely decisions in the absence of accurate business information at the appropriate time.

By exercising adequate management and control mechanisms, a large number of organisations have established information systems within the time and estimated cost. Nevertheless there have also been many failures on this account. Most of the failures are the result of not understanding that developing systems requires a consistent management approach and user involvement in structuring and controlling the process.

To ensure an effective information system, system managers along with the functional heads and management need to ensure that system performance reviews are integrated with planning, that the systems delivered provide value, and that the system outcomes meet internal and external customer needs.

Test Yourself 1

Reliable Ltd is a large chain of department stores in the UK. It has recently set up a large outlet in London, which sells a wide range of products including clothes, electronic equipment, cosmetics, food products, furniture and toys. The management is considering implementing an information system in the new outlet. The information system will enable management to keep track of the day-to-day transactions in order to monitor the performance of the new outlet. The management is required to take a decision regarding the constituents of the information system for the new location.

Required:

What are the considerations that the management of Reliable should take into account, in deciding the constituents of the information system?

---

2. Assess the advantages and disadvantages of using a generic software solution to fulfil those requirements.[2]

[Learning Outcome b]

Newly set-up organisations have to conduct an assessment of their information requirements as well as their information processing and storage requirements. This involves setting up the procedures and practices for conducting the business. The outcomes of processes and the role and responsibilities of the process management function must also be specified.

In the case of an existing organisation which has been operating for several years and now wants to change its processes, it will have to assess the shortcomings in the current information system in terms of quality of information and hardware and software configurations.

If an organisation is not equipped with the organisational setup to conduct the necessary assessments, it may use the services of a professional. Generally, organisations are less inclined towards conducting their own assessments resulting in the minimal involvement of the functional managers. This causes a gap in understanding of the requirements and projects are taken forward on the basis of professional opinions.

In such a situation, the option of off-the-shelf software (generic software) is resorted to. Off-the-shelf software has gone though tremendous developments. New dimensions in generic software include the capability to work with e-commerce and supply chain management involving distributed database management against proprietary database management and use of the internet for communication and conducting processes.

Most vendors of generic software such as SAP, Oracle, Baan, PEOPLESOFT and JD Edward claim that their products have been developed to cater to the needs of a variety of industries or, with slight modifications, they can suit the requirements of any industry. It is claimed that their applications allow companies to specify or modify the flow of control from one module to another and are flexible enough to accommodate the unusual business needs of any industry or production unit.

These appear to be tall claims made by these vendors. Without any information on the process mapping and evaluation carried out by the users, it is not possible to assess the extent of the changes involved in making the software suitable for any industry.

Most of the time, the business process improvement exercise, instead of analysing requirements and designing processes accordingly, takes the reverse route of adopting the readymade processes, inputs and outputs of the given application. The improvement requirements of the organisation are very smartly sidelined by the application vendors and the users' entire efforts are directed towards accommodating the packaged processes.

The software vendors manage to sell their processes without letting the user realise that he has accepted something that does not meet his needs very effectively. Having chosen the option of generic software, organisations have to understand that the packaged applications work within the specified limits. Nevertheless, these applications could help companies to rapidly integrate diverse processes.

Organisations usually find adopting generic software packages cheaper than developing processes Organisations should not attempt to design tailor-made solutions by modifying the off-the-shelf software to suit their needs as this is usually unviable. .The cost and efforts involved are prohibitive in comparison to the cost of purchase and installation.

Modification to generic software has an additional limitation. The upgraded version of the generic software is not compatible with the modified version of the same software. To make it compatible, it has to be modified to incorporate the changes made in the earlier version.

Example

The purchase module which the organisation purchased earlier was not able to evaluate and accept inputs from the material indenting departments. Hence the software has been modified it to accept these inputs. . The latest version of the same module (software) will have to include the modified process again in the same format or a modified format to suit the revised software version functioning.

The advantages and disadvantages of choosing **generic software** are summarised below:

Advantages

1. It is cheaper than developing tailor-made processes and modifying generic software processes to meet the specific needs of the particular industry.
2. The software is simpler to use and can be implemented faster.
3. Although packaged applications work within specified limits, they can still help companies to rapidly integrate diverse processes.

Disadvantages

1. Generic software is not designed for a specific industry or organisation. The business processes covered in generic software are meant for generalised use. If an industry involves processes which are very specific to that industry, adoption of generic software solution is likely to make business processes difficult and ineffective. This adoption of generic software could be risky if it used without a trial version.
2. If a company is using different systems for different functional areas, it is not economically possible to integrate the processes across multiple operational areas. The company will not obtain a complete, integrated view of its operations through different systems in use at its end. The company will require data from many systems to be pooled. Integration of such systems is prohibitively expensive for small and medium-sized companies.
3. As integration of such systems is expensive, it is not desirable for fast growing or fast changing business organisations. It may cause interruptions or bottlenecks.
4. Although there have been substantial developments in generic software, they are generally not scalable and there is a lack of focus on business intelligence. Most generic software is designed for transaction and data processing.
5. This business is handled by large business houses which do not respond promptly to service needs. This creates greater dependability on an organisation's own employees to preserve critical knowledge.
6. In spite of claims of best processes by many well known brands of generic software, they have been found to be, in reality, average processes.

SUMMARY

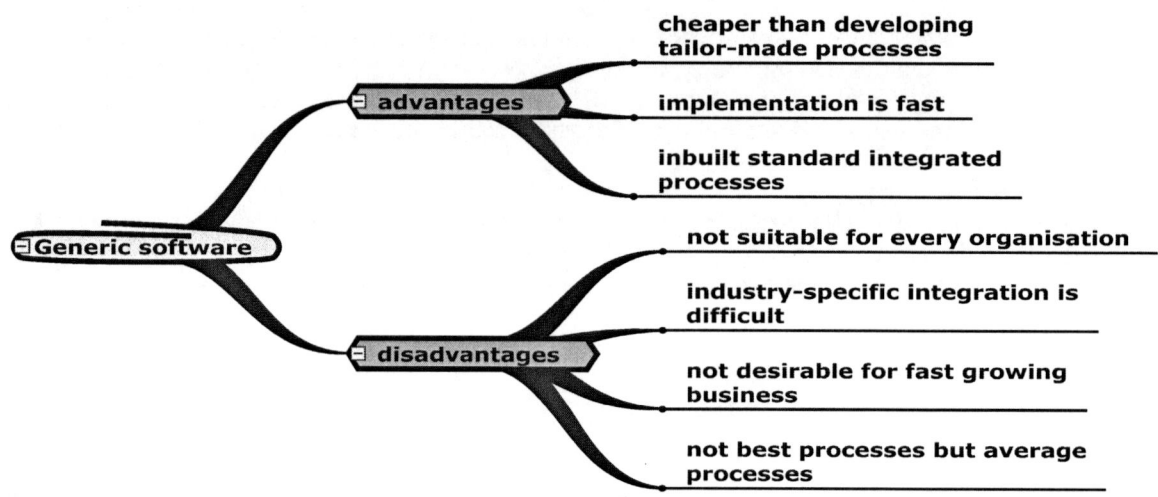

Test Yourself 2

Kula Shaker Ltd is a leading producer of milk products, located in Southport, UK. It is owned by dairy farmers. It has 3 manufacturing units in the UK which employ 1,500 people and the annual turnover of the company is $500 million. A wide range of milk products is manufactured, including milk, cheese, butter, milk powder, ice cream, cheese spread, flavoured milk and flavoured yoghurts.

Kula Shaker has experienced major growth over the last three years. It recently acquired Creamy Dairy Ltd, which manufactures cheese, cream, milk powder, cheese spread and butter.

Kula Shaker's information system operates on software which has been developed in-house, whereas Creamy Dairy Ltd uses a generic software package to meet its information needs. Kula Shaker has now decided to implement the People soft solution system as it was found to be a cost effective solution for Kula Shaker's varied business requirements.

Required:

(a) List the considerations that Kula Shaker should take into account when implementing the People soft solution system.
(b) What are the advantages and disadvantages for Kula Shaker of implementing a generic software solution system to meet its information system requirements?

3. Establish a process for evaluating, selecting and implementing a generic software solution.[2]

[Learning Outcome c]

Consider that an organisation has decided to implement a generic software solution. This may be by way of introducing a new system or improving the current system by using software technology. As seen in the previous section, generic software solutions have certain advantages and disadvantages.

Here, we will study the process or steps involved in the implementation of a generic software solution.

The project commences with management approaching professionals in search of a software solution for the organisation's business process and information needs. On studying the nature and size of the business, the volume of data and the data storage needs, the professionals advise the organisation either to implement specifically developed software or to adopt generic software.

3.1. The steps in detail are as follows:

1. Analyse requirements: this step involves three types of activities.

a) Assessment of requirements: this activity requires the developer to communicate with the users to ascertain their requirements. This is sometimes also called requirements gathering.

b) Analysis of requirements: it is ascertained whether the stated requirements are clear, complete and logical. This will require any ambiguities and contradictions to be removed and any issues resolved. Interviews with the user staff and functional managers prove to be very effective in this regard. Usually, a list of requirements is received from users. This list is used as a guide and by repeatedly raising the question as to 'what purpose is served by the user requirement, actual business processes are discovered and defined.

c) Documentation of requirements: requirements may be documented in various forms, such as natural-language documents and system flow and process specific flow charts. This process of documentation takes into account the weaknesses of the current processes and the problems faced by the organisation.

On analysing the organisation's requirements, the developing team will have to present the document to the users and conduct a meeting of users and functional managers. The aim of the meeting is to provide one or more scenarios to solve the business process or lack of information problems. It is also to communicate how the system should interact with the end user or with another system to achieve a specific business goal. This session helps to clarify matters relating to inter-functional process mismatches or contradictions.

2. Set up the organisation for implementation of the project: the implementation of the project requires decisions to be made from time to time. The decisions in this case are generally guided by the knowledge and experience of the consultants. Hence, in order to reach a consensus and for the decisions to be accepted by management, a committee consisting of management representatives, functional managers and consultants is formed to manage the implementation.

3. Map final processes: in this step, the developers conduct the massive task of mapping the processes to ensure the proper and logical flow of actions and information and defining the objectives of processes.

4. Submit final process documents (maps) to the respective functional staff and managers and invite comments.

5. Discuss with the respective managers and incorporate changes wherever necessary.

6. Determine the business process requirements and the expected objectives and obtain the approval of the committee.for these requirements and objectives.

7. Simultaneously evaluate and shortlist 2-3 likely software packages that have process features similar to those of the organisation. This evaluation is generally conducted along with the functional managers and the outcomes shared with the management representatives.

8. Assess indicative resource requirements including hardware, software, human resources and infrastructure: The exercise may be either to implement a fresh information system or a system improvement project for the organisation. To implement the project, the organisation will have to create new or improved infrastructure and replace or add new hardware and software. The number of staff and their skill-sets may also need to be reviewed to assess the adequacy of numbers and skill-sets in light of the new system.

9. Conduct gap analysis with reference to the final process maps and identify the final two software options which require the fewest modifications. Gap analysis is the comparison between an organisation's ultimate objective and the expected performance from projects both planned and under execution, and the analysis of how any identified difference (i.e. the gap) can be filled. The exercise of gap analysis is a mandatory step for any system and process analysis to determine the gaps between the requirements and the processes available in the software.

10. Prepare consolidated budget with two optional configurations of software and hardware showing comparative cost benefit ratios. The calculations should include the cost of modification, if any.

11. Submit the budget to management for approval. It is not possible to implement any project without the involvement and commitment of management.

12. On budget approval, place orders for hardware and software and make arrangements to procure the manpower and infrastructure needed, if any.

13. On receipt of hardware and software, arrange for installation.

14. Confirm installation of system and commence modifications of software processes as required.

15. Incorporate process modifications in the software.

16. Conduct tests on processes and outcomes with the help of test data.

17. Conduct debugging and confirm functionality: it is likely that some of the processes will fail to give the desired results. These processes need to be changed to ensure functionality conformance.

18. Prepare data templates and conduct data migration for the affected period: the process of the implementation of such projects takes between 8 and 10 months. By the time the implementation of new or improved processes reaches the stage of actual usage, several months may have passed. During this period, the data may be on the old system. The transfer of such data to the new system through a software program is called data migration. If the volume of data is low and therefore manageable, it may be entered afresh in the new system.

19. Handover the system to users: the stage has come when support from consultants will be available only under exceptional circumstances and the organisation shoulders the responsibility of running the system on its own.

20. Monitor system functionality for 1-2 months: the outside consultants usually monitor the system at certain intervals to avoid last moment shocks.

21. Establish post-implementation organisation for system function: the existing management team may not have adequate staff and managers to manage the new system. Care has to be taken to ensure the system is run effectively.

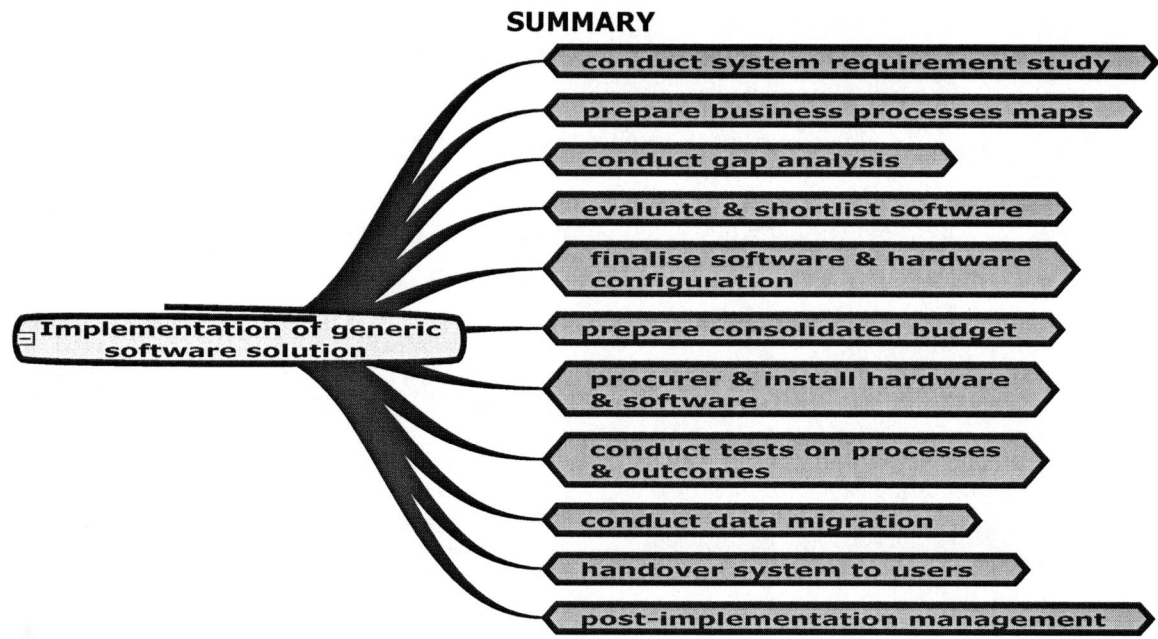

Test Yourself 3

Glasswork Plc is a medium-sized company that manufactures glassware. The company has been in operation for the last two years. Glasswork is now hoping to see a reasonable growth in its business and hence wants to redesign its business processes by introducing computerised business processes, suitable for the process industry. To do so, the company has to choose between the following two options:
- to develop its own processes suitable for the process industry
- to adopt generic software systems available in the market

Option 1 has a long duration and also involves substantially higher costs. Hence it was considered to be an undesirable option, taking into account the size of the organisation.

After examining 3 off-the-shelf generic software systems, the managers selected one, on the basis that it was comparatively cheap. The software vendor promised to incorporate a management information system (MIS) module into the system before delivery to the company. The vendor did so, taking into account the information provided by the managers on the requirements of the organisation.

On implementing the software, the managers found that the processes were incomplete and the MIS module did not meet their expectations.

Required:

Which steps did Glasswork Plc ignore while selecting its software system, which resulted in the company buying undesirable software from the software vendor?

4. Explore the relationship between generic software solutions and business process redesign.[2]

[Learning Outcome d]

If an organisation opts to carry out business process redesign, this implies that it is an ongoing business organisation which already has business processes in place.

When it comes to business process redesign, there might be compelling reasons to undertake the project. For example, business process redesign might be necessary due to technological development, severe competition, low process efficiency or realisation of the need for improved customer care. The reason may be a single reason or a combination of reasons.

Example

One of the leading insurance companies in the UK, Futurma Ltd, offers a wide range of products and services including life insurance, health insurance, retirement benefits plans and coverage plans. The company has been performing very well over recent years. However, it is now facing severe competition from new insurance companies. Customers' expectations have been increasing and the reputation of Futurma Ltd is at stake.

To counter this competition, Futurma Ltd is considering a business process redesign project with the following objectives:

- improve customer service by improving products offered
- increase operational efficiency by using latest information system technology
- minimise operating risks through proper performance monitoring
- reduce operational cost
- reduce customer waiting times in most popular branches

Thus, the implementation of the business process redesign at Futurma Ltd is the result of the severe competition faced by the company and its need to maintain operational efficiency by introducing a modern information system.

It is imperative that any organisation wanting to redesign its business processes must be convinced of the need for process redesign. To ensure that the organisation gains the most from the process redesign project, the project should not be undertaken half-heartedly.

Having decided to undertake a process redesign project, the organisation will have to conduct process analysis of the existing system and processes.

The process specifications of organisations may be available in the form of system manuals, system circulars or through conducting actual processes and user interviews. The process analyser should take note of any weaknesses or measures that have failed to fulfil their objectives and prepare the process requirement documents. The task of evaluating and analysing the requirements of the system is carried out to determine the measures or the process outcomes. It should specify the expected outcomes and measures that processes should meet. This is also termed system evaluation and analysis. These requirements, if transformed into system flow charts and process flow charts, will serve the purpose very effectively. They will form a skeleton of a proposed system and process structure. This is also known as the process requirement document.

Many generic software vendors have developed packages which are meant for standard business processes applicable to most businesses or industries. They generally include processes relating to customer order processing, purchase of raw materials, services, stores and accounting functions. Some generic software has inbuilt business intelligence information modules with varying degrees of versatility.

The organisation should evaluate the processes of at least two alternative software packages in relation to the proposed system and process flow charts. This is known as gap analysis. The gap analysis enables the organisation to ascertain the comparative strengths and weaknesses of the evaluated software and hardware configuration in fulfilling the process redesign objectives of the organisation.

The choice of software as a tool for process redesign will be dominated by the following aspects:

the level of process integration available:
- how far it will help in the intended problem-solving
- functionality of software
- user-friendliness for intended users

This means that before choosing the software, it is necessary to know:

- the tasks that the software performs
- the supporting hardware it will require
- the skills it will demand

In addition, the usual aspects that cannot be ignored are - the cost of the software, the time required for implementation, the cost of implementation, the resource requirements, the cost of the associated hardware, the operational skills required, the training facilities provided by the software vendor, the availability of after sales service and the number of modifications required.

Organisations usually opt for generic software solutions because they are cheaper and, as they are available off-the-shelf, quicker to implement in comparison to the cost and time involved in an organisation developing its own software. They also support most general business process needs, and training needs may be taken care of by the vendors. Implementing a generic software solution is a short time, low workload project and hence does not face any human-related issues.

If an organisation has processes which are very specific to a particular industry, generic software solutions will be found ineffective. Since generic software solutions are in use by a large number of customers, you are likely to adopt the system in use by your competitors and thereby lose the competitive advantage of your information system, if any. Secondly, after-sales support from vendors is also very hard to come by. A few additional factors require attention. Generic software packages have limitations of scalability, which may affect their utility in future. Although they may help organisations to rapidly integrate diverse processes, these applications work within specified limits. Just because generic software is cheaper, organisations should not attempt to design tailor-made solutions by modifying generic software. The costs involved are prohibitive and hence this idea is unviable.

To assist students' understanding of the implementation of a generic software solution, its relationship with business process redesigning and the steps involved in implementation have been shown in the diagram below.

Diagram 1: Implementation of ERP

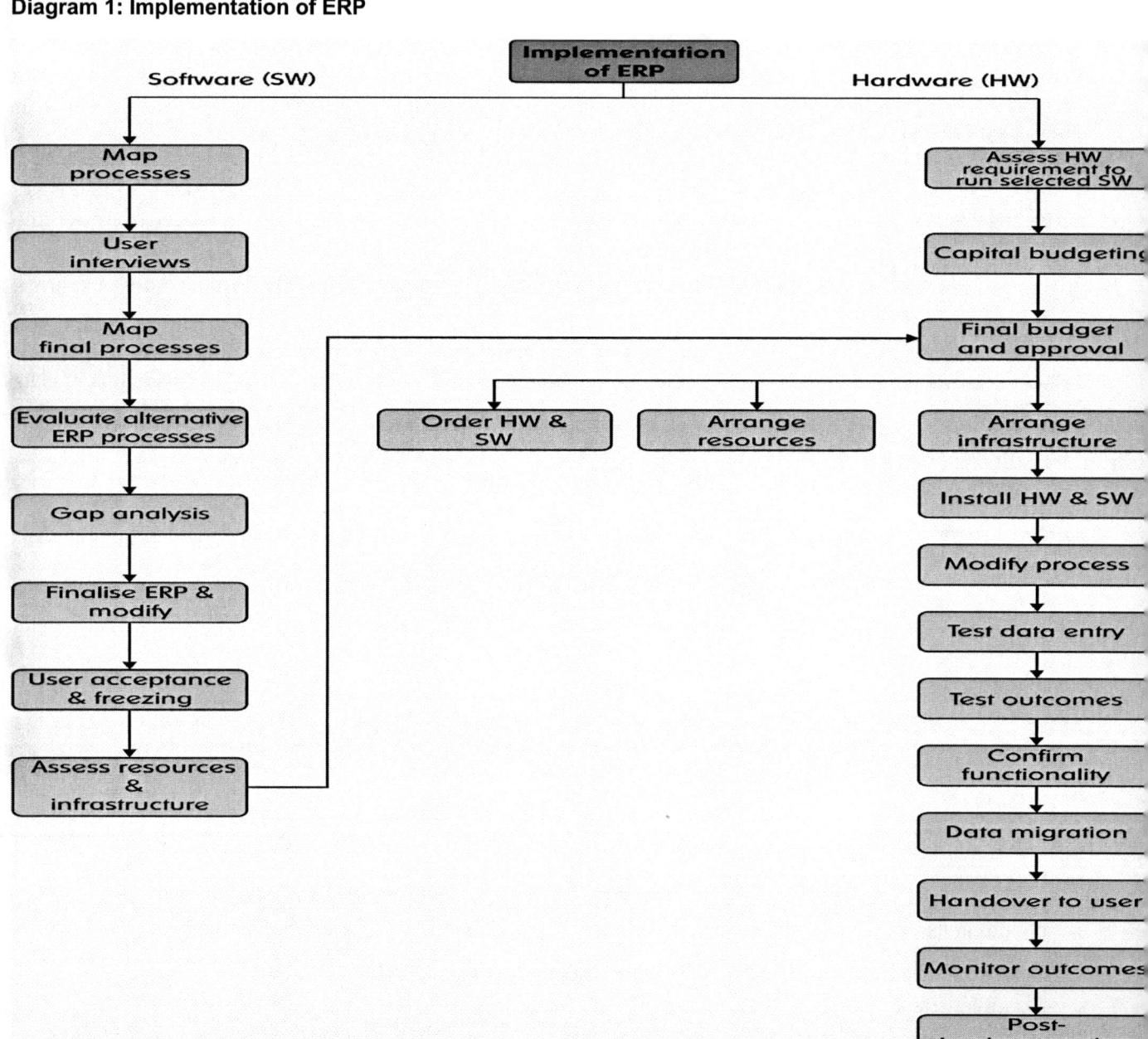

SUMMARY

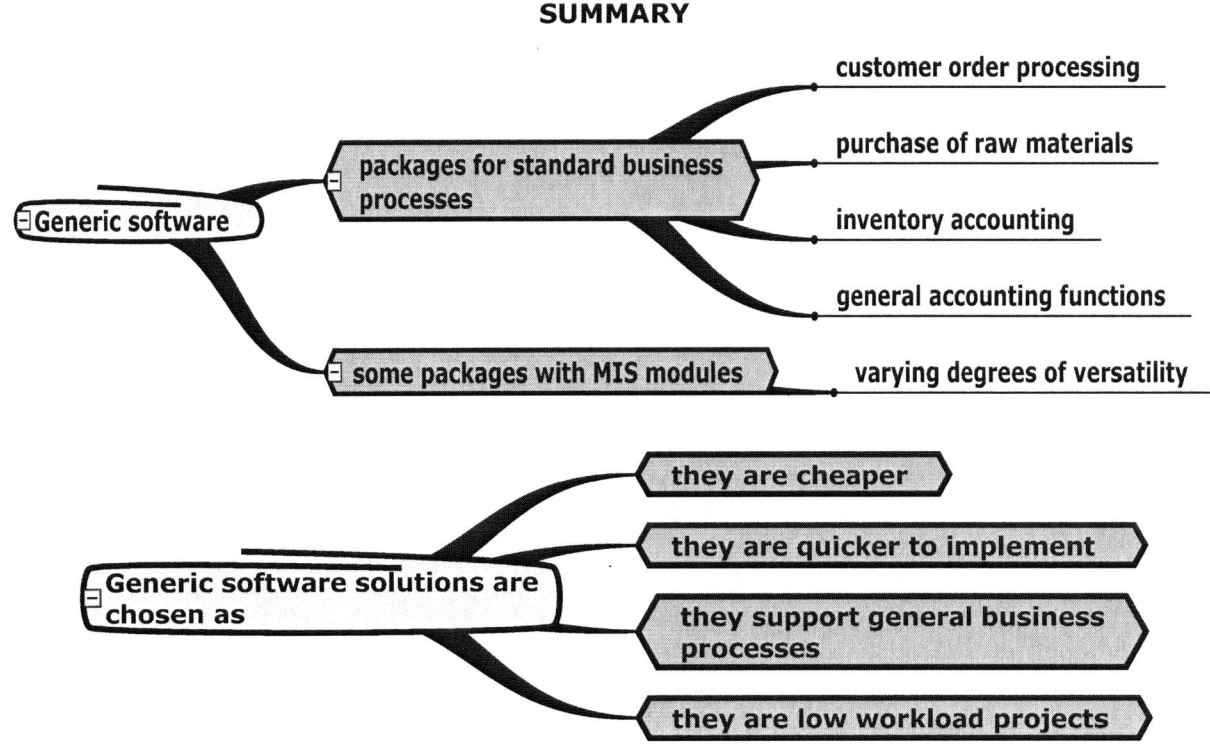

Test Yourself 4

Speed Bikes Ltd, the largest motorcycle company in the world, is trusted by 2 million customers in the UK. The company commands a substantial market share in the industry. This fact, combined with the company's technological excellence, expansive dealer network and reliable after sales service makes Speed Bikes one of the most customer-friendly companies in the world.

Speed Bikes' existing information system operates on different platforms (technologies), which were developed in-house and tailor-made to the company's method of working. The system is responsible for data processing; only some operational reports are generated by the system. The processes are loosely integrated across functional areas. Duplication and inconsistency of information are present in most applications.

The MIS reports are generated in the form of spreadsheets along with different kinds of analysis. Information, therefore, is fragmented and its authenticity is questionable. Speed Bikes lacks access to real time information on product cost, profitability analysis, dispatch and production status. The company is facing operational, management information and management control problems.

The management of Speed Bikes now wants to migrate from fragmented technology to a single, more stable and more modern information system. It has chosen to implement SAP, a well known software solution, to solve the abovementioned problems. The overwhelming presence of SAP in the automotive sector was one of the most important reasons for its selection.

Required:

(a) Establish the limitations of Speed Bikes' information system, their causes and effects.

(b) Establish the relationship between the problems and the proposed solution of SAP implementation.

Answers to Test Yourself

Answer to TY 1

Reliable Ltd is an established organisation. The company is expanding its business by opening a new outlet in London. This is therefore not the first time that the organisation has implemented an information system. The outlet in London being a large operation, the management will have to take the following aspects into account while deciding the constituents of the information system:

Reliable Ltd should consider adopting a client server system at the store to facilitate use of data by the London stores management; although the company will require a Wide Area Network (WAN) to connect the London store to the corporate office in Manchester. WAN requires large investment. The client server arrangement at the London store will enable the corporate office in Manchester to access the London store data on a single server at high speed compared to a decentralised system.

The compatibility of psrocesses, hardware and software will also be important since there has to be an arrangement allowing direct access to the data on the London store server. An arrangement requiring data processing to make the data readable and reformatting of the data to suit the corporate system would not be suitable.

1. In order to decide the server capacity and capability, an accurate estimate will need to be made of the volume of transactions in process at a given point of time, the data processing requirements and the data storage requirements for at least the next five to seven years.

2. Connectivity between the corporate office and individual stores must be ensured through employing a Virtual Private Network (VPN) firm. These firms provide clients with secure, high-performance, fully managed VPNs on privately owned networks. Private internet is secured by a firewall and is expandable to the public internet to make use of the expanded reach of the internet while maintaining privacy and security.

3. The retail store will require barcode readers, digital cameras and close circuit television and may also require touch screens.

4. Teleconferencing and videoconferencing are becoming increasingly popular means of communication and should be given due consideration while deciding the system configuration. The latest computer systems have inbuilt systems to support this equipment in conjunction with the internet.

    It is essential for an organisation to incorporate office automation facilities providing access to e-mail, facsimile (fax), scanners etc. These are comparatively cheap but valuable as they enable businesses to carry out their functions quickly and accurately. These facilities form part of an information system.

5. The budget, the cost and the investment requirements should be given due importance. Efforts should be made to manage the implementation within the budget.

6. The weaknesses of processes and hardware and software noticed at other locations, if any, should be avoided in the London stores as far as possible.

An appropriate information system is necessary, both to conduct the operations at the stores and to monitor these operations against the goals. In order to be successful in deciding the appropriate configuration for its information system, Reliable Ltd should take into account the above considerations.

Answer to TY 2

(a) The biggest challenge for the company is to introduce the new system and new business processes while the company is already going through significant changes including expansion, acquisition and the development of new brands.

Kula Shaker Ltd will have to form a Project Management Team to evaluate the People soft solution for the group. The team will have to hire professionals and together conduct a systematic study of:

➢ the organisation's business process and information needs
➢ the nature and size of the business
➢ the volume of data and the data storage needs
➢ industry-specific business process requirements
➢ the costs and investments involved in introducing industry-specific processes

The People Soft solution has developed integrated processes that can be made applicable to multiple industries with very little changes. Nevertheless, the People soft solution will have to be adapted to include processes designed specifically for the dairy industry such as contract credits and weekly billing for milkmen delivering orders on behalf of Kula Shaker.

The People Soft solution could be changed quickly and easily to incorporate these processes (which are not present in the standard ERP solution). The company will have to ensure that the modules are implemented in phases so that the users understand the processes clearly.

(b) **Advantages**

Having uniform business processes across the group will not only improve the data reliability but will also reduce the possibility of duplication. It will help in providing precise, complete and appropriate information and enable management to take more informed decisions. Other advantages are as follows:

➢ easy and quick customisation and flexibility: the new system can be adapted within very tight timeframes and can go live in just 12 weeks
➢ availability of analysis tools for more powerful business decision making
➢ automation and e-commerce will reduce costs and time spent

Disadvantages

The generic software will be modified to incorporate industry-specific processes. When a newer version of the generic software becomes available and is adopted by Kula Shaker Ltd, the generic software will again have to be modified to include industry-specific processes, which is an expensive task.

Answer to TY 3

Glasswork Plc's decision to adopt generic software systems available in the market was quite reasonable. The option of developing its own system would have a long duration and also involve substantially higher costs.
The software system was selected after examining 2-3 off-the-shelf software packages. The decision has ultimately turned out to be incorrect.

Glasswork Plc's behaviour can be likened to that of a traveller who has neither decided the destinations he wants to visit nor has assessed alternative routes to those destinations. He is depending on fellow travellers and others along the way for guidance. We cannot be certain that he will have an enjoyable journey and will not face problems as a result of being unintentionally misguided by fellow travellers or others. On the other hand, a traveller who has prepared his travel plan in advance cannot be easily misguided by anybody.

So, like the well-planned traveller, Glasswork Plc should have taken certain precautions before implementing its business process redesign project. The company was undertaking a business process design project by introducing computerised processes for the first time. However, even a company which has been in business for some time and now intends to redesign its business processes will have to establish the process deficiencies that it intends to overcome. The organisation should ascertain what it wants to achieve by changing its methods of performing the processes. The organisation should also carry out an evaluation of alternative processes and the implications of these processes.

Glasswork Plc did not carry out a system requirement study, either on its own or by employing the services of professionals. The study should have covered the present business processes, their strengths and weaknesses, the quality of the information generated, the objective of the new or modified system and alternative methods of achieving the objective.

Glasswork Plc should have used the services of a professional to produce a document specifying the revised system and business processes in detail, preferably in the form of system flow charts and business process flow charts (maps). The document should include changes in the methodology of processes and should specify information (data) requirements and information processing and storage requirements (means).

The next step is to evaluate alternative systems by comparing the processes with the required process maps to ascertain gaps between the system and process requirements of the company and the system and processes on offer. The software with the fewest process deviations should have been given priority, even if it is a little more expensive.

Whenever Glasswork Plc has failed to conduct assessments and evaluations of systems and processes, this has almost completely eliminated the involvement of the functional managers in arriving at data requirements, process maps and gaps analysis. This has led to weaknesses in understanding and communicating requirements and excessive dependence on software vendors.

Glasswork Plc appears to have been taken advantage of by the software vendor by being persuaded into buying unsuitable software.

Answer to TY 4

(a) The company is facing a number of multidimensional problems:

➢ It uses multiple software technologies.
➢ The processes are loosely integrated across functional areas.
➢ There is duplication and inconsistency of information in most applications.
➢ Software has been developed in-house for data processing and producing some management information reports.

The problems mentioned in points (1) to (4) above are clear indicators of a casual and negligent management approach towards the information system, business process redesign and improvement aspects. The company has redesigned processes or has attempted coverage of functions from time to time; most probably by opting for cheap and quick development with a very short-term view and lack of foresight. The company has saved little money and has paid a heavy price by creating a deficient information system and business processes.

➢ The majority of the management data is compiled in Excel spreadsheets.
➢ The information is spread over various Excel worksheets and is therefore fragmented.
➢ Speed Bikes lacks real time information on product cost, profitability analysis, dispatch and production status.

(b) These conditions have been created by Speed Bikes' management without realising the limitations of Excel worksheets. In the absence of data compiling modules from the data source, the company is forced to use Excel worksheets. Independent information compilations of this kind will inevitably lack reliability, consistency of report formats, will remain fragmented and, moreover, will make tracing the original worksheets very difficult.

The company is facing serious problems relating to the effectiveness of its business processes, its information system and the availability of timely and reliable management information. Its decision to redesign its processes, improve its information system and make use of the latest information technology is a welcome step, although late.

The solution to these problems lies in the process design of the SAP package. This package has gone through continual improvements. It also said to be the most flexible and versatile package and suitable for a variety of industries. It is claimed to have incorporated best practices in order to meet business needs. It has inbuilt cross-checks and validations for processes involving cross-functional interactions.

The business intelligence module of SAP is claimed to provide real time information of every kind required by business organisations for management control. It is said to be able to be configured to meet the specific needs of a particular industry.

SAP incorporates common processes such as PP with MRP (production planning with material requirement planning), QM (quality management), FI / CO (finance and controller office), SD (sales and distribution) and MM (material management). These are integrated cross-functionally.

The company can make continuous improvements and change the configuration to add more functionality to the systems. SAP has various additional modules such as Plant Maintenance, Human Resources (including Payroll) module, Supply Chain Management project and CRM. The company can choose to implement these modules in phases in accordance with its ability to absorb the technology. These modules can add value in future, as and when implemented. However, this could involve certain implementation problems.

The overwhelming presence of SAP in the automotive sector was one of the most important reasons for its selection. Customers have confirmed that SAP was able to address their needs. Therefore SAP is a much admired solution in the automotive industry.

Therefore we may be confident that SAP will be useful in solving the problems of Speed Bikes Ltd.

Quick Quiz

1. The arrangement of collecting and monitoring business performance data is known as _____ or _____ .

2. What limitations does generic software have during modification?

3. What are the advantages of choosing generic software?

4. 'The first step involved in the implementation of a generic software solution is requirement analysis.' Which types of activities are involved in requirement analysis?

5. Why do organisations opt for generic software solutions?

6. Why do organisations undertake business process redesign projects?

Answers to Quick Quiz

1. management information system, business intelligence mechanism

2. The upgraded version of the generic software and the modified version of the same software are incompatible. In order to make them compatible, the new version of the generic software has to be modified to incorporate the changes effected in the earlier version.

3. The advantages of choosing generic software are:

   A. It is cheaper than developing tailor-made processes and extensively modified generic software processes.
   B. The implementation of generic software is fast.
   C. It helps companies to integrate diverse processes rapidly.

4. Requirement analysis involves three types of activities. These are:

   A. requirement assessment: requires developer to communicate with the user to ascertain the requirements
   B. analysis of requirements: ascertaining whether the stated requirements are clear, complete and logical
   C. documentation of requirements: documenting requirements in various forms, such as natural language documents or system flow and process specific flow charts

5. Organisations often opt for generic software solutions because:

   A. they are available in a short span of time and are cheaper.
   B. the cost and time involved in developing their own software is much more than the cost of buying a generic software solution.
   C. a generic software solution can be implemented quickly
   D. a generic software solution fulfils most business process needs

6. Organisations may have compelling reasons for undertaking a business process redesign project. Organisations undertake business process redesign projects for one or more of the following reasons:

   A. technological development in the product
   B. current use of multiple technologies leading to incompatibility problems
   C. severe competition demanding efficient services
   D. low process efficiency causing low productivity
   E. realisation of need for improved customer care

Self Examination Questions

Question 1

Skyline Towers Plc is a major construction company in the UK. The company has more than 2,500 employees and undertakes large construction projects all over the country. It is required to monitor the progress of each project in terms of work completion and cost incurred in order to ascertain the profitability of the project.

The reporting process system developed by the company has been found to be inefficient and thus makes analysis a difficult task. As a result, the financial results of the projects often turn out to be shocks or surprises.

Required:

(a) Explain the importance of a proper management information system in business performance and management.

(b) State the steps the company should take to establish a proper project management and control system to avoid shocks and surprises regarding the performance of the company.

Question 2

Since 19W5, Jelly Confectionery has been a leading UK manufacturer of chocolate and sugar-based products. Its products include chocolate-coated nuts and raisins, mint flavour chewing gum, sugar-coated almonds, milk chocolates and sugar-coated fruit pulp. Jelly Confectionery markets its products through regional distributors and high street retailers. It exports several products to European and Middle Eastern countries.

Jelly Confectionery has recently acquired Choco Ltd, resulting in the spread of manufacturing to multiple and distant locations. Choco Ltd's information system is quite old and is not compatible with Jelly Confectionery's system. The management of Jelly Confectionery is facing major problems due to the lack of timely and reliable information on the inventory of raw materials and finished products.

Management has realised the urgent need for coordination in manufacturing and distribution activities. Jelly Confectionery is facing a variety of supply chain issues. There is a mismatch between the products manufactured and those in demand. This has led to huge inventories of certain products and shortages of others. Jelly Confectionery is facing a reduction in profitability due to the blockage of capital in undeserving products and loss of market share due to failure to deliver according to demand. Management has also recognised the weaknesses in the current information system as an obstacle to effective management control.

Required:

Describe how Jelly Confectionery can protect itself from the weaknesses generally associated with the use of generic software in resolving information system issues. Also explain the activities required for implementation of a business information system project using generic software (ERP system).

Question 3

STSL is a part of a large business group. The company has recently launched basic telephone services and faces competition from major established operators. It has acquired KSNL, with the intention of benefiting from KSNL's significant presence across the telecom value chain and synergies. STSL is planning to expand the range of its coverage and services. The demand for advanced communication solutions, such as seamless integration of voice, video, data and IP systems, is increasing. As a basic telephone services provider, STSL provides the backbone for major corporate leaders in addition to servicing the telecom needs of retail customers. The company has plans to add advanced communication solutions to its range of products.

STSL is using Oracle Business Suite and has put in place the required equipment and infrastructure. Although the hardware and software in use at STSL are contemporary, STSL is also facing problems due to business process deficiencies. KSNL uses old hardware and software which are not easily compatible with those used by STSL. In order to meet its objectives, STSL needs to create synergy in business processes and simplified management information system (MIS) to fall in line with the group MIS.

Required:

(a) State the vital factors that will determine the information system requirements.

(b) Explain why it is advisable for the company to opt for business process reengineering with an appropriate software solution.

Answers to Self Examination Questions

Answer to SEQ 1

(a) The company has been facing shocks and surprises regarding its profitability due to an inefficient financial reporting and processing system for projects.

Reports on the financial performance of the organisation are of the utmost importance. These reports are of critical financial importance as they enable the company to analyse the cost of each project against the value of the contract and the estimated cost of the remaining work against the unbilled contract value.

Such reports are especially important for companies undertaking construction projects due to the difficulties faced in evaluating the financial performance of projects at intermediary stages.

The objective of every business is to achieve profitable growth. This implies that this objective cannot be achieved if the business grows without a corresponding growth in profits. Likewise, a business will fail to fulfil this objective if it earns a good profit percentage but has a low turnover.

The achievement of this objective is possible by planning, organising, executing and controlling. Controlling is carried out through the management control mechanism. As a part of the long-term strategy, in addition to business volume and profit, management is required to collect and analyse information relating to business trends, raw material price trends, competitor strategies and consumer preferences etc. The financial performance of the project reflects all these elements, which are ascertained by analysing the project reports.

It appears that the inefficiency in project reports originates from weaknesses in the system for generating, processing, analysing, storing and retrieving information as and when required. This is a very important function for the effective management of the business. This function is carried out through a management information system or business intelligence mechanism. A sound business information system is needed to support the management control function and enable effective management of the business.

The company has realised the problem. It now has to conduct an analysis of the current processes involved in data collection, processing, storing and retrieval. Through analysing the reasons for the inaccuracies and inadequacies observed in the reports for the last two quarters, sufficient information can be obtained to identify the corrective actions required.

(b) The company should take the following actions:

- The complete commercial workflow of the project managers should be planned for the project managers' guidance.
- The project report forms should be revised to include valuation of incomplete work and reconciliation with the estimated costs of the remaining work.
- Billing amounts should be decided after reconciliation of the estimated costs of the remaining work.
- An additional report form should be introduced to highlight any eventuality that is likely to impact the profitability of the project by the time the project is completed. This report should be used as an early warning system.
- The report data should be entered into the system after considering any likely increase in cost during the remaining period of the project.
- The financial performance data should be standardised for entry in the system.
- Wherever necessary, new software applications should be developed to ensure speed and accuracy of computation.
- The data retrieval process should be simplified to enable easy access to project reports of previous periods.
- Excel forms used to process data should be standardised for uniformity of reporting.
- Timetables for monthly reporting should be circulated to all project sites to ensure timely reporting.

In this manner, the business management of the company will enhance its efficiency in project reporting on financial performance and minimise the swings in profitability of the company.

Answer to SEQ 2

Jelly Confectionery is facing two problems related to its information system. The first relates to Choco Ltd's old and incompatible information system which requires changes in hardware and software. The second relates to the business processes of production planning and distribution.

The implementation of the business information project should begin with a System Requirement Study to assess the information requirements of Jelly Confectionery's processing hardware and software. The document presenting this assessment is called the SRS document.

It is necessary to study the business processes currently in use and their weaknesses. This assessment should be converted into business processes maps, also referred to as an 'as is' document.

Once the system requirements and weaknesses of the current system and processes have been identified, Jelly Confectionery will be able to derive business process maps of the improved process. These should be discussed with the users and respective functional managers before the final document on process maps is prepared.

Simultaneously, the software options and hardware requirements of the respective software must be assessed to ascertain the cost impact of these options. It is also important to conduct gap analyses in order to identify the off-the-shelf product which requires the fewest possible modifications.

The company is operating from diverse locations. It is not viable to provide connectivity to the system at headquarters through a wide area network (WAN) to facilitate online data transfer. Instead, using the same software at all the locations will be a better option to ensure comparable process results.

The decisions on these matters should be taken after detailed discussions with management.

The results of studies relating to improvements in business processes, selection of suitable software and hardware, resources, investments and time required should be documented and presented to management for approval. This document, when approved by management (with or without changes), is known as the 'to be' document. The signing of the 'to be' document by management representatives, service vendors and consultants is the act of 'freezing the requirements'.

Creating an implementation team involving top management, functional managers and operating staff is the next milestone. Hardware and software should be ordered and resources and infrastructure provided to ensure timely delivery and completion of work.

The system will start to be used after the outcomes of the gap analysis and final process maps of significant processes have been presented to the implementation team. This presentation will clear any doubts in the minds of team members, giving them an understanding of the expected outcomes of various processes and gaining their acceptance.

Clearly there is a time gap between the original proposal to adopt ERP and its availability for conducting business processes. During this period, transactions are entered into the old systems. If the time elapsed is, for example, 1-2 months of the new accounting year and the number of transactions is limited, they are entered afresh in the new system. Whenever the elapsed time and volume of transactions are large, the data migration from old to new is done through application programs.

The system is put to use by conducting transactions on the new system from a predetermined cut-off date. The outcomes are closely monitored to ensure that the system is functioning correctly before replicating it at all locations.

With the implementation of the ERP solution, Jelly Confectionery can achieve the following major objectives:

- efficient processes on contemporary hardware and software
- replication of system at all locations and generation of comparable process results
- improvement in process efficiencies
- better inventory management processes
- meeting market demand effectively by delivering appropriate products
- improved delivery schedule
- improved profits

Answer to SEQ 3

(a) The solution to the problem lies in focusing on introducing best practices, improving business processes and ensuring the uniformity of the group's information system.

The company's information system requirements will be determined by the following major factors:

- the ability of the information system to meet the data processing and storage needs of the merged organisations
- the fact that the hardware and software in use at STSL are comparatively modern
- the compatibility between the business processes and constituents of the information systems of the two former entities (this is already a problematic area)

The company will have to determine its business process and management information system needs afresh. It should conduct gap analysis to ascertain the changes required. Next, the changes should be confirmed with the functional heads and the final changes incorporated into the business processes and management information system. These improved processes can be replicated at all locations of STSL and KSNL.

(b) Fortunately, STSL is using Oracle Business Suite and has put in place the required equipment and infrastructure. The capabilities of this system can be increased to meet the increased needs of the combined entity.

However, STSL is also facing business process deficiencies. For STSL, business process improvement will be a major exercise involving the addition of new business processes and the improvement of deficient business processes.

From KSNL's point of view, it should carry out the business process reengineering exercise involving the adoption of new business processes, hardware and software from scratch.

Therefore the implementation of a uniform information system will involve a major revamp of business processes and the creation of additional processes. Instead of splitting the implementation into two parts for the requirements of STSL and KSNL, the combined organisation should undertake business process reengineering to ensure uniformity in its business processes and information system.

SECTION E: INFORMATION TECHNNOLOGY

E1

STUDY GUIDE 1: PRINCIPLES OF E-BUSINESS

Get Through Intro

Wherever you live in the world, you cannot ignore the advent of computers and the age of E-business. Some gurus say that if a medium sized business does not have an E-business and an E-strategy, the business is doomed to failure. Is this true? Does it depend on your business?

Imagine you have a number of restaurants around the country. Could E-business cause your business to fail? Possibly – if your competitor restaurants adopt better strategies that can help them maximise revenues and minimise costs by using computers. For example, all food purchases for all the restaurants could be streamlined through a computer system, in order to take advantage of discounts. A just-in-time system could be developed; to ensure all food arriving is fresh. Of course, deliveries could also be made through ordering on the web. So if your competitors become E-business aware, your restaurant chain could suffer.

This Study Guide will explain the important points of E-business and show you how you could effectively implement it in your business to streamline your business and maximise revenues. Do not be one of the failures that the gurus doom to failure!

Learning Outcomes

a) Discuss the meaning and scope of e-business.
b) Advise on the reasons for the adoption of e-business and recognise barriers to its adoption.
c) Evaluate how e-business changes the relationships between organisations and their customers.
d) Discuss and evaluate the main business and marketplace models for delivering e-business.
e) Advise on the hardware and software infrastructure required to support e-business.
f) Advise on how the organisation can utilise information technology to help it deliver a selected strategy.

Introduction

Case Study

Implementing E Business - Dubarry Ltd is a company which sells clothes and equipment for sailing. They wanted to provide a catalogue on-line and also find ways of interacting more with customers and distributors. Dubarry were already operating in 18 markets and needed to streamline the way they were collecting orders.

They analysed competitor web sites and looked on the web at other sites, to get an idea of what other companies were using the internet and e-business for.

"After conducting their research, the company identified three very clear strategies – a business to business aimed at its international distributors; a business to consumer element aimed at consumers in areas where it didn't have market representation and a more general aim to promote and assist in the marketing of the brand whether to consumer or trade," according to the Enterprise Ireland site.

The company firmly believes that the intial researching stage was crucially important and they spent time making flowcharts to ensure that system would give them the results that they wanted.

(Enterprise Ireland – Case Studies: Dubarry Ltd)

The above case study should give you an idea of how E business can help you gain a competitive advantage. This Study Guide will deepen your understanding.

> 1. Discuss the meaning and scope of e-business. [2]
>   Advise on the reasons for the adoption of e-business and recognise barriers to its adoption. [3]
>
>   [Learning Outcomes a and b]

In the emerging global economy, e-commerce and e-business have become an essential component of business strategy for organisations. The relationships within organisations and between organisations and individuals have been revolutionised by integrating the information and communication technologies (ICT) in business. Besides reducing costs, the use of ICT in business has enabled:

➢ higher client participation

➢ enhanced productivity

➢ mass customisation: i.e. delivering customised content to a group of users through web pages or e-mail

With recent developments in Internet and web-based technologies, the differences between traditional markets and the global electronic marketplace have lessened gradually. Apart from providing a level playing field, e-commerce, coupled with the appropriate strategy and policy approach, enables smaller organisations to compete with their large-scale counterparts.

1.1. E-business

IBM has defined e-business as the transformation of key business processes by an organisation through the use of Internet technologies. E-business refers to the application of ICT to business processes in order to reduce costs, improve customer value and to find new markets for products and services.

The terms e-commerce and e-business are often used interchangeably. However, e-commerce involves buying and selling transactions which are conducted online, whereas e-business is a broader concept because it encompasses the integration of ICT into the business processes of companies. Moreover, e-business involves varied business dealings which can be done over the Internet, whereas e-commerce is more specialised and encompasses things such as ordering, invoicing, payments and receipts for goods or services.

Diagram 1: E-business (using ICT)

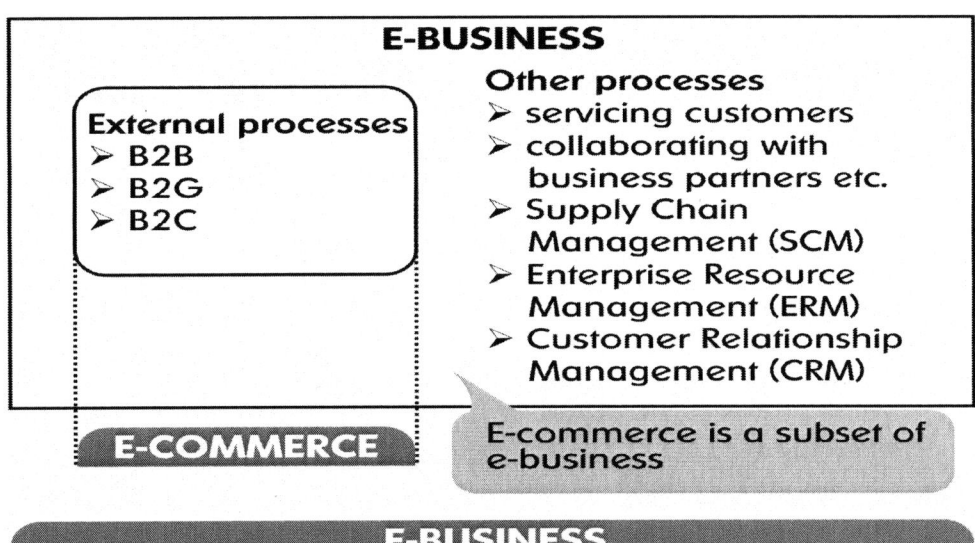

1.2 E-commerce

Definitions

E-commerce refers to any activity involving an organisation's interactions and business dealings either with clients within the organisation or between various organisations through electronic means.

In simpler terms, e-commerce refers to any kind of business transaction in which the parties interact electronically rather than through direct contact.

1.3 Features of e-commerce

1. E-commerce is usually associated with buying and selling over the Internet, or conducting any transaction involving the transfer of ownership or rights for using goods or services through a computer-mediated network.

2. E-commerce encompasses electronic ordering of goods and services which are delivered using traditional channels such as couriers, online ordering, electronic share trading and electronic fund transfers.

3. E-commerce is sometimes classified as buy-side e-commerce and sell-side e-commerce. Buy-side e-commerce refers to transactions relating to the procurement of resources by an organisation from its suppliers, whereas sell-side e-commerce refers to transactions relating to the selling of products by an organisation to its customers.

1.4 Types of e-commerce

Diagram 2: Types of e-commerce

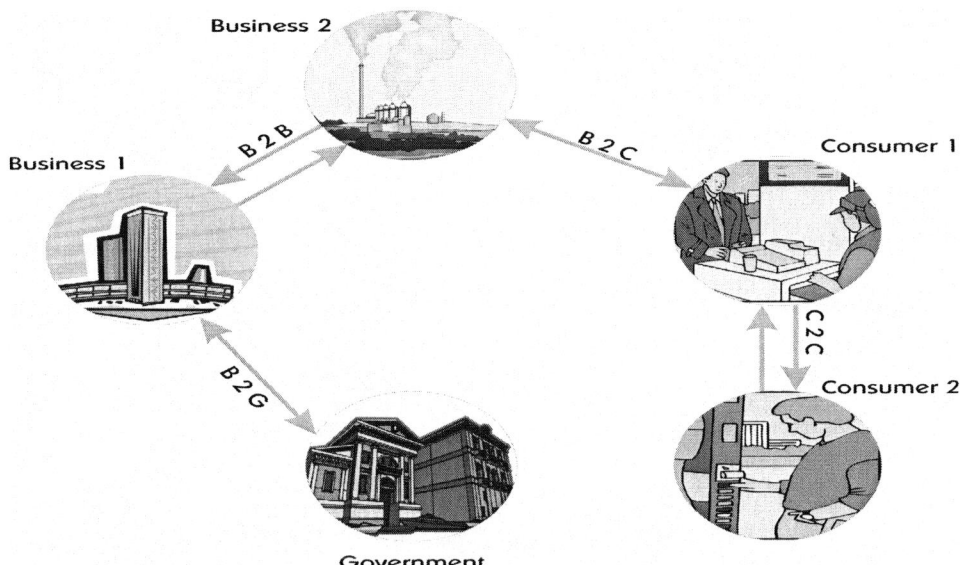

The e-commerce activity can be activated either by organisations or their customers. The main types of e-commerce are:

1. Business-to-business (B2B)

B2B e-commerce is the e-commerce that exists between companies. It deals with relationships between and amongst businesses. It forms the majority of the transactions conducted through e-commerce when compared to the B2G and the B2C segments.

Example

A commonly used example of B2B e-commerce is Dell Inc, which deals in computer hardware and software. It offers a range of products including laptops, desktops and printers and has a diversified client base which includes many multinational companies and retail clients. It receives a large majority of its orders over the Internet. The dealings between Dell and the companies represent B2B e-commerce.

Most B2B applications are in the areas of:

a) supplier management (e.g. purchase order processing)

b) inventory management (e.g. managing order-ship-bill cycles)

c) distribution management (e.g. transmission of shipping documents)

d) channel management (e.g. information dissemination on changes in operational conditions)

e) payment management (e.g. electronic payment systems or EPS)

2. Business-to-consumer (B2C)

Business-to-consumer e-commerce is the commerce that exists between companies and consumers. The more common B2C business models are the online retailing companies such as Amazon.com and E-Trade for information regarding goods.

Common applications for this type of e-commerce deal with the purchasing of products and information.

3. Business-to-government (B2G)

Business-to-government e-commerce or B2G is generally defined as the commerce between companies and the public sector. It refers to the use of the Internet for public procurement, licensing procedures, and other government-related operations. This kind of e-commerce has two features:

➤ The public sector assumes a leading role in establishing e-commerce.
➤ It is assumed that the public sector has the greatest need for making its procurement system more effective.

4. Consumer-to-consumer (C2C)

Consumer-to-consumer e-commerce or C2C is simply commerce between private individuals or consumers. This type of e-commerce is characterised by the growth of electronic marketplaces and online auctions.

Example

Many people trade on www.eBay.com and use the website as a source of secondary income. Trade occurs mainly by way of an auction. Since the trade takes place through a website, only a computer and access to the Internet is required. After the deal is finalised over the Internet, the physical exchange of the product takes place through courier or postal services. Therefore, the need for having a showroom is eliminated.

5. Mobile commerce (M-commerce)

M-commerce is the buying and selling of goods and services through wireless technology i.e., handheld devices such as cellular telephones and personal digital assistants (PDAs). Financial services and telecommunications are examples of industries using M-commerce.

6. Government-to-Government (G2G)

G2G e-commerce is the online non-commercial interaction between government organisations, departments, and authorities within a country or between the governments of different countries.

7. Government-to-business (G2B)

G2B e-commerce is the online non-commercial interaction between the government and the commercial business sector (excluding private individuals).

8. Not-for-profit to consumer (NFP2C)

This refers to the e-commerce between not-for-profit organisations and the customer. Examples include donations by individuals to the Cancer Research Institute, UK.

1.5 Convergence technology

Convergence technology refers to the use of technology that is created by combining two or more technologies. Examples include the use of audio, video and Internet technologies in mobile phones which has enabled the use of mobiles for financial services and telecommunications. Virgin and Orange have introduced convergence technologies into the enterprise world.

SUMMARY

- **E-business** — transformation of key business processes through use of ICT which enables organisation to
  - reduce cost
  - improve customer value
  - find new markets for products and services

- **E-commerce** — refers to any form of business transaction in which parties interact electronically rather than directly
  - **features**
    - is associated with buying & selling over the Internet
    - encompasses electronic ordering of goods & services which are delivered by traditional channels
    - buy-side e-commerce - transactions related to procurement
    - sell-side e-commerce - transactions related to selling product / services to customers
  - **types**
    - B2B - business to business
    - B2C - business to consumer
    - B2G - business to consumer
    - C2C - consumer to consumer
    - M-commerce - using wireless technology
    - G2G - government to government
    - G2B - government to business
    - NFP2C - not-for-profit to consumer

1.6 Scope of e-business

1. The following are some of the activities covered by e-business:

a) **Supply Chain Management (SCM):** includes logistics, warehouse management and distribution.

b) **Enterprise Resource Management (ERM):** includes human resource management, finance and administration.

c) **Customer Relationship Management (CRM):** includes channel sales management and marketing.

2. **Variants of e-business:** There is no single standard or best way of doing e-business. It can be done through different modes using the Internet. The following are some of the variants of e-business:

a) **Business models:** e-business models cover the exchange of goods and services between the supplier and the customer. The customers contribute their feedback or participate in the solutions development processes. An example of this model is the Just-In-Time (JIT) delivery model in which the customer provides feedback. E-commerce business models could also be classified on the basis of revenue models, market opportunity or value proposition. The scope for the use of revenue models is higher because there are several options for different performance units, such as pay by time.

b) **Market-based models:** these models are also known as marketplace channel structures. These structures describe the way in which the seller distributes its products to its customers. Channel structures are mainly in the form of disintermediation, reintermediation and countermediation which will be discussed later in this Study Guide.

c) **Range of industries:** e-business is particularly useful in media and communication industries since these industries don't offer a physical product, thereby avoiding logistics problems. However, for the manufacturing industries, e-business is not highly relevant because these involve only a few processes, such as contracting and billing.

d) **Use of digital products:** with the use of digital products, almost all business processes can be run through the Internet. This means that contracting, communication, billing, etc. can all be done using the click of a computer mouse. The other variants of e-business have a lower digitisation capability. This is due to modelling problems or specification issues relating to the goods or services in question. Examples include consulting and construction businesses.

e) **Customisation:** e-business models can enable mass customisation of content which could be in the form of e-mail alerts or web pages.

SUMMARY

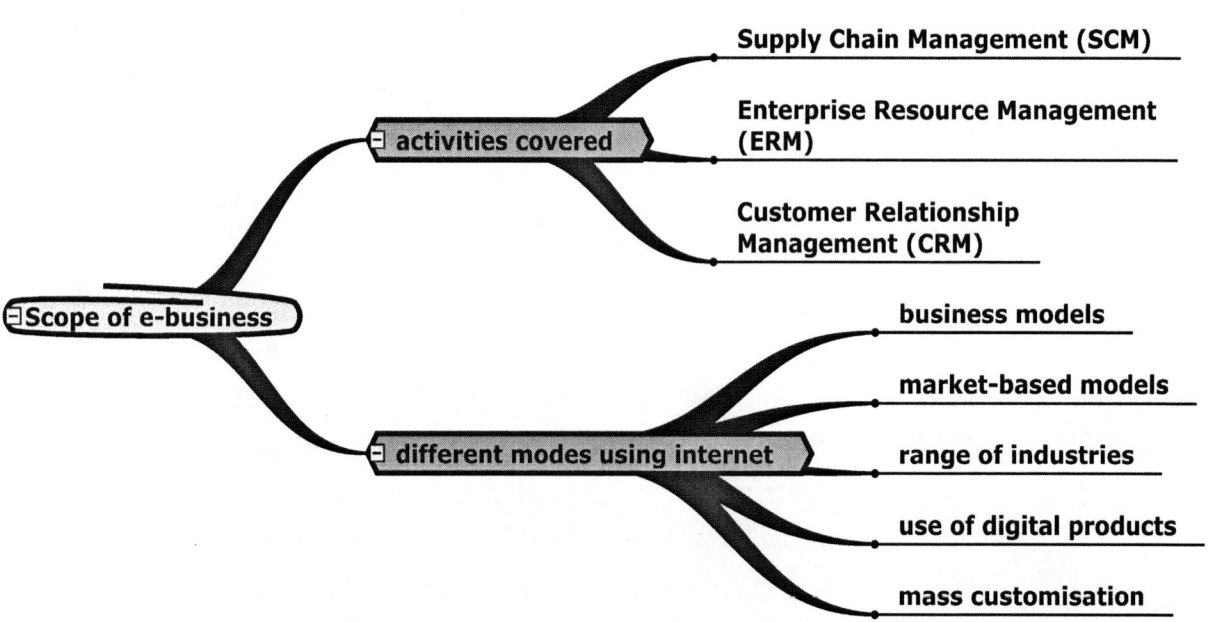

1.7 Reasons for the adoption of e-business

The adoption of e-commerce and e-business is driven by their benefits to different parts of the organisation. Managers are concerned about how the benefits of e-business will impact their earnings. Two general benefits arising out of e-business, which can affect earnings are:

1. **Higher customer reach:** potential for higher sales is achieved by expanding the reach to a large number of customers and opening up new customer segments (e.g. online retail customers). It also encourages loyalty and repeat orders from existing customers.

2. **Cost reduction:** e-business helps in reducing marketing costs, administrative costs and supply chain costs. Reduction in costs can be achieved through electronic delivery of goods or services.

   Marketing cost reductions arise from online sales and reduced printing and distribution costs. Administrative cost reductions arise from more efficient routine processes such as billing and supply chain cost reductions arise from reduced inventory requirements.

3. In addition to these reasons, **other reasons for the possible adoption of e-business are:**

a) **Operational efficiencies:** e-business enables an organisation to reap the benefits arising from replacing manual processes with automated systems. This results in a range of efficiencies like getting paid more quickly.

b) **Improved marketing and promotion:** e-business is a promotional tool that complements other forms of sales promotion. A properly designed and maintained website can be an excellent promotional tool.

c) **Convenience in conducting business:** an organisation with a well planned and designed e-business model can conduct business operations with its customers, suppliers and other associates with relative ease. In addition, customer websites have the effect of creating a retail outlet which is available 24 hours a day, 7 days a week.

d) **Meeting customer expectations:** a well planned and designed website and e-mail enable a firm to meet the expectations of its customers via on-line customer care programmes, etc

e) **Brand enhancement:** a well planned e-business strategy plays a big role in enhancing the brand value of an organisation by influencing customer perceptions about the perceived quality of the products.

f) **Improvement of security position:** e-business improves the security of the organisation's business information, records and contracts by reducing the vulnerability of paper-based records.

g) **Improvement of legal position:** an organisation can improve its legal position in case any disputes or obligations arise. This can be done by data encryption standards.

h) **Competitive advantage:** the use of e-business is essential for organisations in terms of the long-term competitive point of view, as it enables organisations to expand their business into new territories. It also helps develop cost leadership strategies by lowering the cost base and also differentiation strategies by offering increased efficiency and better service such as 24/7 operations.

SUMMARY

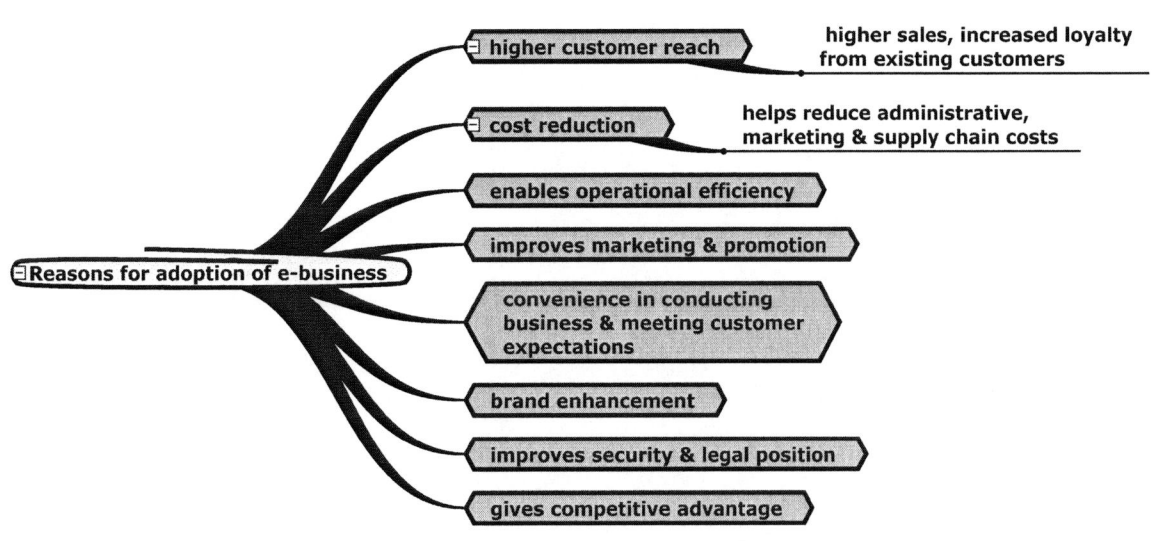

1.8 Barriers to the adoption of e-business

A successful e-business depends on a critical threshold of online users. This means that, as more people go online, the value of the whole network and the opportunities for e-business increase. However, if only a few people are online, the success of e-business is limited. Therefore, it is important to have a higher number of people online for an e-business to be successful. This is known as network effects.

1. **Infrastructure:** inadequate infrastructure is one of the major bottlenecks affecting e-business globally. Problems with Internet access and hardware and software are major hindrances to e-business. For example, in some countries, the infrastructure is so vastly undeveloped that it would take years for an average citizen to benefit from e-commerce.

2. **Higher costs:** the costs of staying connected, typically through telephone lines, are another obstacle in e-business. Government policies can adversely affect e-business to a large extent. In some countries, there is a monopoly resulting in limited choices, high fees, and historically poor service.

3. **Economic and security issues:** non-execution of credit transactions is a major barrier to e-commerce. Until credit cards become more prevalent or new methods of payment are introduced, e-commerce transactions cannot be successful. Issues of transaction security and privacy protection over the Internet are of concern to many consumers. Digital signatures and other authentication procedures can help to protect privacy and personal data.

4. **Cultural issues:** culture and sensitivity to cultural differences are crucial for successful e-business. An understanding of how the Internet can be sensitive to a country's culture is necessary for forming successful customer relations. Different languages and cultural platforms add to the complexity of doing e-business internationally. However, the attitude and culture of business and government entities could be a greater barrier to e-business.

5. **Other issues:** adverse tariffs, different regulations, languages, and higher return rates on international shipments could adversely affect e-business. Address verification may be difficult, which increases the risk of fraud in non-credit card transactions. Often it is also quite difficult to estimate the changes in the demand patterns of customers and to determine the amount of inventory in the channels of distribution.

6. **Business ethics:** businesses conducting B2B e-business globally often partner with foreign firms, which require that they open themselves up to various types of scrutiny and share sensitive information. In modern business ethics, network relationships are highly valued and trust becomes a critical factor, without which firms may be deliberately excluded from e-business opportunities.

SUMMARY

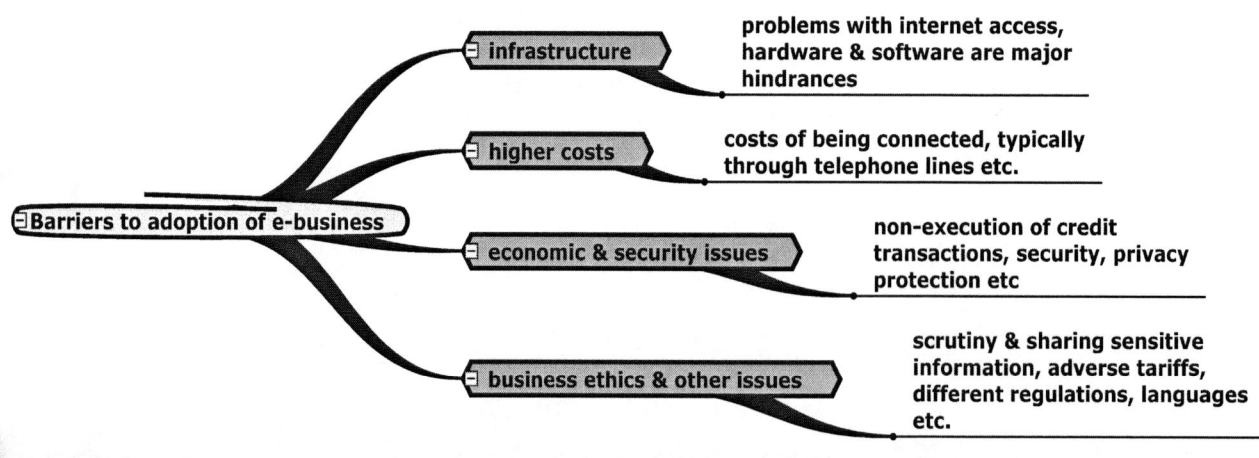

Test Yourself 1

Buildon Ltd is engaged in the business of commercial construction. The CEO of the company, Mark Douglas, is considering the adoption of e-business, mainly for document management, tender management and the purchasing requirements for ongoing projects.

A Explain how e-business can help the company to coordinate its business processes better, and state the possible advantages for Buildon Ltd of adopting e-business.

B What barriers might Buildon Ltd face in its adoption of e-business?

2. Evaluate how e-business changes the relationships between organisations and their customers.[3]

[Learning Outcome c]

As business environments become more dynamic, organisations should think in terms of resetting their customers' expectations and experiences. E-business changes the way organisations operate by enhancing their scope of giving clients a greater understanding of their business. It establishes different types of e-commerce relationships among trading partners. These relationships are mainly categorised as:

1. Transactional relationships

These relationships include the electronic execution of transactions between the buyer and seller and usually involve electronically transmitted forms. A common example of such relationships is the EDI (electronic data interchange) where many companies use established document formats for transmitting transactions. EDI facilitates business transactions, improves accuracy, eliminates paperwork and reduces costs.

2. Information-sharing relationships

In these relationships, one partner transmits information to the other partner or the partner is given access to certain information. These are the next leg of relationships after purely transactional relationships. In these relationships, the trading partners might be given access to web systems that share information about product specifications, prices, etc. An example of this can be found in the automobile industry in which some of the Original Equipment Manufacturers (OEMs) electronically transmit design and information regarding the specifications of the components to some of their suppliers. An OEM is a company that supplies equipment to other companies to resell or incorporate into another product using the reseller's brand name.

3. Collaborative relationships

Collaboration enables trading partners to gain a better understanding of the demand for products and implement more realistic programmes to satisfy that demand. These relationships are useful for the trading partners as they reduce the uncertainty in determining the future demand for raw materials, finished goods etc. An example of this is when buyers and suppliers work jointly in order to promote a new product design, or to forecast consumer demand.

The following are a few illustrative examples of how e-business changes the relationships between an organisation and its customers:

a) It provides a certain amount of extra value to their clients which in turn helps the organisation to expand its client base.

b) It transforms old economy relationships (vertical/linear relationships) to new economy relationships characterised by end-to-end relationship management solutions (integrated or extended relationships).

c) It facilitates organisational networks, in which small firms depend on their 'partner' firms for supplies and product distribution in order to address customer demands more effectively.

d) E-business offers several intangible benefits to the organisations and its customers, such as:

- more responsive marketing communication
- feedback from customers on the organisation's products
- improvement in customer support
- timely management of customers' needs

SUMMARY

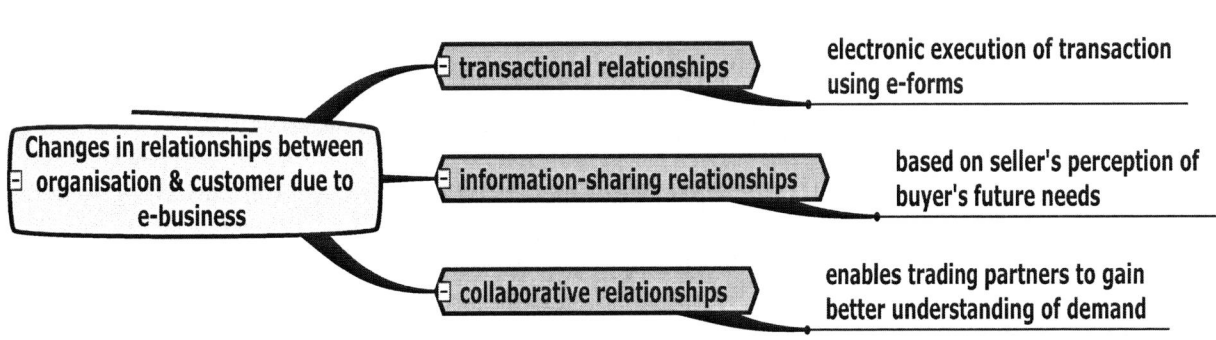

Test Yourself 2

Mall-Water, a retail supermarket chain of stores, has retail outlets in a few select cities. Mall-Water has several suppliers with whom it has regular transactions. In order to increase operational flexibility on the supply side, and to avoid excess inventories, Mall-Water grants a few of its suppliers access to a database for storing a minimum level of sale data. Suppliers are sent a forecast of material requirements to help them plan their schedule of operations. Moreover, Mall-Water electronically transfers some specific information to its suppliers. Electronic catalogues represent a newer form of information sharing.

Recent analysis of customer feedback and market research prompted the management to come up with an expansion plan. Mall-Water now plans to double the number of outlets over the next two years; at the same time, Mall-Water will not increase its number of suppliers in order to cope with the increased demand, but intends to implement new and improved e-business technology for making the expansion plan more cost effective.

Required:

A Explain how adopting e-commerce has changed the relationship between Mall-Water and its trading partners.

B Explain how a collaborative relationship can help to improve the relationship between Mall-Waters and its trading partners for the fulfilment of its strategic goals.

---

3. Discuss and evaluate the main business and marketplace models for delivering e-business.[3]

[Learning Outcome d]

An e-business model consists of costs and expected revenues. Even free web pages and e-mail services have a business model. Each website has different business models. Generally, there are five distinct business models for e-business. Although not all these models derive revenue directly, they all incur costs. In addition, many websites combine several of the five identified business models. Each of the five models has certain unique characteristics which make it different from the other models.

3.1. Business models

1. Advertising model

Advertising through websites is one of the most common features of e-commerce. A website offers free access to certain information and could possibly display advertisements on every page. When a user clicks on an advertisement, he goes to an advertiser's page. The advertiser pays the site operator for showing his advertisement every time someone clicks on the advertisement.

> **Example**
>
> www.chainreaction.co.uk is a cycle based portal which has sponsored listings of certain websites on each web page. The website sponsor pays www.chainreaction.com every time a user clicks on the sponsored website.

2. Subscription model

This model is typically used when accessing databases with news, articles, etc. In order to induce users into subscribing, certain selective web pages could be made available for free and thus act as a taster of the full service.

> **Example**
>
> www.ft.com is a website which displays financial news and articles. A user can subscribe to the website for free daily financial news through email.

3. Community model

This involves a group of users with a common interest who work together on the site. Typically, users share information and contribute to the website in any form.

> **Example**
>
> www.getthroughguides.com is a community-based model that has interactive forums in which students appearing for the ACCA exams can interact with each other and various trainers.

4. Information model

An infomediary collects, analyses and sells information about consumers and their buying behaviour to other parties who want to reach those consumers. Typically, the infomediary offers the consumers something for free, such as free hardware or free Internet access. The latter is especially useful, since it allows the infomediary to control and monitor the user's online activities. After all, the consumer connects through the infomediary's network. The information which the infomediary collects is extremely valuable for marketing.

The infomediary model is useful in combination with the community model, since it offers the ability to organisations to collect the necessary information.

Example
Market research organisations act as infomediaries. They undertake market research according to the client's requirements in return for a fee.

5. Brokerage model

Brokers or intermediaries play the role of bringing the buyers and sellers together and facilitate transactions between them. These transactions can be business-to-business (B2B), business-to-consumer (B2C), or consumer-to-consumer (C2C) transactions. A broker earns his income by charging a fee based on a certain percentage of the price of every facilitated transaction.

Example
www.eBay.com conducts auctions for individuals and merchants and charges the seller a listing fee and commission in accordance with the value of the transaction.

6. Merchant model

A merchant is usually a wholesaler or retailer of goods and services. The merchant provides a website with product information and an online ordering mechanism. Users select the products they want to buy and place an order. The product price can be fixed or negotiable. The merchant earns an income through the profit margin in the product price. This model is mainly suited for physical goods and services, such as books, computers or a delivery service.

Example
www.bestbuy.com is a website which sells various products such as mobile phones, laptops and cameras of various brands.

7. Auction model

In an auction, the price of a product depends on what buyers are willing to pay. The two most popular models for performing auctions are 'open' auction and the 'reverse' auction.

In the 'open' auction, participants repeatedly place higher bids for a product under auction. The person who places the highest bid is awarded the product. An example of an online open auction is eBay.

In a 'reverse' or 'Dutch' auction, the price is initially set at a very high level, and reduces at regular intervals.

SUMMARY

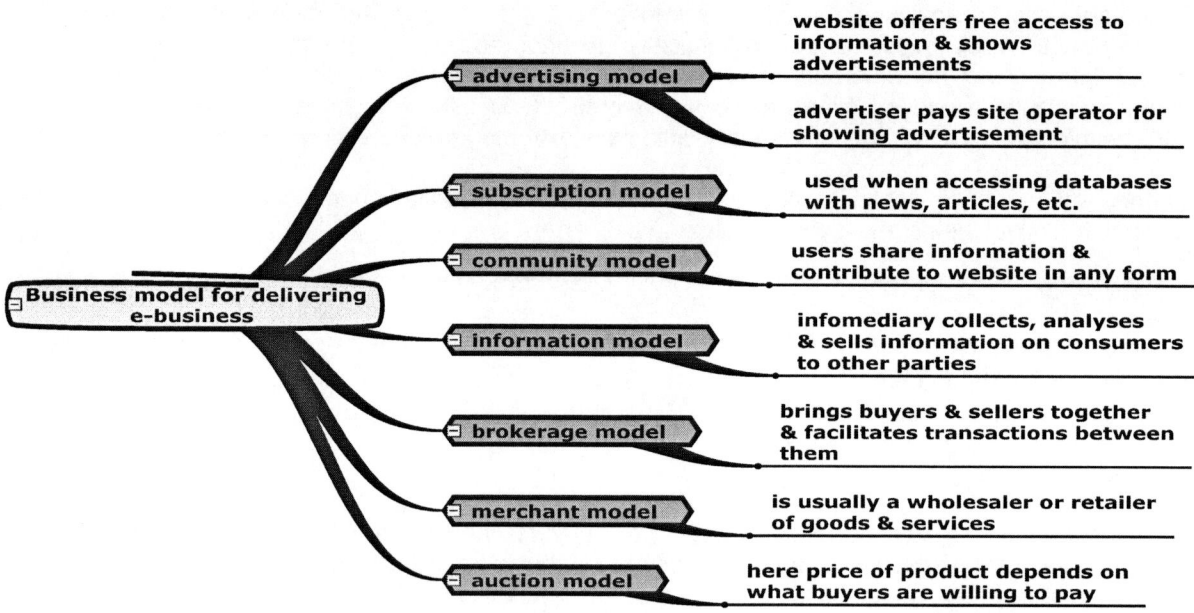

3.2. Marketplace channel structures

From a micro perspective, the e-business environment for an organisation consists of customers, suppliers, competitors and intermediaries. Channel structures are the modes in which a manufacturer or a selling firm delivers products or services to its customers. The distribution channel could consist of one or more intermediaries (such as wholesalers or retailers) in the supply chain. Apart from wholesalers and retailers, the intermediaries include traders, agents, brokers, dealers and distributors who provide specialised information (with the difference being that distributors hold inventory). The relationship between the channel partners and the organisation can be vastly influenced by the Internet because the Internet bypasses some of the channel partners.

1. Disintermediation

This is the process of removing intermediaries in the supply chain that previously linked a company to its customers. Organisations can now deal with their customers directly instead of dealing with intermediaries who have in turn dealt with the customers. This reduces the selling costs and infrastructure costs of selling through a channel. Disintermediation is also closely associated with the just-in-time (JIT) manufacturing approach since removing the need for inventory removes one of the functions of an intermediary.

Diagram 3: Disintermediation

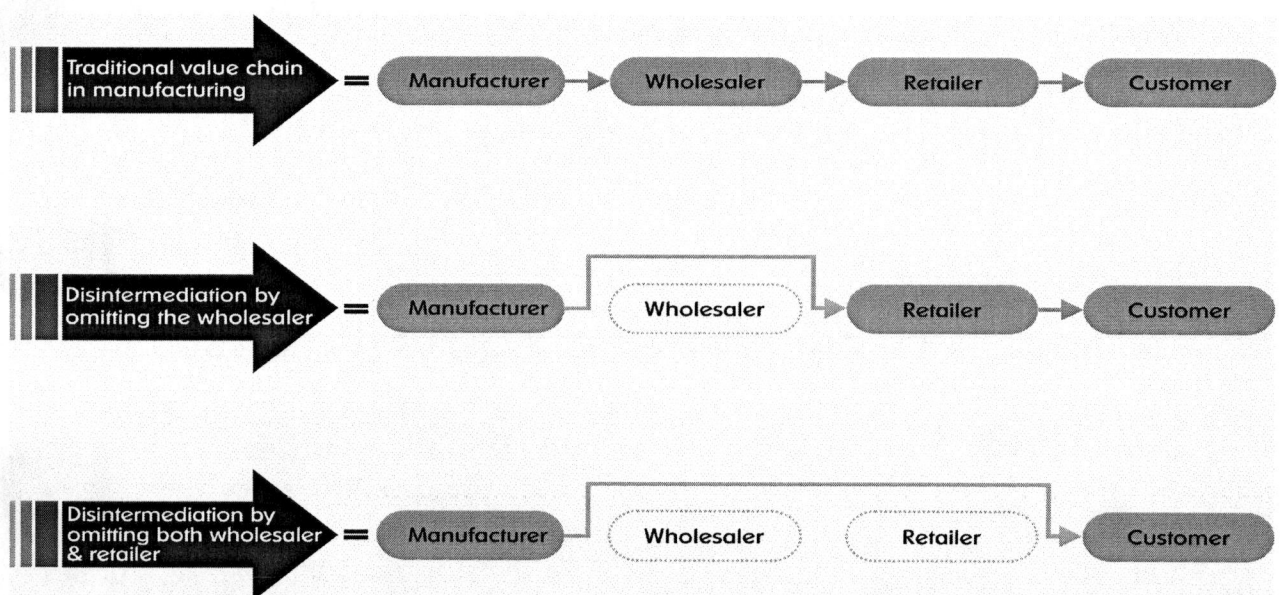

Example

A noteworthy example of disintermediation through the use of the Internet is Dell, Inc, which sells most of its products directly to the customer, and bypasses the traditional retail chains. Another example of disintermediation without using the Internet is Wal-Mart, which reduces its prices by reducing the number of intermediaries between the supplier and the customer.

2. Reintermediation

Reintermediation can be defined as the reintroduction of an intermediary between the manufacturer and the customer. It applies especially to instances in which disintermediation has occurred first. Initially, disintermediation was a way of cutting costs or increasing profits, since it was believed that the Internet would remove the middlemen and drive them out of business by having the manufacturers sell directly to customers.

Diagram 4 (a): Reintermediation without intermediary

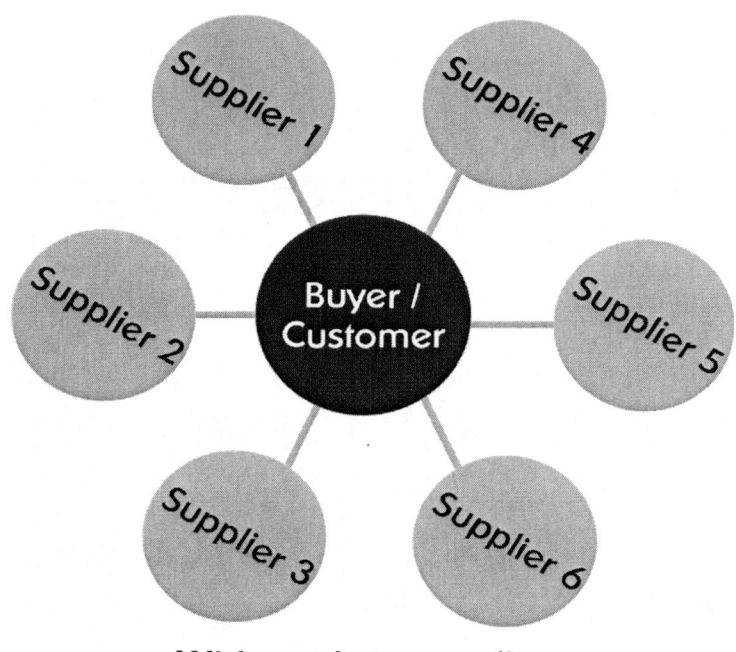

Without intermediary

Diagram 4 (b): Reintermediation with intermediary

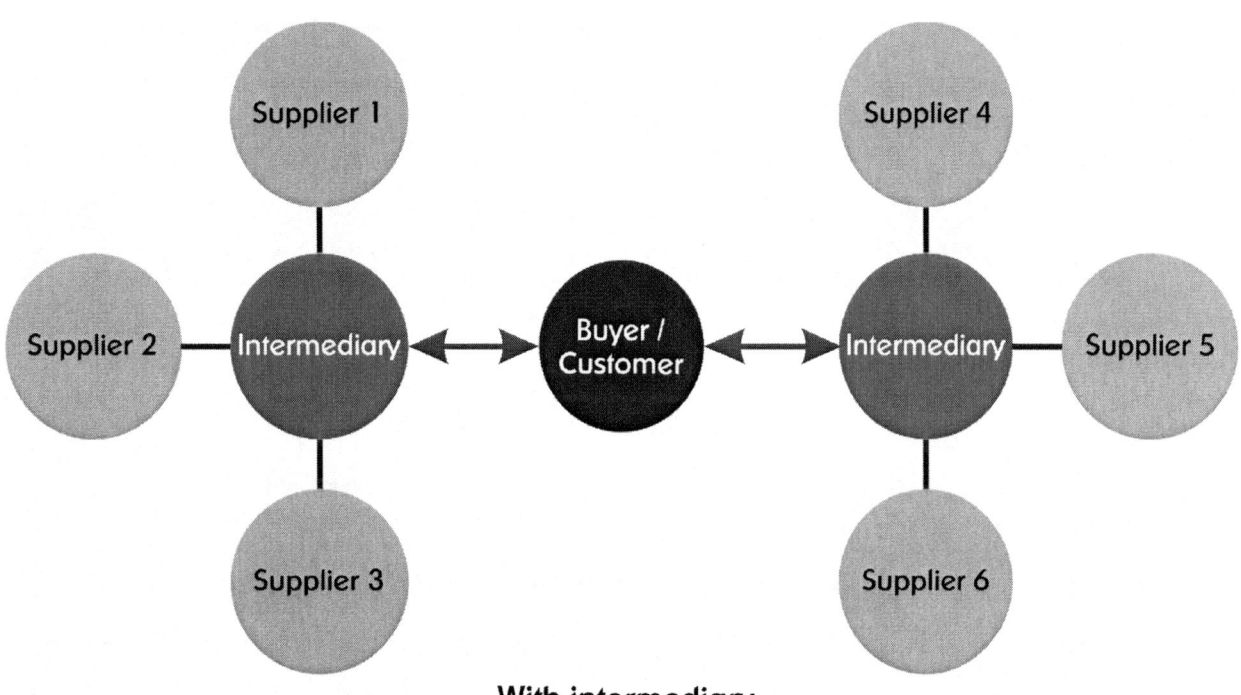

With intermediary

However, the removal of intermediaries brought problems such as the higher cost of handling the shipping of small orders, having to deal with several customer service issues, and confrontations with the retailers and other channel partners. Manufacturers had to incur huge costs for handling post-sales and pre-sales issues. In addition to this, e-business also involved high costs. Reintermediation removes these drawbacks by placing an intermediary between the buyer and the seller. The intermediary provides customers with certain important value added services which are unavailable in the new direct buyer-seller relationship.

Example

The intermediary performs the price evaluation function, since the intermediary has certain links which are updated from prices contained in different suppliers' databases.

3. Countermediation

Countermediation is the creation of a new intermediary by an established organisation so as to enable it to compete with established intermediaries. Countermediation is carried out through e-business. Countermediation also refers to possible partnerships with another independent intermediary e.g. a mortgage broker.

SUMMARY

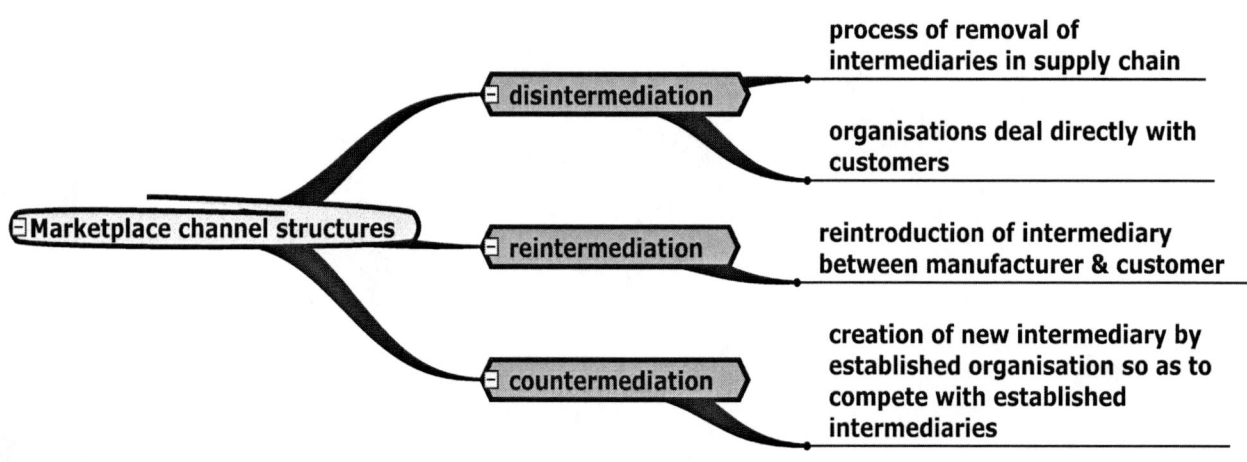

Test Yourself 3

State the marketplace models that deliver e-business. Explain why organisations reintroduce intermediaries between the manufacturer and the customer.

---

4. Advise on the hardware and software infrastructure required to support e-business. [3]
Advise on how the organisation can utilise information technology to help it deliver a selected strategy. [3]

[Learning Outcomes e and f]

4.1. Introduction

An organisation adopting e-business should define its e-business infrastructure adequately. This would include a combination of hardware such as servers and client PCs, and software applications to support the e-business.

1. Electronic mail (E-mail)

a) E-mail is the exchange of electronic messages using computers. It offers ease in communication, particularly when compared with post, fax or phone.

b) It provides the cheapest, quickest and most reliable way for an organisation to exchange business information with its customers, suppliers, etc.

c) It allows a variety of information to be sent, including messages, documents, photographs and drawings.

d) Messages can easily be protected, recorded and organised. In addition, messages can easily be sent to multiple recipients.

e) In order to use e-mail, enterprises need access to a network / Internet-linked computer. Alternatively, e-mail services can be accessed from shared Internet facility providers e.g. Internet cafes.

f) Messages can be read and written in a special program such as Microsoft Outlook Express, or Novell in the case of a large company. Users can even chat using the messenger services provided by Yahoo.com or Skype.

g) Certain websites such as Gmail and Yahoo offer free e-mail services for their registered users.

2. Transmission control protocol / Internet protocol (TCP/IP)

TCP/IP (also referred to as an 'Internet protocol suite') is the set of communications protocols that implement the protocol stack upon which the Internet and other commercial networks run. The data transmissions standards of the Internet are part of a larger set of standards known as the Open Systems Interconnection (OSI) model, which defines a layered model that enables servers to communicate with other servers and clients.

TCP provides the reliable delivery of a stream of bytes, making it suitable for applications like file transfer and e-mail.

TCP is used extensively by the World Wide Web, E-mail and the File Transfer Protocol (FTP).

3. File transfer protocol (FTP)

File Transfer Protocol is used to transfer data from one computer to another over the Internet, or through a network. It is a commonly used protocol for exchanging files over any network that supports the TCP/IP protocol (such as the Internet or an intranet).

The client computer that runs the FTP client software initiates a connection to the server. Once connected, the client can perform many operations such as uploading files to the server, downloading files from the server, renaming or deleting files on the server and so on. FTP uses TCP/IP for transferring data.

4. The Internet and World Wide Web (WWW)

a) The Internet enables communication between computers that are connected via telecommunication links. It consists of a global network of servers and telecommunication links between them which are used to access and transfer information between computers and web servers.

b) The computers in offices and homes can be connected to the Internet via local Internet Service Providers (ISPs), who in turn are connected to global / international ISPs.

c) The World Wide Web is a navigation system based within the Internet and uses a technology called hypertext that allows the web documents stored on host computers on the Internet to be linked with each other. This provides a standard method for exchanging and publishing information on the Internet.

d) A web browser is a software that is used to access information on the WWW stored on web servers.

e) The Internet use of organisations is growing very fast but is still limited.

f) A website contains pages of data (words, pictures, sounds, and video) that are linked together electronically.

g) A website can be accessed by anybody who has access to the Internet, and it links an organisation to a potential worldwide market – e-business.

h) The web is used for information dissemination, transactions and sales support.

i) Organisations can promote business, process enquiries and orders, and can accept payments using debit or credit cards. They can also receive and process relevant information from other organisations' websites.

5. Intranet

An intranet is a private web technologies network that uses Internet protocols and network connectivity for sharing some part of an organisation's information or operations with its staff and corporate management. This can be compared to a private version of the Internet or a version of the Internet which is restricted within an organisation.

Intranets differ from 'extranets' in that intranets are generally restricted to the employees of an organisation while extranets can generally be accessed by customers, suppliers, or other approved parties. Increasingly, intranets are being used to facilitate working in groups, teleconferencing, project management, etc.

The following are some of the other benefits of an intranet:

a) Communication: intranets can serve as powerful tools for communication within an organization, vertically and horizontally.
b) Business operations and management: intranets can be used as a platform for developing and deploying applications to support business operations.
c) Cost-effective: users can view information using a web-browser rather than keeping physical documents such as procedure manuals, internal phone lists and requisition forms. It minimises the usage of paper thereby helping the organisation to fulfil its corporate social responsibility.
d) Provide culture change platforms and enable teamwork: a large number of employees discussing key issues in an online forum can bring up new ideas. The fact that information is easily accessible to all authorised users allows for greater teamwork.

6. Extranet

An extranet is a private web technologies network that uses Internet protocols and network connectivity for sharing part of an organisation's information or operations with its suppliers, customers, partners or other businesses. It can be compared to an intranet that is extended to users outside the company.

An extranet can be used for a variety of commercial applications. Some of the common applications are file management and certain higher project management applications. Companies can use an extranet to:

a) Collaborate with other companies on common development efforts
b) Share product catalogues and price lists exclusively with wholesalers
c) Develop and use training programs jointly with other companies
d) Exchange large volumes of data using Electronic Data Interchange (EDI)
e) Share news on common interests exclusively with business partners
f) Allow access to services provided by one company to a group of other companies, such as an online banking application managed by one company on behalf of affiliated banks
g) Use networking sites such as www.linkedin.com wherein a company can maintain professional contacts and information of other companies or individuals. The users of the website can contact each other.
h) Enable customer care and empowerment by enabling online ordering, complaints, etc.

SUMMARY

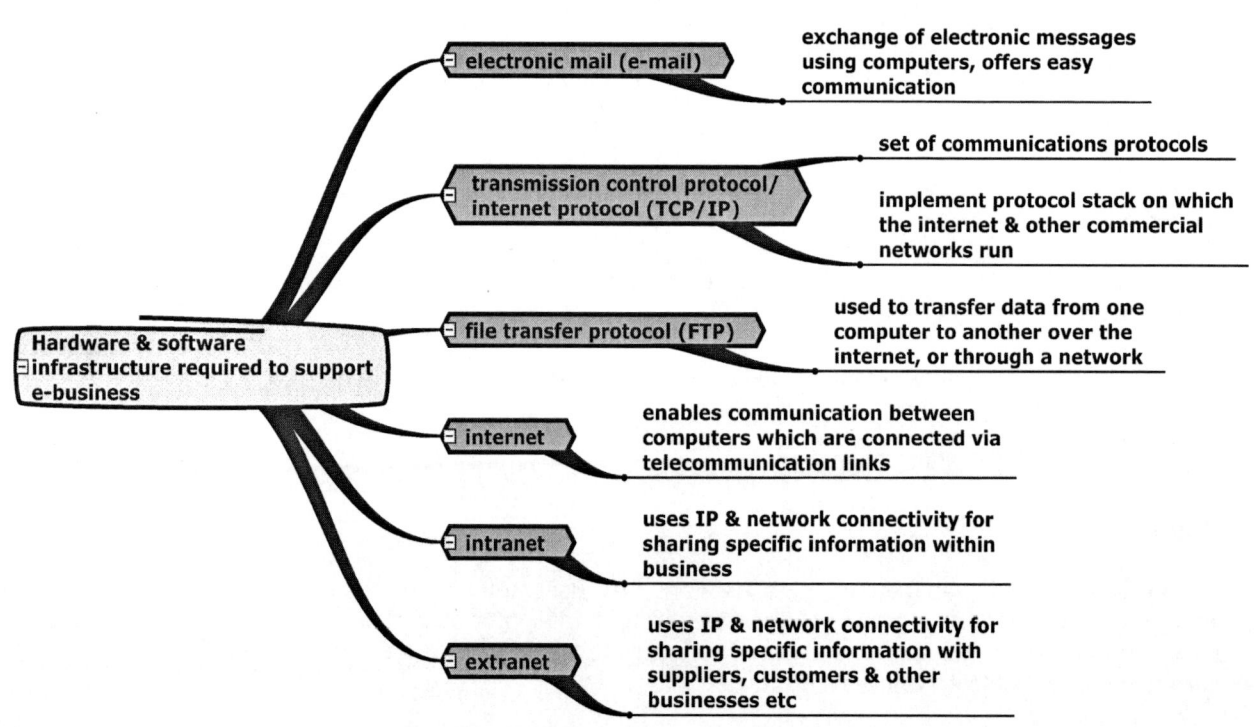

4.2. E-business strategy

An e-business strategy has wide implications for the business of an organisation, as it affects more than one department within the organisation. Therefore, it should be considered by the highest level of management in the organisation. E-business is not simply developing a website but rather involves changing a company's business model to adapt to the new economy.

1. Traditional strategy and e-business strategy

Before e-business became popular, many strategy models had been developed for the corporate strategy, supply chain management strategy, marketing strategy, etc. Many of these models can be applied to the e-business strategy. However, there are certain differences between traditional business strategy and an e-business strategy. These are:

a) Traditional business strategy requires a single development effort as opposed to an e-business strategy, which requires an iterative development effort because technological changes happen rapidly.

b) Traditional business strategy assumes that it is possible to forecast the future and then to develop long-term plans. However, an e-business strategy has limited predictability and focuses on adaptability and responsiveness.

c) Traditional business strategy focuses on production and factory goods whereas e-business strategy is customer-oriented.

2. Strategy model of continuous planning and feedback

Kalakota and Robinson have suggested a dynamic and emergent strategy process specific to e-business. They have emphasised that continuous planning with feedback is essential in any e-business strategy. The method of continuous planning with feedback is structured around the following steps:

a) **Knowledge building and evaluation of capabilities:** this involves understanding the customer's needs comprehensively and developing a clear understanding of the capabilities needed to address those needs.

b) **Development of the e-business design:** this involves developing competence for addressing customer needs.

c) **E-business blueprint:** this is the vital link between the e-business design, organisational goals and technology. The e-business design should be linked to the overall corporate objectives of an organisation.

d) **Application development and deployment:** this involves the translation of key objectives and projects into integrated applications.

3. Development of e-business strategy

Before developing any type of strategy, the management should agree the process they intend to follow for developing and implementing that strategy. While developing an e-business strategy, an organisation should take a combined view of its existing approaches to business, marketing, supply chain management and the development of an IT strategy. An organisation's e-business strategy should meet the following criteria:

a) It should be based on the organisation's current performance in the marketplace, its strengths and weaknesses, products and distribution channels, competition, opportunities, etc

b) It should define how the organisation would meet its objectives. This involves mapping a path to implement the strategy which would put an emphasis on quality service to the organisation's customers, channel partners and others. The strategy should focus on a more personalised approach than is used in traditional technical support.

c) It should allocate the resources required to meet objectives.

d) It should provide a long-term plan for the development of the organisation.

e) The strategy should be flexible and have a scalable architecture which allows the system to adapt to the changing needs of the future.

Lastly, the e-business strategy should conform to the standard criteria of acceptability, suitability and feasibility:

i. **Acceptability:** the e-business strategy should be acceptable to the shareholders and the business groups which deal with the company.

ii. **Suitability:** e-business supplements the other business strategies of an organisation and should be part of the overall corporate strategy of an organisation.

iii. **Feasibility:** resources such as skilled manpower and funds are essential for setting up an effective e-business strategy. These resources should be obtained feasibly by the management.

Ideally, an e-business strategy should be incorporated into the information systems (IS) strategy. However many organisations, such as GE and Dell Inc, consider e-business strategy to be part of their corporate strategy.

Example

Many stock brokerage firms have adopted IT in a support role. Earlier, dealing with brokers involved tremendous paperwork, such as maintaining several paper forms, contract notes for trades executed and daily ledgers. In order to save costs and provide a better service to their customers, many brokerage firms have started issuing digital contract notes through e-mails, electronic forms and scanning those forms to the back-office, as well as maintaining electronic records, margin account summaries through e-mails, online trading platforms, etc. The adoption of IT has resulted in the reduction of a lot of paperwork and ease in conducting transactions.

SUMMARY

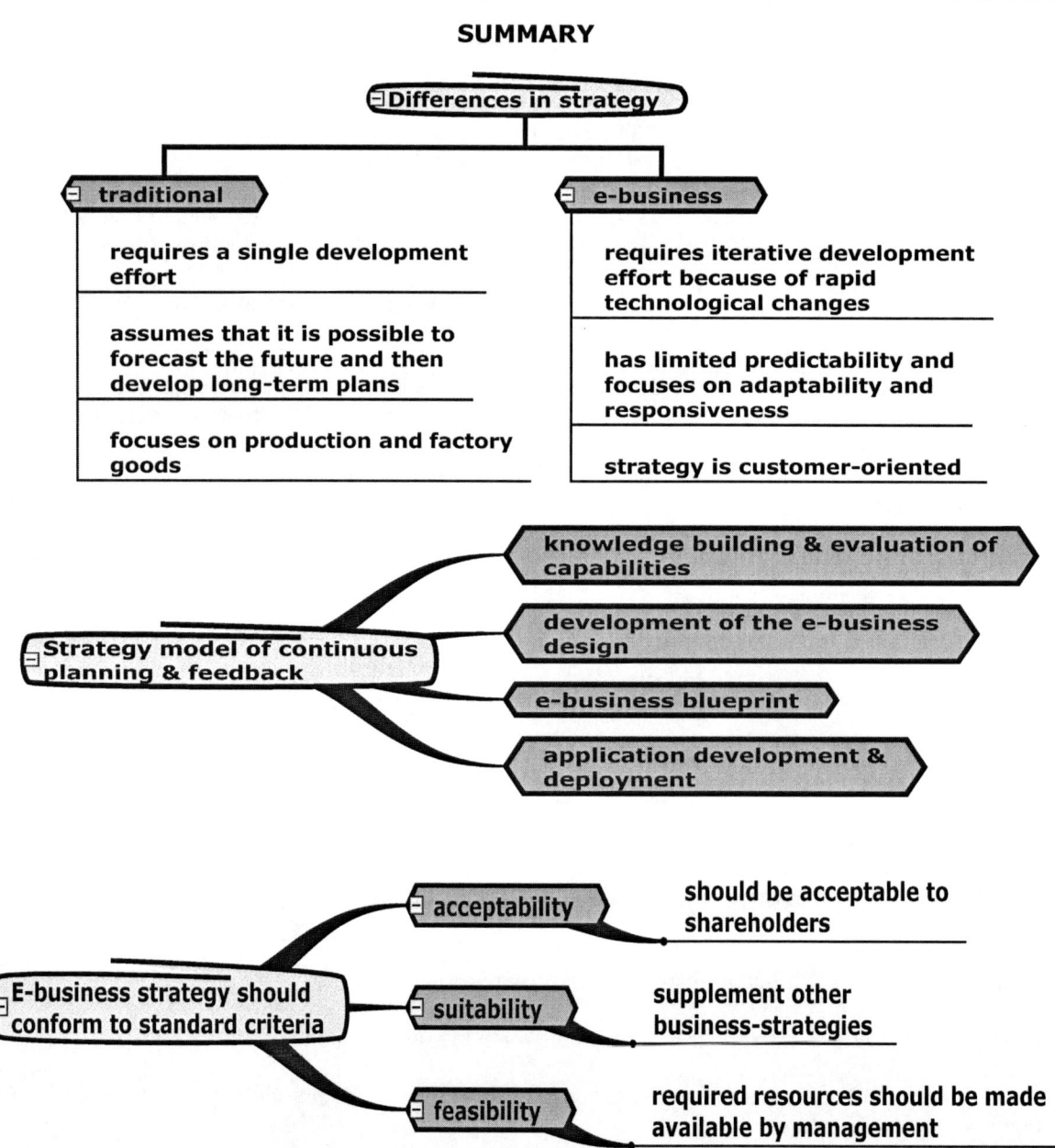

Test Yourself 4

Use of IT in an e-business strategy

Speedex Ltd is a medium-sized manufacturer of automotive components. The CEO of the company feels that in order to gain a competitive advantage over the other medium-sized companies in this area, the company should deploy Internet and e-business technologies and create Internet-enabled business processes. This would not replace the traditional manufacturing and selling of automotive components, but would make it more efficient, flexible and customer-centric. The company also wants to create integrated business processes in order to lower transaction costs across the value chain, increase the company's responsiveness, and decrease inventories.

After conducting an initial study of its business operations, the company is in a dilemma over which processes, it should deploy e-business for, and how it should deploy e-business technologies.

Required:

Explain the importance of information technology and how it can be used for successfully deploying an e-business strategy for Speedex Ltd.

Answers to Test Yourself

Answer to TY 1

A E-business includes a broader spectrum of functionalities than e-commerce because it encompasses the integration of ICT into the business processes of companies. It uses technology and e-commerce processes to build better customer relationships and create new value propositions for the customer.

In order to co-ordinate its business processes better, the organisation should deliver an end-to-end service to customers and link its back office operations to the front office through the application of e-business. The idea behind this is to create a unifying and holistic source of information that allows the business to understand the needs of its customers and thereby provide customer satisfaction.

Advantages of adopting e-business:

An e-business strategy would enable Buildon Ltd to gain a competitive advantage over its rival firms. It would also benefit the company in the following ways:

➤ reduction in operational costs
➤ improvement in existing business processes as well as creation of more efficient new processes
➤ improvement in the security of business information, records and contracts
➤ improvement in the legal position of the business in disputes and obligations
➤ easy for customers and suppliers to access relevant information as nowadays there are various customer care tools provided by a lot of websites
➤ effective co-ordination with major construction industry clients, contractors and suppliers

B Barriers to the adoption of e-business:

Higher costs

➤ The costs associated with impementing e-business (hardware, software, cost of being online, web design for secure and public interactions)
➤ Government policies can sometimes adversely affect e-business to a large extent. Examples include financial services regulations (such as KYC norms) which have to be adhered to by the mutual funds and brokerage houses while conducting e-business.

Infrastructure
Inadequate infrastructure is one of the major bottlenecks affecting e-business for any business. Problems with Internet access and hardware and software are major hindrances to e-business.

Security issues

➤ The issues of security of transactions and privacy protection over the Internet are of concern to many consumers.
➤ Digital signatures and other authentication procedures such as data encryption standards, two-way encryption for security and public key encryption rules should be helpful in protecting privacy and personal data.

Other issues

➢ Adverse tariffs, different regulations, languages, and higher return rates on international shipments could adversely affect e-business.
➢ Address verification may be difficult, which increases the risk of fraud in non-credit card transactions.

Business ethical issues

In modern business ethics, the network relationship is highly valued and trust becomes a critical factor, without which firms may be deliberately excluded from e-business opportunities.

Answer to TY 2

A Trading partnerships using e-business typically evolve in three stages. They start on a transactional level and then move towards information sharing. The third stage, namely collaborative relationships, build upon the transactional and information-sharing relationships.

By adopting e-business, the relationship with the trading partners will definitely change. There are different stages of the relationship according to the organisation's growth patterns, as follows:

Transactional relationship: Electronic Data Interchange (EDI) facilitates business transactions, improves accuracy, eliminates paperwork and reduces costs. This is the routine process for Mall-Water as it already practices e-business.

Information sharing: this is the next step in the evolutionary process of data exchange. Typically, a partner is given access to information, or one partner transmits information to the other. This is the next leg of relationships after purely transactional relationships.

In the given situation, Mall-Water exercises an information-sharing relationship with its trading partners for managing relationships with its suppliers and avoiding excess inventory handling cost by timely and specific procurements.

Collaborative relationship: opportunities for collaboration among trading partners will vary depending upon organisations' respective roles in the supply chain.

Mall-Water has to establish a collaborative relationship with its trading partners based on consumer requirements. An example of this is when the trading partners work jointly on new product designs and on forecasting consumer demand.

When striving to achieve a demand-supply balance, the trading partners could decide quantities and timescales for the products that are to be produced. Collaborative planning efforts can help Mall-Water and its suppliers to focus on new demand forecasting, product planning, package design, and category management, amongst other things.

B Information-sharing relationships do not contribute much towards the reduction of the uncertainty faced by trading partners in determining the future product supply / demand. To enhance the buyer-seller relationship further, many trading partners choose to adopt a more collaborative approach.

The three major types of buyer-seller collaborative relationships are:

Manufacturer-supplier collaboration

Collaborative product development, enabled by sharing and modifying design documents, helps manufacturers to develop products in a better and faster way. Similarly, sharing supplier production schedules helps ensure that future material needs are satisfied. This, in turn, results in improved order fulfilment and increased capacity utilisation.

Manufacturer-customer collaboration

The collaborative opportunities between manufacturers and customers are based on demand planning and inventory replenishment. The thrust is on joint estimation of demand at the point of consumption, followed by the creation of a mutually agreed plan for replenishment. This approach helps ensure that consumer requirements are met efficiently. In order to collaborate on demand planning successfully, trading partners need to share and modify each other's demand plans and forecasts electronically.

Collaboration with third-party logistics providers

Collaboration between Mall-Water and third-party logistics focuses on the joint planning of logistics activities. In terms of transportation services, collaboration results in equipment utilisation, by enabling the consolidation of inbound, interfacility, and outbound shipments amongst trading partners. This can be accomplished through electronic sharing of information on shipment plans and availability of transportation resources.

All forms of e-business relationships, namely the transactional, information-sharing, and collaborative, offer opportunities to improve supply chain performance by reducing costs, improving asset utilisation, and increasing customer service and sales.

Mall-Water needs to keep itself abreast of developments in e-commerce and be flexible in trying new collaborative techniques. There is a tremendous increase in profitability, and a great deal of customer-service performance improvement results from collaboration.

Answer to TY 3

The marketplace models for delivering e-business are:

- disintermediation
- reintermediation
- countermediation

The reintroduction of an intermediary between the manufacturer and the customer applies especially to instances in which disintermediation has occurred first. Initially, disintermediation was resorted to as a way of cutting costs or increasing profits, because it was believed that the Internet would disintermediate the middlemen and drive them out of business by allowing manufacturers to sell directly to customers.

However, the removal of intermediaries brought problems such as the higher cost of handling the shipment of small orders, as well as dealing with several customer service issues and confrontations with retailers and other channel partners. Manufacturers incurred large costs for handling post-sales and pre-sales issues. In addition to this, e-business also involved high costs.

Reintermediation removes these drawbacks by placing an intermediary between the buyer and the seller. The intermediary provides customers with certain important value added services which are not available in the new direct buyer-seller relationship.

Answer to TY 4

The e-business system is a combination of technologies, applications, processes, business strategies and practices that are necessary in order to do business electronically. Information technology is evolving at a rapid pace and plays a large role in determining the corporate strategy of the company. Internet technology coupled with e-business technology, can be used judiciously to improve coordination and communication to solve many problems and to perform complex, collaborative tasks faster and reliably.

IT can enable Speedex Ltd to respond to the existing competition by creating barriers that are difficult to overcome by the new entrants. This could be done by adopting unique technologies that are difficult to emulate. It can also increase the economies of scale by using automated production techniques. The more difficult the services are to imitate, the higher the barrier for new entrants becomes. Alternatively, IT can also help in overcoming certain entry barriers for a business.

Since e-business technologies are very new, the management should bear the following points in mind while framing the strategy:

- How should the company deploy e-business technologies in order to gain access to its customers' preferences?
- How should the company deploy e-business technologies to retain its old customers?
- What kind of strategic deployment of e-business technologies would enable a reduction in procurement, production and distribution costs, and ensure maximum revenue?
- What changes are necessary to stay in business and beat the competition?
- Has the company got the necessary technical, financial and managerial competencies?

The company can deploy an e-business strategy using the following steps:

1. **Internet facility:** the company should successfully perform all community-oriented business communication and co-ordination using an Internet facility. This will enable the company to randomly seize the business opportunities in the industry.
2. **Intranet and extranet facility:** in order to obtain seamless integration of information and workflow across the various locations of the company and outside the company, it should use intranet and extranet facilities. This will enable the company to achieve operational efficiencies across multiple locations.
3. **Setting-up of the e-business structure:** by implementing the above steps, the company creates a virtual organisation that provides around-the-clock interactive services to its customers.

Quick Quiz

1. Explain why e-commerce is associated with doing business electronically.

2. Explain buy-side and sell side e-commerce?

3. Explain how infrastructure and other costs obstruct the adoption of e-business?

4. What is a collaborative relationship and why is it necessary to adopt it even if an information-sharing relationship enables supply / demand coordination between its partners?

5. What is an extranet and how is it different from an intranet?

Answers to Quick Quiz

1. E-commerce (electronic commerce) is associated with buying and selling using information and communication technology e.g. Internet. Any transaction involving the transfer of ownership or rights to use goods or services through a computer-mediated network comes under the scope of e-commerce.

    Although e-commerce encompasses the electronic ordering of goods and services, delivery of goods is carried out by the same traditional channels, such as through couriers, on-line ordering, electronic share trading and electronic fund transfers.

2. **Buy-side e-commerce:** buy-side e-commerce refers to transactions relating to procurement of resources by an organisation from its suppliers

    Sell-side e-commerce: sell-side e-commerce refers to transactions related to the selling of products by an organisation to its customers.

3. Although e-business is a cost effective tool for businesses of all sizes, and has a host of advantages, the major factors which can be viewed as barriers to its adoption are:

i. **Infrastructure:** electronic base i.e. the basic requirement of the ICT, such as problems with Internet access, and the hardware and software and the available skills essential for the e-business setup are major hindrances to the adoption of e-business.

    One model does not fit all businesses, as the requirement, type and size of every business are not the same.

ii. **High cost:** there is always an additional cost associated with the adoption of e-business, and they are:

- cost of infrastructure to set up e-business e.g. Internet access, hardware and software requirement
- security, system administration and maintenance cost
- comparably higher cost of shipment in low quantity
- cost of training people to use software which could lead to a step increase in fixed costs.

4. **Collaborative relationship:** although information-sharing relationships enable supply / demand synchronisation between business / partners, a collaborative relationship is adopted since:

- information-sharing relationships do little to help reduce the uncertainty that trading partners face in determining future product supply / demand
- collaborative relationship enhance the buyer-seller relationship further
- collaboration enables partners to jointly develop a better understanding for future product demands and implementation moves towards this, which helps both the organisations' programs to more realistically satisfy that demand

5. **Extranet:** is a private web technologies network that uses Internet protocols and network connectivity for sharing part of an organisation's information or operations with its suppliers, customers, partners or other businesses. It could be compared to an intranet that is extended to users outside the company.

    Extranet can be used for a variety of commercial applications. Some of the common applications are file management and certain higher project management applications.

Self Examination Questions

Question 1

Markus Ltd is in the business of marketing and distributing FMCG goods. It has witnessed a tremendous rise in its business activities over the past few years. The company is currently using traditional channels for conducting business in which the company has to manually place its orders with its suppliers, and its customers also have to rely on manual systems while doing business with the company.

The company's competitors have recently adopted e-business and have been performing better ever since its adoption. The company is currently unsure how an e-business strategy would help it to face the stiff competition and maintain its market share.

Required:

Explain some of the essential components of an e-business strategy which need to be considered by Marcus Ltd if it decides to implement e-business for its operations.

Question 2

Martin Pringle is the managing director of Martinex, a company that has several outlets which sell jewellery. The company faces intense competition from its larger competitors in its core markets. It has difficulties in diversifying into other segments. The company has a responsive customer care unit and is currently considering the option of introducing an online shopping service, from which customers can specify designs from the comfort of their homes and have their jewellery delivered to their homes.

Martin recognises that for developing an online shopping service, the company would require significant investment in new technology and support systems. He hopes a significant proportion of existing customers and, most importantly, new customers will be attracted to the new service.

Required:

Explain whether the online shopping service segment is profitable enough to commit to the required investment.

Answers to Self Examination Questions

Answer to SEQ 1

E-business is not just about developing a website but about changing the entire business model of the company in order to adapt to the changing economy.

The company should consider whether its current business model can be improved in order to take care of new e-business opportunities. This means that if the company has regional distribution centres throughout the country, e-business can speed up the communication between these centres.

1. The company should **first develop a macro level e-business strategy** that provides a roadmap for adapting its business to e-business. The development of the e-business strategy should start with considering:

   - the company's current position in the market
   - its products and distribution channels
   - the challenges posed by the competition
   - new opportunities in the market
   - a resource audit that would enable the company to choose the best alternative resources available within the resource constraints of the company

2. The next step is to **chart a plan** to implement the strategy. While doing this, the company should mainly focus on delivering excellent services to its customers, the channel partners and other business groups. This would also require the managers to take a 'big picture' perspective and would require the involvement of the senior management as an integrating force.

3. **Customer evaluation:** customers should be allowed to evaluate the existing web site and incorporate their opinion on whether the website meets their needs.

4. **Flexibility:** an e-business strategy should be flexible enough to keep pace with rapid technological developments. Therefore, it is essential to develop a flexible and scalable architecture that allows the system to easily adapt to the future.

5. **Information Technology:** IT is essential for the day-to-day operations of an organisation although it is not the main function fundamental to the growth of an organisation. An organisation should carefully plan its IT development, since IT is essential for creating a competitive advantage in the organisation's future.

Answer to SEQ 2

E-commerce is transforming several traditional relationships between the supplier and customer, and retailing is no exception. Broadly speaking, electronic commerce refers to any activity which involves interactions and business dealings by an organisation with its clients, within the organisation, or between various organisations by electronic means. For tangible goods, such as jewellery shopping, it enables online ordering and delivery direct to the customer and changes well-established methods for doing business in retail business models. In a significant sized business like Martinex, investment costs are high, which could affect profit margins.

B2C e-commerce faces more barriers to growth than B2B e-commerce and is still in the earlier stages of its lifecycle. The retail e-commerce market is still plagued with issues such as high potential for fraud and insecurity of payments. In order for online shopping to be successful for Martinex, it should increase the customer base that can be persuaded to use the service. This, in turn, will reflect the number of homes that have computers and Internet access. However, an established retail firm with a trusted brand and reputation is often in a better position than an online retail firm with no physical stores. This is because it can create a better shopping experience.

The company will have to assess the size and define the characteristics of the customer segment that is likely to use the online shopping service. The following factors should be considered by the company:

➤ The age of consumers is an important factor since electronic retailing is more highly favoured by younger customers who are familiar with using IT.

➤ Income could be an important way of segmenting the market since online shopping is more highly favoured by families with a high disposable income, access to computers, etc.

➤ Geo-demographic segmentation, which is the combination of where a customer lives and the stage of their particular shopping lifecycle, will provide real insights into customers' buying behaviour and their willingness to use electronic shopping.

Martin should consider a combination of the above factors when deciding whether investing in the online structure would be worthwhile for his company.

SECTION E: INFORMATION TECHNOLOGY

E2

STUDY GUIDE 2: E-BUSINESS APPLICATION: UPSTREAM SUPPLY CHAIN MANAGEMENT

■ Get Through Intro

Customers are increasingly demanding – they wish to have products as quickly as possible. In order to give goods to the customers as soon as possible, manufacturers need to work with their suppliers, in order to ensure that they have all the products they need for manufacture available when needed.

Let us take the example of a pizza delivery company called Pizza-so-fast. The customer would like her Pizza to come as quickly as possible. This is only possible if the pizza is made as quickly as possible and sent over to her as quickly as possible. What could Pizza-so-fast do to speed up making the pizzas? It could speak to its food suppliers and ask them to pre-cut all the toppings which go on the pizza. These could be sent over fresh (every day) and in resalable vacuum packed bags to retain freshness. It could also ask its tomato sauce base manufacturer to add all the herbs and salt and cook the sauce, so it is ready to go straight on to the pizza. Finally, instead of making the dough for the pizza itself, it could ask another company to make it for them and deliver it in a similar way to the toppings.

The examples given above are of upstream supply management – Pizza-so-fast's suppliers are providing the goods to the company in such a way that pizzas can be made more quickly, with the minimum of hassle, without compromising on quality.

This Study Guide will show you how you can implement effective upstream supply chain management to minimise costs and time, leading to higher profits and hopefully higher bonuses for you!

■ Learning Outcomes

a) Analyse the main elements of both the push and pull models of the supply chain.
b) Discuss the relationship of the supply chain to the value chain and the value network.
c) Assess the potential application of information technology to support and restructure the supply chain.
d) Advise on how external relationships with suppliers and distributors can be structured to deliver a restructured supply chain.
e) Discuss the methods, benefits and risks of e-procurement.
f) Assess different options and models for implementing e-procurement.

Introduction

Example

Wal-Mart: harnessing the power of e-business

Wal-Mart is a dominant player in the supermarket business in the US. It has successfully used e-business and e-procurement to gain an advantage in the market. Wal-Mart has revolutionised supply chain management into that of a "pull" model in which suppliers are driven by consumer demands. The suppliers are responsive to the purchasing trends of the consumers. Employees in each store can immediately order the appropriate inventory electronically since the procurement processes are decentralised. This, in turn, requires the suppliers to supply the products rapidly. This timely replenishment system, coupled with the correct inventory forecast, helps Wal-Mart to reduce its overall costs.

The company has established new standards for B2B e-commerce.

The above case study gives you an idea of how companies can implement e-business supply chain management to improve costs and meet customer's needs. This Study Guide will show you how you can implement up stream supply chain management both in real life and in the exam!

1. Analyse the main elements of both the push and pull models of the supply chain.[2]
[Learning Outcome a]

1.1 Supply chain

Definition

A supply chain is a network of facilities and distribution options that deals with:
- Procurement of materials
- Transformation of these materials into finished products
- Distribution of the finished products to the consumers

1.2 Supply Chain Management

Definition

Supply Chain Management (SCM) can be defined as the process of influencing the behaviour of the supply chain in order to get the desired results.

However, SCM is different from the traditional concept of logistics. Traditional logistics is associated with activities such as procurement, distribution and inventory management. SCM encompasses these activities and, in addition, also includes activities such as the development of a new product, marketing and finance.

The supply chain is primarily divided into an upstream supply chain and a downstream supply chain. The upstream supply chain includes the processes involved in transforming the inputs into outputs whereas the downstream supply chain includes the processes involved in delivering the products to the final customer.

E-commerce and the Internet are changing the way SCM functions and redefining the manner in which customers choose, purchase and use various products and services. This has resulted in the emergence of new B2B supply chains that are more consumer-focused than product-focused and that provide customised products and services.

1. Push model of supply chain

The push model of the supply chain refers to the push of materials through the supply chain to the end consumer and is associated with forecasting demand by an organisation. An interconnected network of manufacturers and distributors is connected to the consumer through a sales channel. Suppliers and vendors push their products or services through the supply chain to the end customer. Costs are accumulated throughout the supply chain and the end customer incurs most of the cost.

Example

Highly automated service platforms that are supported by standardised processes and which deliver resources to the right places at fixed time schedules. In the case of information technology, large enterprise applications state the activities to be performed and the resources to be deployed for meeting the expected demand.

The core assumptions of push models are:

- that organisations can anticipate demand, and
- mobilising scarce resources is the most efficient and reliable way to meet that demand.

Diagram 1: Push model of SCM

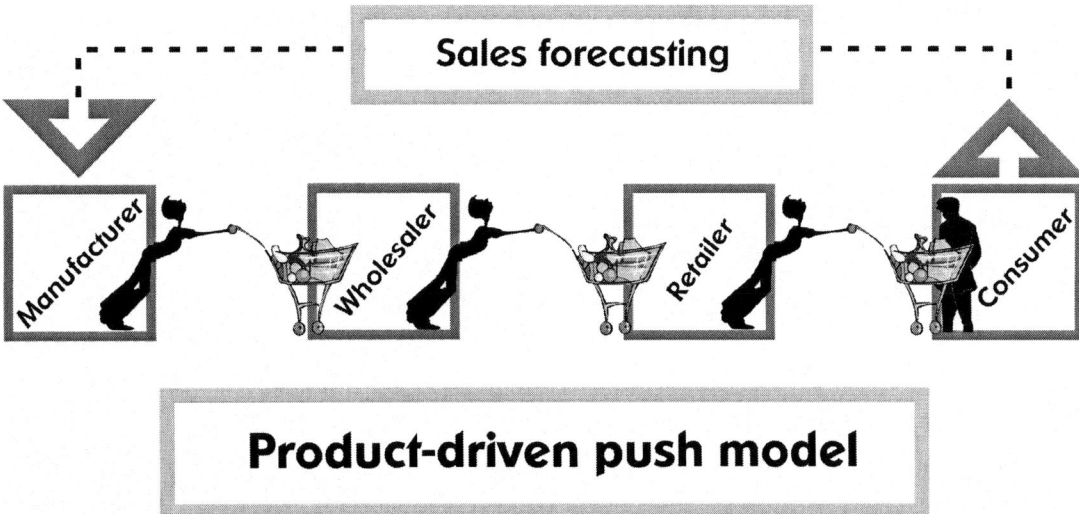

Push models are highly centralised and restrictive in nature, which prevents organisations from experimenting, improvising, and learning as quickly as possible.

2. Pull model of supply chain

The pull model of the supply chain refers to the end customer's pull of finished goods and is associated with responding to the actual consumer demand rather than forecasting demand by organisations. Many companies are moving from the traditional push models to a consumer-driven pull model. The pull models are driven by the capabilities of e-commerce for empowering clients and are less product-driven and more consumer-focused.

Diagram 2: Pull model of SCM

Pull-based models offer the following benefits

- enhanced innovation capabilities
- increased opportunities for collaboration
- better relationships with customers and suppliers
- prompt feedback
- greater scalability

> **Example**
>
> The current position of the media business reflects modern methods for accessing content for users. Instead of waiting for the media companies to push their content, the consumers can pull content at their will. Another example of pull models is where users can pull content in from a broad range of sources and publish their own writings, photographs, etc. using blogging tools and comment options.

3. Distinction between Push and Pull Strategies

Push models	Pull models
Their objective is to minimise cost and focus on efficiency	Their objective is to maximise service levels and focus on innovation
The main business driver of these models is maximum utilisation of resources at the least cost	The main business driver of these models is high customer service levels and flexibility to meet uncertain customer demand
These are complex in nature because they require organisations to specify, monitor and enforce detailed activities and tasks	These are simple as compared to the push models because the consumers can use electronic connections to pull their requirements from the system.
Demand can be anticipated in advance by the suppliers	Demand is highly uncertain since these models are based on actual demand
Push models are product-driven	Pull models are consumer-driven

Diagram 3: Distinction between Push and Pull Strategies

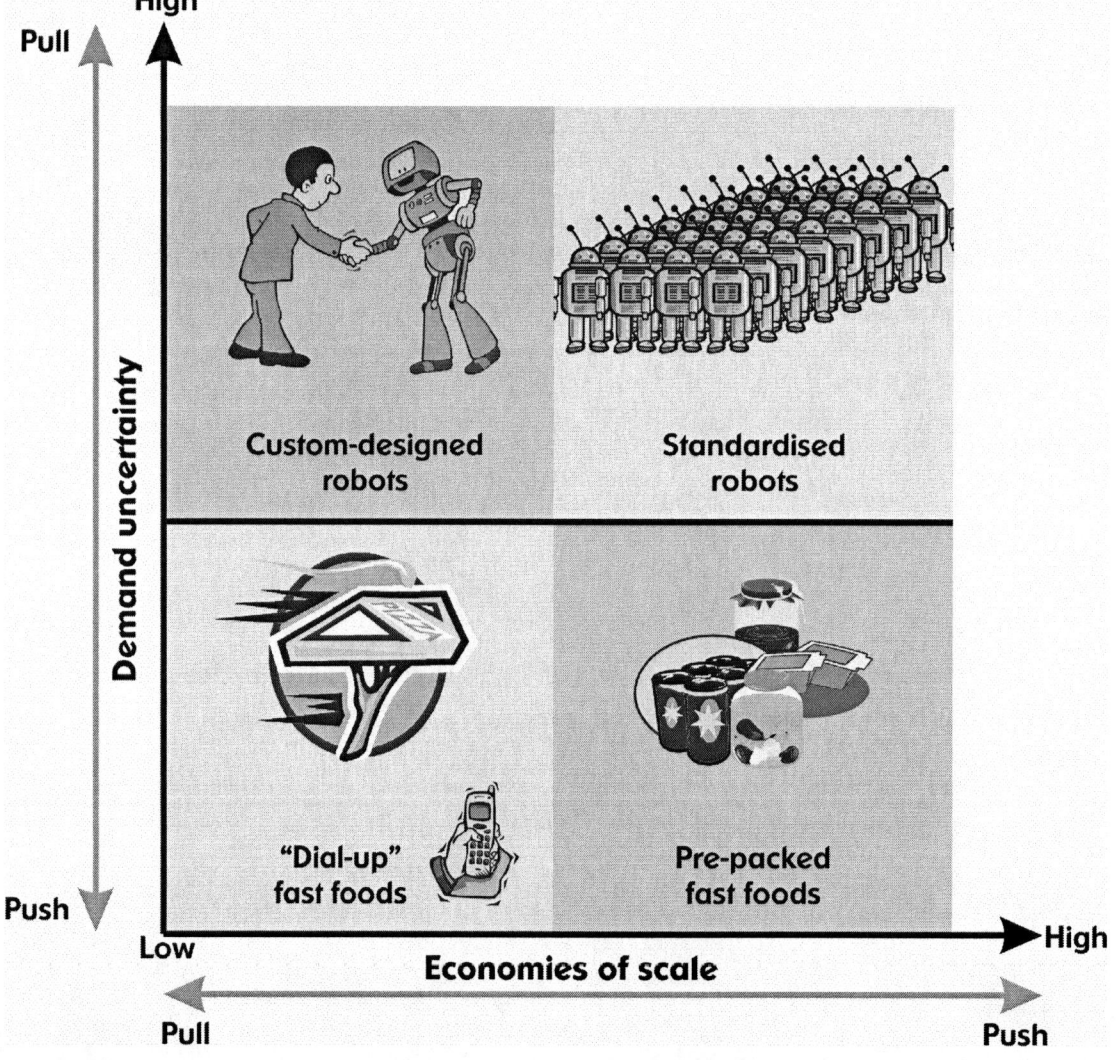

SUMMARY

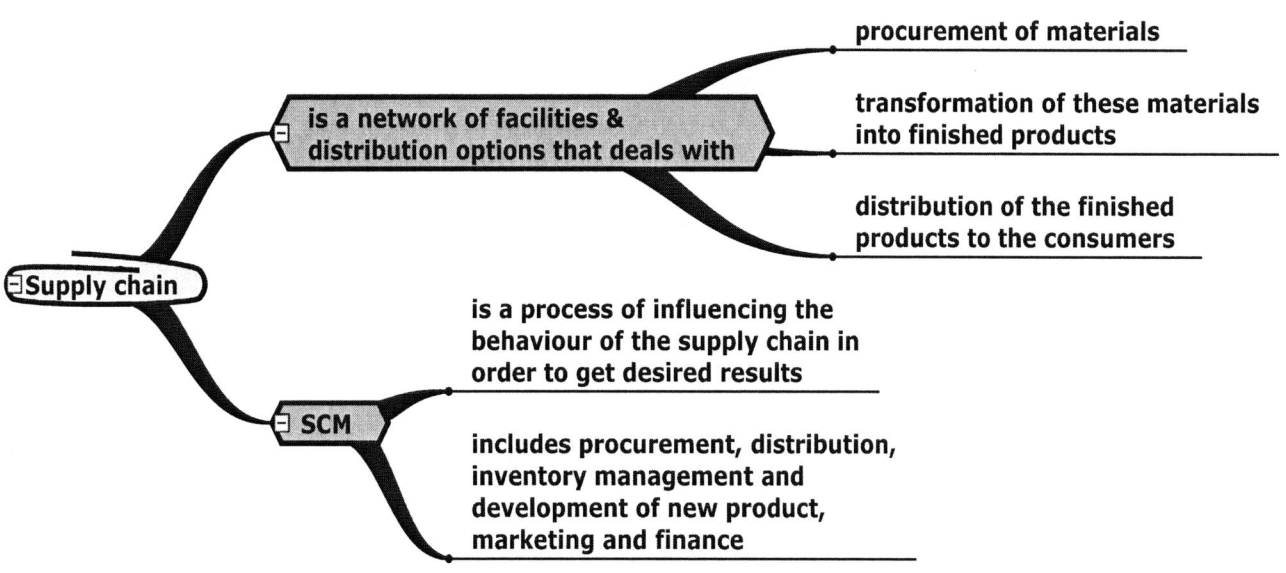

Test Yourself 1

Hugestorage Ltd is in the business of designing, manufacturing and marketing a wide range of electronic components which are used in PCs, notebooks and other consumer electronics applications. The company is dedicated to maintaining high quality performance, customer support and reliability.

In order to meet the growing demand for its products and to maintain its competitive position in the market, the management of the company has identified the following key challenges:
The challenges are:

➢ transition from a build-to-forecast to a build-to-demand execution process
➢ streamlining its demand forecasting process steps

The company aims to overcome these challenges by creating a more responsive supply chain that would support business practices, such as vendor-managed inventory, JIT replacements and build-to-demand manufacturing.

Required:

A Identify which supply chain model the company is using and explain the possible benefits that the company could enjoy if it adopted an alternative supply chain model.

B Suggest how Hugestorage should deal with challenges to gain long-term competitive advantage.

2. Discuss the relationship of the supply chain to the value chain and the value network.[2]
[Learning Outcome b]

The concept of a value chain was first described and popularised by Michael Porter in 1985. The value chain framework is considered a strong analysis tool for strategic planning. Products pass through all activities of the chain in order and gain some value at each activity. This chain of activities gives the products more added value than the sum of the added values of all activities.

Example

In the case of the diamond-cutting business, the cutting activity could be made less costly, but the activity adds to the value of the end product, since a rough diamond is much cheaper than a cut diamond.

2.1 The value chain

In order to analyse the specific activities which enable organisations to create a competitive advantage, it is useful to model the firm as a chain of value-creating activities. Michael Porter identified certain interrelated generic activities common to a wide range of firms. The resulting model is known as the value chain and is depicted below.

Diagram 4: Primary and support activities of value chain

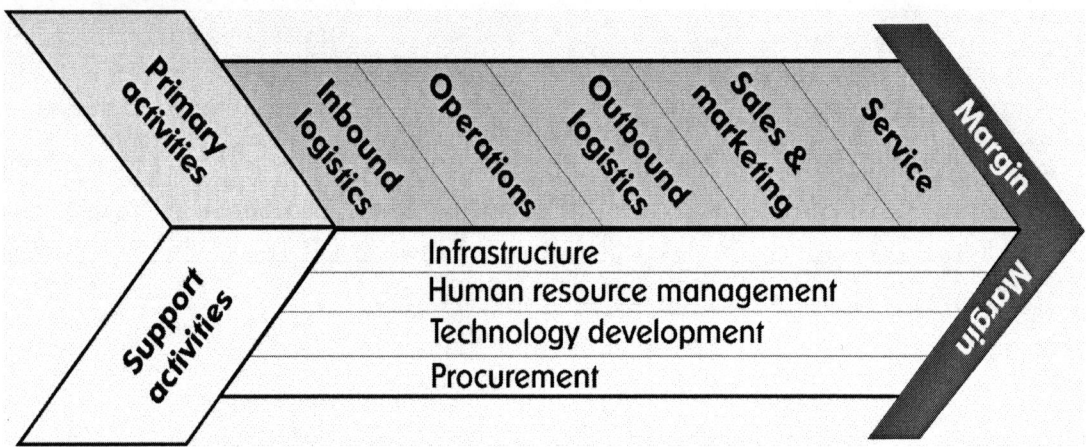

1. Primary value chain activities

The generic value-adding activities of an organisation could be categorised using the value chain. These activities are mainly classified as primary activities and support activities.

The goal of the primary activities is to create value that exceeds the cost of providing the product or service, therefore generating a profit margin.

a) **Inbound logistics** primarily include the receiving, warehousing, and inventory control of input materials.

b) **Operations** are the value-creating activities that transform inputs into the final product. Examples include manufacturing and assembly.

c) **Outbound logistics** are the activities required to get the finished product to the customer, including warehousing, order fulfilment, etc.

d) **Marketing & sales** involve those activities associated with getting buyers to purchase the product, including channel selection, advertising, pricing, etc.

e) **Service activities** are those that maintain and enhance the product's value, including customer support, repair services, etc.

The primary activity or activities can be essential in developing a competitive advantage for an organisation.

> **Example**
> Logistics activities are critical for a provider of distribution services, and service activities may be the key focus for a firm offering on-site maintenance contracts for office equipment.

The primary activities mentioned above are generic in nature and each generic activity includes specific activities that vary by industry.

2. Support Activities

The primary value chain activities described above are facilitated by support activities. Porter identifies four generic categories of support activities, and they are as follows:

a) **Procurement:** the function of purchasing the raw materials and other inputs used in value-creating activities.

b) **Technological development:** includes research and development, process automation, and other technological developments used to support the value-chain activities. It includes the activities related to Information Systems.

c) **Human resource management:** the activities associated with the recruiting, development, and compensation of employees.

d) **Firm infrastructure:** includes activities such as finance, legal and quality management as well as the general administrative activities of the firm.

Support activities are often considered overhead activities, but some firms have successfully used them to develop a competitive advantage. An example of this would include developing a cost advantage through the innovative management of information systems.

An organisation's value chain links to the value chains of its upstream suppliers and downstream buyers. This results in a larger stream of activities known as the "**value system**". The development of a competitive advantage depends not only on the value chain of an organisation, but also on the value system which the organisation is a part of. The value chain concept is also discussed in learning outcome C of Study Guide A4.

3. Value networks

The value network includes the organisations, groups, and individuals that are involved in the development, marketing, and use of a particular type of technology. The value network is derived from the value chain concept. Value networks can be thought of as a set of relatively autonomous units that can be managed independently but operate in a framework of common principles. The value network concept is also discussed in learning outcome D of Study Guide A4.

A value network can also be considered a web of relationships that generates economic or social value by exchanging tangible and intangible benefits in an organisation. Value networks consist of complementary nodes and links. A service delivered over the value network requires the use of two or more network components. By understanding an organisation's relationships with other network members, the following can be ascertained:

a) Where does value lie in the network?

b) How do the activities of the organisation affect the network?

c) How are the other members of the network likely to respond?

SUMMARY

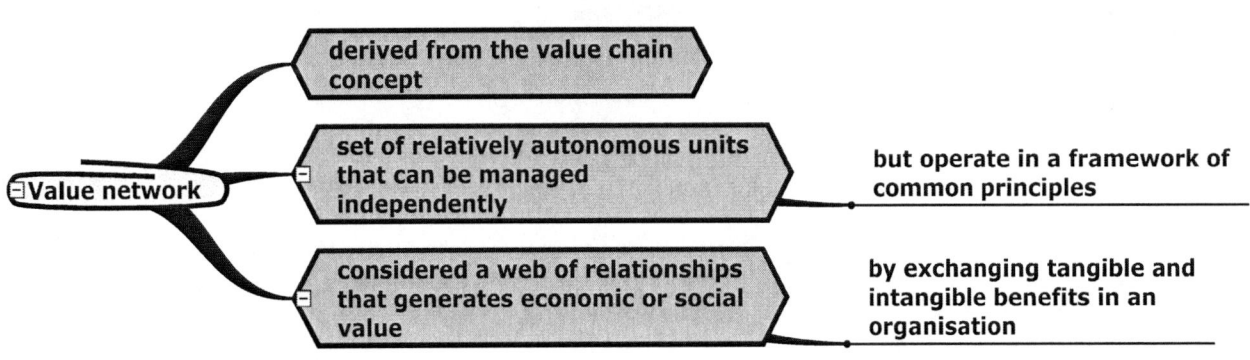

Test Yourself 2

Value chain activities are related to each other. Rather, one value chain activity often affects the cost or performance of the others. Linkages could exist between primary activities and also between primary and support activities.

"An organisation's value chain is part of a larger system that includes the value chains of upstream suppliers and downstream channels and customers. It is the whole value system that competes with other value systems and not simply the firms. The organisation's success in developing and sustaining a competitive advantage depends not only on its own value chain, but also on its ability to manage the value system which it is part of."

Required:

A Explain, with an example, how one value chain activity can affect the cost or performance of other value chain activities.

B "A firm's success depends not only on its own value chain, but on its ability to manage the value system which it is a part of." Justify this statement.

> 3. **Assess the potential application of information technology to support and restructure the supply chain.**[3]
> **Advise on how external relationships with suppliers and distributors can be structured to deliver a restructured supply chain.**[3]
>
> [Learning Outcomes c and d]

3.1. Supply chain restructuring

Supply chain restructuring is a broader concept than changes in the supply chain function. It includes vendor managed inventories or employing electronic reverse auctions. Supply chain restructuring results in fundamental alterations in the supply chain activities of an organisation and affects all functions and activities. Restructuring of the supply chain needs to be viewed as a process of fundamental rejuvenation throughout the organisation and requires an understanding of:

- the reasons and constraints for change
- the paradigm shift required (this includes changing product lines, implementing e-business, increasing the operating hours to 24/7)
- the process of implementation
- the problems that require solutions

1. The Internet

Using the Internet in supply chain management improves communication and collaboration between businesses along the supply chain. Using the Internet has a number of benefits, which include:

a) **cost reduction** by eliminating paper transactions, purchases orders, invoices, consignment notes, and speeding up response times

b) **reduction of errors** in the information passed along the supply chain by avoiding hand-written or faxed documents

c) **improving the satisfaction** of customers or suppliers by 'real time' delivery of information (i.e. the point at which a product is moved)

d) **achieving real cost savings** by the integration of dispatch and distribution data with product development data at each node of the supply chain

2. Technology and the value chain

Since technology is used to some degree in every value-creating activity, changes in technology can increase competitive advantage by making marginal changes to the activities themselves or by constructing possible new configurations of the value chain.

The following technologies are used in both primary value activities and support activities:

a) **Inbound logistics technologies**
- material handling
- transportation
- communications
- material storage
- testing
- information systems

b) **Operations technologies**
- machine tools
- material handling
- process
- packaging
- materials
- maintenance
- testing
- building design & operation
- information systems

c) **Outbound logistics technologies**
   - transportation
   - packaging
   - communications
   - material handling
   - information systems

d) **Marketing & sales technologies**
   - media
   - communications
   - audio/video
   - information systems

e) **Service technologies**
   - communications
   - Internet and broadband
   - mobile technologies
   - convergence systems
   - testing
   - Information Systems

It is important to note that many of these technologies are used across the value chain. For example, information systems are present in every activity. Similar technologies are also used in support activities. In addition, technologies related to training, computer-aided design, and software development are also employed in support activities. Technologies enable an organisation to gain a competitive advantage to the extent that they make an impact on cost drivers.

SUMMARY

3.2. Impact of e-commerce on supply chain management

E-commerce impacts supply chain management in a variety of ways. These include:

1. Cost efficiency

E-commerce enables shippers, freight forwarders, etc., to streamline document handling without the costly and time-consuming formalities required by traditional document delivery systems. By using e-commerce, companies can:

- reduce costs
- improve data accuracy
- streamline business processes
- accelerate business cycles
- enhance customer service

2. Changes in the distribution system

E-commerce provides organisations greater flexibility in managing the highly complex movement of products and information between businesses, their suppliers and customers. It eliminates the link between consumers and distribution centres.

3. **Customer orientation:** using the Internet for e-commerce allows customers to:

- access price information
- place delivery orders
- track shipments
- pay freight bills

E-commerce makes it easier for customers to do business with organisations. Organisations can make their websites a place where customers can not only get detailed information about the services the company offers, but also where they can actually conduct business with the company, thereby providing a universal self-service system for customers.

4. **Shipment tracking**

E-commerce allows users to obtain real-time information about cargo shipments. They may also:

- create and submit bills of lading
- place a cargo order
- submit a freight claim
- carry out several other functions

5. **Shipping documentation and online shipping enquiry**

The need for manual intervention is reduced, as standard bills of lading and shipping labels can be used.

Online shipping enquiry gives instant shipping information access to anyone in the company, from any location.

SUMMARY

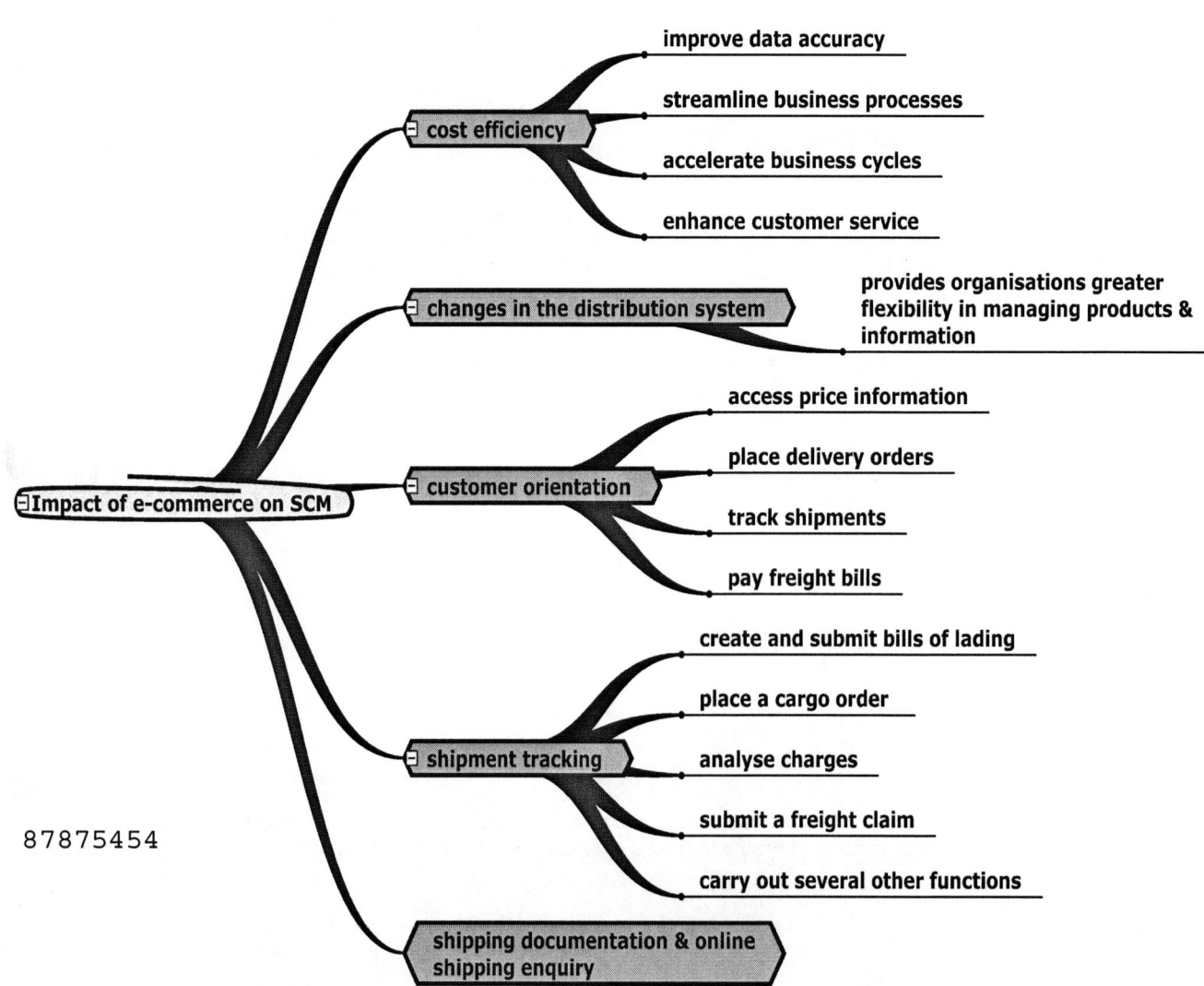

3.3. Supply chain relationships

A supply chain can be viewed as a set of relationships amongst suppliers, manufacturers and distributors, which facilitates the transformation of raw materials into finished goods. Therefore, such relationships are important in determining the effectiveness of an organisation's supply chain. These can be determined by a number of factors such as:

- industry structure
- competitive rivalries
- number of buyers and suppliers
- nature of products and services
- organisational cultures

Different supply chain strategies require an organisation to have different types of relationships with its suppliers and distributors. The principles of supply chain advocate the involvement of all the players in the supply chain. The following are the types of relationships and their impact on the supply chain of an organisation:

1. **Collaborative relationships:** these require the sharing of demand and supply information in order to reduce the excess inventory requirement. Several core suppliers have access to the buyer's data, which enables them to plan and co-ordinate resources for efficient and effective supplies. A company could also collaborate with a strategic supplier for its raw material requirements.

2. **Co-operative relationships:** these relationships enhance the competitive positions of both the manufacturer and the supplier, resulting in benefits for both partners. Such relationships are based on trust, information sharing, shared goals, culture and understanding.

3. **Power based relationships:** certain large organisations (due to their volume of business) are in a position to use market power amongst trading partners in order to get a good price and preferential treatment.

Example

A large automobile company can use its market strength when negotiating with its suppliers for getting good prices and other benefits, such as flexibility in getting good production and delivery lead times.

4. **Arm's length relationships:** these relationships are also known as win-lose relationships and they often involve conflict negotiating techniques. In such relationships, the price is the key negotiating point and there is no sharing of information amongst the partners. Production is based entirely on orders and tenders.

SUMMARY

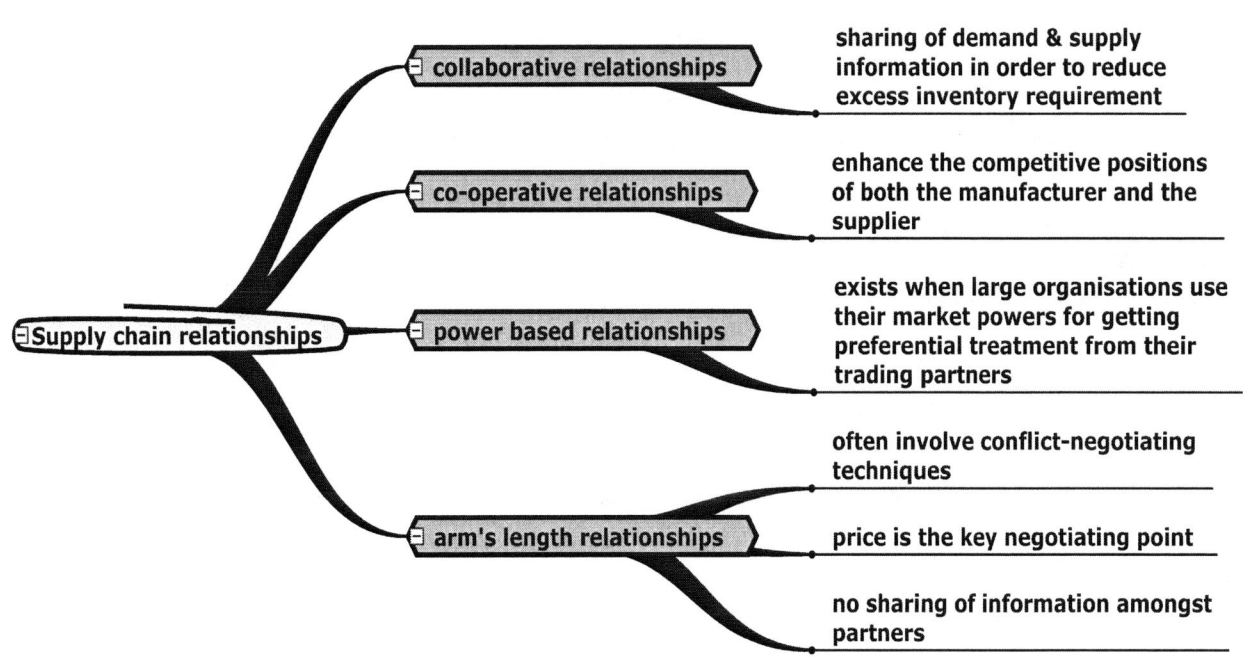

3.4. Effective relationships

For an organisation to establish the right kind of relationships with its suppliers, it is essential to first ascertain what the organisation needs from its suppliers. Examining the interaction variables gives insight into buyer-supplier relationships. Such relationships are influenced by several organisational factors such as technology, strategy and structures, and also by individual factors such as experience and objectives.

All relationships in this context should be based on commercial needs and will inevitably revolve around the needs of the different parties at a particular point of time.

Example

If the buying organisation is an MNC and the supplier is a small firm, it means that there are several alternative suppliers that are willing to meet the demands of the large organisation. This also means that the supplier is at an obvious disadvantage and might compromise on pricing in order to get the order from the MNC.

Traditional supplier relationships could be considered buyer-seller relationships which are typically observed in commodity markets. These relationships are characterised by a single one-to-one relationship between two organisations. In such relationships, neither the buyer, nor the supplier works together for eliminating the redundant costs in the supply chain.

In more complex buyer-seller relationships, several people in either company are in contact with each other. These relationships are characterised by relationship marketing and supply chain relationships. The concept of relationship marketing has been discussed in learning outcome 1 of Study Guide E4.

Test Yourself 3

Emmex Ltd is in the business of distributing tools and spare parts to small scale industries. The company has recently expanded its product range to over 10,000 items and it supplies electronic and computer components to several organisations. The range of components includes small fuses and computer chips for complicated electrical assemblies which require specialist knowledge for installation.

The organisation is sensitive to the specific requests of its customers and prides itself on the personal and friendly service provided by its staff. Recent customer surveys show that a significant amount of repeated business is generated by good customer care, even though the prices charged by Emmex Ltd are higher than those charged by its competitors.

The organisation is planning to introduce its first website. A review of competitors' sites has revealed that the information they provide is a little more than an electronic catalogue. Regular visits to competitors' website show the same home page, whilst most of the information provided on web pages appears to be out-of-date.

Emmex Ltd currently supplies a catalogue every three months in a paper format.

Required:

A   Explain the advantages and disadvantages of Emmex Ltd providing information through a website rather than in a paper-based catalogue.

B   Explain the information that Essex Ltd could provide on its website in order to help its customers install and use its products.

> **4. Discuss the methods, benefits and risks of e-procurement.[2]**
> **Assess different options and models for implementing e-procurement.[2]**
> **[Learning Outcomes e and f]**

Procurement is the process through which organisations purchase goods and services from various suppliers. It includes everything from indirect goods like uniforms, toilet paper, stationery and office supplies, to the raw materials used for manufacturing products. Procurement also involves the purchase of temporary labour, energy, etc. Procurement policies could play an essential role in reducing costs for an organisation. Historically, the procurement manager of an organisation placed orders via telephone, fax, or post.

E-procurement (also known as Internet-based procurement), is a technology solution that facilitates buying over the Internet. E-procurement radically streamlines the procurement process through the use of on-line catalogues that allow users to select items or services that they need with an approval process, using internal e-mail systems.

Diagram 5: E-procurement process

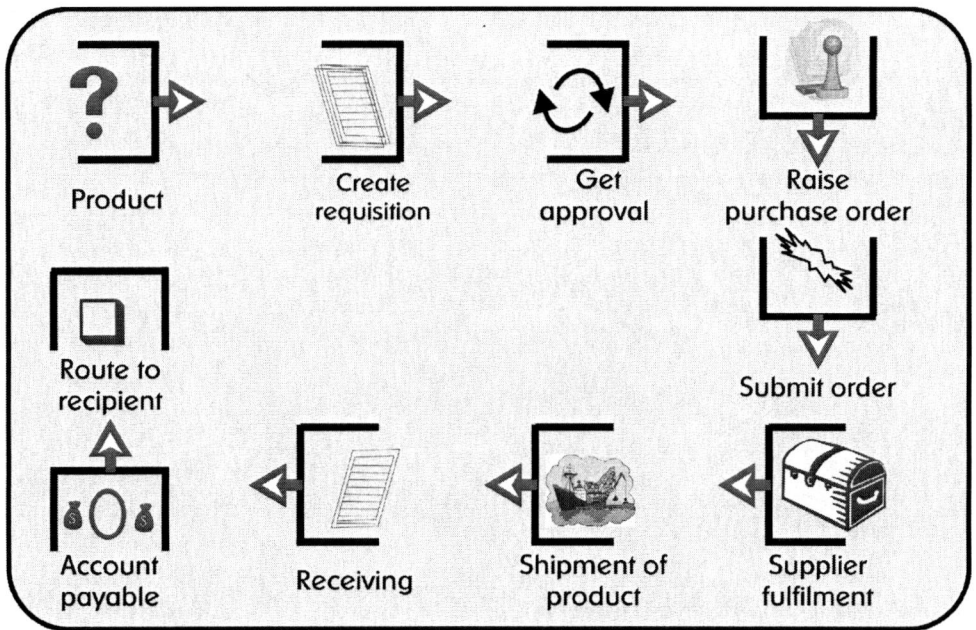

4.1. E-procurement methods

E-procurement solutions / models fall into one of three categories:

- solutions hosted by the buying organisation
- solutions hosted by the selling organisations
- third-party service that brings buyers and sellers together

E-procurement methods allow the procurement process to be carried out in a more efficient manner, and with fewer errors. These **methods** include:

1. Electronic Data Interchange (EDI)

EDI refers to the electronic exchange of business information in the form of purchase orders, invoices, bills of lading, inventory data, and other information between organisations or trading partners in standardised formats. EDI is also used within individual organisations for transferring data between different divisions or departments, such as finance, purchasing, and shipping. EDI is more concerned with the way information is communicated during procurement than with linking buyers and suppliers. It differs from other ways of exchanging information in two ways:

a) EDI only involves B2B transactions. This means that individual consumers do not directly use EDI to purchase goods or services.
b) EDI is associated with transactions between computers or databases and not individuals. Therefore, individuals sending e-mail messages or sharing files over a network do not constitute EDI.

2. Online marketplaces (or e-marketplaces)

Online marketplaces bring buyers and sellers together in an online environment and act as intermediaries between the two parties. In addition to connecting buyers and sellers, online marketplace providers add value to the procurement process by offering various services, which range from inventory management and process improvement to tracking shipments and arranging for funds. Apart from adding value, online marketplaces simplify the process of procurement. For example, allowing suppliers to choose the manner in which they receive orders from purchasers, such as XML, fax, e-mail, or EDI.

3. Online auctions

These are used by companies to procure goods and services for both contract and spot buys. Factors which are critical to the success of online auctions include the kind of bidders involved, the number of bidders, and the length of the bidding periods.

4. Software applications

These allow the procurement personnel to establish systems for managing invoices, purchase orders, receipts, etc. These applications also enable companies to place orders for products from many different suppliers through a single interface.

Different companies use different blends of traditional and electronic procurement methods and these blends vary from industry to industry.

Example

A company could develop software to automate its procurement systems and customise it to manage its routine purchasing functions such as generating purchase orders and receipts.

SUMMARY

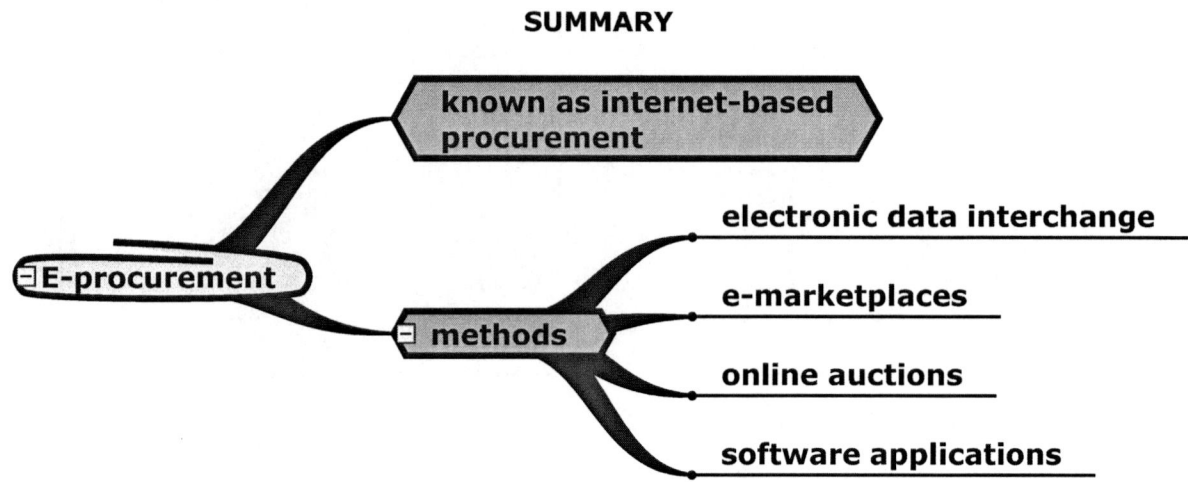

4.2. Benefits of e-procurement

Using **e-procurement** systems offers several advantages when compared to systems involving paper-based forms or oral communication. The main benefits are increased efficiency and cost savings. For example, business transactions can be conducted in less time and with fewer errors than the traditional, paper-based methods. This reduces the amount of inventory that companies must invest in by closely linking manufacturing to actual demand, allowing for 'just-in-time' delivery. It also reduces postage costs and the expenses and space considerations surrounding paper-based record storage.

The other benefits of e-procurement can be summarised as follows:

1. E-procurement enables a company to consolidate orders for similar items with one supplier which results in deeper volume discounts and cost savings.
2. E-procurement allows a company to simplify its purchasing process by reducing the number of variables (available products) involved. Instead of having to sort through large volumes of paper or electronic catalogues, procurement managers can build custom catalogues that include only the items the company is interested in.
3. Improves manufacturing cycles, reduces the overheads of purchase agents and allows effective control over inventory.
4. Enables a higher amount of budgetary control which can be achieved through limited spending and improved reporting facilities.
5. Eliminates administrative errors
6. Empowers the line staff
7. Improves information management.
8. Enables strategic purchasing by buyers.

4.3. Risks of e-procurement

As with every developing technology, e-procurement introduces certain risks which are as follows:

1. There is a lack of experience and skills, particularly in procurement and IT. The reasons for this are numerous.
2. Potential conflicts with other priorities, or a change of policy and direction distort the procurement process.

3. Sharing resources can often result in problems, particularly if multiple parties demand the same materials at the same time.
4. Involvement of people is another area for concern. E-Procurement might be important to a few people in an organisation, but for some people (particularly those in operational / service departments), it is a drain on time.
5. If expectations are not met and things go wrong, people become disillusioned and sometimes this can lead to a withdrawal of resources.
6. If the eventual users do not like the e-procurement system or are unable to use it, they may be able to use spreadsheets and paper systems to do the job. They may, therefore, be reluctant to use the system.
7. An e-procurement system could be quite expensive and could result in the destabilisation of the working system. It might not work for all types of products.

4.4. E-procurement model

Three basic e-procurement **models** have evolved over a period of time. These can be broadly described as buyer-centric, seller-centric and e-marketplace models. These electronic procurement **models** are based on a 'hub and spokes' approach (the hub being the organisation at the centre of the system, while the spokes are the buyers and/or suppliers who interact with the system).

1. Buyer-centric e-procurement model

In a buyer-centric e-procurement model, the buying organisation:
- implements software in order to support its procurement processes
- obtains catalogue data from its suppliers
- aggregates the catalogue data into a single internal catalogue for the use of its procurement officers

In terms of a 'hub and spokes' model, the buyer is the hub, with suppliers connected to the buyer as spokes.

Benefits

- The primary benefit to the buying organisation is that tight control can be maintained over the procurement software, catalogue data and processes.
- Solutions can be highly customised in order to meet the buyer's needs.
- This provides buyers with access to the offerings of several suppliers and can usually make price comparisons.

2. Seller-centric e-procurement model

In a seller-centric procurement model, the seller is at the hub of the model, with the buyers connected to the buyer as spokes. Buyers have access to the supplier's system for browsing the supplier's catalogue and placing orders. An example of such a model is business-to-consumer (B2C) selling, although increasingly, B2B trading is also occurring on these sites.

Benefits

- For the buyer, these models generally offer the lowest investment cost.
- For suppliers these solutions may be optimal in terms of control, cost, maintenance and functionality. However, customers should know where to locate suppliers, otherwise their use may be limited.

3. E-marketplace (or third party-managed) e-procurement model

In this model, a system provided by a third party is at the hub, with the buyers and sellers trading with each other through the common marketplace. The marketplace hosts supplier catalogues, and provides electronic transactional capabilities of different sophistication levels to the buyers and suppliers.

Benefits

- E-marketplaces enable extended trading and are particularly useful for both the buyers and the sellers.
- These models are usually least expensive from the perspectives of both the buyers and the sellers.

4. Developing an open trading environment

All the three **models** discussed above have certain limitations, mainly because they generally involve closed communities. These models are based on one hub that establishes the trading rules for the system, and this limits the flexibility of the other participants. However, these limitations could be overcome in an open trading environment that allows the buyers and sellers to establish systems that are flexible enough to meet their requirements.

Under an open trading model, buyers use software that allows them to create and maintain local internal catalogues according to their requirements. In addition, it also provides access to e-marketplaces and the supplier's stand-alone catalogues. Suppliers have the liberty to choose whether to host their own catalogues or to use such marketplaces. Open trading models benefit buyers by offering them flexibility in accessing supplier catalogues in addition to benefiting the suppliers, who can showcase their catalogues to a wide range of participants.

SUMMARY

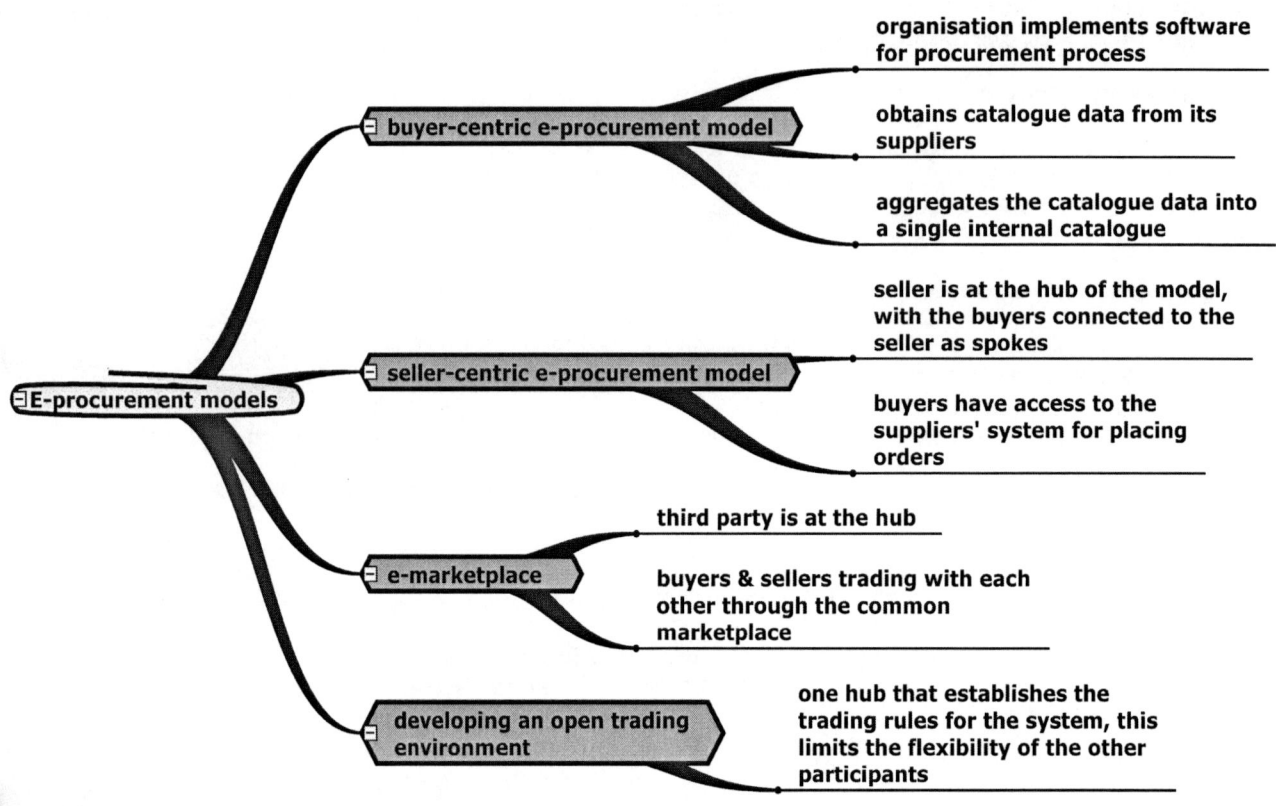

Test Yourself 4

Readers Tonic is a publishing company which provides all kinds of publication services. It includes book publishing, a monthly magazine, translation, editing, DTP, printing and all other publications-related services.

The company is currently following traditional methods of procurement.

In order to leverage the advantages of the Internet and electronic business, Readers Tonic plans to implement an e-procurement system for the organisation.

Required:

A   What are the possible benefits that the company could reap by implementing an e-procurement system? Explain the impact of this on the relationship between the company and its suppliers.

B   State the challenges that Readers Tonic could face while delivering its services through e-procurement.

Answers to Test Yourself

Answer to TY 1

A   From the present scenario, it is clear that the company is using a push strategy which is basically a product-driven model of a supply chain.

Generally, the traditional push model helps organisations to set their objectives of minimising costs and focusing on efficiencies which overlook certain key factors, such as uncertainty in demands, and customer service and retention. The traditional push model lacks innovation.

The pull strategy model, which is driven by e-commerce capabilities, empowers the client with innovative options. By adopting the pull strategy, Hugestorage could reap the following benefits:

- **High levels of customer service:** this relates to a constant web presence.
- **Responsiveness**: the pull model has the flexibility to meet uncertain customer demands
- **Shorter lead time:** this results in the timely delivery of the product
- **Pricing strategy:** in the case of pull models, pricing does not normally impact short-term demand, whereas in push models pricing is a key factor in balancing the supply and demand
- **Manufacturing strategy:** short and flexible production runs can help to reducing costs.
- **Inventory:** the inventory required is typically low in comparison with push models and is therefore advantageous from the point of view of cost
- **Easy and customer driven:** consumers can use electronic connections to pull their requirements from the system

B Push business models incorporate many positive features in order to gain some of the advantages that apply to demand pull models and also to manage the uncertainties of customer demand. These include:

i. eliminating non-value adding processes in order to reduce the lead-times within various process
ii. implementing collaborative planning with suppliers to gain more certainty about customer demand
iii. Hugestorage needs to identify the business segments for which demand pull can be created and segments for which it cannot; then, the company needs to separate supply chain channels and different business units to manage demand
iv. blending a few production processes and applying the principles of postponement

The demand pull supply chains reduce waste and inventory and are more prone to meeting the needs of the end customers. However, certain supply chain participants will almost certainly feel the burden of maintaining inventory, particularly if remotely located from end customers. Therefore, the company should strive to create best practice business models appropriate to its business conditions, including a model with managed elements of push and pull strategies.

Answer to TY 2

A Consider a case in which the design of a product is changed in order to reduce manufacturing costs. In case the new product design results in increased service costs; the cost reduction could be less than anticipated. There could be a net cost increase.

However, sometimes an organisation can reduce cost in one activity and consequently enjoy a cost reduction in another activity, such as when a change in design simultaneously reduces manufacturing costs and improves reliability, resulting in the reduction of service costs. Through such improvements, the organisation can develop a competitive advantage.

Tangible interrelationships provide direct opportunities for creating synergy among business units. This means that, if multiple business units require a particular raw material, the procurement of that material can be shared amongst different business units. This sharing of the procurement activity could reduce costs significantly.

However, achieving synergy from the interrelationships amongst different business units often does not achieve the anticipated results due to the varying needs of different organisations. The costs of coordination, reduced flexibility, and organisational practicalities should be analysed when devising a strategy bases on synergies.

B The value chain is a sequence of activities during which value is added to a new product or service as the product makes its way from invention to final distribution.

The value chain is composed of several linked stages, which can then be grouped into the following three stages:

Stage 1: research, development, design (inbound logistics)
Stage 2: production (operations)
Stage 3: marketing, sales, distribution, services (outbound logistics)

One key way to navigate the value chain is through partnerships and collaborations. Organisations that specialise in one phase of the value chain could partner with other organisations that specialise in another phase of the process.

For example, large businesses that are not very strong in innovation could partner with small or medium-sized firms that have unique innovative capabilities and intellectual talent.

Answer to TY 3

A Advantages and disadvantages of Emmex Ltd providing information on a website

Advantages

- A website is far easier to update. Changes can be made quickly to the Hyper Text Markup Language (HTML) that is used to create the site.
- It is much cheaper over the long term. Since products supplied by Emmex Ltd have many customers and a catalogue is provided four times a year, it makes economic sense to create and maintain a website. By doing this, the printing, postage and stationery costs each year can be avoided.
- A website can be more dynamic than a paper-based catalogue. For example, it can use text, pictures, graphs, cartoons, diagrams and moving images as well as sound to more fully illustrate the appeal of various products. Additional ways of attracting customers can be found by providing further information or installation instructions on receipt of an e-mail address from an enquirer or potential customer.
- The website can potentially reach millions of people, thereby increasing the awareness of both the company and its products. Again, prompts for e-mail addresses can be included in the site, so that Emmex Ltd can build up an electronic mailing list and special offers could be sent out.

Disadvantages

- Creation of a fully dynamic multi-media site requires sufficient preparation and planning. This could be time-consuming, if not done properly. It could also involve some extra security requirements, including additional equipment and software.
- Keeping the website up-to-date is another software maintenance task, i.e. it could turn out to be a chore unless it is properly documented and supported by appropriate resources. The site could lead to further developments building on the same Internet protocols and both intranet and extranet could be created. This would lead to the projects becoming more expensive than they should be.
- There is a popular misconception that once a website has been created then that is the end of the involvement. However, in reality, it is more likely just the beginning of the process, particularly with e-business just around the corner.

B Information EMMEX Ltd can provide on its website to help customers

- With over 10,000 items, electrical engineers will quite often need help with installation. If the installers have portable computers, they can either log on or download the instructions so that information is available. This will reduce training requirements, as the instructions can be provided in words and pictures, and a 'frequently asked questions' (FAQ) section can be incorporated.
- Information about product sizes, quantities, delivery and suitable applications can be provided so that the customers can view everything they need to know about the product ranges at the click of a computer mouse. The website would facilitate future linkages such as intranets and extranets, which provide additional facilities and information required for electronic trading.
- The website is a ready source of reference for specification details, industry and legal standards, etc. So instead of having to refer to several books and/or catalogues, engineers simply require one source of comprehensive information. This information could be made country-specific and could possibly attract a subscription premium because of its potential savings.

Answer to TY 4

A The possible benefits that the company could reap by implementing e-procurement are:

1. **Cost savings:** e-procurement would enable the company to consolidate orders for similar items with one supplier which would result in deeper volume discounts and cost savings.

2. **Process efficiencies:** e-procurement allows a company to simplify its purchasing process by reducing the number of available products involved.

3. **Intangible benefits:**

- allowing staff to concentrate on their primary functions
- enabling a higher amount of budgetary control which can be achieved through limited spending and improved reporting facilities
- eliminating administrative errors
- improving information management
- meeting prompt payment targets and achieving financial transparency and accountability

Readers Tonic's relations with its suppliers would improve in the following aspects if Readers Tonic adopts an e-procurement system:

- order processing would be easy and streamlined
- numerous benefits from Internet and electronic business, especially through prompt and timely deliveries
- reduced supply chain costs
- increased profitability
- faster process improvements

B The challenges that Readers Tonic has to face while delivering benefits from e-procurement are:

- implementing good procurement practice in order to maximise the benefits of e-procurement & reduce costs
- identifying opportunities for delivering the expected benefits; this requires time to be invested
- achieving process efficiencies is critically dependent upon automation
- delivering the benefits of e-procurement could involve a combination of different models e.g. e-marketplace models for ordering goods and procurement cards for payment
- successful implementation of e-procurement would depend upon updating current practices towards best practice adoption

Quick Quiz

1. What do you mean by a value network?
2. List out characteristics of **Pull Strategy.**
3. Which are the major types of supply chain relationships?
4. What do you mean by the term e-procurement?
5. List some of the benefits of **Buyer-centric e-procurement model.**

Answers to Quick Quiz

1. A value network can also be considered a web of relationships that generates economic or social value by exchanging tangible and intangible benefits in an organisation.

2. Following are the characteristics of pull model:

- objective is to maximise service levels and focus on innovation
- main business driver of these models is high customer service levels and flexibility to meet uncertain customer demand
- simple as compared to the push models because the consumers can use electronic connections to pull their requirements from the system
- demand is highly uncertain since these models are based on actual demand
- pull models are consumer-driven

3. The major types of supply chain relationships are:

- Collaborative relationships
- Co-operative relationships
- Power based relationships
- Arm's length relationships

4. E-procurement (also known as Internet-based procurement), is a technology solution that facilitates buying over the Internet.

5. Following are the **benefits of the buyer-centric e-procurement model:**

   ➢ The primary benefit to the buying organisation is that tight control can be maintained over the procurement software, catalogue data and processes.

   ➢ Solutions can be highly customised in order to meet the buyer's needs.

   ➢ It provides buyers with access to the offerings of several suppliers and can usually make price comparisons.

Self Examination Questions

Question 1

Rockine Ltd is a trading company based in the USA. It is in the business of importing cables and selling them after re-branding and re-packaging them as Rockine products. It procures the cables from Cords LLC, based in the UAE, and regularly transacts with Cords LLC through the Internet. On confirmation of the payment, Cords LLC sends an email confirmation of the order to the company. Cords LLC currently manages all shipping-related activities. The products are trans-shipped to MPX logistics, which then delivers the products to Rockine's factory. Once the goods reach Rockine Ltd, they are tested for quality. After that, the cables that pass the tests are re-branded as Rockine cables (by adding appropriate logos) and packed in specially fabricated Rockine boxes, after which these products are ready for sale. The products that fail the inspection tests are returned to Cords LLC.

Presently, 40% of Rockine's total sales are made in the local markets. A vast majority of the company's local customers physically collect their products from the company. Rockine currently advertises its products in local and regional newspapers. Rockine also has a website which provides product details on all its different types of cables. Interested customers can enquire about the availability of products through the e-mail facility on the website. Currently, customers cannot pay for Rockine's products through the website.

Rockine Ltd now plans to increase its domestic and international market share. For this purpose, it needs to increase its imports. It plans to increase its turnover from $1m per annum to $10m per annum over the next three years. Mark Stevens, the CEO of Rockine, believes that the company needs to change its business model if it plans to achieve this growth. He believes that these changes will also have to tackle problems associated with shipments and unpredictable deliveries.

Mark recognises that for achieving growth, the company will have to focus on exports. At the same time, he does not intend to build or invest in assembly plants overseas or to commit to a long-term contract with one supplier.

Required:

(a) Explain the primary activities of Rockine Ltd based on the value chain.

(b) Explain how the company could re-structure its upstream supply chain in order to achieve its targeted growth.

Question 2

The key aspects of executing a supply chain strategy are knowledgeable people, accurate data and analytical tools. Explain the practical methodology of restructuring the supply chain using these aspects.

Answers to Self Examination Questions

Answer to SEQ 1

(a) A simple value chain of the primary activities of Rockine is shown below.

➢ **Inbound logistics:** this requires excellent quality assurance which is essential where customers have high expectations of reliability. In addition to contributing to customer satisfaction, high quality also reduces service costs.

➢ **Operations:** this is a relatively small component in the Rockine value chain and actually adds little value to its customers. Rockine could consider modifying its repackaging arrangement.

- **Outbound logistics:** these are activities required to move the finished product to the customer, including warehousing, order fulfilment. Rockine will have to re-consider this in case it plans to increase its supplies outside its geographical region. The company will also need to maintain the quality of the products during shipment.

- **Marketing and sales:** This should be developed if the company wants to achieve the desired growth. Presently, very little value is offered by the company to its customers.

- **Service:** these maintain and enhance the product's value, including customer support, repair services, etc.

(b) Rockine's website has limited functionality. When it places the order, it is not aware of the expected delivery date until it receives the confirmation email from Cords LLC. It is also unable to track the status of its order until it receives a despatch email from Cords LLC. Since Rockine is not the owner of the shipment, it is unable to track the delivery and therefore, it cannot ascertain the physical arrival of goods. The company does not wish to build or invest in assembly plants in other countries. However, it could possibly consider the following changes to its upstream supply chain:

- Identification of a wider range of suppliers and trade through other sell-side websites. However, there are costs associated with this. Suppliers need to be identified and evaluated and financial and trading arrangements would have to be established. Nevertheless, it eliminates the risk of single-sourcing and other suppliers could possibly have better systems in place for supporting order and delivery tracking.

- Consider negotiating long-term contracts with suppliers (including Cords LLC) thereby exploring the possibility of favourable payment terms.

- Identification of suppliers (including Cords LLC) who can provide information about the delivery dates well before procurement and who are able to provide Internet-based order tracking systems. This would enable efficient planning and supplier monitoring.

- Replacement of the shipment supplier with a contracted logistics company which would collect the goods from the supplier and transport the goods directly to Rockine. This would reduce the problems in physical shipment and enable monitoring of the progress of the order from despatch to arrival. It will also allow Rockine to plan for the arrival of goods and to schedule its re-packaging operations.

Rockine could possibly consider two other procurement models, namely, the buyer centric model and the independent marketplace model.

Buyer centric model

In this model, Rockine would use its website to invite potential suppliers to bid for contract requirements posted on the site. It would attract a much wider range of suppliers than would have been possible with Rockine searching sell-side sites for potential suppliers. If the company is unable to host such a model, it could possibly check a prototype to see if it is viable and whether it uncovers potential suppliers who have not been found in sell-side website searches.

Independent marketplace model

Using this model, Rockine could place its requirements on intermediary web sites. These are essentially B2B electronic marketplaces that allow potential customers to search products being offered by suppliers on one hand and customers to place their requirements and be contacted by potential suppliers on the other hand. Such marketplaces result in a wide choice of suppliers with reduced costs. The independent marketplace model could prove to be a useful approach for Rockine.

Answer to SEQ 2

1. **Identify and select the project team participants:** the project leader should have a great deal of experience in how supply chains operate, and in the linkage of business processes to finance, sales and IT.

2. **Document the service requirements:** the primary reason for the existence of a supply chain is to support a business plan. The business plan should identify market segments and their respective customer service requirements.

3. **Identify internal sources of information:** this includes quantifying cost elements such as inbound and outbound transportation costs, inventory carrying costs, operating costs of distribution and marketing costs.

4. **Collect information:** after identification of the sources of information, the next crucial step is to gather the information.

5. **Identify potential opportunities for improvement:** the next task should be conduct a brainstorming session, and then the project manager should identify and summarise specific actions.

6. **Conduct detailed analysis:** this step is aims to quantify the costs and service impact of the actions summarised in the previous step.

7. **Summarise preliminary results:** this step is aims to achieve a consensus around the short listed alternatives that carry meaningful business benefits. All other alternatives should be scrapped.

8. **Develop a framework of business risk:** this step aims to develop a consistent framework that can be applied to the alternatives by the team.

SECTION E: INFORMATION TECHNOLOGY

E3

STUDY GUIDE 3: E-BUSINESS APPLICATION: DOWNSTREAM SUPPLY CHAIN MANAGEMENT

Get Through Intro

From the Get Through Intro in the last Study Guide, E2, we saw how Pizza-so-fast could utilise upstream supply chain management to help prepare Pizzas faster. Now we look at what Pizza-so-fast can do to increase the no of pizzas sold and ensure the customer gets her pizza as soon as possible.

E-marketing could be used – if someone is surfing the net and is looking for pizza delivery companies, Pizza-so-fast could arrange to advertise to come up near the top in internet searches. The customer could be directed to a website where she could order her perfect pizza, e.g. choose all the toppings she wanted, the type of crust, deep pan or thin crust, and any other food/drink to accompany the pizza e.g. garlic bread and cola. Then she could pay on-line and then sit back and dream of her perfect pizza which will be with her shortly.

E-marketing could take this one stage further. The preferences of the customer could be saved and emails/suggestions could be sent to her for other combinations that she may like. For example, if she ordered a pizza with spicy pepperoni, she may enjoy a pizza with jalapeno peppers. This could be sent to her with a picture of a steaming hot pizza showing the jalapeno peppers. This may encourage her to order again.

If your mouth is now watering at the thought of having a pizza, how about studying this Study Guide and then ordering one as a treat for all your hard work?

Learning Outcomes

a) Define the scope and media of e-marketing.
b) Highlight how the media of e-marketing can be used when developing an effective e-marketing plan.
c) Explore the characteristics of the media of e-marketing using the '6I's of Interactivity, Intelligence, Individualisation, Integration, Industry structure and Independence of location.
d) Evaluate the effect of the media of e-marketing on the traditional marketing mix of product, promotion, price, place, people, processes and physical evidence.
e) Describe a process for establishing a pricing strategy for products and services that recognises both economic and non-economic factors.
f) Assess the importance of on-line branding in e-marketing and compare it with traditional branding.

Introduction

Case Study

Who has not heard of Google - Google's main source of income is advertising revenue shown when people carry out internet searches or send emails. This is a form of e-marketing.

Google's commitment can be seen from its SEC filing:

We will do our best to provide the most relevant and useful advertising. Advertisements should not be an annoying interruption. If any element on a search result page is influenced by payment to us, we will make it clear to our users.

Google had revenues of $5.19 billion for the quarter ended March 31, 20X8. This represented an increase of 42% over the first quarter of 20X7. it was also an increase of 7% over the fourth quarter of 20X7. Google reports its revenues, consistent with GAAP, on a gross basis without deducting traffic acquisition costs, or TAC. In the first quarter of 20X8, TAC totalled $1.49 billion, or 29% of advertising revenues.

From the above case-study, it can be seen that this is a multi-billion dollar industry. If Google are making this much revenue, its clients must see a benefit to the targeted advertising they are doing through Google and equally must be making money too! The customers of Google's clients must therefore be clicking on the sites and exploring opportunities with Google's clients. This Study Guide will help explain why this is so, so you can implement this in your business too.

1. Define the scope and media of e-marketing.[2]

[Learning Outcome a]

1.1. Introduction

E-marketing is a blend of modern communication technologies and the age old marketing principles that human beings have always applied. It is a broader term than online marketing, which is limited to the use of the internet for achieving marketing objectives. The terms e-marketing, internet marketing and online marketing are frequently interchanged, and are often synonymous.

Definition

E-marketing is a kind of e-commerce that aims to achieve marketing objectives through the use of ICT such as the Internet, e-mail, interactive digital TV and mobile marketing, together with other technological approaches such as database marketing and electronic customer relationship management (CRM).

The scope of e-marketing includes the tools that enable interactions with individuals in digitally networked and interactive environments. This interaction can extend to the actual delivery of a number of digital products, such as maps, art, news, software, photographs, tickets, written materials, information, music, films etc.

As with traditional marketing, e-marketing does not affect the entire value chain but only the marketing oriented process of an organisation such as sales or advertising. Since e-marketing uses the internet, the characteristics and advantages of the internet contribute to the strengths of e-marketing.

Example

Internet features allow information and services to be accessed worldwide at any time.

1.2. The benefits of e-marketing as opposed to traditional marketing

1. Reach

The Internet enables businesses to expand their global reach. E-marketing opens up new avenues for smaller businesses to access potential consumers from all over the world. It also provides organisations with more segments to serve.

2. Scope

Internet marketing allows businesses to reach consumers in a variety of ways and enables them to offer a wider range of products and services than is possible with traditional media. This includes:

- information management
- public relations
- customer service and sales

This is expected to grow in the future, in line with the pace of technological growth.

3. Immediacy

Internet marketing is able to provide immediate impact to business dealings. With e-marketing, business dealings can be conducted at the click of a mouse.

Example
Customers can order a laptop or a mobile phone at any time, regardless of normal working hours.

4. Interactivity

Whereas traditional marketing is largely focused on communicating a brand's message, e-marketing goes one step further and facilitates conversations between businesses and their customers. With a two-way communication channel, organisations can learn from the responses of their consumers, which make organisations more dynamic and allows them to develop a new core competence.

E-marketing gives organisations of any size access to the mass market at an affordable price, and facilitates personalised marketing unlike the print media or TV advertising. The Internet can be used by companies as an integral part of the modern marketing concept. The Internet offers companies the following **marketing advantages:**

a) It can be used to support the full range of organisational functions and processes that deliver products and services to customers and other key stakeholders.

b) It is a powerful communications medium that integrates the different functional parts of an organisation.

c) It facilitates information management, which is a critical marketing support tool for strategy formulation and implementation.

5. The other benefits of e-marketing include

a) **Lower cost:** with the help of a properly planned and effectively targeted e-marketing campaign, target customers can be reached at a cost that is lower than those associated with traditional marketing methods.

b) **Personalisation:** by linking the customer database to the website, companies can greet their customers with targeted offers whenever they visit the company's website.

c) **World-wide reach:** a website can reach anyone who has internet access, in any part of the world. This allows organisations to find new markets and compete globally in return for a small investment.

d) **24-hour marketing:** through a website, customers can access product details outside office hours.

e) **One-to-one marketing and interactive campaigns:** e-marketing enables instant access to a large number of people. For example, many people communicate using mobile phones and Personal Digital Assistants (PDAs). These, coupled with personalised e-marketing features, can create effective and targeted campaigns. E-marketing also enables organisations to create interactive campaigns using music, graphics and videos. In this way, companies can send their customers information about things that interest them. This is linked to the modern day practice of convergence in which phones can serve as televisions and computers.

f) **Better client conversion rate:** through a website, customers can be converted more quickly since purchases can be made at the click of a mouse. The traditional media require people to make a phone call, post a letter or go to a shop, whereas e-marketing is conveniently available in people's homes.

SUMMARY

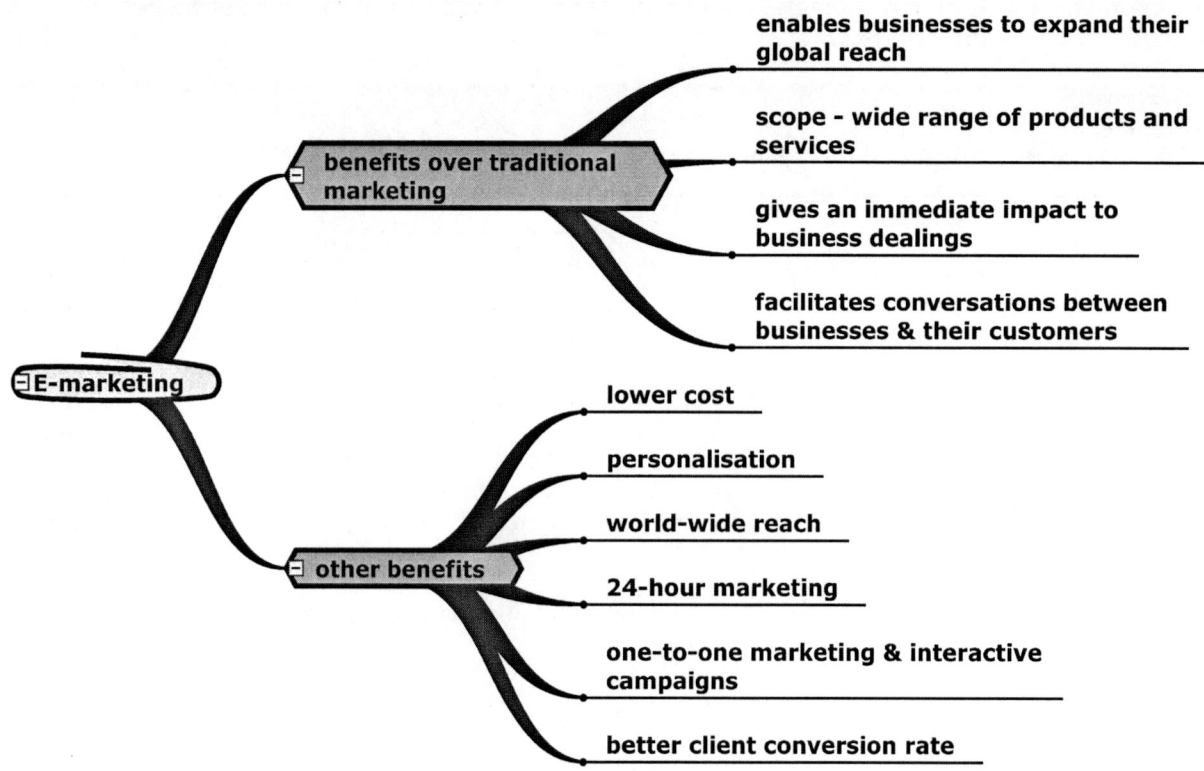

1.3 Media of e-marketing

Digital media continue to grow rapidly in importance as a means by which customers and businesses are made aware of products. **E-marketing media** include the Internet, print media, direct mail and keyword advertising.

Diagram 1: Media of e-marketing

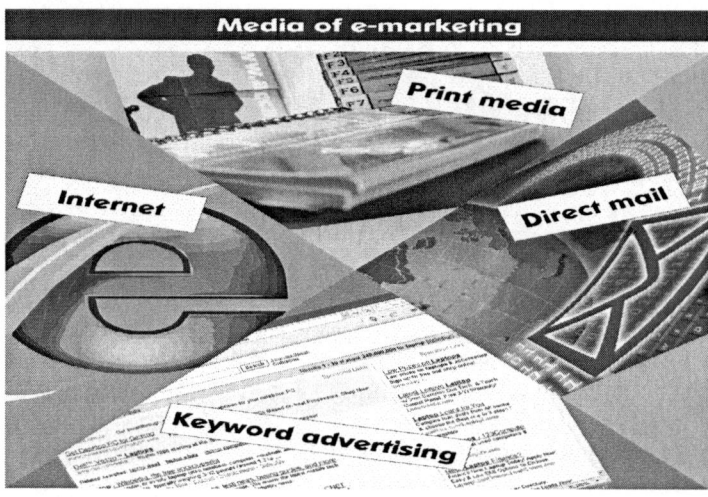

1. Internet

The Internet is the first electronic medium to allow active, self-paced viewing (similar to print media), and it is the best medium for interactivity. In fact, with the Internet, users can create their own content. Streaming audio and video technologies, together with speedy delivery channels, make the presentation of sound, music, and visual imagery easily accessible.

a) The strengths of the Internet:

- selective targeting with e-mail and Web content by using databases
- ability to track advertising effectiveness
- flexibility of message length and delivery timing
- ability to reach global markets with one advertising campaign (e.g., the Yahoo! portal), and interactive features

b) **The weaknesses of the Internet:**

➢ The Internet is unable to reach mass audiences since the Internet by its very nature is a passive medium of marketing unlike the traditional marketing media such as television and radio.
➢ The video delivery is slow due to differences in broadband penetration in different countries.
➢ Spam mail often becomes a problem as the advertiser sends emails to a large database of potential customers and the receiver receives the mail as spam.

2. Print Media

Print media include newspapers and magazines. The Internet is often compared to the print media since its content is text and graphic heavy and also since many traditional publishers of print media maintain online versions. Unlike television and radio, print media allow for active viewing.

3. Direct Mail

Direct mail offers the following benefits:

➢ allows for more selective targeting than any other mass medium
➢ is more personalised
➢ has a good message and timing flexibility
➢ is excellent for measuring effectiveness because of response tracking capability

However, direct mail suffers from junk mail and high costs for production and postage. Conversely, e-mail involves lower costs than postal mail.

4. Keyword advertising

Using this, an advertiser can pay for the word 'laptop' so that when users search using that word, the advertiser's message or banner appears on the resulting webpage. Usually keyword advertising is expensive since they deliver a more highly targeted audience.

SUMMARY

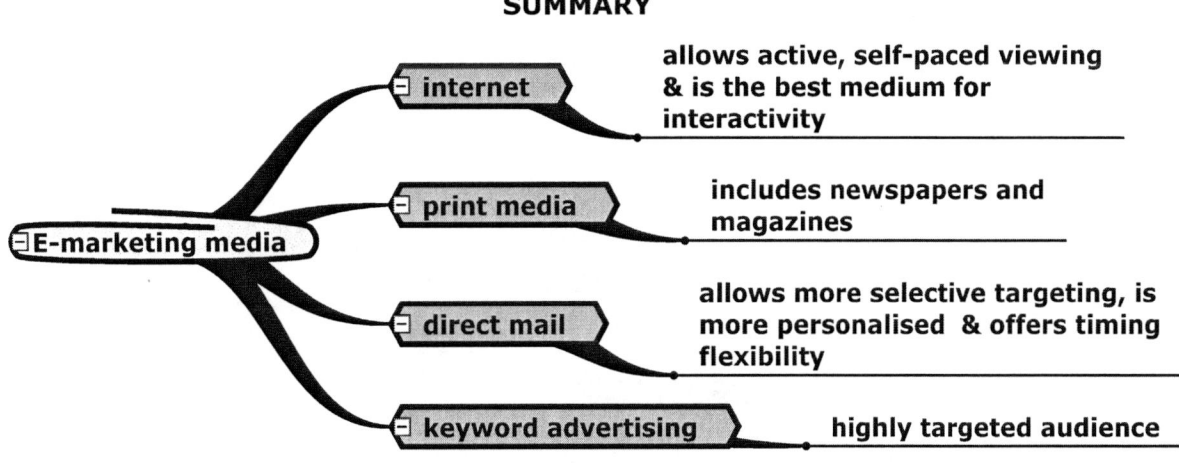

Test Yourself 1

Guide You Best is a UK based global publishing company that specialises in marketing and finance publications. The company has been in the content development business for a host of subjects in the marketing and finance domains.

The VP of publication and marketing, Colin Thompson, recently discovered that the company is gaining popularity not only in the UK but also in some Asian and African countries. Recent management reports show a sharp increase in orders from these countries.

The books published by Guide You Best are self-explanatory. The well-structured presentation of the content is one of the key attributes to the success of the company. In addition to students, many educational institutes have shown a keen interest in buying Guide You Best published books for their customised short courses.

The management of the company has welcomed this opportunity as a way of spreading its business globally and intends to come up with the best strategy to grab this opportunity.

Continued on the next page

Required:

Explain how e-marketing can help Guide You Best to spread its operations globally. Explain the role of the Internet in e-marketing.

---

2. Highlight how the media of e-marketing can be used when developing an effective e-marketing plan.[2]

[Learning Outcome b]

2.1 Developing an e-marketing plan

It is important to recognise that planning for e-marketing does not mean starting from scratch. Any online e-communication should be consistent with the overall marketing goals and current marketing efforts of a business.

Managers often face a dilemma in relation to how they should create the right media mix for an integrated campaign and whether it will work in practice. Answering these questions entails:

➢ looking at the media landscape in a new way, and
➢ going beyond demographics for ascertaining how people respond to different media based on the media's characteristics

This requires careful consideration regarding the media's characteristics, costs, reach, effectiveness, etc. The Internet provides excellent opportunities to companies for bolstering their marketing-related plans. When building integrated marketing campaigns, companies should consider the following:

➢ the target customers
➢ where they are physically when they see the message
➢ the underlying objective

2.2 Steps for creating an effective e-marketing plan

Diagram 2: Steps for creating an effective e-marketing plan

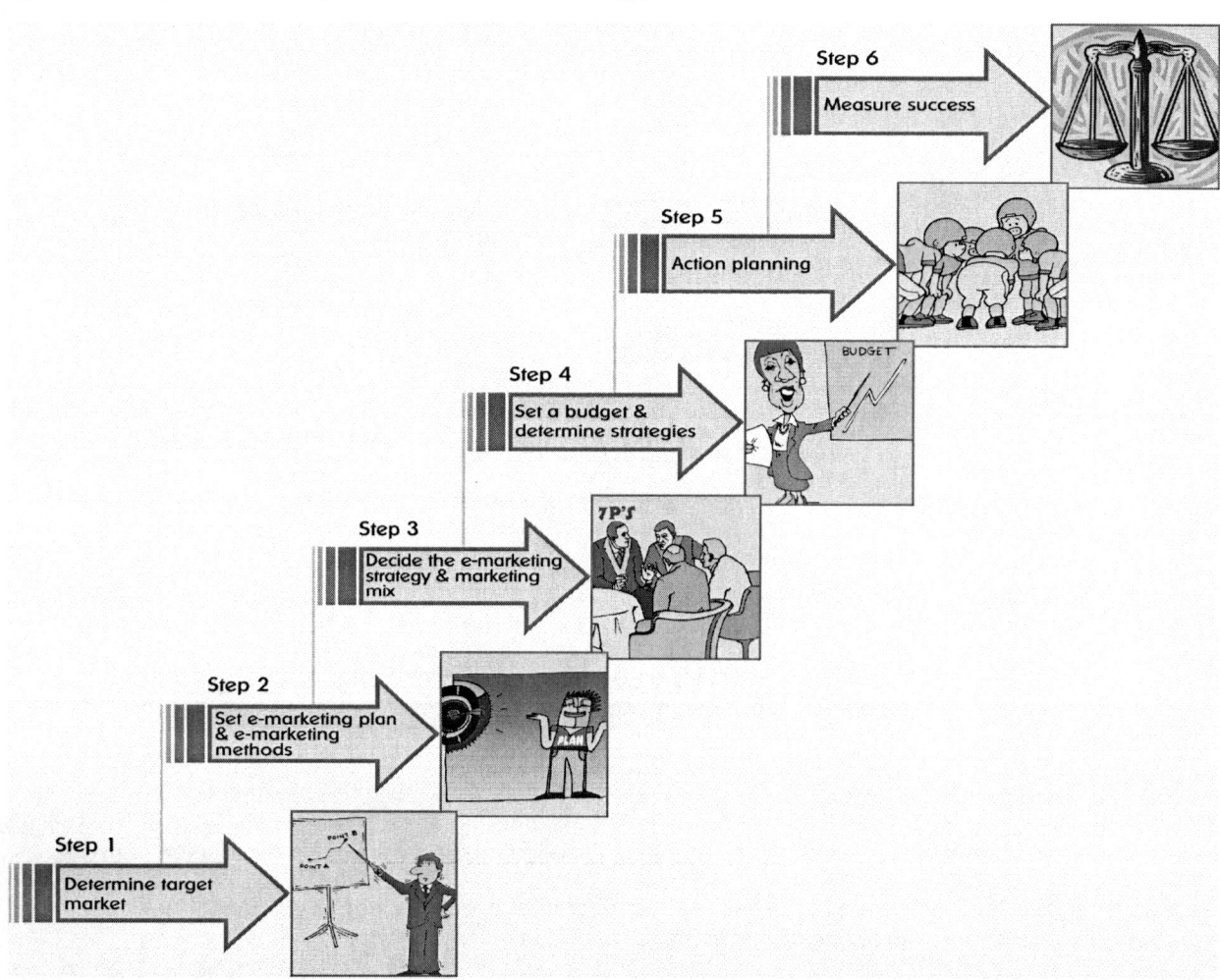

Step 1: Determine the target market

First and foremost, a company should identify its market. This involves ranking and profiling them accordingly and assigning resources to each target segment. Companies should know their customers' expectations, requirements for making an effective sales pitch, and determining its costs and expected benefits. It is equally important to study the market environment and the marketing strategies of competitors. In case multiple targets are identified, these should be ranked in order of their importance so that appropriate resources can be allocated. It is also important to study the market environment and the marketing strategies of the competitors.

Step 2: Set e-marketing plan objectives and e-marketing methods

The next step is to set the objectives for the marketing campaign. Possible objectives could include:

- increasing product or business awareness
- entering new markets
- launching a new product
- achieving higher website traffic
- focusing on sales or internal efficiency
- differentiation of services

After determining the objectives, the company should establish the e-marketing methods it intends to use for achieving its objectives. It is always advisable to use multiple e-marketing methods because the company can reap the advantages of a combination of methods.

Step 3: Decide the e-marketing strategy and marketing mix

The company should identify the strategies and techniques to be used to launch its e-marketing campaign. The company should formulate strategies that focus on capturing the attention of its target customers.

Step 4: Set a budget and determine the strategies

It is also very important to carefully budget expenses, regardless of the objective that has been set and the methods that are formulated to achieve them. Effective budgeting allows for controlling costs. The benefits should more than compensate for marketing costs.

Step 5: Action planning

The company should determine the tactics to be used for implementing the e-marketing methods. The plan should also cover other non-Internet marketing activities that need to be completed.

Step 6: Measure the success

The company should build in feedback mechanisms and regular reviews for enabling an assessment of the success of e-marketing activities.

Test Yourself 2

Leading fast food chain restaurant, Quick-meals, recently witnessed a decrease in sales due to a lack of innovative products. Quick-meals identified this fact and came up with a new range of products in both vegetarian and non-vegetarian fast food categories.

Daniel Smith, the CEO of the company, noted that the launch of products should be successful since it incorporates new and creative concepts. The marketing manager, Jim, suggested to the CEO, that the newly launched products should be marketed using the company's website, which features a creative and user-friendly interface that could make ordering fast foods very convenient. Users can book their orders online. Jim stated: "The success of the new launch depends on the popularity of the websites".

Required:

Considering the above situation, suggest a possible e-marketing plan for the new products to be launched.

> 3. Explore the characteristics of the media of e-marketing using the '6I's of Interactivity, Intelligence, Individualisation, Integration, Industry structure and Independence of location.[2]
> Evaluate the effect of the media of e-marketing on the traditional marketing mix of product, promotion, price, place, people, processes and physical evidence.[3]
>
> [Learning Outcomes c and d]

3.1. Introduction

A useful summary of the differences between new media and traditional media has been formulated by Wilson and McDonald as the '6 Is' of e-marketing. These are useful since they highlight factors that apply to the practical aspects of Internet marketing such as personalisation, direct response and marketing. By considering each of these facets of new media, marketing managers can develop plans that accommodate the characteristics of new media.

Diagram 3: '6I's

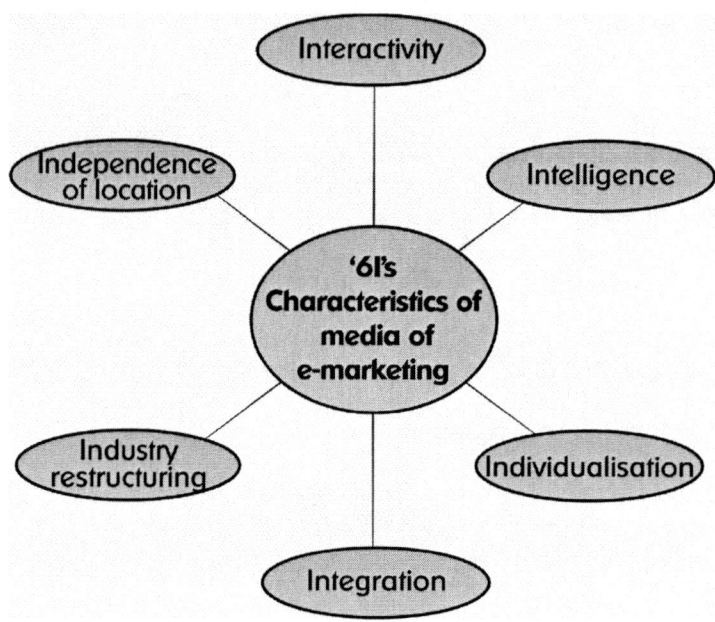

1. Interactivity

This involves ascertaining whether the interactive media allows an organisation to communicate with its customers and respond appropriately to their concerns in a continuing dialogue. Using traditional media, the marketing message can be broadcasted from a company to its customers, stakeholders, etc., and there is limited interaction between the two. However, using the Internet, the customer can initiate contact and seek information on a website.

> **Example**
>
> Certain educational institutions use their website as a means of interaction by providing incentives such as free online tests. This enables them to encourage students to respond to their relevant details and profile them according to study courses.

2. Intelligence

The Internet can be used as a cheaper means of collecting information about the client's perceptions of the goods and services supplied by an organisation. It creates a two-way feedback which does not usually occur in other media. Every time a user clicks on a link, the website records information and the analysts can ascertain the preferences of customers and study their demand patterns. However, this involves certain data protection issues.

> **Example**
>
> Architects and interior designers who purchase books on interior design from Amazon are profiled according to their profession. Amazon could send a standard e-mail to all the architects in its database to advertise its latest books on architecture.

3. Individualisation

A noteworthy feature of the interactive media is that it can be tailored to the needs of particular individuals or segments. In the case of traditional media, the same message is broadcasted to several people. Personalisation is the tailoring of interactive marketing communications to the needs of the individual and delivering the individualised content through web pages or e-mail. Personalisation enables customers who access the company's system to be profiled according to their interests, thereby enabling a display of the products that match their interests.

4. Integration

The Internet could be used as an integrated communications tool that enables its customers to respond to offers and promotions publicised in other media. It could have a direct response or a built-in call back facility.

5. Industry restructuring

While developing an e-marketing strategy, a company should consider the key concepts of disintermediation and reintermediation. Disintermediation and reintermediation have been discussed in Study Guide E2. Industry structuring essentially involves redesigning the business processes, adopting IT enabled services (ITeS) and expanding the boundaries of marketing.

6. Independence of location

The electronic media of communication gives organisations the opportunity to sell in untapped markets without a local sales or customer service department.

3.2. Introduction

Marketing mix is the set of marketing tools used by an organisation to pursue its marketing objectives for a target market. It reflects a conceptual framework which highlights the principal decisions to be taken by executives in configuring their offerings to suit the needs of their customers. The term four Ps was coined by Jerome McCarthy in the early 1960s. These four Ps, namely product, price, place, and promotion, are controllable variables which, when combined, constitute the marketing mix. However, it was argued that the four Ps were more relevant to the products than to services. Later, in 1981, the term 'seven Ps' was developed by Booms and Bitner which was also known as the service mix. They considered the additional Ps, namely people, processes and physical evidence, to be crucial in service delivery.

Diagram 4: seven Ps of marketing mix

refers to goods or services that an organisation produces or offers to its customers. It is a source of differentiation. The use of the Internet has resulted in the creation of new virtual service offerings, such as online news, real time stock quote, etc. The product management and product marketing aspects of marketing deal with how the specifications of the actual goods or services relates to the end-user's requirements and specifications.

2. Promotion

Activities such as sales promotion, advertising, personal and mass selling, constitute promotion. The successful promotion of a product requires, at the very least, that a positive message be received by the potential customers of the organisation that is conducting the promotion. Compared to traditional marketing, target groups can be defined and addressed more precisely.

Every year, an organisation usually sets an advertising budget to spend on advertisements and allocates it to the existing advertising mediums including online advertising, newspapers, magazines etc. Using the Internet for promoting products is relatively low cost and is highly effective.

3. Price

The pricing of goods and services refers to the process that determines the amount to be charged for a specific physical product or service that is acceptable to the customer and maximises profits for the company. The price is an important element in achieving marketing objectives such as customer acquisition and retention for particular target markets.

The Internet offers a new venue for considering a variety of attractive pricing strategies. Certain websites provide free services for visitors in order to create a community for which they can sell advertising space. By using a search engine technique, customers can easily compare prices of goods offered for sales on the Internet.

Example

An airline company could allow its buyers to request their own price for airline tickets, hotel reservation, cars and financing. Requests are binding if they are accepted.

4. Place

Placement involves moving the product from the manufacturer to the customer and primarily deals with outbound logistics or distribution. The product can move directly from the manufacturer to the customer or it could be channelled through intermediaries, such as wholesalers, warehouses, and retailers. E-commerce involving the sales of physical goods can be quite useful in exchanging information between businesses and delivery companies. The interface of the selling or purchasing system that is set up with delivery companies enables faster delivery of goods from warehouses and shop floors to the customer. The Internet is a new channel.

5. People

The personnel dealing with the customers can have an impact on customers' overall satisfaction. People are particularly important, whether as a part of a support function or the overall service, since they are generally inseparable from the total service in the eyes of the customer. Therefore, they should be appropriately trained, well-motivated and used in the right places.

6. Processes

Processes refer to the transactions and the internal communications that are required for running an organisation. Processes are involved in providing a service and could be crucial to overall customer satisfaction e.g. invoicing. An efficient process is a marketing advantage in itself.

7. Physical evidence

A service is intangible since it cannot be experienced before it is delivered. Therefore, it implies that potential customers perceive greater risk while deciding whether or not to use a service. In order to achieve success, it is often vital to offer potential customers the chance to see what a service would be like. This could be done by providing physical evidence, such as case studies, or testimonials.

Test Yourself 3

What do you understand by the traditional marketing mix? Explain, how the Internet media provide opportunities for changing the marketing mix to access the future e-marketing opportunities?

---

4. Describe a process for establishing a pricing strategy for products and services that recognises both economic and non-economic factors.[2]

[Learning Outcome e]

All organisations, whether new or well established, require a proper pricing strategy to be able to have a sustainable growth. Organisations thrive on revenues and the revenues are always dictated by the prices the firms charge for products and services that they sell or want to sell. Setting a price for a product or service is not a static phenomenon, but a very dynamic management function. It is a continuous process that is impacted by many economic and non-economic factors.

The strategic objectives of an organisation form the very basis of the pricing policy it may pursue. However, practically it must have an end-to-end process for developing a pricing strategy that will serve as a conduit between the strategic objectives and the ground zero level activities performed by managers.

Before discussing the process of pricing strategy development, let's revise the knowledge of various factors that can affect price. This was discussed at length in the Study Text for paper F5 Performance Management.

Factors affecting prices:

a) Objectives of the firm: e.g. profit maximisation, or revenue maximisation
b) Market conditions: monopolistic, perfect competition or imperfect competition
c) Customer preferences: quality, technology
d) Cost of manufacturing the product or service
e) Price elasticity of the product
f) Stage of the product life cycle
g) Government control: e.g. administered price
h) Product features

Process for establishing a pricing strategy

Pricing strategy is not about deciding a product specific price at a particular point in time. Basically, the pricing strategy will provide a guideline for setting prices. It is a framework of actions to be taken and factors to be considered when setting the initial price of a new product, making price adjustments during various phases of the product life cycle and generally closing transactions based on a price-discount structure. A firm may decide to adopt different strategies for the different products it manufactures. A few well established pricing strategies are pricing skimming, penetrative pricing, competition matching pricing etc.

The process of pricing is not driven by a single individual or a department in the organisation. A series of steps are needed to be performed at various levels of the organisation across the functional domains. Furthermore, the steps in the overall process should include aspects that are intrinsic to the product or service and also external to the organisation such as competition, customers, environment etc.

The process of establishing the pricing strategy would comprise the following steps:

a) **Understand the company objectives:** the pricing strategy will need to be built upon the strategic objectives of the organisation e.g. if the organisation embarks on a very high volume-driven sales strategy, itmay have to adopt a penetration pricing strategy. If the company aims at achieving a certain rate of return, the pricing strategy will concentrate on this objective.

b) **Corporate brand position:** the comparative positioning of the corporate brand will provide the basis for setting the price strategy.

c) **Consider the product or service features:** the pricing strategy will depend upon distinctive product features via-a-vis the competitors' products. A unique set of product attributes may enable the company to command a premium.

d) **Understand the stage of product life cycle:** the company must decide the pricing strategy for the product over its life cycle. The idea is to ensure that the life cycle costs are recovered and the profitability is ensured.

e) **Analyse demand for the product or service:** the total market for the product or service must be estimated and continuously examined over a longer term. Then based on the objectives, the market share expected by the firm is to be decided. The revenue and profitability will depend upon the demand the product or service generates. Practically it could be the other way round. A firm may have to simulate demand quantities for different price levels.

f) **Decide the pricing structure to be followed:** companies need to decide whether to follow a fixed price strategy or to have MRP with stage-wise discount structure. The firm may decide to adopt differential pricing for retail, institutional and wholesale customers.

g) **Evaluate ethical considerations:** companies must pursue ethical pricing policies e.g. a company manufacturing life-saving drugs should not set very high prices just because customers have no choice but to buy.

h) **Study competition:** a firm's pricing strategy will be largely governed by the competition. A new entrant in the market would want to fight the existing players whereas the existing players would set price barriers for the new entrant.

i) **Study customer needs:** if the product does not suit customer needs, it won't fetch the price the company expects. Hence, to develop the pricing strategy, assessment of whether the product features match the customer needs is essential.

j) **Study cost structure:** the pricing strategy depends upon cost structure of the organisation. A company having higher fixed costs may set the price levels high to bring down the break even point.

SUMMARY

Pricing strategy
- knowing objectives of the organisation
- position of the corporate brand
- features of the product
- product life cycle
- demand for the product
- pricing structure: fixed price / MRP based
- product price competition
- customer needs
- organisation cost structure

---

5. Assess the importance of, on-line branding in e-marketing and compare it with traditional branding.[2]

[Learning Outcome e]

5.1 Introduction to online branding

The tremendous growth of the Internet has huge implications on how people perform their tasks in newer ways. Recently, organisations have started using the Internet to build brands.

The unique nature of the Internet has induced companies to find modern ways to build their brands. Several strategies can be used for creating effective online branding.

Definitions

A brand can be defined as a name, term, sign, symbol, or design, or a combination of these, intended to identify and differentiate the goods or services supplied by an organisation from those of its competitors.

The brand is used to give consumers a sense of the value and feeling of a product in order to set it apart from other similar products. A strong brand can increase market awareness and acceptance of a product while reducing the risk of product failure. The end goal of branding is to influence customers to buy a product or service because the brand represents the value, lifestyle, image, and price that the customers seek.

The brand image and values could be communicated to consumers through:

> **its name:** can be used to portray the product's value and can facilitate the recognition of the brand

> **product packaging:** this could also be used to portray a certain image of the company or its product; the actual product itself, through its usage, creates an image of a brand

> **communicating to the customer:** communication about a product through marketing campaigns can provide an image of the product before a customer actually sees it. Reputation, celebrity endorsement, CSR, etc. can be communicated in this way.

1. **E-brand**

As opposed to a brick-and-mortar company's brand in the real world, an e-brand represents the brick-and-mortar company's brand on the web space. It is designed in cyberspace through e-marketing. The Internet can help in building brands by:

> facilitating marketing communications
> giving name recognition to the products sold by the company
> providing a way to access products through the use of web

The use of websites is the primary way in which companies communicate their brand online.

2. **Online branding**

Branding is one of the most important facets of any organisation beyond its products, distribution, pricing, or location. A brand signifies a company's product position in the marketplace e.g.

> what the product stands for
> what level of quality it has
> what personality it has

The Internet certainly provides a means to build the brand, but it is important to understand different elements of marketing on the Internet and the different channels available for supporting that brand. The online brand has to be treated carefully since online loyalty could be lost at the click of a PC mouse. Branding is a marketing tool, and thus, it is a deliberate act. It is a deliberate attempt to create awareness of the business, product or service to the prospective market or buyer. It involves portraying what makes the business, product or service distinctive and also communicating its intrinsic usefulness.

3. **Importance of online branding**

A brand creates a lasting impression over and above all the other elements of an organisation, such as technology, patents, etc. Such value is often called **brand equity**. Brand equity, unlike other abstract marketing notions, can be quantified. The importance and value of branding becomes apparent when an entrepreneur wants to sell his or her company or approach the stock exchange for a public offering. It is often the brand that a business owner has to sell in such cases.

In the modern era, virtually all of the world's leading brands have embraced the Internet as an important communications vehicle. Today we see an online emporium of branded goods marketing themselves over the Web from Amazon.com to more "traditional brands" such as GE, who are using the Internet to create a more efficient learning and purchasing tool.

4. **Online branding and traditional branding**

In a brick-and-mortar environment, branding is concerned with how the customer is welcomed into the store and how products are packaged and presented whereas, in an online environment, branding is more fragmented and difficult to manage e.g. blogs, online editorials, products reviews, search listings, etc. A robust website could help in the creation of effective brands since a website can build better relationships than any other form of marketing communication.

SUMMARY

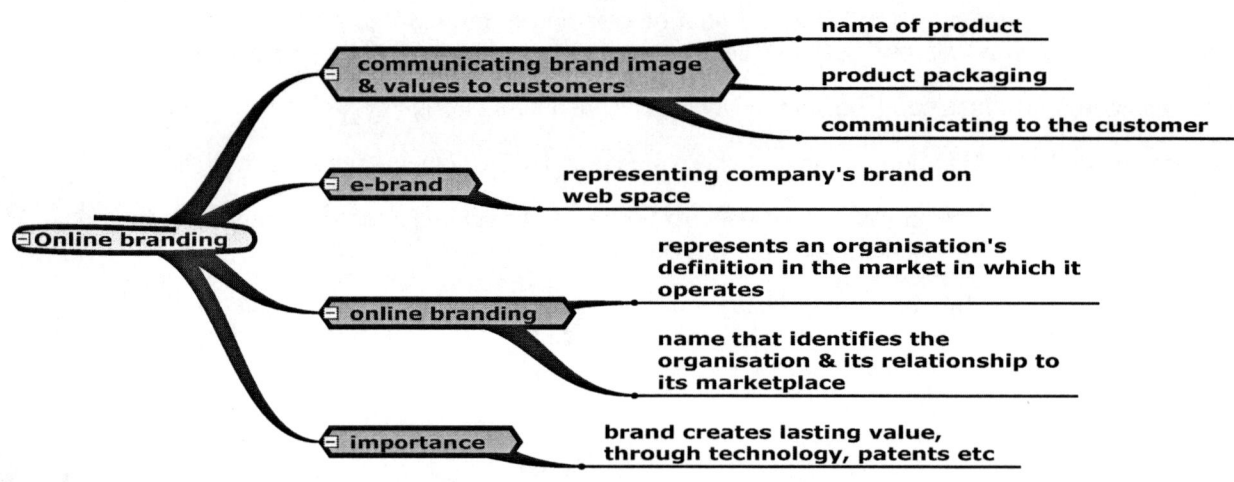

Test Yourself 4

Wesco Ltd has gained a long-standing reputation in the public mind as a trusted provider of traditional phone services. So far the company was considered to be a key player in delivering land-line phone services. With the progress of telecommunications technology, Wesco has broadened its gamut of services to consumers and businesses providing services, in areas such as wireless, broadband and satellite TV. The CEO of the company is facing the challenge of repositioning Wesco as an organisation that is more than just another phone company.

Part of this challenge is to convince all the business and retail customers of the company to readily associate the Wesco brand with their lists of convergent communication services. This includes everything from high speed Internet services to Wesco's mobility wireless services. Wack Jones, the chief strategist of the company, feels online branding campaigns would result in improved customer impact and higher sales. Wesco aims to reposition itself in the public mind and convey a sense of itself as a contemporary service provider.

Required:

State the factors that Wesco Ltd should consider for developing an influential brand.

Answers to Test Yourself

Answer to TY 1

The Internet, being a visual interfacing medium, is an integral part of e-marketing. It connects the potential demand with the company's website. Using robust and interactive websites, consumers can be attracted from across the globe. With the Internet, users can create their own content. Streaming audio and video technologies, together with speedy delivery channels, make the presentation of sound, music, and visual imagery easily accessible.

The **strengths** of the Internet include:

- selective targeting with e-mail and Web content by using databases
- ability to track advertising effectiveness
- flexibility of message length and delivery timing
- ability to reach global markets with one advertising purchase (e.g., the Yahoo! portal) and interactivity
- opens up new market segments

E-marketing offers a wide scope for applying strategies to target customers, for which, an effective, interactive and user-friendly website should be in place. This stage in the implementation of e-marketing is one of the 'sure steps' towards the success of spreading globally.

A website can reach anyone who has Internet access, in any part of the world. It allows organisations to find new markets and compete globally in return for a small investment. In addition to this, the company may reap benefits like low cost marketing, 24-hour online presence, higher conversion rate of customers, etc.

A website should be developed after considering the services offered by the company and the company's target customer profile. The content of the website should be easy to access. Complexities in the website should be avoided for making it user-friendly. In the case of Guide You Best publishers, the website needs frequent updates since the product is revised and changed according to requirements of the readers.

Answer to TY 2

General overview of e-marketing plan

Company Name	Objectives	Target customer	Marketing methods / actions	Aim
Quick-meals	➤ Launch new products ➤ Boost sales of offline stores	➤ Common people who can use the Internet	Create an interactive, user-friendly and creative website specially designed to launch new products on the company website	Using creative website to attract customers to new products and retain them for the long term

Implementing the e-marketing plan is the responsibility of a dedicated management team. Firstly, the team should establish proper short-term and long-term goals which should be in line with the core marketing strategies of the company. The objectives must be clearly stated and should be measurable so that they can be evaluated against determined goals.

Even though there are several approaches to developing an e-marketing plan, depending on different business situations and specific objectives, the following steps are required to develop an e-marketing plan for Quick-meals:

Step 1: Determine the target market

In this step, Quick-meals should:

➤ identify its target market

➤ ascertain its customers' expectations its requirements for making an effective sales pitch and determine its costs and expected benefits

➤ study the market environment and the marketing strategies of its competitors

Step 2: Set e-marketing plan objectives and e-marketing methods

The next step is to set the objectives for the marketing campaign. Possible objectives could include:

➤ **entering new markets:** this requires an interactive website to attract customers

➤ **launching a new product:** using innovative ideas to launch products in different ways for an effective start

➤ **achieving higher website traffic:** creative, user-friendly websites would serve this purpose

➤ **focusing on sales or internal efficiency:** readiness to tackle any situation by correct resource allotment

After determining its objectives, the company should establish the e-marketing methods it intends to use for achieving those objectives. It is always advisable to use multiple e-marketing methods since the company can reap the advantages of multiple approaches.

Step 3: Decide the e-marketing strategy and marketing mix

Step 4: Set a budget and determine the strategies

Step 5: Action planning

The company should determine the tactics to be used for implementing e-marketing methods. The plan should also cover other non-Internet marketing activities that need to be completed, e.g. TV spot, news papers, consumer inboxes, branding product, etc.

Step 6: Measure the success

The company should build in feedback mechanisms and regular reviews for enabling assessment of the success of its e-marketing activities, e.g. use of web analytical tools to identify the scope of improvement and to enable continuous betterment.

Answer to TY 3

A The traditional mix of marketing consists of tools that help promote sale of a product by an organisation. Traditionally, four elements were distinguished (called the 4Ps) and they are:

- **Product:** getting the product with the right features and benefits into the market
- **Place:** selling the product through the right sales channels
- **Promotion:** ensuring that the promotion is done through the right techniques such as advertising
- **Price:** setting the right price for the product

In short, the 4Ps relate to marketing the product in such a way that the product is distributed to the most convenient place for customers to buy the product at the appropriate price.

B Internet media have changed the traditional methods of selling goods and services. Marketing strategies to attract and retain customers are now more connected to online media. The Internet provides various opportunities for assessing the current and future Internet marketing strategy. The traditional marketing mix can be influenced by using the Internet in the following ways:

- **Product:** the Internet provides easy opportunities for altering / changing the product through information-based services.
- **Price:** the Internet facilitates price transparency which ultimately leads to lower prices since the costs of selling through the intermediaries are eliminated.
- **Place:** by using the Internet, it is convenient to locate the desired product i.e. seller-site, buyer-site or intermediary. Flexible channel structures can be adopted either by direct sales or by introducing an intermediary.
- **Promotion.** e-communication promotional methods are faster and more secure e.g. e-mail.

The additional Ps can be influenced in the following ways:

- **Process:** proper delivery of the products is important in the online business in the same way as it is in traditional business. The online process helps to revise processes and streamline efforts so that the potentially large volume of support processes can be easily managed in order to maintain satisfaction among the various people connected to the business.
- **People:** people are an inseparable part of the total service in the eyes of the customers.
- **Physical evidence:** providing physical evidence, such as case studies or testimonials, is often vital for achieving success for a marketing strategy.

Answer to TY 4

Building a new brand is not an easy task and requires long-term dedicated efforts with a commitment of value to the consumer and robust marketing and customer relationship skills. In order to create a successful brand, Wesco should note the following:

- **Only quality products make brands:** this involves delivering a product that fulfils customers' expectations about the product. Competitors could take advantage of false commitments to quality, and an inferior quality product does not make a successful brand.
- **Positioning a brand online:** online brand development is an essential factor for Wesco. All well-established brands such as Toyota, Motorola, Pepsi, etc., have a presence on the Web. Well-established brands also need to maintain their brand image.
- **Repositioning a brand:** in order to satisfy the changing trends of the telecommunications market, Wesco needs to introduce new products. Therefore, it is extremely imperative to reposition its brand regularly. While implementing this, Wesco should consult its consumer relations department or public relations experts.
- **Communication of the brand:** communicating a brand is a vital aspect since communication plays an important role in building up a brand. Organisations develop a brand personality by communicating clearly.

Continued on the next page

- **Long-term planning:** gaining customer loyalty requires a lot of time and unless Wesco satisfies its customers, it cannot acquire a good brand name. Taking initiatives to build a brand is a long-term affair and requires dedicated effort and long-term planning.
- **Internal brand building:** the entire staff of the company should be aware of the brand it is working for and should know the value of it. Developing this awareness among staff is important since the employees represent the company's brand when they interact with clients and the public.

Quick Quiz

1. How e-marketing over traditional marketing offers better scope for organisation?
2. Enumerate strengths of internet as effective e-marketing media?
3. What could be the possible objectives of the organisation that is planning to implement e-marketing?
4. What do you mean by Interactivity in relation to the characteristics of the media of e-marketing?

Answers to Quick Quiz

1. E-marketing allows businesses to reach consumers in a variety of ways and enables them to offer a wide range of products and services than is possible with the traditional media. It includes business information management, improved public relations and effective customer service and sales

2. **The strengths of the Internet include:**
- selective targeting with e-mail and Web content by using databases
- ability to track advertising effectiveness
- flexibility of message length and delivery timing
- ability to reach global markets with one advertising buy (e.g., the Yahoo! portal), and interactivity

3. **Possible objectives could include;**
- increase product or business awareness
- entering new markets
- launching a new product
- achieving higher website traffic
- focusing on sales or internal efficiency

4. Interactivity is a characteristic of the media of e-marketing. this involves ascertaining whether the interactive media allows an organisation to communicate with its customers and respond appropriately to their concerns in a continuing dialogue. Using the traditional media, the marketing message can be broadcast from a company to its customers, stakeholders, etc and there is limited interaction between the two. However, using the Internet, the customer can initiate the contact and seek information on a web site

Self Examination Questions

Question 1

Supertech is a Russian company that provides import and export logistics services for its local and international customers. Due to increase in competition, the company has realised the importance of an e-marketing plan as a part of its long term growth strategy. Although Supertech is a small company, the management team is aware that marketing is not merely advertising.

Mr Jack Dennis, the CEO of the company has noticed that Internet portal firms and B2B service firms are also providing new e-marketing channels that include cost control mechanisms. Supertech's management team is currently focusing on the Russian market and urgently need a systematic and practical e-marketing plan for improving the company's marketing capability and control costs.

Required:

State some of the benefits of e-marketing and broadly outline the key areas to be considered for developing an e-marketing strategy.

Question 2

"A website is an effective brand building device for a company". Comment and suggest how online branding helps companies to improve customer relationships.

Answers to Self Examination Questions

Answer to SEQ 1

E-marketing shares the same fundamental concepts with the traditional marketing mix of the four Ps: product, place, price and promotion. The other Ps are also relevant in this regard. The Internet is a true multimedia medium which allows us to combine text, pictures, moving images, audio and video, along with almost anything. Most importantly, it is interactive and functional.

E-marketing enjoys a unique set of characteristics that help in dominating business marketing these days. These include:

- round-the-clock availability
- reach (as there are no geographical barriers online)
- cost effectiveness
- measurable results
- speed
- flexible and dynamic
- targeting potential and interactivity

E-marketing has immensely changed the consumer research process, interaction and functionality. It has enriched both, the consumer and business practices and created a true global market in a real sense.

Although there are serious challenges for Supertech, the company has a great opportunity for restructuring its current marketing strategy in order to gain a competitive edge over its peers. The management of Supertech should consider the following in order to develop an e-marketing strategy:

- Outline the main objectives for designing an effective e-marketing strategy.
- Ascertain the current position of the company.
- Ascertain what the company intends to do in future. This could be done by analysing the objectives.
- Enumerate the benefits of an e-marketing plan and analyse if it is really justified.
- What tangible and intangible benefits are expected to be generated by implementing this e-marketing plan?
- Whether the plan would generate savings in transaction costs, time and efforts?

Answer to SEQ 2

A website can be the most effective brand building device because a website can enhance relationships more effectively than any other form of marketing communication with customers of any company.

Generally, web surfers are not very interested in reading about a company's structure or why it is a strong player in the market. A website should identify and clearly present the information that customers are looking for. It should reflect the business style or personality of a company in addition to what makes the company unique.

By providing customers with brand-based value, a company can increase the depth and 'stickiness' of its customer relationships.

SECTION E: INFORMATION TECHNOLOGY

STUDY GUIDE E4: E-BUSINESS APPLICATION: CUSTOMER RELATIONSHIP MANAGEMENT

Get Through Intro

Customers are one of the most important, if not the most important element in any business. The more we understand our customer – her wants, needs and budgets, the more we can tailor our services to meet her needs.

Take us at Get Through Guides – we created an online forum to hear what your views are about our materials. We have our tutors on standby to answer your questions. You tell us what improvements we can make and what other services we can provide. You are not a number to us – you are a name and we try to support you. We hope that you like what you see and will recommend what we do to other friends studying ACCA. That is certainly happening as forum members are increasing day by day and so are book orders.

So if you have any suggestions about how we can improve our customer relationship management, please do let us know on-line!

In the mean time, hopefully you have an idea of why CRM is so important to a company and this Study Guide will cement this!

Learning Outcomes

a) Define the meaning and scope of customer relationship management.
b) Explore different methods of acquiring customers through exploiting electronic media.
c) Evaluate different buyer behaviour amongst on-line customers.
d) Recommend techniques for retaining customers using electronic media.
e) Recommend how electronic media may be used to increase the activity and value of established, retained customers.
f) Discuss the scope of a representative software package solution designed to support customer relationship management.

Introduction

Case Study

Supermarkets are tracking you

Those of us that are fortunate to be able to buy our weekly shopping on-line, tend to stick to using one e-retailer. This is partly because we find the service good and partly the retailer has the majority, if not all the goods we need.

Generally when you shop on-line with a supermarket, their systems will make a note of what you have bought this time. They will collate the data for future trips until they have an accurate picture of what your likes and dislikes are (products you buy again and again, against products that you bought once and have not tried again). They will know whether you have pets, children and potentially from nappy sizes, how old your children are. They will also be able to guess at how wealthy you are, by looking at the brands you buy, the amount of fresh produce and where you live. In short, they have now a digital personal profile of your shopping habits and you as a person.

The supermarkets can use this data to tempt you to try products you have not tried before e.g. send you a 20% discount voucher for a new pasta sauce. Or they could try to get you to try products which are complementary to your usual purchasing habits e.g. if you usually buy fresh pasta and sauce, they could encourage you to buy garlic bread or olives.

If you have not ticked a declaration asking them to keep this information confidential, they could potentially sell your data to third parties who could then send you information about loans, or holidays – again targeted to whether you appear to be single, with kids etc.

Remember, this could be very helpful for you and help save your time, so it may not be necessarily bad. However, many people do feel that this is starting to invade their privacy.

The above case study should highlight that customer relationship management can be excellent for managing relationships. Equally there are some downsides too. As you read through this Study Guide you can weigh up if the benefits outweigh the negatives.

1. Define the meaning and scope of customer relationship management.[2]

[Learning Outcome a]

1.1 Customer Relationship Management (CRM)

Customer Relationship Management, also known as relationship marketing or customer management, refers to the methodologies, strategies, and software capabilities used to help an organisation organise and manage its customer relationships. It is an approach to acquiring customers and then retaining them in order to develop a higher lifetime value for each customer. E-CRM refers to managing customers on-line. It draws upon the basic principles of CRM; namely relationship marketing and database marketing.

1. The goal of CRM is to assist organisations in:

   - understanding each customer's value to the company
   - improving the efficiency and effectiveness of communication

Example

Airline companies practise CRM. The customers who are the most loyal and profitable to the airlines get preferential treatment. Frequent flyer programmes are developed in order to promote brand loyalty.

Traditional marketing techniques focused on key marketing mix elements such as price, product, promotion and place. Since these techniques were too functionally-based, they neglected the customer in the after-sales process and failed to meet customers' requirements. CRM emphasises customer retention over customer acquisition and is considered one of the most viable tools used by companies to achieve success in the highly competitive marketplace.

In the modern business scenario, CRM has become an essential part of business strategy, since the development of new technologies has increased the possible benefits for companies tremendously. Today, CRM is essential for:
a) improving the service delivered to customers
b) acquiring and retaining clients
c) identifying and classifying customers based on their behaviour
d) optimising the processes of customer interactions thereby reducing costs
e) helping customers to access information instantly and providing solutions instantaneously
f) managing sales force effectively
g) providing employees with information regarding customers and their needs and building effective relationships with customers.

CRM systems should provide:

- contact management,
- report writing,
- campaign management and
- Integration with other systems

2. **CRM focuses on the following areas for customer satisfaction**:

Diagram 1: Primary areas that focus on customer satisfaction

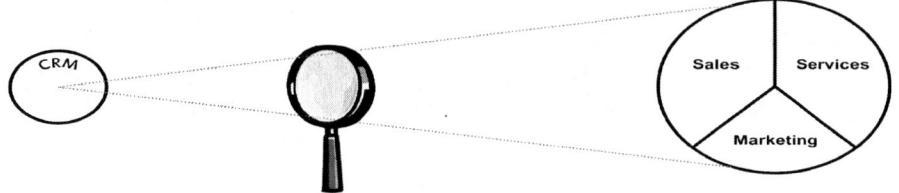

a) **Sales:** the professional sales force predicts and proposes the real-time analysis of information and distributes this information to an organisation and its business partners.
b) **Marketing:** marketing is associated with personalising customer preferences and offering them valuable experiences.
c) **Service:** service is associated with an organisation's call centres and coordinates interaction between Web, e-mail and other communication media.

These areas can be developed further with the help of CRM automation. It is often observed that 80% of profits are derived from just 20% of customers. Therefore it is better to retain existing customers than to acquire new ones. Retaining customers is also more cost effective.

SUMMARY

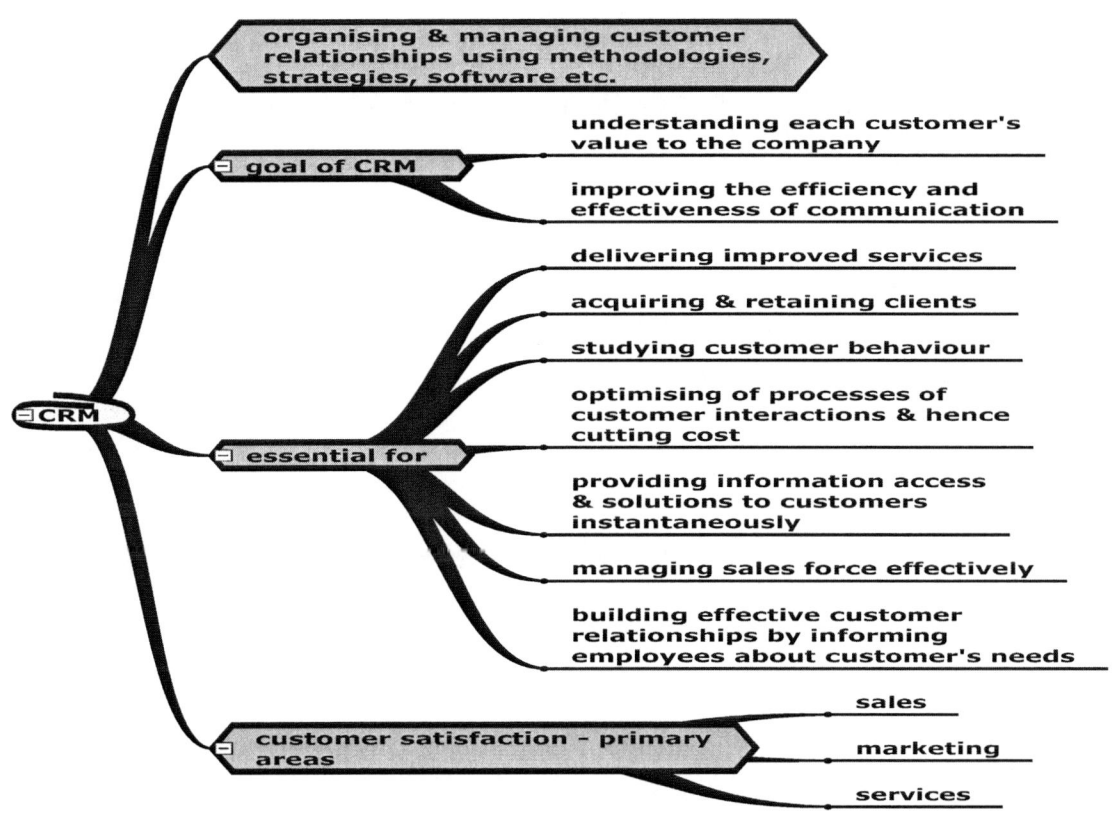

3. Benefits of CRM

a) Cost reduction

Reducing costs or controlling costs is one of CRM's main benefits. Since acquiring a new customer is far more expensive than retaining an existing customer, more and more companies are turning to CRM as it is able to achieve this. A reduction in operating and marketing costs is one of the main benefits of CRM implementation.

b) Customer-focused

CRM understands, anticipates and manages the needs of an organisation's customers. CRM enables an organisation to make quick decisions and offers personalised customer care. It can improve an organisation's service to its employees and help to attract customers, resulting in the creation of a competitive advantage for the organisation as it stimulates growth and customer / employee retention.

CRM helps to retain customers by ensuring that customers are happy and that they keep coming back again and again, thus contributing to the long-term profitability of the organisation.

c) Centralised information

CRM collates information from all data sources within an organisation. It also collects information about the customer from outside resources and gives an overall view of the customers purchasing patterns, likes, dislikes, etc. This helps front office employees to solve customer-oriented issues. It also enables the sales and marketing team to learn more about customer needs and behaviours in order to develop strong relationships with them. It enables an organisation to create detailed profiles such as customer likes / dislikes.

d) Increase in efficiency

CRM manages to bring change into the organisation and its business processes. CRM enables targeting more customers and thus assists the sales and marketing department. CRM enables a company to build a customer database which provides information to management, salespeople etc., enabling them to access information, match customer needs with plans and offerings, provide better customer service etc. Organisations implementing CRM improve their understanding of their customers' needs, allowing them to simplify their marketing and sales processes.

e) Creation of a competitive advantage

CRM offers the opportunity to provide better products for the customer at lower costs. It also generates lifetime value for the customers.

f) Market segmentation

It enables an accurate segmentation of markets and so tailored marketing campaigns can be developed for each market segment.

4. Problems with CRM

Certain organisations experience a lot of confusion about the attributes of CRM and what it really is. Some define it as a business strategy while others view it as something associated with technology. In spite of providing cost effective customer strategies, CRM suffers from the following limitations.

a) Complex systems

The CRM packages available in the market could be highly complex. The employees could find it difficult to cope with these complexities and would require sufficient training in order to overcome these difficulties.

b) Excessive dependence on technology

One of the biggest errors committed by some organisations is allowing the technology to drive their CRM functionality. Organisations go to the industry leaders, gain the technology needed and then apply it to their business problems. This may not be wise and could result in the failure of CRM. Instead the organisations should first analyse their business problems and then find the appropriate CRM solution for them.

c) Excessive costs

CRM involves maintaining a customer database which requires a huge investment in computer hardware, software, personnel etc. The expenditure involved is substantial and the resultant return on investment from the CRM implementation could be insufficient to cover the costs involved. This could lead to a negative feeling within the organisation implementing CRM.

d) Lack of customer focus by employees

CRM plays a vital role in customer-oriented strategies. However, to make its employees more customer-oriented, an organisation needs to motivate its employees. This requires an incredible effort from the organisation. Problems could arise in CRM due to the reluctance of employees to be more customer-focused. This could result in a highly expensive customer strategy being adopted by the organisation in an effort to retain customers but being implemented by reluctant and unfocused employees.

e) Inadequate focus on organisational goals

While deciding a CRM strategy, the objectives should be clearly established and followed. The management and employees of the organisation should be fully aware of the role of CRM in achieving the organisational goals. Sometimes organisational goals lose their importance e.g. the organisation works towards goals that are less important and ignores the organisational goals. This could create problems in CRM.

f) Sluggish returns

CRM is unable to provide speedy returns on investment. It takes years before organisations are able to see actual returns on their investment which tests patience and leads to both the employees and the management relaxing their efforts during the implementation.

g) Inappropriate metrics

One of the main reasons for CRM failures is an inability to choose the right method of implementation. It is necessary to use different metrics to calculate different goals. Organisations may therefore use the wrong metric, resulting in faulty calculations and CRM failures. Further, not all the processes are suited to CRM and the customers could find them quite unfriendly.

h) Insufficient resources

When CRM is implemented in phases, if the internal or external circumstances of an organisation deteriorate, the organisation reduces its budgets for the following phases. When the budgets are strained, the necessary expenditure required for CRM success is not employed. The insufficiency of the necessary resources could result in the failure of CRM implementation.

The majority of the issues with CRM can be mitigated, resolved and ultimately eliminated. However, in order to do this, an organisation must:

i. be able to focus on the business needs

ii. choose a CRM package that works towards fulfilling these needs

iii. employ the right resources

iv. assume the right metrics

SUMMARY

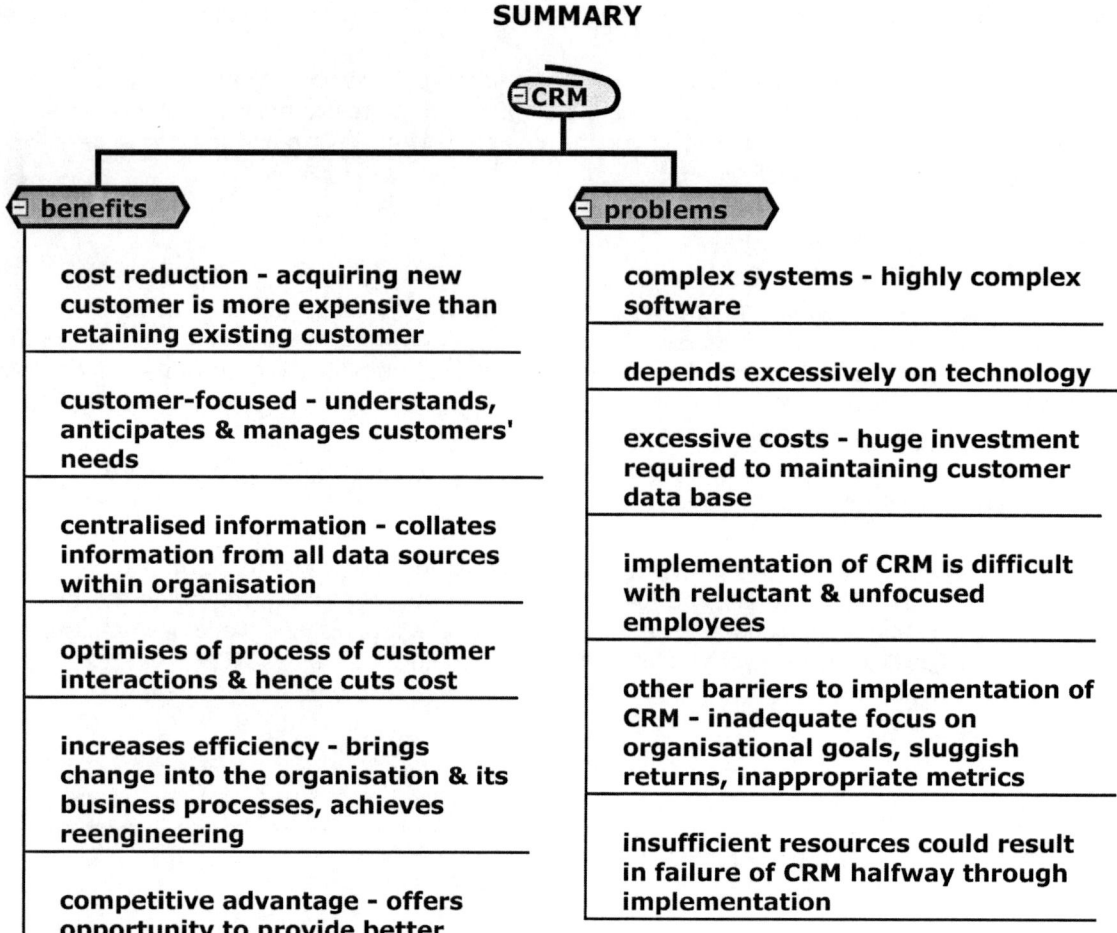

Test Yourself 1

Merry Blue Ocean is a cruise agency which has been providing cruises for the last three years. The luxury treatment offered by the company to its customer right from the enquiry stage until the end of the holiday has proved to be a key aspect for attracting new customers. The company recently spent heavily on promoting and marketing its holiday packages. However, the company's strategy of attracting customers through large promotional and marketing activities resulted in the company's profit margin being lower than its competitors because of the huge marketing expenses.

Merry Blue Ocean consulted Mr Tom Guild, a CRM specialist. Tom recommended the use of a CRM strategy that would enable the company to reduce its current marketing cost by 60%. He also suggested that an effective CRM strategy would enable the company to attract new customers and reduce marketing expenses thereby increasing the profit margin.

Required:

Explain how the implementation of CRM would help to improve the financial position of Merry Blue Ocean.

---

2. **Explore different methods of acquiring customers through exploiting electronic media.**[2]
   Recommend techniques for retaining customers using electronic media.[2]

   [Learning Outcomes b and d]

2.1 Introduction

In order to find new clients, a company needs good, up-to-date address and contact details. On the basis of this information, it should be able to select and communicate with particular target segments. This information should be easily integrated into a single system and not contained in separate lists and tables. After selecting a target group of customers, the company should determine how it wishes to approach these potential clients (called prospects). This can be done via the Internet, e-mail, telemarketing, direct mail or by sending sales staff into the market.

Lifestyle segmentation is a key component of the customer analysis phase and helps a company to identify its customers:

- life stages
- income ranges
- education levels
- media preferences

A company should recognise which line of products fits its customers' lifestyles best in order to enable more precise planning of cross-sell promotions. Cross selling is the selling of an additional product or service to an existing customer.

Diagram 2: Acquiring customers through exploiting electronic media

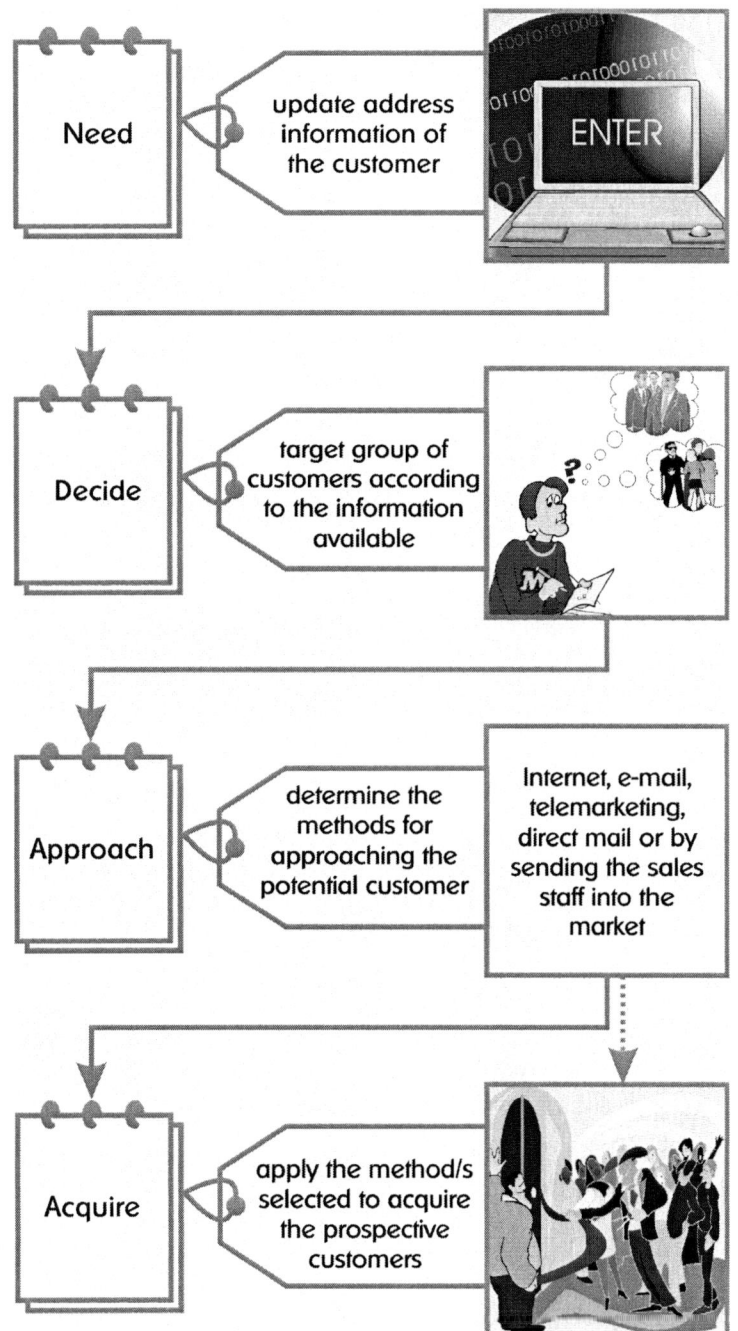

1. On-line customer acquisition

On-line customer acquisition employs the methods used for forming relationships with new customers in order to make an on-line sale.

a) Customer acquisition

i. Customer acquisition is essential for organisations in the following situations:

- for new business start-ups
- when entering new customer market segments
- for exploiting new applications of an existing product or service
- for launching a new product, etc.

ii. The Internet enables a company to attract customers in the following ways:

- by getting the customers using search engines, links, and alliances with other sites
- by proactively finding the customers and sending material electronically

The best way to find on-line business is through search engines. A company can get itself registered with several general purpose engines such as Google, Yahoo and MSN.

A company should find the search engines that focus on its specific industry. Different search engines specialise in information focused on different markets such as telecommunications, oil and gas.

2. Successful customer acquisition and customer retention marketing strategies

Targeted marketing is a vital element for achieving success in marketing. Attracting and retaining profitable customers and converting potential customers into actual customers are immensely important for companies. A comprehensive knowledge of their customers is useful for companies. By understanding the demographic characteristics, lifestyle behaviours and purchase preferences that influence the buyer behaviour, companies can successfully tailor their marketing strategies to:

a) reach their customers;
b) increase customer loyalty; and
c) improve customer profitability.

Example

If the CRM solution indicates that the best customers typically like buying 'electronic goods' in November for an average sale price of $10, an electronic gods company can prepare a marketing approach that is sent out to its customers prior to November that will induce them to buy $20 worth of electronic goods.

3. Techniques for acquiring customers through electronic media

Electronic media can be used to acquire customers in many ways. These techniques include the traditional online mass media techniques and sophisticated online techniques.

a) **Web banners / banner advertising:** a web banner or banner ad is a type of on-line advertising. It entails embedding an advertisement into a web page. It is intended to attract traffic to a website. The website contains images that are usually placed on web pages that have interesting content, such as a newspaper article or report.

b) **Search engine optimisation (SEO):** SEO is a set of methodologies aimed at improving the ranking of a website in search engine listings. Using search engines, visitors can find sites in a variety of ways including:
- paid for advertisements in the search engine results pages (SERPs)
- third parties who are listed in the search engines
- "organic" listings (i.e. the results the search engine's present users)

c) **E-mail**: electronic mail is a push medium of on-line marketing which enables a targeted message to be sent to a prospective customer to inform them or remind about a product or service. Before starting e-mail communications, companies should give their prospective customers, the option of receiving product details through e-mail. This approach is also known as **permission marketing.** Companies sending e-mails to a large database of prospective customers should ensure that they are not sent to customers who prefer not to receive them; this would constitute spamming (also referred to as 'spam e-mails').

Example

In the case of the airline industry, the marketing team can send out lucrative offers through e-mail and give their customers membership cards so that they can receive preferential treatment.

d) **Viral marketing:** viral marketing and viral advertising refer to marketing techniques that produce exponential increases in brand awareness by creating a buzz about the products or services. The term 'viral' is used as product awareness through this type of marketing spreads like a virus. It is word-of-mouth delivered and enhanced on-line. The primary benefit of viral marketing is its potential to target a large number of prospective customers at a low cost.

Example

Hotmail includes a small advertisement at the bottom of all users' outgoing e-mail. This advertisement induces more users to open up a Hotmail account for free. These new users send out e-mails and at the same time send out the same advertisement to others.

Viral marketing is popular due to:

- ease of executing the marketing campaign
- relatively lower cost as compared to direct mail
- better targeting
- fast response rate

e) **Newsletters:** a newsletter is a regularly distributed publication generally about one main topic that is of interest to its subscribers. Newsletters enable an organisation to send news about the company, products or services to its subscribers / prospective customers.

f) **Link campaign:** a link campaign is a form of on-line marketing and is a part of SEO. An organisation seeking to increase the number of visitors to its website can ask its strategic partners, professional organisations, chambers of commerce, suppliers and customers to add links from their websites. A typical link campaign involves mutual links back and forth between related sites. The importance of a website can be judged by the search engines with reference to the number of other sites that link to it and the number of visitors moving from the linking site to the target site using the additional links.

Example

If a user has identified ten target websites which he intends to link back to his website, he can use a link campaign to set up links.

g) **Cool tool:** a cool tool is a video clip, standalone software or a device that appears on the user's computer screen and is often used for a specific purpose. Examples include 3Ms post-it notes and cartoon characters.

SUMMARY

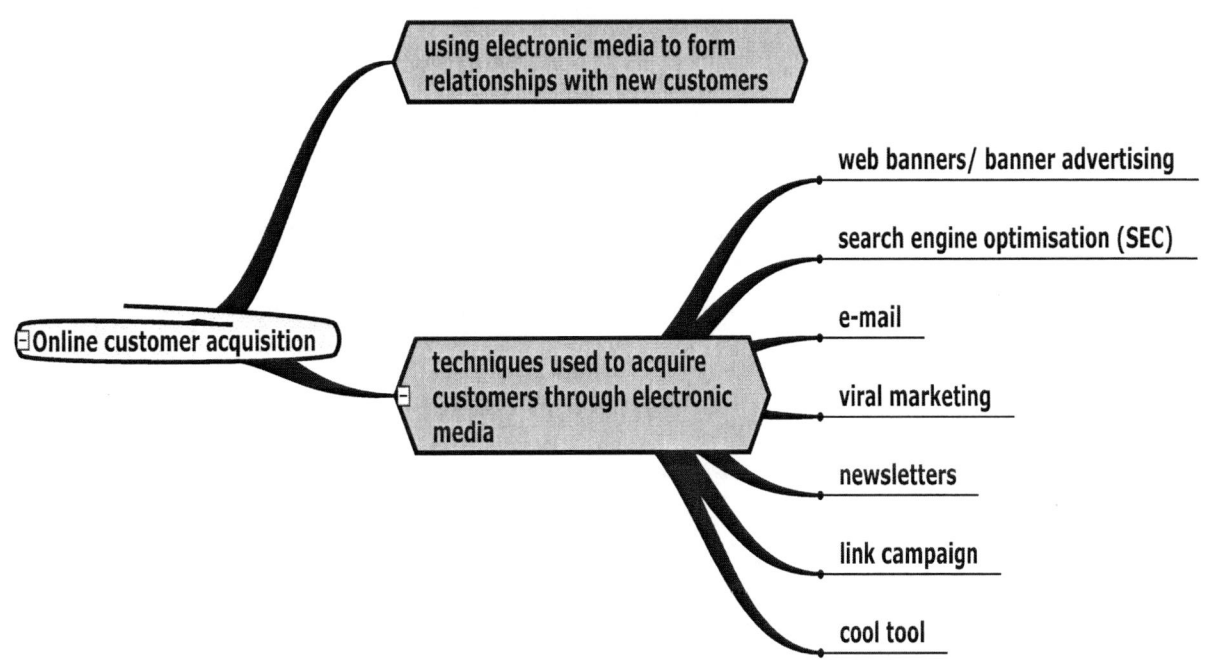

2.2 Successful customer acquisition and retention

An organisation can apply the following marketing techniques to develop the best customer acquisition and customer retention solutions and to tackle specific marketing challenges:

1. **Understanding the customers**

An organisation should begin with a complete examination of both its customer base and its market in order to identify its highest value customer segments and new sales opportunities. This link between the company's internal information and the marketplace provides a valuable insight into its customers' buying behaviour and preferences. This reveals which customer is likely to buy which products or services. Such information enables a company to increase customer profitability and improve customer loyalty.

2. **Develop effective strategies**

After identifying the key customer segments, the company should develop targeting strategies that address customer needs and take full advantage of the present and the future opportunities. This phase focuses on the three core areas, namely customers, markets and delivery channels that are essential for successful customer acquisition and retention.

3. **Implementing the plan**

The knowledge acquired from the analysis and strategic planning phases can be used to implement an effective and targeted, marketing plan. A company should target its prospects precisely, choosing segments that match its customer base and media channels that match their preferences.

4. **Measuring the performance**

The company should set performance benchmarks to assess the effectiveness of its strategies and implementation tactics. This assessment would give a company certain valuable insights, enabling it to:

- make improvements
- implement cost savings
- accurately assess gains or losses

SUMMARY

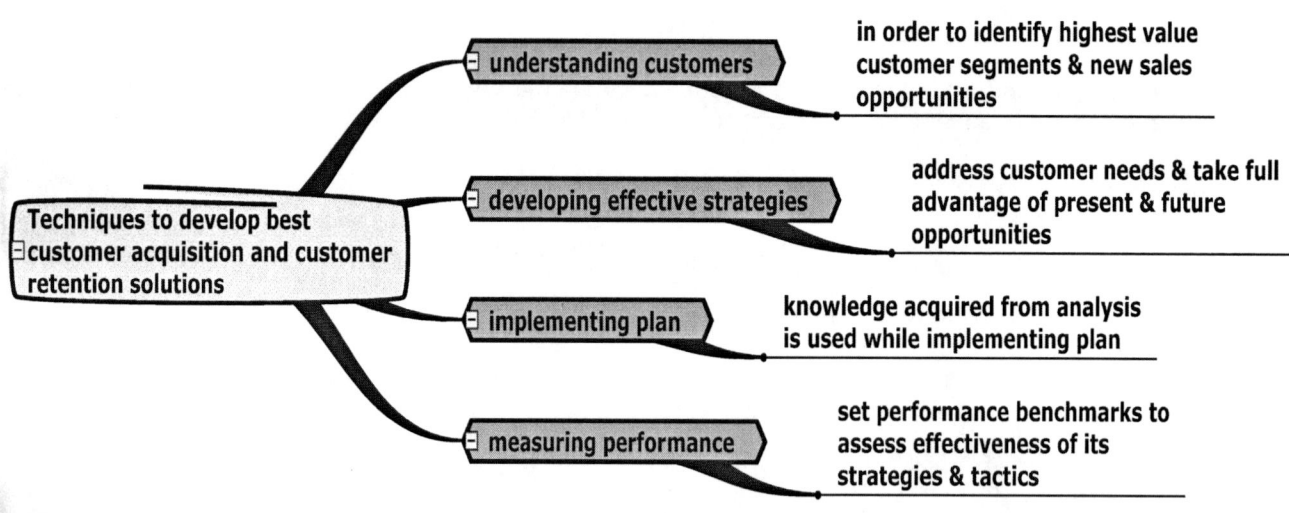

Test Yourself 2

Wellworth Ltd is an established company which specialises in trading steel bars. The company has built an excellent customer base which comprises mainly of automotive companies. Most of the company's transactions take place online.

The board of directors of the company is planning to enter into the manufacturing of certain steel sheets to meet rising demand from the capital goods and the infrastructure sector. The directors are not sure if the Internet would enable them to attract new customers and retain them.

Required:

Explain the benefits of using the Internet to acquire and retain customers.

3. Evaluate different buyer behaviour amongst on-line customers.[3]

[Learning Outcome c]

3.1 Introduction

Buyer behaviour is one of the primary determinants of an organisation's e-business strategy. The present day on-line buyer expects higher standards in terms of service and speed of delivery as well as competitive prices. Buyers also highly regard security, safety and control aspects. The following are some of the expectations of on-line customers:

1. Buying behaviour

Buying behaviour refers to the decision processes and acts of people involved in buying and using the products i.e. the ultimate consumer. Organisations should understand:

➢ the reasons why customers buy
➢ the factors that influence buying decisions
➢ the changing variables in the society

Buyers generally tend to be value-maximisers and would therefore analyse which offer will deliver the greatest perceived value and act on it. Customers today are more educated and informed than ever, and they have the tools necessary to verify companies' claims and seek better alternatives.

Providing good service is an important part of customer satisfaction. Customers are more sophisticated and articulate and have higher aspirations. They respond promptly if companies are unable to meet their expectations.

In off-line business transactions, the buyer can interact with the seller in order to gain information and service. In the case of service failure, the seller can take the necessary action to resolve any defects. However, an on-line buyer interacting with a mediating environment might be unable to detect service failures. Although the Internet gives customers the opportunity to find information without any personal help from the employees of the company, on-line companies need to be aware of the need for personal communication in order to achieve customer satisfaction.

The types of buying behaviour are influenced by the following factors:

➢ The buyer's level of involvement in a buying decision i.e. why he / she is motivated to seek information about only certain products or brands and ignores the others.
➢ Websites are often used to complement physical stores rather than being stores in their own right.
➢ On-line customers demand quick responses to the questions they ask on-line, in order to stay interested.
➢ Personalisation of websites is essential for creating trust and building on-line relationships.
➢ In order for a website to enhance customer satisfaction, it should be fully integrated in the company's marketing strategy.

2. Types of buying behaviour

Diagram 3: Types of buying behaviour

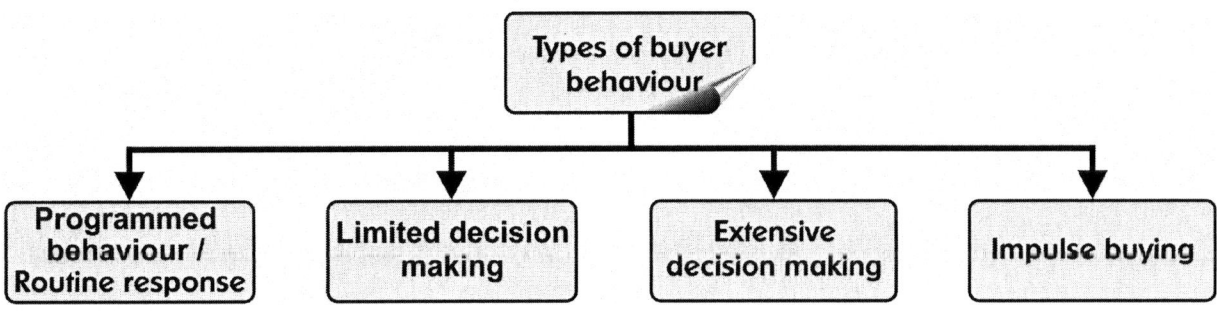

The four types of consumer buying behaviour are:

a) **Routine response / programmed behaviour:** this involves buying frequently purchased low cost items that require very little effort to find and decide on and can be purchased routinely. Examples are grocery items and soft drinks.

b) **Limited decision making:** products that are needed occasionally require a moderate amount of time for gathering information.

Example

Buying clothes requires limited decision making because, when buying clothes, a customer knows the product class but requires time to finalise the brand.

c) **Extensive decision making:** buying products that are expensive and not frequently required takes more time for gathering information and decision making. Examples are computers and consumer durable product buyers.

d) **Impulse buying:** the buyers falling in this category are characterised by a lack of conscious planning. Examples include clothing and cosmetics.

SUMMARY

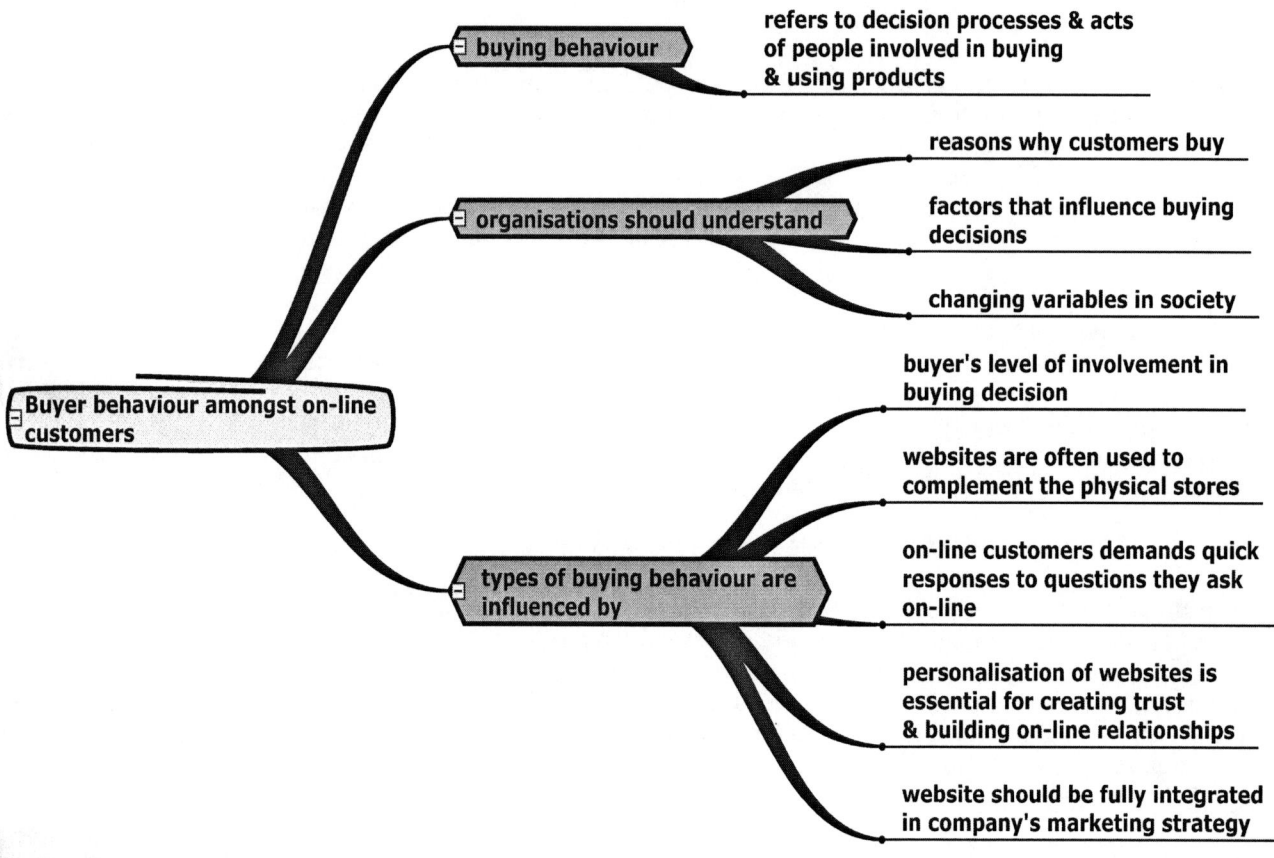

Test Yourself 3

Play Games Ltd is an animation and gaming company. It recently conducted a survey on the on-line purchase behaviour of its customers within the age group of 16 to 30 years. This survey was conducted to give inputs to the marketing department for planning its strategy of exploring new markets.

The survey revealed that around 65% of Internet buyers sought information on the products on-line before making a purchase. This group was mostly made up of well-educated buyers and buyers in high income groups. It was also revealed that female students were using the Internet more frequently to make on-line assessments than male students

The average on-line spending on the surveyed product was reported as $100.20 for one month. This is 30% higher than the last year. Over 80% of the users surveyed were found to be satisfied with their on-line purchase and they were most likely to purchase on-line again.

Required:

Explain, with reference to Play Games Ltd, the importance of on-line buying in customer satisfaction. State the determinants of on-line buying behaviour.

> **4. Recommend how electronic media may be used to increase the activity and value of established, retained customers.**[2]
>
> [Learning Outcome e]

4.1 Introduction

Acquiring new customers is an expensive affair and therefore retaining them is of utmost importance. Customers that are satisfied with the products, prices, service provided, etc. can be retained for longer time periods. A CRM system enables the staff that interacts with customers to see what is going on at the client's end. This enables immediate action to be undertaken if a client has a question or complaint. Using electronic media, every telephone call, incoming e-mail, etc. is registered thereby improving the organisation's knowledge about its customers. This knowledge helps in building a customer database so that the records can be retrieved at any time, even if the concerned staff leaves the organisation.

1. Adopting more targeted customer approach

In order to optimise customer relationships, the information they need should be provided appropriately and promptly. This could be easily achieved by means of an e-mail newsletter. This would also enable the clients' link clicking behaviour in the CRM system to be recorded, resulting in a better understanding of the clients' preferences. Based on this understanding, organisations can communicate with their customers using a more targeted approach, thereby increasing their satisfaction.

2. Building long-term relationships

After gaining sufficient experience with on-line services, a company could use more sophisticated methods to build customer loyalty and strong relationships. Developing customised or personalised sites for customers would provide both value-added services and induce customers to conduct e-business with the company.

3. Improving customer retention on-line

Customer retention is vital to the profitability of any business organisation. Building long-term relationships with customers is essential for improving customer retention on-line.

4. Relationship marketing

Relationship marketing deals with building relationships with all the external parties involved in marketing. Since CRM is customer-oriented, it helps companies by specifically focusing on the long lasting relationships with their customers. E-CRM focuses on the electronic relationship between the organisation and its customers. E-CRM makes the CRM:

- **more flexible:** since CRM systems can be readily updated to accommodate new products and new promotion techniques for new media,
- **faster:** since responses can be instantaneous using e-CRM

5. Database marketing

The customer database is the driving force of modern CRM systems. A customer database is a repository of information about the customers from all sources including websites, sales staff and customer service associates.

Definition

Database marketing is a form of direct marketing which uses databases of customers or potential customers to generate personalised communications in order to facilitate the marketing of a product or a service. It involves gathering all available customers and prospective customers' information into a central database and uses statistical techniques to develop customer behaviour models, which are then used to select customers.

SUMMARY

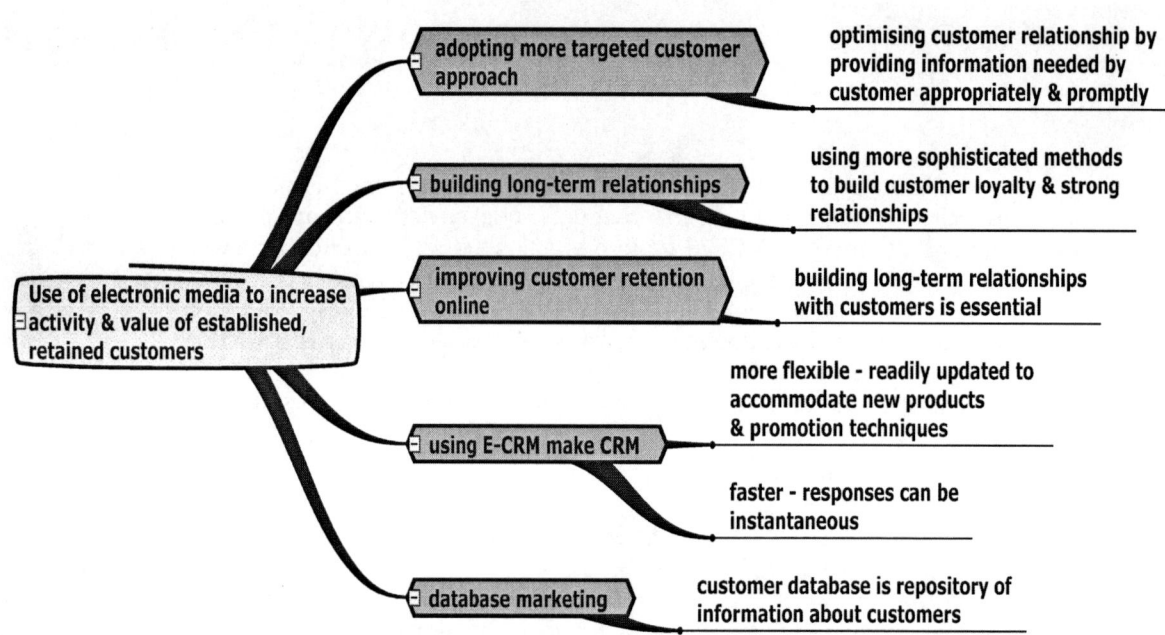

Test Yourself 4

Continuing the example of Wellworth in Learning Outcome 2

Wellworth is able to successfully acquire and retain customers.

Required:

Explain how the company can enhance its client relationships using e-mail as a medium.

---

5. Discuss the scope of a representative software package solution designed to support customer relationship management.[2]

[Learning Outcome f]

CRM software

The process of selecting CRM software is difficult since CRM software is highly complex and consists of several processes. A wide variety of CRM software is available in the market with almost the same advantages and disadvantages. A prerequisite for selecting a particular CRM software system is identifying the needs of the business.

There are different approaches to CRM. At present there is no one software package that allows all of these approaches to be applied.

1. Guidelines for choosing appropriate CRM software

While choosing appropriate CRM software, companies should ensure that the software has the following features:

- It should be productive from the marketing perspective i.e. it should assist the marketing department in all its marketing efforts.
- It should not require extensive customisation and should be easy to customise.
- It should be capable of creating and maintaining a relationship with the customers and analysing customer preferences thereby contributing to customer retention.
- It should have analytical capabilities in order to classify the customers and provide services according to the classifications.
- It should support the sales function. The sales staff should be sufficiently trained in the CRM process since it is they who deal directly with the customers. In this respect they play a significant role in converting sales leads.
- It should enable relevant data to be presented in an easily comprehensible manner since it facilitates easier and faster work.

2. Essentials of an effective CRM system

- Organisations should endeavour to establish clear business objectives and a business plan that is synchronised with the CRM goals. The CRM solution should aid the overall organisational objectives. The existing processes should also be integrated with the CRM software.

- Organisations should conduct an assessment of the data quality issues and ensure that the required measures are undertaken before implementing CRM.
- Organisations should endeavour to understand the customers' problems in order to maximise the benefits of CRM.
- It is essential to maintain all the information available about a customer in the system and make this information available to the concerned staff in the organisation.
- IT enables dynamic changes, since it facilitates change within the organisation and enables it to adapt to changing requirements.
- Organisations should obtain the acceptance of their employees for the implementation of CRM.
- Organisations also need to involve top management in the implementation of CRM in order for it to be successful.
- CRM systems should be able to run campaigns and generate reports
- Organisations should hire CRM consultants / experts since their expertise will go a long way towards reaping the benefits of CRM.

3. Role of Information Technology in CRM

- **Implementation support:** this aims at providing 24/7 service using IT applications. Networked computers with data communication devices help in providing better implementation support.
- **Data mapping:** with this technique, data can be mapped to devise a system that better suits the requirements of the customers.
- **Interface design and development**: a superior interface design and development is a prerequisite for interacting with the customers in order to provide better services to them and also to provide a better interface amongst the various departments of the organisation.
- **Report design and development**: it is essential that reports are properly designed in CRM since reports exist at various levels right from the initial stage where the customer makes a complaint to the final stage of problem resolution. A well-designed report format using IT is useful for organisations.
- **Graphic User Interface (GUI) design and customisation**: it is essential that the format for customer complaints is user-friendly and interactive. With the help of multimedia applications such as graphics, which make use of the GUI, various formats can be customised for different applications.
- **System testing**: the CRM system developed using IT applications should be thoroughly tested before it is fully implemented.
- **Operation and support**: an important feature of CRM is that it should operate effectively and provide better client support.
- **Knowledge management**: the combination of IT and CRM is capable of retaining customers and disseminating the knowledge and expertise acquired amongst all sections of the business. Knowledge Management Services (KMS):

- helps the staff to develop new skills and learn from earlier experiences,
- builds up corporate and customer information,
- helps in saving time in the future by using past processes.

SUMMARY

Role of IT in CRM:
- implementation support — aims to provide 24/7 service
- data mapping — mapping of data to devise system that better suits customers' requirements
- interface design & development — enables interactions with customers to provide better services to customers & better interface amongst various departments
- report design & development — essential that reports are well designed because they exist at various levels
- GUI design & customisation — forms can be customised for different applications
- operation & support — provides better client support
- knowledge management — helps development of new skills & learning from earlier experience

Test Yourself 5

Explain the essential factors that an organisation must consider while evaluating CRM software.

Answers to Test Yourself

Answer to TY 1

Cruise customers are very particular about their safety needs and the reputation of and quality of service provided by the cruise company.

The company should implement CRM to establish, develop, maintain and optimise long-term customer relationships. CRM could result in the following benefits for the company:

1. Reduction in cost

Effective CRM would enable the front office staff of the company to perform marketing tasks in a cost effective manner. Merry Blue Ocean Ltd would be able to reduce its marketing costs since most of the marketing would be done on-line.

2. Enable effective customer service

CRM would give the organisation a broader view of each customer and provide a consistent and unified contact whenever any person in the company deals with that customer. This is because all key customer data such as past history, payment history, customer preferences are accessible to the relevant customer service staff.

3. Customer-focused approach

- CRM would help the company to personalise its relationships with customers using an integrated customer database.
- CRM would help the company to treat individual customers uniquely and employees would be well informed about the needs of each customer.
- Better customer service leads to customer loyalty and repeated business.
- CRM enables better communication and follow up of customers which would help the company to receive continuous feedback from its customers.

4. Other benefits of CRM

- CRM helps in providing cost effective solutions, which would give the company a competitive advantage.
- CRM simplifies the marketing and sales process in the company and achieves operational efficiencies by integrating with other systems such as invoices.

Answer to TY 2

The Internet would enable the company to attract customers in two ways:

- through search engines, links and alliances with other sites
- through proactively finding them and sending material electronically

The best way to find on-line businesses is through search engines. There are a number of general purpose engines such as Google, Yahoo and MSN which are useful in this regard.

Since each search engine indexes information differently, the company should engage a person or company that has experience in this activity. A knowledgeable service provider would provide useful links in the searches.

After acquiring the customer, it is important to add value to the relationship. The company should find out what its customers perceive to be valuable by surveying them either on-line, by phone or by regular mail. Although on-line techniques can be used, the company should also use other ways to connect with customers. Another way to add value is to develop newsletters that can be delivered on-line or by mail. Newsletters could relate to a product or a service announcement and contain general industry information. E-newsletters are simple and inexpensive to develop and send to customers.

As the company builds its relationships with its on-line customers, it will be able to obtain more information about product preferences. Amazon.com is one of the best examples of matching customers' preferences. Once this website knows the book that the customer is searching for or has ordered in the past, it suggests other related books that could be of interest to the customer.

Answer to TY 3

The increase in the on-line customers and their expense patterns confirms that the possibilities for value creation are much higher using the Internet. E-commerce marketplaces (buying and selling through the Internet) are becoming more popular than traditional marketplaces. Understanding and reacting to customer behaviour is the number one resource for acquiring and retaining customers.

Most on-line sellers use search engines as the main tool to improve site navigation and drive sales. Play Games seems to have deployed powerful search solutions which have considerably improved its customer satisfaction and the performance of its on-line businesses.

Easy on-line purchase options are helping buyers to take quick decisions. This is supported by the fact that 65% of buyers reported that they had made their final decision about the product while on-line.

The types of buying behaviour are determined by the buyer's level of involvement in a buying decision, which in turn is determined by the reasons for seeking information about selecting a few products or brands and ignoring the others.

Answer to TY 4

E-mail offers more effective direct marketing campaigns, since it is possible to send more messages at lower cost (there are no costs of printing and postage).

An effective method of formulating an e-mail marketing strategy is to apply it to achieving customer lifecycle objectives as part of CRM. The customer lifecycle objectives are:

- **Retention** – How can Wellworth manage inbound e-mail service quality to increase its customers?
- **Extension** – How can direct e-mail campaigns be used to extend the range and depth of products?

The best practices for effective e-mail campaigns are as follows:

1. Review the full range of options for the type of outbound e-mail and integrate them into the communications mix. Options include:

- Regular newsletter e-mail to keep customers informed about the metal industry or product news.
- E-mail discussion list, perhaps about product support.
- Small Message Service (SMS) messages to mobile phones can be used in a similar way to standard e-mail for a direct response approach.

2. **Choosing the optimum time:** a monthly offer or newsletter could be released on a regular date such as the first of the month. Response rates may differ through the week, for example some B2B agencies send out e-mails between 11am and 3pm since people are most likely to be at their desk.

3. **E-mail communications should be relevant and targeted:** as for any direct marketing effort the offer should be relevant to the recipient.

4. **Consider web response:** here the power of e-mail and the web are integrated. The web page can be used to enable customers to respond directly to the e-mail offer, in the same way a television advertisement provides toll-free phone numbers.

5. **Tracking**: the company should measure response and conversion rates in order to follow up actions such as sales.

Answer to TY 5

Before selecting a CRM software solution, the project team should first list all the eligible vendors and formally evaluate the short-listed vendors. A formal evaluation should evolve around key questions related to CRM software. These include:

1. **Support of core processes**: is the vendor able to support the core processes in a particular industry or company? Is the CRM solution capable of handling special issues related to selling and marketing, service related issues, etc?

2. **Cost of implementing the software**: what is the estimated total cost of ownership of the CRM solution over the expected useful life of the solution?

3. **Relative ease of usage**: how will the key user groups such as sales, marketing and support staff respond to the CRM solution? Do they regard it as cumbersome and unproductive? Does the CRM solution offer any possibilities for increasing the user adoption rate?

4. **Enable transfer of knowledge**: the CRM system should enable the internal staff to assume ownership of the solution. They should be able to create additional functionality or process flows, and provide the solutions to new user groups, etc.

5. **Integration**: the CRM software should support automated workflows and processes involving non-CRM applications, such as applications related to:

- order management
- billing
- accounts receivable
- inventory
- service management

6. **Support business intelligence**: the CRM solution should have analytical and reporting capabilities. The managers should be able to develop the required reports and alerts easily.

7. **Security**. the CRM system should protect confidential customer information from both internal and external threats.

Quick Quiz

1. Explain how CRM leads to a better understanding of customers' needs.
2. How do successful customer acquisition and customer retention marketing strategies help an organisation?
3. What is meant by a cool tool?
4. Explain impulse buying and give an example of how web-based marketing strategies could result in impulse buying?
5. What is database marketing?

Answers to Quick Quiz

1. CRM collects and collates information about customers from various data sources such as:

    - internal data sources within an organisation
    - external sources

    Analysing this data gives the organisation an overview of customers' purchasing patterns, likes, dislikes, etc., leading to a better understanding of the customer. This helps the front office employees to solve customer-oriented issues. It also enables the sales and marketing team to learn more about the customer needs and behaviours in order to develop strong relationships with them. It enables an organisation to create detailed customer profiles on the basis of customer likes / dislikes etc.

2. Attracting and retaining profitable customers and converting potential customers into actual customers are immensely important for organisations. Successful customer acquisition and customer retention help organisations in:

    - reaching customers,
    - increasing customer loyalty
    - improving customer profitability

3. A cool tool is a video clip, standalone software or a device that appears on the user's computer screen and is often used for a specific purpose.

4. Impulse buying means purchasing a product without careful consideration or logical reasoning. It occurs when a buyer purchases a product in excitement (or on an impulse).

    An example of web-based impulse buying is when a user is checking personal e-mails on the Internet and suddenly sees an advertisement showing a watch of his favourite brand with a huge discount if he purchases it on that day. He might simply buy the product without much thought.

5. **Database marketing** is a form of direct marketing using databases of customers or potential customers to generate personalised communications in order to facilitate the marketing of a product or a service. It involves gathering all available customers and prospective customers' information into a central database and uses statistical techniques to develop customer behaviour models, which are then used to select customers.

Self Examination Questions

Question 1

Martin Growell is the managing director of Martinex, a medium-sized supermarket chain that is facing intense competition from its larger counterparts in its core food and drink markets. It is also finding it difficult to respond to these competitors moving into the sale of clothing and household goods. Martinex is known in the marketplace for its friendly customer care and is considering the introduction of an on-line shopping service. This would enable its customers to order products from the comfort of their home and have them delivered to their home, for a small charge.

Martin is aware of the fact that the move to develop an on-line shopping service would require substantial investment in an electronic CRM technology and support systems. He hopes to attract a large proportion of the existing and, more importantly, new customers to the new service.

Required:

a) Briefly assess the likely strategic impact of the CRM system on Martinex's activities and its ability to differentiate itself from its competitors.
b) Explain the guidelines which the company should follow for successful implementation of CRM.

Question 2

Explain the meaning of E-CRM.

Question 3

The Gauge Groups Ltd provides software solutions for various SMEs. Their applications cover a wide range of business requirements which includes accounting, human resources and warehouse management among others.

The CEO has now decided to enter into the development of CRM software for SMEs. He believes that the CRM solutions provided by the company will enable easy access to centralised customer information.

Required:

Explain any two benefits of CRM for small and medium-sized organisations.

Answers to Self Examination Questions

Answer to SEQ 1

(a) The introduction of a CRM system has the potential to have a major strategic impact on the company and its relationship with its customers. The investment in Internet-based technology will affect both the cost and revenue sides of the business. In terms of operations, the company will need to decide how to integrate the new method of customer buying with its traditional methods.

The new on-line system would have an immediate impact on marketing and sales. It would create opportunities for direct marketing to individual customers and enable customisation. The introduction of the on-line shopping system would offer an opportunity for Martinex to differentiate itself from its aggressive competitors. The on-line service is likely to appeal to a limited but growing segment of its customers. Improved levels of customer retention and the attraction of customers who formerly shopped with its competitors would positively impact the profitability.

(b) The following are some of the guidelines for the successful implementation of CRM:

Identification of business needs: The company should first establish its business needs. It is preferable to opt for a phased CRM implementation. This will ensure an adequate return on investment and considerable cost reduction and efficiency.

Balance between CRM solution and business processes: The company should aim to strike a balance between the proposed CRM solution and the business processes. Often organisations adjust their business processes and goals to the CRM package and vice versa. The organisation should make use of the CRM tools to the best of its ability while at the same time accommodating business processes.

Management involvement: The top management and the CRM personnel should be involved in implementing CRM since their participation is critical to the achievement of the CRM objectives. The CRM manager should actively participate in all aspects of the CRM implementation from the inception to the deployment. The CRM implementation team should work actively with the employees so as to achieve the best results from the CRM.

Training: It is important to plan for individual training within the organisation so as to enable the employees to gain the necessary skills required for the job. This is an important part of CRM implementation. Employees should be encouraged to provide feedback on whether the CRM training has been effective i.e. whether they need further help.

Future focus: Since the CRM implementation would result in new challenges, it is essential that the resources in hand be used to deal adequately with the possible change. Sufficient room for modifications and the possibility of failure of plans should be provided while planning. The organisation implementing CRM should be well equipped to deal with these changes.

Get feedback from users: Obtaining user feedback is crucial for the success of the CRM project. Getting feedback would help the organisation to:

- boost its marketing activities
- follow up sales leads
- secure customer retention

Measurement of the results: The company should ensure that the appropriate quantitative and qualitative metrics are established for measuring the CRM results.

Answer to SEQ 2

E-CRM refers to customer management for e-business. It deals with managing customer related issues using the electronic media.

The various methods of communication for servicing the customers in E-CRM include the Internet, e-mail, chat programmes, video interface and voice communication.

E-CRM integrates all the electronic media used throughout the entire value chain and focuses on engaging the customer and the staff who deal with the customers.

Answer to SEQ 3

Increase in sales: As more consumers get to know a company and are satisfied with the quality of its services relative to that of its competitors, they will tend to give more of their business to the company.

Lower costs: It is an established fact that retaining old customers is cheaper than acquiring new customers. For example, early in a relationship, a customer is likely to have questions and encounter more problems as he or she learns to use the service. With the passage of time, the customer will have fewer doubts or questions and will make fewer mistakes (assuming that the quality or service is maintained at a high level) and the service provider will incur fewer costs in serving the customer.

SECTION F: PROJECT MANAGEMENT

STUDY GUIDE F1: THE NATURE OF PROJECTS

Get Through Intro

Projects are now a way of life. By now, the chances are that you have worked on a project, although you may not formally have called it that. For example, you best friend's birthday is coming up and you want to organise a surprise birthday party for her. You may decide to do this jointly with some other friends. In this case, you will probably get together and work out where the party should be, who should be invited, what drinks and food will be available and what entertainment will be organised. You will also divide up the tasks between all of you, with one person as the main co-ordinator. Welcome to the world of project planning!

By planning the birthday party project properly and managing it effectively, you can be sure that your best friend will have the party of her life and all of you attending will also have fun. However, planning and managing the whole process is not easy. You will have to think about the risks too – what happens if the food does not arrive on time, or the DJ does not turn up? What if one of your friends lets you down with bringing something, like the birthday cake?? You need to have contingency plans to manage the risks.

This Study Guide will teach you the importance of project planning, so that any event you organise is a success and any project you undertake, whether for yourself or for work will be meticulously planned, on time and within budget!

Learning Outcomes

a) Determine the distinguishing features of projects and the constraints they operate in.
b) Discuss the implications of the triple constraint of scope, time and cost
c) Discuss the relationship between organisational strategy and project management.
d) Identify and plan to manage risks.
e) Advise on the structures and information that have to be in place to successfully initiate a project.
f) Explain the relevance of projects to process re-design, e-business systems development and quality initiatives.

420: Project Management

Introduction

Case Study

PLANNING TO START FOR KOLB ROAD EXTENSION - ARIZONA DAILY STAR

Planning for the contentious Kolb Road extension to Sabino Canyon Road is scheduled to get under way in the next six months. The project is part of the Regional Transportation Plan, and it involves construction of a new road connecting North Kolb and North Sabino Canyon roads on the city's East Side.

The city Transportation Department plans to ask for bids from design contractors in the next few months, then begin the planning process, said Michael Graham, department spokesman.

Planning includes the creation of a citizens advisory committee made up of representatives of area groups, such as nearby neighbourhoods and businesses. The city follows this community-input model for most of its road-project planning.
And the cost of the project, which is scheduled to receive $9 million in RTA funds, has been questioned.

Joan Lionetti, Udall Park Neighbourhood Association secretary, said the $9 million figure is so low that it's "absolutely ridiculous."

The city is scheduled to get $420,000 in RTA funds for the fiscal year beginning Tuesday.
Construction on the project is scheduled to begin in 2011, before the first five-year segment of the RTA plan has passed, Graham said.

The project has been through many phases. At one point during the planning process years ago, it would have included a grade-separated interchange at Kolb and Speedway, which would have been much more expensive, said Jim Glock, city transportation director.

The above case study should give you an idea of what needs to be considered when planning a project. The road project above includes internal and external stakeholders and has an estimated cost. The following Study Guide will give you ideas of what needs to be taken into account when planning and managing a project.

---

1. **Determine the distinguishing features of projects and the constraints they operate in.** [2]
   Discuss the implications of the triple constraint of scope, time and cost. [2]

   [Learning Outcomes a and b]

Definition

A project can be defined as a temporary endeavour undertaken to create a particular product or service, termed a project objective. A project comprises:

a) collaborative actions, planned activities designed to achieve a project objective
b) a start, middle and end and consumes resources

Example

A company is planning to build a new factory to produce its new product. In this example, the particular aim is to construct a building. The project will end when the factory receives a completion certificate.

SUMMARY

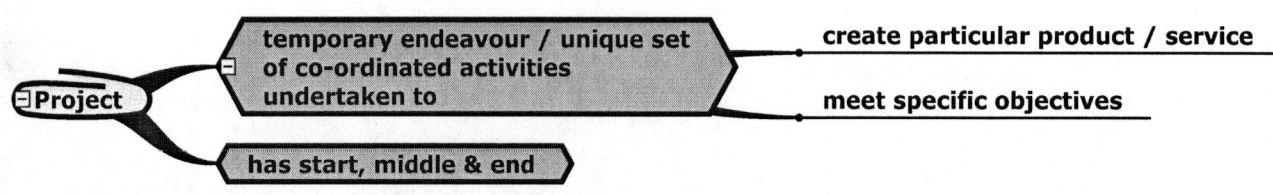

1.1 Project features

A project can be of any size and duration. It may have a budget of $1,000 or $10,000 billion. It may last from a few days to a few years. The following are the attributes of a project. .

1. **A unique purpose:** every project is aimed at achieving some unique objective. If the objective is the same, it is not necessary to carry out another project to achieve the same objective.

> **Example**
>
> An example of this kind of situation is a project to develop an automated response system for handling customers' phone calls. Here the objective is to develop an automated response system. If another project is developed which has the same objective for the same stakeholders then there will be repetition of the tasks required to achieve the objective.

2. **Temporary nature:** every project has an end. When the project objective is achieved or when the project is terminated, it ends. Projects may last for a few days or a few years.

> **Example**
>
> The life of the Y2K project was a few years. Projects are not like operations. Operations are daily activities conducted in the normal course of business and therefore their life is as long as the life of the business.

3. **A project is developed by gradually refining the objectives**: when a project is designed, it begins with broad objectives and as time passes, the objectives become more specific.

> **Example**
>
> A company begins a project to upgrade its infrastructure. It begins with the broad idea of upgrading the infrastructure. After receiving approval from the steering committee, a decision is made on whether to buy or develop the required infrastructure. Afterwards, a detailed plan of development or what needs to be bought is made. Later on, as time passes and the project progresses, many specifications are added to the project plan.

4. **Resource requirement:** a project requires various types of resources in terms of people, financial resources, software, hardware, other assets etc.

5. **Primary sponsor:** every project has several beneficiaries or interested parties. However, each project needs to have one project sponsor / sponsors or primary customer / customers. The sponsor provides the necessary funding and direction for the project.

6. **Uncertainty:** as a project is designed using the subjective judgement of an individual, there could be uncertainty with respect to the **scope, time and cost** of the project. The following events might cause such uncertainties to materialise:

a) Project objectives have not been written clearly.

b) Wrong estimates have been made about the time required to complete the project.

c) Wrong estimates have been made about the cost of the project.

d) External factors such as a supplier going out of business or software becoming obsolete due to advancement in technology.

e) Human resource management problems such as an employee taking unplanned leave.

Projects are **different from operations**. Operations are work carried out in an organisation to sustain the business. These activities are fundamental to the existence of the business. Operations do not have an end date. On the other hand, projects have different start dates. They end when the project objective is achieved or when the project is terminated.

SUMMARY

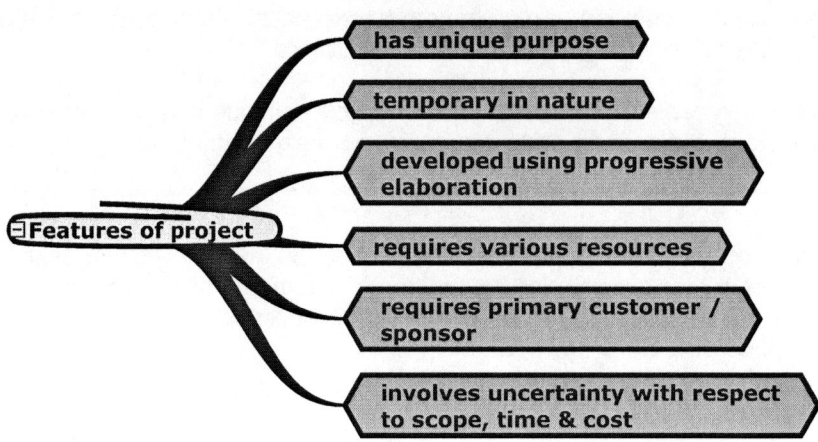

1.2 Project constraints

Every project has three dimensions or three constraints in the form of scope, time and cost.

1. **Scope**
   - Scope can be defined as a certain number of tasks required to achieve a particular objective.
   - Scope can be measured in terms of quality and quantity.
   - The project manager can change the composition of these two elements to successfully manage the project within its triple constraints. Increased scope means the project needs more time and/or increased cost.

2. **Time**
   - What is the time needed to complete the project successfully?
   - How much human resources will be available to complete the project?

Answers to these questions help the project manager to understand all the aspects of the project. A tight time constraint could cause the costs to increase and might reduce the scope of the project.

3. **Cost:** On the basis of the scope and time discussed above, the project manager has to **manage the cost of the project within the approved budget**. If he thinks that it is impossible to adjust the time and scope factors of the triple constraints, he needs to ask for an increase in the budget. A tight budget could mean reduced scope and time.

See the following graphical presentation of these triple constraints to understand this concept more clearly.

Diagram 1: Triple constraints

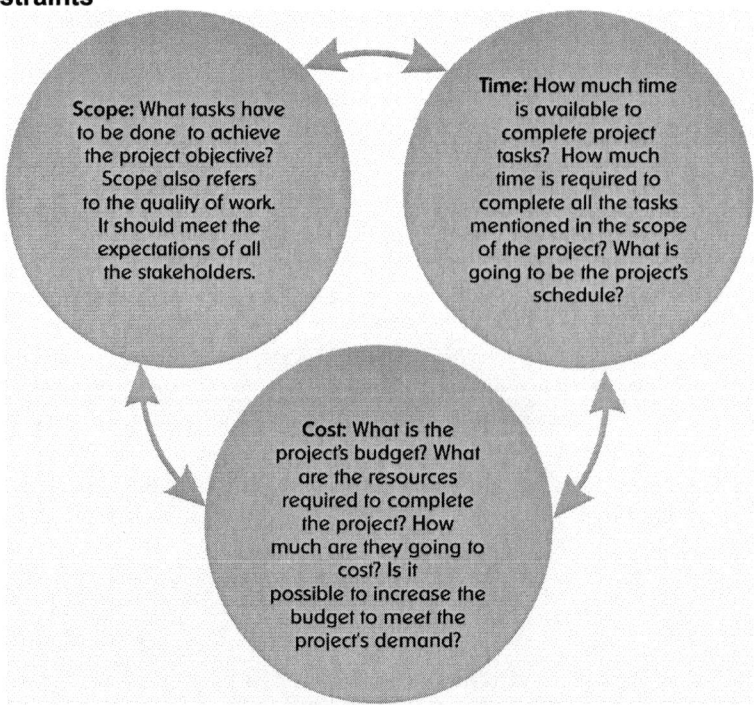

- Each constraint is dependent on the others.
- If scope is the project's primary constraint, the project manager can adjust the cost and time factors accordingly. The scope of the project also refers to quality considerations and customer satisfaction.
- If cost is the project's primary constraint, the project manager can adjust the scope and time required to complete the project.
- If time is the project's primary constraint, e.g. the project manager wants introduce the product in the market before a certain date, the scope and cost factors must be adjusted accordingly.

A good project manager knows what is important to **keep all the stakeholders happy** and **adjusts these triple constraints** accordingly. These constraints are also referred to as the **Project Management Triangle**. If one side of the triangle is changed, the other two sides are changed automatically.

Example

A company has to develop an online billing system which it plans to start using from the next financial year. It has 6 months left. The company has approved $200,000 for this project. Here the objective is to develop an online billing system within 6 months. The project manager needs to outline the tasks to be completed to achieve this objective. After outlining the tasks, he has to allocate the resources needed to complete these tasks, and calculate how much it will cost.

If the human resources needed to complete this project is scarce, to achieve the objective the project manager will need to be a little more flexible about the cost. Alternatively, he can compromise on quality although, in doing so, he must ensure that all the stakeholders are satisfied. If he wants to complete the project without increasing the cost or compromising on quality, he can change the duration of the project, which is not possible in this case.

Test Yourself 1

1. CompOne Ltd is a medium-sized company which manufactures and sells computer hardware. The company also provides after sales services to its customers. In order to improve its after sales service function and resolve customer complaints effectively, CompOne has decided to establish an "Online Complaint System". The finance department has approved an initial budget of $500,000 for this project. The finance department is ready to approve a further budget if needed. The project manager has to set the quality measures and specifications in consultation with the after sales service and marketing department. The project manager has predicted the time frame to complete the project as 5 months with a team of 10 members. The management of CompOne wants the project to be completed within 3 months as it is planning to pursue substantial expansion plans in the coming quarter.

Required:

Identify the primary constraint for CompOne's "Online Complaint System" project and suggest how the other constraints can be adjusted to make the project successful.

2. Discuss the relationship between organisational strategy and project management. [2]
[Learning Outcome c]

2.1 Organisational strategy

Before we discuss the relationship between organisational strategy and project management, let us understand both these terms.

Every organisation has a vision i.e. an idea of where it wants to be in the long run. To achieve its aims, it decides to follow a certain path, use a certain vehicle and makes plans about its speed, time etc. All these different factors (i.e. path, vehicle, plans regarding speed, time etc.) are collectively referred to as the organisational strategy.

> **Definition**
>
> **Organisational strategy** can be defined as follows:
> Strategy is an organisation's long-term plan of action designed to achieve the organisation's objective of being a successful organisation or to achieve a milestone towards this objective. Strategy is different from day-to-day business activities or short-term goals as it is extensively pre-planned or well-narrated. Strategy is the path leading the enterprise to achieve its long-term objective.

2.2 Project management

> **Definition**
>
> Project management can be defined as the activity of managing project activities by facilitating the required resources and demonstrating the required skills of management to achieve the project objective.

Project managers need to implement the project to achieve the project objective and keep all the stakeholders happy. Project managers have to achieve these goals by keeping the project within its triple constraints (cost, time and scope). It is the project manager who, once appointed, facilitates and directs the flow of project activities to meet the demands of the project.

Project management involves the management of the following activities:

a) **Scope:** managing the activities required to achieve the project objective.
b) **Time:** managing the project within the available project time.
c) **Cost:** managing the cost of the project within its budget.
d) **Quality:** managing the quality of work at an acceptable level.
e) **Human resource:** managing the project team and internal and external stakeholders.
f) **Communication:** effective communication at all levels of the management.
g) **Risk:** identifying and managing the risk.
h) **Procurement of resources:** making the make / buy decisions, source selections, supplier overvaluation etc.
i) **Integration of project's activities:** this includes project selection method, project management methodology, stakeholder analysis, project charters, project management plans, project management software, change control boards, project review meetings and lessons learned report.

2.3 Relationship between organisational strategy and project management

Every business has a **vision** i.e. where it sees itself in the future. **Strategies** are developed to achieve this vision. From strategies, **business objectives** are defined. From business objectives, **critical success factors** are identified. Finally, **projects are identified to achieve these critical success factors**.

> **Example**
>
> FunToys Ltd is a supplier of toys for children. It wants to become the top international supplier of toys within the next 10 years. Its strategy is to manufacture and sell toys according to the particular preferences of the consumers of each country. Here the business objective is to expand the business internationally. The critical success factors for this objective are finding new markets, developing new toys for manufacture, automating factories, improving quality and developing a worldwide image. On the basis of these critical success factors, projects such as process redesign, undertaking a marketing campaign, developing the design of the new toy are identified.

The following process diagram shows the connection between an organisation's vision and its projects.

Diagram 2: Organisational strategy and project management

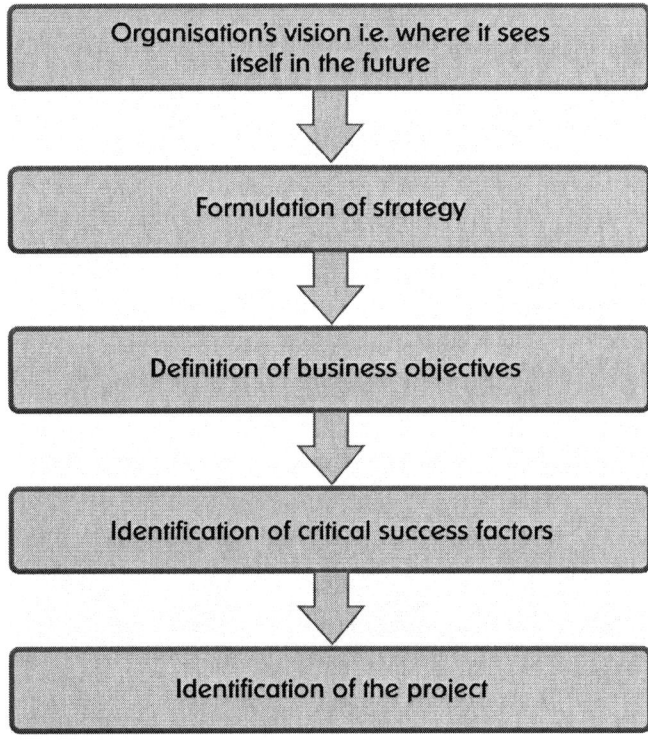

1. Organisational strategy has an **influence** on project management. An organisational strategy has its own attributes with respect to cost, quality and time to market. A project **derives its constraints** from the business / organisational strategy.

Example

Silverline Ltd is introducing a new line of clothing in the market. The company is planning to gain a major share of the clothing market within the next five years. In view of the competition, Silverline wants to introduce its clothing at the same time as its competitor launches its range of branded clothing in the market. The project manager who has been appointed for this project needs to align the project with the organisational strategy. For example, if the competitor is going to launch its clothing range in three months' time, Silverline's project manager has only three months to complete the project.

1. Every business has some motive, such as maximising profit or achieving its socio-economic objective. Organisations operate to make profit and there are also some non-profit organisations which operate to achieve a social objective. Whatever work these organisations undertake is aimed at making profit or achieving a socio-economic objective. These organisations spend their money on projects which contribute to their objective. Hence the project manager needs to **align the scope, time and cost factors with the organisational strategy** and plan the strategy accordingly. Implementing the project outside the scope of the business strategy will not be in stakeholders' interests. Stakeholders are interested in or create the project as the process towards aligning the project objective with the business objective which is derived from the organisational strategy. Sometimes the project manager needs to show the significance of the project objective in view of the organisational strategy.

2. A project is created to achieve goals which, in turn, transform the business. It's not one project but the **integration of all the projects that transforms the business**

Example

A company's projects include developing online accounting systems; developing an online sales service, collecting market data to assist management's decision making and expanding the business. Once these goals have been achieved, the business will be transformed i.e. it will take a new shape.

3. Organisations **prioritise their projects** according to their importance in achieving the organisational objectives. Business strategy is implemented through project management. Projects with strategic importance and competitive value get more attention from management.

4. **SWOT analysis** is one of the tools for aligning organisational strategy with project management. Project managers need to understand the **strengths and weaknesses** the project has in relation to its external and internal environment, and the **opportunities and threats** the project has both within the organisation and outside the organisation. A good project manager should have knowledge of SWOT analysis (explained later on in this Study Guide) in order to know the total rational value of the project. This will help him to identify the goals and objectives of the project more clearly and he can develop strategies to implement the project successfully.

5. Aligning the organisational strategy with project management ensures that the work of the people in the organisation occurs at a **strategic level**. It ensures that everyone is working in the best interests of the organisation.

6. By implementing the organisational strategy in project management, project management becomes **organisational project management** rather than individual project management.

Once the goal or objective has been achieved, an organisation can measure how far it is from its goal. It can measure where it stands in terms of strategy.

Example

Cheap-Mart is working on a strategy to provide low cost goods. As part of this strategy, let's say, Cheap-Mart is setting up a project which involves building a new shop. Here the project manager needs to link the project objective with the overall business strategy. He needs to make sure that the layout of the building accommodates as many goods as possible. The store should meet the objective of selling goods at a low cost. The project manager needs to select a location in which he can attract people who want value for money. (He should not select a location in which the population is wealthy and more interested in the status value of products.)

---

7. Aligning project management with organisational strategy **turns traditional project management into strategic project management**. Traditional project management techniques can be summarised as:

   - stating the project objective
   - defining the project scope and inter-relationships
   - setting the cost and time constraints
   - planning and scheduling the work of the project
   - arranging for resources
   - monitoring the progress over a given timescale

The strategic parts of the project management process include:

   - identifying the problem
   - finding out the alternatives
   - managing stakeholders
   - envisaging a strategic vision for the project
   - visualising possible implementation difficulties

A project manager must have core project management skills. He must be able to manage the project within its life cycle. He must be able to define a project's objective and outline the scope of the project within its triple constraints (quality, time and cost). He must plan the project by breaking tasks down into activities, timescales and priorities. He needs to review the progress of the project, monitoring the time, cost, and scope constraints, which may need to be redefined. The project manager needs to implement corrective actions if required. He needs to see that the project objective has been achieved and that stakeholders are satisfied. He also needs to measure the extent to which stakeholders' expectations have been met.

In strategic project management the project manager has to do more than what is required in traditional project management. He needs to have **leadership skills**, not just to lead the project team members who have come from different functional departments and parts of the company, but to influence the internal and external stakeholders. A project manager should have good **communication skills** and he must be diplomatic i.e. he should know how to get the work done. He needs to show the internal stakeholders who challenge the significance of the project how the project fits in the overall strategy of the organisation. **Review and learning** are two essential aspects of post-review of the project. An organisation has to review the way in which key stakeholders are managed and the extent to which they are satisfied with the project objective. Finally, it needs to review and **improve the project management process**.

SUMMARY

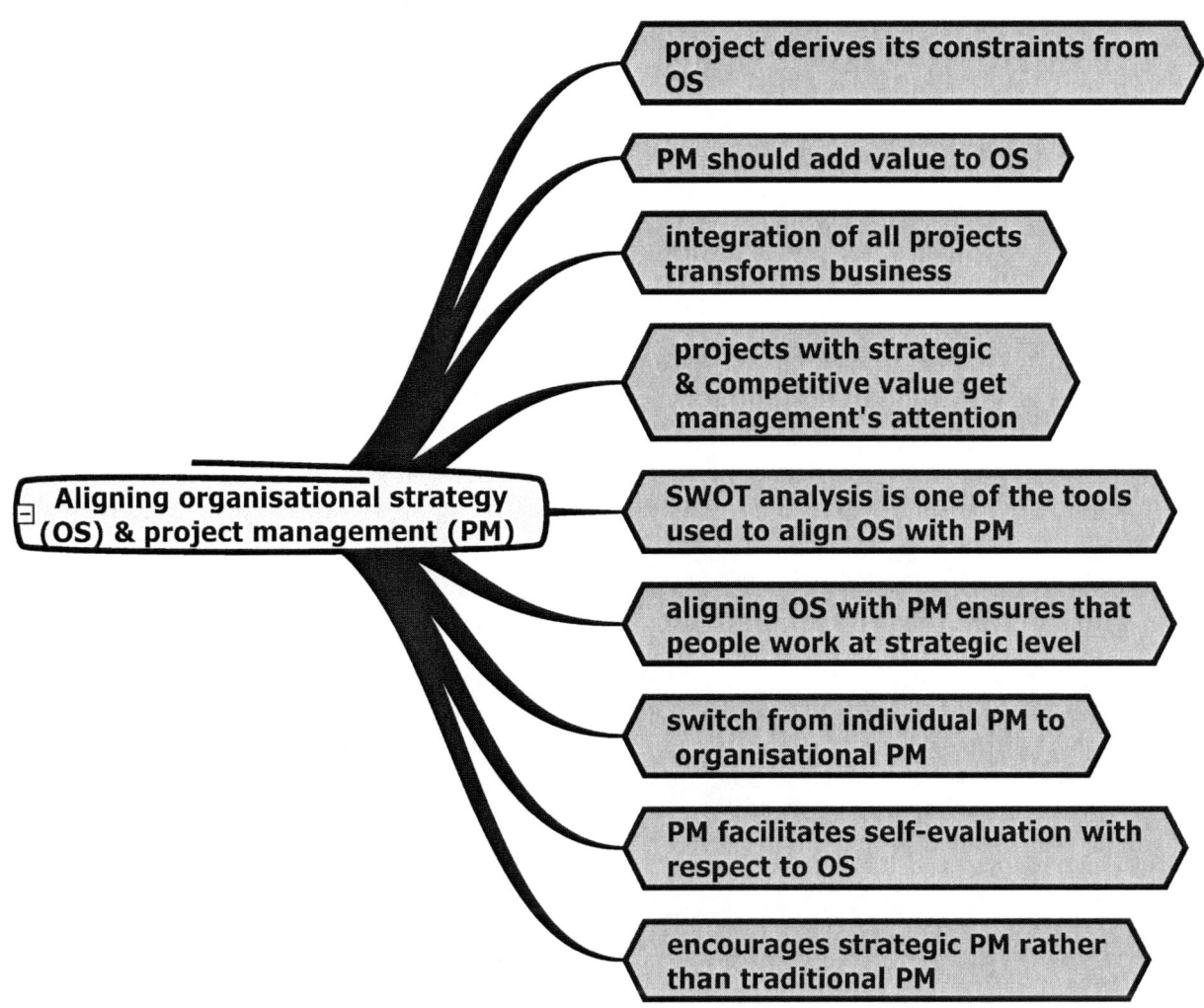

Test Yourself 2

Health Care Ltd is a large company which has been manufacturing medicines and vaccines for the last ten years. Health Care's business objective is to become the market leader in the pharmaceutical industry within the next five years. Health Care's strategy for achieving this objective is to increase its market share and gain a competitive advantage. The company has researched and developed projects for discovering new drugs and improving existing drugs.

Required:

Describe how the R&D projects can be aligned with Health Care's organisational strategy to achieve its business objective, and how Health Care's strategy can influence its projects.

---

3. **Identify and plan to manage risks.** [2]

[Learning Outcome d]

Definition

Project risk can be defined as probability that an event or uncertainty will exploit the asset or group of assets or will cause loss or damage to project objective or project sponsor.

In simple words, risk can be defined as the possibility of something happening or likely deviation from the expectation, which could change the project environment or affect the project outcome in a negative or positive way.

3.1 Risk can be categorised as:

1. **Inherent risk:** this risk arises because of the **nature of the work**. Every project has some inherent risk, as project conception and planning is based on human judgement.

2. **Hazard risk:** this type of risk covers **natural disasters** like earthquakes, fire and floods.

3. **Financial risk:** this type of risk covers **financial problems** which the business faces, such as bankruptcy, bad debts, currency and fluctuations in interest rates.

4. **Operating risk:** this type of risk covers **day-to-day operations,** such as business workers going on strike, computer system failure (e.g. virus problems) or problems with transportation which is supplying goods to customers.

5. **Strategic risk:** this type of risk can be explained as a **threat to the existing strategy,** because of which the business has to change the existing strategy or it will be in danger of losing many of its customers to its competitors. The best example of a strategic risk is if a competitor is automating all its operations, which imposes the risk of losing customers to the competitor.

Risk has the following **three elements**:

- Threats to and weaknesses of an asset exposed to risk
- Impact of this event on assets / project objectives / project sponsors
- Likelihood and frequency of its occurrence

3.2 Features of the risk

1. Business risk has a **negative impact** on the processes, assets or business objectives of an organisation.

2. This impact might be **financial, operational or regulatory**.

3. Risk arises as a result of the interaction between a business or organisation and its environment; sometimes it is just an outcome of the strategies, systems, processes, technology, procedures and information used by the business. Risk also arises as a result of the **existence of uncertainty** in the above elements. When the uncertainty can be quantified, it is known as a risk.

4. Risk can be categorised as **high / medium / low** on the basis of its impact on assets, its likelihood and its frequency. Risk under the high / medium category gets attention from management.

Example

Examples of risk in view of project management:
- missed deadline
- poor quality
- unsatisfied stakeholders
- cost overruns

SUMMARY

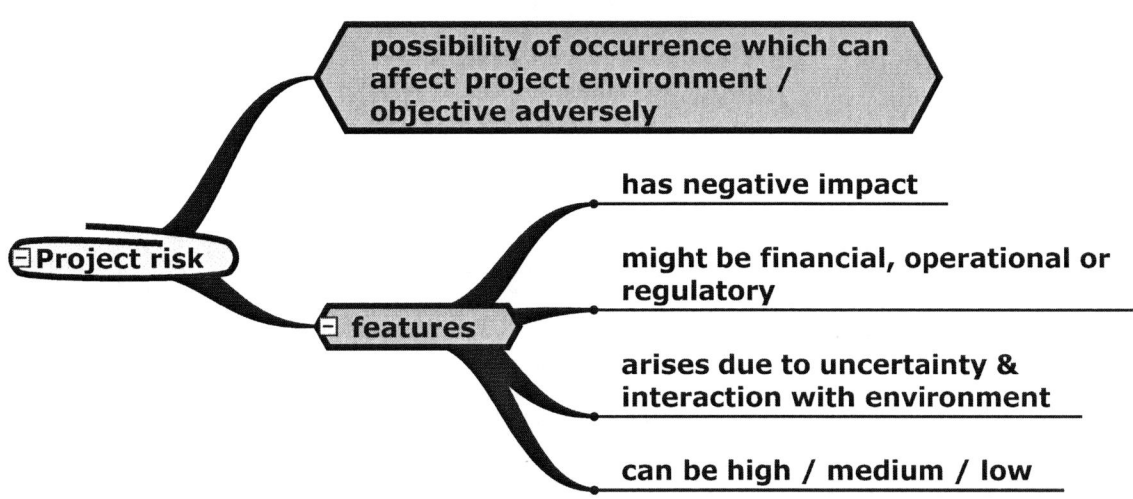

3.3 Risk management

Definition

Risk management can be defined as the process of identifying the parts of the business exposed to risk and threats to the business assets or resources used by an organisation in achieving the business objective, and defining what actions are necessary to mitigate those risks to an acceptable level depending upon the value of the negative impact to the organisation.

1. **Risk assessment (risk identification and risk analysis)**

a) **Risk identification: identifying and classifying the underlying risk events** of the project is the first step in a risk management process. A project is exposed to many uncertainties. These risks may occur as a project progresses.

Example

Performance failure showing an inability to meet the project objective, results which are not according to stakeholders' expectations, delays in completing the work schedule, increase in costs, supply shortages, litigations, strikes etc.

The purpose of classification is to **club similar types of risks together** to enable further analysis, prioritise risks, identify appropriate protection or use a standard protection model.

Generally, project stakeholders identify underlying risk events and rate them as high, medium or low based on the probability of occurrence and the level of impact. The ratings have to be decided keeping in mind the management's risk appetite i.e. management's willingness to take risk.

Example

A loss of $1,000 for a multibillion dollar company can be rated as low whereas it can be rated as high for a company with a turnover of $50,000.

Based upon this, the project manager prepares a **probability and impact matrix**.

b) **Risk analysis**: preparing the **risk register** is the second step in the risk management process. On the basis of the risk probability and impact matrix, the project manager (with the help of his team members) plans possible responses to risks with high / moderate impacts. He then documents the following information in the risk register, for each risk event:

i. an identification number for the risk event
ii. a rank for the risk event
iii. the name of the risk event
iv. a description of the risk event
v. the category under which the risk event falls
vi. the root cause of the risk event
vii. the triggers for the risk event (triggers are the indicators or symptoms of actual risk events)

Example

A change in project scope while the project is progressing might indicate poor scope planning or technology change. There is a possibility that a project is already exposed to scope creep. Cost overruns might indicate poor cost estimates.

viii. potential responses / countermeasures to each risk event

Tip

Scope creep arises due to uncontrolled changes in the project scope. Scope creep can occur when the project's scope is not properly defined, documented and controlled. To tackle the risk of scope creep, the project manager can decide a point/stage, after which he should not allow any changes in project scope.

ix. the risk owner or person who will own or take responsibility for the risk event
x. the probability of the risk event occurring
xi. the impact on the project if the risk event occurs, and the contingency measures required to reduce the impact of such risk
xii. the status of the risk event

2. Risk control (risk planning and risk monitoring)

The project manager needs to choose ways to reduce the risk to an acceptable level. He needs to look for **alternative plans of action** to implement the project. A project manager should try to incorporate clauses in the contractual agreement in order to reduce or to transfer the risk which has negative effects.

Example

In an agreement to buy a product or service, the project manager can make the seller take the responsibility for certain negative risks and make him responsible for any costs that are incurred. He can obligate the seller to deliver a certain quality for a given price. He can add an incentive and penalty clauses. He can even introduce a contract termination clause.

Depending on the type of risk and its significance to the business and the management, a project manager may choose to:
a) **Avoid** i.e. using alternative processes or actions that would incur less risk.
b) **Mitigate** i.e. putting controls in place to protect business assets and the project objective.
c) **Transfer** i.e. transferring risk by outsourcing some work, or by sharing it with partners, or by taking out insurance cover against it.
d) **Accept** i.e. accepting the existence of the risk and monitoring it.
e) **Eliminate** i.e. removing the source of the risk where possible.
f) **Ignore** i.e. ignoring it (this could be dangerous).
g) **Prepare contingency plans:**

- A project manager has to make some contingency plans to reduce the impact of the risk if it actually materialises.
- Fall back plans can also be prepared to supplement the preventive efforts that have a high impact on meeting the project objective. Fall back plans are put into effect when the efforts to reduce the risk are not effective.
- The project manager can maintain contingency reserves which can be used if an unexpected risk materialises, in order to meet the additional demands of the project.

> **Example**
>
> The best example of this kind of plan is the disaster recovery plan. Now day's organisations prepare disaster recovery plan as the part of the Business continuity planning. Disaster recovery plan includes the processes, procedures one should follow to cope up with the unexpected or sudden emergency and for restoring the operations required for the resumption of business including the recovery of data, software and hardware.

SUMMARY

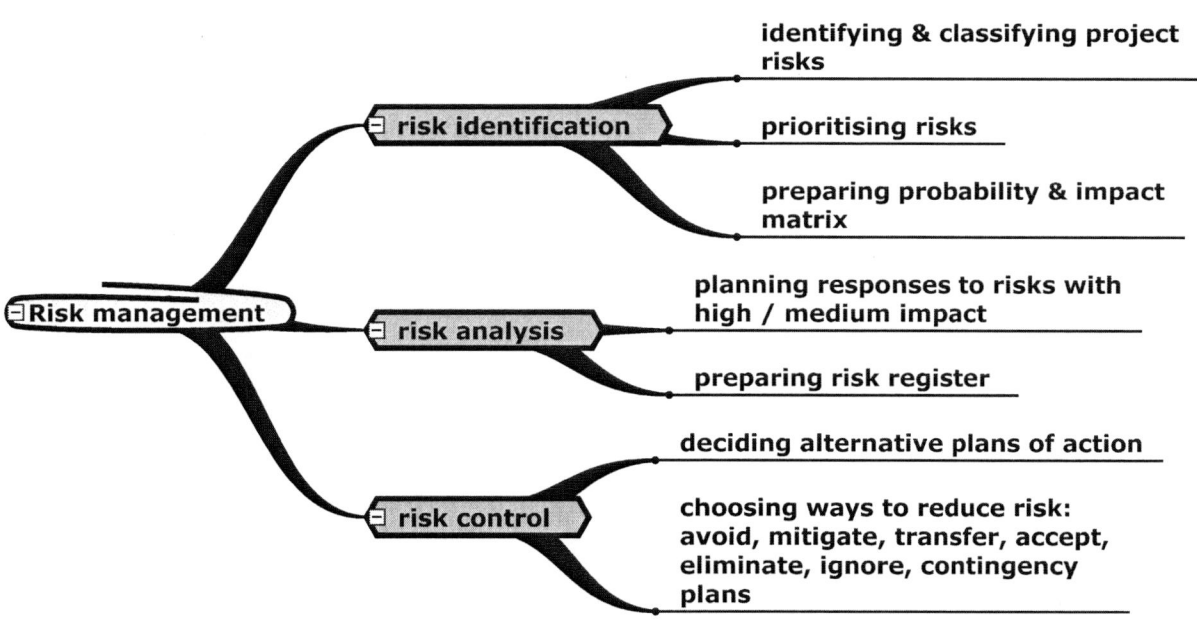

In the context of the project, risk might cause the project to suffer in the following ways:

- project termination
- delays in delivering the project benefits (in other words, an increase in project duration)
- reduction in the quality of benefits
- cost overruns

3.4 In the context of project management, the following attributes **increase the probability of risk**:

1. **Lack of leadership skills**

Many project leaders / project managers do not have the necessary management skills although they might be good at the technical aspects of the project. They need to have **formal training** on project management and some **practical experience** in handling smaller and less critical projects.

2. **Lack of sufficient funds**

Some projects do not get the funds required to carry out the project. Due to this they appoint less qualified staff, buy sub-standard material, and make compromises. This, in turn, affects the **quality of the project objective**. The project objective might not serve the purpose for which the project is created or add the value expected from it. This can be avoided by **breaking down the whole project** into a number of projects and carrying out only the projects that will **fit into the available budget**. The remaining projects can be carried out when cash resources are available.

3. **Scope creep**

Scope creep arises due to **uncontrolled changes** in the project scope. Scope creep can occur when the project's scope is not properly defined, documented and controlled. The project's time is estimated and the budget is approved for the original budget. Any changes later on might lead to the project overrunning its budget and/or deadline. To tackle the risk of scope creep, the project manager can **define the line** after which he should not allow any changes in project scope. If the project scope changes continuously, even after the project work has started, then it might affect the project's success in terms of quality, cost and time.

4. Lack of proper judgement in estimating the time and cost

While breaking down the scope in terms of activities and scheduling those activities, the project manager has to use **proper planning and scheduling techniques** that are available like PERT and Gantt Charts which are explained later on in this Study Guide. If he has not done this, he might come up with **inaccurate estimates** that will affect the project's success in terms of quality, time and cost.

5. Unrealistic deadlines

Sometimes because of competition, or to align the project with the organisation's strategy, the project manager feels the pressure to complete the project within **unrealistic time limits,** with limited resources. Sometimes, to succeed against competitors, project managers quote an unrealistic time, which might affect the project in terms of cost and quality. The project manager should carry out a **critical path analysis** (explained later on in this Study Guide) and see that the activities on this path are not compromised.

Below are a few examples of risks and their countermeasures in a project which involves building a commercial complex in a period of 2 years:

Risk	Probability	Impact	Countermeasure
Expected cash flow may not be realised	High	High	Plan for emergency cash flow which can be used in such a case, or build contingency reserve
Labour may go on strike	Low	High	Have a list of alternative labour supplying agencies
Material may not be received on time	High	Medium	Keep sufficient material in stock and fill in the purchase order well in advance
Quality of the construction may turn out to be substandard	Low	High	Offer some amenities free of cost, or offer some luxury amenities either free of cost or at a concessionary rate

SUMMARY

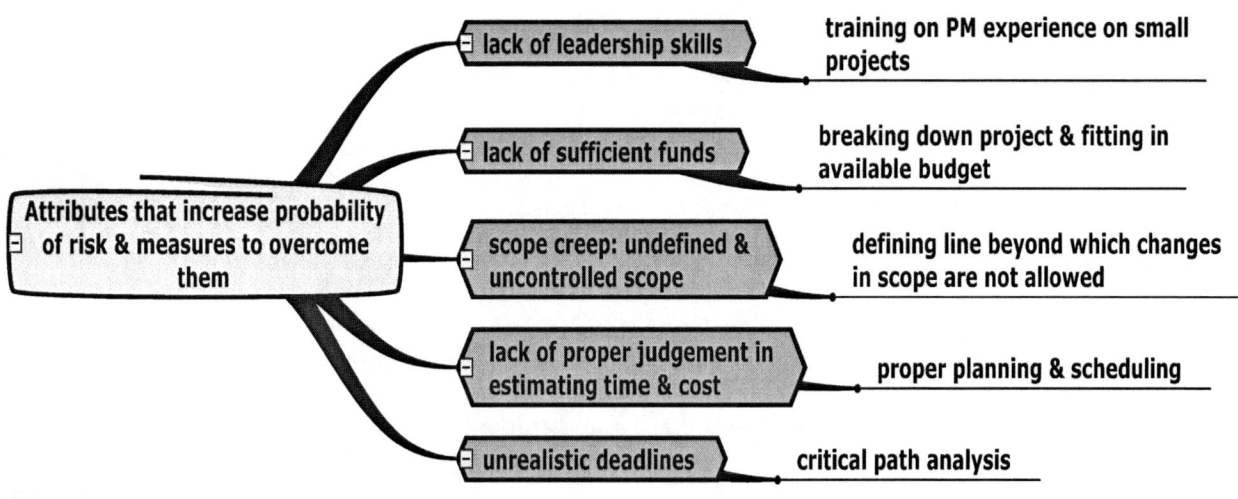

Test Yourself 3

Datasys Ltd is in the consultancy business, providing solutions for the management of databases and information systems. Datasys has received a project from Acme Plc for developing a database design system. The nature of Acme's business is complex due to the diversity and interlinks between its different businesses at different levels. Clara has been promoted to the position of a project manager for this project. Clara is technically proficient but has not handled any projects before. Under normal circumstances, the project would take 6 months to complete. Acme and Datasys's marketing division is pressurising Clara to finish the project within 5 months.

Continued on the next page

Required:

Identify and explain the main factors that could prevent Datasys's software development project from meeting its original objectives.

> **4. Advise on the structures and information that have to be in place to successfully initiate a project.** [3]
>
> **[Learning Outcome e]**

Some initial work needs to be carried out before starting a project. The project champion (senior manager), project sponsor or project manager needs to have some information that can be presented in terms of the project charter and project objective, in a **project initiation document (PID)**. Upon approval of this document, the project will formally begin. One of the techniques to evaluate the project's usefulness is to carry out a SWOT analysis. After doing the SWOT analysis, if the project sponsors and senior managers feel that the project would bring more benefits than the costs required to complete the project, then the project will get the necessary approval.

Initiation of the project

1. **The pre-initiating actions of senior managers** can be summarised as:

   a) Identifying project sponsor / sponsors who will provide the funding and direction for the project.
   b) Determining the scope, time and cost constraints of the project. In order to find out the estimated cost of the project, **work breakdown structures** and **cost breakdown structures** are prepared. To find out the time required, network diagrams like CPA and PERT are used.
   c) Selecting the project manager.
   d) Reviewing the process and expectations of the project sponsor with the project manager.
   e) Deciding whether to do the project as a one big project or divide it into a few smaller projects.

   The senior manager can follow standard processes and procedures set by the organisation for initiating and managing projects. He can give directions or suggestions and act as a mentor to the project manager.

2. **Identifying and understanding project stakeholders**

   A project manager has to build relationships with project stakeholders and project sponsors. He needs to identify their interests in and expectations of the project.

   The people who are going to benefit from this project like customers, employees (especially those who are responsible for the custody of documents and users of these documents), members (who will get an extra share of profit) and management could be considered stakeholders of this project.

   In order to do this, a stakeholders' analysis is undertaken. **The stakeholders' analysis** includes the following points:
   a) names and organisation of the key stakeholders
   b) their roles in the project
   c) characteristics of each stakeholder
   d) the nature of their interest in the project and their exact expectations from it
   e) their influence in the creation / execution / direction of the project
   f) suggestions for managing relationships with each of them

   The stakeholders' analysis is not the official project document as it includes sensitive information. Generally, this is not available to stakeholders for review.

3. **Identifying user requirements**

   Users might be different to stakeholders, so it is essential to know their requirements. This helps the project manager to meet their expectations of the project. It increases the common understanding of the project objective.

4. **Preparing a business case**

   A business case is a document that provides **significance or validity** and justification to the project being undertaken. It states the reasons that led to the birth of the project.

5. Finding alternative solutions

The project manager, along with the project sponsor, project stakeholders and users, should try to find other solutions to the problem.

6. Preparing a project charter

A project charter is a document showing the **plans of the project**. It contains the following points

a) project title
b) date of authorisation
c) project schedule including its start and end date
d) budget allocated to the project and possibility of getting more funds sanctioned for contingencies
e) name and contact information of the project manager
f) description of the project objectives
g) plans made to meet the project objective, assumptions, if any, and references to the relevant documents where possible
h) roles allocated to individuals, their names and positions, contact information etc.
i) project chart - final approval
j) stakeholders' comments

7. **A tasks list and resources required** to complete the project are identified and collected.

Example
(continuing the example of Bro Ltd)

The tasks list will include tasks such as acquiring the necessary software and hardware and finding the required team members and resources. The resource list could include details such as the names of IT professionals and other project team members, hardware and software platforms, other materials and finances required to carry out the project.

8. A project kick-off meeting

The next step in initiating a project is to hold a project kick-off meeting. This is generally used to start the project formally.

a) The kick-off meeting explains the project, its objective, and the roles and responsibilities of those involved in the project. Generally, other than the project manager, the project sponsor, stakeholders, and the team members assigned to the project are invited.
b) A chain of command is established.
c) The senior manager who carries out the pre-initiating tasks will start the meeting by introducing the project manager and project sponsor.
d) The senior manager will try to persuade anyone who challenges the need for the project.

9. Scope statement

The initial-stage scope statement is prepared at this time. Detailed iterations of the scope statement are prepared later on as the project progresses.

The scope statement
a) Outlines the work to be done in order to achieve the project objective. This is written down in order to avoid scope creep.
b) Ensures a common understanding of the scope of the project amongst the project sponsor, project manager and project team members.
c) The scope statement includes:

   ➢ the product / service requirement (in terms of its characteristics)
   ➢ a summary of project outputs / deliverables
   ➢ criteria for the project's success
   ➢ details of the information provided in the business case and project charter
   ➢ specifications of the products and relevant policies, procedures and standards

Summary of documents required for initiating a project

1. project initiation document
2. work breakdown structure (initial stage)
3. cost breakdown structure (initial stage)
4. project's schedule (initial stage)
5. business case
6. budget approval
7. project charter
8. task list and list of resources required to complete the project
9. scope statement

Depending on the organisation's policies, the **following work / tasks have to be documented** in a standard format:

- SWOT analysis
- cost-benefit analysis
- risk analysis
- network diagrams
- stakeholders' analysis
- agenda and minutes of the kick-off meeting

Test Yourself 4

Elegant Jewellers produces jewellery which it sells through ten large showrooms. The showrooms carry a range of designer gold, silver, platinum and diamond jewellery. The company has a centralised IT system for accounting and inventory control. Elegant Jewellers is facing a new challenge due to the emergence of e-shopping, which is quickly becoming popular among customers and being adopted by its competitors. Elegant's management have realised the potential of the concept of e-commerce and have decided to start selling jewellery online.

Required:

State the information that needs to be in place for Elegant Jewellers' e-commerce project to be initiated successfully.

---

5. Explain the relevance of projects to process redesign and e-business systems development. [2]

[Learning Outcome f]

5.1 Process redesign

Business process redesign is **itself a project** with the aim of **process improvement**. Organisations have to look at their processes from a fresh perspective and try to come up with solutions to improve these processes, in order to best suit them to the way the organisation does its business, or to improve the way business is conducted.

Example

KBT Ltd is an automobile manufacturing company which began operating 50 years ago. As the company has a long history, its processes are also old-fashioned. The management at KBT realises that technology has advanced and that they should introduce process redesign efforts by incorporating automation, although they already introduced automation of processes a few years ago. The management thinks it could save on production cost and sell automobiles at a lower cost by taking advantage of mass production.

Apart from the normal steps involved in a project, the following specific work needs to be carried out in a process design project:

Steps involved in a business process redesign

1. defining the areas where business processes change or where improvement is sought

2. developing a project plan for business process redesign
   - For an effective assessment of business process, **process decomposition** to the lowest level possible has to be done in order to reach the elementary process i.e. the unit of work which has a definite input and output.
   - It is necessary to identify the process owners, managers and customers who are involved in the processes from beginning to end

3. understanding and reviewing current processes
   - Process related information is documented.
   - Flow charts are prepared for the baseline processes and related profile documents.
   - New flow charts are prepared with the profile documents after the process redesign.
   - The whole project is aligned with the organisational strategy with respect to culture, structure, direction and components of change.
   - New business priorities are fixed.

4. redesigning and streamlining processes
   - implementing and monitoring new processes to judge their effectiveness
   - Processes are implemented keeping in mind improvements in products / services and profitability.
   - New approaches to organisation are formed.
   - Technology is used to develop and deliver products / services.
   - There are changes in job description and job profiles due to changed processes.

5. establishing a continuous improvement process

SUMMARY

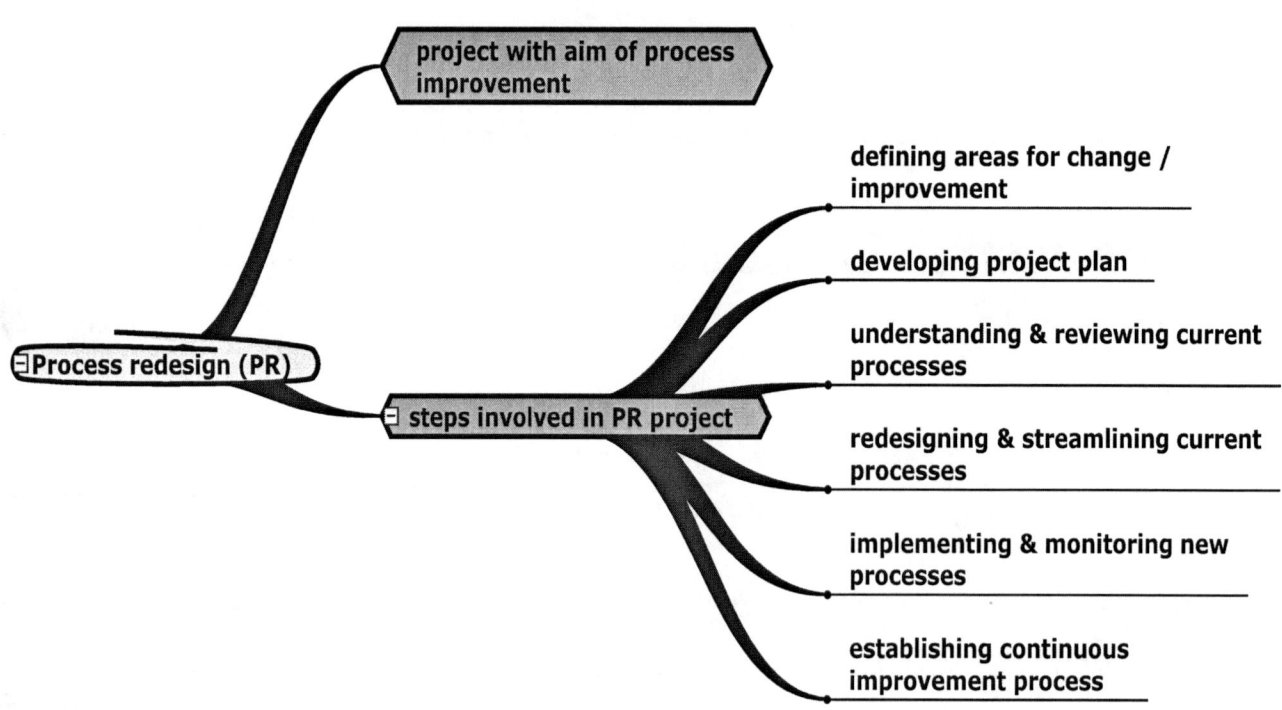

5.2 E-business systems development

As the name suggests, these are electronic business systems comprising **buying and selling online** (using internet technology as a means) as well as other aspects of online business such as customer support and relationships between businesses, office systems and processes that support e-business activities.

In e-business, all key business processes are transformed into electronic systems using internet technology. To transform a traditional business into an e-business, the entity has to undertake a **systems development project**.

Example

Some good examples of e-businesses are amazon.com, ebay.com or priceline.com, where all business-to-business, business-to-customer, customer-to-business and customer-to-customer interactions are online. , Airlines today also provide e-tickets to their customers, and this could be taken as an example of e-business.

The lifecycle of projects initiated for systems development is the same as any other project. E-commerce i.e. e-business requirements include:

1. Building a business case qualifying internet technology as a means for carrying out the project.
2. Developing a clear business purpose.
3. Using the technology to reduce cost.
4. A business case has to be built taking into consideration customers, costs, competitors and capability.
5. Top level commitment: considering the wide scope of the project and the number of changes required; strong commitment and clear vision from the top level is essential to a project's success.
6. Business process reconfiguration: apart from using technology for innovation, inventiveness is required to envisage how this technology could enable the organisation to reconfigure some of its basic processes.
7. Understanding the customer's needs, envisaging their future requirements and assessing how much value these services can bring to customers.
8. Links to legacy systems: the new technology should effectively communicate with the existing database and systems for customer service and order processing. Accelerating response times and providing real interactions to customers is important.
9. Any risk associated with electronic data interchange should be reduced to an acceptable level.

SUMMARY

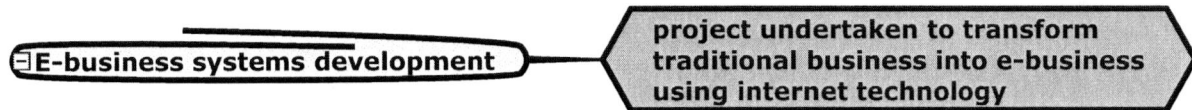

Test Yourself 5

Persona Ltd is a company offering a wide range of personal care products. Its operations are spread across several countries. The company has decided to expand by following a strategy of mergers and acquisitions. However, Persona has to face some challenges due to this strategy. The operating costs are high. Different processes are followed across Persona's operating units which are not aligned with its overall strategic goals. There are difficulties in collecting accurate data from different operating units, which often result in delayed and inefficient operational and strategic decision-making. The management of Persona has realised that it needs to undertake a business process redesign (BPR) project.

Required:

State the steps that need to be taken for successful implementation of Persona Ltd's BPR project.

Answers to Test Yourself

Answer to TY 1.

The project manager needs to decide the most important constraint for his project. Time is the primary constraint in the case of CompOne's "Online Complaint System" project. The time required for completion of the project is 5 months, which is 2 months more than the time limit set by the management. The project manager of this project can change and adjust the scope and/or cost goals to meet the schedule. Cost seems to be the least important constraint as the finance department is ready to provide additional funds. So, by employing additional resources and scaling back on quality measures to the limit acceptable by the sales service and marketing department, the project manager can complete the "Online Complaint System" project within 3 months.

Answer to TY 2.

Every project in an organisation should contribute to the organisation's strategic objectives. All the R&D projects of Health Care need to be integrated with its strategic plan so as to achieve its business objective of becoming the market leader. The scope, time and cost factors of these projects should be aligned with its organisational strategy. SWOT analysis is one of the tools for aligning organisational strategy with project management. Health Care can get to know the total rational value of its different R&D projects through SWOT analysis.

Health Care can increase its sales volume by selling medicines at a lower price than its competitors and by providing better, more innovative medicines to customers than its competitors. In this way it can increase its market share and gain a competitive advantage. The scope of R&D projects should be decided accordingly. The cost of manufacturing the drug should also be controlled accordingly. The R&D fund should be used in the most cost effective manner.

Health Care can gain a competitive advantage by getting new medicines into the market before its competitors. So the time constraint for R&D projects should be managed accordingly. The R&D team should look for the side effects of its competitors' bestselling drugs and try to invent the same drugs without those side effects. By implementing the correct marketing strategy, Health Care can capture the market.

Health Care needs to prioritise its projects according to their importance in achieving the organisational objective. The projects that enable it to get the product out more quickly to market and produce better products than its competitors are going to be the most critical ones for the success of its strategy. Such projects should be given more attention from Health Care's management.

Answer to TY 3.

Risk identification and management are the main concerns in any project. There are a number of factors that can prevent Datasys's software development project from being successfully completed. A common complaint made by many project managers is that clients frequently alter their specifications. Clara needs to be ready to adapt to changing requirements from Acme and unexpected project scope expansions. This may result in an increase in costs and the project taking longer to complete than anticipated. Clara can avoid this situation by having a discussion with the client and fixing a point in advance, after which there should be no changes in the scope of the project. Clara is technically proficient but may not have leadership skills and capabilities to manage the project. Her role should focus on supervision, planning and control and not on detailed operations.

There is also some risk associated with inaccurate planning and control. Without accurate planning it is difficult to assess costs and lead times. Consequently, unattainable deadlines might be agreed upon. The pressure for unrealistic deadlines may lead to dangerous shortcuts which may damage quality. This may also result in incorrect and optimistic status reporting. The problem could become worse if there is no control, i.e. there are no performance reviews and so the management of the project becomes non-existent.

It is also critical for the project to have sufficient and appropriate resources. A lack of certain specialists or finances can result in poor quality output. The project seems to be complex due to complexities in the nature of Acme's business. This is a technical risk that may result in a failure to identify complex functionalities and the time required to develop those functionalities.

Answer to TY 4.

Before starting the e-commerce project, Elegant Jewellers must assess whether it has efficient information technology (IT) solutions to execute its online operations. In addition, Elegant needs to make sure that the following information is in place before initiating the e-commerce project:

1. **SWOT analysis:** evaluation of the e-commerce project on the basis of its strengths, weaknesses, opportunities and threats.

2. **Cost-benefit analysis:** assessment of costs and benefits (both tangible and intangible).

3. **Stakeholders' analysis:** a list of stakeholders, e.g. customers, management and staff, and their interests in and expectations from the project. Customers are the key stakeholders as well as the end users of the project outcome, so a lot of research is required to understand their requirements.

4. **Risk analysis:** possible changes in circumstances, possible problems and an action plan for correcting problems e.g. security issues such as cyber attacks or frauds.

5. **Purpose statement / business case:** the reasons why the project is being undertaken e.g. growing popularity for e-shopping.

6. **Scope statement:** this will set the boundaries for the e-commerce project e.g. decisions about whether to conduct only sales transactions, such as allowing customers to search for, order and pay for products online, or whether to integrate sales transactions with back-office systems such as accounting, inventory and sales.

7. **Cost and time estimates:** cost estimates based on the need for additional IT investment to upgrade existing systems. To know the estimated cost of the project, a work breakdown structure and cost breakdown structure need to be prepared. The project's timescale should be stated clearly.

8. **List of tasks and resources** required to complete the project. Such tasks include selecting a domain name for Elegant Jewellers' website, registering with search engines, choosing a web host for the website, and developing website contents. Resources include funds, hardware and software, as well as the IT team.
9. **Project organisation structure:** chain of command, and the roles and responsibilities assigned to managers and teams.

Answer to TY 5.

Business process redesign (BPR) is a project which starts with the idea of process improvement. The first step is to define the areas in which business processes change or improvement is sought. In the case of Persona Ltd, areas where improvement is needed are: processes followed by its different operating units, adopted cost control techniques and Persona's current information systems.

The next step is to develop a project plan for business process redesign. Persona's project plan will state the steps to be taken for process improvement, such as setting up uniform processes across its operating units and improving information systems to support effective operational and strategic decisions.

The next step is to review current processes to find the disconnects. After this, Persona must look at redesigning and streamlining the processes. This includes introducing revised and standardised process flows across Persona's operating units, organisational restructuring to suit the re-engineered workflows, introducing new processes leading to better cost control, restructuring human resources, changing job descriptions and job profiles according to changed processes, reducing operating costs and building information systems that will avoid delay and build accuracy and reliability. The last two steps will involve implementing and monitoring the new processes in order to judge their effectiveness, and establishing a continuous improvement process.

Quick Quiz

Question 1.

Decide whether the activity is an operation or a project.

A. A company starting a new line of business
B. A couple constructing a new house
C. An organisation working to fight poverty
D. An organisation working for the protection of orphans

Question 2.

The project manager needs to align the scope, time and cost factors with the _____.

Question 3.

Which are the two steps involved in risk management?

Question 4.

The_____ is a document showing the plans of the project.

A. Work breakdown structure
B. Scope statement
C. Project charter
D. Business case

Question 5.

It is necessary to develop a project plan to ensure that the project is progressing in the right direction.
   (a) True
   (b) False

Question 6.

What is meant by quality initiatives?

Answers to Quick Quiz

1.
   A. Project: starting up a new line of business is a one time activity. It's not like an operational activity conducted throughout the life of the business.
   B. Project: construction of a new house is a one time activity.
   C. Project: this is bit difficult as the duration of the project is uncertain. It might take more than a century. But this project will end when the objective of the elimination of poverty is achieved.
   D. Operations: here the objective of working for the protection of orphans does not have any duration.

2. organisational strategy

3. Risk management involves the following steps:

   A. Risk assessment (risk identification and risk analysis)
   B. Risk control (risk planning and risk monitoring)

4. (c) Project charter

5. (a) True – a project plan helps the project manager to make sure that all the project activities are directed towards achieving the project objective.

6. Quality initiatives are initiatives adopted with the aim of quality improvement. These include tools like quality control, TQM, Zero Defects and Six Sigma.

Self Examination Questions

Question 1

S & S Ltd is a milk distribution chain, which distributes milk to the majority of the supermarkets in its country of operation. Many competitors have entered this business over the last 5 years and have started eating into S & S's market share. In order to stay competitive and maintain its previous profitability and future prospects, S & S has initiated a project to add a new line of business: selling automobile accessories.

S & S has appointed Mark as the project manager for this project. The finance provided by management for this project is not sufficient. In addition, a competitor has already opened a shop selling automobile accessories in the location management had earmarked for this project. The prices of land have gone up in other areas.

Required:

(a) Identify and explain the key issues which Mark must take into account when managing the automobile accessories project.
(b) Identify and state the main factors that can cause a project to fail to meet its original objectives.

Question 2

Tim Hack is the director of CC Ltd, a company engaged in the production of cement. It has branches in all major cities of the country and owns a major share of the market. The company's factories produce a lot of pollutants.

CC Ltd is under pressure from the neighbourhoods in the area where its factories are situated. Due to this pressure, and in order to distinguish CC Ltd from its competitors, Tim has initiated a project to plant 1000 trees in each neighbourhood in order to reduce pollution and be environmentally friendly. Tim has been challenged on his decision to start this project, as some of the board members think it is a waste of company money which could be utilised elsewhere.

Tim has proposed the appointment of a project manager for this project.

Required:

Discuss the skills which the project manager for CC Ltd's project would require.

Question 3

Tara Ltd is in the business of designing and developing microprocessors. Tara Ltd was a subsidiary company of Sitara Corp. Recently, Tara separated from Sitara as a part of Sitara's strategy of focusing on its core business area of software development. Tara Ltd was acquired through a management buyout led by the existing general manager of Tara, Stephen Edwards. The aim is for all the operations of Tara and Sitara to be separated, and for Tara to start operating as a completely independent entity within a span of 6 months.

Although the business operations of each company are different and detached from each other, Stephen is concerned about the fact that Tara's existing accounting system is totally integrated into Sitara's systems. Tara does not have a separate financial information system to support decision-making at various levels. Its internal management accounts are almost non-existent. Most management reports are directed to Sitara's management team, not to Tara's management. Budget responsibility has never been delegated to Tara's key line managers in operations and maintenance.

Tara's management is aware that it must now implement its own financial systems. The separation schedule means that Tara only has a few months to set up these new computer-based systems. The requirement is for a project management process which can deal with tight timescales involving a complicated set of interrelated decisions and actions. Tara's management must realise that effective project planning and control need different management skills to those required running operational processes.

This is the immediate requirement, but in the longer term Tara must put in place a strategy for managing information resources in ways which enable it to make efficient and effective strategic decisions, and to achieve a competitive advantage over its competitors.

Required:

State the features of the project and examine the constraints of a project management process for changeover by Tara Ltd to new financial systems.

Answers to Self Examination Questions

Answer to SEQ 1

(a) S & S is a distribution chain distributing a perishable product, milk. This project was initiated to add a new line of products which is not perishable. After studying the strengths and weaknesses as well as the opportunities and threats this business might face, the management has decided to explore this new market.

Mark should take into account following key issues when managing the automobile accessories project:

Scope: the scope of the project should be clear. There should be a point accepted by all, after which the project manager should not allow any changes in the scope of the project. This will help him to avoid scope creep. Selling non-perishable goods will require a different infrastructure. Building such an infrastructure will also come under the project's scope.

Objective: the project manager should understand the objective for starting the project, such as the circumstances under which the project is created and the expectations of the project's stakeholders. This understanding will give the project manager an idea of their expectations from the project. In the given case, maximising profit and being competitive are the two objectives of the project.

Cost: the finances available for the project are limited. Mark should not make any compromises which will harm the main purpose of the project. If, to save money, he ends up choosing land which is located in front of the competitor's land, this would affect the objective of the project. The project manager should try to get additional funding for this project.

Time: time is also a crucial element of the management triangle. Scope and cost constraints have an impact on the time constraint. In this case Mark has a lot of flexibility with respect to time, although finances are limited.

Quality: the project's triple constraints always affect the quality of the project. The time constraint may mean sacrificing the quality, or cost constraints may mean buying low quality inputs which affect the quality of the project. Mark should not in any way compromise on the quality of the project's work as it would affect the ultimate aim of the management and would not justify the investment in the project. The project manager does have some flexibility with respect to the trade-off between the cost, time and scope of the project.

(b) The following are factors that can cause a project to fail to meet its original objective:

- If a project is working on unproven technology then it might cause an increase in cost and time, which may cause the project to exceed its budget and affect the ultimate objective of the project.
- Frequent change in the project's specifications is also a reason for increase in the project's cost and duration.
- Changes in technical platforms (or when technology permits more than one approach to solve a particular issue) can also affect the success of a project. These changes in the technical platform or technical approaches might mean an increase in the cost and time required to complete the project.

- Project managers focusing heavily on technology may forget the operational aspects of the project, and may end up estimating unrealistic time and cost deadlines.

- Again, if the project planning is carried out without using CRM, PERT and Gantt Charts, the project manager might end up making inaccurate cost and time estimates.

- There is always pressure from the competitor, and in an attempt to gain a project, unrealistic estimates for costs and time may be agreed upon. In some cases, even before involving technical experts, commitments are made. The pressures of reputation and competition make it hard to communicate real estimates to the client. This ultimately affects the quality of the project work and may harm the project objective.

- Generally, project managers come from a technical background and know little about management and cost control. Such people might give more attention to the operational / technical aspects of the project rather than management aspects such as supervision, control and monitoring.

- Restrictions on resources might produce substandard results. Limitations on costs can result in following low cost alternatives, like buying substandard material. Pressure on time may lead to compromises in quality.
- Last but not the least is the senior management's support. With the help of the senior management, the project manager can overcome problems which may otherwise seem impossible to solve. Again, if the senior management takes too much interest in operational activities, this could reduce the quality of the entity's management as the managers would not be able to devote much time to the strategically important aspects, which could affect the overall progress of the entity.

Answer to SEQ 2

A project can be defined as a temporary endeavour undertaken to create a particular product or service, which is termed a project objective. A project comprises:

(a) collaborative actions and planned activities designed to achieve a project objective
(b) a start, middle and end process which consumes resources

In CC Ltd's case, the particular objective / aim is 'being environmentally friendly to reduce the pollution created by the cement factories.' By carrying out a SWOT analysis of the project, it emerges the project does not have strong management support, although it has the support of the director of the company. There are insiders challenging the project's existence and outsiders who would love to see the project materialise. This project has strategic importance: being environmentally friendly is a strategy which has not yet been adopted by the company. However, from an operational and administrative point of view, this project does not have much importance. Considering the project's circumstances, the project manager appointed for this project should have both traditional and strategic management skills.

Traditional project management techniques are:

- stating the project objective
- defining the project scope and interrelationships
- setting the cost and time constraints
- planning and scheduling the work of the project
- arranging for the resources
- monitoring the progress over the timescale

Strategic parts of the project management process include:

- identifying the problem
- finding out the alternatives
- managing stakeholders
- envisaging a strategic vision for the project
- visualising possible difficulties in implementation

The project manager is expected to work in the two fields mentioned above. The project manager should be proficient in traditional as well as strategic project management skills. He must be able to manage the project within its lifecycle. He has to define the project's objective and outline the scope of the project within its triple constraints (quality, time and cost). He has to plan the project by breaking down project tasks in terms of activities, time and priorities. He needs to review the progress of the project, checking the time, cost, scope constraints, redefining them if required and taking corrective actions. He needs to see whether the project objective is achieved and stakeholders are satisfied, as well as the extent to which their expectations have been met.

The strategic aspect of project management requires the project manager to do more than just what is needed in traditional project management. He needs to have leadership skills, not just to lead the project team members who have come from different functional departments and parts of the company but to influence the internal and external stakeholders. A project manager should have good communication skills and he must be political. He needs to show the internal stakeholders who are challenging the significance of the project how this project fits the overall strategy of the business. The success of the project could change the company's image or it could distinguish the company from its competitors. The project manager needs to make internal stakeholders aware of the outside pressure on the company to be environmentally-friendly and set up support networks and alliances. The organisation has to learn from every project; reviewing and learning are two essential aspects of the post-review of the project. The organisation has to review how key stakeholders are managed and how much they are satisfied with the project objective. Finally, they need to improve the project management process from the lessons they have learned.

Answer to SEQ 3

A project is a unique set of co-ordinated activities, with definite starting and finishing points, undertaken by an individual or team to meet specific objectives within defined time, cost and performance parameters. The management of Tara Ltd has realised that it needs to undertake a project to set up its own computer-based financial systems. This project has a unique purpose / objective of setting up and implementing separate computer-based financial systems for Tara. The project is temporary and will terminate once the changeover to a new financial system is complete. This project will require various types of resources, such as people, finance, hardware and software. The sponsor and primary customer for this project is the management of Tara.

The project implementation processes for the changeover to a new financial system differ from routine operational activities and pose different management problems. Projects are, in effect, separate one-off activities through which the organisation implements its strategy. Given this strategic link, it follows that it is critical to achieve a successful execution of the project within the set of constraints imposed by scope, time and cost. These constraints collectively define the attributes of a specific project:

Scope: can be defined as a certain number of tasks which need to be completed to achieve the project objective. Scope sets and establishes the boundary and objectives of the specific project. Defining the scope will be relatively easy for Tara as the requirements for operational financial systems are well understood by the management.

Scope can be measured in terms of quality and quantity. Quality is specified in relation to project outputs, fitness for purpose and performance criteria. In the case of a changeover to new computer-based systems, quality should be assimilated into the project through data integrity, systems documentation and the quality assurance process.

Time: every project has defined start and completion dates. The time required for successful completion of the project may vary, but all projects face some kind of time constraint. Time is the key constraint at Tara for this particular project. According to the separation schedule, Tara needs to start operating independently within 6 months. So the changeover to the new financial systems should also be completed within 6 months.

Cost: on the basis of the scope and time, the project manager has to manage the cost of the project within the approved budget. Project costs can be identified as direct costs and indirect costs. Cost includes both capital and revenue expenditure allocated to the project. Depending on Tara's accounting policies, project costs will be either treated as revenue expenditure or capitalised in the period of completion. The financial and economic feasibility of larger projects are generally evaluated using capital investment appraisal techniques such as discounted cash flow analysis.

The three project constraints mentioned above are dependent on each other. This is known as a project management triangle. If one side of the triangle changes, the other two sides will automatically change. For example, increasing the quality specification may in turn increase the cost and time elements of the project, while on the other hand, allowing a project more time may permit costs to be reduced. The combination of these project elements must be determined clearly before starting the project. This is the first key task for Tara in initiating the new system development. If this is not done, it may lead to problems such as a scope creep, or cost and time overruns during project implementation.

Tara needs to decide the most important constraint for its project. Time is the key constraint for the changeover to new financial systems. The time constraint is such that the scope of the project may be reduced and costs may be increased to achieve target implementation.

The project involves a degree of uncertainty with respect to its scope, time and cost. Risk identification and management are the main concerns in any project. Any project has a specific risk profile attached to it. Risk, in effect, relates to the degree of uncertainty surrounding each of the elements of the project. Each project will have different risk characteristics. For example, a project to upgrade or change an existing computer-based system is likely to be subject to less uncertainty than a project to completely revise and re-program an existing system.

When dealing with computer operational systems, neither quality nor the acceptable level of risk should be compromised upon. Successful project planning and control will require Tara to manage each of the project's attributes. Project management tools and techniques that have been developed in order to address the specific requirements of each scope should be laid down in the project specification, which is drawn up at the very beginning of the project planning. This needs to be properly defined, documented and controlled to avoid scope creep. Preparing a work breakdown structure helps in defining the scope, preparing the cost breakdown structure and planning the time and costs elements of the project. It involves breaking down the project work in terms of activities, and activities into sub-activities until the smallest activities are identified. The cost breakdown structure involves estimating the cost required to complete each task in the work breakdown structure.

SECTION F: PROJECT MANAGEMENT

STUDY GUIDE F2: BUILDING THE BUSINESS CASE

■ Get Through Intro

Projects are intended to deliver change and benefits to an organisation and its clients. At the start of a project companies often take significant efforts in defining and gaining agreement to a business case to justify the investment. However, visibility of the "benefits" and disclosures as to how they are to be delivered are often restricted to a relatively small group. As the focus on project delivery takes centre stage, the proposed aims and defined benefits of the project investment are often ignored or even forgotten.

This Study Guide is aimed at improving your understanding of benefits management and benefits realisation.

■ Learning Outcomes

a) Describe the structure and contents of a business case document.
b) Analyse, describe, assess and classify benefits of a project investment.
c) Analyse, describe, assess and classify the costs of a project investment.
d) Evaluate the costs and benefits of a business case using standard techniques.
e) Establish responsibility for the delivery of benefits.
f) Explain the role of a benefits realisation plan.

...er needs to have confidence about the outcome of a project - whether it should earn or save ... should be interested in the net benefits and the amount that will be left after all costs have been ...

...scribe the structure and contents of a business case document.[2]
...Analyse, describe, assess and classify benefits of a project investment.[3]

[Learning Outcomes a and b]

Before we discuss the structure and contents of a business case, it is necessary to understand benefits management.

Benefits management ensures that the desired business change or policy outcomes have been clearly defined, are measurable, and provide a convincing case for investment. This should ultimately result in the achievement of that change or policy outcome.

A generic benefits management process typically includes:

1. **Defining the benefits:** this involves ascertaining the types of benefits desired by investing in the project.

2. **Specifying the benefits:** this involves defining the precise financial and non-financial benefit metrics, which can be delivered in relation to the project.

3. **Benefits realisation:** this refers to the delivery of the benefits, as demonstrated through benefit metrics tracking. The benefits could be realised either during or following the completion of the project.

1.1 Business case

The business case provides a rationale for investment and as such should support robust analysis and rational decision-making. The development of project benefits criteria revolves primarily around the business case.

The purpose of the business case is to establish why the project should go ahead. As in the case of a project, the business case also follows a development cycle as the project evolves from idea to formal proposal.

Traditionally, the reason for developing a business case for a project was to obtain funding for a large financial investment. However, when considered in a broad sense, the business case is intended to realise benefits by implementing a project. In addition, a business case is also necessary:

➢ to enable priorities to be set among different investments for funds and resources;

➢ to identify how the benefits identified will be delivered – a benefit realisation plan;

➢ to ensure commitment from the business managers to achieve the intended investment benefits; and importantly

➢ to create a basis for review of the realisation of the proposed business benefits when the investment is complete.

A typical business case document consists of:

➢ executive summary
➢ introduction
➢ project scope and organisation
➢ benefit and cost
➢ timing
➢ certain other items

The executive summary, project benefits and costs are the sections that are usually read first and so it is essential that these sections:

➢ capture the attention of the reader;
➢ convince them of the suitability of the project; and
➢ request for the resources (money, manpower, machinery, materials, etc.)

The remainder of the business case document should discuss how the project will be delivered, the alternatives, risk factors etc.

1. Executive summary

This section provides an opportunity to capture the attention of the reader. It comprises the main purpose and benefits of the project. The executive summary should be precise, written in two or three paragraphs and ideally fit in half a page.

2. Introduction

This section provides the problem statement, the background to the project, reasons for its selection, impact on business and so on. It should be established that a suitable option has been selected after identifying a number of options that arose from consideration of the needs of the business.

3. Project scope and organisation

The scope of the project should be defined in such a way that it is easy to understand. The major deliverables and activities should be briefly discussed rather than detailing too much since the objective is to present a 'feel' of the overall project.

Project organisation should consider the nature of resources required (internal and external) to deliver the project.

4. Project delivery strategy

The strategy for delivering a project is mainly concerned with how the project will be delivered as opposed to why it should be delivered. The overall approach to delivering the project should be considered within the business case. A formal Project Delivery Plan (PDP) should be in place.

It should include:

- a project roadmap (key stages and gateways)
- project controls (cost, scope, time, risk, change)
- benefits management
- engagement of the business

The discussion here should be limited to the extent of establishing how the project will be delivered when it is approved. Too many details should not be discussed here.

5. Benefit and cost

The project approvers would, in the first instance, be interested in knowing whether the benefit is greater than the cost (within some defined business criteria). The benefit/cost statement should be mentioned in the beginning of this section.

Example

The estimated project costs are $10 million with an anticipated payback of 3 years.

In addition to the above statement, there should be a summary of the benefit and cost data. It should contain a summary table of both the key cost and benefit areas. It should also explain how the estimates have been made (with reference to quotations for cost and data assembled for benefits). Figures should be used to illustrate the cost-benefit analysis.

The costs and benefits analysis should also consider sensitivity within the calculations. Sensitivities are different from risk factors. Sensitivities refer to variables that are outside the control of the project manager that will impact the returns from the project investment. Risk factors may be controllable, are internal to the project (even if they arise due to external factors) and impact the ability of the project to deliver.

6. Timing

This section should contain a top level plan of the project indicating the key milestones and deliverables.

7. Others

The key issues that should be considered are:
- The alternatives that could be considered if no project is undertaken (if nothing is to be done, this should be highlighted in the business case).
- The risks such as potential impact on production and failure to meet specific deadlines should be considered.

1.2 Benefits of a project investment

In reality, not all benefits can be measured financially. In addition to financial benefits expected from a project, qualitative or less tangible benefits, which are often more difficult to measure, will also need to be identified and tracked. The types of benefits of a project investment are:

1. Observable benefits

These are benefits that are capable of being measured by opinion or judgement. These benefits are also often characterised as subjective, intangible or qualitative benefits. These benefits should not be regarded as trivial or ignored even if they play a negligible role in the project investment case.

2. Measurable benefits

A measurable benefit is one where there is already an identified measure for the benefit or where one can be easily put in place. This enables current performance to be determined as the baseline prior to the investment. However, the extent of improvement in performance after the investment is completed cannot be estimated.

In order to measure the benefits, the existing measures should be used and more so when they are part of the organisation's performance measurement system or its KPIs (key performance indicators).

3. Quantifiable benefits

These are similar to measurable benefits. However, in addition to being able to measure performance before the investment is made, the size or extent of the benefit can also be reliably projected. In order to proceed with the business case, there should be sufficient evidence provided to substantiate any assumptions that are made in quantifying the benefits. Quantification of benefit is necessary in order to agree a realistic financial value and thereby convert a qualitative argument into an acceptable economic case for investment.

4. Financial benefits

These are benefits that are capable of being expressed in financial terms. A benefit falls in the category of financial benefits only if it arises as a result of application of a financial value or formula to a 'proven' quantifiable benefit. The financial benefits are useful in calculating the rate of return on investment or payback. Any financial assessment of the return or payback is sensitive to incorrect data being used. Therefore, the underlying data on which the financial calculations are based should be reliable and should also be capable of being verified.

Financial benefits are not the primary reason for proceeding with a project. Organisations may proceed with an unprofitable project for reasons other than financial ones (such as social, environmental, strategic or organisational considerations).

2. Analyse, describe, assess and classify the costs of a project investment.[3]

[Learning Outcome c]

Estimating the benefits, both quantitative and financial, is complex and difficult. Equally, predicting the costs associated with an investment is often a difficult task.

2.1 Capital and revenue expenditure

Definition

Capital expenditure is the expenditure incurred to acquire, make or improve long-term assets.

Capital expenditure is the cost involved to improve the earning capacity of a business. It is incurred either by acquiring a new asset or by improving the performance of an existing asset.

An asset usually held by a business for more than twelve months is considered a long-term asset.

1. **Capital expenditure**

As defined, capital expenditure includes:

a) **Acquisition of a long-term tangible asset**

Expenditure which brings in or acquires a long-term tangible asset is capital expenditure.

> **Example**
> - Purchase of a car
> - Purchase of a machine
> - Erection of a building

b) **Improvement of long-term tangible assets**

Improvement of a long-term asset may lead to an increase in its life or its utility.

> **Example**
> - Increasing the seating capacity of a theatre.
> - Replacing the engine of a car, to increase its fuel efficiency.

c) **Acquisition or improvement of long-term intangible assets**

It is not necessary that all the capital expenditure should be on tangible assets such as cars and machinery. Expenditure on an intangible asset is also called capital expenditure.

> **Example**
> - Purchase of a licence
> - Expenditure on developing a patent

d) **Acquisition of a business**

It increases the earnings of an entity.

> **Example**
> Appearance Inc is a textile company. It acquires another textile company. The acquisition will increase the earnings of Appearance.

2. **Revenue expenditure**

> **Definition**
> Revenue expenditure is the cost of resources consumed for the purpose of generating revenue.

This is an expenditure incurred on recurring items to obtain immediate benefits. The benefits of this expenditure are expected to be consumed within one year.

2.2 Classification of expenditure

a)	Purchase of fixed assets e.g. a computer	Capital expenditure	Computer will be used in the business for long term.
b)	Salaries to staff	Revenue expenditure	It is an expenditure of a regular nature.
c)	Installation cost of a computer server	Capital expenditure	It is expenditure of a capital nature.
d)	Extension of office building	Capital expenditure	It increases the value of non-current assets and provides benefits of an enduring nature i.e. for more than one accounting period.
e)	Interest on bank loan	Revenue expenditure	It is an expenditure of a regular nature.
f)	Rent on computers	Revenue expenditure	It is an expenditure of a regular nature.
g)	Purchase of vehicle	Capital expenditure	Purchase of non-current assets is capital expenditure.
h)	Fees paid to directors	Revenue expenditure	It is an expenditure of a regular nature.
i)	Construction cost of new building	Capital expenditure	It increases the value of non-current assets and includes expenditure that provide benefits of an enduring nature i.e. for more than one accounting period.

3. Evaluate the costs and benefits of a business case using standard techniques.
[Learning Outcome d]

The appraisal of capital investments on financial grounds prior to acceptance is essential. This is because heavy outflows of cash are usually required for these investments, which will be tied up for a relatively long period of time. Managers will need to ensure that they select investments that have the potential to earn maximum returns so as to maximise shareholder wealth.

Example

The overall project cost benefit analyses could be summarised as follows:
➢ The IRR is 25%.
➢ Payback of this investment is 2 years after project completion.

The impact on unit cost of the product is:
➢ The overall cost impact of the improvements on unit cost of product is a 5.3% reduction of the cost of making product Amorax next year.
➢ Benefits amounting to approximately $1.5 million at forecast rates will contribute a 5% reduction to the site's total cost of goods next year.

The techniques such as Accounting Rate of Return (ARR) and the payback period ignore time value of money. This means that these techniques treat the value of an amount of money to be received after a period of five years as equal to the value of the same amount to be received after one year.

The techniques, namely **Net Present Value** and **Internal Rate of Return,** consider the time value of money while appraising investment projects. Discounting the cash flows reflects the fact that money has a time value.

3.1 Techniques of investment appraisal

1. Payback period

The time taken by a project to recover its initial investment is known as the payback period of the project.

Definition

The payback period of a capital investment project is the number of years it takes the investor to recover their original investment from the net cash flows that are obtained from the capital investment.

This method can be used for **conventional projects** which need an initial outlay followed by successive cash inflows during the life of the project. Unconventional cash flows may involve intermittent cash outflows and inflows. The payback method is not suitable for such projects.

An organisation decides a certain 'target payback period' e.g. two years, three years, five years etc. for appraising its capital investment projects. The organisation:

➢ accepts projects with payback period less than the organisation's target payback period; and
➢ rejects projects with payback period more than the organisation's target payback period.

2. Accounting rate of return (ARR)

Any capital investment is made in order to earn a good return and maximise shareholders' value. It is necessary to check how this is achieved in practice. ARR is one of the ways of measuring the return on an investment in terms of profitability.

ARR measures the percentage of accounting profits (profits after depreciation) over the capital employed. A widely used formula to calculate this is as follows:

$$ARR = \frac{\text{Average annual accounting profits}}{\text{Average investment}} \times 100$$

Accounting profits will be calculated after deducting depreciation from the cash profits.

As in other ratio calculations, slightly different formulae are sometimes used for ARR. Hence, in place of average investment, initial or final investment may be used.

a) Average investment

The investment at the beginning of the project is the initial cost. The investment at the end of the project is the disposable value or scrap value. If we want an average, we have to take the total of the two items and divide it by two.

The formula will be:

$$\text{Average investment} = \frac{(\text{Initial investment} + \text{Scrap value})}{2}$$

Method of applying ARR

A target or hurdle rate is decided beforehand. The projects that give an ARR higher than the decided rate are accepted. If there are two or more competing proposals out of which only one is to be selected, then the project with the highest ARR is selected.

Diagram 1: NPV and IRR

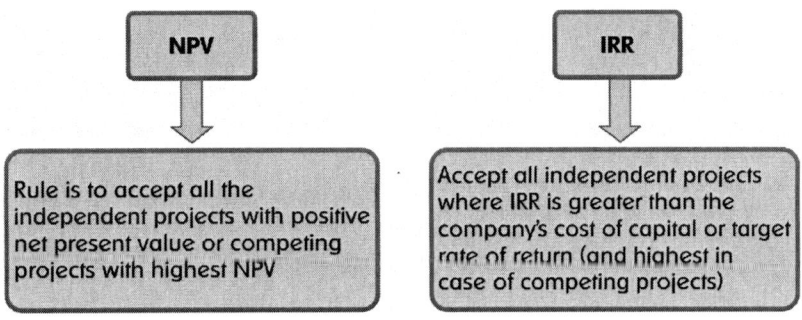

3. Net Present Value

Definition

The net present value (NPV) of an investment (project) is the difference between the present value of cash inflow and the present value of cash outflow.

452: Project Management

The present value can be either positive (cash inflow greater than outflow), negative (cash outflow greater than inflow) or zero (cash outflow and inflow exactly equal). The rule is to accept all the independent projects with positive net present value or in the case of competing projects, the one with the highest NPV.

4. Internal Rate of Return

Definition

An investment project's internal rate of return is the required rate of return or cost of capital which produces a net present value of zero when used to discount the project's cash flows.

In other words, **when internal rate of return is used to discount the cash flows, the present value of outflows and the present value of inflows will be equal.**

Decision Rule

Accept all independent projects where the IRR is greater than the company's cost of capital or target rate of return.

SUMMARY

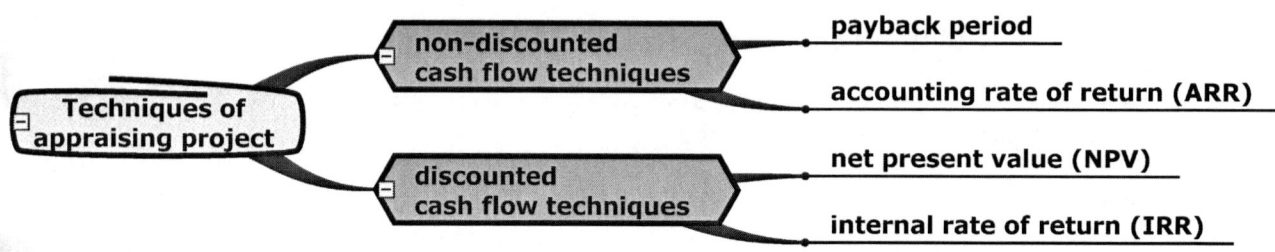

Test Yourself 1

Brambling (Electronics) Ltd is a research-led business that specialises in the development of surveillance equipment. The company has recently developed a new form of camera with a powerful fibre-optic lens and is currently considering whether or not to produce the camera. The board of directors will soon meet to make a final decision and has the following information available to help it decide:

(i) The cost of developing the camera has been $1,400,000 to date, and the company is committed to spending a further $350,000 within the next two months.

(ii) The company has spare production capacity and can produce the camera using machinery that will cost $4,700,000, which can be purchased immediately. It is expected to be sold at the end of four years for $800,000.

(iii) Total fixed costs identified with the production of the camera are $1,725,000 per year. This includes a depreciation expense in respect of the machinery of $975,000 per year and an expense allocated to represent a fair share of the fixed costs of the business as a whole of $250,000 per year.

(iv) The cameras are expected to sell for $10,000 each and the marketing department believes that the business can sell 800 cameras per year over the next four years.

(v) The variable costs of production are $7,000 per camera.

(vi) If the business decides not to produce the camera it can sell the patents immediately for $1,300,000. The company has a cost of capital of 12%.

Note: ignore taxation.

Required:

Calculate the net present value of producing and selling the new camera versus the alternative of selling the patent.

4. Establish responsibility for the delivery of benefits. [2]
Explain the role of a benefits realisation plan. [2]

[Learning Outcomes e and f]

Before we discuss the role of a benefits realisation plan and benefits delivery, it is worthwhile to understand the meaning of the term **'benefits realisation'**.

Benefits realisation is concerned with tracking whether the benefits are delivered after the project scope has been delivered.

Since the realisation of the benefits is closely aligned to the business change, engagement with the customer is essential while planning for realisation of benefits.

Realisation planning should cover both the explicit benefits that the project is expected to deliver and those implicit in the change that the project will introduce.

A benefits realisation plan is used to define the benefits expected from executing a project and the responsibilities for their realisation, measurement and reporting.

It defines all the activities, interdependencies, timing and responsibilities involved in realising the benefits.

Role of the benefits realisation plan

The **purpose of the benefits realisation plan** is to ensure that the project implementation team members should:

- understand the expected strategic outcomes of the project;
- identify the primary and secondary outcomes expected from implementation of the project, accountability of those expected to deliver the benefits and their measurement criteria;
- record the initiatives that will be required to ensure the delivery of the expected outcomes, accountability for their implementation and their completion timeframe; and
- identify the major risks that may impact the delivery of the expected outcomes, the strategies that could be implemented to mitigate those risks and those who will be accountable to implement those strategies.

The **benefits delivery plan deals with the delivery of benefits and outlines** for each major project outcome / benefit:

- the baseline and targets to be achieved;
- a description of how each benefit will be measured;
- the likely delivery schedule for each benefit;
- an outline of the monitoring skills required to measure each specified benefit; and
- the risks that may adversely impact the achievement of each benefit along with how the risk will be mitigated.

Answer to Test Yourself

Answer to TY 1

Annual operating cash flows can be calculated as follows:

	$m
Sales (800 x $10,000)	8·0
Less	
Variable costs (800 x $7,000)	(5.6)
Fixed costs (1.725 – 0.975 – 0.250)	(0.5)
Net cash inflows	**1·9**

Cash flows relating to the project are as follows:

Year	0	1	2	3	4
	$m	$m	$m	$m	$m
Machinery	(4·7)				0.8
Opportunity cost (patent)	(1·3)				
Annual cash flows		1·9	1·9	1·9	1·9
	(6·0)	1·9	1·9	1·9	2·7

The net present value of the project is:

	$m	$m	$m	$m	$m
Cash flows	(6·0)	1·90	1·90	1·90	2·70
Discount rate (12%)	1·0	0·89	0·80	0·71	0·64
Present value	(6·0)	1·69	1·52	1·35	1·73

NPV is equal to $1.69 + $1.52 + $1.35 + $1.73 – $6.0 = **$290,000**

Quick Quiz

1. Business case document consists of:

   A. Introduction
   B. Executive summary
   C. Scope of the project
   D. All of the above

2. Revenue expenditure is the cost involved for improving the earning capacity of a business.

   A. True
   B. False

3. Investment appraisal techniques such as ARR and the payback period ignore _____.

   A. Time value of money
   B. Rate of interest
   C. Useful life of an asset
   D. None of the above

4. The _____ of a project is the difference between the present value of cash inflow and the present value of cash outflow.

   A. Intrinsic value
   B. Cost
   C. Net present value
   D. None of the above

Answers to Quick Quiz

1. The correct option is **D**.

2. The correct option is **B**.

   Capital expenditure is the cost involved to improve the earning capacity of a business.

3. The correct option is **A**.

   Investment appraisal techniques such as ARR and the payback period ignore **time value of money**.

4. The correct option is **C**.

   The **net present value** of a project is the difference between the present value of cash inflow and the present value of cash outflow

Self Examination Question

Question 1

Xylum Ltd had recently concluded the ABC Accounting System Project. This project delivered a fully functional accounting system, with installed software, upgraded hardware, new procedures and employee training on the new system.

The projected benefit to Xylum was reduced transaction costs.

However, solely relying on the project outputs did not deliver the benefits expected.

The transaction costs actually reduced when the staff working in the finance department followed the new procedures and applied their training in using the new accounting system software.

Mr Xylo, the managing director of the company, commented that "changing people's behaviour is not easy".

Required:

Explain how the business benefits can be realised through planning and managing the organisational change required.

Answer to Self Examination Question

Answer to SEQ 1

Managing change in order to realise the benefits requires planning and action in the following areas:

- agreeing and setting measurable goals;
- specifying roles and responsibilities;
- providing on-going support of the executive leadership;
- designing and implementing a system of rewards;
- developing a strategy to deal with those resisting the change.

Some of these areas will come within the scope of the project manager.

In planning for realising the business benefits for the project, one should begin with the end in mind, i.e. the business outcomes intended, and then proceed backwards. In deciding the scope of the project, the desired organisational outcomes should be agreed in measurable terms.

The next step is to decide the organisational processes and systems required to achieve these outcomes. Then the actual outputs that the project will need to deliver to the business for it to achieve these outcomes should be thought of. The planning process is important in fully realising the outcomes intended.

After the scope of project is decided, the benefits realisation plan should be created. The benefits realisation plan should clearly identify the business owner responsible for realising the business benefits.

In addition to specifying accountabilities, the plan should also detail the timeframe for achieving the outcomes and the method by which they will be realised and measured.

Lastly, the following deliverables should be defined:

- design and rollout of training to be conducted;
- revisions to procedures and role descriptions; and
- modifications to systems of reward and remuneration.

SECTION F: PROJECT MANAGEMENT — F3

STUDY GUIDE F3: MANAGING AND LEADING PROJECTS

■ Get Through Intro

Following on from the Get Through Intro for F1, you have decided to take on the task of co-ordinating your best friend's surprise birthday party. After all, it was your idea! So as a project manager what will you have to do? Well the first point is to remember, not everyone will be as excited as you are about organising the party. You may have to get everyone together and stir up some excitement in them! By doing this, you will hopefully get their interest in the party and will encourage them not leave their tasks to the last minute. If the party is 4 weeks away, you may decide to hold weekly update meetings, to see how everyone is doing with their responsibilities, or at least call everyone each week. Emma may be responsible for the food, Jay for arranging the music, Zara for finding the venue and Sam for arranging the cake. In addition Cyrus said he would design an invite and send it out to the final list of friends. Who will you follow up with first? The chances are it will be Zara as she has to find the venue. Without the venue, a few of the other tasks may not be possible. For example, you can not send an invite with no venue on it! Also, certain venues may insist that you use certain caterers or that you buy drinks from them. So this is the most important task to be completed first.

This Study Guide will teach you how to manage the project and lead it without causing tension or you being accused of being a control freak!

■ Learning Outcomes

a) Discuss the organisation and implications of project-based team structures.
b) Establish the roles and responsibilities of the project manager and the project sponsor.
c) Identify and describe typical problems encountered by a project manager when leading a project.
d) Advise on how these typical problems might be addressed and overcome.

1. Discuss the organisation and implications of project-based team structures. [2]

[Learning Outcome a]

Definition

An organisation can be defined as a structure in which people come together to perform the work of the business in an orderly manner.

1.1 An organisation can also be described as the way in which the business is organised or formed or the methodologies used to set up the business' activities so that together they can contribute to the organisation's main objective. An organisation could be described as a production system which interacts with its environment by taking some inputs from the environment and offering the outputs to the environment. Achievement of its strategic objective is dependent on how efficiently this production system operates. The production system consists of four subsystems

- the **economic system** which includes the interaction of the commercial sector with the organisation's economic system which deals with its purchasing and marketing functions
- the **technological system** which is responsible for the transformation processes used to convert the inputs into outputs
- the **socio-cultural system** which looks after the personnel and the public relations functions of the organisation
- the **politico-legal system** which looks after the flow of information within the organisation and its interaction with the outside environment

1. Organisation Structure

People from different departments and functional units come together to conduct project work. They each have authorities and responsibilities in their departments. They represent their functional units in the project team. They communicate the views of the project team back to their functional units. They work in two capacities; one assigned to them by their own units and the other assigned to them by the project manager.

An organisational structure comprising these horizontal and vertical lines of reporting is known as a **matrix structure**. In matrix structures, project team members report to two managers; one from the functional side and the project manager.

Organisational structure was looked at in detail in Study Guide F1.

1.2 The project-based team structure of a typical software company is depicted below:

Diagram 2: Project-based team structure

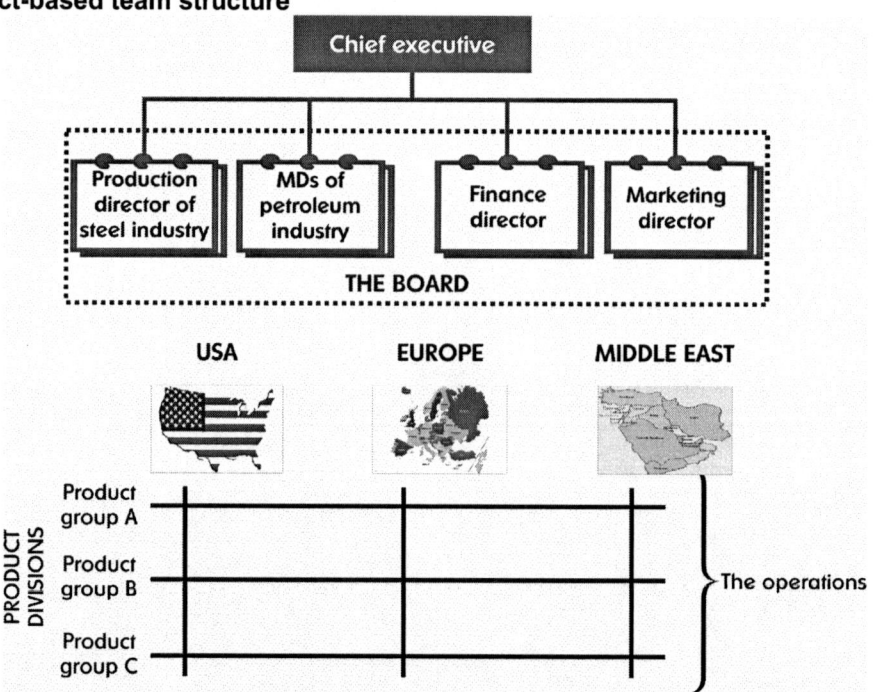

A matrix structure is a combination of organisational and project structures.

The implications of project-based team structures can be summarised in terms of the advantages and disadvantages of the matrix structure.

SUMMARY

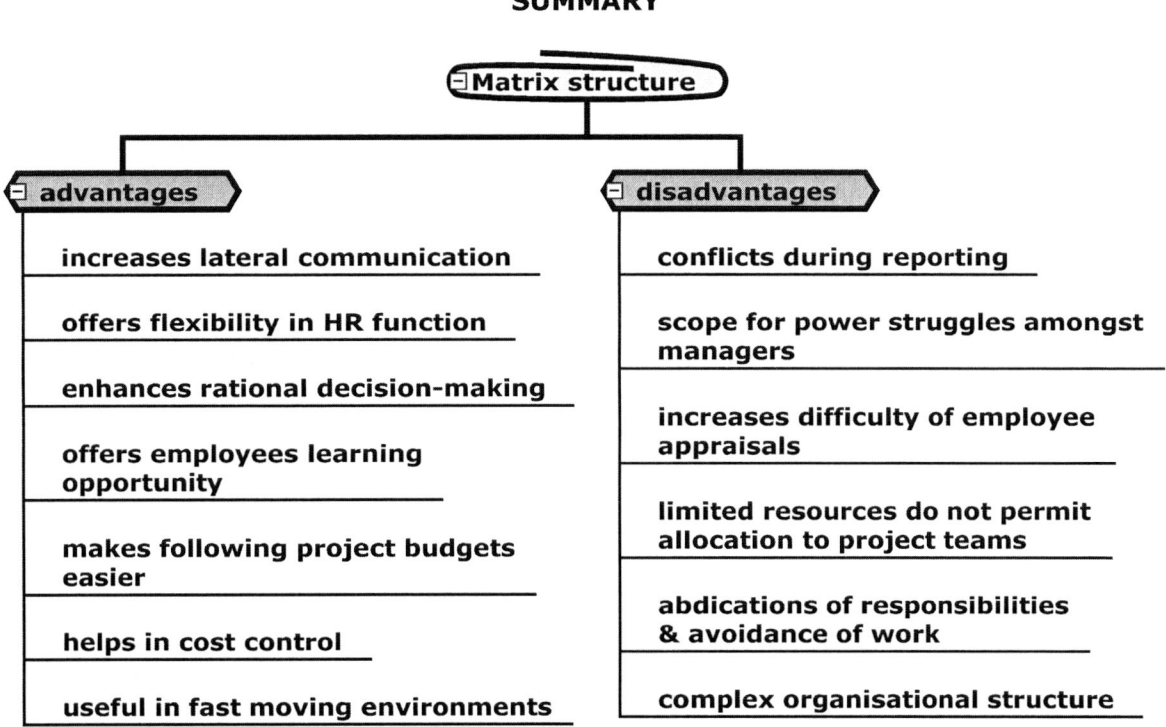

2. Establish the role and responsibilities of the project manager and project sponsor. [2]
[Learning Outcome b]

2.1 Project manager

The project manager is in charge of the project and is responsible for the overall management and execution of the project. Generally, the project sponsor or the steering committee appoints the project manager. The project manager is responsible for delivering the project objective within its triple constraints. The project manager has to lead, motivate, direct and monitor the project team members. Project manager is accountable for the quality of the project's objective and matters related to project assigned to project manager by the project sponsor.

1. **The responsibilities of the project manager can be summarised as follows**

   - delivering the project objective within its triple constraints and satisfying the project's stakeholders
   - providing directions to the project team including effective communication to achieve a common understanding of the project's objectives
   - monitoring the project's work including the work of project team members
   - documenting the project plan, risk register, project completion report and lesson's learned report and other project related documentation
   - capturing the project's requirements as understood by the project sponsor and the business team
   - understanding the acceptance criteria as defined by the project sponsor and stakeholders
   - implementing the organisation's strategy through the project's work as approved by the steering committee

Example

Rapo Ltd has implemented a hiring freeze due to the current recession in the market. The project manager of xyz project must follow the company's policy of not hiring any outside personnel and must complete the project by utilising the company's existing personnel.

The project manager can only recruit external personnel if the steering committee expressly allows it for this project.

- reporting the direction in which the project is heading to the steering committee to ensure overall integrity
- identifying, documenting and planning in order to mitigate risks that might arise during the project
- preparing contingency plans to keep the consequences of a risk event at an acceptable level should those risk events actually take occur
- managing changes in the project's execution;
- managing or solving problems as they arise

A project manager's responsibilities incur various roles such as mentor, team leader, monitor and channel of communication to provide information to and from the project sponsor and steering committee to and from the project team and project stakeholders.

Example

Rachel is the senior manager of Finance. She suspects some malfunctioning in her department and wants to undertake an audit to ensure the reliability of the records. She has appointed Louise as the project manager.

In this case, Rachel is the project sponsor who will benefit the most from the project. There could have been more than one sponsor. For example, if senior management had initiated the project, the members of the management could be the project sponsors.

2. **To fulfil their responsibilities, project managers should have the following skills**
   - communication
   - leadership
   - team building
   - problem solving
   - technical knowledge of the assigned project
   - flexibility and patience
   - managerial skills

SUMMARY

Responsibilites of project manager
- deliver project objective
- provide direction to project team
- monitor project work
- document project plan
- meet project requirements
- understand acceptance criteria
- implement strategy
- plan to mitigate risk
- manage change in project's execution

2.2 Project sponsor

1. **A project sponsor is**

   - the project owner
   - the provider of the funding required for the project
   - the person who has initiated the project
   - one of the project stakeholders and the beneficiary of the project
   - usually one of the members of senior management who acts as a link between the project manager / team and the upper echelons of the firm

2. **The responsibilities of the project sponsor can be summarised as follows**

a) Ensuring that the project management framework is in place for the project under consideration.

b) Prioritising projects and selecting only the projects which have strategic importance.

c) Preparing a project initiation document and valid business case on the basis of SWOT analysis.

d) Evaluating and selecting the best alternative to solve the problem leading to the project under consideration.

e) Coordinating and directing or guiding the required inputs from the business' side or client's side.

f) Organising the funding for the project and fixing the budget. Some contingency funds should be kept aside to finance the risk mitigation actions initiated by the risk triggers.

g) Obtaining benefits from the project using the least amount of funds.

h) Monitoring and controlling the changes, along with the project manager.

i) Performing risk management (jointly with the project manager).

j) The project sponsor and project manager are the main points of contact for the project under consideration.

k) Developing and coordinating teamwork is also the joint responsibility of the project sponsor and project manager.

l) Reviewing the work of the project manager and acting as a mentor to him/her. The project sponsor should receive the project's progress reports from the project and review them.

m) Setting up the formal communication lines including reporting systems in the project's organisation. This also includes communication from project stakeholders and sponsors to the project manager. Project managers also facilitate communication with other senior managers informing them with regards to progress on the project.

n) Guiding the project manager on the standard performance measures expected from the project to facilitate control and management of project's work.

o) Achieving the business objective is the project sponsor's responsibility.

p) Mentoring and assisting the project manager in resolving project-related issues / problems.

q) Taking decisions that are outside the scope of the project such as whether to abandon the project where circumstances make it difficult to continue the project.

Example

PPT has started a project to construct a new building as a result of its plans for expansion. Their project manager, Caroline has discovered that cement prices have increased threefold from last year, which will make it difficult to complete the project within budget. Caroline approaches Peter, the senior manager, to ask for the necessary additional funds. Here, as the project sponsor, it is Peter's responsibility to take the decision regarding the extra fund allocation.

The role of the project sponsor is to give directions regarding the project objective and problems which are outside of the scope of the project manager. Managing the project is the project manager's role. In this way, the two roles can be distinguished.

SUMMARY

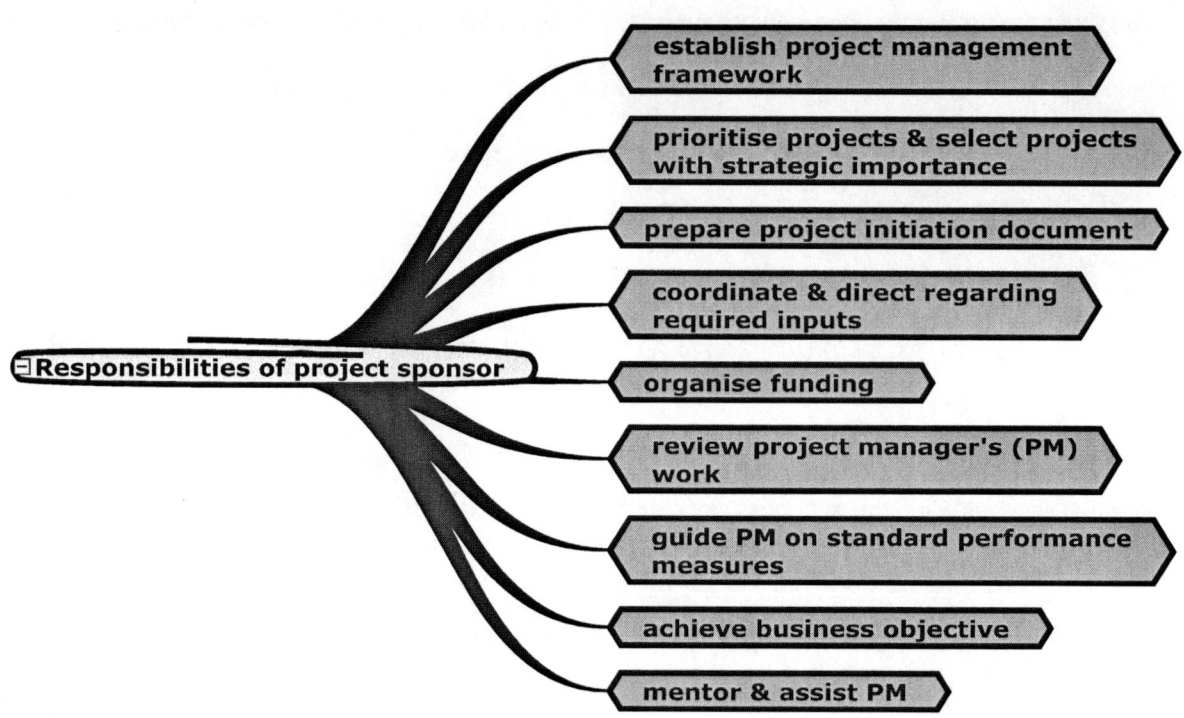

Test Yourself 1

Wonder Ltd is a world class producer of cosmetics. Wonder Ltd's collection meets the needs of fashion with an impressive range of colours and shades and exclusive packaging.

Wonder is a well known brand and would like to expand into online sales through its website to enable customers to buy its products more easily. As the brand is widely known, it has a responsibility to meet the requirements of its customers. John is the manager of Wonder Ltd's production team and has been assigned the project of applying an efficient software solution to facilitate the move into online shopping. The software must ensure secure transactions in order to maintain customer satisfaction. The entire website needs to be designed in a manner that will promote the brand and also increase customer loyalty.

Required:

Distinguish between John's roles as production manager and project manager.

---

3. Identify and describe typical problems encountered by a project manager when leading a project [2]
   Advise on how these typical problems might be addressed and overcome. [3]

   [Learning Outcomes c and d]

Study Guide G1 discussed the problems encountered by project managers while leading a project and their counter measures.

Additional problems encountered by project managers while leading a project and ways to overcome these problems are as follows:

1. **Scope creep:** Clients frequently change their requirements, which increases project costs and delays project completion. Scope creep was discussed earlier in Study Guide 1. This issue can be avoided by setting a date after which no change in the project's scope is allowed.

2. **Delay in delivering the project objective due to hardware or software defects:** A bug or defect in externally purchased software or hardware can cause delays to project completion. These delays could be reduced by ensuring that software and hardware is purchased from a reputed company, reducing the chance of defects or by inserting penalties into the contract should a bug or defect in the software be found.

3. **Lack of common understanding of the project's scope or objective:** The project manager and project team might not achieve what the project sponsor and project stakeholders are expecting. This can be avoided by ensuring proper communication and by appointing a project manager with some technical experience.
4. **Changes in the applicable law:** Laws which apply to the entity might change. Such changes could affect the scope, cost and time constraints of the project.

Example

When the US government introduced the Sarbanes-Oxley Act, companies resisted it, as the costs of compliance with this law are huge. However, companies do not have any choice; they must incorporate procedures as laid down by Sarbanes-Oxley. This changed the scope of some existing projects.

5. **Problems in integrating the new system with the old one:** New systems might not be properly interfaced with old systems, which may necessitate changes in one or other of the systems. Problems such as this can be avoided by accommodating such changes at the design phase.

Example

Express Ltd has automated most of its operations by carrying out its own in-house software development. Express Ltd has now undertaken the final project which is to develop the accounts payable register. The project manager appointed for this project must design the project carefully to ensure that the accounts payable register works properly (unit testing) and that its results are linked properly to the rest of the general ledger and financial documents (interface system).

6. **Project's dependency on external parties:** When a project is dependent on external parties for delivery, failure to receive material on time could create a problem. This problem could be avoided by ordering material well in advance.
7. **Lack of judgement with respect to estimation and decision-making:** If the WBS (work breakdown structure) is not done properly; it could create problems in computing the estimated cost and time for the project. Such problems could be avoided by working out a detailed WBS.
8. **Resource scarcity:** It is sometimes difficult to know what resources will be required for the project, such as skilled personnel or additional funds required to carry out the project. These problems could be avoided by arranging the resources in advance.
9. **Human resource problems**

➢ Often project managers do not possess as much technical expertise as the technical experts on project teams. The project manager might find it difficult to deal with such skilled team members, leading to conflicts and resentment.
➢ The project manager might face other problems associated with human relationships, particularly with the heads of those departments from which the team members have been taken. These situations might arise particularly when the team member is only working on the project part time.

Managing a project team with multiple resources is a difficult task. These problems can be avoided by effective communication.

To resolve unexpected problems, organisation's project management should have predefined processes. By following these processes problems will be resolved more efficiently.

SUMMARY

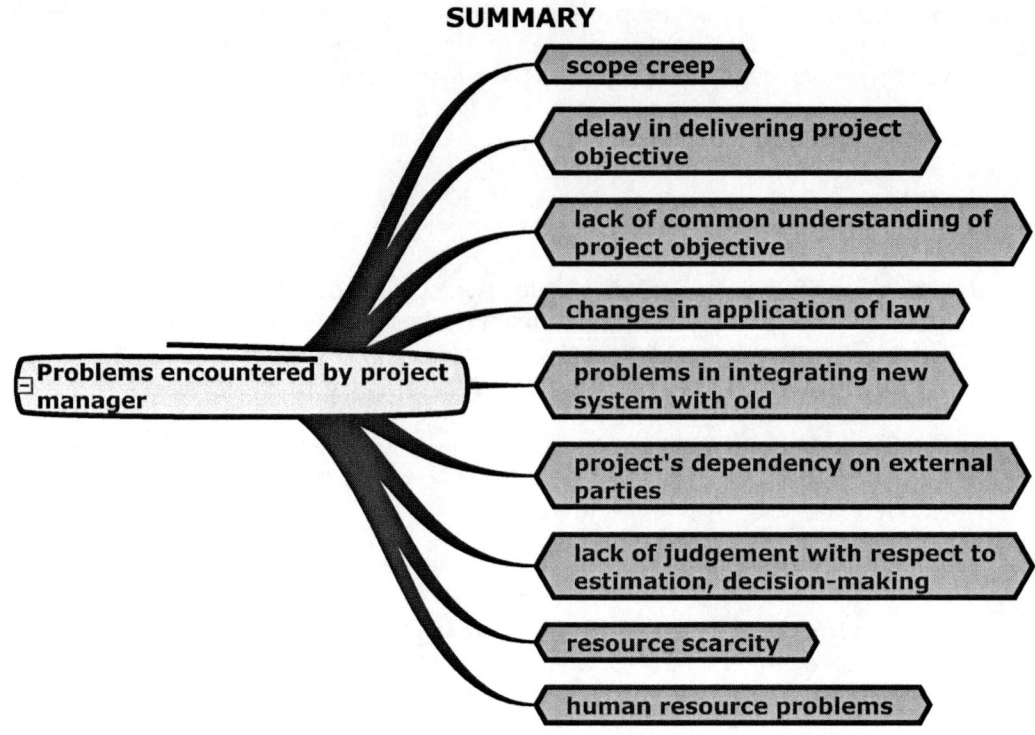

Test Yourself 2

Huda Ltd is a large four-wheeler company, trusted by millions of customers in the UK. The product range commands a market share of 50%. The product quality, expanded dealer network and after-sales service has made Huda a very customer-friendly company. Huda's management information system is dependent on its accounting system; Data is available to the management for decision making only after the data have been processed.

Previously, Huda's Management Information System (MIS) provided different kinds of analysis for the company. Over a period of time, the systems underwent changes, additions and modifications. These were not properly incorporated across functional areas. There was repetition and information irregularity with most legacy applications. It was therefore important to migrate from this stage to something more reliable and innovative.

Senior management supported an IT system which was not limited to data processing. This helped in improving the business processes and covered supply chain. The company chose SAP as it acted as the backbone for the company's growth. Huda assigned the project to Joy as project manager. To help in the implementation of the project, about 100 of the company's executives were given training.

The training helped to improve the quality of the service, access and usage of transactional data and eliminated multiple entries. This meant that there was no longer any need for manual reconciliation.

Required:

Discuss the general problems that the project manager, Joy, may face while implementing this project.

Answers to Test Yourself

Answer to TY 1

John is the production manager of Wonder Ltd, managing the requirements of the production department alone. However, he has now been assigned a project to apply an efficient software solution to promote the company's brand and increase customer loyalty. Now John must perform the role of production manager as well as the role of project manager. The following points distinguish John's two roles:

1. **As production manager, John**

   - represents the specific area in which he is specialised
   - meets the requirements of the production department
   - takes responsibility for every activity required for efficient production
   - enjoys direct authority over his production team

2. **As project manager, John**

   ➤ represents the assigned project
   ➤ is responsible for delivering the project objective
   ➤ gives directions to the project team members
   ➤ observes and monitors each team member's work as well as the project as a whole
   ➤ is responsible for documenting the project's plan, risk, completion report and other project related document
   ➤ implements the organisation's strategy
   ➤ manages all project-related problems as they arise
   ➤ manages all financial as well as technical issues related to the project
   ➤ has limited authority to monitor the work of each project team member

Answer to TY 2

The following are the general problems which Joy may face while implementing the project:

1. **Scope creep:** Scope creep occurs when there are changes to the project scope. Joy may face this problem if the project's objective is not defined properly.

   One way to tackle this problem is to set a deadline after which no changes are permitted to the project.

2. **Delays in delivering the project objective due to defects in hardware / software:** There may be delays to the implementation of the project due to defects in hardware or software.

   The project manager should always purchase hardware and software from a reputed company and under an agreement requiring twenty-four hour backup and maintenance service. This will save time and reduce the possibility of defected hardware / software requirement affecting the project delivery. He can also insert penalty clauses in the agreement to protect the company from defects which are found later on or delay in delivery.

3. **Lack of common understanding of the project's scope or objective:** It may be that the project assigned to Joy and the team is not clearly communicated. This could cause delays to the implementation of the project.

   This problem could be solved if the project sponsor appoints someone who possesses sufficient technical expertise to understand the project's objective and if there is proper communication between the project manager and the project sponsor.

4. **Problems in integrating the new system with the old one:** It might happen that the new system does not interface property with the old system and requires alterations after the new system has been implemented.

   Joy should accommodate such changes at the designing phase of the project.

5. **Project's dependency on external parties:** A project may be adversely affected if there is too much reliance on external parties, who may deliver the required components on time.

   Joy ensures that all necessary requirements are ordered well in advance and that the other party delivers on time.

6. **Lack of judgement with respect to estimates and decision-making:** It might happen that due to improper Work Breakdown Structure (WBS), Joy is unable to make clear decisions about the estimated cost and time of the project.

   If the project manager implements the proper WBS, it should clearly estimate the time and the cost necessary for the completion of the project.

7. **Resources:** Resources are one of the most important aspects to get right in order for a project to be successful. During project implementation, Joy might realise that she requires further skilled staff and additional funds, which may not be possible at such short notice and will lead to delays in the project.

   Joy, therefore, should arrange the necessary resources before implementing the project.

8. **Human resources:** Joy might not possess sufficient technical expertise on the project team. She might also face problems with relationships with departmental heads.

   To prevent this problem from occurring, Joy should appoint a technical expert to the team to ensure that the work is completed in a timely and efficient manner.

466: Project management

Quick Quiz

1. An organisational structure comprising horizontal and vertical lines of reporting is known as a _____.

2. What skills does the project manager need in order to fulfil his/her responsibilities?

3. How can the role of project sponsor be distinguished from that of project manager?

Answers to Quick Quiz

1. Matrix structure.

2. The skills a project manager needs to fulfil his/her responsibilities are

   - good communication
   - good leadership
   - good management
   - good problem solving
   - technical knowledge of the assigned project
   - flexibility

The differences between the roles of project sponsor and project manager are as follows:

Project sponsor	Project manager
1. Gives only direction for a particular project	1. Manages the assigned project
2. Acts as a mentor for project manager	2. Implements the organisation's strategy
3. Reviews the work of project manager	3. Manages and solves problems as they arise
4. Provides funding for the project and acts as a link between the upper echelons of the entity and the project manager	

Self Examination Questions

Question 1.

Eastern Education (EE) has undertaken a project to bring all educational institutes and schools in the region to a national information network, called "EduWorld". George is the senior management accountant of one of the educational institutes, Brainpower Institute, and is also part of the project team. He is responsible for communication between all the education institutes and schools concerning the progress of the project.

EE is a government-controlled authority, responsible to the central educational department. Each government-controlled authority manages and controls the educational institutes for the public in its local area. EE is responsible for 50 education institutions and 50 schools in its region. EE has been set a target by the government to ensure that at least 50 to 70 per cent of the institutions and schools in its region should be connected to the national information network i.e. to "EduWorld" within two years. To facilitate the project, most information about educational institutions and schools was collected manually and was paper-based. Data were exchanged by telephone.

EE's senior management established a project team to oversee and communicate the progress of the project.

Required:

George has been asked to prepare a memorandum of his work to discuss the relationship of the project manager to the project sponsor and the project team. He is also required to discuss the conflicting project objectives of the stakeholders.

Question 2.

For the above case, explain the role of the project manager in respect of the people, process and product involved in the project.

Question 3

Medicare is the largest manufacturer of chemicals and drugs in the UK. Recently, Medicare developed a new inventory processing system. After the system had been in use for a few months, it was observed that it was failing to meet the purpose for which it was designed and had become unreliable.

The failure of the inventory processing system led to a major analysis of the project which led to the conclusion that project management procedures were not being followed properly and it would take at least 3 years to overcome this problem.

Due to the interdependent tasks and responsibilities involved in the project, there were a number of small oversights and failures which led to the failure of the system.

After the analysis, it was decided to restructure the IT department and to implement an information system strategy. This strategy would include monitoring the procedures for the project and starting procedures for employing an external consultant to overlook the process and also to build trust between various departments.

The following observations were made
- New computer systems were purchased without proper budgeting, buy or do analysis or cost calculations.
- The team was moved to new manufacturing unit that was not equipped with the necessary tools.
- The project manager was changed more than twice and no one from senior management took responsibility for the project.
- Several senior members resigned.
- Operational policies for the administrative work were not followed.
- Unrealistic time limits were set for the project.

Required:

Discuss the reasons for the failure of Medicare's project.

Answers to Self Examination Questions

Answer to SEQ 1

1. Relationship of project manager with project sponsor and project team

Brainpower Institute is responsible for carrying out a project that was started by the government - the project sponsor. The project manager has to work according to the government's i.e. the project sponsor's instructions. He has to look at all the communications between Brainpower, the organisation he is representing and the project sponsor. The project sponsor is responsible for ensuring that the project has sufficient funds and resources. Therefore, the project manager needs to communicate with the project sponsor to solve conflict over project costs. There is also a lack of frequent communication and reporting between the project manager and the project sponsor regarding the progress of the project.

The project sponsor is the person who has benefited from the achievement of the project objectives. He/she also evaluates the strategic level of the objectives to ensure that the project utilises available resources and that the resources are not wasted.

The team is responsible for the achievement of the project objectives, for the overall running of the project without being distracted from their own business objectives. There should be direct communication between the project manager and the team to ensure regular reporting of the project.

2. Conflicting project objectives of the stakeholders

The government's (project sponsor) main objective for this project is to improve the education facility for students. The employees' objective is to minimise their workload and, at the same time, provide a good education system. There may be conflict between the objective of the sponsor and the employees. Employees are concerned about implementing the workload, costs and education facility.

There may be conflict between the sponsor and the project team members over funding. It has been observed that improper funding has created a financial burden upon EE and individual educational institutes and schools. The project is to cover at least 50 to 70 per cent of the educational institutes and schools in the region under the education programme and connect them to "EduWorld". Many teachers have expressed concern about resources being spent on the new system and not on students' education. The government has made it clear that the project is not flexible although the sponsors have allowed institutes and schools to implement their own methods of operation.

The project sponsor and the project team have concerns about the funding requirement and cost minimisation of the project, but, at the same time, stakeholders may cut costs and reduce the value of the project. For a public sector project, quality and customer opinions are more important to the stakeholders than the project team members' problems as public funds should be used effectively.

Answer to SEQ 2

The project manager's role is to guarantee the project's success, which requires considerable project management skills to do the following:

1. People

It is the project manager's duty to manage the people involved in the project. This does not only mean the project team, but also staff working with the project team. The manager will need to allocate and monitor the work of subordinate project team members and must provide strategic progress reports for decision makers. This job demands good human resource management skills.

2. Process

The project manager must be involved with setting the project objective and then have systems in place to monitor the project's progress. The use of system diagrams will help with this.

3. Product

The product is the outcome of the project and will involve the installation of a new or revised system. Complete monitoring of the project is directed to ensure that the project provides the finished product. Therefore, the project manager will be involved in checking the specifications that are to be completed.

Answer to SEQ 3

The following are the reasons for the failure of the project

1. Improper utilisation of project resources

Without effective cost calculation and a proper funding source, the company purchased a new computer system. As a result, the project's financial resources were not allocated properly and this increased the cost of the project.

There was failure of budgeting for this project. The proper business scenario would present a clear picture for stakeholders to obtain proper resources for the implementation of the project.

2. Lack of project planning

Implementation of the new inventory control system was not successful because the project team was moved to a new manufacturing unit that was not properly equipped. Therefore, there was a lack of planning for the basic tools required by the project team to conduct their day-to-day work.

3. Lack of proper project management and accountability

The project manager was changed twice which had a disruptive effect on the project team. Moreover, senior management did not take responsibility for the project.

One of the main reasons for the failure of the project was a lack of senior management support. The senior management is responsible for giving support throughout the project and needs to ensure that the problems are tackled as and when they arise.

4. Lack of unexpected plans

When administrative employees do not follow the operational system, the work is not properly performed and this leads to tension between employees but there is no alternative action. This leads to failure of risk management.

If there is a parallel running of old and new systems, the employees can work within the old system and can fix problems faced by the new system.

5. Unrealistic limit

The original limit for the project was rigidly adhered to, despite the fact that it could have been postponed as several senior project team members had resigned creating various problems such as disruption of the work flow, skill shortages and low morale of the existing staff. Some project team members questioned the viability of the go-live date.

Effective planning and monitoring includes being able to realise when changes are required and re-planning is necessary. Good risk management and unexpected event planning might have mitigated this problem but the unexpected c

SECTION F: PROJECT MANAGEMENT

STUDY GUIDE F4: PLANNING, MONITORING AND CONTROLING PROJECTS

■ Get Through Intro

So we are now 2 weeks away from the birthday party of your best friend (started in the Get Through Intro for F1). She still has no idea that you are planning it. Zara has found a great venue. Unfortunately Sam has not found a baker for the cake, as he is insisting it is in the shape of a champagne bottle and no one wants to do that. Cyrus has still not finished designing the card – he is a perfectionist. No one else has got back to you with details of how their part is progressing. You call an emergency meeting and motivate the team. You remind them that it is your best friend, Katerina's 21st birthday and you all want it to be a party to remember. So you re-energise everyone and agree that you are going to send a daily email round to get a progress report that everyone has to fill in.

The following 2 weeks go quickly and everything seems to be happening on schedule. The night before the party, you have a final meeting and confirm everyone's responsibilities. You are pretty sure you have thought of everything. The night of the party comes and you realise that no one had been given the responsibility of decorating the hall! So you call a few friends to come early to help you. You manage to get the decorations up at the last minute. The night is a huge success and Katerina is thrilled with what you did. At the party, another friend, Pete congratulates you on the job and asks you if you would consider organising his engagement party – what's more he will pay you!

So after the event, you decide to sit down with the others involved and think of all the things that did go wrong and how they could be prevented in the future. After all, if you are going into the event management business, you need to have sharp project management skills and that involves learning from your mistakes!

■ Learning Outcomes

a) Discuss the principles of a product breakdown structure
b) Assess the importance of developing a project plan and discuss the work required to produce this plan.
c) Monitor the status of a project and identify project risks, issues, slippage and changes.
d) Formulate responses for dealing with project risks, issues, slippage and changes.
e) Discuss the role of benefits management and project gateways in project monitoring

1. Discuss the principles of a product breakdown structure.[2]

[Learning Outcome a]

This learning outcome has been discussed in Study Guide F5, Learning Outcome b.

2. Assess the importance of developing a project plan and discuss the work required to produce this plan.[3]

[Learning Outcome b]

Definition

A project plan is a tool of project execution and project control which can be defined as a statement about:
- the project objective
- the means that are going to be used to achieve this objective
- when the objective is going to be achieved
- the assumptions and decisions used to prepare it
- the scope, time and cost boundaries of the project

The project plan should reflect the expectations of the project sponsor and the stakeholders. It contains a list of milestones, activities and resources required for the project.

A project plan can be used as a guide to justify the reasons for a project's existence. It can be used in a cost-benefit analysis at a high level or it can be used as a detailed plan of project execution and control.

2.1 The importance of developing a project plan

As discussed earlier, every project has a project objective. All project activities should be **directed to achieve this project objective**. Strategy is implemented through the project. All project activities are bound by the triple constraints of the project. If these activities cross the boundaries of the project triangle, there is a high probability of not meeting the project objective in time, and the project not meeting the expectations of stakeholders. The project manager needs to make sure that the project is **progressing in the right direction**. To do this, he has to engage in project planning. There is an old saying that if you do not plan, you plan to fail.

Example

Express Ltd has initiated a project to produce and sell T-shirts which carry advertisements for a cold drink. It plans to sell these T-shirts at the Olympics, which are 6 months away. If the project manager does not plan carefully, the T-shirts might not be ready by the required date, and the project might not achieve the objective for which it was started.

Planning facilitates the following

1. **It facilitates the monitoring of the project**: the project manager can compare the actual work with the planned work, make an analysis of the variances and take corrective action.

2. **It gives the project manager a list of the resources which are required to carry out the project activities**: in simple words, the materials and structures required to complete the project tasks. This helps the project manager when searching for a source or making arrangements to obtain resources.

3. **It enables timely supply of resources for project activities**: this means arranging for resources when required so that the project work does not stop because of the unavailability of resources.

4. **It helps the project manager to manage the time requirement of the project**: every project has to be done keeping in mind the time factor. Gantt Charts and critical path evaluation, program evaluation and review techniques can help the project manager to estimate the time required for the project, identify overlapping activities and make the schedule for the project.

Example

(continuing the example of Express Ltd)

With proper planning, the project manager was able to monitor the project to see that it stayed within the time constraint of the project. The project manager could arrange for required inputs at the right time. By using scheduling techniques like Pert, CPM and Gantt Charts, he could plan the project's schedule and provide the required inputs to complete it within 6 months.

5. **It checks whether targets are realistic:** after making a detailed plan of the estimated time to complete the project, and the resources required to complete the project tasks, the project manager can judge whether the targets of the project are achievable with given constraints.

6. **It checks whether the project aligns with the organisational strategy:** the project manager can judge whether the project outcome is in accordance with the organisational strategy.

7. **It allows forward-thinking so the project manager can see the possibility of project success:** after doing the planning, if the project manager thinks that everything can go forward as planned, he can visualise the project's success or he can take the necessary actions required to ensure success.

8. **It allows for common understanding of the project objective among the project team:** while planning, the project manager needs to interact with the project team. In doing so, the project team also becomes aware of the project objective.

9. **Communication flow within internal and external environment:** a project manager has to plan each level of the project starting from scope, time, cost, human resources, communication, risk and procurement, and ending with integration management. In doing this he needs to interact with internal project team members and outside functional side members of the organisation, as well as outside entities.

10. **Interactions with the project stakeholders and project sponsor regarding their expectations:** if the expectations of the project sponsor and stakeholders do not match realistic estimates, then the project manager needs to coordinate with them to explain his concern.

11. **Helps to set the milestones of the project:** the project manager could set the milestones for the project and compare the results with the planned outcome.

Example

(continuing the example of Express Ltd)

The project manager could set a milestone for when designing of the advertising brand is complete and 50% of the targeted T-shirts have been produced. At this point, he could compare the progress of the project with the plan and take corrective actions to bring it on track, if needed.

---

12. **Helps to reduce risk to an acceptable level:** as uncertainty is a part of life, there is a probability that it may affect project execution. Uncertainty might affect the project objective and satisfaction levels of the stakeholders. By planning properly, the project manager can keep the project's consensuses at an acceptable level.

Project planning has to be done for all the key elements of project management. It starts from the conception and initiation of the project and ends with the handover and evaluation.

2.2 Work required to plan at project execution stage

1. Gathering the project team members

The first task is to build the project team. These team members come from different functional groups from different parts of the organisation. At this stage they are introduced to the project objective and goals expected from each functional side member.

2. Preparing the work breakdown structure

The project team has to list the work that is required in order to achieve and deliver the project objective. The team has to **break the work down into activities, then activities into sub-activities, until the smallest activities** are identified. These plans are then used for defining scope, assigning work responsibilities, comparing the performance of each activity and preparing a cost breakdown structure. These plans also facilitate the identification of risk and identification of the person responsible for risk and help in measuring the overall project risk.

Example

When applied to a project to prepare financial statements for a client, work breakdown structure includes first collecting data, then recording the transactions in a unit-wise manner (such as cash, A/R, A/P, expenses), preparing a profit and loss account, and then preparing the statement of financial position. After estimating the cost required to complete each activity, the overall costs to complete the project can also be estimated.

3. Listing required resources

The project manager needs to list the resources required in order to complete the activities in the work breakdown structure. He has to arrange the required resources in advance so that the flow of activities is not interrupted.

4. Calculating the time required to complete project activities

On the basis of the work breakdown structure, the project manager has to make a critical path analysis, prepare the Gantt Chart, apply program evaluation and review techniques. This will give him an idea of how activities are related to each other, such as the dependency of activities on each other, overlapping activities and handovers. The project manager can estimate a realistic time to complete the project and do a sequencing of project activities. This will help in identifying the changes that could occur if any of the activities are changed.

a) Critical path analysis (CPA)

CPA is a statistical technique used to calculate the interdependencies of the project's activities on each other. Different scheduling paths are calculated in terms of time, which can be followed to complete the project and the lead time available between the two activities. The project manager could change the human resources and/or scope of the activities on these paths to evaluate the effects of his decisions regarding inputs to the project time. The longest path on this analysis is called the critical path for the project. The activities that lie on the critical path should be completed first in order to complete the project in time.

Diagram: CPA analysis of different activities

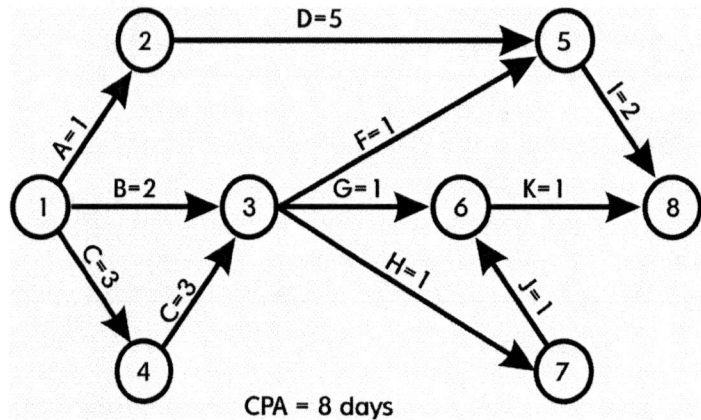

b) Program evaluation and review technique

This is also a statistical technique used to calculate the project duration when there is uncertainty about the individual duration of activities. Individual activity duration is calculated using the PERT weighted average.

PERT weighted average = Optimistic time + 4 x Most likely time + Pessimistic time/6

The technique addresses the risk associated with the duration of each activity.

5. Preparing the cost breakdown structure

On the basis of the work breakdown structure and resources required to complete the activities listed in the work breakdown structure, the project manager has to prepare a cost breakdown structure. The cost breakdown structure means **estimating the cost required to complete each task in the work breakdown structure**. It identifies costs as direct costs such as labour, material, and indirect costs such as factory and administrative overheads.

6. Stakeholders' analysis

The project manager has to carry out a stakeholders' analysis by looking at the role of stakeholders in the project's conception and execution, their position or influence in the organisation, and their respective interest in the project etc.

7. Risk management

The project manager needs to list possible uncertainties or risks that could affect the project's success. The project manager needs to rate the **severity** of their impact and the **probability** of their occurrence. The project manager has to come up with a plan or countermeasures to **reduce the risk to an acceptable level** in case the risk materialises.

> **Example**

The project manager of a market research team needs to list the risks a project might face (such as selecting a sample or collection of samples which is not representative of the population). He also needs to introduce some measures to reduce those risks to an acceptable level (such as composing samples carefully by involving representatives from each group of the population that has the same characteristics).

8. Standards to measure the quality of work

The project manager needs to specify standards against which the performance of the project work is going to be measured.

> **Example**

The project manager should specify the standards of performance, e.g. the performance rating / tolerance limits for a design of an electronic chip required for a television, DVD player or VCR. He can specify that chips having a tolerance of 1 or performance rating of 4 on a scale of 1 to 5 should be discarded. Although performance rating is 5/ o tolerance i.e.100% is strongly recommended.

9. Intellectual property rights

If the project manager decides to outsource all the work or part of the work to a third party, the project manager has to put clauses in the contract agreement with respect to who is going to own intellectual property rights, and how and when they can be accessed and used.

> **Example**

When the entity decides to buy a software product from outside, generally a clause is added to the agreement to buy, to clarify that the source code would be kept in an escrow account (account created with a third party who upon satisfaction of contractual contingency or condition will release it to the party mentioned in the contract.) where it would be accessible to the buyer in case the selling entity does not exist.

10. Gates and milestones

The project manager has to fix the milestones for the project. After achieving these milestones, he can compare the real results of the project with the planned ones in terms of scope, time and cost. Milestones can be described **as check points or the interim goals of the project**. Gates are the **tests or reviews included in the project plan** to assess work in accordance with the planned work. Examples of gates are audits, quality assurance testing, technical reviews, risk assessment and completion reviews. Gates also include the **performance measures** that are used for quality testing.

11. How the deliverables will be delivered

The project manager needs to clarify how he is going to deliver the deliverables on their respective dates. He must decide the actions he will take to meet the project objective.

> **3. Monitor the status of a project and identify project risks, issues, slippage and changes.** [2]
> **Formulate responses for dealing with project risks, issues, slippages and changes.** [2]
> [Learning Outcomes c and d]

3.1 Monitoring a project's progress is essential in ensuring the timely delivery of the quality project objective, which must meet the expectations of project stakeholders.

Monitoring work requires:
i. measuring the performance

ii. comparing the work done with:
    ➢ the pre-established standards of performance agreed at the time of planning
    ➢ milestones that have been fixed
    ➢ quality attributes of the project objective as stated in the scope statement

iii. analysing problems using techniques such as fishbone analysis or gap analysis

SUMMARY

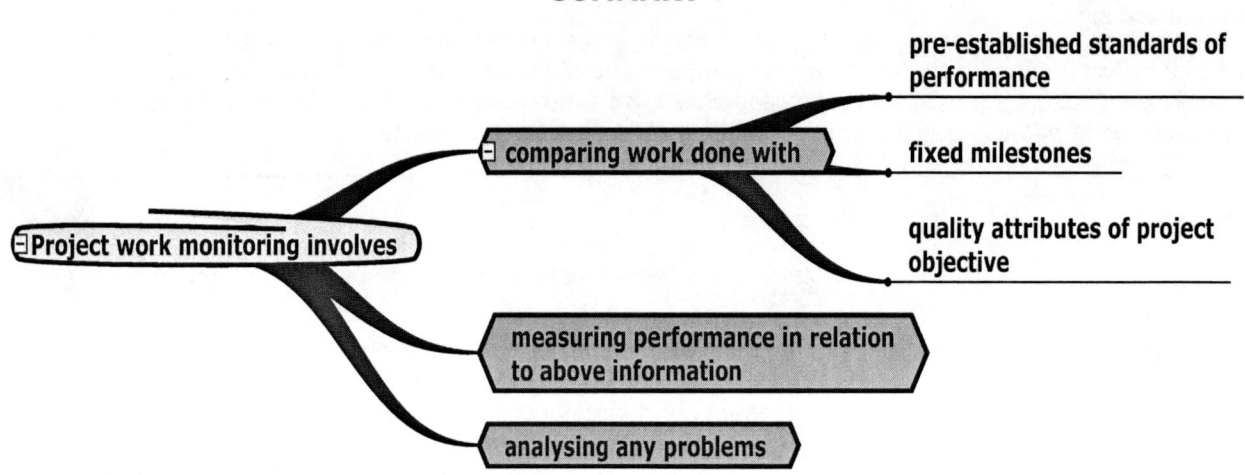

3.2 Steps involved in measuring current performance

Information about current performance should always be present in the progress report. Progress reports are written by the project manager for the project sponsor and project stakeholders. These reports detail the current status of the project in terms of cost, time, scope and quality.

Methods used to measure performance:

- indicators of performance, such as colour indicators in project management software
- reaching milestones
- morale and discipline of workers
- performance review meetings and tracking Gantt Chart, CPA and PERT

1. Scope monitoring

Scope monitoring requires the verification of the scope by the project sponsor and project stakeholders by formally signing:

- the project scope statement
- the document stating the WBS (work breakdown structure)
- the project's scope management plans
- deliverables

On the basis of these documents, the work done and the scope of the remaining project are measured. Any changes to the scope statement should be monitored. There should be a procedure which allows changes in the scope statement which was originally verified by the project sponsor and project stakeholders.

Scope also refers to the quality of the work that is done and the extent to which specifications of the project objective (as stated in the scope statement) are achieved. Quality should be measured by setting up tolerance limits and comparing the actual results with predefined tolerance limits. Below are few tools used for quality control purposes.

- Cause and effect diagrams: these diagrams help in identifying the root causes of quality problems.

- Control charts: control charts are a graphical representation of data. Control charts are used to identify activities that are out of control.

- Run charts: run charts are used to show the history and variations of a process over a time curve.

- Scatter diagrams: scattered diagrams are used to see if there is any relationship between two variables.

- Histogram: a histogram is a graphical representation of problems in terms of their attributes, characteristics and frequency. Below is a graphical representation of a histogram for a process redesign project.

Diagram 1: Histogram for a project redesign

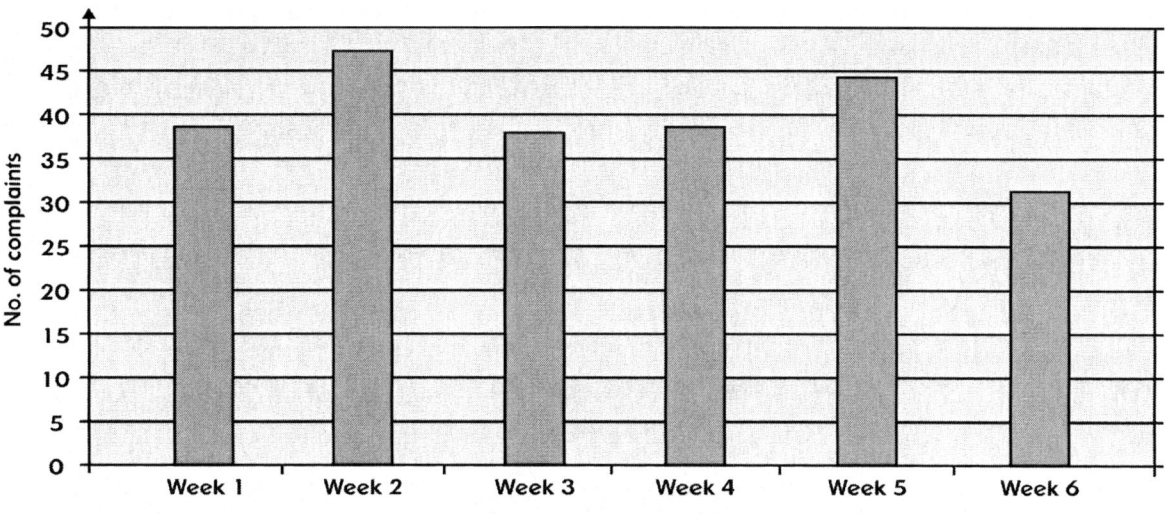

No. of product failures for new process

Slippage

Any slippage in this area could be reduced by measures such as employing additional resources to improve quality, by reducing the scope of the project, or by using quality material. Any slippage which cannot be corrected should be brought to the attention of the project sponsor and project stakeholders. It may be that the original project objective or specifications are invalid and need to be modified.

Example

Tran Ltd has started a project in business re-engineering. While monitoring the project, the project manager, Kelly, notices that the quality assurance procedures that should have been included in the project's original scope (outlined by the project sponsor) are missing in the scope statement and WBS.

To bring the project back on track, Kelly hires additional project team members. Since reducing the quality of the project objective in a core strategy project is not recommended, Kelly decides to spend more on resources and on giving the existing team incentives which would help the project. She also discusses this with the senior management and asks for extra time for completing this project.

SUMMARY

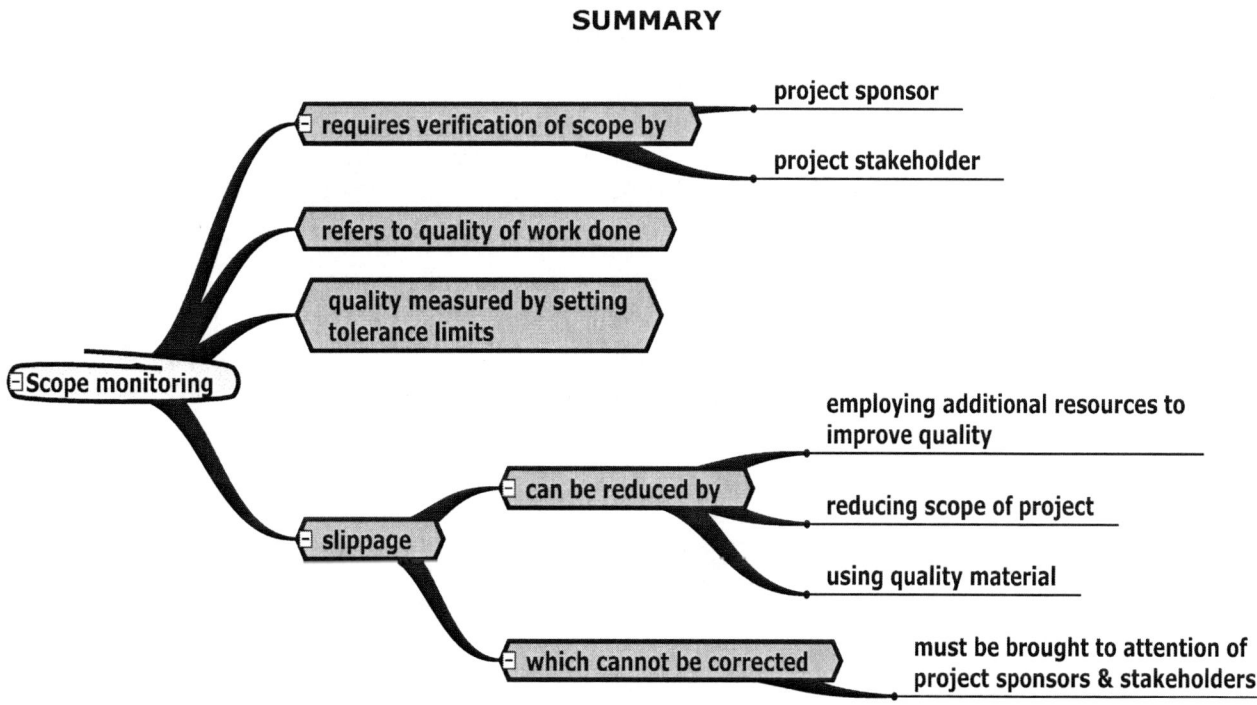

2. Time monitoring

Time monitoring refers to the completion of the work mentioned in the project's schedule. Any variances in the schedule which have an impact on the timely delivery of the project objective should be calculated. Work that has already been done should be compared with the milestones stated in the project plan.

Slippage

Any slippage in this area should be addressed with corrective actions such as:

- deploying additional resources
- revising previous planning to consider the possibility of subcontracting
- introducing incentives to staff
- rescheduling activities by conducting activities in parallel
- changing the method of doing the work and seeking other options.

SUMMARY

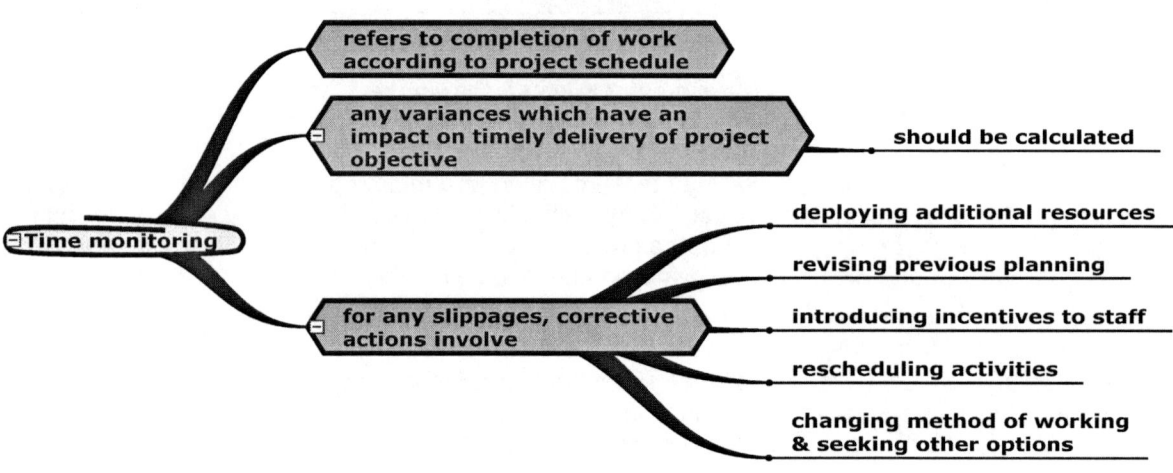

3. Cost

Cost should be monitored by comparing the costs incurred with the budgeted costs. Decisions about project processes, procurement of inputs and design should be monitored for cost. An estimate should be made of the funds available from the budget to carry out the remaining project including the funds required for corrective actions. Any variances should be reported to the project sponsor or to senior management. Earned value management is one of the tools for implementing cost control.

Slippage

Slippage in this area could be compensated by taking cost-cutting measures such as sacrificing quality to some extent, or reducing work incentives. Additional funding for the project could be obtained from senior management.

SUMMARY

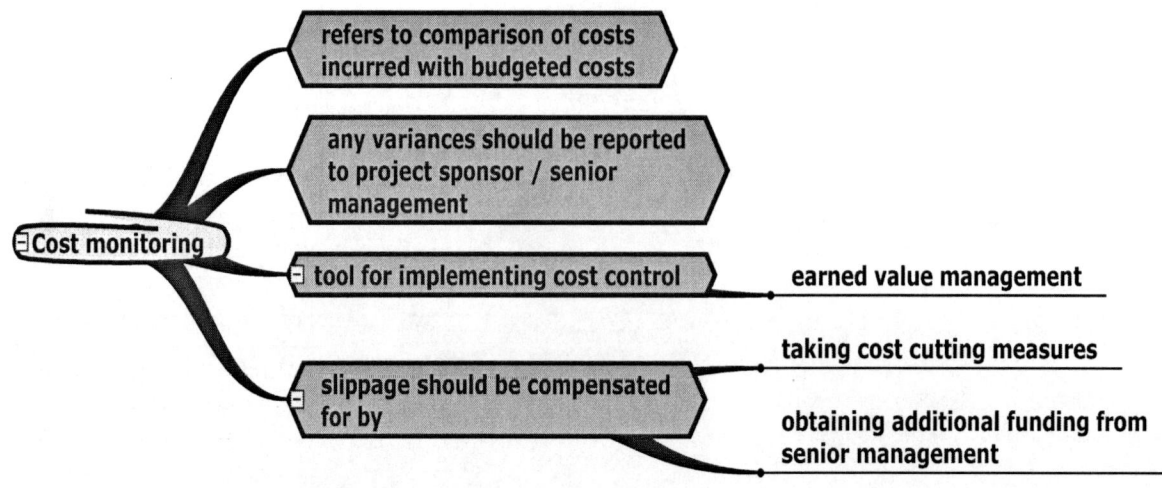

4. Resolution of problems

Monitoring the resolution of problems includes problem identification and its subsequent resolution. Problems do arise while executing a project; examples include communication gaps and human resource problems such as high turn over of human resource. These problems might have an impact on the delivery of the project objective within its time, cost, scope and quality constraints.

Slippage

Any slippage in handling problems should be avoided by taking immediate action at the inception of the problem. Procedures should be set out in order to reduce the occurrence of problems, such as setting up formal communication lines in order to prevent communication gaps.

SUMMARY

```
                          ┌─ includes problem identification & resolution
Resolution of problem ────┤
monitoring                │                                    ┌─ taking immediate action at inception of problem
                          └─ any slippage should be avoided by ┤
                                                               └─ setting up procedures to reduce occurrence of problems
```

5. Satisfaction of project's stakeholders

The project manager needs to understand the project stakeholders' views about, and satisfaction with, the way in which the project is progressing

Slippage

If stakeholders are not satisfied, it is necessary to identify the reasons for that and take corrective actions to close the gap between the desired output and the current predicted output.

SUMMARY

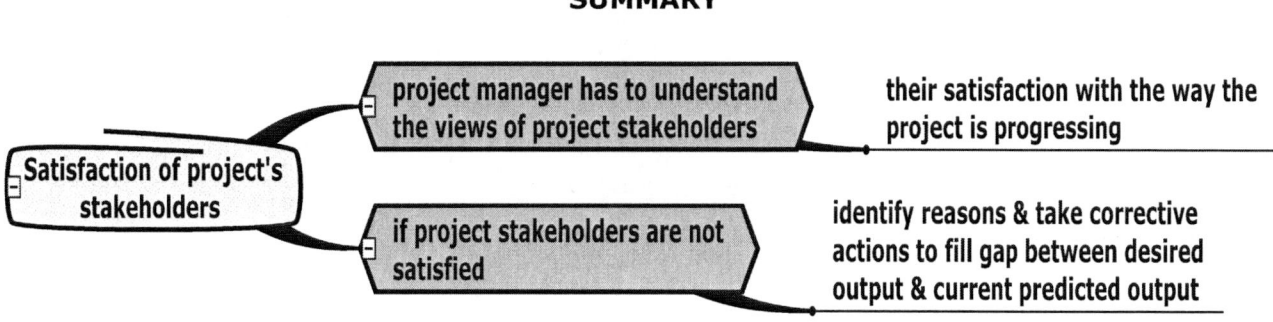

3.2 Some techniques used to diagnose or solve a problem are:

1. Fishbone analysis

A fishbone analysis could be described as a root cause analysis. In this approach, a problem is analysed by looking beyond the immediate problem. A problem forensic is carried out to identify the main cause of the problem. Then, instead of dealing with the symptoms of a problem, the root cause of the problem is identified, and measures to remove the root cause (and its symptoms) are put into place. Grundy Brown explains this analysis as being the same as the cause-effect analysis, except that in the cause-effect analysis there is a single cause with many effects, whereas in a fishbone analysis there are many effects with one cause.

2. Gap analysis

Gap analysis is a technique used to measure the difference between the desired future strategic performances (could be interpreted as the desired project objective for project monitoring) and the likely future performance (could be interpreted as the likely future performance of the project objective). The project manager could use this technique to monitor the project's future performance i.e. projecting the project's future performance (feed-forward) using the feedback on the work which has already been done.

Diagram 2: Graphical representation of gap analysis

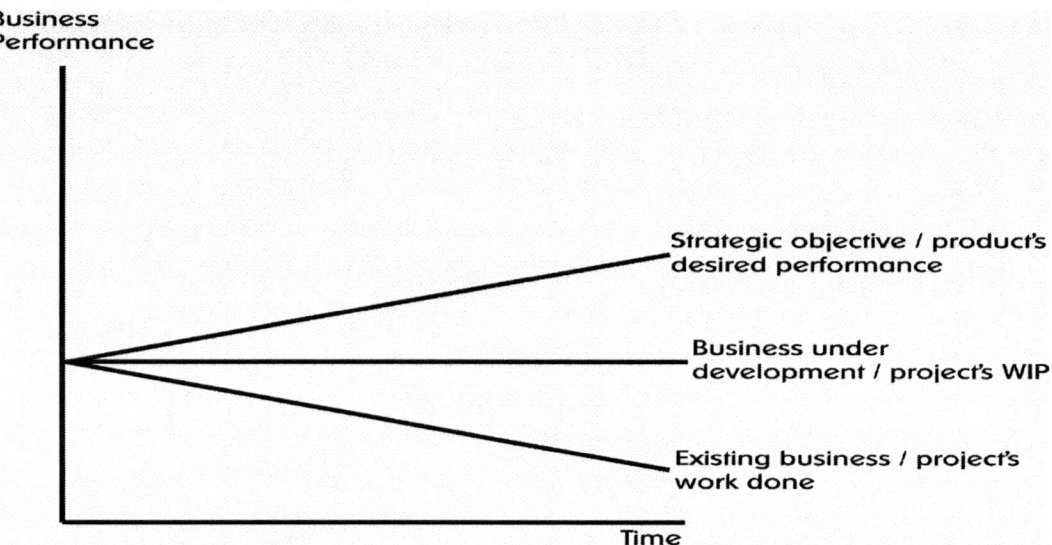

3. From-to analysis

From-to analysis can be used to measure the current state or definition of 'From' i.e. where you are right now and of 'To' i.e. where you want to go. After defining the above terms, the work required to achieve the desired future objective is listed. The factors responsible for the difference should be analysed, and efforts and plans to resolve issues should be activated.

4. Force field analysis

Force field analysis, as explained by Grundy and Brown, is one of the strategic management tools used especially for planning. This tool can also be used in the project monitoring stage. Force field analysis envisages possible future problems generating from the materialisation of risks. By predicting problems in advance, methods can be developed to reduce risk to an acceptable level. Grundy and Brown state that it is necessary to identify and manage enablers, forces which push success, and constraints which hold the project back from its objective.

Project management is a continuous process starting from the project's inception and ending with the delivery of the project objective. The project manager needs to evaluate enablers and constraints throughout the project management process. As this is a continuous process, it could be termed a project management monitoring tool.

Since we have discussed risk in the previous Study Guide, P3 G1, we shall now look at **project change procedures**.

Sometimes there are changes in the project's execution due to a change in scope, time, cost, or in the methods and technology used for implementing the project.

SUMMARY

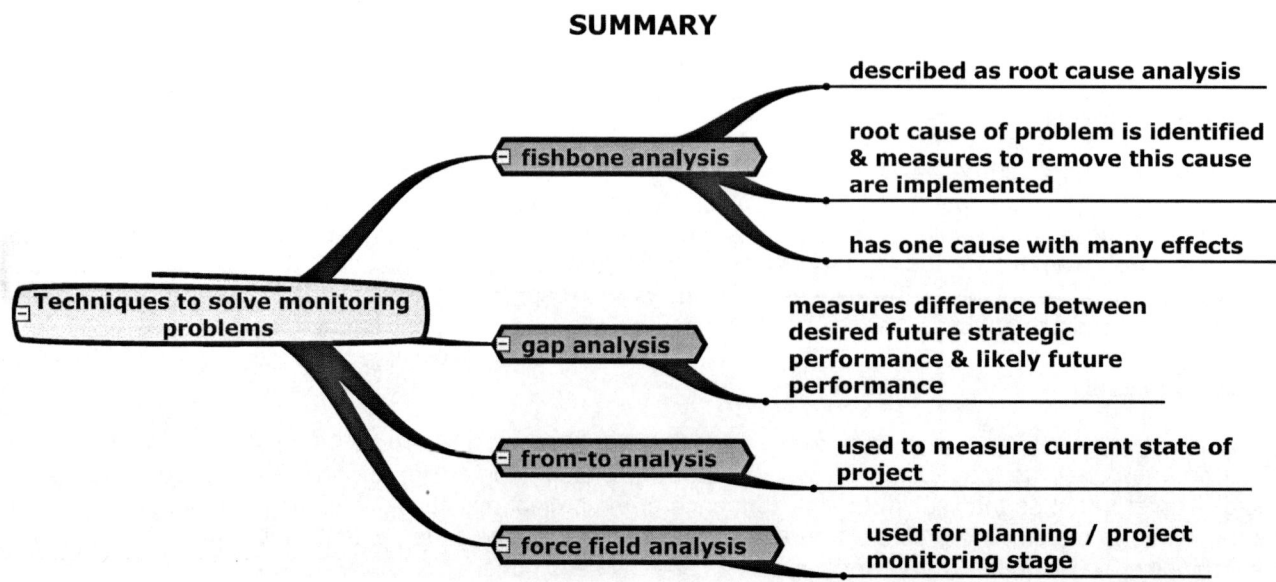

3.3 Factors responsible for change

1. adoption of new or better technology
2. changes in the composition of the team, including changes in personnel
3. team's perception of the scope and the project objective being different from those of the project sponsor and project stakeholders
4. introduction of new legislation, such as the introduction of Sarbanes-Oxley in 2002
5. changes in the business environment, such as a merger with another business

These changes have their impact on the project's triangle. The project manager is responsible for successfully handling such changes. Change control, i.e. configuration management, is also a part of project management.

The project manager must be very careful while allowing such changes. He should assess the following points:
- What is the cost of not implementing the change?
- What is the cost of implementing the change?
- Is the change justifiable, taking into account cost-benefit analysis?
- What is the risk associated with implementing the change?
- What is the reaction of the project sponsor or of the project stakeholders towards the proposed change?

Example

Dash Ltd started a software development project to support its main business of insurance two months ago. The marketing manager, Bob, has told one of the prospective clients that the company is developing a system which will become effective in the following year.

The client is significant and could account for up to 50% of Dash's turnover. The client is interested in using online transactions. The current structure does not support online transactions.

After considering the huge turnover the client could bring to Dash Ltd, the company decides to expand its scope to include the development of online business in its current project. The project manager, Tom, has to put change control procedures into place, which include re-planning the project in terms of time, cost and scope, and conducting a risk assessment for the project.

SUMMARY

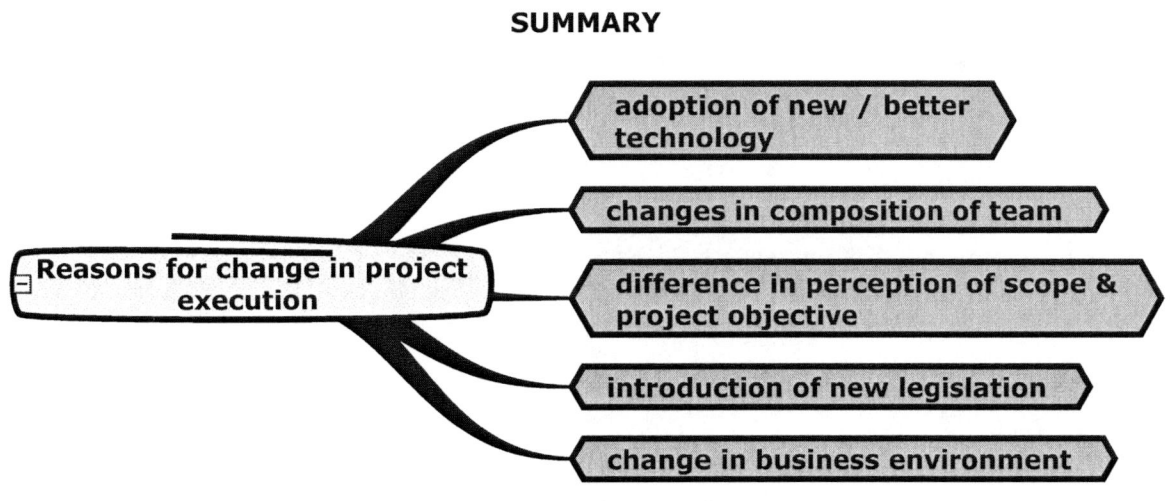

Test Yourself 1

Amazing Ltd, a car manufacturing company, has decided to introduce a new car into the market. The planning and production departments have set their targets according to the schedule given by the top management. The top management has already declared the launch date of the car.

After the project work begins, the technical and engineering department finds some faults in the car model, so the designing department has to redesign the model. Due to this, it is difficult for the project manager to complete the project in the given time.

Required:

Explain the steps a project manager can take if the project is not on schedule.

4. Discuss the role of benefits management and project gateways in project monitoring
[Learning Outcome e]

Project gateways examine a project at critical stages (or gates) in its lifecycle to provide assurance that the project can progress successfully to the next stage. Gateways verify whether the project is still on track.

Gateway 1 – Concept appraisal

This gateway simply consists of the management's approval to a project idea, confirming that it is in line with the organisational objectives and current priorities, and commissioning the next stage of project development work. Sign off at gateway 1 means that the concept of the project is sound and appears viable and deliverable.

Gateway 2 – Project Evaluation

In this stage, detailed planning takes place with the development of a robust business case scaled appropriately to reflect the size of the project. This stage will involve submitting project documentation for review, consultation and input from various areas.

Sign off at gateway 2 means that detailed plans are in place to assure that the project will deliver on time, remain within budget and meet the standards expected.

Gateway 3 – Business case

In this stage, detailed **project planning** is done. The work undertaken includes the following elements (which collectively comprise the business case):

- appraisal of project delivery options;
- planning for resources;
- developing budgets for project development and delivery (both revenue and capital)
- detailed risk and stakeholder analysis; and
- value for money assessment.

Sign off at gateway 3 means that sources of finance are available and the project will be formally accepted on completion of this stage.

Gateway 4 – Delivery & Assurance

In this stage, milestones are identified that enable **reviews** to be scheduled at appropriate points during project delivery. However, if the project does not progress as planned or exceeds the agreed timescales/budget tolerances, project reviews can be carried out in addition to the ones scheduled as above.

Sign off at gateway 4 means that the project can enter the practical completion and financial closure stage.

Scope creep

In project management parlance, the term **project scope** refers to the work that needs to be accomplished to deliver a product, service, or result with the specified features and functions.

Scope creep occurs when the scope of a project expands incrementally. This means that the project scope acquires more requirements that may not have been a part of the initial planning of the project.

Scope creep can occur when the scope of a project is not properly defined, documented, or controlled. It is generally considered an adverse happening that should be avoided, and sometimes causes cost overrun.

PROJECT GATEWAY LIFECYCLE

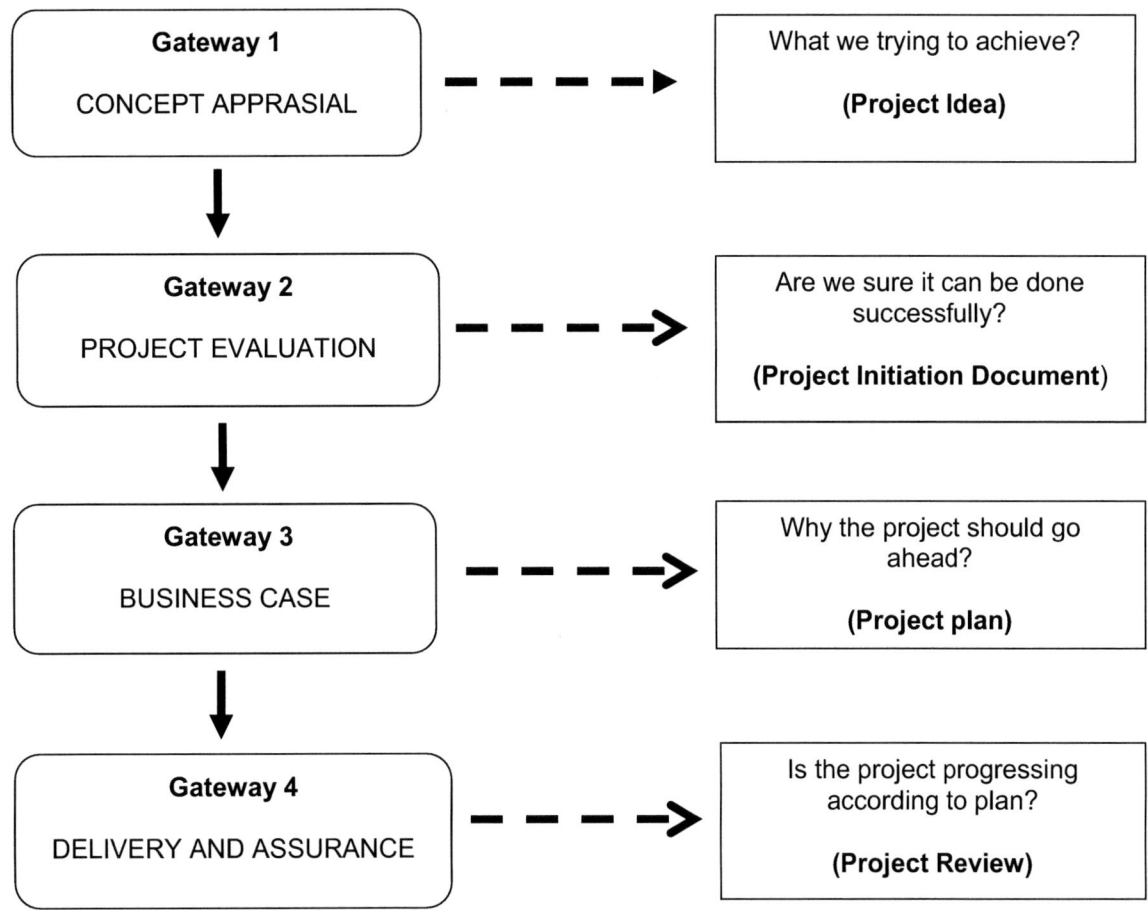

Answer to Test Yourself

Answer to TY 1

As soon as the project manager realises that the project is not on schedule, he should start evaluating the scope statement. He should analyse whether the project is on track in relation to the objectives set in the scope statement and evaluate the remaining work in terms of the available funds. He will need to assess the reasons for the project not being on schedule. Once he has discovered the root cause of the project's problems, he should look for solutions.

Progress reports are written by the project manager to report the current status of the project in terms of cost, time, scope and quality. This is reported to the project sponsor and project stakeholders.

To bring the project on track the project manager can hire additional project team members. He should also discuss this with the senior management and ask for extra time to complete the project

The project manager of Amazing Ltd will need to assess the situation and discuss it with management. Management can hire more designers as well as skilled employees which will improve the quality and quantity of the production. These steps may increase the cost of the product but will help the project manager to complete the product on time.

Quick Quiz

1. State the different types of techniques used for solving monitoring problems.
2. State the four project gateways in project monitoring.

Answers to Quick Quiz

1. The different types of techniques used for solving monitoring problems are:
    - fishbone analysis
    - gap analysis
    - from- to analysis
    - force field analysis

2. The four project gateways in project monitoring are:
   A. Concept appraisal
   B. Project evaluation
   C. Business case
   D. Delivery and assurance

Self Examination Question

Question 1.

Glamorous is a New York-based cosmetics company, which is listed on the New York Stock Exchange. Glamorous markets a large range of cosmetic products in 59 countries globally.

Glamorous is committed to conducting its business in a manner which demonstrates respect for the environment.

All Glamorous's products are manufactured in accordance with Good Environmental Practices and in compliance with all relevant national and local regulations.

Glamorous is fully committed to continuous improvement in environmental management and is constantly looking for more eco-friendly methods to use in the manufacturing of its varied products.

Recently, its R&D department has discovered a new chemical formula which is very beneficial for the user's skin. Glamorous is in the process of setting up a laboratory for further research and development and for the production of a new product, 'Smooth Skin', which will be made using this discovery

The project manager needs to ensure smooth execution of the project and the launch of the new product into the market.

Required:

Advice the project manager on the risks involved in this project's execution.

Answer to Self Examination Question

Answer to SEQ 1

This project is crucial for Glamorous Ltd due to its use of a new ingredient. The project could be a breakthrough for the R&D team working on it. The R&D team is responsible for product enhancement. The target market for this product is teenagers and so the project manager has to keep a close eye on the budgets of various departments, i.e. research, HR, advertising and marketing. The successful launch of the new product, "Smooth Skin", will help Glamorous to increase its market share and share value.

1. **Evaluation of project risks:** The role of the project manager is to evaluate the risks involved in the project. He needs to look at the risks involved in developing the product whilst considering the following:
2. **Environmentally-friendly image:** The company needs to maintain its reputation as an environmentally-friendly company. The product needs to be a safe and environmentally-friendly product. The research work carried out for the project must follow the guidelines set by the government and must not cause any harm to the ecological environment.
3. **Dermatological test:** The project manager needs to ensure that all tests carried out are successful and that the product is safe to use and ready for launch, so that he can avoid project failure. The product must be beneficial to all types of skin. The product must also bear a warning if it is not suitable for children or the elderly.
4. **Government policies:** The project manager needs to ensure that project execution is in accordance with the policies and regulations of local governing bodies and industry councils. The project manager has to keep himself updated in case there are any changes in the rules and policies of local and national legislation.
5. **Patents:** The product needs to be patented before its launch.
6. **Against animal testing:** The project manager needs to ensure that the project team follows the company policy of avoiding animal testing.
7. **Funding and costs:** The project manager needs to ensure that sufficient funds are available for smooth execution of the project.
8. **Estimated period for project execution:** The project needs to be completed within a stipulated period. The manager has to ensure adherence to the deadlines. Non-adherence could lead to competitors launching similar products into the market.
9. **Timely launch of product:** The project manager needs to ensure a successful and timely launch for the product in order for the company to become the market leader for this product.
10. **Pricing:** The pricing of the product plays a very important role in the success of its launch. The product targets teenagers and policies for the price promotion must be fixed accordingly.

The project manager will have to make sure he and his team are well-prepared for the execution of the project. They are the people responsible for the timely and efficient delivery of the project.

SECTION F: PROJECT MANAGEMENT

STUDY GUIDE F5: CONCLUDING A PROJECT

■ Get Through Intro

Once satisfied that the product/service works, the project is effectively over. Concluding the project involves gaining stakeholder and customer acceptance of the final product/service and bringing the project to an orderly end.

It is extremely important to formally close projects (whether completed or cancelled) and reflect on what are the key takeaways from the projects. Equally important is to plan for and execute a smooth transition of the project into the normal operations of the company.

This Study Guide discusses how you can conclude a project successfully and avoid mistakes in future by understanding what went wrong.

■ Learning Outcomes

a) Establish mechanisms for successfully concluding a project.
b) Discuss the relative meaning and benefits of a post-implementation and a post-project review
c) Discuss the meaning and value of benefits realisation.
d) Evaluate how project management software may support the planning and monitoring of a project.
e) Apply 'lessons learned' to future business case validation and to capital allocation decisions

> **1. Establish mechanisms for successfully concluding a project.** [2]
>
> [Learning outcome a]

Upon completion of project work, every project objective has to be delivered to the project sponsor. The project sponsor will benefit more than the other project stakeholders from the successful delivery of the project objective.

Procedure to deliver project objective

1. **Unit testing**

Each unit of the project is tested for its efficiency and effectiveness. The main purpose of this test is to see whether a unit achieves the purpose for which it was developed. This testing is done before integrating all parts of the WBS.

2. **Systems testing**

The project objective is tested to see whether the project has achieved the purpose for which it was created. This includes testing the effectiveness of all the characteristics of the project objective as mentioned in the original scope statement.

3. **Interface testing**

The new system or part of the new system is then tested for its integration with the existing system. If there are any problems, they must be resolved immediately.

4. **Project completion report:**

This report is addressed to the project sponsor / project stakeholders, and it states

a) the project's outcome against the outcome stated in the scope statement

b) any unresolved issues which are related to the project, such as if the response time for a software program is more than expected, but it does not affect the project's objective

c) time taken to complete the project objective in relation to the original schedule

d) costs incurred in relation to budgeted costs

e) procedures that have been put into place in case a problem relating to project objective occurs after the project objective is applied to production or to day-to-day operations (responsibilities for such procedures need to be set out in the report)

The project sponsor or the project stakeholders need to sign this document.

The completion report represents the formal delivery of the project. After delivery, the project objective is actually merged into the existing system.

Example

The lifecycle of a software development project always ends with unit tests, systems testing and interface testing, and is followed by the formal release of the project.

SUMMARY

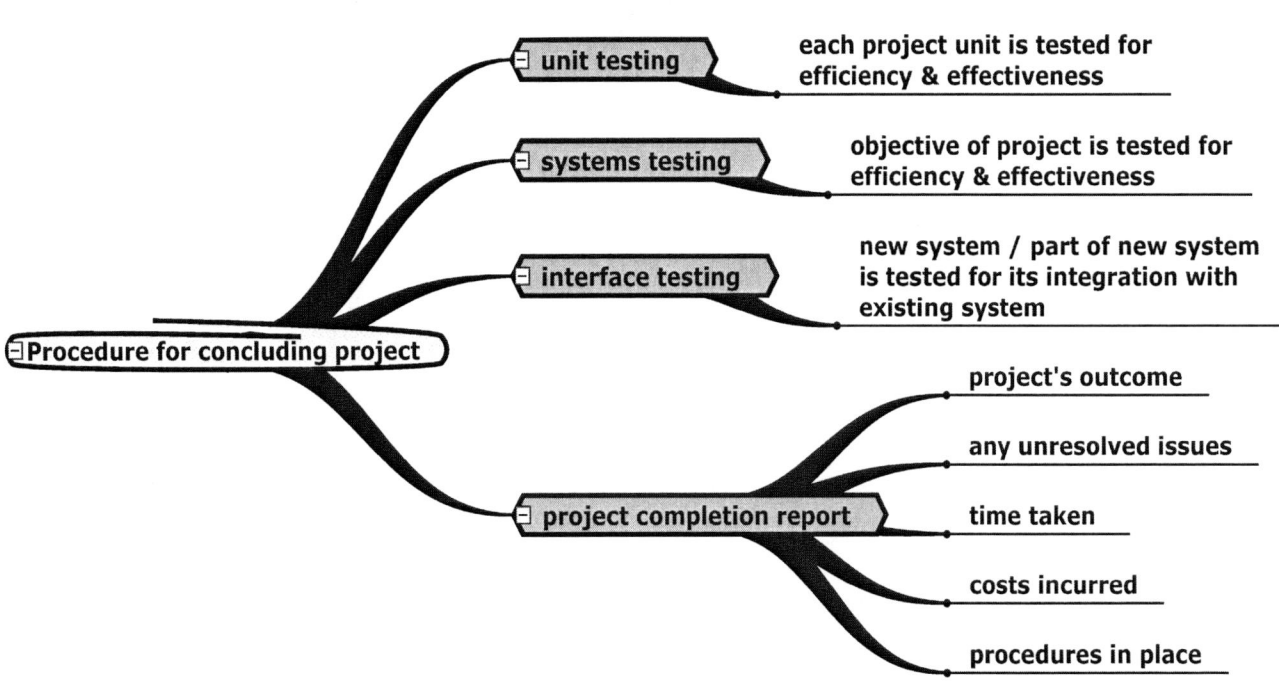

Test Yourself 1

2. Angels Ltd is a software development company which has accepted a project to prepare an accounting system for Asterix Ltd. The team of software engineers has prepared the program for the general ledger, purchase ledger and sales ledger as well as for the SOCI (income statement) and SOFP (balance sheet).

Required:

Explain the tests Angels needs to perform once the project has been completed.

---

2. **Discuss the relative meaning and benefits of a post-implementation and a post-project review.**[2]
   Apply 'lessons learned' to future business case validation and to capital allocation decisions.[2]

   [Learning Outcomes b and e]

Post-project review

A post-project review is a review of the **project.** The purpose of this review is to determine whether the benefits, including those set out in the business case, have been achieved and to identify opportunities for further improvement. The review also looks at whether the project produced the required deliverables within the agreed time frame.

This review involves the sponsor, the project team and those affected by the project. The review is performed to identify:

- what was done well
- what didn't go well
- whether the expected benefits were delivered
- whether the cost and time budgets were met
- what needs to be done to improve the outcome of the project

The advantages of undertaking the post-project review include:

- identifying ways to improve the functional value of a project
- increasing user morale through continuous improvement in the way projects are managed
- identifying opportunities for further improvement
- determining cost efficiencies resulting from improved project performance
- improved decision-making.

Post-implementation review

A post-implementation review is primarily a review of the product produced by the project. Its purpose is to check whether the delivered product meets the needs of the users.

The end-product is the overall deliverable of the project. A product may be a physical component, software, intellectual property, documentation etc. A product may itself be a collection of other products, thereby giving rise to a Product Breakdown Structure (PBS).

Product Breakdown Structure (PBS)

Before we understand the meaning of a PBS, it is important to understand the term 'Work Breakdown Structure (WBS)'. In project management parlance, WBS is a technique that breaks down a project into 'manageable components'.

A PBS is a type of application of WBS. In general, a PBS is a structure that identifies the products to be delivered by a project and is displayed in a logical hierarchy. The need for PBS emanates in the case of large projects where WBS based on 'products' is needed. The need also arises if the project:

- is relatively large in value and of a higher duration
- involves several geographical regions
- is complex with multiple components or systems

Generally, the PBS describes the object that is intended to be created.

Lessons learned

Capturing lessons learned from projects is essential for any organisation in order to ensure efficiencies over time and development of best practices.
The purpose of lessons learned is to bring together any insights gained during a project that can be usefully applied to future projects.

However, in reality, project teams usually move quickly from project to project. Therefore, capturing lessons learned is often forgotten at the end of the project. It is essential to capture the lessons learned on your projects. Effective transfer of knowledge from what is learned does not apply solely to other project teams, but also to the organisation as a whole. There should be a formal process for capturing what is learned to ensure consistency among all project teams.

An individual who is trained in capturing what is learned should track the project throughout all its stages. The lessons learned should not be captured just from the project team, but also from customers and other employees.

A log of lessons learned should be created. Such a log should comprise the following things, amongst others:

- How did the lesson arise?
- What are the key things learnt from the lesson?
- What can other people do to recreate that situation or avoid it from happening?

Test Yourself 2

Destiny Ltd plays a dominant role in the construction sector. It has accepted several construction projects for apartment blocks as well as for business premises. Destiny has also constructed a bridge in the city. While inspecting the bridge, John, the project manager, finds that the bridge is unstable.

Required:

(a) What is the significance of a lessons learned report?

(b) How will a lessons learned report help John to overcome the situation?

3. Discuss the meaning and value of benefits realisation.[2]

[Learning outcome c]

This Learning Outcome has been discussed in Study Guide F2, Learning Outcomes e and f.

4. Evaluate how project management software may support the planning and monitoring of a project. [3]

[Learning outcome d]

With the evolution of computer technology, the need to do a lot of things manually has reduced. Technology has also affected the project management field and now, with the help of project management software tasks, project planning and monitoring have become much easier, allowing the project manager to exercise more control on planning and monitoring tasks. The role of project management software in project management depends upon the size of the project under consideration.

4.1 Small businesses

The project manager of a small business does not always need to carry out project portfolio management and controlling and monitoring projects is relatively easy. It does not make sense to invest a lot of money in buying expensive software. Project managers who want to be precise about their cost and time estimates are interested in using software. Low-end project management software tools that are suitable for small businesses facilitate the computerised project management planning process and the preparation of status reports, and provide tools for project scheduling such as preparation of Gantt Charts and PERT Charts. Turbo project, milestone simplicity and quick Gantt are some examples of low-end project management software.

4.2 Medium-sized businesses

As a business increases in size, the size of the area covered by the project also increases, demanding a higher quality of project management skills which can often be supplemented by the correct project management software. Some software packages provide simulation and adjustment to a project in case of changes in any one variable, such as rescheduling an activity on PERT. Processes for calculating critical path, slack, delay reports and resource level capacity are computerised. This also causes a change in the project budget, since every decision to change the inputs or scope of the project affects cost.

Example

The project manager of a building construction project decided to create a modern interior for the building. Once the project manager has modified the data inputs to the project management software, the software will provide the new estimate of costs or the new budget. This will help the project manager to calculate the cost of his decision and, therefore, it will help him to make quick decisions.

This software provides scheduling techniques which schedule internal as well as external consultants. These tools are expensive and buying such tools demands a big investment decision based upon proved cost-benefit analysis. Mid-end software is generally recommended for businesses in this category.

4.3 Large businesses

This means organisations which are in level 4 or 5 of the project management capabilities maturity model. Project managers at senior levels need to manage a large portfolio of projects. Accountability for project portfolios is fixed among the executives. This increases the importance of presenting consolidated and individual project data with a consistent flow of information so that executives can prioritise projects, allocate resources for projects, and manage the human resources for projects. High-end project management software tools are suitable for such organisations. These help executives to manage the complex demands of resources and also help to prioritise projects. Here, software can provide cost data much more quickly than the company's accounting system, which provides a base for timely decisions. Software such as SAP and Oracle Financials could be considered suitable for large companies. Due to their advanced features, the cost of buying such software packages is very high.

Case Study

MS Office project -
Mec Engineering is a medium size company. It uses MS Office Project Professional 2007 and Microsoft Office Project Web Access while managing its projects. With the use of these software packages, Mec Engineering can coordinate its work effectively, ranging from single projects to complex programmes throughout the life of the project.

These software packages can help a project manager in the following ways:
- These packages make it easier to track budgets and cost resources, enabling better financial insight.
- MS Office Web Access also offers the facility to evaluate proposals by managing plans and activities prior to project approval.
- MS Office Web Access helps Mec Engineering to manage ongoing operations after the completion of the project.
- Common business reporting tools such as Microsoft Office Share Point Server 2007 make reporting data easier.

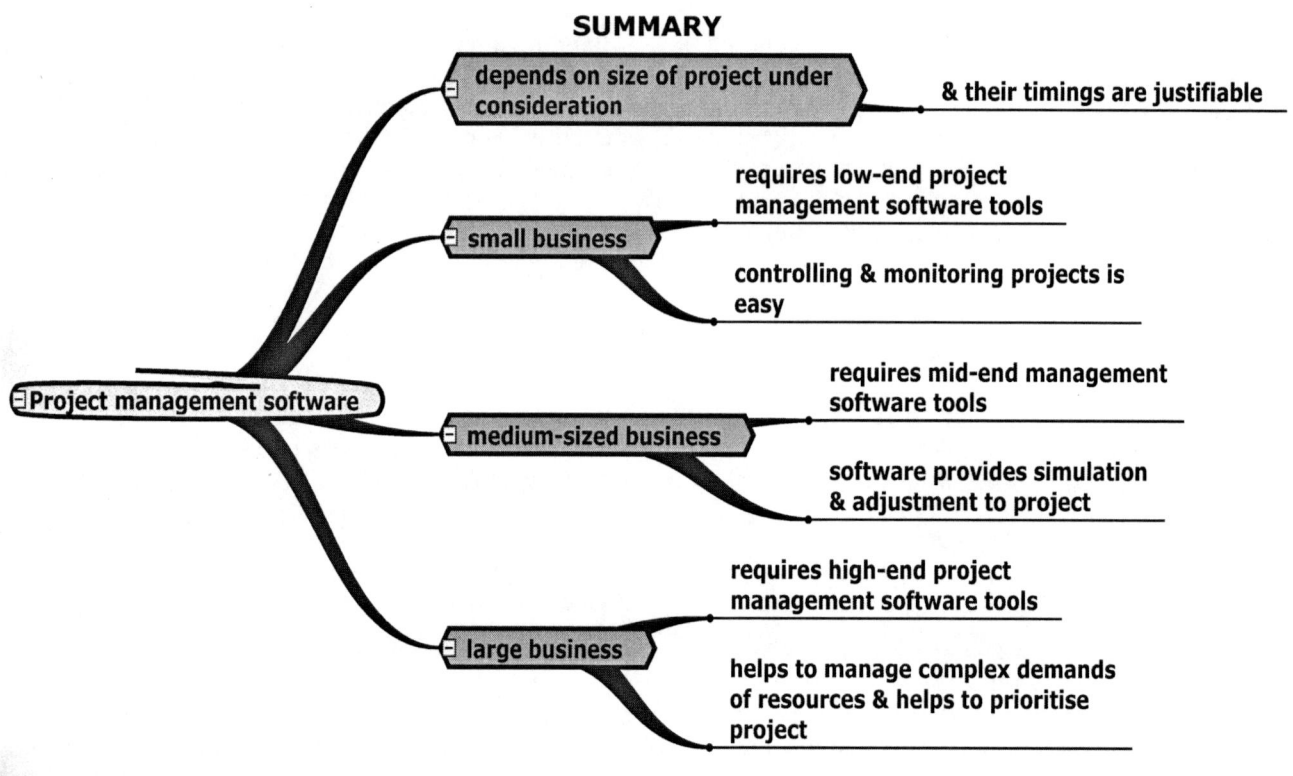

Test Yourself 3

4. Pager Co is a medium-sized company. The manager of Pager Co, Stephen, wants to install project monitoring software to monitor the company's projects.

Required:

Inform Stephen of the software available in the market and recommend which software would be suitable for Pager Co.

Answers to Test Yourself

Answer to TY 1

Once the project has been completed, the following tests need to be performed:

1. unit tests
2. systems testing
3. interface testing
4. formal release of the project

The project manager of Angels will need to carry out **unit testing** to see whether a unit achieves the purpose for which it has been developed. All the ledger entries should be correctly recorded by the accounting system.

The project manager then needs to check the **systems testing** to see whether the project has achieved the purpose for which it was created. Systems testing shows the effectiveness of all the characteristics of the project objectives as mentioned in the original scope statement and gives the final effect to accounts as required. For example, if stock is purchased and recorded in the purchase ledger, the second effect of the purchase needs to be shown in inventory by increasing the stock.

After that, the project manager will need to carry out **interface testing** to check the integration with the existing systems i.e. the client's existing systems. Such systems might be the payroll system or sales invoicing.

The project manager will need to obtain satisfactory results from all the above tests before submitting the **project completion report.** The project manager will also need to resolve any unresolved issues such as unsatisfactory project quality.

Answer to TY 2

(a) A lessons learned report is a project review report. It is prepared once the project is complete. It includes the company's review of the project. It consists of all the lessons the team learned while working on the project, whether they related to human resources, cost or time-keeping. The report mentions the problems that the project faced and solutions that were applied to those problems.

Therefore, the lessons learned report helps the organisation to refer back to the problems faced by a particular team on a project. If, in future, another team faces similar kinds of problems, it can refer to this report and follow the same solution, or modify the solution to suit the requirements of its own problems. The report also prevents the organisation from repeating the mistakes that were committed during previous projects.

(b) The lessons learned report will help John to evaluate the project and assess the problems by considering the causes of the problems. The report will also give recommendations of how to solve the problems and give John an idea of the cost that this may involve.

Answer to TY 3

Project management software helps an organisation to plan and monitor a project's tasks more easily. With the advancement of technology, more and more corporate activities are becoming automated. More machines are being used to obtain effective and accurate results.

The role of the project management software depends upon the size of the project under consideration.

1. **Small businesses:** The projects undertaken by small businesses are smaller in nature. Project management software is expensive in nature. Therefore, small businesses should not make high investments in project management software.

   Low-end project management software tools are available for small businesses. This software facilitates the computerised project management planning process, preparation of status reports and provides tools for project scheduling, such as preparing Gantt Charts or PERT Charts.

2. **Large businesses:** Project managers at senior levels need to manage a large portfolio of projects.

   High-end project management software tools are suitable for large businesses. These help the executives in managing the complex demands of the project's resources and help in prioritising the project. Such software provides cost data much more quickly than the company's accounting system and provides the base for timely decisions.

   Due to their advanced features, the costs of buying such software packages are very high.

3. **Medium-sized businesses:** The size of projects undertaken in a medium-sized business is larger than in a small business but smaller than in a large business. The project manager of a project undertaken by a medium-sized business needs software for planning and scheduling purposes. He will be interested in getting auto generated Gantt Charts, CPA and PERT.

   Mid-end software is generally recommended for businesses in this category. This software provides scheduling techniques which offer scheduling of internal as well as external consultants. These tools are expensive and buying such tools demands a big investment decision based upon proved cost-benefit analysis. The cost of the human resources used for preparing statistical techniques such as Gantt Charts and CPA and the potential benefits from the timely availability of such data should be compared. Milestone simplicity and Turbo project are some examples of the software suitable for medium-sized businesses.

   According to the above information, mid-end project management software would be most suitable for Pager Co. Stephen should purchase this type of software to meet his requirements.

490: Project Management

Quick Quiz

1. State the different types of techniques used for solving monitoring problems.
2. Configuration management is a part of project management. Is this statement true or false?
3. What are the goals of a project review?
4. What is benefits realisation?

Answers to Quick Quiz

1. The different types of techniques used for solving monitoring problems are:
   - fishbone analysis
   - gap analysis
   - from- to analysis
   - force field analysis

2. True

3. The goals of a project review are:
   - to prepare a set of well-documented procedures
   - to ensure that the benefits received from the review are more than the costs incurred to conduct those reviews

4. Benefits realisation is the process of assessing whether the estimated benefits of a project are actually realised at the end of the project, and whether their timings are justifiable to the project sponsors and stakeholders.

Self Examination Question

Question 1

Venus Ltd is a textile company. It is about to launch a new project. The project manager, Danny, is new to this process and has little knowledge of how to prepare project reports.

Required:

Advise Danny on how he should write his project report.

Answer to Self Examination Question

Answer to SEQ 1

Concluding a project report is as crucial as preparing a project report. Concluding a project report involves certain important tests that need to be conducted before submitting the final report to the authorities.

Delivering a project to the client according to the client's specifications and requirements is the ultimate goal of any project undertaken by an organisation.

Danny will have to follow the steps outlined below in order to conclude his project in a satisfactory manner:

1. **Unit testing:** Each unit of the project needs to be tested for efficiency and effectiveness. It is important to know that every unit produced has achieved the objective it was produced for.
2. **Systems testing:** The complete project objective is tested to see whether it has achieved the purpose for which it was created. This also includes testing for the effectiveness of each characteristic of the project objective, as mentioned in the original scope statement.
3. **Interface testing:** The new system or new part of the system created by the project team is then tested for its integration with the existing system. If there are any problems, they should be resolved immediately.
4. **Project completion report:** This report is addressed to the project sponsor / project stakeholders, and it states:

- the project's outcome in relation to the outcome stated in the scope statement
- whether there are any unresolved issues which relate to the project, such as if the response time for a software program is more than the expected time, but this in no way affects the project's objective
- the time taken to complete the project objective in relation to the original schedule
- the costs incurred as against the budgeted costs
- the responsibilities for post-production problems and the procedures to handle these problems

Danny needs to make sure that he follows all the above steps in order to submit a complete report to the management.

SECTION G: FINANCIAL ANALYSIS

STUDY GUIDE G1: THE LINK BETWEEN STRATEGY AND FINANCE

Get Through Intro

Imagine you have a business idea. You want to develop a resort on the moon. You have spoken friends and they think it is an excellent idea. They said if it was reasonable in price, they would all want to visit it and would consider buying an apartment. You write your business plan and work out it will cost several trillion dollars. The project will take about 20 years to complete. You know that Richard Branson's Virgin Group have also said they will start flights into space, so you think it is just a matter of time until he starts fully fledged flights to the moon.

You work out that in order to make it cost effective for people to visit, the payback time is approximately 300 years. Do you think anyone is likely to invest in your project? It is unlikely! Perhaps a silly example, but it helps you understand that whilst you may have an innovative strategy, if you have not got the finance, you will not be able to deliver the strategy.

Many projects are turned down every day by companies and banks. It is because the finance providers do not feel that the strategy is sound. This chapter will help you understand what financial stakeholders are looking for and how to ensure you have the best chances of obtaining funding for your ventures in the future!

Learning Outcomes

a) Explain the relationship between strategy and finance:
   i. Managing for value
   ii. Financial expectations of stakeholders
   iii. Funding strategies

Introduction

Case Study

Drilling for oil - In early July, Associated Press reported that whilst previously it had been considered uneconomical to drill for oil in the waters off the coast of Florida, it is now potentially profitable. With the cost of oil soaring in 2008, it is likely that research and development will re-start in certain places.

According to the article published on 4th July, drilling can take up to 2 years and engineers need to drill more than 3 miles below the surface of the ocean floor to extract oil. An oil expert was quoted as saying that they could have around $200 million invested before they know whether it will be profitable in the long run

It could cost up to $4 billion and take 5 years to see a return on investment.

However, many green organisations are extremely concerned as they believe there will be a huge dame to the environment, which could prove to cost much more in the long term.

The above case study will hopefully show you that calculations need to be made carefully when assessing future projects. Also, to some stakeholders, a project will be acceptable and to others it will not. The purpose of this chapter is to give you an idea about what stakeholders could be concerned about and how they can potentially evaluate future strategies.

> 1. **Explain the relationship between strategy and finance:** [3]
>   i. Managing for value
>   ii. Financial expectations of stakeholders
>   iii. Funding strategies
>
> [Learning Outcome a]

A detailed explanation of strategy can be found in Study Guide A1.

Finance is one of the branches of economics, and it deals with the **management of money and other assets**. Finance is related to determining value or decision-making. It also deals with matters related to money and the market. The finance branch of an organisation distributes the resources required for purchasing goods or services, and for investing or managing activities in an organisation. Finance is one of the most important activities in an organisation because the **funding requirements** of other departments are met by the finance department. Moreover, if adequate financial planning is not undertaken, the organisation cannot function smoothly.

1.1 Relationship between strategy and finance

The relationship between strategy and finance is explained by analysing the reasons why some strategies are more effective than others. Every strategy must possess the following three features to be successful:
- suitability
- acceptability
- feasibility

These features are explained further below:

1. Suitability

Suitability refers to the strategy's **appropriateness** to the organisation's operations. An organisation's management plans the strategy according to the goals of the organisation. The strategies are suitable to the organisation but they must be analysed to verify whether they take account of **environmental changes**, **strategic capabilities** and **stakeholders' expectations**.

The suitability criteria are assessed for the various strategic options available and are measured in terms of environmental change, capabilities and the expectations of stakeholders. The policy to be implemented by management is first checked for suitability and only then implemented.

There are some situations in which strategies are found to be unsuitable for an organisation:.
- Managers may select a strategy which may not take all three factors into consideration. They may select a strategy which considers environmental change but not the capabilities of the organisation.
- There are situations in which more than one strategic option can be suitable for the organisation. In such cases, only one option is adopted by the management and the other options become unsuitable.

The suitability of different strategic options can be evaluated through the following methods:

- The available options are analysed by giving them **ranks**. This ranking is done by taking into consideration environmental changes, strategic capabilities and stakeholder expectations.
- The options are analysed by using **decision trees**. Decision trees are the tools that help to eliminate options which are not useful and add the needs that must be met in future.

2. Acceptability

Acceptability refers to how satisfying a strategy is. The strategy must be acceptable to stakeholders. The most significant stakeholders are the shareholders. The shareholders value those strategies which are **financially beneficial** and profitable to them. The stakeholders measure the performance of the strategy on the basis of return, risk and stakeholder reactions.

a) Returns

It is important to note that stakeholder groups have differing needs. Shareholders, for example, are primarily interested in profitability, as this provides them with dividends and capital growth in their shareholding. Other stakeholder groups may have needs that are non-financial, for example, the local community may be interested in ensuring that the organisation does not damage the environment.

The stakeholders measure these benefits from an angle of profitability, cost-benefit ratio and increase in their wealth.

b) Risk

Risk refers to the danger of a strategy failing in an organisation. When a strategy is being implemented, management should consider that the strategy could fail: there is an element of risk involved in the strategy implementation. Managers are expected to analyse the risk as a way of improving the means of achieving the organisation's goals. They must possess innovative skills and abilities to manage risk.

i. **Sensitivity analysis:** sensitivity analysis refers to the methods adopted by managers for **evaluating the consequences** of implementing a particular strategy. This analysis explains the risks involved in applying the strategy. Sensitivity analysis is used to calculate the outcome of a strategy and whether it is beneficial for an organisation or not. For example, a discounted cashflow can be used to measure sensitivity to discount rate by altering the discount rate and then observing the effect on net present value.

ii. **Financial ratios:** financial ratios are an important mode of evaluating the risk involved in an organisation's strategy. These ratios provide an organisation's financial status. With the help of various ratios, managers can evaluate whether or not the implementation of a particular strategy would be beneficial to the organisation. An organisation's management plans various strategies, but the strategy that is most financially viable or beneficial to the organisation will be implemented by them. The financial ratio analysis is explained in further detail in Study Guide H3.

c) Stakeholder reactions

Another method of evaluating the risk involved in strategy implementation is stakeholder reaction. Whenever a strategy receives a favourable reaction from stakeholders, it implies that the stakeholders agree to the decision and the strategy. On the other hand, when stakeholders give no reaction or a negative reaction, it implies that they are not in favour of the implementation of that particular strategy. In every organisation, stakeholders play an important role in decision-making. Hence, the reactions of the stakeholders are vital for strategic action.

3. Feasibility

Here, feasibility refers to the **viability of a strategy**. Feasibility indicates how practical it is to implement the strategy with the available resources and skills. There are different ways of measuring the feasibility of the strategy. One is to evaluate whether the organisation has sufficient **finances** to conduct the strategy effectively. All aspects relating to fund management must be evaluated by the organisation's management.

A second way of evaluating the feasibility of a strategy is to assess whether there are sufficient **resources** at the organisation's disposal. Managers must assess the extent to which the resources available to the organisation need to be adjusted in order to meet the demands of the strategy. Moreover, managers have to evaluate whether the available resources are sufficient to gain a share of the market with the implementation of the strategy and whether the available resources are capable of sustaining a competitive advantage in the industry.

For an organisation, one of the significant elements in the success of a strategy is **'finance'**. Efficient management of finance means leads an increased likelihood that the strategy will be effective. Finance is the source of the implementation of every strategy. A strategy is successful if it is both beneficial for the organisation and also financially viable.

All stakeholders are keen to know whether they will receive financial benefits (returns) from the implementation of a strategy. They are also interested in whether they will receive regular returns such as dividends for shares held.

The relationship between strategy and finance can be explained with the help of the diagram below:

Diagram 1: Relationship between strategy and finance

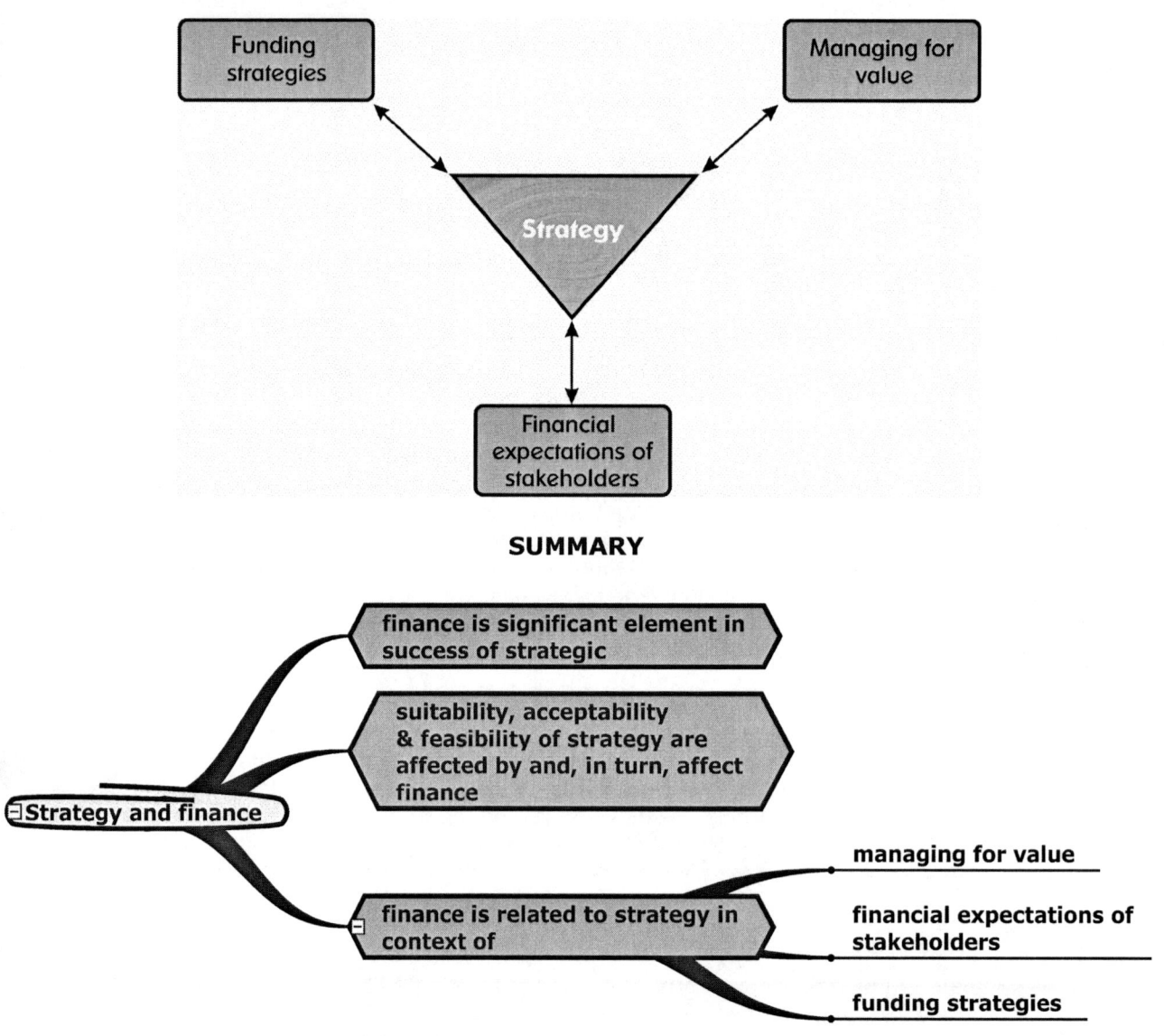

Test Yourself 1

Robust Equipment Ltd is a medium sized company involved in equipment manufacturing and sales. The company is looking to expand and grow. As a part of this strategy, Robust's management is considering a major upgrade in its information technology support for office staff. Currently, the company's administrative operations are inconsistent and uncoordinated. The proposed upgrade will enable office staff to perform their day-to-day functions more efficiently and accurately. The transfer of information between staff members will be faster and information will be more readily available to management for decision-making. This should improve the overall efficiency and effectiveness of Robust. Under the upgrade, it is proposed that each of the hundred and fifty staff members will have a high specification personal computer (PC) with associated software (word processing, spreadsheets etc.). All the PCs will be linked into a local area network comprising several fileservers to handle shared applications, plus network links into internet services. There is a substantial capital cost involved in the proposed upgrade.

Required:

Explain how you might undertake an evaluation of the proposed strategy for upgrading the office information technology of Robust Equipment Ltd. Your evaluation should cover both financial and non-financial criteria.

1.2 What is managing for value?

Managing for value is one of the elements of **value based management**. Value based management refers to the management approach which ensures that the organisation is structured and managed on the basis of **shareholder's value**.

The elements of value based management are:

- creating value
- managing for value
- measuring value

Any strategy which creates value for its stakeholders is considered successful. One of the major stakeholders of any organisation is its shareholders. The value is created for shareholders by ensuring large **returns** to them. The returns to the shareholders are in the form of timely dividends.

Managing for value is one of the key elements of a manager's task in an organisation for the success of a strategy. Managing for value relates to **maximising the long-term cash generating capacity** of an organisation.

Here, 'long-term cash generating capacity' refers to the ability of an organisation to earn increased funds for use in the future.

In an organisation, value creation is essential because an organisation has to maintain its status in a developing market; it also has **to gain competitive advantages** over other market players. The organisation has to add certain value to its business **to sustain itself in the market**.

There are various factors of value creation in an organisation, such as operations, financing and investments:

a) Funds generated from the operations

Operations refer to the functioning of the organisation. There are two aspects to operations: **revenue and cost**. Revenue leads to increased shareholder value and costs lead to a reduction in shareholder value. Funds are generated from sales revenue, which depends on the volume of sales and the selling price.

Operational costs include various costs such as production, selling and distribution costs, administration costs, overheads or other indirect costs.

b) Financing

Financing costs is the cost of capital. Cost of capital is composed of two main elements: equity and debt. In case of external loans, the organisation must pay interest, which would lead to a reduction in funds and ultimately a reduction in shareholder value.

c) Investments

Organisations block their funds in assets. If the investment leads to a generation of funds, it creates value for the shareholder.

On the other hand, if the investment is such that it reduces funds, then it leads to reduction in the value creation for the shareholder.

The increase and reduction in shareholder value can also be termed **value drivers** (increase) or **cost drivers** (reduction). These drivers are the main source of value creation for an organisation. These drivers are presented diagrammatically below:

Diagram 2: Value and cost drivers

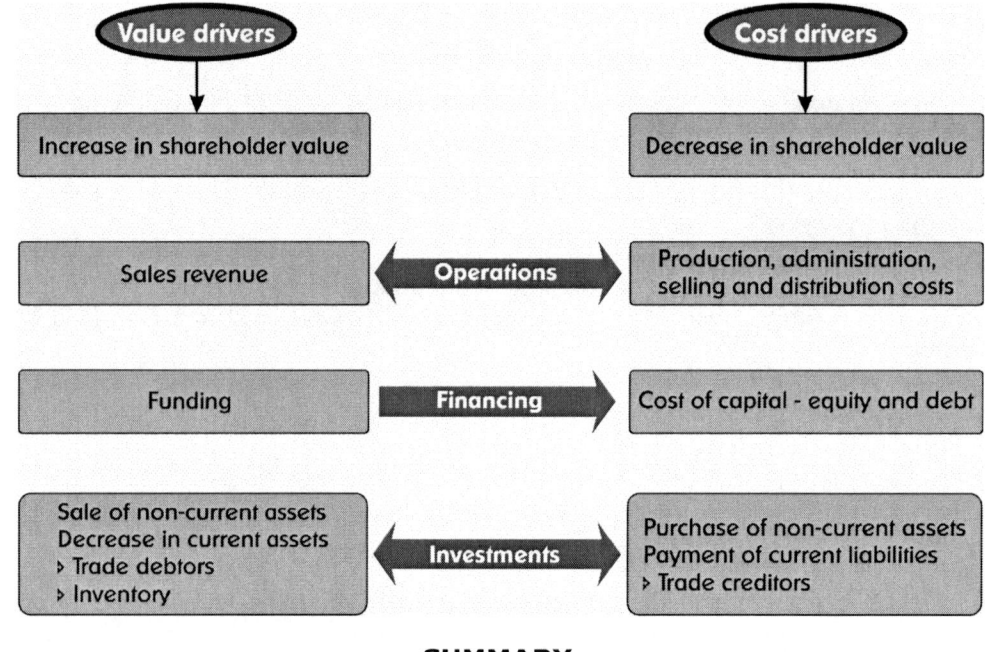

SUMMARY

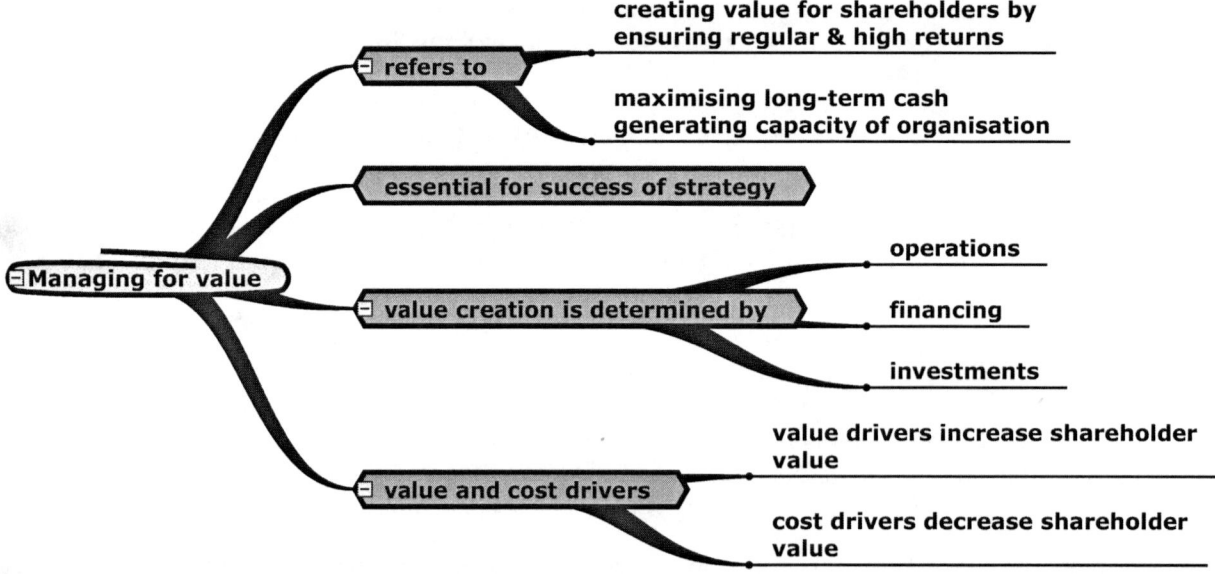

1.3 Financial expectations of stakeholders

Management has to develop and sustain stakeholder relationships while it tries to meet its objectives of maximising shareholder wealth. This can, however, be difficult in the event of **conflicting objectives** among stakeholder groups. Consensus theory recognises that each organisation represents a coalition of shareholders, directors, employees, customers etc. each having different and sometimes opposing goals. Since it is difficult to meet the objectives of each group completely, political compromise results from each party settling for less than their ideal. In this case, shareholder wealth is not maximised, other stakeholder groups will also settle for less.

The financial expectations of different stakeholders will vary according to their circumstances. The expectations are:

1. **Suppliers and employees**

These stakeholders expect **timely payment** from the organisation. The suppliers expect the organisation to **pay their dues within the credit limit** granted to the organisation. They will often also want to maximise their payments,.

The employees expect the organisation to pay their **salary / wages on time**. They should expect **incentives** for good work. These incentives can be financial in nature, e.g. bonuses, commissions, etc., or non-financial, e.g. promotions, job enrichment, autonomy, good working conditions, etc.

2. **Bankers**

Banks are interested in the organisation's ability to **repay the loan along with the interest**. Banks may consider the organisation's **capital gearing** ratio because it provides the relationship between the debt and equity in an organisation. Moreover, the **interest cover** ratio also indicates the capacity of the organisation to pay interest.

3. **Shareholders**

They expect the organisational strategy to be such that it gives them **regular dividends** and that the organisation has **sufficient funds for its long-term commitments**. If the organisation intends to reorganise its business through mergers or acquisitions, the strategy adopted or to be adopted by the organisation should safeguard the interests of the shareholders. The shareholders of the organisation also desire capital growth in their shareholdings.

4. **Customers**

Customers expect the organisation to provide **value for the money** they pay. They also expect **high quality goods and services** if there is extensive competition among market players, which means that customers have the option of selecting the seller who satisfies their demands.

5. **Community**

The organisation's strategy should be capable of providing employment for the community; concern should be given to controlling pollution and other potentially harmful effects on the environment; it should also take care of **ethical considerations** in the community such as abiding by the law and order of society.

While implementing strategies, management should pay attention to the financial effects of the strategy on all stakeholders.

SUMMARY

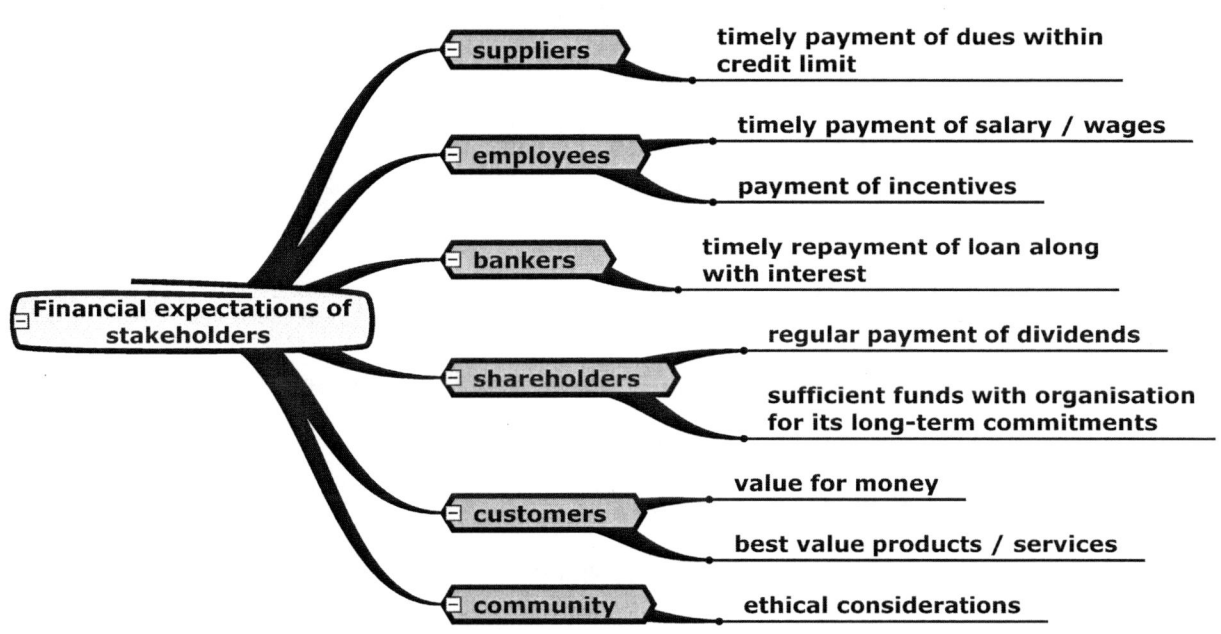

Test Yourself 2

Baby-Cosset Inc is a medium sized privately owned company which has produced baby-care products for the last ten years. It has achieved a steady market share for its products. The company is aspiring to grow and expand. As part of this strategy, Baby-Cosset has decided to expand its operations into new markets. It has also decided to add baby clothes to its line of products. The capital investment required for existing facilities, setting up new facilities for the production of baby clothes and for expansion into new markets is expected to be substantial. Management has approached the company's bank to obtain the required funding for its proposed expansion.

Required:

Explain what the different financial expectations of Baby-Cosset's stakeholders could be in relation to its proposed growth strategy and what possible conflicts could be involved in those expectations.

1.4 Funding strategies

The organisation's funding strategies depend on factors such as whether or not the organisation is **owned privately** or **publicly and** the **goals** of the organisation. The organisation's goals decide how much funding is required. Managers develop a strategy of obtaining funds from different sources depending upon the company's goals, such as different funding strategies to be adopted in case of acquisition, mergers or improvement in the product features.

The organisation's different funding strategies can be explained with the help of the **growth / share matrix**, which shows the different phases of business development. This matrix is explained in detail in Study Guide B1.

The type of funding strategy to be implemented by the organisation depends on the **risk and return factors**. It is a general principle that higher the risk, the higher the return. Moreover, the organisation's plan to obtain funds through loans from outside agencies will also incur interest charges to be paid to the money lenders. So, debts create more risks.

Answers to Test Yourself

Answer to TY 1

In an organisation, one of the most significant elements in a strategy's success is 'Finance'. Finance is the source for every strategy's implementation. Every strategy must possess three main features to be successful: suitability, acceptability and feasibility. These three aspects have an effect on and are affected by finance. Robust's proposed office support system can be evaluated on the basis of these aspects. The following are some of the criteria that can be considered:

1. **Suitability:** refers to the appropriateness of the strategy in the organisation's operations.

    - Is the IT support upgrade in alignment with Robust's strategic goals?
    - Will there be a measurable change to information quality (timeliness, relevance and accuracy) after the implementation of the new office support system?
    - Is the new office support system appropriate for future trends and changes in the external and internal environment of Robust?
    - Will the proposed strategy give Robust the edge over competitors?

2. **Acceptability:** refers to the performance outcomes of a strategy. The strategy must be acceptable to the stakeholders.

    - Will the new office support system benefit Robust's shareholders and other stakeholders financially or otherwise?
    - What are stakeholders' (employees, suppliers, customers) reactions to the proposed office support system? Are these favourable or unfavourable?

3. **Feasibility:** refers to the viability of the strategy.

    - Does Robust have sufficient financing for the upgrade in its information technology support?
    - To what extent can the present staff members adjust to the new office support system?
    - Do the staff members possess the requisite skills to use the new office support system? If no, is it possible to train the staff?
    - Is there the possibility that complications may arise in the implementation of the new office support system such as disruption, change management, cultural and industrial relations?
    - Is the proposed upgrade technically feasible for Robust?
    - How will the new system integrate with existing technologies?

Answer to TY 2

Different stakeholders have different, often contradictory, financial expectations from the organisation. Management has to address these expectations while it tries to meet its overriding objective of creating value for shareholders. The financial expectations of the different stakeholders of Baby-Cosset Inc relating to its proposed growth strategy and the possible conflicts could be as follows:

1. **Suppliers and employees:** likely to be concerned with the liquidity position of Baby-Cosset. Suppliers would expect that the proposed growth strategy would not have any adverse impact on Baby-Cosset's ability to meet its short-term commitments towards creditors and the credit limit offered to it. Employees will be concerned about timely payment of their salaries and wages.

    However, there may be a decrease in profitability and cash flow during and after the expansion. This may have an adverse impact on Baby-Cosset's short-term commitments to its suppliers and employees.

2. **Bank:** Baby-Cosset's bank will be concerned about the risk attached to the loan that is being demanded for the proposed expansion. It would expect be timely repayment of its loan along with interest. To ensure this, it would check Baby-Cosset's previous record with the bank and its capital gearing and interest cover ratios.

3. **Shareholders:** would expect that the proposed growth strategy will ensure regular dividends for them and will also further increase returns to them.

    However, the loan taken from the bank might affect Baby-Cosset's ability to pay dividends as the company will have to make regular loan repayments along with interest before paying dividends to its shareholders. A possible decrease in short-term profitability and cash flow during and after the expansion process would also affect dividends. However, the growth strategy may lead to higher share prices and capital growth for the shareholders.

4. **Customers:** Baby-Cosset's customers would expect that the baby products and cloths produced by the company should be the best value products available in the market.

    However, expanding into different markets may result in a decline in product quality. Also, as 'baby cloth' is the company's new product, it may not be of sufficient quality to satisfy customer demands.

5. **Community:** the community is likely to be concerned that the growth strategy of Baby-Cosset should benefit the whole community. The proposed expansion is likely to provide new employment opportunities. However, the community will also expect the company to take account of the ethical and environmental impact, such as pollution control and preservation of environment.

    As it is difficult to satisfy each group completely, political compromise results when each part settles for less than their ideal outcome. The company should attempt to identify its most important stakeholders in terms of their centrality to the corporate mission and strategy.

Quick Quiz

1. In order to be successful, a strategy must be:
    A. suitable to management
    B. acceptable to stakeholders
    C. feasible to customers
    D. none of the above

2. Managing for value relates to maximising the _____ of an organisation.

3. Revenue generated from the organisation's operations is a _____ (value / cost) driver.

4. What can the financial expectations of shareholders be from an organisation?

Answers to Quick Quiz

1. **B** Acceptability to stakeholders is one of the three features of successful strategy. In addition to this, a successful strategy must also be suitable to the goals of the organisation and feasible to the organisation.

2. Long-term cash generating capacity

3. Revenue generated from the organisation's operations is a value driver as it leads to an increase in shareholder value.

4. Shareholders expect the organisational strategy to be such that they receive regular dividends and also that the organisation has sufficient funds for its long-term commitments.

Self Examination Question

Question 1

Star-Folders is a recently established firm which manufactures document folders. Andrew Carlson is the founder and owner of Star-Folders. Andrew has spotted an opportunity to manufacture a new type of presentation folder. The folder possesses a new and unique feature which makes it unlike standard presentation folders; it can be folded and used for two different sizes – letter size and legal size according to the user's requirement. Apart from this, the folder possesses different sections in which to keep different things such as papers, pens, cards and CDs. The material used for these folders is a high quality, waterproof material. The folder can be made with attractive pre-printed or custom-made material. The customer's design and logo can be printed on a folder, which creates an opportunity for organisations to build their brand identity and make an impact at conferences and other high profile events.

The potential market for the product is huge as this type of folder is currently unavailable in the market. It is expected to have a high demand for these folders, particularly from the corporate sector. Andrew plans to introduce some innovative products in the future. He anticipates rapid growth for Star-Folders as its innovative products become more widely known and appreciated. The key issue is the funding required to support Star-Folders' growth and development. Andrew has estimated that the funding required is £1 million to support the company's development over the next two years. However, he is unsure about the type of funding which would be most appropriate for the expected rapid growth. Some of Andrew's friends have shown interest in providing the funds; but Andrew prefers not to borrow from family and friends and is keen to broaden the financial support for his business. He seeks advice on how he should organise the funding of the business.

Required:

Explain how Andrew Carlson should develop a funding strategy for the growth and development of Star-Folders.

Answer to Self Examination Question

Answer to SEQ 1

Andrew Carlson has identified a real business opportunity with his unique type of folder and expects to have a high demand for his product. The future growth of Star-Folders seems to depend on the sale of this new product. He needs funds to bring this product to the market and to support the expected growth of his business. However, there is a business as well as a financial risk involved in turning this opportunity into reality. The key issue is what type of strategy should be developed to help the funding of Star-Folders' growth and development.

The funding strategies that could be adopted by the organisation can be explained through the growth / share matrix. The growth / share matrix shows the different phases of business development. The type of funding strategy to be implemented in the organisation depends upon the risk and return factors. Linking business risk to financial risk is important. Star-Folders is a recently established firm. The new type of folder that Andrew wants to introduce is not yet established in the market and so he will have very little market share. It is also at the beginning phase of a product life cycle. Therefore, it falls under the question mark category in terms of BCG growth / share matrix. A new business venture such as this could be seen as a problem child with a non-existent market share but high growth potential. The investment requirements of these units are very high as they will have to undergo intensive research and development, sales promotion etc. In the early stages of a business, the business risk is high and consequently there is a need to select low financial risk option.

Funding the business is essentially a process of deciding the balance between debt and equity finance. Equity offers the low risk that Andrew should be looking for. The advantages of exercising equity finance are that the organisation does not have to bear interest costs. However, there are some disadvantages, such as loss of control, or sharing of profits. Andrew is aware of the need to avoid reliance on friends and family for funding. He should also avoid taking on large amounts of debt with a commitment to service the debt. Investors are willing to accept the risks associated with a new business venture. It is a general principle that the higher the risk, the higher the return. Investors in equity accept the higher risks associated with putting money into equity capital but may expect a significant share in the returns of the business. They will seek to realise this once the business is successfully established.

The balance between debt and equity will change as the organisation grows and develops. As the business moves into the growth (stars) and maturity (cash cows) phases of its life cycle, the business risks will reduce and access to debt finance becomes more feasible and cost effective. In maturity, the business should be able to generate significant retained earnings in order to finance further development. In the declining phase (dogs), it becomes more difficult for the organisation to find its required funds from equity sources.

Therefore, Andrew should raise funds through equity source to fulfil the current funding requirements of Star-Folders.

SECTION G: FINANCIAL ANALYSIS

STUDY GUIDE G2: FINANCE DECISIONS TO FORMULATE AND SUPPORT BUSINESS STRATEGY

Get Through Intro

OK, after realising that the resort on the moon will not work, you have a more realistic idea. You notice that young people love going out in the evening and like to stay up late. You also know that many of them like drinking alcohol which can make them sleepy. You hit on the idea of making an alcoholic coffee drink as there is not one on the market – you call it Cofahol. You want to aim it at young people so you have thought about the 4 Ps of marketing and come up with a trendy design for the bottle and a colourful label.

You have written your business plan and you have run some focus groups where young people at bars have tried Cofahol and they really liked it. The payback period is 3 years and it will cost you $1.5m to manufacture and market the product.

Now you have to work out how you are going to finance the venture. A bank is unlikely to loan you this full amount, as it may be too risky and also there are few assets the loan can be secured on. A venture capitalist will probably be ready to give you the money, but is likely to want a large stake in the business. So what alternatives could you have? What are the relative advantages or disadvantages? Find out by reading this chapter!

Learning Outcomes

a) Determine the overall investment requirements of the business.
b) Evaluate alternative sources of finance for these investments and their associated risks.
c) Efficiently and effectively manage the current and non-current assets of the business from a finance and risk perspective.

Introduction

Case Study

In the early 1990s, many investors invested in start-up companies such as software companies. These companies invested heavily in advertising to increase their customer base. They received a lot of venture capital funding from venture capitalists that had **expectations of receiving large** returns in a short period. These companies followed the strategy of operating at a loss or bottom line to earn a large market share. They showed that large, but short-term earnings are not sustainable enough to attract investment. This led to rapidly increasing stock prices, individual speculation in stock and availability of venture capital that made companies abandon the standard business model of gaining market share by operating at a loss. This bubble burst in 2000 and led most of the companies into bankruptcy.

Investors learned a lesson from this that every business should be judged on its own merit and there should be realistic time limits for judging the start of the pay back period. Making investments on the basis of short-term results is unwise; this taught companies how not to make business investments.

The above case study shows you that you need to think carefully about who invests and what they are looking for in their investment. The chapter will further enlighten you!

> 1. **Determine the overall investment requirements of the business.** [2]
> **Efficiently and effectively manage the current and non-current assets of the business from a finance and risk perspective.** [2]
>
> [Learning Outcomes a and c]

1.1 Investment requirements of the business

The investment requirements of businesses vary from one business to the next. A business receives its funding through capital contribution and debt.
These funds are:
- invested in non-current assets used in the business; and
- used to meet the working capital requirements
- business directors or entrepreneurs might invest some of these funds in investments outside of the organisation

1. Investments made in non-current assets

While making investments in non-current assets, the following points should be considered:

- whether a non-current asset considered for purchase with business funds can contribute to an increase in production
- whether a non-current asset could contribute to a reduction in the unit cost of production by atomising some operations or through the cost benefits of mass production
- whether a non-current asset considered for purchase will generate revenue
- whether a non-current asset could replace an old non-current asset whose useful life is over

2. Investments made in working capital

Below are some points that should be considered:

- The working capital requirements of any business depend on the nature of the cost structure and its relative importance to the total cost. Therefore, performing the cost benefit analysis of these costs to value creation is very important.

Example

For a manufacturing company, labour costs and the cost of purchase of different materials are high. They consume a lot of working capital and should therefore be monitored. Sometimes, decisions such as undertaking 'in house' production instead of outsourcing in the event of rising labour costs are recommended to avoid over investments in working capital. Also, saved funds could be utilised for investments in other strategically important projects or in external investments.

- If the current assets are twice the value of the current liabilities, it is considered good. If they are less than twice the value, the company requires more short-term capital i.e. working capital and if it is more than twice the value, this means that the company has unnecessarily invested more in working capital. The company could take out the non-yielding portion of working capital and invest it in other income producing activities.

3. **Investments which are made outside of the organisation:** an organisation could invest its excess funds in any external venture, associate or subsidiary. The organisation might invest these funds in money market investments or fixed deposits.

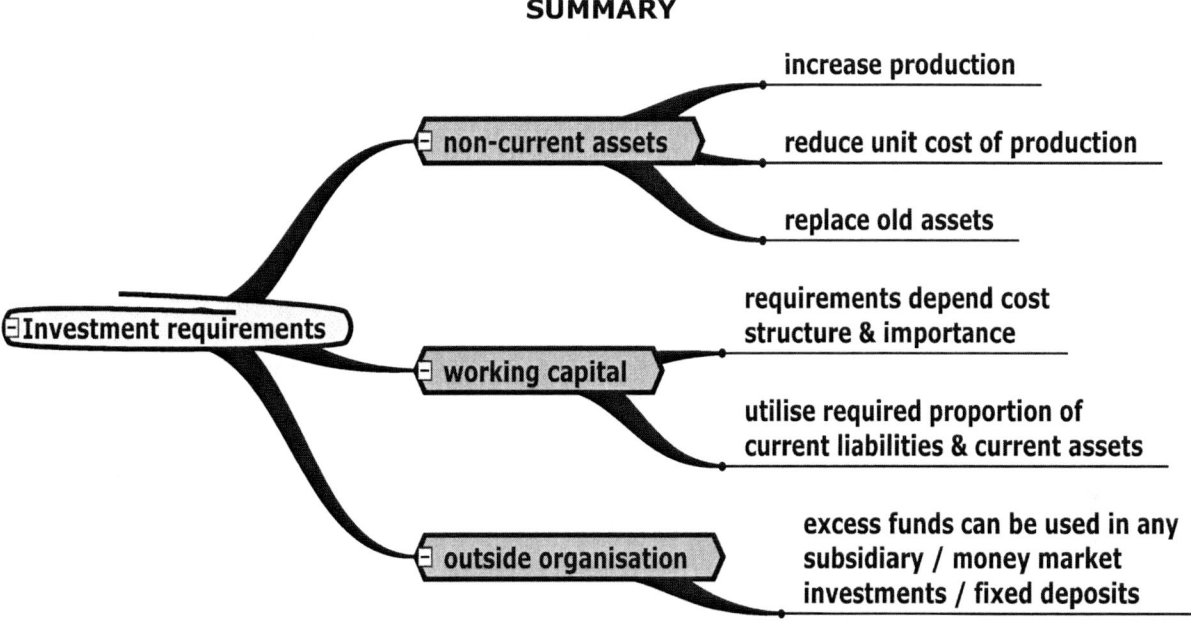

SUMMARY

1.2 Questions to be considered when making an investment decision:

- Can the company afford to invest?
- When is the investment going to give a return?
- What is the payback period?
- What is the profile of the income?
- Is there any alternative opportunity to generate more income which the organisation could explore?
- What is the net present value of all the options?

1.3 Distinguishing features of investment decisions taken by the organisation:

- Investments should maximise share value.
- A formal risk assessment must be undertaken: both the risk of losing the investment opportunity and of the threat involved should be assessed
- The possibility of something happening to damage or harm the possible outcome of an investment should be assessed.
- The individuals responsible for investment-related decisions should have a good understanding of the organisation's strategic position. Different aspects of strategy can influence investment decisions.
- It is necessary to assess investment decisions over key cost and value drivers which change over the time curve.

> **Example**
>
> Gem Engineering has completed the development of its new product. At this stage of the product introduction, the production of sales volume and the establishment of sales are the two most important factors. There are more investment requirements and the risk is high. In the case of an established product, prices and unit costs are the cost and value drivers that influence investment decisions. In case of declining demand, improving cash flow through stock and debt reduction may be required to encourage the introduction of the next generation of products.

- While comparing the return on investments, the net present value of cash flows or IRR should be used.
- Dividend: companies need to calculate their investment requirements before declaring any dividend. Companies might want to invest these funds in venture capital projects, associates or subsidiaries. Company shareholders who have invested with the expectation of earning income would not invest in the company if they do not get any income. This situation should be resolved if the company wants to raise additional finance by issuing equity shares. Such an incident will reduce share prices in the stock market.

To conclude, the obligation to pay the dividend reduces the company's short-term ability to obtain investment, but in the long run it increases investment potential by maintaining or increasing prices and demand for shares.

Test Yourself 1

Cruise Ltd manufactures spare parts for machines. It has raised $20,000 from the following sources:

- Equity share capital $12,000
- 10% Debentures $8,000

Cruise has the following investment options:

- Purchase plant and machinery of $15,000.
- Purchase raw materials (inventory) of $18,000 for production process (company has sufficient inventory but wants to purchase more because prices may rise in the near future).
- Reinvest the same amount in 11% of bonds of Ship Ltd for five years.

Assume that:
- Cruise Ltd want to invest its funds in plant and machinery as its present non-current assets' useful life will be over in the next two years.
- Cruise Ltd's current ratio for the financial year is 2.6:1.

Required:

As an expert, advise Cruise Ltd about efficient and effective management of the business's current and non-current assets from a finance and risk perspective.

---

2. Evaluate alternative sources of finance for these investment and their associated risks. [3]
[Learning Outcome b]

Every business needs finance to support its business strategy. It is the business strategy that defines the business's investment requirements. A business's financial strategy should be aligned to its business strategy as they depict the relationship between financial risk and financial returns to investors.

The organisation could obtain the required finance either from public or private parties. Below is the list of sources from which the organisation could raise the finance.

Equity sources of finance:

2.1 Venture capital

Venture capitalists (VCs) provide finance to small and medium-sized businesses that do not have access to stock markets. VCs tend to invest in new businesses and specific expansion schemes. They tend to be attracted to businesses that will eventually be listed on the stock exchange, both because businesses of this size will generate the largest profits and because this also gives them an exit route in the future. VCs will only invest in businesses with good growth potential and will expect the owners and managers to have the drive and ambition to achieve this growth. The investment made in a business may take the form of share capital and/or loan capital and will normally be for a reasonably long period (five years or more).

Venture capitalists provide equity and loan finance for different types of business situations including:
- start-up capital for new business ventures.
- growth capital to help expanding businesses to fund growth plans.
- share purchase capital to help finance the acquisition of an existing ownership interest.
- refinancing bank debt to help a business reduce the burden of gearing.

2.2 Equity capital

Raising finance through equity share capital is one of the ways of raising finance. Venture capital, leverage buyouts and growth capital are types of private equity. Finance can be raised by issuing equity to the public. Higher levels of security and governance are attached to the public issues of equity.

- The company's ordinary shareholders represent ownership restricted to the percentage they own.
- These shares have a nominal value or face value usually £1 or 50 pence.
- These shares might not have any face value outside the UK.
- The issue price of these shares may be more than or equal to their face value

Venture capital has been discussed earlier in this learning outcome.

1. **Leverage buy-outs:** is one of the ways of obtaining equity finance. This type of finance is sought only as a last resort as, along with obtaining the finance, the company has to transfer the business assets or the company itself to the lender along with its financial control.
2. **Growth capital:** this is also one way of obtaining private finance. Here the financer gets a minority share in the equity of the company. There is no change of control as is the case in leverage buy-outs.

Funds raised from equity issue can be used to finance the company's investment needs as explained in Study Guide H, Section 2.1. Companies might want to issue equity share capital to get listed on the stock market. According to the stock exchange rules, when a UK company is floated, it is compulsory to issue at least the minimum of its shares to the public.

Disadvantages of raising capital through issuing equity share capital

- Once becoming publicly limited, companies must follow the regulations regarding the issue of information to the general public. Some companies might view it as a way of reducing the company's competitive advantage and may not like it.
- As this option gives a percentage ownership and voting rights to shareholders i.e. it offers a share in the company's profits and results in dilution of control, a company might prefer the alternative of obtaining finance through bank loans.

Advantages of raising capital through issuing equity share capital

- As the finance is raised by giving equity rights, the company does not have to return the money raised nor is it under any obligation to pay interest. The company needs to pay the dividend but only if it earns sufficient profits.

New shareholders may bring extra skills which the company could use.

2.3 Preference share capital

The company could raise funds through preference share capital. This resource is similar to raising share capital through equity issue except that the dividend payable requirements are different. Preference shareholders have preference over equity shareholders (but after debt holders) for the receipt of dividend.

2.4 Debt sources:

Issue of debentures or bonds (loan stock)

The company might take loans by issuing loan stock. These stocks also possess some nominal value such as equity shares. Some interest rates are always affixed to it such as 12% bonds i.e. company will pay 12% per annum on the stated face value of the bonds.

a) Bonds may be redeemable in that case they are repaid to the lenders with interest.
b) There could be irredeemable bonds which form the long-term liability with the stated amount of interest payable on these bonds.
c) There might be convertible bonds which will be converted to equity shares on their maturity.
d) Although the face value of these bonds remains the same, their market value may vary.
e) The entity and the bond holder may agree on the interest moratorium issues in the early years of the bond's tenure.
f) Most of the time bonds / debentures are backed by the sinking funds in which the entity has to set aside some funds each year to reduce the financial impact on maturity.
g) An issue of bonds may include a guarantee in terms of charges over the assets.

The advantages and disadvantages of debentures have been discussed in detail in Study Guide F4 learning outcome 2. The relevant text has been reproduced below.

Advantages

- The cost of debt capital represented by debentures is much lower than the cost of preference or equity capital.
- Debenture financing does not result in dilution of control since debenture holders are not entitled to vote.
- The call provision found in many debenture issues provides flexibility in changing the capital structure.
- In a period of rising prices, debenture issue is advantageous. The burden of servicing debentures, which entails a fixed monetary commitment for repayment of interest and principal, decreases in real terms as the price level increases.

Disadvantages

- Debenture interest and capital repayments are obligatory payments. Failure to meet these payments jeopardises the solvency of the company.
- Various provisions are associated with a debenture issue in order to protect the interests of debenture holders. Some of these provisions are registration of charges, maintaing debenture holders registers and adherence to the provisions of the company's Articles and Memorandum. The protective covenants associated with a debenture issue may prove restrictive.

This is considered a source of finance as public finance is raised without issuing ownership rights.

2.5 Bank loans

Companies could approach the bank to meet their finance needs. Companies prefer to take bank loans in the following situations:
- When they want to borrow any non-current assets. These loans are known as term loans.
- When a company needs to finance its working capital to carry out day to day operations. Such loans can be taken through an overdraft facility.

1. Term loan

A 'term loan' is taken by a company from a bank in order to purchase non-current assets. The company repays the loan in agreed instalments with interest fixed at the time of issue.

a) Care should be taken with respect to the term of the loan. The term should not be more than the useful life of the asset purchased as repayments are generally made from the cash inflows generated from using the asset.
b) There is a longer payback time than other forms of loan.
c) As cash inflow and outflow are easily measured, cash planning i.e. budgeting is easy.

2. Bank overdraft

Borrowing through a bank overdraft is a method of short-term borrowing. Companies in need of money for a short period of time and who are expecting cash inflow at various points of time, especially within a short period, often opt for a bank overdraft.

a) In a bank overdraft, a limit is sanctioned by the bank and a borrower is able to withdraw money up to that limit and deposit the cash inflow and take benefit of the interest.
b) A bank overdraft is one of the ways to finance the business' working capital needs. It comes under current liabilities or is shown as a negative figure in the current assets section on the SOFP (balance sheet), which is an advantage as there is no long-term obligation on the SOFP (balance sheet).
c) The disadvantages associated with overdrafts are that overdrafts can be recalled at anytime and bear high interest rates.

The process of taking a bank loan has the following advantages over the process of raising finance through the public issue of bonds:

- Banks ask for collateral when giving a loan, which is not case with the issue of bonds or debentures. Although there could be bonds guaranteed by the collateral.
- Bank terms can be altered more easily than the terms of the issue of bonds.
- Following a bank's monitoring is easier than following the security board's norms for public raising of debt.
- It is a cheap and fast way of raising finance.

2.6 Retaining business profits

Funding can be obtained by retaining the accumulated profits from the business.

- It could be described as self-financing. Although this has disadvantages in terms of the company's inability to declare sufficient dividends to meet shareholders' expectations as the company has diverted funds to other investments.
- Shareholders are not motivated to invest in a particular company if they do not get the expected returns.
- This might dilute the company's ability to raise future funding through the issue of equity.

Diagram 1: Alternative sources of raising finance

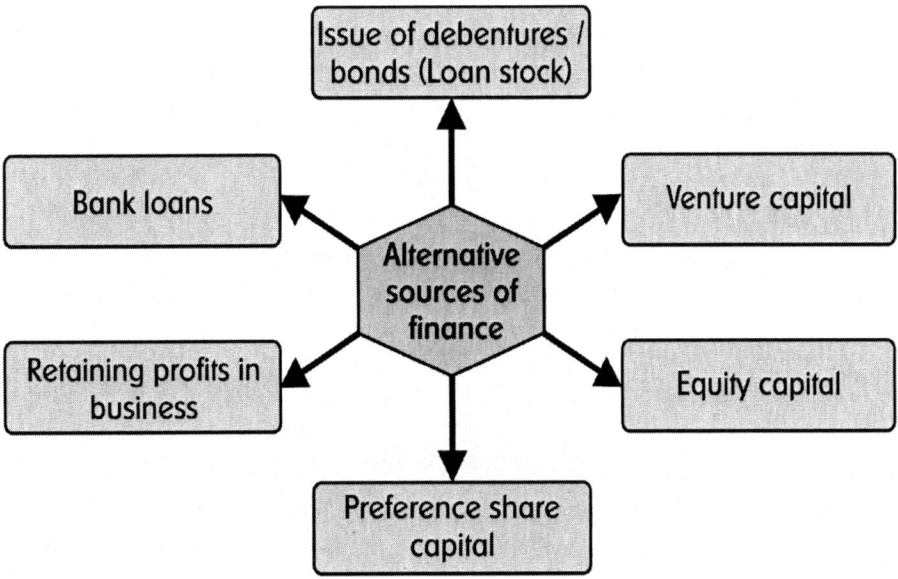

Answers to Test Yourself

Answer to TY 1.

Here, Cruise Ltd has obtained funds through capital of $12,000 and debt of $8,000.

Investment requirements and investment decisions vary from business to business.

Cruise Ltd has three investment options:
- $15,000 in non-current assets
- $18,000 in current assets
- $20,000 outside the interest in order to gain 11% interest per annum

Cruise Ltd should take the following points into consideration in order to make a proper investment decision from a finance and risk perspective.

Non-current assets	Current assets	Outside the business
➢ Purchased non-current assetsshould contribute to either increasing production or to reducing the per unit cost of production. ➢ It should provide the benefits of mass production. ➢ Whether the non-current asset considered for purchase will generate any revenue or it could replace the old non-current assets whose useful life is over.	➢ Working capital requirements depend upon the nature of cost structure and its relative importance to the total cost. ➢ Current ratio i.e. proportion of current assets and liabilities should be 2:1 (applicable to this industry) If current assets are less than twice that of current liabilities then Cruise Ltd is in need of short-term capital. In such circumstances, Cruise Ltd should choose the second investment option of investing their funds in spare parts. ➢ If the current ratio shows that the current assets are more than twice the value of current liabilities then Cruise Ltd has unnecessarily invested more than the required amount in current assets. In such circumstances the company could take out the non-yielding portion of working capital and invest it in other income generating activities.	➢ Cruise Ltd could invest the gathered funds in money market investments. ➢ By investing money in Ship Ltd, Cruise Ltd will get 11% interest on the amount invested. This rate of interest is higher than rate of debenture interest which shows that company would get financial benefits from investing in Ship Ltd.

Conclusion

1. **If Cruise Ltd invests funds in a non-current asset of $15,000:** non-current assets that are in use will no longer be useful in two years time. This shows that Cruise Ltd is in need of plant and machinery to continue smooth production. If money / funds are not invested in the necessary plant and machinery, there are chances of production delays because of outdated machinery.
2. **If Cruise Ltd invests funds in a current asset of $18,000:** current ratio shows that Cruise Ltd has invested more than the required amount in working capital. It shows that either Cruise Ltd has invested money in inventories or that it is inefficient when collecting dues from receivables. In the given scenario, Cruise Ltd wants to invest in inventories because of the market assumption that prices will rise in the near future.
3. **If Cruise Ltd invests funds of $20,000 outside the business at 11% interest per annum:** the company has raised funds from both equity and debt. Cruise Ltd must pay 10% interest on debt. If it invests funds in Ship Ltd, it would benefit financially as the rate of interest on the investment is higher than the rate of interest on the incurred debt. The company might enjoy the benefits of trading on equity by following this investment option.

Cruise Ltd should not invest in current assets. The current ratio shows that the investment in current assets is higher than recommended Cruise Ltd should give priority to purchasing non-current assets i.e. plant and machinery. The company has raised funds of $20,000 and the required investment amount for plant and machinery is only $15,000. If Cruise Ltd invests that amount it can also invest the remaining amount in Ship Ltd to earn interest. Cruise Ltd should try to get a bank loan overdraft for $15,000 in order to purchase plant and machinery, but only if it is available at less than 11% interest rate. If Cruise Ltd can do so, it will benefit from paying less interest on the outstanding loan and by earning more interest on investments.

Quick Quiz

1. State the alternative sources of finance for the investment requirements of a business.
2. Define 'venture capital'.

Answers to Quick Quiz

1. Venture capital, equity capital, preference share capital, issue of debentures / bonds, bank loans, bank overdrafts and retaining the profits of business are sources of finance for investment requirements of the business.
2. Venture capital is a private source of finance suitable for small to medium-sized organisations. It is pooled investment. A venture capitalist generally invests in businesses which are considered too risky by the banks.

Self Examination Questions

Question 1

Welcome Ltd is a small company which produces water pumps. Welcome Ltd's capital structure consists of equity capital and 8% debentures. The current ratio shows a balanced situation of working capital. It wants to raise funds for investment purposes in non-current assets.

Briefly describe the benefits and risks of various sources of finance.

Required:

Which source is most suitable for Welcome Ltd?

Question 2

Patro Ltd is a car company earning a 50% profit. According to its business policy it reinvests 25% of its profit back into the business and the surplus amount is invested outside the business.

Required:

Explain the points which Patro will need to consider before investing.

Answers to Self Examination Questions

Answer to SEQ 1

Before raising funds, Welcome Ltd should be aware of the advantages and disadvantages of each available source of funding. Welcome Ltd can either raise its funds from private or public sources.

1. **Benefits and risks of public finance**

a) **Equity share capital**

Benefits of equity share capital:
  i. Ordinary shareholders represent ownership according to the percentage of shares they own.
  ii. The company can raise capital from a large number of investors through issuing shares. New shareholders may bring expertise to the business.
  iii. Funds raised from equity issue could be used to finance the company's investment needs.
  iv. If company earns a sufficient profit then it only needs to pay dividend and not interest on debt.

Risks of equity share capital
  i. Entity has to be big enough to afford the public issue of shares. On becoming a public limited company, it has to follow the norms of a public limited company regarding the issue of information to the general public. It has to follow the legal and public governance requirements. Some companies may not like it as they might find it as a way of reducing the company's competitive.
  ii. Companies have to publish a lot of information including financial data which a competitor could compare against its own data.
  iii. Equity capital gives ownership rights along with voting rights to shareholders. This results in the dilution of control and sharing of profits.

b) **Preference share capital**

Benefits and risks of preference share capital:
  This resource is almost the same as raising share capital through an equity issue. Only the dividend payable requirements are different. Preference shareholders have preference for the receipt of dividend over the equity shareholders

c) Issue of debentures / bonds

Benefits of issuing debentures / bonds:
   i. Some many consider it the best source of finance as no ownership rights are issued yet public finance is raised.
   ii. They might be converted into equity share capital on their maturity, if they are issued as convertible debentures / bonds.
   iii. The entity and the bond holder may agree on the interest moratorium issues in the early years of the bond's tenure.
   iv. Most of the time, bonds / debentures are backed by sinking funds in which the entity has to set aside some funds each year to reduce the financial impact on maturity.
   v. The issue of bonds may include a guarantee in terms of charges over the assets.

Risks of issuing debentures / bonds:
   i. Redeemable debentures / bonds are repaid to the lenders with interest.
   ii. To pay interest on debentures is compulsory every year.
   iii. Bond holders do not bring expertise to the entity.

d) Bank loans / bank overdraft / term loan

Benefits and risks of bank finance:
   i. Term loans are generally taken for non-current assets but their duration should not be more than the useful life of the asset. It will be suitable for Welcome Ltd, but only after ensuring loan duration and useful life of that non-current asset.
   ii. A bank overdraft is a short-term finance solution which directly fulfils the needs of working capital. In the case of Welcome Ltd, the current ratio is sound so there is no need to disturb the working capital by taking a bank overdraft as it is for short-term finance.
   iii. Bank terms can be altered more easily than the terms of the bonds issue. However, banks ask for collateral when giving the loan.

2. Benefits and risks of private finance

a) Venture capital

Venture capital is more suitable for small companies, such as Welcome Ltd. However, venture capital is a pooled investment and is mainly invested in those businesses that are considered too risky by the standard capital markets and bank loans. Venture capitalists can influence company decisions and they receive some portion of equity and some share in the profits of the company which is not the case when raising a debt.

b) Retaining profits in the business

Ploughing profit back into the business is one of the best sources of raising finance. It is an easier and simpler way of obtaining finance. However, it is not suitable for small companies and newly established companies. For the purpose of retaining profits, shareholders become discouraged if they do not get the expected returns on their investment.

Considering the probable risks and benefits described above, Welcome Ltd should choose the option of **public finance** through bank loan or by issuing debentures / bonds. If the useful life of an asset is not less than the duration of term loan, then it is the best option for Welcome Ltd.

Answer to SEQ 2

While making an outside investment, Patro Ltd should ask itself the following questions:

1. Does the company have sufficient funds to invest in the market?
2. After investing the money, will the company make a profit?
3. What is the period of time the company needs to wait for the profit?
4. Does the company want to invest money for a short or long period of time? Can the company afford to invest that much money for that period of time?
5. What are the options available in the market for investing money?

Patro should keep the following points in mind while taking the decision:

➢ The organisation needs to think about how to increase shareholders' value in the market.
➢ The investment risk needs to be considered while investing money in markets. Markets affect the value of investments.
➢ Before investing, the company needs to conduct market research to find out more about market positions and the eventual returns.
➢ The company should consider market risks and changes in market situations.

SECTION G: FINANCIAL ANALYSIS

STUDY GUIDE G3: THE ROLE OF COST AND MANAGEMENT ACCOUNTING IN STRATEGIC PLANNING AND DECISION-MAKING

Get Through Intro

Careful planning and effective decision making is vital to the health of the organisation. Strategic management aims at setting the approach and roadmap for the growth of the organisation. The role of Cost and Management Accounting is to provide both financial and non-financial information and also the supporting strategic (planning), operational (operating), and control (performance evaluation) management decision making. Thus management accounting information is pervasive and purposeful, and is intended to meet specific decision making needs at all levels of the organisation.

Corporate or strategic planning is a step-by-step, systematised procedure involving:

- identification of the mission (purpose of the existence) of the organisation and its objectives;
- corporate appraisal (Strengths, Weaknesses, Opportunities and Threats analysis); and
- analysis of the gap between corporate objectives and the envisaged ability.

The process of strategic planning typically deals with allocating the available resources and directing the efforts in achieving the unified corporate objective. Thus, the strategic plan of an organisation is the bridge which attempts to connect the available resources with the corporate objectives.

Strategic management accounting is a set of tools that provide the planners with all-important inputs - facts, figures and documents, which form the basis of their plans. The distinguishing feature of strategic management accounting (SMA) is that it focuses on the organisation's internal as well as external business environment. Over the years, SMA has become a specialist function and professional accounting institutions provide technical education in this field. The role of management accountant is particularly crucial in providing management with analysis and evaluation of performance using techniques such as budgeting, standard costing, marginal costing etc. The management accountant contributes in a big way in assisting the management to evaluate decision variables in situations of risk and uncertainty.

This Study Guide explains the role of management accountant in strategic planning and decision making, which happens to be a favourite topic of the examiner! By understanding this Study Guide, you will be able to apply strategic management accounting to your business and see how you can improve profits!

Learning Outcomes

a) Explain the role, advantages and possible limitations of a budgetary process.
b) Explain the principles of standard costing, its role in variance analysis and suggest possible reasons for identified variances.
c) Evaluate strategic and operational decisions taking into account risk and uncertainty using decision trees.
d) Evaluate the following strategic options using marginal and relevant costing techniques
　i. Make or buy decisions
　ii. Accepting or declining special contracts
　iii. Closure or continuation decision
　iv. Effective use of scarce resources.

Introduction

Strategic Management and Planning

Strategic management can be defined as "the art and science of formulating, implementing and evaluating cross-functional decisions that enable an organisation to achieve its objective." The planning process identifies the goals or objectives to be achieved, formulates strategies to achieve them, arranges or creates the means required, and implements, directs, and monitors all steps in their proper sequence.

The following diagram describes the interrelation between Strategic Plan and Budgeting:

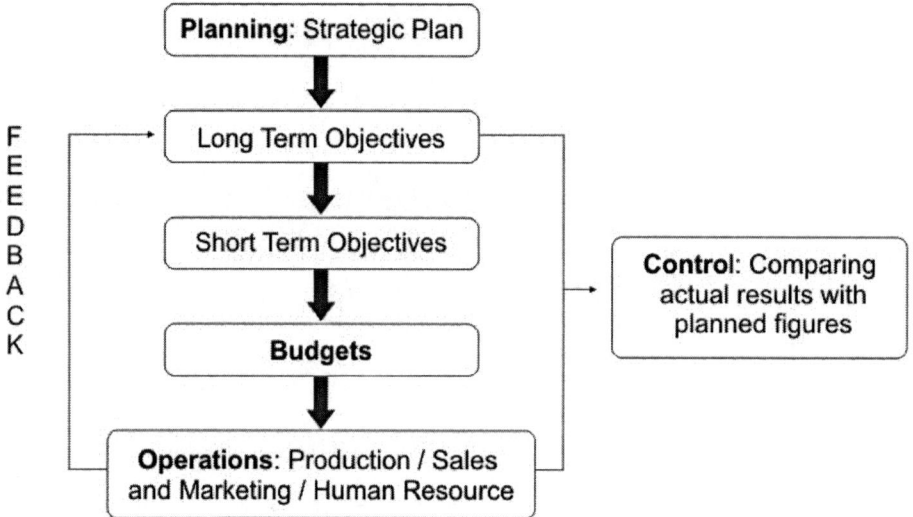

The above diagram shows the interrelationship between Budget and Planning, Operations and Control. Budgets usually evolve from the long term objectives of an organisation; they form the basis of operations and control is exercised through a process of comparison of budgeted values with the planned figures. This process not only provides feedback to the operations but also helps in setting budgets for the future.

Strategic management involves streams of decisions and actions with a view to develop effective long term and short term plans and policies that would help the organisation to achieve its desired objectives. Strategic management includes vision and mission formulation, strategic analysis, strategy formulation, strategic choice, strategy implementation and control strategic decision for an organisation to deploy resources to new opportunities.

One sure-fire way to improve the profitability of an organisation is to dust off a timeless tool — the strategic plan. No one strategic model fits all organisations, but the planning process includes certain basic elements that all businesses can use to explore their vision, goals, and the next steps for an effective strategic plan.

Plans could be of two types, viz. long term plan and short term plan. Long term planning is a systematic and formalised process for directing and controlling future operations towards desired objectives to be achieved over a period, normally beyond one year. This is also known as strategic or corporate planning. The long term plans of an organisation are based on the corporate strategy with respect to key functions such as production, marketing, finance, research and development, human resource etc. and they cover projections with respect to revenues, expenses, capital expenditure, man power planning and other resources.

Long term plans evaluate the future implications associated with present decisions and help management in making present decisions and selecting the most optimum alternative. Long term plans are prepared keeping in mind the opportunities and core strength of an organisation, and also the risks associated with allocation and commitment of the resources.

Short term plans are prepared for a period ranging from one year to three years. Usually, the short term plan period will typically depend upon the production cycle, seasonal cycle, financing or working capital cycle etc. Short term plans or budgets are prepared with precision, based on the current business environment and are normally phased, on a monthly or quarterly basis.

An organisation consists of various functions, processes and activities. In order to accomplish the business objectives, effective planning processes should be in place. Management planning and control has been recognised as one of the most important approaches for ensuring effective performance of the management process.

The strategic planning process involves determining the answers to the following questions:

1. Where are we now? This involves situational analysis of the environment in which an organisation is operating. The relative market position is determined by carrying out Strengths, Weaknesses, Opportunities and Threats (SWOT) analysis.

2. Where do we want to be? This is an important stage for formulating the strategy framework of an organisation. The corporate objectives, vision and mission statements are finalised. A strategic vision is the roadmap for the future of the organisation. It focuses on the customer, products and geographical markets to be pursued. The mission statement deals with the core purpose of existence of an organisation.

3. How do we get there? This stage involves deciding various strategic alternatives to achieve the corporate goals.

4. Which is the best fit? This stage involves deciding the best alternative. Success isn't a matter of chance but rather a matter of choice.

5. How do we ensure that we reach there? This stage deals with continuous situational analysis, monitoring the performance, taking corrective action if necessary, and ensuring that the corporate objectives are achieved.

1. Explain the role, advantages and possible limitations of a budgetary process.[2]

[Learning Outcome a]

In the Papers F2 and F5, you have already learnt the basics of the budgetary process. You are advised to revise those concepts. This Study Guide will help you to revisit the concepts from an organisation's strategic perspective. In the earlier sections, the steps in the strategic planning were fully explained. One of the important steps in strategy implementations is converting strategic plans into clear cut operating plans that can be executed by the operating management.

A budget is a short term business plan expressed in monetary terms. Budgets are, however, different from forecasts. Forecasts relate to the predictions about the future state of business environment and are used for developing the budgets.

Definition

A financial and / or quantitative statement prepared and approved prior to a defined period of time, of the policy to be pursued during that period for the purpose of attaining the given objectives.

It may include revenue, costs and the employment of capital and other resources.

Budgeting is an integral part of the management function of planning, organising, motivating and controlling. One of the central tools used to carry out the management function is a budget.

All organisations attempt to use the available scarce resources to achieve their goals. To achieve long term goals (of usually five to ten years) it is necessary to develop long term strategic plans. These plans are concerned with broad objectives and goals. To achieve long term goals we need to develop short term strategies that are incorporated into annual budgets. These short term plans are more detailed and consider the means to attain the goals. The means by which these short term plans are converted into action is through the budgeting process. Short term plans tend to use more of quantitative data to estimate the future. This includes dollar values, sales quantities, production units, inventory levels, number of personnel, financial ratios etc.

Whether planning is done formally (by the use of budgets) or informally it does not in itself guarantee business success, as it needs to be monitored and adjusted. This function of monitoring and adjustment is called controlling. Keeping in mind that all plans (budgets) are best estimates of the future, management needs to monitor its progress at regular intervals. It needs feedback on achievements and shortfalls so that it can take remedial action. To facilitate this process of monitoring, yearly budgets are broken down into smaller chunks such as months or even weeks so that if remedial action needs to be taken it will not be too late. The promptness and accuracy of feedback reports is essential to the whole process of controlling. The reports should compare actual results against the budget. These reports are known as variance reports. They require analysis to assess the progress of budget outcomes. Minor variances are usually ignored but significant variances must be investigated so that appropriate corrective action can be taken.

Budgets are prepared for all areas of the organisation, and all levels of management are responsible for their success. Managers at the lowest level must be given some basic information about their area of operations if they are to be held accountable for their department or unit. There is also an accompanying need to supply the manager with details of both actual performance and the criteria by which the budget performance was calculated. Where budgetary control systems are used, management reporting will be able to highlight those exceptions.

Budgeting is a method of communicating the goals of the organisation to the appropriate managers so that, with their involvement and participation, the desired budget outcomes are achieved. The level of support and participation depends on the management's approach to budgeting. Under the **'top-down' approach** (i.e. the traditional model) budgets are the targets and standards that are imposed by top management onto workers. The assumptions under the traditional model are that the employee cannot be relied upon to be self-motivated or innovative. While budget outcomes are only achieved by strict adherence to budgetary controls, the employee is likely to be lazy and wasteful and require constant supervision.

On the other end of the continuum, management adopts a **participative approach**. Under this approach management realises that individuals play the most important part in the budgetary process. It is recognised that workers typically have access to information concerning the operation of their areas of responsibility that is not available to their superiors. By having their subordinates participating in budget setting, superiors have the opportunity to incorporate that information into budgets to enhance accuracy. This approach is typically known as the **'bottom-up' approach**. The bottom-up approach enhances employees' motivation and commitment to goals and targets. When subordinates are asked to participate in setting budgets, the goals of the organisation are internalised, that is they become the individual employee's goals.

1.1 Budgeting or Budgetary Process

Budgeting or budgetary process is the process of established short-term financial plans, designed to meet definite goals by making available adequate financial resources to match projected activities.

The process of preparation of budgets is called budgeting or budgetary process. Management planning and control means the development and acceptance of business objectives and goals and successfully directing the efforts towards achieving the desired results. The management system comprises activities such as planning, co-ordination and control.

1. Role of Budgetary Process

a) **Translating strategic plan into executable actions:** a budget is a quantitative statement for a defined period of time, usually a year, (and broken down into manageable time periods such as a month or a quarter) which may include planned revenues, expenses, assets, liabilities and cash flows. At an organisational level, the budget aims at planning to achieve goals and objectives that emanate from the strategic plans. For example, if the strategic plan is to achieve market share of 10% over a three year period, the first year budget would be a step to achieve this strategic goal and it will provide for various actions in furtherance thereof. The functional budgets will be drawn to support this premise. For example, it will include planning for resources for marketing, production, customer service etc. which will help the organisation reach the desired targets.

b) **Tracking the actual performance vis-à-vis the budgeted targets:** the budgeting process has an inbuilt component of comparing actual performance with the budget, followed by variance analysis. This forms the basis for performance measurement and paves the way for enterprise performance management. Organisations put in robust systems to drive this at various levels of management. The budgeting process is expected to provide alerts and signals for shortfalls in achievement of budgeted results, so that corrective action can be initiated in time.

c) **Control:** the budgets provide a performance framework to the managers highlighting the resources they are authorised to acquire and use. Managers can exercise effective control by keeping the costs within the allowed budgets. The zero based budgeting model provides a sound basis to controlling.

d) **Motivating the team:** as it lays down the targets to which the reward system is linked, the budgetary process keeps the managers motivated to work to achieve the set targets. The overall targets for the organisation are broken down division/department-wise to ensure no conflicts occur due to individual managers taking decisions.

2. Advantages of Budgetary Process

A budget is the principal document prepared and approved by management, with the following advantages:

a) **Budgets promote a forward-thinking attitude:** a budget is a blue print of the desired plan of action or operation. Plans covering the entire organisation and all its functions such as purchase, production, sales, financial management, research and development etc. are expressed through budgets. Many a times, budgets help in early identification of the potential problems.

b) **Budgets can be used for directing the efforts towards a unified goal**: budgets provide a means of co-ordination of the business as a whole. In the process of establishing budgets, various factors such as production capacity, sales possibilities and procurement of material, labour, etc. are balanced and co-ordinated so that all the activities proceed according to the objective.

c) **Budgets act as a device for communicating management philosophy and plans**: the budget serves as a declaration of policies and also defines the objective for executives at all levels of management. Complex plans laid down by the top management are passed on to those who are responsible for putting them into action.

d) **Budgets are used as a benchmark or target:** against which the actual performance is compared, monitored and controlled (system of control). Budgets facilitate centralised control with delegated authority and responsibility. Grouped according to the responsibilities of different executive levels, they facilitate decentralisation of work.

e) **Budgets are used as a motivating tool:** for managers for achieving better performance. Budgets are instruments of managerial control by means of which management can measure performances in every part of the concern and take corrective action as soon as any deviations from the budgets come to light.

3. Limitations of the Budgetary Process:

a) Budgets can be perceived to be a tool for management to pressurise labour by imposing 'difficult to achieve' objectives / targets. In such a case, the budgets would prove to be non-motivating and would result in stressed relations with labour (in the case of top down approach).

b) Non achievement of set goals or targets may result in inter departmental / inter functional conflicts and disputes.

c) Budgets are to be aligned with the corporate goals and strategic objectives. Many a times individual objectives assume top priorities and strategic alignment with corporate objectives may be difficult to achieve.

d) The budgeting process may be dominated by the influential people in the organisation. This may result in unrealistic estimation of revenue or expenses.

e) Budgets cannot deal with sudden changes in the economic environment.

f) The budgeting process is quite time consuming.

g) Budgets are usually based on traditional business functions and use past data; hence they do not go beyond certain boundaries.

h) Budgets are used for controlling the costs rather than reducing them.

Some European companies have decided to abandon the use of the budget on account of centralisation, inflexible planning, command and control. The '**beyond budgeting**' movement advocates that budgeting should be replaced with rolling forecasts that embrace key performance indicators (KPI) and incorporate exception based monitoring and benchmarking. However, budgeting still is widely practised despite the criticisms.

1.2 The Behavioural Dimension of Budgeting

One of the key objectives of management accounting is to influence the behaviour of the employees in order to maximise their efficiency and attain the corporate goals. It is absolutely necessary that the organisational goals are congruent with the aspiration levels of individual managers. This is usually achieved by responsibility accounting. Responsibility accounting is a system of accounting whereby managers are made responsible for items of costs and revenues so that their performance can be assessed and evaluated. Responsibility must be matched with control, otherwise managers will be de-motivated. Controls are determined by the level of authority of the manager i.e. his power to influence the costs and revenues.

The success of a budgetary system depends on how seriously human factors are considered. Budgets are often used to judge the actual performance of managers. Bonuses, salary increases, incentives and promotions are all affected by a manager's ability to achieve or exceed budgeted goals. Since a manager's financial status and career can be affected, favourably or unfavourably, budgets can have a significant behavioural effect. Whether that effect is positive or negative depends to a large extent on how budgets are used. Positive behaviour occurs when the goals of individual managers are aligned with the strategic objectives of the organisation and the manager is motivated to drive, stretch and excel to reach there. The alignment of managerial and organisational goals is known as goal congruence.

If the budget is improperly communicated or administered, the reaction of managers may be negative. This negative behaviour can be manifested in numerous ways, but certainly it will result in subversion of the organisation's goals. For example, a manager who deliberately underestimates sales and overestimates costs for the purpose of making the budget easier to achieve, is engaging in unethical behaviour. It is the responsibility of the organisation to create budgetary incentives that do not encourage unethical behaviour.

To discourage dysfunctional behaviour, organisations should avoid overemphasising budgets as a control mechanism. Other areas of performance should be evaluated in addition to budget adherence.

Budgets can be improved as **performance measures**:
- by the use of participative budgeting and other non-monetary incentives;
- by providing frequent feedback on performance;
- by the use of flexible budgeting;
- by ensuring that the budgetary objectives reflect reality; and
- by holding managers accountable for only controllable costs.

Test Yourself 1

You are the budget controller of a large organisation and are primarily concerned with budgetary control of large scale administrative expenses.

(a) Indicate broadly what sort of data you would require from the administrative department to be included in an annual budget.
(b) In the context of management motivation and involvement, explain what is meant by lack of goal congruence, giving two examples.
(c) Explain what other problems you might expect in administrative expenses budgets that would not normally be present if you were controlling operating expenses budgets.

2. Explain the principles of standard costing, its role in variance analysis and suggest possible reasons for identified variances.[3]

[Learning Outcome b]

Budgets help managers in **planning**, and at the same time, **setting standards** that are used to **control and evaluate managerial performance**.

For the purpose of planning and control, costs have been classified as historical costs and standard costs. Historical costs are the costs which have been incurred and are not relevant for decision making. These costs are used as the basis for estimating the future costs and thus they provide a basis for comparison with budgeted information in order to highlight areas where control may be necessary. **Standard costs** are predetermined (planned) cost estimates for a unit of output in order to provide a basis for comparison with actual costs. Standards are the building blocks, which are used to compile budgets. The term **'budgeted costs'** is a total concept i.e. the budgeted cost of material is $10,000, if 10,000 units are to be produced and the standard cost of material is $1 per unit.

Definition

Standard cost can be defined as "a pre-determined cost which is calculated from management's standard of efficient operation and relevant necessary expenditure". It may be used as a basis for price fixing and for control through variance analysis.

Hence, we can say that standard cost is a pre-determined estimate of cost of a single unit or a number of units of a product service.

2.1 Uses of standard cost

1. Use of standard cost is an effective way of planning and controlling costs.

2. Pricing decisions and decisions involving submission of quotations, answering tenders etc. are also facilitated by the use of standard costs.

3. Identification and measurement of variances from standards have been made possible with the use of standard cost, with a view to improve performance or to correct loose standards, if any.

4. It facilitates Management By Exception (MBE).

Definition

Standard costing is defined by the CIMA, UK as "the preparation and uses of standard costs, their comparison with actual costs and the analysis of variance to their causes and point of incidence."

In other words, standard costing is a method of preparation of standards and their uses for comparison with actual costs by variance analysis.

It involves the following steps:

1. setting up of the standard;
2. ascertainment of actual costs;
3. comparison of actual cost with standard cost to determine the variance; and
4. investigation of variance and taking appropriate action thereon wherever necessary.

2.2 Setting up of the standard

In order to use a predetermined standard cost, a standard has to be set for each element of cost (i.e. material, labour and overhead) for each line of product manufactured or service supplied. Standard cost shows what the cost should be keeping in mind the most favourable production conditions and on the assumption that the plant will operate at the maximum possible efficiency.

The integration of all functional departments is a must for setting standards. The quantities, price and rates, qualities and grades, terms of purchases, product substitution etc. have to be kept in mind while setting standards.

The success of a standard cost system depends upon the accuracy and reasonableness while defining standards.

1. **Role of Standard Costs**

Standard cost systems aid in planning operations and gaining insights into the probable impact of managerial decisions on cost levels and profits.

2. **Standard costs are used for the following:**

a) **Establishing budgets:** budgets are compiled from standards.
b) **Standard costing highlights the areas of strengths and weaknesses.**
c) **Controlling costs, directing and motivating employees and measuring efficiencies:** actual cost can be compared with standard cost in order to evaluate performance.
d) **Promoting possible cost reduction:** the setting of standards should result in the utilisation of best resources and methods being used, thereby increasing efficiency. It adds to management effectiveness and efficiency. It reduces clerical record keeping and aids cost reduction.
e) **Costs can be assigned** to materials, work in process and finished goods inventories.
f) It helps in **product pricing**.
g) It is a method for **valuation of stock** and provides a basis for setting wages, incentive schemes etc.
h) It provides a basis for **establishing bids** and contracts and for **setting sales prices**.

So we can say that a good standard costing system has many advantages, and increases the working capacity of a firm.

3. Problems faced while setting standards

a) Deciding how to incorporate inflation into planned unit costs
b) Agreeing a labour efficiency standard (for example, should current time, expected time or idle time be used in the labour efficiency standard)
c) Deciding on the quality of material to be used, because a better quality of material will cost more but may reduce the material wastage.
d) Estimating materials prices where seasonal price variations or bulk price discount may be significant.
e) Possible 'behavioural' problems: managers responsible for the achievement of standard costing control may fear being 'blamed' for any adverse variance.
f) Considerable cost is involved in setting up and maintaining a system for establishing standards.

There are many advantages of a standard costing system, so despite these disadvantages, this system is widely used.

SUMMARY

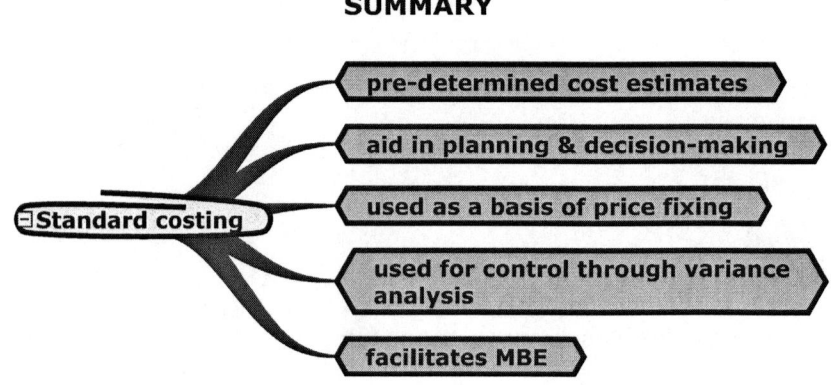

2.3 Variance analysis

We have already seen that standard costing involves setting of pre-determined cost estimates so as to provide a basis for comparison with actual costs. A standard cost is a **planned cost** of a unit of product or service.

Variance analysis is designed to identify management areas of weakness or poor control within the operations of the company. It can also identify areas of planning weaknesses. It will not, however, provide the outcome or a direction for change; it will merely highlight areas that require further management attention. While this, in itself, is an important management tool for decision making, variance analysis would normally be used in conjunction with other decision-making techniques.

Basic variance analysis has already been covered in Paper F5. The variance analysis at the profit and loss statement level is important, and can be useful for management decision making to provide further detail on financial areas of key importance to the business.

Variance analysis is also useful in determining the difference between operating and planning variances. For example, if sales were reported as 10 per cent less than planned, the variance analysis should tell management whether this was due to genuine poor sales or inadequate planning.

This is a step further than traditional variance analysis which implies that any variance is due to performance issues only.

Variances denote the differences between actual costs / revenue and the expected costs / revenue. The variances are of two types - **Favourable (F)** or **Unfavourable / Adverse (A)**.

Variances are not ends in themselves but springboards for further analysis, investigation, and action. A variance provides the yardstick to measure the fairness of the standard, allowing management to redirect its effort and to make reasonable adjustments.

Action to eliminate the causes of undesirable variances and to encourage and reward desired performance lies in the field of management, but supervisory and operating personnel rely on the accounting information system for facts which facilitate intelligent action towards the control of costs.

1. Reasons for variances

Given below is a summary of reasons for different variances. The list is not exhaustive, however, would provide a brief insight into the causes of variances.

Type of Variance	Reason for variance
a) Material Price Variance	➢ Procurement policy with respect to quantity and quality of material to be procured ➢ Material price inflation ➢ Occasional opportunities for sourcing at a discounted price
b) Material Usage Variance	➢ Consumption of higher / lower quality of material as compared to standard ➢ Efficiency of labour with regard to usage of material (control over wastages) ➢ Quality assurance and control over incoming material
c) Labour Rate Variance	➢ Deployment of higher / lower grade of skilled workers than planned ➢ Inflation in the case of wages
d) Labour Efficiency Variance	➢ Use of higher / lower grade of skilled workers than planned ➢ Quality of material used ➢ Errors in allocation of time to jobs
e) Idle Time Variance	➢ Sickness or illness of workers ➢ Machine breakdown ➢ Stoppage of production due to non-availability of material
f) Overhead Expenditure Variance	➢ Higher or lower economical use of services ➢ Alteration in the type of services than planned ➢ Inflation
g) Overhead Capacity Variance	➢ Over / under utilisation of capacity of the plant ➢ Higher idle time
h) Overhead Efficiency Variance	➢ Efficiency of the workers and the plant ➢ Change in technology

2. Problems faced in the interpretation of variances

a) Due to pressures on the budgetary control system, **errors** may arise **in the recording** of actual results. This may undermine the credibility of the variance analysis.
b) Efficiency variances will depend on the **tightness or looseness of the standards set**, and therefore any decisions regarding these variances must be taken in the light of the standard used.
c) There may be **interdependency** between variances e.g. procuring material at a competitive price may result in a favourable material variance, however, it may adversely affect the material usage and labour efficiency variances.
d) If the standards for material prices are based on current prices levels, due to inflation, the standard will have to be continually **reviewed and revised**, else would result in an adverse price variance.
e) Some variances are controllable, so that action can be taken and the system can be brought back on course. Other variances may be uncontrollable, resulting in **revision of the budget.**
f) The **size of the variance** is also important. Tolerance limits are set so that only variances which exceed these limits are reported. Small favourable or unfavourable variances should cancel each other out over a number of control periods.

The following example will illustrate the **importance of identifying the difference between an operational and a planning variance:**

Example

House of Bags Ltd's budget for March 20X0 is to sell 1,000 bags of a new design at $100 each. The variable cost for each bag is $50.

Budget for the month of March 20X0	$
Sales (1,000 bags x $100 per bag)	100,000
Cost of sales (variable cost at $50 per bag)	(50,000)
Gross profit	50,000
Overheads	(30,000)
Operating profit	**20,000**

Continued on the next page

During February 10, it became known to management that there would be a distribution problem and it was estimated that the new bags would not arrive at the retail stores until 15 March. So the company can achieve only half the sales volumes that were originally budgeted. A revised forecast for March was then drawn up as follows:

Forecast for the month of March 20X0	$
Sales (500 units x $100 per bag)	50,000
Cost of sales (variable cost @ $50 per bag)	(25,000)
Gross profit	25,000
Overheads	(30,000)
Operating loss	(5,000)

Overheads are assumed to be fixed and therefore will be incurred, and paid, regardless of sales or production volume.

Actual figures for March 20X0	$
Sales (600 units x $100 per bag)	60,000
Cost of sales (variable cost @ $50 per bag)	(30,000)
Gross profit	30,000
Overheads	(30,000)
Operating loss	NIL

While we can see that the total operating profit variance against the budget was $20,000, it would be useful for management to determine just how much of that variance was due to poor planning and how much was due to normal operational factors. This analysis is carried out using the following planning and operational variances.

Planning variance

The planning variance is designed to compare the revised forecast with the original budget.

Revised forecast sales volume (units)	500	
Less: Original budgeted sales volume (units)	1,000	
Total planning variance (units) - A	500	(Adverse)
Standard gross profit per unit ($) - B	50	
Planning variance (A x B)	25,000	(Adverse)

Operational variance

The operational variance is calculated in the normal way; however, it compares the actual units sold with the revised forecast units:

Actual sales volume (units)	600	
Less: Revised forecast sales volume (units)	500	
Total planning variance (units) – A	100	(Favourable)
Standard gross profit per unit ($) – B	50	
Planning variance (A x B)	5,000	(Favourable)

So, if management were to merely consider the total overall variance, they would know that operating profits showed an adverse variance of $20,000. This effective analysis technique provides management with the additional information that March 10 showed a $25,000 adverse variance due to the planning issue, whereas operationally, the company showed a $5,000 favourable variance. This allows management to focus attention on preventing future planning issues, knowing that the operational performance is in line with the budget.

Example

Bright Company has experienced increased production costs. The primary area of concern identified by the management is direct labour. The company is considering adopting a standard cost system to help control labour and other costs. Useful historical data is not available because detailed production records have not been maintained.

Continued on the next page

To establish labour standards, Bright Company has retained an engineering consulting firm. After a complete study of the work process, the consultants recommended a labour standard of one unit of production every 30 minutes, or 16 units per day for each worker. The consultants further advised that Bright's wage rates were below the prevailing rate per hour.

Bright's production vice-president thought that this labour standard was too tight, and from experience with the labour force, believed that a labour standard of 40 minutes per unit or 12 units per day for each worker would be more reasonable.

The president of Bright Company believed that the standard should be set at a high level to motivate the workers and to provide adequate information for control and reasonable cost comparison. After much discussion, management decided to use a dual standard. The labour standard of one unit every 30 minutes, recommended by the consulting firm, would be employed in the plant as a motivation device, while a cost standard of 40 minutes per unit would be used in reporting. Management also decided that the workers would not be informed of the cost standard used for reporting purposes. The production vice-president conducted several sessions prior to implementation in the plant, informing the workers of the new standard cost system and answering questions. The new standards were not related to incentive pay but were introduced when wages were increased to $7 per hour.

The standard cost system was implemented on January 1, 20X1. At the end of six months of operation, these statistics on labour performance were presented to executive management:

	January	February	March	April	May	June
Production (units)	5,100	5,000	4,700	4,500	4,300	4,400
Direct labour hours	3,000	2,900	2,900	3,000	3,000	3,100
Quantity variances:						
Variance based on labour standard (one unit every 30 minutes)	3150 A	2,800 A	3,850 A	5,250 A	5,950 A	6,300 A
Variance based on cost standard (one unit every 40 minutes)	2,800 F	3,033 F	1,633 F	-0-	933 A	1,167 A

Materials quality, labour mix, and plant facilities and conditions have not changed to any great extent during the six month period.

Required:

(a) Discuss the impact of different types of standards on motivation, specifically the likely effect on motivation of adopting the labour standard recommended for Bright Company by the engineering firm.

(b) Evaluate Bright Company's decision to employ dual standards in its standard cost system.

Solution

(a) Impact of different types of standards

1. Standards which are too loose or too tight will generally have a negative impact on workers' motivation. If too loose, workers will tend to set their goals at this low rate, thus reducing productivity below what is obtainable. If too tight, workers will realise that it is impossible to attain the standard, become frustrated, and will not attempt to meet the standard. An attainable or reasonable standard which can be achieved under normal working conditions is likely to contribute to the worker's motivation to achieve the designated level of activity.

2. If executive management imposes standards, workers and plant management will tend to react negatively because they may feel threatened. If workers and plant management participate in setting the standard, they can more readily identify with it and it could become one of their personal goals

In Bright's case, it appears that the standard was imposed on the workers by management. In addition, management used an ideal standard to measure performance. Both of these actions appear to have had a negative impact on output over the first six months.

(b) Evaluation of decision

Bright made a poor decision to use dual standards. If the workers learn of the dual standards, the company's entire measurement system may become suspect and credibility will be lost. Company morale could suffer because the workers would not know for sure how the company evaluates their performance. As a result, disregard for the present and any future cost control system may develop.

3. Evaluate strategic and operational decisions taking into account risk and uncertainty using decision trees.[3]

[Learning Outcome c]

The process of decision making involves selecting an alternative that is the best fit for the organisation under the circumstances. Most complex decisions are made under risk and uncertainty. Risk is the probability of not achieving the desired objective. Uncertainty is the lack of complete knowledge about the future event, which is required for the purpose of making a decision.

A decision maker is faced with a challenge of making a decision under the circumstances of risk and uncertainty. The risk is usually measured in terms of probability or frequency and the impact or consequence. The decision maker estimates probabilities of various outcomes, based on the past information and the available knowledge about the future. The sum of all probabilities would be 1.0, so that the set of outcomes in a decision problem should be mutually exclusive and collectively exhaustive.

Decision tree is a useful **analytical tool** for classifying the range of alternative courses of action and their possible outcomes. It is a diagram showing several possible courses of action and possible events (i.e. states of nature) and the potential outcomes for each course of action. It depicts in a systematic manner all possible sequences of decisions and consequences. Decision trees are designed to illustrate the full range of alternatives and events that can occur under all envisaged conditions. It brings out logical analysis of a problem and enables a complete strategy to be drawn to cover all eventualities before an organisation becomes committed to a decided course of action.

In the decision tree, various act-event combinations and resulting pay-offs of the problems are considered based on the risks. Decision trees give a clear, concise and meaningful overview of outcomes of various alternatives.

Decision trees provide an **effective method of decision making** because they:

- clearly lay out the problem so that all options can be challenged;
- allow us to fully analyse the possible consequences of a decision;
- provide a framework in which to quantify the values of outcomes and the probabilities of achieving them; and
- help us to make the best decisions on the basis of existing information and best guesses.

Following criteria are used for decision making under conditions of risks and uncertainty:

a) **Expected Monetary Value (EMV);** this is the expected value of a conditional pay off of each action. This is usually done by determining the conditional profit for each act-event combination along with the event probabilities. The act with the optimum EMV is selected, as a decision.

b) **Expected Opportunity Loss (EOL):** expected opportunity loss is calculated first by determining the event conditional opportunity loss values for the most profitable act (maximum pay off). Thereafter difference between conditional profit value and each conditional profit for that event is calculated to determine the expected conditional opportunity loss. The sum of all these values would be expected opportunity loss and the act corresponding to the minimum expected loss is chosen as a decision.

c) **Expected Value of Perfect Information (EVPI):** the expected value of perfect information is the expected average return in the long run, provided we have perfect information available for making the decision. In other words, expected value of perfect information is the amount that one would be willing to pay to obtain the perfect information relating to a future event. It is calculated as follows:

Expected Value of Perfect Information = Expected Pay-off of perfect information – Expected Monetary Value

Advantages of the decision tree method

- Decision trees are able to generate understandable rules.
- Decision trees perform classification without requiring much computation.
- Decision trees are able to handle both continuous and categorical variables.
- Decision trees provide a clear indication of which fields are most important for prediction or classification.

Disadvantages of the decision tree method

➤ Decision trees are less appropriate for estimation tasks where the goal is to predict the value of a continuous attribute.
➤ Decision trees are prone to errors in classification problems with many class and relatively small number of training examples.
➤ The process of developing a decision tree is expensive. At each node, each candidate splitting field must be sorted before its best split can be found. In some algorithms, combinations of fields are used and a search must be made for optimal combining weights. Pruning algorithms can also be expensive since many candidate sub-trees must be formed and compared.
➤ Decision trees are not very effective in the case of non-rectangular regions. Most decision-tree algorithms only examine a single field at a time. This leads to rectangular classification boxes that may not correspond well with the actual distribution of records in the decision space.

Example

Taba Ltd is a shoe manufacturer. In the last two years, the company has not introduced a new variety of shoes. It has $100,000 surplus cash for which the management is exploring introducing three new product lines, each with different levels of price, profitability and sales volumes. Market research has been conducted to estimate customer demand for each type of shoe.

Each type of shoe requires an initial investment of $50,000, so the directors are faced with a decision to choose two out of three options.

The three new shoe products have been named TAA, BAA and DAA. TAA has been estimated as having a 90 per cent take-up from customers as it is a variation of an existing model which has been very successful. BAA has a take-up estimate of 85 per cent; however, DAA has been estimated at only 55 per cent as it is a new design that has been targeted as a diversion away from market trends, as a signature item.

Taba Ltd's marketing department has given the unit sales estimations along with the sales price set for each new product. The finance department has provided the cost estimates of each new shoe to complete the unit profit analysis.

A summary of the data is as follows:

Product	Take Up (%)	No. of Units	Sales Value ($)	Cost ($)	Profit ($)
TAA	90%	10,000	395,000	158,000	237,000
BAA	85%	10,000	445,000	190,000	255,000
DAA	55%	7,500	595,000	190,000	405,000

In case the company decides not to introduce any new product, the management can park the surplus cash in a liquid financial instrument and wait for alternative investment opportunities. The management is also worried that the brand of the company may lose popularity due of lack of innovativeness in introduction of new products in the market.

Construct a decision tree showing various options for enabling the management to arrive at a decision.

Solution

Decision tree (TABA Ltd)

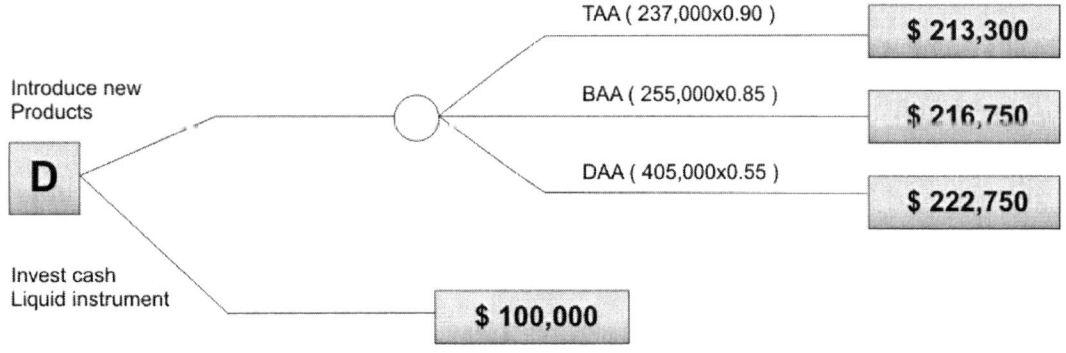

Continued on the next page

524: Financial Analysis

Analysis and conclusion

The output from the decision tree indicates that DAA is the most profitable product per unit, and is estimated to have sufficient take-up to match the overall contribution from TAA and BAA. The financial analysis indicates that the working capital of $100,000 available should then be allocated to investing in DAA and BAA, since the company can introduce two products.

Example

D Risk Limited is currently working on a process which, after paying for direct expenses, would bring a profit of $12,000. The following alternatives are available to the organisation:

a) It can conduct research (R1) which is expected to cost $10000 with 90% chances of success. If it proves to be successful, it can earn a gross income of $25000.

b) It can conduct research (R2) which is expected to cost $8000 with a chance of 60% success; the expected gross income will be $25000.

c) It can pay royalty of $6000 for a new process which will bring a gross income of $20000.

d) It can continue with the current process.

Due to limitation of resources it can conduct only one of the two types of research at a time.

Use decision tree analysis to determine the optimal strategy for the organisation.

Solution

The various activity–event combinations and the resulting pay offs of the problem are given in the following decision tree diagram. The net expected monetary value (EMV) of each event / decision points are also indicated below:

Alternatives

A   Conduct research R 1
B   Conduct research R 2
C   Pay royalty for new process
D   Continue the current process

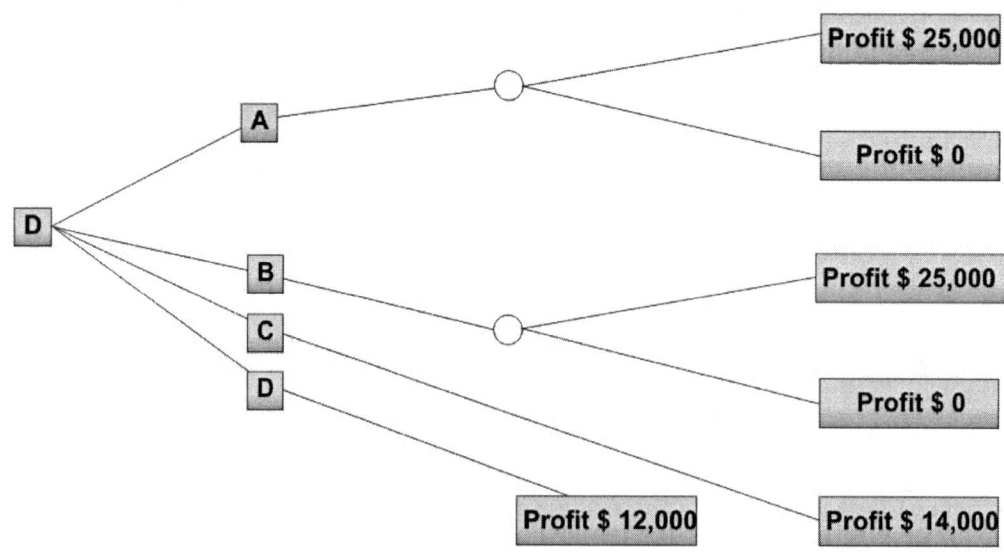

Continued on the next page

Decision analysis at Point D

Decision	Event	Probability	Gross Income($)	Expected Income ($)
1. Conduct Research (R1)	Successful	0.9	25000	22500
	Unsuccessful	0.1	0	0
			Total	22500
			Cost	(10000)
			Net EMV	12500
2. Conduct Research (R2)	Successful	0.6	25000	15000
	Unsuccessful	0.4	0	0
			Total	15000
			Cost	(8000)
			Net EMV	7000
3. Pay Royalty for new process	Certain	1	20000	20000
			Total	20000
			Cost	(6000)
			Net EMV	14000
4. Continue the current process	Certain	1	12000	

As the net EMV is the highest for the alternative **"Pay royalty for the new process"**, the optimal decision would be to introduce the new process on royalty basis.

> 4. **Evaluate the following strategic options using marginal and relevant costing techniques**
>   i. make or buy decisions
>   ii. accepting or declining special contracts
>   iii. closure or continuation decisions
>   iv. effective use of scarce resources.[3]
>
>   **[Learning Outcome d]**

Decision making involves prediction and a forward looking approach, which cannot change the past, but can certainly influence the future of the organisation.

Decision making involves choosing the best course of alternatives based on multiple quantitative and qualitative factors. It can be of two types - long term decisions and short term or operating decisions. The long term decisions relate to a period beyond the current year and therefore cost of investment, time value of money, return on investments etc. are the relevant considerations. On the other hand, short term decisions can be implemented within a period of one year.

The significant inputs for choosing among the alternatives are costs and revenues. The strategic option giving the lowest cost and the highest revenues would be the acceptable alternative to be chosen. It is needless to mention that the decisions must be made within the light of an organisation's overall corporate objectives and strategies.

Cost benefit analysis is an important criterion if profits are to be maximised, incremental costs to be incurred would be compared with the incremental benefits to be derived from the additional expenditure. The decisions would be accepted only when the benefits outweigh the additional outlay.

4.1 Relevant costs for decision making

Identifying and comparing relevant costs and revenues is an important part of the tactical decision making process.

Relevant costs and revenues differ across different alternatives.

Definition

Relevant costs (or revenues) are those that are appropriate to a specific management decision. These are represented by future cash flows whose magnitude will vary depending upon the outcome of the management decision made.

Thus, following are the important points, which emerge from the above definition:

- Relevant costs are future costs.
- Relevant costs are cash flows.
- Relevant costs are incremental costs.

The concept of relevant costs is also explained by describing the following terms:

1. Differential costs
2. Incremental costs
3. Avoidable costs
4. Opportunity costs

1. **Differential costs** are the differences in total costs between alternatives; calculated to assist decision making. Differential costs are relevant costs which are simply additional costs incurred as a consequence of a decision.

Differential cost vs marginal cost: marginal cost is based on the variability. It does not contain fixed cost, whereas differential cost may include fixed cost, if fixed costs change under different alternatives being considered.

2. **Incremental costs** are relevant costs that are simply additional costs incurred as a consequence of a decision. Incremental costs may or may not include fixed costs. If fixed costs do not change as a result of a decision, the incremental costs will be zero.

3. **Avoidable costs** are the specific costs of an activity or sector of a business which would be avoided if that activity or sector did not exist. Avoidable costs are normally associated with shutdown decisions but can also be applied to control decisions. Avoidable costs may be saved by not adopting a given alternative, whereas unavoidable costs cannot be saved. Therefore only avoidable costs are relevant costs for decision making.

4. **Opportunity costs** are the value of benefit sacrificed when one course of action is chosen, in preference to an alternative. The opportunity cost is represented by the foregone potential benefit from the best rejected course of action. Thus opportunity cost measures the opportunity that is lost or sacrificed when the choice of the course of action is given up.

Following costs are **NOT** considered to be relevant for decision making:

1. sunk costs
2. historical costs
3. non relevant variable costs and fixed costs

4.2 Assumption of relevant costing

1. Cost behaviour pattern is known / predictable.
2. The amount of fixed costs, unit variable cost, sales prices and sales demand are known with certainty.
3. The objective of decision making in the short run is to maximise satisfaction.
4. Complete and reliable information is available for decision making.

It is the responsibility of the manager to evaluate the financial implications of decisions that provide trade-offs between the costs and the benefits of different strategic options. Financial information about the different types of costs forms the basis of decisions about an organisation's activities and processes. Whether particular costs and revenues are relevant for decision making depends on the decision context and the strategic options available.

However, choice of the various strategic options would depend upon whether the costs and revenues are relevant. Usually, the costs that would remain the same irrespective of the options chosen are regarded as relevant for the decision. Normally, opportunity costs are also considered to be relevant for many decisions. Costs incurred / committed in the past, however, cannot be charged to any current decision and are called sunk costs. Sunk costs are not relevant for any alternative, as they do not influence choice of any option.

Therefore sunk costs are not considered in evaluating the financial implications of a decision.

4.3 Various decisions using relevant costing and marginal costing

1. **Make or buy:** an organisation is forced to take this decision under the following circumstances:

a) buy certain part or components from outside vendors; or
b) use available in-house capacity for production of the part or component.

Following are the important strategic considerations for taking such a decision:

- Opportunity cost of available capacity is to be considered when there is a possible alternative use of the available capacity.
- The decision to 'make' may involve incurring capital expenditure. This in turn will give rise to increase in fixed costs. However, fixed costs are not normally considered in the 'make or buy' decisions as they are sunk costs.
- In respect of 'buy' decisions, the outright bought out price is compared with the variable / marginal cost of making a product. If the 'bought out price' is lower than the variable cost of making a product then the option of buying the product is chosen.
- Where the 'make or buy' decision is to be taken under the circumstances of scarce resources (limiting factors), due consideration is given to the impact of such scarce resources.
- The most important consideration for make or buy is the volume of production, as fixed costs tend to go up beyond a level of activity.
- Non cost considerations or qualitative factors like price stability from vendors, reliability and adherence to delivery schedule, continuity of supply etc. are equally important.

Example

Bata Auto Components Limited (BACL) is a manufacturer of components for four wheelers. They have introduced a new version of shock absorbers and the product has been well received by Original Equipment Manufacturers (OEM). Each shock absorber requires one unit of the raw materials XEE, YEE and ZEE. All the shock absorbers are currently manufactured in-house and the capacity utilisation of the plant is full.

BACL is considering modifying the existing version of the shock absorber, which will require special machining and fixing of an additional attachment. With this, BACL hopes to double the volume of production.

The cost structure of the modified version of the shock absorber is as follows:

Raw Material	Variable Cost ($) (Per unit)	Fixed Cost ($) (Allocated per unit)	Total Cost ($) (Per unit)	Machine Hours (Per unit)
Xee	50	15	65	16
Yee	56	20	76	24
Zee	54	30	84	32
Special Machining and Additional Attachments	60	45	105	-
Total	220	110	330	
Selling Price			500	

The existing machines in the plant are capable of making all the components i.e. XEE, YEE and ZEE. The additional capacity required cannot be increased in the near future due to capital constraints. BACL has an option of procuring one of the raw materials from outside and do the special machining and assembly of the new shock absorber in-house. The offers received by BACL are as follows:

XEE - $66 per unit
YEE - $78 per unit
ZEE - $94 per unit

BACL is confident of increasing the sales volume by 50 % during the current year and by 75 % in the following year, with little sales promotional support.

You are required to give your recommendations as to which raw materials should be bought from outside, if the production increases by 50 % and 75 % respectively.

Continued on the next page

Solution

From the facts given in the problem, the present capacity of BACL is sufficient for machining and assembly of XEE, YEE and ZEE in house and the capacity utilisation is full. Thus the relevant limiting factor is the available machining hours. Let us compute the extra cost per machine hour for each of the bought out material.

Raw Material	Offer Price ($)	In house Cost ($)	Excess Cost Variable ($)	Machine Hours Released (per unit)	Extra Cost per Machine Hour ($)	Rank
	(A)	(B)	(C)=(A) – (B)	(D)	(E) = (D) / (C)	(F)
XEE	66	50	16	16	1.00	2
YEE	78	56	22	24	0.92	1
ZEE	94	54	40	32	1.25	3

Thus the order of preference would be YEE, XEE and ZEE. Since only one of the materials can be procured from outside, it should be ensured that the machine hours released in each case are sufficient to manufacture 50 % or 75 % more of the remaining materials. The calculation for this is given below:

Raw Material	Machine hours released (When bought from outside)	Total Machine Hours required for other materials for	
		50 % increase ($)	75 % increase ($)
XEE	16	28 (W1)	42 (Note 2)
YEE	24	24 (W1)	36 (Note 2)
ZEE	32	20 (W)	30 (Note 2)

Workings

W1
- When XEE is outsourced, additional machine hours required for YEE and ZEE at 50 % increase would be (50 % * (24 of YEE) + (32 of ZEE) = 28 hours.
- When YEE is outsourced, additional machine hours required for XEE and ZEE at 50 % increase would be (50 % * (16 of XEE) + (32 of ZEE) = 24 hours.
- When ZEE is outsourced, additional machine hours required for XEE and YEE at 50 % increase would be (50 % * (16 of XEE) + (24 of YEE) = 20 hours.

W2
- When XEE is outsourced, additional machine hours required for YEE and ZEE at 50 % increase would be (75 % * (24 of YEE) + (32 of ZEE) = 42 hours.
- When YEE is outsourced, additional machine hours required for XEE and ZEE at 50 % increase would be (75 % * (16 of XEE) + (32 of ZEE) = 36 hours.
- When ZEE is outsourced, additional machine hours required for XEE and YEE at 50 % increase would be
- (75 % * (16 of XEE) + (24 of YEE) = 30 hours.

Recommendation

1. When 50 % increase in sales is realised, buy YEE and make XEE and ZEE in house.
2. When 75 % increase in sales is realised, buy ZEE and make XEE and YEE.

---

2. Accepting or declining special orders

When an organisation is having excess idle production capacity, management may consider the possibility of selling additional products at less than normal selling prices. It is important to note that units sold at lower prices are produced as marginal output (i.e. they are produced in addition to the regular volume of output). The critical consideration is to determine an acceptable price for marginal output. Cost analysis using the contribution approach is a useful technique to determine the short term profit effects of the special order transactions. Pricing analysis concentrates on the recovery of incremental costs caused by accepting the order. The total selling price of the special order must recover at least the variable costs incurred, so as to provide either nil or positive contribution. Thus, as a general principle, the total price for the special order should be the incremental cost plus the desired profit.

Following are the important considerations in accepting / declining a special order:

a) Identification of 'relevant cost and benefit'. The relevant cost and benefits will influence the decision.
b) Specific procurements for the special order. Those that do not have any other use should still be charged to the special order, even though they are lying in stock.
c) Similarly, any additional cost incurred for the special order should be charged to the same order.
d) Loss of contribution of the opportunity foregone is always a relevant consideration.
e) Absorbed overhead or allocated costs are not relevant and should be ignored in the short term decisions.
f) In strategic situations like recession in the economy etc., the price quoted may be well below the marginal cost. However, such pricing will not continue for a long period. In normal circumstances, the lowest price will be equal to the marginal costs.

Example

ABC Limited has idle capacity and has received an offer to supply 2000 units of one of its products to a new customer in a new territory, currently not serviced by the company. The offer price is $10 per unit with a normal selling price of $14. The data extracted from the activity based accounting system of the company is as follows:

Element of cost	Cost driver	Unused capacity	Quantity in demand	Activity rate – Fixed ($)	Activity rate – Variable ($)
Direct Material	No. of Units	0	2,000	0	3.00
Direct Labour	Labour Hours	0	400	0	7.00
Set up time	Hours	0	25	50.00	8.00
Machining	Machine Hours	6,000	4,000	4.00	1.00

Notes:

1. The quantity in demand column shows the resource requirement for the special order of a new customer.
2. Fixed activity rate is the price that must be paid per unit of activity capacity. The variable activity rate is the price per unit of resources, for resources required for special order.

The fixed activity rate for set up is $25 per hour. The additional resources can be acquired in a block of 100 hours. Thus the unit of purchase for set ups is 100 hours of set up servicing. The price per hour is the fixed activity rate.

Required:

1. Compute the change in income for ABC limited if the order is accepted. Comment on whether the order should be accepted considering various strategic issues involved in the decision.
2. Suppose that the set up activity has 50 hours of unused capacity. How will it affect the analysis?

Solution:

	$	$
Revenue		20,000
Increase in cost due to accepting an order		
i) Direct Material 2,000 units x 3 per unit	6,000	
ii) Direct Labour 400 hours x 7 per hour	2,800	
iii) Set up cost (25 x $8) + (100 hours x $50)	5,200	
iv) Matching (4000 hours x $1)	4,000	
Total		18,000
Change in Income		2,000

Thus by accepting the special order, increase in revenue will be $2000. For this order, ABC will have to arrange for 100 hours relating to set up at a cost of $5000. This commitment should be made on the assumption that the company will continue to get such business in future.

In order to accept the special order, following considerations are to be kept in mind:

1. Impact of acceptance of special order on the regular business: the main assumption behind accepting a special order is that the existing business is not adversely affected.
2. Potential opportunity for expanding the market / business in future
3. Accepting a special order in order to use the idle capacity: this is a short term solution and therefore, the company will have to find out an alternative solution for full utilisation of the capacity in the long run.

b) The special order requires only 25 set up hours, whereas the company has 50 hours of excess capacity. In this case, there will be no need for expansion of capacity with increase in fixed costs. The total income will increase by $7000 (i.e. $5000 in addition to the change in income as computed in (a) above).

3. **Closure or continuation of operations:** sometimes management is confronted with the problem of whether to continue or shut down the manufacturing and marketing facilities. Continuation of operations is beneficial for the organisation so long as the sales prices for products or services are able to recover the variable cost and make some positive contribution. The discontinuation or closure of facilities would not eliminate all costs. For example, depreciation, interest, property taxes, insurance etc. would have to be incurred despite complete closure of the facilities. Where operations are continued, some of these expenses would be recovered. Moreover, the cost of reopening the facilities would be saved. Other qualitative aspects like morale of employees, confidence of customers etc. would be adversely affected in the event of closure. Therefore, the organisation should continue operations as long as differential costs can be recovered.

Example

Sun limited manufactures 60000 units of product 'Light' at the normal production capacity. The unit variable costs and fixed costs at this level are $13 and $4 respectively. The selling price of "Light" is $20. Due to recession in the market, it is envisaged that only 6000 units of "Light' would be sold in the next year. The fixed cost for the next year can be reduced to $99000. The management of the company plans to close down the plant, as it was not viable. The cost of closure of the plant would be $36000.

Advise the management whether the plant should be closed down. If yes, what should be the close down point?

Solution

Comparative statement considering both the proposals

Particulars	Plant to continue operations	Plant to close down
Variable cost 6,000 units @ $3 per unit	52,000	-
Fixed cost (60,000 x $4)	240,000	99,000
Additional cost of close down	-	36,000
Total costs	292,000	126,000
Sales (6,000 x $20)	120,000	-
Loss	172,000	126,000

Recommendations
Based on the above comparative statement, it is evident that the loss in the option to close down the operations would be lower by $46000, as compared to continuing the operations. Therefore management should consider closing down the plant, subject to other consequences.

The close down (shut down) point = (Total Fixed Cost – Shut down cost) / Contribution per unit
= ($240,000 - $126,000) / ($20 - $13)
= 16,285 units

---

4. **Effective use of scarce resources:** the effective use of scarce resources would become important in the following circumstances:

- Capacity is being fully utilised.
- Output is restricted by scarce resources like shortage of material, labour or factory space.
- Demand for the product is in excess of the productive capacity of the organisation.

In such circumstances, the management has to decide the best product mix which would generate the highest contribution margin. The key to solve this problem would be to calculate the contribution per unit of the scarce resource and prioritise the products based on the highest contribution per unit of scarce resource. The problem becomes complex where one or more resources are scarce. Such problems are solved by using the linear programming method to determine the optimal product mix.

Example

A company produces three products – Blue, Black and Red. Following information has been made available:

Particulars	Blue	Black	Red
Contribution per unit ($)	12	10	6
Machine hours required per unit	6	2	1
Estimated sales (number of units)	200	200	200

Continued on the next page

The total machine hours available are 1200 and therefore not sufficient for production of all the three products to fulfil the sales demand.

You are required to advise the management as to which products should be produced in the next year so as to maximise the profitability.

Solution:

Let us first calculate the contribution per scarce factor i.e. the machine hours in this case.

Particulars	Blue	Black	Red
Contribution per unit ($)	12	10	6
Machine hours required per unit	6	2	1
Contribution per machine hour	2	5	6
Order of preference	3	2	1

Thus, first preference will be given for manufacturing product Red. For the production of 200 units of Red, 200 machine hours will be required and the balance 1000 machine hours would be available for the production of other products. The next preference will be given to product Black, which will require 400 machine hours. Thus, we are now left with 600 machine hours. By utilising 600 machine hours we can produce 100 units of Blue. Therefore the product-wise optimum allocation of machine hours will be as follows:

Product	Production (Units)	Contribution / Unit	Total Contribution ($)	Machine Hours required
Red	200	6	1,200	200
Black	200	10	2,000	400
Blue	100	12	1,200	600
Total	500	-	4,400	1,200

In addition to the above analysis, other qualitative factors may also have to be considered. They are:

1. loss of customer goodwill / loyalty, if sufficient supply of products is not made available in time
2. implication on future sales
3. whether the sales of products manufactured by the company are complimentary to each other

---

Answers to Test Yourself

a) It is assumed that the budget controller has a critical and / or co-ordinating role, but as an administrative manager he is responsible for:
   - deciding the nature and level of activities of his department; and
   - controlling the cost of providing the services, being a service department.

The following items of data are expected to be included:

b. A statement of the philosophy underlying the existence of the administrative department
c. A statement of responsibilities covered and services provided by the department
d. A statement of costs expected to be incurred in the department for the budgetary period
e. Explanation of change proposed in comparison to the activities of the current year
f. An indication of how cost levels will be expected to respond to the change in the nature or level of the service required or provided

b) Lack of goal congruence occurs when the likelihood of achieving corporate objectives is reduced by the way in which functional budgets are prepared. For example, if the relationship between two departments is not properly "balanced", the conflict arising from it would adversely affect achieving of the corporate objectives.

Following are the two examples of lack of goal congruence:

1. Establishment of levels of cost (manpower, outsourcing of services etc.) in the administrative department for providing service levels more than what is expected by the receiving departments: such kind of "budget padding' would result in lack of goal congruence.

2. Development of the departmental future plans in isolation from the development objectives of the whole organisation: this will lead to imbalance in the growth. Therefore, development plan of administrative department as a service function should be in line with the growth strategy of the whole organisation.

c)
1. It may be difficult to identify a measurable output from the department, being a service department.
2. It may be difficult trying to relate cost inputs to service benefits provided.
3. Difficulty in setting the bases for a flexible budget does not exist and therefore judgment of changes in cost levels is not easy.
4. Cost efficiency as one means of appraising manager performance becomes questionable.

Self-Examination Question

Question 1

One of the purposes of management accounting is to influence the managers' behaviour so that their resulting actions will yield a maximum benefit to the organisation.

In the light of this objective, answer the following questions:

a) How can budgets cause behavioural conflict?
b) How can this behavioural conflict be overcome?
c) What is the importance of feedback of information?
d) What is the purpose of goal congruence?

Answers to Self Examination Question

a) While it is true that management accounting tries to influence the behaviour of managers, this may not always result in the desired outcome. The organisational conflicts are inherent in any organisation and this may set in inefficiencies which would prove to be counter productive for achievement of the corporate goal. While it is understandable that the top management would set the business and the corporate goals at the apex or organisational level, there would also exist divisional, departmental or individual goals. In the absence of proper strategic alignment between these multiple departmental goals and the corporate goal, the collective efforts would fail to produce the desired result.

The budgetary process will aim at reconciling the interest of the various departments and functions and thus help in achieving the corporate goals. Budget preparation is a participatory process and is usually approved by the top management; therefore budgets usually receive buy-in of various functions. Top management, while approving the budgets, would also ensure that they are in line with the strategic / corporate objectives of the organisation and take into account the interests of the various departments, divisions and functions. This helps the efforts directed to achieve the unified objective and would result in goal congruence.

Where budgets are prepared and approved by the top management without recognising the individual interests of the departments or are imposed on them, they will have a negative impact. Employees of the organisation may look upon the budgets as a punitive measure and not as a tool for motivation. The budgetary process also provides and allocates the required resources to various departments and divisions for achieving their objectives, thereby achieving the organisational goals.

b) The top management can overcome the behavioural conflict by taking the following actions:

i. The budgetary process should be transparent and the intentions behind the process should be made known to all those involved in this process.
ii. Budget procedures should be formalised and documented.
iii. Budgetary process should be participatory, that is it should involve the larger stakeholders in the organisation.
iv. A fair system of feedback should be introduced.

c) Feedback is an important element in the control process. It helps in taking corrective action so as to ensure that the performance is within the acceptable levels under the circumstances. Cost control is undoubtedly a managerial responsibility and the sound and fair feedback would go a long way in taking timely corrective action. Sometimes, feedback also helps to confirm that the process is in control.

d) The purpose of goal congruence is to provide a unified goal and the resources required for its achievement. Lack of goal congruence occurs when the likelihood of achieving corporate objectives is reduced by the way in which functional budgets are prepared. If the budgetary process tries to balance the interest and functional objectives of various departments in a conducive manner, the final budget prepared would not only be well accepted but also act as a motivating factor. Thus goal congruence in the budgetary process is the prime responsibility of the top management.

SECTION G: FINANCIAL ANALYSIS

STUDY GUIDE G4: FINANCIAL IMPLICATIONS OF MAKING STRATEGIC CHOICES AND OF IMPLEMENTING STRATEGIC ACTIONS

Get Through Intro

So the Coff-ahol business from the Get Through Intro in G2 is doing well. You decided to go with a venture capitalist partner so you could launch the product as soon as possible. The VC fund has taken 40% of the shares.

You decide to invest in a small bottling plant which has the facilities to mix the drink and then bottle it.

You will now have to show that the business is performing and that it will make money. Ratio analysis will help tell, whether you are on the right lines. It will also help the VC fund decide if you are meeting their targets. And it will also help show up whether you are likely to face any financial difficulties e.g. cash flow issues along the way.

This Study Guide will help you revise ratios and also see the financial implications of the decisions you have.

Learning Outcomes

a) Apply efficiency ratios to assess how efficiently an organisation uses its current resources.
b) Apply appropriate gearing ratios to assess the risks associated with financing and investment in the organisation.
c) Apply appropriate liquidity ratios to assess the organisation's short-term commitments to creditors and employees.
d) Apply appropriate profitability ratios to assess the viability of chosen strategies.
e) Apply appropriate investment ratios to assist investors and shareholders in evaluating organisational performance and strategy.

Introduction

Case Study

Chevron – use of funds and strategic analysis - Chevron – the oil and gas company gives a management discussion and analysis of their 2007 financial statements on their website. Extracts include:

Cash, cash equivalents and marketable securities

Total balances were $8.1 billion and $11.4 billion at December 31, 2007 and 2006, respectively. Cash provided by operating activities in 2007 was $25.0 billion, compared with $24.3 billion in 2006 and $20.1 billion in 2005.

Cash provided by operating activities was net of contributions to employee pension plans of $300 million, $400 million and $1.0 billion in 2007, 2006 and 2005, respectively. Cash provided by investing activities included proceeds from asset sales of $3.3 billion in 2007, $1.0 billion in 2006 and $2.7 billion in 2005.

Cash provided by operating activities and asset sales during 2007 was sufficient to fund the company's $17.7 billion capital and exploratory program, pay $4.8 billion of dividends to stockholders and repay approximately $3.7 billion of debt."

With regards to debt and financing, the report goes on to say:

The company's future debt level is dependent primarily on results of operations, the capital-spending program and cash that may be generated from asset dispositions. The company believes that it has substantial borrowing capacity to meet unanticipated cash requirements and that during periods of low prices for crude oil and natural gas and narrow margins for refined products and commodity chemicals, it has the flexibility to increase borrowings and/or modify capital spending plans to continue paying the common stock dividend and maintain the company's high-quality debt ratings.'

The above case study shows how seriously listed companies take their responsibility to stake holders. They have to explain in detail where the money has come from and what it will be used for. This also helps stakeholders understand the company's strategy. This Study Guide will help you understand how companies can analyse the financial implications of strategic decisions taken.

1. Apply efficiency ratios to assess how efficiently an organisation uses its current resources.[2]

[Learning Outcome a]

1.1 Efficiency ratios

An efficiency ratio measures **how well the organisation uses and manages its business assets**. It helps by measuring how adequately the assets are utilised to earn maximum returns. The efficiency ratios are also called **asset management ratios or working capital ratios**. The different efficiency ratios are:

1. Asset turnover

This calculation is not expressed as a percentage but as a number of times. It shows how much revenue is generated per $1 of assets and is calculated as:

$$\text{Asset turnover} = \frac{\text{Sales revenue}}{\text{Total assets}} \text{ (times p.a.)}$$

This ratio can be further split to calculate non-current asset turnover and current asset turnover:

$$\text{Non-current asset turnover} = \frac{\text{Sales revenue}}{\text{Non-current asset}} \text{ (times p.a.)}$$

$$\text{Current asset turnover} = \frac{\text{Sales revenue}}{\text{Current assets}} \text{ (times p.a.)}$$

> **Tip**
> The higher this ratio, the more efficiently the assets are being used to generate revenues.

The ratio could be unrealistically high if the non-current assets are at the end of their productive lives and have been depreciated to a considerable extent. It could be unrealistically low if they have been recently revalued and there has been a profit on revaluation.

2. Inventory turnover

The inventory turnover ratio helps in measuring the **speed with which an organisation converts its output into revenues** by way of sales.

The inventory turnover ratio is expressed with reference to the cost of sales and is calculated as:

$$\text{Inventory turnover} = \frac{\text{Cost of sales}}{\text{Inventory}} \text{ (times p.a)}$$

This indicates how many times the inventory is being turned over in a year.

The inventory turnover ratio can also be reversed to find the number of days, inventory has been held in the warehouse.

$$\text{Inventory turnover} = \frac{\text{Inventory}}{\text{Cost of sales}} \times 365 \text{ days}$$

> **Tip**
> The lower the number of days, the more quickly inventory is being sold.

The number of days could be unrealistically high if management has stocked more goods in anticipation of a shortage or in order to obtain bulk discounts. It could be unrealistically low if management has just passed on inventory to customers and plans to take it back in the next financial year.

Inventory turnover also impacts on warehouse space and costs of storage because until the inventory is sold, it has to be stored and hence it occupies space in the warehouse. An organisation may have a high inventory which may be expensive because storage of inventory takes up expensive warehouse space and interest charges may also accrue on the costs of storage.

Moreover, the Just in Time (JIT) system increases an organisation's competitiveness. The implementation of the JIT system leads to lower levels of inventory which, in turn, lead to improved performance.

2. Debtors turnover ratio

This ratio shows **how long an organisation takes to collect payments from its debtors**. This ratio indicates the number of times the debtors turnover each year. The higher the debtors turnover ratio, the better the **efficiency of the credit management** in the organisation. This ratio can be calculated as follows:

$$\text{Debtors turnover} = \frac{\text{Credit sales}}{\text{Average debtors}} \text{ (times p.a.)}$$

This ratio helps the management to analyse and compare (with competitors), its **relationship with its customers and cash management systems**.

The average number of days for which the debtors remain outstanding is called the average collection period. It is calculated as follows:

Average collection period

The average collection period reflects the **number of days it takes for a customer to pay**. It is calculated as follows:

$$\text{Average collection period} = \frac{\text{Debtors}}{\text{Credit sales}} \times 365 \text{ days}$$

This ratio can also be calculated using average debtors. In that case, it reflects the number of days it takes for the average customer to pay up.

3. Creditors turnover ratio

This ratio shows **how long does the organisation takes to pay its suppliers**.

$$\text{Creditors turnover} = \frac{\text{Credit purchases}}{\text{Average creditors}} \text{ (times p.a.)}$$

Average payment period

The average payment period reflects the **number of days it takes for a company to settle its bills**. It is calculated as:

$$\text{Average payment period} = \frac{\text{Creditors}}{\text{Credit purchases}} \times 365 \text{ days}$$

This ratio can also be calculated using average creditors. In that case it reflects the average number of days it takes for a company to settle its bills.

> **Tip**
> How an organisation uses these ratios (covered in all the learning outcomes) to assess various situations is explained at the end of the five learning outcomes in this Study Guide.

Diagram 1: Efficiency ratios

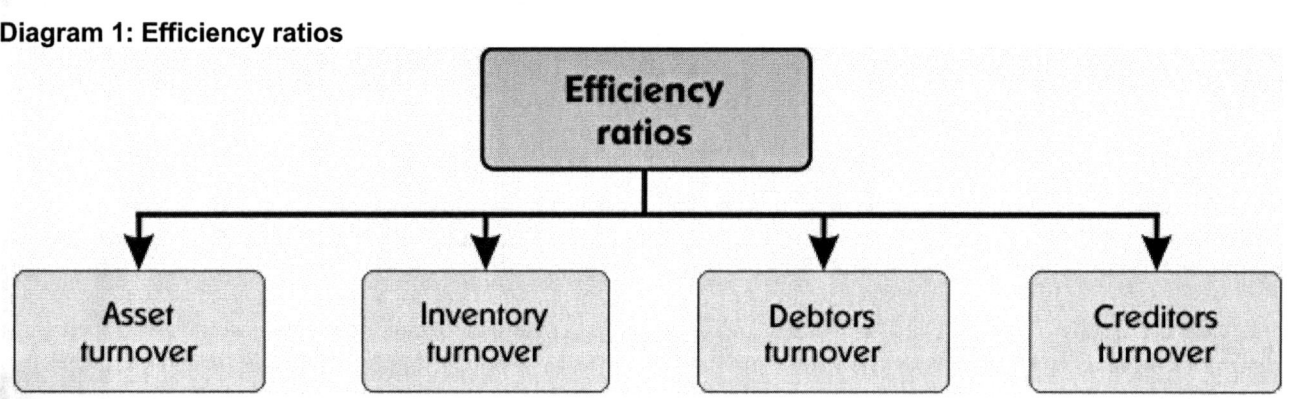

Test Yourself 1

The following ratios are calculated on the basis of the financial statements of Maridon Co for the years 20X6 and 20X7.

	20X7	20X6
Asset turnover	0.70 times	0.75 times
Inventory turnover	48 days	33 days
Average collection period	61 days	54 days
Average payment period	64 days	68 days

Required:

Interpret these ratios and comment on how efficiently Maridon Co uses its current resources.

2. Apply appropriate gearing ratios to assess the risks associated with financing and investment in the organisation. [2]

[Learning Outcome b]

The financial ratio measures the relationship of owner's equity to borrowed funds. A greater proportion of equity indicates that the financial position of the organisation is strong.

Many organisations aim to expand their business or invest in new assets such as highly advanced machinery or equipment. For this purpose, they are in need of funds. They obtain part of these funds from the issue of shares (equity finance), the profits they earn and the remaining requirement of funds is satisfied by borrowing (debt finance). If the organisation borrows money beyond its borrowing capacity then it has to pay more interest. Many analysts are of the opinion that excessive borrowing is always a risk because the funds borrowed may or may not give attractive returns or may even result in loss but, regardless of these possibilities, the organisation has to pay interest on the funds.

Financial gearing can be calculated in a number of different ways as explained below. Some calculations will be based on interest and income figures taken directly from the company's SOCI (income statement), while others will be based on figures taken from the company's SOFP (balance sheet).

2.1 Gearing ratios

Gearing' refers to the proportion of assets invested in a business that is **funded or financed by the borrowing**. Gearing ratios help determine the **stability** of the company and the **ability** of the company to repay its long-term debts.

Diagram 2: Gearing ratios

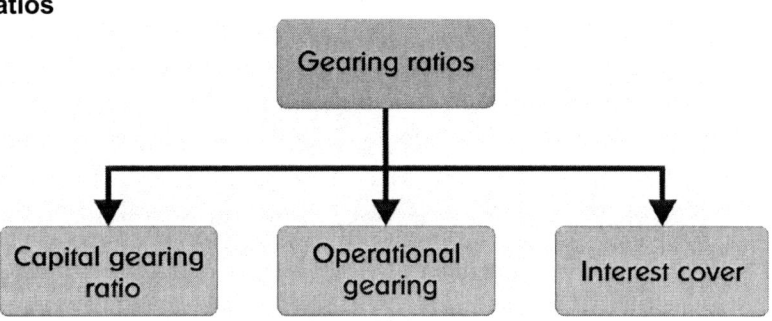

1. Capital gearing ratio

This ratio is an important measure of the company's risk and stability because it expresses the relationship between a **company's borrowings and its own funds**.

It is calculated as:

$$\text{Capital gearing ration} = \frac{\text{Total long - term debts}}{\text{Shareholders' funds}} \times 365 \text{ days}$$

Total long-term debt includes all items that have to be classified as debts according to the requirements of IAS 32 and IAS 39. Debts include long-term borrowings, debentures and preference shares.

Shareholders' funds include all items that have to be classified as equity according to the requirements of IAS 32 and IAS 39. Shareholders' funds include equity share capital and reserves. Note that preference shares are counted as debt not shareholders funds.

Example

The following information is available for Cell Inc.

	$
Ordinary share capita	450,000
8% non-redeemable preference share capital	100,000
Debentures	100,000
Long-term borrowings	400,000
Bank overdraft	50,000
Reserves	125,000

Continued on the next page

In this example:

The 8% non-redeemable preference share capital is to be classified as debt because, even though the preference shares are non-redeemable, they carry a fixed interest charge. (The substance of the transaction is given more importance than its form).

In the absence of information to the contrary, it is assumed that the bank overdraft is a short-term debt and is not to be included in the long-term debt.

Long-term debt	$
8% non-redeemable preference share capital	100,000
Debentures	100,000
Long-term borrowings	400,000
Total Long-term debt	**600,000**
Shareholders' funds	
Ordinary share capital	450,000
Reserves	125,000
Total shareholders' funds	**575,000**

$$\text{Capital gearing ratio} = \frac{\text{Total long - term debt}}{\text{Shareholders' funds}} \times 100$$

$$= \frac{600,000}{575,000} \times 100$$

$$= 104.35\%$$

This ratio shows the relationship between total long-term debt and shareholders' funds. This means that, for every $100 of shareholders' funds, the company has long-term borrowings of $104.35. An organisation with a higher gearing ratio is considered to be riskier than another organisation with a lower gearing ratio.

The capital gearing ratio can also be calculated as a relationship between the long-term debts and the total long-term funds (equity + long-term debts) of a company. This is calculated as:

$$\text{Capital gearing ratio} = \frac{\text{Total long - term debt}}{\text{Shareholders' funds} + \text{Long - term debt}} \times 100$$

In this case, the capital gearing ratio shows how much long-term borrowing the company has for every $100 of shareholders' funds and long-term debt taken together.

Important points for analysis purposes
- There can be no rule of thumb or limit for this ratio. It has to be analysed keeping in mind the circumstances under which a company operates.
- The higher the ratio, the more geared the company is. This means that it relies heavily on debts for conducting its business.

   This is acceptable for a company which is certain of making consistent profits and has an adequate asset base to offer as a security.
   Moreover, different industries have different norms for analysis purposes e.g. fast moving industries can survive even with higher gearing ratios.
- This is essential because a company has to pay interest on its borrowed capital, which will be difficult for a company which is not stable, has irregular sales and hence earns irregular profits. An adequate asset base is needed as it will be required by lending institutions as a security.
- A low capital gearing ratio is suitable for companies which have erratic sales / erratic profits and an insufficient asset base (for example, a consultancy – such companies do not have tangible assets, their main assets are their manpower resources).

Risks of having a high capital gearing ratio

A **high capital gearing ratio** means **more borrowed funds**. The higher the ratio, the more vulnerable the position of shareholders with regard to profits available for distribution.

The profit available for distribution to shareholders depends upon the level of borrowings. Fixed amounts have to be paid as interest and this eats into the amount available for distribution among shareholders.

As a result, there is less money available for distribution as dividends.

Example

Company Hope and Company Wish plan to expand their businesses by expanding their target markets. They plan to enter into foreign markets to attract additional customers. For expansion purposes, they require sufficient funds and hence they decide to obtain loans from financial institutions.

The financial data of the two organisations are presented below. By analysing the relevant facts, state which organisation is likely to obtain funds from financial institutions, and why?

Consider the following information:

Gearing ratio	Company Hope 40% $	Company Wish 60% $
Case 1		
PBIT	60,000	60,000
Interest	(20,000)	(35,000)
Profit after interest	40,000	25,000
Tax at 30%	(12,000)	(7,500)
Profit after tax	28,000	17,500
(available for distribution among shareholders)		
Case 2		
PBIT	50,000	50,000
Interest	(20,000)	(35,000)
Profit after interest	30,000	15,000
Tax at 30%	(9,000)	(4,500)
Profit after Tax	21,000	10,500
(available for distribution among shareholders)		

Conclusion (Case 1 versus Case 2)

Fall in PBIT	10,000	10,000
In % terms	(17%)	(17%)
Fall in profit after tax	(10,000/60,000 x 100)	(10,000/60,000 x 100)
(available for distribution among shareholders)		
In % terms	(25%)	(40%)
	(7,000/28,000 x 100)	(7,000/17,500 x 100)

Here, the more geared the company, the more volatile the effect of changes in levels of PBIT will be on the profits available for distribution among the shareholders. This is primarily because interest paid on borrowed funds is tax-deductible expenditure.

A company that has a high capital gearing (Company Wish) may also find that banks are not willing to lend it any more funds as it has too much debt. The worry is that it will not be able to pay the loan interest or capital.

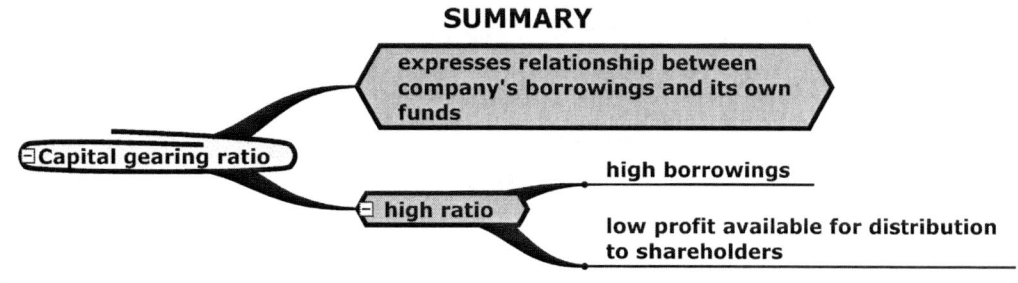

SUMMARY

Capital gearing ratio
- expresses relationship between company's borrowings and its own funds
- high ratio
  - high borrowings
  - low profit available for distribution to shareholders

2. Operational gearing

Operational gearing refers to the **effect of fixed costs** on the relationship between operating profits and sales. Operational gearing can be calculated in several ways. Companies with high fixed costs will show high operational gearing and their earnings will therefore be very sensitive to changes in sales.

$$\text{Operational gearing1} = \frac{\text{Fixed operating costs}}{\text{Variable operating costs}}$$

This ratio shows fixed costs as a proportion of variable costs.

$$\text{Operational gearing 2} = \frac{\text{Fixed operating costs}}{\text{Total operating costs}}$$

This ratio shows what proportion of total operating costs are represented by fixed costs.

$$\text{Operational gearing 3} = \frac{\text{Contribution}}{\text{PBIT}}$$

This ratio is used to show the impact a percentage change in sales will have on profit before interest and tax (PBIT). If this ratio is 1.5 it means that a 1% increase in sales will lead to a 1.5% increase in PBIT.

$$\text{Operational gearing} = \frac{\%\text{ change in PBIT}}{\%\text{ change in sales}}$$

Example

	Alpha Ltd $	Beta Ltd $
Sales revenue	10,000	10,000
Operating costs – Variable	6,000	5,000
Contribution	4,000	5,000
Operating costs – Fixed	2,000	3,000
Earnings before interest and tax (EBIT)	2,000	2,000

Let us assume that there is an increase in activity by 10%. The revised calculations would be:

	$	$
Sales revenue	11,000	11,000
Operating costs – Variable	6,600	5,500
Contribution	4,400	5,500
Operating costs – Fixed	2,000	3,000
Earnings before interest and tax	2,400	2,500
This can also be solved by using the following formula: Contribution/PBIT	1.83	2.20
Increase in EBIT	400	500
% increase in EBIT	20%	25%
Operational gearing (proportion of fixed costs to variable costs).	0.30	0.54

It can be seen that, due to an increase of 10% in revenue, Alpha's EBIT increased by 20% whereas Beta's EBIT increased by 25%. The reason for a higher increase in the case of Beta is that Beta's operational gearing is higher as its fixed costs are higher.

SUMMARY

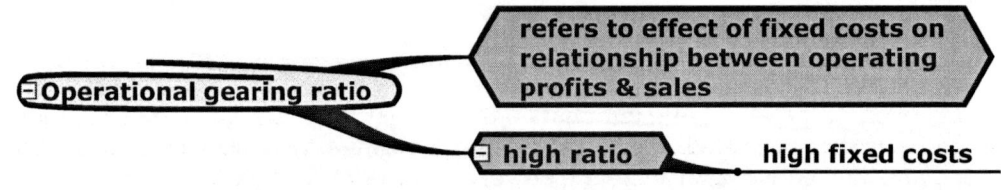

3. Interest cover

This indicates how many times **the profit covers the interest charge**. It measures whether or not the profits are sufficient to pay the interest and other finance costs. It reflects the ability of the organisation to repay its debt.

It is calculated as:

$$\text{Interest cover} = \frac{\text{Profit before interest and tax}}{\text{Interest expense}}$$

Example

The following information is available from Red Inc:

Profit before interest and tax	45,000
Interest	(18,000)
Profit before tax	27,000

In this example; Interest cover is 2.5 times i.e. (45,000/18,000)

Important points for analysis purposes

A higher ratio indicates that the company is in a better position **to pay the fixed charge of interest**.

Test Yourself 2

Fastrack Ltd and Tredest Ltd are two companies with similar business operations. Both companies have approached E-Money Ltd for finance. The financial information related to these companies is given below:

	Fastrack Ltd $m	**Tredest Ltd** $m
Interest	24,000	48,000
Shareholders' funds	425,000	575,000
PBIT	100,250	125,000
Long-term borrowings	265,000	355,000

Required:

Apply appropriate gearing ratios to assess the risks associated with financing Fastrack Ltd and Tredest.

---

3. Apply appropriate liquidity ratios to assess the organisation's short-term commitments to creditors and employees. [2]

[Learning Outcome c]

3.1 Liquidity ratios

Liquidity refers to an organisation's capacity **to pay its short-term obligations**. Short-term obligations refer to obligations which are usually to be paid within a period of up to one year. In order to calculate liquidity ratios, different analysts use different methods. They consider different assets to be relevant in the calculation of the liquidity of an organisation. Some analysts calculate only the sum of cash and equivalents divided by current liabilities as they think that they are the most liquid assets and would be the most significant assets to cover short-term debts in the event of a crisis.

Every organisation is required to maintain **sufficient liquidity** because an organisation has many **financial responsibilities towards its employees and creditors**.

An organisation has responsibilities towards its employees as it has to pay monthly salaries to them. In order to motivate the employees, the organisation has to pay bonuses or other incentives on a timely basis. For these reasons, the organisation is under an obligation to maintain sufficient liquid resources.

Creditors are the persons from whom the organisation purchases goods or materials on a credit basis. The organisation is under an obligation to repay the creditors within its allotted credit limit. So, the organisation has to maintain sufficient liquidity to repay its creditors in time and, in so doing, to maintain a good and lasting relationship with them.

The liquidity ratios are also sometimes called working capital ratios because these ratios show the relationships between the different types of working capital only. The liquidity ratios can be used to assess the **liquidity and cash position** of an organisation. When financial institutions sanction loans to an organisation, they analyse the liquidity ratio of the organisation to find out whether or not the financial position of the organisation is sound. In addition, financial institutions expect the organisation to maintain a certain fixed percentage of the liquidity ratio to ensure timely repayment of the loan. The liquidity ratios are; the current ratio and quick ratio. The detailed explanations of both these ratios are given below.

1. Current ratio

This ratio helps decide whether or not the current assets will be able to generate sufficient cash to pay off the current liabilities as and when they fall due. Here, the liquidity of the current assets and the ability of an organisation to pay its short-term debt obligation are measured. This ratio is calculated as:

$$\text{Current ratio} = \frac{\text{Current assets}}{\text{Current liabilities}}$$

Tip
The higher the current ratio, the greater the organisation's short-term solvency.

An organisation which has a high proportion of current assets in the form of cash and trade debtors is considered to be more liquid than an organisation which has a high proportion of current assets in the form of inventories, even if both the organisations have the same current ratio.

2. Quick ratio or acid test ratio

This is another ratio used to test the liquidity position of a company.

It is generally appreciated that the conversion of inventory into cash can take a considerable amount of time and may result in less money being realised than the face value. The quick ratio is calculated by **removing inventory** from the total amount of current assets. This ratio helps decide whether the quick assets of a company will be able to generate sufficient cash to pay off the current liabilities as and when they fall due.

This is calculated as:

$$\text{Quick ratio} = \frac{\text{Quick assets}}{\text{Current liabilities}}$$

$$\text{Quick assets} = \text{Current assets} - \text{Inventory}$$

Important points for analysis purposes
- The higher the current ratio and the quick ratio, the **better cash flow** the company has.
- High liquidity could indicate a problem of a different kind. It could mean that the company is not able to invest its cash into more profitable investments.

Test Yourself 3

Bright Co has approached Shine Co for the supply of raw material as the Bright Co's contract with its current supplier is about to expire. The credit period requested by Bright Co is higher than that which Shine Co normally extends to its customers. Shine Co is anxious about accepting the credit terms requested by Bright Co since it has no previous dealings with Bright Co.

The following information is available from the financial statements of Bright Co.

	20X7 $
Current assets	
Inventory	310,000
Trade receivables	440,000
Cash	93,250
Total current assets	**843,250**
Current liabilities	
Trade payables	313,500
Bank overdraft	66,500
Total current liabilities	**380,000**

Continued on the next page

Required:

Apply appropriate ratios to help Shine Co in assessing the liquidity position of Bright Co and its short-term commitments to creditors.

---

4. Apply appropriate profitability ratios to assess the viability of chosen strategies.[2]
[Learning Outcome d]

Every organisation is keen to know the amount of profit it is earning every year and the percentage of increase in its profit from the previous year. The organisation plans and implements its strategies to achieve certain goals. Every organisation's main aim is to earn profits. Whether its strategies have been successful or not, can be understood from the analysis of ratios such as profitability ratios and many more.

Profitability ratio analysis is also essential from the viewpoint of stakeholders (It is to be noted here that not all stakeholders invest in cash) because the comparison between the organisation's earnings in the current year with the previous year's earnings will help stakeholders to make better and more efficient investment decisions.

To measure profitability, the ratios which require to be calculated include profitability ratios and the ratios which reflect the relationship of returns to capital employed. Detailed discussions of these ratios are provided in the following paragraphs.

4.1 Profitability ratios

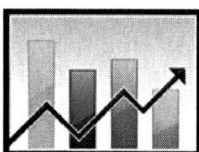

These help in **analysing the profitability of an organisation.** The best way to start an analysis of the profitability of an organisation is by examining the revenue it earns.

1. Gross profit margin

This ratio reflects the **gross margin** that an organisation makes on its **sales** and is calculated as:

$$\text{Gross profit margin} = \frac{\text{Gross profit}}{\text{Sales revenue}} \times 100$$

Some of the variables which affect this ratio are:
- the sales mix, the rise or fall in selling prices, the rise or fall in sales volumes
- the rise or fall in purchase costs
- variations in direct expenses

Important points for analysis purposes

The higher this ratio:
- the more efficient the performance of the organisation
- the more efficient it is in controlling direct costs
- the better is its sales mix and its performance

2. Operating profit (net profit before interest and tax) margin

This ratio reflects the **operating margin** that an organisation makes on its **sales** and is calculated as:

$$\text{Operating profit margin} = \frac{\text{Operating profit}}{\text{Sales revenue}} \times 100$$

The variables which affect this ratio are:
- all variables which affect the gross profit
- variations in selling expenses, distribution expenses and administrative expenses
- changes in depreciation (which depends upon variations in non-current assets, accounting policies etc.)

Important point for analysis purposes

The higher this ratio:
- the more efficient is the performance of the organisation
- the more efficient it is in controlling selling and administrative costs

3. Net profit margin

This ratio reflects the **net margin** that an organisation makes on its **sales** and is calculated as:

$$\text{Net profit margin} = \frac{\text{Net profit}}{\text{Sales revenue}} \times 100$$

The variables which affect this ratio are:

➤ all variables which affect the net profit
➤ variations in finance costs and taxation

Tip
Sometimes, net profit is considered to be the profit before interest and tax and so the operating profit margin is the same as the net profit margin. Remember that in this ratio it is net profit after tax and interest.

Important points for analysis purposes

The higher this ratio:

➤ the more efficient the performance of the organisation
➤ the more efficient it is in controlling its borrowings and borrowing costs

Any late adjustments made by the organisation could lead to a high gross profit margin.

4.2 Return on capital employed ratios

The viability of chosen strategies can be assessed by calculating the ratios which provide the relationships between returns and capital employed and returns and assets. The two ratios are as follows:

1. Return on capital employed

This is the most important ratio as it measures the **overall performance** of the organisation. It reflects the relationship between the **profits earned** by an organisation and the size of the organisation i.e. the **capital employed** by the organisation. It is calculated as:

$$\text{Return on capital employed} = \frac{\text{Operating profit}}{\text{Capital employed}} \times 100$$

Profit used in this calculation is **profit before interest and tax.**

Capital employed includes **shareholders' equity and all long-term borrowings** (non-current liabilities) or **total assets – current liabilities.**

In this ratio, we are measuring the relationship between capital and profit. It is important that the **two are consistent with each other.** We include long-term borrowings in capital, so the profit being used should be before deducting interest as interest is the cost of loan capital.

Important point for analysis purposes

➤ The higher this ratio, the more efficiently the business is being managed to generate profits from the available resources.
➤ Any conscious decisions taken by management which will reduce returns in one year but will prove beneficial in the long term, will reduce this ratio.
➤ Any fresh additions to capital employed at the end of the year will lead to an unnecessary fall in the ratio.

2. Return on assets

This reflects the relationship between the **profits earned** by a company and its **total assets**. It is calculated as:

$$\text{Return on assets} = \frac{\text{Operating profit}}{\text{Total assets}} \times 100$$

Profit used in this calculation is calculated **before interest and tax.** Total assets are the **SOFP (balance sheet) total.**

Important points for analysis purposes

- The higher this ratio, the more efficiently the total assets are being managed to generate profits from the available resources.
- Any conscious decisions taken by the management which reduce returns in one year but will prove beneficial in the long term, will reduce this ratio.
- Any fresh additions to total assets at the end of the year will lead to an unnecessary fall in the ratio.

The return on assets is a combination of two ratios:

Return on assets = Operating profit margin x Asset turnover

This can be explained by showing the formulae used to calculate the two ratios:

$$\frac{\text{Operating profit}}{\text{Total assets}} = \frac{\text{Operating profit}}{\text{Revenue}} \times \frac{\text{Revenue}}{\text{Total assets}}$$

Diagram 3: Ratios to assess viability of chosen strategies

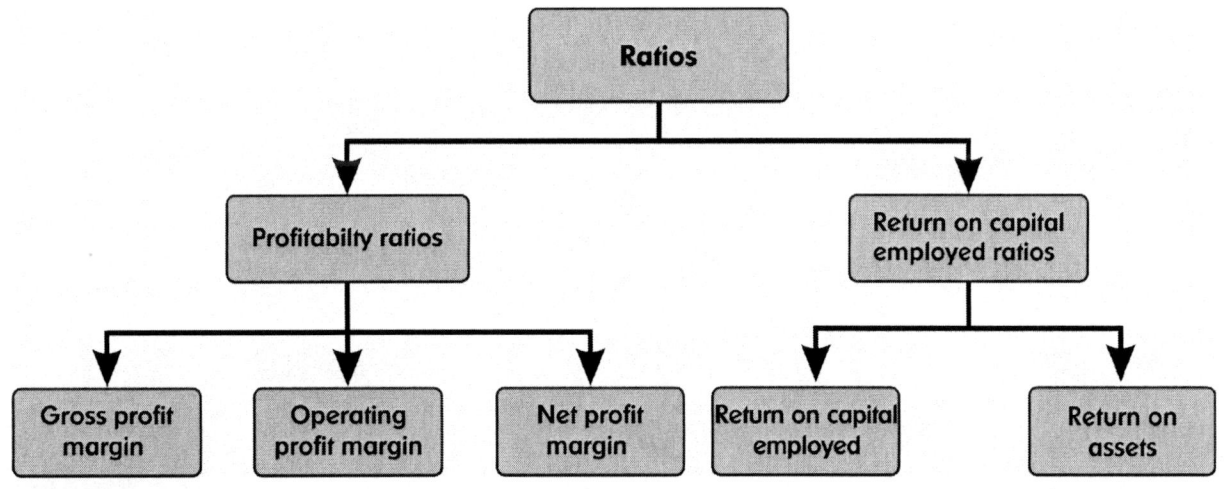

Test Yourself 4

The management of Seemtek Ltd purchased a large number of non-current assets in the year 20X6, to achieve its targeted market share. This helped Seemtek to increase its production, which in turn increased its sales turnover. The profits have increased significantly in 20X7 because of the increase in sales.

The following information related to the last two years is available:

	20X7	20X6
Gross profit margin	53%	64%
Operating profit margin	31%	41%
Net profit margin	24%	40%
Return on capital employed	28%	37%
Return on assets	27%	36%

Continued on the next page

Note: the non-current assets were purchased through a loan from a financial institution.

Required

Report on whether the performance of Seemtek Ltd has improved in the year 20X7 as a result of its investment in non-current assets.

---

5. Apply appropriate investment ratios to assist investors and shareholders in evaluating organisational performance and strategy.[2]

[Learning Outcome e]

Investment ratios measure the **returns** that an investor or shareholder obtains by investing funds in an organisation. Everyone in the world wants to put his money in safe hands. He first evaluates the **risk and returns involved** in the investment proposal and then decides whether or not to invest. Hence, when a prospective investor intends to invest in the organisation, he first evaluates the returns or the liquidity aspects of the proposal applying the various investment ratios.

The risk and returns of the investment proposal largely depend upon the **strategy and performance** of the organisation. An effectively planned strategy helps managers to perform better and to achieve the set goals. When the financial position of an organisation is strong, prospective investors are attracted to invest their funds in the organisation. While making a decision regarding investment, the investment ratios play a vital role in any organisation.

The different investment ratios are:

- Earnings per share (EPS)
- Price / Earnings ratio
- Profit retention ratio
- Dividend yield
- Dividend cover

Diagram 4: Investment ratios

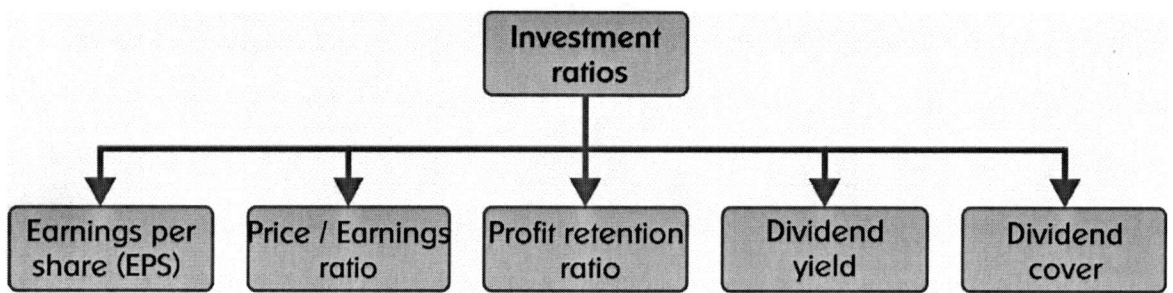

The calculation and analysis of all these ratios are explained in detail in the following paragraphs.

1. Earnings per share (EPS)

EPS represent the amount of **profits attributable to each ordinary share** or, in other words, what each share has generated in profits. This ratio calculates the earnings an organisation makes per share. Investors are interested in knowing the size of **their share in the total earnings** of the organisation. They are keen to know the current EPS as well as the future EPS to plan whether to continue investing in the organisation or to search for other investment options.

Earnings per share are calculated as follows:

$$\text{Earnings per share} = \frac{\text{Profits available for distribution to ordinary shareholders}}{\text{Number of shares}}$$

Example

The following information is available for Maple Inc:

Profits after interest and tax	140,650
Preference dividend	(25,317)
Profits available for distribution to ordinary shareholders	115,333
Number of shares of $1 each	100,000

$$\text{Earnings per share} = \frac{\text{Profits available for distribution to ordinary shareholders}}{\text{Number of shares}}$$

$$= \frac{115,333}{100,000}$$

$$= \$1.15$$

This means that every share of $1 earns a profit of $1.15.

Important point for analysis purposes
- The higher this ratio, the better for the investor.
- It is not an objective measure on which one can depend blindly. The **subjective nature** of the EPS ratio is due to the fact that its numerator is profit and this in turn depends upon the **accounting policies** used and the accounting estimates prepared by management.

Example

In the above example, the profits available for distribution are $115,333. These are arrived at after deducting borrowing costs of $14,667. If these costs were capitalised instead and added to the cost of the asset, then the profits available for distribution would be $130,000 (115,333 + 14,667).

Earnings per share in this case would be:

$$\text{Earnings per share} = \frac{\text{Profits available for distribution to ordinary shareholders}}{\text{Number of shares}}$$

$$= \frac{130,000}{100,000}$$

$$= \$1.30$$

This means that every share of $1 earns a profit of $1.30.

This shows that the EPS is a highly subjective ratio which changes with changes in accounting policies.

Sometimes analysts calculate this ratio by taking the **weighted average number of shares**. The weighted average number of shares is used because the number of shares outstanding can change over time. When the calculation of EPS takes the weighted average number of equity shares outstanding, it considers that the shareholders' capital may differ during the period depending on the number of shares outstanding at any point of time. To calculate the EPS, different (varied) numbers of shares cannot be taken as a denominator and hence a weighted average is calculated which provides a clear understanding of the profitability of the organisation.

$$\text{EPS} = \frac{\text{Profit attributable to ordinary shareholders}}{\text{Weighted average number of ordinary shares}}$$

Example

Toseco gives the following details:

Profit attributable to ordinary shareholders $3b
Weighted average number of ordinary shares outstanding 1.5b
Industry average is $1.5.
The company's previous year's EPS were $1.7, and the target for the current year was $1.9

$$EPS = \frac{3}{1.5} = \$2$$

The company has surpassed its past performance, the industry average and its own target.

SUMMARY

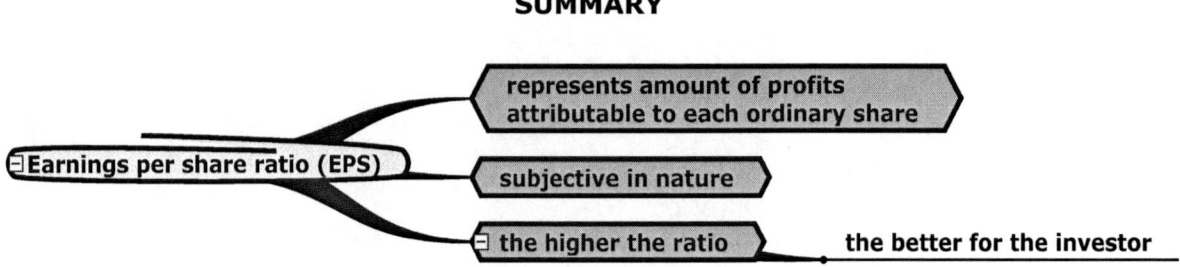

2. Price/Earnings ratio

This ratio can be used to assess the **relative risk** of an investment. This ratio helps a potential investor to form an opinion on whether the organisation is expensive or cheap because with this ratio, any investor can **compare the organisation with other organisations** in the same sector. The analysis is carried out not only on the basis of the current P/E ratio but also the prospective P/E ratio on the basis of expected future financial data. This helps investors to make an analytical judgement of how quickly the organisation's earnings are going to grow in future years and ultimately to make an decision on whether to buy shares of the organisation or not.
It is calculated as:

$$\text{Price/Earnings ratio} = \frac{\text{Current market price per share}}{\text{Earnings per share}}$$

Example

If the current market price of the shares of Maple Inc is $1.75 and the earnings per share are $0.50 then:

$$\text{Price/Earnings ratio} = \frac{\text{Current market price per share}}{\text{Earnings per share}} = \frac{1.75}{0.50} = 3.5$$

Important point for analysis purposes
- The higher this ratio, the more confidence shareholders will have in the organisation's ability to increase EPS, and the less risky the investment. Often this means they are expecting a growth in earnings.
- The parameters used for calculating the numerator and denominator are not consistent. The market price is current and up-to-date whereas the EPS may not necessarily be up-to-date.
- The market price is influenced by factors beyond the control of the organisation.

Example

A key director of Dreams Inc dies of a heart attack. This could lead to a decline in the market price of the organisation, as investors believe the organisation will not perform so well without the director.

SUMMARY

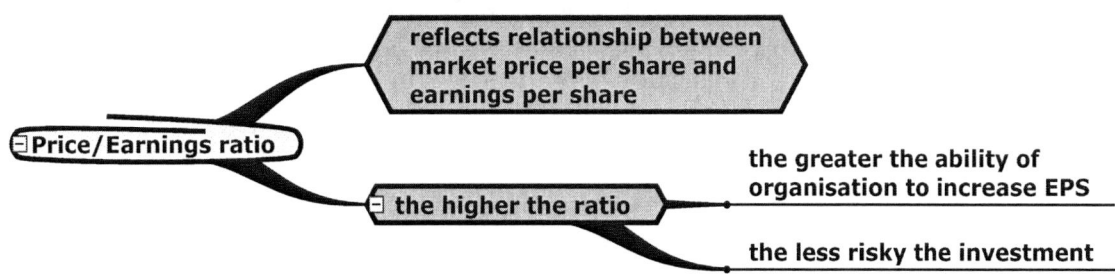

3. Profit retention ratio

This ratio measures how much of the profits earned by the organisation are **retained by it**. It is calculated as:

$$\text{Profit retention ratio} = \frac{\text{Profits after dividend}}{\text{Profits before dividend}} \times 100$$

Example

The following information is available for Maple Inc:

Profits after interest and tax	140,650
Dividend	(25,317)
Profits after dividend	115,333

$$\text{Profit retention ratio} = \frac{\text{Profits after dividend}}{\text{Profits before dividend}} \times 100$$

$$= \frac{115,333}{140,650}$$

$$= 82\%$$

Important points for analysis purposes:

The higher the ratio, the more shareholders expect the organisation to retain the profit for further growth. This means that the higher the ratio, the higher the expected growth.

SUMMARY

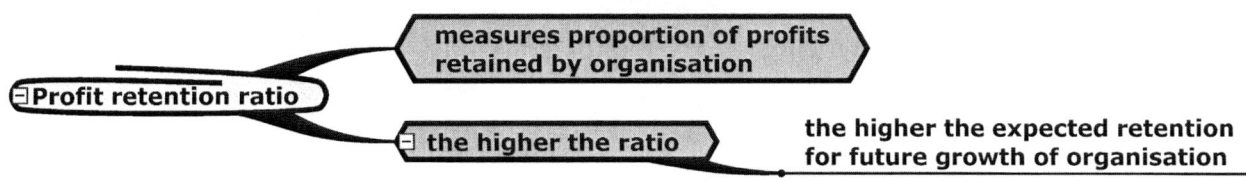

4. Dividend yield

Dividend yield measures the return on capital investment **as a percentage of market price**. It is calculated as:

$$\text{Dividend yield} = \frac{\text{Dividend per share}}{\text{Market price per share}} \times 100$$

Example

The following information is available for Elegant Inc, whose market price per share is $6.5.

Number of shares   500,000
Dividend $725,000

Dividend per share = $1.45 (725,000/500,000)

Continued on the next page

$$\text{Dividend yield} = \frac{\text{Dividend per share}}{\text{Market price per share}} \times 100$$

$$= \frac{1.45}{3.50} \times 100$$

$$= 22.3\%$$

Important points for analysis purposes
- The dividend yield is the return a shareholder expects currently on his investment. The lower the ratio, the lower the return he expects.
- The parameters used for calculating the numerator and denominator are highly subjective in nature.
- It is possible that management may declare a low dividend in spite of the organisation making a sufficient amount of profit as it wishes to retain the profit for expansion purposes.
- Conversely, management could declare a high dividend in spite of the organisation not making sufficient profit as it wishes to maintain the level of dividend declared in previous years.
- The market price is influenced by factors beyond the control of the organisation.

Example

In the above example, it is possible that the management of Elegant Inc has declared a dividend of $725,000 when it could have declared a dividend of $925,000. Management decides to use the difference of $200,000 for its expansion programme.

If, however, Elegant Inc had paid a dividend of $925,000, then the dividend yield would have been:

Dividend per share = $1.85 (925,000/500,000)

$$\text{Dividend yield} = \frac{\text{Dividend per share}}{\text{Market price per share}} \times 100$$

$$= \frac{1.85}{6.50} \times 100$$

$$= 28.5\%$$

This shows that, in spite of the fact that the dividend yield could have been better (28.5%), the management decision to retain funds has led to a lower dividend yield of 22.3%.

SUMMARY

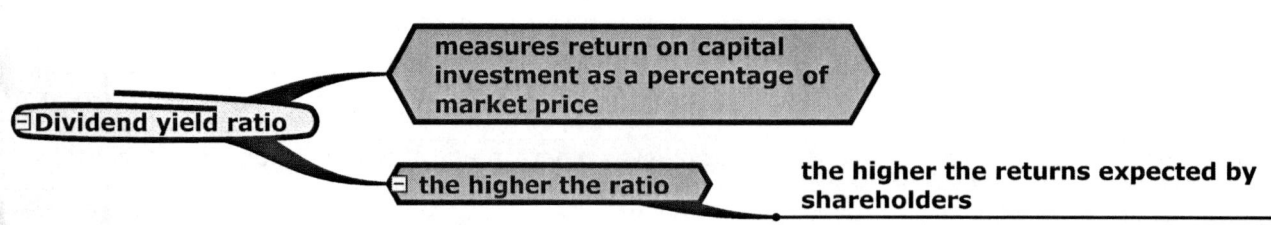

5. Dividend cover

Dividend cover measures the ability of an organisation to **maintain its existing levels of dividends**. It is calculated as:

$$\text{Dividend cover} = \frac{\text{Profit after tax}}{\text{Dividend}}$$

Example

The following information is available for Maple Inc:

Profits after interest and tax	140,650
Dividend	(25,317)
Profits transferred to SOFP (balance sheet)	115,333

$$\text{Dividend cover} = \frac{\text{Profit after tax}}{\text{Dividend}}$$

$$= \frac{115,333}{25,317}$$

$$= 4.6 \text{ times}$$

Important points for analysis purposes

The higher the ratio:

➢ the better the position the organisation is in to pay the fixed charge of interest
➢ the more likely it will be for the organisation to maintain the dividend yield and the level of dividends declared in the past

SUMMARY

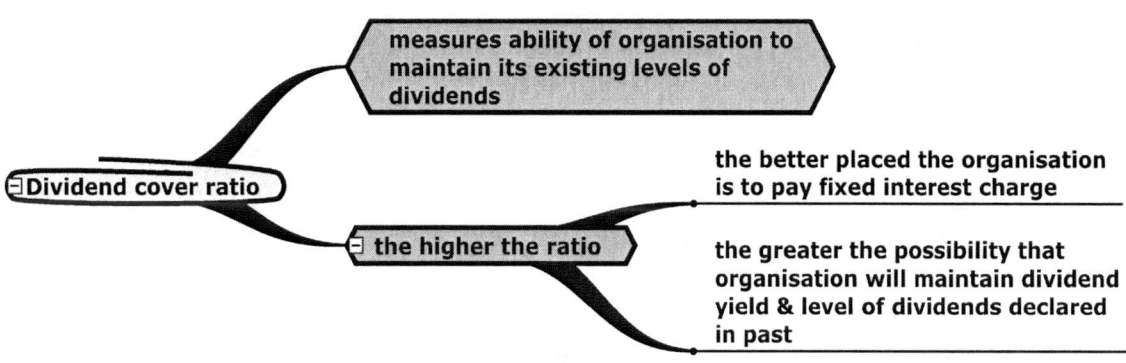

Summary of investment ratios

Ratio	Use
Earnings per share	To find out profits attributable to each ordinary share
Price/Earnings ratio	To assess the relative risk of an investment in relation to current market price per share and earnings per share
Profit retention ratio	To measure how much of the profit earned by the organisation is retained by it
Dividend yield	To measure the return on capital investment as a percentage of market price per share
Dividend cover	To measure the ability of the organisation to maintain its existing levels of dividends

Example

Excellent Inc has been a dealer in consumer goods for the last fifteen years. In 20X6, the directors of Excellent Inc devised a strategy to expand their scope of operations by entering foreign markets in which their competitors are not present. The organisation has been doing very well in the industry for the last ten years. In the last four-five years, the number of competitors has substantially increased and they are also capable of attracting more and more customers by offering additional facilities and price benefits. In response, the managers of Excellent Inc have planned to reduce their cost and sell their products at a low margin to customers to withstand the competition in the market.

Continued on the next page

The creditors of Excellent Inc are concerned about whether their money will be repaid to them or not due to this price reduction strategy and the strategy of market expansion. Moreover, although Excellent Inc's employees are interested in the organisation's expansion plan, they are also worried about the current liquidity position of the organisation and whether they will receive their monthly salary or incentives on time or not.

Excellent Inc has engaged Truth-teller Plc as a financial analyst to analyse the financial statements of the organisation and to give an opinion on the feasibility of the proposed strategy.

The extracts from financial statements of Excellent Inc for the years 20X6 and 20X7 are given below:

SOCI (Income statement)	20X6		20X7	
	$	$	$	$
Sales				
Cash	52,000		54,800	
Credit	388,000	440,000	488,800	543,600
Cost of sales		(340,400)		(427,200)
Gross margin		99,600		116,400
Expenses				
Transportation	8,900		14,500	
Selling expenses	15,900		20,100	
Rent charges	18,700		20,100	
Administrative expenses	27,100		27,100	
Debenture interest	-	(70,600)	3,300	(85,100)
Net profit		29,000		31,300

SOFP (Balance sheet)	20X6		20X7	
	$		$	
Non-current assets		52,000		66,000
Current assets				
Inventory	94,000		141,600	
Debtors	80,000		124,800	
Cash	24,000	198,000	19,800	286,200
Current liabilities		(80,000)		(116,400)
Net current assets		118,000		169,800
Total assets		170,000		235,800
Share capital		115,000		115,000
Reserves		55,000		68,800
Debenture loan		-		52,000
Capital employed		170,000		235,800

Example

From the financial data given above and calculating the relevant ratios:

1. Analyse how efficiently Excellent Inc uses its current resources.
   Applying the various liquidity ratios, assess whether the Excellent Inc has sufficient funds to meet its short-term commitments to creditors and the employees of the organisation.
2. Analyse by calculating the profitability ratios whether the strategy chosen by the directors of the organisation to expand its scope of operation, is viable or not.

Continued on the next page

Analysis of the financial statements using ratio analysis

1. To assess how efficiently Excellent Inc uses its current resources, it will be useful to calculate the relevant **efficiency ratios** of the organisation.

a) $$\text{Inventory turnover ratio} = \frac{\text{Cost of sales}}{\text{Inventory}} \text{ (times p.a.)}$$

20X6	20X7
= 340,400/94,000	= 427,200/141,600
= 3.62 times	= 3.02 times

In the current year, the inventory turnover is **lower** (3.02 times) than in the previous year (3.62 times). This indicates that the number of times the inventory is being turned over in the current year is lower than in the previous year. This may be a concern for management who will need to investigate why.

b) $$\text{Asset turnover} = \frac{\text{Sales revenue}}{\text{Total assets}} \text{ (times p.a.)}$$

20X6	20X7
= 440,000/170,000	= 543,600/235,800
= 2.59 times	= 2.31 times

In the current year, the assets turnover is **lower** than in the previous year. The higher the asset turnover ratio, the more efficiently the assets are being used to generate revenues.

c) $$\text{Debtors turnover} = \frac{\text{Credit sales}}{\text{Average debtors}} \text{ (times p.a.)}$$

20X6	20X7
= 388,000/80,000	= 488,800/124,800
= 4.85 times	= 3.92 times

In the current year, the debtors turnover ratio is lower than in the previous year. This ratio analyses the number of times the debtors turnover each year.

Calculation of the average collection period will provide a fuller analysis:

d) $$\text{Average collection period} = \frac{\text{Debtors}}{\text{Credit sales}} \times 365 \text{ days}$$

20X6	20X7
= 80,000/388,000 x 365	= 124,800/488,800 x 365
= 75.26 days	= 93.19 days

In the current year, the average collection period is longer (93.19 days) than in the previous year (75.26 days). This indicates that the customers of Excellent Inc are taking longer to pay, the credit management of the organisation has increased its credit limit to its debtors / customers, or the credit management company is not being efficient.

Example

To assess whether Excellent Inc has sufficient funds to meet its short-term commitments to creditors and the employees of the organisation, the **liquidity ratios** will have to be calculated and analysed:

a) $$\text{Current ratio} = \frac{\text{Current assets}}{\text{Current liabilities}}$$

20X6	20X7

Continued on the next page

= 198,000/80,000	= 286,200/116,400
= 2.48:1	= 2.46:1

The higher the current ratio, the greater the organisation's short-term solvency. In the current year, the current ratio is lower than the previous year's current ratio. The difference in ratio is nominal. Hence, this ratio indicates the relationship between the current assets and the current liabilities.

b) $$\text{Quick ratio} = \frac{\text{Quick assets}}{\text{Current liabilities}}$$

Quick Assets = Current assets – Inventory

Quick assets for 20X6 = 198,000 – 94,000 = 104,000

Quick assets for 20X7 = 286,200 – 141,600 = 144,600

Quick ratio	20X6	20X7
	= 104,000/80,000	= 144,600/116,400
	= 1.3:1	= 1.24:1

The quick ratio indicates the organisation's liquidity position. It shows the relationship between the quick assets and the current liabilities. In the current year, this ratio is again lower than the previous year's ratio. This indicates that the current year's liquidity position has not strengthened in comparison to the previous year. The difference is of 0.06, which is again nominal.

2. Profitability ratios

e) $$\text{Gross profit margin} = \frac{\text{Gross profit}}{\text{Sales revenue}} \times 100$$

20X6	20X7
= 99,600/440,000 x 100	= 116,400/543,600 x 100
= 22.64%	= 21.41%

The gross profit margin is 1.23% lower in the current year. The gross profit ratio is affected by a rise or fall in the purchase costs or variations in the direct expenses. The strategy which is to be followed by Excellent Inc is to reduce the costs so that they can sell their products at lower prices than their competitors.

f) $$\text{Net profit margin} = \frac{\text{Net profit}}{\text{Sales revenue}} \times 100$$

20X6	20X7
= 29,000/440,000 x 100	= 31,300/543,600 x 100
= 6.59%	= 5.76%

In the current year, the net profit margin is lower than the previous year's ratio. As the GP margin has reduced, the NP margin has also fallen.

Example

g) $$\text{Return on capital employed} = \frac{\text{Operating profit}}{\text{Capital employed}} \times 100$$

20X6	20X7
= 29,000/170,000 x 100	= 31,300/235,800 x 100
= 17.06%	= 13.27%

The return on capital employed is 3.79% lower in the current year. The higher the ratio, the more efficiently the business is being managed to generate profits from the available resources.

Conclusion

Hence, from the above analyses of financial ratios, it appears that all the ratios in the current year are lower than in the previous year. Although the difference from the previous year is nominal in every case, the strategy to expand the scope of the market may lead to benefits and increased goodwill in the near future. It is possible that expanding the market or lowering the prices to attract more customers may not yield huge profits in the first year of operation but may earn a sufficient amount of profits to cover the costs. On the other hand, by implementing the strategy, the organisation can earn a good reputation and create demand in the foreign market.

If there had been enormous differences in the ratios from the previous year, the directors would have to cancel their expansion plans and instead undertake some other strategy for the benefit of the organisation.

Test Yourself 5

Samantha wishes to invest $10,000 in the shares of either White Inc or Black Inc. The current market price per share of both companies is $2. Both the companies are operating in the same sector. She scrutinises the financial statements and calculates the following ratios for both companies:

	White Inc	Black Inc
EPS	$0.56	$0.49
Dividend cover	1 time	3 times
Profit retention ratio	75%	25%

Required

Assist Samantha in evaluating the organisational performance of both companies.

Answers to Test Yourself

Answer to TY 1

All the ratios given in the question fall under the category of efficiency ratios. These ratios help to measure how effectively an organisation manages and applies its current resources.

1. The asset turnover ratio measures the relationship between assets and the sales they generate. The asset turnover ratio of Maridon has declined from 0.75 in the year 20X6 to 0.70 in 20X7. This implies that there has been a decrease in the productivity of Maridon's assets. The efficiency with which the assets were being used to generate revenues has reduced as compared to last year.

2. The inventory turnover ratio helps in measuring the speed with which an organisation converts its output into revenues by way of sales. There has been an increase in inventory turnover by 15 days. This indicates that there has either been a slow down in sales or an increase in inventory levels. This means that the Maridon's effectiveness in managing its investment in inventories has reduced.

3. The debtors turnover ratio measures how long it takes an organisation to collect payments from its debtors or how quickly the organisation can increase its cash supply. Maridon's average collection period has increased by around 10%. In effect, debtors are taking longer to pay. This may be due to complacency on the part of the credit control department or Maridon may have decided to extend longer periods of credit to bring its policies in line with those of its competitors.

4. The creditors turnover ratio measures how long it takes an organisation to settle its creditors. The decrease in the average payable period of Maridon is an encouraging sign. Maridon has managed to reduce its average payable period in spite of an increase in the average receivable period. This implies that suppliers may have imposed stricter credit terms or Maridon may have decided to take advantage of early settlement discounts offered by suppliers.

Answer to TY 2

E-Money Ltd will be primarily interested in determining the risks associated with financing Fastrack Ltd and Tredest Ltd and whether they are in a position to repay their loans along with interest. Gearing ratios help determine the stability of an organisation and its ability to repay long-term debts. These are mostly used by providers of finance to assess the finance risk of the business.

The required ratios are calculated as follows:

1. $$\text{Capital gearing} = \frac{\text{Total long - term debt}}{\text{Shareholders' funds}}$$

Fastrack Ltd	Tredest Ltd
$= \frac{265,000}{425,000} \times 100 = 62.4\%$	$= \frac{355,000}{575,000} \times 100 = 61.7\%$

2. $$\text{Interest cover} = \frac{\text{Profit before interest and tax}}{\text{Interest expense}}$$

Fastrack Ltd	Tredest Ltd
$= \frac{100,250}{24,000} = 4.2 \text{ times}$	$= \frac{125,000}{48,000} = 2.6 \text{ times}$

The capital gearing ratio measures the proportion of an organisation's long-term borrowings to its own funds. The higher the capital gearing, the greater the perceived riskiness of the organisation. In this case, the capital gearing of both the companies is under 100%, which indicates that both the companies are not highly geared. The capital gearing of Fastrack (62.4%) is slightly higher than that of Tredest (61.7%). This means that lending funds to Fastrack will be riskier than lending funds to Tredest. However, taking decisions on the basis of only one ratio may prove to be dangerous. Therefore the other gearing ratio is taken into consideration.

The interest cover ratio measures the ability of an organisation to pay interest and other finance costs. The higher the ratio, the better placed the organisation is to pay the fixed charge of interest. The interest cover of Fastrack (4.2 times) is higher than that of Tredest (2.6 times). This implies that Fastrack's ability to pay interest to its lenders is greater than that of Tredest.

Although the capital gearing of Fastrack is slightly higher (by 0.7%) than that of Tredest, the deciding factor in this case is its higher interest cover. E-Money's main concern is getting back the principal and interest. Fastrack's interest cover of 4.2 times will ensure this.

Answer to TY 3

Shine Co can make use of liquidity ratios in order to assess the short-term commitments of Bright Co to its creditors. The organisation's ability to turn short-term assets into cash to cover debts is of the utmost importance when creditors are seeking payment. Creditors are often interested in liquidity ratios because they show the ability of the organisation to quickly generate the cash needed to pay creditors' bills.

The calculation of the liquidity ratios of Bright Co is given below:

1. **Current ratio** is the ratio of total current assets to total current liabilities. The higher the current ratio, the greater the short-term solvency of an organisation.

$$\text{Current ratio} = \frac{\text{Current assets}}{\text{Current liabilities}}$$

$$= \frac{843,250}{380,000}$$

$$= 2.22 : 1$$

This implies that Bright Co has $2.22 worth of current assets for each $1 worth of current liabilities. In other words, the current assets of Bright Co are more than double its current liabilities. This means that Bright Co has enough current assets to convert into cash to pay its current liabilities. In addition, Bright Co has a high proportion of assets in the form of trade receivables which are considered to be more liquid than inventory, because converting inventory into cash may take a long time as it depends on sale of the inventory. On the contrary, a trade receivable can be converted into money quickly provided the debtors are not bankrupt.

2. **Quick ratio** is the ratio of total quick assets to total current liabilities. Quick assets are calculated by excluding inventory as inventory cannot be turned into cash as and when required. The higher the quick ratio, the better the cash flow of an organisation.

$$\text{Quick ratio} = \frac{\text{Quick assets}}{\text{Current liabilities}}$$

$$= \frac{843{,}250 - 310{,}000}{380{,}000}$$

$$= \frac{533{,}250}{380{,}000}$$

$$= 1.4 : 1$$

This reflects that Bright Co has $1.4 worth of quick assets for each $1 worth of current liabilities. This means that Bright Co has sufficient assets to quickly convert into cash, if its current liabilities fall due. The quick ratio of Bright Co can be considered satisfactory as it is not below 1.

Hence the analysis of both ratios indicates that Bright Co has a strong liquidity position and sound short-term solvency.

Answer to TY 4

The investment made by Seemtek Ltd in non-current assets has helped it to increase production. This, in turn, has resulted in an increase in sales turnover and profits. With the help of profitability ratios it can be further assessed whether this has resulted in an improvement in the performance of the company. Profitability ratios are used to measure the financial performance of an organisation.

1. **Gross profit margin:** measures the gross profit as a percentage of net sales. The gross profit margin of Seemtek has fallen from 64% to 53% in 20X7. This indicates that there has been an increase in the cost of sales. This implies that Seemtek's efficiency in controlling its production costs has reduced. It also implies that the increase in sales may be the effect of a decrease in selling prices.

2. **Operating profit margin:** measures the net operating profit (net profit before interest and tax) as a percentage of net sales. The operating profit margin of Seemtek has fallen from 41% to 31% in 20X7. This implies that the fixed costs have increased for the production volume. This indicates that Seemtek's efficiency in controlling its other operating costs or overheads has decreased.

3. **Net profit margin:** measures the net profit as a percentage of net sales. The net profit margin of Seemtek has fallen from 40% to 24% in 20X7. The net profit margin has reduced considerably because of the increase in interest costs. This increase is a result of increased borrowings to finance the purchase of non-current assets.

4. **Return on capital employed (ROCE):** measures how much profit the capital employed has earned during the period. The ROCE of Seemtek has fallen from 37% to 28% in 20X7. This implies that the efficiency of Seemtek in generating adequate returns on capital employed from the available resources has reduced. One of the reasons for this may be that investment in non-current assets has not yet started to give the required results.

5. **Return on assets (ROA):** measures the relationship between the profits earned by the organisation and its total assets. The ROA of Seemtek has fallen from 36% to 27% in 20X7. This indicates that the efficiency of Seemtek in utilising its total assets for generating profits from the available resources has reduced. This may be because the newly purchased assets are taking a longer time to generate profits from the available resources. After a certain period of time, the new assets purchased may provide high returns and hence may increase the profit generation capacity of Seemtek.

Therefore the analysis of ratios shows that despite the significant increase in sales turnover and profits, the performance of Seemtek has not improved in 20X7. The fall in profitability ratios suggests that the overall efficiency in performance of Seemtek has reduced. A further analysis needs to be undertaken (along the lines suggested above) in order to identify all the causes of the underperformance and to take corrective measures.

Answer to TY 5

Analysing investment ratios is an important way of evaluating organisational performance and determining whether an organisation is a good investment choice.

Higher EPS are regarded as better as this implies that investors are earning higher profits for every share they own. The EPS of White Inc ($0.56) are greater than the EPS of Black Inc ($0.49). However, along with the EPS, Samantha should consider other ratios. It may be possible that the EPS of White Inc are higher because the company's scale of operations is much larger than Black Inc. In addition, not all the profit earned is going to be distributed as dividends.

The low dividend cover of White Inc (1) indicates that its dividend payout might be affected by a short-term fall in profits. The high dividend cover of Black Inc (3) indicates that it is making sufficient profits to sustain the payment of future dividends.

If Samantha is looking for capital appreciation, then the high profit retention ratio (75%) of Black Inc is what she would want, as the retained profits would be used for expansion purpose. However, if she is looking for returns in the form of dividends, then the low profit retention ratio (25%) of Black Inc would suit her as the possibility of earning regular dividends will increase. Therefore the choice between the two companies will depend upon Samantha's perspective.

Apart from the above three ratios, the price/earnings (P/E) ratio can be calculated and analysed from the given information. This ratio helps to assess the relative risk of an investment. With this ratio, an investor can compare an organisation with other organisations in the same sector.

$$\text{P/E ratio} = \frac{\text{Current market price per share}}{\text{Earnings per share}}$$

White Inc

$$= \frac{2}{0.56}$$
$$= 3.6$$

Black Inc

$$= \frac{2}{0.49}$$
$$= 4.1$$

The higher P/E ratio of Black Inc (4.1) indicates that its earnings are growing faster than White Inc and it is less risky to invest in Black Inc than in White Inc.

Quick Quiz

1. Fill in the blanks

    A. The lower the capital gearing, the _____ (more / less) geared the company.

    B. The higher the interest cover, the _____ (better/worse) the position the company is in to pathefixed charge of interest.

    C. The lower the current ratio, the _____ (more / less) liquid the business.

    D. The lower the dividend yield, the _____ (higher / lower) the return a shareholder expects from the shares he holds.

2. What does the acid test ratio indicate?

3. What are the factors to be considered while investing in the short term?

4. What is financial 'gearing'?

Answers to Quick Quiz

1.
   A. less
   B. better
   C. less
   D. lower

2. The acid test ratio indicates whether the liquid current assets will be able to pay off the current liabilities as and when they fall due.

3. The following factors are considered while investing in the short term:

   (a) Liquidity: it should be possible for these investments to be converted into cash as and when required. The company should also check whether there are any penalties for early liquidation.

   (b) Risk: there should be no risk of a capital loss on these investments. In addition, as a means of minimising risk, companies should spread the investments over different banks, so as to avoid concentrating the risks in one place. For this purpose it may be appropriate to fix limits up to which funds can be kept in one bank.

   (c) Return: investments sold should offer a reasonable return; at least higher than returns on the company's current account.

4. It is the amount of debt finance a company uses relative to its equity finance.

Self Examination Questions

Question 1

Tania Jones is the owner and chief executive of a chain of twenty designer-wear retail shops, Allure Apparels. These shops are clustered in the south of the country. The company is privately owned by the family and the freeholds of these shops which the company owns and which are on prime retail sites account for the majority of the assets of Allure Apparels. The company sells a range of designer outfits including formals, casuals, party wear and ethnic wear.

Allure Apparels was founded by Tania's father twenty-five years ago when he opened his first, small shop. Over the next twenty-five years the company grew steadily. However, by late 20X6, there was evidence that Allure Apparels' overall position within the market was weakening. Sales had stabilised, but even more importantly, competition was growing from a number of players who were prepared to operate on low profit margins but with larger volumes. It was at this time that Tania took over the company from her father.

Tania was impatient with the lack of growth. By nature she was an entrepreneur who sought growth. She was not convinced that steady organic growth was appropriate in the current conditions. Her father's policy had been to open a store each year, funding this growth out of current earnings. Tania saw that the market was becoming so competitive that even small markets were proving vulnerable. She believed that only the large, nation-wide retail chains would survive and that the smaller-sized groups would be taken over by the larger chains of clothes retailers who were more profitable and had greater ability to raise finance. She decided that a 'dash for growth' was required if the company was to achieve the critical size to survive in the market place.

At about this time another chain of fifteen fashion clothes shops became available for purchase. This group was in a distinctly separate area of the country – about 150 miles from Allure Apparels' current area of operations. As the overall market was still growing, the price being asked for this acquisition was rather high. However, Tania was convinced that this was too good an opportunity to miss. She believed that Allure Apparels needed this expansion. For an acquisition of this size it was obvious that the growth could not be funded internally so Tania decided to approach a bank for funding. Tania assumed that she might use the freeholds of the properties Allure Apparels owned as securities for the finance the company needed to borrow.

560: Financial analysis

The proposed acquisition was expected to be complete by the end of 20X8 or in early 20X9. Before approaching the bank, Tania discussed this issue with her accountant and offered the following ideas for her proposed expansion. In anticipating the proposed expansion and the need to manage an enlarged group, Tania believes that it is time for a strong and centralised leader. Recognising that the current system of stock ordering is delegated to individual store managers, she proposes to provide a centralised purchasing function based upon a warehouse owned and controlled by Allure Apparels. Individual shop managers will be permitted to decide upon their stock range but they will have to order from the central warehouse set up by Allure Apparels. Tania has also decided to tackle the problem of marketing and, in particular, promotion. The decentralised approach adopted by her father has not brought about the development of a well-known image and therefore the brand of Allure Apparels needs to be strengthened. Under Tania's plan it is proposed to allocate a substantial budget - 15% of sales - to spend on advertising and public relations and this level of commitment will continue for the foreseeable future. The shop managers will be expected to hold much more stock. A criticism of the shops when Tania's father was in charge was that they were often short of variety and stock. Most customers were unwilling to wait and they therefore bought from competitors' shops.

Tania fully understands that the costs incurred in the proposed acquisition involve more than the purchase of the new shops. Modernisation programmes for all the shops, as well as upgrading stock with a wider and more sophisticated range of clothes, will also require funding. Forecasts of immediate future sales appear to be attractive. Tania anticipates that sales per store will rise by about 8% over the next year. She believes that this growth in sales, accompanied by her more aggressive approach to retailing will enable her bold expansion plans for Allure Apparels to be achieved. Above all Tania wishes to see her company become a national company, no longer having to operate as a regional retailer.

The table below shows a summary of the figures that have been prepared by Tania's accountant for discussion. Part of the data has been obtained from trade association statistics.

	20X7 Actual $m	20X8 Budget $m	20X9 Forecast $m	20Y0 Forecast $m
Sales revenue	40	39.3	78.4	77.3
Costs of sales	20	19.7	33.7	33.2
Gross profit	20	19.7	44.7	44.1
Expenses	16	16.7	39.3	39.7
Operating profit	4	3	5.4	4.4
Interest paid	0	0	3.3	3.3
Profit after interest	4	3	2	1.1
Equity	33	32.8	34.9	34.5
Long-term debt	0	0	33.3	33.3
Gross margin	50%	50%	57%	57%
Operating profit margin	10%	7.6%	6.8%	5.7%
Inventory turnover ratio	5.8	3.5	2.1	2.2
Return on assets	14.3%	10.8%	9.2%	7.5%
Return on equity	12.1%	9.2%	5.8%	3%
Capital gearing ratio	0	0	96%	96%
Interest cover	-	-	1.6	1.3
Industry sales	125	135	140	138

Required:

Acting in the position of Tania Jones' accountant, and using the financial data provided, assess the viability of the strategy that has been proposed by her.

Question 2

Two companies Pineapple Co and Pear Co have approached Blue Chip Finance Co for loans.
SOCI (income statements)

	Pineapple Co		Pear Co	
	Y.E. 31.12.20X6 $m	Y.E. 31.12.20X5 $m	Y.E. 31.12.20X6 $m	Y.E. 31.12.20X5 $m
Revenue	1,833	2,000	1,867	2,067
Cost of sales	(933)	(1,000)	(1,057)	(1,087)
Gross profit	900	1,000	810	980
Administration / selling expenses	(350)	(400)	(284)	(300)
PBIT	550	600	526	680
Interest	(60)	(67)	(73)	(73)
Income tax expense	(165)	(180)	(158)	(204)
Net profit	325	353	295	403
Dividends	(100)	(100)	(100)	(100)
Net profit	225	253	195	303

SOFP (balance sheets)

	Pineapple Co		Pear Co	
	As at 31.12.20X6 $m	As at 31.12.20X5 $m	As at 31.12.20X6 $m	As at 31.12.20X5 $m
Non-current assets	2,050	2,000	1,586	1,517
Inventories	225	200	167	183
Trade receivables	248	267	267	300
Cash	20	33	50	50
	2,543	2,500	2,070	2,050
Issued share capital	500	500	367	367
Reserves	1,273	1,200	703	617
	1,773	1,700	1,070	984
Long-term borrowings	500	600	800	800
Current liabilities	270	200	200	266
	2,543	2,500	2,070	2,050

Required:

1. Blue Chip Co has asked you to go through the two sets of financial statements and advise as to which company is more creditworthy.

2. Different categories of users consider and analyse only those ratios relevant to themselves.' Comment.

Answers to Self Examination Questions

Answer to SEQ 1

It is evident that Tania is seeking to expand her business rapidly by acquiring the chain of shops that has become available for purchase. She is not happy with the steady progress that has been achieved over the last twenty-five years and is convinced that this slow rate of growth would not be appropriate in the current highly competitive market. Tania realises that geographic expansion into complementary and uncompetitive markets should increase her market share. This growth, however attractive it may appear, does involve considerable and probably unjustifiable risks. Apart from the potential problems of moving from a decentralised company to a centralised one, the major problem would appear to be one of over-rapid expansion, associated with careless financial control. Most of Tania's proposals have a cost implication.

The size of the acquisition is huge compared to the present size of Allure Apparels. The cost of the acquisition is very high as the price is based on the present growing market. In addition, considerable cost is involved in the proposed store modernisation and upgrading of stock. The amount of funds required for this, which Tania intends to obtain from bank, will also be considerable. Allure Apparels doesn't have any long-term debt at present. Considering this, it may be able to obtain the required finance for the proposed acquisition from the bank. However, in 20X9 and 20Y0, the borrowings are forecasted to be almost equal to shareholders' funds, making Allure Apparels a highly geared company (capital gearing ratio of 96%) as compared to its present debt position. The high borrowings will result in high interest costs. The forecasted interest cover ratio is showing a decline from 1.6 in 20X9 to 1.3 in 20Y0. The interest costs as a result of the high gearing will almost entirely wipe out the profits in 20Y0. In that year, the profits after tax are forecasted to be only $1/4^{th}$ of the profits achieved in 20X7.

The proposed centralised purchasing system could enable Allure Apparels to take advantage of the financial benefits of centralised purchasing and warehousing. The company will be able to control its purchasing, storage and logistics costs more efficiently. This benefit can be seen in the financial forecasts where gross margins have improved by 7% (from 50% to 57%). However, the decision to increase stock levels so as to minimise customer dissatisfaction has resulted in a forecasted decrease in the inventory turnover ratio from 5.8 in 20X7 to 2.2 in 20Y0. This would lead to an increase in the cost of investment in and management of inventory for the company.

The promotional and distribution changes after the proposed acquisition will involve a substantial financial commitment. Moreover Tania proposes to allocate a substantial budget of 15% of sales for advertising and sales promotion. There will also be an increase in administrative expenses due to the expansion and centralisation of the operations of Allure Apparels. This increase could be acceptable if the future sales were optimistic. Unfortunately there appears to be a decline in the forecasted sales of Allure Apparels in 20Y0 due to a forecasted decrease in industry sales. The table shows that expenses will rise considerably faster than the growth in sales, leading to a dramatic fall in the operating profit margin from 10% in 20X7 to a forecasted 5.7% in 20Y0.

A consistent fall in return on assets from 14.3% in 20X7 to a forecasted 7.5% in 20Y0 indicates that the assets acquired after acquisition will not generate adequate profits. A sharp decline in return on equity from 12.1% in 20X7 to 3% in 20Y0 is also forecasted due to an increase in expenditure coupled with a fall in sales in 20Y0.

Therefore from the financial data provided for Allure Apparels it is evident that the strategies proposed by Tania are not viable. The predictions of the future position of Allure Apparels over the next three years suggest that Tania's strategy for rapid expansion is both financially unjustifiable and unsustainable. They indicate that over-optimistic growth and expenditure is likely to lead Allure Apparels into serious difficulties.

Answer to SEQ 2

1. Report on the relative creditworthiness of Pineapple Co and Pear Co

An analysis of the financial statements leads to the following conclusions:

Pineapple Co:

In spite of a marginal increase in the profitability ratios, there is a decline in Return on Capital Employed and Return on Assets. This, together with the fall in Asset Turnover, suggests that the capital and assets are not being used at their optimal level.

It has a low Capital Gearing ratio which has fallen further in 20X6. This low level of borrowings has led to a high Interest Cover – a positive feature.

Pear Co

The reason for the increase in direct costs which has led to a considerable fall in the profitability ratios needs to be investigated. This fall in profitability has led to a fall in all the relevant ratios.

Capital gearing is less than 50%. Interest cover is adequate.

Comparison between the two companies

In spite of the fall in the profitability and its cascading effects on the accounts of Pear Co, it still has a better Return on capital employed and Return on assets than Pineapple Co.

Both companies have low capital gearing and high interest cover.

Conclusion:

If the cause of the fall in profitability of Pear Co can be identified and it can be ascertained that it has been controlled and will not lead to a further loss in the coming years, then Pear Co is more creditworthy than Pineapple Co.

If the 'cause' identified as the reason for fall in profitability cannot be controlled, then it would mean that the company's profitability might decline in the future as well. The profitability of Pineapple Co has remained stable and so, in the situation mentioned above, Pineapple Co would be more creditworthy than Pear Co.

Appendix 1: Calculation of ratios (ratios calculated in $m)

	Pineapple Co		Pear Co	
	20X6	20X5	20X6	20X5
Return on Capital Employed ratios:				
Return on Capital Employed	$\frac{550}{2,273} \times 100 = 24.2\%$	$\frac{600}{2,300} \times 100 = 26.09\%$	$\frac{526}{1,870} \times 100 = 28.13\%$	$\frac{680}{1,784} \times 100 = 38.12\%$
Return on Assets	$\frac{550}{2,543} \times 100 = 21.63\%$	$\frac{600}{2,500} \times 100 = 24\%$	$\frac{526}{2,070} \times 100 = 25.41\%$	$\frac{680}{2,050} \times 100 = 33.17\%$
Profitability ratios:				
Gross Profit Margin	$\frac{900}{1,833} \times 100 = 49.1\%$	$\frac{1,000}{2,000} \times 100 = 50\%$	$\frac{810}{1,867} \times 100 = 43.39\%$	$\frac{980}{2,067} \times 100 = 47.41\%$
Operating Profit Margin	$\frac{550}{1,833} \times 100 = 30.01\%$	$\frac{600}{2,000} \times 100 = 30\%$	$\frac{526}{1,867} \times 100 = 28.17$	$\frac{680}{2,067} \times 100 = 32.9\%$
Net Profit Margin	$\frac{325}{1,833} \times 100 = 17.73\%$	$\frac{353}{2,000} \times 100 = 17.65\%$	$\frac{295}{1,867} \times 100 = 15.80$	$\frac{403}{2,067} \times 100 = 19.5\%$
Activity ratios:				
Asset Turnover	$\frac{1,833}{2,543} = 0.72$ times	$\frac{2,000}{2,500} = 0.8$ times	$\frac{1,867}{2,070} = 0.91$ times	$\frac{2,067}{2,050} = 1.01$ times
Gearing ratios:				
Capital Gearing	$\frac{500}{2,273} \times 100 = 22\%$	$\frac{600}{2,300} \times 100 = 26.09\%$	$\frac{800}{1,870} \times 100 = 42.78\%$	$\frac{800}{1,784} \times 100 = 44.84\%$
Interest Cover	$\frac{550}{60} = 9.17$ times	$\frac{600}{67} = 8.96$ times	$\frac{526}{73} = 7.2$ times	$\frac{680}{73} = 9.32$ times

2. Different categories of users consider and analyse only those ratios relevant to themselves.'

A wide range of users depend upon the information contained in financial statements to make economic decisions. As the financial statements by themselves only present data, they have to be analysed. The tools used for these analyses are accounting ratios.

The different categories of users have different reasons for which they require information.

For instance, a prospective lender of funds would be concerned with the creditworthiness of the company; a prospective supplier will be bothered with its liquidity position.

A supplier would not be bothered about the interest cover that the company has to offer and the lender of funds would not be bothered about the Working Capital Cycle of the company.

This is the reason why different categories of users consider and analyse only those ratios which are relevant to them.

SECTION H: PEOPLE

STUDY GUIDE H1: STRATEGY AND PEOPLE: LEADERSHIP

Get Through Intro

In your working life, you are likely to have many bosses and come into contact with those that actually run the company (e.g. the CEOs and Chairmen). If you look at the best bosses, you will often find that they are often great leaders, who can oversee and motivate teams, in order to get the job done. They are often visionaries, who see the 'bigger picture' and find ways to implement it.

But exactly what makes a good leader? Are they always right? Is a great leader born or made? These questions, amongst others will be answered in this chapter. After all, in 20 years time you may be leading your company. What will make people believe in you and want to emulate you? Read well and learn well – your job could depend on it!

Learning Outcomes

a) Explain the role of visionary leadership and identify the key leadership traits effective in the successful formulation and implementation of strategy and change management.
b) Apply and compare alternative classical and modern theories of leadership in the effective implementation of strategic objectives

Introduction

Case Study

Bob Diamond is President of Barclays PLC and the Chief Executive of Investment Banking and Investment Management, which is made up of Barclays Capital, Barclays Global Investors and Barclays Wealth. He is considered a great inspiration and strong leader of the firm, inspiring his workers to win and be high-achievers. He is amongst those responsible for the position of Barclays Capital as the third largest investment bank in the the UK and it's reputation as the fastest growing investment bank globally, with an average of 25% annual growth from 2000-2007. Year on year Diamond has delivered spectacular growth for Barclays Capital and is known for his meritocratic approach to management which rewards hard working and strong commitment very generously.

---

1. Explain the role of visionary leadership and identify the key leadership traits effective in the successful formulation and implementation of strategy and change management. [3]

(Learning Outcome a)

Every organisation needs one leader to lead it on the path of strategy. A leader needs to have the vision to envisage impossibilities and the power to turn that vision into reality. There can be many leaders in the hierarchy of an organisation. They lead their group on the mission allocated to them by the organisation's main leader.

Example

The marketing executive leads the sales area and the production executive leads the production area in the implementation and formulation of business strategy.

As we have learned, every leader (like the project manager of a project) needs to visualise possible implementation difficulties of a project – he needs to visualise possible difficulties in the area of strategy and implementation. If a leader does not have the ability to envisage, he cannot prepare measures to overcome possible problems. It's hard to progress when they do not have a leader to guide them. A visionary leader creates an understanding about how to progress toward goals.

1.1 Key leadership traits essential for the successful formulation and implementation of strategy and change management are:

1. **Decision-making on the basis of predicted future**: these leaders should be able to look forward and should take decisions on the basis of what they are predicting or envisaging.

2. **Entrepreneurial mind:** someone with an entrepreneurial mind is needed to take decisions in a fast-changing marketplace where it's hard for products or services to adapt to the ever-changing tastes and expectations of customers.

3. **Risk-takers**: to move forward, it is necessary to take some risks. Without taking risks, gains are limited. By following a risky path, it is possible to make large profits or to incur huge losses. Every business has to take some risk to establish itself. Again, each decision needs to be evaluated on the basis of risk and returns.

4. **Effective communication**: effective communication is the key to solving any problems and is important at all the levels of an organisation.

5. **Analytical mind**: a leader needs to have an analytical mind to analyse the root causes of problems and the circumstances that led to the formation of issues and challenges. The leader need to set up responses in terms of actions which yield the maximum benefits for issues and challenges

6. **Creative**: creativity is needed to forge new relationships, alliances and to help explore the new directions the organisation could take i.e. the entrepreneurial qualities.

7. **Diversity:** every leader should have the capacity to effectively handle multiple tasks simultaneously.

SUMMARY

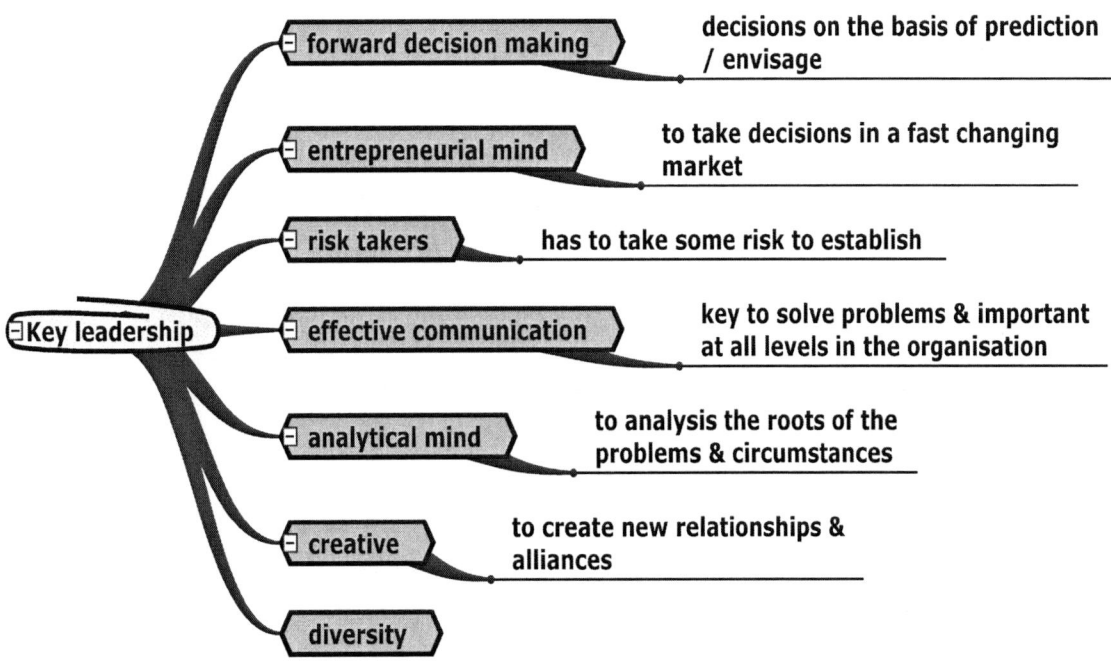

1.2 Barriers for visionary leadership

1. **Time management:** in order to apply bring visionary leadership to reality, a leader needs to do everything he can to achieve maximum effectiveness in his work. This puts pressure on the board as it has to attend meetings, read material and maintain contact with each other. In the absence of effective time management it is impossible to bring visionary leadership into practice.

2. **Reluctant to take risk:** to be innovative and creative, one has to take risks. There is a risk involved in starting any new venture and success is not guaranteed. Most of the leaders are reluctant to take actions beyond rendering their stewardship role of managing organisations. Leaders should try to maintain a balance between taking chances and rendering stewardship.

3. **Non-inclusion of visionary leaders in the formulation and implementation of strategy:** the visionary leadership is a necessary quality for board members, as they are responsible for the successful formulation and implementation of strategy.

4. **Lack of knowledge:** these days the ever-changing environment makes it difficult to stay updated. This lack of knowledge is reflected in reduced levels of confidence and an inability to make authoritative decisions.

5. **Micro management:** visionary leaders need to avoid the temptation to get involved in micro management. Visionary leaders have to deal with other major issues. If they involve themselves in micro management then they would not be able to give the attention required for macro management issues such as growth and development.

6. **Employees' reluctance to change:** sometimes employees prefer to stick to old rules and processes, making it hard for leaders to introduce new ways of doing things.

7. **Clarity of job:** sometimes leaders are not told about their responsibilities towards visionary leadership. Managers might assume that maintaining the current business is their only responsibility. If they are required to implement visionary leadership activities, e.g. business expansion, then their job descriptions must clarify this. Without this, they might say that such activities are not their responsibility.

8. **Lack of awareness:** lack of awareness about the need for changing leadership style when there is a change in the organisation's environment.

SUMMARY

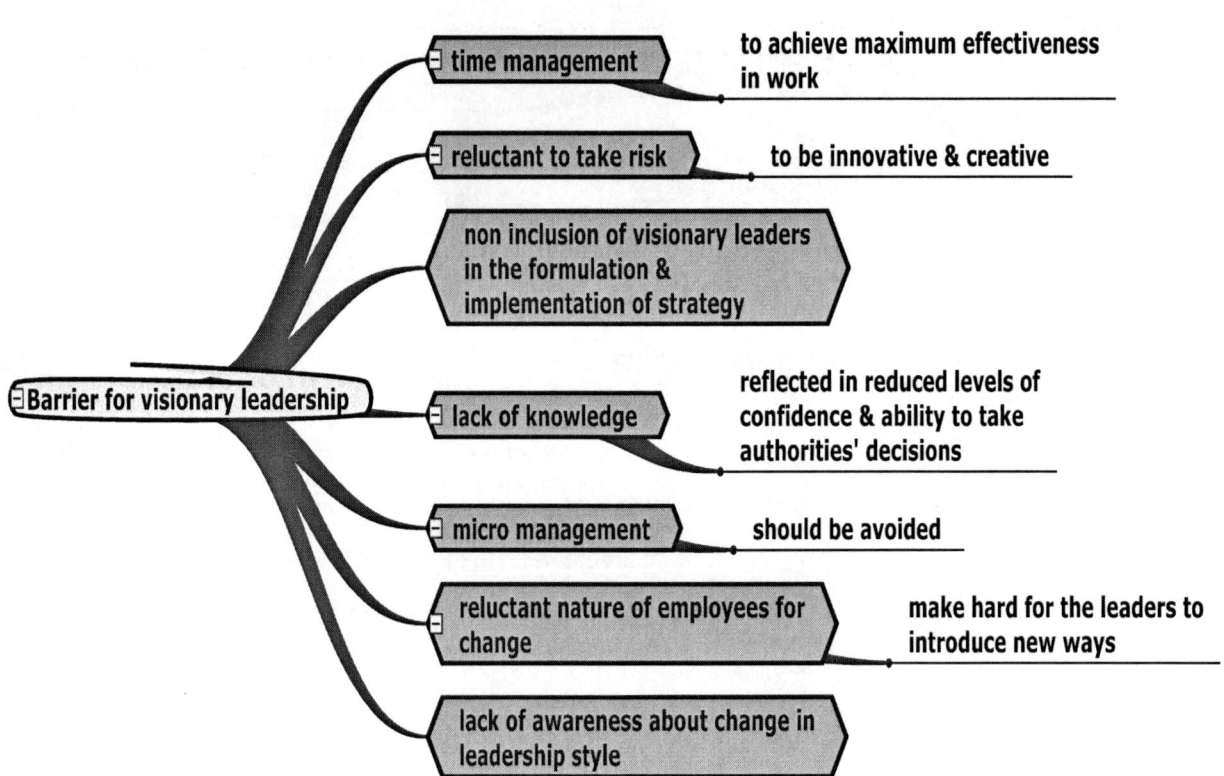

Focusing on the organisation's final aim or objective, and formulating the long-term plans for the development of visionary leadership are the two most important steps needed to turn organisational leadership into visionary leadership.

1.3 The difference between managers and leaders

A manager's job is to maintain the level of business activities within an organisation. A manager looks after managing functions such as assessing the past, forecasting the future and making decisions on the basis of this analysis. A leader takes the organisation forward in terms of growth, change and development. Leaders give guidance to managers.

Example

The electronic and digital world is continuously evolving. Every day we come across new products making the old obsolete. Would it be possible to enjoy laptops, mobile phones and walkmans without someone first imaging these things, which were considered impossible at that time? Without visionary leaders (such as Akio Morita who invented the walkman) the electronic and the digital world would remain stagnant.

Rather than just manufacturing and producing the standard commodities, these leaders had innovative ideas, worked on those ideas and brought them into reality. In doing so, they achieved tremendous success.

2. Apply and compare alternative classical and modern theories of leadership in the effective implementation of strategic objective. [3]

[Learning Outcome b]

The traditional saying, 'Leaders are born not made', is being challenged by the modern generation of academics in the field. Nowadays there are lot of courses that claim to turn a person from a follower to a leader. To some extend this is true. One can learn leadership skills and can come very close to becoming a leader. There are many theories describing different leadership styles.

Below are the eight modern theories of leadership:

1. 'Great Man' theories

This theory is based on the idea that great leaders are born and not made. According to this theory, leadership qualities are inherent in a person and that person can lead others whenever needed. Here, the leader's performance is considered heroic. The difference between Great Man theories and trait theories is that leaders in Great Man theories are recognised as heroes by society, whereas leaders in trait theories are recognised as leaders by their organisations.

> **Example**
>
> George Kennedy or Abraham Lincoln could be seen as examples of this kind of leadership.

2. **Trait theories**

Trait theories are similar to 'great man' theories. Trait theories describe the traits that a leader possesses. These theories also believe that leadership qualities are inherent in a person, but if we say the person possessing these qualities is a leader, this is not true in all cases.

> **Example**
>
> Myers-Briggs Type Indicator (MBTI) is a personality model which is an example of a trait theory. This model classifies personality traits according to different learning styles and individual preferences on the basis of another psychological model. The actions of managers, employees, and individuals are used to judge their personality traits, such as whether they are extroverts or introverts, sensors or intuitors, thinkers or feelers, judgers or perceivers, etc. By looking at different combinations of these traits, theories are formed and taught. This model has been criticised as being commercial pseudo-psychology.

3. **Contingency theories:** not all styles of leadership are suited to all situations. An individual who is a follower in one situation might become a leader in another situation. These theories emphasise the importance of a situation, the variables such as the qualities of a follower, the demands of the situation and leadership styles, such as the leadership style required to tackling the emergency created by unforeseen circumstances.

For example, an emergency situation created by a tsunami or a fire. The qualities of the follower are an important factor as the qualities required by a leader who is tackling a fire with the help of a fire brigade are different from those required by a leader who is tackling a fire with the help of the public. The demands of the situation also play an important part in making a person a leader. For example, in a situation in which someone is drowning, the situation demands the leader to have swimming skills.

> **Example**
>
> Fiedler's theory can be quoted as an example of contingency theories. According to Fiedler, group performance is contingent on the leader's psychological orientation and group atmosphere, task structure and the leader's power position. Again, group performances come from the leadership style and situation. To summarise, the effectiveness of leadership is dependent upon the interaction of the style of leadership and the characteristics of the environment in which the leader works.

Diagram 1: Fiedler's Theory

Fiedler's Theory

Performance	Low to High	High to Medium	Medium to High	High	High	High	Medium to High	Medium
	1	2	3	4	5	6	7	8
Group Atmosphere	Good	Good	Good	Good	Poor	Poor	Poor	Poor
Task Structure	Structured	Unstructured	Structured	Unstructured	Structured	Unstructured	Structured	Unstructured
Leader Position Power	Strong	Weak	Strong	Weak	Strong	Weak	Strong	Weak

4. **Situational theories:** according to these theories, leadership actions are responses to a situation. The styles of leadership required for a situation may change from situation to situation. The qualities and process of decision-making always change whenever there is a change in situation.

> **Example**
>
> Heresy and Blanchard's situation leadership model explains how to analyse the current situation and explains the use of the most appropriate leadership styles for it. In this model, leadership is expressed as the amount of direction and support that a leader gives to followers. The leadership behaviour of the leader and the development level of the follower are presented in a matrix structure and plans to supervise and monitor them are made.

Diagram 2: Hersey and Blanchard leadership Theory

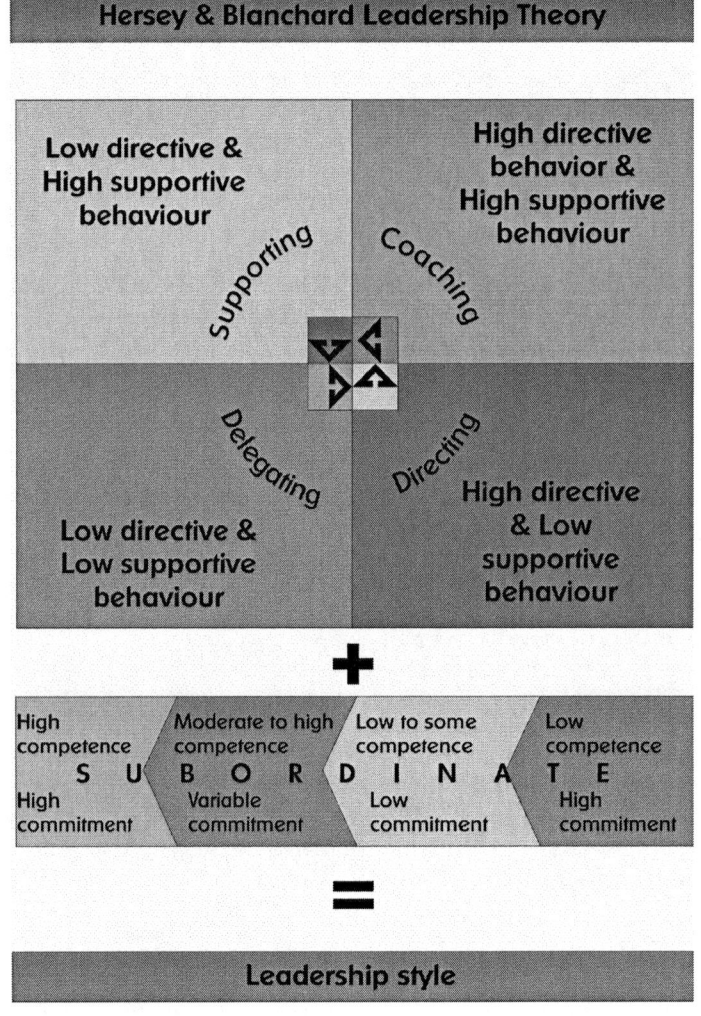

5. **Behavioural theories:** according to these theories, it is not the inherent qualities and traits of a person which make the person a leader. Instead, it is the actions of the leader in response to the situation and circumstances that make him a leader. The methods for taking these actions can be taught to a person. The person can learn leadership skills through formal education and observation. The basic fundamentals of how problems should be dealt with can also be taught.

6. **Participative theory:** relying only on one person's views is risky. This theory outlines the importance of inputs from the team members. A leader generally encourages contribution from group members in the decision-making process. Decisions about which inputs should be considered are made by the leader.

> **Example**
>
> The Path Goal theory, as explained by Robert House, says that a leader can affect the performance, satisfaction and motivation of a group. This can be done by:
> - offering rewards for the performance goals
> - clarifying the path toward these goals
> - removing the obstacles in the performance path
>
> This is done in addition to what is done in the situation theories. One of the leadership styles explained in the path goal theory is participative leadership.

Diagram 3: Path goal theory

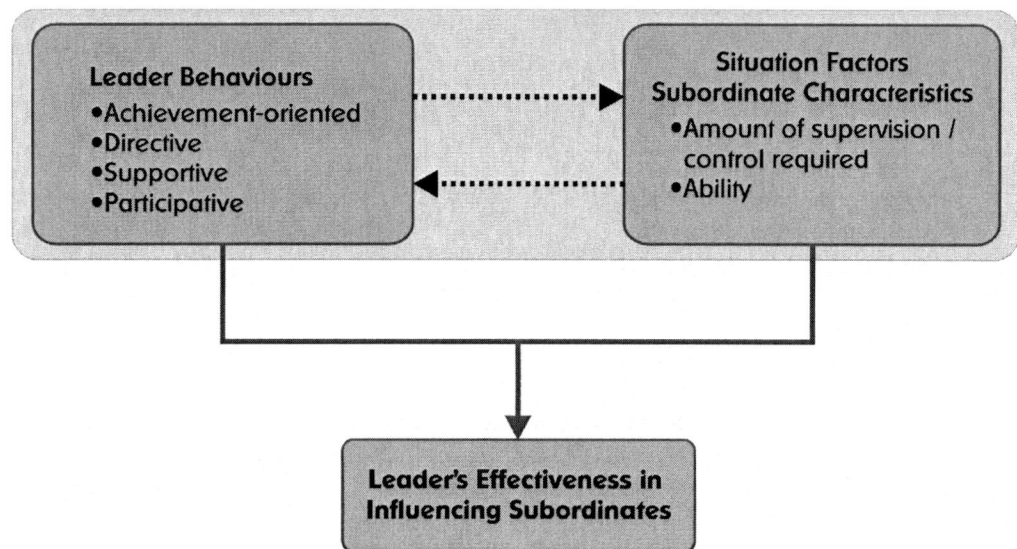

7. **Management theories**: the role of management is to supervise the work of employees and related third-parties and to organise people in an orderly manner to carry out business activities. These styles of leadership generally come from rendering the management role. This is based on rewards for good work and corrective actions for work considered not up to standard or bad. These theories are also known as **transactional theories**. These theories are a contrast to transformational leadership.

8. **Relationship theories:** according to these theories, the relationships between people are integral in creating a leader. A person who generally provides motivation and inspiration to others, and brings out the best in, them becomes the leader. The leader generally helps other people to deliver what is expected from them. These theories demand high ethical and moral standards from the leader. These theories are also known as transformational theories. Maximising the group performance is the aim of these theories.

SUMMARY

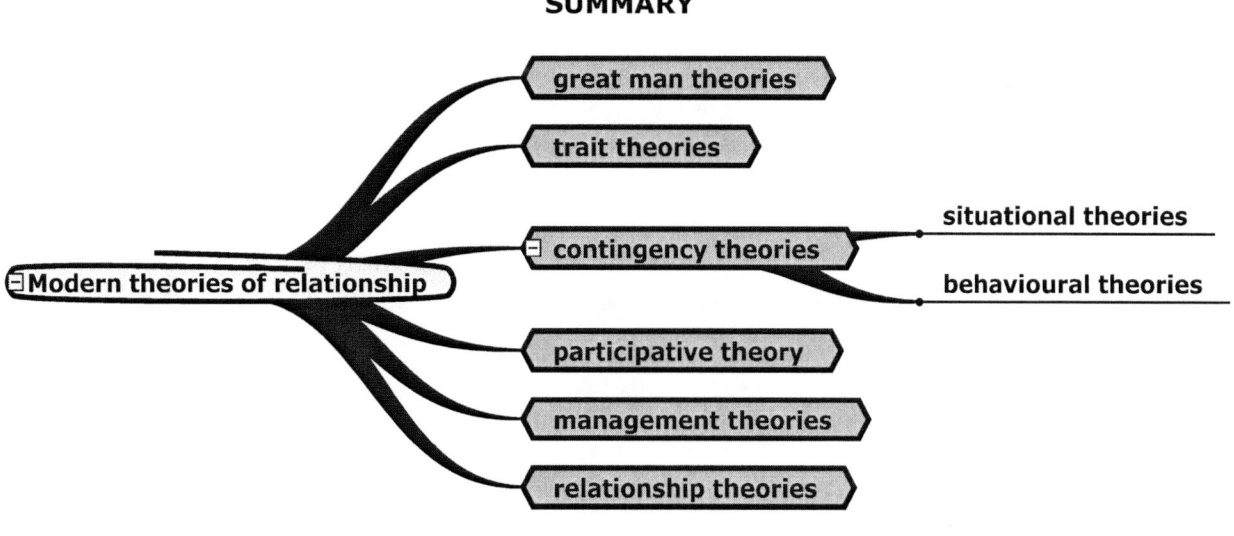

Test Yourself 1

Dennis Ltd is engaged in the business of fashion designing. Sandy is the CEO of Dennis Ltd and also the founder of the company. Until now, Dennis Ltd has been following the relationship theory of leadership.

In recent years, the company has undergone considerable changes. Sales at Dennis Ltd have increased and now it has become difficult for Sandy to manage the business single-handedly. Denis Ltd is considering adopting the management theory of leadership.

Required:

Explain the relationship theory and the management theory in detail.

Also state which theory you think would be beneficial to Dennis Ltd.

Answers to Test Yourself

Answer to TY 1

1. **Relationship theories** are also known as **transformation theories.** According to this theory, one person acts as the leader and motivates and inspires others to deliver work of high quality and quantity. A leader should have high ethical and moral standards.

2. **Management theories** are also known as **transactional theories. According to this theory, the** management monitors the work of the employees and the related third-parties. In this style of leadership, good quality work is rewarded and corrective actions are taken for work considered not up to the standard or bad.

3. In this case, Sandy is the founder of the business organisation and acts as the leader (CEO) of Dennis Ltd. Recently, Dennis Ltd's sales have increased, leading to an increase in Sandy's workload because he is the sole leader of Dennis Ltd. Sandy is responsible for all the tasks that need to be performed and decisions that need to be made for the smooth functioning of the business organisation. Due to his increased workload, Sandy has not been able to devote sufficient quality and quantity time on each of the tasks he performed earlier.

If Dennis Ltd adopts management theories of leadership, Sandy's workload would lessen, as he would be able to organise his work culture systematically by placing responsible individuals in responsible positions. These individuals could then handle their own work effectively and efficiently. Such employees, if they are experts in their fields, can devote quality time to their jobs and lead to an increase in the quality and quantity of the product. Furthermore, Sandy can make more time for other work.

Based on the above explanation, we can conclude that a management theory is more competent than a relationship theory for a large scale organisation.

Quick Quiz

1. Why is an individual reluctant to take risk in the business?
2. What is meant by an "entrepreneurial mind?"
3. Explain the 'Great Man' theory of leadership.
4. What is the participative theory of leadership?

Answers to Quick Quiz

1. Leaders are not willing to take a risk. They want to play safe so that they can ensure that success is guaranteed, or they only want to follow agency theory. Starting a new project always involves risk, which some leaders are not willing to take. This is one of the barriers of visionary leadership.

2. An entrepreneurial mind is one of the qualities a leader should possess. A leader needs to be quick in taking proper decisions according to the change in market trends, surroundings which fulfil the customers' requirements and help the organisation to grow.

3. This theory believes that great leaders are born and not made. A leader's performance represents heroic characteristics which enable him to lead others whenever needed. Leadership qualities are thought to be inherent in a person.

4. Participative theory involves leaders encouraging their team members to actively participate in decision-making; members' views are taken into consideration.

Self Examination Questions

Question 1

Archie Ltd is a multinational firm. The firm manufactures different type of LCDs. The firm has a strong engineering and technical department.

The firm has just employed a new CEO. The new CEO, Ethan, implements a new marketing strategy for the promotion of goods (advertising in professional automobile magazines, brochures etc). To implement this strategy, he purchases some more fixed assets and he increases the current assets. He also increases the budget set for advertising and marketing expenses. Ethan is held in high regard by the firm's senior partner.

With the help of senior partners, Ethan is able to unveil a new strategic plan to increase sales volumes. The plan is drawn up on conditions of secrecy, which involves a collaboration with an advertising agency.

The company could agree to start a customer care centre which includes:

1. Customer service to provide information to customers on:
   - details of the company's showrooms and service provided sectors
   - queries and arrangements for sending service engineers to help the customer etc.
2. Discount offers / gift offers on products that support a sales promotion campaign
3. Raising brand awareness & creating preference
4. Creating positive PR & raising awareness of the organisation as a whole
5. Providing attractive content for a range of products & services
6. Creating internal, emotional commitment to the brand
7. Engaging in corporate hospitality which promotes good relations with clients

With the help of the above strategic plan, Archie Ltd has achieved more than 25% of its targeted profits.

Required:

Explain how the visionary leadership skills of Ethan helped Archie Ltd in achieving its targeted profits?

Question 2

Briefly explain modern theories of leadership.

Answers to Self Examination Questions

Answer to SEQ 1

Archie Ltd appointed a new CEO, Ethan, who had the skills and qualities of a leader. He visualised the future plans of Archie Ltd. Ethan realised that, for any good product, the consumer expects good customer service.

Ethan had qualities like good visualisation and managerial skills, which enabled him to successfully implement a new strategy at Archie. Ethan demonstrated the following qualities:

1. Visionary decision-making

A leader should have the power to make decisions by looking beyond the current situation and acting in a way which would help the organisation in the future. Ethan launched a customer services department, which had not been considered by the organisation's competitors. At the centre, staff provided services to customers according to their requirements and worked on improving business relations with customers.

2. Entrepreneurial mind

An entrepreneurial mind is necessary for making proper decisions in proper timescales which will help the organisation. Ethan made a good decision and tried to create brand awareness for the company's products in the market. His decision initiated a corporate hospitality trend, which promoted the maintenance of good relations with clients. Archie Ltd became the first company in its market to provide customer care services to its consumers. The customer care department helps customers by answering their queries and providing personal attention to customers. Archie Ltd also offers some gifts and discounts on its products, which attracts customers, resulting in increased sales.

3. Risk takers

Rather than playing it safe and thinking about limited growth, the leader needs to take a risk which may result in a gain or a loss for the organisation. His decisions should be backed by proper risk and return analysis. To succeed in business, everybody has to take risks. Ethan, the new CEO of Archie, is ready to take a risk and to introduce new technology, with a range of products and services, into the market by investing in the business. He could either have gained or lost by implementing this marketing strategy. His visionary decision-making helped the organisation. Archie Ltd offered discounts and gifts to customers which increased their expenses. Archie spent a large amount of money on setting up the customer care department and also in marketing and advertising. Archie Ltd bore these expenses because it wanted to be the lead player in the LCDs' market.

4. Effective communication

Ethan coordinated with his senior managers, manager, and other members of the organisation regarding his strategy. This created an internal, emotional commitment to the brand which helped the organisation. The strategy was passed on from the top down and every member of the organisation took responsibility for the work involved. This increased the quality and quantity of the product.

5. Analytical mind

The leader needs to have an analytical mind so that he can look at the root cause of problems and try to overcome the causes or factors which started these problems. Here, Ethan has an analytical mind towards the situation, because he performs the required market research and concludes that the company's competitors also provide as good range a of product as Archie does. Therefore, Archie needs to provide something more than its competitor are offering and something which is needed from the point of view of the customer. Ethan thinks of a customer service which creates goodwill in the market. This also supports sales promotion by providing some discount offers or gift offers to the market.

6. Creative

Creativity is needed to create new relationships. Ethan created positive PR and raised awareness of the organisation. He also helped build the brand position of Archie's LCDs in the market and promoted good relations with the company's clients.

7. Diversity

Every leader should possess the ability to multi-task. This has become a key ingredient for leadership, as this role and responsibility is not only restricted to a particular job or task. A leader has to be able perform various tasks simultaneously.

This is a benefit of the visionary leadership of the CEO, which helps the brand to increase awareness and to generate consumer preference and foster brand loyalty.

Answer to SEQ 2

There are eight modern theories of leadership:

1. 'Great Man' theories

This theory explains that leaders are born and not made. Leaders possess natural qualities of leadership, e.g. George Kennedy, Abraham Lincoln etc.

2. Trait theories

This theory is similar to the Great Man theory in its approach to the leadership qualities in a person, as it assumes that leaders are born and not made.

3. Contingency theories

This theory discusses the way in which leadership qualities change according to different situations. Individuals who are followers in many situations can sometimes become leaders in other situations.

> **Situational theories:** This theory discusses the leadership qualities required in a range of situations. Decision-making is sometimes dependent on the situation.

> **Behavioural theories:** According to this theory, a person can become a leader if he is trained properly. Training must be provided on how to act in particular situations and circumstances. This theory does not believe that leaders are born and not made'

4. Participative theory

This theory explains the importance of inputs from team members. Leaders need to encourage their team members to participate in the decision-making process and their views need to be considered while making decisions.

5. Management theories

This theory is also known as transactional theory, where the management performs the role of a supervisor. The management supervises the efforts and performance of the employees and rewards them for quality, disciplined work.

6. Relationship theories

This theory is also known as transformational theory and tries to increase the active participation of groups and their performance. This theory demands high ethical and moral standards from the leader, as he has to inspire and motivate employees to actively participate and give suggestions which help the management to make decisions.

SECTION H: PEOPLE

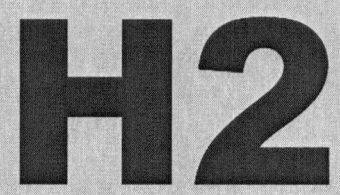

STUDY GUIDE H2: STRATEGY AND PEOPLE: JOB DESIGN

Get Through Intro

Imagine if you had been working for the same company for 5 years and doing the same job. You would probably be quite bored. Alternatively perhaps your job profile had been changed on an annual basis, but you were still quite bored with what you do.

Motivating employees is a core way to improve business. Without motivated employees, work standards often slip and output becomes poorer. There are some simple techniques that you could adopt, which would make your organisation a more motivating one. Try these out and see how things improve!

Learning Outcomes

a) Assess the contribution of four different approaches to job design (scientific management, job enrichment, Japanese management and re-engineering).
b) Explain the human resource implications of knowledge work and post-industrial job design.
c) Discuss the tensions and potential ethical issues related to job design.
d) Advise on the relationship of job design to quality initiatives, process re-design, project management and the harnessing of e-business opportunities.

Introduction

Case Study

Changes in management thinking - Looking after employees and ensuring they are motivated is now a necessity rather than the norm. Japanese companies have been dominating the world for a long time, especially in manufacturing. Toyota has recently taken over as the largest producer of vehicles.

New techniques in job design have helped employees become much more motivated. Whilst previously, job design was just seen as a process of breaking down the roles needed to complete a task (scientific management), it is now accepted that employees can often help create a different way of designing job, in order to complete the task faster, more efficiently and to a better standard.

The Hawthorne experiments (see later) proved that employees liked to be distinguished from each other and valued by the company. If they felt like they were seen as individuals, they performed better.

This Study Guide will help you understand what goes in to job design and how you can improve the process.

> 1. Assess the contribution of four different approaches to job design (scientific management, job enrichment, Japanese management and re-engineering).[3]
>
> [Learning Outcome a]

1.1 Job design

Job design can be defined as:

Definition

The process of combining, splitting and arranging the tasks and responsibilities required to produce or manufacture a product or service into job duties and responsibilities; and defining the relationships between different jobs.

How a job is designed plays a significant role in the level of job satisfaction and the productivity of employees. According to Adam Smith, the founder of modern economics, job design on the basis of division of labour could bring advantages to the organisation in the following ways:
- By concentrating on only one area, workers become more skilled and therefore more productive
- It reduces the time required for each job as a result of reduction in the preparation time and changeover time between the two jobs (e.g. between finishing the manufacturing process and starting the polishing process)
- Introducing specialisation in each job encourages invention of new machinery

There are four different approaches to designing a job. Each one has advantages and disadvantages.
- scientific management
- job enrichment
- Japanese management
- re-engineering

1. Scientific management

a) Taylor's approach

Fredrick Taylor pioneered the scientific management approach. This approach is also recognised as Taylorism. According to Taylor, this approach aims to identify the correct and most efficient way of performing tasks. Henry Ford first implemented the concept of scientific management on a large scale.

b) The principles behind Taylor's approach:

i. **Maximum possible fragmentation of the job:** each task is analysed and divided into several tasks.

ii. **Separating planning and doing roles:** according to Taylor, a worker performing manual tasks is not capable of taking any decisions. All decision making functions are to be taken away from them

iii. **Separating direct and indirect labour:** the worker's roles are divided into skilled and unskilled tasks or semi-skilled tasks, such as preparation and servicing. According to Taylor, skilled workers should be allotted difficult or decision-making tasks; preparation and servicing tasks should be allotted to unskilled workers.

iv. **Reducing skill requirements and job learning time:** if jobs are designed to minimise skill requirements and job learning time, then workers' control over job processes will be reduced.

v. **Reduction in material handling:** it is management's responsibility to introduce machines to perform repetitive tasks and so reduce the time taken to complete the job and the materials required.

c) **Problems or difficulties associated with scientific management:**

i. Performing repetitive tasks for a long time results in a high staff turnover and absenteeism.

ii. Whilst there may be a reduction in the cost of basic labour, overall savings may not be significant as planning and supervision costs increase.

iii. This approach does not consider job satisfaction and may result in a lack of commitment and may give rise to issues of quality as not all the workers are interested in money. Some may prefer intangible benefits such as group working environments.

Diagram 1: Scientific Management

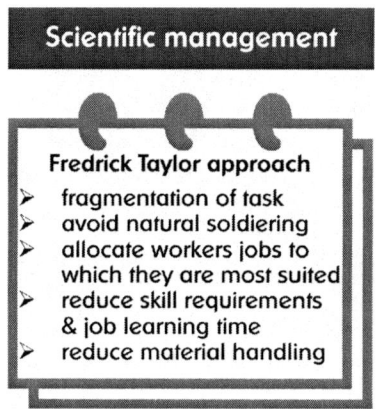

d) **An alternative to scientific management is:**

i. **Human relations movement**: this movement made managers think about their staff's psychological and social needs while designing the job

Hawthorne experiments

The Hawthorne experiments were based on the effects of lighting in the workplace. It was found those changes in lighting as well as other factors such as maintaining a clean work environment, removing obstacles from the floor and frequently relocating the workstations led to a short-term increase in the productivity of the workforce. It was also discovered that workers' productivity increases when they are given attention. The results of these experiments are known as the Hawthorne effects.

Hawthorne's experiments regarding job design and employee productivity came up with the following observations which resulted in improved productivity:

➢ Giving economic incentives encouraged employees to work harder, but so did other factors:
➢ The work environment was important to employees.
➢ Employees worked harder when given recognition, social cohesion, group working, autonomy and decision making powers.
➢ People work harder when shown attention.

ii. **Little and Salaman's five principles** of job design are based on the principle of 'quality of work life'. These principles are:

➢ Scope of the job includes all the tasks to necessary to complete the product or process, satisfying employee's social needs.
➢ Incorporation of control and monitoring with tasks results in taking responsibility for quality control
➢ A variety of tasks makes it possible for staff to acquire different skills
➢ Self-regulation of the speed of the work
➢ This job design offers a work structure that promotes social interaction and co-operation among employees

2. **Job enrichment**

Definition

Job enrichment is a job design approach which is in contrast to the scientific approach and considers the number of processes that a worker has to perform as part of his job i.e. vertical loading. Techniques such as job rotation and aggregation of tasks are used to expose the worker for doing a number of processes.

a) Job rotation

The process of rotation in which the periodic shifting of workers from one job to another is performed. Job rotation aims to reduce the boredom and monotony associated with repetitive tasks and achieves flexibility. It also offers training and promotion opportunities to the employees.

Aggregation of tasks

This is the reverse of the scientific approach. The linked processes are combined in one job i.e. vertical expansion of the job.

b) Hackman and Oldham's job characteristics mode: lists the five core job characteristics that should be used for job design.

i. **Variety of skills:** requires the worker to perform a variety of activities using a variety of talents and skills
ii. **Task Identity:** the inclusion of all tasks required to complete a process or product each task has its own identity e.g. it may be a skilled, semi-skilled or unskilled task. Each task has its own importance in the production process. The value attached to the task gives it a special identity.
iii. **Task significance:** impact of the job on other people's lives or work
iv. **Autonomy:** worker's independence, freedom and discretion with respect to scheduling and determining the procedures to be used while carrying out work
v. **Feedback:** provides information on an individual's work performance

SUMMARY

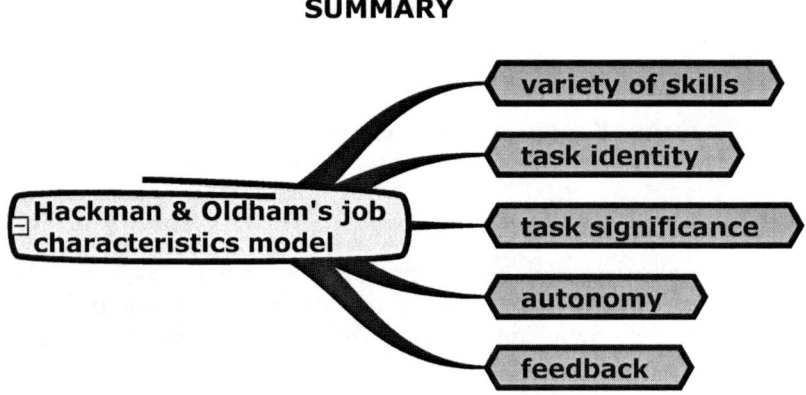

c) Quality of work life is increased by satisfying employee's needs:

i. providing interesting and meaningful work.
ii. assigning responsibility for outcomes
iii. providing information about actual results and performance

d) These principles help in resolving the disadvantages of scientific management by providing:

i. maximising productivity and quality
ii. increasing job satisfaction, resulting in low absenteeism and labour turnover

e) As with scientific management, job enrichment also has problems with implementation. According to the Job Characteristic model, there are **three moderators which define the success of this job model:**

i. Knowledge and skills: level of knowledge and skills possessed by the worker
ii. Growth need strength: workers are motivated by growth needs. Each individual has certain expectations from life. They want advancement in terms of money and career. On the other hand, there are also some people who are satisfied where they are and don't want to put in more efforts in order to earn more.
iii. Context satisfaction: relationship between the context and job satisfaction.

3. Japanese management

Japan has achieved huge economic growth. Japan has used innovative ways of marketing and organisation restructuring to achieve their success. This model is characterised by:
- Employees' interdependency on each other resulting in a high degree of socialisation
- A culture in which the members of the organisation are treated as one community i.e. an organisational culture where the members of the organisation are like a family. This family culture results in cooperation between the members of the organisation. A culture of this sort is suitable for the participative theory Y (explained below) .This culture is in complete contrast to the theory X (explained below) where workers try to avoid their work. Japanese organisational culture is characterised by long-term employment, participative decisions and slow career progress.

a) **Theory X** is based on the authoritarian and hard management approach. Theory X is particularly suitable for large scale operations. Theory X is suitable to lead shop floor and mass production workers. Theory X works under the following assumptions:

i. Workers will try to avoid the work.
ii. Workers need to be controlled and supervised.
iii. Workers need direction.
iv. Workers do not like to take responsibility.
v. Workers need a secure work environment.

b) **Theory Y** is suitable to lead professionals, knowledge workers and managers. Theory Y is based on soft management. Theory Y is based on the following assumptions:

i. People enjoy their work as much as they enjoy play.
ii. People are self-motivated and they will follow self-direction to achieve the organisation's goals.
iii. Employee's commitment is ensured through job satisfaction.
iv. People love to take responsibility.
v. Such workforce is very creative and can be used to solve an organisation's problems.

c) **Theory Z:** William Ouchi combined the American and Japanese style of management. This leadership style is called Theory Z. Theory Z took the following characteristics from Japanese management.

i. long term employment
ii. individual responsibility
iii. collective decision making
iv. slow career progress
v. formalised measures with implicit informal control

d) **Below are the elements of the Japanese model:**

i. flexibility
ii. quality control
iii. minimum waste

i. Flexibility

This is the opposite of the scientific approach and offers job enrichment. This approach offers flexibility by arranging the lay out of the factory in a U-shaped design. This facilitates easy access for the worker to the machinery required to complete the whole component. This model uses a multi-skilled workforce who could work on different machines, which is the opposite of the scientific approach in which a specialised worker works on a specific machine in a one specific workstation. This is also known as cellular manufacturing.

ii. Quality control

The Japanese model adopts an approach of total quality control. This is based on the concept of job enlargement whereby each worker is responsible for quality control. Total Quality Control (TQC) tries to build quality standards into the manufacturing processes. Here, employees undertake the self inspection task and results in savings in labour and raw materials costs.

iii. Minimum waste

The Japanese model developed the 'just in time' production system. This system aims to produce the required quantity of raw material with good quality at the required time. Raw material and stock of components is kept at a minimum level and is delivered to the production system just before their use in the manufacturing process.

SUMMARY

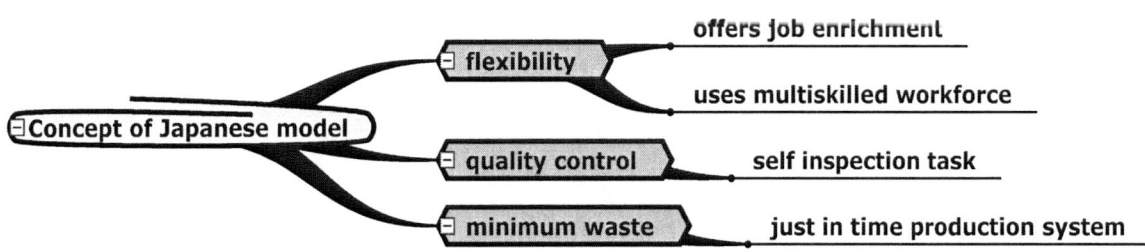

580: People

4. **Re-engineering:** also known as Business process re-engineering (BPR) is discussed in Section D of this Study Guide.

Definition
The re-engineering is a technique used to bring a change in the way business is conducted by improving the efficiency and the effectiveness of the existing processes followed by the organisation.

Business process reengineering aims to redesign the tasks i.e. the existing processes. Such redesigned tasks bring about change in job design. Job design resulted from such business process reengineering comprises the task according to the changed processes.

This approach has led to changes in the traditional organisation structure. Below are some of the advantages of BPR:

➢ Organises work horizontally in self-managed teams; this facilitates an increase in the orientation and adaptation of efforts towards continuous improvement.
➢ Views employees as valuable assets capable of servicing customers' needs without an organisation structure of 'command and control'.
➢ Makes use of the latest technology.

SUMMARY

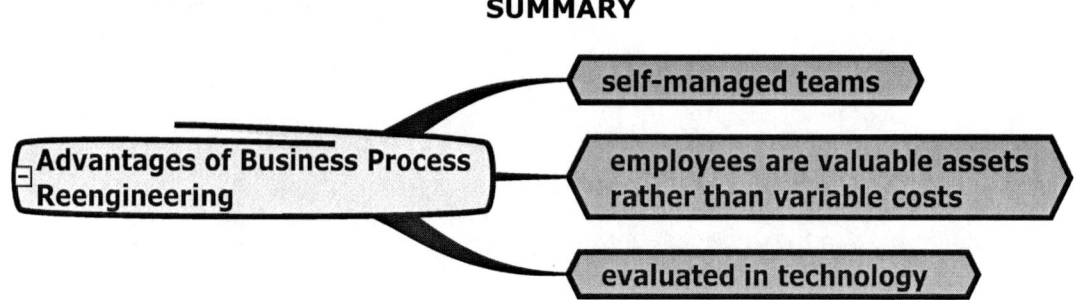

Advantages of Business Process Reengineering
- self-managed teams
- employees are valuable assets rather than variable costs
- evaluated in technology

Test Yourself 1

Serena Ltd is an engineering firm run by Mr. Joseph. During a business tour to Japan, he was impressed by Japan's economic growth.

Mr. Joseph wants to change Serena's way of job designing from traditional to Japanese management.

Required:

Explain to Serena's management the concepts of the Japanese model which will help Serena to improve its working conditions.

---

2. **Explain the human resource implications of knowledge work and post-industrial job design.**[2]

[Learning Outcome b]

2.1 Knowledge work

Definition
Knowledge work is work performed by an individual who has the necessary information or formal knowledge to perform that particular task.

A knowledgeable worker is one who demonstrates knowledge in the workplace

A company can obtain the following benefits from a knowledgeable employee:

➢ developing business intelligence
➢ increase in intellectual capital
➢ gaining insight into customer preferences
➢ a collection of knowledge in other areas of business which is adds to the business's growth.
➢ a knowledge worker is able to work on many projects simultaneously. They can achieve a lot with minimum effort.

> **Example**
>
> Doctors, engineers and lawyers are examples of knowledge workers as they are professionals who have expert knowledge in their fields and apply their knowledge consistently in their jobs every day, to add value to their clients.

2.2 Human resource implications of knowledge work and post industrial job design

- A knowledge worker is an academically capable worker who can apply his knowledge and add value to information within an organisation. Human resource implications indicate there is a greater emotional relationship between the knowledge worker and the organisation. This is because, due to the nature of their work, they need to rely on others within the organisation to help them complete their jobs. For example, a doctor will need to rely on the nurse and her team when doing tests to diagnose a patient.

- Job design comes from the organisational structure. According to Bratton and Gold, organisational structure should be based on the assumptions of McGregor's Theory Y. According to the Theory of Y, people work because they want to work rather than because they have to. This theory assumes that challenging assignments and autonomy over work assignments given to knowledge workers could result in high motivation, a high level of commitment and performance.

- Human resource management includes a reward system. Job design forms the basis for recruitment and selection processes. Job design, which is based on job specification and job description, indicates the need for and offers rewards to the knowledge worker.

- Knowledge is an asset which enhances the organisation's success. Organisations must acquire and manage knowledge.

- An environment of sharing and learning is critical for the business' success.

- Changes in the workforce's knowledge also change the manager's role.

2.3 Level of knowledge work and post industrial job design

As industries evolve, changes occur in job design. Knowledge workers are an important part of the new organisational structure. Features of such organisation structures are:

- efforts to recruit knowledge workers

- increased job security by offering flexibility in work hours and strengthening relationships between employers and employees

- performance incentives

- team structures

- flexible job design that offers flexible working

- multi-skilled employees

> **Example**
>
> it is difficult to write the job description for a research scientist, a knowledge worker, as one cannot set the detail scope for the job. The area of research is related to the organisation's business and, accordingly, job specifications are set. Job designs should include the full scope of how the research should be undertaken. On the other hand, the job design of a shop worker includes a detailed list of activities.

SUMMARY

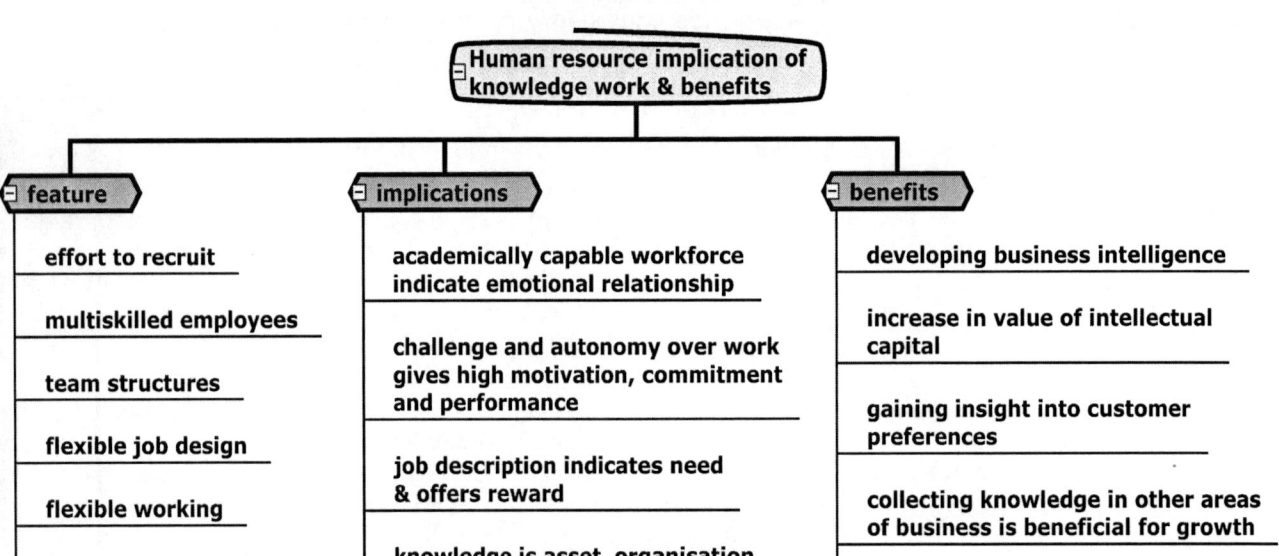

Test Yourself 2

Cheryl Ltd is an engineering company which manufactures electronic chips required in televisions, VCR etc. Cheryl has made a lot of progress in the last few years. Cherly's director, Tom, gives the credit for this to the workforce. Cheryl has followed the policy of appointing only knowledge workers since its inception.

Cheryl's staff consists of 50 electronic engineers. Cheryl's products are famous for their quality. Currently Cheryl is considering business expansion by introducing a new product line. To do this, Cheryl will need to recruit new employees.

Required:

Explain how Cheryl's knowledge workers will be assets for the organisation.

---

3. Discuss the tensions and potential ethical issues related to job design.[2]
[Learning Outcome c]

3.1 Job design creates different tensions for the manager and employee.

Differentiation and integration tension

This tension arises because of management's strategies on the division of labour and the integration of those activities. Managers are concerned with output quality and must apply cost control techniques to activities. It is difficult to achieve quality control when the activities are divided amongst workers.

1. Sometimes jobs are created by for a specific purpose and can lead to undesirable outcomes such as stress or boredom.

2. Modern organisation structures offer employees more initiatives and give scope to their creativity. It is difficult to control the work of such employees.

3. In case of the job redesign and reengineering, job descriptions and specifications are changed. It is possible that employees may be unhappy with their new responsibilities. Such restructuring could also involve reductions in the workforce, which leads to tension between employers and employees.

SUMMARY

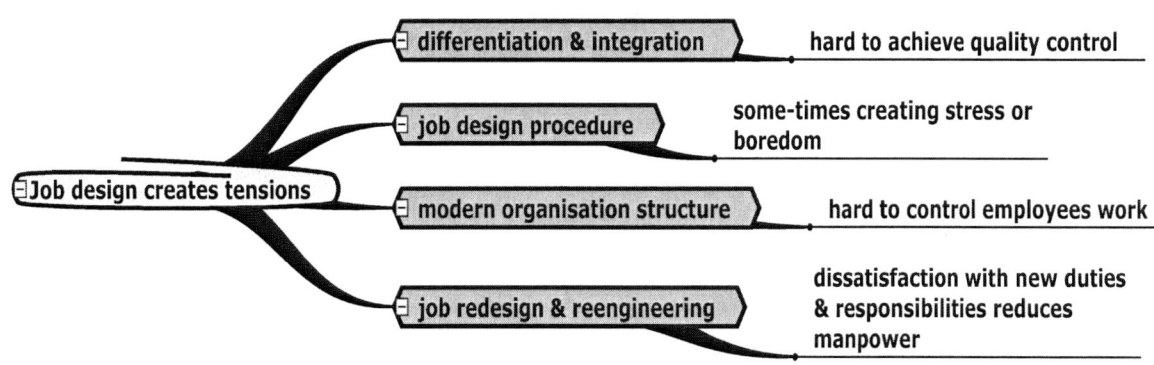

3.2 Ethical issues related to the job design

While designing any job, it is essential to keep the following points in mind:
- workers are human and they should not be treated merely as a means to an end i.e. they are very special assets and should not be treated like any other intangible assets
- rights and responsibilities are delegated along with job duties

Management is mainly concerned with maximising profits and, in the process of reducing and controlling costs, the needs of the workforce could be forgotten.

The following are examples in which management could relegate the needs of their workforce:
- Jobs are designed to maximise productivity and employees' job satisfaction could be compromised by monotonous work.
- Reduction of work force due to process reengineering, automation or outsourcing creates stress on the workforce.
- Restructured, and often reduced, teams are often asked to complete the same amount of work as larger teams.

Test Yourself 3

Jen Ltd is a textile manufacturing company. Jen has never made any change in its processes since it started operation 15 years ago. Jen's new managing director, Bob, wants to keep the company up to date with new technology. He thinks it could save a lot of money if it carries out process redesign and could sell the products at low costs. Jen has decided to undertake process redesign with these benefits in mind. The project manager of this project devises a plan which includes changes in current job designs.

Required:

Explain to Jen's management what kind of tensions could arise between management and the employees from changing job designs.

---

4. Advise on the relationship of job design to quality initiatives, process re-design, project management and the harnessing of the e-business opportunities.[3]

[Learning Outcome d]

4.1 Relationship of job design to quality initiatives, process redesign, project management and the harnessing of the e-business opportunities.

Whenever an organisation takes on a strategically important project, it affects the whole organisation. Examples of such projects are quality initiatives, process redesign and the harnessing of e-business.

While planning such projects, management and the project manager should pay attention to the following points:

1. Such projects generally bring automated and streamlined processes into the organisation. Such changes bring change in processes, job descriptions and specifications. This brings the need for changes in existing job designs.
2. Jobs for which processes are unchanged still need to be reviewed in view of its relation to the new environment.
3. Some changes have an impact on the whole organisation. Even if only one process is changed, other job designs may need to be changed to accommodate the new process.
4. Some changes increase the organisation's existing knowledge base. Such changes require job designs to undergo a variety of changes.

584: People

5. Such projects not only bring about changes in internal processes, but also in the way the organisation interacts with its customers and suppliers.
6. Careful attention to changes in the job design is essential for the successful implementation of change in strategy. The success of the strategic objective depends on the support of individuals.

SUMMARY

Points to be considered by management & project manager while project planning:

- automated streamline processes — require to change existing job design
- need review — although process has not changed
- change in description & specification — impact on whole organisation
- change in job redesign — increase existing knowledge base in organisation
- change in interaction with suppliers & customers — change in internal processes
- change in strategy — essential for successful implementation

Test Yourself 4

Joey Ltd is an interior designing company Joey's competitor has started using the latest technology. With the help of this technology, it is offering better services to its client.

As a result of its competitor's success, Joey has lost almost 20% of its market share. Joey's management has now realised the need to introduce e-packages into the organisation. This will change the current job design.

Required:

Explain to Joey Ltd's management what they will need to consider when planning such changes.

Answers to Test Yourself

Answer to TY 1

Japan has experienced tremendous growth following World War II. Japan has used innovative ways of marketing and organisation restructuring to achieve this success.

There are three elements of the Japanese model:

1. **Flexibility:** the Japanese management approach offers job enrichment. The workers need to have easy access to the required resources e.g. machinery or computers. The organisation needs to use a multi-skilled workforce who can work on different machines.

   To apply Japanese management, Serena's management needs to appoint skilled workers and give them training for the whole production process. This will mean that if the situation demands then the workers will be able to work on any of the production processes.

2. **Quality control:** japanese management adopts a quality control approach. Each worker is responsible for quality control and undertakes self-inspection. This builds quality standards into the manufacturing process and results in reductions in labour and raw materials costs.

   Every employee of Serena will be responsible for his work and will need to carry out self-inspection. This will help to improve the working conditions of the organisation.

3. **Minimum waste:** the Japanese model developed the just-in-time production system. In this system, raw materials and stock of components are kept at a minimum level and are delivered to the production system just before their use in the manufacturing process.

   This approach is very useful for Serena as it will reduce the cost of purchasing and storing the goods and will help Serena to increase its profitability. Serena should also try to enforce Japanese culture such as community spirit, jobs for life and slow career progress.

Answer to TY 2

Knowledge workers could be defined as those who demonstrate knowledge in the workplace.

By recruiting knowledge workers, the company will obtain the following benefits.
- developing business intelligence within the company as all employees will understand all the processes
- increase in value of intellectual capital as again the employees can be asked to work on any part of the process and have the necessary skills to do so
- gaining insight into customer preferences as knowledge workers have better analytical and technical skills than other workers
- collection of knowledge in the other areas of business which will beneficial to the business's growth
- ability to work on several projects simultaneously

These factors will help Cheryl's expansion and future growth. These factors will result in higher levels of motivation, commitment and performance.

Answer to TY 3

Job design will create the following tensions between the manager and employee.

1. Differentiation and integration tension

Management's motivation in applying strategies on division of labour and integration of activities is to reduce costs and maximise profits and not to consider the needs of the workforce.

2. Creating stress or boredom

Jobs are created for some specific purpose, which can lead to undesirable outcomes such as stress or boredom.

3. Modern organisation structure

Modern organisation structures provide employees with more initiatives and increase the scope for their creativity. It is difficult to control the work of these employees.

4. Job redesign and reengineering

Job redesign and reengineering will change job descriptions and specifications, which employees may not be happy with. Such restructuring might involve reductions in human resources, which creates stress for the employer and employee.

Jen's management will need to plan the new job designs and divide work activities and responsibilities to ensure that output quality is not affected. The employees should enjoy their work activities rather than feel stress or boredom. A new organisational structure will provide scope for their creativity and will increase initiative. Management will need to take care of all these situations.

Answer to TY 4

Joey Ltd will need to consider the following points when introducing an e-package and changing job designs in the organisation:

1. **Need for change in existing job designs:** a change in the project will lead to changes in job descriptions and specifications.
2. **Need in review:** though the job processed will not necessarily change, there will need to be a review to accommodate the change in environment.
3. **Change in description and specification:** changes in one process will lead to changes in other related areas of the job.
4. **Change in knowledge base:** changes in the knowledge base will necessitate changes in job design.
5. **Interaction with suppliers and customers:** sometimes a change in a project will lead to changes in interactions with suppliers and customers.
6. **Successful implementation of change in strategy:** changes in job design will bring about changes in strategic objectives.

Joey will introduce an e-package that will require qualified employees with the knowledge to operate it. It will reduce the employees' working time, which will increase production and employees have scope for greater creativity because of availability of time.

Quick Quiz

1. State the names of the different approaches to job design.

2. Explain job rotation.

3. Explain the characteristics of Japanese management.

4. Explain the ethical issues related to job design.

Answers to Quick Quiz

1. There are four different approaches to job designs:
   - scientific management
   - job enrichment
   - Japanese management
   - re-engineering

2. Job rotation is the process involving the periodic shifting of the workers from one job to another.

3. Japanese management has the following characteristics:
   - interdependency of the workers which increases socialisation.
   - socialisation leads to a culture whereby the organisation is treated as one community where there is an emphasis on quality, a job-for-life mentality and relatively slow career progress.

4. The following are the ethnical issues related to the job design:
   - workers should not be treated merely as means to an end
   - rights and responsibilities are attached to duties

Self Examination Questions

Question 1

John has an automotive company. He wants to design job specifications where tasks and responsibilities are combined. John is unsure whether to follow scientific management or job enrichment while carrying out job design.

Required:

(a) Explain to John the scientific management and job enrichment approaches to job design.

(b) Give your opinion on which approach to job design is more suitable for his organisation.

Question 2

Janet Ltd manufactures pipes and wants to begin exporting goods. In order to do this, the company wants to change its job designs and recruit skilled employees. It also wants to introduce e-business.
Required:

(a) Explain to Janet the human resource implications of knowledge work and post industrial job design. Give some example of this.
(b) Explain the human factors the company needs to consider while designing the job.

Answers to Self Examination Questions

Answer to SEQ 1

(a) The scientific management and job enrichment approaches to job design are as follows:

1. Scientific management

Fredrick Taylor is the pioneer of this approach, the characteristics of which are as follows:

- Reengineering, or scientifically analysing, tasks undertaken and redesigning them to eliminate time and motion waste i.e. jobs should be broken down into discrete parts and the workers are trained to do these specialised activities.
- The approach is based on the notion that workers tend not to do a full day's work. Taylor called this 'natural soldiering'. Taylor strongly believed that if an organisation doesn't offer incentives and piece rates to its workers, then the workers tend to avoid working. Workers work harder if offered incentives.
- Training should be given to workers and they should be allocated jobs for which they are most suited. Workers need to be selected carefully before being employed. Training should be given in the best way to perform the tasks.
- Clear division between workers and managers is essential. Careful management and discipline is also necessary in any organisation.
- There is a correct and efficient way of doing all work / tasks which needs to be identified.
- Co-operation and a good relationship between management and staff play an important role.

This approach aims to identify the correct and the most efficient way of performing tasks. Employing the right people and giving them proper training are essential parts of scientific management.

Taylor has some principles behind his scientific approach. According to Taylor the management needs to introduce machinery for repetitive tasks. It needs to analyse and plan the task and separate the labour accordingly. This will minimise skills requirements and job learning time and automatically reduce the workers' control over job process.

2. Job enrichment

Bratton and Gold describe job enrichment as a number of different processes of rotating, enlarging and aggregating tasks.

Hackman and Oldham list five job characteristics that should be used for job design:
- **Variety of skills:** workers should be required to carry out multi-skilled activities.
- **Task identity:** inclusion of all tasks required to complete a process or product.
- **Task significance:** impact of job on other people's lives or work.
- **Autonomy:** workers' freedom to schedule and determine the procedures to be used while carrying out work.
- **Feedback:** providing information about the performance of an individual.

In this process, the quality of employees' work lives is increased by satisfying their needs and providing them with interesting and meaningful work. The responsibility for the outcomes is assigned and information is provided about the actual results and the performance.

Some difficulties are associated with scientific management:
- There is high turnover and absenteeism as workers do repetitive tasks for a long time.
- The overall reduction in costs may not be that considerable as the planning and supervision costs increase.
- Job satisfaction is not considered in this approach and hence may result in a lack of commitment and may give rise to quality issues. Workers may not respond to the incentives. They might demand a good social environment at work.

However, job enrichment helps to reduce these problems by providing maximum productivity and quality. This process also tries to increase the job satisfaction which results in low absenteeism and labour turnover.

According to the Job Characteristic model, there are three moderators which define the success of this job model:
- **Knowledge and skills:** knowledge and skill levels possessed by the worker
- **Growth need strength:** workers are motivated with growth needs.
- **Context satisfaction:** relationship between the context and job satisfaction.

(b) After considering scientific management and job enrichment, John should choose job enrichment, as this approach provides a job design in which tasks and responsibilities are combined by using techniques such as rotation, enlargement and aggregation of tasks. This will help to increase employee satisfaction and skills to do the job. Ultimately, it helps the organisation to increase its output and leads to increased profitability.

Answer to SEQ 2

(a) Janet Ltd needs to consider the following points for the human resource implication of knowledge work and post-industrial job design:
- job design should be based on the job specification and description
- it should indicate the need and offer rewards in order to hire the knowledge worker
- management should analyse the work, plan it and divide the work by considering job descriptions and specifications
- challenging assignments and giving work assignment autonomy to the knowledge workers will result in high motivation, commitment and performance

(b) Janet needs to consider that knowledge is an asset which will lead to the organisation's success. Changes in the workforce's knowledge level change the manager's role. The organisation should acquire and manage the knowledge.

Below are examples which explain the relationship

Job design	Control position	Example where such relationship exist
Low level of knowledge	Manager as controller	Factory level or shop
Reasonable level of skills and knowledge	Manager as coach or co-worker	Professional organisation
Staff's level of knowledge exceeds that of the manager	Manager as servant or facilitator	Research and development centre

Janet's will need to keep the following factors in mind while designing the jobs

- Although the jobs are designed to maximise production, workers are human beings. They are bored by repetitive tasks.
- Janet's will need to develop a good relationship with employees and assure them of their job security.
- The tasks assigned to employees / teams of employees and time allocated to them should be realistic.
- Janet's should keep in mind that rights and responsibilities are attached to duties.

SECTION H: PEOPLE

H3

STUDY GUIDE H3: STRATEGY AND PEOPLE: STAFF DEVELOPEMENT

Get Through Intro

Richard Branson, Donald Trump and Lakshmi Mittal are household names in a global world. However, what will happen when they retire? Does the Virgin Group have someone strong to replace Branson? Can anyone replace Donald Trump at the Trump Organisation? Will Aditya Mittal, Lakshmi's son live up to his father's reputation?

Whilst their plans of succession may not concern you, succession planning as a topic is crucial to the success of an organisation. If you do not train someone up to do your job, how will you ever move up the ladder? This chapter will show you how to develop human resources within your organisation, so you can go on to move further up the career ladder

Learning Outcomes

a) Discuss the emergence and scope of human resource development, succession planning and their relationship to the strategy of the organisation.
b) Advise and suggest different methods of establishing human resource development.
c) Advise on the contribution of competency frameworks to human resource development.
d) Discuss the meaning and contribution of workplace learning, the learning organisation, organisation learning and knowledge management.

Introduction

Case Study

Bye Bye Bill Gate - June 2008 saw the living legend of Bill Gates consigned to the history books of Microsoft. He chose to retire to devote his life to more philanthropic causes through the Gates Foundation which already has assets of $40 billion. He will continue to be a non executive and probably work 1 day a week there.

He had already given his role as Microsoft CEO to Steve Ballmer in 2000, when Gates chose to become chief software architect. Now his role will be split between 2 executives – Ray Ozzie (operational issues) and Craig Mundie (long term planning). The planning had been in the pipeline for a long time so it was expected to be a smooth transition.

The above case study shows that large companies take succession planning very seriously. If Gates had left without clear successors, its share price could have plummeted and employees could have felt unsettled. However, in all size companies, succession is important. This chapter will teach you other areas of human resource management which are equally important.

> 1. Discuss the emergence and scope of human resource development, succession planning and their relationship to the strategy of the organisation.[2]
>
> [Learning outcome a]

1.1 Human resource development

Human resource development relates to the continuous development of the organisation's staff, its management and its directors. Human resources are an intangible asset to the company. Like any other asset, human resources need to be maintained. It is essential, particularly in today's ever-changing markets, for an organisation to keep the knowledge and skills of its human resources up to date. Below are some of the requirements that relate to human resource development within organisations.

- Successful human resource development needs the support of the organisation's leaders and senior managers and a culture that reinforces the management of human resources.
- Workers' readiness to learn and change is preferable. Human resource development can be improved by encouraging employees to teach themselves new skills.
- Adoption of embedded learning in the work place as an ongoing practice.
- Line manager's involvement in the development of subordinates, to the extent that it is hard to differentiate between learning and working.
- Informal learning and appreciation of its value by the line managers.
- Alignment of strategy, culture and commitment.
- Environments outside of the organisation, such as technology advancement and market change, may signal a need for human resource development.
- A culture that nurtures employees by giving them the training to become leaders.
- The senior manager's ability and contribution puts the human resources managements' policies and plans into action.
- Continuous learning creates a flow of knowledge and such interactions can lead to emergent, deliberate strategies.
- Human resource development must reconcile emergent learning with deliberate control i.e. there should be control on the time employees spend on learning and working.

1.2 Succession Planning

Succession planning deals with managing the loss of key persons / managers in the organisation and the identification and development of individuals to fill future vacancies.

- As part of this risk management process, a continuous search for potential key players or managers must be undertaken by the human resources management.
- Addressing the development needs of new recruits to prepare them for such roles is known as succession planning. This is the responsibility of the human resources management department.
- Organisations must find skilled, external workers who can be used for their expertise. Otherwise, skilled workers can be identified early in their career and prepared to take on certain positions through mentoring and providing them with training and new experiences through job rotation.

- The management could benefit from such employees' specialised knowledge of the business. Taking out insurance for the loss of a key person is also becoming common. Funds can be used to cope with the problems raised by the loss of a key person.
- Succession planning involves a periodic review of those who are in the next lower level to identify backups for senior positions.
- Succession planning takes into consideration the course of action that will bring the least possible disruption to the work of the organisation and maintain the effectiveness of its administration.

SUMMARY

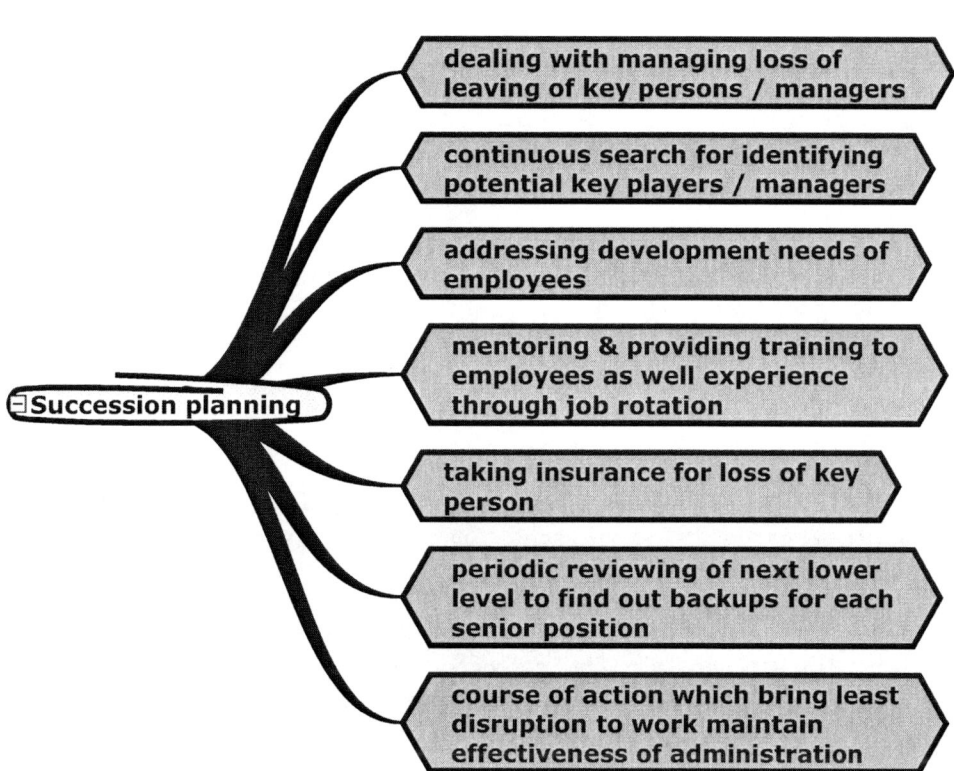

1.3 Relationship of human resource development and succession planning to the strategy of the organisation:

1. McGoldrick and Stewart explain the linking of strategy, culture and the commitment of employees by using the idea of transformational leadership. The idea of transformational leadership consists of four components, namely:
- charisma
- inspiration
- individualised consideration
- intellectual stimulation

Such leadership is capable of aligning an organisation's strategy, culture and the commitment of its employees. Transactional leadership is a contrast of transformational leadership which is explained in Study Guide I_1.

2. Minzberg's design school model of strategic work provides the following features which can lead to the introduction of learning opportunities for employees.
- Assessment of internal and external situations gives the organisation an idea of the future trends of markets and an awareness of where it currently stands.
- Identifying the threats and opportunities that an organisation can explore, such as e-business, this might require employees to learn new skills.
- Identifying strengths and weaknesses: this self-assessment allows employees to learn about and improve upon their weaknesses.
- Declaration of intent, values and visions of the strategy makers.

Succession planning ensures an uninterrupted journey for an organisation on its strategy path.

Test Yourself 1

Betty Ltd is an engineering company. Betty has introduced some new members to its management. The new management wants to change Betty's existing work culture and has taken some initiatives towards changing its work culture, strategy and the level of employees' commitment.

Required:

Advise Betty on how to align its strategy, culture and the commitment of its employees.

> **2. Advise and suggest different methods of establishing human resource development.**[3]
> **[Learning Outcome b]**

2.1 Methods of human resource development

Human resource development and succession planning are necessary for the strategic success of an organisation. An organisation can develop its human resources by following one of the methods below.
- systematic training model
- an integrated approach

1. Systematic training model

As the name suggests, this is a systematic approach towards human resource development. This approach emerged as a result of encouragement from the industrial training board in 1960. The approach can be explained in four stages. This model is based on the theme of rationality and the efficiency. Its theory reflects a mechanistic view.

a) **Identifying training needs and specifying objectives**: According to this approach, the manager needs to identify the training needs of the staff. This approach expects certain standards to be developed by an organisation against which the work of employees can be measured. Employees who do not match the standards that have been set out are considered for training. Managers might come across other training areas which they think will enhance the knowledge of their staff and improve their job performance such as training on project management techniques. Identifying needs and setting the training objective are part of the managers' job. Managers can give on-the-job training or can arrange for outside training. This approach requires a consideration of the cost-effectiveness of training. A justification of how cost-effective the training is must be made before the company incurs any training costs.

b) **Design and implementation of activities:** Designing training activities occurs after identifying the training needs and training objectives have been set. The manager might decide to give on-the-job training, or might ask the external trainer, or arrange the training through e-training software / distance learning. Training activities should achieve their training objectives. Evaluation tests are included at all the levels of the training model.

c) **Evaluation activities:** Evaluation of training activities and the effects that this training has brought in the workplace should be carried out at regular intervals in order to justify the training expenditure. Tests are generally conducted to see whether employees have gained the knowledge and skills stated in the training objective. From the results of these tests, training activities are evaluated for their sufficiency and ability to achieve training objectives.

Diagram 1: Systematic training model

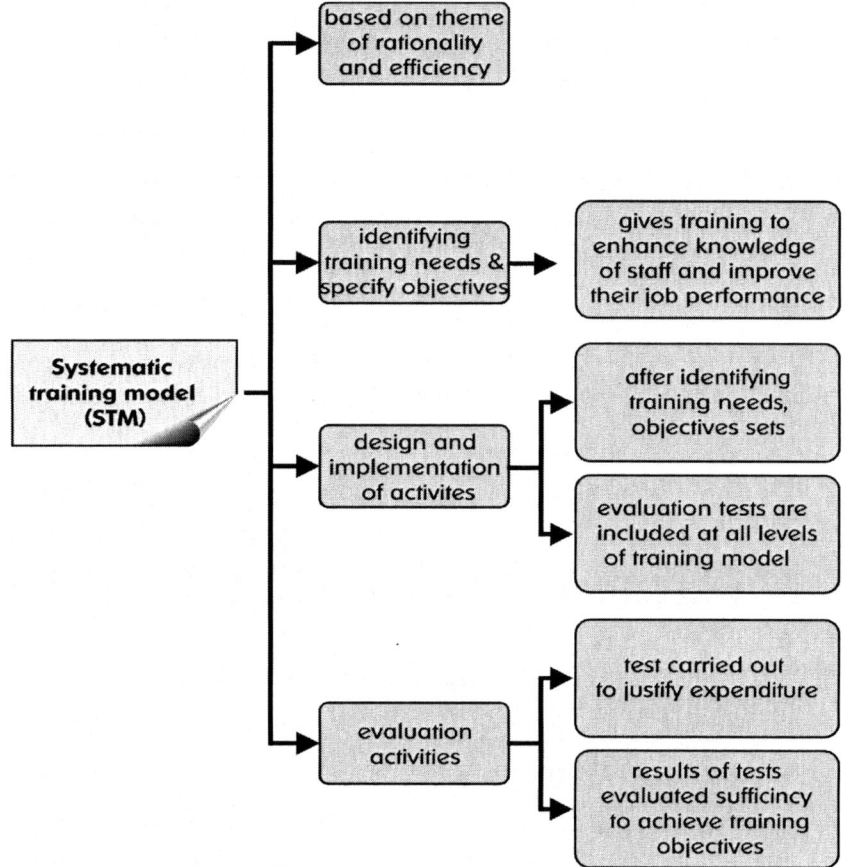

Problems associated with the systematic training model:

- The senior management may delegate the responsibility for training to the training department. This might create a gap between the training offered to the employees and organisational requirements, as the senior management might have a better idea of employees' training needs.
- This model's implementation is dependant on factors such as budget, climate and culture.
- Organisational strategies that give little importance to training, and the tendency of the organisation to emphasise short-term results as opposed to the set standards, act as a barrier to the implementation of this model.
- Managers may refuse to take responsibility for identifying training needs and refuse to support to transfer the learning processes to work experience.
- There could be problems with the refinement of training activities, as the trainers do not have access to the real learning needs of the organisation and the information provided by the senior manager might not be creditable, as there could be differences in perception.
- There may be a divergence of interest between the employer and employee with respect to training needs. Employees might think that their need for training would be seen by the management as a need to change job responsibilities, which would be a threat to their jobs. Employers who are more interested in short-term results could look for other capable human resources in the market. Employees might also see it as a way of increasing their market worth and it may prompt them to change the jobs.

2. An integrated approach

This approach is a contrast to the mechanistic view explained in the systematic approach This approach is considered as the organic approach as per the Burns and Stalker's model. This approach is suitable to organisations that have uncertain or continuously changing environments. Organisations which expect rapid and continuous changes can also adopt this approach.

a) This approach takes into consideration key interdependencies within the organisation. This is based on the existing relationships between strategy, the role of line managers and emergent learning features.

> **Example**

Gateway Ltd is a software company. Employees' work is dependent on each other. Programs written by the employees are integrated into the system by another employee and tested for quality by yet another employee. Employees learn the business logic on which they have to write the programs from other employees and those employees gain knowledge of how the system works from computer professionals.

Human resource development takes place as employees learn about the jobs of other employees through such interdependencies. The strategies of Gateway require its employees to learn about new developments in the software field in order to keep itself competitive. Line managers are aware of the strategic need for learning and encourage their staff to learn new things. Some technical developments are easy to understand and on-the-job training is possible for certain developments.

b) This approach ensures that the organisation's staff is ready to face the challenges of the situation by extending itself beyond their existing capacity of skills, knowledge and abilities.

c) This approach tries to frame a competency framework by linking business objectives to employee performance.

d) This approach recommends the following steps for developing human resources:
   i. competency framework (explained later on in this Study Text)
   ii. performance development plan
   iii. identification of training needs
   iv. development plan

e) Creation of a learning climate that will translate HR policies into employee effectiveness, in terms of improved performance and enhanced knowledge.

f) The manager is responsible for staff development. Coaching and mentoring are considered a way of providing training to staff.

Diagram 2: Integrated approach

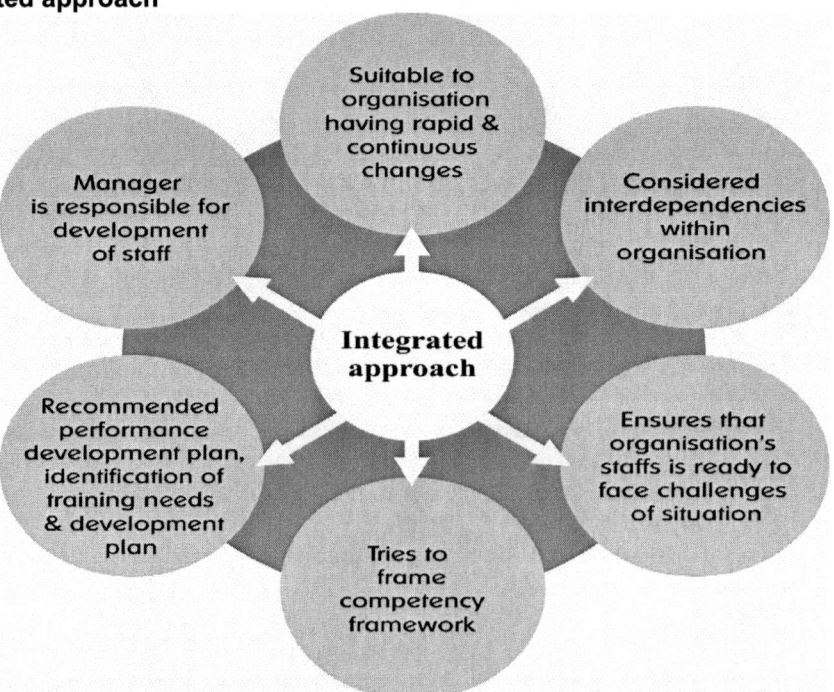

Problems associated with the integrated approach

➢ Competencies of employees are reviewed in the appraisal meetings. Training and development needs are generally identified at this level. Implementation of training for development, however, depends on individual confidence levels and employees' willingness to perform the activities mentioned in the appraisal task.
➢ Physical and psychological variables for employees, such as noise levels in the work environment, norms and attitudes could affect the learning potential of employees.
➢ Managers who are constantly under pressure to achieve performance targets might find it difficult to train their staff.

Test Yourself 2

Pacey, an interior designing firm, is a very small organisation which has become one of the key players in its field due to its CEO, Robert. Robert uses his experience and knowledge very effectively within the organisation.

The management of Pacey knows that to depend on the one person is not good for any organisation, so it decides to implement succession planning in the organisation and considers new ways to introduce programmes which will help of the organisation to achieve strategic success.

Required:

Help Pacey's management to come up with an effective programme.

---

3. Advise on the contribution of competency frameworks to human resource development.[3]
[Learning outcome c]

3.1 Contribution of competency frameworks to human resource development

Competencies are the skills, critical qualities, knowledge base and aptitude which an organisation sees as the qualities required of a competent job holder who has to perform specific job duties.

Types of competencies:
- managerial competencies such as analytical ability, critical thinking, results orientation, people management
- meta or higher competencies such as business focus i.e. understanding of the bigger picture, innovation, creativity and attitudes such as 'make it happen'
- normal competencies such as knowledge and communication skills required to carry out day-to-day jobs

The performance of a competent job holder is analysed by the organisation to identify required competencies in terms of related behaviour, or standards of performance. Competency frameworks are used by an organisation to describe the necessary skills and qualities of prospective employees.

Advantages of using a competency framework (applications of a competency framework)

- Competency frameworks generally outline the essential qualities of the job holder which are necessary to achieve the strategic objectives of the organisation. These essential qualities measure the performance expected from the job holder. In short, competency frameworks try to align the performance of individual employees with the strategy of the organisation.
- These competency frameworks help the HR department in the recruitment and selection process by specifying the required knowledge level and other essential qualities of the candidate. Questions about a candidate's past experience which are related to the required competencies, may be asked in interviews in order to predict the future performance of the candidate or alternatively the psychometric testing may be used for this

Example

Monster.com is an employment website which works as a mediator between employers and prospective employees. Employers publish job advertisements based on the competencies required to perform particular jobs.

- Competency frameworks help to identify the training and development needs of an individual, in order to bring the performance of that individual up to an acceptable level.
- Competency frameworks are a tool for managing the performance of individual employees.
- Competency frameworks facilitate the comparison between the actual performance and the expected performance of an individual. This comparison is then used as a basis for recognising rewards and promotions. If an employee's performance is below standard then the human resources department has to provide training and development opportunities to the employee. Or take corrective actions.

Diagram 3: Advantages of using Competencies framework (Applications of the competency frameworks)

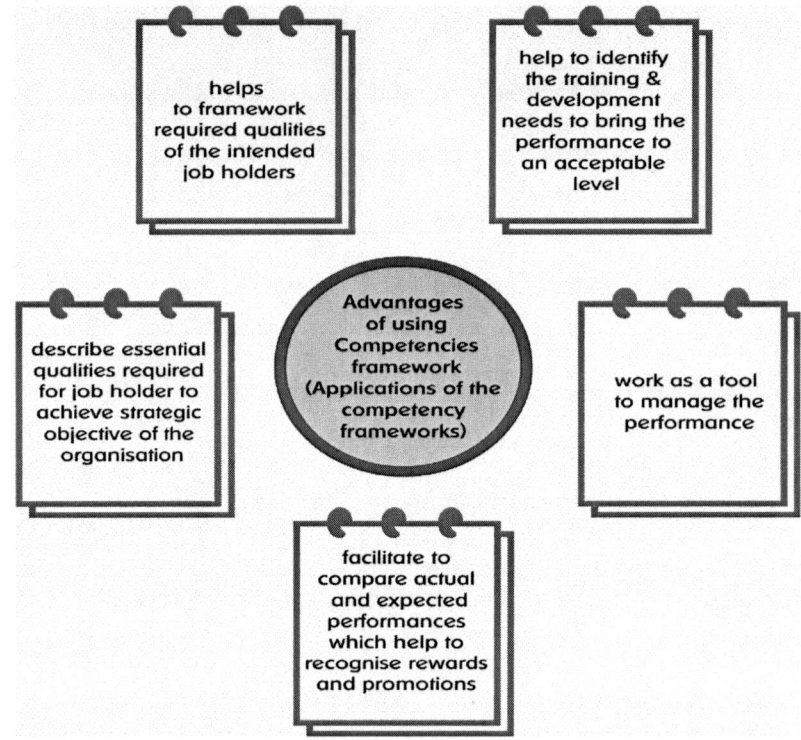

Test Yourself 3

John is a director in Brian Ltd, an advertising company. John wishes to introduce competency frameworks, but before that he needs to explain the advantages of competency frameworks to the management.

Required:

Explain competency frameworks to the management of Brian Ltd and clarify how they can help the organisation.

---

4. Discuss the meaning and contribution of workplace learning, the learning organisation, organisation learning and knowledge management.[3]

[Learning Outcome d]

4.1 Workplace learning

Workplace learning can be described as a theme for human resource development and it differs from mainstream learning in that it is customised to actual work and tasks that normally take place in an organisation. It forms a part of the human resource development, but in the modern era, it is seen as an area of development in itself. According to Bratton and Gold, workplace learning prepares the organisation to cope with the change, complexity and uncertainty in the environment and provides a competitive advantage by filling the gap between reality and an organisation's desired level of knowledge.

Features of workplace learning

1. As discussed above, workplace learning fills the gap between current performance and the performance levels demanded by strategy. As such, learning at the workplace, can be seen as more than a human resource development activity. Such learning can change the strategies of an organisation.
2. Adopting and encouraging the learning climate of the workplace can change an organisation's culture. This could offer the organisation a competitive advantage.

Example

When any technology is introduced into an organisation for the first time, it demands a level of learning at an organisational level. Such learning can change the organisation's culture. For instance, in a situation where an organisation's managers make some time for learning / reading about economic trends, the knowledge these managers gain through such learning could provide the company with a competitive advantage. This could change the organisation's culture, so that managers begin to value their knowledge, and ensure that their learning stays at par with the market.

3. Workplace learning aims to improve generic skills such as communication and problem solving.
4. Workplace learning increases the innovative capacity of the organisation.
5. Learning becomes the integral part of the business and is considered during corporate planning.
6. Learning could result in an increase in work capacity. As the employees learn new ways of working and gain more insights about their work, they are able to increase their work capacity.

4.2 Learning organisation

Organisational learning is different from workplace learning. Employees in an organisation continuously strive to increase their capacity to achieve the organisation's objectives. Such environment nurtures the new thinking and supports the emerging ideas. Workplace learning relates to learning at an individual level whereas learning organisation relates to learning at an organisation level. A learning organisation encourages sharing and integration of knowledge. Learning organisations continuously strive to transform themselves into progressed organisations. Learning organisations are also known as learning companies. Such companies are using information technology infrastructure such as intranets and lotus notes.

Advantages of learning organisations:

- Individual recognition: as the knowledge of the employees is shared, individuals receive recognition for their ideas, values and opinions. This recognition acts as a motivator and results in increased performance.
- Suitable for rapidly changing environment: a learning organisation offers its employees knowledge beyond performing their routine jobs. Such workforces can easily move between different job descriptions. The organisational structure of learning organisations eliminates traditional barriers and brings flexibility to the workforce.
- Just like workforce learning, learning organisations increase the innovative capacity of an organisation by encouraging employees' creativity.
- Improved teamwork: learning organisations try to increase social interactions among their employees which in turn results in increased team work.
- Training: learning organisations allow a transfer of knowledge between the employees, which acts as training and improves employees' knowledge – this helps to reduce work dependencies among employees.
- Learning organisations are benefited from the better reputation and find it easier to attract and retain staff and may attract more investors.
- A learning organisation can provide better customer service than a non-learning organisation. Communication flows more easily in learning organisations, making it easier for customers to interact. Changes in customers' preferences can be recognised more quickly in learning organisations. Mckinsey is a good example of the learning organisation. They keep record of assignments and share them amongst their companies.

SUMMARY

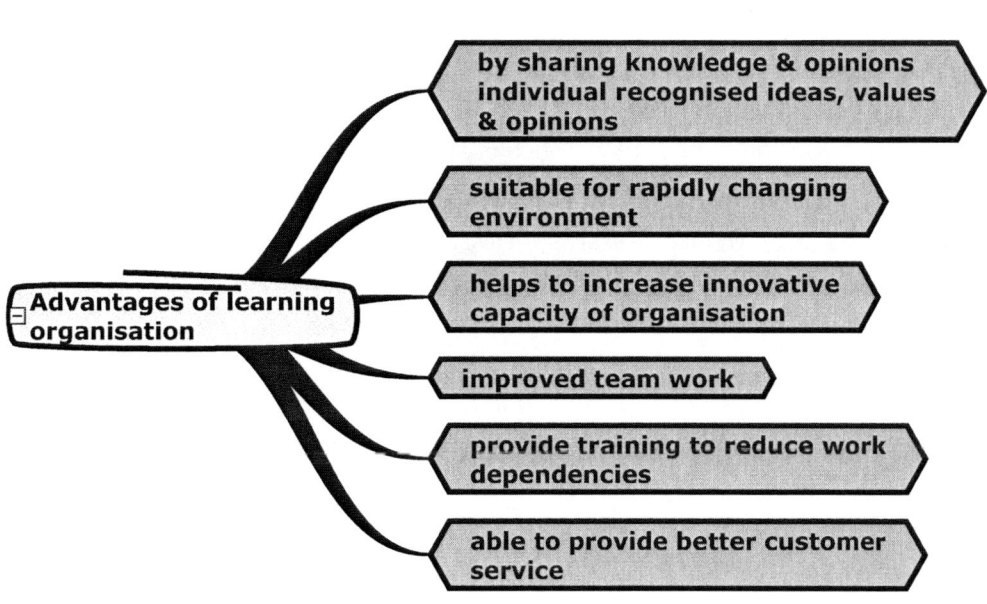

Implementation difficulties in learning organisations

> - Those who are not supportive of this idea may show their resistance to it.
> - Managers who are under constant pressure to meet deadlines find it difficult to provide a scope for learning.
> - Some controllers or private organisations that follow the policy of controlling knowledge flow in the organisation (to keep the whole organisation under their control) act as a barrier for learning organisations.

4.3 Organisational learning

Organisation learning is different from the concept of a learning organisation. A learning organisation can be described as having an organisational structure, whereas organisational learning can be described as the process of learning at an organisational level.

4.4 Knowledge management

Modern organisations consider human resources an asset to the functioning of the organisation as a whole. Like any asset, human resources need to be maintained.

1. Human resources are linked to employees' knowledge levels. Knowledge management involves managing the knowledge of workers.

2. Knowledge comes in a variety of forms – it might be written down or it might be on software, or it may come in tacit form which is in the brains of the people.

3. Knowledge is the intellectual capital which, upon application, becomes the key ingredient in any product or service.

4. Knowledge management deals with the acquisition / retention of knowledge, transforming information into a knowledge base.

5. Knowledge management aims to accumulate the knowledge of capable employees and apply it to knowledge software or to documents which can facilitate knowledge sharing. This sharing helps the organisation to reduce its dependency on key personnel, since their knowledge is available in a knowledge database.

6. Learning is a social activity which is not necessarily productive. So, the knowledge management needs to monitor learning to ensure that the organisation benefits from it without wasting productive time.

7. Big organisations that have realised the importance of knowledge tend to have separate departments to manage knowledge, such as the human resources department, information technology department, etc.

Example

Nowadays many software companies store the knowledge of skilled workers, and transfer their knowledge to software programs. These companies build many kinds of software which provide solutions to various problems. Such software does substitute human resources to some extent. This software does not substitute the tacit knowledge of the individual employee, which requires the involvement of the knowledge worker. Project management software is an example of such software.

8. Knowledge management aims to achieve strategic success. Strategic success could be achieved by:

i. improvement in performance
ii. inventing new solutions for problems or methods
iii. sharing of experiences through a lessons learned report

9. The difference between knowledge management and organisational learning is that the latter is concerned with learning, and knowledge management is concerned with the management of knowledge.

Diagram 4: Meaning and contribution of workplace learning, learning organisation, organisational learning and knowledge management

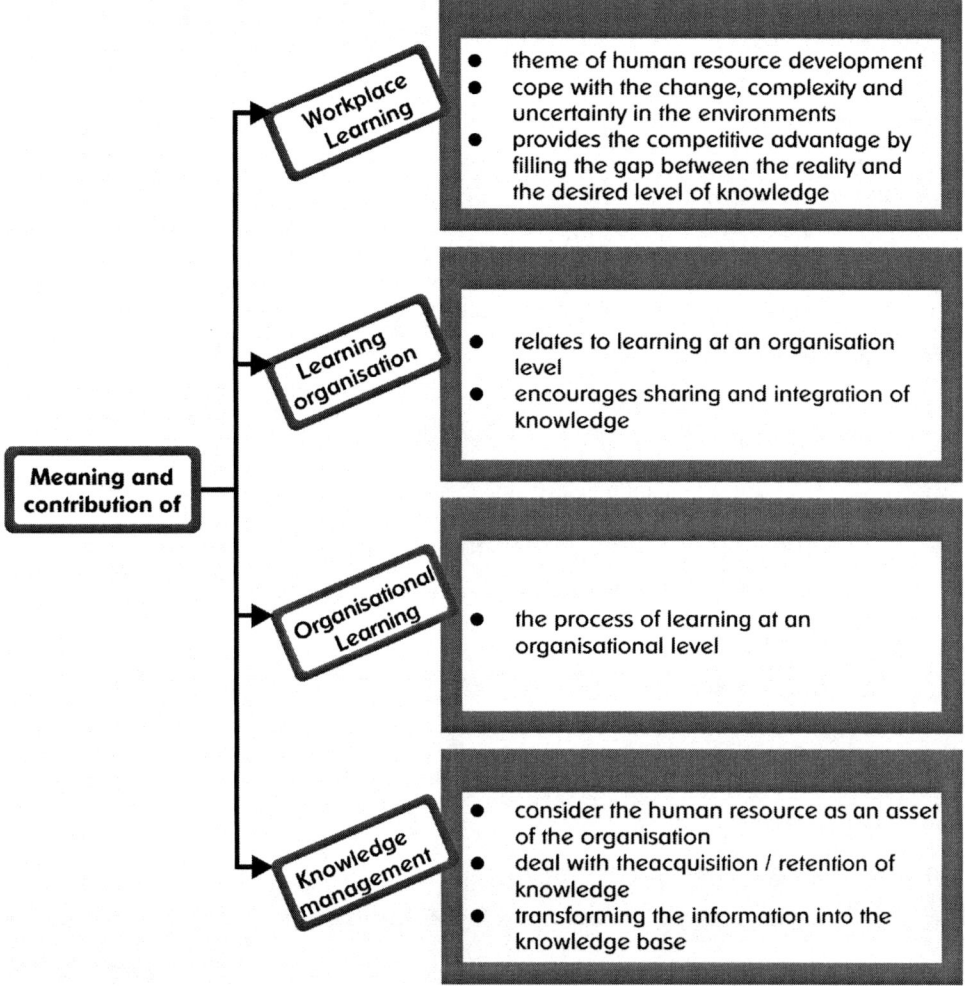

Test Yourself 4

Best Ltd, a garment company, is interested in becoming a learning organisation.

Required:

Help Best Ltd to understand what is meant by a learning organisation. Explain its advantages and the difficulties an organisation may face while implementing this model.

Answers to Test Yourself

Answer to TY 1

McGoldrick and Stewart explain the linking of strategy, culture and the commitment of employees by using the idea of transformational leadership. This idea consists of components such as charisma, inspiration, individualised consideration and intellectual stimulation.

Such leadership is capable of aligning the strategy, culture and commitment of the employees.

Minzberg's design school model of strategic work includes the following features:
- assessment of internal and external situations
- identifying threats and opportunities
- finding strengths and weaknesses
- declaration of intent, values and visions of the strategy makers

Strategies are formed on the basis of the above information. These strategies are meant to address the gap between the perception of the current reality and future goals. According to Minzberg's model, learning and development of staff takes place in order to fill this gap, depending on the market and technical awareness that the management has for new and upcoming environmental trends, and the need to prepare staff. The senior managers support the human resources management's plans and policies because these will help the senior managers to achieve their strategic goals.

Betty's management will need to work according to these features. They will need to asses the situation and collect basic information for the organisation to fill the gap between its current reality and its future ambitions. The management will need to provide training and development opportunities to its staff so that it can cater to new and upcoming trends. The management should provide support for implementation of new plans and policies.

Answer to TY 2

Human resource development and succession planning is necessary for the strategic success.

Pacey will be able to follow a systematic training model. This is a systematic approach towards human resource development. This approach is based on the theme of rationality and efficiency.

> **identifying training needs and specify objectives**

According to this approach, an organisation needs to identify training needs for the development of its staff and provide training to employees in order to enhance their knowledge and improve their job performance.

> **design and implementation of activities**

After identifying the training needs, training objectives need to be set. Evaluation tests will need to be included at all the levels of the training model. Training activities should achieve the training objectives.

> **evaluation activities**

An evaluation of training activities should be carried out in order to justify the expenditure on training. These tests evaluate training activities for their sufficiency and ability to achieve their training objectives.

Pacey's management will be able to identify key employees through succession planning and will be able to develop those employees' skills. Pacey will be able to train and develop employees, and design training activities which are useful for the growth of the organisation. The company can evaluate training activities by assessing its employees. In this way, Pacey can find employees like Robert, who has proved himself as an asset to the organisation.

Answer to TY 3

Competency frameworks are used by an organisation to describe the necessary skills and qualities of prospective employees.

Advantages of using competencies frameworks are:

> they describe the essential qualities required for a job holder to achieve the strategic objective of the organisation
> they frame the required qualities of the intended job holders
> they identify staff training and development needs to bring performance levels to an acceptable level
> they work as a tool to manage performance
> they facilitate the comparison of actual and expected performances, which help to recognise rewards and promotions

Brian will able to recruit employees according to the requirements outlined in job specifications. The organisation can frame jobs according to its requirements and the essential qualities of prospective employees. Brian will analyse the work of the employees and try to give them training to develop their performance to an acceptable level. The company can setup the system to manage the performance of its employees. This will facilitate the comparison between the actual and expected performance of the employees and, accordingly, the company can reward its employees for their efforts.

Answer to TY 4

A learning organisation involves learning at an organisational level. This encourages the sharing and integration of knowledge. This is also known as a learning company which continuously tries its best to transform itself into a progressed organisation.

Advantages of a learning organisation

> Individuals are recognised for their ideas, values and opinions by sharing knowledge and opinions with each other. This act motivates employees and helps them to improve their performance.
> It offers employees knowledge which goes beyond performing their routine jobs and brings flexibility to the workforce and help them get promoted and therefore results in employee retention.
> It increases the innovative capacity of an organisation by encouraging the creativity of employees.
> Sharing of knowledge acts as training which helps to reduce work dependencies as the other person could perform the job of the other person in emergency situations.
> It makes it easier for the customer to interact with the company. This could provide better customer service.

Implementation difficulties of a learning organisation

- It is an idea which requires employees' and top management's support; those who are not supportive may show their resistance.
- Employees who are always under work pressure find it difficult to provide a scope for learning.
- Some organisations follow the policy of controlling the knowledge flow in the organisation to keep the whole organisation under the strict control of the management, which acts as a barrier for learning organisations.

Best Ltd can implement a learning organisational structure. This will help its employees to improve their performance by sharing their ideas and knowledge. It will act as training for employees. This can help Best to reduce work dependencies and encourage its employees' creativity. But, while implementing a learning organisational structure, Best must also keep in mind that implementation will depend on individual attitudes and some employees may show their resistance. Employees who are always under work pressure may not get sufficient time and scope for learning.

Quick Quiz

1. State the concepts explained by McGoldrick and Steward.
2. Name the models that can develop an organisation's human resources.
3. Explain the use of competency frameworks in one sentence.

Answers to Quick Quiz

1. McGoldrick and Steward explain the linking of strategy, culture and the commitment of employees by using the idea of transformational leadership.
2. An organisation can develop its human resources with the help of:
   - a systematic training model
   - an integrated approach
3. Competency frameworks are used by the organisation to describe the necessary skills and qualities of prospective employees.

Self Examination Questions

Question 1

Amazing Ltd is a fashion boutique, which has been operating for five years and is totally dependent on its key employees. Amazing wishes to develop its human resources and is interested in pursuing succession planning.

Required:

Explain which human resource development approach Amazing should follow and how it will help the organisation.

Question 2

Backstreet Ltd is a steel manufacturing company which has become one of the key players in the steel market. Backstreet has set a target to become double in size within the next two years. Backstreet started with only 100 employees and has now become a leading company due to the efforts of John, the director of the company.

Backstreet management now feels the need for more key players like John who can lead the organisation and be able to achieve strategic success for the organisation. The company's management conducts a periodic review of those who are in the next lower level to identify backups for each senior position.

Robert, the managing director and CEO of Backstreet, does not agree with the steps taken by his management. He does not understand the importance of workplace training and knowledge management, and is not aware of how these can help the organisation for in its development and growth of strategy.

Required:

How can Backstreet's management explain the importance of workplace learning and knowledge management to Robert?

Answers to Self Examination Questions

Answer to SEQ 1

Amazing is a fashion boutique which belongs to an industry in which organisations must work in uncertain or continuously changing environments. An integrated approach is the most suitable one for such industries.

The important aspects of an integrated approach

- suitable to organisation that require rapid and continuous changes
- considers interdependencies within an organisation
- ensures that the organisation's staffs is ready to face challenges

- tries to outline a competency framework
- recommends a performance development plan – identification of training needs and development plan
- managers are responsible for staff development

Fashion trends are always changing. Those working for Amazing should be aware that their industry is a rapidly and continuously changing industry. All the employees are linked to each other and depend on each other for their work.

Employees will need to face challenges related to market trends in order to fulfil customers' demands. The manager will need to take responsibility for developing his staff and reviewing their performance. The manager will also need to identify training needs and frame his approach by considering the company's business objective.

While adopting an integrated approach within the organisation, Amazing also needs to be aware of succession planning.

Succession planning deals with managing the loss of key personnel. Human resource management is always:
- performing continuously searches for identifying potential key players / managers
- addressing the development needs of employees
- mentoring and providing training to employees as well experience through job rotation
- taking insurance for the loss of key personnel
- periodically reviewing the next lower level to identify backups for each senior position
- planning processes which bring the least disruption to work and maintain the effectiveness of administration

Amazing's human resources department needs to carry out succession planning.

At the moment, Amazing is totally dependent on its key employees, who have always been part of Amazing's success. Though its existing management performs well, Amazing still needs to adopt succession planning. The company should be continuously searching for potential key players or managers who will be able to address the development needs of the organisation. With the help of key employees' experience and knowledge, an organisation can provide training and development programmes for its other employees. Amazing can achieve this by knowledge sharing and work based learning. Amazing needs to conduct a periodic review of those, who are in the next lower level to identify backups for each senior position. Amazing needs to take into consideration the course of action that will bring the least disruption to the work of the organisations and maintain the effectiveness of its administration.

Answer to SEQ 2

Firstly, Backstreet's management needs to explain the meaning of workplace learning and knowledge management.

Workplace learning can be described as human resource development.

Features of workplace learning
- fills the gap between the current performance and the performance levels demanded by the strategy
- adopting and encouraging a learning climate within the workplace could change the organisation's culture
- improves generic skills such as communication and problem solving skills
- increases the innovative capacity of the organisation

Every organisation should make learning an integral part of its business and needs to give attention to corporate planning. This can help an organisation to increase its work capacity.

Workplace learning will help Backstreet's employees to improve their performance through training and development programmes. This will motivate employees to adapt to changes and new techniques, improve their communication skills and share their knowledge. This will ultimately help Backstreet by increasing the innovative capacity of the organisation.

Knowledge management

Modern organisations see human resource as an asset to the organisation and take special efforts to manage this knowledge held by the staff. This deals with the acquisition / retention of knowledge, and transforming information into a knowledge base. It aims to achieve strategic success which could be an improvement in performance or involve inventing new solutions to problems or methods, or sharing experiences through a lessons learned report.

Backstreet should treat its human resources as an asset because with the help of knowledge management, an organisation can implement new strategies and techniques. The organisation will be able to share employees' knowledge for training and developing the skills and performance of the other employees. This will help Backstreet to achieve strategic success and organisational growth. Backstreet should use information technology such as intranets.

With the help of workplace learning and knowledge management, Backstreet will be able to improve its organisational culture. It may find backups for each senior position. It could also find people with potential, like John, who can later become assets to the organisation. By improving learning and knowledge, and making full use of the capacities of its employees, the organisation can introduce new techniques. The organisation will be able to increase its productivity by motivating employees to work harder, and may, as a result, achieve its set targets within the set time period.

GLOSSARY

A

Ansoff matrix -is in essence a pictorial representation of the strategic options available to an organisation and can be used to help decide upon their strategic choices (i.e. what goods / services to offer and to whom)-197

B

B2B e-commerce-e-commerce that exists between companies. It deals with relationships between and amongst businesses-338

Benefits realization-concerned with tracking whether the benefits are delivered after the project scope has been delivered-453

Brand-name, term, sign, symbol, or design, or a combination of these, intended to identify and differentiate the goods or services supplied by an organisation from those of its competitors-392

Business ethics-the branch of ethics that examines rules and principles within a commercial context.-116

Business process management systems-integrated software solutions or packages that help organisations to set and control the processes that will drive their business-278

Business process outsourcing ("BPO")-occurs when an organisation contracts out an entire business function to an external party-279

Business strategy-is usually at the Strategic Business Unit (SBU) level and involves an organisation asking itself how it can achieve its corporate strategy-7

Business-to-consumer e-commerce-commerce that exists between companies and consumers-338

Business-to-government e-commerce-defined as the commerce between companies and the public sector. It refers to the use of the Internet for public procurement, licensing procedures, and other government-related operations-338

Buying behavior-decision processes and acts of people involved in buying and using the products i.e. the ultimate consumer-409

Buy-side e-commerce-refers to transactions relating to the procurement of resources by an organisation from its suppliers-337

C

Channel structures-modes in which a manufacturer or a selling firm delivers products or services to its customers-346

Collaborative relationships-enables trading partners to gain a better understanding of the demand for products and implement more realistic programmes to satisfy that demand-343

Competences-activities and processes through which an organisation deploys its resources effectively-90

Competitive advantage-higher than the average-183

Consumer-to-consumer e-commerce-commerce between private individuals or consumers-338

Convergence-as occurring "where previously separate industries begin to overlap in terms of activities, technologies, products and customers".-47

Convergence technology-use of technology that is created by combining two or more technologies".-339

Core competences-represent an organisation's ability to conduct business and deploy resources more efficiently and effectively than their competitors-91

Co-operative relationships - based on trust, information sharing, shared goals, culture and understanding. -369

Corporate governance-"the system by which business corporations are directed and controlled-104

Corporate strategy-looks at the overall suite of businesses / products of an organisation.-7

Cost leadership strategy-where an organisation attempts to produce and sell its product / service at a lower price than what its competitors charge-97

Countermediation-creation of a new intermediary by an established organisation so as to enable it to compete with established intermediaries-348

Cross selling-selling of an additional product or service to an existing customer-405

Glossary

Cultural web-representation of the taken-for-granted assumptions, or paradigm, of an organisation and the physical manifestations of organisational culture.-128

Customer Relationship Management-refers to the methodologies, strategies, and software capabilities used to help an organisation organise and manage its customer relationships-400

D

Database marketing-form of direct marketing which uses databases of customers or potential customers to generate personalised communications in order to facilitate the marketing of a product or a service. It involves gathering all available customers and prospective customers' information into a central database and uses statistical techniques to develop customer behaviour models, which are then used to select customers-411

Differentiator strategy-where an organisation attempts to create products / services that are different from ones offered by their competitors.-97

Disintermediation-process of removing intermediaries in the supply chain that previously linked a company to its customers-346

E

E-brand-as opposed to a brick-and-mortar company's brand in the real world, an e-brand represents the brick-and-mortar company's brand on the web space-393

E-business-application of ICT to business processes in order to reduce costs, improve customer value and to find new markets for products and services-336

E-business blueprint-vital link between the e-business design, organisational goals and technology-351

E-commerce-any activity involving an organisation's interactions and business dealings either with clients within the organisation or between various organisations through electronic means-337

E-mail-exchange of electronic messages using computers-348

E-marketing-kind of e-commerce that aims to achieve marketing objectives through the use of ICT such as the Internet, e-mail, interactive digital TV and mobile marketing, together with other technological approaches such as database marketing and electronic customer relationship management (CRM)-382

ERP systems-represent software application packages such as SAP and PeopleSoft which are designed to help an organisation to integrate its various departments / functions by allowing information to freely flow across the business-276

Extranet-private web technologies network that uses Internet protocols and network connectivity for sharing part of an organisation's information or operations with its suppliers, customers, partners or other businesses-350

F

File Transfer Protocol-used to transfer data from one computer to another over the Internet, or through a network-349

Firm infrastructure-includes administration systems, planning, procedures, rules and the finance department of the organization-79

Focus strategy-where an organisation concentrates on servicing a specific market niche and customer segment-97

G

G2B e-commerce-online non-commercial interaction between the government and the commercial business sector (excluding private individuals)-339

G2G e-commerce-online non-commercial interaction between government organisations, departments, and authorities within a country or between the governments of different countries-339

H

Harmon's process-strategy matrix-technique that organisations can use to identify and categorise their various processes as well as ways in which these processes can be improved.-277

I

Infomediary-collects, analyses and sells information about consumers and their buying behaviour to other parties who want to reach those consumers-345

Information-sharing relationships-trading partners might be given access to web systems that share information about product specifications, prices, etc-343

Intranet-private web technologies network that uses Internet protocols and network connectivity for sharing some part of an organisation's information or operations with its staff and corporate management.-349

J

Job design-the process of combining, splitting and arranging the tasks and responsibilities required to produce or manufacture a product or service into job duties and responsibilities; and defining the relationships between different jobs.-576

Job enrichment-job design approach which is in contrast to the scientific approach and considers the number of processes that a worker has to perform as part of his job i.e. vertical loading. Techniques such as job rotation and aggregation of tasks are used to expose the worker for doing a number of processes.-577

K

Knowledge work-work performed by an individual who has the necessary information or formal knowledge to perform that particular task-580

M

Market segment-amarket segment is a group of customers who have similar needs that are different from customer needs in other parts of the market.-63

Marketing mix-set of marketing tools used by an organisation to pursue its marketing objectives for a target market-389

Marketplace channel structures-describe the way in which the seller distributes its products to its customers-340

Matrix structure-is adopted when an organisation combines elements of a functional and customer focused structure-212

M-commerce-buying and selling of goods and services through wireless technology i.e., handheld devices such as cellular telephones and personal digital assistants (PDAs)-338

N

Network-occurs when two or more organisations agree to work upon a particular activity in collaboration-202

Not-for-profit to consumer (NFP2C)-e-commerce between not-for-profit organisations and the customer-339

O

Operational Strategy-Involves an organisation asking itself how it can implement its business strategy-7

Organisation-collection of people working towards achieving a shared objective and purpose-274

Organisation-structure in which people come together to perform the work of the business in an orderly manner.-458

P

Parental developer-corporate parent looking to employ its own competences as a parent to append value to its businesses and construct parenting abilities that are appropriate for its portfolio of business units.-161

Primary activities-functions such as production, marketing, logistics and after sales functions-79

Procurement-based on trust, information sharing, shared goals, culture and understanding-330

push model-process of influencing the behaviour of the supply chain in order to get the desired results-360

Procurement of materials-transformation of these materials into finished products-360

Project-a temporary endeavour undertaken to create a particular product or service, termed a project objective. A project comprises:-420

Project plan-tool of project execution and project control which can be defined as a statement about:-470

pull model-refers to the push of materials through the supply chain to the end consumer and is associated with forecasting demand by an organization-361

R

Reengineering-the fundamental rethinking and redesign of business processes to achieve dramatic improvements in critical, contemporary measures of performance, such as cost, quality, service and speed-275

Re-engineering-a technique used to bring a change in the way business is conducted by improving the efficiency and the effectiveness of the existing processes followed by the organisation.-580

Reintermediation-reintroduction of an intermediary between the manufacturer and the customer-347

Related diversification-strategy development beyond existing products and markets, though within the capabilities or value network of the organisation.-149

Relationship marketing-deals with building relationships with all the external parties involved in marketing-411

S

Search engine optimisation (SEO)-set of methodologies aimed at improving the ranking of a website in search engine listings.-406

Secondary activities-serve as a support function to the organisation's primary activities-79

Glossary

Sell-side e-commerce-refers to transactions relating to the selling of products by an organisation to its customers-337

Strategic alliance-occurs when "two or more organisations share resources and activities to pursue a strategy-202

Strategic capability-the adequacy and suitability of the resources and competences of an organisation for it to survive and prosper-90

Strategic fit-occurs when an organisation adapts or amends its competences and resources (i.e. its strategic capabilities) to meet the new demands and tastes of the changed external environment-92

Strategic position-it is concerned with the impact on strategy of the external environment, an organisation's strategic capability (resources and competences) and the expectations and influence of stakeholders-31

Subcontracting-an organisation typically contracts out part of its work / activities to another organization-202

SWOT analysis-strategic planning tool that organisations use to identify their strengths, weaknesses, opportunities and threats (hence the acronym)-98

T

TCP/IP-set of communications protocols that implement the protocol stack upon which the Internet and other commercial networks run-34

The project objective-the means that are going to be used to achieve this objective-470

Threshold resources-resources that an organisation needs and uses to meet the threshold requirements of its customers-90

TOWS matrix-technique designed to help an organisation match its internal strengths and weaknesses to the threats and opportunities that are present in its external environment-198

Transactional relationships-electronic execution of transactions between the buyer and seller and usually involve electronically transmitted forms-343

V

Value chain-technique that can be used by organisations to identify how the various activities that go into producing a product / service create value-78

Value network-the set of inter-organisational links and relationships that are necessary to create a product or service-81

Value network-network of organisations which have entered into business with each other or have a business relationship with each other so as to create a particular product or service-213

Viral marketing
refer to marketing techniques that produce exponential increases in brand awareness by creating a buzz about the products or services-407

W

Web banners / banner advertising-web banner or banner ad is a type of on-line advertising. It entails embedding an advertisement into a web page-406

Web browser-software that is used to access information on the WWW stored on web servers-349

INDEX

A

Accounting rate of return (ARR)	451
Adhocracy	223
Adoption of e-business	341
Advertising model	344
Ansoff matrix	146, 197
Arm's length relationships	369
Ashridge mission model	130, 143
Auction model	345

B

Back office outsourcing	279
Barriers to the adoption of e-business	342
BCG Matrix	162
Benefits management	446
Best in class benchmarking	83
Brand enhancement	341
Brokerage model	345
Business analysis and strategy	13
Business case	446
Business ethics	342
Business process management systems	278
Business process outsourcing	279
Business process redesign	281
Business Process Reengineering	275
Business Strategy	7
Business units	143
Business-to-business (B2B)	338
Business-to-consumer (B2C)	338
Business-to-government (B2G)	338
Buyer-centric e-procurement model	373
Buying behaviour	409
Buy-side e-commerce	337

C

Capital gearing	538
Carroll's model	121
Centralisation	217
Collaboration?	189
Commoditisation of business processes	278
Community model	344
Competences	90
Competency frameworks	595
Competitive advantage?	183
Consumer-to-consumer (C2C)	338
Convergence	47
Convergence technology	339
Cool tool	407
Core competences	91
Corporate centre	218
Corporate governance	104
Corporate parent	143
Corporate Strategy	7, 144
Cost drivers	496
Cost globalisation	29
Cost reduction	341
Countermediation	348
Critical path analysis	472
CRM software	412
Cultural issues	342
Cultural web	127, 234
Culture	123
Customer acquisition	406, 408
Customer focused structure	212
Customer Relationship Management (CRM)	340, 400
Customer retention	406
Customisation	340

D

Database marketing	400
Database marketing	411
Decentralisation	217
Digital signatures	342
Direct Mail	385
Disintermediation	346
Diversification	146
Drivers of change	28

E

E-business	336
E-business models	340
E-business strategy	351
E-business systems development	436
E-commerce	337
E-CRM	400
Effective relationships	370
Efficiency ratios	534
Electronic Data Interchange (EDI)	371
Electronic mail (E-mail)	348
E-mail	406
E-marketing	382
E-marketing media	384

Index

E-marketing plan	386
E-marketing plan objectives	387
E-marketing strategy	387
E-marketplace	373
Enterprise Resource Management	340
E-procurement	371
E-procurement	372
E-procurement methods	371
E-procurement model	373
E-procurement process	371
Extranet	350

F

File transfer protocol (FTP)	349
Firm infrastructure	79
Fishbone analysis	477
Force field analysis	478
Forecasting	34
Four Ps	389
Franchising	202
Function focused structure	211
Funding strategies	498

G

Gap analysis	477
Gearing ratios	537
Generic strategy	179
Governance chain	105
Government-to-business (G2B)	339
Government-to-Government (G2G)	339
Graphic User Interface (GUI) design	413

H

Handy model	125
Harmon's 5 stage plan for process redesign	281
Harmon's process-strategy matrix	277
Hawthorne experiments	577
Historical benchmarking	82
Horizontal integration	150
Human resource development	590
Hypercompetition	60.186

I

Immediacy	383
Imposed politics	264
Imposed strategy	262
Impulse buying	410
Independence of location	389
Individualisation	389
Industry / sector benchmarking	82
Industry restructuring	389
Information model	345
Information Technology in CRM	413
Integrated approach	593
Integration	389
Intelligence	388
Intended and emergent strategies	256
Interactivity	388
Internal Rate of Return	452
International strategies	156

J

Japanese management	576
Job design	576
job enrichment	576

K

Keyword advertising	385
Knowledge economy	97
Knowledge management	413,598
Knowledge process outsourcing	280
Knowledge work	580
Learning organisation	597

L

Lifecycle model	57
Lifestyle segmentation	405
Link campaign	407
Liquidity ratios	541
Logical incrementalism	263

M

Market globalisation	29
Market segmentation	63,402
Market-based models	340
Marketplace channel structures	346
Matrix structure	212,459
Measurable benefits	448
Merchant model	345
Mintzberg's organisational configurations	222
Missionary	223
Mobile commerce (M-commerce)	338

N

Net Present Value	451
Network effects	342
Network structure	213
Networks	221
Newsletters	407

O

Observable benefits	448
Online auctions	371
Online branding	392,393
On-line customer acquisition	405
Online marketplaces (or e-marketplaces)	371
Open trading environment	373
Operational efficiencies	341
Operational gearing	539
Operational strategy	7
Organisational context	233
Organisational learning	598
Organisational strategy	423
Outsourcing	279

P

Personalisation	383
PESTEL	20
Physical evidence	390
Porter's Diamond	31
Porter's five forces	49
Portfolio analysis	162
Portfolio managers	159
Portfolio models	162
Primary activities	79
Primary value chain activities	364
Print Media	385
Process redesign	435
Process standards	278
Program evaluation and review technique	472
Project	420
Project management software	487
Project Management Triangle	423
Project management	424
Project manager	459
Project sponsor	460
Project-based team structure	458
Pull model	361
Push model	360

R

Re-engineering	576
Reintermediation	347
Relationship marketing	411
Risk management	429
Rummler-Brache Matrix	275

S

Scenario	34
Scientific management	576
Secondary activities	79
Segmentation	74
Seller-centric e-procurement model	373
Sell-side e-commerce	337
SEO	406
Seven Ps	389
Seven Ps of marketing mix	389
Stakeholder mapping	113
Stakeholders	111
Strategic Alliances	202,221
Strategic capability	90,91
Strategic change	230
Strategic Choice	9
Strategic decisions	5
Strategic drift	266
Strategic fit	92
Strategic groups	62
Strategic planning	259
Strategic position	8,30
Strategic position	98
Strategic stretch	92
Strategy canvass	77
Strategy clock	174
Strategy consultants	261
Strategy into action	10
Strategy model of continuous planning Snd feedback	351
Strategy workshops and project teams	260
subcontracting	202
Subscription model	344
Succession Planning	590
Supply chain	360
Supply Chain Management	340,360
Supply chain relationships	369
Supply chain restructuring	366
Support Activities	364
SWOT analysis	98,426
Synergy	93
Synergy managers	160
Systematic training model	592

T

Targeted marketing	406
Theories of leadership	568
Threshold competences	91
Threshold resources	91
Total Quality Management	275
TOWS matrix	198

Index

Traditional marketing	382
Traditional strategy	351
Transmission control protocol / Internet protocol (TCP/IP)	349
Turnaround strategy	244

V

Value chain	78,363
Value drivers	496
Value maximisers	91,93
Value networks	81,365
Venture capital	504
Vertical integration	106,150
Viral advertising	407
Viral marketing	407
Visionary leadership	566